ESSENTIAL ROAD ATLAS
BRITAIN
AND NORTHERN IRELAND

G000299203

Collins

Published by Collins
An imprint of HarperCollins Publishers
Westerhill Road, Bishopbriggs, Glasgow G64 2QT
www.harpercollins.co.uk

HarperCollinsPublishers, 1st Floor,
Watermarque Building, Ringsend Road,
Dublin 4, Ireland

Copyright © HarperCollins Publishers Ltd 2022
Collins® is a registered trademark of HarperCollins Publishers Limited

Mapping generated from CollinsBartholomew digital databases

Contains Ordnance Survey data © Crown copyright and database right (2021)

Printed in Poland

ISBN 9780008447823   10 9 8 7 6 5 4 3 2 1

e-mail: roadcheck@harpercollins.co.uk   facebook.com/collinsref   @collins_ref

© Natural England copyright. Contains Ordnance Survey data © Crown copyright and database right (2020)

Information for the alignment of the Wales Coast Path provided by © Natural Resources Wales. All rights reserved. Contains Ordnance Survey Data. Ordnance Survey Licence number 100019741. Crown Copyright and Database Right (2013).

Information for the alignment of several Long Distance Trails in Scotland provided by © walkhighlands

With thanks to the Wine Guild of the United Kingdom for help with researching vineyards.

For the latest information on Blue Flag award beaches visit www.blueflag.global

MIX
Paper from
responsible sources
FSC
www.fsc.org
FSC™ C007454

This book is produced from independently certified FSC™ paper to ensure responsible forest management.

For more information visit: www.harpercollins.co.uk/green

Contents

Route planning

Route planning maps	ii-vii
Restricted motorway junctions	viii-ix
Motorway services information	x-xi
Orbital motorway maps - M25 & Birmingham	xii-xiii
Crash risk map of Great Britain 2017 to 2019	xiv-xv
Distance chart	xvi

Urban approach maps (1 mile to 1 inch)   1-32

Symbols used on maps / Locator map	1
Plymouth	2
Bournemouth	3
Southampton & Portsmouth	4-5
Swansea	6
Cardiff & Newport	7
Bristol	8
Milton Keynes	9
London	10-13
West Midlands	14-15
Coventry	16
Leicester	17
Derby & Nottingham	18-19
Stoke-on-Trent	20
Sheffield	21
Merseyside	22-23
Greater Manchester	24-25
Leeds & Bradford	26-27
Newcastle upon Tyne & Sunderland	28
Middlesbrough	29
Glasgow	30-31
Edinburgh	32

Street maps   33-91

Symbols used on maps / Locator map	33	Hastings	75
		Hereford	75
Birmingham	34-35	Hull (Kingston upon Hull)	76
Edinburgh	36-37	Inverness	76
Glasgow	38-39	Leicester	77
Leeds	40-41	Lincoln	77
Liverpool	42-43	Middlesbrough	78
London	44-45	Milton Keynes	78
Manchester	46-47	Newcastle upon Tyne	79
Birmingham index	48	Norwich	79
Edinburgh index	49	Nottingham	80
Glasgow index	51	Oxford	80
Leeds index	52	Perth	81
Liverpool index	54	Plymouth	81
London index	56	Portsmouth	82
Manchester index	60	Reading	82
Aberdeen	63	Salisbury	83
Belfast	63	Scarborough	83
Blackpool	64	Sheffield	84
Bournemouth	64	Southampton	84
Bradford	65	Stoke-on-Trent	85
Brighton	65	Stratford-upon-Avon	85
Bristol	66	Sunderland	86
Cambridge	66	Swansea	86
Canterbury	67	Swindon	87
Cardiff	67	Torquay	87
Carlisle	68	Watford	88
Cheltenham	68	Weston-super-Mare	88
Chester	69	Winchester	89
Coventry	69	Windsor	89
Derby	70	Worcester	90
Dover	70	York	90
Dundee	71		
Durham	71	**Airport plans**	
Eastbourne	72	Birmingham	91
Exeter	72	Gatwick	91
Folkestone	73	Glasgow	91
Gloucester	73	Heathrow	91
Guildford	74	Manchester	91
Harrogate	74	Stansted	91

Road maps   92-287

Symbols used on maps & key to map pages	92-93
England, Wales & Southern Scotland (3.2 miles to 1 inch)	94-253
Northern Scotland (4.2 miles to 1 inch)	254-279
Northern Ireland (4.2 miles to 1 inch)	280-287

Index   288-328

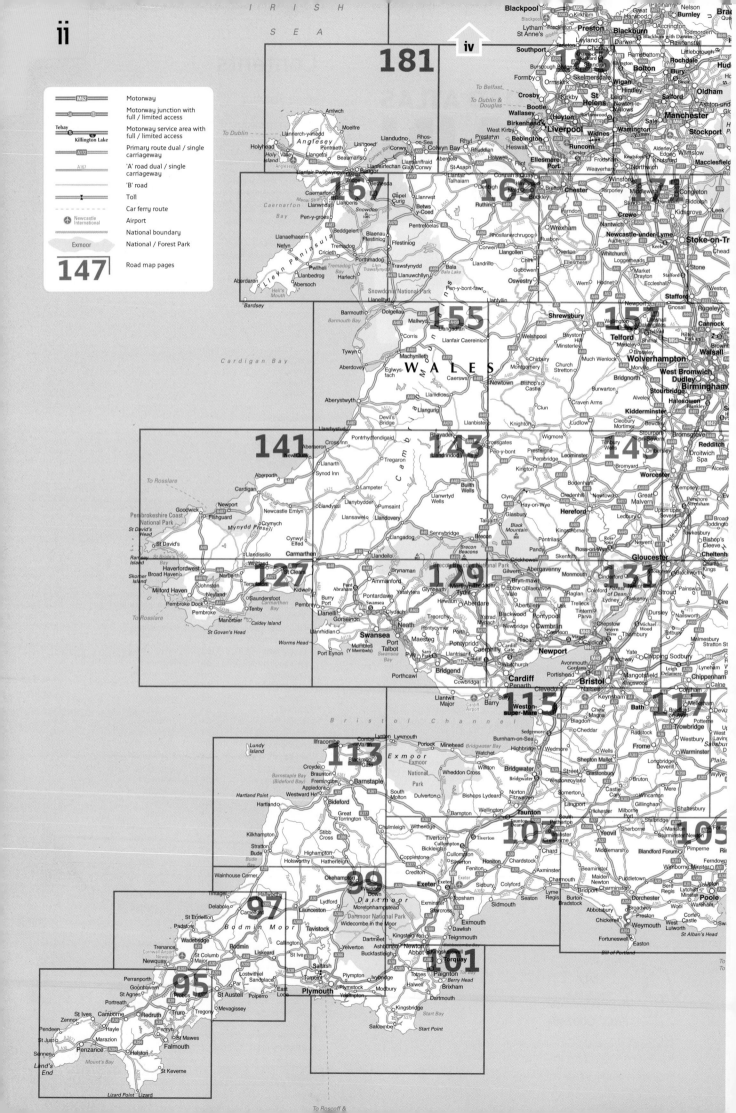

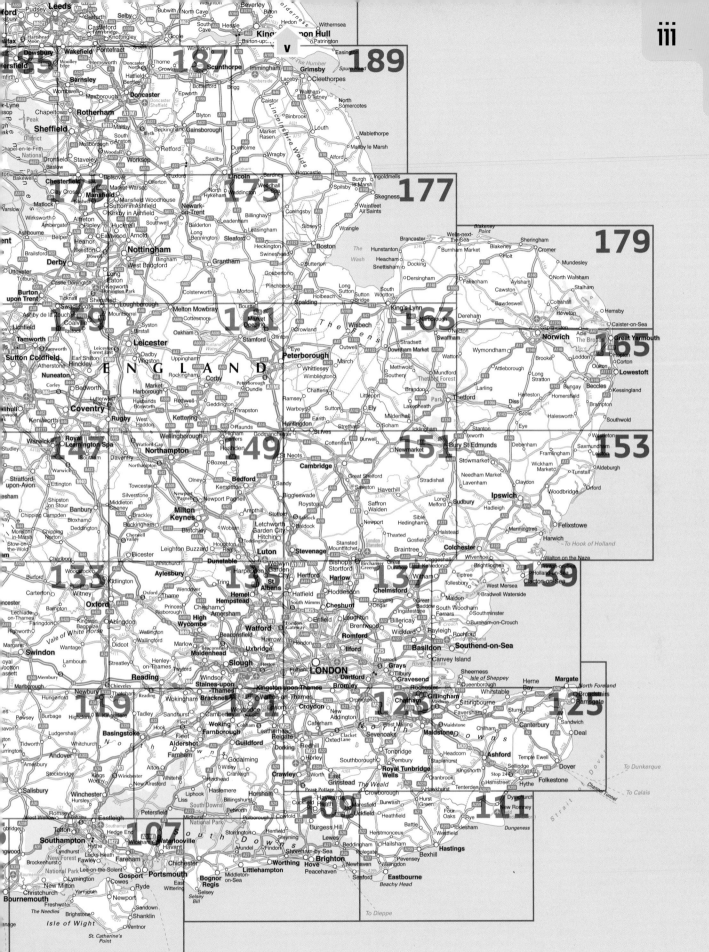

SCALE 1:1,478,872

0   10   20   30   40 miles

0   10   20   30   40   50   60 kilometres

23 miles to 1 inch / 15 km to 1 cm

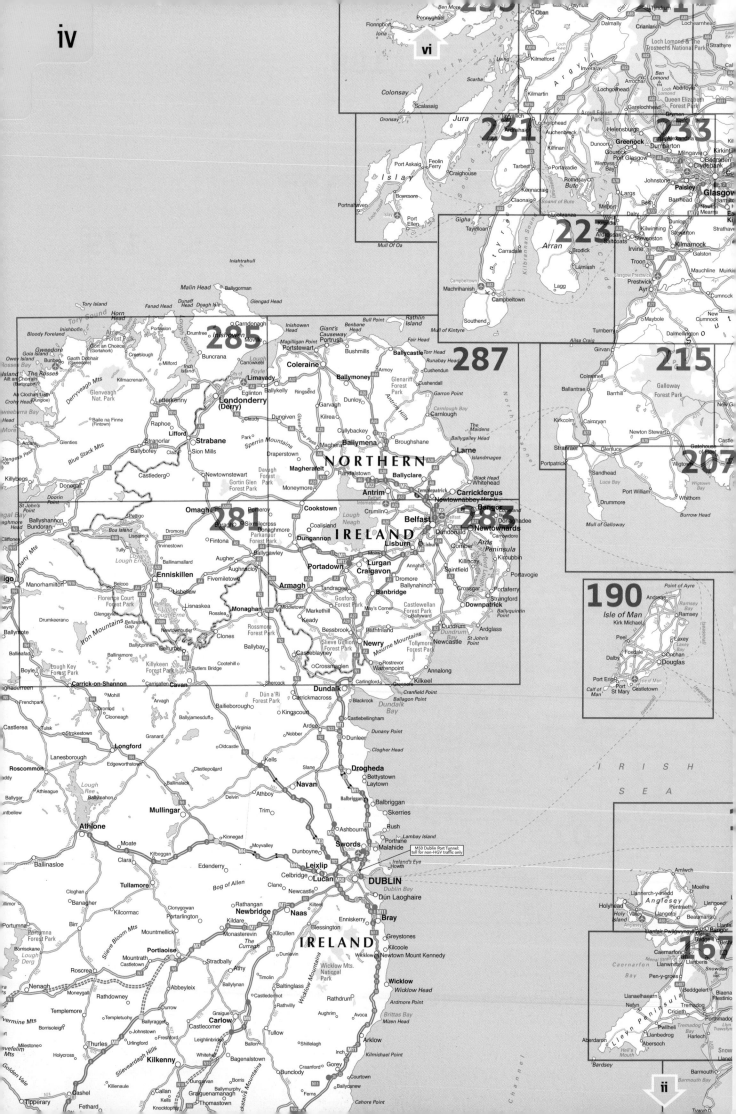

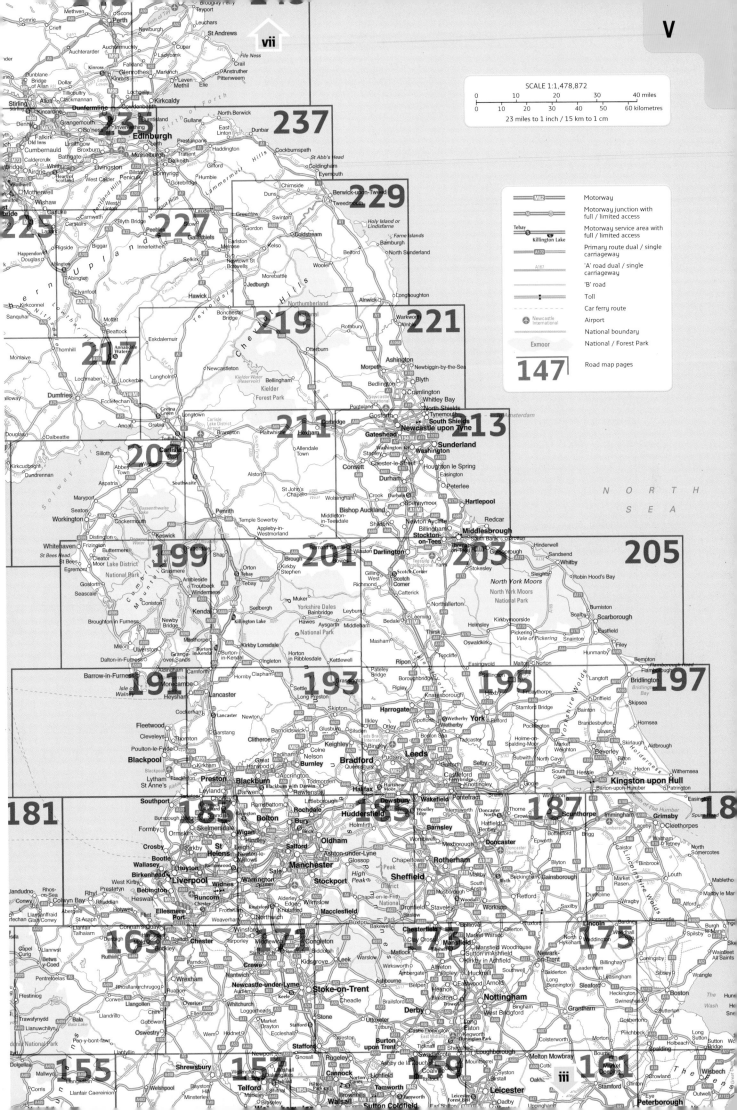

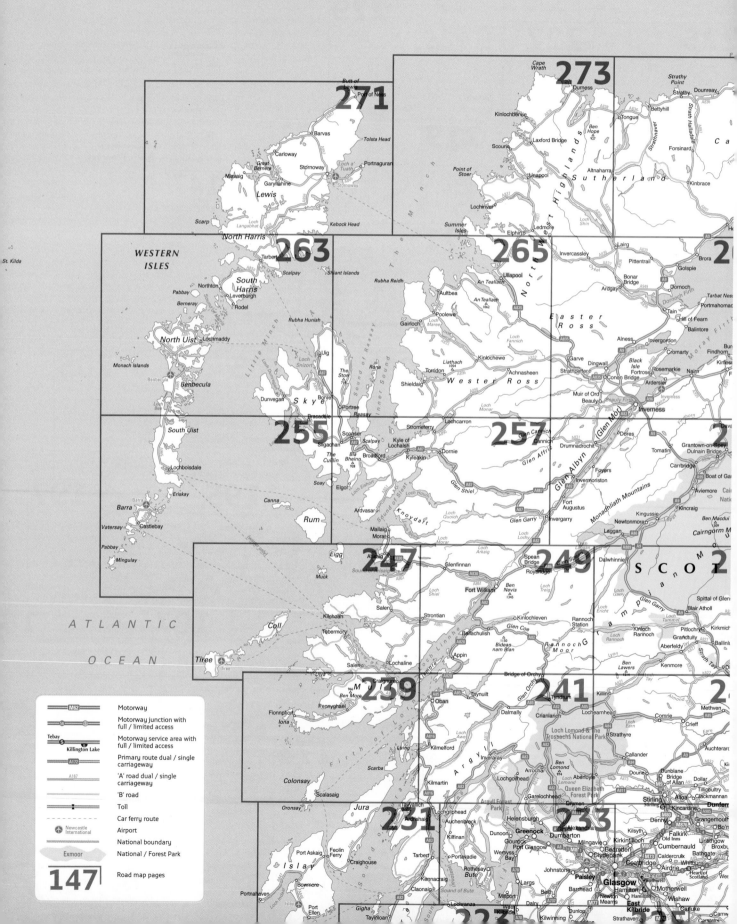

Legend:

M62	Motorway
	Motorway junction with full / limited access
Tebay / Killington Lake	Motorway service area with full / limited access
A172	Primary route dual / single carriageway
A167	'A' road dual / single carriageway
	'B' road
	Toll
	Car ferry route
Newcastle International	Airport
	National boundary
Exmoor	National / Forest Park
147	Road map pages

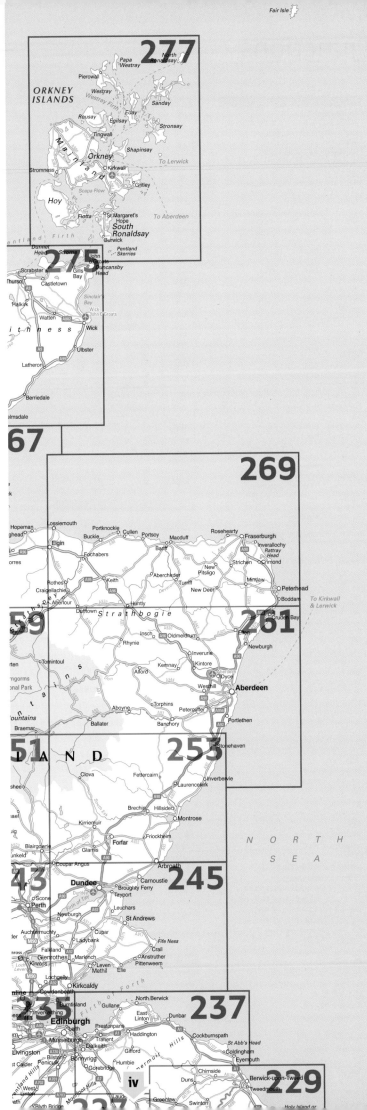

Fair Isle

277

ORKNEY ISLANDS

Papa Westray
North Ronaldsay
Pierowall
Westray
Rousay
Westray Firth
Sanday
Eday
Egilsay
Stronsay
Tingwall
Shapinsay
To Lerwick
Stromness
Orkney
Kirkwall
Kirkwall
Scapa Flow
Gritley
Hoy
To Aberdeen
Flotta
St Margaret's Hope
South Ronaldsay
Burwick
Pentland Skerries

Pentland Firth
275
Dunnet Head
Scrabster
Castletown
John O'Groats
Gills Bay
Duncansby Head
Thurso
Sinclair Bay
Halkirk
Watten
Wick
John O'Groats
Caithness
Wick
Ulbster
Latheron
Berriedale
Helmsdale

67

279
SHETLAND ISLANDS
Unst
Baltasound
Haroldswick
Belmont
Gutcher
Oddsta
Yell
Funzie
Hillswick
Ulsta
Toft
St. Magnus Bay
Vidlin
Out Skerries
Brae
Laxo
Whalsey
Sandness
Aith
Symbister
Walls
Shetland
Sandness
Bressay
Scalloway
Lerwick
Sumburgh
Sumburgh
To Aberdeen & Kirkwall

269
Hopeman
Lossiemouth
Portknockie
Cullen
Portsoy
Rosehearty
Fraserburgh
Elgin
Buckie
Banff
Macduff
Inverallochy
Rattray Head
Fochabers
New Pitsligo
Strichen
Crimond
Forres
Aberchirder
Mintlaw
Keith
Turriff
Peterhead
Rothes
New Deer
Boddam
Craigellachie
Aberlour
Huntly
Cruden Bay
Dufftown
Strathbogie
To Kirkwall & Lerwick
59
Insch
Oldmeldrum
Ellon
Rhynie
Newburgh
Tomintoul
Inverurie
261
Kemnay
Kintore
Alford
Dyce
Westhill
Aberdeen
Cairngorms National Park
Torphins
Aboyne
Petercutter
Mountains
Ballater
Banchory
Portlethen
Braemar
Stonehaven
51
253
LAND
Clova
Fettercairn
Inverbervie
Laurencekirk
Brechin
Hillside
Montrose
Kirriemuir
Friockheim
43
Blairgowrie
Forfar
Glamis
N O R T H
Dunkeld
Coupar Angus
Arbroath
245
Scone
Dundee
Carnoustie
Perth
Dundee
Broughty Ferry
S E A
Newburgh
Tayport
Leuchars
Auchtermuchty
Cupar
St Andrews
Falkland
Ladybank
Fife Ness
Kinross
Glenrothes
Crail
Kinross
Markinch
Anstruther
Loch Leven
Leven
Pittenweem
Methil
Elie
Lochgelly
Cowdenbeath
Kirkcaldy
Dunfermline
Burntisland
235
Inverkeithing
North Berwick
237
Edinburgh
Gullane
Dunbar
Musselburgh
East Linton
Livingston
Prestonpans
Cockburnspath
Tranent
Haddington
St Abb's Head
Dalkeith
Gifford
Coldingham
Bonnyrigg
Humbie
Eyemouth
Penicuik
Gorebridge
iv
Chirnside
Berwick-upon-Tweed
Duns
229
Blyth Bridge
Lauder
Tweedmouth
Greenlaw
Swinton
Holy Island or

To Lerwick
To Aberdeen
To Kirkwall & Lerwick
To Aberdeen & Kirkwall

SCALE 1:1,478,872
0   10   20   30   40 miles
0 10 20 30 40 50 60 kilometres
23 miles to 1 inch / 15 km to 1 cm

Restricted motorway junctions

A1(M) LONDON TO NEWCASTLE

(2)
Northbound : No access
Southbound : No exit

(3)
Southbound : No access

(5)
Northbound : No exit
Southbound : No access
: No exit

(41)
Northbound : No exit to M62 Eastbound

(43)
Northbound : No exit to M1 Westbound

Dishforth
Southbound : No access from A168 Eastbound

(57)
Northbound : No access
: Exit only to A66(M) Northbound
Southbound : Access only from A66(M) Southbound
: No exit

(65)
Northbound : No access from A1
Southbound : No exit to A1

A3(M) PORTSMOUTH

(1)
Northbound : No exit
Southbound : No access

(4)
Northbound : No access
Southbound : No exit

A38(M) BIRMINGHAM

Victoria Road
Northbound : No exit
Southbound : No access

A48(M) CARDIFF

Junction with M4
Westbound : No access from M4 **(29)** Eastbound
Eastbound : No exit to M4 **(29)** Westbound

(29A)
Westbound : No exit to A48 Eastbound
Eastbound : No access from A48 Westbound

A57(M) MANCHESTER

Brook Street
Westbound : No exit
Eastbound : No access

A58(M) LEEDS

Westgate
Southbound : No access
Woodhouse Lane
Westbound : No exit

A64(M) LEEDS

Claypit Lane
Eastbound : No access

A66(M) DARLINGTON

Junction with A1(M)
Northbound : No access from A1(M) Southbound
: No exit
Southbound : No access
: No exit to A1(M) Northbound

A74(M) LOCKERBIE

(18)
Northbound : No access
Southbound : No exit

A167(M) NEWCASTLE

Campden Street
Northbound : No exit
Southbound : No access
: No exit

M1 LONDON TO LEEDS

(2)
Northbound : No exit
Southbound : No access

(4)
Northbound : No exit
Southbound : No access

(6A)
Northbound : Access only from M25 **(21)**
: No exit
Southbound : No access
: Exit only to M25 **(21)**

(7)
Northbound : Access only from A414
: No exit
Southbound : No access
: Exit only to A414

M1 LONDON TO LEEDS *(continued)*

(17)
Northbound : No access
: Exit only to M45
Southbound : Access only from M45
: No exit

(19)
Northbound : Exit only to M6
Southbound : Access only from M6

(21A)
Northbound : No access
Southbound : No exit

(23A)
Northbound : No access from A453
Southbound : No exit to A453

(24A)
Northbound : No exit
Southbound : No access

(35A)
Northbound : No access
Southbound : No exit

(43)
Northbound : No access
: Exit only to M621
Southbound : No exit
: Access only from M621

(48)
Northbound : No exit to A1(M) Southbound
: Access only from A1(M) Northbound
Southbound : Exit only to A1(M) Southbound
: No access

M2 ROCHESTER TO CANTERBURY

(1)
Westbound : No exit to A2 Eastbound
Eastbound : No access from A2 Westbound

M3 LONDON TO WINCHESTER

(8)
Westbound : No access
Eastbound : No exit

(10)
Northbound : No access
Southbound : No exit

(13)
Southbound : No exit to A335 Eastbound
: No access

(14)
Westbound : No access
Eastbound : No exit

M4 LONDON TO SWANSEA

(1)
Westbound : No access from A4 Eastbound
Eastbound : No exit to A4 Westbound

(2)
Westbound : No access from A4 Eastbound
: No exit to A4 Eastbound
Eastbound : No access from A4 Westbound
: No exit to A4 Westbound

(21)
Westbound : No access from M48 Eastbound
Eastbound : No exit to M48 Westbound

(23)
Westbound : No exit to M48 Eastbound
Eastbound : No access from M48 Westbound

(25)
Westbound : No access
Eastbound : No exit

(25A)
Westbound : No access
Eastbound : No exit

(29)
Westbound : No access
: Exit only to A48(M)
Eastbound : Access only from A48(M) Eastbound
: No exit

(38)
Westbound : No access

(39)
Westbound : No exit
Eastbound : No access
: No exit

(41)
Westbound : No exit
Eastbound : No access

(42)
Westbound : No exit to A48
Eastbound : No access from A48

M5 BIRMINGHAM TO EXETER

(10)
Northbound : No exit
Southbound : No access

(11A)
Northbound : No access from A417 Eastbound
Southbound : No exit to A417 Westbound

M6 COVENTRY TO CARLISLE

Junction with M1
Northbound : No access from M1 **(19)** Southbound
Southbound : No exit to M1 **(19)** Northbound

(3A)
Northbound : No access from M6 Toll
Southbound : No exit to M6 Toll

(4)
Northbound : No exit to M42 Northbound
: No access from M42 Southbound
Southbound : No exit to M42
: No access from M42 Southbound

(4A)
Northbound : No access from M42 **(8)**
Northbound
: No exit
Southbound : No access
: Exit only to M42 **(8)**

(5)
Northbound : No access
Southbound : No exit

(10A)
Northbound : No access
: Exit only to M54
Southbound : Access only from M54
: No exit

(11A)
Northbound : No exit to M6 Toll
Southbound : No access from M6 Toll

(24)
Northbound : No exit
Southbound : No access

(25)
Northbound : No access
Southbound : No exit

(30)
Northbound : Access only from M61 Northbound
: No exit
Southbound : No access
: Exit only to M61 Southbound

(31A)
Northbound : No access
Southbound : No exit

M6 Toll BIRMINGHAM

(T1)
Northbound : Exit only to M42
: Access only from A4097
Southbound : No exit
: Access only from M42 Southbound

(T2)
Northbound : No exit
: No access
Southbound : No access

(T5)
Northbound : No exit
Southbound : No access

(T7)
Northbound : No access
Southbound : No exit

(T8)
Northbound : No access
Southbound : No exit

M8 EDINBURGH TO GLASGOW

(6A)
Westbound : No exit
Eastbound : No access

(7)
Westbound : No exit
Eastbound : No access

(7A)
Westbound : No access
Eastbound : No exit

(8)
Westbound : No access from M73 **(2)**
Southbound
: No access from A8 Eastbound
: No access from A89 Eastbound
Eastbound : No access from A89 Westbound
: No exit to M73 **(2)** Northbound

(9)
Westbound : No exit
Eastbound : No access

(13)
Westbound : Access only from M80
Eastbound : Exit only to M80

(14)
Westbound : No exit
Eastbound : No access

(16)
Westbound : No access
Eastbound : No exit

(17)
Eastbound : Access only from A82,
not central Glasgow

M8 EDINBURGH TO GLASGOW *(cont)*

(17)
Eastbound : Exit only to A82,
not central Glasgow

(18)
Westbound : No access
Eastbound : No access

(19)
Westbound : Access only from A814 Eastbound
Eastbound : Exit only to A814 Westbound,
not central Glasgow

(20)
Westbound : No access
Eastbound : No exit

(21)
Westbound : No exit
Eastbound : No access

(22)
Westbound : No access
: Exit only to M77 Southbound
Eastbound : Access only from M77 Northbound
: No exit

(23)
Westbound : No access
Eastbound : No exit

(25A)
Eastbound : No exit
Westbound : No access

(28)
Westbound : No access
Eastbound : No exit

(28A)
Westbound : No access
Eastbound : No exit

(29A)
Westbound : No access
Eastbound : No exit

M9 EDINBURGH TO STIRLING

(2)
Westbound : No exit
Eastbound : No access

(3)
Westbound : No access
Eastbound : No exit

(6)
Westbound : No exit
Eastbound : No access

(8)
Westbound : No access
Eastbound : No exit

M11 LONDON TO CAMBRIDGE

(4)
Northbound : No access from A1400 Westbound
: No exit
Southbound : No access
: No exit to A1400 Eastbound

(5)
Northbound : No access
Southbound : No exit

(8A)
Northbound : No access
Southbound : No exit

(9)
Northbound : No access
Southbound : No exit

(13)
Northbound : No access
Southbound : No exit

(14)
Northbound : No access from A428 Eastbound
: No exit to A428 Westbound
: No exit to A1307
Southbound : No access from A428 Eastbound
: No access from A1307
: No exit

M20 LONDON TO FOLKESTONE

(2)
Westbound : No exit
Eastbound : No access

(3)
Westbound : No access
: Exit only to M26 Westbound
Eastbound : Access only from M26 Eastbound
: No exit

(11A)
Westbound : No exit
Eastbound : No access

Restricted motorway junctions are shown on the maps as:

M23 LONDON TO CRAWLEY

⑦
Northbound : No exit to A23 Southbound
Southbound : No access from A23 Northbound
⑩A
Southbound : No access from B2036
Northbound : No exit to B2036

M25 LONDON ORBITAL MOTORWAY

①B
Clockwise : No access
Anticlockwise : No exit
⑤
Clockwise : No exit to M26 Eastbound
Anticlockwise : No access from M26 Westbound
Spur of M25 ⑤
Clockwise : No access from M26 Westbound
Anticlockwise : No exit to M26 Eastbound
⑲
Clockwise : No access
Anticlockwise : No exit
㉑
Clockwise : No access from M1 ⑥A
Northbound
: No exit to M1 ⑥A Southbound
Anticlockwise : No access from M1 ⑥A
Northbound
: No exit to M1 ⑥A Southbound
㉛
Clockwise : No exit
Anticlockwise : No access

M26 SEVENOAKS

Junction with M25 ⑤
Westbound : No exit to M25 Anticlockwise
: No exit to M25 spur
Eastbound : No access from M25 Clockwise
: No access from M25 spur
Junction with M20
Westbound : No access from M20 ③
Eastbound
Eastbound : No exit to M20 ③ Westbound

M27 SOUTHAMPTON TO PORTSMOUTH

④ West
Westbound : No exit
Eastbound : No access
④ East
Westbound : No access
Eastbound : No exit
⑩
Westbound : No access
Eastbound : No exit
⑫ West
Westbound : No exit
Eastbound : No access
⑫ East
Westbound : No access from A3
Eastbound : No exit

M40 LONDON TO BIRMINGHAM

③
Westbound : No access
Eastbound : No exit
⑦
Eastbound : No exit
⑧
Northbound : No access
Southbound : No exit
⑬
Northbound : No access
Southbound : No exit
⑭
Northbound : No exit
Southbound : No access
⑯
Northbound : No exit
Southbound : No access

M42 BIRMINGHAM

①
Northbound : No exit
Southbound : No access
⑦
Northbound : No access
: Exit only to M6 Northbound
Southbound : Access only from M6 Northbound
: No exit

M42 BIRMINGHAM

⑦A
Northbound : No access
: Exit only to M6 Eastbound
Southbound : No access
: No exit
⑧
Northbound : Access only from M6 Southbound
: No exit
Southbound : Access only from M6 Northbound
: Exit only to M6 Northbound

M45 COVENTRY

Junction with M1
Westbound : No access from M1 ⑰ Southbound
Eastbound : No exit to M1 ⑰ Northbound
Junction with A45
Westbound : No exit
Eastbound : No access

M48 CHEPSTOW

M4
Westbound : No exit to M4 Eastbound
Eastbound : No access from M4 Westbound

M49 BRISTOL

⑱A
Northbound : No access from M5 Southbound
Southbound : No access from M5 Northbound

M53 BIRKENHEAD TO CHESTER

⑪
Northbound : No access from M56 ⑮ Eastbound
: No exit to M56 ⑮ Westbound
Southbound : No access from M56 ⑮ Eastbound
: No exit to M56 ⑮ Westbound

M54 WOLVERHAMPTON TO TELFORD

Junction with M6
Westbound : No access from M6 ⑩A
Southbound
Eastbound : No exit to M6 ⑩A Northbound

M56 STOCKPORT TO CHESTER

①
Westbound : No access from M60 Eastbound
: No access from A34 Northbound
Eastbound : No exit to M60 Westbound
: No exit to A34 Southbound
②
Westbound : No access
Eastbound : No exit
③
Westbound : No exit
Eastbound : No access
④
Westbound : No access
Eastbound : No exit
⑦
Westbound : No access
Eastbound : No exit
⑧
Westbound : No exit
Eastbound : No access
⑨
Westbound : No exit to M6 Southbound
Eastbound : No access from M6 Northbound
⑮
Westbound : No access
: No access from M53 ⑪
Eastbound : No exit
: No exit to M53 ⑪

M57 LIVERPOOL

③
Northbound : No exit
Southbound : No access
⑤
Northbound : Access only from A580 Westbound
: No exit
Southbound : No access
: Exit only to A580 Eastbound

M60 MANCHESTER

②
Westbound : No exit
Eastbound : No access
③
Westbound : No access from M56 ①
: No access from A34 Southbound
: No exit to A34 Northbound

M60 MANCHESTER (continued)

③
Eastbound : No access from A34 Southbound
: No exit to M56 ①
: No exit to A34 Northbound
④
Westbound : No access
Eastbound : No exit to M56
⑤
Westbound : No access from A5103 Southbound
: No exit to A5103 Southbound
Eastbound : No access from A5103 Northbound
: No exit to A5103 Northbound
⑭
Westbound : No access from A580
: No exit to A580 Eastbound
Eastbound : No access from A580 Westbound
: No exit to A580
⑯
Westbound : No access
Eastbound : No exit
⑳
Westbound : No access
Eastbound : No exit
㉒
Westbound : No access
㉕
Westbound : No access
㉖
Eastbound : No access
: No exit
㉗
Westbound : No exit
Eastbound : No access

M61 MANCHESTER TO PRESTON

②
Northbound : No access from A580 Eastbound
: No access from A666
Southbound : No exit to A580 Westbound
③
Northbound : No access from A580 Eastbound
: No access from A666
Southbound : No exit to A580 Westbound
Junction with M6
Northbound : No exit to M6 ㉚ Southbound
Southbound : No access from M6 ㉚ Northbound

M62 LIVERPOOL TO HULL

㉓
Westbound : No exit
Eastbound : No access
㉜A
Westbound : No exit to A1(M) Southbound

M65 BURNLEY

⑨
Westbound : No exit
Eastbound : No access
⑪
Westbound : No access
Eastbound : No exit

M66 MANCHESTER TO EDENFIELD

①
Northbound : No access
Southbound : No exit
Junction with A56
Northbound : Exit only to A56 Northbound
Southbound : Access only from A56 Southbound

M67 MANCHESTER

①
Westbound : No exit
Eastbound : No access
②
Westbound : No access
Eastbound : No exit

M69 COVENTRY TO LEICESTER

②
Northbound : No exit
Southbound : No access

M73 GLASGOW

①
Northbound : No access from A721 Eastbound
Southbound : No exit to A721 Eastbound
②
Northbound : No access from M8 ⑧
Eastbound
Southbound : No exit to M8 ⑧ Westbound

M74 GLASGOW

①A
Westbound : No exit to M8 Kingston Bridge
Eastbound : No access from M8 Kingston Bridge

M74 GLASGOW (continued)

③
Westbound : No access
Eastbound : No exit
③A
Westbound : No exit
Eastbound : No access
⑦
Northbound : No exit
⑨
Northbound : No access
: No exit
Southbound : No access
⑩
Southbound : No exit
⑪
Northbound : No exit
Southbound : No access
⑫
Northbound : Access only from A70 Northbound
Southbound : Exit only to A70 Southbound

M77 GLASGOW

Junction with M8
Northbound : No exit to M8 ㉒ Westbound
Southbound : No access from M8 ㉒
Eastbound
④
Northbound : No exit
Southbound : No access
⑥
Northbound : No exit to A77
Southbound : No access from A77
⑦
Northbound : No access
: No exit
⑧
Northbound : No access
Southbound : No access

M80 STIRLING

④A
Northbound : No access
Southbound : No exit
⑥A
Northbound : No exit
Southbound : No access
⑧
Northbound : No access from M876
Southbound : No exit to M876

M90 EDINBURGH TO PERTH

①
Northbound : No exit to A90
②A
Northbound : No access
Southbound : No exit
⑦
Northbound : No exit
Southbound : No access
⑧
Northbound : No access
Southbound : No exit
⑩
Northbound : No access from A912
: No exit to A912 Southbound
Southbound : No access from A912 Northbound
: No exit to A912

M180 SCUNTHORPE

①
Westbound : No exit
Eastbound : No access

M606 BRADFORD

Straithgate Lane
Northbound : No access

M621 LEEDS

②A
Northbound : No exit
Southbound : No access
⑤
Northbound : No access
Southbound : No exit
⑥
Northbound : No exit
Southbound : No access

M876 FALKIRK

Junction with M80
Westbound : No exit to M80 ⑧ Northbound
Eastbound : No access from M80 ⑧ Southbound
Junction with M9
Westbound : No access
Eastbound : No exit

Motorway services information

X

All motorway service areas have fuel, food, toilets, disabled facilities and free short-term parking

For further information on motorway services providers:

Moto   www.moto-way.com   RoadChef   www.roadchef.com   Welcome Break   www.welcomebreak.co.uk
Euro Garages   www.eurogarages.com   Extra   www.extraservices.co.uk   Westmorland   www.westmorland.com

Motorway	Junction	Service provider	Service name	Fuel supplier	Information	Accommodation	Conference facilities	Showers	M&S Simply Food	Waitrose	Costa Coffee	Starbucks	Burger King	KFC	McDonalds
A1(M)	1	Welcome Break	South Mimms	BP	●	●	●	●			●		●	●	●
	10	Extra	Baldock	Shell	●	●			●			●		●	●
	17	Extra	Peterborough	Shell	●	●			●					●	●
	34	Moto	Blyth	Esso	●	●		●	●						●
	46	Moto	Wetherby	BP	●	●		●	●						●
	53	Moto	Scotch Corner	Esso	●	●		●	●						
	61	RoadChef	Durham	Shell	●	●	●			●					●
	64	Moto	Washington	BP	●	●				●					
A74(M)	16	RoadChef	Annandale Water	BP	●	●				●			●		
	22	Welcome Break	Gretna Green	BP	●	●			●			●			
M1	2-4	Welcome Break	London Gateway	Shell	●	●	●	●			●		●	●	●
	11-12	Moto	Toddington	BP	●	●		●			●				●
	14-15	Welcome Break	Newport Pagnell	Shell	●	●			●			●			●
	15A	RoadChef	Northampton	BP	●					●					●
	16-17	RoadChef	Watford Gap	BP	●	●	●			●					●
	21-21A	Welcome Break	Leicester Forest East	Shell	●	●			●			●			●
	23A	Moto	Donington Park	BP	●	●		●			●				●
	25-26	Moto	Trowell	BP	●	●			●						●
	28-29	RoadChef	Tibshelf	Shell	●	●	●			●					●
	30-31	Welcome Break	Woodall	Shell	●	●		●		●	●		●	●	●
	38-39	Moto	Woolley Edge	BP	●	●		●	●						●
M2	4-5	Moto	Medway	BP		●		●	●			●		●	●
M3	4A-5	Welcome Break	Fleet	Shell	●	●	●	●			●		●	●	●
	8-9	Moto	Winchester	BP	●	●			●			●			●
M4	3	Moto	Heston	BP	●	●		●			●		●	●	●
	11-12	Moto	Reading	BP	●	●	●	●	●			●			●
	13	Moto	Chieveley	BP	●	●		●			●				●
	14-15	Welcome Break	Membury	BP	●	●			●	●		●			●
	17-18	Moto	Leigh Delamere	BP	●	●		●	●			●			●
	23A	RoadChef	Magor	Esso	●	●		●							●
	30	Welcome Break	Cardiff Gate	Shell	●		●				●	●			●
	33	Moto	Cardiff West	Esso	●	●		●			●				
	36	Welcome Break	Sarn Park	Shell	●		●				●				●
	47	Moto	Swansea	BP	●	●		●			●				
	49	RoadChef	Pont Abraham	Esso	●	●		●							●
M5	3-4	Moto	Frankley	BP		●		●	●		●				●
	8	RoadChef	Strensham (South)	BP	●					●					●
	8	RoadChef	Strensham (North)	Texaco	●	●		●			●				●
	11-12	Westmorland	Gloucester	Texaco				●							
	13-14	Welcome Break	Michaelwood	BP	●	●			●			●			●
	19	Welcome Break	Gordano	Shell	●	●		●	●			●			●
	21-22	RoadChef	Sedgemoor (South)	Shell	●	●		●			●				●
	21-22	Welcome Break	Sedgemoor (North)	Shell	●	●		●			●				●
	24	Moto	Bridgwater	BP	●	●		●	●			●			●
	25-26	RoadChef	Taunton Deane	Shell	●	●				●					●
	27	Moto	Tiverton	Shell	●	●			●						
	28	Extra	Cullompton	Shell	●	●			●			●			●
	29-30	Moto	Exeter	BP	●	●		●			●				●
M6 Toll	T6-T7	RoadChef	Norton Canes	BP	●	●	●	●			●				●

Motorway	Junction	Service provider	Service name	Fuel supplier	Information	Accommodation	Conference facilities	Showers	M&S Simply Food	Waitrose	Costa Coffee	Starbucks	Burger King	KFC	McDonalds
M6	1	Moto	Rugby	BP				●	●			●			●
	3-4	Welcome Break	Corley	Shell	●	●		●			●	●			●
	10-11	Moto	Hilton Park	BP	●	●		●	●			●			●
	14-15	RoadChef	Stafford (South)	Esso	●	●	●	●			●				●
	14-15	Moto	Stafford (North)	BP	●	●		●	●						●
	15-16	Welcome Break	Keele	Shell	●	●			●			●	●	●	●
	16-17	RoadChef	Sandbach	BP	●	●		●			●				●
	18-19	Moto	Knutsford	BP	●	●		●	●			●			●
	20	Moto	Lymm	BP	●	●		●	●			●			●
	27-28	Welcome Break	Charnock Richard	Shell	●	●		●		●	●		●	●	●
	32-33	Moto	Lancaster	BP	●	●		●	●			●			●
	35A-36	Moto	Burton-in-Kendal (N)	BP	●	●		●	●						●
	36-37	RoadChef	Killington Lake (S)	BP	●	●		●			●				●
	38-39	Westmorland	Tebay	Total	●	●	●	●							
	41-42	Moto	Southwaite	BP	●	●		●	●			●			●
	44-45	Moto	Todhills	BP/Shell	●										
M8	4-5	BP	Heart of Scotland	BP			●	●	●						
M9	9	Moto	Stirling	BP	●	●			●		●		●		●
M11	8	Welcome Break	Birchanger Green	Shell	●	●	●	●	●			●		●	●
M18	5	Moto	Doncaster North	BP	●	●		●			●				●
M20	8	RoadChef	Maidstone	Esso	●	●		●			●				●
	11	Stop 24	Stop 24	Shell	●	●		●			●				●
M23	11	Moto	Pease Pottage	BP	●				●			●			
M25	5-6	RoadChef	Clacket Lane	BP	●					●					●
	9-10	Extra	Cobham	Shell		●		●	●			●		●	●
	23	Welcome Break	South Mimms	BP	●	●		●	●			●		●	●
	30	Moto	Thurrock	Esso	●	●		●			●				●
M27	3-4	RoadChef	Rownhams	BP	●	●				●					●
M40	2	Extra	Beaconsfield	Shell		●			●			●	●	●	●
	8	Welcome Break	Oxford	BP	●	●		●			●	●			●
	10	Moto	Cherwell Valley	Esso	●	●			●			●			●
	12-13	Welcome Break	Warwick	BP	●	●	●	●			●		●	●	●
M42	2	Welcome Break	Hopwood Park	Shell	●	●		●	●			●			●
	10	Moto	Tamworth	Esso	●	●		●	●						●
M48	1	Moto	Severn View	BP		●		●	●			●			●
M54	4	Welcome Break	Telford	Shell	●	●			●			●			●
M56	14	RoadChef	Chester	Shell		●	●	●							
M61	6-7	Euro Garages	Rivington	BP		●		●	●				●		●
M62	7-9	Welcome Break	Burtonwood	Shell	●						●		●		●
	18-19	Moto	Birch	BP	●	●		●	●	●		●			●
	25-26	Welcome Break	Hartshead Moor	Shell	●	●		●		●			●		●
	33	Moto	Ferrybridge	BP	●	●		●			●				●
M65	4	Extra	Blackburn with Darwen	Shell	●	●	●	●				●			●
M74	4-5	RoadChef	Bothwell (South)	Shell	●	●		●			●				
	5-6	RoadChef	Hamilton (North)	Shell	●	●		●			●				
	11-12	Cairn Lodge	Happendon	Shell	●	●		●			●				
	12-13	Welcome Break	Abington	Shell	●	●		●				●		●	●
M80	6-7	Shell	Old Inns	Shell											
M90	6	Moto	Kinross	BP	●	●		●	●			●			

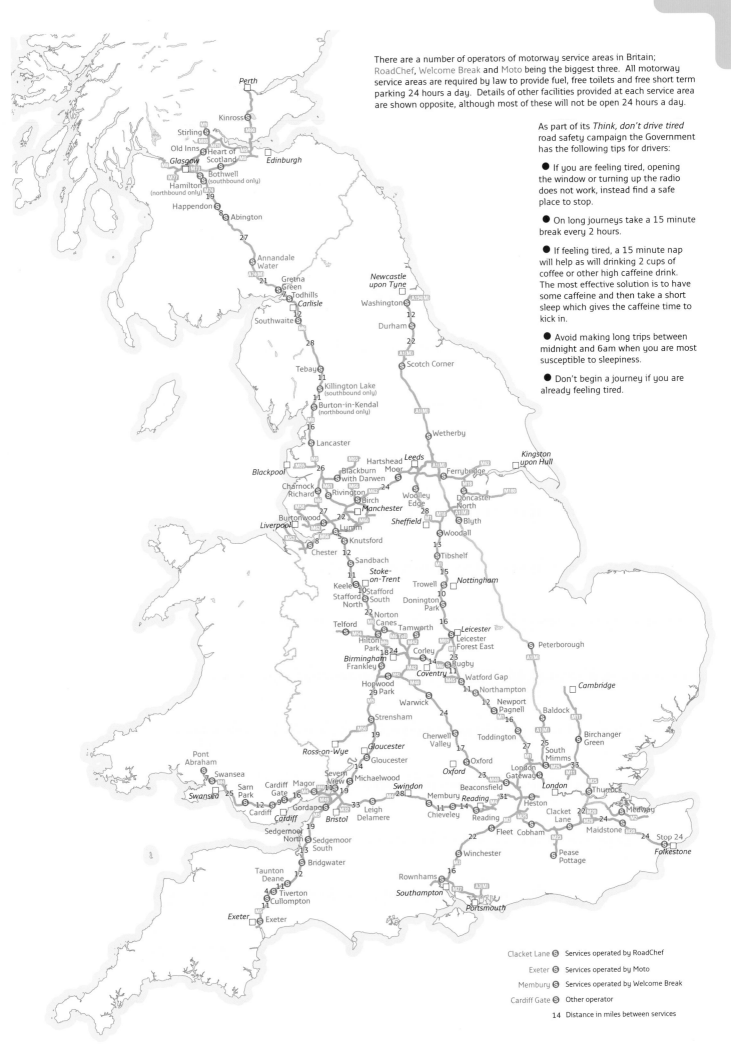

There are a number of operators of motorway service areas in Britain; RoadChef, Welcome Break and Moto being the biggest three. All motorway service areas are required by law to provide fuel, free toilets and free short term parking 24 hours a day. Details of other facilities provided at each service area are shown opposite, although most of these will not be open 24 hours a day.

As part of its *Think, don't drive tired* road safety campaign the Government has the following tips for drivers:

● If you are feeling tired, opening the window or turning up the radio does not work, instead find a safe place to stop.

● On long journeys take a 15 minute break every 2 hours.

● If feeling tired, a 15 minute nap will help as will drinking 2 cups of coffee or other high caffeine drink. The most effective solution is to have some caffeine and then take a short sleep which gives the caffeine time to kick in.

● Avoid making long trips between midnight and 6am when you are most susceptible to sleepiness.

● Don't begin a journey if you are already feeling tired.

Clacket Lane Ⓢ Services operated by RoadChef

Exeter Ⓢ Services operated by Moto

Membury Ⓢ Services operated by Welcome Break

Cardiff Gate Ⓢ Other operator

14 Distance in miles between services

M25 orbital map

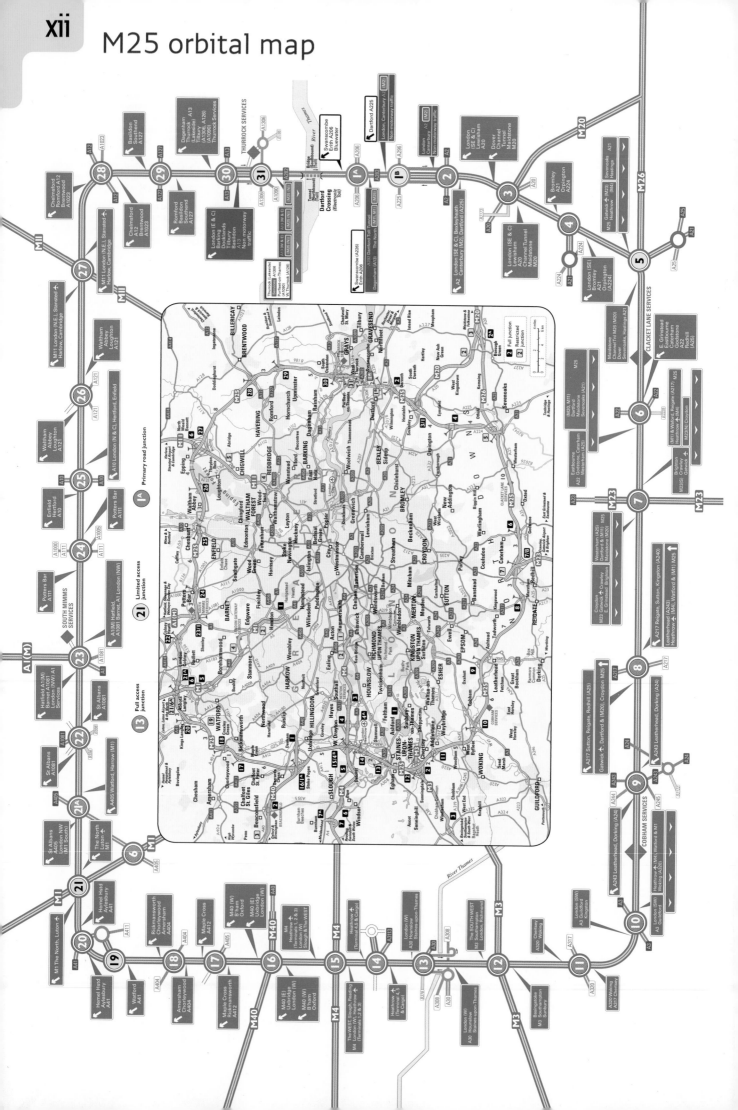

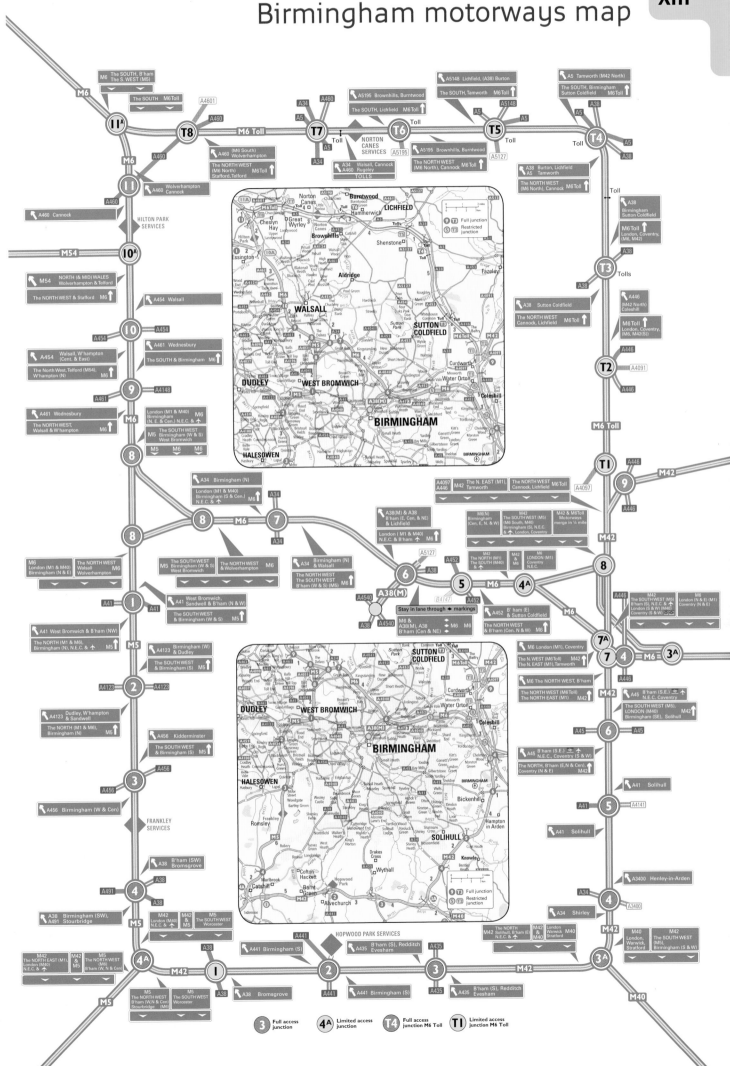

Crash risk map of Great Britain 2017 to 2019

EuroRAP

This map shows the statistical risk of a fatal or serious injury crash occurring on Britain's motorway and 'A' road network from 2017 to 2019, although some of the roads shown have had improvements made to them recently. This network represents less than 15% of Britain's total road length, but around 60% of fatal road crashes, and more than 40% of serious road crashes, occur on these roads.

The risk is calculated by comparing the frequency of road crashes resulting in fatal or serious injury on every stretch of road with how much traffic each road is carrying (although a different scaling factor is used to determine the banding depending on whether the route is primarily rural or primarily urban). Two routes of the same length and with the same number of crashes on them (with the same rurality) may therefore have different levels of risk due to differences in traffic flows: **the risk bandings indicate the individual risk to users of the route.**

The map excludes some roads that are not statistically robust enough for analysis, shown in grey, and minor 'A' roads in central London and roads for which no traffic data are available, both shown in white.

For more information on the Road Safety Foundation go to **www.roadsafetyfoundation.org.**
For more information on the statistical background to this research, visit the EuroRAP website at **www.eurorap.org.**

Road Assessment Programme Risk Rating

- Low risk (safest) roads
- Low–medium risk roads
- Medium risk roads
- Medium–high risk roads
- High risk roads

- Motorway
- Single and dual carriageway

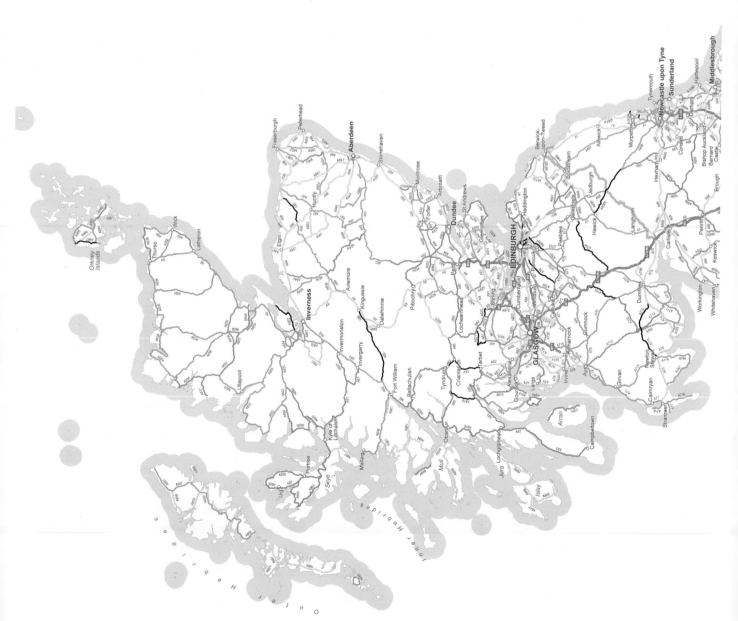

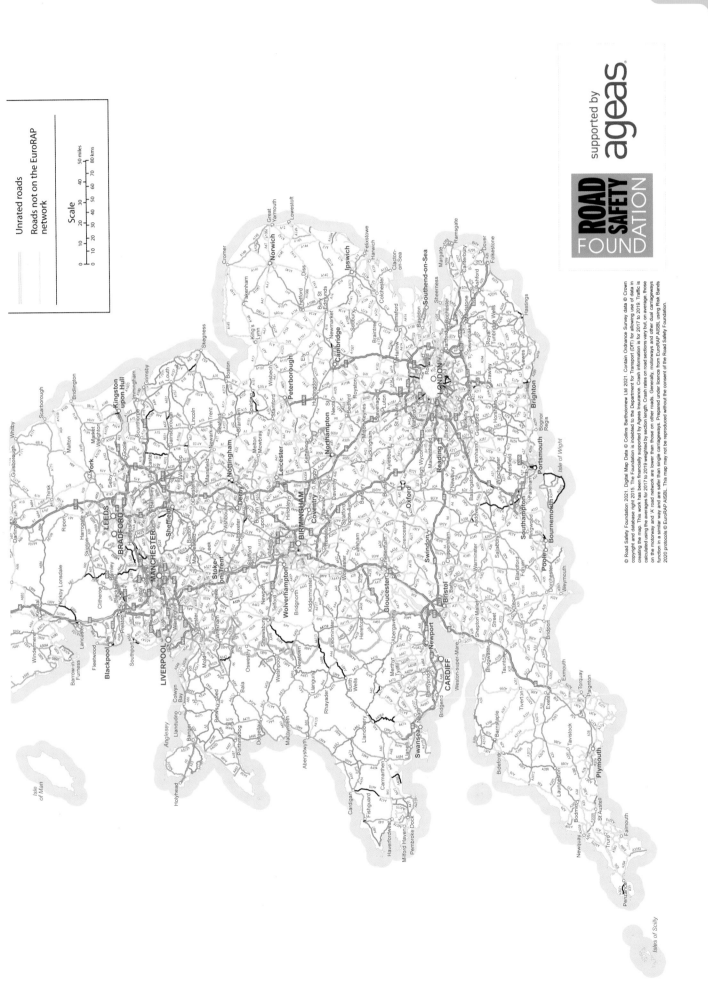

Unrated roads

Roads not on the EuroRAP network

Scale

| 0 | 10 | 20 | 30 | 40 | 50 miles |
| 0 | 10 | 20 | 30 | 40 | 50 | 60 | 70 | 80 kms |

supported by
ageas®

ROAD SAFETY FOUNDATION

Distance chart

Distances between two selected towns in this table are shown in miles and kilometres.
In general, distances are based on the shortest routes by classified roads.

Distance in kilometres

Distance in miles

Symbols used on the map

Blue place of interest symbols e.g ★ are listed on page 93

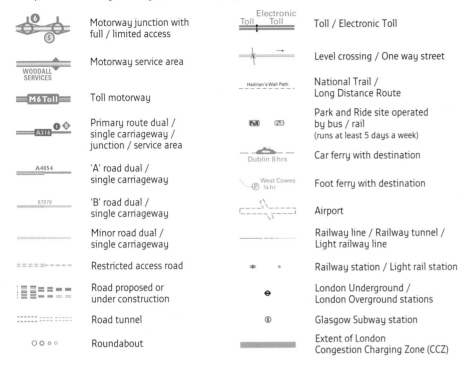

	Motorway junction with full / limited access
WOODALL SERVICES	Motorway service area
M6 Toll	Toll motorway
A316	Primary route dual / single carriageway / junction / service area
A4054	'A' road dual / single carriageway
B7078	'B' road dual / single carriageway
	Minor road dual / single carriageway
	Restricted access road
	Road proposed or under construction
	Road tunnel
○○○○	Roundabout

Toll / Electronic Toll	Toll / Electronic Toll
	Level crossing / One way street
Hadrian's Wall Path	National Trail / Long Distance Route
P&R P&R	Park and Ride site operated by bus / rail (runs at least 5 days a week)
Dublin 8 hrs	Car ferry with destination
West Cowes ¼ hr	Foot ferry with destination
	Airport
	Railway line / Railway tunnel / Light railway line
	Railway station / Light rail station
⊖	London Underground / London Overground stations
Ⓢ	Glasgow Subway station
	Extent of London Congestion Charging Zone (CCZ)

· · · · · · · · ·	Extent of London Low Emission Zone (LEZ)
· · · · · · · · ·	Extent of London Ultra Low Emission Zone (ULEZ)
	Notable building
H	Hospital
362 ▲	Spot height (in metres) / Lighthouse
	Built up area
	Woodland / Park
	National Park
	Heritage Coast
BRISTOL	County / Unitary Authority boundary and name
SEE PAGE 68	Area covered by street map

Locator map

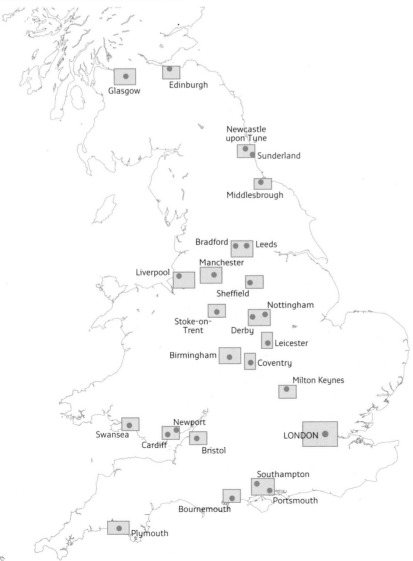

Urban approach maps	
Birmingham	14-15
Bournemouth	3
Bradford	26-27
Bristol	8
Cardiff	7
Coventry	16
Derby	18-19
Edinburgh	32
Glasgow	30-31
Greater Manchester	24-25
Leeds	26-27
Leicester	17
Liverpool	22-23
London	10-13
Manchester	24-25
Merseyside	22-23
Middlesbrough	29
Milton Keynes	9
Newcastle upon Tyne	28-29
Newport	7
Nottingham	18-19
Plymouth	2
Portsmouth	4-5
Sheffield	21
Southampton	4-5
Stoke-on-Trent	20
Sunderland	28-29
Swansea	6
West Midlands	14-15

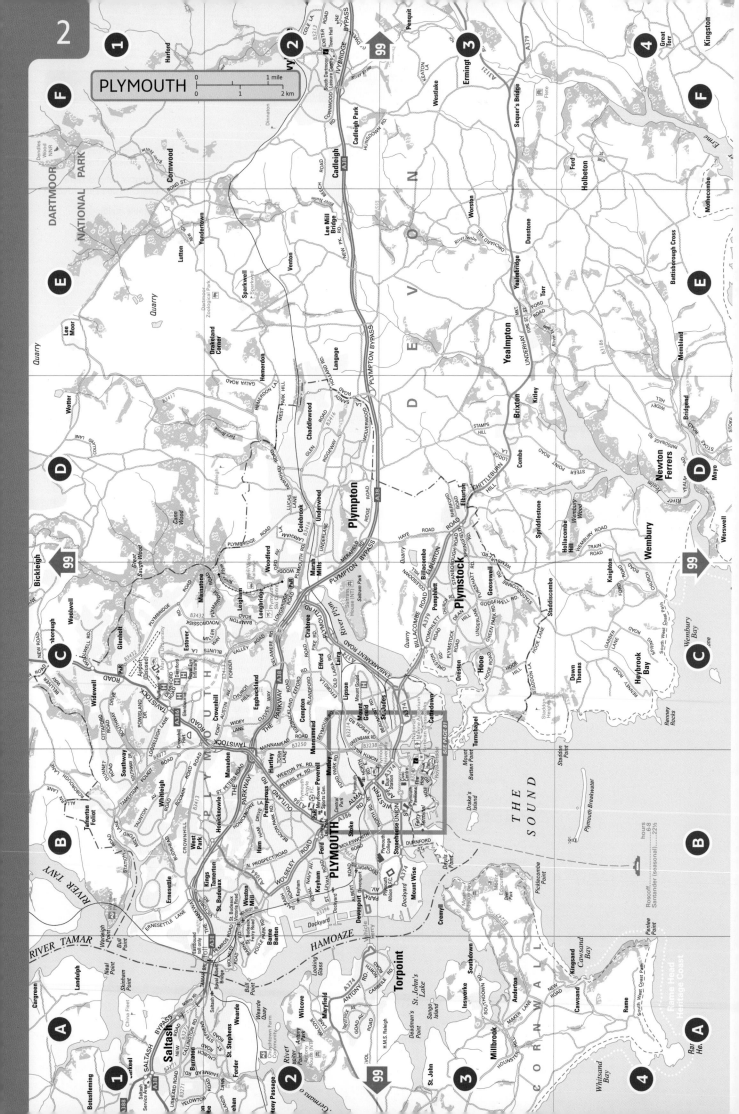

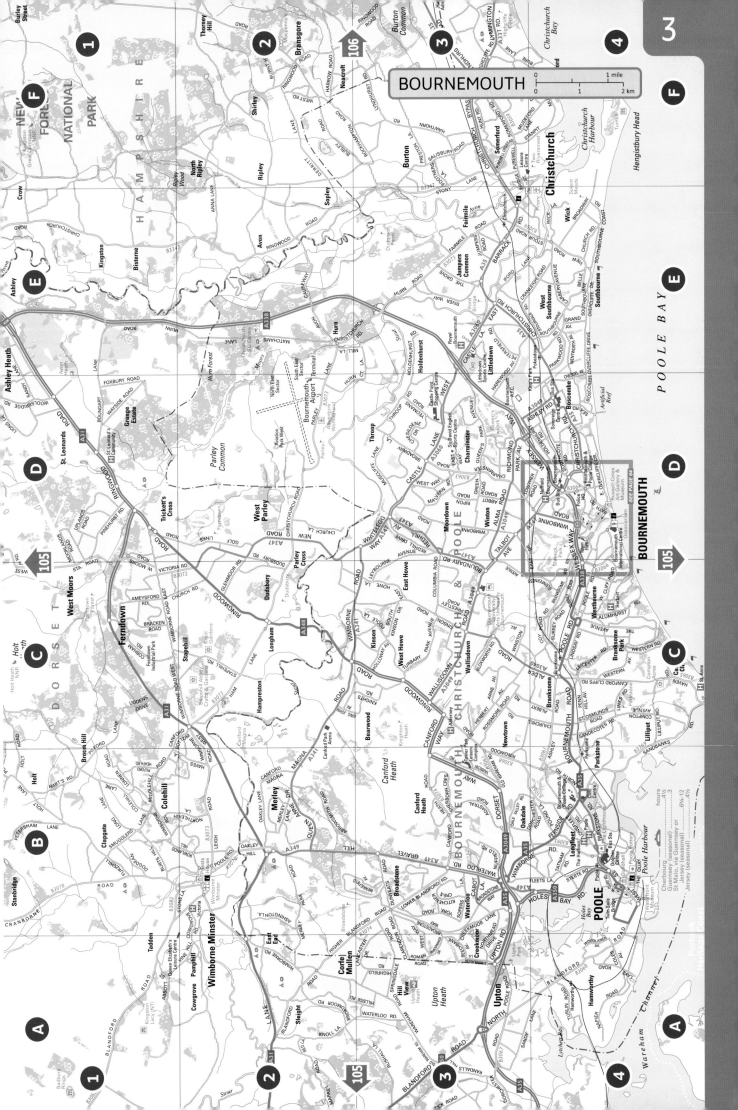

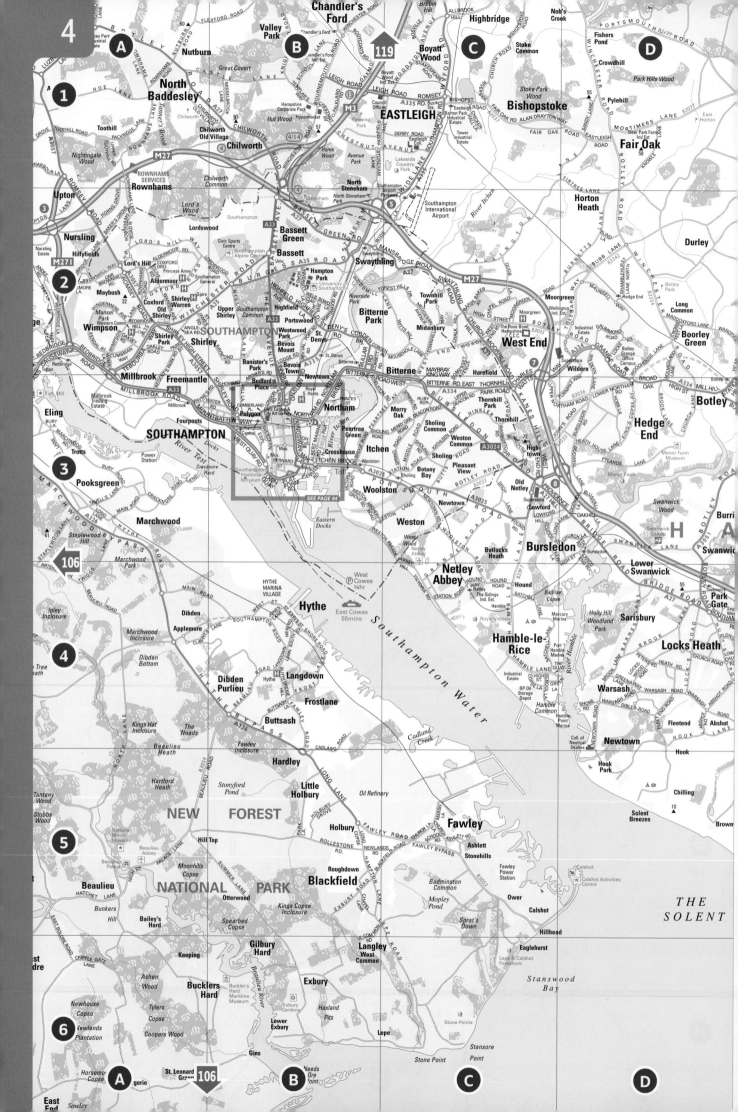

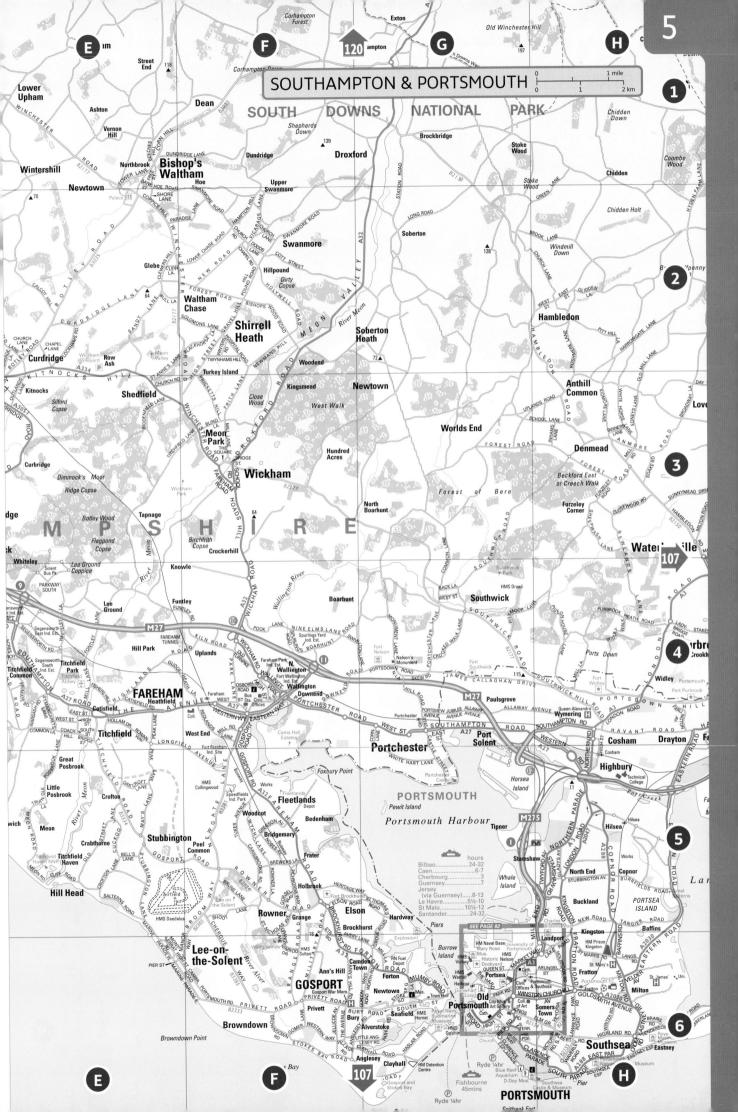

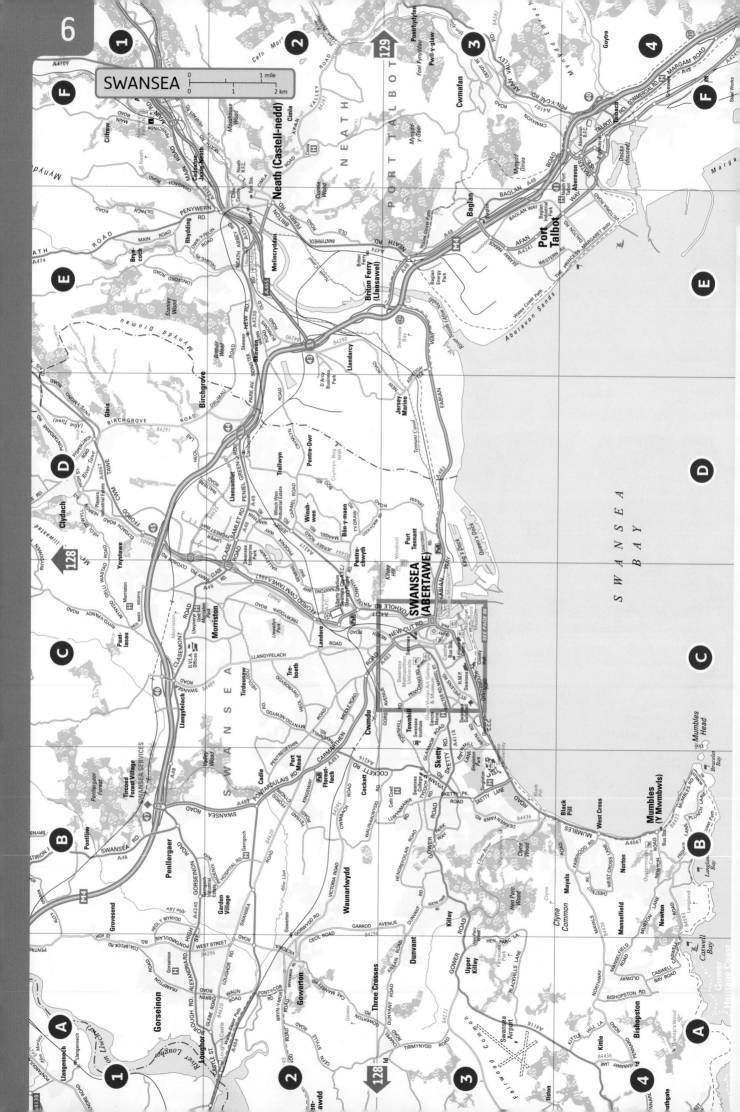

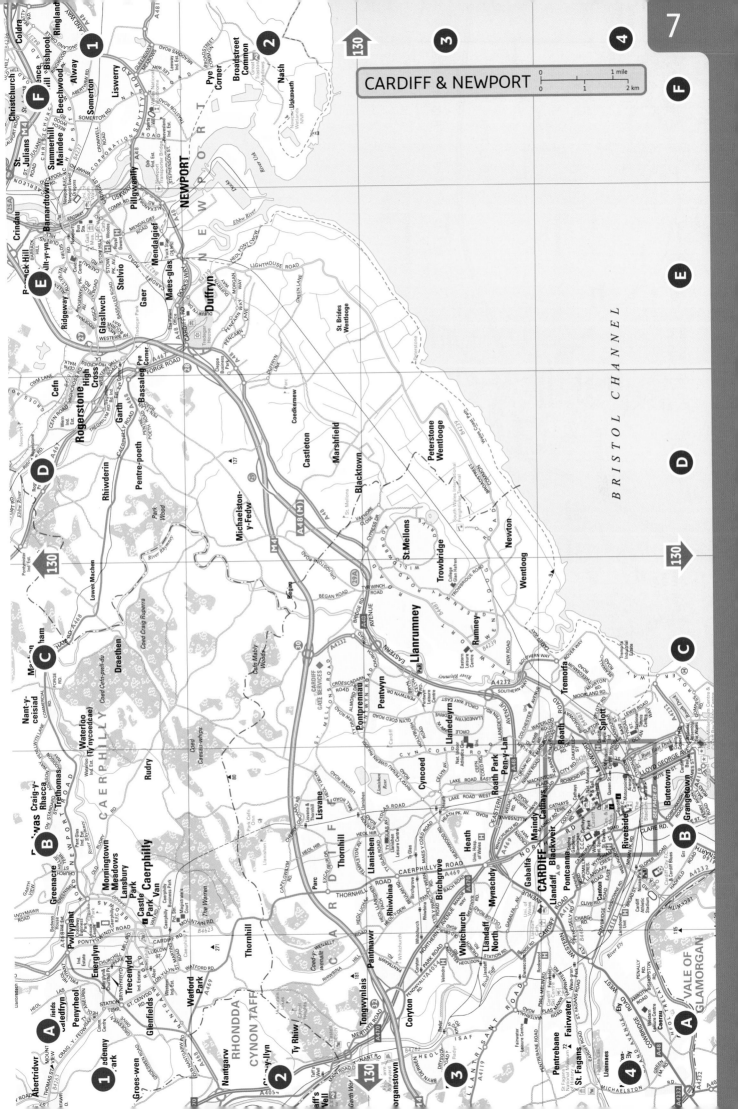

CARDIFF & NEWPORT

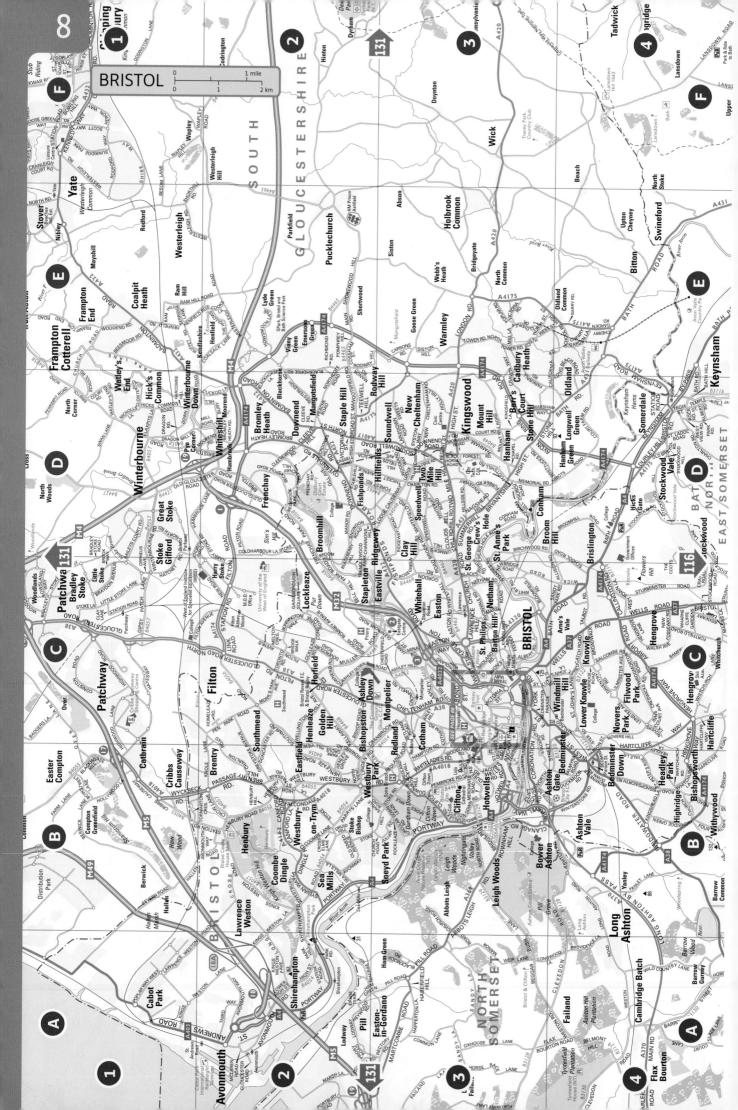

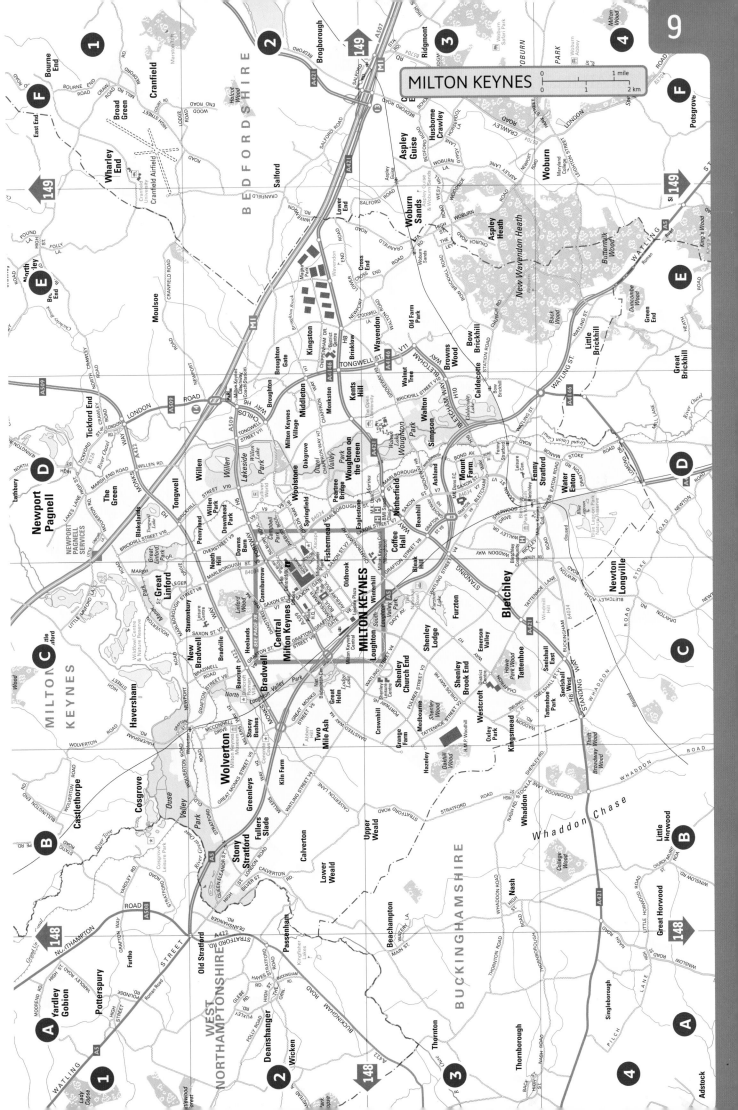

MILTON KEYNES

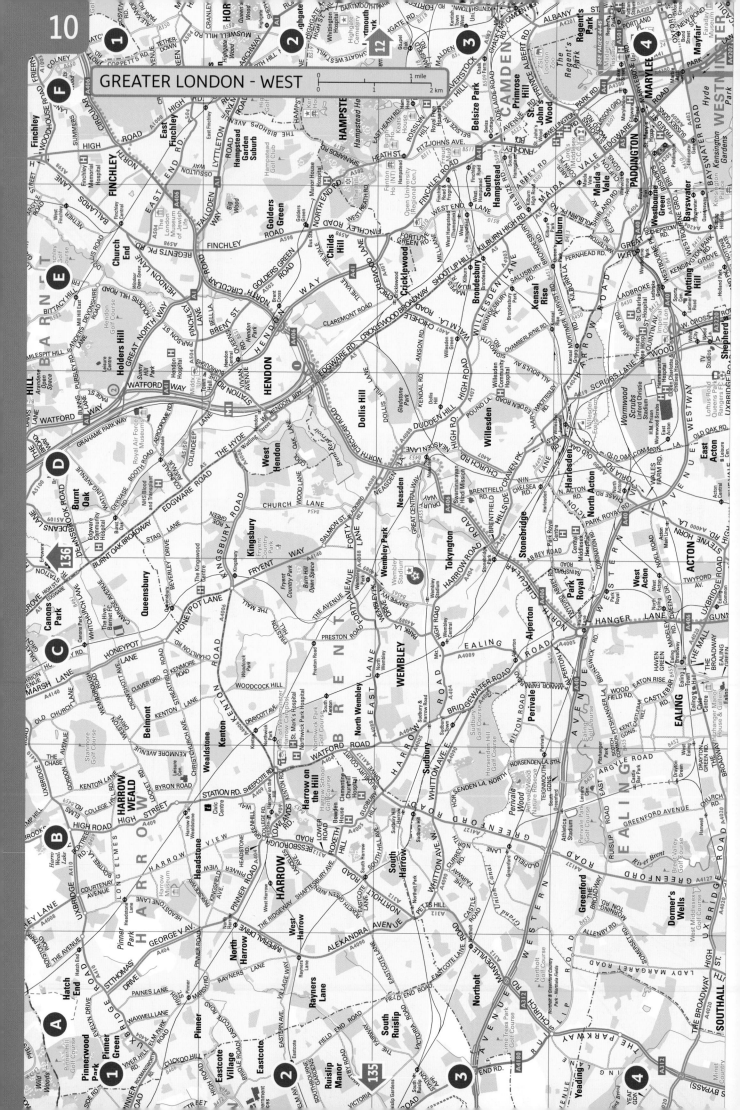

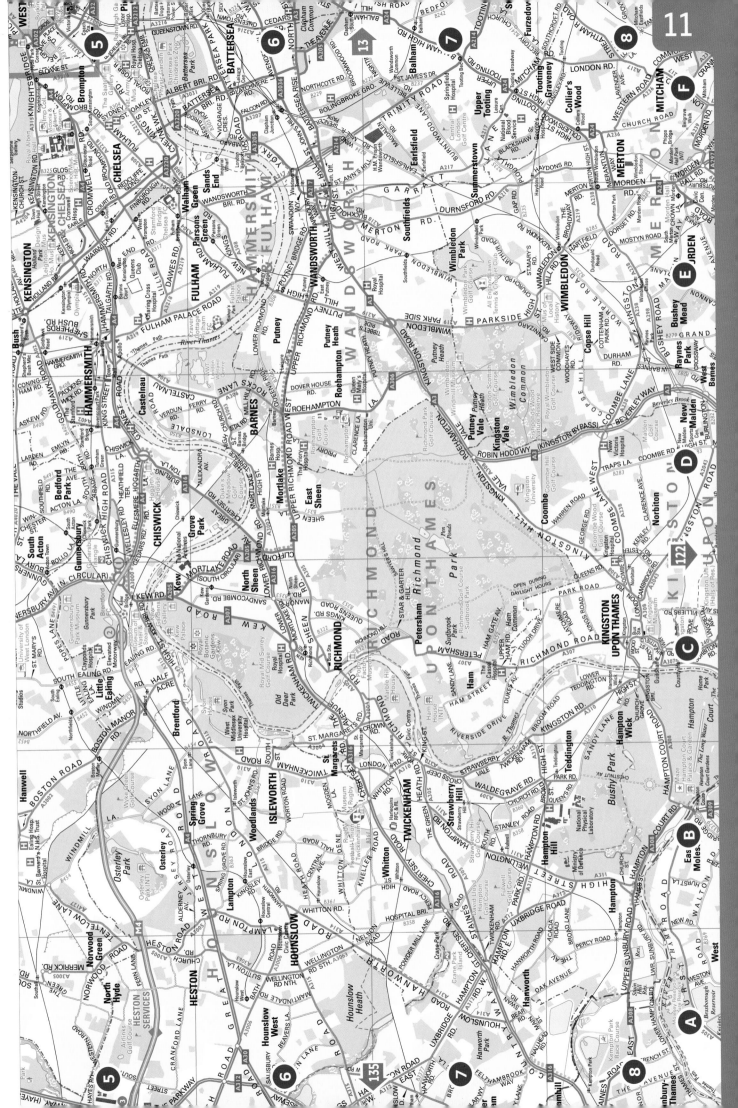

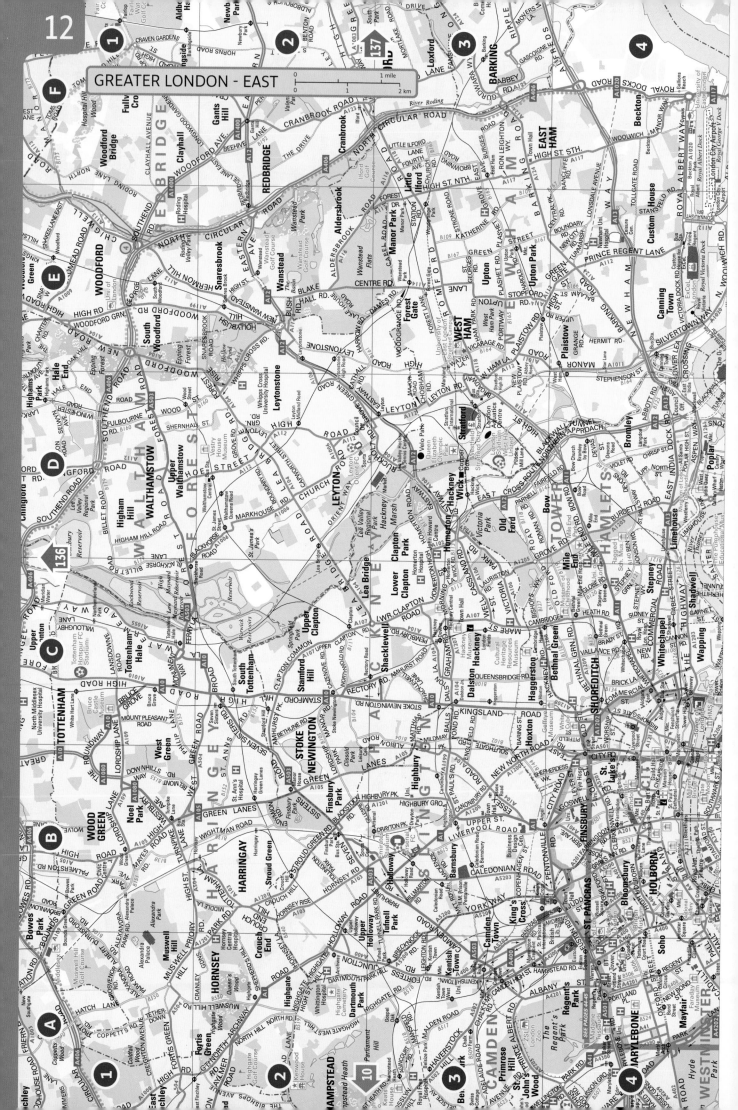

GREATER LONDON - EAST

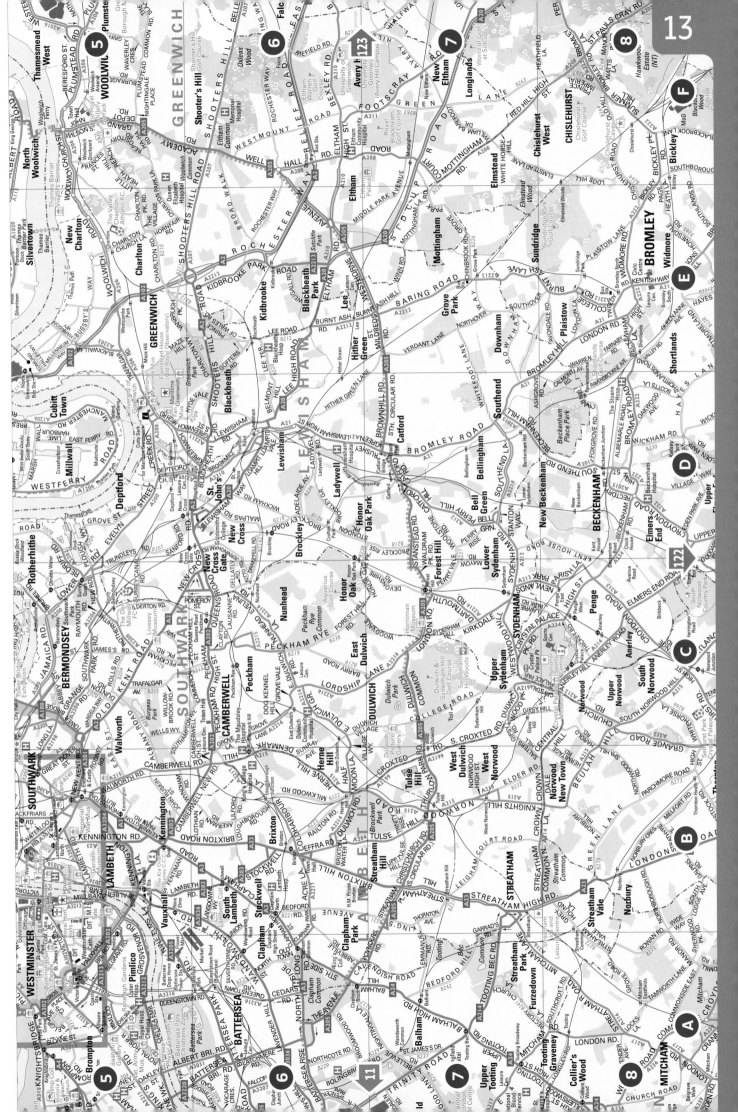

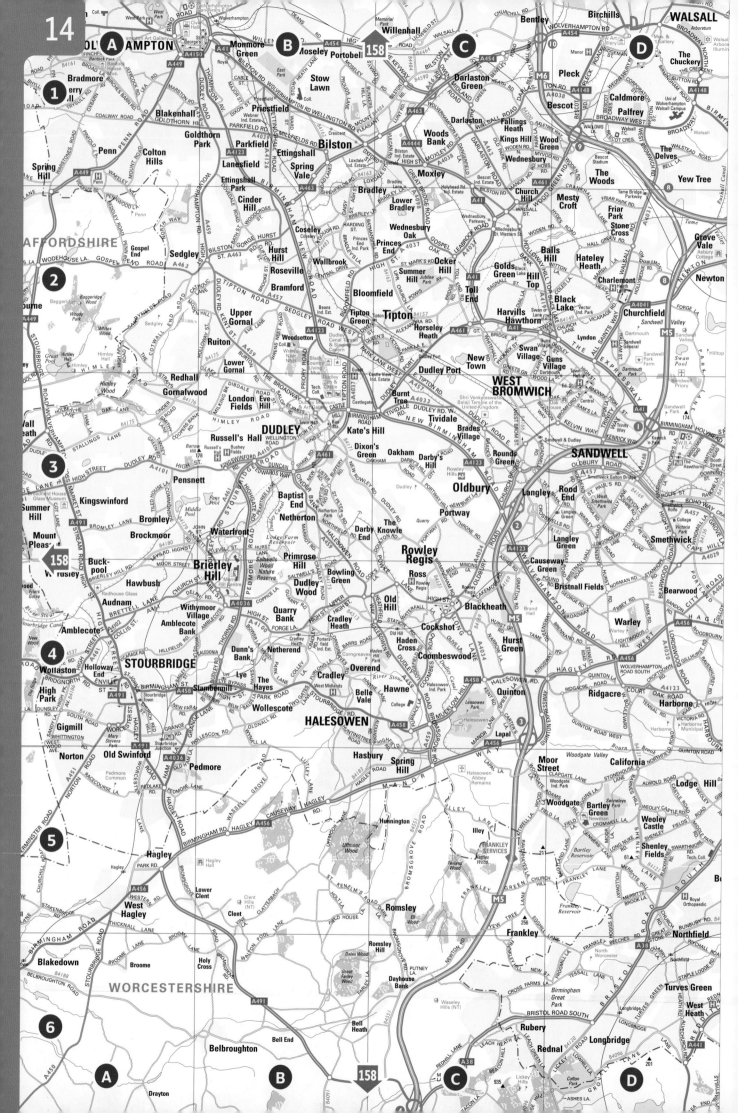

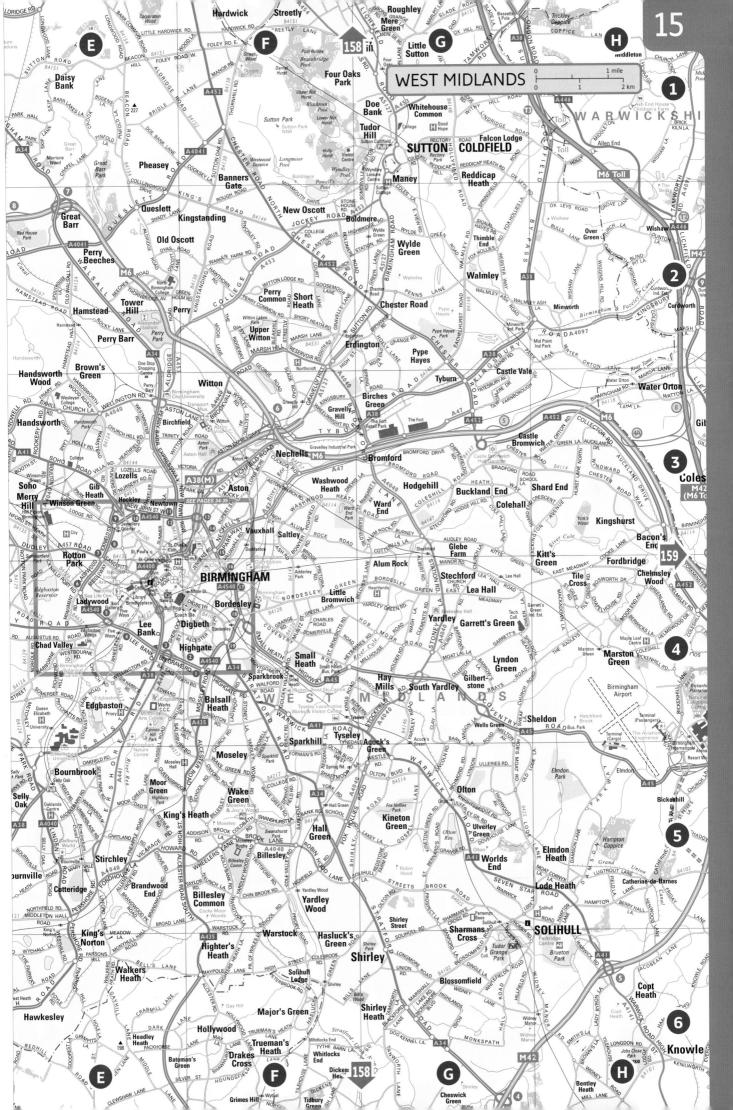

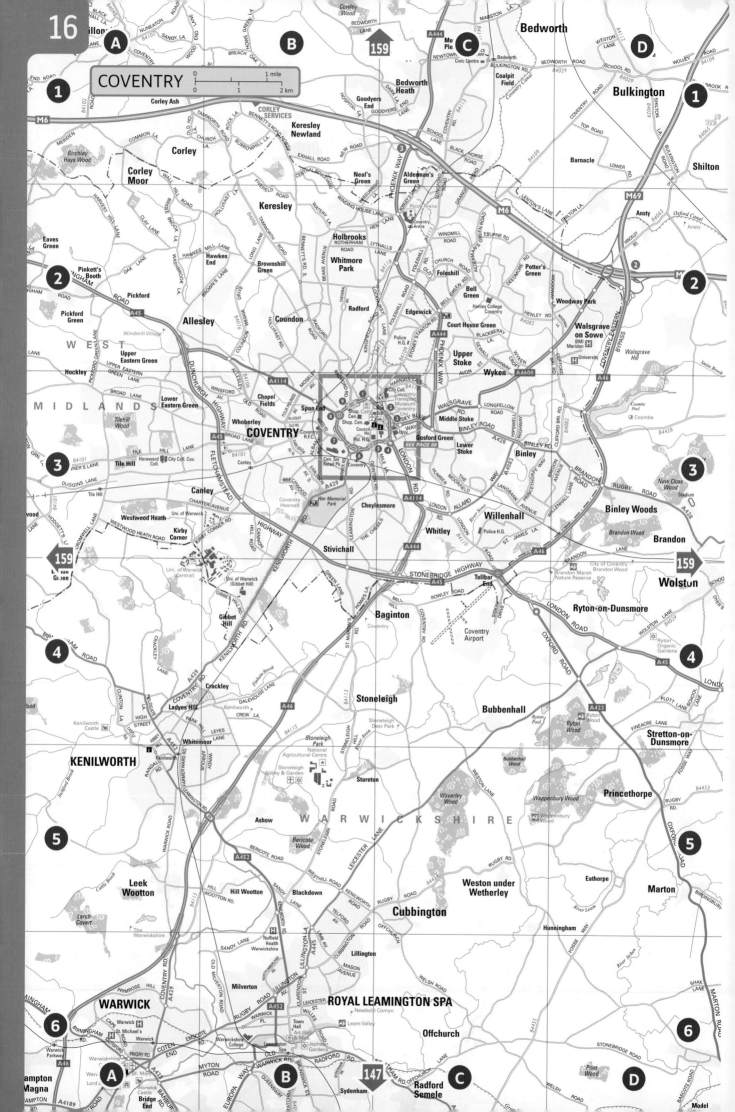

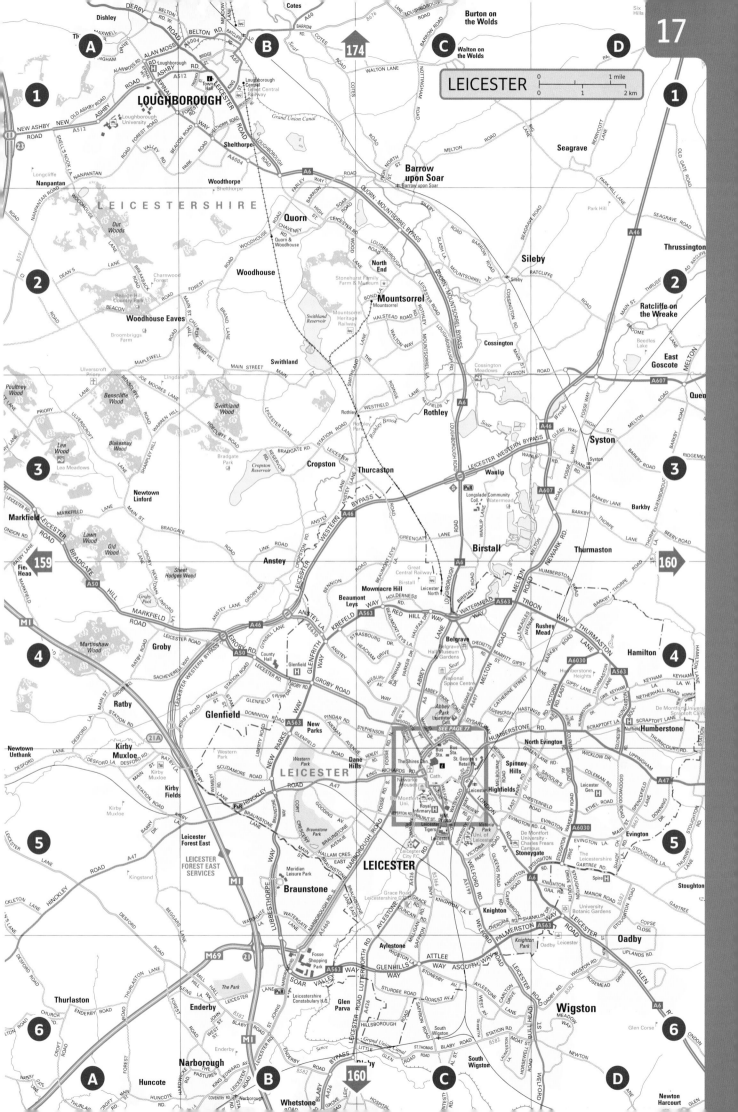

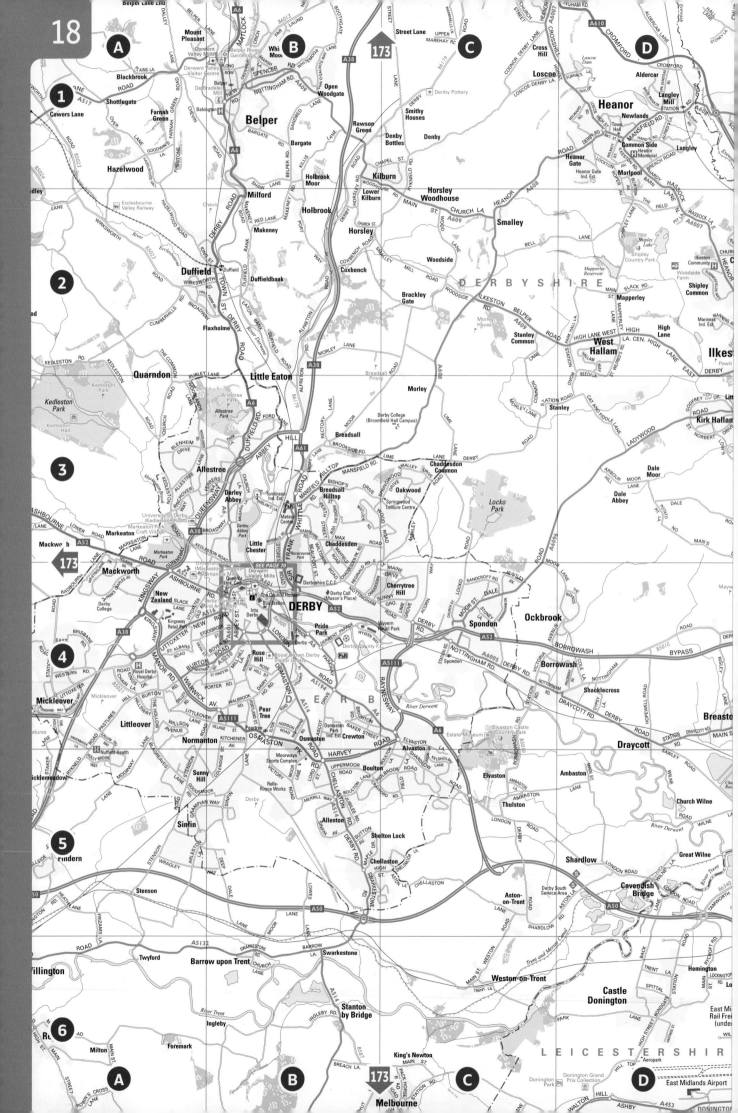

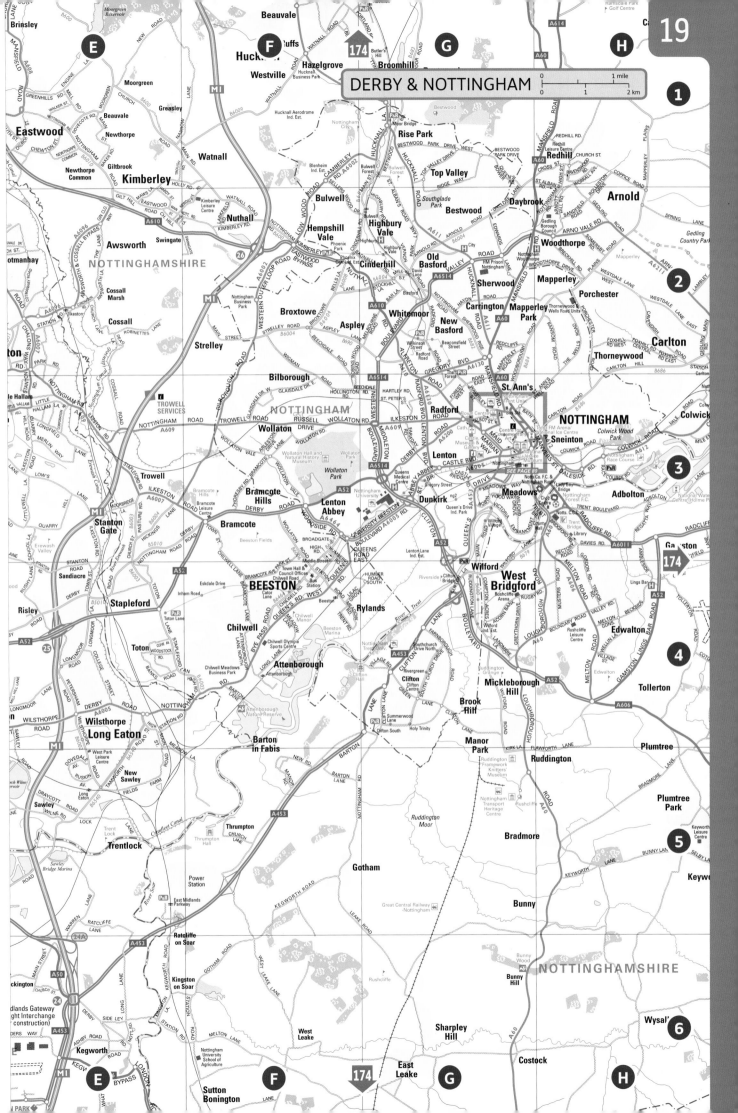

DERBY & NOTTINGHAM

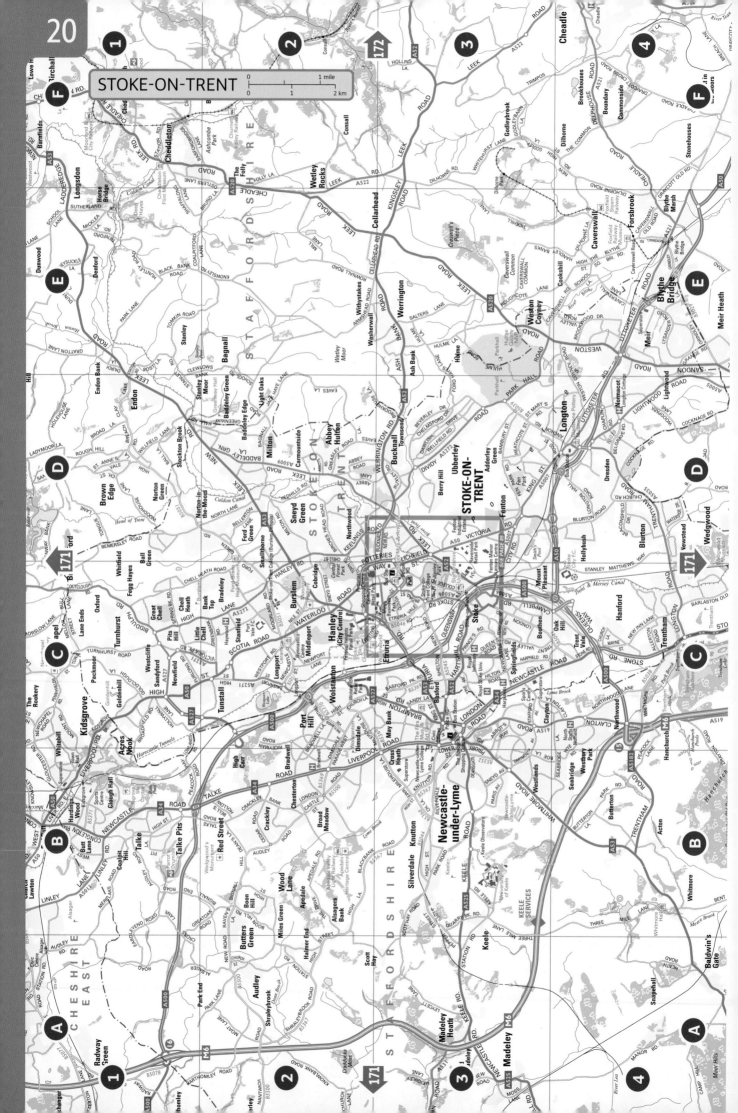

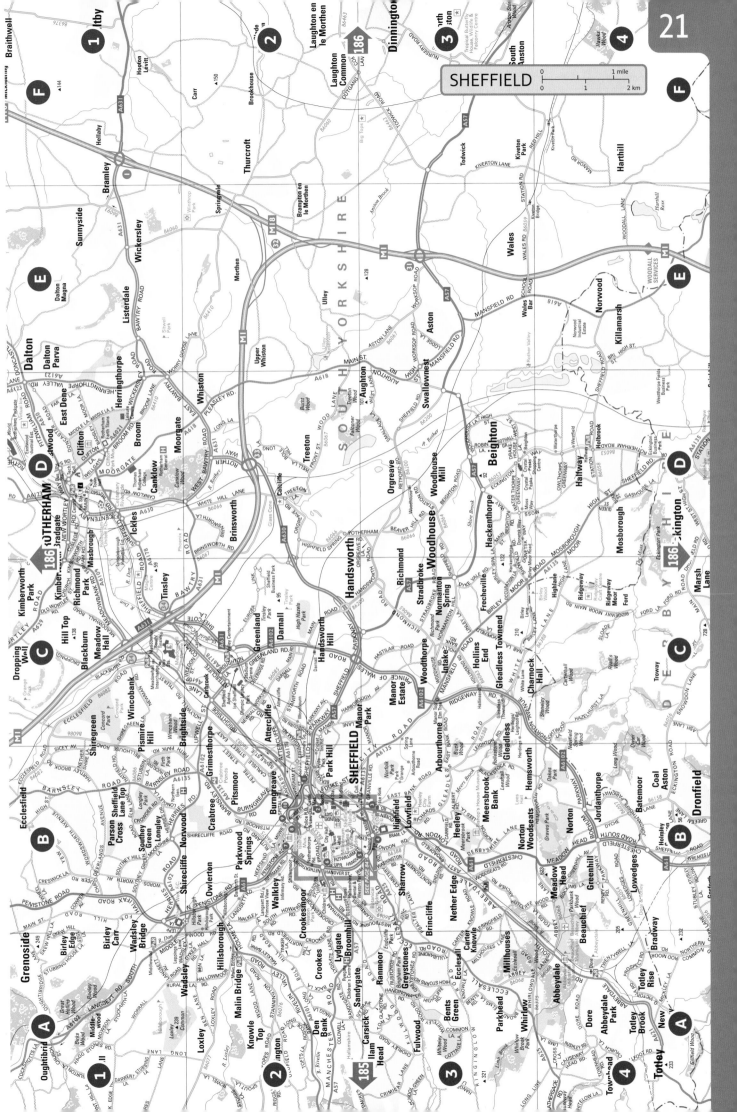

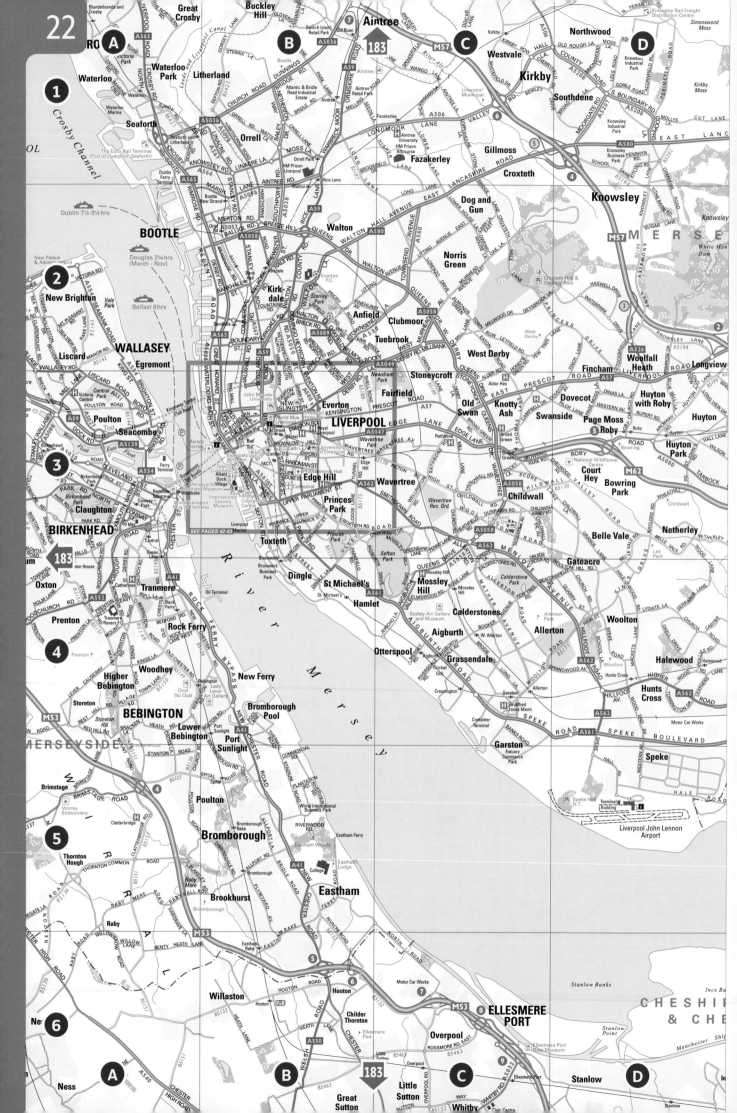

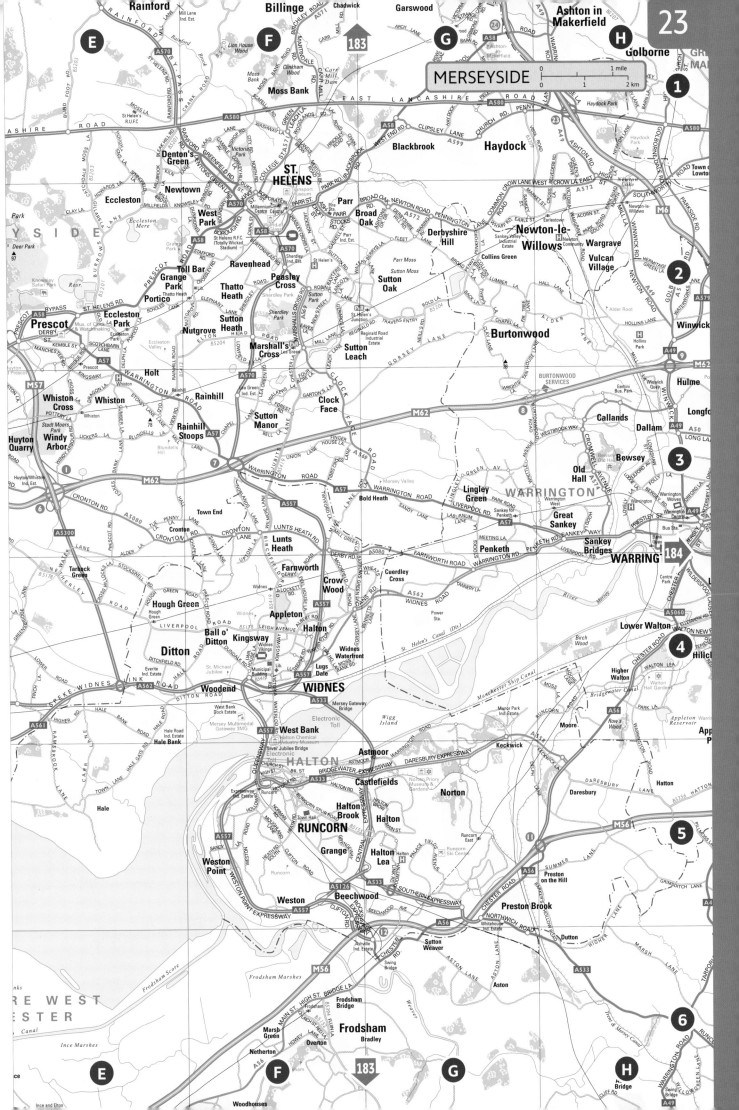

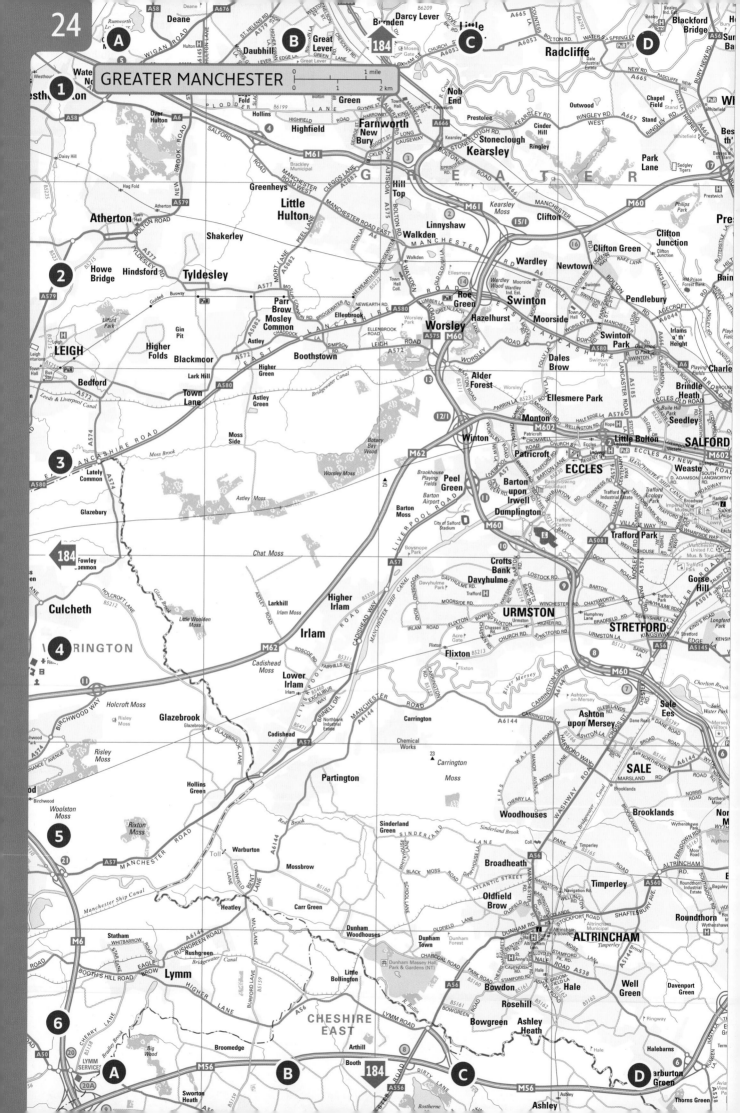

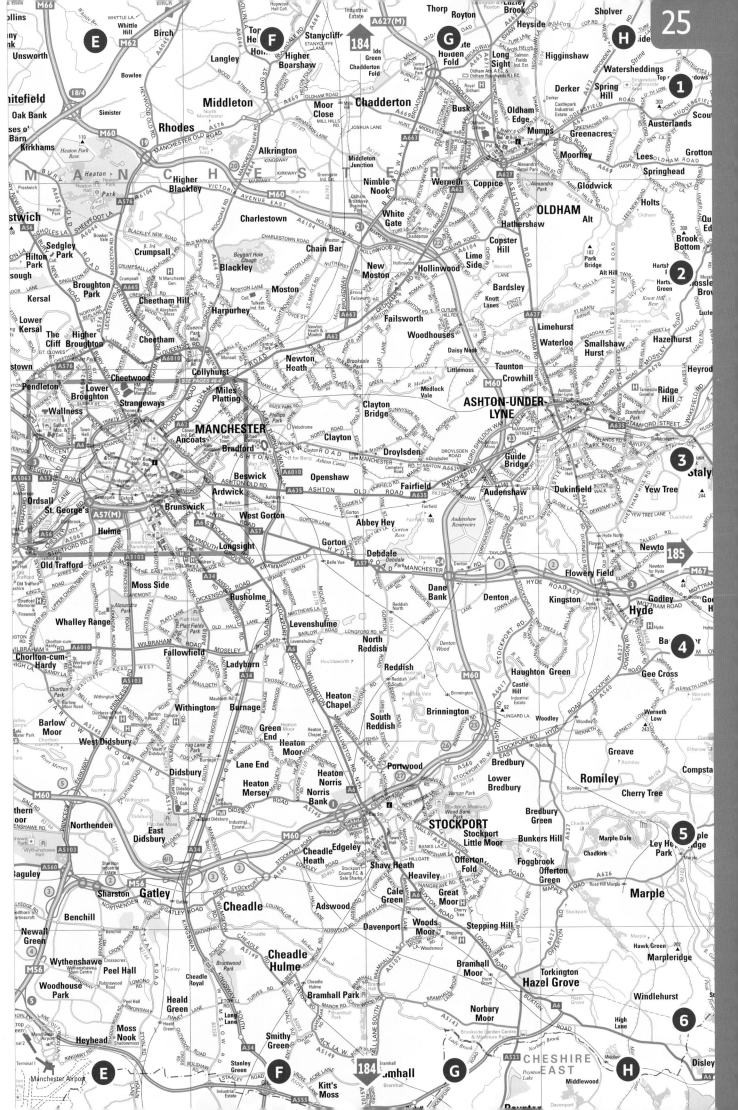

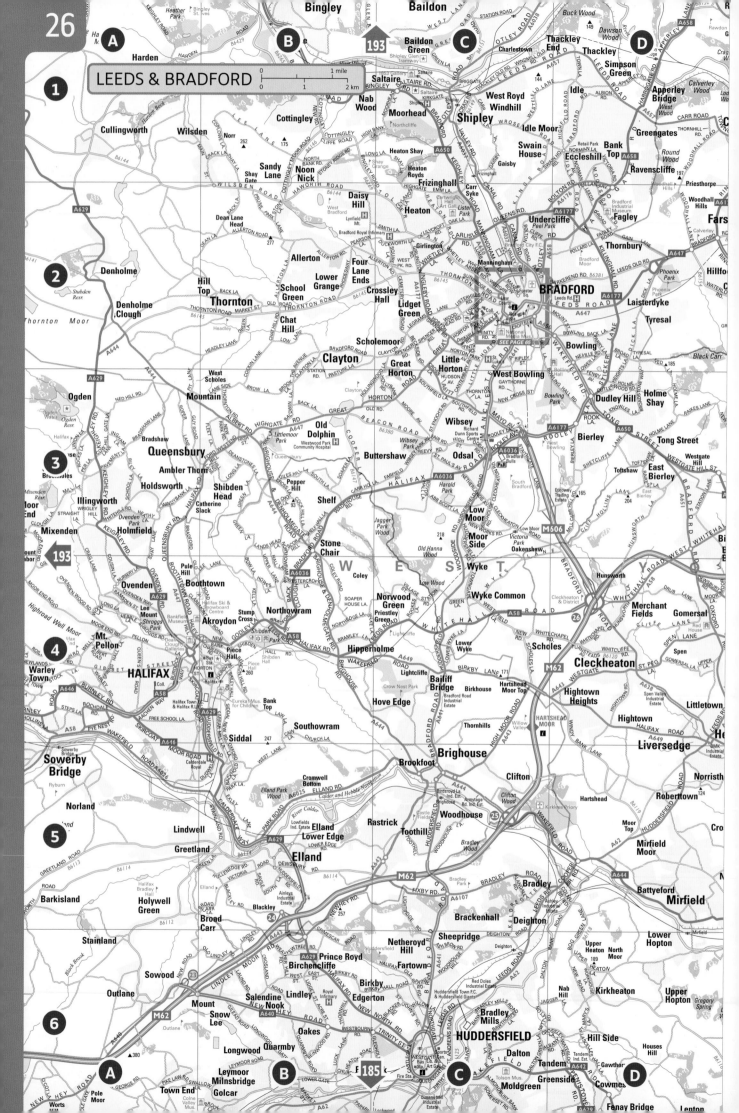

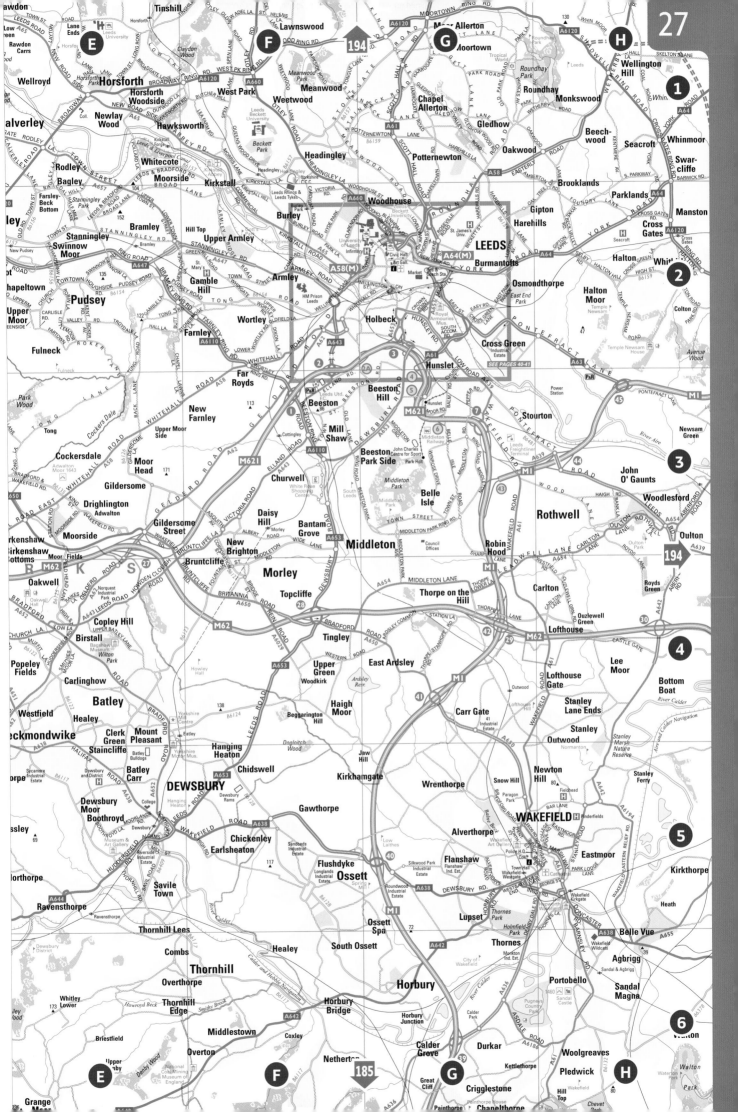

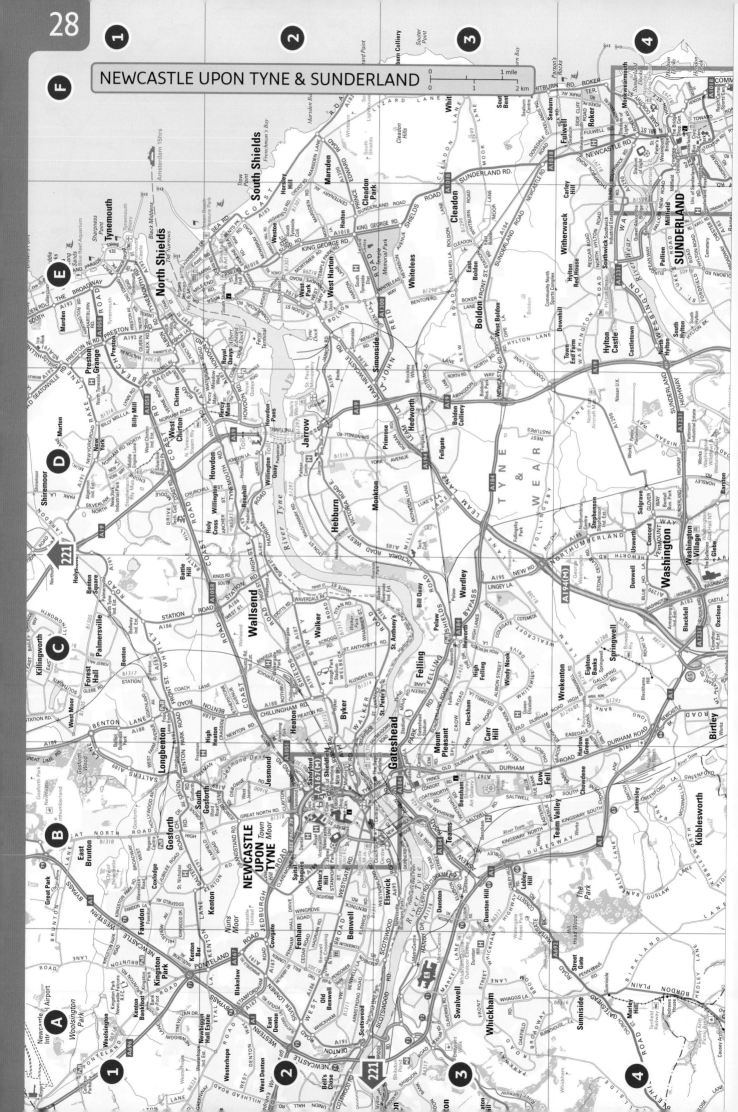

NEWCASTLE UPON TYNE & SUNDERLAND

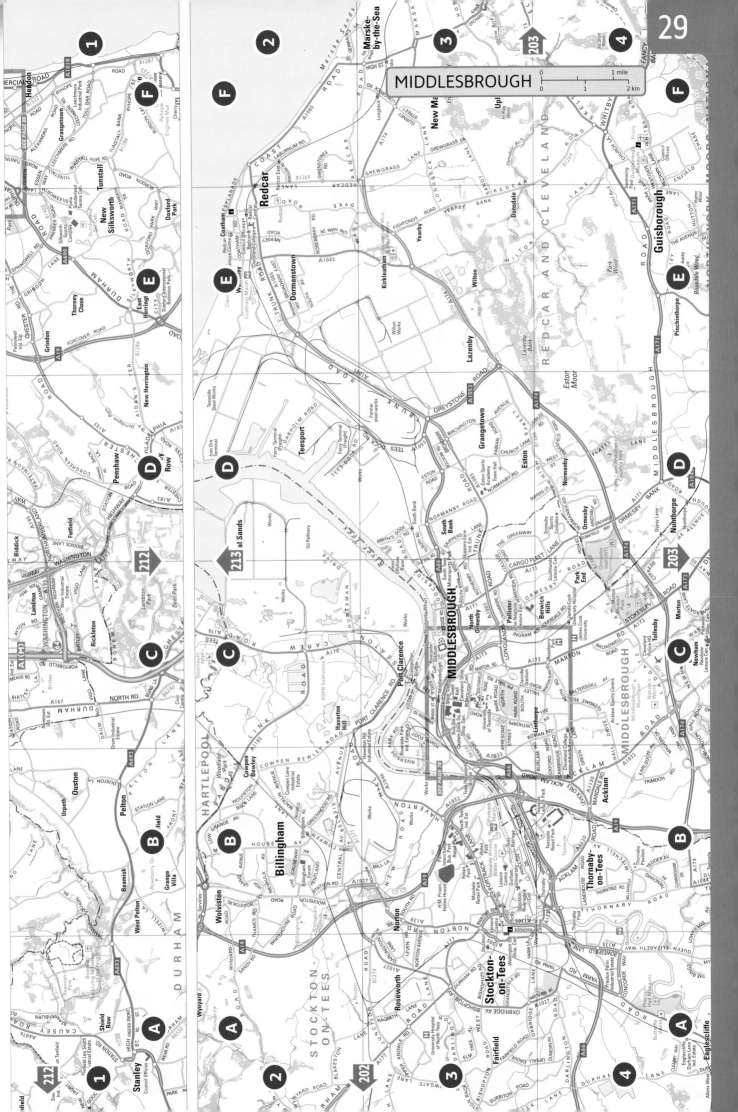

MIDDLESBROUGH

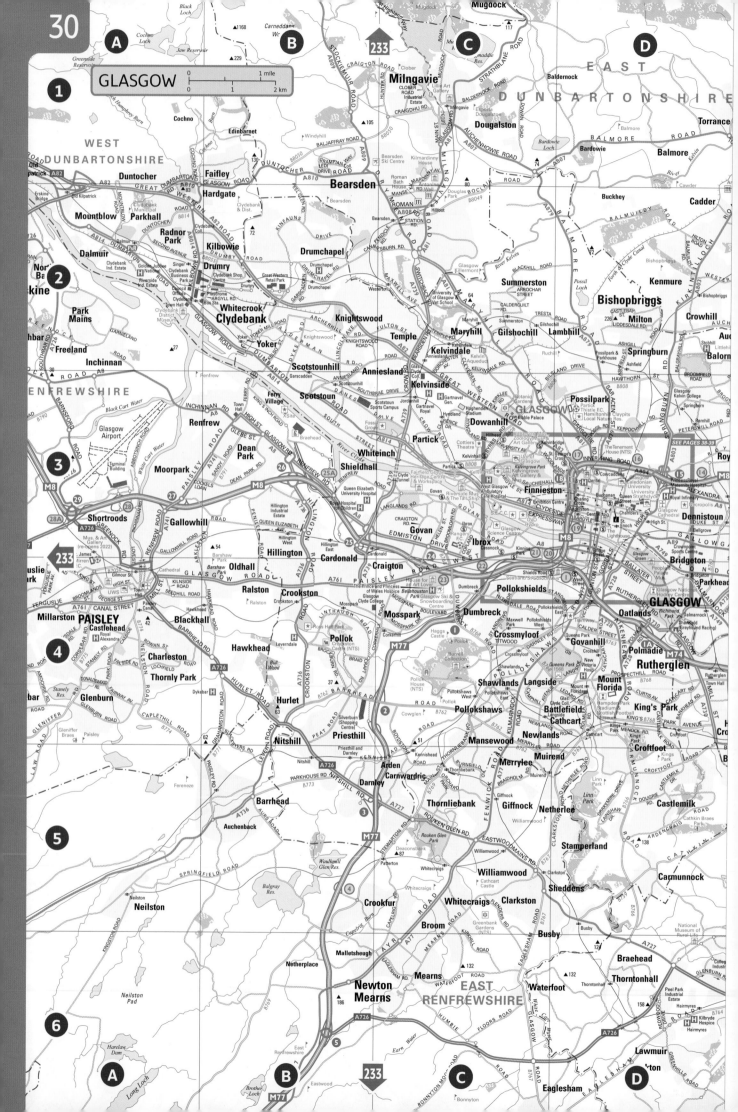

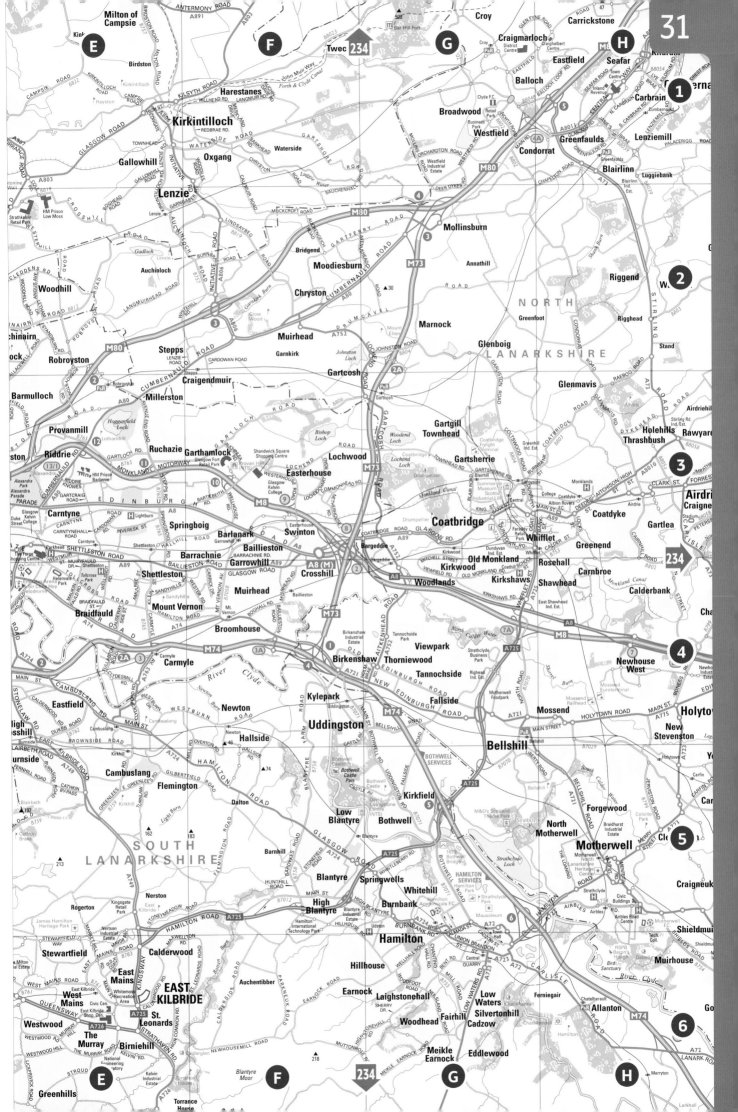

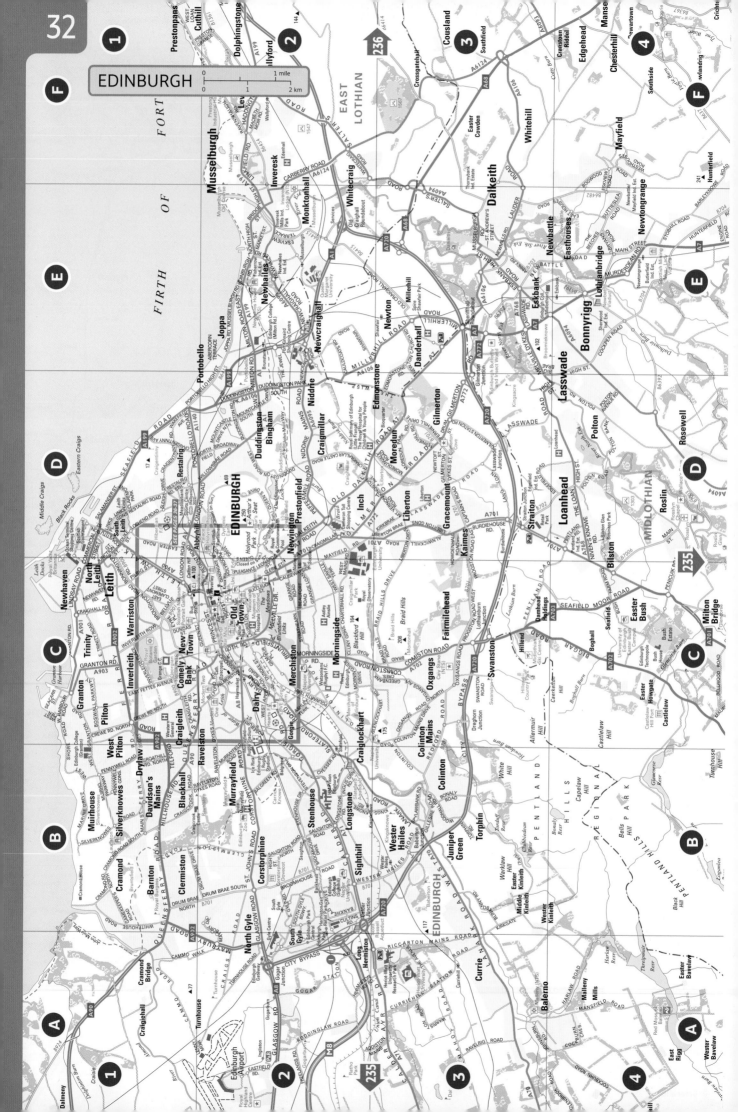

Symbols used on the map

M8	Motorway		Bus / Coach station	JAPAN	Embassy
A4 ❶	Primary route dual / single carriageway / Junction	P&R	Park and Ride site - rail operated (runs at least 5 days a week)		Cinema
A40	'A' road dual / single carriageway		Extent of London congestion charging zone	+	Cathedral / Church
B507	'B' road dual / single carriageway	Douglas 2¾hrs	Vehicle / Pedestrian ferry	☾ ✡ ■ Mormon	Mosque / Synagogue / Other place of worship
Toll	Other road dual / single carriageway / Toll	P P	Car park		Leisure & tourism
→ 7	One way street / Orbital route	☷	Theatre		Shopping
•	Access restriction	☷	Major hotel		Administration & law
	Pedestrian street	◗	Public House		Health & welfare
	Street market	Pol	Police station		Education
	Minor road / Track	Lib	Library		Industry / Office
FB	Footpath / Footbridge	PO	Post Office		Other notable building
	Road under construction	◪ ◪	Visitor information centre (open all year / seasonally)		Park / Garden / Sports ground
⇄ ⇄	Main / other National Rail station	⚇	Toilet	↑↑↑↑	Cemetery
⊖ ⊖	London Underground / Overground station				
Ⓐ	Light Rail / Station				

Locator map

Street maps

Aberdeen	63	Leeds index	52
Belfast	63	Leicester	77
Birmingham	34-35	Lincoln	77
Birmingham index	48	Liverpool	42-43
Blackpool	64	Liverpool index	54
Bournemouth	64	London	44-45
Bradford	65	London index	56
Brighton	65	Manchester	46-47
Bristol	66	Manchester index	60
Cambridge	66	Middlesbrough	78
Canterbury	67	Milton Keynes	78
Cardiff	67	Newcastle upon Tyne	79
Carlisle	68	Norwich	79
Cheltenham	68	Nottingham	80
Chester	69	Oxford	80
Coventry	69	Perth	81
Derby	70	Plymouth	81
Dover	70	Portsmouth	82
Dundee	71	Reading	82
Durham	71	Salisbury	83
Eastbourne	72	Scarborough	83
Edinburgh	36-37	Sheffield	84
Edinburgh index	49	Southampton	84
Exeter	72	Stoke-on-Trent	85
Folkestone	73	Stratford-upon-Avon	85
Glasgow	38-39	Sunderland	86
Glasgow index	51	Swansea	86
Gloucester	73	Swindon	87
Guildford	74	Torquay	87
Harrogate	74	Watford	88
Hastings	75	Weston-super-Mare	88
Hereford	75	Winchester	89
Hull (Kingston upon Hull)	76	Windsor	89
Inverness	76	Worcester	90
Leeds	40-41	York	90

Airport plans

Birmingham	91
Gatwick	91
Glasgow	91
Heathrow	91
Manchester	91
Stansted	91

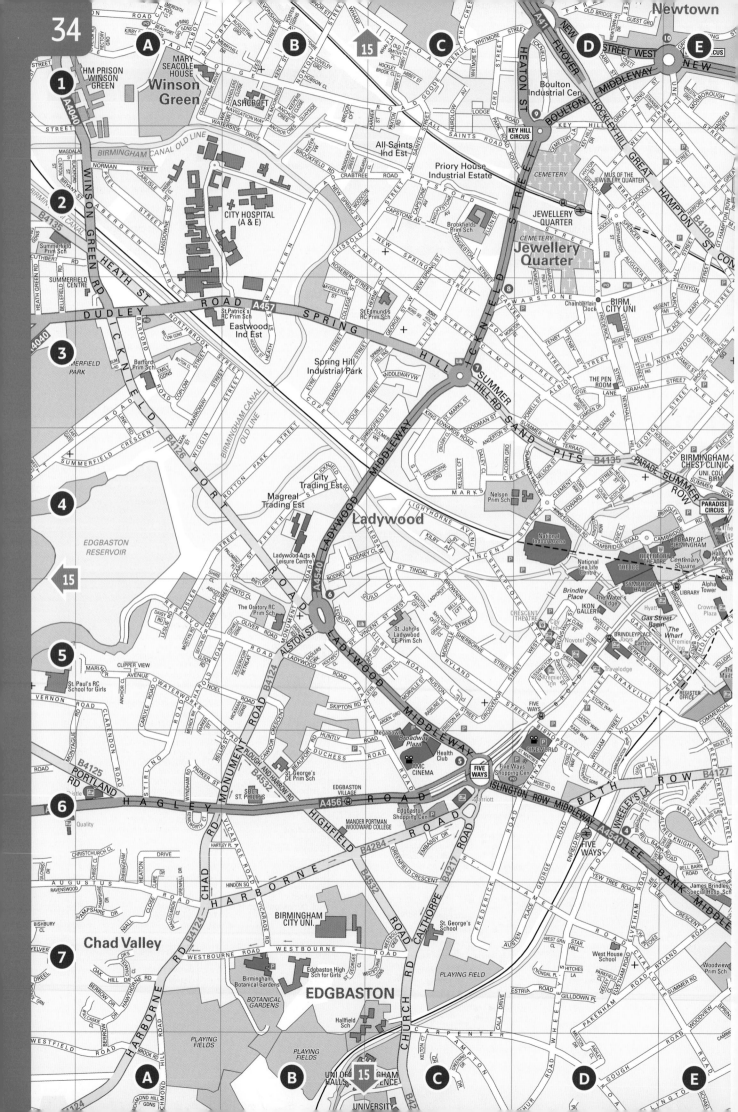

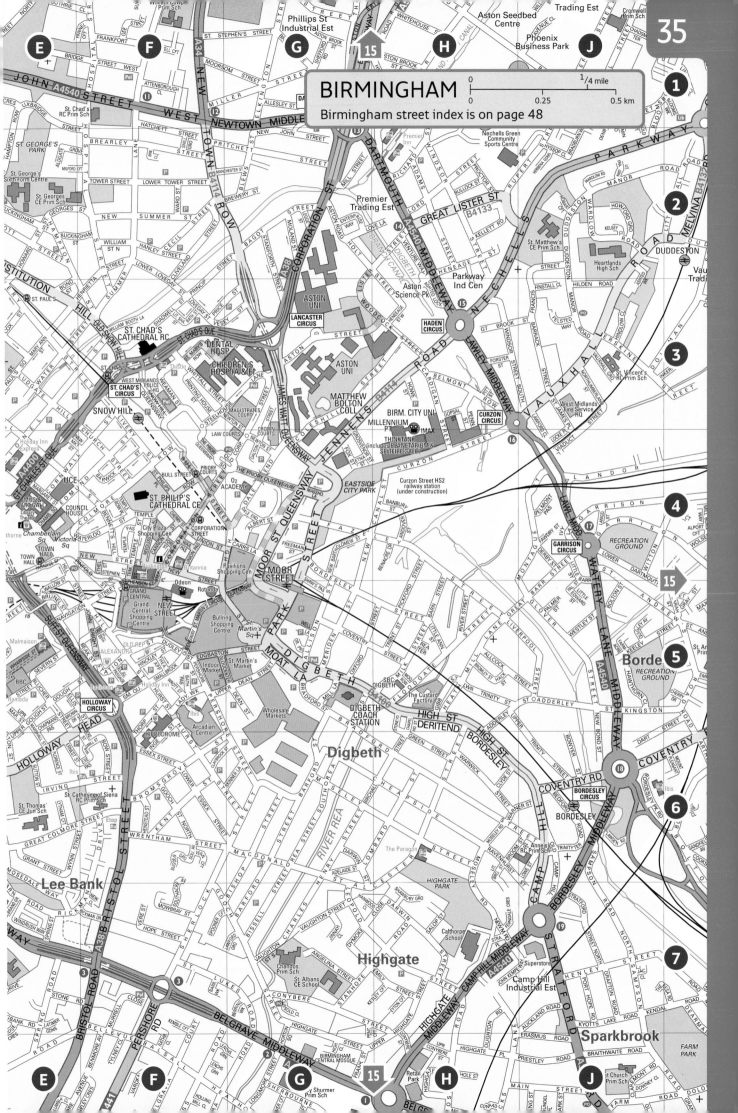

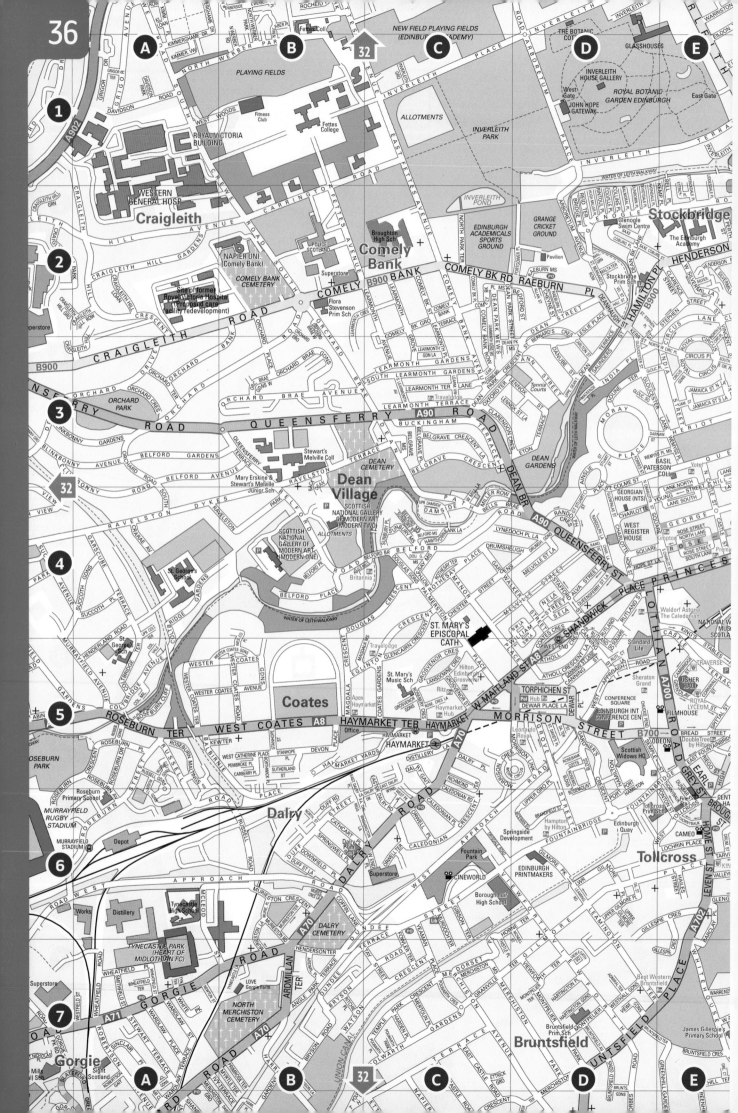

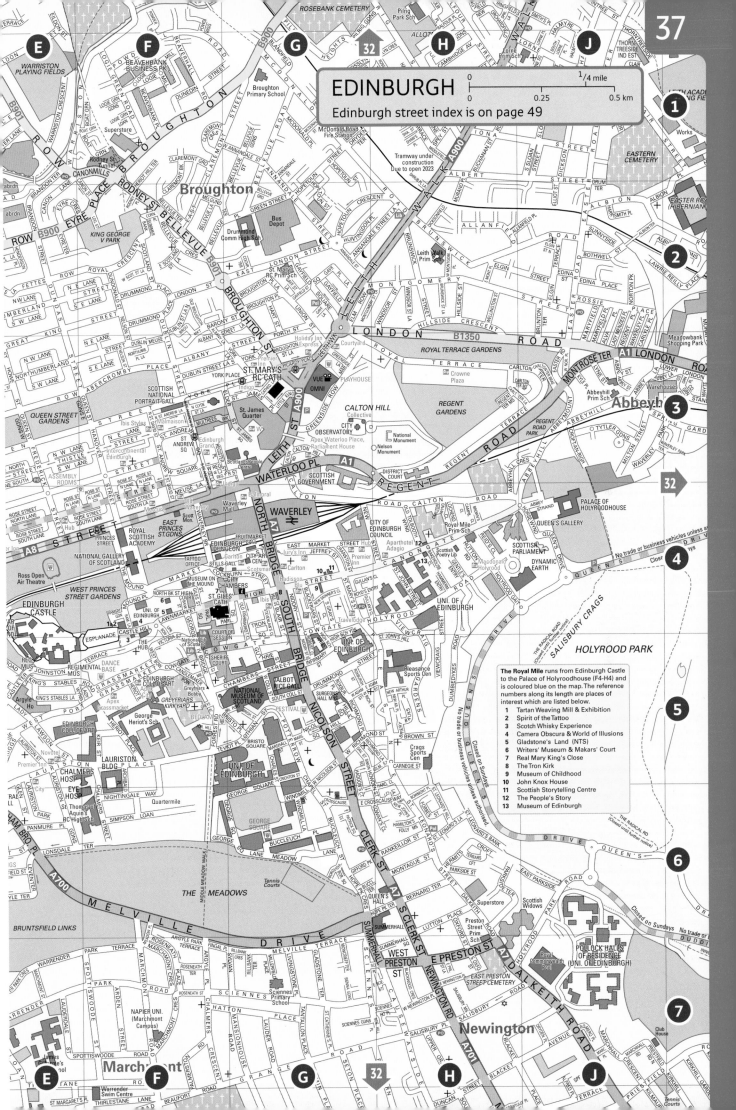

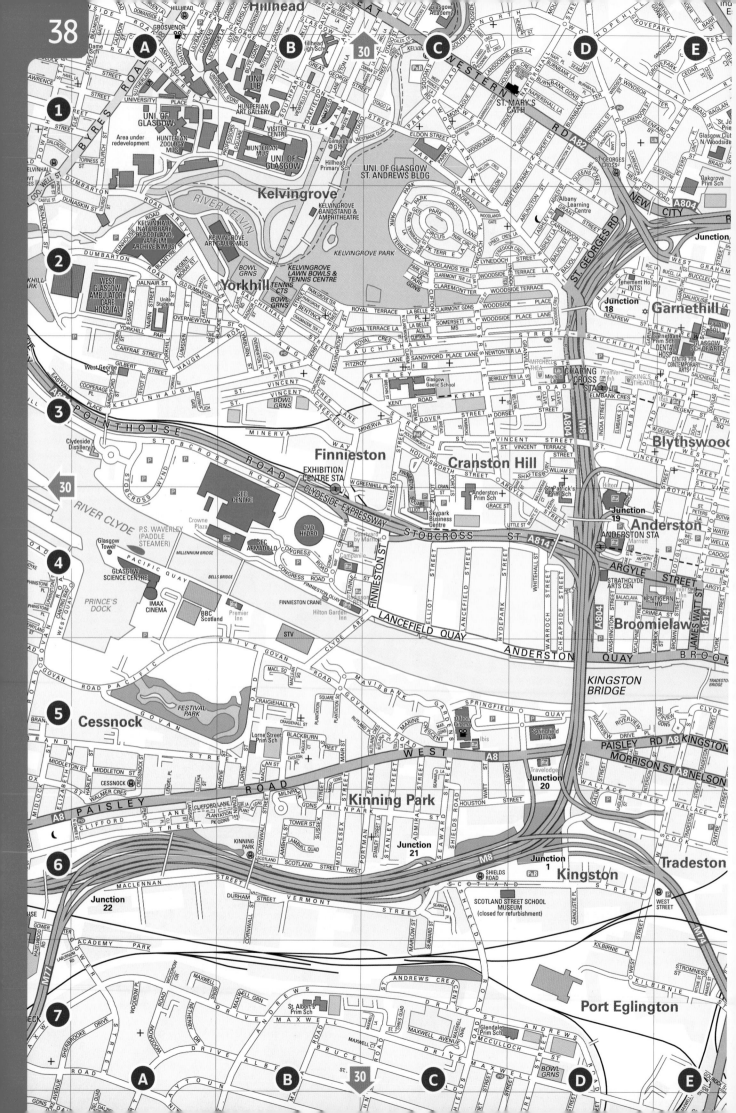

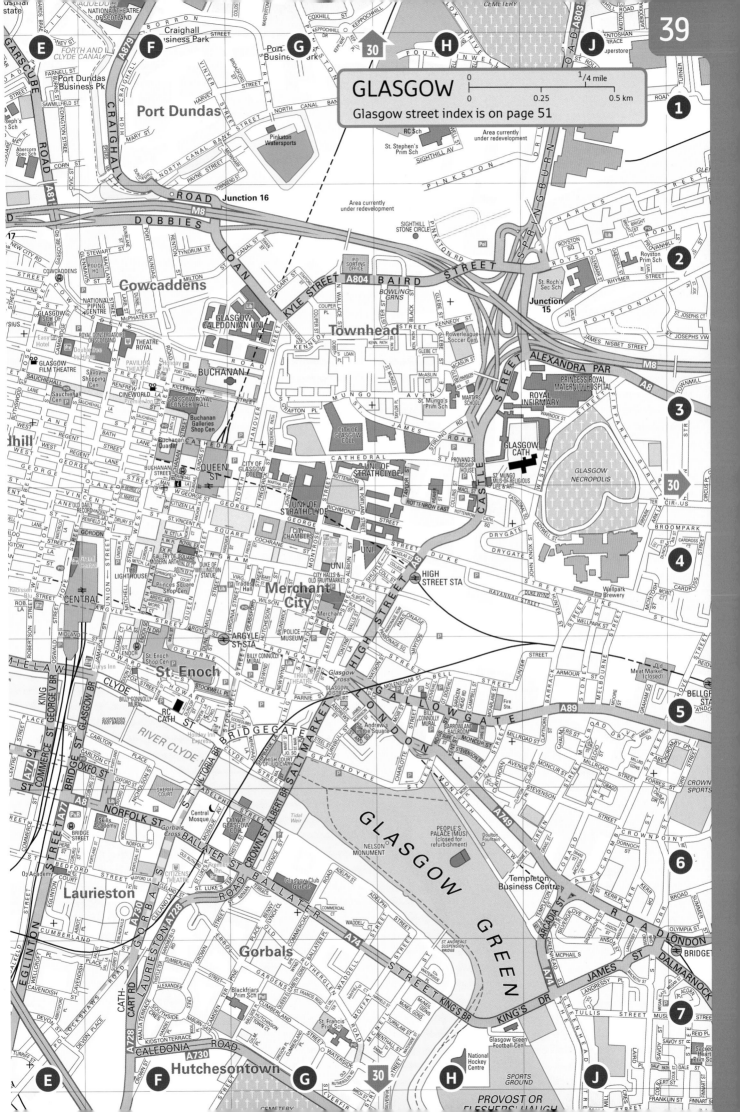

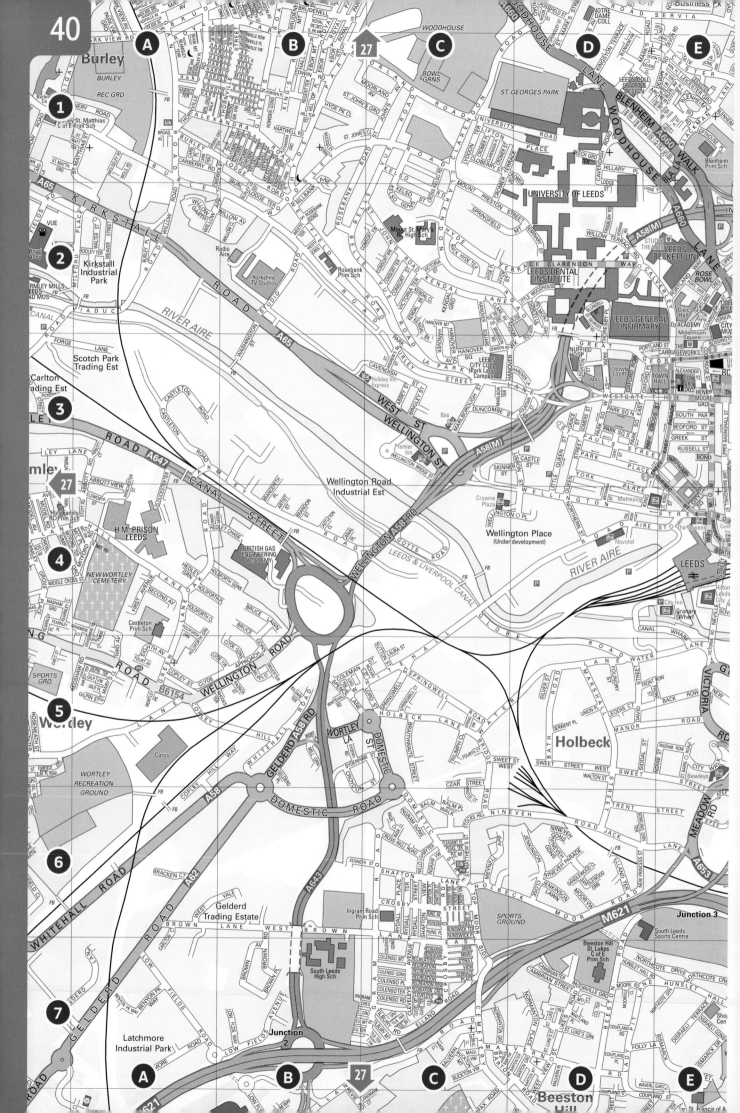

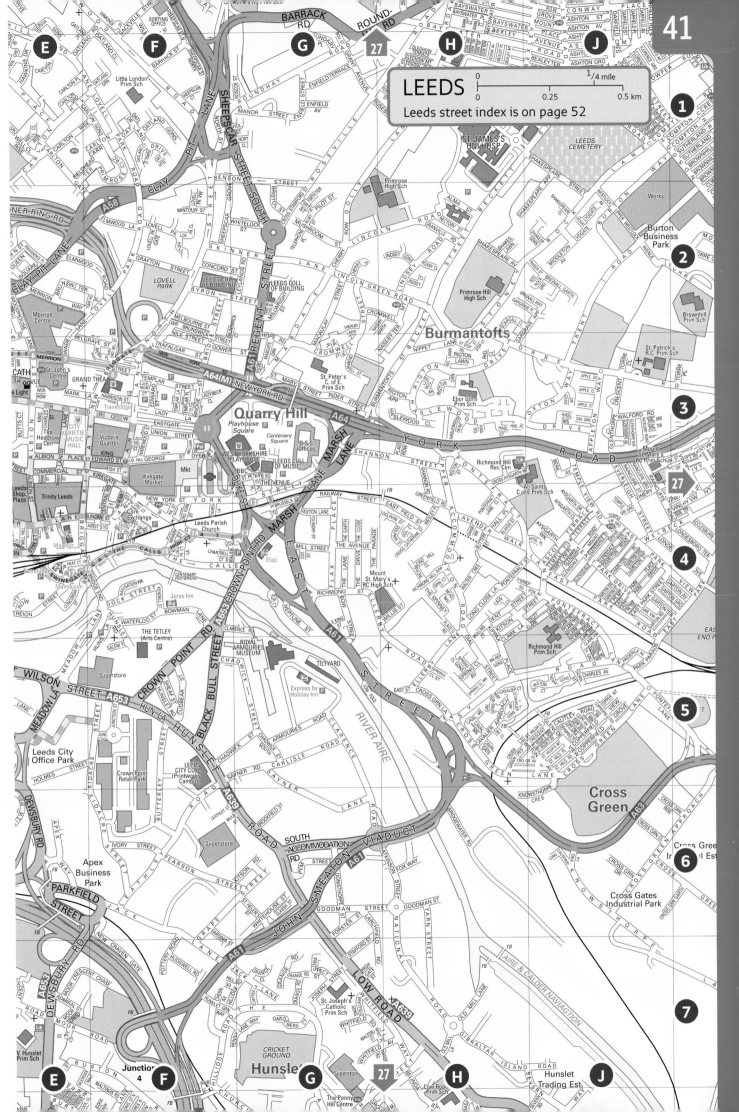

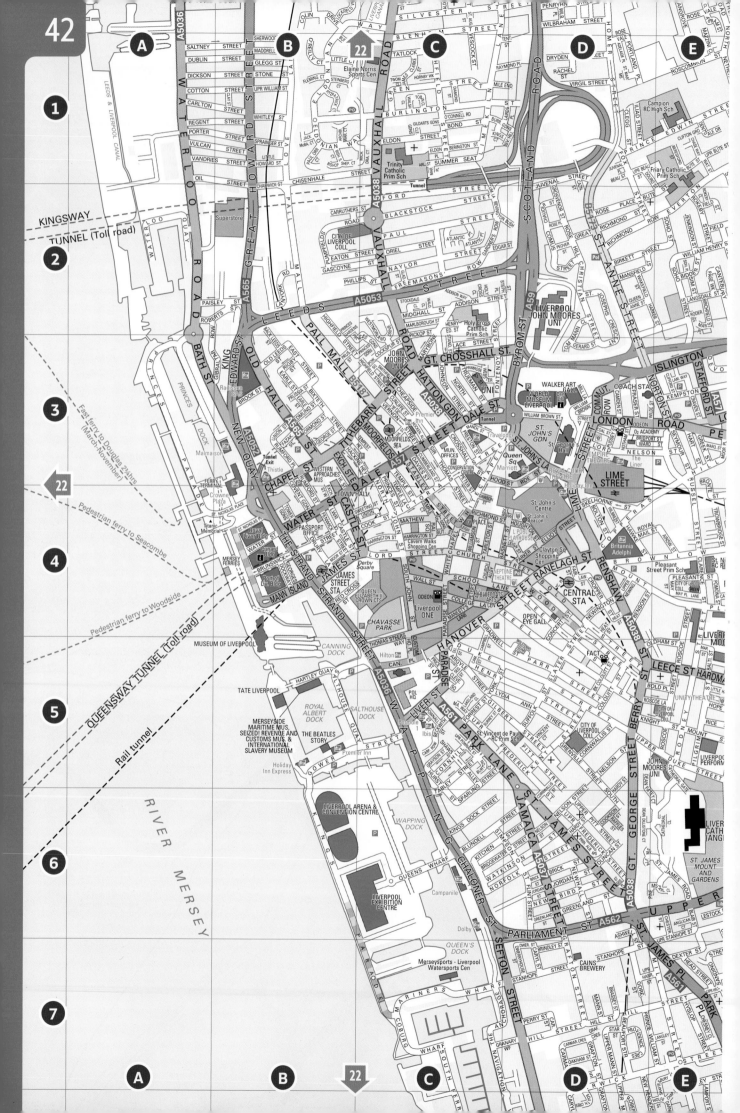

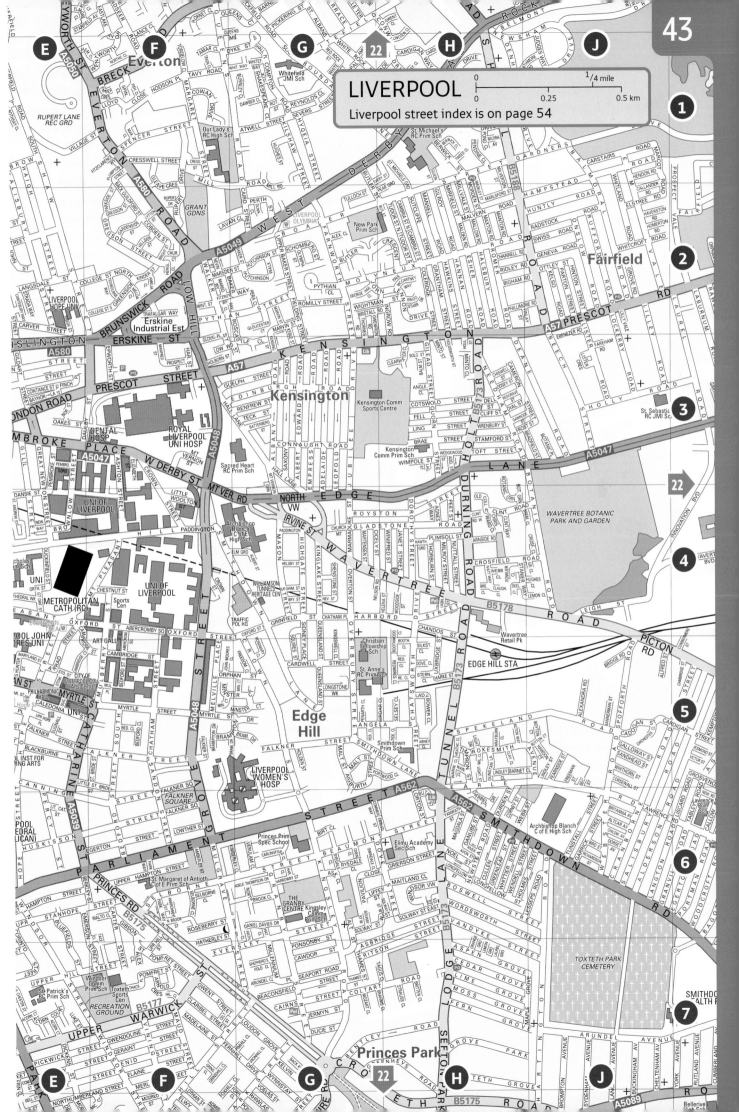

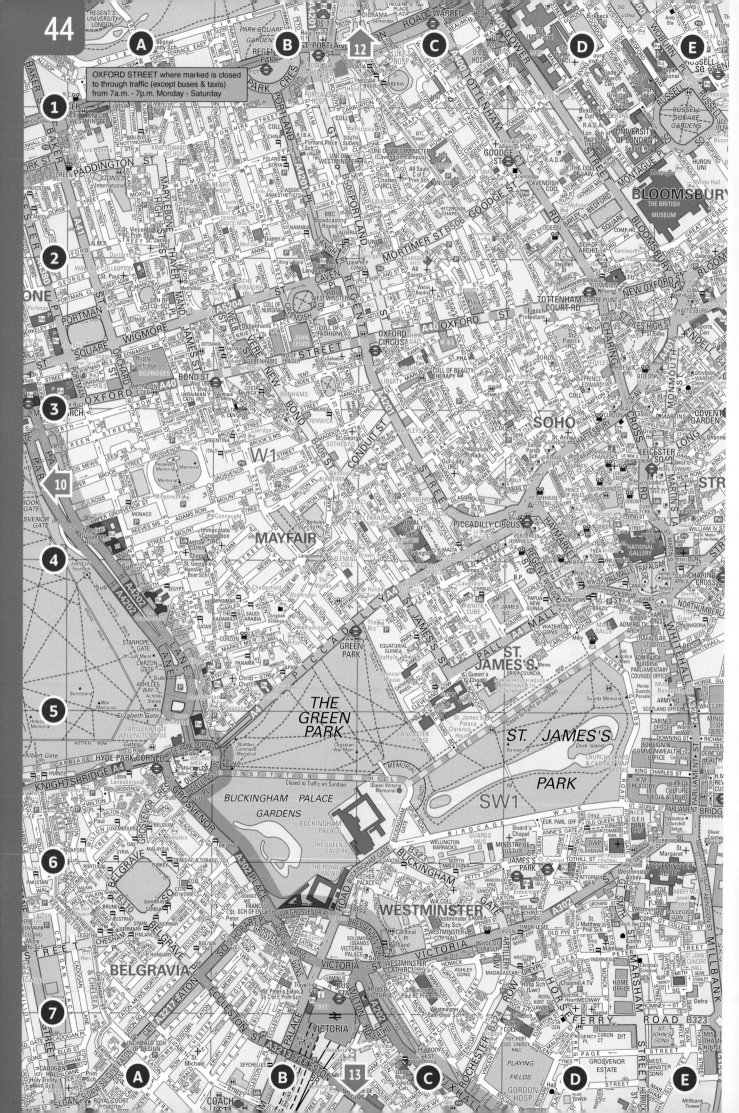

OXFORD STREET where marked is closed to through traffic (except buses & taxis) from 7a.m. - 7p.m. Monday - Saturday

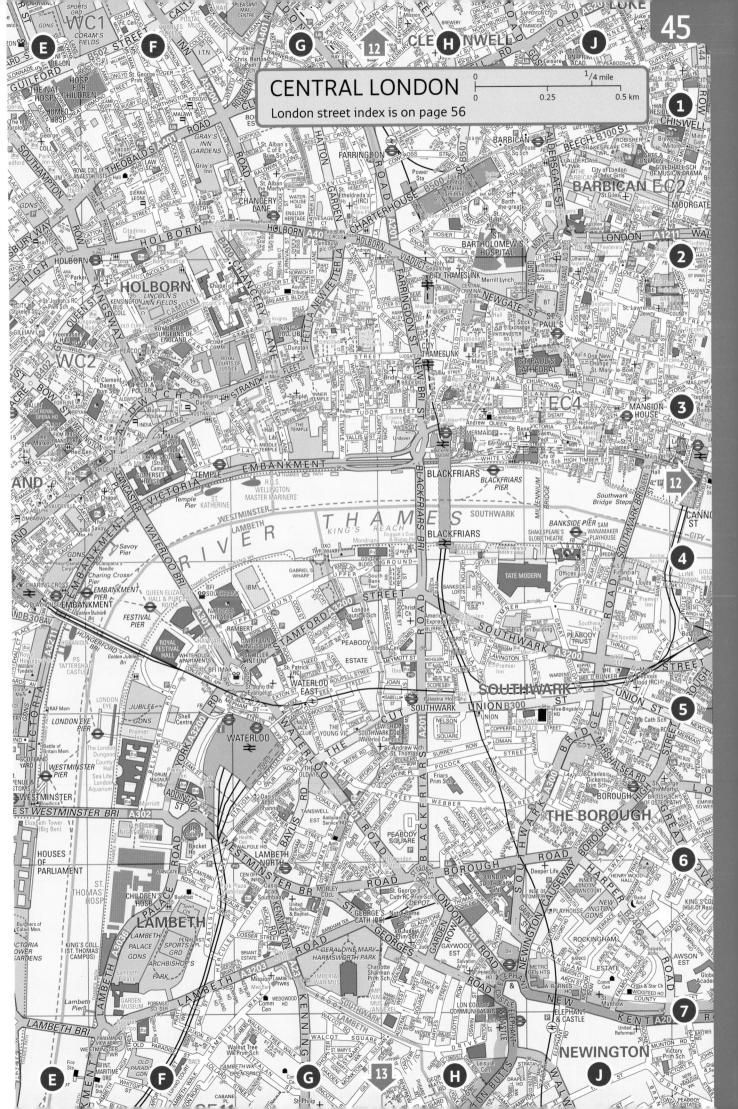

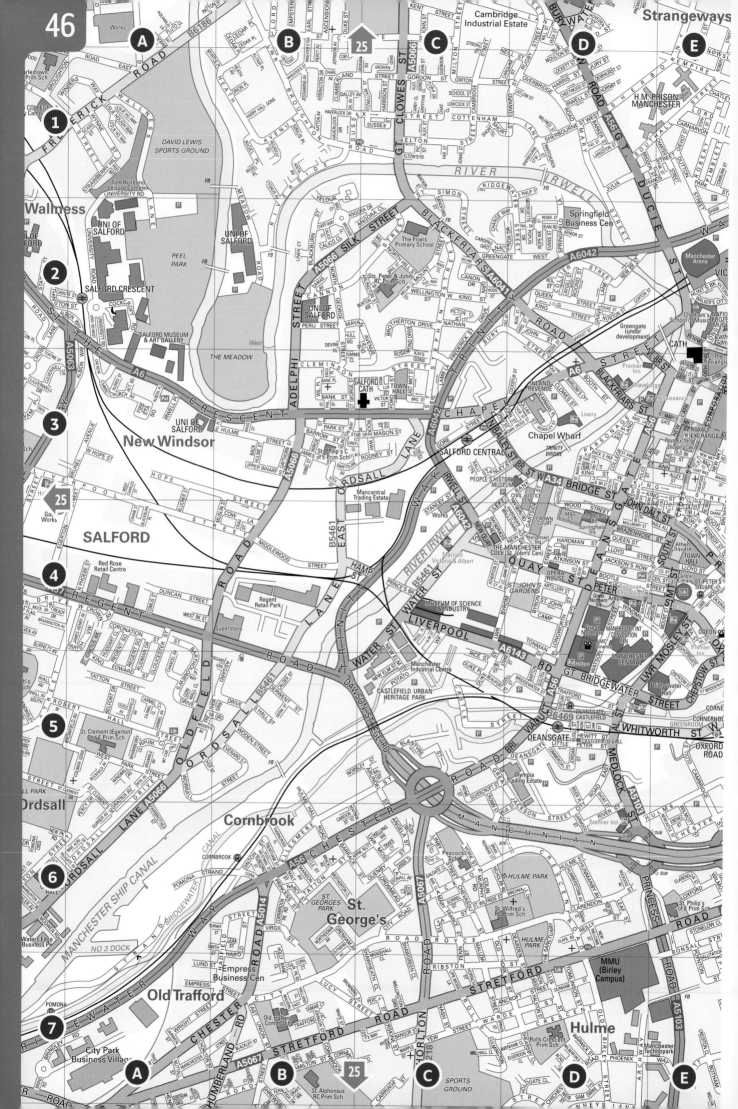

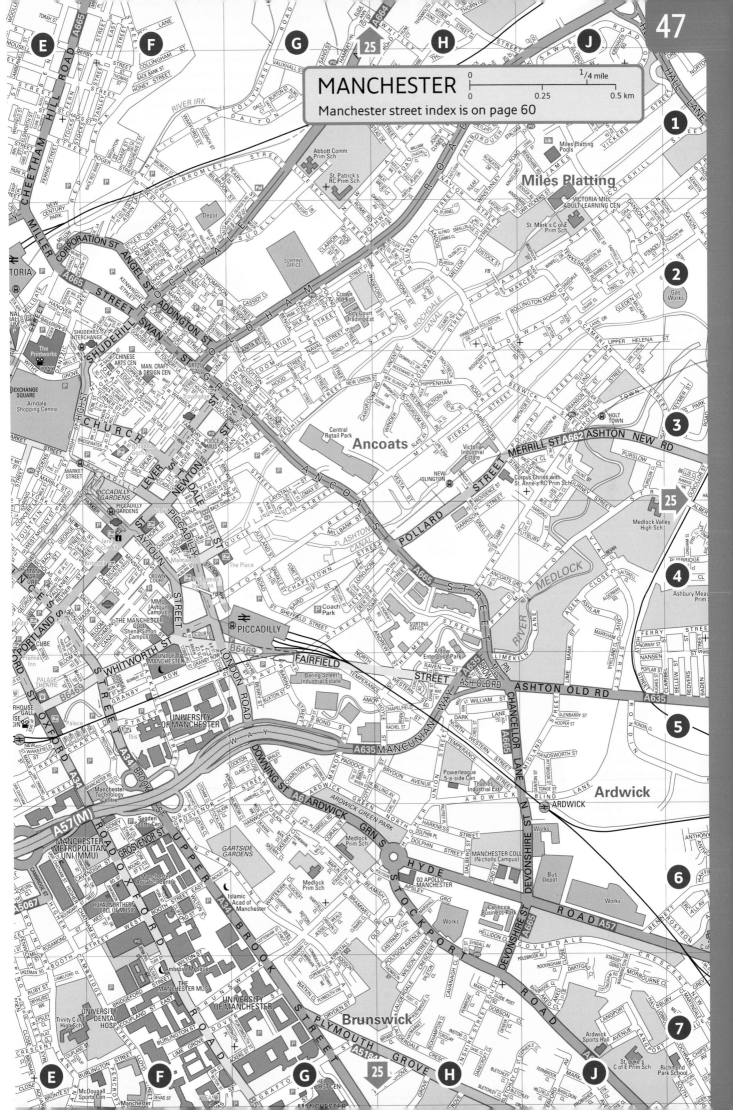

Indexes to street maps

General abbreviations

All	Alley
App	Approach
Arc	Arcade
Av/Ave	Avenue
Bdy	Broadway
Bldgs	Buildings
Br/Bri	Bridge
Cen	Central, Centre
Ch	Church
Chyd	Churchyard
Circ	Circus
Clo	Close
Cor	Corner
Cres	Crescent
Ct	Court
Ctyd	Courtyard
Dr	Drive
E	East
Embk	Embankment
Est	Estate
Flds	Fields
Gdn	Garden
Gdns	Gardens
Grd	Ground
Grn	Green
Gro	Grove
Ho	House
La	Lane
Lo	Lodge
Mans	Mansions
Mkt/Mkts	Market/Markets
Ms	Mews
N	North
Par	Parade
Pas	Passage
Pk	Park
Pl	Place
Rd	Road
Ri	Rise
S	South
Sq	Square
St	Street
St.	Saint
Ter	Terrace
Twr	Tower
W	West
Wf	Wharf
Wk	Walk
Yd	Yard

Place names are shown in bold type

Birmingham street index

A
Abbey St 34 C1
Abbey St N 34 C1
Aberdeen St 34 A2
Acorn Gro 34 C4
Adams St 35 H2
Adderley St 35 H5
Adelaide St 35 G6
Albert St 35 G4
Albion St 34 D3
Alcester St 35 G7
Aldgate Gro 35 E2
Alfred Knight Way 34 E6
Allcock St 35 H5
Allesley St 35 G1
Allison St 35 G5
All Saints Rd 34 C1
All Saints St 34 C2
Alston St 34 B5
Anchor Cl 34 A5
Anchor Cres 34 B1
Anderton St 34 C4
Angelina St 35 G7
Ansbro Cl 34 A2
Arden Gro 34 C5
Arthur Pl 34 D4
Ascot Cl 34 A5
Ashted Lock 35 H3
Ashted Wk 35 J2
Ashton Cft 34 C5
Aston 35 H1
Aston Br 35 G1
Aston Brook St 35 G1
Aston Brook St E 35 H1
Aston Expressway 35 G2
Aston Rd 35 H1
Aston St 35 G3
Attenborough Cl 35 F1
Auckland Rd 35 J7
Augusta St 34 D2
Augustine Gro 34 B1
Austen Pl 34 C7
Autumn Gro 34 E1
Avenue Cl 35 J1
Avenue Rd 35 H1

B
Bacchus Rd 34 A1
Bagot St 35 G2
Balcaskie Cl 34 A7
Banbury St 35 G4
Barford Rd 34 A3
Barford St 35 G6
Barn St 35 H5
Barrack St 35 J3
Barrow Wk 35 F7
Barr St 34 D1
Bartholomew Row 35 G4
Bartholomew St 35 G4
Barwick St 35 F4
Bath Pas 35 F5
Bath Row 34 D6
Bath St 35 F3
Beak St 35 F5
Beaufort Gdns 34 A1
Beaufort Rd 34 B6
Bedford Rd 35 J6
Beeches, The 34 D7
Belgrave Middleway 35 F7
Bell Barn Rd 34 D6
Bellcroft 34 C5
Bellevue 35 F7
Bellis St 34 A6
Belmont Pas 35 J4
Belmont Row 35 H3
Benacre Dr 35 H4
Bennett's Hill 35 F4
Benson Rd 34 A1
Berkley St 34 D5
Berrington Wk 35 G7
Birchall St 35 G6
Bishopsgate St 34 D5
Bishop St 35 G7
Bissell St 35 G7
Blews St 35 G2
Bloomsbury St 35 J2
Blucher St 35 E5
Blyton Cl 34 A3
Boar Hound Cl 34 C3
Bodmin Gro 35 J1
Bolton St 35 J5
Bond Sq 34 C3
Bond St 35 E3
Bordesley 35 J5
Bordesley Circ 35 J6
Bordesley Middleway 35 J7
Bordesley Pk Rd 35 J6
Bordesley St 35 G4
Boulton Middleway 34 D1
Bow St 35 F6
Bowyer St 35 J6
Bracebridge St 35 G1
Bradburn Way 35 J2
Bradford St 35 G5
Branston St 34 D2
Brearley Cl 35 F2
Brearley St 35 F2
Bredon Cft 34 B1
Brewery St 35 G2
Bridge St 34 E5
Bridge St W 35 E1
Brindley Dr 34 D4
Brindley Pl 34 D5
Bristol St 35 F7
Broad St 34 D6
Broadway Plaza 34 C6
Bromley St 35 H5
Bromsgrove St 35 F6
Brookfield Rd 34 B2
Brook St 34 E3
Brook Vw Cl 34 E1
Broom St 35 H6
Brough Cl 35 J1
Browning St 34 C5
Brownsea Dr 35 E5
Brunel St 35 E5
Brunswick St 34 D5
Buckingham St 35 E2
Bullock St 35 H2
Bull St 35 F4

C
Cala Dr 34 C7
Calthorpe Rd 34 C7
Cambridge Rd 34 D4
Camden Dr 34 D3
Camden Gro 34 D3
Camden St 34 B2
Camp Hill 35 J7
Camp Hill Middleway 35 H7
Cannon St 35 F4
Capstone Av 34 C2
Cardigan St 35 H3
Carlisle St 34 A2
Carlyle Rd 34 A5
Caroline St 34 E3
Carpenter Rd 34 C7
Carrs La 35 G4
Carver St 34 C3
Cawdor Cres 34 B6
Cecil St 35 F2
Cemetery La 34 D2
Centenary Sq 34 E4
Central Pk Dr 34 A1
Central Sq 34 E5
Chad Rd 34 A7
Chadsmoor Ter 35 J1
Chad Valley 34 A7
Chamberlain Sq 35 E4
Chancellor's Cl 34 A7
Chandlers Cl 34 B1
Chapel Ho St 35 H5
Chapmans Pas 35 E5
Charles Henry St 35 G7
Charlotte Rd 34 D7
Charlotte St 34 E4
Chatsworth Way 34 E6
Cheapside 35 G6
Cherry St 35 F4
Chester St 35 H1
Chilwell Cft 35 F1
Christchurch Cl 34 A6
Church Rd 34 C7
Church St 35 F3
Civic Cl 34 D4
Clare Dr 34 A7
Clarendon Rd 34 A5
Clark St 34 A5
Claybrook St 35 F6
Clement St 34 D4
Clipper Vw 34 A5
Clissold Cl 35 G7
Clissold St 34 B2
Cliveland St 35 F3
Clyde St 35 H6
Colbrand Gro 35 E7
Coleshill St 35 G4
College St 34 B3
Colmore Circ 35 F3
Colmore Row 35 F4
Commercial St 34 E5
Communication Row 34 D6
Constitution Hill 34 E2
Conybere St 35 G7
Cope St 34 B3
Coplow St 34 A3
Cornwall St 35 E4
Corporation St 35 F4
Coveley Gro 34 B1
Coventry Rd 35 J6
Coventry St 35 G5
Cox St 35 E3
Coxwell Gdns 34 B5
Crabtree Rd 34 B2
Cregoe St 34 E6
Crescent, The 34 C1
Crescent Av 34 C1
Cromwell St 35 J1
Crondal Pl 34 D7
Crosby Cl 34 C4
Cumberland St 34 D5
Curzon Circ 35 H3
Curzon St 35 H4

D
Daisy Rd 34 A5
Dale End 35 G4
Daley Cl 34 C4
Dalton St 35 G4
Darnley Rd 34 B5
Dartmouth Circ 35 G1
Dartmouth Middleway 35 G2
Dart St 35 J6
Darwin St 35 G6
Dean St 35 G5
Deeley Cl 34 D7
Denby Cl 35 J2
Derby St 35 J4
Devonshire Av 34 B1
Devonshire St 34 B1
Digbeth 35 G6
Digbeth 35 G5
Dollman St 35 J3
Dover St 34 B1
Duchess Rd 34 B6
Duddeston Manor Rd 35 J2
Dudley St 35 F5
Dymoke Cl 35 G7

E
Edgbaston 34 B7
Edgbaston St 35 F5
Edmund St 35 E4
Edward St 34 D4
Eldon Rd 34 A5
Elkington St 35 G1
Ellen St 34 C3
Ellis St 35 E5
Elvetham Rd 34 D7
Embassy Dr 34 C6
Emily Gdns 34 A3
Emily St 35 G7
Enfield Rd 34 D6
Enterprise Way 35 G2
Ernest St 35 E6
Erskine St 35 J3
Essex St 35 F6
Essington St 34 D5
Estria Rd 34 C7
Ethel St 35 F4
Exeter Pas 35 F6
Exeter St 35 F6
Eyre St 34 B3
Eyton Cft 35 H7

F
Farmacre 35 J5
Farm Cft 34 D1
Farm St 34 D1
Fawdry St 35 J4
Fazeley St 35 G4
Felsted Way 35 J3
Ferndale Cres 35 H7
Finstall Cl 35 J3
Five Ways 34 C6
Fleet St 34 E4
Floodgate St 35 H5
Florence St 35 E6
Ford St 34 C1
Fore St 35 F4
Forster St 35 H3
Foster Gdns 34 B1
Fox St 35 G4
Francis Rd 34 B5
Francis St 35 J3
Frankfort St 35 F1
Frederick Rd 34 C7
Frederick St 34 D3
Freeman St 35 G4
Freeth St 34 B4
Friston Av 34 C6
Fulmer Wk 34 C4

G
Garrison Circ 35 J4
Garrison La 35 J4
Garrison St 35 J4
Gas St 34 D5
Gas St Basin 34 E5
Geach St 35 F1
Gee St 35 F1
George Rd 34 D7
George St 34 D4
George St W 34 C3
Gibb St 35 H5
Gilby Rd 34 C5
Gilldown Pl 34 D7
Glebeland Cl 34 C5
Gloucester St 35 F5
Glover St 35 J5
Gooch St 35 F7
Gooch St N 35 F6
Goode Av 34 C1
Goodman St 34 C4
Gopsal St 35 H3
Gough St 35 E5
Grafton Rd 35 J7
Graham St 34 D3
Grant St 35 E6
Granville St 34 D5
Graston Cl 34 C5
Great Barr St 35 H5
Great Brook St 35 H3
Great Charles St Queensway 35 E4
Great Colmore St 34 E6
Great Hampton Row 34 E2
Great Hampton St 34 D2
Great King St 34 D1
Great King St N 34 E1
Great Lister St 35 H2
Great Tindal St 34 C4
Greenfield Cres 34 C6
Green St 35 H6
Grenfell Dr 34 A7
Grosvenor St 35 G4
Grosvenor St W 34 C5
Guest Gro 34 D1
Guild Cl 34 B5
Guild Cft 35 F1
Guthrie Cl 35 E1

H
Hack St 35 H5
Hadfield Cft 34 E2
Hagley Rd 34 A6
Hall St 34 E3
Hampshire Dr 34 A7
Hampton St 35 E2
Hanley St 35 F2
Hanwood Cl 35 G7
Harborne Rd 34 A7
Harford St 34 E2
Harmer St 34 C2
Harold Rd 34 A5
Hartley Pl 34 A6
Hatchett St 35 F1
Hawthorn Cl 35 J5
Hawthorne Rd 34 A7
Heath Mill La 35 H5
Heath St S 34 B3
Heaton Dr 34 A7
Heaton St 34 D1
Helena St 34 D4
Heneage St 35 H2
Heneage St W 35 H3
Henley St 35 J7
Henrietta St 35 F3
Henstead St 35 F6
Herne Cl 34 C3
Hickman Gdns 34 B5
Highfield Rd 34 B6
Highgate 35 H7
Highgate St 35 G7
High St 35 G4
Hilden Rd 35 J3
Hill St 35 E4
Hinckley St 35 F5
Hindlow Cl 35 J3
Hindon Sq 34 B7
Hingeston St 34 C2
Hitches La 34 D7
Hobart Cft 35 J2
Hobson Cl 34 B1
Hockley Brook Cl 34 B1
Hockley Cl 35 F1
Hockley Hill 34 D1
Hockley St 34 D2
Holland St 34 D4
Holliday Pas 34 E5
Holliday St 34 E5
Holloway Circ 35 F5
Holloway Head 35 E6
Holt St 35 G2
Holywell Cl 34 B5
Hooper St 34 B3
Hope St 35 F7
Hospital St 35 F1
Howard St 35 E2
Howe St 35 H3
Howford Gro 35 J2
Hubert St 35 H1
Hunter's Vale 34 D1
Huntly Rd 34 B6
Hurdlow Av 34 C2
Hurst St 35 F5
Hylton St 34 D2
Hyssop Cl 35 J2

I
Icknield Port Rd 34 A3
Icknield Sq 34 B4
Icknield St 34 C3
Inge St 35 F6
Inkerman St 35 J3
Irving St 35 E6
Islington Row Middleway 34 C6
Ivy La 35 J4

J
Jackson Cl 35 J7
James St 34 E3
James Watt Queensway 35 G3
Jennens Rd 35 G4
Jewellery Quarter 34 D2
Jinnah Cl 35 G7
John Bright St 35 F5
John Kempe Way 35 H7

K
Keeley St 35 J5
Keepers Cl 34 B1
Kellett Rd 35 H2
Kelsall Cft 34 C4
Kelsey Cl 35 J2
Kemble Cft 35 F7
Kendal Rd 35 J7
Kenilworth Ct 34 A6
Kent St 35 F6
Kent St N 34 B1
Kenyon St 34 E3
Ketley Cft 35 G7
Key Hill 34 D2
Key Hill Dr 34 D2
Kilby Av 34 C4
King Edwards Rd 34 D4
Kingston Rd 35 J5
Kingston Row 34 D4
Kirby Rd 34 A1
Knightstone Av 34 C2
Kyotts Lake Rd 35 J7

L
Ladycroft 34 C5
Ladywell Wk 35 F5
Ladywood 34 C4
Ladywood Middleway 34 B5
Ladywood Rd 34 B5
Lancaster Circ 35 G3
Landor St 35 J4
Langdon St 35 J4
Lansdowne St 34 A2
Latimer Gdns 35 E7
Lawden Rd 35 J6
Lawford Cl 35 J3
Lawford Gro 35 G7
Lawley Middleway 35 H3
Ledbury Cl 34 B5
Ledsam St 34 C4
Lee Bk 35 E7
Lee Bk Middleway 34 D6
Lee Cres 34 D7
Lee Mt 34 D7
Lees St 34 B1
Legge La 34 D3
Legge St 35 G2
Lennox St 35 E1
Leopold St 35 G7
Leslie Rd 34 A5
Leyburn Rd 34 C5
Lighthorne Av 34 C4
Link Rd 34 A3
Lionel St 34 E4
Lister St 35 G3
Little Ann St 35 H5
Little Barr St 35 J4
Little Broom St 35 H6
Little Edward St 35 J5
Little Francis Grn 35 J2
Little Shadwell St 35 F3
Liverpool St 35 H5
Livery St 35 F3
Locke Pl 35 J4
Lodge Rd 34 A1
Lombard St 35 G6
Longleat Way 34 D6
Lord St 35 H2
Louisa St 34 D4
Loveday St 35 F3
Love La 35 G2
Lower Dartmouth St 35 J4
Lower Essex St 35 F6
Lower Loveday St 35 F2
Lower Severn St 35 F5
Lower Temple St 35 F4

Street	Ref
Lower Twr St	35 F2
Lower Trinity St	35 H5
Lowe St	35 J6
Ludgate Hill	35 E3
Lytham Cft	35 E6
M	
Macdonald St	35 G6
Malcolmson Cl	34 A7
Manchester St	35 F2
Margaret St	35 E4
Mariner Av	34 A5
Marroway St	34 A3
Marshall St	35 E5
Mary Ann St	35 E3
Mary St	34 E3
Mason Way	34 E6
Masshouse La	35 G4
Mearse Cl	34 C2
Melton Dr	34 D7
Meredith Pool Cl	34 A1
Meriden St	35 G5
Merryhill Dr	34 A1
Meyrick Wk	34 A6
Middleway Vw	34 C3
Midford Grn	34 E6
Milford Cft	35 E2
Milk St	35 H5
Miller St	35 F1
Mill La	35 G5
Mill St	35 G2
Milton St	35 F1
Moat La	35 G5
Moland St	35 G2
Montague St	35 J4
Monument Rd	34 B6
Moore's Row	35 H5
Moorings, The	34 B1
Moorsom St	35 F1
Moor St Queensway	35 G4
Moreton St	34 C3
Morville St	34 C5
Mosborough Cres	34 E1
Mosedale Way	35 E6
Moseley Rd	35 H6
Moseley St	35 G6
Moss Ho Cl	34 D6
Mostyn Rd	34 A5
Mott St	34 E2
Mowbray St	35 F7
Murrell Cl	35 F7
Musgrave Rd	34 A1
Myddleton St	34 B3
N	
Navigation St	35 E5
Navigation Way	34 B1
Nechells Parkway	35 H3
Needless All	35 F4
Nelson St	34 D4
New Bartholomew St	35 G4
Newbold Cft	35 J1
New Bond St	35 J5
New Canal St	35 G4
Newhall Hill	34 D3
Newhall St	34 E3
Newhope Cl	35 F7
New John St	35 G2
New John St W	34 E1
New Mkt St	35 E4
New Moseley Rd	35 H7
New Spring St	34 C2
New Spring St N	34 B2
New St	35 F4
New Summer St	35 F2
Newton St	35 G4
Newtown	34 E1
Newtown Dr	34 D1
Newtown Middleway	35 F1
New Town Row	35 F1
Niall Cl	34 A7
Noel Rd	34 A5
Norman St	34 A2
Northampton St	34 D2
Northbrook St	34 A3
Northumberland St	35 J3
Northwood St	34 D3
Norton St	34 B1
Nova Scotia St	35 G4
Nursery Rd	34 D1
O	
Oak Hill Dr	34 A7
Old Br St	34 D1
Old Camp Hill	35 J6
Old Smithy Pl	34 C1
Old Snow Hill	35 F3
Old Sq	35 F4
Oliver Rd	34 B5
Oliver St	35 J1
Oozells St	34 D5
Orchid Dr	35 E1
Orwell Pas	35 G5
Osler St	34 A5
Oxford St	35 G5
P	
Paddocks Grn	34 B2
Pakenham Rd	34 D7
Palmer St	35 J5
Palomino Pl	34 B4
Pannel Cft	35 F1
Parade	35 E4
Paradise Circ	34 E4
Paradise St	35 E4
Parker St	34 A6
Parkfield Cl	34 D7
Park Rd	34 C1
Park Rd S	34 C1
Park St	35 G5
Paxton Rd	34 C2
Peel St	34 A2
Pemberton St	34 D2
Penn St	35 H3
Pershore St	35 F5
Pickford St	35 H5
Pinfold St	35 E4
Pinto Cl	34 B5
Pitsford St	34 C2
Pitt St	35 H3
Plough & Harrow Rd	34 B6
Pool St	35 G1
Pope St	34 C3
Port Hope Rd	35 J7
Powell St	34 D3
Power Cres	34 C5
Price St	35 F3
Princip St	35 F3
Printing Ho St	35 F3
Priory Queensway, The	35 G4
Pritchett St	35 F2
Proctor St	35 H2
Q	
Quayside	34 B1
Queens Hosp Cl	34 D6
Quigley Av	35 J5
R	
Radnor St	34 B1
Radshaw Cl	34 D6
Rake Way	34 D5
Rann Cl	34 C5
Ravenhurst St	35 H6
Rawlins St	34 C5
Rea St	35 G6
Rea St S	35 G6
Rea Ter	35 H5
Rectory Gro	34 A1
Regent Par	34 D3
Regent Pl	34 D3
Regent St	34 D3
Reservoir Retreat	34 B5
Reservoir Rd	34 A5
Richard St	35 H2
Rickman Dr	35 E7
Ridley St	34 E6
River St	35 H5
Rocky La	35 J1
Rodney Cl	34 B4
Rosebery St	34 B2
Roseland Way	34 D6
Rotton Pk St	34 B4
Rupert St	35 H2
Ruston St	34 C5
Ryland Rd	34 D7
Ryland St	34 C5
S	
Sadlers Wk	34 B5
St. Andrew's Rd	35 J4
St. Chad's Queensway	35 F3
St. Georges Cl	34 B7
St. Georges St	35 E2
St. Helen's Pas	34 D3
St. James Pl	35 J3
St. James Rd	34 C6
St. Jude's Pas	35 F5
St. Lukes Rd	35 F7
St. Marks Cres	34 C4
St. Marks St	34 C3
St. Martin's Circ Queensway	35 F5
St. Martin's Sq	35 G5
St. Martin's St	34 D6
St. Mary's Row	35 F3
St. Paul's Sq	34 E3
St. Phillips Pl	35 F4
St. Stephen's St	35 F1
St. Vincent St	34 C4
St. Vincent St W	34 B5
Salop St	35 H7
Sampson Rd	35 J7
Sampson Rd N	35 J6
Sand Pits	34 C3
Sandy Way	34 D5
Scotland St	34 D4
Sefton Rd	34 A5
Severn St	35 E5
Shadwell St	35 F3
Shawbury Gro	35 H7
Shaw's Pas	35 G4
Sheepcote St	34 C4
Shefford Rd	35 G1
Shepherds Gdns	34 D6
Sherborne Gro	34 C4
Sherborne St	34 C5
Sheringham	34 A6
Sherlock St	35 F7
Shetland Cl	34 B5
Shillcock Gro	35 F2
Shire Cl	34 A4
Shyltons Cft	34 C5
Skinner La	35 G6
Skipton Rd	34 B5
Sloane St	34 D4
Smallbrook Queensway	35 F5
Smith St	34 E1
Snow Hill Queensway	35 F3
Soho Pool Way	35 B1
Southacre Av	35 F7
South Rd	35 J7
Spencer St	34 D2
Spooner Cft	35 F7
Springbank Rd	34 E7
Springfield St	34 B4
Spring Gro Gdns	34 A1
Spring Hill	34 B3
Spring Hill Pas	34 C3
Spring St	35 E7
Stainsby Av	34 D1
Stanhope Rd	35 G7
Staniforth St	35 G2
Star Hill	34 D7
Station St	35 F5
Steelhouse La	35 F3
Stephenson Pl	35 F5
Stephenson St	35 F4
Steward St	34 B3
Stirling Rd	34 A6
Stoke Way	34 D5
Stone Rd	35 E7
Stone Yd	35 H5
Stour St	34 B3
Stratford Pl	35 H7
Stratford Rd	35 J7
Stratford St N	35 J7
Suffolk St Queensway	35 E5
Sugden Gro	35 F6
Summer Cft	35 F1
Summerfield Rd	34 A3
Summer Hill Rd	34 D4
Summer Hill St	34 D4
Summer Hill Ter	34 D3
Summer La	35 F3
Summer Rd	34 E7
Summer Row	34 E4
Sutton St	35 E6
Swallow St	35 E5
T	
Talbot St	34 A1
Temple Pas	35 F4
Temple Row	35 F4
Temple Row W	35 F4
Temple St	35 F4
Tenby St	34 D3
Tenby St N	34 D3
Tennant St	34 D6
Theatre App	35 F5
Theresa Rd	35 J7
Thomas St	35 G1
Thorp St	35 F6
Tower St	35 F2
Townsend Way	34 D4
Trent St	35 H5
Trinity Ter	35 J6
U	
Unett St	34 E1
Union Pas	35 F4
Union St	35 F4
Upper Dean St	35 F5
Upper Gough St	35 E6
Upper Marshall St	35 E5
Upper Trinity St	35 H5
Uxbridge St	35 E1
V	
Vaughton St	35 G7
Vaughton St S	35 G7
Vauxhall Gro	35 J3
Vauxhall Rd	35 J3
Venture Way	35 H2
Verbena Gdns	35 J2
Vere St	35 F7
Vernolds Cft	35 F6
Vesey St	35 F3
Viaduct St	35 J4
Vicarage Rd	34 B6
Victoria Sq	35 E4
Victor Rd	34 A1
Vittoria St	34 D3
Vyse St	34 D3
W	
Walter St	35 J1
Wardlow Rd	35 J2
Ward St	35 F2
Warner St	35 H6
Warstone La	34 C3
Warstone Par E	34 D2
Warwick Pas	35 F4
Warwick St	35 H6
Washington St	34 E5
Waterloo St	35 E4
Waterside Dr	34 A1
Waterside Vw	34 B2
Water St	35 E3
Waterworks Rd	34 A5
Watery La Middleway	35 J4
Weaman St	35 F3
Well La	35 G5
Well St	34 D2
Westbourne Cres	34 C7
Westbourne Gdns	34 B7
Westbourne Rd	34 A7
Western Rd	34 B3
West Grn Cl	34 D7
Westhorpe Gro	34 E1
Westley St	35 J5
Wharf, The	34 E5
Wharf La	34 C1
Wharfside St	35 E5
Wharf St	34 B1
Wheeler St	35 E1
Wheeley's La	34 D6
Whitehouse St	35 H1
Whitmore St	34 C1
Whittall St	35 F3
Wiggin St	34 A4
William Booth La	35 F3
William Henry St	35 J1
William St	34 D6
William St N	35 F2
Willow Gdns	34 A3
Windmill St	35 F6
Windrush Way	35 E7
Windsor St	35 H2
Windsor St S	35 H3
Winson Grn	34 A1
Witton St	35 J4
Woodcock St	35 G3
Woodcote Way	34 B2
Woodview Dr	34 E7
Wrentham St	35 F6
Wrottesley St	35 F5
Wyndham Rd	34 A6
Wynn St	35 E6
Y	
Yew Tree Rd	34 D6

Edinburgh street index

Street	Ref
A	
Abbeyhill	37 J3
Abbeyhill	37 J3
Abbeyhill Cres	37 H4
Abbey La	37 J3
Abbeymount	37 J3
Abbey Strand	37 J4
Abbey St	37 J3
Abercromby Pl	37 F3
Admiral Ter	36 D7
Ainslie Pl	36 D3
Albany La	37 F2
Albany St	37 F3
Albany St La	37 F3
Albert St	37 H1
Albion Gdns	37 J2
Albion Pl	37 J2
Albion Rd	37 J2
Albion Ter	37 J2
Alfred Pl	37 J7
Allanfield	37 H2
Allanfield Pl	37 H2
Allan St	36 D2
Alva Pl	37 J3
Alva St	36 D4
Angle Pk Ter	36 B7
Annandale St	37 G1
Annandale St La	37 G2
Ann St	36 D3
Arboretum Av	36 D2
Arboretum Pl	36 D1
Archibald Pl	37 F6
Arden St	37 F7
Ardmillan Pl	36 B7
Ardmillan Ter	36 B7
Argyle Pk Ter	37 F7
Argyle Pl	37 F7
Arthur St	37 H1
Arthur St La	37 H1
Atholl Cres	36 D5
Atholl Cres La	36 D5
Avondale Pl	36 D1
B	
Back Dean	36 B4
Bakehouse Cl	37 H4
Balbirnie Pl	36 A5
Balmoral Pl	36 D2
Bank St	37 F4
Barclay Pl	36 E7
Barony St	37 F2
Beaverbank Pl	37 F1
Beaverhall Rd	37 F1
Bedford St	36 D2
Belford Av	36 A3
Belford Br	36 C4
Belford Gdns	36 A3
Belford Ms	36 C4
Belford Pk	36 B4
Belford Pl	36 B4
Belford Rd	36 B4
Belgrave Cres	36 C3
Belgrave Cres La	36 C3
Belgrave Ms	36 C3
Belgrave Pl	36 C3
Bellevue	37 F2
Bellevue Cres	37 F2
Bellevue Gdns	37 G1
Bellevue Gro	37 G2
Bellevue La	37 F2
Bellevue Pl	37 F2
Bellevue Rd	37 G2
Bellevue St	37 G2
Bellevue Ter	37 F2
Bell Pl	36 E1
Bells Brae	36 C4
Bell's Mills	36 B4
Bernard Ter	37 H6
Blacket Av	37 H7
Blacket Pl	37 H7
Blackfriars St	37 G4
Blackwood Cres	37 H7
Blair St	37 G4
Blandfield	37 G1
Boat Grn	37 F1
Boroughloch	37 G6
Boroughloch Sq	37 G6
Borthwick Pl	36 B5
Bothwell St	37 J2
Bowmont Pl	37 H6
Boyd's Entry	37 G4
Brandfield St	36 D6
Brandon St	37 E2
Brandon Ter	37 E2
Bread St	36 E5
Bridge Pl	36 D2
Briery Bauks	37 H5
Brighton St	37 G5
Bristo Pl	37 F5
Bristo Port	37 F5
Brougham Pl	37 E6
Brougham St	36 E6
Broughton	37 F1
Broughton Mkt	37 F2
Broughton Pl	37 G2
Broughton Pl La	37 G2
Broughton Rd	37 F1
Broughton St	37 G2
Broughton St La	37 G3
Brown's Cl	37 H4
Brown St	37 H5
Brunswick Rd	37 H2
Brunswick St	37 H2
Brunswick St La	37 H2
Brunton Ter	37 J3
Bruntsfield	36 D7
Bruntsfield Av	36 D7
Bruntsfield Cres	36 E7
Bruntsfield Gdns	36 D7
Bruntsfield Ter	36 D7
Bryson Rd	36 B7
Buccleuch Pl	37 G6
Buccleuch St	37 G6
Buccleuch Ter	37 G6
Buchanan St	37 H1
Buckingham Ter	36 C3
C	
Caledonian Cres	36 C6
Caledonian Pl	36 C6
Caledonian Rd	36 C6
Calton Hill	37 G3
Calton Rd	37 G3
Cambridge Av	37 H1
Cambridge Gdns	37 H1
Cambridge St	36 E5
Campbell's Cl	37 H4
Candlemaker Row	37 F5
Canning St	36 D5
Canning St La	36 D5
Canongate	37 G4
Canon La	37 F2
Canonmills	37 E1
Canon St	37 E1
Carberry Pl	36 B5
Carlton St	36 D3
Carlton Ter	37 H3
Carlton Ter Brae	37 J3
Carlton Ter La	37 H3
Carlton Ter Ms	37 H3
Carlton Wynd	37 H4
Carlyle Pl	37 J3
Carnegie St	37 H5
Carrington Rd	36 B2
Castle Hill	37 F4
Castle St	36 E4
Castle Ter	36 E4
Cathcart Pl	36 B6
Cathedral La	37 G3
Causewayside	37 H7
Chalmers Cres	37 F7
Chalmers St	37 F5
Chambers St	37 F5
Chapel St	37 G5
Charles St	37 G5
Charlotte La	36 D4
Charlotte Sq	36 D4
Chester St	36 C4
Chuckie Pend	36 D5
Circus Gdns	36 E3
Circus La	36 E3
Circus Pl	36 E3
Claremont Bk	37 F2
Claremont Cres	37 F1
Claremont Gro	37 F1
Clarence St	37 E2
Clarendon Cres	36 C3
Clerk St	37 G6
Coates	36 B5
Coates Cres	36 D5
Coates Gdns	36 C5
Cochran Ter	37 G2
Cockburn St	37 F4
Coffin La	36 B6
Collins Pl	36 D2

Coltbridge Av 36 A5
Coltbridge Gdns 36 A5
Coltbridge Millside 36 A5
Coltbridge Ter 36 A5
Coltbridge Vale 36 A5
Colville Pl 36 D2
Comely Bk 36 C2
Comely Bk 36 B2
Comely Bk Av 36 C2
Comely Bk Gro 36 C3
Comely Bk Pl 36 C2
Comely Bk Pl Ms 36 C2
Comely Bk Rd 36 C2
Comely Bk Row 36 C6
Comely Bk St 36 C2
Comely Bk Ter 36 C2
Conference Sq 36 D5
Cornwallis Pl 37 F2
Cornwall St 36 E5
Cowan's Cl 37 G6
Cowgate 37 F5
Cowgatehead 37 F5
Craigleith 36 A2
Craigleith Hill
  Cres 36 A2
Craigleith Hill
  Gdns 36 A2
Craigleith Hill Ln 36 A2
Craigleith Hill Row 36 A2
Cranston St 37 G4
Crarae Av 36 A4
Crewe Rd S 36 A1
Crichton St 37 G5
Croft-an-Righ 37 J3
Cumberland St 36 E2
Cumberland St
  N E La 37 E2
Cumberland St
  N W La 37 E2
Cumberland St
  S E La 37 E2
Cumberland St
  S W La 37 E2
Cumin Pl 37 G7

D
Dalkeith Rd 37 H6
Dalmeny St 37 H1
Dalry 36 B6
Dalry Gait 36 C5
Dalry Pl 36 C5
Dalry Rd 36 B7
Damside 36 C4
Danube St 36 D3
Darnaway St 36 D3
Davidson Pk 36 A1
Davidson Rd 36 A1
Davie St 37 G5
Dean Bk La 36 D2
Dean Br 36 C3
Deanhaugh St 36 D2
Dean Pk Cres 36 C3
Dean Pk Ms 36 C2
Dean Pk St 36 C2
Dean Path 36 C3
Dean St 36 D3
Dean Ter 36 D3
Dean Village 36 B4
Devon Pl 36 B5
Dewar Pl 36 D5
Dewar Pl La 36 D5
Dicksonfield 37 H2
Dickson St 37 J1
Distillery La 36 C5
Dorset Pl 36 C7
Douglas Cres 36 B4
Douglas Gdns 36 C4
Douglas Gdns Ms 36 C4
Doune Ter 36 D3
Downfield Pl 36 B6
Drumdryan St 36 E6
Drummond Pl 37 F2
Drummond St 37 G5
Drumsheugh Gdns 36 C4
Drum Ter 37 J2
Dryden Gait 37 G1
Dryden Gdns 37 G1
Dryden Pl 37 J7
Dryden St 37 G1
Dryden Ter 37 G1
Drysdale Rd 36 C6
Dublin Meuse 37 F3
Dublin St 37 F2
Dublin St La N 37 F2
Dublin St La S 37 F3
Duff Rd 36 B6
Duff St 36 B6
Duff St La 36 B6
Dumbiedykes Rd 37 H5
Dunbar St 36 E5
Dundas St 37 E2
Dundee St 36 B7
Dundee Ter 36 B7
Dundonald St 37 F2

Dunedin St 37 F1
Dunrobin Pl 36 D2

E
Earl Grey St 36 E5
East Adam St 37 G5
East Castle Rd 36 C7
East Claremont St 37 F2
East Crosscauseway 37 G6
Easter Dalry Dr 36 B6
Easter Dalry Pl 36 B5
Easter Dalry Rigg 36 B6
Easter Dalry Wynd 36 C6
Easter Rd 37 J3
East Fettes Av 36 C1
East
  Fountainbridge 36 E5
East London St 37 G2
East Mkt St 37 G4
East Montgomery Pl 37 H2
East Newington Pl 37 H7
East Parkside 37 H6
East Preston St 37 H7
East Preston St La 37 H7
East Scienne St 37 G7
East Scotland St La 37 F2
East Silvermills La 37 E2
Edina Pl 37 J2
Edina St 37 J2
Edinburgh Quay 36 D6
Eglinton Cres 36 B5
Eildon St 37 E1
Eildon Ter 36 E1
Elder St 37 F3
Elgin St 37 H2
Elgin St N 37 J2
Elgin Ter 37 J2
Elliot St 37 J2
Elm Row 37 G2
Eton Ter 36 D3
Ettrickdale Pl 36 E1
Ettrick Gro 36 C7
Eyre Cres 37 E2
Eyre Pl 37 E2
Eyre Ter 37 E2

F
Fettes Av 36 B2
Fettes Row 37 E2
Findhorn Pl 37 G7
Fingal Pl 37 F7
Forbes St 37 H6
Forres St 36 D3
Forrest Hill 37 F5
Forrest Rd 37 F5
Forth St 37 G3
Fountainbridge 36 D6
Fowler Ter 36 C6
Frederick St 37 E3

G
Gardner's Cres 36 D5
Garscube Ter 36 A4
Gayfield La 37 G2
Gayfield Pl La 37 G2
Gayfield Sq 37 G2
Gayfield St 37 G2
Gayfield St La 37 G2
Gentle's Entry 37 H4
George IV Br 37 F4
George Sq 37 F6
George Sq La 37 F6
George St 36 E4
Gibson Ter 36 C6
Gifford Pk 37 G6
Gillespie Cres 36 D6
Gillespie St 36 D6
Gilmore Pk 36 D6
Gilmore Pl 36 D7
Gilmour St 37 G5
Gladstone Ter 37 G7
Glencairn Cres 36 C5
Glenfinlas St 36 D4
Glengyle Ter 36 E6
Glenogle Rd 36 D2
Glen St 37 E5
Gloucester La 36 D3
Gloucester Pl 36 D3
Gloucester Sq 36 D3
Gloucester St 36 D3
Gorgie Rd 36 A7
Grange Rd 37 F7
Granville Ter 36 C7
Grassmarket 37 F5
Great King St 37 E3
Great Stuart St 36 D4
Greenhill Ct 36 E7
Greenhill Gdns 36 E7
Greenhill Pl 36 E7
Greenhill Ter 36 E7
Greenside La 37 G3
Greenside Row 37 G3
Green St 37 G2

Greyfriars Pl 37 F5
Grigor Av 36 A1
Grigor Dr 36 A1
Grigor Gdns 36 A1
Grigor Ter 36 A1
Grindlay St 36 E5
Grosvenor Cres 36 C5
Grosvenor Gdns 36 C5
Grosvenor St 36 C5
Grove St 36 D5
Gullan's Cl 37 G4
Guthrie St 37 G5

H
Haddon's Ct 37 G5
Hailes St 36 E6
Halmyre St 37 J1
Hamilton Pl 36 D2
Hamilton's Folly Ms 37 H6
Hammermen's Entry 37 H4
Hanover St 37 F3
Harden St 36 C7
Hardwell Cl 37 H6
Harrismith Pl 37 J2
Harrison La 36 B7
Harrison Rd 36 B7
Hartington Gdns 36 D7
Hartington Pl 36 D7
Hart St 37 G2
Hatton Pl 37 F7
Haugh St 36 D2
Hawthornbank La 36 C4
Hawthornden Pl 37 H1
Haymarket 36 C5
Haymarket Ter 36 B5
Haymarket Yards 36 B5
Henderland Rd 36 A5
Henderson Pl 37 E2
Henderson Pl La 36 E2
Henderson Row 36 E2
Henderson Ter 36 B7
Heriot Br 37 F5
Heriot Hill Ter 37 F2
Heriot Pl 37 F5
Heriot Row 37 E3
Hermits Cft 37 H6
High Riggs 36 E5
High Sch Wynd 37 G4
High Sch Yards 37 G5
High St 37 F4
Hill Pl 37 G5
Hillside Cres 37 H2
Hillside St 37 H2
Hill Sq 37 G5
Hill St 36 E3
Hill St La N 36 E3
Hill St La S 36 E4
Holyrood Gait 37 H4
Holyrood Pk Rd 37 H7
Holyrood Rd 37 G4
Home St 36 E6
Hope Pk Cres 37 G6
Hope Pk Ter 37 G6
Hope St 36 D4
Hope St La 36 D4
Hopetoun Cres 37 G2
Hopetoun St 37 G2
Horne Ter 36 C6
Horse Wynd 37 J4
Howden St 37 G5
Howe St 37 E3
Hugh Miller Pl 36 D2
Hunter Sq 37 G4
Huntingdon Pl 37 G2
Hutton Rd 37 H4

I
India Pl 36 D3
India St 36 E3
Infirmary St 37 G5
Inverleith 36 C1
Inverleith Gro 36 C1
Inverleith Pl 36 C1
Inverleith Ter 36 D1
Inverleith Ter La 36 E1
Iona St 37 H1
Ivy Ter 36 A7

J
Jamaica St 36 E3
Jamaica St N La 36 E3
Jamaica St S La 36 E3
Jameson Pl 37 H1
Jeffrey St 37 G4
Johnston Ter 37 E5

K
Keir St 37 F5
Kemp Pl 36 D1
Kerr St 36 D2
Kew Ter 36 A5
Kimmerghame Dr 36 A1
Kimmerghame Vw 36 A1
King's Stables La 37 E5

King's Stables Rd 36 E4
Kirkhill Rd 37 J7
Kyle Pl 37 J3

L
Lady Lawson St 37 E5
Lady Menzies Pl 37 J3
Lady Wynd 37 F5
Lamb's Cl 37 H6
Lansdowne Cres 36 C5
Lauderdale St 37 E7
Lauder Rd 37 G7
Lauriston Gdns 37 E5
Lauriston Pk 37 E5
Lauriston Pl 36 E6
Lauriston St 37 E5
Lawnmarket 37 F4
Lawrie Reilly Pl 37 J2
Leamington Rd 36 D6
Leamington Ter 36 D6
Learmonth Av 36 B2
Learmonth Cres 36 B3
Learmonth Gdn La 36 C3
Learmonth Gdns 36 C3
Learmonth Gdns Ms 36 C3
Learmonth Gro 36 C2
Learmonth Pl 36 C2
Learmonth Ter 36 C3
Learmonth Ter La 36 C3
Learmonth Vw 36 C3
Leith St 37 G3
Leith Wk 37 G3
Lennox St 36 C3
Lennox St La 36 C3
Leslie Pl 36 D3
Leven St 36 E6
Leven Ter 37 E6
Liddesdale Pl 36 E1
Little King St 37 G3
Livingstone Pl 37 G7
Lochend Cl 37 H4
Lochrin Pl 36 E6
Logan St 37 F2
Logie Grn Gdns 37 F1
Logie Grn Ln 37 F1
Logie Grn Rd 37 F1
Logie Mill 37 F1
London Rd 36 D4
London St 37 F2
Lonsdale Ter 37 E6
Lorne Pl 37 J1
Lorne Sq 37 J1
Lorne St 37 J1
Lothian Rd 36 D4
Lothian St 37 G5
Lower Gilmore Pl 36 D6
Lower London Rd 37 J3
Lutton Pl 37 H6
Lynedoch Pl La 36 C4
Lyne St 37 J3

M
McDonald Pl 37 G1
McDonald Rd 37 G1
McDonald St 37 G1
McEwan Sq 36 D6
Mackenzie Pl 36 D3
McLeod St 36 A6
McNeill St 36 D6
Magdala Cres 36 B5
Magdala Ms 36 B5
Malta Grn 36 D2
Malta Ter 36 D2
Manor Pl 36 C4
Mansionhouse Rd 37 G7
Marchhall Cres 37 J7
Marchhall Pl 37 J7
Marchhall Rd 37 J7
Marchmont Cres 37 F7
Marchmont Rd 37 F6
Marchmont St 37 E7
Market St 37 F4
Marshall's Ct 37 G3
Marshall St 37 G5
Maryfield 37 J3
Maryfield Pl 37 J3
Meadow La 37 G6
Meadow Pl 37 F7
Melgund Ter 37 F2
Melville Dr 37 E6
Melville St 36 C4
Melville St La 36 C4
Melville Ter 37 G7
Merchant St 37 F5
Merchiston Av 36 C7
Merchiston Gro 36 A7
Merchiston Ms 36 C7
Merchiston Pk 36 C7
Mertoun Pl 36 C7
Meuse La 37 F4
Middlefield 37 H1
Millerfield Pl 37 G7
Miller Row 36 C4
Milton St 37 J3

Minto St 37 H7
Moncrieff Ter 37 G7
Montague St 37 H6
Montgomery St 37 G2
Montgomery St La 37 G2
Montpelier 36 D7
Montpelier Pk 36 D7
Montpelier Ter 36 D7
Montrose Ter 37 J3
Moray Pl 36 D3
Morrison Circ 36 C5
Morrison Cres 36 D5
Morrison Link 36 D5
Morrison St 36 C5
Mound, The 37 F4
Mound Pl 37 F4
Multrees Wk 37 F3
Murano Pl 37 H2
Murdoch Ter 36 C6
Murieston Cres 36 B6
Murieston Cres La 36 B6
Murieston La 36 B7
Murieston Pl 36 B6
Murieston Rd 36 B6
Murieston Ter 36 B6
Myrtle Ter 36 B7

N
Napier Rd 36 C7
Nelson St 37 F2
New Arthur Pl 37 H5
Newington Rd 37 H7
New John's Pl 37 H6
New Skinner's Cl 37 G4
New St 37 G4
Newton St 36 A7
Nicolson Sq 37 G5
Nicolson St 37 G5
Niddry St 37 G4
Niddry St S 37 G5
Nightingale Way 37 F6
North Bk St 37 F4
North Br 37 G4
North Castle St 36 E3
North Charlotte St 36 D3
North Clyde St La 37 F3
Northcote St 36 B6
North E Circ Pl 36 E3
North Pk Ter 36 C2
North Richmond St 37 G5
North St. Andrew La 37 F3
North St. Andrew St 37 F3
North St. David St 37 F3
Northumberland
  Pl La 37 F3
Northumberland St 37 E3
Northumberland
  St N E La 37 F3
Northumberland
  St N W La 37 E3
Northumberland
  St S E La 37 F3
Northumberland
  St S W La 37 E3
North Werber Pk 36 A1
North Werber Pl 36 B1
North W Circ Pl 36 D3
Norton Pk 37 J2

O
Old Broughton 37 F2
Old Fishmarket Cl 37 G4
Old Tolbooth Wynd 37 H4
Orchard Bk 36 A3
Orchard Brae 36 B2
Orchard Brae Av 36 B3
Orchard Brae Gdns 36 B3
Orchard Brae
  Gdns W 36 B3
Orchard Brae W 36 B2
Orchard Cres 36 A3
Orchard Dr 36 A3
Orchard Gro 36 B2
Orchard Pl 36 B2
Orchard Rd 36 A3
Orchard Rd S 36 A3
Orchard Ter 36 A3
Orwell Pl 36 C6
Orwell Ter 36 C6
Oxford St 37 H6
Oxford Ter 36 C3

P
Palmerston Pl 36 C4
Panmure Pl 37 E6
Papermill Wynd 37 G1
Parkside St 37 H6
Parkside Ter 37 H6
Parliament Sq 37 F4
Pembroke Pl 36 B5
Perth St 36 E2
Picardy Pl 37 G3
Pilrig Gdns 37 G1
Pilrig Glebe 37 H1

Pleasance 37 G5
Polwarth Cres 36 C7
Polwarth Gdns 36 C7
Polwarth Pk 36 C7
Polwarth Pl 36 C7
Ponton St 36 D6
Portgower Pl 36 D2
Port Hamilton 36 D6
Potterrow 37 G5
Powderhall Rd 37 F1
Priestfield Rd N 37 J7
Primrose Ter 36 B7
Princes St 36 D4

Q
Queen's Dr 37 H5
Queensferry Rd 36 B3
Queensferry St 36 D4
Queensferry St La 36 D4
Queensferry Ter 36 B3
Queen St 36 E3
Queen St Gdns E 37 F3
Queen St Gdns W 37 E3

R
Raeburn Ms 36 D2
Raeburn Pl 36 D2
Raeburn St 36 D2
Ramsay Gdn 37 F4
Ramsay La 37 F4
Randolph Cres 36 D4
Randolph La 36 D4
Randolph Pl 36 D4
Rankeillor St 37 H6
Ravelston Dykes 36 A4
Ravelston Pk 36 A4
Ravelston Ter 36 B4
Regent Pl 37 J3
Regent Rd 37 G3
Regent Ter 37 H3
Regent Ter Ms 37 H3
Register Pl 37 F3
Reid's Cl 37 H4
Reid Ter 36 D2
Richmond La 37 G5
Richmond Pl 37 G5
Richmond Ter 36 C5
Riego St 36 E5
Rillbank Cres 37 G7
Rillbank Ter 37 G7
Rintoul Pl 36 D2
Ritchie Pl 36 B7
Robertson Av 36 A7
Robertson Gait 36 A7
Robertson's Cl 37 G5
Rodney Pl 37 F2
Rodney St 37 F1
Romero Pl 37 J7
Rosebank Cotts 36 D5
Rosebery Cres 36 C5
Rosebery Cres La 36 C5
Roseburn Av 36 A5
Roseburn Cliff 36 A5
Roseburn Dr 36 A5
Roseburn Gdns 36 A5
Roseburn Maltings 36 A5
Roseburn Pl 36 A5
Roseburn Ter 36 A5
Rosemount Bldgs 36 D6
Roseneath Pl 37 F7
Roseneath St 37 F7
Roseneath Ter 37 F7
Rose St 36 E4
Rose St N La 36 E4
Rose St S La 36 E4
Rossie Pl 37 J2
Rosslyn Cres 37 G1
Rosslyn Ter 37 H1
Rothesay Ms 36 C4
Rothesay Pl 36 C4
Rothesay Ter 36 C4
Roxburgh Pl 37 G5
Roxburgh St 37 G5
Royal Circ 36 E3
Royal Cres 37 F2
Royal Ter 37 G3
Russell Gdns 36 A5
Russell Rd 36 A5
Rutland Ct La 36 D5
Rutland Sq 36 D4
Rutland St 36 D4

S
St. Andrew Sq 37 F3
St. Bernard's Cres 36 D3
St. Bernard's Row 36 D2
St. Catherine's Pl 37 G7
St. Clair Av 37 J1
St. Clair Pl 37 J1
St. Clair Rd 37 J1
St. Clair St 37 J1
St. Colme St 36 D4
St. David's Pl 36 D5
St. David's Ter 36 D5

St. Giles St 37 F4
St. James Pl 37 G3
St. James Sq 37 G3
St. John's Hill 37 H5
St. John St 37 H4
St. Leonard's Bk 37 H6
St. Leonard's Hill 37 H6
St. Leonard's La 37 H6
St. Leonard's St 37 H6
St. Mary's St 37 G4
St. Patrick Sq 37 G6
St. Stephen Pl 36 D2
St. Stephen St 36 D3
St. Vincent St 36 E2
Salisbury Ms 37 H7
Salisbury Pl 37 H7
Salisbury Rd 37 H7
Saunders St 36 D3
Saxe Coburg Pl 36 D2
Saxe Coburg St 36 D2
Sciennes 37 G7
Sciennes Gdns 37 G7
Sciennes Hill Pl 37 G7
Sciennes Ho Pl 37 G7
Sciennes Pl 37 G7
Sciennes Rd 37 F7
Scotland St 37 F2
Semple St 36 D5
Seton Pl 37 G7
Shandwick Pl 36 D5
Shaw's Pl 37 H1
Shaw's St 37 H1
Shaw's Ter 37 H1
Shrub Pl La 37 H1

Sienna Gdns 37 G7
Silvermills 36 E2
Simon Sq 37 G5
Simpson Loan 37 F6
Sinclair Cl 36 A7
Sinclair Gdns 36 A7
Sinclair Pl 36 A7
Sloan St 37 J1
Smithfield St 36 A7
South Br 37 G4
South Charlotte St 36 E4
South Clerk St 37 H6
South Coll St 37 G5
South E Circ Pl 36 E3
South Gray's Cl 37 G4
South Learmonth Av 36 C3
South Learmonth Gdns 36 C3
South Lorne Pl 37 J1
South Oxford St 37 H7
South St. Andrew St 37 F3
South. St. David St 37 F3
South Sloan St 37 J1
Spence St 37 J7
Spey St 37 H1
Spey St La 37 H1
Spey Ter 37 H1
Spittal St 36 E5
Spottiswoode Rd 37 E7
Spottiswoode St 37 F7
Spring Gdns 37 J3
Springwell Pl 36 B6
Stafford St 36 D4
Stanhope Pl 36 B5

Stanhope St 36 B5
Stevenlaw's Cl 37 G4
Stewart Ter 36 A7
Stockbridge 36 E2
Succoth Gdns 36 A4
Succoth Pl 36 A4
Summer Bk 37 F2
Summerhall 37 G6
Summerhall Sq 37 H7
Sunbury Ms 36 C4
Sunbury Pl 36 C4
Sunbury St 36 C4
Sunnyside 37 J2
Sutherland St 36 B5
Sylvan Pl 37 G7

T
Tantallon Pl 37 G7
Tarvit St 37 E6
Tay St 36 C7
Temple Pk Cres 36 C7
Terrars Cft 37 H6
Teviotdale Pl 36 D1
Teviot Pl 37 F5
Thirlestane Rd 37 E7
Thistle Pl 36 C7
Thistle St 37 E3
Thistle St N E La 37 F3
Thistle St N W La 37 E3
Thistle St S W La 37 E3
Tollcross 36 D6
Thornybauk 36 E6
Torphichen St 36 D5
Tron Sq 37 G4

Tynecastle La 36 B7
Tynecastle Ter 36 A7
Tytler Gdns 37 J3

U
Union St 37 G2
Upper Bow 37 F4
Upper Coltbridge Ter 36 A4
Upper Damside 36 C4
Upper Dean Ter 36 D3
Upper Gilmore Pl 36 D6
Upper Gilmore Ter 36 D6
Upper Gray St 37 H7
Upper Gro Pl 36 D6

V
Valleyfield St 36 E6
Veitch's Sq 36 D2
Victoria St 37 F5
Viewcraig Gdns 37 H4
Viewcraig St 37 H5
Viewforth 36 C6
Viewforth Gdns 36 D7
Viewforth Sq 36 D7
Viewforth Ter 36 D7

W
Walker St 36 C4
Wardlaw Pl 36 A7
Wardlaw St 36 A7
Warrender Pk Cres 36 E7
Warrender Pk Rd 36 E7
Warrender Pk Ter 37 E7
Warriston Cres 37 E1

Warriston Rd 37 E1
Washington La 36 B6
Waterloo Pl 37 G3
Watson Cres 36 B7
Waverley Br 37 F4
Waverley Pk 37 J3
Waverley Pk Ter 37 J3
Waverley Pl 37 J3
Wellington St 37 H2
Wemyss Pl 36 E3
Wemyss Pl Ms 36 D3
West Adam St 37 G5
West Annandale St 37 F1
West App Rd 36 D5
West Bow 37 F5
West Bryson Rd 36 B7
West Castle Rd 36 C7
West Catherine Pl 36 B5
West Coates 36 A5
West Coll St 37 G5
West Crosscauseway 37 G6
West End Pl 36 C6
Wester Coates Av 36 A5
Wester Coates Gdns 36 A5
Wester Coates Pl 36 B5
Wester Coates Rd 36 B5
Wester Coates Ter 36 A5
Westfield St 36 A7
Westhall Gdns 36 D7
West Maitland St 36 C5
West Mill La 36 C4
West Montgomery Pl 37 H2
West Newington Pl 37 H7
West Nicolson St 37 G5

West Norton Pl 37 J3
West Pk Pl 36 C6
West Port 37 E5
West Preston St 37 H7
West Register St 37 F3
West Register St La 37 F3
West Richmond St 37 G5
West Scotland St La 37 F2
West Silvermills La 36 E2
West Tollcross 36 E6
West Wds 36 A1
Wheatfield Pl 36 A7
Wheatfield Rd 36 A7
Wheatfield St 36 A7
Wheatfield Ter 36 A7
Whitehouse Ln 36 E7
White Pk 36 A7
William St 36 C5
William St N E La 36 D4
William St N W La 36 D4
William St S E La 36 D4
William St S W La 36 D5
Windmill La 37 G6
Windmill St 37 G6
Windsor St 37 H2
Windsor St La 37 H2

Y
Yeaman Pl 36 C6
York La 37 G3
York Pl 37 F3
Young St 36 D4
Young St La N 36 E4
Young St La S 36 E4

Glasgow street index

A
Abbotsford Pl 39 E7
Abercromby Dr 39 J5
Abercromby Sq 39 J5
Abercromby St 39 J6
Academy Pk 38 A7
Adams Ct La 39 F5
Adelphi St 39 F6
Admiral St 38 C6
Aird's La 39 G5
Albert Br 39 G6
Albert Dr 38 B7
Albion Gate 39 G4
Albion St 39 G5
Alexander Cres 39 F7
Alexandra Par 39 J3
Anchor La 39 F4
Anderston 38 E4
Anderston Quay 38 C5
Anson St 39 J7
Anthony St 38 D4
Arcadia Pl 39 J6
Arcadia St 39 J6
Argyle St 39 F4
Argyll Arc 39 F4
Ark La 39 J4
Arlington St 38 D2
Armour St 39 J5
Arthur St 38 A2
Ashley La 38 D2
Ashley St 38 D2
Ashton La 38 A1
Ashton Rd 38 A1
Auchentoshan Ter 39 J1

B
Bain St 39 H5
Baird St 39 H2
Balaclava St 38 D4
Baliol La 38 D2
Baliol St 38 D2
Ballantrae Ct 38 D4
Ballater Pl 39 G7
Ballater St 39 F6
Bank St 38 B1
Barrack St 39 J5
Barrington Dr 38 C1
Bath La 38 D3
Bath St 38 D3
Beaumont Gate 38 A1
Bedford La 39 F6
Bedford St 39 E6
Bell St 39 G4
Beltane St 38 D3
Benny Lynch Ct 39 G6
Benthall St 39 G7
Bentinck St 38 B2
Berkeley St 38 C3
Berkeley Ter La 38 C3
Binnie Pl 39 H6

Bishop St 38 D4
Blackburn St 38 B5
Blackfriars St 39 G4
Blackie St 38 B3
Black St 39 H2
Blantyre St 38 A2
Blythswoodhill 38 E3
Blythswood Sq 38 E3
Blythswood St 38 E4
Bothwell La 38 E4
Bothwell La (Hillhead) 38 C1
Bothwell St 38 E4
Braid Sq 38 E1
Braid St 38 E1
Breadalbane St 38 C3
Brechin St 38 C3
Bridgegate 39 F5
Bridge St 39 E6
Bridgeton Cross 39 J6
Bright St 39 J2
Broadford St 39 G1
Broomielaw 38 E5
Broompark Dr 39 J4
Brown St 38 E5
Bruce Rd 38 B7
Brunswick St 39 G4
Buccleuch La 38 E2
Buccleuch St 38 D2
Buchanan St 39 F4
Bunhouse Rd 38 A2
Burnbank Gdns 38 D1
Burnbank La 38 D1
Burnbank Pl 38 D1
Burnbank Ter 38 D1
Burns St 39 E1
Bute Gdns 38 B1
Bute La 38 B1

C
Cadogan St 38 E4
Cadzow St 38 D4
Caledonian Cres 38 C1
Caledonia Rd 39 F7
Caledon La 38 A1
Caledon St 38 A1
Calgary St 39 G2
Cambridge St 39 E3
Camden Ter 39 F7
Canal St 39 G2
Candleriggs 39 G5
Cardwell St 38 E7
Carfrae St 38 A3
Carlton Ct 39 E5
Carlton Pl 39 F5
Carnarvon St 38 D2
Carnoustie Pl 38 D6
Carnoustie St 38 D6
Carrick St 38 E5
Carrington St 38 D1

Castle St 39 H4
Cathcart Rd 39 F7
Cathedral Sq 39 H4
Cathedral St 39 F3
Cavendish Pl 39 E7
Cavendish St 39 E7
Cecil St 38 B1
Cedar Ct 38 E1
Cedar St 38 E1
Centre St 38 E6
Cessnock 38 A5
Chalmers St 39 J5
Charles St 39 J2
Charlotte St 39 H5
Cheapside St 38 D5
Chisolm St 39 G5
Church St 38 A2
Circus Dr 39 J4
Citizen La 39 F4
Civic St 39 E2
Clairmont Gdns 38 C2
Claremont Pl 38 C2
Claremont St 38 C3
Claremont Ter 38 C2
Claremont Ter La 38 C2
Clarendon Pl 38 D1
Clarendon St 38 D1
Clayslaps Rd 38 B2
Claythorn Av 39 H6
Claythorn Circ 39 H5
Claythorn Pk 39 H6
Claythorn St 39 J5
Claythorn Ter 39 J5
Cleland La 39 F6
Cleland St 39 F6
Cleveland La 38 D3
Cleveland St 38 D3
Clifford La 38 A6
Clifford Pl 38 A6
Clifford St 38 A6
Cliff Rd 38 C1
Clifton Pl 38 C3
Clifton St 38 C2
Clutha St 38 A6
Clyde Arc 38 B5
Clyde Pl 38 E5
Clydeside Expressway 38 B4
Clyde St 39 F5
Cobden Rd 39 J1
Coburg St 39 E6
Cochrane St 39 G4
College La 39 H4
College St 39 G4
Collins St 39 H4
Commerce St 39 E5
Commercial Ct 39 G6
Commercial Rd 39 G7
Congress Rd 38 B4
Congress Way 38 B4

Cook St 38 E6
Cooperage Pl 38 A3
Corn St 39 E1
Cornwall St S 38 B7
Corunna St 38 B3
Couper Pl 39 G2
Couper St 39 G2
Cowan La 38 C1
Cowan St 38 B1
Cowcaddens 39 F2
Cowcaddens Rd 39 E2
Cownwall St 38 B6
Cragmaddie Ter La 38 B2
Craighall Rd 39 F1
Craigiehall Pl 38 B5
Craigiehall St 38 B5
Cranston Hill 38 C3
Cranston St 38 C4
Cressnock St 38 A5
Crimea St 38 D4
Cromwell La 38 D1
Cromwell St 38 D1
Crownpoint Rd 39 J6
Crown St 39 F7
Cumberland Pl 39 G7
Cumberland St 39 E6

D
Dale Path 39 J7
Dalhouse St 38 E3
Dalhousie St 38 E2
Dalintober St 38 D6
Dalmarnock Rd 39 J7
Dalnair St 38 A2
Derby St 38 B3
Devon Pl 39 E7
Devon St 39 E7
Dixon St 39 F5
Dobbies Ln 39 F2
Dobbie's Ln Pl 39 G3
Dornoch St 39 J6
Dorset St 38 C3
Douglas La 38 E3
Douglas St 38 E4
Dover St 38 C3
Drake St 39 J6
Drury St 39 F4
Drygate 39 H4
Duke St 39 H4
Duke Wynd 41 J4
Dunblane St 39 F2
Dunchattan Pl 39 J5
Dundashill 39 F1
Dundas La 39 F3
Dundas St 39 F3
Dunearn St 38 D1
Dunlop St 39 F5
Durham St 38 B6

E
Eaglesham Ct 38 B5
Eaglesham Pl 38 B5
Eagle St 39 F1
Earlston Av 39 J2
Earlston Pl 39 J2
East Bath La 39 F3
East Campbell St 39 H5
Edington St 39 E1
Edwin St 38 B6
Eglinton Ct 39 E6
Elcho St 39 J5
Elderslie St 38 C2
Eldon St 38 C1
Elie St 38 A1
Elliot Pl 38 C4
Elliot St 38 C4
Elmbank Cres 38 D3
Elmbank St 38 D3
Elmbank St La 38 D3
Errol Gdns 39 F6
Esmond St 38 A2
Eton La 38 B1
Exchange Pl 39 F4

F
Falfield St 38 E7
Farnell St 39 E1
Finnieston 38 B3
Finnieston Quay 38 B4
Finnieston Sq 38 C3
Finnieston St 38 C4
Firpark St 39 J3
Firpark Ter 39 J4
Fitzroy La 38 B3
Florence St 39 G6
Forbes Dr 39 J6
Forbes St 39 J5
Fountainwell Dr 39 H1
Fountainwell Gdns 39 H1
Fountainwell Gro 39 H1
Fountainwell Rd 39 H1
Fountainwell St 39 H1
Fox St 39 F5
Francis St 38 E7

G
Gadshill St 39 J2
Gallowgate 39 H5
Garnethill 38 E2
Garnethill St 38 E2
Garnet St 38 D3
Garscube Rd 39 E2
Garth St 39 G4
George Sq 39 F4
George St 39 G4
Gibson St 39 H5
Gibson St (Hillhead) 38 B1
Gilbert St 38 A3
Gilmour Pl 39 G7

Gladstone St 38 D1
Glasgow Br 39 F5
Glassford St 39 G4
Glebe Ct 39 H3
Glebe St 39 H2
Glenbarr St 39 J2
Glenfarg St 38 D1
Glenmavis St 39 E2
Gloucester St 38 D6
Goosedubbs 39 G5
Gorbals 39 G7
Gorbals St 39 F7
Gordon La 39 F4
Gordon St 39 E4
Gourock St 38 E7
Govan Rd 38 A5
Grace St 38 C4
Grafton Pl 39 G3
Graham Sq 39 J5
Graignestock St 39 J6
Granby La 38 B1
Grant St 38 D2
Granville St 38 D3
Gray St 38 B3
Great Dovehill 39 H5
Great George St 38 B1
Green, The 39 J7
Greendyke St 39 G5
Greenhead St 39 J6
Green St 39 J6
Grovepark Ct 38 D1
Grovepark Gdns 38 D1

H
Hallside Pl 39 G7
Handel Pl 39 F7
Hanover St 39 F4
Harley St 38 A6
Harvey St 39 F1
Harvie St 38 B5
Hastie St 38 A2
Haugh Rd 38 A3
Havannah St 39 H4
Hayfield Ct 39 G7
Hayfield St 39 G7
Herbertson St 39 E6
High Craighall Rd 39 F1
High St 39 G5
Hillhead St 38 B1
Hill St 38 D2
Holland St 38 D3
Holm St 38 E4
Holyrood Cres 38 C1
Holyrood Quad 38 D1
Hopehill Rd 38 D1
Hope St 39 E4
Houldsworth La 38 C3
Houldsworth St 38 C3
Houston Pl 38 C5
Houston St 38 C6

Street	Ref		Street	Ref		Street	Ref
Howard St	39 F5		Lynedoch Cres La	38 C2		Napiershall Pl	38 D1
Hunter St	39 H5		Lynedoch Pl	38 C2		Napiershall St	38 D1
Huntingdon Rd	39 H1		Lynedoch St	38 C2		Nelson Mandela Pl	39 F4
Hutcheson St	39 G5		Lynedoch Ter	38 D2		Nelson St	38 E5
Hutchesontown	39 G7					Netherby Dr	38 A7
Hutchison Town Ct	39 G7		**M**			New City Rd	38 D2
Hydepark St	38 C5		Mcalpine St	38 D5		Newton St	38 D2
			McAslin Ct	39 H3		Newton Ter La	38 C3
I			Mcaslin St	39 H3		New Wynd	39 G5
India St	38 D3		McCulloch St	38 C7		Nicholas St	39 H4
Ingram St	39 G4		Mcfarlane St	39 H5		Nicholson St	39 F6
			McIntosh Ct	39 J4		Norfolk Ct	39 F6
J			McIntosh St	39 J4		Norfolk St	39 F6
Jamaica St	39 F5		Mcintyre St	38 D4		North Canal Bk	39 G1
James Morrison St	39 G5		MacKeith St	39 J7		North Canal Bk St	39 F1
James Nisbet St	39 J3		MacKinlay St	39 E7		North Claremont St	38 C2
James St	39 J7		Maclean Sq	38 B5		North Ct	39 F4
James Watt St	38 E5		Maclean St	38 B5		North Ct La	39 F4
Jocelyn Sq	39 G5		Maclennan St	38 A6		North Dr	39 F4
John Knox St	39 J4		Macleod St	39 H4		North Frederick Path	39 G3
John St	39 G4		McNeil Gdns	39 H7		North Frederick St	39 G4
			McNeil St	39 G7		North Gower St	38 A6
K			McPhail St	39 J7		North Hanover St	39 G4
Kelvingrove	38 B2		McPhater St	39 F2		North Portland St	39 G4
Kelvingrove St	38 B3		Mair St	38 B5		North St	38 D2
Kelvinhaugh	38 A3		Maitland St	39 F2		North Wallace St	39 G2
Kelvinhaugh Gate	38 A3		Malta Ter	39 F7			
Kelvinhaugh Pl	38 B3		Manresa Pl	39 E1		**O**	
Kelvinhaugh St	38 A3		Marine Cres	38 C5		Oakfield Av	38 B1
Kelvin Way	38 B2		Marine Gdns	38 C5		Oakfield La	38 B1
Kennedy Path	39 G3		Marlow St	38 C7		Oak St	38 D4
Kennedy St	39 G3		Martha St	39 G3		Old Dumbarton Rd	38 A2
Kent Rd	38 C3		Mart St	39 G5		Old Rutherglen Rd	39 G6
Kent St	39 H5		Mary St	39 F1		Old Wynd	39 G5
Keppochhill Pl	39 G1		Mauchline St	38 E7		Oregon Pl	39 G7
Keppochhill Way	39 G1		Mavisbank Gdns	38 B5		Orr St	39 J6
Kerr Dr	39 J6		Maxwell Av	38 C7		Osborne St	39 F5
Kerr Pl	39 J6		Maxwell Ct	38 B7		Oswald St	39 E5
Kerr St	39 J6		Maxwell Dr	38 B7		Otago La	38 C1
Kidston Pl	39 F7		Maxwell Gdns	38 A7		Otago La N	38 C1
Kidston Ter	39 F7		Maxwell Grn	38 B7		Otago St	38 B1
Kilbarchan St	39 E6		Maxwell La	38 C7		Overnewton Pl	38 B3
Kilbirnie Pl	38 D7		Maxwell Oval	38 C7		Overnewton Sq	38 A3
Kilbirnie St	38 D7		Maxwell Rd	38 C7		Overnewton St	38 A2
Killermont St	39 F3		Maxwell St	39 F5		Oxford La	39 F6
King George V Br	39 E5		Megan Gate	39 J7		Oxford St	39 E5
King's Br	39 H7		Megan St	39 J7			
King's Dr	39 H7		Melbourne St	39 J5		**P**	
Kingston	38 D6		Melrose St	38 D1		Pacific Dr	38 A5
Kingston St	38 E5		**Merchant City**	39 G4		Pacific Quay	38 A4
King St	39 G5		Merchant La	39 G5		Paisley Rd	38 D5
Kinning Pk	38 B6		Metropole La	39 F5		Paisley Rd W	38 C5
Kinning St	38 D6		Middlesex Gdns	38 B6		Palmerston Pl	38 B3
Kyle St	39 G2		Middlesex St	38 B6		Parnie St	39 G5
			Middleton St	38 A5		Park Av	38 C1
L			Midland St	39 E4		Park Circ	38 C2
La Belle Allee	38 C2		Midwharf St	39 F1		Park Circ La	38 C2
La Belle Pl	38 C2		Miller St	39 F4		Park Circ Pl	38 C2
Ladywell St	39 J4		Millroad Dr	39 J5		Park Dr	38 C1
Laidlaw St	38 D6		Millroad Gdns	39 J5		Park Gdns	38 C2
Laird Pl	39 J7		Millroad St	39 H5		Park Gdns La	38 C2
Lambhill Quad	38 B6		Milnpark Gdns	38 B6		Park Gate	38 C2
Lambhill St	38 B6		Milnpark St	38 B6		Parkgrove Ter	38 B2
Lanark St	39 H5		Milton St	39 F2		Parkgrove Ter La	38 B2
Lancefield Quay	38 C4		Minerva St	38 B3		Park Quad	38 C2
Lancefield St	38 C4		Minerva Way	38 B3		Park Rd	38 C1
Landressy Pl	39 J7		Mitchell La	39 F4		Park St S	38 C2
Landressy St	39 J7		Mitchell St	39 F4		Park Ter	38 C2
Langshot St	38 A6		Moffat St	39 G7		Park Ter E La	38 C2
Lansdowne Cres	38 C1		Moir St	39 H5		Park Terrrace La	38 C2
Lansdowne Cres La	38 C1		Molendinar St	39 H5		Parsonage Row	39 H4
Larbert St	39 F2		Moncur St	39 H5		Parsonage Sq	39 H4
Laurieston	39 F6		Montague St	38 C1		Parson St	39 H3
Laurieston Rd	39 F7		Monteith Pl	39 H6		Paterson St	38 D6
Lendel Pl	38 A6		Monteith Row	39 H5		Payne St	39 F1
Lilybank Gdns	38 A1		Montrose St	39 G4		Pembroke St	38 C3
Lilybank Gdns La	38 A1		Moore St	39 J5		Percy St	38 A6
Lilybank Ter	38 B1		Morrison Ct	39 F4		Perth St	38 D4
Lister St	39 H2		Morrison St	38 D5		Piccadilly St	38 D4
Little Dovehill	39 H5		Mosque Av	39 F6		Pine Pl	39 G7
Little St	38 C4		Muslin St	39 J7		Pinkston Dr	39 H2
London Rd	39 G5					Pinkston Rd	39 H2
Lorne St	38 B5		**N**			Pitt St	38 E4
Lumsden St	38 A3		Naburn Gate	39 F7		Plantation Pk Gdns	38 A6
Lymburn St	38 B2		Nairn St	38 A2		Plantation Sq	38 B5
Lynedoch Cres	38 C2		Napiershall La	38 D1		**Port Dundas**	38 D1

Street	Ref		Street	Ref		Street	Ref
Port Dundas La	39 F3		St. Vincent Ter	38 C3		Tullis St	39 J7
Port Dundas Rd	39 F2		Salisbury La	39 F7		Tunnel St	38 B4
Port Eglington	38 D7		Salisbury St	39 F7		Tureen St	39 J5
Portman St	38 C6		Salkeld St	38 E7		Turnbull St	39 G5
Port St	38 C3		Saltmarket	39 G5		Turnlaw St	39 H7
Portugal St	39 F6		Sandiefield Rd	39 F6		Turriff St	39 E7
Possil Rd	39 E1		Sandyford Pl La	38 C3		Tyndrum St	39 F2
Professors Sq	38 B1		Sandyford St	38 A3			
Provanhill St	39 J2		Saracen Head Rd	39 H5		**U**	
			Sauchiehall La	38 E3		Union Pl	39 F4
Q			Sauchiehall St	38 B2		Union St	39 F4
Queen Elizabeth Gdns	39 G7		Savoy St	39 J7		Unity Pl	38 E1
Queens Cres	38 D1		Sawmillfield St	39 E1		University Av	38 A1
Queen St	39 F4		Scotland St	38 C6		University Gdns	38 A1
			Scotland St W	38 B6		University Pl	38 A1
R			Scott St	38 E3			
Radnor St	38 B2		Seamore St	38 D1		**V**	
Raglan St	38 E1		Seaward La	38 C5		Vermont St	38 B6
Regent Moray St	38 A2		Seaward Pl	38 C6		Victoria Br	39 F5
Renfield La	39 E4		Seaward St	38 C6		Viewfield La	38 B1
Renfield St	39 F4		Shaftesbury St	38 D3		Vinter St	39 F1
Renfrew Ct	39 F3		Shamrock St	38 E2		Virginia Pl	39 G4
Renfrew La	39 F3		Shields Rd	38 C6		Virginia St	39 G4
Renfrew St	38 D2		Shipbank La	39 G5			
Renton St	39 F2		Shuttle St	39 G4		**W**	
Rhymer St	39 J2		**Sighthill**	39 H1		Waddell Ct	39 G6
Richmond St	39 G4		Sighthill Av	39 H1		Waddell St	39 G7
Ritchie St	38 E7		Silverfir St	39 G7		Wallace St	38 D5
Riverview Dr	38 D5		Silvergrove St	39 J6		Walls St	39 G4
Riverview Gdns	38 E5		Snowdon St	39 G7		Walmer Cres	38 A6
Riverview Pl	38 D5		Somerset Pl Ms	38 C2		Warnock St	39 J3
Robertson La	38 E4		South Ex Ct	39 F4		Warroch St	38 D5
Robertson St	38 E5		South Frederick St	39 G4		Washington St	38 D5
Rodney St	39 E1		Southpark Av	38 B1		Waterloo La	39 E4
Ropework La	39 F5		Southpark La	39 F5		Waterloo St	38 E4
Rose St	39 E3		South Portland St	39 F5		Waterside Pl	39 H7
Ross St	39 H5		Southside Cres	39 F7		Waterside St	39 G7
Rottenrow	39 G3		South Woodside Rd	38 C1		Watson St	39 G5
Rottenrow E	39 H4		Spiers Wf	39 F1		Watt St	38 C6
Royal Bk Pl	39 F4		Spoutmouth	39 H5		Weaver St	39 H4
Royal Cres	38 B3		Springburn Rd	39 J2		Wellcroft Pl	39 E7
Royal Ex Ct	39 F4		Springfield Ct	39 F4		Wellington La	38 E4
Royal Ex Sq	39 F4		Springfield Quay	38 C5		Wellington St	39 E4
Royal Ter	38 B2		Spring Wynd	39 G7		Wellpark St	39 J4
Royal Ter La	38 B2		Stafford St	39 G2		Westbank La	38 B1
Royston	39 J2		Stanley St	38 C6		Westbank Quad	38 B1
Roystonhill	39 J2		Stanley St La	38 C6		West Campbell St	38 E4
Royston Rd	39 J2		Steel St	39 G5		West End Pk St	38 C2
Royston Sq	39 J2		Stevenson St	39 J6		West George La	38 E3
Rupert St	38 D1		Stewart St	39 F2		West George St	39 E3
Rutland Ct	38 C5		Stirlingfauld Pl	39 F7		West Graham St	38 E2
Rutland Cres	38 C5		Stirling Rd	39 H3		West Greenhill Pl	38 B3
Rutland Pl	38 B5		Stobcross Rd	38 A3		West Nile St	39 F4
			Stobcross St	38 C4		West Prince's La	38 C1
S			Stobcross Wynd	38 A3		West Princes St	38 C1
St. Andrews Cres	38 C7		Stockwell Pl	39 F5		West Regent La	39 E3
St. Andrew's La	39 G5		Stockwell St	39 F5		West Regent St	39 E3
St. Andrews Rd	38 C7		Stromness St	38 E7		West St	38 D7
St. Andrews Sq	39 G5		Suffolk St	39 H5		Whitehall St	38 D3
St. Andrews St	39 G5		Surrey St	39 F7		William St	38 D3
St. Clair St	38 D1		Sussex St	38 B6		Willowbank Cres	38 C1
St. Enoch	39 F5		Sutherland La	38 A1		Willowbank St	38 C2
St. Enoch Sq	39 F4		Swan St	39 G2		Wilson St	39 G4
St. Francis Rigg	39 G7		Sydney St	39 J5		Windsor St	38 D1
St. Georges Rd	38 D2					Windsor Ter	38 D1
St. Georges Rd	38 D2		**T**			Wishart St	39 J4
St. James Rd	39 G3		Taylor Pl	39 H3		Woodlands Dr	38 C1
St. John's Ct	38 B7		Taylor St	39 H4		Woodlands Gate	38 C1
St. John's Quad	38 C7		Templeton St	39 J6		Woodlands Rd	38 C1
St. Josephs Vw	39 J2		Teviot St	38 A3		Woodlands Ter	38 C2
St. Luke's Pl	39 F6		Thistle St	39 G6		Woodrow Circ	38 A7
St. Luke's Ter	39 F6		Thistle Ter	39 F7		Woodrow Pl	38 A7
St. Margaret's Pl	39 G5		Thornbank St	38 A3		Woodrow Rd	38 A7
St. Marys La	39 F4		Thurso St	38 A2		Woodside Cres	38 D2
St. Mungo Av	39 G3		Tobago Pl	39 J5		Woodside Pl	38 C2
St. Mungo Pl	39 H3		Tobago St	39 J6		Woodside Pl La	38 C2
St. Ninian Ter	39 F6		Toll La	38 C5		Woodside Ter	38 C2
St. Peters La	38 E4		Tontine La	39 G5		Woodside Ter La	38 C2
St. Peters St	38 E2		Torness St	38 A1			
St. Rollox Brae	39 J1		Tower St	38 B6		**Y**	
St. Valentine Ter	39 G7		**Townhead**	39 G2		**Yorkhill**	38 B2
St. Vincent Cres	38 B3		Townsend St	39 F2		Yorkhill Par	38 A2
St. Vincent Cres La	38 B3		**Tradeston**	38 E6		Yorkhill St	38 A3
St. Vincent La	38 E3		Tradeston St	38 E6		York St	38 E5
St. Vincent Pl	39 F4		Trongate	39 G5			
St. Vincent St	38 C3		Tullis Ct	39 J7			

Leeds street index

Street	Ref		Street	Ref		Street	Ref
A			Albion St	41 E3		Apex Way	41 E6
Abbey St	40 C3		Alexander St	40 E3		Appleton Cl	41 J3
Abbott Ct	40 A3		Alexandra Gro	40 B1		Appleton Ct	41 J3
Abbott Rd	40 A4		Alexandra Rd	40 A1		Appleton Sq	41 J3
Abbott Vw	40 A3		Alma St	41 H2		Appleton Way	41 J3
Admiral St	41 E7		Anderson Av	41 H1		Archery Pl	40 D1
Aire St	40 D4		Anderson Mt	41 H1		Archery Rd	40 D1
Albion Pl	41 E3		Apex Vw	40 E6		Archery St	40 E1

Street	Ref		Street	Ref		Street	Ref
Archery Ter	40 E1		Ashton Av	41 J1		Atkinson St	41 G6
Armley Rd	40 A3		Ashton Gro	41 J1		Autumn Av	40 B1
Armouries Rd	41 G5		Ashton Mt	41 J1		Autumn Gro	40 B1
Artist St	40 B4		Ashton Pl	41 J1		Autumn Pl	40 B1
Ascot Ter	41 J4		Ashton Ter	41 J1		Autumn St	40 B1
Ashley Av	41 J1		Ashton Vw	41 J1		Autumn Ter	40 B1
Ashley Rd	41 J1		Ashville Vw	40 A1		Avenue, The	41 G4
Ashley Ter	41 J1		Assembly St	41 F4		Aysgarth Cl	41 J4

Aysgarth Dr	41 J4	Burley Lo Pl	40 B2	Colenso Pl	40 C7	Duxbury Ri	40 E1	Glensdale Gro	41 J4	Ingram Rd	40 C7
Aysgarth Pl	41 J4	Burley Lo Rd	40 A1	Colenso Rd	40 C7	Dyer St	41 F3	Glensdale Mt	41 J4	Ingram Row	40 E5
Aysgarth Wk	41 J4	Burley Lo St	40 B2	Colenso Ter	40 C7			Glensdale Rd	41 J4	Ingram St	40 E5
		Burley Lo Ter	40 B1	Colville Ter	40 D7	**E**		Glensdale St	41 J4	Ingram Vw	40 C6
B		Burley Pl	40 A2	Commercial St	41 E3	East Fld St	41 H4	Glensdale Ter	41 J4	Inner Ring Rd	40 E2
Back Ashville Av	40 A1	Burley Rd	40 A1	Compton Av	41 J1	Eastgate	41 F3	Glenthorpe Av	41 J3	Ivory St	41 F6
Back Hyde Ter	40 C2	Burley St	40 C3	Compton Cres	41 J1	East King St	41 G4	Glenthorpe Cres	41 J3		
Back Row	40 E5	**Burmantofts**	41 H3	Compton Gro	41 J1	East Par	40 E3	Glenthorpe Ter	41 J3	**J**	
Balm Pl	40 C6	Burmantofts St	41 G3	Compton Mt	41 J1	East Pk Dr	41 J4	Globe Rd	40 C4	Jack La	40 D6
Balm Wk	40 C6	Burton Row	41 E7	Compton Pl	41 J1	East Pk Gro	41 J4	Gloucester Ter	40 A4	Jenkinson Cl	40 D6
Bank St	41 E4	Burton St	41 E7	Compton Rd	41 J1	East Pk Mt	41 J4	Goodman St	41 G6	Jenkinson Lawn	40 D6
Baron Cl	40 C7	Burton Way	41 J2	Compton St	41 J1	East Pk Par	41 J4	Gotts Rd	40 C4	John Smeaton	
Barrack St	41 F1	Butterfield St	41 H4	Compton Ter	41 J1	East Pk Pl	41 J4	Gower St	41 F3	Viaduct	41 G6
Barran Ct	41 H1	Butterley St	41 F6	Compton Vw	41 J1	East Pk Rd	41 J4	Grace St	40 D3	Joseph St	41 G7
Barton Gro	40 D7	Butts Ct	41 E3	Concordia St	41 E4	East Pk St	41 J4	Grafton St	41 F2	Junction St	41 F5
Barton Mt	40 D7	Byron St	41 F2	Concord St	41 F2	East Pk Ter	41 J4	Grange Cl	41 G7		
Barton Pl	40 C7			Consort St	40 C2	East Pk Vw	41 J4	Grange Rd	41 G7	**K**	
Barton Rd	40 C7	**C**		Consort Ter	40 C2	Easy Rd	41 H5	Grant Av	41 G4	Keeton St	41 H3
Barton Ter	40 D7	Cain Cl	41 H4	Consort Vw	40 B2	Ebor Mt	40 B1	Granville Rd	41 H2	Kelsall Av	40 B1
Barton Vw	40 C7	Call La	41 F4	Consort Wk	40 C2	Ebor Pl	40 B1	Grape St	41 F7	Kelsall Gro	40 B2
Bath Rd	40 D5	Calls, The	41 F4	Constance Gdns	40 E1	Ebor St	40 B1	Grasmere Cl	40 A5	Kelsall Pl	40 B1
Bayswater Vw	41 H1	Calverley St	40 D2	Constance Way	40 E1	Edgware Av	41 H1	Grassmere Rd	40 A5	Kelsall Rd	40 B1
Beamsley Gro	40 A1	Cambrian St	40 D7	Cookridge St	40 E3	Edgware Gro	41 H1	Great George St	40 D3	Kelsall Ter	40 B1
Beamsley Mt	40 A1	Cambrian Ter	40 D7	Copley Hill	40 A5	Edgware Mt	41 H1	Great Wilson St	40 E5	Kelso Gdns	40 C1
Beamsley Pl	40 A1	Canal Pl	40 A1	Copley Hill Way	40 A6	Edgware Pl	41 H1	Greek St	40 E3	Kelso Rd	40 C1
Beamsley Ter	40 A1	Canal St	40 A3	Copley St	40 A5	Edgware Row	41 H1	Greenfield Rd	41 H4	Kelso St	40 C2
Beckett St	41 H3	Canal Wf	40 D4	Copperfield Av	41 J5	Edgware Ter	41 H1	Green La	40 A5	Kendal Bk	40 C2
Bedford St	40 E3	Carberry Pl	40 A1	Copperfield Cres	41 J5	Edgware Vw	41 H1	Grosvenor Hill	41 E1	Kendal Cl	40 C2
Beech Gro Ter	40 D1	Carberry Rd	40 A1	Copperfield Gro	41 J5	Edward St	41 F3			Kendal Gro	40 C2
Belgrave St	41 E3	Carberry Ter	40 A1	Copperfield Mt	41 J5	Edwin Rd	40 B1	**H**		Kendal La	40 C2
Belinda St	41 H7	Carlisle Rd	41 G5	Copperfield Pl	41 J5	Eighth Av	40 A5	Hall Gro	40 B1	Kendell St	41 F4
Belle Vue Rd	40 B2	Carlton Carr	41 E1	Copperfield Row	41 J5	Elland Rd	40 C7	Hall La	40 A4	Kenneth St	40 B6
Bell St	41 G3	Carlton Ct	40 A7	Copperfield Ter	41 J5	Elland Ter	40 D6	Hall Pl	41 H4	Kepler Gro	41 H1
Belmont Gro	40 D2	Carlton Gdns	41 E1	Copperfield Vw	41 J5	Ellerby La	41 H5	Hanover Av	40 C2	Kepler Mt	41 H1
Benson St	41 F1	Carlton Gate	41 E1	Copperfield Wk	41 J5	Ellerby Rd	41 G4	Hanover La	40 D3	Kepler Ter	41 H1
Benyon Pk Way	40 A7	Carlton Gro	41 E1	Copperfiield Dr	41 J5	Elmtree La	41 G7	Hanover Mt	40 C2	Kidacre St	41 F5
Berking Av	41 J3	Carlton Hill	41 E1	Cotton St	41 G4	Elmwood La	41 F2	Hanover Sq	40 C2	Kildare Ter	40 B5
Bertrand St	40 C6	Carlton Pl	41 E1	Coupland Pl	40 D7	Elmwood Rd	41 E2	Hanover St	40 C3	King Charles St	41 E3
Bexley Av	41 H1	Carlton Ri	41 E1	Coupland Rd	40 D7	Elsworth St	40 A4	Hanover Wk	41 F3	King Edward St	41 F3
Bexley Gro	41 J1	Carlton Vw	41 E1	Cowper Av	41 J1	Enfield Av	41 G1	Harewood St	41 F3	Kings Av	40 B2
Bexley Mt	41 H1	Castle St	40 D3	Cowper Cres	41 J1	Enfield St	41 G1	Harold Av	40 A1	King's Rd	40 B1
Bexley Pl	41 H1	Castleton Cl	40 B4	Cowper Rd	40 A3	Enfield Ter	41 G1	Harold Gro	40 A1	Kingston Ter	40 D1
Bexley Rd	41 J1	Castleton Rd	40 A3	Cromer Pl	41 J5	Euston Gro	40 C1	Harold Mt	40 A1	King St	40 D4
Bexley Ter	41 J1	Cautley Rd	41 J5	Cromer Rd	40 C1	Euston Mt	40 C1	Harold Pl	40 A1	Kippax Pl	41 H4
Bingley St	40 C3	Cavalier App	41 H5	Cromer St	40 C1	Euston Ter	40 C2	Harold Rd	40 A1	Kirkgate	41 F4
Bishopgate St	40 E4	Cavalier Cl	41 H5	Cromer Ter	40 C2	Everleigh St	41 J3	Harold St	40 A1	Kirkstall Rd	40 A2
Bismarck Dr	40 E7	Cavalier Ct	41 H5	Cromwell Mt	41 G2			Harold Ter	40 A1	Kitson Rd	41 G6
Bismarck St	40 E7	Cavalier Gdns	41 H5	Cromwell St	41 G3	**F**		Harold Vw	40 A1	Kitson St	41 H4
Black Bull St	41 F5	Cavalier Gate	41 H5	Crosby Pl	40 C6	Far Cft Ter	40 A5	Harold Wk	40 A1	Knowsthorpe Cres	41 H5
Blackman La	40 E1	Cavalier Ms	41 H5	Crosby Rd	40 C7	Fewston Av	41 H5	Harper St	41 F4	Knowsthorpe La	41 J6
Blandford Gdns	40 D1	Cavalier Vw	41 H5	Crosby St	40 C6	Fewston Ct	41 J5	Harrison St	41 F3		
Blandford Gro	40 D1	Cavendish Rd	40 D1	Crosby Ter	40 C6	Fieldhead Ter	40 E1	Hartwell Rd	40 B1	**L**	
Blayds St	41 H4	Cavendish St	40 C3	Crosby Vw	40 C6	Finsbury Rd	40 D2	Haslewood Cl	41 H3	Ladybeck Cl	41 F3
Blayd's Yd	41 E4	Cemetery Rd	40 C7	Cross Aysgarth Mt	41 H4	First Av	40 A4	Haslewood Ct	41 H3	Lady La	41 F3
Blenheim Av	40 E1	Central Rd	41 F4	Cross Belgrave St	41 F3	Firth St	41 J6	Haslewood Dene	41 H3	Lady Pit La	40 D7
Blenheim Ct	40 E1	Central St	40 D3	Cross Catherine St	41 H4	Firth Ter	41 J6	Haslewood Dr	41 H3	Lands La	41 E3
Blenheim Cres	40 E1	Chadwick St	41 F5	**Cross Grn**		Fish St	41 H5	Haslewood Ms	41 J3	Lane, The	41 G4
Blenheim Gro	40 E1	Chadwick St S	41 G5	Cross Grn App	41 J6	Flax Pl	41 G4	Haslewood Pl	41 H3	Larchfield Rd	41 G6
Blenheim Sq	40 E1	Chantrell Ct	41 F4	Cross Grn Av	41 J6	Florence Av	41 J1	Haslewood Sq	41 H3	Latchmore Rd	40 A7
Blenheim Vw	40 D1	Charles Av	41 J5	Cross Grn Cl	41 J6	Florence Gro	41 J1	Hawkins Dr	40 D3	Laura St	40 C5
Blenheim Wk	40 D1	Charlton Gro	41 J4	Cross Grn Cres	41 H5	Florence Mt	41 J1	Headrow, The	40 E4	Lavender Wk	41 H4
Blundell St	40 D2	Charlton Pl	41 J4	Cross Grn Dr	41 J6	Florence Pl	41 J1	Heaton's Ct	41 E4	Leathley Rd	41 F6
Boar La	40 E4	Charlton Rd	41 J4	Cross Grn Garth	41 J6	Florence St	41 J1	Hedley Chase	40 A4	Leathley St	41 F6
Bodley Ter	40 A2	Charlton St	41 J4	Cross Grn La	41 H5	Folly La	40 D7	Hedley Gdns	40 A4	Leicester Cl	40 E1
Bond St	40 E3	Cherry Pl	41 G2	Cross Grn Ri	41 J6	Forster St	41 G6	Hedley Grn	40 A4	Leicester Gro	40 E1
Boundary Pl	41 G1	Cherry Row	41 G2	Cross Grn Way	41 J6	Foundry St		High	41 G7	Leicester Pl	40 D1
Boundary St	41 G1	Chesney Av	41 F7	Cross Ingram Rd	40 C6	(Holbeck)	40 D5	High Ct	41 F4	Leighton St	40 D3
Bourse, The	41 E4	Chiswick St	40 A2	Cross Kelso Rd	40 C2	Foundry St		High Ct La	41 F4	Leodis Ct	40 D5
Bowling Grn Ter	40 D6	Chorley La	40 D2	Cross Mitford Rd	40 A4	(Quarry Hill)	41 G4	Hillary Pl	40 D1	Leylands Rd	41 G2
Bowman La	41 F4	Churchill Gdns	40 E1	Cross Stamford St	41 G2	Fountain St	40 D3	Hillidge Rd	41 F7	Lifton Pl	40 C1
Bow St	41 G4	Church La	41 F4	Cross York St	41 F4	Fourteenth Av	40 A5	Hillidge Sq	41 F7	Lincoln Grn Rd	41 G2
Bracken Ct	40 A6	City Sq	40 E4	Crown Ct	41 F4	Fourth Ct	40 A5	Hill Top Pl	40 B1	Lincoln Rd	41 G2
Braithwaite St	40 C5	City Wk	40 E5	Crown Pt Rd	41 F5	Fourth Ct	40 C5	Hill Top St	40 B1	Lindsey Ct	41 H2
Brancepeth Pl	40 B4	Claremont Av	40 C2	Crown St	41 F4	Fox Way	40 B5	Hirst's Yd	41 F4	Lindsey Gdns	41 H2
Brandon Rd	40 C2	Claremont Gro	40 C2	Croydon St	40 B5	Fraser St	41 F5	**Holbeck**	40 D5	Lindsey Rd	41 H2
Brandon St	40 B4	Claremont Vw	40 C2	Cudbear St	41 G5	Frederick Av	41 J5	Holbeck La	40 C5	Lisbon St	40 D3
Branksome Pl	40 B1	Clarence Rd	41 G6	Czar St	40 C5	Front Row	40 D5	Holbeck Moor Rd	40 C6	Little King St	40 E4
Brick St	41 G4	Clarendon Pl	40 C1			Front St	40 D5	Holdforth Cl	40 A4	Little Queen St	40 D4
Bridge Ct	40 C5	Clarendon Rd	40 C1	**D**				Holdforth Gdns	40 A4	Little Woodhouse St	40 D2
Bridge End	41 E4	Clarendon Way	40 D2	Danby Wk	41 H4	**G**		Holdforth Grn	40 A4	Livinia Gro	40 E1
Bridge Rd	40 C5	Clark Av	41 J4	David St	40 D5	Gardeners Ct	41 G7	Holdforth Pl	40 A4	Lodge St	40 E1
Bridge St	41 F3	Clark Cres	41 J4	Dene Ho Ct	40 E1	Gargrave App	41 H3	Holmes St	41 E5	Lofthouse Pl	40 E1
Bridgewater Rd	41 H6	Clark Gro	41 J5	Denison Rd	40 C3	Gargrave Pl	41 H2	Holroyd St	41 G1	Londesboro Gro	41 J4
Briggate	41 E4	Clark La	41 H5	Dent St	41 H4	Garth, The	41 G4	Hope Rd	41 G3	Long Causeway	41 H6
Brignall Garth	41 J2	Clark Mt	41 J4	Derwent Pl	40 D5	Garton Av	41 J4	Howden Gdns	40 B1	Long Cl La	41 H4
Brignall Way	41 H2	Clark Rd	41 J5	Devon Cl	40 D1	Garton Gro	41 J4	Howden Pl	40 B1	Lord St	40 C5
Bristol St	41 G2	Clark Row	41 J5	Devon Rd	40 D1	Garton Rd	41 E6	Hudson Rd	41 J1	Lord Ter	40 B5
Britannia St	40 D4	Clark Ter	41 J4	Dewsbury Rd	40 E6	Garton Ter	41 H5	Hudswell Rd	41 F7	Lovell Pk Cl	41 F2
Broadway Av	40 A1	Clark Vw	41 J5	Dial St	41 H5	Garton Vw	41 J4	**Hunslet**	41 G7	Lovell Pk Gate	41 F2
Brookfield St	41 G6	Clay Pit La	41 E2	Disraeli Gdns	40 E7	Gelderd Pl	40 B5	Hunslet		Lovell Pk Hill	41 F2
Brown Av	40 B7	Cleveleys Av	40 C7	Disraeli Ter	40 E7	Gelderd Rd	40 A7	Grn Way	41 F7	Lovell Pk Rd	41 F2
Brown La E	40 B6	Cleveleys Mt	40 C7	Dock St	41 F4	George St	41 F3	Hunslet Hall Rd	40 E7	Lovell Pk Vw	41 F2
Brown La W	40 A6	Cleveleys Rd	40 C7	Dolly La	41 G2	Gibralter Island Rd	41 H7	Hunslet La	41 F5	Lower Basinghall St	40 E3
Brown Pl	40 B7	Cleveleys St	40 C7	Dolphin Ct	41 H4	Gilpin Pl	40 A5	Hunslet Rd	41 F4	Lower Brunswick St	41 F2
Brown Rd	40 B7	Cleveleys Ter	40 C7	Dolphin St	41 H4	Gilpin St	40 A5	Hyde Pk Cl	40 B1	Low Flds Av	40 B7
Bruce Gdns	40 B4	Cloberry St	40 C1	Domestic Rd	40 B6	Gilpin Ter	40 A5	Hyde Pk Rd	40 C2	Low Flds Rd	40 A7
Bruce Lawn	40 B4	Close, The	41 G4	Domestic St	40 C5	Gilpin Vw	40 A5	Hyde Pl	40 C2	Low Flds Way	40 B7
Brunswick Ct	41 F3	Cloth Hall St	41 F4	Donisthorpe St	41 G6	Glasshouse St	41 G6	Hyde St	40 C2	Low Fold	41 G5
Brunswick Ter	41 E2	Clyde App	40 A5	Drive, The	41 G4	Gledhow Mt	41 H1	Hyde Ter	40 C2	Low Rd	41 G7
Brussels St	41 G4	Clyde Gdns	40 B5	Driver Ter	40 B5	Gledhow Pl	41 H1			Low Whitehall Row	41 G6
Buckton Cl	40 C7	Clyde Vw	40 A5	Dudley Way	41 E3	Gledhow Rd	41 H1	**I**		Ludgate Hill	41 F3
Buckton Mt	40 C7	Coleman St	40 C5	Duke St	41 F3	Gledhow Ter	41 H1	Infirmary St	40 E3	Lyddon Ter	40 C1
Buckton Vw	40 C7	Colenso Gdns	40 C7	Duncan St	41 E4	Gledhow Vw	41 H1	Ingram Cl	40 C6	Lydgate	41 J2
Burley	40 A1	Colenso Mt	40 C7	Duncombe St	40 C3	Glencoe Vw	41 J5	Ingram Cres	40 B7	Lydia St	41 F3
								Ingram Gdns	40 C6		

M
Mabgate 41 G3
Mabgate Grn 41 G3
Macaulay St 41 G3
Maitland Pl 40 D7
Maltings Rd 41 F7
Malvern Gro 40 D7
Malvern Ri 40 D7
Malvern Rd 40 C7
Malvern St 40 C7
Malvern Vw 40 C7
Manor Rd 40 D5
Manor St 41 G1
Mark La 41 E3
Marlborough Gdns 40 D1
Marlborough Gro 40 D1
Marlborough St 40 C3
Marlborough Twrs 40 C3
Marshall St 40 D5
Marsh La 41 G4
Maude St 41 F4
May Ter 41 H5
Meadowcroft Ms 41 H4
Meadow La 41 E5
Meadow Rd 40 E6
Melbourne St 41 F2
Merrion Pl 41 F3
Merrion St 41 E3
Merrion Way 41 E2
Meynell App 40 C6
Middleton Av 41 J2
Milford Pl 40 A2
Millgarth St 41 F3
Mill Grn 40 B5
Mill Hill 41 E4
Mill St 41 G4
Millwright St 41 G2
Milner Gdns 41 H5
Milnes St 40 B5
Mitford Rd 40 A4
Mitford Vw 40 A4
Moor Cres 41 E7
Moor Cres Chase 41 E7
Moorland Av 40 B1
Moorland Rd 40 B1
Moor Rd 41 E7
Moorside Maltings 41 E7
Moor Vw 40 D6
Moorvile Cl 40 D7
Moorville Ct 40 D7
Moorville Gro 40 D7
Moorville Rd 40 D7
Mount Preston St 40 C2
Mulberry St 41 F6
Mullins Ct 41 H5
Mushroom St 41 G2

N
Naseby Garth 41 G2
Naseby Ter 41 H3
National Rd 41 H6
Navigation Wk 41 F4
Neptune St 41 G4
Neville St 40 E4
New Briggate 41 F3
New Craven Gate 41 F6
New La 40 E5
New Mkt St 41 F4
New Princess St 40 D6
New Sta St 40 E4
New York Rd 41 G3
New York St 41 F4
Nickleby Rd 41 J3
Nile St 41 F3

Nineveh Gdns 40 D6
Nineveh Par 40 D6
Nineveh Rd 40 C6
Nippet La 41 H3
Normanton Gro 40 C7
Normanton Pl 40 D7
Nortech Cl 41 G1
Northcote Cres 40 E7
Northcote Dr 40 D7
Northcote Grn 40 D7
North Ct 41 F3
Northern St 40 D4
North St 41 F3

O
Oak Rd 40 A4
Oatland Cl 41 F1
Oatland Ct 41 F1
Oatland Dr 41 F1
Oatland Gdns 41 F1
Oatland Grn 41 F1
Oatland Hts 41 F1
Oatland La 41 E1
Oatland Rd 41 E1
Oatland Twrs 41 F1
O'Grady Sq 41 H4
Old Mill La 41 H7
Oval, The 41 G7
Oxford Pl 40 D3
Oxford Row 40 D3
Oxley St 41 J4
Oxton Mt 41 J3
Oxton Way 41 J3

P
Parade, The 41 G4
Park Cross St 40 D3
Parkfield St 41 E6
Park La 40 C3
Park Par 41 J5
Park Pl 40 D3
Park Row 40 E3
Park Sq E 40 D3
Park Sq N 40 D3
Park Sq S 40 D3
Park Sq W 40 D3
Park St 40 D3
Park Vw Rd 40 A1
Pearson St 41 F6
Penny La Way 41 F7
Pilot St 41 G2
Pitt Row 41 E4
Place's Rd 41 H4
Plaid Row 41 H3
Playhouse Sq 41 G3
Pleasant Mt 40 C6
Pleasant Pl 40 C6
Pleasant Ter 40 C6
Pontefract Av 41 J4
Pontefract La 41 H3
Pontefract La Cl 41 H4
Pontefract St 41 H4
Portland Cres 40 E2
Portland Gate 40 E2
Portland St 40 D3
Portland Way 40 E2
Pottery Rd 41 F7
Primrose Circ 41 F1
Prosper St 41 G7
Providence Pl 41 E2
Pym St 41 G6

Q
Quarry Hill 41 G3
Quebec St 40 D3

Queen Sq 41 E2
Queens Rd 40 B1
Queen St 40 D4

R
Radnor St 40 B5
Railway St 41 G4
Raincliffe Gro 41 J3
Raincliffe Rd 41 J3
Raincliffe St 41 J3
Recreation Cres 40 C7
Recreation Gro 40 C7
Recreation Mt 40 C7
Recreation Pl 40 C7
Recreation Row 40 C7
Recreation St 40 C7
Recreation Ter 40 C7
Recreation Vw 40 C7
Rectory St 41 H2
Redshaw Rd 40 A5
Regent St 41 G3
Regent Ter 40 B1
Rhodes Ter 40 A5
Richmond Hill App 41 H4
Richmond Hill Cl 41 H4
Richmond St 41 G4
Rickard St 40 C5
Rider St 41 G3
Rigton App 41 H3
Rigton Cl 41 H3
Rigton Dr 41 H3
Rigton Grn 41 H3
Rigton Lawn 41 H3
Rigton Ms 41 H3
Rillbank La 40 B2
Roscoe St 41 G1
Rosebank Gdns 40 B2
Rosebank Rd 40 B2
Rosebud Wk 41 G1
Roseville Rd 41 G1
Roseville St 41 H1
Rossington St 40 E3
Roundhay Rd 41 G1
Roxby Cl 41 H2
Royal Pk Av 40 B1
Royal Pk Gro 40 B1
Royal Pk Rd 40 A1
Royal Pk Ter 40 B1
Ruby St 41 G2
Runswick Av 40 C6
Runswick Pl 40 C6
Runswick St 40 C6
Runswick Ter 40 C6
Russell St 40 E3
Rydall Pl 40 C6
Rydall St 40 C6
Rydall Ter 40 C6

S
Sackville St 41 F1
St. Andrew's St 40 C3
St. Barnabas Rd 40 E5
St. Georges Rd 40 D2
St. Helen's St 41 G6
St. Hilda's Av 41 J5
St. Hilda's Cres 41 H5
St. Hilda's Gro 41 J5
St. Hilda's Mt 41 J5
St. Hilda's Pl 41 J5
St. Hilda's Rd 41 J5
St. John's Av 40 C1
St. John's Cl 40 B1
St. John's Gro 40 B1
St. John's Rd 40 B2
St. Luke's Cescent 40 D7
St. Luke's Cres 40 D7
St. Luke's Grn 40 D7
St. Luke's Rd 40 D7
St. Luke's St 40 D7
St. Mark's Av 40 D1
St. Mark's Rd 40 D1
St. Mark's St. 40 D1
St. Mary's Cl 40 A5
St. Mary's St 41 G3
St. Matthew's St 40 C6
St. Matthias St 40 A1
St. Matthias Ter 40 A1
St. Paul's St 40 D3
St. Peter's Ct 41 E7
St. Peter's Pl 41 G3
St. Peter's Sq 41 G3
St. Stephen's Ct 41 H3
St. Stephen's Rd 41 H3
Salem Pl 41 F5
Sandlewood Cl 40 D6
Sandlewood Grn 40 D6
Sardinia St 41 F6
Saville Grn 41 J3
Saxton La 41 G4
Sayner La 41 G5
Sayner Rd 41 F5
Scargill Cl 41 H2
Scarth Av 41 J1
Second Av 40 A4
Seminary St 40 D2
Severn Way 41 H7
Shafton La 40 C6
Shafton Pl 40 C6
Shafton St 40 C6
Shafton Vw 40 C6
Shakespeare App 41 H2
Shakespeare Av 41 H2
Shakespeare Cl 41 J2
Shakespeare Gdns 41 J2
Shakespeare Lawn 41 H2
Shakespeare St 41 J1
Shannon Rd 41 H3
Shannon St 41 G3
Sheaf St 41 F5
Sheepscar Ct 41 F1
Sheepscar Gro 41 F2
Sheepscar St N 41 F1
Sheepscar St S 41 F1
Siddal St 40 D5
Sidney St 41 F3
Silver St 40 D5
Skinner La 41 F2
Skinner St 40 C3
Somers St 40 D3
South Accommodation Rd 41 G6
South Par 40 E3
Sovereign St 40 E4
Spence La 40 B5
Spenceley St 40 D1
Spinney, The 41 H4
Spinneyfield Ct 41 H4
Spring Cl Av 41 H5
Spring Cl Gdns 41 H5
Spring Cl St 41 H5
Spring Cl Wk 41 H5
Springfield Mt 40 C2
Spring Gro Ter 40 A1
Spring Gro Vw 40 B1
Spring Gro Wk 40 A1
Springwell Ct 40 C5
Springwell Rd 40 C5
Springwell St 40 C5
Springwell Vw 40 C5
Stafford St 41 G7

Stanley Av 41 J1
Stanley Pl 41 J1
Stanley Rd 41 J1
Stanley Ter 41 J1
Stocks Hill 41 C6
Stoney Rock Gro 41 J2
Stoney Rock La 41 H2
Stott Rd 40 A4
Studio Rd 40 B2
Sutton St 40 C5
Sweet St 40 D5
Sweet St W 40 C5
Swinegate 41 E4
Sydenham Rd 40 B5
Sydenham St 40 B5

T
Telephone Pl 41 G2
Templar La 41 F3
Templar Pl 41 F3
Templar St 41 F3
Temple Vw Gro 41 J4
Temple Vw Pl 41 J4
Temple Vw Rd 41 J3
Temple Vw Ter 41 J4
Thealby Cl 41 G3
Thealby Lawn 41 G2
Thealby Pl 41 G3
Third Av 40 A5
Thirsk Row 40 D4
Thoresby Pl 40 D3
Thornleigh Gdns 41 J5
Thornleigh Gro 41 J5
Thornleigh Mt 41 J5
Thornleigh St 41 J5
Thornleigh Vw 41 J5
Thornville Pl 40 B1
Thornville Rd 40 A1
Thornville Row 40 B1
Thornville St 40 B1
Thornville Vw 40 B1
Tilbury Av 40 C7
Tilbury Gro 40 C7
Tilbury Mt 40 C7
Tilbury Par 40 C7
Tilbury Rd 40 C7
Tilbury Ter 40 C7
Tilbury Vw 40 C7
Tong Rd 40 A5
Top Moor Side 40 C6
Torre Cl 41 J3
Torre Dr 41 J2
Torre Rd 41 H3
Tower Ho St 41 F2
Trafalgar St 41 F3
Trent Rd 41 J3
Trent St 40 D6
Trinity St 41 E3
Triumph Cl 40 C5
Turlow Ct 41 G4

U
Union Pl 40 D5
Union St 41 F3
University Rd 40 C1
Upper Accommodation Rd 41 H3
Upper Basinghall St 40 E3
Upper N St 40 E2
Upper Westlock Av 41 J2

V
Vernon Rd 40 D2
Vernon St 40 E2
Vicar La 41 F3

Victoria Rd 40 E5
Victoria Sq 40 D3
Victoria St 40 C2
Victoria Ter 40 C2
Village Ter 40 A1
Vinery Mt 41 J4
Vinery Pl 41 J4
Vinery St 41 J3
Vinery Ter 41 J4

W
Wade La 41 E3
Walford Gro 41 J3
Walford Rd 41 J3
Walford Ter 41 J3
Walter Cres 41 H4
Walter St 40 A2
Walton St 40 D5
Washington St 40 B3
Water La 40 C5
Waterloo Rd 41 G7
Waterloo St 41 F4
Waverley Garth 40 D7
Weaver St 40 A2
Welbeck Rd 41 J4
Well Cl Ri 41 E1
Wellington Br St 40 C3
Wellington Pl 40 C4
Wellington Rd 40 B4
Wellington St 40 D4
Wesley Pl 41 H4
Westfield Cres 40 B2
Westfield Rd 40 B2
Westfield Ter 40 B2
Westgate 40 D3
Westlock Av 41 J2
West St 40 C3
West Vale 40 A6
Wharf St 41 F4
Whitehall Rd 40 B5
Whitehouse St 41 G7
Whitelock St 41 F2
Whitfield Av 41 G7
Whitfield Gdns 41 G7
Whitfield Pl 41 G7
Whitfield Sq 41 G7
Whitfield Way 41 G7
Willis St 41 H4
Willoughby Ter 40 C6
Willow App 40 A2
Willow Av 40 A2
Willow Cl 40 B2
Willow Garth 40 A2
Willow Rd 40 A2
Willow Ter Rd 40 D2
Wilmington St 41 F1
Winchester St 40 A4
Winfield Gro 40 E1
Winfield Pl 40 E1
Winfield Ter 40 E1
Wintoun St 41 F2
Wolseley Rd 40 A1
Woodhouse La 40 D1
Woodhouse Sq 40 D3
Woodsley Grn 40 B1
Woodsley Rd 40 B2
Wormald Row 41 E3
Wortley La 40 B5
Wortley Pk 40 A5

Y
Yarn St 41 H6
York Pl 40 D3
York Rd 41 H3
York St 41 F4

Liverpool street index

A
Abercromby Sq 43 F4
Abney Cl 43 H5
Acorn Ct 43 E7
Acton Way 43 H5
Adderley St 43 H3
Addison St 42 C2
Addison Way 42 C2
Adelaide Pl 42 D1
Adelaide Rd 43 G4
Adele Thompson Dr 43 F6
Agnes Way 43 H4
Aigburth St 43 G5
Ainsworth St 42 E4
Albany Rd 43 G3
Albert Edward Rd 43 G3
Albert St 43 G4
Alderson Rd 43 J6
Alexandra Cl 43 G2

Alexandra Rd 43 J5
Alex Cl 43 J7
Alfred Ms 42 D6
Alfred St 43 J5
Altcar Av 43 J6
Alt St 43 G6
Amberley St 43 F6
Amelia Cl 43 F2
Amethyst Cl 43 G1
Anchorage, The 42 C7
Angela St 43 G5
Anglezark Cl 43 H3
Anglican Ct 42 E6
Archbishop Warlock Ct 42 B1
Argyle St 42 C5
Arley St 42 C1
Arnold Cres 43 F7
Arnside Rd 43 H4

Arrad St 43 E5
Arundel Av 43 J7
Arundel Cl 43 G7
Asbridge St 43 G7
Ashton St 42 D6
Ashwell St 42 D6
Askham Cl 43 G6
Aspen Gro 43 H7
Atlantic Pt 42 C2
Atwell St 43 G1

B
Back Colquitt St 42 D5
Back Guildford St 43 F1
Back Kelvin Gro 43 G7
Back Leeds St 42 B2
Baker St 43 G2
Baker Way 43 F2
Balmoral Rd 43 J1

Balm St 43 H3
Baltimore St 42 E5
Bannerman St 43 J5
Barnet Cl 43 H5
Basnett St 42 C4
Bath St 42 A3
Battenberg St 43 G3
Bayhorse La 43 E3
Beaconsfield St 43 G7
Beaufort St 42 D7
Beaumont St 43 G6
Beau St 42 D1
Beckwith St 42 C5
Bective St 43 J5
Bedford Cl 43 F5
Bedford St S 43 F6
Beech St 43 J3
Benson St 42 D4
Bentley Rd 43 G7

Beresford St 42 E1
Berington St 42 C1
Berkley St 43 E6
Berry St 42 D5
Berwick Cl 43 H1
Berwick St 43 H1
Bevington Bush 42 C2
Bevington Hill 42 C1
Bidder St 42 E2
Bigham Rd 43 H2
Birchfield St 42 E2
Bird St 43 J6
Birkett St 42 D2
Birstall Rd 43 G2
Birt Cl 43 G6
Bishop Sheppard Ct 42 B1
Bixteth St 42 B3
Blackburne Pl 43 E5

Blackstock St 42 C2
Blair St 42 E6
Blenheim St 42 C1
Bluefields St 43 E6
Blundell St 42 C6
Boaler St 43 G2
Bold Pl 42 D5
Bold St 42 D4
Bolton St 42 D4
Bond St 42 C1
Boothwood Cl 43 H5
Boswell St 43 H6
Botanic Grn 43 H3
Botanic Pl 43 J3
Botanic Rd 43 J3
Boundary La 43 G1
Boyton Ct 43 J5
Bradfield St 43 H3
Brae St 43 H3

Brahms Cl	43	G7
Brampton Dr	43	F5
Brassey St	42	D7
Breames Cl	43	H4
Breck Rd	43	F1
Bremner Cl	43	H4
Brick St	42	D6
Bridge Rd	43	J5
Bridgewater St	42	C6
Bridport St	42	D3
Bright St	43	F2
Brindley St	42	D7
Britannia Av	43	J6
Britten Cl	43	H7
Bronte St	42	E3
Brook St	42	B3
Brownlow Hill	42	D4
Brownlow St	43	E4
Brow Side	43	E1
Brunswick Rd	43	F3
Brunswick St	42	B4
Bryges St	43	G4
Brythen St	42	C4
Burlington St	42	C1
Burnley Cl	43	G1
Burroughs Gdns	42	C1
Burrows Ct	42	B1
Burton Cl	42	C5
Bute St	42	D2
Bute St (Edge Hill)	43	H6
Butler Cres	43	G2
Butler St	43	G1
Button St	42	C4
Byrom St	42	D3

C

Cadogan St	43	J5
Caird St	43	G2
Cairns St	43	G7
Caledonia St	43	E5
Callander Rd	43	J2
Cambria St N	43	H2
Cambria St S	43	H2
Cambridge Ct	43	E5
Cambridge St	43	E4
Camden St	42	D3
Cameo Cl	43	G1
Cameron St	43	H3
Campbell St	42	C5
Canada Boul	42	B4
Canning Pl	42	C4
Canning St	43	E5
Cantebury St	42	E2
Cantebury Way	42	E2
Cardigan St	43	J5
Cardigan Way	43	H1
Cardwell St	43	G5
Carlingford Cl	43	G6
Carlton St	42	A1
Carmarthen Cres	42	D7
Carpenters Row	42	C5
Carruthers St	42	B2
Carstairs Rd	43	J1
Carter St	43	F6
Carver St	43	E2
Caryl St	42	D7
Castle St	42	B4
Catharine St	43	F5
Cathedral Cl	42	E6
Cathedral Gate	42	E5
Cathedral Wk	42	E4
Cawdor St	43	G7
Cazneau St	42	D1
Cedar Gro	43	H7
Celtic St	43	F7
Chadwick St	42	B2
Chaloner St	42	C6
Chandos St	43	H4
Channell Rd	43	H2
Chapel St	42	B4
Chase Way	42	E1
Chatham Pl	43	G4
Chatham St	43	F5
Chatsworth Dr	43	H5
Chaucer St	42	D2
Cheapside	42	C3
Chesney Cl	42	E7
Chesterfield St	42	E6
Chester St	42	E7
Chestnut St	43	F4
Chichester Cl	43	J6
Childwall Av	43	J6
Chisenhale St	42	B1
Chiswell St	43	H3
Christian St	42	D2
Chris Ward Cl	43	H4
Church All	42	C4
Church Mt	43	G4
Church St	42	C4
Churton Ct	43	F2
Cicely St	43	G4
Clarence St	42	E4
Claribel St	43	F7
Claughton Cl	43	H4
Claypole Cl	43	H5
Clay St	42	B1
Clearwater Cl	43	H3
Clegg St	42	D1
Clement Gdns	42	C1
Cleveland Sq	42	C5
Clifford St	42	E3
Cliff St	43	H3
Clifton Gro	42	E1
Clint Rd	43	H4
Clint Rd W	43	H4
Clint Way	43	H4
Coal St	42	D3
Cobden St	43	F2
Cockspur St	42	C7
Coleridge St	43	H2
College La	42	C4
College St N	42	E2
College St S	43	F2
Colquitt St	42	D5
Coltart Rd	43	G7
Comberme St	43	E7
Commerce Way	43	G6
Commutation Row	42	D3
Compton Rd	43	G1
Comus St	42	D2
Concert St	42	D5
Connaught Rd	43	G3
Contance St	43	E3
Cookson St	42	D6
Cook St	42	C4
Copperas Hill	42	D4
Corinto St	42	E6
Corney St	43	H6
Cornhill	42	C5
Cornwallis St	42	D5
Corsewall St	43	J5
Cotswold St	43	H3
Cotton St	42	A1
Covent Gdn	42	B3
Cowan Dr	43	F1
Cranborne Rd	43	J6
Craven St	42	E3
Cresswell St	43	F1
Cropper St	42	D4
Crosfield Cl	43	J4
Crosfield Rd	43	H4
Crosshall St	42	C3
Crown St	43	F3
Croxteth Gro	43	H7
Croxteth Rd	43	G7
Crump St	42	D6
Cullen St	43	H6
Cumberland St	42	C3
Cunliffe St	42	C3
Custom Ho Pl	42	C5

D

Dale St	42	B4
Daniel Davies Dr	43	G6
Dansie St	43	E4
Danube St	43	H6
Darrel Dr	43	H6
Daulby St	43	F3
Davies St	42	C3
Dawber Cl	43	G1
Dawson St	42	C4
Dean Dillistone Ct	42	D6
Deane Rd	43	H3
Dean Patey Ct	43	H4
Deeley Cl	43	H4
Dell St	43	H3
Denham Dr	43	H1
Denham Way	43	H1
Dentdale Dr	42	E1
Devon St	42	E3
Dexter St	42	E7
Dial St	43	H3
Diamond St	42	C1
Dickens St	43	E7
Dickson St	42	A1
Dombey St	43	E7
Dorothy St	43	H4
Dorrit St	43	E7
Dorset Av	43	J6
Douro St	42	D1
Dove St	43	H5
Dovestone Cl	43	H5
Drury La	42	B4
Dryden St	42	D1
Dublin St	42	A1
Ducie St	43	G7
Duckinfield St	43	E4
Duke St	42	C5
Duncan St	42	D6
Dunkeld Cl	43	G2
Dunstan La	43	H5
Durden St	43	H6
Durning Rd	43	H3
Dwerryhouse St	42	D7
Dyke St	43	H5

E

Earle Rd	42	D1
Earle St	42	C1
East St	42	C5
Eaton St	42	E3
Ebenezer Rd	43	H3
Eden St	42	E1
Edgar St	43	H4
Edge Hill	43	H4
Edge La	42	D3
Edinburgh Rd	43	F2
Edmund St	42	C7
Egerton St	42	C3
Elaine St	43	H2
Eldonian Way	42	C4
Eldon Pl	42	C1
Eldon St	42	C1
Elizabeth St	43	F3
Elliot St	42	D4
Elm Gro	43	F4
Elm Vale	43	J1
Elstree Rd	43	J2
Ember Cres	43	F1
Embledon St	43	G6
Emerson St	43	E6
Empress Rd	43	G4
Enid St	43	F7
Epworth St	43	F3
Erin Cl	43	E7
Erskine St	43	F3
Esher Rd	43	H2
Eversley St	43	F7
Everton Brow	42	E2
Everton Rd	43	F1
Every St	43	G1
Exchange St E	42	B3
Exchange St W	42	B3

F

Fairclough St	42	D4
Fairfield	43	J2
Falkland St	43	E3
Falkner Sq	43	F6
Falkner St	43	E5
Fareham Rd	43	J3
Farnworth St	43	G2
Fazakerley St	42	B3
Fearnside St	43	J5
Fell St	43	H3
Fenwick St	42	B4
Fern Gro	43	H7
Fernhill Dr	43	F7
Fielding St	43	G2
Field St	42	E2
Finch Pl	43	E3
Finlay St	43	H2
Fishguard Cl	43	F1
Fitzclarence Way	43	F1
Fitzpatrick Ct	42	B1
Fitzroy Way	43	F2
Fleet St	42	D4
Fleming Ct	42	B1
Flint St	42	D6
Fontenoy St	42	C3
Ford St	42	C2
Forrest St	42	C5
Fowler Cl	43	H4
Foxhill Cl	43	F7
Fox St	42	D1
Fraser St	42	D3
Freedom Cl	43	G5
Freeman St	43	J5
Freemasons' Row	42	C2
Frost St	43	H3

G

Galloway St	43	J5
Gannock St	43	H3
Gardenside St	43	F2
Gardners Dr	43	H1
Gardner's Row	42	C2
Garrick St	43	J6
Gascoyne St	42	B2
Geneva Rd	43	J2
George Harrison Cl	43	G2
Georges Dockway	42	B4
George St	42	B3
Geraint St	43	F7
Gerard St	42	D3
Gibraltar Row	42	B3
Gibson St	43	F6
Gilbert St	42	C5
Gildarts Gdns	42	C1
Gildart St	43	E3
Gilead St	43	H3
Gill St	43	E3
Gilroy Rd	43	H2
Gladstone Rd	43	G4
Gladstone St	42	C2
Gleave Cres	43	F1
Glegg St	42	B1
Gloucester Ct	43	G2
Gloucester Pl	43	F1
Gore St		
Gower St		
Gradwell St	43	H6
Grafton Cres	42	B3
Grafton St	42	B3
Granary Wf	42	B2
Granby St	43	J3
Grantham St	43	H6
Granville Rd	42	C2
Grayson St	43	G5
Great Crosshall St	43	G4
Great George Pl	43	G3
Great George St	42	B3
Great Howard St	43	E6
Great Nelson St	43	F7
Great Newton St	42	B1
Great Orford St	42	C1
Great Richmond St	42	C1
Greek St	43	F3
Greenheys Rd	43	D4
Greenland St	43	F4
Green La	43	J1
Greenleaf St	43	J2
Greenside	43	F1
Green St	43	G6
Gregson St	43	E6
Grenville St S	43	F2
Gresley Cl	43	F3
Grierson St	43	E7
Grinfield St	43	H2
Grinshill Cl	43	F7
Grosvenor St	43	E2
Grove Pk	43	F1
Grove Rd	43	G1
Grove St	42	B3
Guelph St	43	G1
Guion St	42	B3
Gwendoline St		
Gwenfron Rd		
Gwent St		

H

Hackins Hey	42	B3
Haigh St	43	E1
Hale St	42	C3
Hall La	43	F3
Halsbury Rd	43	H2
Hampstead Rd	43	J2
Hampton St	43	J5
Hannan Rd	43	H3
Hanover St	42	B4
Harbord St	43	H7
Hardman St	43	F7
Hardy St	43	G2
Harewood St	42	E2
Harker St	43	E3
Harke St	43	H2
Harper St	43	F1
Harrington St	43	F1
Harrowby Cl	42	B1
Harrowby St	43	F2
Hartley Quay	42	D4
Hart St	42	B1
Hatherley Cl	42	D6
Hatherley St	42	C3
Hatton Gdn	42	C2
Haverston Rd	42	C5
Hawdon Ct	43	H4
Hawke St	43	F7
Hawkins St	42	D1
Hawthorn Gro	42	D3
Head St	43	G5
Heathcote Cl	43	J5
Heathfield St	42	C2
Helena St	43	H3
Helsby St		
Hendon Rd		
Henglers Cl	43	J5
Henry Edward St	43	H3
Henry St	43	F2
Hewitts Pl	43	H1
Highfield St	42	C2
Highgate St	43	J6
High St	42	B2
Hilbre St	43	J2
Hillaby Cl	43	G2
Hillside St	42	B4
Hill St	42	B3
Hinton St	43	F7
Hockenhall All	42	D3
Hodson Pl	42	B3
Holborn St	43	F6
Holden St	42	C5
Holdsworth St	42	C1
Holly Rd	43	E3
Holmes St	43	H3
Holt Rd	43	H3
Holy Cross Cl	43	H2
Homerton Rd	43	G4
Hood St	42	C2
Hope Pl	43	F1
Hope St	43	E6
Hornby Wk	42	C1
Hotham St	43	F3
Houghton St	42	D7
Houlton St	43	H3
Hughes Cl	42	C4
Hughes St	42	D7
Huntly Rd	42	D6
Hurst St	42	C7
Huskisson St	43	G6
Hutchinson St	43	H2
Hutchinson Wk	43	J6
Hygeia St	42	C5
Hyslop St	42	C3

I

Iliad St	42	B2
Ingrow Rd	42	D1
Innovation Bvd	43	E3
Irvine St	43	E4
Irwin St	42	D2
Islington	42	E3
Ivatt Way	43	H4

J

Jack McBain Ct	42	B1
Jade Rd	43	H1
Jamaica St	42	D6
James Clarke St	42	C1
James St	42	B4
Janet St	43	H4
Jasmine Cl	43	E1
Jenkinson St	42	E2
Jermyn St	43	G7
Jet Cl	43	H1
John Lennon Dr	43	G2
John Moores Cl	43	F5
Johnson St	42	C3
John St	42	E2
Jordan St	42	D6
Jubilee Dr	43	G3
Judges Dr	43	J1
Judges Way	43	J1
Juvenal Pl	42	D1
Juvenal St	42	D2

K

Keble St	43	E1
Kelso Rd	43	J2
Kelvin Gro	43	G7
Kempston St	42	E3
Kenley Cl	43	H1
Kensington	43	G3
Kensington St	43	G2
Kent St	42	D5
Kilshaw St	43	G1
Kimberley Cl	43	F6
Kinder St	43	F2
King Edward St	42	B3
Kinglake St	43	H5
Kings Dock St	42	C6
Kingsley Rd	43	G6
Kings Par	42	B5
Kingsway Ct	42	C1
Kingswell Cl	43	G4
Kitchen St	42	C6
Knight St	42	D5

L

Lace St	42	C3
Ladybower Cl	43	H5
Laggan St	43	H3
Lairds Pl	42	C1
Lakeland Cl	42	C5
Lambert Way	42	E3
Lamport St	42	E7
Lance Cl	43	H4
Langley St	42	E7
Langsdale St	42	E2
Langton Rd	43	J6
Lanyork Rd	42	B2
Laurel Gro	43	H7
Lavan Cl	43	F2
Lawrence Rd	43	J6
Lawton St	42	D4
Laxey St	42	E7
Leece St	42	E5
Leeds St	42	B2
Leigh St	42	C4
Leigh St (Edge Hill)	42	D7
Lemon Cl	43	H4
Lemon Gro	43	H7
Leopold Rd	43	G4
Lesseps Rd	43	F1
Lestock St	43	F3
Liffey St	43	G5
Lightbody Dr	43	H3
Lightwood St	43	J3
Lilley Rd	43	H6
Lilly Vale	43	H3
Lime Gro	43	G2
Limekiln La	42	C1
Lime St	42	D4
Lincoln Cl	43	H1
Lindley Cl	43	H5
Lindley St	42	C1
Ling St	43	H3
Lister Cres	43	J3
Lister Rd	43	J2
Little Catherine St	43	E6
Little Ct	42	B1
Little Hardman St	42	E5
Little Howard St	42	B1
Little St. Bride St	43	E5
Little Woolton St	43	F4
Liver St	42	C5
Lloyd St	43	F1
Lockerby Rd	43	J2
Lodge La	43	H7
London Rd	42	D3
Longfellow St	43	H6
Longstone Wk	43	G5
Lord Nelson St	42	D3
Lord St	42	C4
Lorton St	43	H6
Lothian St	43	F7
Loudon Gro	43	G7
Love La	42	B1
Lower Castle St	42	B4
Low Hill	43	F2
Lowther St	43	F6
Low Wd St	43	F3
Luke St	43	E7
Lyceum Pl	42	D4
Lydia Ann St	42	C5
Lytton St	43	F2

M

Maddrell St	42	B1
Madelaine St	43	F7
Madeley St	43	H1
Magdala St	43	H6
Maitland Cl	43	H6
Malden Rd	43	H2
Mallow Rd	43	H2
Malt St	43	G5
Malvern Rd	43	H2
Manchester St	42	C3
Manesty's La	42	C4
Manfred St	43	F3
Mann Island	42	B4
Mann St	42	D7
Mansell Rd	43	H2
Mansfield St	42	D2
Manton Rd	43	H2
Maple Gro	43	H7
Marathon Cl	43	F1
Marcot Rd	43	J1
Margaret St	43	F1
Mariners Wf	42	C7
Maritime Pl	43	F6
Maritime Way	42	C5
Marlborough St	42	C2
Marlsford St	43	H2
Marmaduke St	43	G4
Marquis St	42	E3
Marsden St	43	F2
Marsden Way	43	F2
Marshall Pl	42	C1
Martensen St	43	G4
Marvin St	43	G2
Marybone	42	C3
Maryland St	43	E5
Mason St	43	G4
Mathew St	42	C4
Maud St	43	F7
Maxton Rd	43	H2
Mayfair Cl	43	H1
May Pl	42	E4
May St	42	E4
Melda Cl	43	F2
Melville Pl	43	F5
Merlin St	43	F7
Michael Dragonette Ct	42	C1
Midghall St	42	C2
Mile End	42	C1
Millennium Pl	43	G7
Mill La	42	D3
Mill Rd	43	F1
Mill St	42	E7
Millvale St	43	H1
Milroy St	43	H4
Milverton St	43	H1
Minshull St	43	F4
Minster Ct	43	F5
Minto Cl	43	H3
Minto St	43	H3
Mirfield St	43	H2
Molyneux Rd	43	G2
Montgomery Way	43	H1
Moorfields	42	C3
Moor Pl	42	E3
Moor St	42	B4
Morden St	43	H1
Moss Gro	43	H7
Mount Pleasant	42	D4
Mount St	42	E5
Mount Vernon Grn	43	G3

Street	Page	Grid
Mount Vernon Rd	43	F4
Mount Vernon St	43	F3
Mozart Cl	43	G7
Muirhead Av	43	H1
Mulberry Pl	43	F5
Mulberry St	43	F5
Mulgrave St	43	F6
Myrtle St	43	E5

N

Street	Page	Grid
Navigation Wf	42	C7
Naylor St	42	C2
Needham Rd	43	H3
Nelson Rd	43	G4
Nelson St	42	D6
Netherfield Rd S	42	E1
Nevin St	43	F2
Nevison St	43	G4
New Bird St	42	D6
New Grey Rock Cl	43	G1
Newhall St	42	D6
New Henderson St	42	D7
Newington	42	D4
New Quay	42	B3
New Red Rock Vw	43	G1
Newsham Dr	43	H1
Newstead Rd	43	H6
Newton Way	43	E4
Noel St	43	H6
Norfolk St	42	C6
Norman St	42	E3
Northbrook Cl	43	G6
North Brook St	43	F6
Northcote Cl	43	F1
North John St	42	C3
North St	42	C3
North Vw	43	G4
Norton St	42	D3
Norwood Gro	43	H1
Nuttall St	43	H4

O

Street	Page	Grid
Oakes St	43	E3
Oakham St	42	D7
O'Connell Rd	42	C1
Odsey St	43	H3
Oil St	42	A1
Old Coll Pl	43	H4
Old Hall St	42	B3
Oldham St	42	D5
Old Leeds St	42	B3
Olympia St	43	G2
Onslow Rd	43	J2
Opal Cl	43	G1
Orange Gro	43	H7
O'Reilly Ct	42	B1
Oriel Steet	42	C2
Ormond St	42	B3
Orphan St	43	F5
Orthes St	43	E4
Ottley St	43	J2
Overbury St	43	G4
Overton St	43	G4
Oxendale Cl	43	G6
Oxford St	43	E4
Oxford St E	43	G4

P

Street	Page	Grid
Paddington	43	F4
Page Wk	42	E2
Paisley St	42	A2
Pall Mall	42	B2
Paradise St	42	C5
Parker St	42	D4
Park La	42	C5
Park Pl	42	E7
Park Rd	43	E7
Parkside St	43	F2
Park Way	43	F6
Parliament Cl	42	E6
Parliament St	42	D6
Parr St	42	D5
Parton St	43	J2
Paul McCartney Way	43	H2
Paul Orr Ct	42	B1
Paul St	42	C2
Pavilion Cl	43	G6
Pear Gro	43	H2
Pearl Way	43	G1
Peet St	43	H4
Pembroke Gdns	43	E3
Pembroke Pl	42	E3
Pembroke St	43	E4
Penarth Cl	43	G5
Pendine Cl	43	H1
Penlinken Dr	43	H1
Penvalley Cres	43	H1
Peover St	42	D2
Pera Cl	43	G2
Percy St	43	E6
Perrygate Cl	43	G5
Perry St	42	D7
Perth St	43	G2
Peter's Arcade	42	C4
Peter St	42	C3
Phillimore Rd	43	H2
Pickop St	42	C3
Pickwick St	43	E7
Picton Rd	43	J5
Pilgrim St	42	E5
Pimhill Cl	43	G7
Pine Ms	42	E6
Pinetop Cl	43	H1
Pitt St	42	D5
Pleasant St	42	E4
Plimsoll St	43	H4
Plumpton St	43	F1
Pomfret St	43	F7
Pomona St	42	E4
Pond Cl	43	H1
Ponsonby St	43	G7
Porter St	42	A1
Portland Pl	42	D1
Portwood Cl	43	G5
Pownall Sq	42	C3
Pownall St	42	C5
Prescot Rd	43	J2
Prescot St	43	F3
Preston St	42	C3
Price St	42	C5
Primrose Hill	42	C3
Prince Albert Ms	42	D6
Prince Edwin St	42	D1
Princes Av	43	F6
Princes Gdns	42	B2
Princes Par	42	A3
Princes Pk	43	G7
Princes Rd	43	F6
Princes St	42	C3
Prince William St	42	D7
Prospect St	43	F3
Providence Cres	43	H2
Prussia St	42	B3
Pudsey St	42	D3
Pumpfields Rd	42	B2
Pythian Cl	43	G2
Pythian St	43	F2

Q

Street	Page	Grid
Queen Anne St	42	D2
Queensland St	43	G4
Queens Sq	42	D3
Queens Wf	42	C6
Quorn St	43	H3

R

Street	Page	Grid
Rachel St	42	D1
Radstock Rd	43	J2
Raffles St	42	D6
Rainford Gdns	42	C4
Rainford Sq	42	C4
Ranelagh St	42	D4
Raven Cl	43	F2
Raymond Pl	42	C1
Red Cross St	42	B4
Redgrave St	43	H3
Redmires Cl	43	H5
Red Rock St	43	G1
Regent St	42	A1
Renfrew St	43	G3
Renshaw St	42	D4
Reservoir St	43	F1
Reynolds Cl	43	G1
Rialto Cl	43	F6
Rice St	42	E5
Richardson St	43	J6
Richmond Row	42	D2
Richmond St	42	C4
Ridley Rd	43	H2
Rigby St	42	B3
Ringo Starr Dr	43	H2
Ritson St	43	G7
River Avon St	43	H6
Roberts St	42	A2
Roderick St	42	E2
Rodney St	42	E5
Roe St	42	D3
Rokeby Cl	42	E2
Rokeby St	42	E2
Rokesmith Av	43	H5
Romer Rd	43	H2
Romilly St	43	G2
Roscastle Cl	43	G2
Roscoe La	42	D5
Roscoe St	42	E4
Roscommon St	42	D1
Roseberry St	43	F6
Rose Hill	42	D2
Rosemary Cl	43	G4
Rose Pl	42	D2
Rothsay Cl	42	E1
Rothwell St	43	G1
Royal Mail St	42	D4
Royston St	43	G4
Rufford Rd	43	J2
Rumford Pl	42	B3
Rumford St	42	B3
Rupert Dr	43	F2
Russel St	42	E3
Ryedale Cl	43	G6

S

Street	Page	Grid
St. Andrew St	42	E4
St. Anne St	42	D2
St. Bride St	43	F5
St. James Pl	42	D6
St. James Rd	42	E6
St. James St	42	D6
St. John's La	42	D3
St. Josephs Cres	42	D2
St. Martins Ms	42	D1
St. Michaels Gro	43	H1
St. Nicholas Pl	42	A4
St. Stephen's Pl	42	C2
Salisbury Rd	43	J6
Salisbury St	42	E1
Salthouse Quay	42	B5
Saltney St	42	A1
Sandhead St	43	J5
Sandino St	42	E7
Sandon St	43	F5
Saxon Cl	43	G1
Saxony Rd	43	G3
Schomberg St	43	G2
School La	42	C4
Scotland Rd	42	D2
Seaport Rd	43	G7
Seddon St	42	C5
Seel St	42	C4
Sefton Pk Rd	43	H7
Sefton St	42	C6
Selborne Cl	43	F6
Selborne St	43	F6
Selsey Cl	43	H5
Severs St	43	G1
Seymour St	42	E3
Shakespeare Cl	43	G1
Shallcross Pl	43	G1
Shaws All	42	C5
Shaw St	43	E1
Sheil Rd	43	H1
Shenstone St	43	G4
Shepherd's Fold Cl	43	G7
Sherwood St	42	B1
Shimmin St	43	G4
Sidney Pl	43	G4
Silkstone Cl	43	H5
Simpson St	42	C6
Sim St	42	E2
Sirdar Cl	43	H5
Sir Thomas St	42	C3
Skelhorne St	42	D4
Slater St	42	D5
Smithdown La	43	F4
Smithdown Rd	43	H6
Smithfield St	42	C3
Soho Pl	42	E2
Soho St	42	E2
Solomon St	43	H3
Solway St E	43	H6
Solway St W	43	G6
South Chester St	42	E7
Southern Cres	42	D7
South Ferry Quay	42	C7
South Hunter St	42	E5
South John St	42	C4
Sparling St	42	C6
Spekeland Rd	43	H5
Spencer St	43	F1
Spindle Cl	43	F1
Spofforth Rd	43	J5
Sprainger St	42	B1
Springfield	42	D2
Squires St	43	G4
Stafford St	42	E3
Stamford St	43	H3
Standish St	42	C3
Stanhope St	42	D7
Stanier Way	43	H4
Stanley St	42	C3
Star St	42	D7
Steinberg Ct	42	B1
Sterndale Cl	43	H5
Stockdale Cl	42	C2
Stone St	42	B1
Stowell St	43	E5
Strada Way	43	E2
Strand, The	42	B4
Strand St	42	B4
Strathmore Rd	43	H1
Strauss Cl	43	H7
Suffolk St	42	D5
Sugnall St	43	E5
Summer Seat	42	C1
Surrey St	42	C5
Sutcliffe St	43	H2
Sweeting St	42	B4
Swindale Cl	43	G6
Swiss Rd	43	J2

T

Street	Page	Grid
Tabley St	42	C6
Tace Cl	43	F6
Tagus Cl	43	G7
Tamar Cl	43	F1
Tarleton St	42	C4
Tatlock St	42	C1
Tavy Rd	43	F1
Teck St	43	G3
Teign Cl	43	F1
Tempest Hey	42	B3
Temple Ct	42	C4
Temple La	42	C3
Temple St	42	C3
Tenterden St	42	C1
Thackeray Pl	43	F7
Thames St	43	G7
Thomas St Way	42	C5
Thorburn St	43	H4
Thornes Rd	43	G2
Tichbourne Way	43	F2
Tideswell Cl	43	H5
Timpron St	43	H5
Titchfield St	42	C1
Tithebarn St	42	B3
Tobin Cl	42	C1
Toft St	43	H3
Tom Mann Cl	42	B4
Tordelow Cl	43	F1
Tower Gdns	42	B4
Trafalgar Way	43	F2
Trowbridge St	42	E4
Trueman St	42	C3
Tudor St N	43	H2
Tudor St S	43	H2
Tulloch St	43	G2
Tunnel Rd	43	H5
Tunstall St	43	J6
Tweed Cl	43	H1
Twomey Cl	42	C1

U

Street	Page	Grid
Union Ct	42	C4
Union St	42	B3
Upper Baker St	43	G2
Upper Beau St	42	D1
Upper Bute St	42	E1
Upper Duke St	42	D5
Upper Frederick St	42	C5
Upper Hampton St	43	F6
Upper Harrington St	42	D7
Upper Hill St	43	E7
Upper Hope Pl	43	E5
Upper Mann St	42	D7
Upper Mason St	43	G4
Upper Newington	42	D4
Upper Parliament St	42	D6
Upper Pitt St	42	D6
Upper Pownall St	42	C5
Upper Stanhope St	43	E6
Upper Warwick St	43	E7
Upper William St	42	B1
Uxbridge St	43	H5

V

Street	Page	Grid
Vandries St	42	A1
Vandyke St	43	H6
Vauxhall Rd	42	C2
Vernon St	42	C3
Verulam Cl	43	G6
Victoria St	42	C4
Village St	43	E1
Vincent Ct	42	D5
Vining St	43	F7
Virgil St	42	D1
Voelas St	43	G7
Vronhill Cl	43	G7
Vulcan St	42	A1

W

Street	Page	Grid
Wainwright Cl	43	H5
Wakefield St	42	D2
Waldron St	42	C2
Walker St	43	F2
Wall St	42	C4
Walsh Cl	42	C1
Wapping	42	C5
Ward St	42	D3
Warwick St	42	E7
Waterloo Quay	42	A2
Water St	42	B4
Watkinson St	42	C6
Watmough St	42	E1
Wavertree Bvd	43	K4
Wavertree Rd	43	G4
Webb Cl	43	H4
Webb St	43	H6
Webster Rd	43	J6
Webster St	42	C3
Wedgewood St	43	H3
Wendell St	43	H6
Wentworth Dr	43	F1
West Derby Rd	43	G2
West Derby St	43	F3
Westmorland Dr	42	C2
Whitcroft Rd	43	J2
Whitechapel	42	C4
Whitefield Rd	43	G1
Whitefield Way	43	G1
White Rock Ct	43	G1
White Rock St	43	G1
Whithorn St	43	J5
Whitland Rd	43	J1
Whitley St	42	B1
Whittier St	43	H6
Wightman St	43	G2
Wilde St	42	D3
Wilfer Cl	43	H5
William Brown St	42	D3
William Henry St	42	E2
Williamson St	42	C4
Wimpole St	43	H3
Windsor St	43	E6
Windsor Vw	43	H6
Winifred St	43	H4
Winter St	43	F2
Wolstenholme Sq	42	D5
Woodside St	43	H4
Wood St	42	D4
Wordsworth St	43	H6
Wrayburn Cl	43	H5
Wrenbury St	43	H3
Wynnstay St	43	G7

Y

Street	Page	Grid
Yanwath St	43	H6
York St	42	C5

London street index

A

Street	Page	Grid
Abbey Orchard St SW1	44	D6
Abingdon St SW1	44	E6
Achilles Way W1	44	A5
Adam & Eve Ct W1	44	C2
Adams Row W1	44	A4
Adam St WC2	45	E4
Addington St SE1	45	F6
Addle Hill EC4	45	H3
Adelaide St WC2	45	E4
Adeline Pl WC1	44	D2
Adelphi Ter WC2	45	E4
Agar St WC2	44	E4
Air St W1	44	C4
Alaska St SE1	45	G5
Albany W1	44	C4
Albany Ctyd W1	44	C4
Albemarle St W1	44	B4
Albemarle Way EC1	45	H1
Albert Barnes Ho SE1	45	J7
Albion Pl EC1	45	H1
Albion Way EC1	45	J2
Aldburgh Ms W1	44	A2
Aldermanbury EC2	45	J2
Aldermanbury Sq EC2	45	J2
Aldersgate St EC1	45	J2
Aldford St W1	44	A4
Aldwych WC2	45	F3
Alfred Ms W1	44	D1
Alfred Pl WC1	44	D1
All Souls Pl W1	44	B2
Ambassador's Ct SW1	44	C5
Ambrosden Av SW1	44	C7
Amen Cor EC4	45	H3
Amen Ct EC4	45	H2
America St SE1	45	J5
Andrew Borde St WC2	44	D2
Andrewes Ho EC2	45	J2
Andrews Crosse WC2	45	G3
Angel Ct SW1	44	C5
Angel St EC1	45	J2
Apothecary St EC4	45	H3
Apple Tree Yd SW1	44	C4
Apsley Way W1	44	A5
Aquinas St SE1	45	G4
Arch St SE1	45	J7
Archer St W1	44	D3
Arches, The WC2	45	E4
Archibald Ms W1	44	A4
Argyll St W1	44	C3
Aria Ho WC2	45	E2
Arlington St SW1	44	C4
Arne St WC2	45	E3
Arneway St SW1	44	D7
Arrol Ho SE1	45	J7
Artillery Mans SW1	44	D6
Artillery Pl SW1	44	D7
Artillery Row SW1	44	D7
Arundel Gt Ct WC2	45	F3
Arundel St WC2	45	F3
Ashentree Ct EC4	45	G3
Ashland Pl W1	44	A1
Ashley Gdns SW1	44	C7
Ashley Pl SW1	44	C7
Astbury Ho SE11	45	G7
Audley Sq W1	44	A4
Austral St SE11	45	H7
Ave Maria La EC4	45	H3
Avery Row W1	44	B3
Avonmouth St SE1	45	J6
Avon Pl SE1	45	J6
Aybrook St W1	44	A2
Aylesbury St EC1	45	H1
Ayres St SE1	45	J5

B

Street	Page	Grid
Babmaes St SW1	44	D4
Back Hill EC1	45	G1
Bainbridge St WC1	44	D2
Baker's Ms W1	44	A2
Baker's Row EC1	45	G1
Baker's Yd EC1	45	G1
Balderton St W1	44	A3
Baldwin's Gdns EC1	45	G1
Balfour Ms W1	44	A4
Balfour Pl W1	44	A4
Baltic St E EC1	45	J1
Baltic St W EC1	45	J1
Banbury Ct WC2	44	E3
Bank End SE1	45	J4
Banks Ho SE1	45	J7
Bankside SE1	45	J4
Bankside Lofts SE1	45	H4
Banner St EC1	45	J1
Barbican EC2	45	J2
Barbican, The EC2	45	J2
Barbon Cl WC1	45	E1
Barge Ho St SE1	45	G4
Barkham Ter SE1	45	G6
Barley Mow Pas EC1	45	H2
Barlow Pl W1	44	B4
Barnard's Inn EC1	45	G2
Barons Pl SE1	45	G6
Barrett St W1	44	A3
Barter St WC1	45	E2
Bartholomew Cl EC1	45	J2
Bartholomew Pl EC1	45	J2

Bartlett Ct EC4 45 G2
Bartletts Pas EC4 45 G2
Barton St SW1 44 E6
Bastion Highwalk EC2 45 J2
Bateman's Bldgs W1 44 D3
Bateman St W1 44 D3
Bath Ct EC1 45 G1
Bath Ter SE1 45 J7
Bayley St WC1 44 D2
Baylis Rd SE1 45 G6
Beak St W1 44 C3
Bear All EC4 45 H2
Bear Gdns SE1 45 J4
Bear La SE1 45 H4
Bear St WC2 44 D3
Beauchamp St EC1 45 G2
Beaumont Ms W1 44 A1
Beaumont St W1 44 A1
Bedford Av WC1 44 D2
Bedfordbury WC2 44 E3
Bedford Ct WC2 44 E4
Bedford Pl WC1 44 E1
Bedford Row WC1 45 F1
Bedford Sq WC1 44 D2
Bedford St WC2 44 E3
Bedford Way WC1 44 D1
Bedlam Ms SE11 45 G7
Beech St EC2 45 J1
Beeston Pl SW1 44 B7
Belgrave Ms N SW1 44 A6
Belgrave Ms S SW1 44 A6
Belgrave Ms W SW1 44 A6
Belgrave Pl SW1 44 A6
Belgrave Sq SW1 44 A6
Belgrave Yd SW1 44 B7
Belgravia SW1 44 A7
Bell Wf La EC4 45 J4
Bell Yd WC2 45 G2
Belvedere Bldgs SE1 45 H6
Belvedere Pl SE1 45 H6
Belvedere Rd SE1 45 F5
Benjamin St EC1 45 H1
Bennet's Hill EC4 45 H3
Bennet St SW1 44 C4
Bennett St SW1 44 C4
Bennetts Yd SW1 44 D7
Bentinck Ms W1 44 A2
Bentinck St W1 44 A2
Berkeley Sq W1 44 B4
Berkeley St W1 44 B4
Bernard St WC1 44 E1
Berners Ms W1 44 C2
Berners Pl W1 44 C2
Berners St W1 44 C2
Berwick St W1 44 D3
Betterton St WC2 44 E3
Bingham Pl W1 44 A1
Binney St W1 44 A3
Birdcage Wk SW1 44 C6
Bird St W1 44 A3
Bishop's Ct EC4 45 H2
Bishop's Ct WC2 45 G2
Bishops Ter SE11 45 G7
Bittern St SE1 45 J6
Blackburne's Ms W1 44 A3
Blackfriars Br EC4 45 H3
Blackfriars Br SE1 45 H3
Blackfriars Ct EC4 45 H3
Black Friars La EC4 45 H3
Blackfriars Pas EC4 45 H3
Blackfriars Rd SE1 45 H6
Bleeding Heart Yd EC1 45 G2
Blenheim St W1 44 B3
Bloomfield Pl W1 44 B3
Bloomsbury WC1 44 D2
Bloomsbury Ct WC1 45 E2
Bloomsbury Pl WC1 45 E1
Bloomsbury Sq WC1 45 E2
Bloomsbury St WC1 44 D2
Bloomsbury Way WC1 44 E2
Blore Ct W1 44 D3
Blue Ball Yd SW1 44 C5
Bolsover St W1 44 B1
Bolt Ct EC4 45 G3
Bolton St W1 44 B4
Book Ms WC2 44 D3
Booth La EC4 45 J3
Booth's Pl W1 44 C2
Borough, The SE1 45 J6
Borough High St SE1 45 J6
Borough Rd SE1 45 H6
Borough Sq SE1 45 J6
Boscobel Pl SW1 44 A7
Boswell Ct WC1 45 E1
Boswell St WC1 45 E1
Boundary Row SE1 45 H5
Bourchier St W1 44 D3
Bourdon Pl W1 44 B3
Bourdon St W1 44 B3
Bourlet Cl W1 44 C2
Bourne Est EC1 45 G1
Bouverie St EC4 45 G3

Bow Chyd EC4 45 J3
Bow La EC4 45 J3
Bow St WC2 45 E3
Boyce St SE1 45 F5
Boyfield St SE1 45 H6
Boyle St W1 44 C3
Brackley St EC1 45 J1
Brad St SE1 45 G5
Bread St EC4 45 J3
Bream's Bldgs EC4 45 G2
Bressenden Pl SW1 44 B6
Brewer's Grn SW1 44 D6
Brewers Hall Gdns EC2 45 J2
Brewer St W1 44 C3
Briant Est SE1 45 G7
Briant Ho SE1 45 F7
Brick Ct EC4 45 G3
Brick St W1 44 B5
Bride Ct EC4 45 H3
Bride La EC4 45 H3
Bridewell Pl EC4 45 H3
Bridford Ms W1 44 B1
Bridge Pl SW1 44 B7
Bridge St SW1 44 E6
Bridgewater Sq EC2 45 J1
Bridgewater St EC2 45 J1
Bridle La W1 44 C3
Brinton Wk SE1 45 H5
Briset St EC1 45 H1
Britton St EC1 45 H1
Broadbent St W1 44 B3
Broad Ct WC2 45 E3
Broad Sanctuary SW1 44 D6
Broadstone Pl W1 44 A2
Broad Wk W1 44 A4
Broadwall SE1 45 G4
Broadway SW1 44 D6
Broadwick St W1 44 C3
Broad Yd EC1 45 H1
Brockham St SE1 45 J6
Broken Wf EC4 45 J3
Bromley Pl W1 44 C1
Brook Dr SE11 45 G7
Brooke's Ct EC1 45 G1
Brookes Mkt EC1 45 G1
Brooke St EC1 45 G2
Brook's Ms W1 44 B3
Brook St W1 44 A3
Brown Hart Gdns W1 44 A3
Browning Ms W1 44 B2
Brownlow Ms WC1 45 F1
Brownlow St WC1 45 F2
Brunswick Sq WC1 45 E1
Bruton La W1 44 B4
Bruton Pl W1 44 B4
Bruton St W1 44 B4
Brydges Pl WC2 44 E4
Buckingham Arc WC2 45 E4
Buckingham Gate SW1 44 C6
Buckingham Ms SW1 44 C6
Buckingham Pl SW1 44 C6
Buckingham St WC2 45 E4
Buckley St SE1 45 G5
Bucknall St WC2 44 D2
Bull Inn Ct WC2 45 E4
Bulstrode Pl W1 44 A2
Bulstrode St W1 44 A2
Burdett St SE1 45 G6
Burgon St EC4 45 H3
Burleigh St WC2 45 F3
Burlington Arc W1 44 C4
Burlington Gdns W1 44 C4
Burrell St SE1 45 H4
Burrows Ms SE1 45 H5
Bury Pl WC1 44 E2
Bury St WC1 44 C4
Butler Pl SW1 44 D6
Byng Pl WC1 44 D1
Bywell Pl W1 44 C2

C
Cadogan La SW1 44 A7
Cahill St EC1 45 J1
Caleb St SE1 45 J5
Cambridge Circ WC2 44 D3
Candover St W1 44 C2
Cannon St EC4 45 J3
Canon Row SW1 44 E6
Canterbury Ho SE1 45 F6
Canvey St SE1 45 H4
Capener's Cl SW1 44 A6
Capper St WC1 44 C1
Carburton St W1 44 B1
Carey La EC2 45 J2
Carey St WC2 45 F3
Carlisle La SE1 45 F7
Carlisle Pl SW1 44 C7
Carlisle St W1 44 D3
Carlos Pl W1 44 A4
Carlton Gdns SW1 44 D5
Carlton Ho Ter SW1 44 D5
Carlton St SW1 44 D4

Carmelite St EC4 45 G3
Carnaby St W1 44 C3
Carpenter St W1 44 B4
Carrington St W1 44 B5
Carteret St SW1 44 D6
Carter La EC4 45 H3
Carthusian St EC1 45 J1
Carting La WC2 45 E4
Castle Baynard St EC4 45 H3
Castlebrook Cl SE11 45 H7
Castle La SW1 44 C6
Castle Yd SE1 45 H4
Cathedral Piazza SW1 44 C7
Cathedral Wk SW1 44 C7
Catherine Pl SW1 44 C6
Catherine St WC2 45 F3
Catherine Wheel Yd SW1 44 C5
Catton St WC1 45 F2
Cavendish Ms N W1 44 B1
Cavendish Ms S W1 44 B2
Cavendish Pl W1 44 B2
Cavendish Sq W1 44 B2
Caxton St SW1 44 C6
Cecil Ct WC2 44 D4
Centaur St SE1 45 F6
Centrepoint WC1 44 D2
Chadwick St SW1 44 D7
Chancel St SE1 45 H4
Chancery La WC2 45 G2
Chandos Pl WC2 44 E4
Chandos St W1 44 B2
Chapel Pl W1 44 B3
Chapel St SW1 44 A6
Chaplin Cl SE1 45 G5
Chapone Pl W1 44 D3
Chapter Ho Ct EC4 45 J3
Charing Cross SW1 44 D4
Charing Cross Rd WC2 44 D2
Charles II St SW1 44 D4
Charles St W1 44 B4
Charlotte Ms W1 44 C1
Charlotte Pl W1 44 C2
Charlotte St W1 44 C1
Charterhouse, The EC1 45 H1
Charterhouse Bldgs EC1 45 H1
Charterhouse Ms EC1 45 H1
Charterhouse Sq EC1 45 H1
Charterhouse St EC1 45 G2
Cheapside EC2 45 J3
Chenies Ms WC1 44 D1
Chenies St WC1 44 D1
Chequer St EC1 45 J1
Cherry Tree Wk EC1 45 J1
Chesham Cl SW1 44 A7
Chesham Ms SW1 44 A6
Chesham Pl SW1 44 A7
Chesham St SW1 44 A7
Cheshire Ct EC4 45 G3
Chester Cl SW1 44 A6
Chesterfield Gdns W1 44 B4
Chesterfield Hill W1 44 B4
Chesterfield St W1 44 B4
Chester Ms SW1 44 B6
Chester Sq SW1 44 B7
Chester Sq Ms SW1 44 B7
Chester St SW1 44 A6
Chicheley St SE1 45 F5
Chichester Rents WC2 45 G2
Chiltern St W1 44 A1
Ching Ct WC2 44 E3
Chiswell St EC1 45 J1
Chitty St W1 44 C1
Christ Ch Pas EC1 45 H2
Church Entry EC4 45 H3
Church St W1 44 C4
Churchyard Row SE11 45 H7
Clare Mkt WC2 45 F3
Clarges Ms W1 44 B4
Clarges St W1 44 B4
Clarke's Ms W1 44 A1
Clement's Inn WC2 45 F3
Clement's Inn Pas WC2 45 F3
Clennam St SE1 45 J5
Clerkenwell EC1 45 H1
Clerkenwell Grn EC1 45 G1
Clerkenwell Rd EC1 45 G1
Cleveland Ms W1 44 C1
Cleveland Pl SW1 44 C4
Cleveland Row SW1 44 C5
Cleveland St W1 44 C1
Clifford's Inn Pas EC4 45 G3
Clifford St W1 44 C4
Clink St SE1 45 J4
Clipstone Ms W1 44 C1
Clipstone St W1 44 B1
Cliveden Pl SW1 44 A7

Cloak La EC4 45 J3
Cloth Ct EC1 45 H2
Cloth Fair EC1 45 H2
Cloth St EC1 45 J1
Coach & Horses Yd W1 44 B3
Coburg Cl SW1 44 C7
Cock La EC1 45 H2
Cockpit Steps SW1 44 D6
Cockpit Yd WC1 45 F1
Cockspur Ct SW1 44 D4
Cockspur St SW1 44 D4
Coin St SE1 45 G4
Cole St SE1 45 J6
Coley St WC1 45 F1
College Hill EC4 45 J3
College Ms SW1 44 E6
College St EC4 45 J3
Collinson St SE1 45 J6
Collinson Wk SE1 45 J6
Colnbrook St SE1 45 H7
Colombo St SE1 45 H5
Colonnade WC1 44 E1
Colville Pl W1 44 C2
Computer Pass EC2 45 J2
Concert Hall App SE1 45 F5
Conduit Ct WC2 44 E3
Conduit St W1 44 B3
Cons St SE1 45 G5
Constitution Hill SW1 44 B5
Conway Ms W1 44 C1
Conway St W1 44 C1
Cooper Cl SE1 45 G6
Copeland Ho SE11 45 F7
Copperfield St SE1 45 H5
Coptic St WC1 44 E2
Coral St SE1 45 G6
Coram St WC1 44 E1
Cork St W1 44 C4
Cork St Ms W1 44 C4
Corner Ho St WC2 44 E4
Cornwall Rd SE1 45 G4
Cosmo Pl WC1 45 E1
Cosser St SE1 45 G6
Cottesloe Ms SE1 45 G6
County St SE1 45 J7
Covent Gdn WC2 45 E3
Covent Gdn Mkt WC2 45 E3
Coventry St W1 44 D4
Cowcross St EC1 45 H1
Cowley St SW1 44 E6
Craig's Ct SW1 44 E4
Cramer St W1 44 A2
Cranbourn St WC2 44 D3
Crane Ct EC4 45 G3
Cranfield Row SE1 45 G6
Craven Pas WC2 44 E4
Craven St WC2 44 E4
Crawford Pas EC1 45 G1
Creed La EC4 45 H3
Crescent Row EC1 45 J1
Cripplegate St EC2 45 J1
Cromwell Twr EC2 45 J1
Cross Keys Cl W1 44 A2
Cross Keys Sq EC1 45 J2
Crown Ct EC2 45 J3
Crown Ct WC2 45 E3
Crown Office Row EC4 45 G3
Crown Pas SW1 44 C5
Cubitts Yd WC2 45 E3
Culross St W1 44 A4
Cursitor St EC4 45 G2
Curzon Gate W1 44 A5
Curzon Sq W1 44 A5
Curzon St W1 44 A5
Cut, The SE1 45 G5
Cypress Pl W1 44 C1

D
Dacre St SW1 44 D6
Dane St WC1 45 F2
Dansey Pl W1 44 D3
Dante Pl SE11 45 H7
Dante Rd SE11 45 H7
D'Arblay St W1 44 C3
Dartmouth St SW1 44 D6
Davidge St SE1 45 H6
Davies Ms W1 44 B3
Davies St W1 44 B3
Dean Bradley St SW1 44 E7
Deanery Ms W1 44 A4
Deanery St W1 44 A4
Dean Farrar St SW1 44 D6
Dean Ryle St SW1 44 E7
Deans Ct EC4 45 H3
Deans Ms W1 44 B2
Dean Stanley St SW1 44 E7
Dean St W1 44 D2
Dean's Yd SW1 44 D6
Dean Trench St SW1 44 E7
Denman St W1 44 D4
Denmark Pl WC2 44 D2
Denmark St WC2 44 D3

Derby Gate SW1 44 E5
Derby St W1 44 A5
Dering St W1 44 B3
Devereux Ct WC2 45 G3
Devonshire Cl W1 44 B1
Devonshire Ms N W1 44 B1
Devonshire Ms S W1 44 B1
Devonshire Ms W W1 44 B1
Devonshire Pl W1 44 A1
Devonshire Pl Ms W1 44 A1
Devonshire Row Ms W1 44 B1
Devonshire St W1 44 A1
De Walden St W1 44 A2
Diadem Ct W1 44 D3
Dickens Ms EC1 45 H1
Dickens Sq SE1 45 J6
Disney Pl SE1 45 J5
Disney St SE1 45 J5
Distaff La EC4 45 J3
Doby Ct EC4 45 J3
Dodson St SE1 45 G6
Dolben St SE1 45 H5
Dombey St WC1 45 F1
Doon St SE1 45 G5
Dorrington St EC1 45 G1
Dorrit St SE1 45 J5
Dorset Bldgs EC4 45 H3
Dorset Ms SW1 44 B6
Dorset Ri EC4 45 H3
Doughty Ms WC1 45 F1
Dover St W1 44 B4
Dover Yd W1 44 B4
Downing St SW1 44 E5
Down St W1 44 B5
Down St Ms W1 44 B5
Doyce St SE1 45 J5
D'Oyley St SW1 44 A7
Drake St WC1 45 F2
Draper Ho SE1 45 H7
Drury La WC2 45 E3
Dryden St WC2 45 E3
Duchess Ms W1 44 B2
Duchess St W1 44 B2
Duchy Pl SE1 45 G4
Duchy St SE1 45 G4
Duck La W1 44 D3
Dufferin St EC1 45 J1
Dufour's Pl W1 44 C3
Dugard Way SE11 45 H7
Duke of Wellington Pl SW1 44 A5
Duke of York St SW1 44 C4
Duke's Ms W1 44 A2
Duke St SW1 44 C4
Duke St W1 44 A2
Duke's Yd W1 44 A3
Duncannon St WC2 44 E4
Dunns Pas WC1 45 E2
Dunstable Ms W1 44 A1
Durham Ho St WC2 45 E4
Dyer's Bldgs EC1 45 G2
Dyott St WC1 44 E2

E
Eagle Ct EC1 45 H1
Eagle Pl SW1 44 C4
Eagle St WC1 45 F2
Earlham St WC2 44 D3
Earnshaw St WC2 44 D2
Easley's Ms W1 44 A2
Eastcastle St W1 44 C2
East Harding St EC4 45 G2
East Pas EC1 45 H1
East Poultry Av EC1 45 H2
Eaton Gate SW1 44 A7
Eaton La SW1 44 B7
Eaton Ms N SW1 44 A7
Eaton Ms S SW1 44 A7
Eaton Ms W SW1 44 A7
Eaton Pl SW1 44 A7
Eaton Row SW1 44 B6
Eaton Sq SW1 44 B6
Eaton Ter SW1 44 A7
Eaton Ter Ms SW1 44 A7
Ebury Ms SW1 44 A7
Ebury Ms E SW1 44 B7
Ebury St SW1 44 B7
Eccleston Br SW1 44 B7
Eccleston Ms SW1 44 A6
Eccleston Pl SW1 44 B7
Eccleston St SW1 44 B7
Edwards Ms W1 44 A3
Elba Pl SE17 45 J7
Elephant & Castle SE1 45 H7
Elephant Rd SE17 45 J7
Elizabeth Ct SW1 44 D7
Elizabeth St SW1 44 A7
Ellington Ho SE1 45 J6
Elliotts Row SE11 45 H7
Elm Ct EC4 45 G3
Elm St WC1 45 F1
Elverton St SW1 44 D7

Ely Ct EC1 45 G2
Ely Pl EC1 45 G2
Embankment Pier WC2 45 F4
Embankment Pl WC2 45 E4
Emerald St WC1 45 F1
Emerson St SE1 45 J4
Emery Hill St SW1 44 C7
Emery St SE1 45 G6
Endell St WC2 44 E2
Errol St EC1 45 J1
Essex Ct EC4 45 G3
Essex St WC2 45 G3
Euston Rd NW1 44 B1
Evelyn Yd W1 44 D2
Ewer St SE1 45 J5
Excel Ct WC2 44 D4
Exchange Ct WC2 45 E4
Exeter St WC2 45 E3
Exton St SE1 45 G5
Eyre St Hill EC1 45 G1

F
Falconberg Ct W1 44 D2
Falconberg Ms W1 44 D2
Falcon Ct EC4 45 G3
Falmouth Rd SE1 45 J6
Fann St EC1 45 J1
Fann St EC2 45 J1
Fareham St W1 44 D2
Farm St W1 44 B4
Farnham Pl SE1 45 H5
Farringdon La EC1 45 G1
Farringdon St EC4 45 H2
Faulkner's All EC1 45 H1
Ferrybridge Ho SE11 45 F7
Fetter La EC4 45 G3
Field Ct WC1 45 F2
Fisher St WC1 45 E2
Fitzalan St SE11 45 G7
Fitzhardinge St W1 44 A3
Fitzmaurice Pl W1 44 B4
Fitzroy Ct W1 44 C1
Fitzroy Ms W1 44 C1
Fitzroy Sq W1 44 C1
Fitzroy St W1 44 C1
Fives Ct SE11 45 H7
Flaxman Ct W1 44 D3
Fleet St EC4 45 G3
Flitcroft St WC2 44 D2
Floral St WC2 44 E3
Florin Ct EC1 45 J1
Foley St W1 44 C2
Fore St EC2 45 J2
Fortune St EC1 45 J1
Forum Magnum Sq SE1 45 F5
Foster La EC2 45 J2
Foubert's Pl W1 44 C3
Fountain Ct EC4 45 G3
Fountain Sq SW1 44 B7
Fox & Knot St EC1 45 H1
Francis St SW1 44 C7
Frazier St SE1 45 G6
Friars Cl SE1 45 H5
Friar St EC4 45 H3
Friary Ct SW1 44 C5
Friday St EC4 45 J3
Frith St W1 44 D3
Fulwood Pl WC1 45 F2
Furnival St EC4 45 G2
Fynes St SW1 44 D7

G
Gabriel's Wf SE1 45 G4
Gage St WC1 45 E1
Galen Pl WC1 45 E2
Gambia St SE1 45 H5
Ganton St W1 44 C3
Garbutt Pl W1 44 A1
Garden Row SE1 45 H7
Gardners La EC4 45 J3
Garlick Hill EC4 45 J3
Garrick St WC2 44 E3
Garrick Yd WC2 44 E3
Gate Ho Sq SE1 45 J4
Gate St WC2 45 F2
Gaunt St SE1 45 H6
Gayfere St SW1 44 E7
Gaywood Est SE1 45 H7
Gaywood St SE1 45 H7
Gees Ct W1 44 A3
George Ct WC2 45 E4
George Mathers Rd SE11 45 H7
George Yd W1 44 A3
Geraldine St SE11 45 H7
Gerald Ms SW1 44 A7
Gerald Rd SW1 44 A7
Gerrard Pl W1 44 D3
Gerrard St W1 44 D3
Gerridge St SE1 45 G6
Gilbert Pl WC1 44 E2
Gilbert St W1 44 A3

Gildea St W1 44 B2
Gillingham Row SW1 44 C7
Gillingham St SW1 44 B7
Giltspur St EC1 45 H2
Gladstone St SE1 45 H6
Glasshill St SE1 45 H5
Glasshouse St W1 44 C4
Glasshouse Yd EC1 45 J1
Globe St SE1 45 J6
Globe Yd W1 44 B3
Godliman St EC4 45 J3
Golden Jubilee Br SE1 45 F5
Golden Jubilee Br WC2 45 E4
Golden La EC1 45 J1
Golden La Est EC1 45 J1
Golden Sq W1 44 C3
Goldsmith St EC2 45 J2
Goodge Pl W1 44 C2
Goodge St W1 44 C2
Goodwins Ct WC2 44 E3
Gordon Sq WC1 44 D1
Gosfield St W1 44 C1
Goslett Yd WC2 44 D3
Goswell Rd EC1 45 J1
Gough Sq EC4 45 G2
Gower Ms WC1 44 D2
Grafton Ms W1 44 C1
Grafton St W1 44 B4
Grafton Way W1 44 C1
Grafton Way WC1 44 C1
Granby Pl SE1 45 G6
Grand Av EC1 45 H1
Grange Ct WC2 45 F3
Grantham Pl W1 44 B5
Granville Pl W1 44 A3
Grape St WC2 44 E2
Gray's Inn WC1 45 F1
Gray's Inn Pl WC1 45 F2
Gray's Inn Sq WC1 45 G1
Gray St SE1 45 G6
Gray's Yd W1 44 A3
Great Arthur Ho EC1 45 J1
Great Castle St W1 44 B2
Great Chapel St W1 44 D2
Great Coll St SW1 44 E6
Great Dover St SE1 45 J6
Great George St SW1 44 D6
Great Guildford St SE1 45 J4
Great James St WC1 45 F1
Great Marlborough St W1 44 C3
Great New St EC4 45 G2
Great Ormond St WC1 45 E1
Great Peter St SW1 44 D7
Great Portland St W1 44 B1
Great Pulteney St W1 44 C3
Great Queen St WC2 45 E3
Great Russell St WC1 44 D2
Great St. Thomas Apostle EC4 45 J3
Great Scotland Yd SW1 44 E5
Great Smith St SW1 44 D6
Great Suffolk St SE1 45 H5
Great Sutton St EC1 45 H1
Great Titchfield St W1 44 C2
Great Trinity La EC4 45 J3
Great Turnstile WC1 45 F2
Great Windmill St W1 44 D3
Greek Ct W1 44 D3
Greek St W1 44 D3
Green Arbour Ct EC1 45 H2
Greencoat Pl SW1 44 C7
Greencoat Row SW1 44 C7
Greenham Cl SE1 45 G6
Greenhill's Rents EC1 45 H1
Green's Ct W1 44 D3
Greenwell St W1 44 B1
Greet St SE1 45 G5
Grenville St WC1 45 E1
Gresham St EC2 45 J2
Gresse St W1 44 D2
Greville St EC1 45 G2
Greycoat Pl SW1 44 D7
Greycoat St SW1 44 D7
Greyfriars Pas EC1 45 H2
Greystoke Pl EC4 45 G2
Grindal St SE1 45 G6
Groom Pl SW1 44 A6
Grosvenor Cotts SW1 44 A7
Grosvenor Cres SW1 44 A6
Grosvenor Cres Ms SW1 44 A6
Grosvenor Est SW1 44 D7
Grosvenor Gdns SW1 44 B6
Grosvenor Gdns Ms E SW1 44 B6
Grosvenor Gdns Ms N SW1 44 B7
Grosvenor Gdns Ms S SW1 44 B7
Grosvenor Hill W1 44 B3
Grosvenor Pl SW1 44 A6
Grosvenor Sq W1 44 A3
Grosvenor St W1 44 B3
Grotto Pas W1 44 A1
Groveland Ct EC4 45 J3
Guildhall Yd EC2 45 J2
Guildhouse St SW1 44 C7
Guilford Pl WC1 45 F1
Guilford St WC1 45 E1
Gunpowder Sq EC4 45 G2
Gutter La EC2 45 J2

H

Half Moon Ct EC1 45 J2
Half Moon St W1 44 B4
Halkin Arc SW1 44 A6
Halkin Ms SW1 44 A6
Halkin Pl SW1 44 A6
Halkin St SW1 44 A6
Hallam Ms W1 44 B1
Hallam St W1 44 B1
Hamilton Ms W1 44 B5
Hamilton Pl W1 44 A5
Ham Yd W1 44 D3
Hand Ct WC1 45 F2
Hanging Sword All EC4 45 G3
Hanover Pl WC2 45 E3
Hanover Sq W1 44 B3
Hanover St W1 44 B3
Hanson St W1 44 C1
Hanway Pl W1 44 D2
Hanway St W1 44 D2
Hare Ct EC4 45 G3
Hare Pl EC4 45 G3
Harewood Pl W1 44 B3
Harley Pl W1 44 B2
Harley St W1 44 B2
Harmsworth Ms SE11 45 H7
Harp All EC4 45 H2
Harper Rd SE1 45 J6
Harpur Ms WC1 45 F1
Harpur St WC1 45 F1
Hat & Mitre Ct EC1 45 H1
Hatfields SE1 45 G4
Hatton Gdn EC1 45 G1
Hatton Pl EC1 45 G1
Hatton Wall EC1 45 G1
Haunch of Venison Yd W1 44 B3
Hay Hill W1 44 B4
Hayles St SE11 45 H7
Haymarket SW1 44 D4
Haymarket Arc SW1 44 D4
Hayne St EC1 45 H1
Hay's Ms W1 44 B4
Hayward's Pl EC1 45 H1
Headfort Pl SW1 44 A6
Heddon St W1 44 C3
Hedger St SE11 45 H7
Hen & Chicken Ct EC4 45 G3
Henrietta Pl W1 44 B3
Henrietta St WC2 45 E3
Herald's Pl SE11 45 H7
Herbal Hill EC1 45 G1
Hercules Rd SE1 45 F7
Herrick St SW1 44 D7
Hertford St W1 44 B4
High Holborn WC1 45 E2
High Timber St EC4 45 J3
Hilary Ms SE1 45 J5
Hills Pl W1 44 C3
Hill St W1 44 A4
Hind Ct EC4 45 G3
Hinde St W1 44 A2
Hindon Ct SW1 44 C7
Hobart Pl SW1 44 B6
Holborn EC1 45 G2
Holborn WC2 45 F2
Holborn Circ EC1 45 G2
Holborn Pl WC1 45 F2
Holborn Viaduct EC1 45 G2
Holland St SE1 45 H4
Hollen St W1 44 D2
Holles St W1 44 B2
Holmes Ter SE1 45 G5
Holsworthy Sq WC1 45 F1
Holyoak Rd SE11 45 H7
Honey La EC2 45 J3
Hood Ct EC4 45 G3
Hop Gdns WC2 44 E4
Hopkins St W1 44 C3
Hopton's Gdns SE1 45 H4
Hopton St SE1 45 H4
Hornbeam Cl SE11 45 G7
Horse & Dolphin Yd W1 44 D3
Horseferry Rd SW1 44 D7
Horse Guards Av SW1 44 E5
Horse Guards Rd SW1 44 D5
Horsemongers Ms SE1 45 J6
Horse Ride SW1 44 D5
Hosier La EC1 45 H2
Houghton St WC2 45 F3
Howick Pl SW1 44 C7
Howland Ms E W1 44 C1
Howland St W1 44 C1
Hudson's Pl SW1 44 B7
Huggin Ct EC4 45 J3
Huggin Hill EC4 45 J3
Hulme Pl SE1 45 J6
Hungerford Br SE1 45 E4
Hungerford Br WC2 45 E4
Hungerford La WC2 44 E4
Huntley St WC1 44 C1
Hunt's Ct WC2 44 D4
Hutton St EC4 45 G3
Hyde Pk Cor W1 44 A5

I

India Pl WC2 45 F3
Ingestre Pl W1 44 C3
Ingram Cl SE11 45 F7
Inigo Pl WC2 44 E3
Inner Temple La EC4 45 G3
Invicta Plaza SE1 45 H4
Ireland Yd EC4 45 H3
Irving St WC2 44 D4
Isaac Way SE1 45 J5
Isabella St SE1 45 H5
Ivybridge La WC2 45 E4

J

Jacob's Well Ms W1 44 A2
James St W1 44 A2
James St WC2 45 E3
Jermyn St SW1 44 C4
Jerusalem Pas EC1 45 H1
Jervis Ct W1 44 B3
Joan St SE1 45 H5
Jockey's Flds WC1 45 F1
Johanna St SE1 45 G6
John Adam St WC2 45 E4
John Carpenter St EC4 45 H3
John Milton Pass EC2 45 J3
John Princes St W1 44 B2
John's Ms WC1 45 F1
John St WC1 45 F1
Jones St W1 44 B4
Jubilee Mkt Hall WC2 45 E3
Juxon St SE11 45 F7

K

Kean St WC2 45 F3
Keeley St WC2 45 F3
Kell St SE1 45 H6
Kemble St WC2 45 F3
Kemp's Ct W1 44 C3
Kendall Pl W1 44 A2
Kennet Wf La EC4 45 J3
Kennington Rd SE1 45 G6
Kennington Rd SE11 45 G7
Kenrick Pl W1 44 A1
Keppel Row SE1 45 J5
Keppel St WC1 44 D1
Keyworth Pl SE1 45 H6
Keyworth St SE1 45 H6
King Charles St SW1 44 D5
King Edward St EC1 45 J2
King Edward Wk SE1 45 G6
Kinghorn St EC1 45 J2
King James Ct SE1 45 H6
King James St SE1 45 H6
Kingly Ct W1 44 C3
Kingly St W1 44 C3
Kings Bench St SE1 45 H5
Kings Bench Wk EC4 45 G3
Kingscote St EC4 45 H3
King's Ms WC1 45 F1
Kings Pl SE1 45 J6
King's Reach Twr SE1 45 G4
King's Scholars' Pas SW1 44 C7
King St EC2 45 J3
King St SW1 44 C5
King St WC2 44 E3
Kingsway WC2 45 F2
Kinnerton St SW1 44 A6
Kirby St EC1 45 G1
Kirkman Pl W1 44 D2
Kirk St WC1 45 F1
Knightrider St EC4 45 J3

L

Lambeth SE1 45 F7
Lambeth Br SE1 45 E7
Lambeth Br SW1 45 E7
Lambeth Hill EC4 45 J3
Lambeth Palace Rd SE1 45 F7
Lambeth Pier SE1 45 E7
Lambeth Rd SE1 45 F7
Lambeth Rd SE11 45 F7
Lambeth Twrs SE11 45 G7
Lambeth Wk SE1 45 F7
Lambeth Wk SE11 45 F7
Lambs Conduit Pas WC1 45 F1
Lamb's Conduit St WC1 45 F1
Lamlash St SE11 45 H7
Lamp Office Ct WC1 45 F1
Lancashire Ct W1 44 B3
Lancaster Pl WC2 45 F3
Lancaster St SE1 45 H6
Lanesborough Pl SW1 44 A5
Langham Pl W1 44 B2
Langham St W1 44 B2
Langley Ct WC2 44 E3
Langley St WC2 44 E3
Lansdowne Row W1 44 B4
Lansdowne Ter WC1 45 E1
Lant St SE1 45 J5
Lauderdale Twr EC2 45 J1
Launcelot St SE1 45 G6
Lavington St SE1 45 H5
Lawrence La EC2 45 J3
Laystall St EC1 45 G1
Laytons Bldgs SE1 45 J5
Lazenby Ct WC2 44 E3
Leake St SE1 45 F5
Leather La EC1 45 G2
Lees Pl W1 44 A3
Leicester Ct WC2 44 D3
Leicester Pl WC2 44 D3
Leicester Sq WC2 44 D4
Leicester St WC2 44 D3
Leigh Hunt St SE1 45 J5
Leigh Pl EC1 45 G1
Leopards Ct EC1 45 G1
Leo Yd EC1 45 H1
Lewisham St SW1 44 D6
Lexington St W1 44 C3
Library St SE1 45 H6
Lily Pl EC1 45 G1
Limeburner La EC4 45 H3
Lincoln's Inn WC2 45 F2
Lincoln's Inn Flds WC2 45 F2
Lindsey St EC1 45 H1
Lisle St WC2 44 D3
Litchfield St WC2 44 D3
Little Argyll St W1 44 C3
Little Britain EC1 45 J2
Little Chester St SW1 44 A6
Little Coll St SW1 44 E6
Little Dean's Yd SW1 44 E6
Little Dorrit Ct SE1 45 J5
Little Essex St WC2 45 G3
Little George St SW1 44 E6
Little Newport St WC2 44 D3
Little New St EC4 45 G2
Little Portland St W1 44 C2
Little Russell St WC1 44 E2
Little St. James's St SW1 44 C5
Little Sanctuary SW1 44 D6
Little Smith St SW1 44 D6
Little Titchfield St W1 44 C2
Little Trinity La EC4 45 J3
Little Turnstile WC1 45 F2
Livonia St W1 44 C3
Lollard St SE11 45 F7
Loman St SE1 45 H5
Lombard La EC4 45 G3
London Cen Mkts EC1 45 H1
London Rd SE1 45 H6
London Silver Vaults WC2 45 G2
London Trocadero, The W1 44 D4
London Wall EC2 45 J2
Long Acre WC2 44 E3
Long La EC1 45 H1
Longridge Ho SE1 45 J7
Long's Ct WC2 44 D3
Longstone Ct SE1 45 J6
Longville Rd SE11 45 H7
Long Yd WC1 45 F1
Lord N St SW1 44 E7
Love La EC2 45 J2
Lover's Wk W1 44 A4
Lower Belgrave St SW1 44 B7
Lower Grosvenor Pl SW1 44 B6
Lower James St W1 44 C3
Lower John St W1 44 C3
Lower Marsh SE1 45 G6
Lower Rd SE1 45 G5
Lowndes Cl SW1 44 A7
Lowndes Ct W1 44 C3
Lowndes Pl SW1 44 A7
Ludgate Bdy EC4 45 H3
Ludgate Circ EC4 45 H3
Ludgate Hill EC4 45 H3
Ludgate Sq EC4 45 H3
Lumley Ct WC2 45 E4
Lumley St W1 44 A3
Luxborough St W1 44 A1
Lyall Ms SW1 44 A7
Lyall Ms W SW1 44 A7
Lyall St SW1 44 A7
Lygon Pl SW1 44 B7

M

McAuley Cl SE1 45 G6
Macclesfield St W1 44 D3
McCoid Way SE1 45 J6
Macfarren Pl NW1 44 A1
Macklin St WC2 45 E2
Mac's Pl EC4 45 G2
Maddox St W1 44 B3
Magpie All EC4 45 G3
Maiden La SE1 45 J4
Maiden La WC2 45 E4
Maidstone Bldgs Ms SE1 45 J5
Maldonado Wk SE1 45 J7
Malet Pl WC1 44 D1
Malet St WC1 44 D1
Mall, The SW1 44 C5
Maltravers St WC2 45 F3
Manchester Ms W1 44 A2
Manchester Sq W1 44 A2
Manchester St W1 44 A2
Mandeville Pl W1 44 A2
Manette St W1 44 D3
Mansfield Ms W1 44 B2
Mansfield St W1 44 B2
Maple Pl W1 44 C1
Maple St W1 44 C1
Margaret Ct W1 44 C2
Margaret St W1 44 B2
Marigold All SE1 45 H4
Market Ct W1 44 C2
Market Ms W1 44 B5
Market Pl W1 44 C2
Marlborough Ct W1 44 C3
Marlborough Rd SW1 44 C5
Marshall St W1 44 C3
Marshalsea Rd SE1 45 J5
Marsham St SW1 44 D7
Martin Ho SE1 45 J7
Martlett Ct WC2 45 E3
Marylebone High St W1 44 A1
Marylebone La W1 44 B3
Marylebone Ms W1 44 B2
Marylebone Pas W1 44 C2
Marylebone St W1 44 A2
Masons Arms Ms W1 44 B3
Mason's Yd SW1 44 C4
Matthew Parker St SW1 44 D6
Matthews Yd WC2 44 E3
Maunsel St SW1 44 D7
Mayfair W1 44 B4
Mayfair Pl W1 44 B4
Mays Ct WC2 44 E4
Meadow Row SE1 45 J7
Mead Row SE1 45 G6
Meard St W1 44 D3
Medway St SW1 44 D7
Melbourne Pl WC2 45 F3
Memel Ct EC1 45 J1
Memel St EC1 45 J1
Mepham St SE1 45 F5
Mercer St WC2 44 E3
Merrick Sq SE1 45 J6
Metro Cen Hts SE1 45 J7
Meymott St SE1 45 H5
Middlesex Pas EC1 45 H2
Middle St EC1 45 J1
Middle Temple EC4 45 G3
Middle Temple La EC4 45 G3
Middleton Pl W1 44 C2
Midford Pl W1 44 C1
Milcote St SE1 45 H6
Milford La WC2 45 F3
Milk St EC2 45 J3
Millbank SW1 44 E7
Millbank Ct SW1 44 E7
Millennium Br EC4 45 J3
Millennium Br SE1 45 J3
Miller Wk SE1 45 G5
Millman Ms WC1 45 F1
Millman St WC1 45 F1
Mill St W1 44 B3
Milroy Wk SE1 45 H4
Minera Ms SW1 44 A7
Mint St SE1 45 J5
Mitre Ct EC2 45 J2
Mitre Rd SE1 45 G5
Monck St SW1 44 D7
Monkton St SE11 45 G7
Monkwell Sq EC2 45 J2
Monmouth St WC2 44 E3
Montague Pl WC1 44 D1
Montague St EC1 45 J2
Montague St WC1 44 E1
Montreal Pl WC2 45 F3
Montrose Pl SW1 44 A6
Moor St W1 44 D3
Morley St SE1 45 G6
Morpeth Ter SW1 44 C7
Mortimer Mkt WC1 44 C1
Mortimer St W1 44 C2
Morton Pl SE1 45 G7
Morwell St WC1 44 D2
Mount Pleasant WC1 45 F1
Mount Row W1 44 B4
Mount St W1 44 A4
Mount St Ms W1 44 B4
Moxon St W1 44 A2
Munton Rd SE17 45 J7
Murphy St SE1 45 G6
Museum St WC1 44 E2

N

Nag's Head Ct EC1 45 J1
Nassau St W1 44 C2
Neal St WC2 44 E3
Neal's Yd WC2 44 E3
Neathouse Pl SW1 44 C7
Nelson Sq SE1 45 H5
Newall Ho SE1 45 J6
New Bond St W1 44 B3
New Br St EC4 45 H3
Newburgh St W1 44 C3
New Burlington Ms W1 44 C3
New Burlington Pl W1 44 C3
New Burlington St W1 44 C3
Newbury St EC1 45 J2
Newcastle Cl EC4 45 H2
New Cavendish St W1 44 B1
New Change EC4 45 J3
New Compton St WC2 44 D3
New Fetter La EC4 45 G2
Newgate St EC1 45 H2
New Globe Wk SE1 45 J4
Newington SE1 45 J7
Newington Causeway SE1 45 H7
New Inn Pas WC2 45 F3
New Kent Rd SE1 45 J7
Newman Pas W1 44 C2
Newman's Row WC2 45 F2
Newman St W1 44 C2
Newman Yd W1 44 C2
Newnham Ter SE1 45 G6
New N St WC1 45 F1
New Oxford St WC1 44 D2
Newport Ct WC2 44 D3
Newport Pl WC2 44 D3
New Row WC2 44 E3
New Sq WC2 45 F2
New St Sq EC4 45 G2
Newton St WC2 45 E2
New Turnstile WC1 45 F2
Nicholson St SE1 45 H5
Nightingale Ms SE11 45 G7
Noble St EC2 45 J2
Noel St W1 44 C3
Norfolk Row SE1 45 F7
Norris St SW1 44 D4
North Audley St W1 44 A3
North Cres WC1 44 D1
Northington St WC1 45 F1
North Ms WC1 45 F1
Northumberland Av WC2 44 E4
Northumberland St WC2 44 E4
Norwich St EC4 45 G2
Nottingham Ct WC2 44 E3
Nottingham Pl W1 44 A1
Nottingham St W1 44 A1
Nottingham Ter NW1 44 A1

O

Oakden St SE11 45 G7
Oakey La SE1 45 G6
Oat La EC2 45 J2
Odhams Wk WC2 45 E3
Ogle St W1 44 C1
Old Bailey EC4 45 H3
Old Barrack Yd SW1 44 A5
Old Bond St W1 44 C4
Old Brewers Yd WC2 44 E3
Old Bldgs WC2 45 G2
Old Burlington St W1 44 C3
Oldbury Pl W1 44 A1
Old Cavendish St W1 44 B2
Old Compton St W1 44 D3
Old Fish St Hill EC4 45 J3
Old Fleet La EC4 45 H2
Old Gloucester St WC1 45 E1

Old Mitre Ct EC4 **45** G3
Old N St WC1 **45** F1
Old Palace Yd SW1 **44** E6
Old Paradise St SE11 **45** F7
Old Pk La W1 **44** A5
Old Pye St SW1 **44** D6
Old Queen St SW1 **44** D6
Old Seacoal La EC4 **45** H2
Old Sq WC2 **45** F2
O'Meara St SE1 **45** J5
Onslow St EC1 **45** G1
Ontario St SE1 **45** H7
Orange St WC2 **44** D4
Orange Yd W1 **44** D3
Orchard St W1 **44** A3
Orde Hall St WC1 **45** F1
Orient St SE11 **45** H7
Ormond Cl WC1 **45** E1
Ormond Ms WC1 **45** E1
Ormond Yd SW1 **44** C4
Osnaburgh St NW1 **44** B1
Ossington Bldgs W1 **44** A1
Oswin St SE11 **45** H7
Outer Circle NW1 **44** A1
Oxendon St SW1 **44** D4
Oxford Circ Av W1 **44** C3
Oxford St W1 **44** C2
Oxo Twr Wf SE1 **45** G4

P

Paddington St W1 **44** A1
Pageantmaster Ct EC4 **45** H3
Page St SW1 **44** D7
Palace Pl SW1 **44** C6
Palace St SW1 **44** C6
Pall Mall SW1 **44** C5
Pall Mall E SW1 **44** D4
Palmer St SW1 **44** D6
Pancras La EC4 **45** J3
Panton St SW1 **44** D4
Panyer All EC4 **45** J3
Paris Gdn SE1 **45** H4
Park Cres W1 **44** B1
Park Cres Ms E W1 **44** B1
Park Cres Ms W W1 **44** B1
Parker Ms WC2 **45** E2
Parker St WC2 **45** E2
Park La W1 **44** A5
Park Pl SW1 **44** C5
Park Sq Ms NW1 **44** B1
Park St SE1 **45** J4
Park St W1 **44** A3
Parliament Sq SW1 **44** E6
Parliament St SW1 **44** E6
Parliament Vw Apts SE1 **45** F7
Passing All EC1 **45** H1
Pastor St SE11 **45** H7
Paternoster Row EC4 **45** J3
Paternoster Sq EC4 **45** H3
Paul's Wk EC4 **45** H3
Peabody Est EC1 **45** J1
Peabody Est SE1 **45** G5
Peabody Est SW1 **44** C7
Peabody Sq SE1 **45** H6
Peabody Trust SE1 **45** J5
Pearman St SE1 **45** G6
Pear Pl SE1 **45** G5
Pearson Sq W1 **44** C2
Pear Tree Ct EC1 **45** G1
Pemberton Row EC4 **45** G2
Pembroke Cl SW1 **44** A6
Penhurst Pl SE1 **45** F7
Pepper St SE1 **45** J5
Percy Ms W1 **44** D2
Percy Pas W1 **44** C2
Percy St W1 **44** D2
Perkin's Rents SW1 **44** D6
Perkins Sq SE1 **45** J4
Perrys Pl W1 **44** D2
Peters Hill EC4 **45** J3
Peter's La EC1 **45** H1
Peter St W1 **44** C3
Petty France SW1 **44** C6
Phipp's Ms SW1 **44** B7
Phoenix St WC2 **44** D3
Piccadilly W1 **44** B5
Piccadilly Arc SW1 **44** C4
Piccadilly Circ W1 **44** D4
Piccadilly Pl W1 **44** C4
Pickering Pl SW1 **44** C5
Pickwick St SE1 **45** J6
Picton Pl W1 **44** A3
Pilgrim St EC4 **45** H3
Pineapple Ct SW1 **44** C6
Pitt's Head Ms W1 **44** A5
Playhouse Yd EC4 **45** H3
Plaza Shop Cen, The W1 **44** C2
Pleydell Ct EC4 **45** G3
Pleydell St EC4 **45** G3
Plough Pl EC4 **45** G2
Plumtree Ct EC4 **45** G2
Pocock St SE1 **45** H5
Poland St W1 **44** C3
Pollen St W1 **44** B3
Polperro Ms SE11 **45** G7
Pontypool Pl SE1 **45** H5
Pooles Bldgs EC1 **45** G1
Poppins Ct EC4 **45** H3
Porter St SE1 **45** J4
Portland Ms W1 **44** C3
Portland Pl W1 **44** B1
Portman Ms S W1 **44** A3
Portman St W1 **44** A3
Portpool La EC1 **45** G1
Portsmouth St WC2 **45** F3
Portugal St WC2 **45** F3
Powis Pl WC1 **45** E1
Pratt Wk SE11 **45** F7
Price's St SE1 **45** H5
Priest Ct EC2 **45** J2
Primrose Hill EC4 **45** G3
Prince's Arc SW1 **44** C4
Princes Pl SW1 **44** C4
Princess St SE1 **45** H7
Princes St W1 **44** B3
Princeton St WC1 **45** F1
Printers Inn Ct EC4 **45** G2
Printer St EC4 **45** G2
Procter St WC1 **45** F2
Providence Ct W1 **44** A3
Prudent Pas EC2 **45** J2
Puddle Dock EC4 **45** H3

Q

Quadrant Arc W1 **44** C4
Quality Ct WC2 **45** G2
Queen Anne Ms W1 **44** B2
Queen Anne's Gate SW1 **44** D6
Queen Anne St W1 **44** B2
Queenhithe EC4 **45** J3
Queen's Head Pas EC4 **45** J2
Queen Sq WC1 **45** E1
Queen Sq Pl WC1 **45** E1
Queen St EC4 **45** J3
Queen St W1 **44** B4
Queen St Pl EC4 **45** J4
Queen's Wk SW1 **44** C5
Queen's Wk, The SE1 **45** F5
Queens Yd WC1 **44** C1
Queen Victoria St EC4 **45** H3
Quilp St SE1 **45** J5

R

Ramillies Pl W1 **44** C3
Ramillies St W1 **44** C3
Rathbone Pl W1 **44** D2
Rathbone St W1 **44** C2
Raymond Bldgs WC1 **45** F1
Ray St EC1 **45** G1
Ray St Br EC1 **45** G1
Redcross Way SE1 **45** J5
Red Lion Ct EC4 **45** G2
Red Lion Sq WC1 **45** F2
Red Lion St WC1 **45** F1
Red Lion Yd W1 **44** A4
Red Pl W1 **44** A3
Reeves Ms W1 **44** A4
Regency Pl SW1 **44** D7
Regency St SW1 **44** D7
Regent Pl W1 **44** C3
Regent St SW1 **44** D4
Regent St W1 **44** B2
Remnant St WC2 **45** F2
Renfrew Rd SE11 **45** H7
Rennie St SE1 **45** H4
Rex Pl W1 **44** A4
Richardson's Ms W1 **44** C1
Richbell Pl WC1 **45** F1
Richmond Bldgs W1 **44** D3
Richmond Ms W1 **44** D3
Richmond Ter SW1 **44** E5
Ridgmount Gdns WC1 **44** D1
Ridgmount Pl WC1 **44** D1
Ridgmount St WC1 **44** D1
Riding Ho St W1 **44** C2
Risborough St SE1 **45** H5
Rising Sun Ct EC1 **45** H2
River Ct SE1 **45** H4
Robert Adam St W1 **44** A2
Roberts Ms SW1 **44** A7
Robert St WC2 **45** E4
Rochester Row SW1 **44** C7
Rochester St SW1 **44** D7
Rockingham Est SE1 **45** J7
Rockingham St SE1 **45** J7
Rodney Pl SE17 **45** J7
Rodney Rd SE17 **45** J7
Roger St WC1 **45** F1
Rolls Bldgs EC4 **45** G2
Rolls Pas EC4 **45** G2
Romilly St W1 **44** D3
Romney Ms W1 **44** A1
Romney St SW1 **44** D7
Roscoe St EC1 **45** J1
Rose All SE1 **45** J4
Rose & Crown Ct EC2 **45** J2
Rose & Crown Yd SW1 **44** C4
Rosebery Av EC1 **45** G1
Rosebery Sq EC1 **45** G1
Rose St EC4 **45** H2
Rose St WC2 **44** E3
Rotary St SE1 **45** H6
Rotherham Wk SE1 **45** H5
Rotten Row SW1 **44** A5
Roupell St SE1 **45** G5
Royal Arc W1 **44** C4
Royal Ms, The SW1 **44** B6
Royal Opera Arc SW1 **44** D4
Royal St SE1 **45** F6
Royalty Ms W1 **44** D3
Rugby St WC1 **45** F1
Rupert Ct W1 **44** D3
Rupert St W1 **44** D3
Rushworth St SE1 **45** H5
Russell Ct SW1 **44** C5
Russell Sq WC1 **44** E1
Russell St WC2 **45** E3
Russia Row EC2 **45** J3
Rutherford St SW1 **44** D7
Rutland Pl EC1 **45** J1
Ryder Ct SW1 **44** C4
Ryder St SW1 **44** C4
Ryder Yd SW1 **44** C4

S

Sackville St W1 **44** C4
Saddle Yd W1 **44** B4
Saffron Hill EC1 **45** G1
Saffron St EC1 **45** G1
Sail St SE11 **45** F7
St. Albans Ct EC2 **45** J2
St. Albans St SW1 **44** D4
St. Alphage Gdn EC2 **45** J2
St. Andrew's Hill EC4 **45** H3
St. Andrew St EC4 **45** G2
St. Anne's Ct W1 **44** D3
St. Ann's La SW1 **44** D6
St. Ann's St SW1 **44** D6
St. Anselm's Pl W1 **44** B3
St. Brides Av EC4 **45** H3
St. Bride St EC4 **45** H2
St. Christopher's Pl W1 **44** A2
St. Clement's La WC2 **45** F3
St. Cross St EC1 **45** G1
St. Ermin's Hill SW1 **44** D6
St. Georges Circ SE1 **45** H6
St. Georges Ct EC4 **45** H2
St. Georges Ms SE1 **45** G6
St. Georges Rd SE1 **45** G6
St. George St W1 **44** B3
St. Giles High St WC2 **44** D2
St. Giles Pas WC2 **44** D3
St. James's SW1 **44** D5
St. James's Ct SW1 **44** C6
St. James's Mkt SW1 **44** D4
St. James's Palace SW1 **44** C5
St. James's Pk SW1 **44** D5
St. James's Pl SW1 **44** C5
St. James's Sq SW1 **44** C4
St. James's St SW1 **44** C4
St. John's La EC1 **45** H1
St. John's Path EC1 **45** H1
St. John's Pl EC1 **45** H1
St. John's Sq EC1 **45** H1
St. John St EC1 **45** H1
St. Margaret's Ct SE1 **45** J5
St. Margaret's St SW1 **44** E6
St. Martin's La WC2 **44** E3
St. Martin's-le-Grand EC1 **45** J2
St. Martin's Ms WC2 **44** E4
St. Martin's Pl WC2 **44** E4
St. Martin's St WC2 **44** D4
St. Mary's Gdns SE11 **45** G7
St. Mary's Wk SE11 **45** G7
St. Matthew St SW1 **44** D7
St. Olaves Gdns SE11 **45** G7
St. Paul's Chyd EC4 **45** H3
St. Vincent St W1 **44** A2
Salisbury Ct EC4 **45** H3
Salisbury Sq EC4 **45** G3
Sanctuary, The SW1 **44** D6
Sanctuary St SE1 **45** J6
Sandell St SE1 **45** G5
Sandland St WC1 **45** F2
Saperton Wk SE11 **45** F7
Sardinia St WC2 **45** F3
Savile Row W1 **44** C3
Savoy Bldgs WC2 **45** F4
Savoy Ct WC2 **45** E4
Savoy Hill WC2 **45** F4
Savoy Pl WC2 **45** E4
Savoy Row WC2 **45** F3
Savoy St WC2 **45** F3
Savoy Way WC2 **45** F4
Sawyer St SE1 **45** J5
Scala St W1 **44** C1
Scoresby St SE1 **45** H5
Scotland Pl SW1 **44** E4
Scovell Cres SE1 **45** J6
Scovell Rd SE1 **45** J6
Secker St SE1 **45** G5
Sedding St SW1 **44** A7
Sedley Pl W1 **44** B3
Sekforde St EC1 **45** H1
Serjeants Inn EC4 **45** G3
Serle St WC2 **45** F2
Sermon La EC4 **45** J3
Seymour Ms W1 **44** A2
Shaftesbury Av W1 **44** D3
Shaftesbury Av WC2 **44** D3
Shakespeare Twr EC2 **45** J1
Shavers Pl SW1 **44** D4
Sheffield St WC2 **45** F3
Shelton St WC2 **44** E3
Shepherd Mkt W1 **44** B4
Shepherd's Pl W1 **44** A3
Shepherd St W1 **44** B5
Sheraton St W1 **44** D3
Sherlock Ms W1 **44** A1
Sherwood St W1 **44** C3
Shoe La EC4 **45** G2
Shorts Gdns WC2 **44** E3
Short St SE1 **45** G5
Shropshire Pl WC1 **44** C1
Sicilian Av WC1 **45** E2
Sidford Pl SE1 **45** F7
Silex St SE1 **45** H6
Silk St EC2 **45** J1
Silver Pl W1 **44** C3
Silvester St SE1 **45** J6
Skinners La EC4 **45** J3
Slingsby Pl WC2 **44** E3
Smart's Pl WC2 **45** E2
Smeaton Ct SE1 **45** J7
Smithfield St EC1 **45** H2
Smith's Ct W1 **44** C3
Smith Sq SW1 **44** E7
Smokehouse Yd EC1 **45** H1
Snow Hill EC1 **45** H2
Snow Hill Ct EC1 **45** H2
Soho W1 **44** C3
Soho Sq W1 **44** D2
Soho St W1 **44** D2
Southampton Bldgs WC2 **45** G2
Southampton Pl WC1 **45** E2
Southampton Row WC1 **45** E1
Southampton St WC2 **45** E3
South Audley St W1 **44** A4
South Cres WC1 **44** D2
South Eaton Pl SW1 **44** A7
South Molton La W1 **44** B3
South Molton St W1 **44** B3
South Sq WC1 **45** G2
South St W1 **44** A4
Southwark SE1 **45** H5
Southwark Br EC4 **45** J4
Southwark Br SE1 **45** J4
Southwark Br Rd SE1 **45** H6
Southwark St SE1 **45** H4
Spanish Pl W1 **44** A2
Spenser St SW1 **44** C6
Spring Gdns SW1 **44** D4
Spur Rd SE1 **45** G5
Spur Rd SW1 **44** C6
Stable Yd SW1 **44** C5
Stable Yd Rd SW1 **44** C5
Stacey St WC2 **44** D3
Stafford Pl SW1 **44** C6
Stafford St W1 **44** C4
Staining La EC2 **45** J2
Stamford St SE1 **45** G5
Stangate SE1 **45** F6
Stanhope Gate W1 **44** A4
Stanhope Row W1 **44** B5
Staple Inn WC1 **45** G2
Staple Inn Bldgs WC1 **45** G2
Star Yd WC2 **45** G2
Station App SE1 **45** F5
Stedham Pl WC1 **44** E2
Stephen Ms W1 **44** D2
Stephen St W1 **44** D2
Stew La EC4 **45** J3
Stillington St SW1 **44** C7
Stone Bldgs WC2 **45** F2
Stonecutter St EC4 **45** H2
Stones End St SE1 **45** J6
Store St WC1 **44** D2
Storey's Gate SW1 **44** D6
Strand WC2 **44** E4
Strand WC2 **44** E4
Strand La WC2 **45** F3
Stratford Pl W1 **44** B3
Stratton St W1 **44** B4
Streatham St WC1 **44** D2
Strutton Grd SW1 **44** D6
Stukeley St WC1 **45** E2
Stukeley St WC2 **45** E2
Sturge St SE1 **45** J5
Sudrey St SE1 **45** J6
Suffolk Pl SW1 **44** D4
Suffolk St SW1 **44** D4
Sullivan Rd SE11 **45** G7
Summers St EC1 **45** G1
Sumner St SE1 **45** H4
Surrey Row SE1 **45** H5
Surrey St WC2 **45** F3
Sutton La EC1 **45** H1
Sutton Row W1 **44** D2
Sutton's Way EC1 **45** J1
Sutton Wk SE1 **45** F5
Swallow Pl W1 **44** B3
Swallow St W1 **44** C4
Swan St SE1 **45** J6
Swiss Ct W1 **44** D4
Sycamore St EC1 **45** J1

T

Tachbrook Ms SW1 **44** C7
Tallis St EC4 **45** G3
Tanswell Est SE1 **45** G6
Tanswell St SE1 **45** G6
Tarn St SE1 **45** J7
Tavistock St WC2 **45** E3
Telford Ho SE1 **45** J7
Temple Av EC4 **45** G3
Temple La EC4 **45** G3
Temple Pl WC2 **45** F3
Temple W Ms SE11 **45** H7
Tenison Ct W1 **44** C3
Tenison Way SE1 **45** G5
Tenterden St W1 **44** B3
Terminus Pl SW1 **44** B7
Thavies Inn EC1 **45** G2
Thayer St W1 **44** A2
Theed St SE1 **45** G5
Theobald's Rd WC1 **45** F1
Thirleby Rd SW1 **44** C7
Thomas Doyle St SE1 **45** H6
Thorney St SW1 **44** E7
Thornhaugh Ms WC1 **44** D1
Thornhaugh St WC1 **44** D1
Thrale St SE1 **45** J5
Three Barrels Wk EC4 **45** J4
Three Cups Yd WC1 **45** F2
Three Kings Yd W1 **44** B3
Tilney St W1 **44** A4
Tiverton St SE1 **45** J7
Took's Ct EC4 **45** G2
Torrington Pl WC1 **44** C1
Torrington Sq WC1 **44** D1
Tothill St SW1 **44** D6
Tottenham Ct Rd W1 **44** C1
Tottenham Ms W1 **44** C1
Tottenham St W1 **44** C2
Toulmin St SE1 **45** J6
Tower Ct WC2 **44** E3
Tower Royal EC4 **45** J3
Tower St WC2 **44** D3
Trafalgar Sq SW1 **44** D4
Trafalgar Sq WC2 **44** D4
Trebeck St W1 **44** B4
Treveris St SE1 **45** H5
Trig La EC4 **45** J3
Trinity Ch Sq SE1 **45** J6
Trinity St SE1 **45** J6
Trio Pl SE1 **45** J6
Trump St EC2 **45** J3
Trundle St SE1 **45** J5
Tudor St EC4 **45** G3
Tufton St SW1 **44** D6
Turk's Head Yd EC1 **45** H1
Turnagain La EC4 **45** H2
Turnmill St EC1 **45** G1
Tweezer's All WC2 **45** G3
Twyford Pl WC2 **45** F2
Tyler's Ct W1 **44** D3

U

Ufford St SE1 **45** G5
Ulster Pl NW1 **44** B1
Ulster Ter NW1 **44** B1
Union Jack Club SE1 **45** G5
Union St SE1 **45** H5
University St WC1 **44** C1
Upper Belgrave St SW1 **44** A6
Upper Brook St W1 **44** A4
Upper Grosvenor St W1 **44** A4
Upper Grd SE1 **45** G4
Upper James St W1 **44** C3
Upper John St W1 **44** C3
Upper Marsh SE1 **45** F6
Upper St. Martin's La WC2 **44** E3
Upper Tachbrook St SW1 **44** C7
Upper Thames St EC4 **45** H3
Upper Wimpole St W1 **44** B1

V

Valentine Pl SE1 **45** H5
Valentine Row SE1 **45** H6
Vandon Pas SW1 **44** C6
Vandon St SW1 **44** C6
Vane St SW1 **44** C7
Vauxhall Br Rd SW1 **44** C7
Vere St W1 **44** B3
Vernon Pl WC1 **45** E2
Verulam Bldgs WC1 **45** F1
Verulam St WC1 **45** G1
Vesage Ct EC1 **45** G2
Victoria Embk EC4 **45** F4
Victoria Embk SW1 **45** E5
Victoria Embk WC2 **45** F4
Victoria Pl SW1 **44** B7
Victoria Sq SW1 **44** B6
Victoria Sta SW1 **44** B7
Victoria St SW1 **44** C7
Vigo St W1 **44** C4
Villiers St WC2 **44** E4
Vincent Sq SW1 **44** C7
Vincent St SW1 **44** D7
Vine Hill EC1 **45** G1
Vine St W1 **44** C4
Vine St Br EC1 **45** G1
Vine Yd SE1 **45** J5
Vintners Ct EC4 **45** J3
Virgil St SE1 **45** F6
Viscount St EC1 **45** J1

W

Waithman St EC4 **45** H3
Walcot Sq SE11 **45** G7
Walcott St SW1 **44** C7
Walkers Ct W1 **44** D3
Wallis All SE1 **45** J5
Wallside EC2 **45** J2
Walnut Tree Wk SE11 **45** G7
Walworth Rd SE1 **45** J7
Walworth Rd SE17 **45** J7
Wardens Gro SE1 **45** J5
Wardour Ms W1 **44** C3
Wardour St W1 **44** D3
Wardrobe Ter EC4 **45** H3
Warner St EC1 **45** G1
Warner Yd EC1 **45** G1
Warren Ms W1 **44** C1
Warren St W1 **44** B1
Warwick Ct WC1 **45** F2
Warwick Ho St SW1 **44** D4
Warwick La EC4 **45** H3
Warwick Pas EC4 **45** H2
Warwick Row SW1 **44** B6
Warwick Sq EC4 **45** H2
Warwick St W1 **44** C3
Warwick Yd EC1 **45** J1
Watergate EC4 **45** H3
Watergate Wk WC2 **45** E4
Waterhouse Sq EC1 **45** G2
Waterloo Br SE1 **45** F4
Waterloo Br WC2 **45** F4
Waterloo Pl SW1 **44** D4
Waterloo Rd SE1 **45** G5
Waterloo Sta SE1 **45** G5
Water St WC2 **45** F3
Watling Ct EC4 **45** J3
Watling St EC4 **45** J3
Waverton St W1 **44** A4
Webber Row SE1 **45** G6
Webber St SE1 **45** G5
Wedgwood Ho SE11 **45** G7
Wedgwood Ms W1 **44** D3
Weighhouse St W1 **44** A3
Welbeck St W1 **44** B2
Welbeck Way W1 **44** B2
Well Ct EC4 **45** J3
Weller St SE1 **45** J5
Wellington St WC2 **45** E3
Wells Ms W1 **44** C2
Wells St W1 **44** C2
Wesley St W1 **44** A2
West Cen St WC1 **44** E2
West Eaton Pl SW1 **44** A7
West Eaton Pl Ms SW1 **44** A7
West Halkin St SW1 **44** A6
West Harding St EC4 **45** G2
Westminster SW1 **44** C6
Westminster Br SE1 **45** E6
Westminster Br SW1 **45** E6
Westminster Br Rd SE1 **45** F6
Westminster Gdns SW1 **44** E7
Westmoreland St W1 **44** A2

West One Shop Cen W1 44 A3
West Poultry Av EC1 45 H2
West Smithfield EC1 45 H2
West Sq SE11 45 H7
West St WC2 44 D3
Weymouth Ms W1 44 B1
Weymouth St W1 44 A2
Wheatley St W1 44 A2
Whetstone Pk WC2 45 F2
Whichcote St SE1 45 G5
Whitcomb St WC2 44 D4
Whitefriars St EC4 45 G3

Whitehall SW1 44 E4
Whitehall Ct SW1 44 E5
Whitehall Gdns SW1 44 E5
Whitehall Pl SW1 44 E5
White Hart St EC4 45 H2
White Horse All EC1 45 H1
White Horse Ms SE1 45 G6
White Horse St W1 44 B5
White Lion Hill EC4 45 H3
White Lyon Ct EC2 45 J1
Whitfield Pl W1 44 C1
Whitfield St W1 44 D2
Whitgift St SE11 45 F7

Whittlesey St SE1 45 G5
Whitworth Ho SE1 45 J7
Wickstead Ho SE1 45 J7
Wigmore Pl W1 44 B2
Wigmore St W1 44 A3
Wilcox Pl SW1 44 C7
Wild Ct WC2 45 F2
Wild St WC2 45 E3
Wilfred St SW1 44 C6
William IV St WC2 44 E4
Willoughby St WC1 44 E2
Willow Pl SW1 44 C7
Wilton Cres SW1 44 A6

Wilton Ms SW1 44 A6
Wilton Pl SW1 44 A6
Wilton Rd SW1 44 B7
Wilton Row SW1 44 A6
Wilton St SW1 44 B6
Wilton Ter SW1 44 A6
Wimpole Ms W1 44 B1
Wimpole St W1 44 B2
Wincott St SE11 45 G7
Windmill St W1 44 D2
Windmill Wk SE1 45 G5
Windsor Pl SW1 44 C7
Wine Office Ct EC4 45 G2

Winnett St W1 44 D3
Winsley St W1 44 C2
Woburn Sq WC1 44 D1
Wollaston Cl SE1 45 J7
Woodstock Ms W1 44 A2
Woodstock St W1 44 B3
Wood St EC2 45 J3
Wootton St SE1 45 G5

Y
Yarmouth Pl W1 44 B5
York Bldgs WC2 45 E4
York Gate NW1 44 A1

York Pl WC2 45 E4
York Rd SE1 45 F5
Yorkshire Grey Yd WC1 45 F2
York Ter E NW1 44 A1
York Ter W NW1 44 A1

Z
Zoar St SE1 45 J4

Manchester street index

A
Abingdon St 47 E4
Academy Wk 46 D7
Ackers St 47 F7
Acton Sq 46 A3
Adair St 47 G4
Addington St 47 F2
Addison Cl 47 G7
Adelphi St 46 B3
Aden Cl 47 J4
Adlington St 47 H5
Adstone Cl 47 J3
Adswood St 47 J3
Airton Cl 47 H1
Aked Cl 47 J7
Albion Pl 46 A3
Albion St 46 D5
Albion Way 46 A3
Alderman Sq 47 J4
Aldred St 46 A3
Alexander Gdns 46 C1
Alexandra St 46 C1
Alfred James Cl 47 H2
Alker Rd 47 J2
Alley St 46 E3
Almond St 47 G1
Altair Pl 46 B1
Amory St 47 G5
Anaconda Dr 46 C2
Ancoats 47 G3
Ancoats Gro 47 H4
Ancroft St 46 C7
Angela St 46 C6
Angel St 47 F2
Angora Cl 46 B2
Angora Dr 46 B2
Anita St 47 G3
Anne Nuttall St 46 B5
Anscombe Cl 47 H1
Antares Av 46 B1
Apsley Gro 47 H6
Aquarius St 47 E7
Archway 46 D7
Ardwick 47 J5
Ardwick Grn N 47 G5
Ardwick Grn S 47 G5
Arlington St 46 C2
Arnott Cres 46 E7
Artillery St 46 D4
Arundel St 46 C5
Asgard Dr 46 B5
Asgard Grn 46 B5
Ashlar Dr 47 J4
Ashley St 47 F2
Ashton New Rd 47 J3
Ashton Old Rd 47 H5
Aspin La 47 F2
Atherton St 46 C4
Atkinson St 46 D4
Atwood St 47 E5
Auburn St 47 F4
Audlem Cl 47 J2
Augustus St 47 E1
Avenham Cl 46 D7
Aytoun St 47 F4

B
Back Acton St 47 F4
Back Ashley St 47 F2
Back Bk St 47 F1
Back Br St 46 D3
Back China La 47 F4
Back Coll Land 46 D3
Back George St 47 E4
Back Hampson St 47 H1
Back Hulme St 46 B3
Back Junct St 47 G4
Back Piccadilly 47 F3
Back Pool Fold 47 F3
Back Red Bk 47 F1
Back St. George's Rd 47 G2
Back S Par 46 D3
Back Thomas St 47 F3

Back Turner St 47 F3
Badby Cl 47 J3
Bainbridge Cl 47 J7
Baird St 47 G4
Bale St 46 E4
Balloon St 47 E2
Balmforth St 46 C5
Balsam Cl 47 G6
Bangor St 46 C7
Bankmill Cl 47 G6
Bank Pl 46 B3
Bank St 46 B3
Baptist St 47 F2
Baring St 47 G5
Barker St 46 D1
Barlow Pl 47 G6
Barlow's Cft 46 D3
Barnett Dr 46 C2
Barrack St 46 B6
Barrhill Cl 46 C6
Barrow St 46 B3
Barton St 46 D5
Basildon Cl 47 J7
Beamish Cl 47 G6
Beattock St 46 C6
Beaufort St 46 C5
Beaver St 47 E5
Beckhampton Cl 47 H7
Bednal Av 47 J1
Beechcroft Cl 47 H2
Belfort Dr 46 A5
Bendix St 47 F2
Bengal St 47 G2
Bennett St 47 J6
Bentinck St 46 B6
Bent St 47 E1
Berkshire Rd 47 J1
Berry St 47 G5
Beswick Row 47 E2
Beswick St 47 H3
Betley St 47 G4
Bevan Cl 47 J4
Bilbrook St 47 F1
Billing Av 47 G5
Binns Pl 47 G3
Birchin La 47 F3
Birchvale Cl 46 D6
Birt St 47 H1
Bishopsgate 46 E4
Blackburn Pl 46 A4
Blackburn St 46 B2
Blackfriars Rd 46 C2
Blackfriars St 46 D3
Blackhill Cl 47 G6
Blackley St 46 B7
Blacklock St 46 E1
Blantyre St 46 C5
Bletchley Cl 47 H7
Blind La 47 J5
Blisworth Cl 47 J3
Bloom St 47 F4
Blossom St 46 D2
Blossom St (Ancoats) 47 G3
Blucher St 46 A4
Blyton St 47 F7
Boad St 47 G4
Bollington Rd 47 H2
Bombay St 47 F5
Bond St 47 G5
Bonsall St 46 E7
Boond St 46 D2
Booth St 46 E4
Booth St (Salford) 46 D3
Booth St E 47 F6
Booth St W 47 E7
Bootle St 46 D4
Botham Cl 46 E7
Bothwell Rd 47 G2
Boundary La 47 E6
Boundary St E 47 F6
Boundary St W 47 E6
Bourdon St 47 J2

Bow La 46 E4
Bow St 46 D4
Brackley Av 46 B6
Bradford Rd 47 H3
Bradleys Ct 47 F3
Braley St 47 G5
Bramble Av 46 A5
Bramwell Dr 47 G6
Brancaster Rd 47 F5
Branson St 47 J3
Brazennose St 46 D4
Brazil St 47 F5
Brennan Cl 47 E7
Brewer St 47 F3
Brian Redhead Ct 46 C6
Brickley St 47 E1
Brick St 47 F3
Briddon St 46 D1
Bridgeford St 47 F7
Bridge St 46 D3
Bridge St W 46 D3
Bridgewater Pl 47 E3
Bridgewater St 46 D5
Bridgewater St (Salford) 46 C1
Bridgewater Viaduct 46 D5
Briggs St 46 C2
Brighton Pl 47 F7
Brighton St 47 F1
Brindle Pl 47 E7
Brocade Cl 46 B2
Brock St 47 G3
Bromley St 47 F1
Bronte St 47 E7
Brook St 47 F5
Brotherton Cl 46 B6
Brotherton Dr 46 C2
Browfield Av 46 A5
Brown Cross St 46 C3
Browning St 46 B7
Browning St (Salford) 46 C3
Brown St 46 E4
Brunel Av 46 A3
Brunswick 47 G7
Brunswick St 47 F7
Bryant Cl 47 H7
Brydon Av 47 H5
Buckfield Av 46 A5
Bugle St 46 D5
Bunsen St 47 F3
Burlington St 47 E7
Burnell Cl 47 H2
Burstock St 47 F1
Burton St 47 G1
Burton Wk 46 B2
Bury St 46 C2
Butler La 47 H2
Butler St 47 H2
Butter La 46 D3
Buxton St 47 G5
Byrcland Cl 47 J5
Byron St 46 D4

C
Cable St 47 F2
Cabot St 47 G6
Cakebread St 47 G5
Calder St 46 B5
Calico Cl 46 B2
Camberwell St 47 E1
Cambrian St 47 J2
Cambridge St 46 E5
Cambridge St (Salford) 46 C1
Camelford Cl 47 E7
Cameron St 47 D5
Canal St 47 F4
Cannon St 46 B2
Canon Grn Dr 46 C2
Carding Gro 46 C2
Cardroom Rd 47 G3
Carey Cl 46 C1

Carib St 46 D7
Carmel Av 46 A5
Carmel Cl 46 A5
Carnarvon St 46 E1
Caroline St 46 C1
Carpenters La 47 F3
Carriage St 46 C7
Carruthers St 47 H3
Cassidy Cl 47 G2
Castle St 46 C5
Caterham St 47 J4
Cathedral Gates 46 E3
Cathedral St 46 E3
Cathedral Yd 46 E3
Catlow La 47 F3
Catlow St 46 D1
Cavalier St 47 J3
Cavanagh Cl 47 H7
Cavell St 47 F3
Cavendish St 46 E6
Cawdor St 46 B6
Caxton St 46 D3
Caygill St 46 D2
Cedar Pl 46 B1
Central St 46 E4
Century St 46 D5
Chadderton St 47 F2
Chain St 47 E4
Chancel Av 46 A5
Chancellor La 47 H5
Chancery La 46 E4
Change Way 46 C2
Chapelfield Rd 47 H5
Chapel St 46 C3
Chapeltown St 47 G4
Chapel Walks 46 E3
Charles St 47 E5
Charley Av 46 B1
Charlotte St 47 E4
Charlton Pl 47 G5
Charnley Cl 47 J2
Charter St 46 D1
Chase St 46 E1
Chatford Cl 46 C1
Chatham St 47 F4
Chatley St 46 E1
Cheapside 46 E3
Cheetham Hill Rd 47 E2
Cheetwood St 46 D1
Chepstow St 46 E5
Cherryton Wk 47 G7
Chesshyre Av 47 J3
Chester Rd 46 B6
Chester St 46 E6
Chevassut St 46 C6
Cheviot St 46 E1
Chevril Cl 47 E6
Chichester Rd 46 D7
Chiffon Way 46 B2
China La 47 F4
Chippenham Rd 47 H3
Chorlton Rd 46 C7
Chorlton St
Chorlton St (Old Trafford) 46 A7
Christchurch Av 46 A3
Churchgate Bldgs 47 G4
Church St 47 F3
Cinder St 47 G2
Cipher St 47 G2
City Rd 46 B7
City Rd E 46 D6
Clarence St 46 E4
Clarendon St 46 D6
Clare St 47 G5
Clarion St 47 G2
Clayburn Rd 46 D6
Cleminson St 46 B3
Cleworth St 46 B6
Clifford St 47 F6
Clifton Gro 46 B7
Clifton St 46 B7
Clive St 47 F2

Cloak St 47 F5
Cloughfield Av 46 A5
Clowes St 46 D3
Cobourg St 47 F4
Coburg Av 46 B1
Cockcroft Rd 46 A2
Cockspur St 46 D3
Coleshill St 47 J1
Colin Murphy Rd 46 C6
College Land 46 D3
Collier St 46 D5
Collier St (Salford) 46 D2
Collingham St 47 F1
Collyhurst Rd 47 G1
Colman Gdns 46 A5
Comet St 47 G4
Commercial St 46 D5
Comus St 46 A4
Concert La 47 E4
Congou Av 47 G4
Cooper St 46 E4
Coop St 47 F3
Copeman Cl 47 G7
Copperas St 47 F3
Coral St 47 G6
Cork St 47 J4
Cornbrook 46 B6
Cornbrook Ct 46 B7
Cornbrook Gro 46 B7
Cornbrook Pk Rd 46 B6
Cornbrook St 46 B7
Cornell St 47 G2
Coronation Sq 47 H5
Coronation St 46 A4
Corporation St 46 E3
Cottenham La 46 C1
Cottenham St 47 G6
Cotter St 47 G5
Cottingham Rd 47 J7
Cotton St 47 G3
County St 46 E4
Coupland St 46 E6
Coupland St E 47 E7
Coverdale Cres 47 H6
Cowan St 47 J3
Cow La 46 B4
Cowburn St 46 E1
Crabbe St 46 E1
Cranbourne St 46 A4
Crane St 47 H5
Cranfield Cl 47 J2
Craven St 46 B4
Crediton Cl 46 E7
Cresbury St 47 H5
Crescent, The 46 A2
Cross Keys St 47 F2
Crossley Ct 47 J3
Cross St 46 E4
Cross St (Salford) 46 D3
Crown La 47 F2
Crown St 46 C5
Crown St (Salford) 47 F4
Culmington Cl 46 C7
Cumberland St 46 B1
Cumbrian Cl 47 G6
Cunard Cl 47 G6
Cygnus Av 46 B1
Cyrus St 47 J3

D
Dainton St 47 J5
Daintry Cl 47 G6
Dalberg St 47 H6
Dale St 47 F3
Dalley Av 46 B1
Dalton Ct 47 G1
Dalton St 47 G1
Damask Av 46 B2
Danebank Wk 47 G6
Danecroft Cl 47 H7
Danson St 47 J2
Dantzic St 47 E3

Dark La 47 H5
Dartford Cl 47 J7
Darton Av 47 J2
Darwen St 46 A7
Davy St 47 G1
Dawson St 46 B5
Dean Rd 46 D2
Deansgate 46 D4
Dean St 47 F3
Deanwater Cl 47 G6
Dearden St 46 D6
Dearmans Pl 46 D3
Deer St 47 G4
Denewell Cl 47 H7
Denver Av 47 J1
Derby St 47 E1
Derwent St 46 B5
Devas St 47 F7
Devine Cl 46 B2
Devonshire St 47 H7
Devonshire St N 47 J6
Devonshire St S 47 H7
Dewhurst St 46 D1
Dickinson St 46 E4
Dilston Cl 47 H7
Dinsdale Cl 47 J2
Dinton St 46 B6
Dobson Cl 47 H7
Dolefield 46 D3
Dolphin Pl 47 H6
Dolphin St 47 H6
Donald St 47 F5
Dorsey St 47 F3
Dover St 47 F7
Downing St 47 G5
Downley Dr 47 H3
Drayton Wk 46 B7
Droitwich Rd 47 H1
Dryden St 47 G7
Dryhurst Wk 47 E7
Ducie St 47 F4
Duke Pl 46 C5
Duke St 46 C5
Duke St (Salford) 46 D2
Dulwich St 47 F1
Duncan St 46 A4
Dun Cl 46 B3
Dunham St 46 D7
Dunlop St 46 D3
Durant St 47 F2
Durling Av 47 H6
Dutton St 46 E1
Dyche St 47 F2
Dyer St 46 A5

E
Eagle St 47 F2
Eastburn Av 47 H1
Eastfield Av 47 J2
Eastleigh Dr 47 H1
East Mkt St 46 C3
East Newton St 47 H2
Eastnor Cl 46 B7
East Ordsall La 46 B4
Eastpark Cl 47 H6
East Philip St 46 D1
East Union St 46 B7
Ebden St 47 F4
Ebenezer St 46 E6
Echo St 47 F5
Eden Cl 46 E7
Edgehill St 47 F3
Edge St 47 F3
Edward St 46 D1
Egerton Rd 46 C5
Egerton St 46 C5
Elbe St 47 H5
Eliza St 46 C6
Ellesmere St 46 B6
Ellis St 46 D7
Elsworth St 47 E1
Elton St 46 C1
Elton's Yd 46 C1

Elverdon Cl 46 D7
Empire St 46 E1
Empress St 46 A7
Encombe Pl 46 B3
Epping St 46 E6
Epsley Cl 47 E7
Epworth St 47 H4
Errington Dr 46 B1
Erskine St 46 C7
Essex St 46 E4
Essex Way 46 C7
Etruria Cl 47 J7
Evans St 46 D2
Everard St 46 B5
Every St 47 H4
Exford Cl 47 H2
Eyre St 47 E7

F
Fairbrother St 46 A6
Fairfield St 47 G5
Fair St 47 G4
Falkland Av 47 J1
Faraday St 47 F3
Farnborough Rd 47 H1
Farrell St 46 C1
Farwood Cl 46 B7
Faulkner St 47 E4
Federation St 47 E2
Fennel St 46 E2
Fenn St 46 C7
Fenwick St 47 E6
Ferdinan St 47 H1
Fernbrook Cl 47 J7
Fernie St 47 E1
Fernleigh Dr 46 B7
Fern St 47 E1
Ferry St 47 J4
Filby Wk 47 J1
Firbeck Dr 47 H2
Firefly Cl 46 B3
Fire Sta Sq 46 A3
Fir St 47 H1
Fitzwilliam St 46 C1
Flatley Cl 47 E7
Flora Dr 46 C1
Ford St 47 H6
Ford St (Salford) 46 C3
Foundry La 47 F3
Fountain St 47 E4
Four Yards 46 E4
Frances St 47 G6
Francis St 46 D1
Frederick St 46 C3
Freeman Sq 47 E7
Freya Gro 46 A5
Frobisher Cl 47 J7
Frost St 47 J3
Fulmer Dr 47 H2

G
Gaitskell Cl 47 J4
Galgate Cl 46 C6
Garden La 46 D3
Garden St 46 D2
Garden Wall Cl 46 A5
Garforth Av 47 H2
Gartside St 46 D4
Garwood St 46 D6
Gateaton St 46 E3
Gaythorn St 46 B3
George Leigh St 47 F3
George St 47 E4
Georgette Dr 46 D2
Gibbs St 46 B3
Gibson Pl 47 E1
Girton St 46 C1
Glasshouse St 47 G2
Gleden St 47 J2
Glenbarry Cl 47 G7
Glenbarry St 47 J5
Gloucester St 46 E5
Gloucester St (Salford) 46 A5
Goadsby St 47 F2
Gold St 47 F4
Gordon St 46 C1
Gore St 47 F4
Gore St (Salford) 46 C3
Gorton St 46 D2
Goulden St 47 F2
Gould St 47 F1
Grafton St 47 G7
Granby Row 47 F5
Granshaw St 47 J2
Gratrix Av 46 A6
Gravell La 46 D2
Grear Ducie St 46 E2
Great Ancoats St 47 F3
Great Bridgewater St 46 D5
Great Clowes St 46 C1
Great Ducie St 46 D1
Great George St 46 B3
Great Jackson St 46 C5
Great John St 46 C4

Great
    Marlborough St 47 E5
Greek St 47 F6
Greengate W 46 C2
Grenham Av 46 B6
Griffiths Cl 46 C1
Groom St 47 F6
Grosvenor Gdns 46 C1
Grosvenor Sq 46 C1
Grosvenor St 47 F6
Guide Post Sq 47 H7
Gunson St 47 H2
Gun St 47 G3
Gurner Av 46 A6
Gurney St 47 J3

H
Hackleton Cl 47 J3
Hadfield St 46 B7
Half St 46 D2
Hall St 46 E4
Halmore Rd 47 H2
Halsbury Cl 47 J7
Halston St 46 D7
Hamerton Rd 47 G1
Hamilton Gro 46 B7
Hamilton St 46 B7
Hampson St 47 H1
Hamsell Rd 47 G6
Handsworth St 47 J5
Hanging Ditch 46 E3
Hanover St 47 E2
Hanworth Cl 47 G6
Harding St 47 J4
Hardman Sq 46 D4
Hardman St 46 D4
Hardshaw Cl 47 G6
Harehill Cl 47 G5
Hare St 47 F3
Hargreave's St 47 F1
Harkness St 47 H6
Harold St 46 B7
Harriett St 47 H2
Harrison St 47 H4
Harris St 46 C1
Harry Hall Gdns 46 B1
Harter St 47 E4
Hartfield Cl 47 G6
Hart St 47 F4
Hatter St 47 F2
Hatton Av 46 B1
Haverlock Dr 46 B1
Haymarket Cl 47 H7
Heath Av 46 B1
Helga St 47 H1
Hellidon Cl 47 H6
Helmet St 47 H5
Henry St 47 G3
Henry St
    (Old Trafford) 46 A7
Hewitt St 46 D5
Heyrod St 47 G4
Higher Ardwick 47 H6
Higher Cambridge St 47 E6
Higher Chatham St 47 E6
Higher Ormond St 47 F6
Higher Oswald St 47 F2
Higher York St 47 F6
High St 47 E3
Hillcourt St 47 F6
Hillfield Cl 47 J7
Hillkirk St 47 J3
Hilton St 47 F3
Hinton St 47 G2
Hodson St 46 C2
Holdgate Cl 46 D7
Holkham Cl 47 H3
Holland St 47 H2
Holly Bk Cl 46 B6
Holly St 47 J4
Holt Town 47 J3
Honey St 47 F1
Hood St 47 G3
Hooper St 47 F4
Hope St 46 A3
Hope St (Salford) 46 A3
Hornby St 46 D1
Hornchurch St 46 C7
Horne Dr 47 H3
Houldsworth St 47 F3
Hoyle St 47 H5
Huddart Cl 46 A5
Hughes St 47 J5
Hull Sq 46 B2
Hulme 46 D7
Hulme Ct 46 C6
Hulme Hall Rd 46 B5
Hulme Pl 46 B3
Hulme St 46 D6
Hulme St (Salford) 46 B3
Humberstone Av 46 D6
Hunmanby Av 46 D6
Hunt's Bk 46 E2

Hyde Gro 47 G7
Hyde Pl 47 H7
Hyde Rd 47 H6
Hyde St 46 C7

I
Inchley Rd 47 F6
Instow Cl 47 H7
Ionas St 46 C1
Irk St 47 F1
Iron St 47 J2
Irwell Pl 46 A3
Irwell St 46 D1
Irwell St (Salford) 46 C3
Islington Way 46 B3

J
Jackson Cres 46 C6
Jackson's Row 46 D4
James Henry Av 46 A4
James St 47 J1
James St (Salford) 46 B3
Jenkinson St 47 F6
Jersey St 47 G3
Jerusalem Pl 46 D4
Jessamine Av 46 B1
Jessel Cl 47 G6
Joddrell St 46 D4
John Clynes Av 47 H1
John Dalton St 46 D3
Johnson Sq 47 H1
Johnson St 46 B7
Johnson St (Salford) 46 C3
John St 47 F3
John St
    (Lower Broughton) 46 C1
John St (Salford) 46 D2
Joiner St 47 F3
Jordan St 46 D5
Joynson Av 46 B1
Julia St 46 D1
Jury St 46 D1
Justin Cl 47 F6
Jutland St 47 G4

K
Kale St 47 G6
Kays Gdns 46 C3
Keele Wk 47 H1
Kelling Wk 46 C6
Kelvin St 47 F3
Kennedy St 46 E4
Kenwright St 47 F2
Kincardine Rd 47 F6
King Edward St 46 A5
Kingham Dr 47 H2
Kingsfold Av 47 H1
Kingsland Cl 47 H1
King St 46 D3
King St (Salford) 46 D2
King St W 46 D3
Kirkgate Cl 47 H2
Kirkhaven Sq 47 J1
Kirkstall Sq 47 G7
Kirkwood Dr 47 H1

L
Lackford Dr 47 H1
Lamb La 46 C3
Lamport Cl 47 F5
Lanchester St 47 J2
Landos Rd 47 H2
Langholme Cl 46 C6
Langport Av 47 J7
Langston St 46 D1
Lanstead Dr 47 J2
Lauderdale Cres 47 H7
Laystall St 47 G3
Layton St 47 J2
Leaf St 46 D6
Leak St 46 B6
Ledburn Ct 46 C6
Left Bk 46 C4
Lena St 47 F4
Leslie Hough Way 46 A1
Lever St 47 F3
Lewis St 47 J1
Leycroft St 47 G4
Lidbrook Wk 47 J7
Lime Bk St 47 J5
Lime Gro 47 F7
Limekiln La 47 H5
Linby St 46 C6
Lind St 47 J3
Linen Ct 46 B2
Linsley St 46 D2
Linton Cl 47 H4
Litcham Cl 47 F5
Little Ancoats St 47 F3
Little Holme St 47 J3
Little John St 46 C4
Little Lever St 47 F3
Little Nelson St 47 F2
Little Peter St 46 D5

Little Pit St 47 G7
Little Quay St 46 D4
Liverpool Rd 46 C4
Livesey St 47 G1
Lizard St 47 F3
Lloyd St 46 D4
Lloyd St N 47 F7
Lockett St 46 D1
Lockton Cl 47 G5
Lomax St 47 G3
London Rd 47 F4
Longacre St 47 G4
Long Millgate 46 E2
Longworth St 46 D4
Loom St 47 G3
Lordsmead St 46 C6
Lord St 46 E1
Lostock St 47 H2
Lowcock St 46 C1
Lower Byrom St 46 C4
Lower Chatham St 47 E6
Lower Mosley St 46 D5
Lower Moss La 46 C6
Lower Ormond St 47 E5
Lower Vickers St 47 J2
Lowndes Wk 47 G6
Loxford St 47 E6
Lucy St 46 B7
Ludgate Hill 47 F2
Ludgate St 47 F2
Luna street 47 F3
Lund St 46 A7
Lupton St 46 C3
Lyceum Pl 47 E6

M
Maidford Cl 47 J3
Major St 47 E4
Makin St 47 E5
Mallard St 47 E5
Mallow St 46 C6
Malta St 47 H3
Malt St 46 B6
Malvern St 46 B7
Manchester St 46 A7
Mancunian Way 46 C6
Mangle St Street 47 F3
Manor St 47 G5
Manson Av 46 B6
Maplin Cl 47 G6
Marble St 47 F3
Marcer Rd 47 H2
Marchmont Cl 47 H7
Market St 47 E3
Markfield Av 47 J7
Markham Cl 47 J4
Marple St 46 C7
Marsden St 46 E3
Marshall St 47 F2
Marshall St (Ardwick) 47 H6
Marsworth Dr 47 H3
Mary France St 46 C6
Mary St 46 D1
Mason St 47 F2
Mason St (Salford) 46 C3
Massey St 46 B3
Mayan Av 46 B2
Mayes St 47 E2
Mayo St 47 H5
Mays St 47 F2
Meadow Rd 46 B1
Medlock St 46 D5
Melbourne St 46 C6
Mellor St 47 J7
Melville St 46 D1
Merrill St 47 H3
Middlewood St 46 B4
Midland St 47 J5
Miles Platting 47 J1
Milk St 47 E3
Millbank St 47 G4
Millbeck St 47 E6
Miller St 47 E2
Mill Grn St 47 H5
Millhall Cl 46 C7
Millhead Av 47 J2
Millow St 47 E2
Milnrow Cl 47 F5
Milton St 46 C1
Mincing St 47 F2
Minshull St 47 F4
Minshull St S 47 F4
Mistletoe Grn 46 C2
Moorhead St 47 G2
Morbourne Cl 47 J7
Mosley St 47 E4
Mosscott Wk 47 G5
Mosshall Cl 46 C7
Moulton St 46 D1
Mouncey St 47 E5
Mount Carmel Cres 46 A4
Mount St 46 E4
Mount St (Salford) 46 C2
Mozart Cl 47 H2

Mullberry St 46 D4
Munday St 47 J5
Munster St 47 E2
Murrey St 47 G3
Museum St 47 E4
Muslin St 46 B4
Myrtle Pl 46 A1

N
Nancy St 46 B6
Nansen St 47 J5
Naples St 47 F2
Nash St 46 C7
Nathan Dr 46 D4
Naval St 47 G3
Naylor St 47 H1
Neild St 47 G5
Neill St 46 C1
Nelson St 47 J1
Nether St 47 G5
New Allen St 47 G2
Newbeck St 47 F2
Newcastle St 46 E6
New Cath St 46 E3
New Century Park 47 E2
Newcombe St 46 E1
New Elm St 46 C4
New Gartside St 46 D4
New Islington 47 H3
New Mkt 46 E3
New Mkt St 46 E3
New Mt St 47 F2
New Quay St 46 C4
Newton St 47 F3
New Union St 47 G3
New Vine St 46 D6
New Wakefield St 47 E4
New Welcome St 46 D6
New Windsor 46 A3
New York St 46 C6
Nicholas St 47 E4
Nine Acre Dr 46 A6
Niven St 47 G5
North Bailey St 46 C3
Northdown Av 46 B6
North George St 46 B2
North Hill St 46 C2
North Phoebe St 46 A4
North Star Dr 46 B3
Northumberland Cl 46 A7
Northumberland
    Cres 46 A7
North Western St 47 G5
North W Services Rd 46 D3
Norton St 46 D2
Norway St 47 J4
Nuneaton Dr 47 H1
Nuttall St 46 A7

O
Oakford Av 47 G1
Oak St 47 F3
Old Bk St 46 E3
Old Birley St 46 D7
Old Elm St 47 G6
Oldfield Rd 46 A5
Oldham Rd 47 F3
Oldham St 47 F3
Old Medlock St 46 C4
Old Mill St 47 G3
Old Mt St 47 F2
Old Trafford 47 H2
Old York St 46 C6
Oliver St 47 F7
Ordsall Dr 46 A6
Ordsall La 46 A5
Oregon Cl 47 G6
Orion Pl 46 B1
Ormsgill St 46 D7
Orsett Cl 47 H1
Osborne St 47 G1
Oswald St 47 F2
Oswald St (Ancoats) 47 H4
Overbridge Rd 46 D1
Oxford Rd 47 E5
Oxford St 46 E4

P
Paddock St 47 G5
Palfrey Pl 47 H6
Pall Mall 46 E4
Palmerston St 47 H4
Parish Vw 46 A4
Parker St 47 F3
Park Pl 47 E1
Park St 47 E1
Park St (Salford) 46 B3
Parsonage 46 D3
Parsonage La 46 D3
Parsonage Way 46 A5
Paton St 47 F4
Pattishall Cl 47 J4

Peak St 47 G3
Peary St 47 G1
Peel Mt 46 A1
Pegasus Sq 46 B1
Pembroke Cl 47 H7
Pencroft Way 47 F7
Penfield Cl 47 F5
Percy Dr 46 A6
Percy St 46 C7
Peru St 46 B2
Peter St 46 D4
Phoenix St 47 E3
Phoenix Way 46 D7
Piccadilly 47 F3
Pickford St 47 G3
Picton Cl 46 C2
Picton St 46 C1
Piercy Av 46 B1
Piercy St 47 H3
Pigeon St 47 G3
Pimblett St 46 E1
Pine St 47 E4
Pin Mill Brow 47 H5
Pittbrook St 47 J5
Plymouth Gro 47 G7
Plymouth Vw 47 G7
Pochin St 47 J1
Poland St 47 G2
Polebrook Av 47 H7
Police St 46 D3
Pollard St 47 H4
Pollard St E 47 H3
Polygon Av 47 H7
Polygon St 47 G6
Pomona Strand 46 A6
Poplar St 47 J5
Poplin Dr 46 D2
Portland St 47 E5
Portsmouth St 47 G7
Port St 47 F3
Portugal St 47 G2
Portugal St E 47 G4
Postal St 47 G3
Postbridge Cl 47 H7
Potato Wf 46 C5
Poynton St 46 E6
Price St 47 J3
Primrose St 47 G2
Prince's Br 46 C4
Princess Rd 46 D6
Princess St 46 E4
Princess St
    (Cornbrook) 46 B6
Pritchard St 47 F5
Providence St 47 H4
Pryme St 46 C5
Purslow Cl 47 J3

Q
Quay St 46 C4
Quay St (Salford) 46 D3
Queen St 46 D4
Queen St (Salford) 46 D2
Quenby St 46 C6
Quendon Av 46 C1

R
Rachel St 47 H5
Radium St 47 G2
Ralli Cts 46 C3
Randerson St 47 G5
Rankin Cl 46 D7
Raven St 47 H5
Reather Wk 47 H1
Red Bk 47 E2
Redfern St 47 E2
Redhill St 47 G3
Red Lion St 47 F3
Regent Sq 46 A5
Reilly St 46 D6
Reservoir St 46 D2
Reyner St 47 E4
Rial Pl 47 E7
Ribston St 46 C7
Rice St 46 C5
Richmond St 47 F4
Richmond St
    (Salford) 46 C2
Ridgefield 46 D3
Ridgeway St E 47 H3
Ridgway St 47 H3
Riga St 47 F2
Rigel Pl 46 B1
Rigel St 47 H2
Rimworth Dr 47 H1
Ringstead Dr 47 G1
Ripley Cl 47 H4
River Pl 46 D5
Riverside 46 B2
River St 46 D6
River St (Ardwick) 47 H5
Robert St 46 E1
Roby St 47 F4
Rochdale Rd 47 F2

Rockdove Av 46 D6
Rocket Way 46 C3
Rockingham Cl 47 J7
Rodney St 47 H2
Rodney St (Salford) 46 C3
Roe St 47 G2
Roger St 47 F1
Rolla St 46 D2
Rolleston Av 47 H2
Rolls Cres 46 C7
Roman St 47 F3
Rome Rd 47 G2
Rondin Cl 47 J5
Rondin Rd 47 J5
Rope Wk 46 D2
Rosamond Dr 46 C3
Rosamond St W 47 E6
Rosewell Cl 47 J1
Rostron Av 47 J6
Rowendale St 46 D5
Royce Rd 46 C6
Roydale St 47 J2
Royds Cl 47 J7
Ruby St 47 E7
Rudcroft Cl 47 G6
Rudman Dr 46 A5
Rugby St 46 D1
Runcorn St 46 B6

S
Sackville St 47 E4
Sagar St 46 D1
St. Andrew's Sq 47 H4
St. Andrew's St 47 G4
St. Ann's Sq 46 D3
St. Ann St 46 D3
St. Bartholomew's Dr 46 A4
St. Chad's St 47 E1
St. Clement's Dr 46 A5
St. George's 46 B6
St. Ignatius Wk 46 A5
St. James's Sq 46 E4
St. James St 47 E4
St. John St 46 D4
St. Mary's Gate 46 E3
St. Mary's
    Parsonage 46 D3
St. Mary's St 46 C3
St. Nicholas Rd 46 C6
St. Philip's St 46 B3
St. Simon St 46 C1
St. Stephen's Cl 47 H7
St. Stephen St 46 C3
St. Thomas St 47 F1
St. Vincent St 47 H3
St. Wilfrids St 46 C6
Salford 46 A4
Salmon St 47 F3
Saltford Av 47 H3
Salutation St 46 E7
Samouth Cl 47 H2
Sam Swire St 46 D7
Samuel Ogden St 47 F5
Sanctuary, The 46 D7
Sandal St 47 J2
Sandford St 46 C1
Sand St 47 G1
Sawley Rd 47 J1
Scarsdale St 46 A1
School Ct 47 G3
School St 47 F2
School St (Salford) 46 C1
Scotporth Cl 46 C6
Sefton Cl 47 G6
Senior St 46 D2
Seymour Cl 46 A7
Sharp St 47 F2
Shaw Cres 46 E2
Shawgreen Cl 46 C6
Shawheath Cl 46 C6
Shearsby Cl 46 D7
Sheffield St 47 G4
Sherborne St 46 D1
Sherbourne St W 46 D1
Sherratt St 47 G2
Shetland Rd 47 H1
Shilford Dr 47 G2
Shortcroft St 46 D5
Short St 47 F3
Short St (Salford) 46 C1
Shrewsbury St 46 B7
Shudehill 47 F3
Sidney St 47 F6
Sidney St (Salford) 46 C3
Silkin Cl 47 F6
Silk St 47 G2
Silk St (Salford) 46 B2
Silvercroft St 46 C5
Silver St 47 F4
Simeon St 47 F2
Simms Cl 46 B3
Simpson St 47 F2
Sirius Pl 46 B1
Skerry Cl 47 G6

Skip Pl 47 E1
Slate Av 47 H3
Sleaford Cl 47 H1
Smallridge Cl 47 H2
Smith St 46 A6
Smithy La 46 D3
Snell St 47 H4
Soar St 47 F3
Sorrel St 46 C6
Southall St 46 D4
Southall St
    (Strangeways) 46 D1
Southend Av 46 B7
Southern St 46 D5
Southgate 46 D3
South Hall St 46 B5
South King St 46 D3
Southmill St 46 E4
South Pump St 47 F4
South W Services Rd 46 C4
Sparkle St 47 G4
Spaw St 46 C3
Spa St 47 F7
Spear St 47 F3
Spectator St 47 H3
Springfield La 46 D2
Springfield Sq 46 D4
Spring Gdns 47 E4
Spruce St 46 C7
Stalham Cl 47 H1
Stanley Rd 46 B7
Stanley St 47 F1
Stanley St (Salford) 46 C4
Stansby Gdns 47 J7
Station App (for
    Oxford Road
    Station) 47 E5
Station App (for
    Piccadilly Station) 47 F4
Staverton Cl 47 G6
Stephen St 46 E1
Stevenson Pl 47 F3
Stevenson Sq 47 F3
Stevenson St 46 B3
Stockland Cl 47 F6
Stockport Rd 47 H6
Stocks St 47 E1
Stocks St E 47 E1
Stonall Av 46 C6
Stonelow Cl 46 E6
Stone St 46 C5
Store St 47 F4
Stracey St 47 J2
Strawberry Hill 46 A1
Stretford Rd 46 B7
Style St 47 F2
Sudbury Cl 46 B7
Sudell St 47 G2
Sussex St 46 B1
Swan St 47 F2
Swiftsure Av 46 B3
Syndall Av 47 H6
Syndall St 47 H6

T
Talgarth Rd 47 G1
Tamar Ct 46 B7
Tame St 47 H4
Tariff St 47 F3
Tasle All 46 D4
Tatton St 46 B6
Tatton St (Salford) 46 A5
Taunton St 47 J3
Tavery Cl 47 H3
Tebutt St 47 G2
Teer St 47 J3
Temperance St 47 G5
Tewkesbury Rd 47 J2
Thirsk St 47 G5
Thomas St 47 F3
Thompson St 47 F2
Thompson St
    (Strangeways) 46 D1
Thomson St 47 H7
Thor Grn 46 B5
Thornage Dr 47 H1
Thorncross Cl 46 B6
Thornden Rd 47 J1
Thornley Brow 47 E2
Thornton St 47 H1
Tib La 46 E4
Tib St 47 F3
Tideswell Av 47 H2
Tidworth Av 47 H3
Tinsley Cl 47 J2
Tivoli St 46 D4
Todd St 47 E2
Tomlinson St 46 D7
Tonge St 47 G5
Tonman St 46 D4
Torquay Cl 47 H7
Towcester Cl 47 J3
Town Hall La 46 E3
Trafford Bk Rd 46 A7

Trafford Ct 46 C6
Trafford Pl 46 B7
Trafford St 46 D5
Travis St 47 G5
Trentham St 46 B6
Trinity Way 46 B5
Tristam Cl 47 G6
Troutbeck Av 47 H3
Trumpet St 46 D5
Tudbury Way 46 C2
Tuer St 47 F7
Turner St 47 F3
Turner St
    (Old Trafford) 46 A6
Tutbury St 47 H4
Twillbrook Dr 46 D2

U
Union St 47 F3
Union St (Ardwick) 47 H5
University Rd 46 A2
University Rd W 46 A2
Upper Brook St 47 F6
Upper Cyrus St 47 J3
Upper Helena St 47 J2
Upper Kirby St 47 H3
Upper Moss La 46 C7
Upper Wf St 46 B3

V
Varley St 47 J1
Vauxhall St 47 G1
Velour Cl 46 B1
Vesta St 47 H3
Viaduct St 47 J4
Viaduct St (Salford) 46 D2
Vickers St 47 J1
Victoria Br St 46 D3
Victoria Sta App 46 E2
Victor St 47 G1
Victor St (Salford) 46 C3
Virgil St 46 B6

W
Wadeford Cl 47 G2
Wadeson Rd 47 G5
Wadlow Cl 46 C2
Walker's Cft 46 E2
Wallness 46 A1
Wallness La 46 A1
Warde St 46 C7
Wardle St 47 J2
Warford St 47 F1
Warmington Dr 47 J7
Warwick St 47 F3
Warwick St (Hulme) 46 D7
Waterloo St 47 E4
Water St 46 B5
Water St (Ardwick) 47 H5
Watkin Cl 47 G7
Watkin St 46 C1
Watson St 46 D5
Weald Cl 47 G6
Weir St 46 D7
Welland Cl 46 B7
Wellhead Cl 46 E7
Wellington Grn 46 C7
Wellington St 46 C2
Well St 47 E3
West Bk St 46 A4
West Charles St 46 A3
West Crown Av 46 A4
West Hope St 46 A3
West King St 46 C2
Westminster St 46 B6
West Mosley St 47 E4
Weston St 47 J3
West Pk St 46 A5
Weybridge Rd 47 H3
Whalley St 47 H2
Wheater's Cres 46 B1
Wheater's St 46 B1
Wheater's Ter 46 B1
Whimberry Cl 46 A5
Whitchurch St 46 D1
Whitekirk Cl 47 G6
White St 46 B7
Whitfield St 47 E1
Whittle's Cft 47 G4
Whittle St 47 F3
Whitworth St 47 F5
Whitworth St W 46 D5
Wilberforce Cl 46 D7
Wilfred St 46 D1
William Chadwick Cl 47 H1
Williamson St 47 F1
William St 47 H5
Wilmott St 46 E6
Wilson St 47 H7
Wilton Pl 46 B3
Wilton St 47 F6
Winder Dr 47 H3
Windmill Av 46 A5
Windmill St 46 D4

Winfell Dr 47 J2
Winscombe Dr 47 H1
Winser St 47 E5
Winstanley Rd 47 H2
Withy Gro 47 E3
Woden's Av 46 A5
Woden St 46 B5
Woodlark Cl 46 B3
Wood St 46 D4
Woodward Pl 47 H3
Woodward St 47 H3
Woollam Pl 46 C4
Worrall St 46 A5
Worsley St 46 B5
Worsley St (Salford) 46 D3
Wright St 46 A7
Wroe St 46 B3
Wyatt Av 46 A5
Wynne St 46 A1
Wyre St 47 G5

Y
Yew St 46 C7
Yorkshire St 46 D3
York St 47 E3
York St (Hulme) 46 C6
York St (off Charles
    Street) 47 E5
York St E 47 F6

Z
Zion Cres 46 D7

Tourist Information Centre: 23 Union Street
Tel: 01224 269180

Albert Quay	C3	Hutcheon Street	B2
Albert Street	B2	Justice Mill Lane	B3
Albury Road	B3	King's Crescent	C1
Albyn Place	A3	King Street	C1
Argyll Place	A2	Langstane Place	B3
Ashgrove Road	A1	Leadside Road	B2
Ashgrove Road West	A1	Leslie Terrace	B1
Ash-hill Drive	A1	Links Road	C2
Ashley Road	A3	Linksfield Road	C1
Back Hilton Road	A1	Loch Street	B2
Baker Street	B2	Maberly Street	B1
Beach Boulevard	C2	Market Street	C3
Bedford Place	B1	Menzies Road	C3
Bedford Road	B1	Merkland Road East	C1
Beechgrove Terrace	A2	Mid Stocket Road	A2
Belgrave Terrace	A2	Mile-end Avenue	A2
Berryden Road	B1	Miller Street	C2
Blaikie's Quay	C3	Mount Street	B2
Bon-Accord Street	B3	Nelson Street	C1
Bonnymuir Place	A2	North Esplanade East	C3
Bridge Street	B2	North Esplanade West	C3
Brighton Place	A3	Orchard Street	C1
Cairncry Road	A1	Osborne Place	A3
Canal Road	B1	Palmerston Road	C3
Carden Place	A3	Park Road	C1
Carlton Place	A3	Park Street	C2
Cattofield Place	A1	Pittodrie Place	C1
Causewayend	B2	Pittodrie Street	C1
Chapel Street	A3	Powis Place	B1
Claremont Street	A3	Powis Terrace	B1
Clifton Road	A1	Queens Road	A3
College Bounds	B1	Queens Terrace	A3
College Street	C3	Regent Quay	C2
Commerce Street	C2	Rosehill Crescent	A1
Commercial Quay	C3	Rosehill Drive	A1
Constitution Street	C2	Rosemount Place	A2
Cornhill Drive	A1	Rose Street	B2
Cornhill Road	A1	Rubislaw Terrace	B3
Cornhill Terrace	A1	St. Swithin Street	A3
Cotton Street	C2	Schoolhill	B2
Cromwell Road	A3	Seaforth Road	C1
Desswood Place	A3	Sinclair Road	C3
Devonshire Road	A3	Skene Square	B2
Elmbank Terrace	B1	Skene Street	B2
Esslemont Avenue	B2	South Crown Street	B3
Ferryhill Road	B3	South Esplanade West	C3
Fonthill Road	B3	Spital	C1
Forest Road	A3	Springbank Terrace	B3
Forest Avenue	A3	Spring Gardens	B2
Fountainhall Road	A2	Stanley Street	A3
Froghall Terrace	B1	Sunnybank Road	B1
Gallowgate	C2	Sunnyside Road	B1
George Street	B1	Union Glen	B3
Gillespie Crescent	A1	Union Grove	A3
Gladstone Place	A3	Union Street	B3
Golf Road	C1	Urquhart Road	C2
Gordondale Road	A2	Victoria Bridge	C3
Great Southern Road	B3	Victoria Road	C3
Great Western Road	A3	Walker Road	C3
Guild Street	C3	Waterloo Quay	C2
Hamilton Place	A2	Waverley Place	B3
Hardgate	B3	Well Place	C3
Hilton Drive	A1	Westburn Drive	A1
Hilton Place	A1	Westburn Road	A2
Hilton Street	A1	West North Street	C2
Holburn Road	B3	Whitehall Place	A2
Holburn Street	B3	Whitehall Road	A2
Holland Street	B1	Willowbank Road	B3

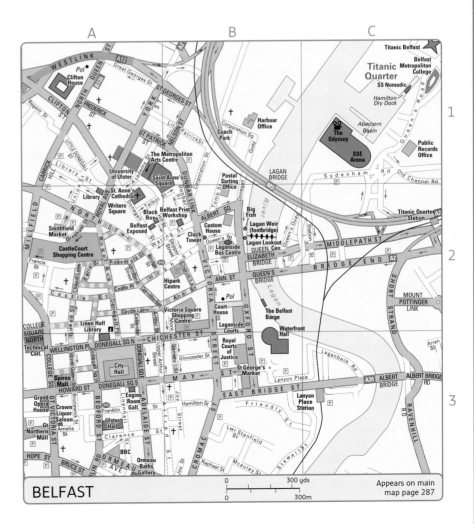

ABERDEEN

0   500 yds
0   500m

Appears on main
map page 261

Tourist Information Centre: 9 Donegall Square North
Tel: 028 9024 6609

Academy Street	A1	Millfield	A2
Adelaide Street	A3	Montgomery Street	B2
Albert Bridge	C3	Mount Pottinger Link	C2
Albert Bridge Road	C3	Nelson Street	B1
Albert Square	B2	North Queen Street	A1
Alfred Street	A3	North Street	A2
Amelia Street	A3	Old Channel Road	C1
Ann Street	B2	Ormeau Avenue	A3
Arran Street	C3	Oxford Street	B2
Arthur Street	A2	Queen Elizabeth Bridge	B2
Bedford Street	A3	Queen Street	A3
Berry Street	A2	Queen's Bridge	B2
Bridge End	C2	Queen's Quay	B2
Bridge Street	A2	Queen's Road	C1
Bruce Street	A3	Queen's Square	B2
Brunswick Street	A3	Raphael Street	B3
Callender Street	A2	Ravenhill Road	C3
Carrick Hill	A1	Regent Street	A1
Castle Place	A2	Rosemary Street	A2
Castle Street	A2	Royal Avenue	A2
Chapel Lane	A2	Short Strand	C2
Chichester Street	A3	Skipper Street	B2
Church Lane	B2	Stanhope Street	C2
Clarence Street	A3	Stewart Street	B3
Clifton Street	A1	Sydenham Road	C1
College Square	A2	Talbot Street	A2
College Square North	A2	Tomb Street	B2
Cornmarket	A2	Union Street	A2
Corporation Square	B1	Upper Arthur Street	A3
Corporation Street	B2	Upper Queen Street	A3
Cromac Street	B3	Victoria Street	B2
Donegall Place	A2	Waring Street	A2
Donegall Quay	B2	Wellington Place	A3
Donegall Square East	A3	Westlink	A1
Donegall Square North	A3	York Street	A1
Donegall Square South	A3		
Donegall Square West	A3		
Donegall Street	A2		
Dunbar Link	B1		
Dunbar Street	B1		
East Bridge Street	B3		
Francis Street	A2		
Franklin Street	A3		
Frederick Street	A1		
Friendly Street	B3		
Gloucester Street	B3		
Great Georges Street	A1		
Great Patrick Street	A1		
Great Victoria Street	A3		
Gresham Street	A2		
Hamilton Street	B3		
High Street	A2		
Hill Street	A2		
Hope Street	A3		
Howard Street	A3		
Joy Street	B3		
Laganbank Road	C3		
Lanyon Place	B3		
Library Street	A1		
Linenhall Street	A3		
Little Donegall Street	A1		
Little Patrick Street	B1		
Lombard Street	A2		
Lower Stanfield Street	B3		
May Street	B3		
Middlepath Street	C2		

BELFAST

0   300 yds
0   300m

Appears on main
map page 287

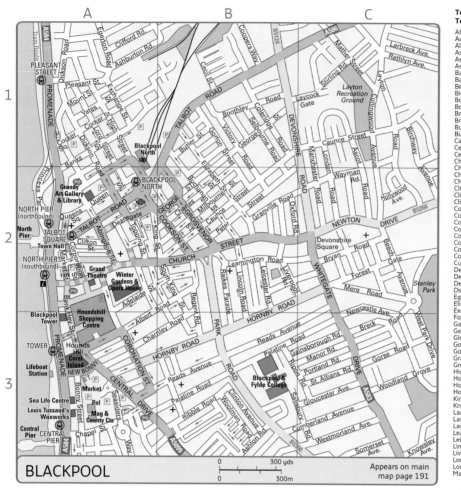

BLACKPOOL

0   300 yds
0   300m

Appears on main
map page 191

Tourist Information Centre: Festival House, Promenade
Tel: 01253 478222

Abingdon Street	A2
Adelaide Street	A2
Albert Road	A3
Ascot Road	C1
Ashburton Road	A1
Ashton Road	B3
Bank Hey Street	A2
Banks Street	A1
Beech Avenue	C2
Birchway Avenue	C1
Bonny Street	A3
Boothley Road	B1
Breck Road	C3
Bryan Road	C2
Buchanan Street	B2
Butler Street	B1
Caunce Street	B2/C1
Cecil Street	B1
Central Drive	A3
Chapel Street	A3
Charles Street	B2
Charnley Road	A3
Church Street	B2
Clifford Road	A1
Clifton Street	A2
Clinton Avenue	B3
Cocker Square	A1
Cocker Street	A1
Coleridge Road	B1
Collingwood Avenue	C1
Cookson Street	B2
Coopers Way	B1
Coronation Street	A3
Corporation Street	A2
Cumberland Avenue	C3
Deansgate	A2
Devonshire Road	B1
Devonshire Square	C2
Dickson Road	A1
Egerton Road	A1
Elizabeth Street	B1
Exchange Street	A1
Forest Gate	C2
Gainsborough Road	B3
George Street	B2/B1
Gloucester Avenue	C3
Gorse Road	C3
Gorton Street	B1
Granville Road	B2
Grosvenor Street	B2
High Street	A1
Hollywood Avenue	C2
Hornby Road	A3
Hounds Hill	A3
King Street	A2
Knowsley Avenue	C3
Larbreck Avenue	C1
Laycock Gate	C1
Layton Road	C1
Leamington Road	B2
Leicester Road	B2
Lincoln Road	B2
Liverpool Road	B2
London Road	C1
Lord Street	A1
Manchester Road	C1

Manor Road	C3
Market Street	A2
Mather Street	C1
Mere Road	C2
Milbourne Street	B2
Mount Street	A1
New Bonny Street	A3
Newcastle Avenue	C2
Newton Drive	C2
Oxford Road	B2
Palatine Road	B3
Park Road	B2
Peter Street	B2
Pleasant Street	A1
Portland Road	C3
Princess Parade	A2
Promenade	A1
Queens Square	A2
Queen Street	A2
Rathlyn Avenue	C1
Reads Avenue	B3
Regent Road	B2
Ribble Road	B3
Ripon Road	B3
St. Albans Road	C3
Salisbury Road	C3
Seasiders Way	A3
Selbourne Road	B1
Somerset Avenue	C3
South King Street	B2
Stirling Road	C1
Talbot Road	A2/B1
Talbot Square	A2
Topping Street	A2
Victory Road	B1
Wayman Road	C2
Westmorland Avenue	C3
West Park Drive	C2
Whitegate Drive	C2/C3
Woodland Grove	C3
Woolman Road	B3
Yates Street	A1

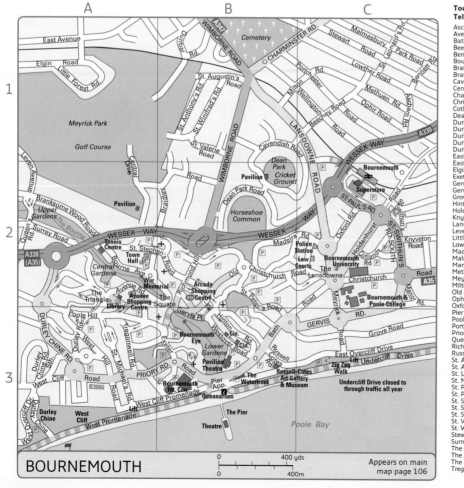

BOURNEMOUTH

0   400 yds
0   400m

Appears on main
map page 106

Tourist Information Centre: Pier Approach
Tel: 01202 451781

Ascham Road	C1
Avenue Road	A2
Bath Road	B3
Beechey Road	C1
Bennett Road	C1
Bourne Avenue	A2
Braidley Road	B2
Branksome Wood Road	A2
Cavendish Road	B1
Central Drive	A1
Charminster Road	B1
Christchurch Road	C2
Cotlands	C2
Dean Park Road	B2
Dunbar Road	B1
Durley Chine	A3
Durley Chine Road	A3
Durley Chine Road South	A3
Durley Road	A3
East Avenue	A1
East Overcliff Drive	C3
Elgin Road	A1
Exeter Road	B3
Gervis Place	B3
Gervis Road	C3
Grove Road	C3
Hinton Road	B3
Holdenhurst Road	C2
Knyveton Road	C2
Lansdowne Road	B1
Leven Avenue	A1
Little Forest Road	A1
Lowther Road	C1
Madeira Road	B2
Malmesbury Park Road	C1
Manor Road	C2
Methuen Road	C1
Meyrick Road	C2
Milton Road	B1
Old Christchurch Road	C2
Ophir Road	C1
Oxford Road	C2
Pier Approach	B3
Poole Hill	A3
Portchester Road	C1
Priory Road	A3
Queen's Road	A2
Richmond Hill	B2
Russell Cotes Road	B3
St. Augustin's Road	B1
St. Anthony's Road	B1
St. Leonard's Road	C1
St. Michael's Road	A3
St. Pauls' Road	C2
St. Peter's Road	B2
St. Stephen's Road	A2
St. Swithun's Road	C2
St. Swithun's Road South	C2
St. Valerie Road	B1
St. Winifred's Road	B1
Stewart Road	C1
Surrey Road	A2
The Lansdowne	C2
The Square	B2
The Triangle	A2
Tregonwell Road	A3

Undercliff Drive	C3
Wellington Road	C1
Wessex Way	A2/C1
West Cliff Promenade	A3
West Cliff Road	A3
West Hill Road	A3
West Overcliff Drive	A3
West Promenade	A3
Westover Road	B3
Wimborne Road	B2

Tourist Information Centre: Britannia House, Broadway
Tel: 01274 433678

Akam Road	A1
Ann Place	A3
Ashgrove	A3
Balme Street	B1
Bank Street	B2
Baptist Place	A1
Barkerend Road	C1
Barry Street	A2
Bolling Road	C3
Bolton Road	C1
Brearton Street	A1
Bridge Street	B2
Britannia Street	B3
Broadway	B2
Burnett Street	C2
Caledonia Street	B3
Canal Road	B1
Captain Street	C1
Carlton Street	A2
Carter Street	C3
Centenary Square	B2
Chain Street	A1
Channing Way	B2
Chapel Street	C2
Charles Street	B2
Cheapside	B2
Chester Street	A3
Churchbank	C2
Claremont	C1
Croft Street	B3
Darfield Street	A1
Darley Street	B1
Drake Street	B2
Drewton Road	A1
Dryden Street	C3
Duke Street	B1
Dyson Street	A1
East Parade	C2
Edmund Street	A3
Edward Street	C3
Eldon Place	A1
Fairfax Street	C3
Filey Street	C2
Fitzwilliam Street	C3
Fountain Street	A1
George Street	C2
Godwin Street	B2
Gracechurch Street	A1
Grafton Street	A3
Grattan Road	A2
Great Horton Road	A3
Grove Terrace	A3
Guy Street	C3
Hall Ings	B2
Hall Lane	C3
Hallfield Road	A1
Hamm Strasse	B1
Hammerton Street	C2
Hanover Square	A1
Harris Street	C2
Heap Lane	C1
Houghton Place	A1
Howard Street	A3
Hustlergate	B2
Ivegate	B2
James Street	B2

John Street	B2
Kirkgate	B2
Leeds Road	C2
Little Horton Lane	A3
Lower Kirkgate	B2
Lumb Lane	A1
Manchester Road	B3
Manningham Lane	A1
Mannville Terrace	A3
Manor Row	B1
Melbourne Place	A3
Midland Road	B1
Moody Street	C3
Morley Street	A3
Neal Street	A3
Nelson Street	B3
North Parade	B1
North Street	C1
North Wing	C1
Nuttall Road	C1
Otley Road	C1
Paradise Street	A1
Park Road	B3
Peckover Street	C2
Prince's Way	B2
Prospect Street	C3
Radwell Drive	A3
Rawson Place	B1
Rawson Road	A1
Rebecca Street	A1
Rouse Fold	C3
Russell Street	A3
Salem Street	B1
Sawrey Place	A3
Sedgwick Close	A1
Sharpe Street	B3
Shipley Airedale Road	C1
Simes Street	A1
Snowden Street	A1
Sunbridge Road	A1
Sylhet Close	A1
Ternhill Grove	B3
Tetley Street	A2
The Tyrls	B2
Thornton Road	A2
Trafalgar Street	A3
Trinity Road	A3
Tumbling Hill Street	A3
Valley Road	B1
Vaughan Street	A3
Vicar Lane	C2
Vincent Street	C3
Wakefield Road	C3
Wapping Road	C1
Water Lane	A2
Westgate	A1
Wigan Street	A2

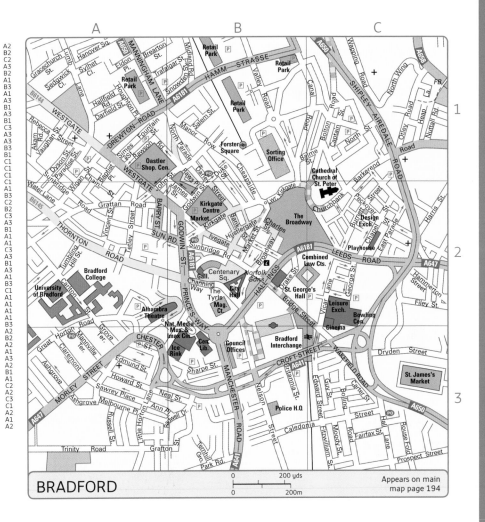

BRADFORD

200 yds
200m

Appears on main map page 194

Tourist Information Centre: The Brighton Centre
Tel: 01273 290337

Addison Road	A1
Albion Hill	C2
Beaconsfield Road	B1
Brunswick Square	A2
Buckingham Place	B1
Buckingham Road	B2
Carlton Hill	C2
Cheapside	B2
Church Street	B2
Churchill Square	B3
Clifton Hill	A2
Clyde Road	B1
Davigdor Road	A1
Ditchling Rise	B1
Ditchling Road	C1
Dyke Road	B2
Dyke Road Drive	B1
Eastern Road	C3
Edward Street	C3
Elm Grove	C1
Fleet Street	B2
Florence Road	B1
Freshfield Road	C3
Furze Hill	A2
Gloucester Road	B2
Grand Junction Road	B3
Hamilton Road	B1
Hanover Street	C2
Highdown Road	A1
Holland Road	A2
Hollingdean Road	C1
Howard Place	B1
Islingword Road	C2
John Street	C2
King's Road	A3
Lansdowne Road	A2
Lewes Road	C1
London Road	B1
Lyndhurst Road	A1
Madeira Drive	C3
Marine Parade	C3
Montefiore Road	A1
Montpelier Road	A2
New England Road	B1
New England Street	B1
Nizells Avenue	A1
Norfolk Terrace	A2
North Road	B2
North Street	B2
Old Shoreham Road	A1
Old Steine	C3
Park Crescent Terrace	C1
Park Street	C2
Port Hall Road	A1
Preston Circus	B1
Preston Road	B1
Preston Street	A3
Prince's Crescent	C1
Queen's Park Road	C2
Queen's Road	B2
Richmond Place	C2
Richmond Road	C1
Richmond Street	C2
Richmond Terrace	C2
St. James's Street	C3
Somerhill Road	A2

Southover Street	C2
Springfield Road	B1
Stafford Road	A1
Stanford Road	B1
Sussex Street	C2
Terminus Road	B2
The Lanes	B3
The Upper Drive	A1
Trafalgar Street	B2
Union Road	C1
Upper Lewes Road	C1
Upper North Street	A2
Upper Rock Gardens	C3
Viaduct Road	B1
Victoria Road	A2
Waterloo Street	A2
Wellington Road	C2
West Drive	C2
West Street	B3
Western Road	A2
Wilbury Crescent	A1
York Avenue	A2
York Place	C2

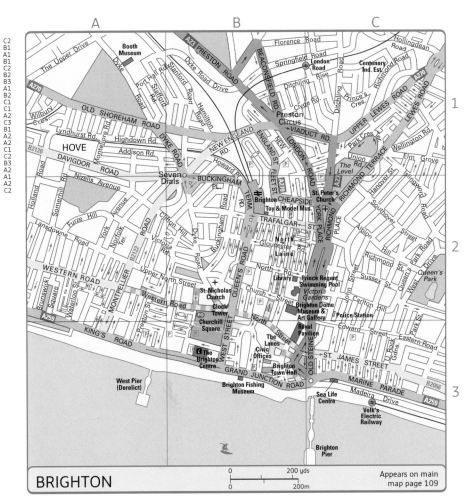

BRIGHTON

200 yds
200m

Appears on main map page 109

BRISTOL

Tourist Information Centre: E Shed 1, Canons Road
Tel: 0906 711 2191

Alfred Hill	A1	Redcliffe Bridge	B3
Anchor Road	A3	Redcliffe Parade	B3
Avon Street	C2	Redcliff Hill	B3
Baldwin Street	A2	Redcliff Mead Lane	C3
Bath Road	C3	Redcliff Street	B2
Bond Street	B1	Redcross Street	C1
Bridge Street	B2	River Street	C1
Brigstowe Street	C1	Rupert Street	A1
Bristol Bridge	B2	St. James Barton	B1
Broadmead	B1	St. Matthias Park	C1
Broad Quay	A2	St. Michael's Hill	A1
Broad Street	B2	St. Nicholas Street	A2
Broad Weir	C1	St. Thomas Street	B2
Brunswick Square	B1	Small Street	A2
Cannon Street	B1	Somerset Street	C3
Canon's Road	A3	Southwell Street	A1
Canon's Way	A3	Station Approach Road	C3
Castle Street	C2	Straight Street	C2
Charles Street	B1	Surrey Street	C1
Cheese Lane	C2	Temple Back	C2
Christmas Steps	A1	Temple Gate	C3
Church Lane	C2	Temple Street	B2
College Green	A2	Temple Way	C3
Colston Avenue	A2	Terrell Street	A1
Colston Street	A2	The Grove	A3
Concorde Street	C1	The Haymarket	B1
Corn Street	C1	The Horsefair	B1
Countership	B2	Thomas Lane	B2
Eugene Street	A1	Trenchard Street	A2
Fairfax Street	B1	Tyndall Avenue	A1
Frogmore Street	A2	Union Street	B1
George White Street	C1	Unity Street	A2
High Street	B2	Unity Street	C2
Horfield Road	A1	Upper Maudlin Street	A1
Houlton Street	C1	Victoria Street	B2
John Street	B2	Wapping Road	A3
King Street	A2	Water Lane	C2
Lewins Mead	A1	Welsh Back	B2
Lower Castle Street	C1	Wilder Street	B1
Lower Maudlin Street	B1	Wine Street	B2
Marlborough Street	B1		
Marsh Street	A2		
Merchant Street	B1		
Nelson Street	B1		
Newfoundland Street	C1		
Newgate	B2		
New Street	C1		
North Street	B1		
Old Bread Street	C2		
Old Market Street	C2		
Park Row	A2		
Park Street	A2		
Passage Street	C2		
Penn Street	C1		
Pero's Bridge	A3		
Perry Road	A2		
Pipe Lane	A2		
Portwall Lane	B3		
Prewett Street	B3		
Prince Street	A3		
Prince Street Bridge	C1		
Quakers' Friars	B1		
Queen Charlotte Street	B2		
Queen Square	A3		
Queen Street	C2		
Redcliff Backs	B3		

Appears on main map page 131

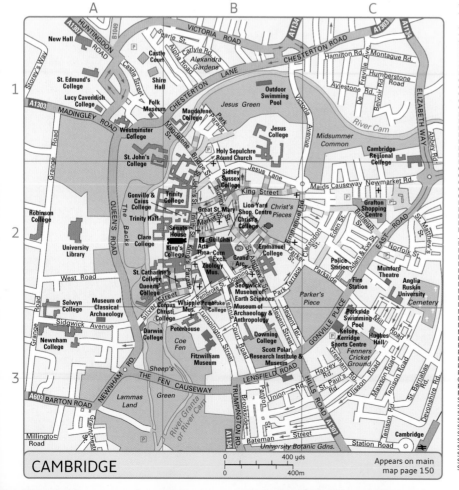

CAMBRIDGE

Tourist Information Centre: The Guildhall, Peas Hill
Tel: 01223 791500

Adam and Eve Street	C2	Tenison Road	C3
Alpha Road	B1	Tennis Court Road	B2
Aylestone Road	C1	Trinity Street	B2
Barton Road	A3	Trumpington Road	B3
Bateman Street	B3	Trumpington Street	B3
Belvoir Road	C1	Union Road	B3
Brookside	B3	Victoria Avenue	B1
Burleigh Street	C2	Victoria Road	B1
Carlyle Road	B1	West Road	A2
Castle Street	A1		
Chesterton Lane	B1		
Chesterton Road	B1		
Clarendon Street	C2		
De Freville Avenue	C1		
Devonshire Road	C3		
Downing Street	B2		
East Road	C2		
Eden Street	C2		
Elizabeth Way	C1		
Emmanuel Road	B2		
Fen Causeway, The	A3		
Glisson Road	C3		
Gonville Place	C3		
Granchester Street	A3		
Grange Road	A3		
Gresham Road	C3		
Hamilton Road	C1		
Harvey Road	C3		
Hills Road	C3		
Humberstone Road	C1		
Huntingdon Road	A1		
Jesus Lane	B2		
King's Parade	B2		
King Street	B2		
Lensfield Road	B3		
Madingley Road	A1		
Magdalene Bridge Street	B1		
Maids Causeway	C2		
Market Street	B2		
Mawson Road	C3		
Millington Road	A3		
Mill Road	C3		
Montague Road	C1		
Newmarket Road	C2		
Newnham Road	A3		
Norfolk Street	C2		
Panton Street	B3		
Parker Street	B2		
Park Parade	B1		
Parkside	C2		
Park Terrace	B2		
Pembroke Street	B2		
Queen's Road	A2		
Regent Street	B2		
Regent Terrace	B2		
St. Andrew's Street	B2		
St. Barnabas Road	C3		
St. John's Street	B2		
St. Matthew's Street	C2		
St. Paul's Road	C3		
Searce Street	A1		
Sidgwick Avenue	A3		
Sidney Street	B2		
Silver Street	A3		
Station Road	C3		
Storey's Way	A1		

Appears on main map page 150

Canterbury

Tourist Information Centre: 18 The High Street
Tel: 01227 862162

Best Lane	B2	Watling Street	B2
Borough Northgate	B1	Whitehall Gardens	A2
Broad Street	C1	Whitehall Road	A2
Burgate	B2	Wincheap	A3
Castle Row	A3	York Road	A3
Castle Street	A3		
College Road	C1		
Cossington Road	C3		
Craddock Road	C1		
Dover Street	C2		
Edgar Road	C1		
Ersham Road	C3		
Forty Acres Road	A1		
Gordon Road	A3		
Havelock Street	C1		
Hawk's Lane	B2		
High Street	B2		
Ivy Lane	C2		
King Street	B1		
Kirby's Lane	A1		
Lansdown Road	B3		
Longport	C2		
Lower Bridge Street	C2		
Lower Chantry Lane	C2		
Marlowe Avenue	B3		
Martyrs' Field Road	A3		
Mead Way	A2		
Military Road	C1		
Monastery Street	C2		
New Dover Road	C3		
North Holmes Road	C1		
North Lane	A1		
Nunnery Fields	C3		
Oaten Hill	C3		
Old Dover Road	C3		
Orchard Street	A1		
Oxford Road	B3		
Palace Street	B2		
Pin Hill	A3		
Pound Lane	A1		
Puckle Lane	C3		
Rheims Way	A2		
Rhodaus Town	B3		
Roper Road	A1		
Rose Lane	B2		
St. Dunstan's Street	A1		
St. George's Lane	B2		
St. George's Place	C2		
St. George's Street	B2		
St. Gregory's Road	C1		
St. Margarets Street	B2		
St. Peter's Lane	B1		
St. Peter's Place	A2		
St. Peter's Street	A1		
St. Radigund's Street	B1		
St. Stephen's Road	B1		
Simmonds Road	A3		
Station Road East	A3		
Station Road West	A1		
Stour Street	A2		
The Causeway	B1		
The Friar's	B2		
Tourtel Road	C1		
Tudor Road	A3		
Union Street	C1		
Upper Bridge Street	B3		

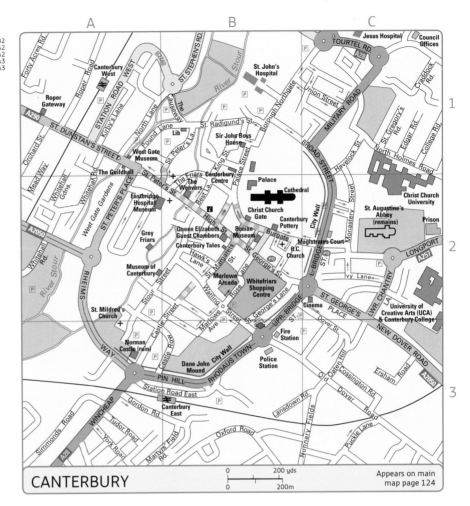

CANTERBURY

Appears on main map page 124

Cardiff

Tourist Information Centres: Cardiff Castle Visitor Centre,
Castle Street   Tel: 029 2087 8101
Old Library The Hayes   Tel: 029 2087 2167

Adam Street	C3	Moira Place	C2
Albany Road	C1	Moira Terrace	C2
Allerton Street	A3	Moy Road	C1
Arran Place	C1	Museum Avenue	B1
Arran Street	C1	Neville Street	A2
Basil Place	B1	Newport Road	C2
Bedford Street	C1	Newport Road Lane	C2
Boulevard de Nantes	B2	Ninian Park Road	A3
Bridge Street	B3	North Road	A1
Brook Street	A3	Oxford Lane	C1
Bute Street	B3	Park Grove	B2
Bute Terrace	B3	Park Place	B1
Castle Street	A2	Park Street	B3
Cathays Terrace	B1	Partridge Road	C1
Cathedral Road	A2	Penarth Road	B3
Celerity Drive	C3	Pendyris Street	A3
Central Link	C3	Pitman Street	A2
Charles Street	B2	Planet Street	C2
Churchill Way	C2	Queen Street	B2
City Road	C1	Rhymney Street	B1
Clare Road	A3	Richard Street	B1
Clare Street	A2	Richmond Road	C1
Claude Road	C1	Ryder Street	A2
Coburn Street	B1	St. Mary Street	B3
College Road	B2	St. Peters Street	C2
Colum Road	A1	Salisbury Road	B1
Corbett Road	B1	Schooner Way	C3
Cornwall Street	A3	Senghennydd Road	B1
Cottrell Road	C1	Stafford Road	A3
Cowbridge Road East	A2	Strathnairn Street	C1
Craddock Street	A3	Stuttgarter Strasse	B2
Craiglee Drive	C3	Taffs Mead Embankment	A3
Croft Street	C1	Talbot Street	A2
Crwys Road	B1	Thesiger Street	B1
Cyfartha Street	C1	The Parade	C2
De Burgh Street	A2	The Walk	C1
Despenser Street	A3	Tudor Street	A3
Duke Street	B2	Tyndall Street	C3
Dumfries Place	C2	Wedmore Road	A3
Ellen Street	C3	Wells Street	A3
Elm Street	C1	West Grove	C2
Fanny Street	B1	Westgate Street	B2
Fitzhamon Embankment	A3	Windsor Place	B2
Flora Street	B1	Windsor Road	C2
Glossop Road	C2	Wood Street	B3
Gordon Road	C1	Woodville Road	B1
Greyfriars Road	B2	Wordsworth Avenue	C2
Hamilton Street	A2	Working Street	B2
Harriet Street	B1	Wyeverne Road	B1
Herbert Street	C3		
High Street	B2		
Hirwain Street	B1		
Keppoch Street	C1		
Kingsway	B2		
Lewis Street	A2		
Longcross Street	C2		
Maindy Road	A1		
Mardy Street	A3		
Mark Street	A2		
Merches Gardens	A3		
Merthyr Street	B1		
Meteor Street	C2		
Mill Lane	B3		
Minny Street	B1		
Miskin Street	B1		

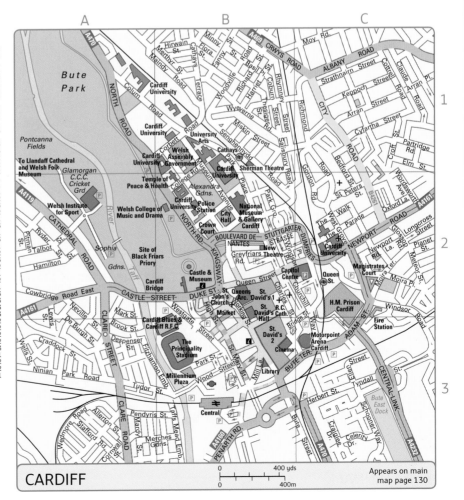

CARDIFF

Appears on main map page 130

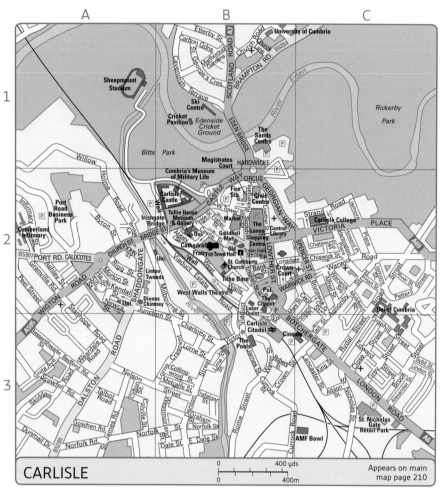

CARLISLE

Appears on main map page 210

Tourist Information Centre: Old Town Hall, Green Market
Tel: 01228 598596

Abbey Street	B2	Lancaster Street	C3
Aglionby Street	C2	Lime Street	B3
Albion Street	C3	Lindon Street	C3
Alexander Street	C3	Lismore Place	C2
Alfred Street	C2	Lismore Street	C2
Ashley Street	A2	London Road	C3
Bank Street	B2	Lonsdale	B2
Bassenthwaite Street	A3	Lorne Crescent	B3
Bedford Road	A3	Lorne Street	B3
Botchergate	B3	Lowther Street	B2
Brampton Road	B1	Marlborough Gardens	C1
Bridge Lane	A2	Mary Street	B2
Bridge Street	A2	Metcalfe Street	B3
Broad Street	C2	Milbourne Street	B2
Brook Street	C3	Morton Street	A2
Brunswick Street	C2	Myddleton Street	C2
Byron Street	A2	Nelson Street	A3
Caldcotes	A2	Newcastle Street	A2
Carlton Gardens	B1	Norfolk Road	A3
Castle Street	B2	Norfolk Street	A3
Castle Way	B2	Peel Street	A2
Cavendish Terrace	B1	Petteril Street	C2
Cecil Street	C2	Port Road	A2
Charlotte Street	B3	Portland Place	C3
Chatsworth Square	C2	Rickergate	B2
Chiswick Street	C2	Rigg Street	A2
Church Lane	B1	River Street	C2
Church Road	B1	Robert Street	B3
Church Street	A2	Rome Street	B3
Clifton Street	A3	Rydal Street	C3
Close Street	C3	St. George's Crescent	B1
Collingwood Street	B3	St. James Road	A3
Colville Street	A3	St. Nicholas Street	C3
Crown Street	B3	Scawfell Road	A3
Currock Road	B3	Scotch Street	B2
Currock Street	B3	Scotland Road	B1
Dale Street	B3	Shaddongate	A2
Denton Street	B3	Silloth Street	A2
Dunmail Drive	A3	Skiddaw Road	A3
East Dale Street	B3	Spencer Street	C2
East Norfolk Street	B3	Stanhope Road	A2
Eden Bridge	B1	Strand Road	C2
Edward Street	C3	Sybil Street	C3
Elm Street	B3	Tait Street	C3
English Street	B2	Talbot Road	A3
Etterby Street	B1	Trafalgar Street	B3
Finkle Street	B2	Viaduct Estate Road	B2
Fisher Street	B2	Victoria Place	C2
Fusehill Street	C3	Victoria Viaduct	B3
Georgian Way	B2	Warwick Road	B2
Goschen Road	A3	Warwick Square	C2
Graham Street	B3	Water Street	B3
Granville Road	A2	Weardale Road	A3
Greta Avenue	A3	West Tower Street	B2
Grey Street	C3	West Walls	B2
Hardwicke Circus	B1	Westmorland Street	B3
Hart Street	C2	Wigton Road	A2
Hartington Place	C2	Willow Holme Road	A1
Hawick Street	A2		
Howard Place	C2		
Infirmary Street	A2		
James Street	B3		
John Street	A2		
Junction Street	A2		
Kendal Street	A2		
King Street	C3		

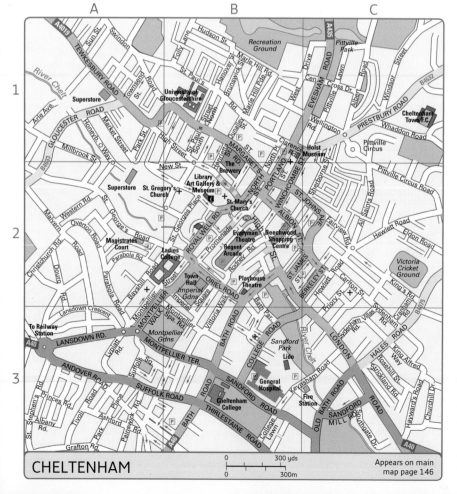

CHELTENHAM

Appears on main map page 146

Tourist Information Centre: The Wilson, Cheltenham Art Gallery and Museum, Clarence Street   Tel: 01242 387492

Albany Road	A3	Portland Street	B2
Albert Road	C1	Prestbury Road	C1
Albion Street	B2	Princes Road	A3
All Saints Road	C2	Priory Street	C3
Andover Road	A3	Promenade	B2
Arle Avenue	A1	Rodney Road	B2
Ashford Road	A3	Rosehill Street	C3
Bath Parade	B2	Royal Well Road	B2
Bath Road	B3	St. George's Place	B2
Bayshill Road	A2	St. George's Road	A2
Berkeley Street	B2	St. James Street	B2
Brunswick Street	B1	St. Johns Avenue	B2
Carlton Street	C2	St. Margaret's Road	B1
Central Cross Drive	C1	St. Paul's Road	B1
Christchurch Road	A2	St. Paul's Street North	B1
Churchill Drive	C3	St. Paul's Street South	B1
Clarence Road	B2	St. Stephen's Road	A3
College Lawn	B3	Sandford Mill Road	C3
College Road	B3	Sandford Road	B3
Cranham Road	C3	Sherborne Street	C2
Douro Road	A2	Southgate Drive	C3
Dunalley Street	B1	Strickland Road	C3
Eldon Road	C2	Suffolk Road	A3
Evesham Road	C1	Suffolk Square	A3
Fairview Road	C2	Sun Street	A1
Folly Lane	B1	Swindon Road	A1
Gloucester Road	A2	Sydenham Road	C2
Grafton Road	A3	Sydenham Villas Road	C3
Hales Road	C3	Tewkesbury Road	A1
Hanover Street	B1	Thirlestaine Road	B3
Hayward's Road	C3	Tivoli Road	A3
Henrietta Street	B2	Townsend Street	A1
Hewlett Road	C2	Vittoria Walk	B3
High Street	B1	Wellington Road	B3
Honeybourne Way	A1	West Drive	B1
Hudson Street	B1	Western Road	A2
Imperial Square	B2	Whaddon Road	C1
Keynsham Road	B3	Winchcombe Street	B2
King Alfred Way	C3	Windsor Street	C1
King's Road	C2		
Lansdown Crescent	A3		
Lansdown Road	A3		
London Road	C3		
Lypiatt Road	A3		
Malvern Road	A2		
Market Street	A1		
Marle Hill Parade	B1		
Marle Hill Road	B1		
Millbrook Street	A1		
Montpellier Spa Road	B3		
Montpellier Street	A3		
Montpellier Terrace	A3		
Montpellier Walk	A3		
New Street	A2		
North Place	B2		
North Street	B2		
Old Bath Road	C3		
Oriel Road	B2		
Overton Road	A2		
Painswick Road	A3		
Parabola Road	A2		
Park Place	A3		
Park Street	A1		
Pittville Circus	C1		
Pittville Circus Road	C2		
Pittville Lawn	C1		

Chester

Tourist Information Centre: Town Hall, Northgate Street
Tel: 0845 647 7868

Bath Street	C2	Queen's Park Road	B3
Bedward Row	A2	Queen's Road	C1
Black Diamond Street	B1	Queen Street	B2
Black Friars	A3	Raymond Street	A1
Bold Square	B2	Russel Street	C1
Boughton	C2	St. Anne Street	B1
Bouverie Street	A1	St. George's Crescent	C3
Bridge Street	B2	St. John's Road	C3
Brook Street	B1	St. John Street	B2
Canal Street	A1	St. Martins Way	A1
Castle Drive	A3	St. Oswalds Way	B1
Charles Street	B1	St. Werburgh Street	B2
Cheyney Road	A1	Seller Street	C2
Chichester Street	A1	Sibell Street	C1
City Road	C2	Souter's Lane	B3
City Walls Road	A2	Stanley Street	A2
Commonhall Street	A2	Station Road	C1
Cornwall Street	B1	Steam Mill Street	C2
Crewe Street	C1	Talbot Street	B1
Cuppin Street	A3	The Bars	C2
Dee Hills Park	C2	The Groves	B3
Dee Lane	C2	Trafford Street	B1
Deva Terrace	C2	Union Street	A2
Duke Street	B3	Upper Northgate Street	A1
Eastgate Street	B2	Vicar's Lane	B2
Edinburgh Way	C3	Victoria Crescent	C3
Egerton Street	B1	Victoria Place	B2
Elizabeth Crescent	C3	Victoria Road	A1
Foregate Street	B2	Walker Street	C1
Forest Street	B2	Walpole Street	A1
Francis Street	C1	Walter Street	B1
Frodsham Street	B2	Watergate Street	A2
Garden Lane	A1	Water Tower Street	A2
George Street	B1	Weaver Street	A2
Gloucester Street	B1	White Friars	A3
Grey Friars	A3	York Street	B2
Grosvenor Park Terrace	C2		
Grosvenor Road	A3		
Grosvenor Street	A3		
Handbridge	B3		
Hoole Road	B1		
Hoole Way	B1		
Hunter Street	A2		
King Street	A2		
Leadworks Lane	C2		
Lightfoot Street	C1		
Louise Street	A1		
Love Street	B2		
Lower Bridge Street	B3		
Lower Park Road	C3		
Mill Street	C2		
Milton Street	B1		
Newgate Street	B2		
Nicholas Street	A2		
Nicholas Street Mews	A2		
Northern Pathway	C3		
Northgate Avenue	B1		
Northgate Street	A2		
Nun's Road	A3		
Old Dee Bridge	B3		
Pepper Street	B3		
Phillip Street	C1		
Prince's Avenue	C1		
Princess Street	A2		
Queen's Avenue	C1		
Queen's Drive	C3		

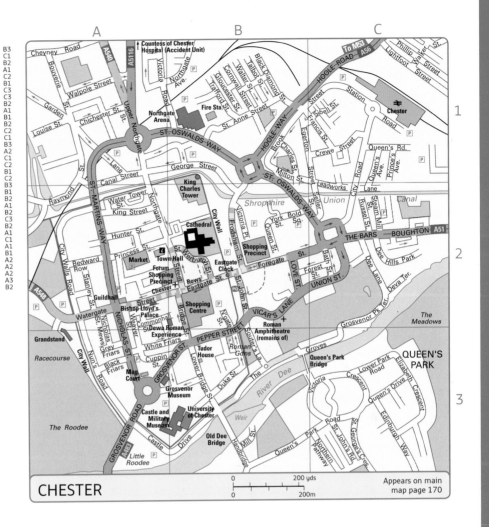

CHESTER

0 — 200 yds
0 — 200m

Appears on main map page 170

Coventry

Tourist Information Centres: St. Michael's Tower, Coventry Cathedral Tel: 024 7622 5616
Herbert Art Gallery & Museum, Jordan Well
Tel: 024 7623 7521

Abbott's Lane	A1	Minster Road	A2
Acacia Avenue	C3	Much Park Street	B2
Albany Road	A3	New Union Street	B2
Alma Street	C2	Norfolk Street	A2
Asthill Grove	B3	Oxford Street	C2
Barker's Butts Lane	A1	Park Road	B3
Barras Lane	A2	Parkside	B3
Berry Street	C1	Primrose Hill Street	C1
Bishop Street	B1	Priory Street	B2
Blythe Road	C1	Puma Way	B3
Bond Street	A2	Quarryfield Lane	C3
Bramble Street	C2	Queen's Road	A3
Bretts Close	A3	Queen Street	C1
Broadway	B2	Queen Victoria Road	A2
Burges	B2	Quinton Road	B3
Butts Road	A2	Radford Road	A1
Cambridge Street	C1	Raglan Street	C2
Canterbury Street	C1	Regent Street	A3
Clifton Street	C1	Ringway Hill Cross	A2
Colchester Street	C1	Ringway Queens	A2
Cornwall Road	C3	Ringway Rudge	
Corporation Street	B2	A2	
Coundon Road	A1	Ringway St. Johns	B3
Coundon Street	A1	Ringway St. Nicholas	B1
Cox Street	C2	Ringway St. Patricks	B3
Croft Road	A2	Ringway Swanswell	
Drapers Fields	B1	B2	
Earl Street	B2	Ringway Whitefriars	C2
East Street	C2	St. Nicholas Street	B1
Eaton Road	B3	Sandy Lane	B1
Fairfax Street	B2	Seagrave Road	C3
Far Gosford Street	C2	Silver Street	B1
Foleshill Road	B1	Sky Blue Way	C2
Fowler Road	A1	South Street	C2
Gordon Street	A3	Spencer Avenue	A3
Gosford Street	C2	Spon Street	A2
Greyfriars Road	A2	Srathmore Avenue	C3
Gulson Road	C2	Stoney Road	B3
Hales Street	B2	Stoney Stanton Road	B1
Harnall Lane East	C1	Swanswell Street	B1
Harnall Lane West	B1	Tomson Avenue	A1
Harper Road	C2	The Precinct	B2
Harper Street	B2	Trinity Street	B2
Hertford Street	B2	Upper Hill Street	A2
Hewitt Avenue	A1	Upper Well Street	B2
High Street	B2	Vauxhall Street	C2
Hill Street	A2	Vecqueray Street	C2
Holyhead Road	A2	Victoria Street	C1
Hood Street	C2	Vine Street	C1
Howard Street	B1	Warwick Road	A3
Jordan Well	B2	Waveley Road	A2
King William Street	C1	Westminster Road	A3
Lamb Street	B2	White Street	B1
Leicester Row	B1	Windsor Street	A2
Leigh Street	C1	Wright Street	C1
Little Park Street	B3		
London Road	C3		
Lower Ford Street	C2		
Market Way	B2		
Meadow Street	A2		
Michaelmas Road	A3		
Middleborough Road	A1		
Mile Lane	B3		
Mill Street	A1		

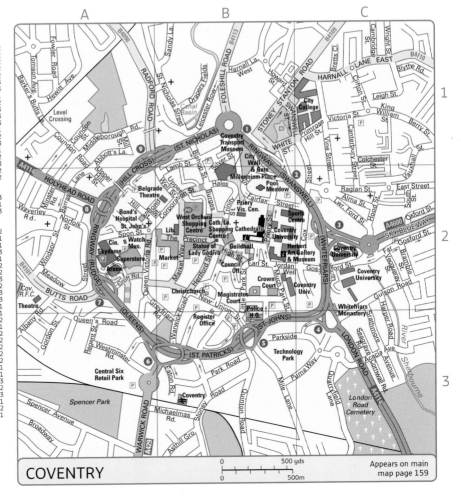

COVENTRY

0 — 500 yds
0 — 500m

Appears on main map page 159

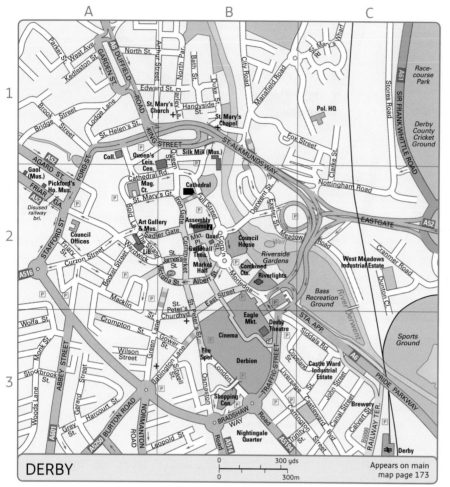

DERBY

0   300 yds
0   300m

Appears on main
map page 173

Tourist Information Centre: Assembly Rooms, Market Place
Tel: 01332 643411

Abbey Street	A3
Agard Street	A1
Albert Street	B2
Arthur Street	A1
Babington Lane	A3
Bath Street	B1
Becket Street	A2
Bold Lane	A2
Bradshaw Way	B3
Bridge Street	A1
Brook Street	A1
Burton Road	A3
Calvert Street	C3
Canal Street	C3
Carrington Street	B3
Castleward Boulevard	C3
Cathedral Road	A2
City Road	B1
Clarke Street	C2
Copeland Street	B3
Cornmarket	B2
Corporation Street	B2
Cranmer Road	C2
Crompton Street	A3
Curzon Street	A2
Darley Lane	B1
Derwent Street	B2
Duffield Road	A1
Duke Street	B1
Dunton Close	C2
Eastgate	C2
East Street	B2
Edward Street	A1
Exeter Street	B2
Ford Street	A2
Fox Street	B1
Friar Gate	A2
Friary Street	A2
Full Street	B2
Garden Street	A1
Gerard Street	A3
Gower Street	B3
Green Lane	A3
Grey Street	A3
Handyside Street	B1
Harcourt Street	A3
Iron Gate	B2
John Street	C3
Kedleston Street	A1
King Street	A1
Leopold Street	A3
Liversage Street	B3
Lodge Lane	A1
London Road	B3
Macklin Street	A2
Mansfield Road	B1
Market Place	B2
Meadow Road	B2
Monk Street	A3
Morledge	B2
Normanton Road	A3
North Parade	B1
North Street	A1
Nottingham Road	C2
Osmaston Road	B3
Parker Street	A1
Pride Parkway	C3
Queen Street	B1
Railway Terrace	C3
Sadler Gate	B2
St. Alkmunds Way	B1
St. Helen's Street	A1
St. James Street	B2
St. Mary's Gate	A2
St. Mary's Wharf Road	C1
St. Peter's Churchyard	B3
St. Peter's Street	B2
Siddals Road	C3
Sir Frank Whittle Road	C1
Sitwell Street	B3
Stafford Street	A2
Station Approach	C2
Stockbrook Street	A3
Stores Road	C1
The Strand	A2
Traffic Street	B3
Trinity Street	B3
Victoria Street	A2
Wardwick	A2
West Avenue	A1
Wilson Street	A3
Wolfa Street	A3
Woods Lane	A3

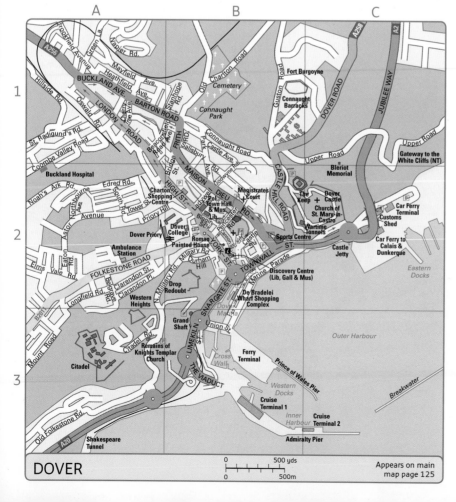

DOVER

0   500 yds
0   500m

Appears on main
map page 125

Tourist Information Centre: Dover Museum, Market Square
Tel: 01304 201066

Astor Avenue	A2
Barton Road	A1
Beaconsfield Avenue	A1
Beaconsfield Road	A1
Belgrave Road	A2
Biggin Street	B2
Bridge Street	B2
Brookfield Avenue	A1
Buckland Avenue	A1
Cannon Street	B2
Canons Gate Road	B2
Castle Avenue	B1
Castle Hill Road	B2
Castle Street	B2
Cherry Tree Avenue	A1
Citadel Road	A3
Clarendon Place	A2
Clarendon Street	A2
Connaught Road	B1
Coombe Valley Road	A2
Dover Road	C1
Durham Hill	B2
Eaton Road	A2
Edred Road	A2
Elms Vale Road	A2
Folkestone Road	A2
Frith Road	B1
Godwyne Road	B2
Green Lane	A1
Guston Road	B1
Heathfield Avenue	A1
High Street	B2
Hillside Road	A2
Jubilee Way	C1
Ladywell	B2
Limekiln Street	B3
London Road	A1
Longfield Road	A2
Maison Dieu Road	B2
Marine Parade	B2
Mayfield Avenue	A1
Military Road	B2
Mount Road	A3
Napier Road	A1
Noah's Ark Road	A2
Northbourne Avenue	A2
North Military Road	A2
Old Charlton Road	B1
Old Folkestone Road	A3
Oswald Road	A1
Park Avenue	B1
Pencester Road	B2
Priory Hill	A2
St. Radigund's Road	A1
Salisbury Road	B1
Snargate Street	B3
South Road	A2
Stanhope Road	B1
The Viaduct	B3
Tower Street	A2
Townwall Street	B2
Union Street	B3
Upper Road	C1
York Street	B2

Tourist Information Centre: 16 City Square
Tel: 01382 527527

Adelaide Place	A1
Albany Terrace	A1
Albert Street	C2
Alexander Street	B1
Ann Street	B2
Arbroath Road	C2
Arklay Street	C1
Arklay Terrace	C1
Arthurstone Terrace	C2
Barrack Road	A2
Blackness Road	A2
Blinshall Street	A2
Brewery Lane	A2
Brook Street	A2
Broughty Ferry Road	C2
Brown Street	A2
Bruce Street	A1
Byron Street	A1
Canning Street	B1
City Square	B3
Clepington Road	C1
Constitution Road	B2
Constitution Street	B1
Court Street	C1
Cowgate Street	B2
Dens Road	B1
Douglas Street	A2
Dudhope Street	A1
Dudhope Terrace	C1
Dundonald Street	C1
Dura Street	C2
East Dock Street	C2
East Marketgait	B2
Fairbairn Street	B1
Greenmarket	B3
Guthrie Street	A2
Hawkhill	A2
High Street	B3
Hill Street	B1
Hilltown	B1
Kenmore Terrace	A1
Killin Avenue	A1
Kinghorne Road	A1
King Street	B2
Larch Street	A2
Law Crescent	A1
Lawside Avenue	A1
Law Street	A1
Leng Street	A1
Lochee Road	A2
Lower Princes Street	C2
Mains Road	B1
Main Street	B1
Meadowside	B2
Morgan Street	C2
Murraygate	B2
Nelson Street	B2
Nethergate	A3
North Marketgait	A2
Perth Road	A3
Polepark Road	A2
Princes Street	C2
Riverside Drive	A3
Roseangle	A3
Rosebank Road	B2
Seagate	B2
South Marketgait	B3
South Tay Street	A3
Strathmartine Road	B1
Tannadice Street	B1
Tay Road Bridge	B3
Trades Lane	B2
Upper Constitution Street	A1
Victoria Road	B2
Victoria Street	C2
Ward Road	A2
West Marketgait	A2
West Port	A2
William Street	C2

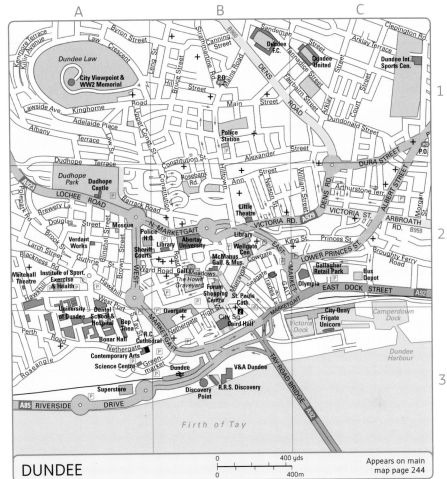

Tourist Information: Telephone Service
Tel: 03000 262626

Aykley Heads	A1
Church Street	B3
Clay Lane	A3
Claypath	B2
Crossgate	B2
Crossgate Peth	A3
Darlington Road	A3
Dryburn Road	A1
Durham Road	A1
Fieldhouse Lane	A1
Framwelgate	B2
Framwelgate Peth	B1
Framwelgate Waterside	B2
Gilesgate	C2
Great North Road	A1
Green Lane	C2
Grove Street	B3
Hallgarth Street	C3
Hawthorn Terrace	A2
Leazes Road	B2
Margery Lane	B3
Market Place	B2
Millburngate Bridge	B2
Newcastle Road	A1
New Elvet	B2
North Bailey	B2
North End	A1
North Road	B2
Old Elvet	C2
Pity Me Bypass	A1
Potters Bank	A3
Quarryheads Lane	B3
Providence Row	B2
Redhills Lane	A2
St. Monica Grove	A2
Sidegate	B2
Silver Street	B2
South Bailey	B3
South Road	B3
South Street	B3
Southfield Way	A1
Stockton Road	B3
Sutton Street	B2
The Avenue	A3
Toll House Road	A2
Western Hill	A2
Whinney Hill	C3
Whitesmocks	A1

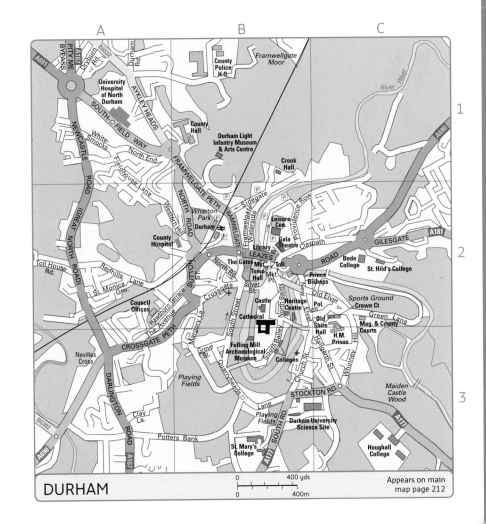

Eastbourne Exeter

Edinburgh street map on pages 36-37

EASTBOURNE

Tourist Information Centre: 3 Cornfield Road
Tel: 01323 415415

Arlington Road	A2	The Avenue	B2
Arundel Road	B1	The Goffs	A1
Ashford Road	B2/C2	Trinity Trees	C2
Avondale Road	B1	Upper Avenue	B1
Bedfordwell Road	B1	Upperton Lane	B2
Belmore Road	C1	Upperton Road	A1
Blackwater Road	B3	Watts Lane	A1
Borough Lane	A1	Whitley Road	A1
Bourne Street	C2	Willingdon Road	A1
Carew Road	A1/B1	Winchcombe Road	C1
Carlisle Road	A3		
Cavendish Avenue	C1		
Cavendish Place	C2		
College Road	B3		
Commercial Road	B2		
Compton Place Road	A2		
Compton Street	B3		
Cornfield Terrace	B2		
Denton Road	A3		
Devonshire Place	B2		
Dittons Road	A2		
Dursley Road	C2		
Enys Road	B1		
Eversfield Road	B1		
Fairfield Road	A3		
Firle Road	C1		
Furness Road	B3		
Gaudick Road	A3		
Gilbert Road	C1		
Gildredge Road	B2		
Gorringe Road	B1		
Grand Parade	C3		
Grange Road	B3		
Grassington Road	B3		
Grove Road	B2		
Hartfield Road	B1		
Hartington Place	C2		
High Street	A1		
Hyde Gardens	B2		
King Edward's Parade	B3		
Langney Road	C2		
Lewes Road	B1		
Marine Parade	C2		
Mark Lane	B2		
Meads Road	A3		
Melbourne Road	C1		
Mill Gap Road	A1		
Mill Road	A1		
Moat Croft Road	A1		
Moy Avenue	C1		
Ratton Road	A1		
Royal Parade	C2		
Saffrons Park	A3		
Saffrons Road	A2		
St. Anne's Road	A1		
St. Leonard's Road	B2		
Seaside	C2		
Seaside Road	C2		
Selwyn Road	A1		
Silverdale Road	B3		
South Street	B2		
Southfields Road	A2		
Station Parade	B2		
Susan's Road	C2		
Sydney Road	C2		
Terminus Road	B2		

Appears on main map page 110

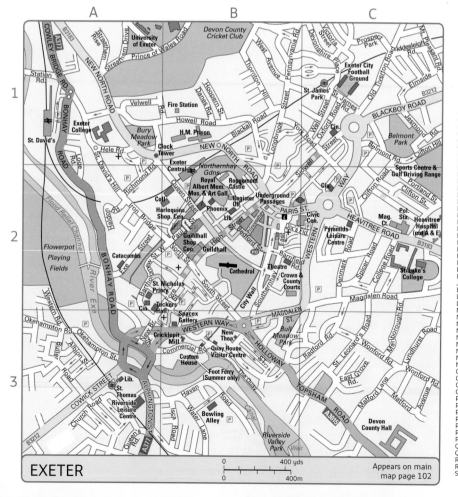

EXETER

Tourist Information Centre: Dix's Field
Tel: 01392 665700

Albion Street	A3	St. James' Road	C1
Alphington Street	A3	St. Leonard's Road	C3
Barnfield Road	B2	Sidwell Street	B2
Bartholomew Street West	A2	Southernhay East	B2
Bedford Street	B2	South Street	B2
Belmont Road	C1	Spicer Road	C2
Blackboy Road	C1	Station Road	A1
Blackall Road	B1	Streatham Drive	A1
Bonhay Road	A2	Streatham Rise	A1
Buller Road	A3	The Quay	B3
Church Road	A3	Thornton Hill	B1
Clifton Hill	C1	Topsham Road	B3
Clifton Road	C2	Velwell Road	A1
Clifton Street	C2	Victoria Street	C1
College Road	C2	Water Lane	B3
Commercial Road	B3	Well Street	C1
Cowick Street	A3	West Avenue	B1
Cowley Bridge Road	A1	Western Road	A2
Danes Road	B1	Western Way	C2
Denmark Road	C2	Wonford Road	C3
Devonshire Place	C1	York Road	B1
Dix's Field	B2		
East Grove Road	C3		
Elmside	C1		
Exe Street	A2		
Fore Street	B2		
Haldon Road	A2		
Haven Road	B3		
Heavitree Road	C2		
Hele Road	A1		
High Street	B2		
Holloway Street	B3		
Hoopern Street	B1		
Howell Road	B1		
Iddesleigh Road	C1		
Iron Bridge	A2		
Isca Road	B3		
Jesmond Road	C1		
Longbrook Street	B1		
Looe Road	A1		
Lyndhurst Road	C3		
Magdalen Road	C2		
Magdalen Street	B3		
Marlborough Road	C3		
Matford Avenue	C3		
Matford Lane	C3		
Mount Pleasant Road	C1		
New Bridge Street	A3		
New North Road	A1/B1		
North Street	B2		
Okehampton Road	A3		
Okehampton Street	A3		
Old Tiverton Road	C1		
Oxford Road	C1		
Paris Street	B2		
Paul Street	B2		
Pennsylvania Road	B1		
Portland Street	C2		
Prince of Wales Road	A1		
Princesshay	B2		
Prospect Park	C1		
Queen's Road	A3		
Queen Street	B2		
Radford Road	C3		
Richmond Road	A2		
St. David's Hill	A1		

Appears on main map page 102

Tourist Information Centre: Town Hall, 1-2 Guildhall Street
Tel: 01303 257946

Alder Road	B2
Archer Road	C2
Bathurst Road	A2
Beatty Road	C1
Black Bull Road	B2
Bournemouth Road	A3
Bouverie Road West	B2
Bradstone Road	A3
Broadfield Road	A2
Broadmead Road	B2
Brockman Road	B2
Canterbury Road	C1
Castle Hill Avenue	B3
Cheriton Gardens	B3
Cheriton Road	A2/B2
Cherry Garden Avenue	A1
Christ Church Road	B3
Churchill Avenue	B1
Clifton Crescent	A3
Coniston Road	A1
Coolinge Road	B2
Cornwallis Avenue	A2
Dawson Road	B2
Dixwell Road	A3
Dolphins Road	B1
Dover Hill	C1
Dover Road	C1
Downs Road	B1
Earles Avenue	A3
Foord Road	B2
Godwyn Road	A3
Grimston Avenue	A3
Grimston Gardens	A3
Guildhall Street	B2
Guildhall Street North	B2
Harbour Way	C1
Hill Road	C1
Ivy Way	C1
Joyes Road	B2
Linden Crescent	A1
Links Way	A3
Lower Sandgate Road	A3
Lucy Avenue	A1
Manor Road	B3
Marine Parade	B3
Marshall Street	C1
Mead Road	B2
Old High Street	C3
Park Farm Road	B1
Pavilion Road	B2
Radnor Bridge Road	C2
Radnor Park Avenue	A2
Radnor Park Road	B2
Radnor Park West	A2
Sandgate Hill	A3
Sandgate Road	B3
Shorncliffe Road	A2
Sidney Street	C2
The Leas	B3
The Stade	C3
The Tram Road	C2
Tontine Street	C2
Turketel Road	A3
Tyson Road	C1
Wear Bay Crescent	C2
Wear Bay Road	C1
Westbourne Gardens	A3
Wingate Road	B1
Wood Avenue	C1
Wilton Road	A2

FOLKESTONE

0 200 yds
0 200m

Appears on main
map page 125

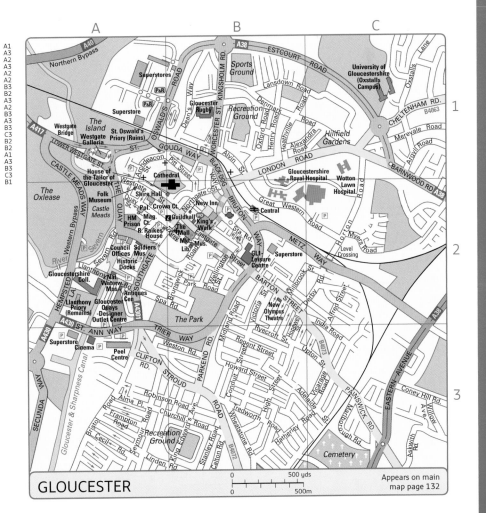

Tourist Information Centre: 28 Southgate Street
Tel: 01452 396572

Adelaide Street	B3
Alexandra Road	B1
Alfred Street	C2
Alma Place	A3
Alvin Street	B1
Archdeacon Street	A1
Argyll Road	C1
Askwith Road	C3
Barnwood Road	C1
Barton Street	B2
Black Dog Way	B1
Bristol Road	A3
Brunswick Road	B2
Bruton Way	B2
Calton Road	B3
Castle Meads Way	A1
Cecil Road	A3
Cheltenham Road	C1
Churchill Road	A3
Clifton Road	A3
Conduit Street	B3
Coney Hill Road	C3
Dean's Way	B1
Denmark Road	B1
Derby Road	B2
Estcourt Road	B1
Eastern Avenue	C3
Eastgate Street	B2
Frampton Road	A3
Gouda Way	A1
Great Western Road	B2
Greyfriars	B2
Hatherley Road	B3
Heathville Road	B1
Hempsted Lane	A2
Henry Road	B1
High Street	B3
Hopewell Street	B3
Horton Road	C2
Howard Street	B3
India Road	C2
King Edward's Avenue	B3
Kingsholm Road	B1
Lansdown Road	B1
Linden Road	A3
Llanthony Road	A2
London Road	B1
Lower Westgate Street	A1
Marlborough Road	C3
Merevale Road	C1
Metz Way	B2
Midland Road	B3
Millbrook Street	B2
Myers Road	C2
Northgate Street	B2
Oxford Road	B1
Oxstalls Lane	C1
Painswick Road	C3
Park Road	B2
Parkend Road	B3
Pitt Street	B1
Quay Street	A2
Regent Street	B3
Robinson Road	A3
Ryecroft Street	B3
St. Ann Way	A3
St. Oswald's Road	A1
Secunda Way	A3
Severn Road	A2
Seymour Road	A3
Southgate Street	A2
Spa Road	A2
Stanley Road	B3
Station Road	B2
Stroud Road	A3
The Quay	A2
Tredworth Road	B3
Trier Way	A3
Upton Street	B3
Vicarage Road	C3
Victoria Street	B2
Wellington Street	B2
Westgate Street	A1
Weston Road	A3
Wheatstone Road	B3
Willow Avenue	C3
Worcester Street	B1

GLOUCESTER

0 500 yds
0 500m

Appears on main
map page 132

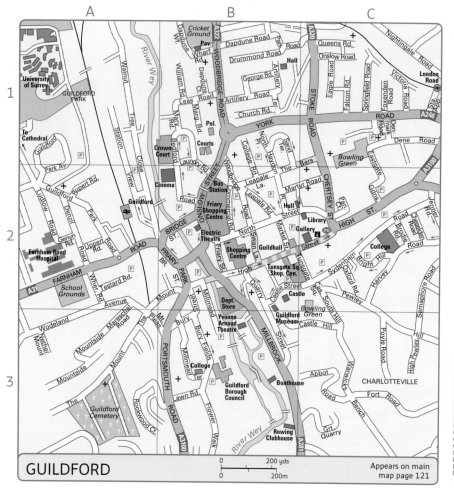

GUILDFORD

0 200 yds
0 200m

Appears on main
map page 121

Tourist Information Centre: 155 High Street
Tel: 01483 444333

Abbot Road	C3	Portsmouth Road	B3
Artillery Road	B1	Poyle Road	C3
Artillery Terrace	B1	Quarry Street	B2
Bedford Road	B1	Queens Road	C1
Bridge Street	B2	Rookwood Court	A3
Bright Hill	C2	Rupert Road	A2
Brodie Road	C2	Sand Terrace	B1
Bury Fields	B3	Semaphore Road	C3
Bury Street	B3	South Hill	C2
Castle Hill	C3	Springfield Road	C1
Castle Square	C2	Station Approach	A1
Castle Street	B2	Station View	C1
Chertsey Street	C1	Stoke Road	B1
Cheselden Road	C2	Swan Lane	B2
Commercial Road	B2	Sydenham Road	C2
Dapdune Court	B1	Testard Road	A2
Dapdune Road	B1	The Bars	B2
Dapdune Wharf	B1	The Mount	A3
Dene Road	C1	Tunsgate	C2
Denmark Road	C1	Upperton Road	A2
Denzil Road	A2	Victoria Road	C1
Drummond Road	B1	Walnut Tree Close	A1
Eagle Road	C1	Warwicks	C3
Eastgate Gardens	C1	Wharf Road	B1
Falcon Road	C1	Wherwell Road	A2
Farnham Road	A2	William Road	B1
Flower Walk	B3	Wodeland Avenue	A3
Fort Road	C3	Woodbridge Road	B1
Foxenden Road	C1	York Road	B1
Friary Bridge	B2		
Friary Street	B2		
Genyn Road	A2		
George Road	B1		
Great Quarry	C3		
Guildford Park Avenue	A1		
Guildford Park Road	A2		
Harvey Road	C2		
Haydon Place	B1		
High Pewley	C3		
High Street	B2/C2		
Laundry Road	B1		
Lawn Road	B3		
Leap Lane	B2		
Leas Road	B1		
Ludlow Road	A2		
Mareschal Road	A3		
Margaret Road	B1		
Market Street	B2		
Martyr Road	B2		
Mary Road	B1		
Millbrook	B3		
Millmead	B2		
Millmead Terrace	B3		
Mount Pleasant	A3		
Mountside	A3		
Nether Mount	A3		
Nightingale Road	C1		
North Place	B1		
North Street	B2		
Onslow Road	C1		
Onslow Street	B2		
Oxford Road	C2		
Pannells Court	C2		
Park Road	B1		
Park Street	B2		
Pewley Hill	C2		

HARROGATE

0 150 yds
0 150m

Appears on main
map page 194

Tourist Information Centre: Royal Baths, Crescent Road
Tel: 01423 537300

Ainsty Road	C1	Regent Grove	C1
Albert Street	B2	Regent Parade	C1
Alexandra Road	B1	Regent Street	C1
Arthington Avenue	B2	Regent Terrace	C1
Beech Grove	A3	Ripon Road	A1
Belford Road	B2	Robert Street	B3
Bower Road	B1	St. James Drive	C3
Bower Street	B2	St. Mary's Walk	A3
Cambridge Street	B2	Skipton Road	C1
Cavendish Avenue	C3	South Park Road	B3
Chelmsford Road	B2	Springfield Avenue	A1
Cheltenham Mount	B1	Spring Grove	A1
Chudleigh Road	C1	Spring Mount	A1
Clarence Drive	A2	Station Avenue	B2
Claro Road	C1	Station Parade	B2
Cold Bath Road	A3	Stray Rein	B3
Commercial Street	B1	Stray Walk	C3
Coppice Drive	A1	Studley Road	B1
Cornwall Road	A2	Swan Road	A2
Crescent Gardens	A2	The Grove	C1
Dragon Avenue	B1	Tower Street	B3
Dragon Parade	B1	Trinity Road	B3
Dragon Road	B1	Valley Drive	A2
Duchy Road	A1	Victoria Avenue	B2
East Parade	B2	Victoria Road	A3
East Park Road	B2	West End Avenue	A3
Franklin Mount	B1	West Park	B2
Franklin Road	B1	Woodside	B2
Gascoigne Crescent	C1	York Place	B3
Glebe Avenue	A2	York Road	A2
Glebe Road	A3		
Grove Park Terrace	C1		
Grove Road	B1		
Harcourt Drive	C2		
Harcourt Road	C1		
Heywood Road	A3		
Hollins Road	A1		
Homestead Road	B2		
James Street	B2		
Kent Road	A1		
King's Road	A2		
Knaresborough Road	C2		
Lancaster Road	A3		
Leeds Road	B3		
Lime Grove	C1		
Lime Street	C1		
Mayfield Grove	B1		
Montpellier Hill	A2		
Montpellier Street	A2		
Mowbray Square	C1		
North Park Road	C2		
Oatlands Drive	C3		
Otley Road	A3		
Oxford Street	B2		
Park Chase	C1		
Park Drive	B3		
Park Parade	C2		
Park Road	A3		
Park View	B2		
Parliament Street	A2		
Princes Villa Road	B2		
Providence Terrace	B1		
Queen Parade	C2		
Queen's Road	A3		
Raglan Street	B2		
Regent Avenue	C1		

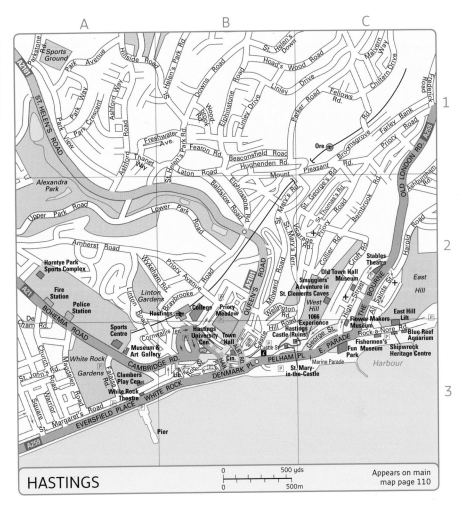

Tourist Information Centre: Muriel Matters House, 2 Breeds Pl
Tel: 01424 451111

Albert Road	B3	St. Margaret's Road	A3
All Saints Street	C2	St. Mary's Road	B2
Amherst Road	A2	St. Mary's Terrace	B2
Ashburnham Road	C2	St. Thomas's Road	C2
Ashford Road	A1	Thanet Way	A1
Ashford Way	A1	The Bourne	C2
Baldslow Road	B2	Upper Park Road	A2
Beaconsfield Road	B1	Vicarage Road	B2
Bembrook Road	C2	Warrior Square	A3
Bohemia Road	A2	Wellington Road	B2
Braybrooke Road	B2	White Rock	A3
Broomsgrove Road	C1	Woodbrook Road	B1
Cambridge Road	A3	Wykeham Road	A2
Castle Hill Road	B3		
Castle Street	C1		
Chiltern Drive	A3		
Church Road	C2		
Collier Road	C2		
Cornwallis Terrace	A3		
Croft Road	A3		
De Cham Road	A3		
Denmark Place	B3		
Downs Road	B1		
East Parade	C3		
Elphinstone Road	B1		
Eversfield Place	A3		
Falaise Road	A3		
Farley Bank	C1		
Fearon Road	B1		
Fellows Road	C1		
Frederick Road	C1		
Freshwater Avenue	A1		
George Street	C3		
Harold Place	B3		
Harold Road	C2		
High Street	C2		
Hillside Road	A1		
Hoad's Wood Road	B1		
Hughenden Road	B1		
Laton Road	B1		
Linley Drive	B1		
Linton Road	A2		
Lower Park Road	A2		
Magdalen Road	A3		
Malvern Way	C1		
Marine Parade	C3		
Milward Road	B2		
Mount Pleasant Road	B1		
Old London Road	C2		
Park Avenue	A1		
Park Crescent	A1		
Park View	A1		
Park Way	A1		
Parker Road	B1		
Parkstone Road	A1		
Pelham Place	B3		
Priory Avenue	B2		
Priory Road	C2		
Queen's Road	B2		
Robertson Street	B3		
Rock-a-Nore Road	C3		
St. George's Road	C2		
St. Helen's Down	B1		
St. Helen's Park Road	B2		
St. Helen's Road	A1		
St. John's Road	A3		

HASTINGS

Appears on main map page 110

Tourist Information Centre: The Butter Market, High Town,
Maylord St Tel: 01432 370514

Aubrey Street	B2	Vaughan Street	C2
Barrs Court Road	C1	Victoria Street	A2
Barton Road	A2	West Street	B2
Barton Yard	A2	Widemarsh Street	B2
Bath Street	C2	Wye Street	B3
Belmont Avenue	A3		
Berrington Street	B2		
Bewell Street	B2		
Blackfriars Street	B1		
Blueschool Street	B1		
Brewers Passage	B2		
Bridge Street	B2		
Broad Street	B2		
Canonmoor Street	A1		
Cantilupe Street	C2		
Castle Street	B2		
Catherine Street	B1		
Central Avenue	C2		
Church Street	B2		
Commercial Road	C1		
Commercial Street	B2		
Coningsby Street	B1		
East Street	B2		
Edgar Street	B1		
Eign Gate	B2		
Eign Street	A2		
Ferrers Street	B2		
Friars Street	A2		
Gaol Street	C2		
Green Street	C3		
Grenfell Road	C3		
Greyfriars Avenue	A3		
Greyfriars Bridge	B2		
Grove Road	C3		
Harold Street	C3		
High Street	B2		
High Town	B2		
King Street	B2		
Kyrle Street	B2		
Maylord Street	B2		
Mill Street	C3		
Monkmoor Street	C1		
Moorfield Street	A1		
Moor Street	B1		
Mostyn Street	A1		
Nelson Street	C3		
Newmarket Street	B1		
Park Street	C3		
Penhaligon Way	A1		
Plough Lane	A1		
Portland Street	A1		
Quay Street	B2		
Ryeland Street	A2		
St. Guthiac Street	C2		
St. James Road	C3		
St. Martin's Avenue	B3		
St. Martin's Street	B3		
St. Owen Street	C2		
Station Approach	C1		
Station Road	A2		
Stonebow Road	C1		
Symonds Street	C2		
The Atrium	B1		
Turner Street	C3		
Union Street	B2		
Union Walk	C1		

HEREFORD

Appears on main map page 145

Leeds street map on pages 40-41

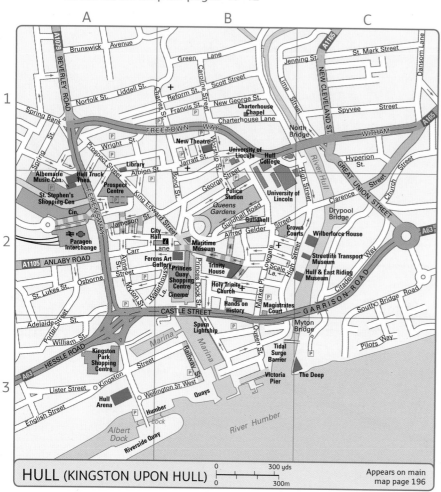

HULL (KINGSTON UPON HULL)

0 ____ 300 yds
0 ____ 300m

Appears on main map page 196

Tourist Information Centre: Hull City Hall, 1 Paragon Street
Tel: 01482 223559

Adelaide Street	A3
Albion Street	A2
Alfred Gelder Street	B2
Anlaby Road	A2
Anne Street	A2
Beverley Road	A1
Bond Street	B2
Brunswick Avenue	A1
Caroline Street	B1
Carr Lane	A2
Castle Street	B2
Charles Street	B1
Charterhouse Lane	B1
Church Street	C2
Citadel Way	C2
Clarence Street	C2
Cleveland Street	C1
Dansom Lane	C1
English Street	A3
Ferensway	A2
Francis Street	B1
Freetown Way	A1
Garrison Road	C2
George Street	B2
Great Union Street	C1
Green Lane	B1
Guildhall Road	B2
Hessle Road	A3
High Street	C1
Hyperion Street	C1
Jameson Street	A2
Jarratt Street	B1
Jenning Street	B1
King Edward Street	A2
Kingston Street	A3
Liddell Street	A1
Lime Street	B1
Lister Street	A3
Lowgate	B2
Market Place	B2
Myton Street	A2
New Cleveland Street	C1
New George Street	B1
Norfolk Street	A1
North Bridge	B1
Osborne Street	A2
Pilots Way	C3
Porter Street	A3
Princes Dock Street	B2
Prospect Street	A1
Queen Street	B3
Reform Street	B1
St. Lukes Street	A2
St. Mark Street	C1
Scale Lane	B2
Scott Street	B1
Scott Street Bridge	B1
South Bridge Road	C2
Spring Bank	A1
Spring Street	A2
Spyvee Street	C1
Waterhouse Lane	A2
Wellington Street West	A3
William Street	A3
Witham	C1
Worship Street	B1
Wright Street	A1

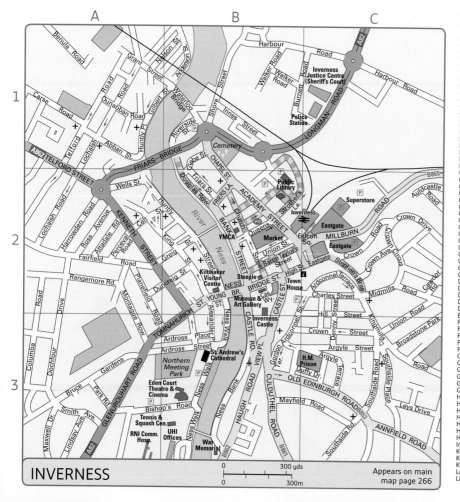

INVERNESS

0 ____ 300 yds
0 ____ 300m

Appears on main map page 266

Tourist Information Centre: 36 High Street
Tel: 01463 252401

Abban Street	A1	Lochalsh Road	A1
Academy Street	B2	Longman Road	C1
Alexander Place	B2	Maxwell Drive	A3
Anderson Street	B1	Mayfield Road	B3
Ardconnel Street	B3	Midmills Road	C2
Ardconnel Terrace	C2	Millburn Road	C2
Ardross Place	B3	Montague Row	A2
Ardross Street	B3	Muirfield Road	C3
Argyle Street	C3	Nelson Street	A1
Argyle Terrace	C3	Ness Bank	B3
Attadale Road	A2	Ness Bridge	B2
Auldcastle Road	C2	Ness Walk	B3
Bank Street	B2	Old Edinburgh Road	B3
Baron Taylor's Street	B2	Park Road	A3
Benula Road	A1	Perceval Road	A2
Bishop's Road	A3	Planefield Road	A2
Bridge Street	B2	Queensgate	B2
Broadstone Park	C3	Rangemore Road	A2
Bruce Gardens	A3	Riverside Street	B1
Burnett Road	C1	Ross Avenue	A2
Carse Road	A1	Shore Street	B1
Castle Road	B2	Smith Avenue	A3
Castle Street	B2	Southside Place	C3
Castle Wynd	B2	Southside Road	C3
Cawdor Road	C2	Stephen's Brae	C2
Celt Street	A2	Strother's Lane	B2
Chapel Street	B1	Telford Road	A1
Charles Street	C2	Telford Street	A1
Church Street	B2	Tomnahurich Street	A3
Columba Road	A3	Union Road	C3
Crown Avenue	C2	Union Street	B2
Crown Circus	C2	View Place	B3
Crown Drive	C2	Walker Road	B1
Crown Road	C2	Waterloo Bridge	B1
Crown Street	C3	Wells Street	A2
Culduthel Road	B3	Young Street	B2
Denny Street	C3		
Dochfour Drive	A3		
Douglas Row	B1		
Duffy Drive	B3		
Duncraig Street	A2		
Eastgate	C2		
Fairfield Road	A2		
Falcon Square	B2		
Friars Bridge	A1		
Friars Lane	B2		
Friars Street	B2		
Gilbert Street	A1		
Glebe Street	B1		
Glen Urquhart Road	A3		
Gordon Terrace	B3		
Grant Street	A1		
Greig Street	A2		
Harbour Road	B1		
Harrowden Road	A2		
Haugh Road	B3		
High Street	B2		
Hill Street	C2		
Huntly Place	A1		
Huntly Street	A2		
Innes Street	B1		
Kenneth Street	A2		
Kingsmills Road	C2		
King Street	A2		
Leys Drive	C3		
Lindsay Avenue	A3		

Liverpool street map on pages 42-43, London street map on pages 44-45

LEICESTER

Tourist Information Centre: 51 Gallowtree Gate
Tel: 0116 299 4444

Abbey Street	B1	Market Place South	B2
Albion Street	B2	Market Street	B2
All Saints Road	A2	Mill Lane	A3
Aylestone Road	B3	Millstone Lane	B2
Bassett Street	A1	Montreal Road	C1
Bath Lane	A2	Morledge Street	C2
Bedford Street North	C1	Narborough Road	A3
Belgrave Gate	B1	Narborough Road North	A2
Bell Lane	C1	Nelson Street	C3
Belvoir Street	B2	Newarke Close	A3
Braunstone Gate	A2	Newarke Street	B2
Burgess Street	B1	Northgate Street	A1
Burleys Way	B1	Ottawa Road	C1
Byron Street	B1	Oxford Street	B2
Cank Street	B2	Pasture Lane	A1
Castle Street	A2	Peacock Lane	B2
Charles Street	C2	Pocklingtons Walk	B2
Christow Street	C1	Prebend Street	C3
Church Gate	B1	Princess Road East	C3
Clarence Street	B1	Pringle Street	A1
Clyde Street	C1	Queen Street	B3
College Street	C2	Regent Road	C3
Colton Street	C2	Regent Street	C3
Conduit Street	C2	Repton Street	A1
Crafton Street East	C1	Rutland Street	C2
Cravan Street	A1	Samuel Street	C2
De Montfort Street	C3	Sanvey Gare	A1
Deacon Street	B3	Saxby Street	C3
Dryden Street	B1	Slater Street	A1
Duns Lane	A2	Soar Lane	A1
Dunton Street	A1	South Albion Street	C2
Eastern Boulevard	A3	Southampton Street	C2
Friar Lane	B2	Sparkenhoe Street	C2
Friday Street	B1	St. George Street	C2
Frog Island	A1	St. George's Way	C2
Gallowtree Gate	B2	St. John's Street	B1
Gaul Street	A3	St. Margaret's Way	A1
Glebe Street	C2	St. Matthew's Way	C1
Gotham Street	C3	St. Nicholas Circle	A2
Granby Street	B2	Swain Street	C2
Grange Lane	B3	Swan Street	A1
Grasmere Street	A3	Taylor Road	C1
Great Central Street	A1	Thames Street	B1
Halford Street	B2	The Gateway	A3
Havelock Street	B3	The Newarke	A2
Haymarket	B1	Tigers Way	B3
High Street	B2	Tower Street	B3
Highcross Street	A1	Tudor Road	A1
Hobart Street	C2	Ullswater Street	A3
Horsfair Street	B2	University Road	C3
Humberstone Gate	B2	Upperton Road	A3
Humberstone Road	C1	Vaughan Way	A1
Infirmary Road	B3	Vestry Street	C2
Jarrom Street	A3	Walnut Street	A3
Jarvis Street	A2	Waterloo Way	C3
Kamloops Crescent	C1	Welford Road	B2
Kent Street	C1	Wellington Street	B2
King Richard's Road	A2	West Street	B2
King Street	B2	Western Boulevard	A3
Lancaster Road	B3	Western Road	A3
Lee Street	B1	Wharf Street North	C1
Lincoln Street	C2	Wharf Street South	C1
London Road	C3	Wilberforce Road	A3
Loseby Lane	B2	Windermere Street	A3
Lower Brown Street	B2	Woodboy Street	B1
Manitoba Road	C1	Yeoman Street	B2
Mansfield Street	B1	York Road	B2

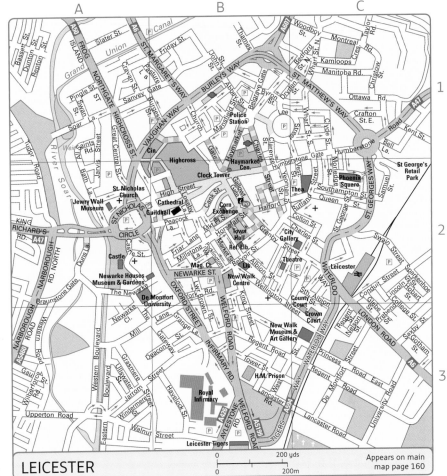

LEICESTER

Appears on main map page 160

LINCOLN

Tourist Information Centre: 9 Castle Hill
Tel: 01522 545458

Alexandra Terrace	A2	Spa Road	C3
Bagholme Road	C2	St. Anne's Road	C2
Bailgate	B1	St. Giles Avenue	C1
Beaumont Fee	B2	St. Mark Street	B3
Beevor Street	A3	St. Mary's Street	B3
Brayford Way	A3	St. Rumbold Street	B2
Brayford Wharf North	A2	Stamp End	C3
Broadgate	B2	Steep Hill	B2
Broadway	B1	The Avenue	A2
Bruce Road	C1	Tritton Road	A3
Burton Road	A1	Union Row	B2
Canwick Road	B3	Upper Lindum Street	C2
Carholme Road	A2	Upper Long Leys Road	A1
Carline Road	A1	Vere Street	B1
Carr Street	A2	Vine Street	C2
Cheviot Street	C2	Waterside North	B3
Church Lane	B1	Waterside South	B3
Clasketgate	B2	West Parade	A2
Croft Street	B2	Westgate	B1
Cross Street	B3	Wigford Way	A2
Curle Avenue	C1	Wilson Street	A1
Drury Lane	B2	Winn Street	C2
East Gate	B2	Wragby Road	C2
Firth Road	A3	Yarborough Road	A1
George Street	C3		
Great Northern Terrace	B3		
Greetwell Close	C1		
Greetwell Road	C2		
Gresham Street	A2		
Hampton Street	A2		
Harvey Street	A2		
High Street	B3		
John Street	C2		
Langworthgate	B1		
Lee Road	C1		
Lindum Road	B2		
Lindum Terrace	C2		
Long Leys Road	A1		
Mainwaring Road	C1		
Mill Road	A1		
Milman Road	C2		
Monks Road	C2		
Monson Street	B3		
Moor Street	A2		
Mount Street	A1		
Nettleham Road	B1		
Newland	A2		
Newland Street West	A2		
Newport	B1		
Northgate	B1		
Orchard Street	A2		
Pelham Bridge	B3		
Portland Street	B3		
Portland Street	B3		
Pottergate	B2		
Queensway	B1		
Rasen Lane	B1		
Richmond Road	A2		
Ripon Street	B3		
Rope Walk	A3		
Rosemary Lane	B2		
Ruskin Avenue	C1		
Saltergate	B2		
Sewell Road	C2		
Silver Street	B2		
Sincil Bank	B3		

LINCOLN

Appears on main map page 187

Middlesbrough   Milton Keynes

Manchester street map on pages 46-47

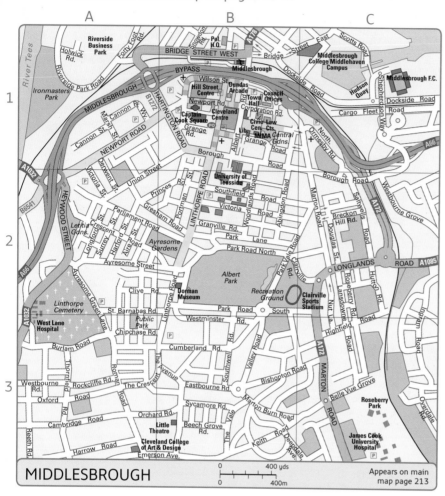

MIDDLESBROUGH

Abingdon Road	B2
Aire Street	A2
Albert Road	B1
Ayresome Green Lane	A2
Ayresome Street	A2
Beech Grove Road	B3
Belle Vue Grove	C3
Bishopton Road	B3
Borough Road	B1/C3
Breckon Hill Road	C2
Bridge Street East	B1
Bridge Street West	B1
Burlam Road	A3
Cambridge Road	A3
Cannon Park Way	A1
Cannon Street	A1
Cargo Fleet Road	C1
Chipchase Road	A3
Clairville Road	B2
Clive Road	A2
Corporation Road	B1
Crescent Road	A2
Cumberland Road	B3
Deepdale Avenue	B3
Derwent Street	A1
Dockside Road	B1/C1
Douglas Street	C2
Eastbourne Road	B3
Emerson Avenue	B3
Forty Foot Road	A1
Grange Road	B1
Granville Road	B2
Gresham Road	A2
Harford Street	A2
Harrow Road	A3
Hartington Road	A1
Heywood Street	A2
Highfield Road	C3
Holwick Road	A1
Hudson Quay	C1
Hutton Road	C2
Ingram Road	C2
Keith Road	B3
Lansdowne Road	C2
Linthorpe Road	B3
Longford Street	A2
Longlands Road	C2
Marsh Street	A1
Marton Burn Road	B3
Marton Road	C2/C3
Newport Road	A1/B1
North Ormesby Road	C1
Nut Lane	C2
Orchard Road	A3
Overdale Road	C3
Oxford Road	A3
Park Lane	B2
Park Road North	B2
Park Road South	B2
Park Vale Road	B2
Parliament Road	A2
Portman Street	B2
Princes Road	A2
Reeth Road	A3
Riverside Park Road	A1
Rockcliffe Road	A3

Roman Road	A3
Roseberry Road	C2
Saltwells Road	C2
Scotts Road	C1
Sheperdson Way	C1
Snowdon Road	B1
Southfield Road	B2
Southwell Road	B3
St. Barnabas Road	A2
Surrey Street	A2
Sycamore Road	B3
The Avenue	B3
The Crescent	A3
The Vale	B3
Thornfield Road	A3
Union Street	A2
Valley Road	B3
Victoria Road	B2
Victoria Street	A1
Westbourne Grove	C2
Westbourne Road	A3
Westminster Road	B3
Wilson Street	B1
Woodlands Road	B2

Appears on main map page 213

MILTON KEYNES

Tourist Information Centre: Silbury Arcade
Tel: 01908 688293

Avebury Boulevard	B2/C1
Boycott Avenue	B3
Bradwell Common Boulevard	A1
Bradwell Road	A3
Burnham Drive	A1
Chaffron Way	C3
Childs Way	A3/C2
Conniburrow Boulevard	B1
Dansteed Way	A1
Deltic Avenue	A2
Elder Gate	A2
Evans Gate	B3
Fennel Drive	B1
Fishermead Boulevard	C2
Fulwoods Drive	C3
Gibsons Green	A1
Glovers Lane	A1
Grafton Gate	A2
Grafton Street	A1/B3
Gurnards Avenue	C2
Hampstead Gate	A1
Harrier Drive	C3
Leys Road	A3
Lloyds	C3
Mallow Gate	B1
Marlborough Street	C1
Mayditch Place	A1
Midsummer Boulevard	B2/C1
Oldbrook Boulevard	B3
Patriot Drive	A2
Pentewan Gate	C2
Portway	B2/C1
Precedent Drive	A2
Quinton Drive	A1
Redland Drive	A3
Saxon Gate	B2
Saxon Street	B1/C3
Secklow Gate	C1
Silbury Boulevard	B2/C1
Skeldon Gate	C1
Snowdon Drive	B3
Stainton Drive	A1
Strudwick Drive	C3
Trueman Place	C3
Underwood Place	B3
Witan Gate	B2

MILTON KEYNES

Appears on main map page 149

Newcastle upon Tyne

Albert Street	C2
Ancrum Street	A1
Argyle Street	C2
Askew Road	C3
Barrack Road	A1
Barras Bridge	B1
Bath Lane	A2
Bigg Market	B2
Blackett Street	B2
Byron Street	C1
Chester Street	C1
City Road	C2
Claremont Road	B1
Clarence Street	C2
Clayton Road	B2
Clayton Street West	A3
Corporation Street	A2
Coulthards Lane	C3
Crawhall Road	C2
Dean Street	B2
Diana Street	A2
Elswick East Terrace	A3
Eskdale Terrace	C1
Essex Close	A3
Falconar Street	C1
Forth Banks	B3
Forth Street	A3
Gallowgate	A3
Gateshead Highway	C3
George Street	A3
Gibson Street	C2
Grainger Street	B2
Grantham Road	C1
Grey Street	B2
Hanover Street	B3
Hawks Road	C3
Helmsley Road	C1
High Street	C3
Hillgate	C3
Howard Street	C2
Hunters Road	A1
Ivy Close	A3
Jesmond Road	C1
Jesmond Road West	B1
John Dobson Street	B2
Kelvin Grove	C1
Kyle Close	A3
Lambton Street	C3
Mansfield Street	A2
Maple Street	A3
Maple Terrace	A3
Market Street	B2
Melbourne Street	C2
Mill Road	C3
Neville Street	A3
New Bridge Street	C2
Newgate Street	B2
Northumberland Road	B2
Northumberland Street	B1
Oakwellgate	C3
Orchard Street	B3
Oxnam Crescent	A1
Park Terrace	B1
Percy Street	B2
Pilgrim Street	B2
Pipewellgate	B3
Pitt Street	A2
Portland Road	C1
Portland Terrace	C1
Pottery Lane	A3
Quarryfield Road	C3
Quayside	C3
Queen Victoria Road	B1
Railway Street	A3
Redheugh Bridge	A3
Richardson Road	A1
Rye Hill	A3
St. James Boulevard	A3
St. Mary's Bridge	B1
St. Thomas Street	B1
Sandyford Road	B1/C1
Scotswood Road	A3
Skinnerburn Road	B3
South Shore Road	C3
Stanhope Street	A2
Starbeck Avenue	C1
Stodart Street	C1
Stowell Street	A2
Strawberry Place	A2
Summerhill Grove	A2
Swing Bridge	B3
The Close	C3
Tyne Bridge	C3
Union Street	C2
Warwick Street	C1
Wellington Street	A2
West Street	C3
Westgate Road	A2
Westmorland Road	A3
Windsor Terrace	B1
York Street	A2

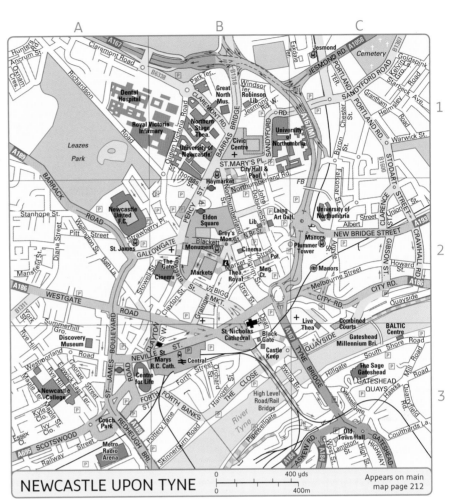

NEWCASTLE UPON TYNE

0 ——— 400 yds
0 ——— 400m

Appears on main
map page 212

Norwich

Tourist Information Centre: The Forum, Millennium Plain
Tel: 01603 213999

Albion Way	C3
All Saints Green	B3
Ashby Street	B3
Bakers Road	A1
Bank Plain	B2
Barker Street	A1
Barn Road	A2
Barrack Street	B1
Bedford Street	B2
Ber Street	B3
Bethel Street	A2
Bishopbridge Road	C2
Bishopgate	C2
Botolph Street	B1
Brazen Gate	B3
Britannia Road	C1
Brunswick Road	A3
Bullclose Road	B1
Canary Way	C3
Carrow Hill	C3
Carrow Road	C3
Castle Meadow	B2
Chapel Field Road	A2
Chapelfield North	A2
City Road	B3
Clarence Road	C3
Colegate	B1
Coslany Street	A2
Cowgate	B1
Dereham Road	A2
Duke Street	B1
Earlham Road	A2
Edward Street	B1
Elm Hill	B2
Fishergate	B1
Gas Hill	C1
Grapes Hill	A2
Grove Avenue	A3
Grove Road	A3
Grove Walk	A3
Gurney Road	C1
Hall Road	B3
Hardy Road	C3
Heathgate	C1
Heigham Street	A1
Horns Lane	B3
Ipswich Road	A3
Ketts Hill	C1
King Street	B3
Koblenz Avenue	C3
Lothian Street	A1
Lower Clarence Road	C2
Magdalen Street	B1
Magpie Road	B1
Market Avenue	B2
Marlborough Road	B1
Mountergate	B2
Mousehold Street	C1
Newmarket Road	A3
Newmarket Street	A3
Oak Street	A1
Orchard Street	A1
Palace Street	B2
Pitt Street	B1
Pottergate	A2
Prince of Wales Road	B2
Queens Road	B3
Rampant Horse Street	B2
Recorder Road	C2
Red Lion Street	B2
Riverside	C3
Riverside Road	C2
Rosary Road	C2
Rose Lane	B2
Rouen Road	B3
Rupert Street	A3
Russell Street	A1
St. Andrew's Street	B2
St. Augustine's Street	A1
St. Benedict's Street	A2
St. Crispin's Road	A1
St. Faiths Lane	B2
St. George's Street	B1
St. Giles Street	A2
St. James Close	C1
St. Leonards Road	C2
St. Martin's Road	A1
St. Stephen's Road	A3
St. Stephen's Street	B3
Silver Road	B1
Silver Street	B1
Southwell Road	B3
Surrey Street	B3
Sussex Street	A1
Theatre Street	A2
Thorn Lane	B3
Thorpe Road	C2
Tombland	B2
Trinity Street	A3
Trory Street	A2
Union Street	A3
Unthank Road	A3
Vauxhall Street	A3
Victoria Street	A3
Wensum Street	B1
Wessex Street	A3
Westwick Street	A1
Wherry Road	C3
Whitefriars	B1
Wodehouse Street	B1
York Street	A3

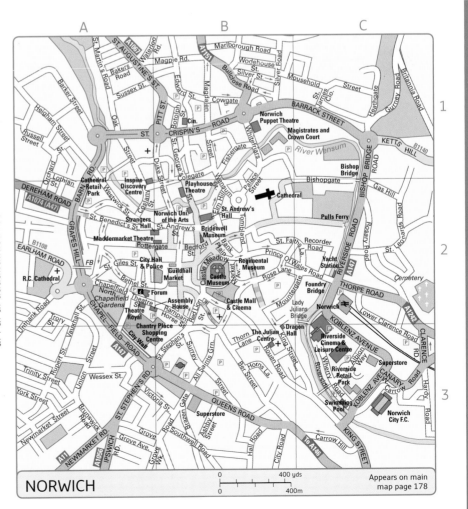

NORWICH

0 ——— 400 yds
0 ——— 400m

Appears on main
map page 178

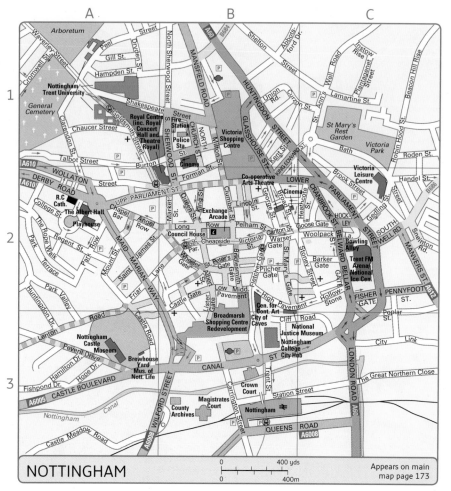

NOTTINGHAM

0   400 yds
0   400m

Appears on main
map page 173

Tourist Information Centre: 1-4 Smithy Row
Tel: 0844 477 5678

Abbotsford Drive	B1
Albert Street	B2
Angel Row	A2
Barker Gate	C2
Bath Street	C1
Beacon Hill Rise	C1
Bellar Gate	C2
Belward Street	C2
Bridlesmith Gate	B2
Broad Street	B2
Brook Street	C1
Burton Street	A1
Canal Street	B3
Carlton Street	B2
Carrington Street	B3
Castle Boulevard	A3
Castle Gate	B2
Castle Meadow Road	A3
Castle Road	A3
Chapel Bar	A2
Chaucer Street	A1
Cheapside	B2
City Link	C3
Clarendon Street	A1
Cliff Road	B3
Clumber Street	B2
College Street	A2
Cranbrook Street	C2
Cromwell Street	A1
Curzon Street	B1
Derby Road	A2
Dryden Street	A1
Fisher Gate	C2
Fishpond Drive	A3
Fletcher Gate	B2
Forman Street	B2
Friar Lane	A2
Gedling Street	C2
George Street	B2
Gill Street	A1
Glasshouse Street	B1
Goldsmith Street	A1
Goose Gate	C2
Hamilton Drive	A3
Hampden Street	A1
Handel Street	C2
Heathcote Street	B2
High Pavement	B2
Hockley	C2
Hollowstone	C2
Hope Drive	A3
Huntingdon Drive	A2
Huntingdon Street	B1
Instow Rise	C1
Kent Street	B1
King Edward Street	B2
King Street	B2
Lamartine Street	C1
Lenton Road	A3
Lincoln Street	B2
Lister Gate	B3
London Road	C3
Long Row	B2
Low Pavement	B2
Lower Parliament Street	B2
Maid Marian Way	A2
Mansfield Road	B1
Manvers Street	C2
Market Street	B2
Middle Pavement	B2
Milton Street	B1
Mount Street	A2
North Church Street	B1
North Sherwood Street	B1
Park Row	A2
Park Terrace	A2
Park Valley	A2
Peel Street	A1
Pelham Street	B2
Pennyfoot Street	C2
Peveril Drive	A3
Pilcher Gate	B2
Plantagenet Street	C1
Poplar Street	C2
Queens Road	B3
Queen Street	B2
Regent Street	A2
Robin Hood Street	C1
Roden Street	C1
St. Ann's Well Road	C1
St. James Street	A2
St. Mary's Gate	B2
St. Peter's Gate	B2
Shakespeare Street	A1
Shelton Street	B1
Sneinton Road	C2
South Parade	B2
South Sherwood Street	B1
Southwell Road	C2
Station Street	B3
Stoney Street	C2
Talbot Street	A1
The Great Northern Close	C3
The Rope Walk	A2
Trent Street	B3
Union Road	B1
Upper Parliament Street	A2
Victoria Street	B2
Warser Gate	B2
Waverley Street	A1
Wheeler Gate	B2
Wilford Street	A3
Wollaton Street	A2
Woolpack Lane	C2

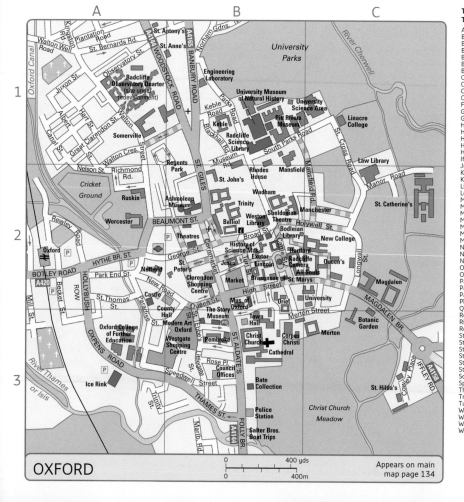

OXFORD

0   400 yds
0   400m

Appears on main
map page 134

Tourist Information Centre: 15-16 Broad Street
Tel: 01865 686430

Albert Street	A1
Banbury Road	B1
Beaumont Street	A2
Becket Street	A2
Blackhall Road	B1
Botley Road	A2
Broad Street	B2
Canal Street	A1
Cattle Street	B2
Cornmarket	B2
Cowley Place	C3
Folly Bridge	B3
George Street	A2
Great Clarendon Street	A1
Hart Street	A1
High Street	B2
Hollybush Row	A2
Holywell Street	B2
Hythe Bridge Street	A2
Iffley Road	C3
Juxon Street	A1
Keble Road	B1
Kingston Road	A1
Littlegate Street	B3
Longwall Street	C2
Magdalen Bridge	C2
Manor Road	C2
Mansfield Road	C1
Marlborough Road	B3
Merton Street	B3
Mill Street	A2
Museum Road	B1
Nelson Street	A2
New Road	A2
Norham Gardens	B1
Observatory Street	A1
Oxpens Road	A3
Paradise Street	A2
Park End Street	A2
Parks Road	B1
Plantation Road	A1
Queen Street	B2
Rewley Road	A2
Richmond Road	A2
Rose Place	B3
St. Aldate's	B3
St. Bernards Road	A1
St. Cross Road	C1
St. Ebbe's Street	B3
St. Giles	B1
St. Thomas' Street	A2
South Parks Road	B1
Speedwell Street	B3
Thames Street	B3
Trinity Street	A3
Turl Street	B2
Walton Crescent	A1
Walton Street	A1
Walton Well Road	A1
Woodstock Road	A1

PERTH

Tourist Information Centre: 45 High Street
Tel: 01738 450600

Abbot Crescent	A3
Abbot Street	A3
Albany Terrace	A1
Atholl Street	B1
Balhousie Street	B1
Barossa Place	B1
Barossa Street	B1
Barrack Street	B1
Bowerswell Road	C2
Caledonian Road	B2
Canal Street	B2
Cavendish Avenue	A3
Charlotte Street	B1
Clyde Place	A3
Darnhall Drive	A3
Dundee Road	C2
Dunkeld Road	A1
Edinburgh Road	B3
Feus Road	A1
Friar Street	A3
George Street	C2
Glasgow Road	A2
Glover Street	A2
Gowrie Street	C1
Gray Street	A2
Graybank Road	A2
Hay Street	B1
High Street	B2
Isla Road	C1
Jeanfield Road	A2
King's Place	B3
King James Place	B3
King Street	B2
Kinnoull Street	B1
Kinnoull Terrace	C2
Knowelea Place	A3
Leonard Street	B2
Lochie Brae	C1
Long Causeway	A1
Main Street	C1
Manse Road	C2
Marshall Place	B3
Melville Street	B1
Mill Street	B2
Milne Street	B2
Murray Crescent	A3
Needless Road	A3
New Row	B2
North Methven Street	B1
Park Place	A3
Perth Bridge	C1
Pickletullum Road	A2
Pitcullen Terrace	C1
Pitheavlis Crescent	A3
Princes Street	C3
Priory Place	B3
Queen Street	A3
Queens Bridge	C2
Raeburn Park	A3
Riggs Road	A2
Rose Crescent	A2
Rose Terrace	B1
St. Catherines Road	A1
St. John Street	C2
St. Leonard's Bank	B3
Scott Street	B2
Shore Road	C3
South Methven Street	B2
South Street	B2
Strathmore Street	C1
Stuart Avenue	A3
Tay Street	C2
Victoria Street	B2
Watergate	C2
Whitefriars Crescent	A2
Whitefriars Street	A2
William Street	B2
Wilson Street	A3
Young Street	A3
York Place	A2

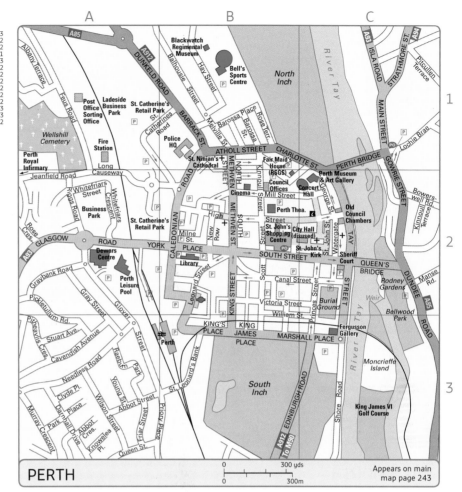

PERTH

0   300 yds
0   300m

Appears on main
map page 243

PLYMOUTH

Tourist Information Centre: Plymouth Mayflower Centre,
3-5 The Barbican   Tel: 01752 306330

Alexandra Road	C1
Alma Road	A1
Armada Street	B2
Armada Way	B2
Ashford Road	C1
Barbican Approach	C3
Beaumont Road	C2
Beechwood Avenue	B1
Belgrave Road	C1
Bretonside	B2
Buckwell Street	B3
Camden Street	B2
Cattledown Road	C3
Cecil Street	A2
Central Park Avenue	A1
Charles Street	B2
Citadel Road	A3
Clarence Place	A2
Cliff Road	A3
Clifton Place	B1
Clovelly Road	C3
Cobourg Street	B2
Coleridge Road	C1
Connaught Avenue	C1
Cornwall Street	B2
Dale Road	B1
De-La-Hay Avenue	A1
Desborough Road	C2
Drake Circus	B2
East Street	A3
Ebrington Street	B2
Elliot Street	A3
Embankment Road	C2
Exeter Street	B2
Ford Park Road	B1
Furzehill Road	C1
Gdynia Way	C3
Glen Park Avenue	B1
Grand Parade	A3
Greenbank Avenue	C2
Greenbank Road	C1
Grenville Road	C2
Harwell Street	A2
Hill Park Crescent	B1
Hoe Road	B3
Houndiscombe Road	B1
James Street	B2
King Street	A2
Knighton Road	C2
Lipson Hill	C1
Lipson Road	C2
Lisson Grove	C1
Lockyer Street	B3
Looe Street	B2
Madeira Road	B3
Manor Road	A2
Martin Street	A3
Mayflower Street	B2
Millbay Road	A3
Mount Gould Road	C1
Mutley Plain	B1
New George Street	A2
North Cross	B2
North Hill	B2
North Road East	B2
North Road West	A2
North Street	B2
Notte Street	B3
Oxford Street	A2
Pentillie Road	B1
Ponsonby Road	A1
Princess Street	B3
Queen's Road	C1
Royal Parade	B2
Salisbury Road	C2
Saltash Road	A1
Seaton Avenue	B1
Seymour Avenue	C2
Southside Street	B3
Stoke Road	A2
Stuart Road	A1
Sutton Road	C2
Sydney Street	A2
Teats Hill Road	C3
The Crescent	A3
Tothill Avenue	C2
Tothill Road	C2
Union Street	A2
Vauxhall Street	B3
West Hoe Road	A3
Western Approach	A2
Whittington Street	A1
Wilton Street	A2
Wyndham Street	A2

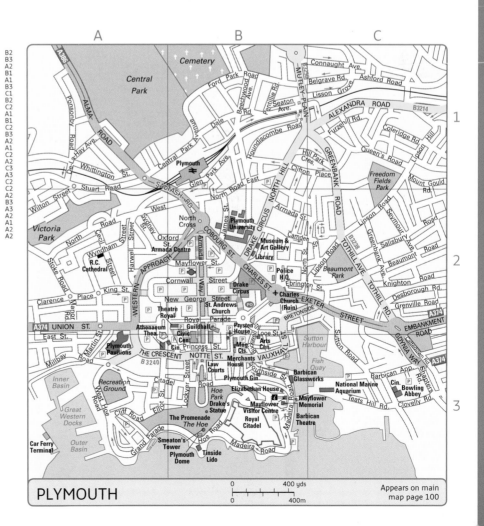

PLYMOUTH

0   400 yds
0   400m

Appears on main
map page 100

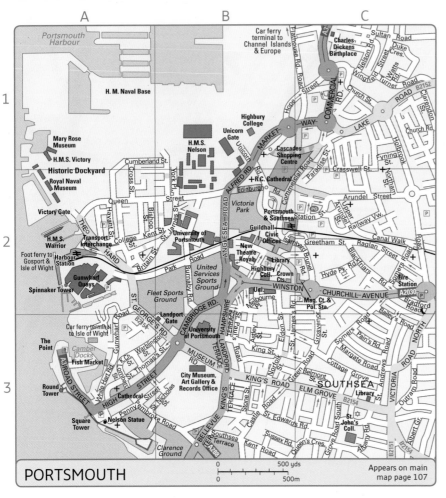

PORTSMOUTH

Albany Road	C3	Penny Street	A3
Albert Grove	C3	Queen's Crescent	C3
Alfred Road	B2	Queen Street	A2
Anglesea Road	B2	Raglan Street	C2
Arundel Street	C2	Railway View	C2
Astley Street	B3	St. Andrews Road	C3
Bailey's Road	C2	St. Edward's Road	B3
Bellevue Terrace	B3	St. George's Road	A2
Belmont Street	B3	St. James Road	B3
Bishop Street	A1	St. James Street	B3
Blackfriars Road	C2	St. Paul's Road	B3
Bradford Road	A2	St. Thomas's Street	A3
Britain Street	A2	Somers Road	C2
Broad Street	A3	Southsea Terrace	B3
Burnaby Road	B2	Station Street	C2
Cambridge Road	B3	Stone Street	B3
Canal Walk	C2	Sultan Road	C1
Castle Road	B3	Sussex Street	B3
Church Road	C1	The Hard	A2
Church Street	C1	Turner Road	C1
Clarendon Street	C1	Unicorn Road	B1
College Street	A2	Upper Arundel Street	C2
Commercial Road	B2	Victoria Road North	C3
Cottage Grove	C3	Warblington Street	A3
Crasswell Street	C1	Watts Road	C1
Cross Street	A1	White Hart Road	A3
Cumberland Street	A1	Wingfield Street	C1
Duke Crescent	C1	Winston Churchill Avenue	B2
Edinburgh Road	B2	York Place	B2
Eldon Street	B3		
Elm Grove	C3		
Flathouse Road	C1		
Fyning Street	C1		
Green Road	B3		
Greetham Street	C2		
Grosvenor Street	C3		
Grove Road South	C3		
Gunwharf Road	A3		
Hampshire Terrace	A2		
Havant Street	A2		
High Street	A3		
Holbrook Road	C1		
Hope Street	B1		
Hyde Park Road	C2		
Isambard Brunel Road	B2		
Kent Road	B3		
Kent Street	A1		
King Charles Street	A3		
King's Road	B3		
King's Terrace	B3		
King Street	B3		
Lake Road	C1		
Landport Terrace	B3		
Lombard Street	A3		
Margate Road	C3		
Market Way	B1		
Melbourne Place	B2		
Museum Road	B3		
Nelson Road	C1		
Norfolk Street	B3		
Northam Street	C2		
Outram Road	C3		
Pain's Road	C3		
Paradise Street	C1		
Park Road	B2		
Pembroke Road	A3		

Appears on main map page 107

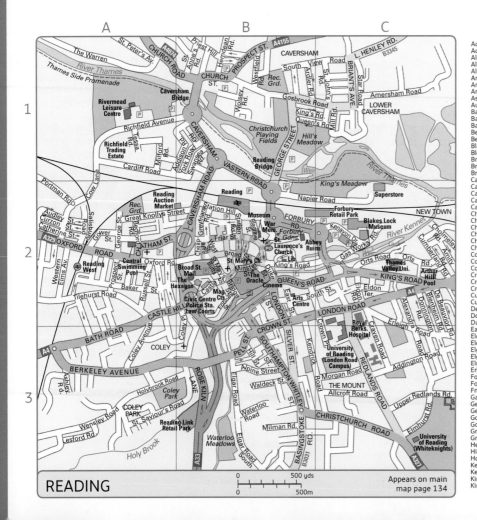

READING

Addington Road	C3	Lesford Road	A3
Addison Road	A1	London Road	C2
Alexandra Road	C2	London Street	B2
Allcroft Road	C3	Lower Henley Road	C1
Alpine Street	B3	Mill Road	C1
Amersham Road	C1	Milford Road	A1
Amity Road	A2	Milman Road	B3
Ardler Road	B1	Minster Street	B2
Ashley Road	A3	Morgan Road	C3
Audley Street	A2	Napier Road	B2
Baker Street	A2	Orts Road	C2
Basingstoke Road	B3	Oxford Road	A2
Bath Road	A3	Pell Street	B3
Bedford Road	A2	Portman Road	A1
Berkeley Avenue	A3	Priest Hill	B1
Blagrave Street	B2	Prospect Street *Caversham*	B1
Blenheim Road	C2	Prospect Street *Reading*	A2
Briant's Avenue	C1	Queen's Road *Caversham*	B1
Bridge Street	B2	Queen's Road *Reading*	B2
Broad Street	B2	Richfield Avenue	A1
Cardiff Road	A1	Rose Kiln Lane	B3
Castle Hill	A2	Russell Street	A2
Castle Street	B2	St. Anne's Road	B1
Catherine Street	A2	St. John's Road	C1
Caversham Road	A2	St. Mary's Butts	B2
Chatham Street	A2	St. Peters Avenue	A1
Cheapside	B2	St. Saviours Road	A3
Cholmeley Road	C2	Silver Street	B3
Christchurch Road	C3	South Street	B2
Church Road	A1	Southampton Street	B3
Church Street	B2	South View Road	B1
Coley Avenue	A3	Star Road	C1
Coley Place	B2	Station Hill	B2
Cow Lane	A2	Station Road	B2
Craven Road	C2	Swansea Road	B1
Crown Place	C2	Tessa Road	A1
Crown Street	B3	The Warren	A1
Cumberland Road	C2	Tilehurst Road	A2
Curzon Street	A2	Upper Redlands Road	C3
De Beauvoir Road	C2	Vastern Road	B1
Donnington Road	B2	Waldelk Street	B3
Duke Street	B2	Waterloo Road	B3
East Street	B2	Wensley Road	A3
Eldon Road	B3	Western Elms Avenue	A2
Eldon Terrace	C2	Westfield Road	B1
Elgar Road	B3	West Street	B2
Elgar Road South	B3	Whitley Street	B3
Elmhurst Road	C2	Wolsey Road	B1
Erleigh Road	C2	York Road	B1
Fobney Street	B2		
Forbury Road	B2		
Friar Street	B2		
Gas Work Road	C2		
George Street *Caversham*	B1		
George Street *Reading*	A2		
Gosbrook Road	B1		
Gower Street	A2		
Great Knollys Street	A2		
Greyfriars Road	B2		
Hemdean Road	B1		
Hill Street	B3		
Holybrook Road	A3		
Kenavon Drive	C2		
Kendrick Road	B3		
King's Road *Caversham*	B1		
King's Road *Reading*	B2		

Appears on main map page 134

Tourist Information Centre: Fish Row
Tel: 01722 342860

Albany Road	B1	Salt Lane	B2
Ashley Road	A1	Scots Lane	B2
Avon Terrace	A1	Silver Street	B2
Barnard Street	C2	Southampton Road	C3
Bedwin Street	B1	Swaynes Close	B1
Belle Vue Road	B1	Tollgate Road	C2
Bishops Walk	B3	Trinity Street	C2
Blackfriars Way	C3	Wain-a-long Road	C1
Blue Boar Row	B2	West Walk	B3
Bourne Avenue	C1	Wilton Road	A1
Bourne Hill	C1	Winchester Street	B2
Bridge Street	B2	Windsor Road	A2
Brown Street	B2	Wyndham Road	B1
Butcher Row	B2	York Road	A1
Carmelite Way	B3		
Castle Street	B1		
Catherine Street	B2		
Chipper Lane	B2		
Churchfields Road	A2		
Churchill Way East	C2		
Churchill Way North	B1		
Churchill Way South	C3		
Churchill Way West	A1		
Clifton Road	A1		
College Street	C1		
Crane Bridge Road	A2		
Crane Street	B3		
De Vaux Place	A1		
Devizes Road	A1		
Elm Grove Road	C2		
Endless Street	B1		
Estcourt Road	C1		
Exeter Street	B3		
Fairview Road	C1		
Fisherton Street	A2		
Fowlers Hill	C2		
Fowlers Road	C2		
Friary Lane	C3		
Gas Lane	A1		
Gigant Street	C2		
Greencroft Street	C1		
Hamilton Road	B1		
High Street	B2		
Ivy Street	B2		
Kelsey Road	C1		
Laverstock Road	C2		
Manor Road	C1		
Marsh Lane	A1		
Meadow Road	A1		
Milford Hill	C2		
Milford Street	B2		
Mill Road	A2		
Millstream Approach	B1		
Minster Street	B2		
New Canal	B2		
New Street	B2		
North Walk	B3		
Park Street	C1		
Pennyfarthing Street	B2		
Queens Road	B1		
Rampart Road	C2		
Rollestone Street	B1		
St. Ann Street	C3		
St. John's Street	B2		
St. Marks Road	C1		
St. Paul's Road	A1		

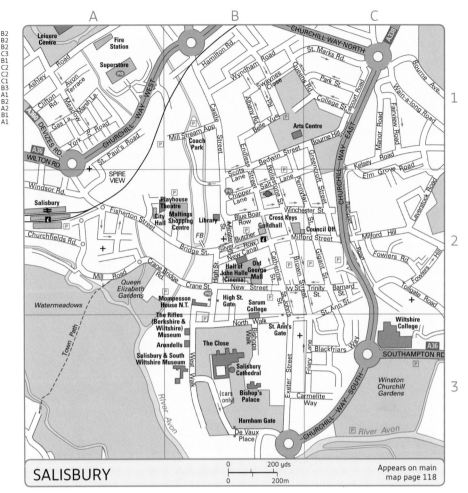

SALISBURY

0   200 yds
0   200m

Appears on main
map page 118

Tourist Information Centre: Brunswick Shopping Centre,
Unit 15a, Westborough Tel: 01723 383636

Aberdeen Walk	B2	Valley Bridge Road	B2
Albion Road	B3	Valley Road	A3
Ashville Avenue	A2	Vernon Road	B2
Avenue Road	A3	Victoria Park Mount	A1
Belmont Road	B3	Victoria Road	A3
Candler Street	A2	Victoria Street	B2
Castle Road	B2	West Street	B3
Chatsworth Gardens	A1	Westborough	A3
Columbus Ravine	A2	Westbourne Grove	B3
Commercial Street	A3	Westover Road	A3
Cross Street	B2	Westwood	A3
Dean Road	A2	Westwood Road	A3
Eastborough	B2	Weydale Avenue	A1
Esplanade	B3	Wykeham Street	A3
Falconers Rd	B2		
Falsgrave Road	A3		
Foreshore Road	B2		
Franklin Street	A2		
Friargate	B2		
Friarsway	B2		
Garfield Road	A2		
Gladstone Road	A2		
Gladstone Street	A2		
Gordon Street	A2		
Grosvenor Road	B3		
Highfield	A3		
Hoxton Road	A2		
Longwestgate	C2		
Manor Road	A2		
Marine Drive	C1		
Mayville Avenue	A2		
Moorland Road	A1		
New Queen Street	B1		
Newborough	B2		
North Marine Road	B1		
North Street	B2		
Northstead Manor Drive	A1		
Northway	A2		
Norwood Street	A2		
Oak Road	A3		
Peasholm Crescent	A1		
Peasholm Drive	A1		
Peasholm Road	A1		
Prince Of Wales Terrace	B3		
Princess Street	C2		
Prospect Road	A2		
Queen Street	B2		
Queen's Parade	B1		
Raleigh Street	A2		
Ramshill Road	B3		
Roscoe Street	A3		
Rothbury Street	A2		
Royal Albert Drive	B1		
Royal Avenue	B3		
Sandside	C2		
Seamer Road	A3		
St. James Road	A3		
St. John's Avenue	A3		
St. John's Road	A3		
St. Thomas Street	B2		
Tollergate	B1		
Trafalgar Road	A1		
Trafalgar Square	B1		
Trafalgar Street West	A2		
Trinity Road	A3		
Valley Bridge Parade	B3		

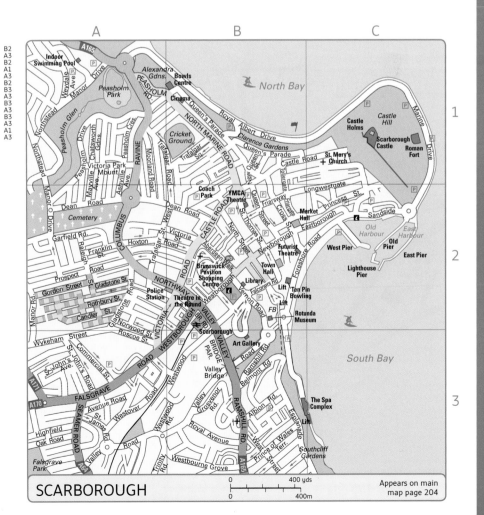

SCARBOROUGH

0   400 yds
0   400m

Appears on main
map page 204

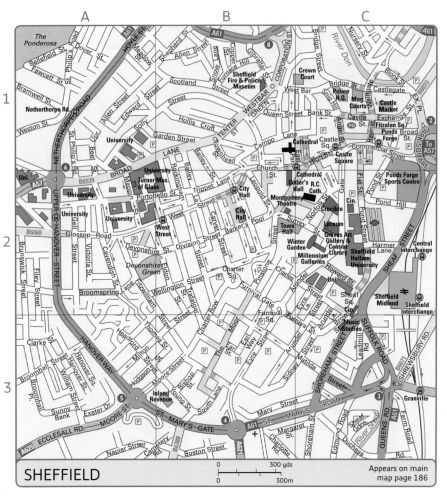

SHEFFIELD

0 ___ 300 yds
0 ___ 300m

Appears on main map page 186

Allen Street	B1	Hanover Square	A3
Angel Street	C1	Hanover Street	A3
Arundel Gate	B2	Hanover Way	A3
Arundel Lane	C3	Harmer Lane	C2
Arundel Street	B3	Haymarket	C1
Bailey Lane	B1	Headford Street	A3
Bailey Street	B1	High Street	C1
Bank Street	C1	Hodgson Street	A3
Barker's Pool	B2	Hollis Croft	B1
Beet Street	A1	Howard Street	C2
Bellefield Street	A1	Hoyle Street	A1
Bishop Street	B3	Leadmill Road	C3
Blonk Street	C1	Leopold Street	B2
Boston Street	B3	Mappin Street	A2
Bower Street	B1	Margaret Street	B3
Bramwell Street	A1	Mary Street	B3
Bridge Street	C1	Matilda Street	C3
Broad Lane	A2	Meadow Street	A1
Broad Street	C1	Milton Street	A3
Broomhall Street	A3	Moore Street	A3
Broomhall Place	A3	Napier Street	A3
Broomspring Lane	A2	Netherthorpe Road	A1
Brown Street	C3	Norfolk Street	C2
Brunswick Street	A2	Nursery Street	C1
Campo Lane	B1	Pinstone Street	B2
Carver Street	B2	Pond Hill	C2
Castle Square	C1	Pond Hill	C2
Castle Street	C1	Pond Street	C2
Castlegate	C1	Portobello Street	A2
Cavendish Street	A2	Queen Street	B1
Cemetery Road	A3	Queens Road	C3
Charles Street	B2/C2	Rockingham Street	B2
Charlotte Road	B3	St. Mary's Gate	B3
Charter Row	B3	St. Mary's Road	B3
Charter Square	B2	St. Philip's Road	A1
Church Street	B1	Scotland Street	B1
Clarke Street	A3	Sheaf Gardens	C3
Commercial Street	C1	Sheaf Square	C2
Copper Street	B1	Sheaf Street	C2
Corporation Street	B1	Shepherd Street	B1
Devonshire Street	A2	Shoreham Street	C3
Division Street	B2	Shrewsbury Road	C3
Dover Street	A1	Sidney Street	B3
Duchess Road	C3	Snig Hill	C1
Earl Street	B3	Snow Lane	B1
Earl Way	B3	Solly Street	A1
East Parade	C1	South Lane	B3
Ecclesall Road	A3	Spring Street	B1
Edmund Road	C3	Suffolk Road	C3
Edward Street	A1	Sunny Bank	A3
Eldon Street	B2	Surrey Street	B2
Exchange Street	C1	Tenter Street	B1
Exeter Drive	A3	The Moor	B3
Eyre Lane	C2	Thomas Street	A3
Eyre Street	B3	Townhead Street	B1
Farm Road	C3	Trafalgar Street	B2
Fawcett Street	A1	Trippet Lane	B2
Filey Street	A2	Upper Allen Street	A1
Fitzwilliam Street	A2	Upper Hanover Street	A2
Flat Street	C1	Victoria Street	A2
Furnace Hill	B1	Waingate	C1
Furnival Gate	B2	Wellington Street	B2
Furnival Square	B2	West Bar	B1
Furnival Street	B2	West Street	B2
Garden Street	A1	Westbar Green	B1
Gell Street	A2	Weston Street	A1
Gibraltar Street	B1	William Street	A3
Glossop Road	A2	Young Street	B3

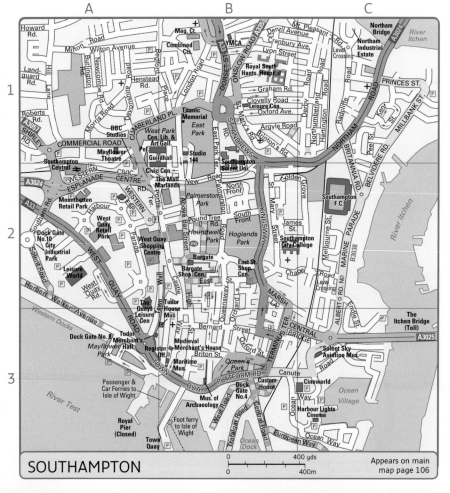

SOUTHAMPTON

0 ___ 400 yds
0 ___ 400m

Appears on main map page 106

Above Bar Street	B2	Queensway	B3
Albert Road North	C3	Radcliffe Road	C1
Argyle Road	B1	Roberts Road	A1
Bedford Place	A1	St. Andrews Road	B1
Belvidere Road	C2	St. Mary's Road	B1
Bernard Street	B3	St. Mary Street	B2
Brintons Road	B1	Shirley Road	A1
Britannia Road	C1	Solent Road	A2
Briton Street	B3	Southern Road	A2
Burlington Road	A1	South Front	B2
Canute Road	B3	Terminus Terrace	B3
Castle Way	B2	Town Quay	A3
Central Bridge	B3	Trafalgar Road	B3
Central Road	B3	West Quay Road	A2
Chapel Road	B2	West Road	B3
Civic Centre Road	A2	Western Esplanade	A2
Clovelly Road	B1	Wilton Avenue	A1
Commercial Road	A1		
Cranbury Avenue	B1		
Cumberland Place	A1		
Denzil Avenue	B1		
Derby Road	C1		
Devonshire Road	A1		
Dorset Street	B1		
East Park Terrace	B1		
East Street	B2		
Endle Street	C2		
European Way	B3		
Golden Grove	B2		
Graham Road	B1		
Harbour Parade	A2		
Hartington Road	C1		
Henstead Road	A1		
Herbert Walker Avenue	A2		
High Street	B2		
Hill Lane	A1		
Howard Road	A1		
James Street	B2		
Kent Street	C1		
Kingsway	B1		
Landguard Road	A1		
London Road	B1		
Lyon Street	B1		
Marine Parade	C2		
Marsh Lane	B2		
Melbourne Street	C2		
Millbank Street	C1		
Milton Road	A1		
Morris Road	A1		
Mount Pleasant Road	B1		
Newcombe Road	A1		
New Road	B2		
Northam Road	C1		
North Front	B2		
Northumberland Road	C1		
Ocean Way	B3		
Onslow Road	B1		
Orchard Lane	B3		
Oxford Avenue	B1		
Oxford Street	B3		
Palmerston Road	B2		
Peel Street	C1		
Platform Road	B3		
Portland Terrace	A2		
Pound Tree Road	B2		
Princes Street	C1		

Tourist Information Centre: The Potteries Museum & Art Gallery, Bethesda Street   Tel: 01782 236000

Albion Street	B1	Snow Hill	B2
Ashford Street	B2	Stafford Street	B1
Avenue Road	B2	Station Road	B3
Aynsley Road	B2	Stoke	B3
Bedford Road	B2	Stoke Road	B3
Bedford Street	A2	Stone Street	A3
Belmont Road	A1	Stuart Road	C2
Beresford Street	B2	Sun Street	B1
Berry Hill Road	C2	Trentmill Road	C2
Boon Avenue	A3	Victoria Road	C2
Botteslow Street	C1	Warner Street	B1
Boughey Road	B3	Waterloo Street	C1
Broad Street	B1	Wellesley Street	B2
Bucknall New Road	C1	Wellington Road	C1
Bucknall Old Road	C1	West Avenue	A3
Cauldon Road	B2	Westland Street	A3
Cemetery Road	A2	Yoxall Avenue	A3
Church Street	B3		
Clough Street	A1		
College Road	B2		
Commercial Road	C1		
Copeland Street	B3		
Dewsbury Road	C3		
Eagle Street	C1		
Eastwood Road	C1		
Elenora Street	B3		
Etruria Road	A1		
Etruria Vale Road	A1		
Etruscan Street	A2		
Festival Way	A1		
Forge Lane	A1		
Garner Street	A2		
Glebe Street	B3		
Greatbatch Avenue	A3		
Hanley	B1		
Hartshill Road	A3		
Hill Street	A3		
Honeywall	A3		
Howard Place	B2		
Ivy House Road	C1		
Leek Road	B3		
Lichfield Street	C1		
Liverpool Road	B3		
Lordship Lane	B3		
Lytton Street	B3		
Manor Street	C3		
Marsh Street	B1		
Newlands Street	B2		
North Street	A2		
Old Hall Street	B1		
Oxford Street	A3		
Parliament Row	B1		
Potteries Way	B1		
Potters Way	C1		
Prince's Road	A3		
Quarry Avenue	A3		
Quarry Road	A3		
Queen's Road	A3		
Queensway	A2		
Rectory Road	B2		
Regent Road	B2		
Richmond Street	A3		
Ridgway Road	B2		
Seaford Street	B2		
Shelton New Road	A2		
Shelton Old Road	A3		

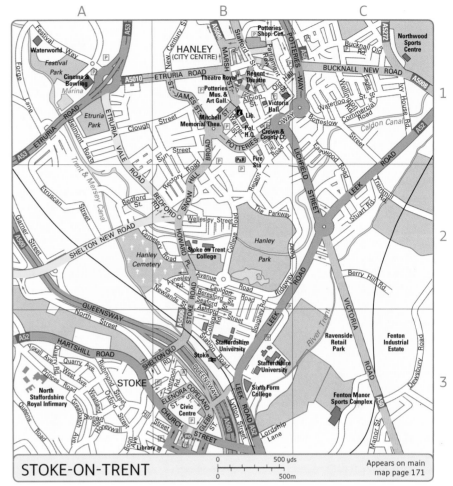

STOKE-ON-TRENT

| 0 | 500 yds |
| 0 | 500m |

Appears on main map page 171

Tourist Information Centre: Bridgefoot   Tel: 01789 264293

Albany Road	A2	Swan's Nest Lane	C2
Alcester Road	A1	The Waterways	A1
Arden Street	A1	Tiddington Road	C2
Avonside	B3	Trinity Street	B3
Banbury Road	C2	Tyler Street	B1
Bancroft Place	C2	Union Street	B2
Birmingham Road	A1	Warwick Court	B1
Brewery Street	B1	Warwick Crescent	C1
Bridgefoot	C2	Warwick Road	C1
Bridge Street	B2	Waterside	B2
Bridgeway	C2	Welcombe Road	C1
Bridgetown Road	C3	Westbourne Grove	A2
Broad Street	A3	Western Road	A1
Broad Walk	A3	West Street	A3
Bull Street	A3	Wharf Road	A1
Chapel Lane	B2	Windsor Street	B2
Chapel Street	B2	Wood Street	B2
Cherry Orchard	A3		
Chestnut Walk	A2		
Church Street	B2		
Clopton Bridge	C2		
Clopton Road	B1		
College Lane	B3		
College Street	B3		
Ely Street	B2		
Evesham Place	A3		
Evesham Road	A3		
Great William Street	B1		
Greenhill Street	A2		
Grove Road	A2		
Guild Street	B1		
Henley Street	B1		
High Street	B2		
Holtom Street	A3		
John Street	B1		
Kendall Avenue	B1		
Maidenhead Road	B1		
Mansell Street	A1		
Meer Street	B2		
Mill Lane	B3		
Mulberry Street	B1		
Narrow Lane	A3		
New Street	B3		
Old Town	B3		
Old Town Square	B3		
Old Tramway Walk	C3		
Orchard Way	A3		
Payton Street	B1		
Red Lion Court	B2		
Rother Street	A2		
Ryland Street	B3		
St. Andrews Crescent	A2		
St. Gregory's Road	B1		
Sanctus Drive	A3		
Sanctus Road	A3		
Sanctus Street	A3		
Sandfield Road	A3		
Scholar's Lane	A2		
Seven Meadow Road	A3		
Shakespeare Street	B1		
Sheep Street	B2		
Shipston Road	C3		
Shottery Road	A2		
Shrieve's Walk	B2		
Southern Lane	B3		
Station Road	A1		

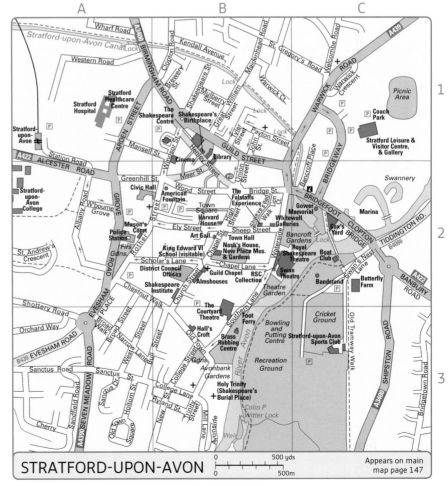

STRATFORD-UPON-AVON

| 0 | 500 yds |
| 0 | 500m |

Appears on main map page 147

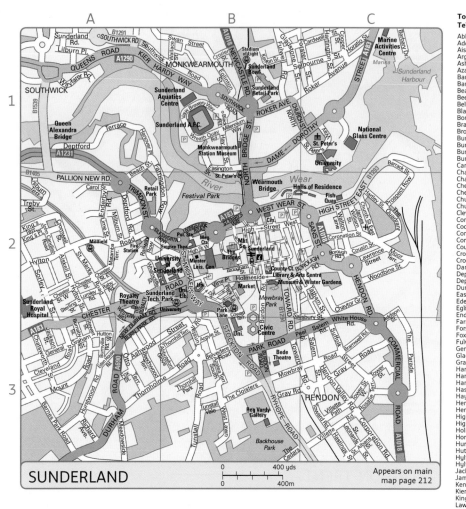

Tourist Information Centre: 50 Fawcett Street
Tel: 0191 553 2000

Abbotsford Grove	B3	Lime Street	A2
Addison Street	C3	Livingstone Road	B2
Aiskell Street	A2	Lumley Road	A2
Argyle Street	B3	Matamba Terrace	A2
Ashwood Street	A3	Milburn Street	A2
Azalea Terace South	B3	Millennium Way	B1
Barnes Park Road	A3	Moor Terrace	C2
Barrack Street	C1	Mount Road	A3
Beach Street	A2	Mowbray Road	B3
Beechwood Terrace	A3	New Durham Road	A3
Belvedere Road	B3	Newcastle Road	B1
Black Road	B1	North Bridge Street	B1
Borough Road	B2/C2	Otto Terrace	A3
Bramwell Road	C3	Pallion New Road	A2
Brougham Street	B2	Park Lane	B2
Burdon Road	B3	Park Road	B3
Burn Park Road	A3	Peel Street	B3
Burnaby Street	A3	Prospect Row	C2
Burnville Road	A3	Queens Road	A1
Carol Street	A2	Raby Road	A2
Chatsworth Street	A2	Railway Row	A1
Chaytor Grove	C2	Roker Avenue	B1/C1
Chester Road	A2	Rosalie Terrace	C3
Chester Street	A2	Ryhope Road	B3
Church Street East	C3	St. Albans Street	C3
Church Street North	B1	St. Leonards Street	C3
Cleveland Road	A3	St. Marks Road	A2
Commercial Road	C3	St. Mary's Way	B2
Cooper Street	C1	St. Michaels Way	B2
Coronation Street	C2	St. Peter's Way	C1
Corporation Road	C3	Salem Road	C3
Cousin Street	C2	Salem Street	C3
Cromwell Street	A2	Salisbury Street	B2
Crozier Street	B1	Sans Street	C2
Dame Dorothy Street	B1	Selbourne Street	B1
Deptford Road	A2	Silksworth Row	A2
Deptford Terrace	A1	Sorley Street	A2
Durham Road	A3	Southwick Road	A1
Easington Street	B1	Southwick Road	B1
Eden House Road	A3	Stewart Street	A3
Eglinton Street	B1	Stockton Road	B3
Enderby Road	A2	Suffolk Street	C3
Farringdon Row	A1	Sunderland Road	A1
Forster Street	C1	Swan Street	B1
Fox Street	A3	Tatham Street	C2
Fulwell Road	B1	The Cedars	B3
General Graham Street	A3	The Cloisters	B3
Gladstone Street	B1	The Parade	C3
Gray Road	B3/C3	The Quadrant	C2
Hanover Place	A1	The Royalty	A2
Hartington Street	C1	Thornhill Park	B3
Hartley Street	C2	Thornhill Terrace	B3
Hastings Street	C3	Thornholme Road	A3
Hay Street	B1	Toward Road	B2/C3
Hendon Road	C2	Tower Street	C3
Hendon Valley Road	C3	Tower Street West	C3
High Street East	C2	Trimdon Street	A2
High Street West	B2	Tunstall Road	B3
Holmeside	B2	Tunstall Vale	B3
Horatio Street	C1	Vaux Brewery Way	B1
Hurstwood Road	A3	Villette Road	C3
Hutton Street	A3	Vine Place	B2
Hylton Road	A2	Wallace Street	B1
Hylton Street	A2	West Lawn	B3
Jackson Street	A3	West Wear Street	B2
James William Street	C2	Western Hill	A2
Kenton Grove	B1	Wharncliffe Street	A2
Kier Hardy Way	A1	White House Road	C3
King's Place	A2	Woodbine Street	C2
Lawrence Street	C2	Wreath Quay Road	B1

SUNDERLAND

0 ——— 400 yds
0 ——— 400m

Appears on main map page 212

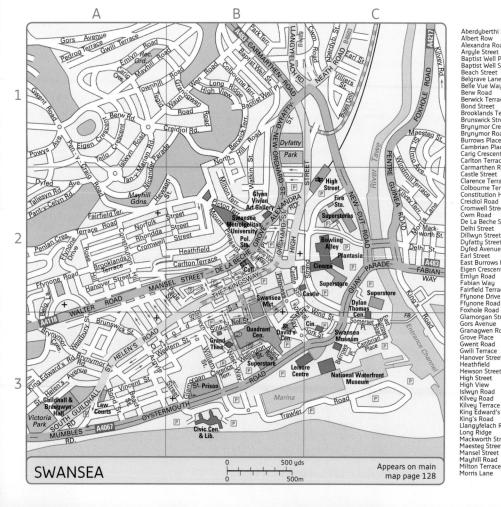

Aberdyberthi Street	C1	Mount Pleasant	B2
Albert Row	B3	Mumbles Road	A3
Alexandra Road	B2	Neath Road	C1
Argyle Street	A3	Nelson Street	B3
Baptist Well Place	B1	New Cut Road	C2
Baptist Well Street	B1	New Orchard Street	B1
Beach Street	A3	Nicander Parade	A2
Belgrave Lane	A3	Norfolk Street	A2
Belle Vue Way	B2	North Hill Road	B1
Berw Road	A1	Orchard Street	B2
Berwick Terrace	B1	Oxford Street	A3
Bond Street	A3	Oystermouth Road	A3
Brooklands Terrace	A2	Page Street	B2
Brunswick Street	A3	Pant-y-Celyn Road	A2
Brynymor Crescent	A3	Park Terrace	B1
Brynymor Road	A3	Pedrog Terrace	A1
Burrows Place	C3	Penlan Crescent	A2
Cambrian Place	C3	Pentre Guinea Road	C1
Carig Crescent	A1	Pen-y-Craig Road	A1
Carlton Terrace	B2	Picton Terrace	B2
Carmarthen Road	B1	Powys Avenue	A1
Castle Street	B2	Princess Way	B2
Clarence Terrace	B3	Quay Parade	C2
Colbourne Terrace	B1	Rhondda Street	A2
Constitution Hill	A2	Rose Hill	A2
Creidiol Road	A1	St. Elmo Avenue	C1
Cromwell Street	A2	St. Helen's Avenue	A3
Cwm Road	C1	St. Helen's Road	A3
De La Beche Street	B2	St. Mary Street	B2
Delhi Street	C2	Singleton Street	B3
Dillwyn Street	B3	Somerset Place	C3
Dyfatty Street	B1	South Guildhall Road	A3
Dyfed Avenue	A2	Strand	C2
Earl Street	C1	Taliesyn Road	A2
East Burrows Road	C3	Tan-y-Marian Road	A2
Eigen Crescent	A1	Tegid Road	A1
Emlyn Road	A1	Teilo Crescent	A1
Fabian Way	C2	Terrace Road	A2
Fairfield Terrace	A2	The Kingsway	B2
Ffynone Drive	A2	Townhill Road	A1
Ffynone Road	A2	Trawler Road	B3
Foxhole Road	C1	Villiers Street	C1
Glamorgan Street	B3	Vincent Street	A3
Gors Avenue	A1	Walter Road	A3
Granagwen Road	B1	Watkin Street	B1
Grove Place	A1	Waun-Wen Road	B1
Gwent Road	A1	Wellington Street	B3
Gwili Terrace	A1	West Way	B3
Hanover Street	A2	Westbury Street	A3
Heathfield	B2	Western Street	A3
Hewson Street	A2	William Street	B3
High Street	B2	Windmill Terrace	C1
High View	B1	York Street	C3
Islwyn Road	A1		
Kilvey Road	C1		
Kilvey Terrace	C2		
King Edward's Road	A3		
King's Road	C1		
Llangyfelach Road	B1		
Long Ridge	B1		
Mackworth Street	C1		
Maesteg Street	C1		
Mansel Street	A2		
Mayhill Road	A1		
Milton Terrace	B2		
Morris Lane	C2		

SWANSEA

0 ——— 500 yds
0 ——— 500m

Appears on main map page 128

Tourist Information Centre: Central Library, Regent Circus
Tel: 01793 466454

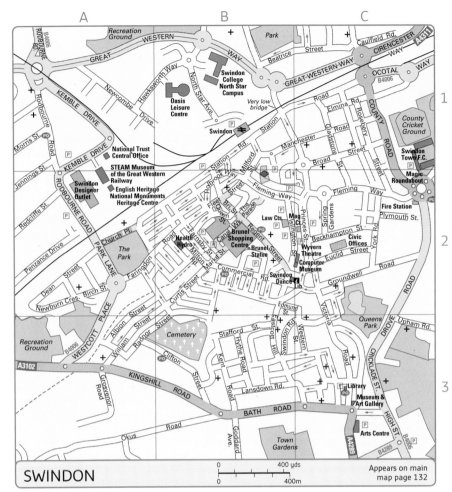

SWINDON

0   400 yds

0   400m

Appears on main map page 132

Tourist Information Centre: 5 Vaughan Parade
Tel: 01803 211211

TORQUAY

0   400 yds

0   400m

Appears on main map page 101

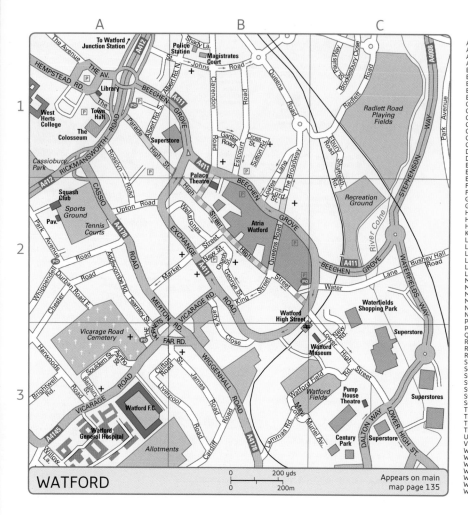

WATFORD

Scale: 0 200 yds / 0 200m

Appears on main map page 135

Addiscombe Road	A2
Albert Road North	A1
Albert Road South	A1
Aynho Street	A3
Banbury Street	A3
Beechen Grove	A1/C2
Brightwell Road	A3
Brocklesbury Close	C1
Bushey Hall Road	C2
Cardiff Road	B3
Cassio Road	A2
Chester Road	A2
Church Street	B1
Clarendon Road	B1
Clifton Road	A3
Cross Street	B1
Dalton Way	C3
Durban Road East	A2
Ebury Road	C1
Estcourt Road	B1
Exchange Road	A2
Farraline Road	A3
Fearnley Street	A2
Garlet Road	B1
George Street	B2
Harwoods Road	A3
Hempsted Road	A1
High Street	A1/B2
King Street	B2
Lady's Close	B2
Lammas Road	B3
Liverpool Road	A3
Loates Lane	B2
Lord Street	B2
Lower High Street	C3
Market Street	A2
May Cottages	B3
Merton Road	A2
Muriel Avenue	B3
New Road	C3
New Street	B2
Park Avenue	C1
Park Avenue	A2
Queens Road	B1/B2
Radlett Road	C1
Rickmansworth Road	A2
Rosslyn Road	A1
Shaftesbury Road	C1
Souldern Street	A3
St. James Road	B3
St. Johns Road	A1
St. Pauls Way	C1
Stephenson Way	C2
Sutton Road	B1
The Avenue	A1
The Broadway	B2
The Hornets	A3
The Parade	A1
Upton Road	A2
Vicarage Road	A3/B2
Water Lane	C2
Waterfields Way	C2
Watford Field Road	B3
Wellstones	B2
Whippendell Road	A2
Wiggenhall Road	B3
Willow Lane	A3

WESTON-SUPER-MARE

Scale: 0 400 yds / 0 400m

Appears on main map page 115

**Tourist Information Centre: Tropicana, Marine Parade
Tel: 01934 888877**

Addicott Road	B3
Albert Avenue	B3
Alexandra Parade	B2
Alfred Street	B2
All Saints Road	B1
Amberey Road	C3
Arundell Road	B1
Ashcombe Gardens	C1
Ashcombe Road	C2
Atlantic Road	A1
Baker Street	B2
Beach Road	B3
Beaconsfield Road	B2
Birnbeck Road	A1
Boulevard	B2
Brendon Avenue	C1
Bridge Road	C2
Brighton Road	B3
Bristol Road	B1
Carlton Street	B2
Cecil Road	B1
Clarence Road North	B3
Clarendon Road	C2
Clevedon Road	B3
Clifton Road	B3
Drove Road	C3
Earlham Grove	C2
Ellenborough Park North	B3
Ellenborough Park South	B3
Exeter Road	B3
George Street	B2
Gerard Road	B1
Grove Park Road	B1
High Street	B2
Highbury Road	A1
Hildesheim Bridge	B2
Hill Road	C1
Jubilee Road	B2
Kenn Close	C3
Kensington Road	C3
Knightstone Road	A1
Langford Road	C3
Lewisham Grove	C2
Locking Road	C2
Lower Bristol Road	C1
Lower Church Road	A1
Manor Road	C1
Marchfields Way	C3
Marine Parade	B3
Meadow Street	B2
Milton Road	C2
Montpelier	B1
Neva Road	B2
Norfolk Road	C3
Oxford Street	B2
Queen's Road	B1
Rectors Way	C3
Regent Street	B2
Ridgeway Avenue	B3
Royal Crescent	A1
St. Paul's Road	B3
Sandford Road	C2
Severn Road	B3
Shrubbery Road	A1
South Road	A1
Southside	B1

Stafford Road	C2
Station Road	B2
Sunnyside Road	B3
Swiss Road	C2
The Centre	B2
Trewartha Park	C1
Upper Church Road	A1
Walliscote Road	B3
Waterloo Street	B2
Whitecross Road	B3
Winterstoke Road	C3

Tourist Information Centre: Guildhall, High Street
Tel: 01962 840500

Alison Way	A1	St. Peter Street	B2
Andover Road	A1	St. Swithun Street	B3
Archery Lane	A2	St. Thomas Street	B3
Bar End Road	C3	Saxon Road	B1
Barfield Close	C3	Silver Hill	B2
Beaufort Road	A3	Southgate Street	A3
Beggar's Lane	C2	Staple Gardens	B2
Blue Ball Hill	C2	Station Road	A1
Bridge Stret	C2	Step Terrace	A1
Broadway	B2	Stockbridge Road	A1
Canon Street	B3	Sussex Street	A2
Chesil Street	C3	Swan Lane	B1
Christchurch Road	A3	Symond's Street	B3
City Road	A1	Tanner Street	C2
Clifton Hill	A2	The Square	B2
Clifton Road	A1	Tower Street	A2
Clifton Terrace	A2	Union Street	C2
Colebrook Street	B2	Upper Brook Street	B2
College Street	B3	Upper High Street	A2
College Walk	B3	Wales Street	C2
Compton Road	A3	Water Lane	C2
Cranworth Road	A1	Wharf Hill	C3
Culver Road	B3	Worthy Lane	A1
Domum Road	C3		
Durngate	C3		
East Hill	C3		
Eastgate Street	C2		
Easton Lane	C1		
Ebden Road	C1		
Edgar Road	A3		
Elm Road	A1		
Fairfield Road	A1		
Friarsgate	B2		
Gordon Road	B1		
Great Minster Street	B2		
Hatherley Road	A1		
High Street	B2		
Hyde Abbey Road	B1		
Hyde Close	B1		
Hyde Street	B1		
Jewry Street	B2		
King Alfred Place	B1		
Kingsgate Street	B3		
Little Minster Street	B2		
Lower Brook Street	B2		
Magdalen Hill	C2		
Market Lane	B2		
Middle Brook Street	B2		
Middle Road	A2		
Milland Road	C3		
North Walls	A1		
Parchment Street	B2		
Park Avenue	B1		
Peninsula Square	A2		
Portal Road	C3		
Quarry Road	C3		
Romans' Road	A3		
Romsey Road	A2		
St. Catherine's Road	C3		
St. Cross Road	A3		
St. George's Street	B2		
St. James Lane	A2		
St. James Villas	A3		
St. John's Street	C2		
St. Michael's Road	A3		
St. Paul's Hill	A1		

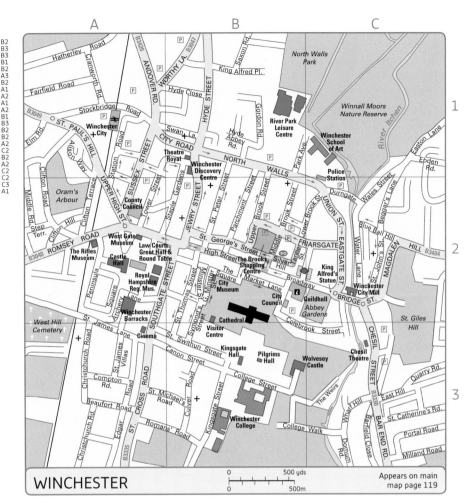

WINCHESTER

0   500 yds

0   500m

Appears on main
map page 119

Tourist Information Centre: Old Booking Hall, Central Station
Tel: 01753 743900

Adelaide Square	C3
Albert Street	A2
Alexandra Road	B3
Alma Road	B2/B3
Arthur Road	B2
Barry Avenue	B1
Bexley Street	B2
Bolton Avenue	B3
Bolton Crescent	B3
Bolton Road	B3
Bulkeley Avenue	A3
Castle Hill	C2
Charles Street	B2
Clarence Crescent	B2
Clarence Road	A2
College Crescent	A3
Dagmar Road	B2
Datchet Road	C1
Frances Road	B3
Goslar Way	A2
Goswell Road	B2
Green Lane	A2
Grove Road	B2
Helston Lane	A2
High Street (Eton)	B1
High Street (Windsor)	C2
Imperial Road	A3
King Edward VII Avenue	C1
Kings Road	C3
Meadow Lane	B1
Mill Lane	A1
Osborne Road	B3
Oxford Road	B2
Park Street	C2
Parsonage Lane	A2
Peascod Street	B2
Peel Close	A3
Princess Avenue	A3
Romney Lock Road	C1
St. Leonards Road	B3
St. Marks Road	B2
Sheet Street	C2
South Meadow Lane	B1
Springfield Road	A3
Stovell Road	A1
Thames Street	C1
The Long Walk	C3
Upcroft	A3
Vansittart Road	B2
Victoria Street	B2
Victor Road	A3
Westmead	A3
Windsor & Eton Relief Road	A2
York Avenue	A3
York Road	A3

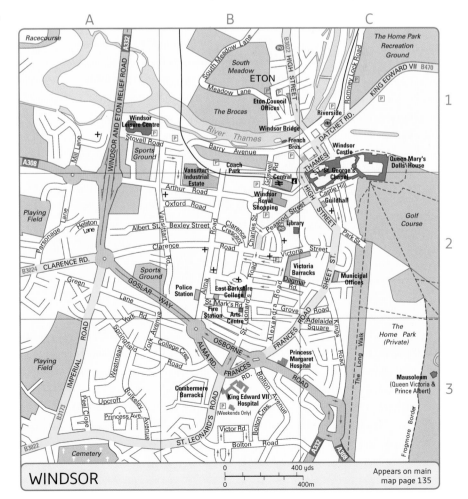

WINDSOR

0   400 yds

0   400m

Appears on main
map page 135

A B C

WORCESTER

0   200 yds
0   200m

Appears on main
map page 146

Tourist Information Centre: The Guildhall, High Street
Tel: 01905 726311

Albany Terrace	A1	Sherriff Street	C1
Albert Road	C3	Shrub Hill	C2
Angel Place	A2	Shrub Hill Road	C2
Angel Street	B2	Sidbury	B3
Arboretum Road	B1	Southfield Street	B1
Back Lane South	A1	Spring Hill	C2
Bath Road	B3	Stanley Road	C3
Bridge Street	A2	Tallow Hill	C2
Britannia Road	A1	Tennis Walk	A1
Britannia Square	A1	The Butts	A2
Broad Street	A2	The Cross	B2
Carden Street	B3	The Moors	A1
Castle Street	A2	The Shambles	B2
Charles Street	B3	The Tything	A1
Chestnut Street	B1	Tolladine Road	C1
Chestnut Walk	B1	Trinity Street	B2
City Walls Road	B2	Upper Tything	A1
Cole Hill	C3	Vincent Road	C3
College Street	B3	Washington Street	B1
Compton Road	C3	Westbury Street	B1
Copenhagen Street	A3	Wyld's Lane	C3
Croft Road	A2		
Deansway	A2		
Dent Close	C3		
Dolday	A2		
Farrier Street	A2		
Foregate Street	B2		
Fort Royal Hill	C3		
Foundry Street	B3		
Friar Street	B3		
George Street	C2		
Grand Stand Road	A2		
High Street	B2		
Hill Street	C2		
Hylton Road	A2		
Infirmary Walk	A2		
Kleve Walk	B3		
Lansdowne Crescent	B1		
Lansdowne Walk	C1		
London Road	B3		
Loves Grove	A1		
Lowesmoor	B2		
Lowesmoor Place	B2		
Midland Road	C3		
Moor Street	A1		
Newport Street	A2		
New Road	A3		
New Street	B2		
Northfield Street	B1		
North Quay	A2		
Padmore Street	B2		
Park Street	B3		
Park Street	C3		
Pheasant Street	B2		
Pump Street	B3		
Rainbow Hill	B1		
Richmond Hill	C3		
St. Martin's Gate	B2		
St. Mary's Street	A1		
St. Oswalds Road	A1		
St. Paul's Street	B2		
Sansome Street	B2		
Sansome Walk	B1		
Severn Street	B3		
Severn Terrace	A1		
Shaw Street	A2		

A B C

YORK

0   400 yds
0   400m

Appears on main
map page 195

Tourist Information Centre: 1 Museum Street
Tel: 01904 550099

Abbey Street	A1	Paragon Street	B3
Albermarle Road	A3	Park Grove	B1
Aldwark	B2	Park Street	A3
Barbican Road	C3	Penley's Grove Street	B1
Bishopthorpe Road	B3	Petergate	B2
Bishopgate Street	B3	Piccadilly	B2
Blossom Street	A3	Queen Street	A2
Bootham	A1	Rougier Street	A2
Bootham Crescent	A1	St. Andrewgate	B2
Bridge Street	B2	St. John Street	B1
Bull Lane	C1/C2	St. Maurice's Road	B2
Burton Stone Lane	A1	St. Olave's Road	A1
Cemetery Road	C3	Scarcroft Hill	A3
Charlotte Street	C2	Scarcroft Road	A3
Church Street	B2	Shambles	B2
Clarence Street	B1	Sixth Avenue	C1
Clifford Street	B2	Skeldergate	B2
Clifton	A1	Southlands Road	A3
Coney Street	B2	Station Road	A2
Dale Street	A3	Terry Avenue	B3
Dalton Terrace	A3	The Avenue	A1
Dodsworth Avenue	C1	The Mount	A3
East Parade	C1	The Stonebow	B2
Eldon Street	B1	Thorpe Street	A3
Fairfax Street	B3	Tower Street	B2
Fifth Avenue	C1	Vine Street	B3
Fishergate	B3	Walmgate	B2
Foss Bank	C2	Water End	A1
Fossgate	B2	Watson Street	A3
Foss Islands Road	C2	Wellington Street	C3
Fourth Avenue	C2	Westminster Road	A1
Gillygate	B2	Wigginton Road	B1
Goodramgate	B2		
Grange Garth	B3		
Grosvenor Road	A1		
Grosvenor Terrace	A1		
Hallfield Road	C2		
Haxby Road	B1		
Heslington Road	C3		
Holgate Road	A3		
Hope Street	B3		
Huntington Road	C1		
Irwin Avenue	C1		
James Street	C2		
Kent Street	C3		
Lawrence Street	C3		
Layerthorpe	C2		
Leeman Road	A2		
Lendal	B2		
Longfield Terrace	A1		
Lord Mayor's Walk	B1		
Lowther Street	B1		
Malton Road	C1		
Marygate	A2		
Maurices Road	B2		
Micklegate	A2		
Monkgate	B1		
Moss Street	A3		
Mount Vale	A3		
Museum Street	B2		
Navigation Road	C2		
North Street	B2		
Nunnery Lane	A3		
Nunthorpe Road	A3		
Ousegate	B2		

Key to map symbols

🅿 Short stay car park 🅿 Mid stay car park 🅿 Long stay car park 🅿 Other car park ▭ Airport terminal building

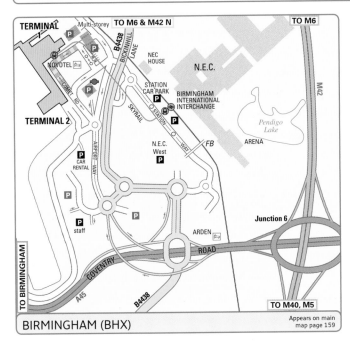

BIRMINGHAM (BHX)

Appears on main map page 159

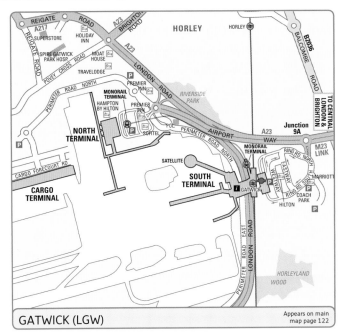

GATWICK (LGW)

Appears on main map page 122

GLASGOW (GLA)

Appears on main map page 233

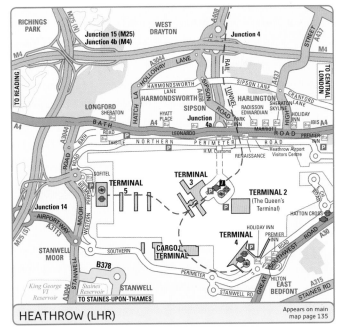

HEATHROW (LHR)

Appears on main map page 135

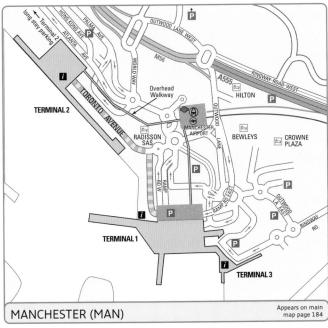

MANCHESTER (MAN)

Appears on main map page 184

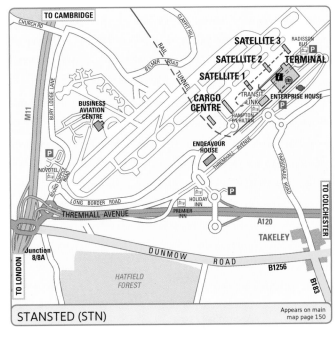

STANSTED (STN)

Appears on main map page 150

Symbols used on the map

M5 — Motorway

M6Toll — Toll motorway

8 / **9** — Motorway junction with full / limited access (in congested areas there is just a numbered symbol)

Maidstone / Birch / Sarn — Motorway service area with off road / full / limited access

A556 — Primary route dual / single carriageway

S — 24 hour service area on primary route

Peterhead — Primary route destination
Primary route destinations are places of major traffic importance linked by the primary route network. They are shown on a green background on direction signs.

A30 — 'A' road dual / single carriageway

B1403 — 'B' road dual / single carriageway

— Minor road

========= — Road with restricted access

— Roads with passing places

— Road proposed or under construction

33 — Multi-level junction with full / limited access (with junction number)

— Roundabout

4 — Road distance in miles between markers

— Road tunnel

— Steep hill (arrows point downhill)

Toll / Electronic Toll — Toll / Electronic Toll

— Level crossing

St Malo 8 hrs — Car ferry route with journey times

— Railway line / station / tunnel

Wales Coast Path — National Trail / Long Distance Route

✈ — Airport with / without scheduled services

(H) — Heliport

P&R / P&R — Park and Ride site operated by bus / rail (runs at least 5 days a week)

— Built up area

□ □ ▫ — Town / Village / Other settlement

Hythe — Seaside destination

–·–·–·– — International boundary

–·–·– — National boundary

KENT — County / Unitary Authority boundary and name

— Heritage Coast

National Park

Regional / Forest Park boundary

Woodland

Danger Zone — Military range

·468 ▲941 — Spot / Summit height (in metres)

— Lake / Dam / River / Waterfall

— Canal / Dry canal / Canal tunnel

— Beach / Lighthouse

SEE PAGE 3 — Area covered by urban area map

0	150	300	500	700	900	metres
water 0	490	985	1640	2295	2950	feet

Land height reference bar

Reading our maps

Multi-level junctions Non-motorway junctions where slip roads are used to access the main roads.

Distances Blue numbers give distances in miles between junctions shown with a blue marker.

Park & Ride Sites are shown that operate at least 5 days a week. Bus operated sites have a yellow symbol and rail operated sites a pink symbol.

Motorway service area

World Heritage site Places of interest defined by UNESCO as special on a world scale.

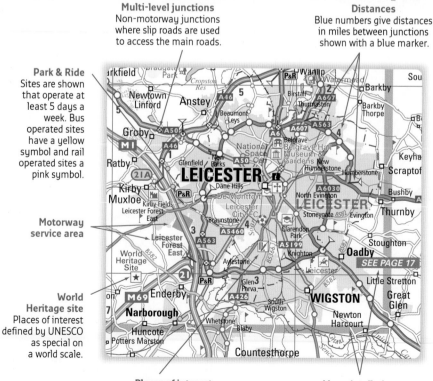

Places of interest Blue symbols indicate places of interest. See the section at the bottom of the page for the different types of feature represented on the map.

More detailed maps Green boxes indicate busy built-up areas. More detailed mapping is available.

Places of interest

A selection of tourist detail is shown on the mapping. It is advisable to check with the local tourist information centre regarding opening times and facilities available.

Any of the following symbols may appear on the map in maroon ★ which indicates that the site has World Heritage status.

i (black)	Tourist information centre (open all year)
i	Tourist information centre (open seasonally)
𝕞	Ancient monument
	Aquarium
	Aqueduct / Viaduct
	Arboretum
⚔ 1643	Battlefield
	Blue flag beach
▲ ⌖	Camp site / Caravan site (England, Wales and Scotland only)
	Castle
	Cave
	Country park
	County cricket ground
	Distillery
✝	Ecclesiastical feature
	Event venue
	Farm park
❈	Garden
⚑	Golf course
🏛	Historic house
	Historic ship
⚽	Major football club
£	Major shopping centre / Outlet village
	Major sports venue
	Motor racing circuit
	Mountain bike trail
🏛	Museum / Art gallery
	Nature reserve (NNR indicates a National Nature Reserve)
	Racecourse
	Rail Freight Terminal
	Ski slope (artificial / natural)
	Spotlight nature reserve (Best sites for access to nature)
	Steam railway centre / preserved railway
	Surfing beach
	Theme park
	University
	Vineyard
	Wildlife park / Zoo
	Wildlife Trust nature reserve
★	Other interesting feature
(NT) (NTS)	National Trust / National Trust for Scotland property

Map scale

A scale bar appears at the bottom of every page to help with distances.

```
0        2        4      6 miles
|--|--|--|--|--|--|--|--|--|--|
0    2    4    6    8   10 km
```

England, Wales & Southern Scotland are at a scale of 1:200,000 or 3.2 miles to 1 inch
Northern Scotland & Northern Ireland are at a scale of 1:263,158 or 4.2 miles to 1 inch.

Map pages

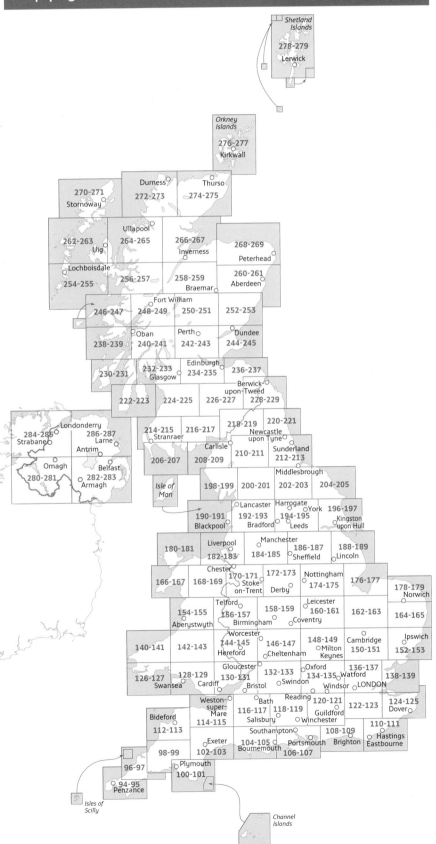

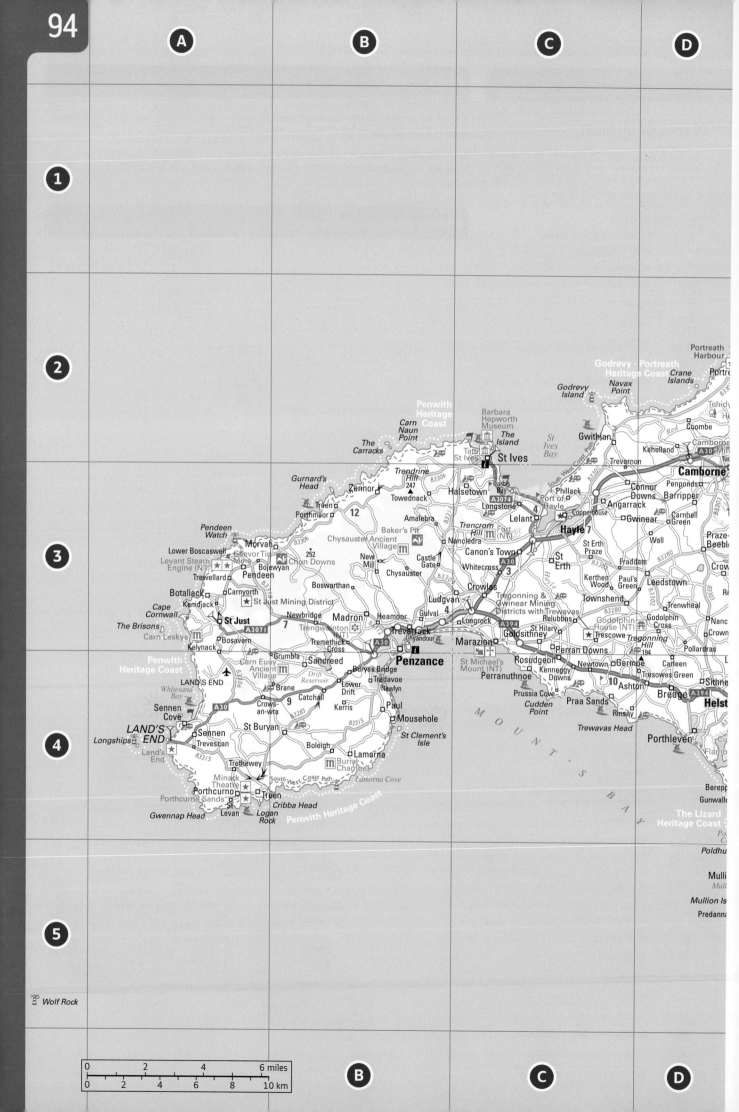

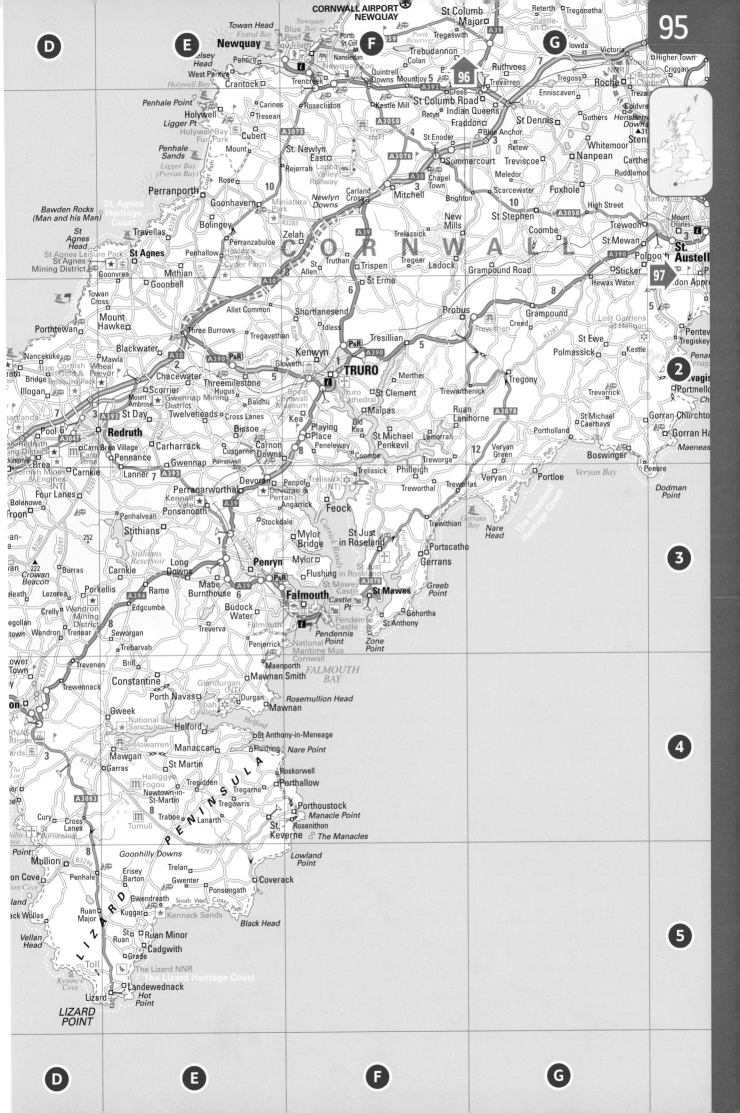

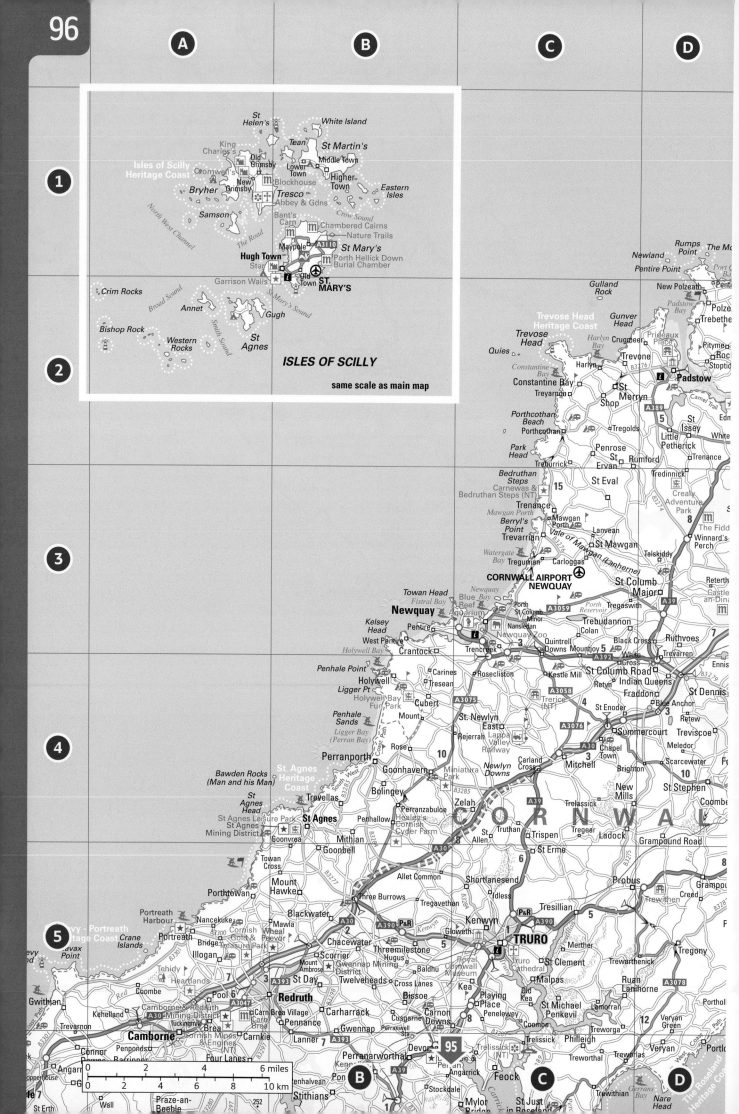

A　　**B**　　**C**　　**D**

1

2

3

4

5

Isles of Scilly (inset)

Isles of Scilly Heritage Coast

St Helen's
White Island
King Charles's
Tean
Old Grimsby
St Martin's
Cromwell's
Middle Town
Lower Town
Higher Town
New Grimsby
Blockhouse
Tresco
Bryher
Abbey & Gdns
Eastern Isles
Samson
Bant's Carn
Crow Sound
Chambered Cairns
Nature Trails
Maypole
A3110
St Mary's
Hugh Town
Porth Hellick Down Burial Chamber
Star
Old Town
ST. MARY'S
Garrison Walls

North West Channel
The Road

Crim Rocks
Broad Sound
Annet
St Mary's Sound
Bishop Rock
Smith Sound
Western Rocks
Gugh
St Agnes

ISLES OF SCILLY

same scale as main map

Main map — Cornwall

Rumps Point
Newland
The Mouls
Pentire Point
New Polzeath
Port Quin Bay
Polzeath
Gulland Rock
Trebetherick
Padstow Bay
Prideaux Place
Pityme
Trevose Head Heritage Coast
Gunver Head
Harlyn Bay
Crugmeer
Rock
Quies
Trevose Head
Harlyn
Stoptide
Constantine Bay
Trevone
B3276
St Merryn
Padstow
Treyarnon
Shop
A389
Camel Trail
Porthcothan Beach
Tregolds
St Issey
Porthcothan
Rumford
Trenance
Little Petherick
Park Head
Treburrick
Ervan
Tredinnick
St Eval
Crealy Adventure Park
Bedruthan Steps
Carnewas & Bedruthan Steps (NT)
15
B3274
Trenance
8
Mawgan Porth
St Mawgan
Talskiddy
The Fidd
Berryl's Point
Mawgan Porth
Lanvean
Winnard's Perch
Trevarrian
Vale of Mawgan (Lanhernel)
St Mawgan
Watergate Bay
Tregurrian
Carloggas
CORNWALL AIRPORT NEWQUAY
Reterth
Towan Head
Fistral Bay
Newquay Blue Bay
Porth
St Columb
Tregaswith
Castle-an-Dinas
Newquay Beef Aquarium
Porth Reservoir
A39
Minor
A3059
Trebudannon
Kelsey Head
Pentire
Nansledan
Colan
St Columb Major
West Pentire
Newquay Zoo
Quintrell Downs
Mountjoy
5
Black Cross
Ruthvoes
Holywell Bay
Crantock
Trencreek
Ennis
Penhale Point
3
5
Retyn
B3279
Carines
Tresean
Rosecliston
Kestle Mill
Indian Queens
St Dennis
Holywell
Roseclisto
Trerice (NT)
4
Fraddon
Ligger Pt
Cubert
A3075
St Enoder
Blue Anchor
Holywell Bay Fun Park
3
Retew
Penhale Sands
Mount
3058
Summercourt
Treviscoe
Ligger Bay (Perran Bay)
Rose
St Newlyn East
A3076
Chapel Town
Meledor
Perranporth
Rejerrah
Lappa Valley Railway
Carland Cross
Brighton
Scarcewater
Goonhaven
Newlyn Downs
Mitchell
New Mills
St Stephen
Bawden Rocks (Man and his Man)
Miniatura Park
3
Coombe
St. Agnes Heritage Coast
Bolingey
B3285
Zelah
Trelassick
St Agnes Head
Trevellas
Perranzabuloe
Healey's Cornish Cyder Farm
10
8
Trispen
Tregear
Ladock
Grampound Road
St Agnes
Penhallow
Allen
St Erme
Goonvrea
St Agnes Leisure Park
Mithian
C O R N W A L L
B3284
St Agnes Mining District
Goonbell
Truthan
Probus
Towan Cross
Allet Common
6
Trewithen
Creed
Grampou
Mount Hawke
Shortlanesend
Idless
Grampou
Porthtowan
Three Burrows
Tregavethan
Tresillian
B3275
Portreath Harbour
Blackwater
A390
Kenwyn
P&R
A390
Merther
Tregony
Nancekuke
Mawla
Gloweth
Trewarthenick
A3078
Tehidy Heartlands
Wheal Peevor
P&R
Chacewater
Kenwyn
Portreath
Cornish Gold & Treasure Park
Scorrier
Threemilestone
5
TRURO
St Clement
Crane Islands
Bridge
Gwennap Mining District
Hugus
Royal Cornwall Museum
Malpas
Ruan Lanihorne
Illogan
Baldhu
Truro Cathedral
Lamorran
Pool
St Day
Twelveheads
Cross Lanes
Kea
Old Kea
St Michael Penkevil
Trewarthenick
Camborne & Redruth Mining District
A3047
Carn Brea
Bissoe
Playing Place
Penelewey
Veryan Green
Gwithian
Kehelland
A30
Redruth
Brea Village
Carharrack
Cusgarne
Carnon Downs
Coombe
Trewiarlas
Veryan
Trevarnon
Brea
Pennance
Perranwell Sta
Trelissick
Phillleigh
Camborne
Cornish Mines & Engines
Carnkie
Gwennap
8
Treworga
12
Veryan
Connor Downs
Penponds
Tuckingmill
A393
Perranwell
Trewithan
Portloe
Barripper
Four Lanes
Lanner
7
Devoran
95
Feock
Nare Head
Stithians
Kenwyn
Perran
Angarrick
St Just in Roseland
Gerrans Bay
B

0   2   4   6 miles
0 2 4 6 8 10 km

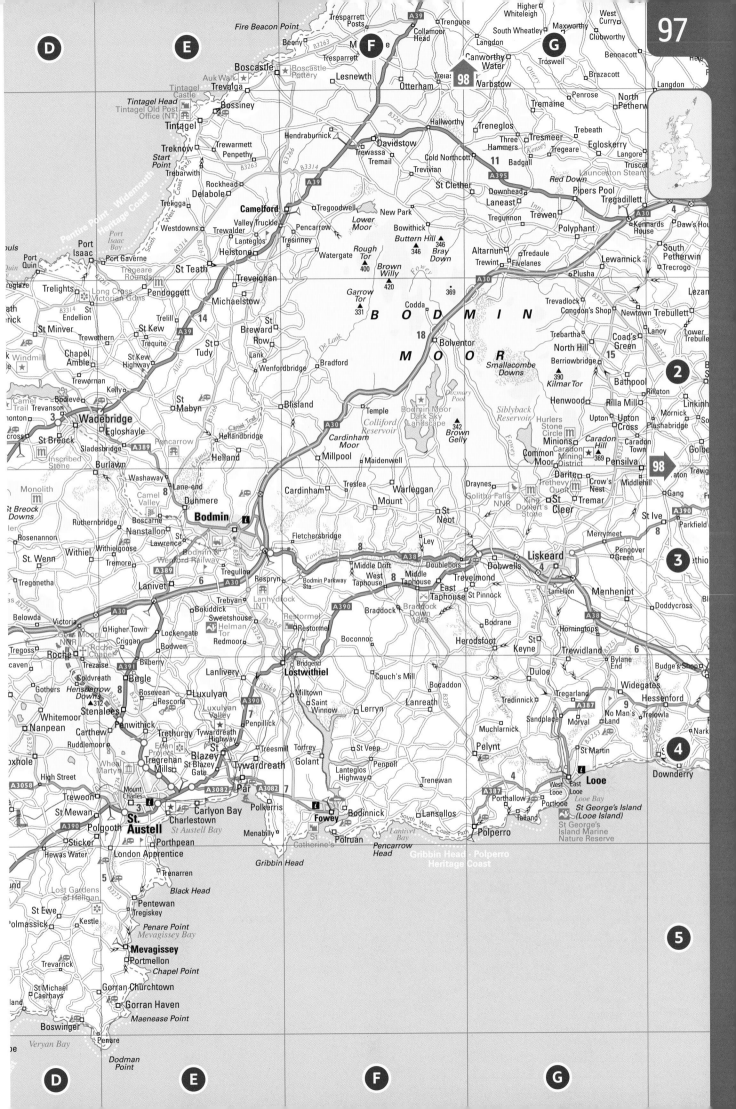

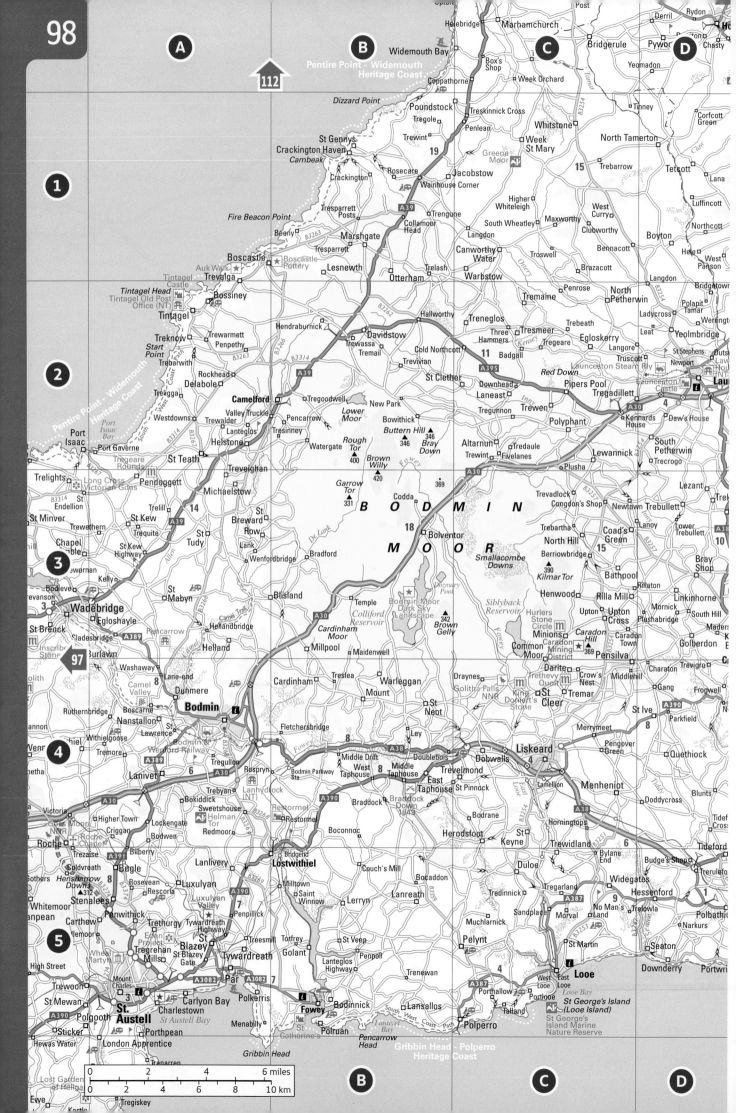

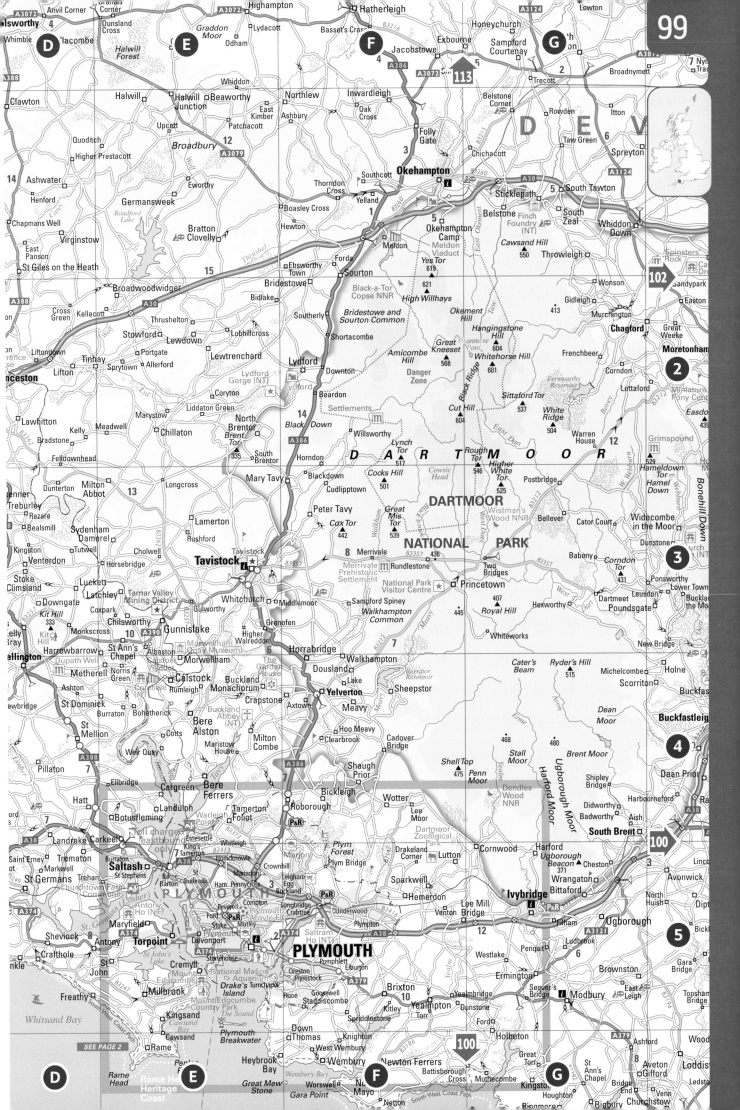

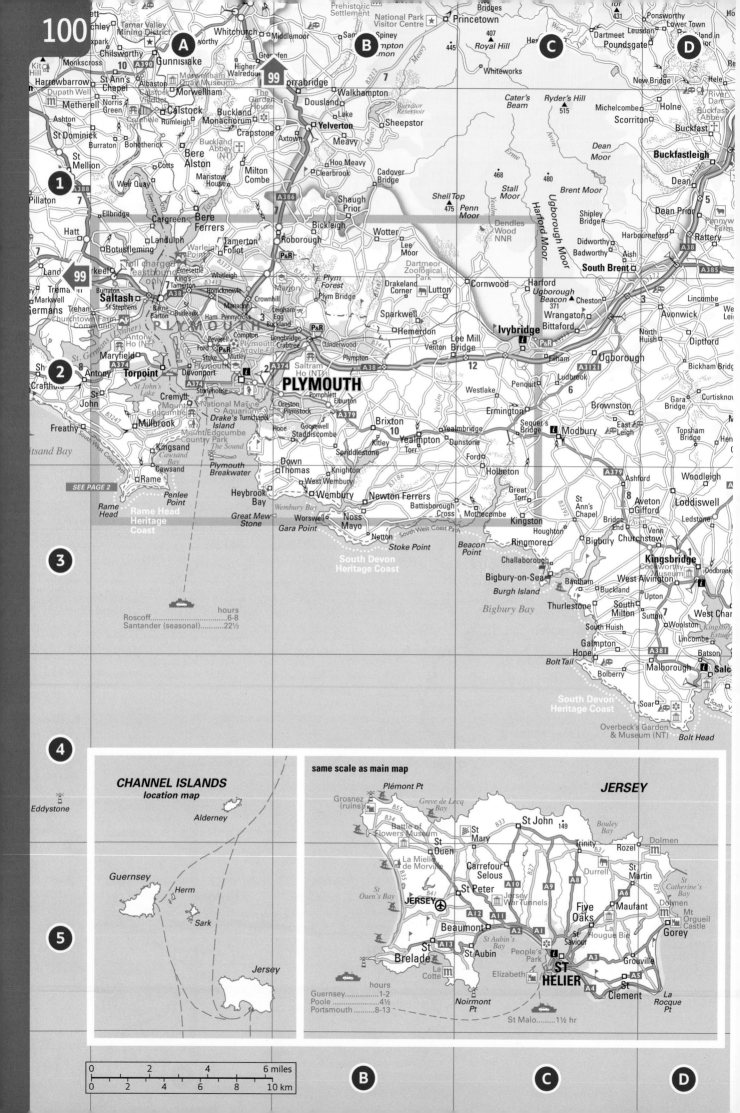

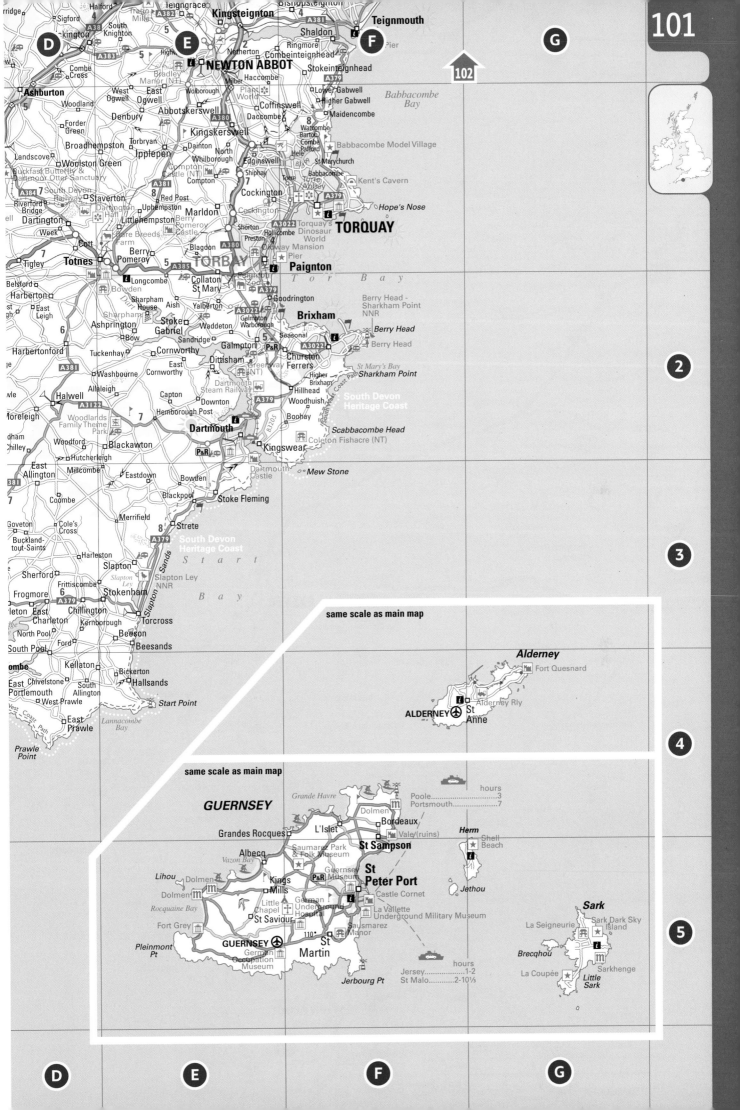

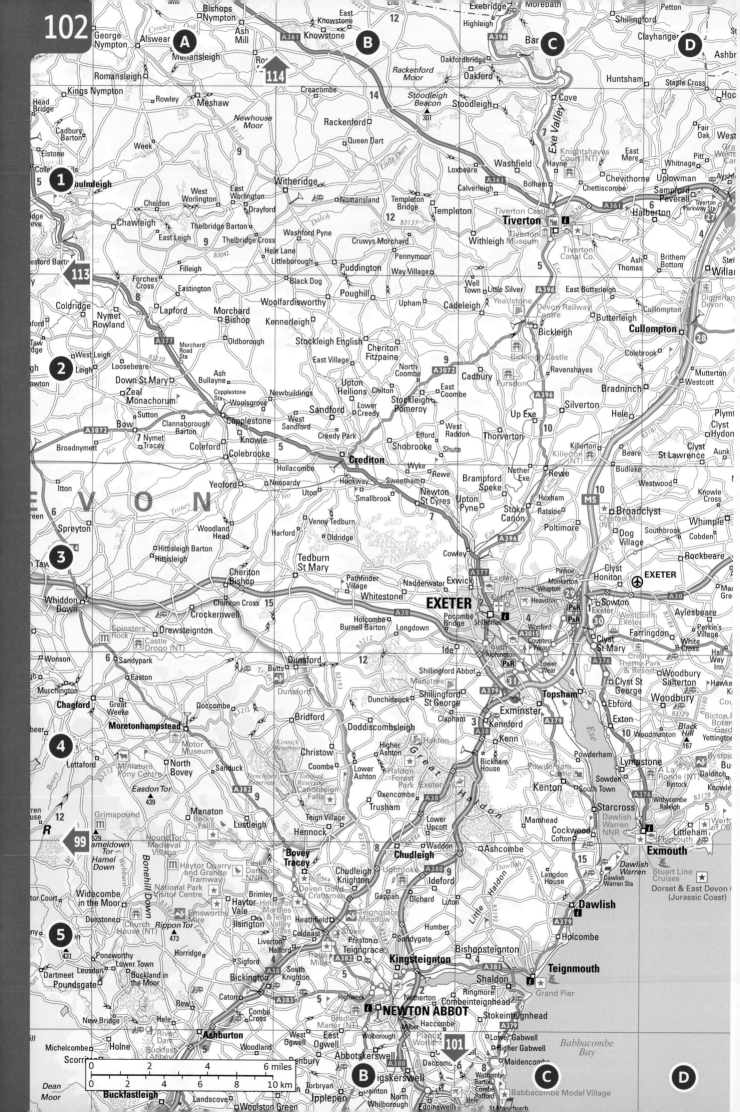

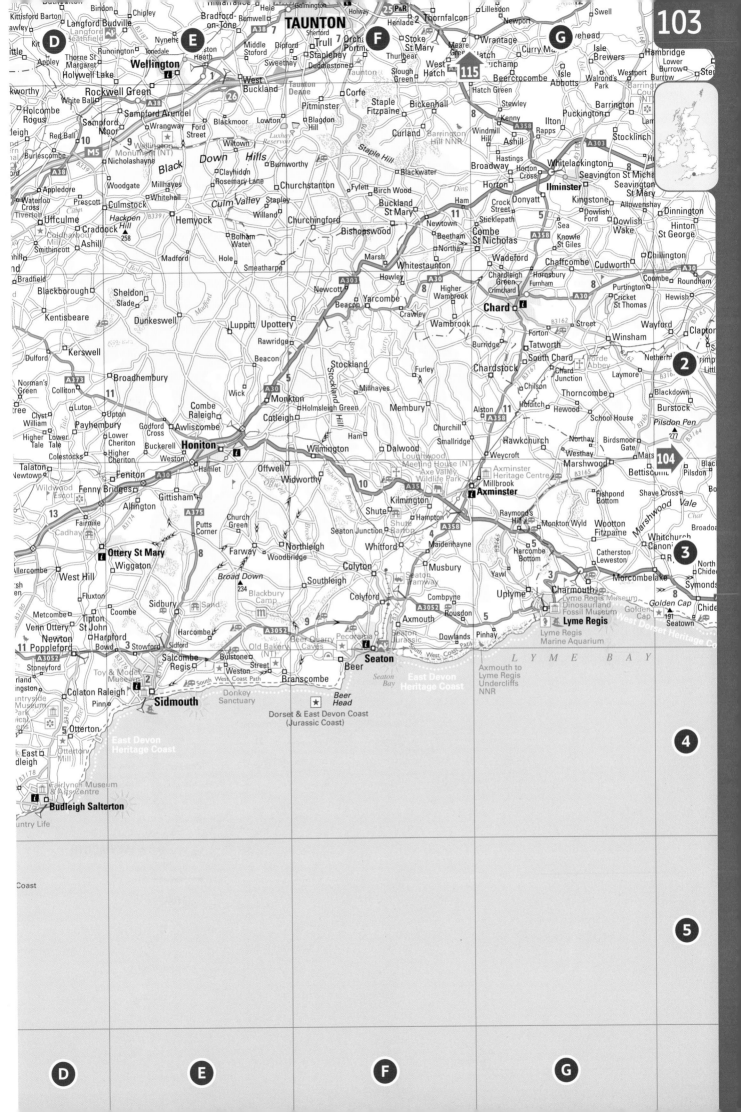

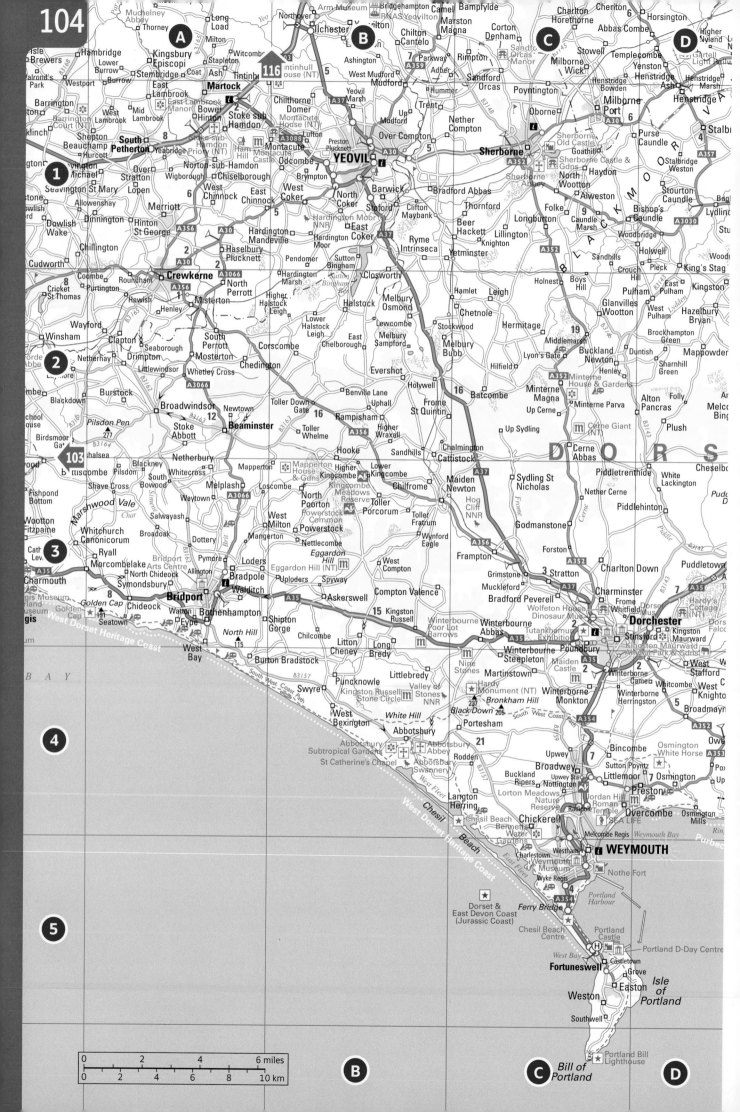

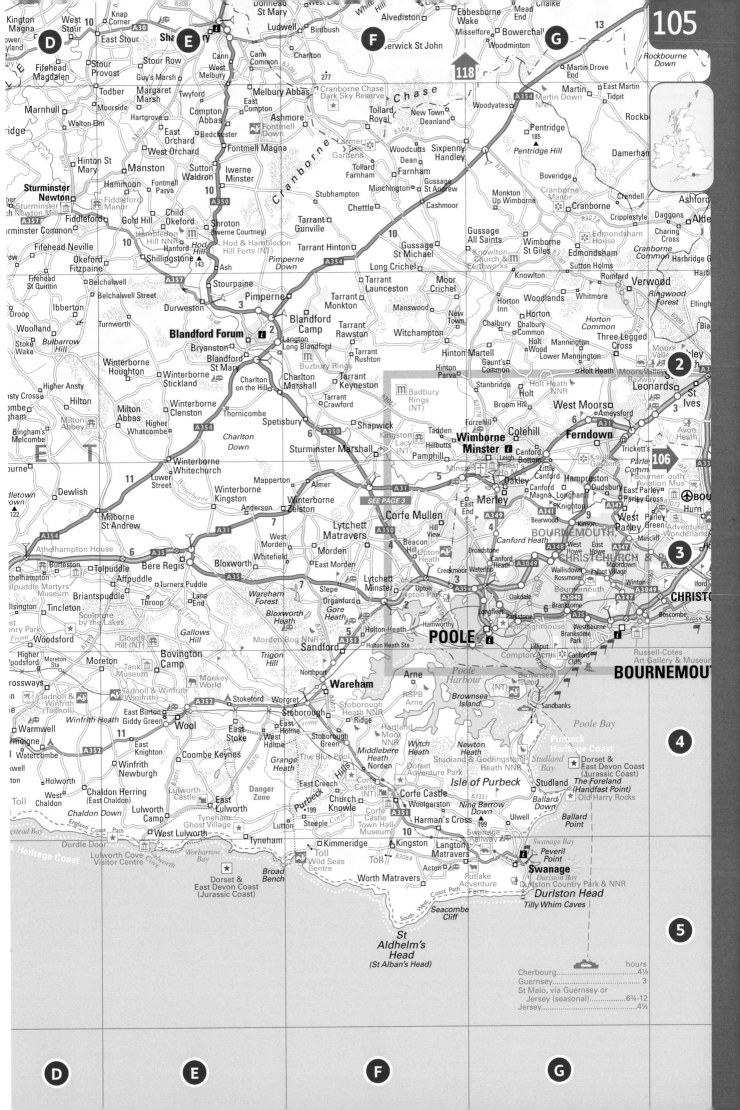

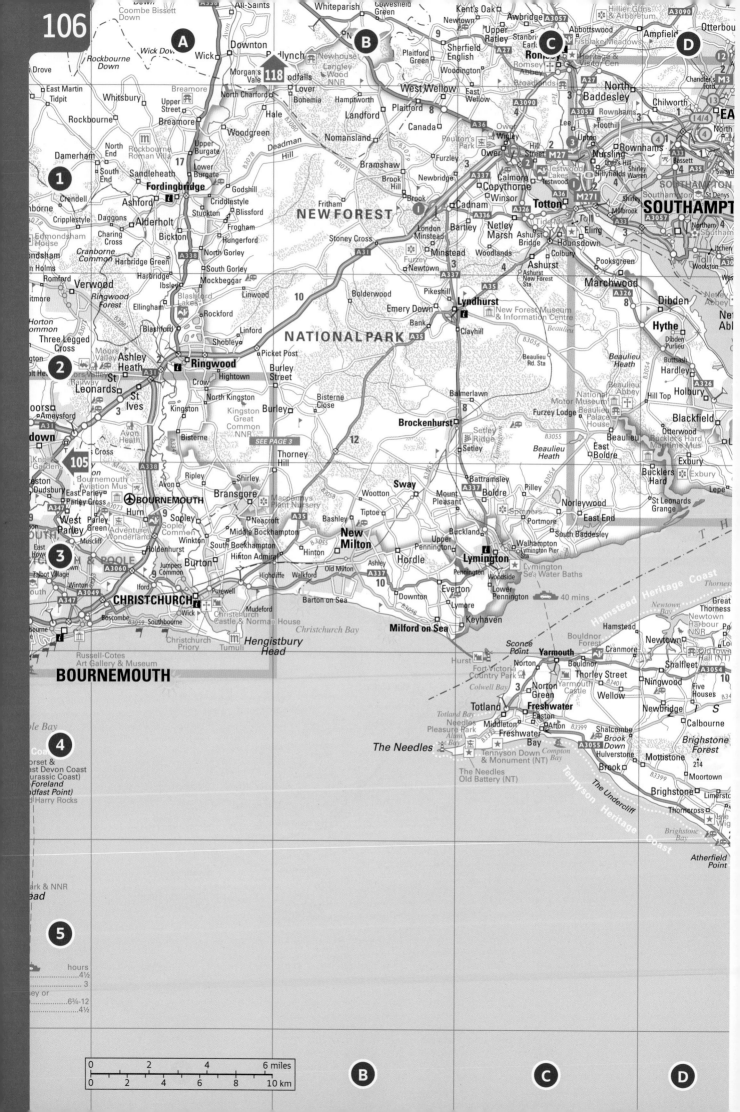

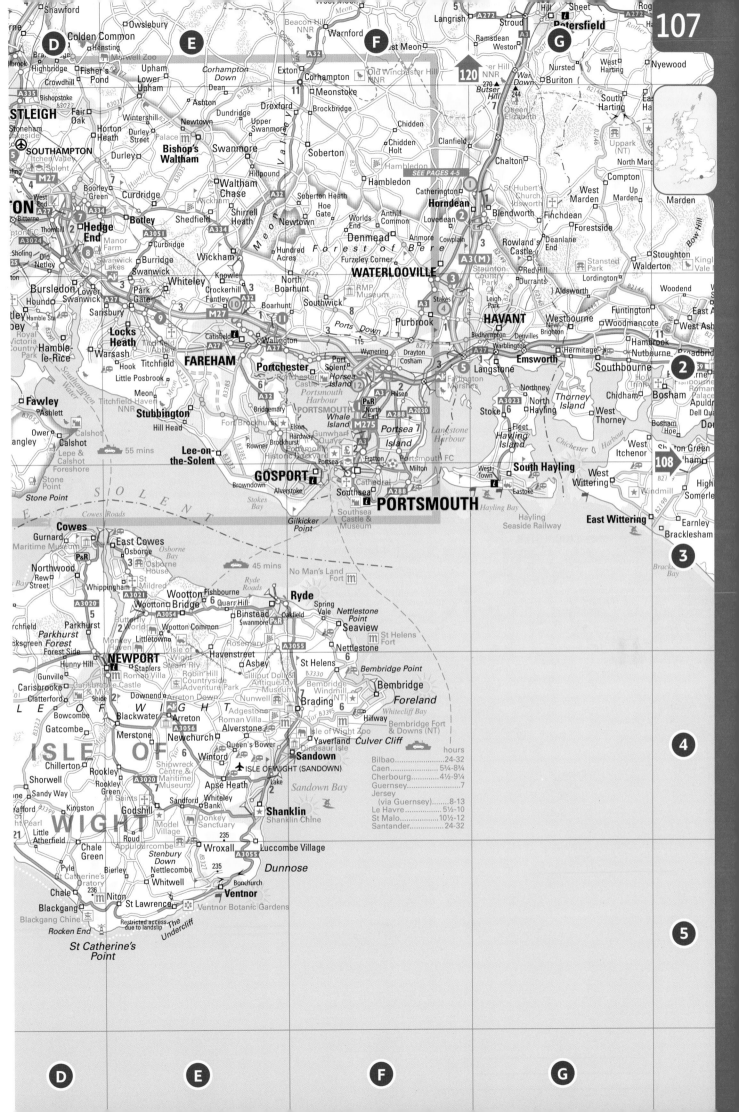

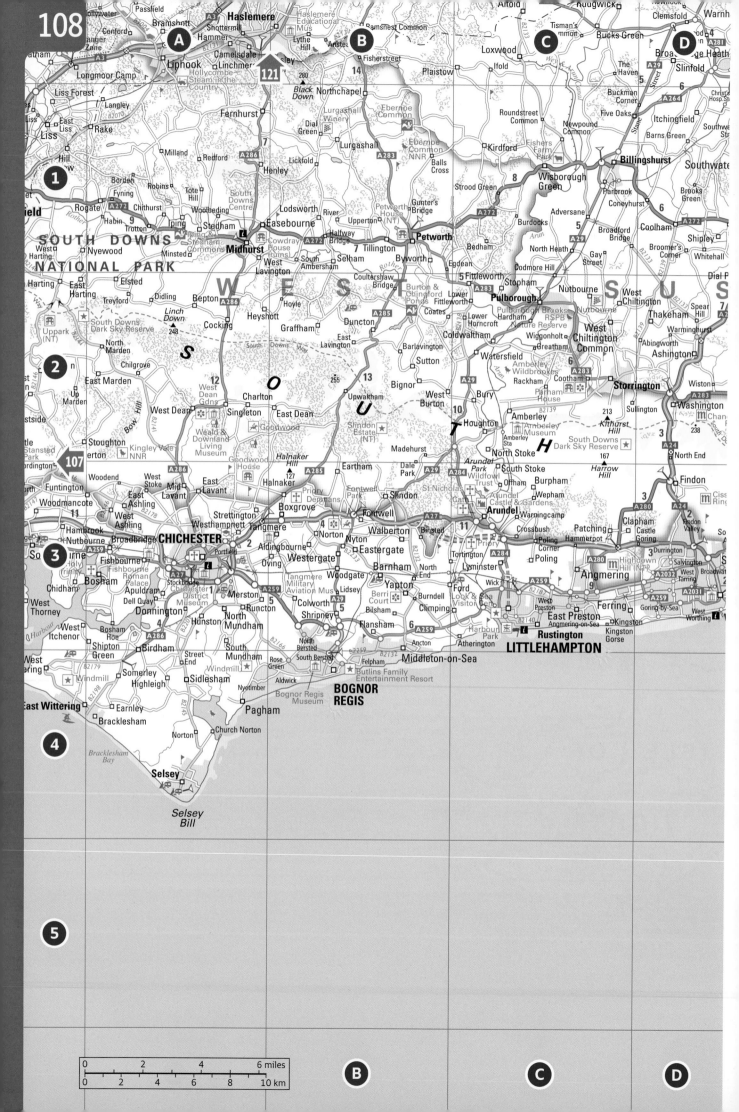

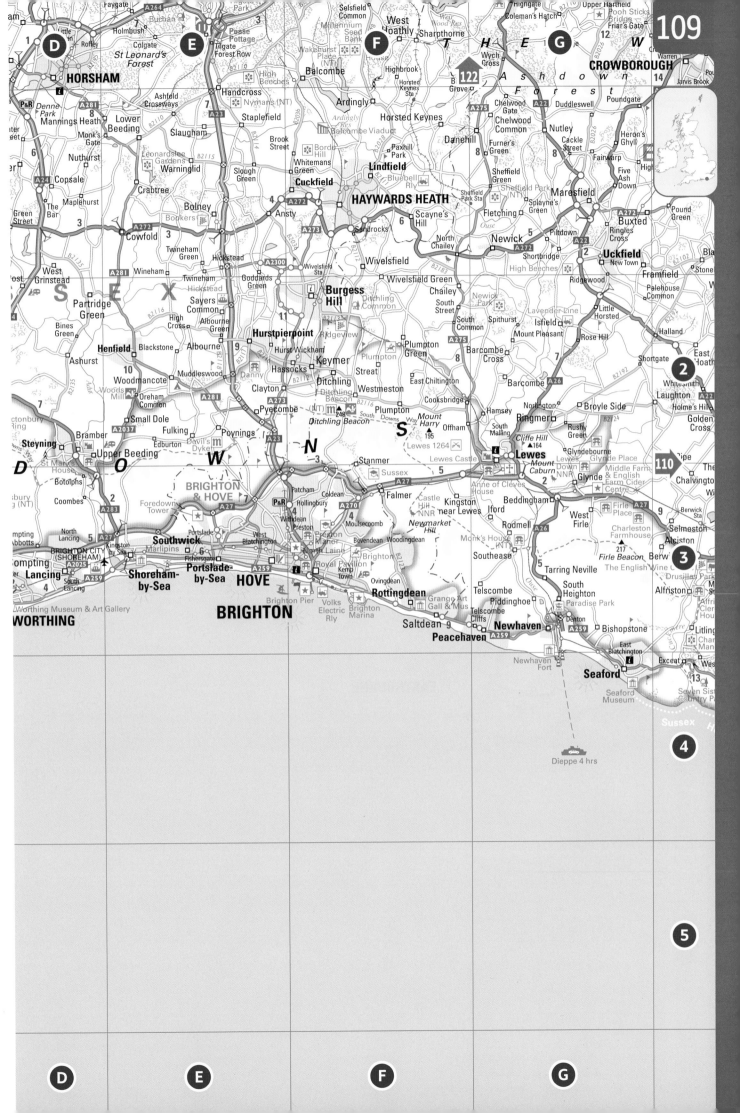

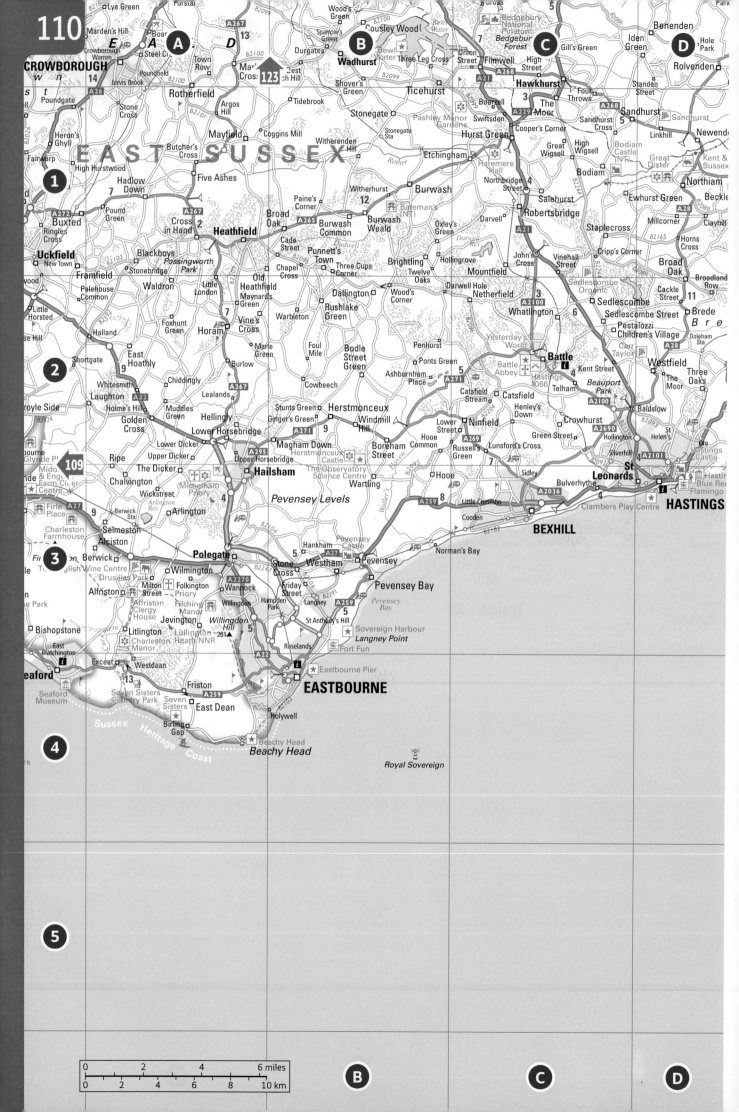

Channel Tunnel terminal maps

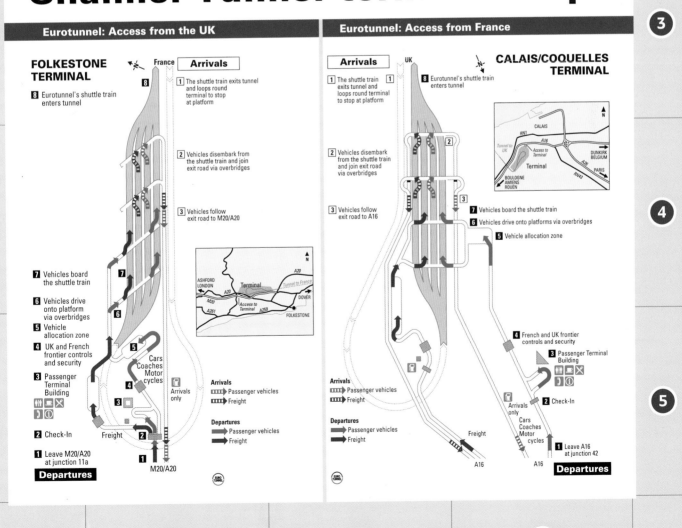

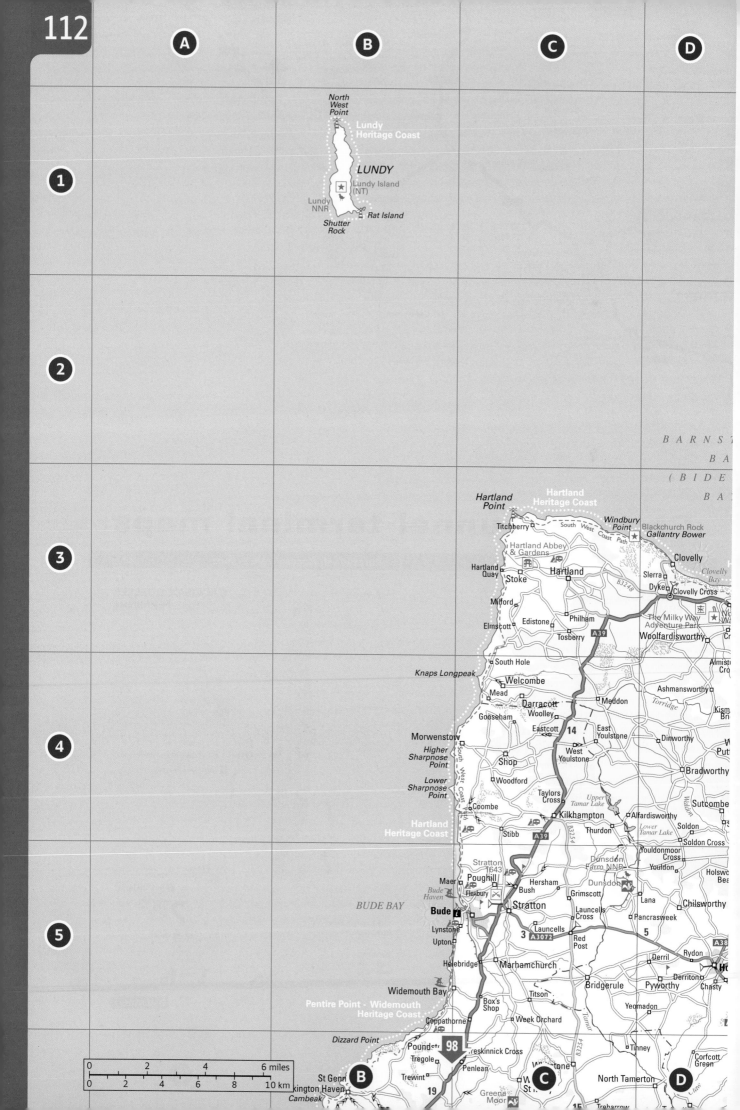

A   B   C   D

1

2

3

4

5

North West Point

Lundy Heritage Coast

LUNDY

Lundy Island (NT)

Lundy NNR

Rat Island

Shutter Rock

BARNST

BA

(BIDE

BA

Hartland Point

Hartland Heritage Coast

Windbury Point

Blackchurch Rock

Gallantry Bower

Titchberry

South West Coast Path

Hartland Abbey & Gardens

Clovelly

Clovelly Bay

Hartland Quay

Stoke

Hartland

Slerra

Dyke

Clovelly Cross

Milford

Philham

The Milky Way Adventure Park

Elmscott

Edistone

Tosberry

A39

Woolfardisworthy

Cr

Almist Cr

South Hole

Ashmansworthy

Torridge

Knaps Longpeak

Welcombe

Kism Br

Mead

Darracott

Meddon

Woolley

Gooseham

Eastcott

14

East Youlstone

Dinworthy

Putt

Morwenstow

West Youlstone

Bradworthy

Higher Sharpnose Point

Shop

Woodford

South West Coast

Taylors Cross

Upper Tamar Lake

Alfardisworthy

Sutcombe

Lower Sharpnose Point

Coombe

Kilkhampton

Lower Tamar Lake

Soldon

Soldon Cross

Hartland Heritage Coast

Stibb

A39

Thurdon

B3254

Waldon

Holsw

Stratton 1643

Dunsdon Farm NNR

Youldonmoor Cross

Bea

Maer

Poughill

Hersham

Dunsdon

Youldon

Bude Haven

Flexbury

Bush

Grimscott

Lana

Chilsworthy

BUDE BAY

Bude

Stratton

Launcells Cross

Pancrasweek

A38

Lynstone

Launcells

3

A3072

Red Post

5

Rydon

Derril

Upton

Marhamchurch

Titson

Bridgerule

Pyworthy

Chasty

Helebridge

Box's Shop

Derriton

H

Yeomadon

Tamar

Widemouth Bay

Pentire Point - Widemouth Heritage Coast

Week Orchard

Treskinnick Cross

North Tamerton

Corfcott Green

Dizzard Point

Coppathorne

98

Tinney

Claw

Pound

Tregole

Penlean

W

St

B3254

St Genn

Trewint

19

C

D

Greena Moor

15

kington Haven

Cambeak

Troharow

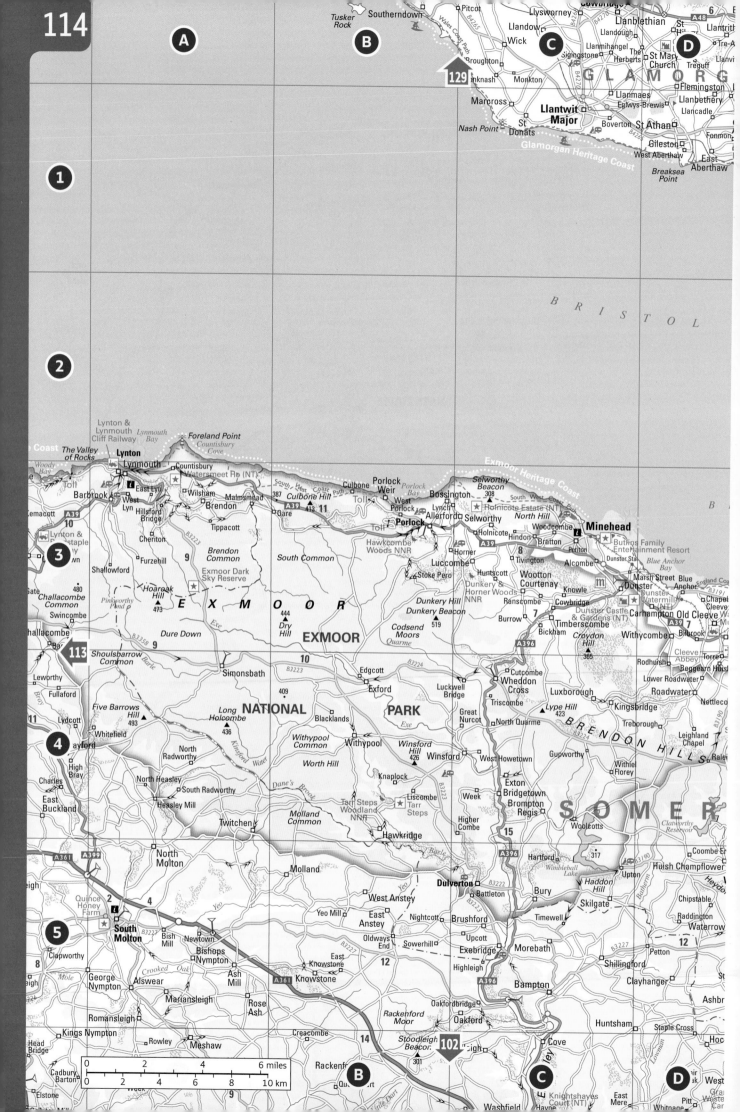

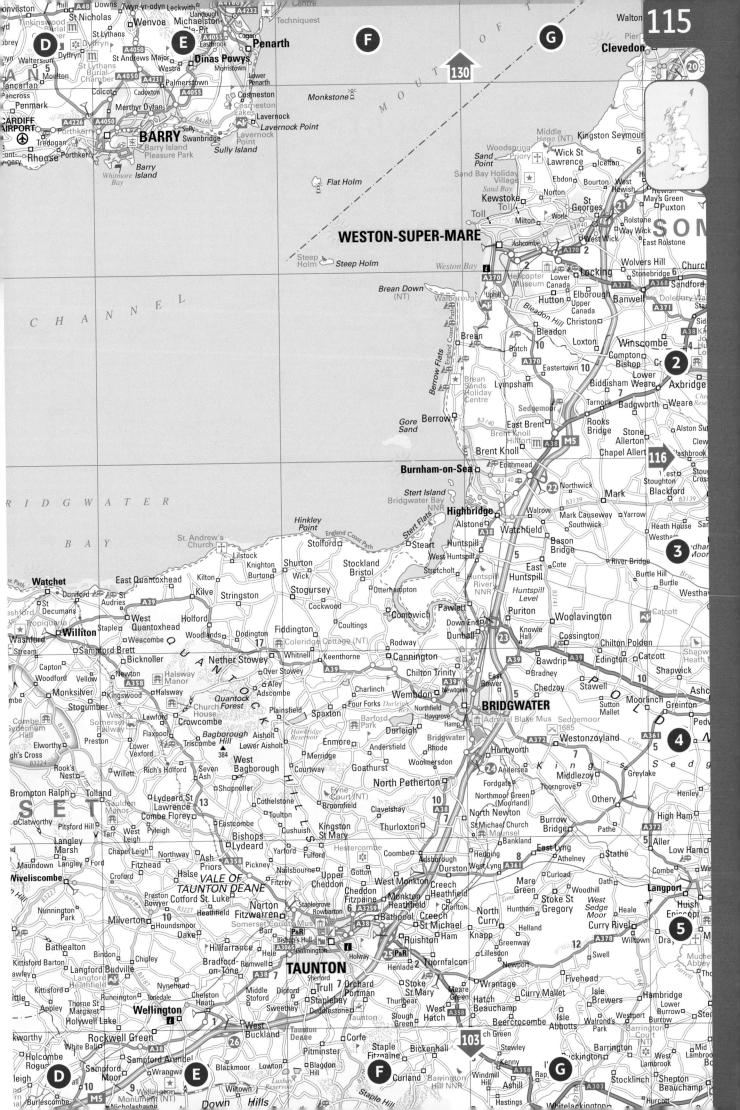

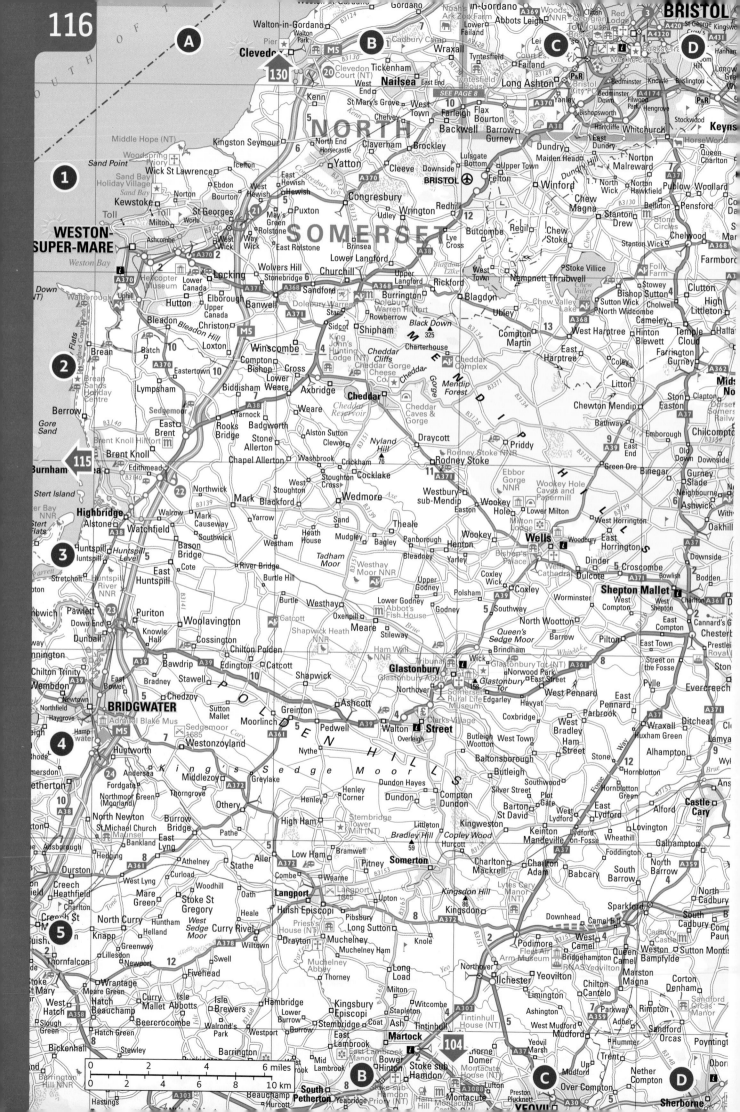

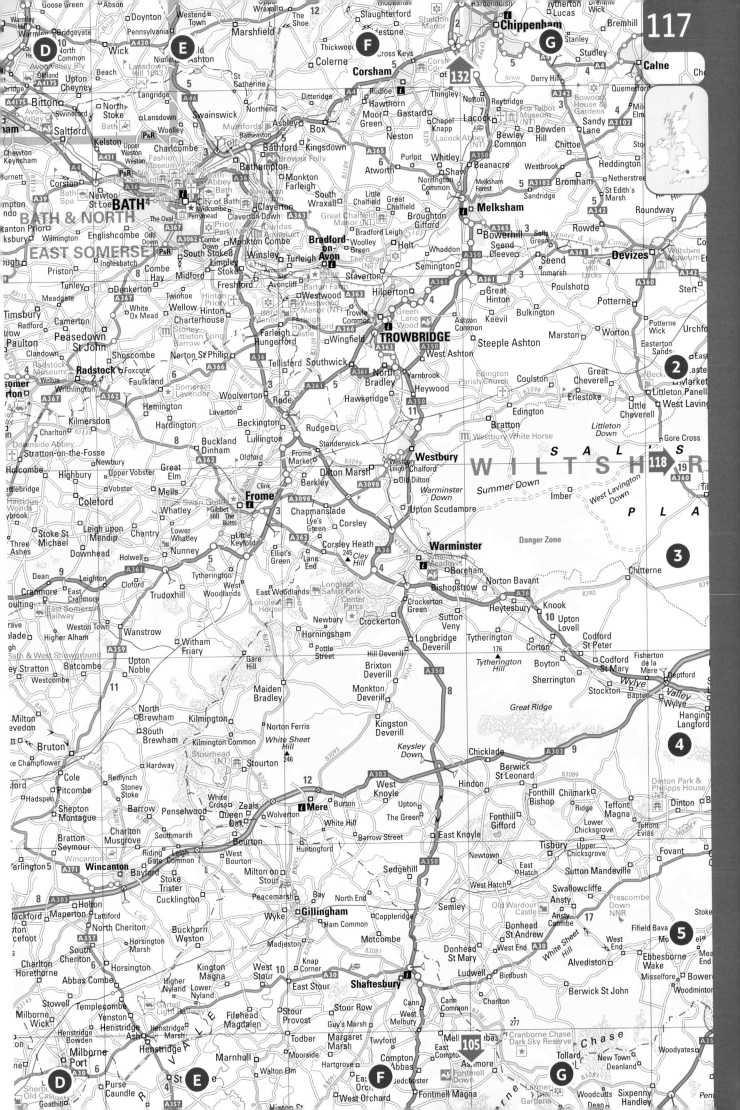

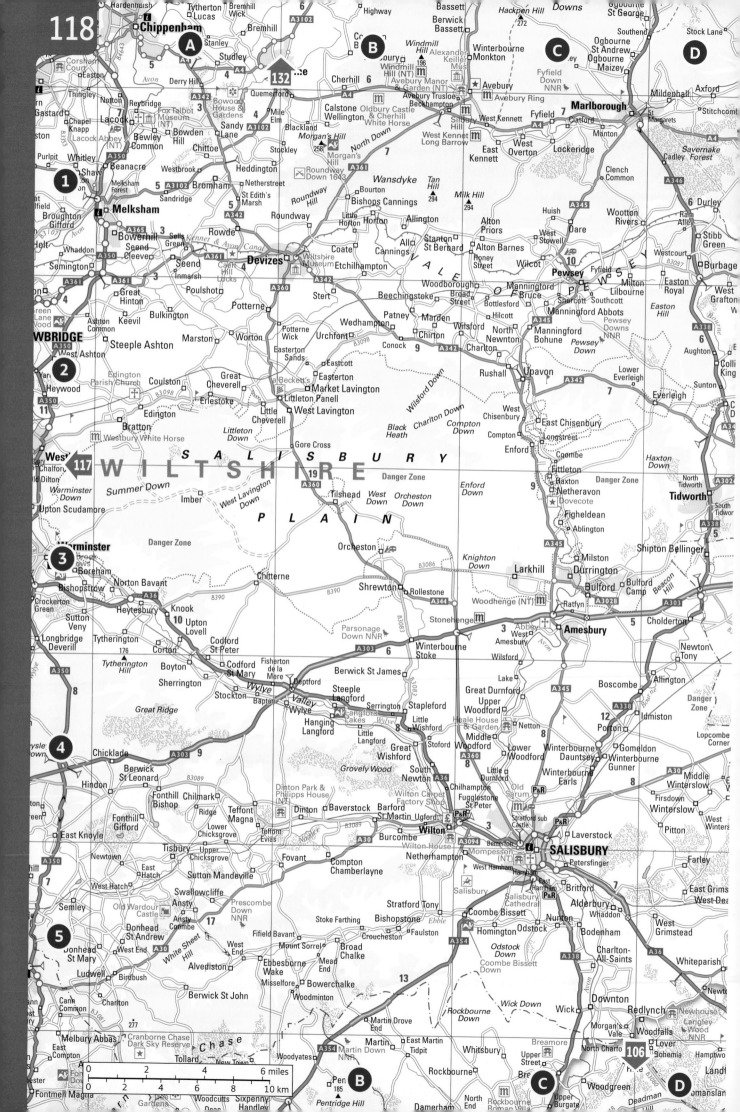

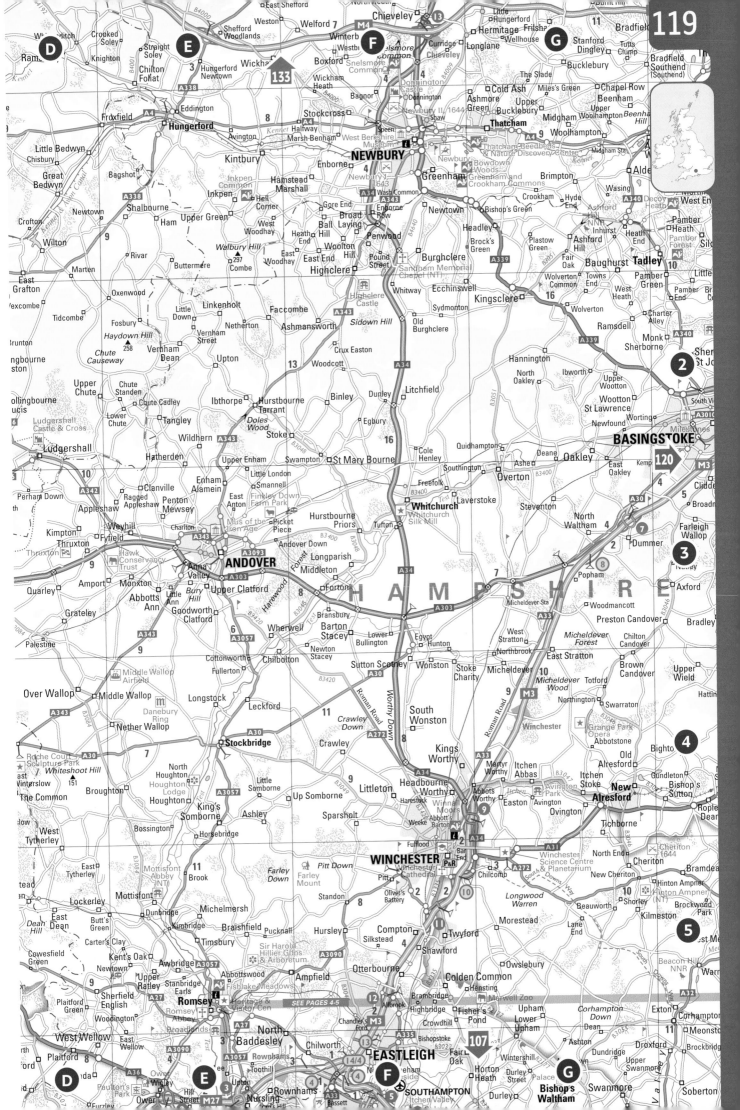

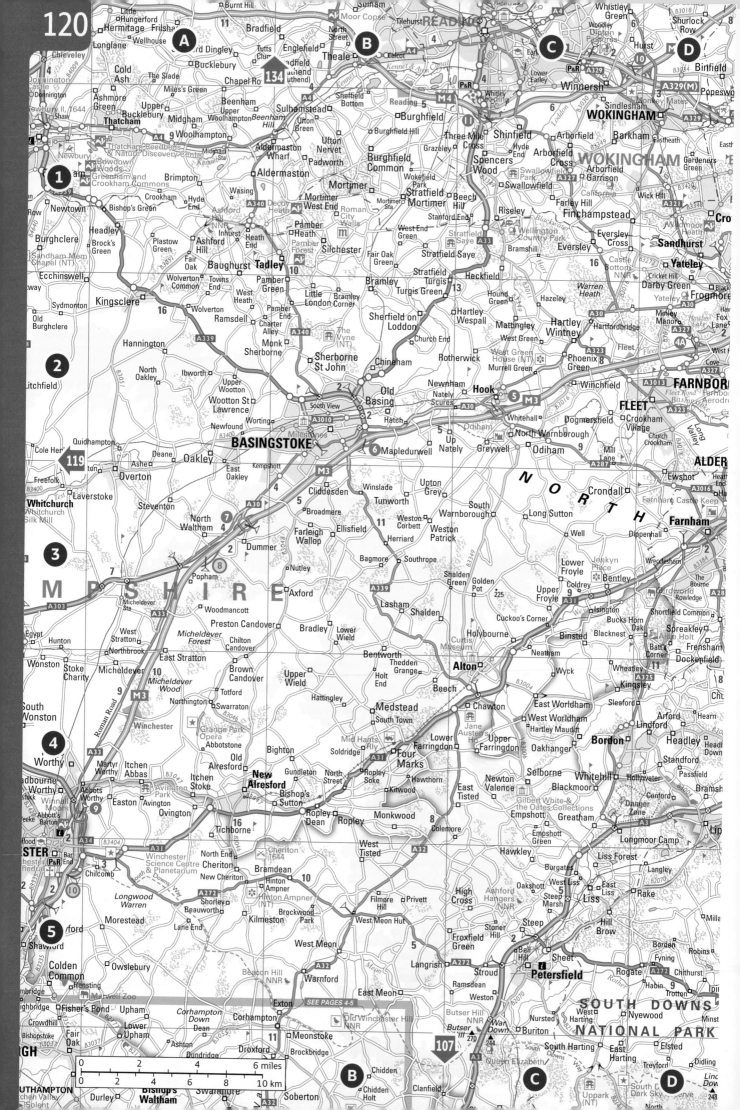

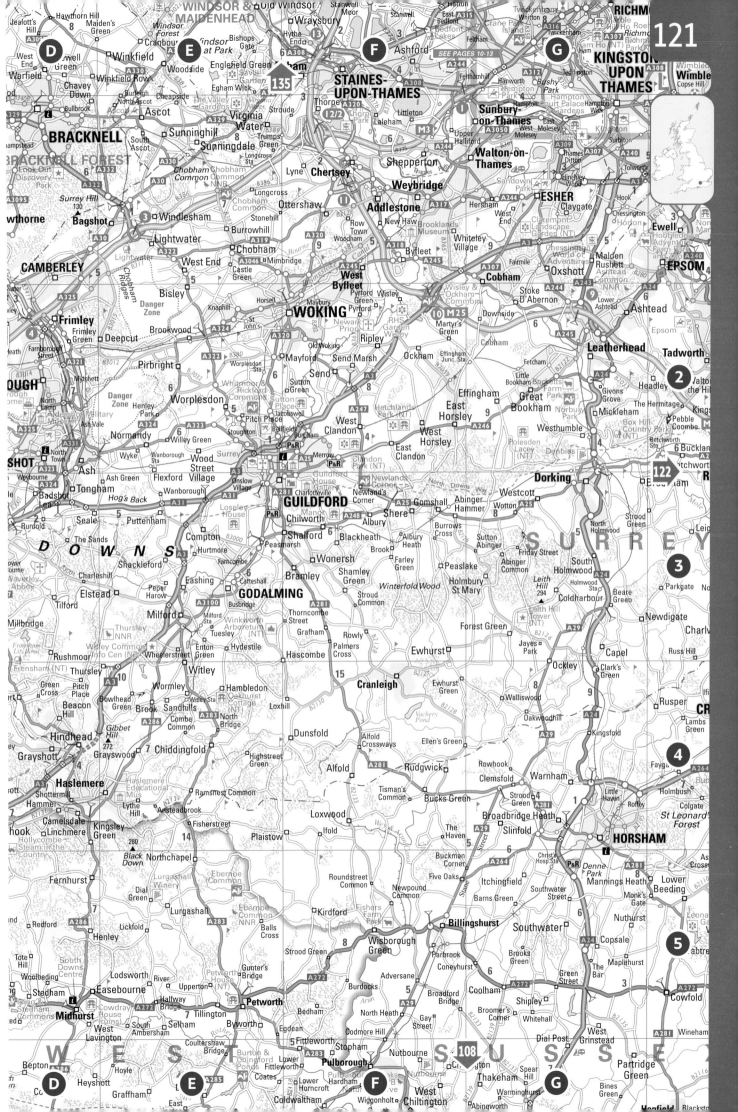

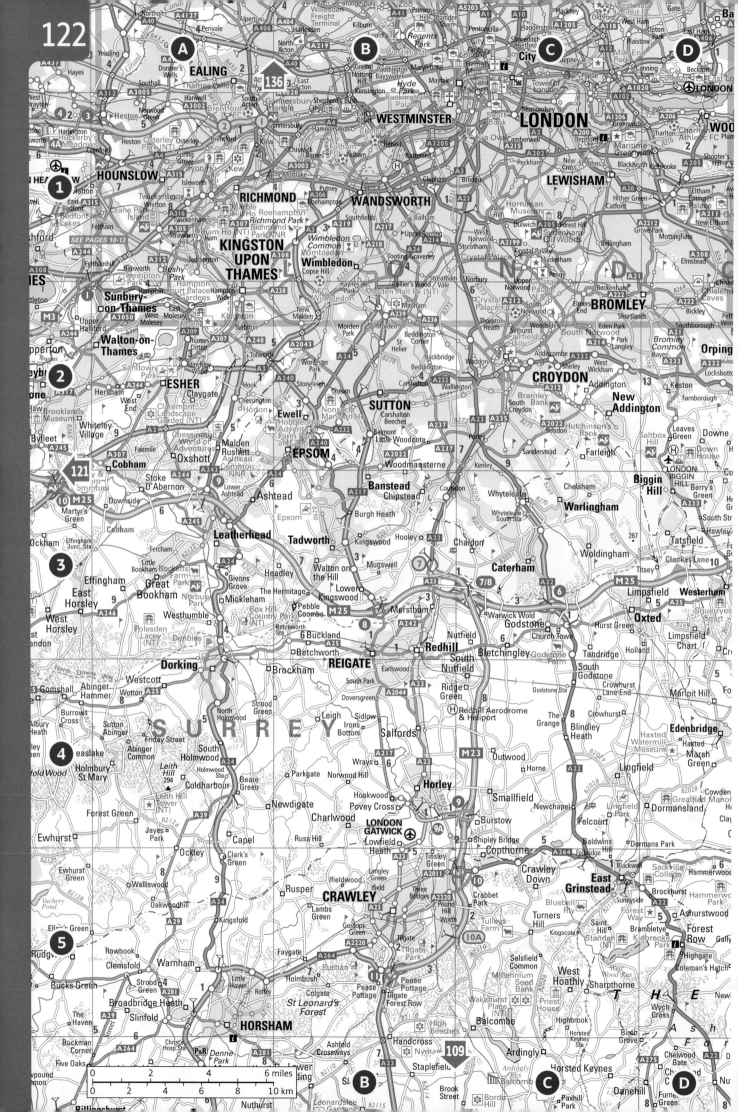

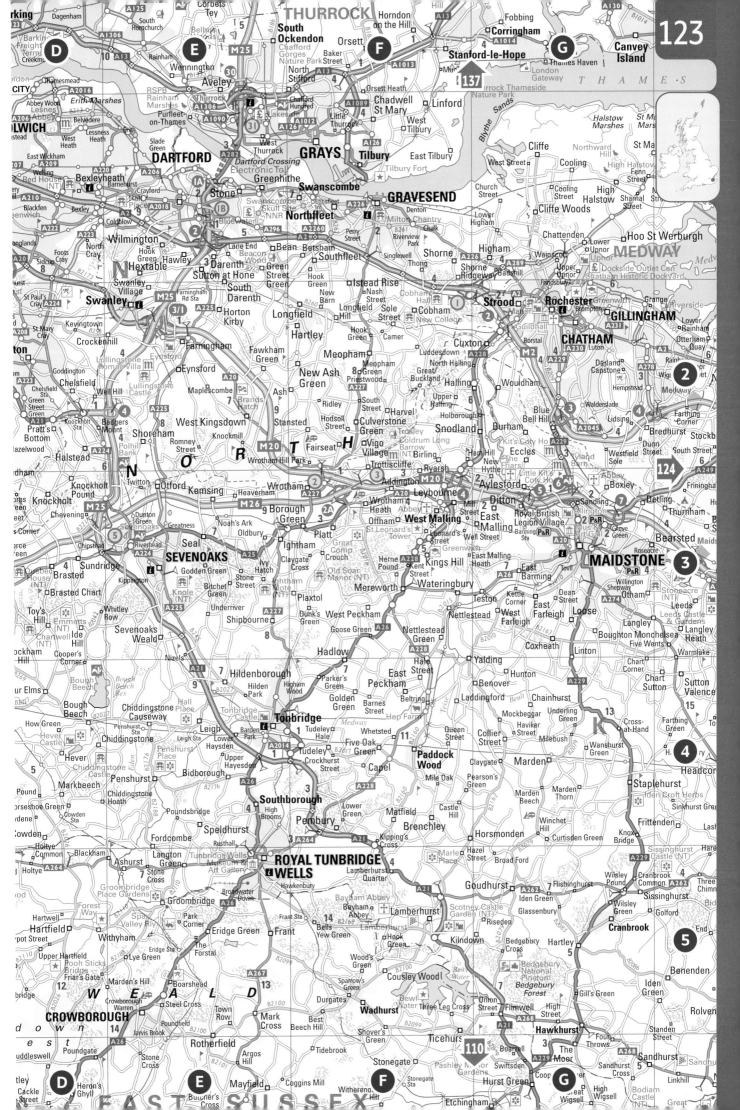

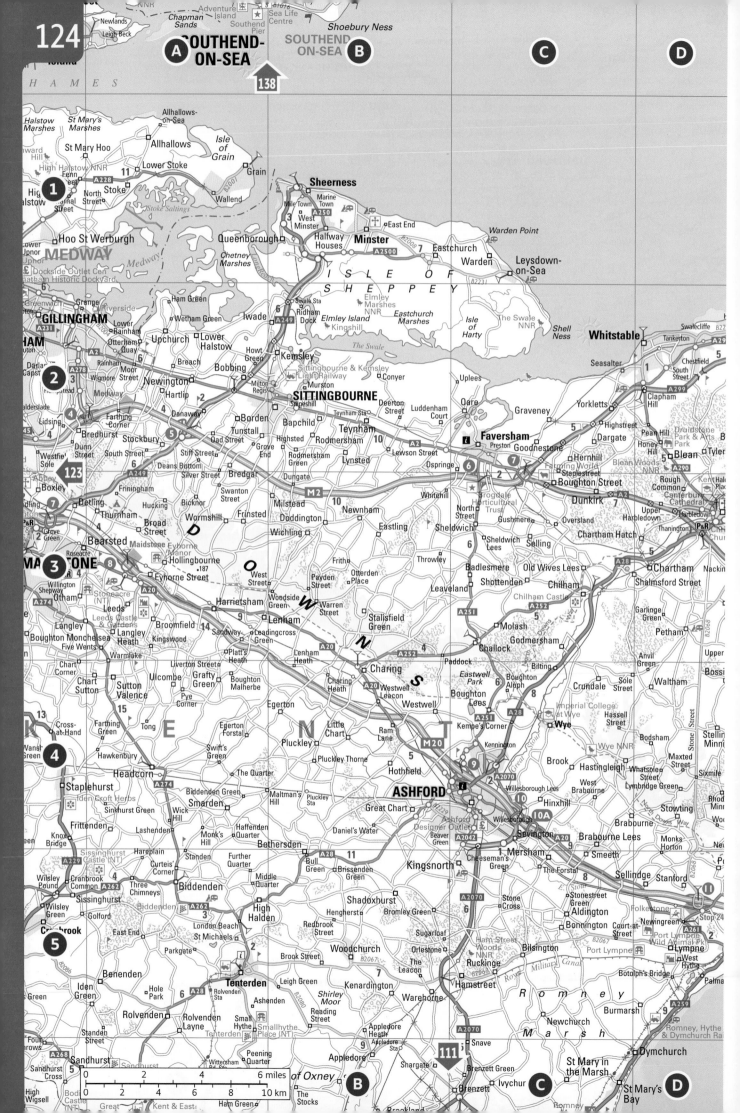

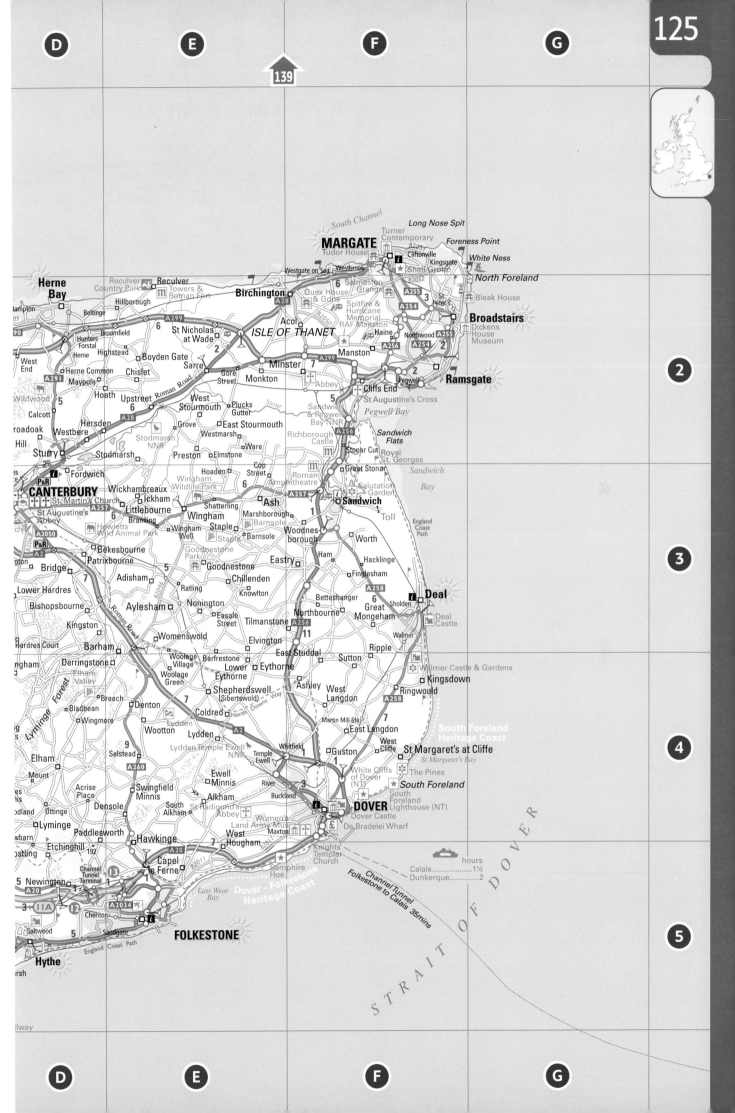

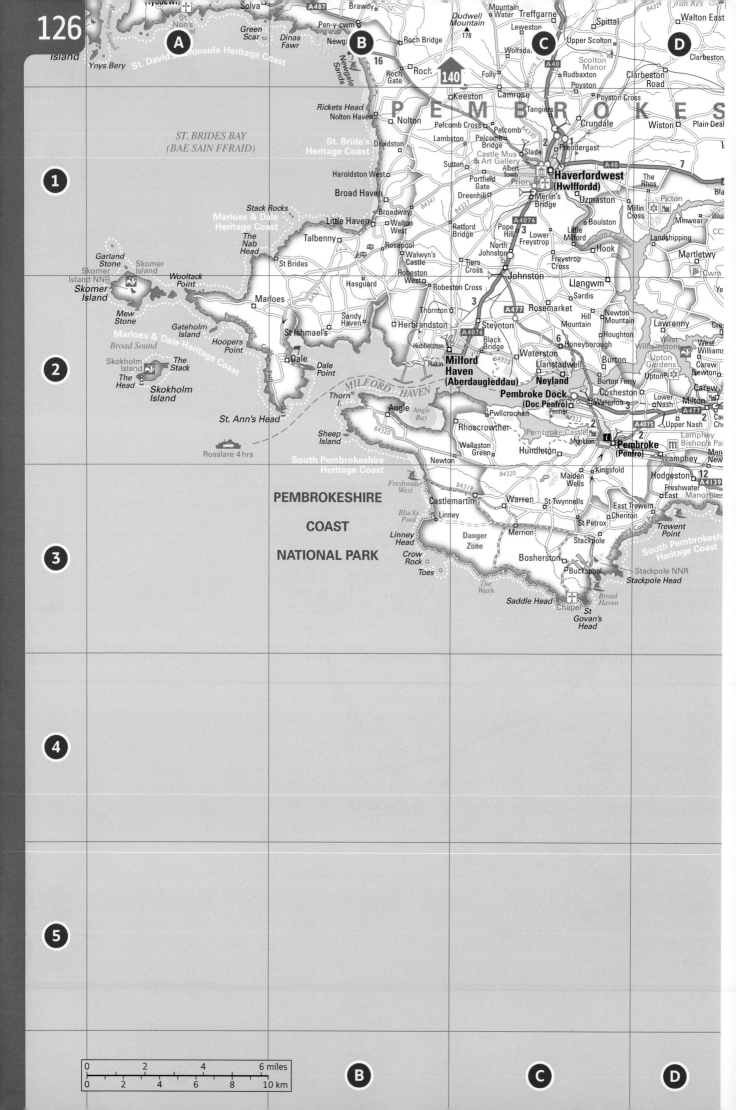

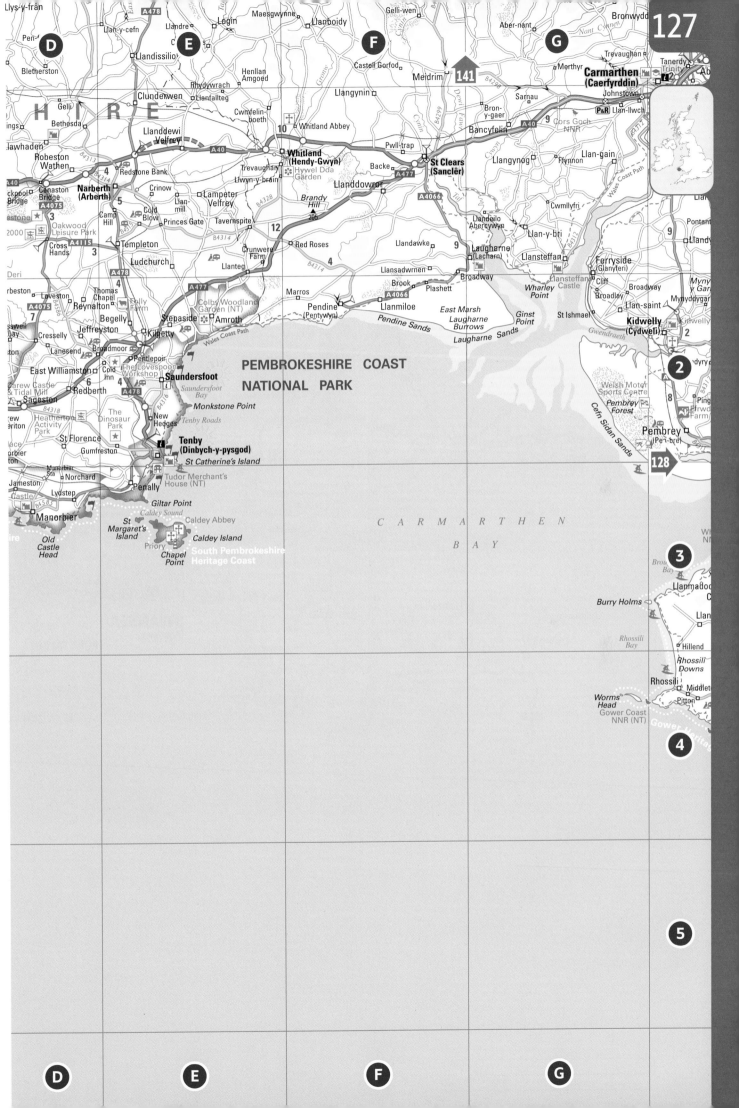

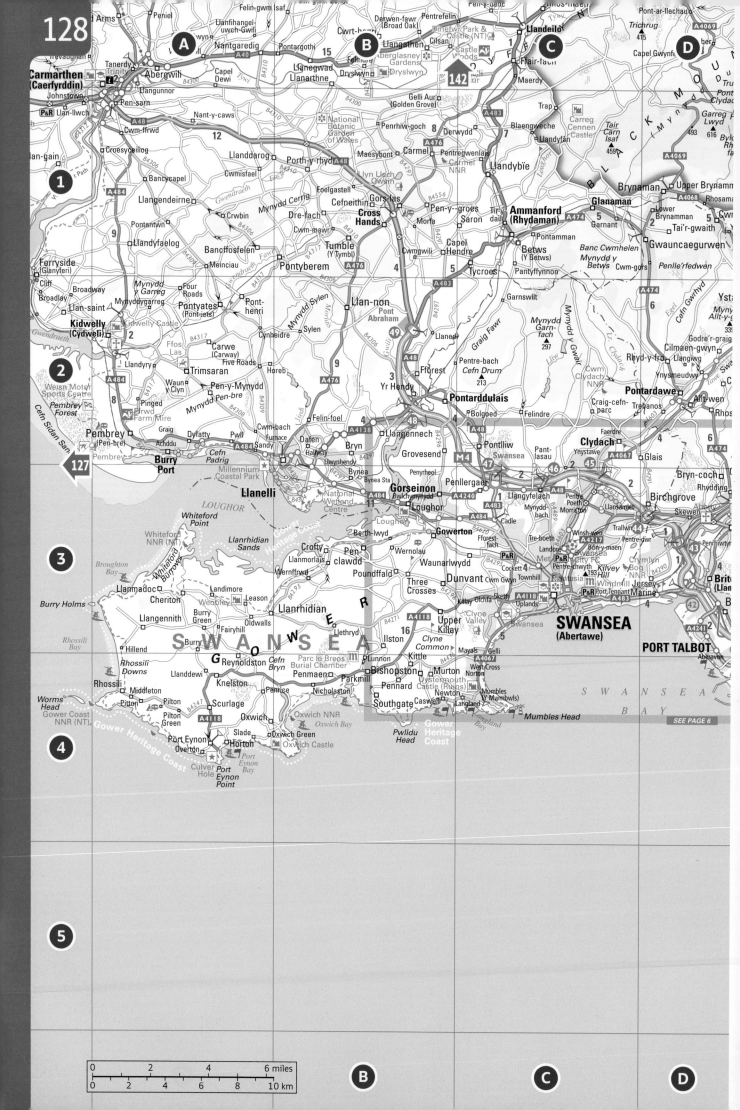

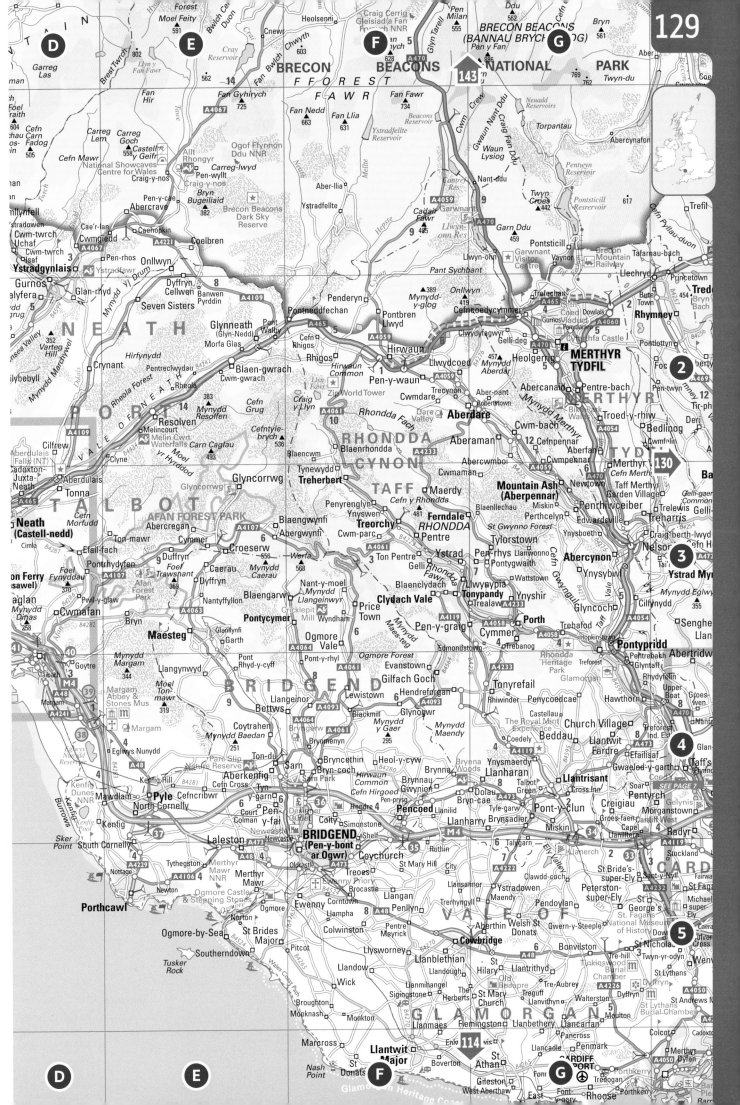

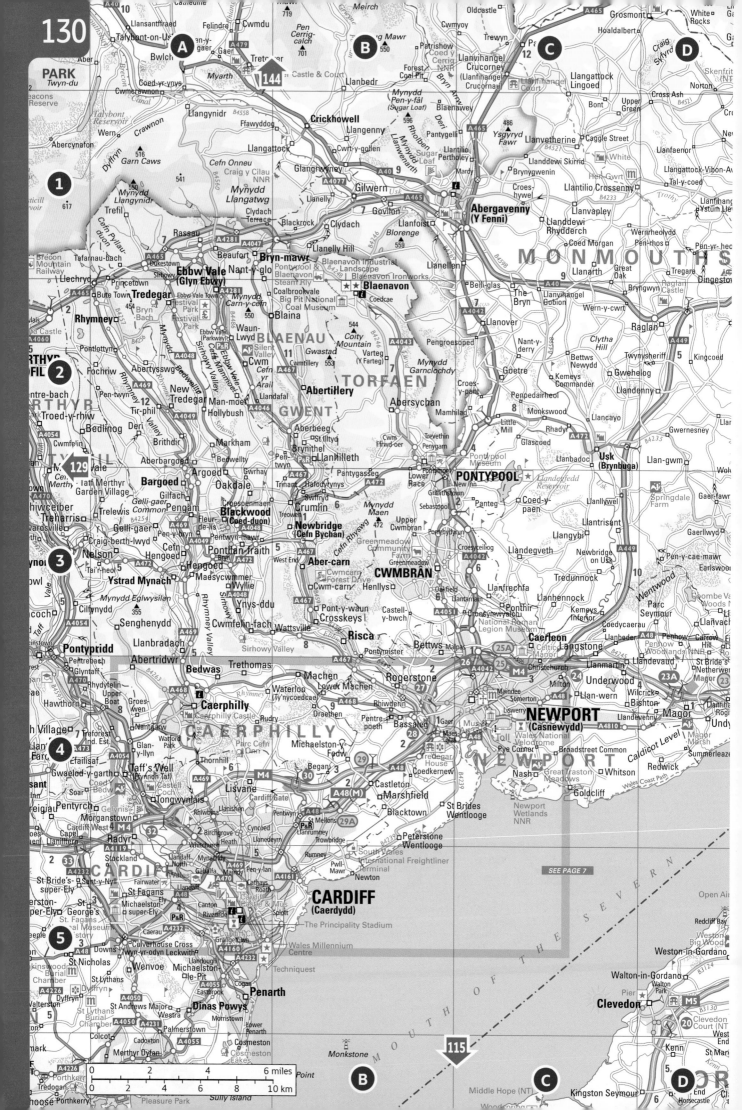

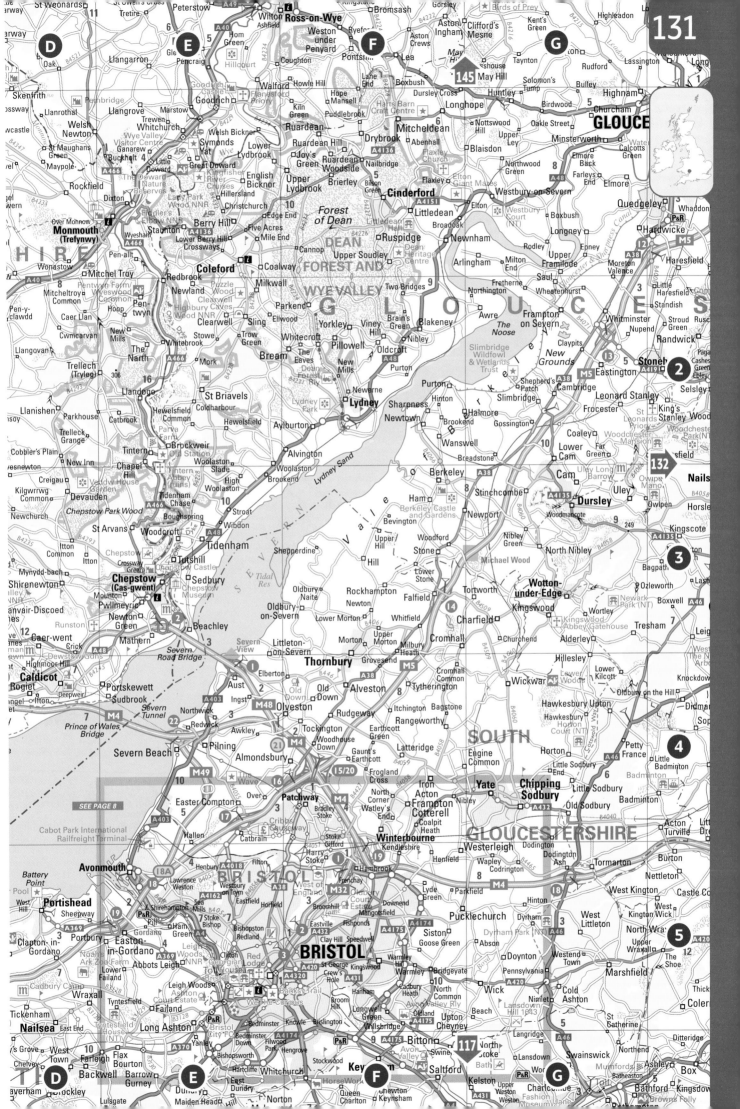

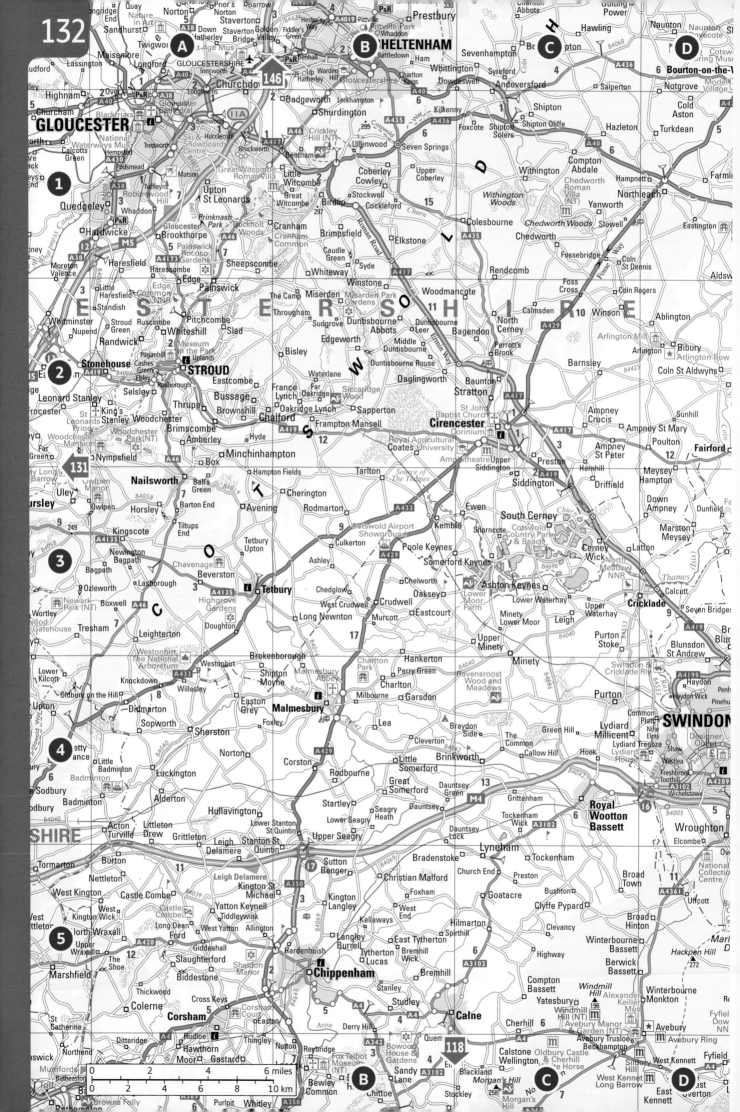

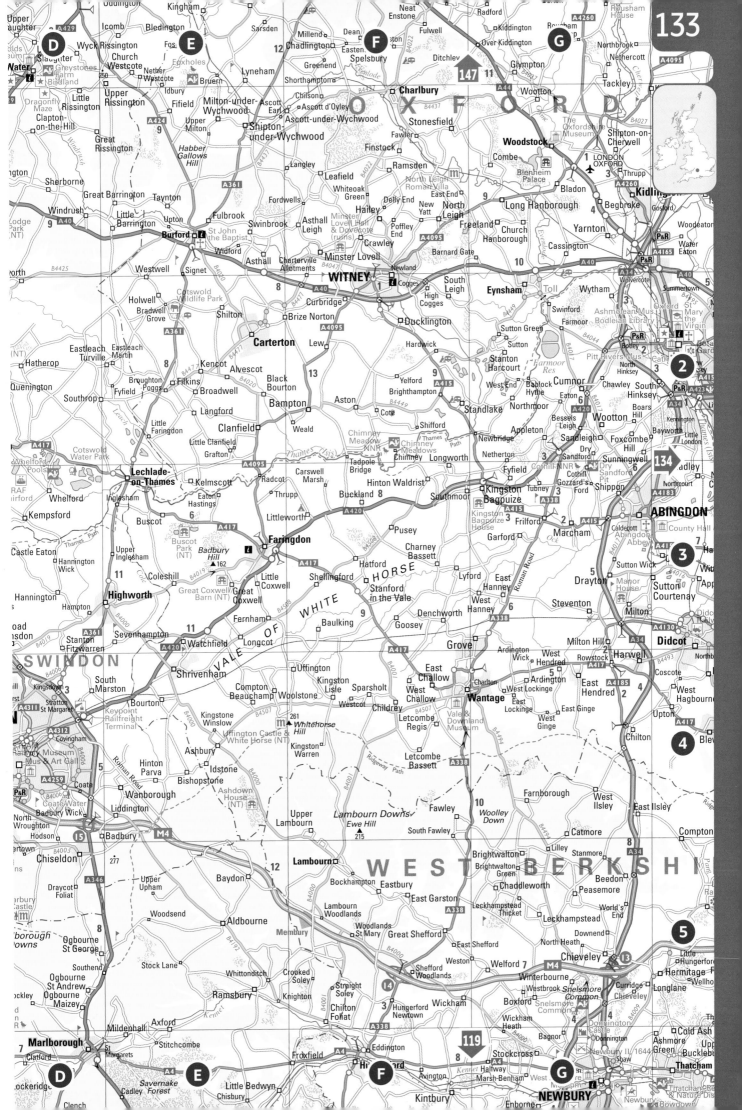

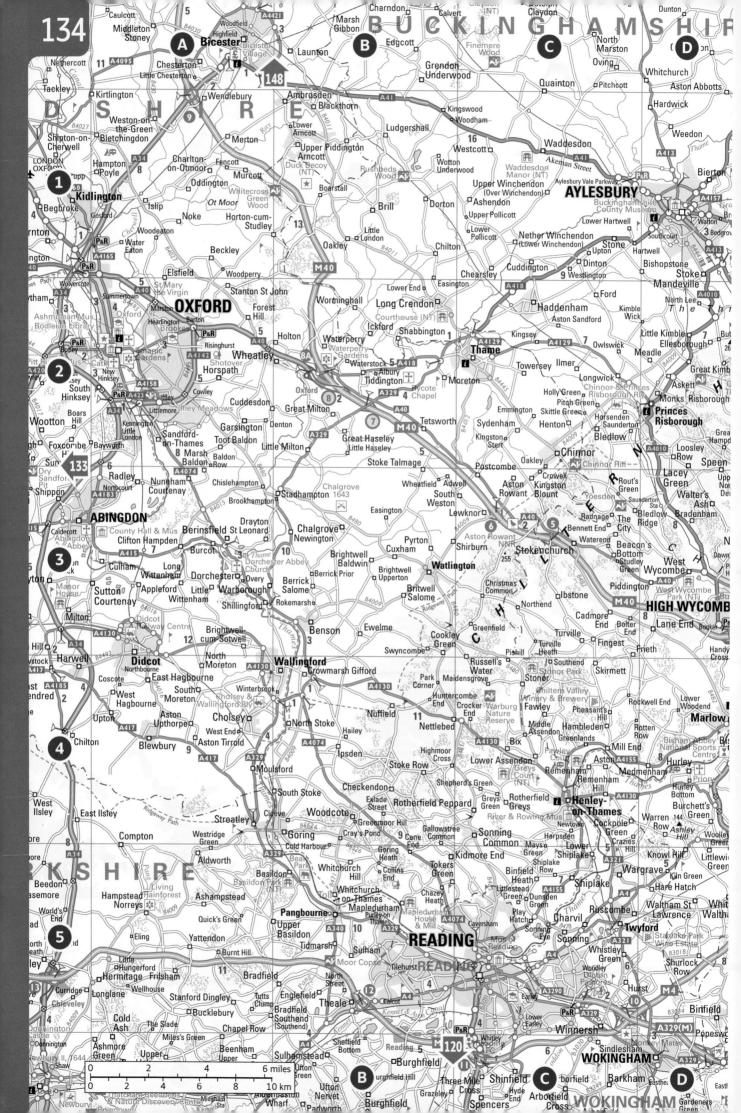

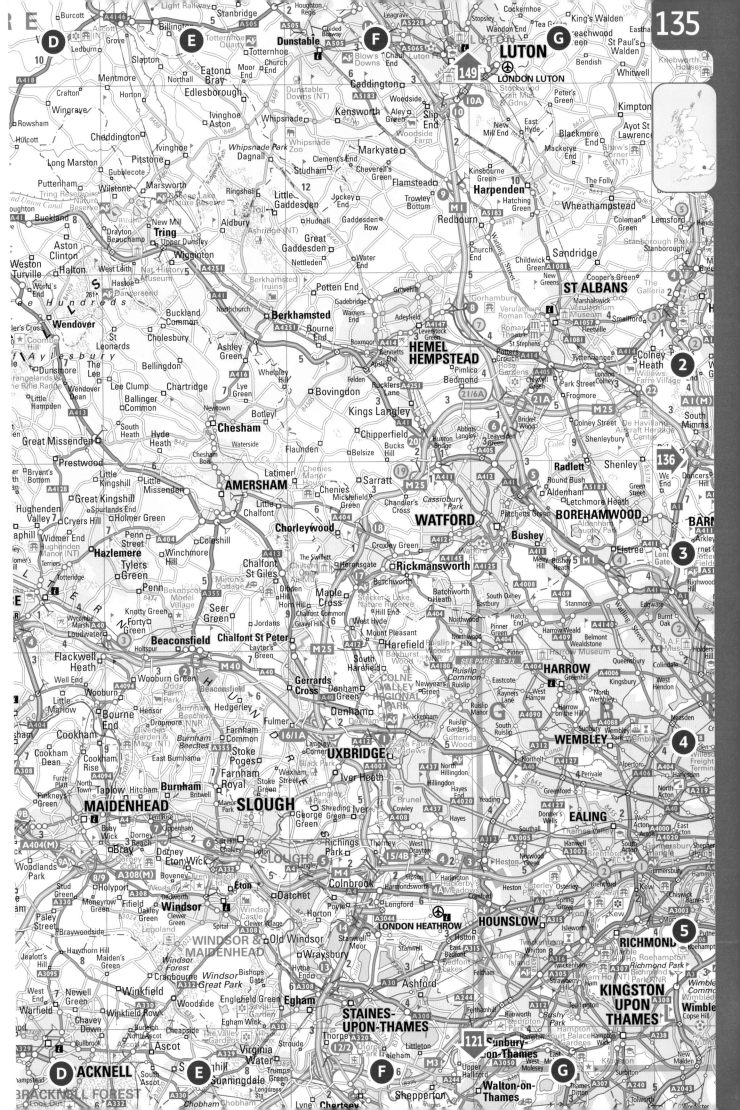

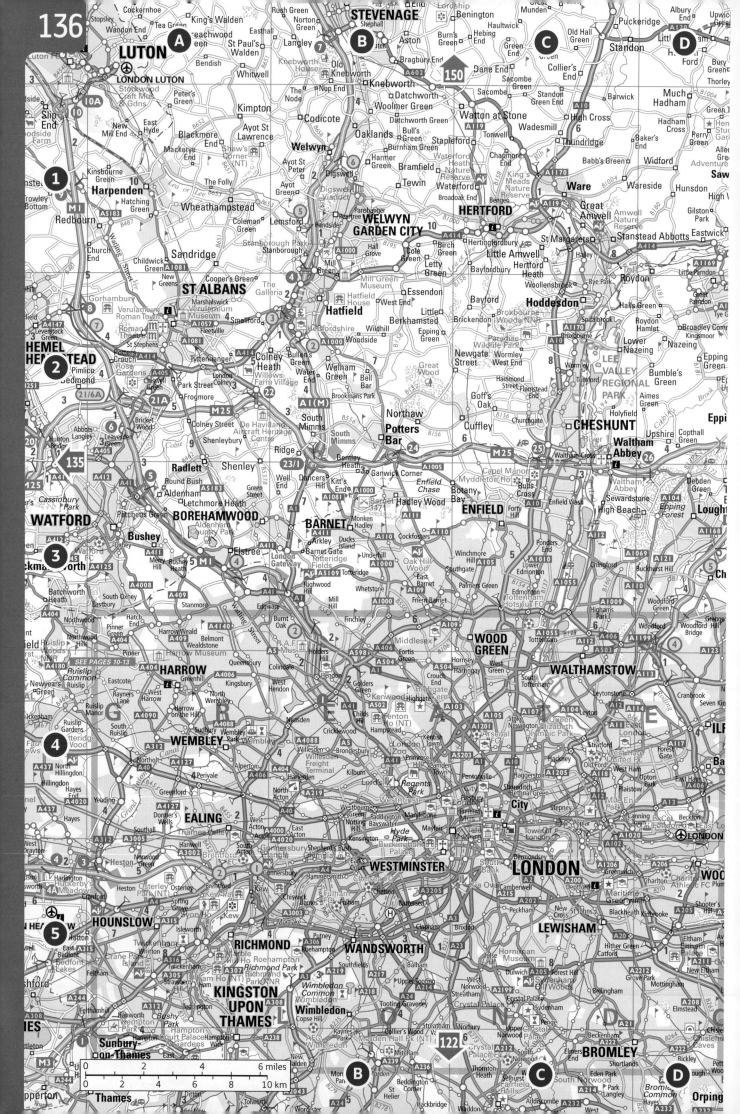

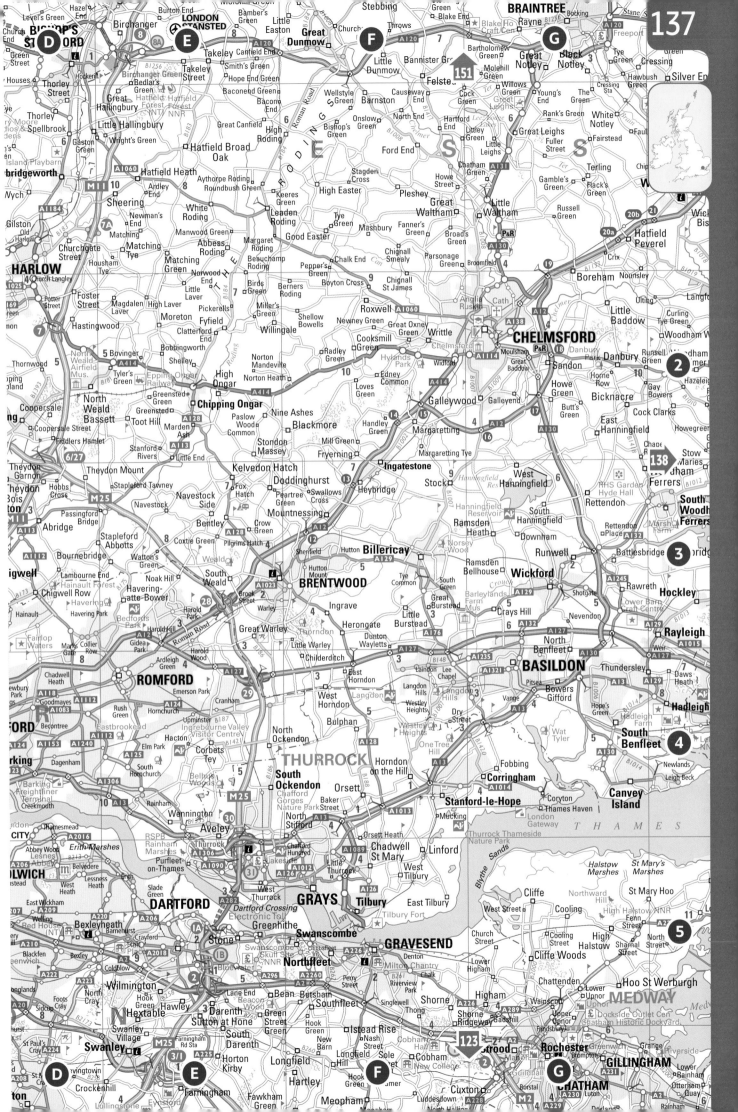

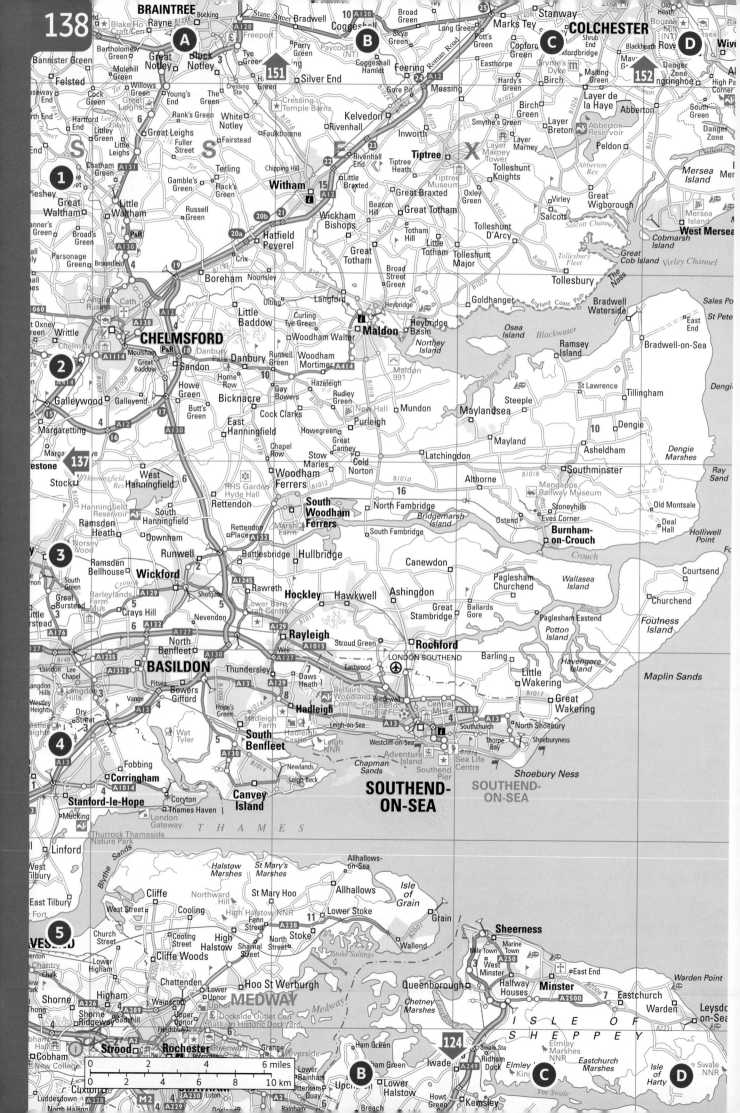

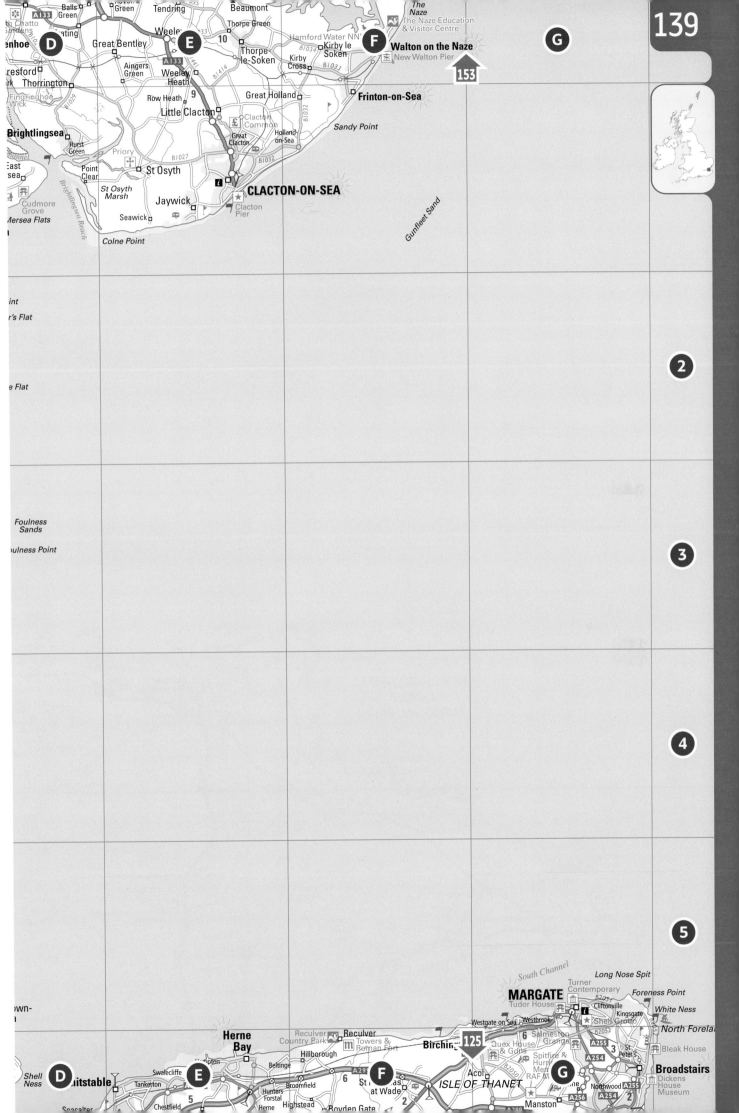

A　B　C　D

1

2

3

Rosslare 3¼–4¼ hrs

Strumble Head
St. David's Peninsula
Heritage Coast

Carregwastad
Point

Crincoed
Point

*Trwyn
Bwa*

Dinas
Head

Dinas Head
Heritage
Coast

*Newport
Bay*

Tresinwen

Pen Brush
Garn Fawr

Pen Caer

Llanwnda

*Fishguard
Bay*

Dinas
Island

Cwm-yr-Eglwys

Trefasser

Rhosycaerau

Goodwick
(Wdig)

Fishguard
(Abergwaun)

Brynhenllan

Parrog

PEMBROKESHIRE
COAST
NATIONAL PARK

Penbwchdy

Dyffryn

A487

A487

Dinas
Cross

*Myn
Carr*

St Nicholas

Manorowen

Lower
Town

Llanychaer
(Llanychâr)

*Mynydd
Melyn*

307

311

34

Penmorfa

Granston

Scleddau

Cilrhedyn Bridge

*Mynydd
Caregog*

4

Ynys Deullyn

Abercastle

Llangloffan

Jordanston

A40

Trecwn

Newbridge

Pont-faen

Cwm Gwau

Penclegyr

Tre-fin

Porth-gain

Mathry

Llanvirn

Coedydd
Llangloffan
NNR

*Mynydd
Cilciffeth*

334

B4313

Morvil

St. David's Peninsula
Heritage Coast

Abereiddy

Carreg-
gwylan-fach

Penclegyr

Penllechwen

St David's Head

North
Bishop

St David's
Head

Bishops & Clerks

on

Point
St John

Llanrhian

Berea

Penparc

Croes-goch

14

Western Cleddau

Llangloffan
Fen

Castle
Morris

B4331

Mynydd Castleby

347

Treglemais

Treffynnon

Treddiog

Letterston

Little
Newcastle

Puncheston

Castlebythe

Tufton

M

Tretio

Treleddyd-fawr

Carnhedryn

Llanreithan

B4330

15

Sealyham

St Dogwells

Castlebythe

Whitesands Bay
(Porth-mawr)

St David's Cathedral
& Bishop's Palace

Rhodiad-
y-brenin

Caerfarchell

A487

Newton

Welsh
Hook

Wolf's
Castle

Ford

Rinaston

Ambleston

Wallis

Woodstock

Rhosson

Whitchurch

Middle Mill

Llandeloy

Hayscastle

Hayscastle
Cross

Brimaston

Llys-y-
frân Res

Ramsey
Island NNR

St David's
(Tyddewi)

Solva

Trefgarn
Owen

Brawdy

Mountain
Water

Treffgarne

Spittal

Walton East

Ramsey
Sound

St
Non's
Chapel

Green
Scar

Dinas
Fawr

Pen-y-cwm

*Dudwell
Mountain*

178

Leweston

Upper Scolton

Clarbeston

*Ramsey
Island*

Ynys Bery

St. David's Peninsula Heritage Coast

Newgale

Roch Bridge

Wolfsdale

A40

Scolton
Manor

Clarbeston
Road

Newgale
Sands

16

Roch
Gate

Roch

Folly

Rudbaxton

Poyston

Poyston Cross

Rickets Head
Nolton Haven

PEMBROKES

126

Camrose

Crundale

Wisto

Plain Deal

Nolton

Tangiers

Pelcomb Cross

Pelcomb

St. Bri
Heritage Coast

Druidston

Lambston

Pelcomb
Bridge

Castle Mus
& Art Gallery

Slade

Prendergast

1

A40

7

Sutton

Albert

0　2　4　6 miles
0　2　4　6　8　10 km

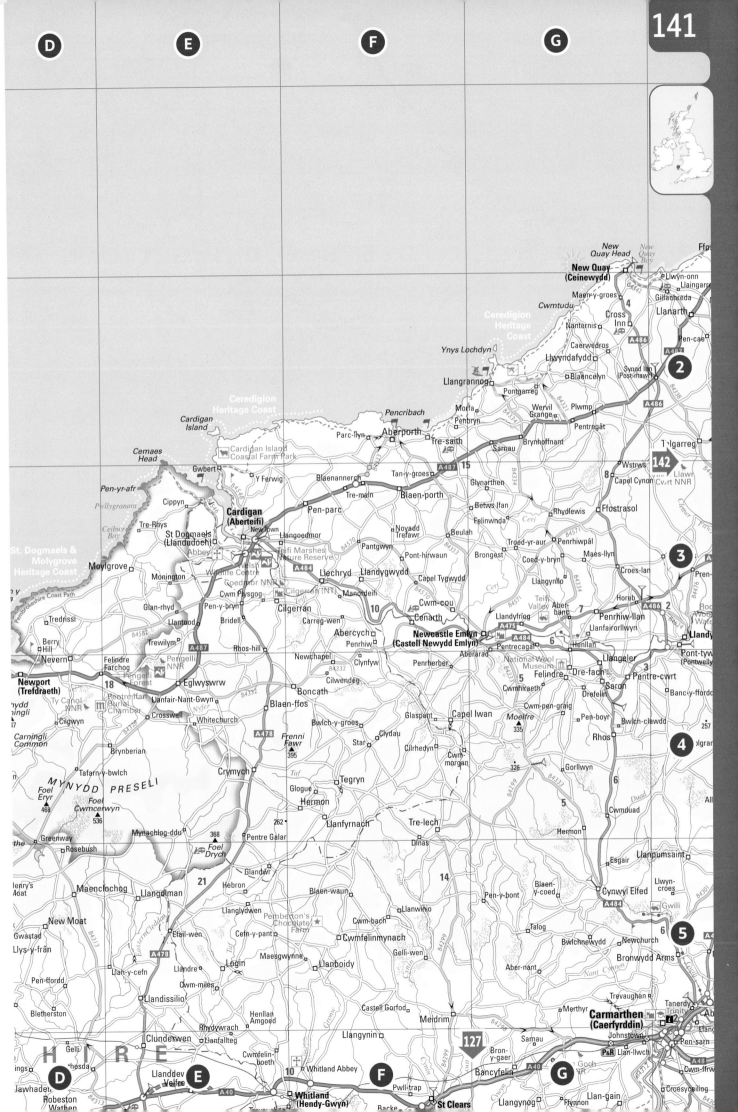

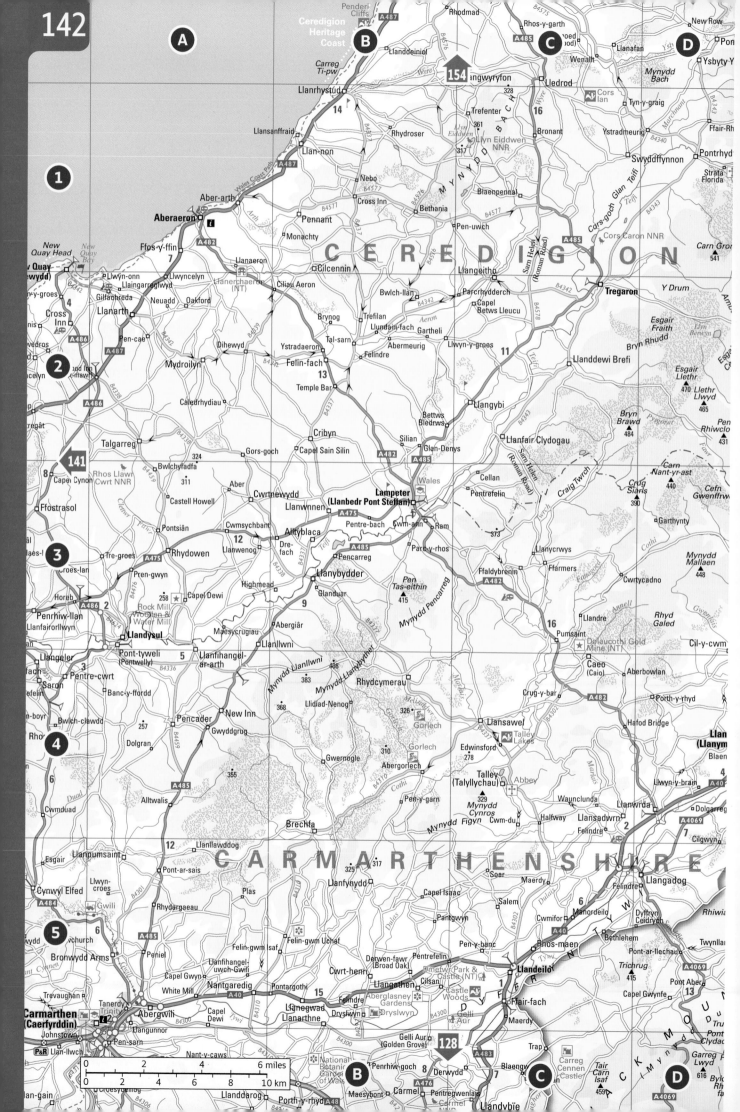

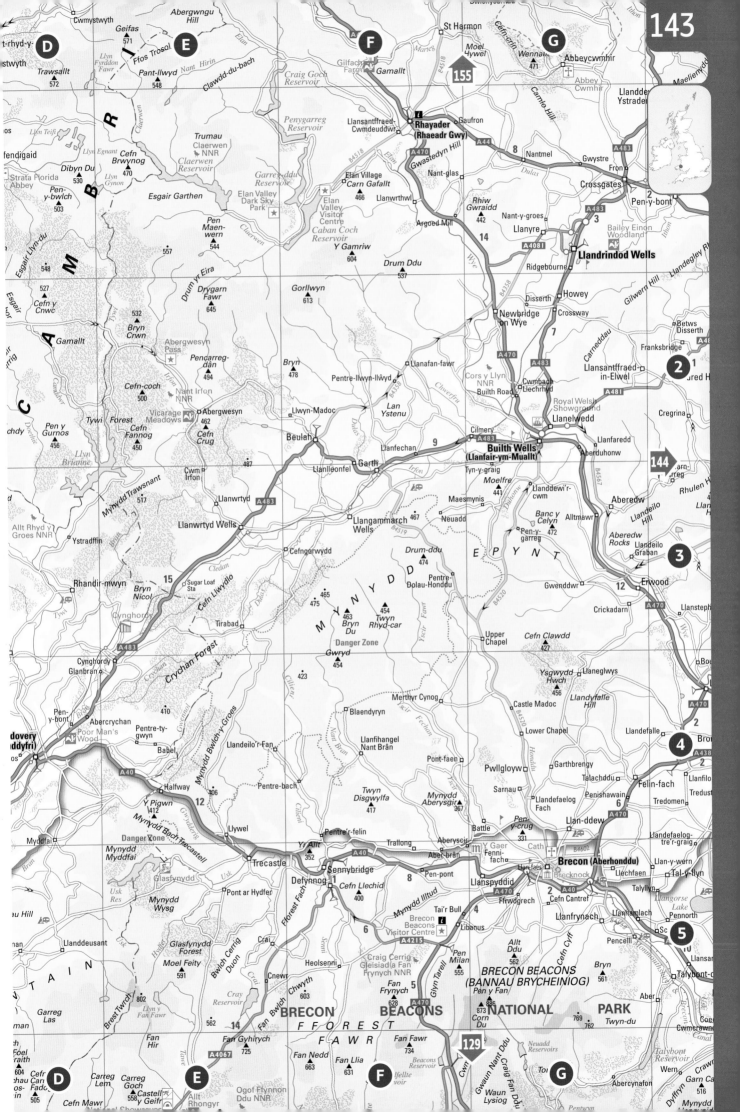

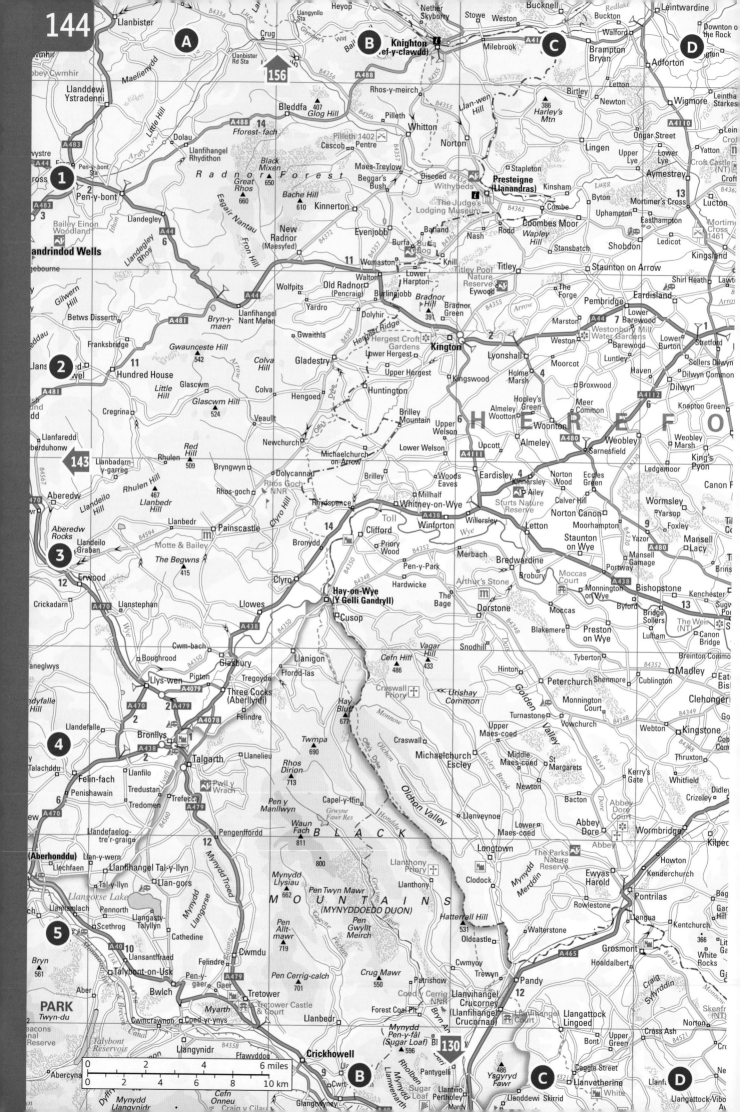

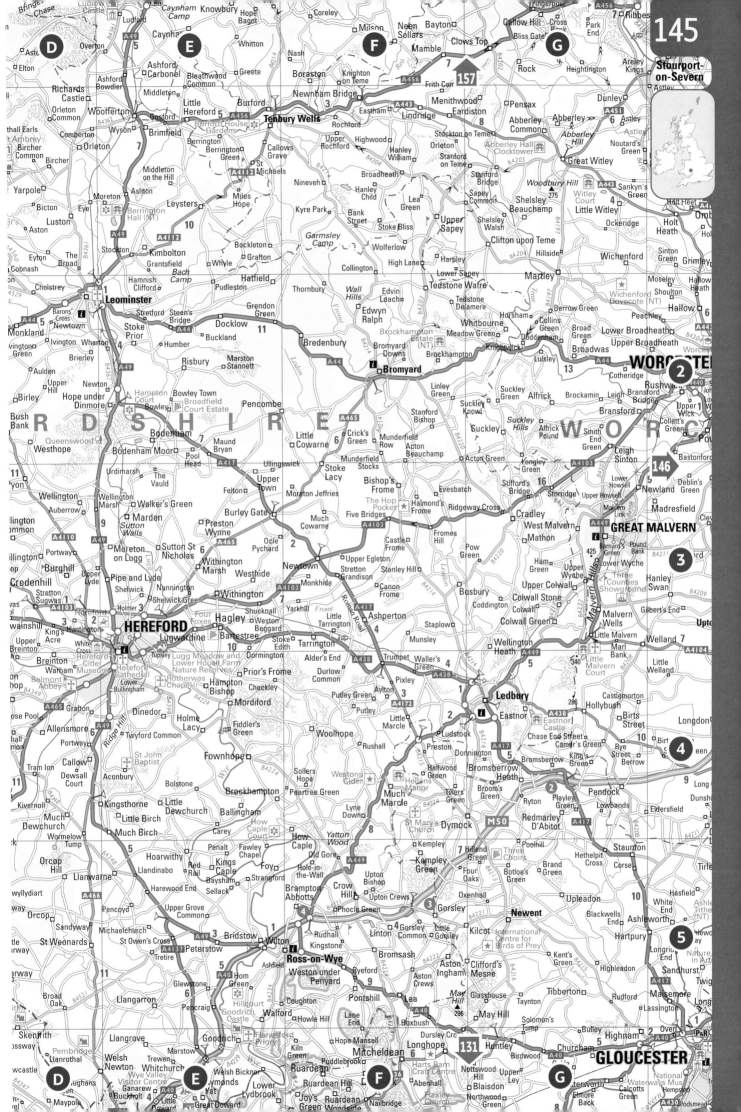

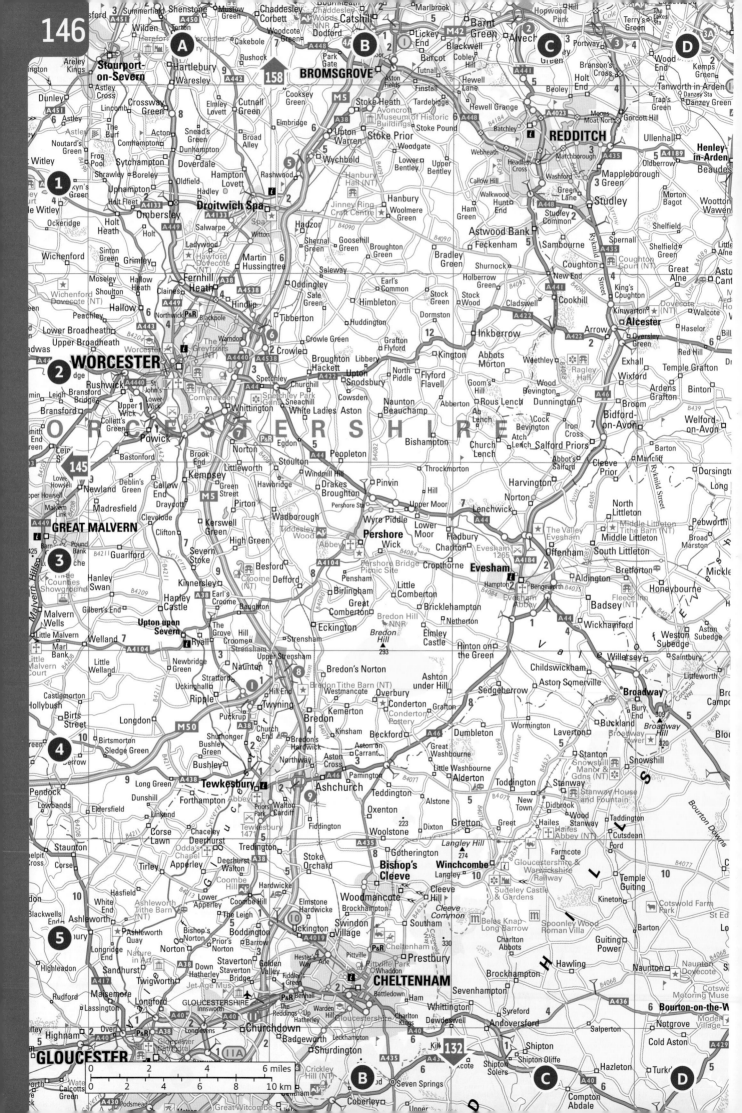

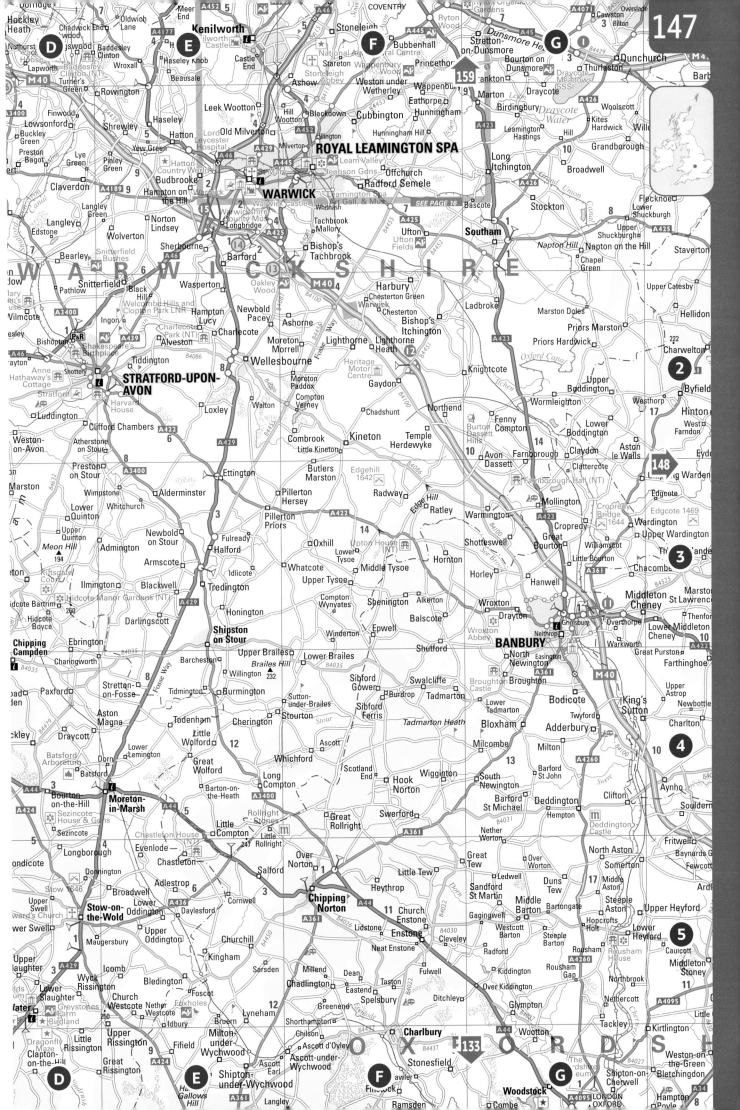

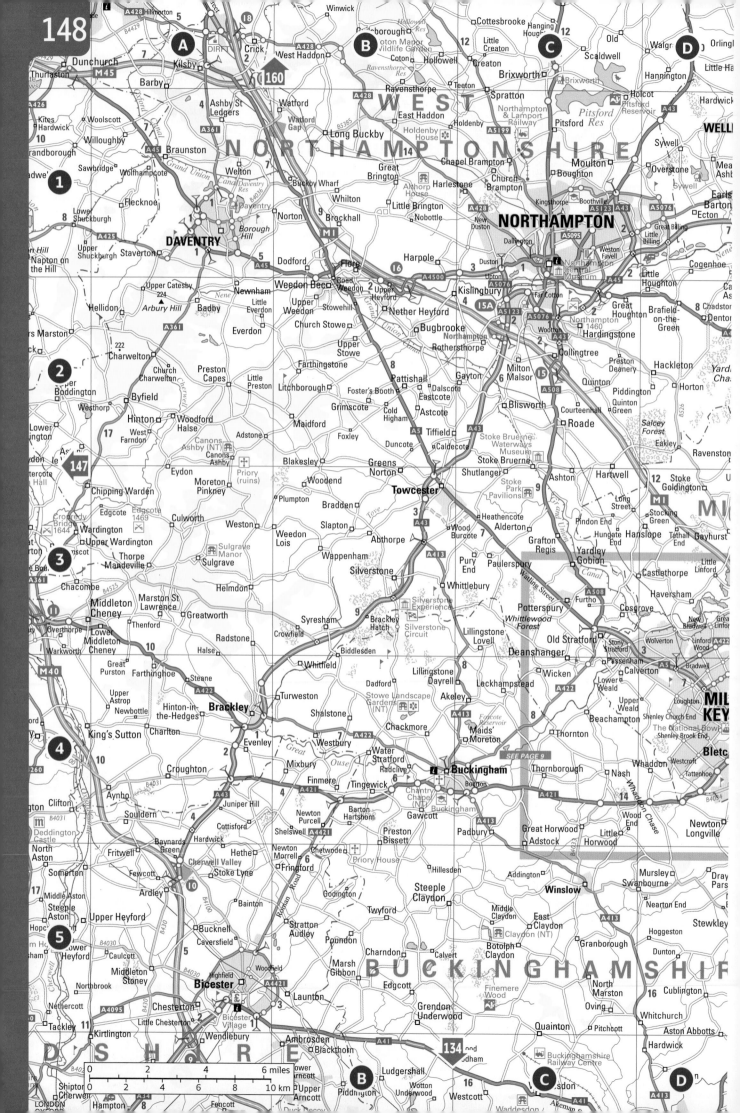

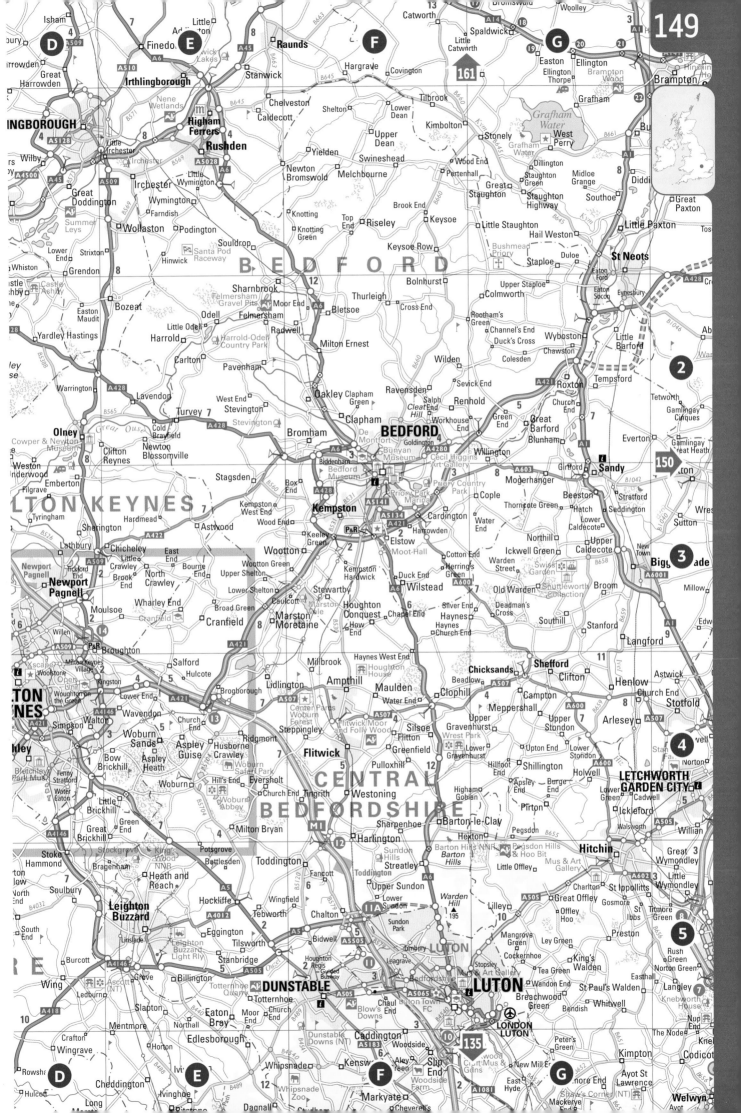

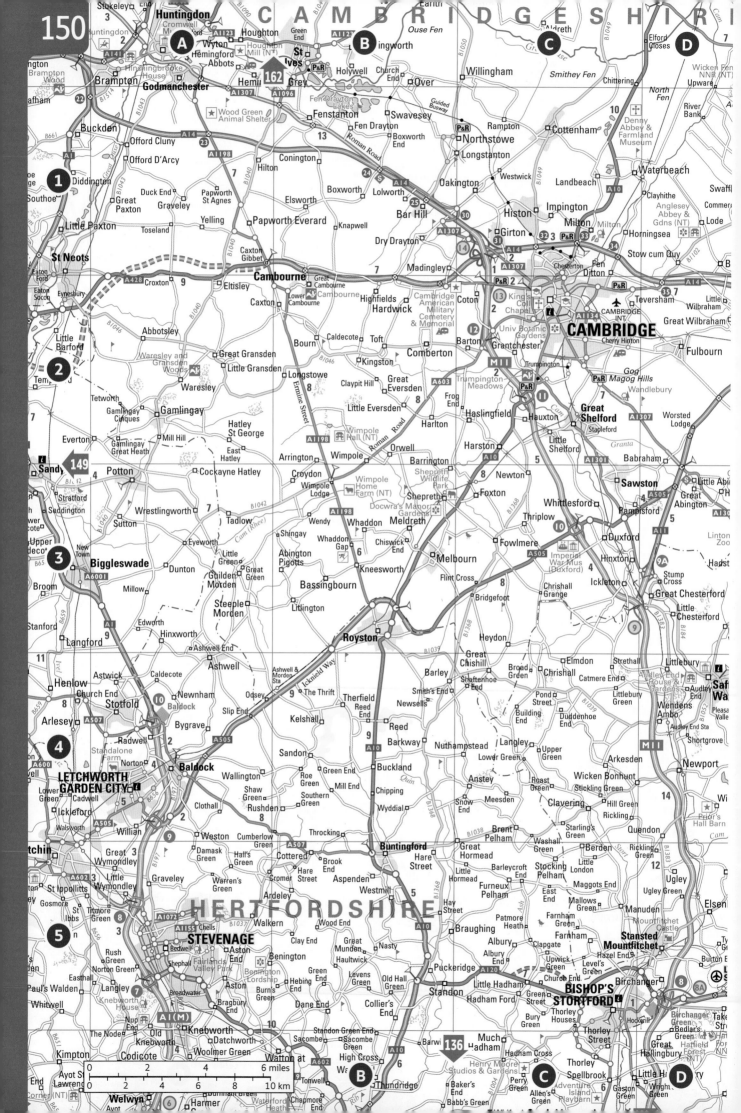

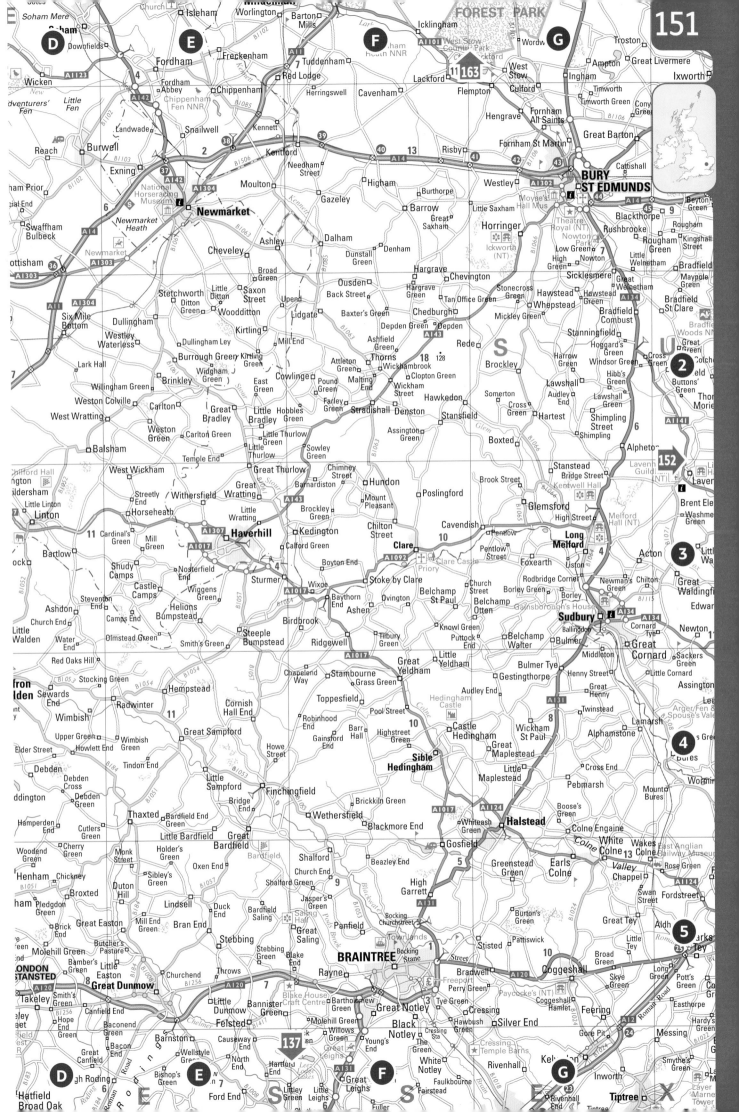

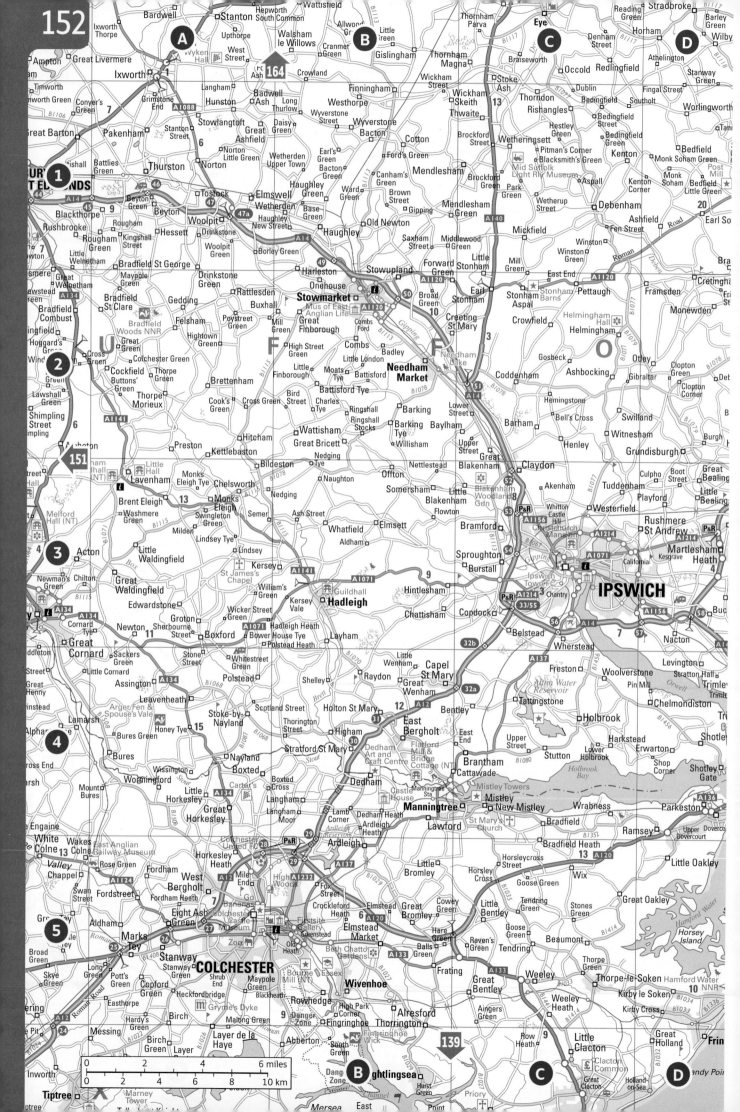

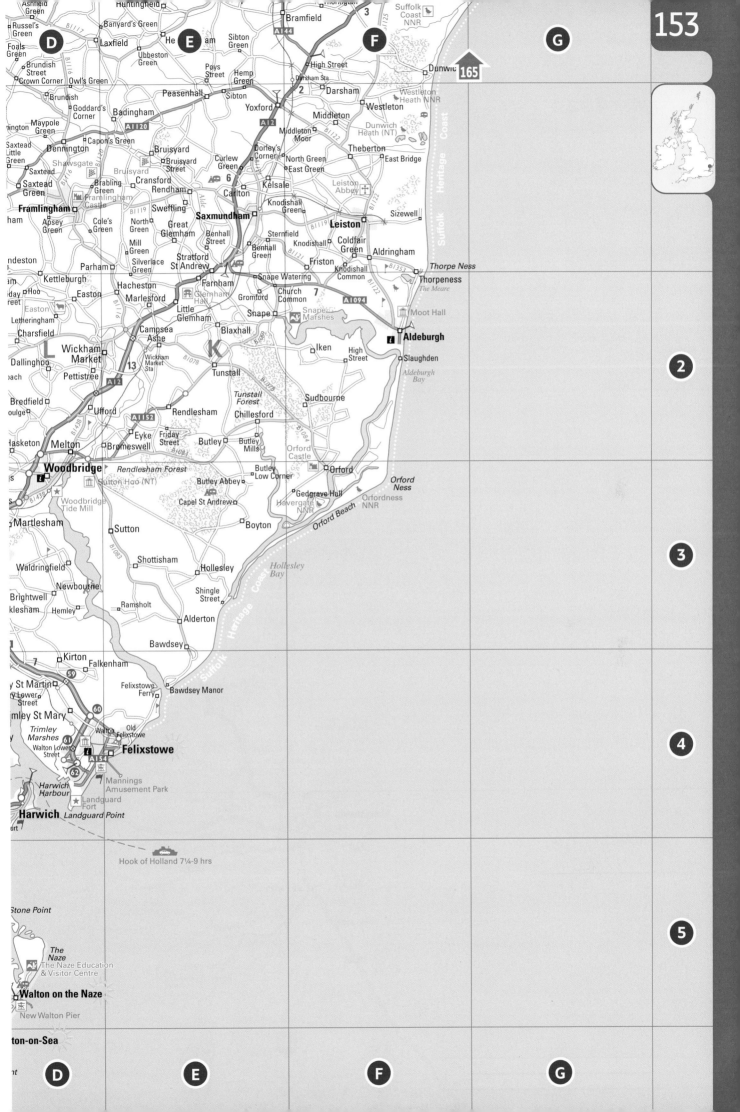

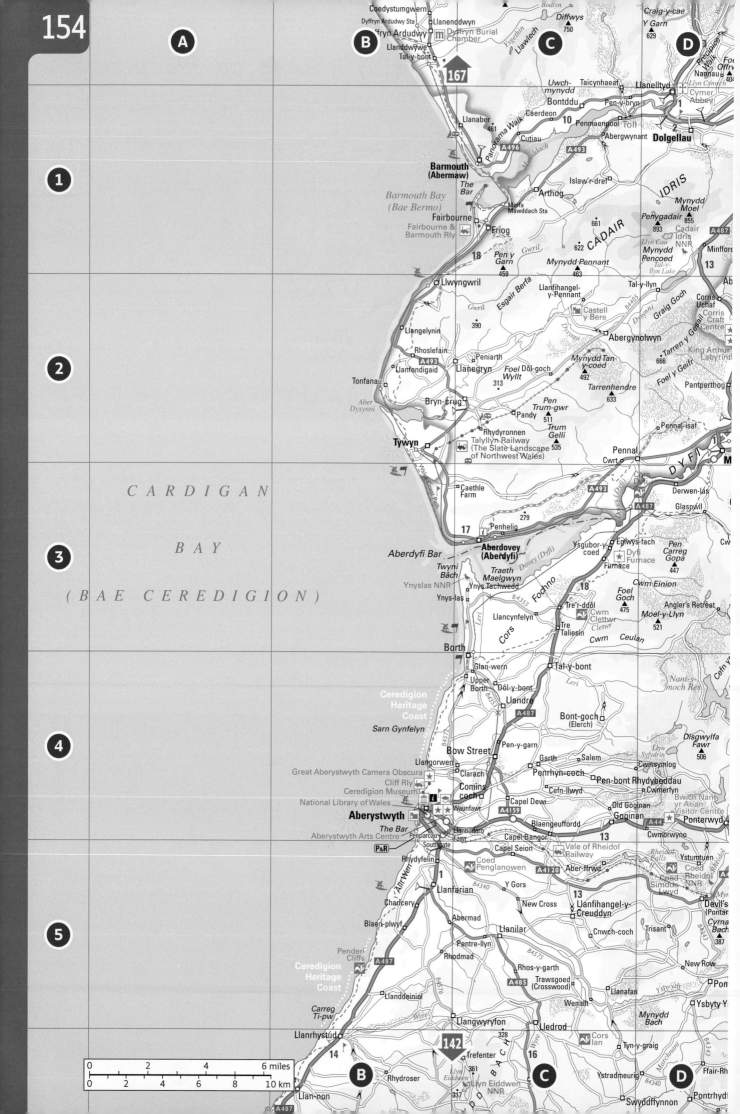

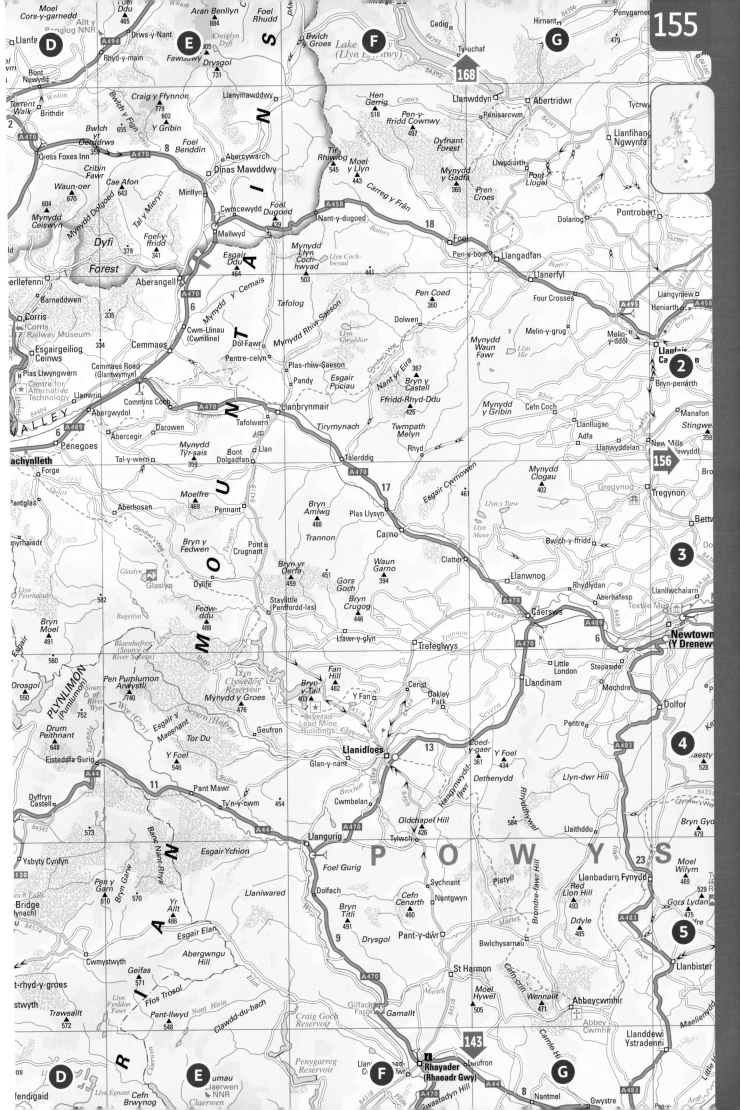

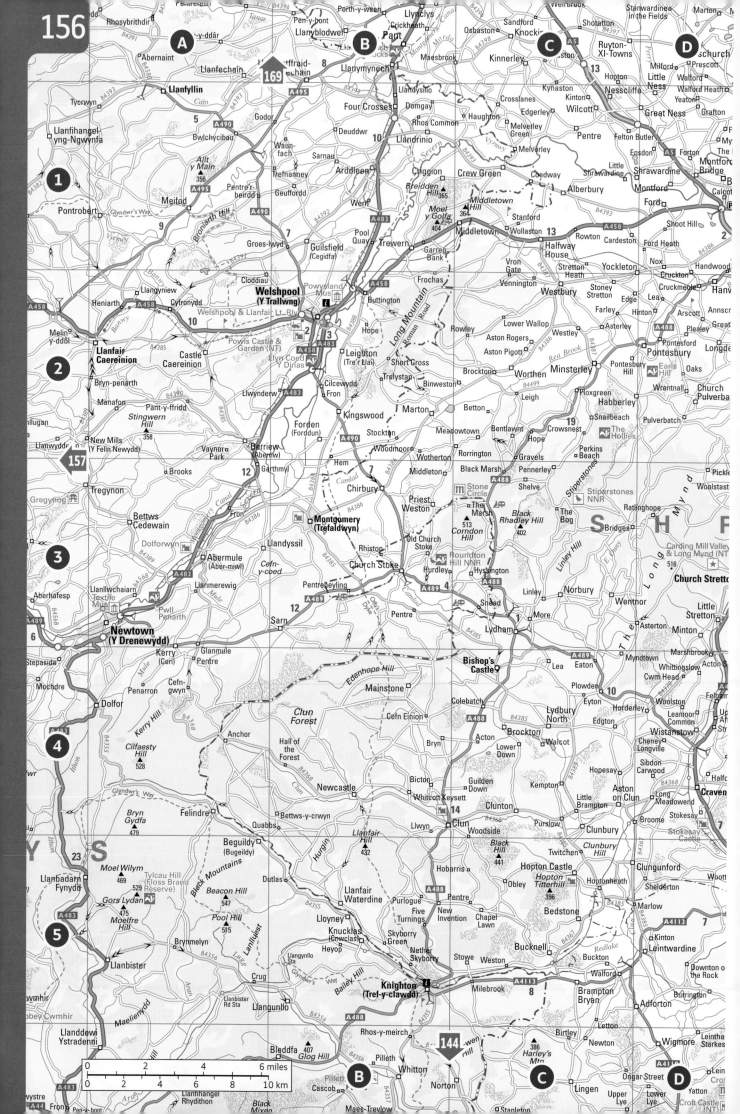

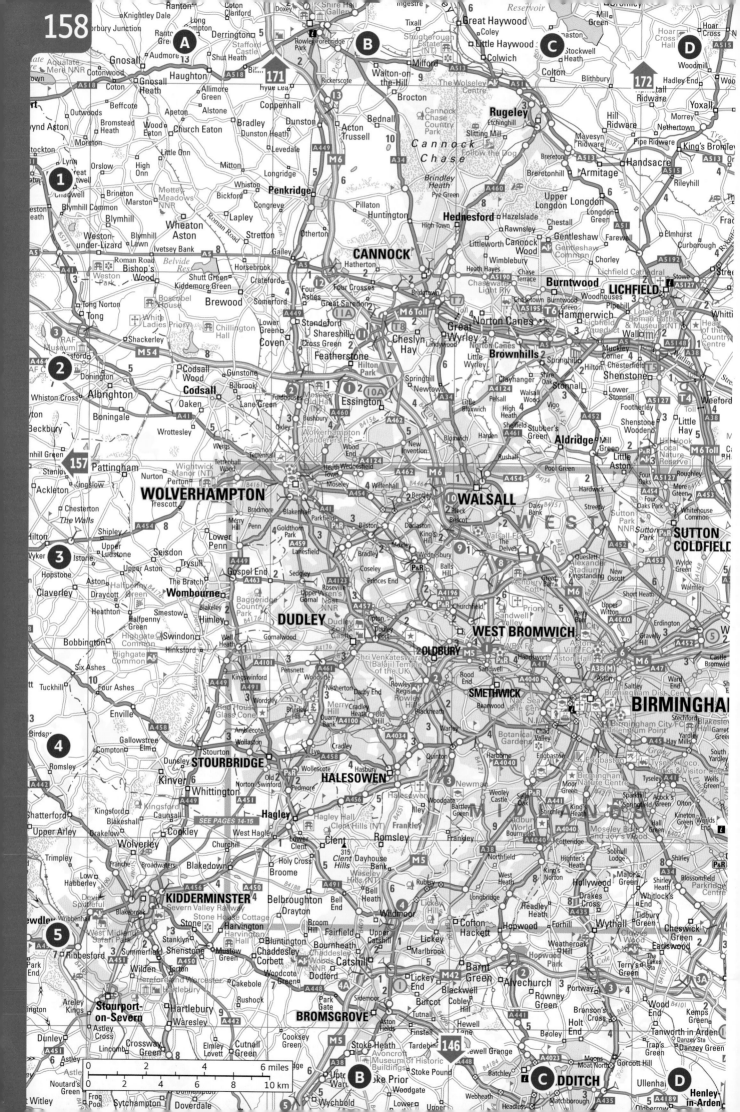

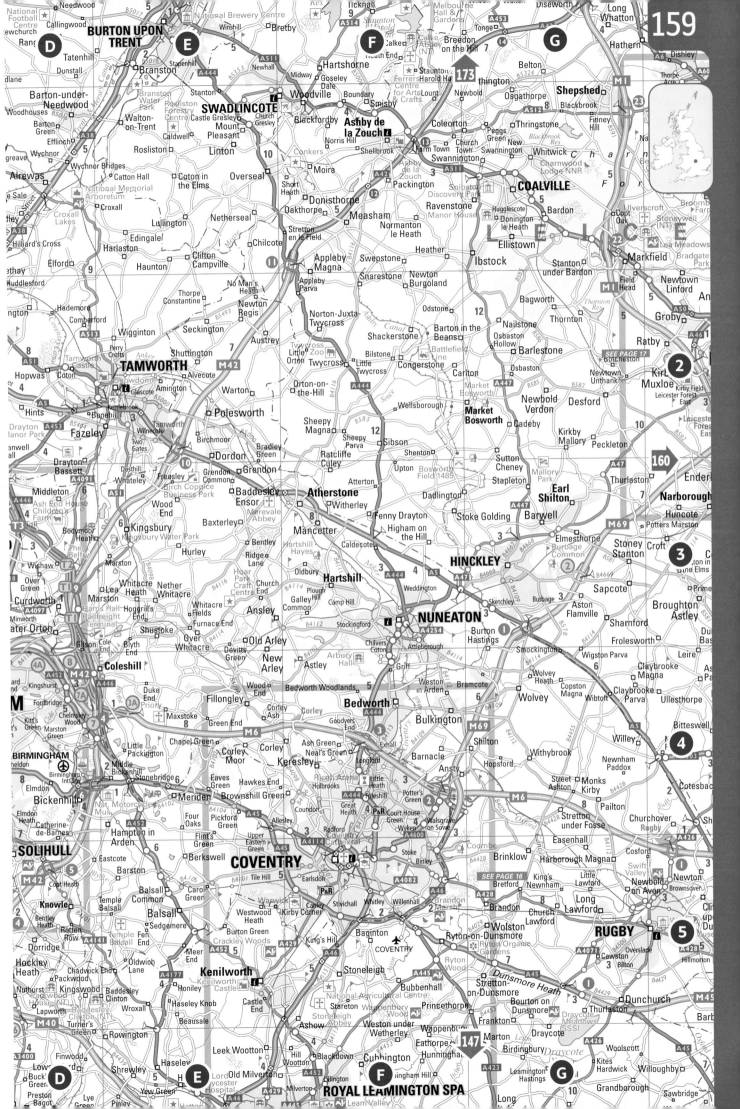

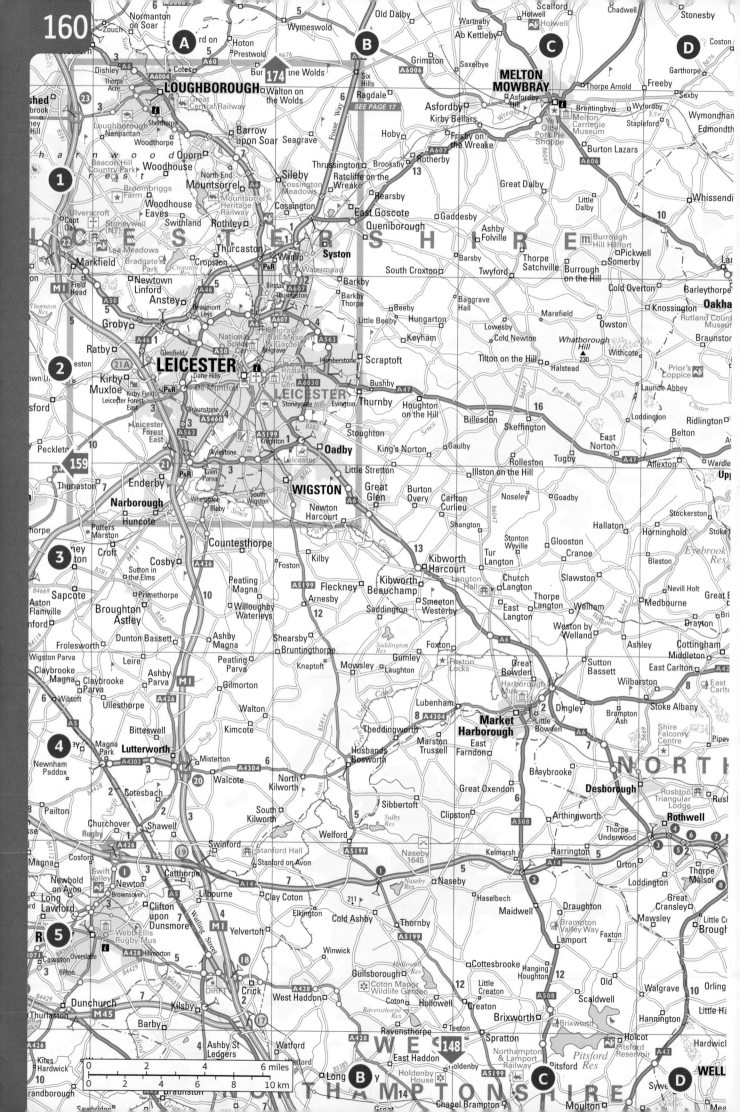

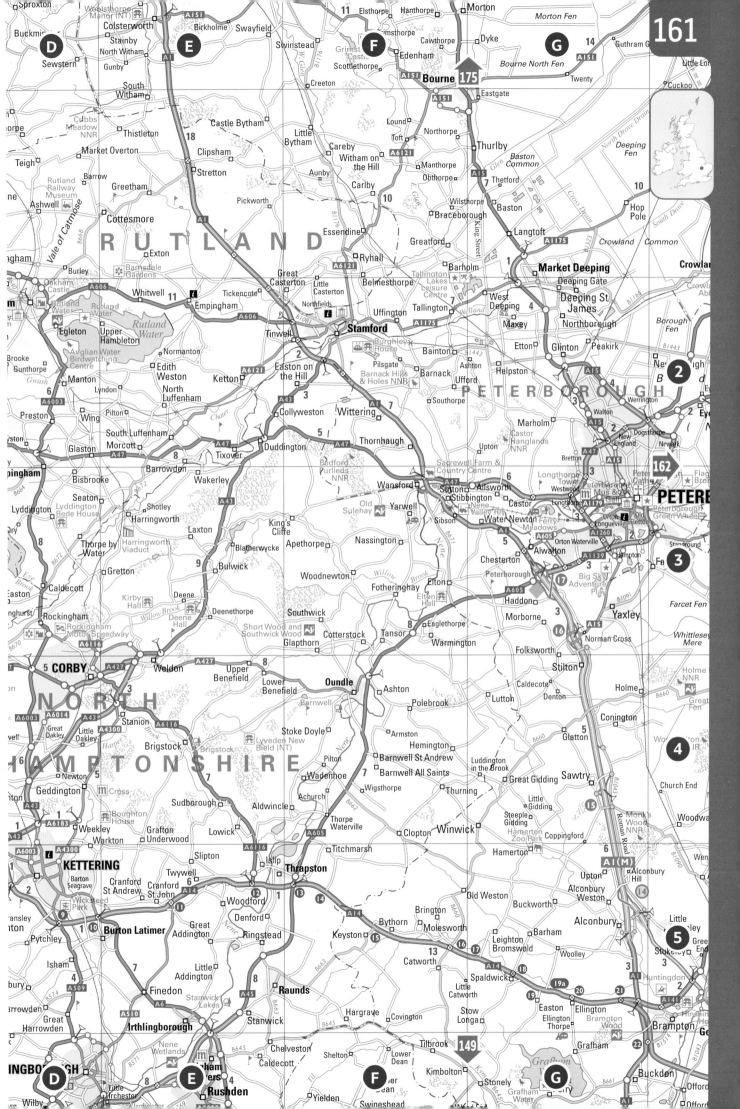

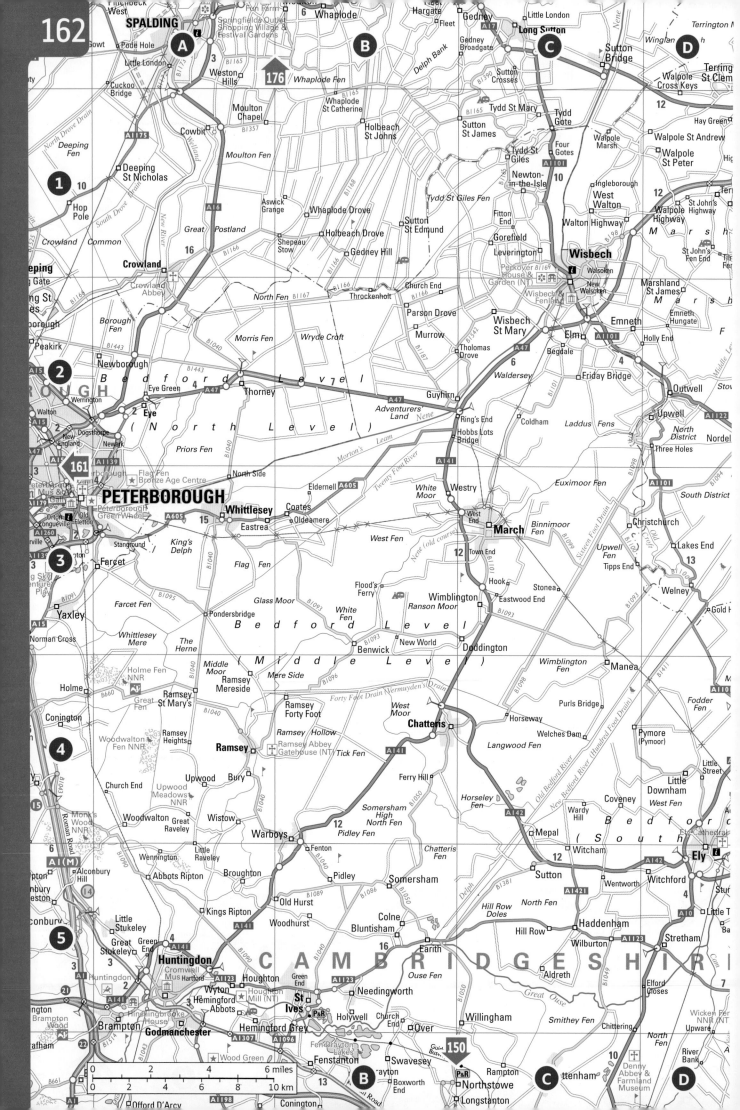

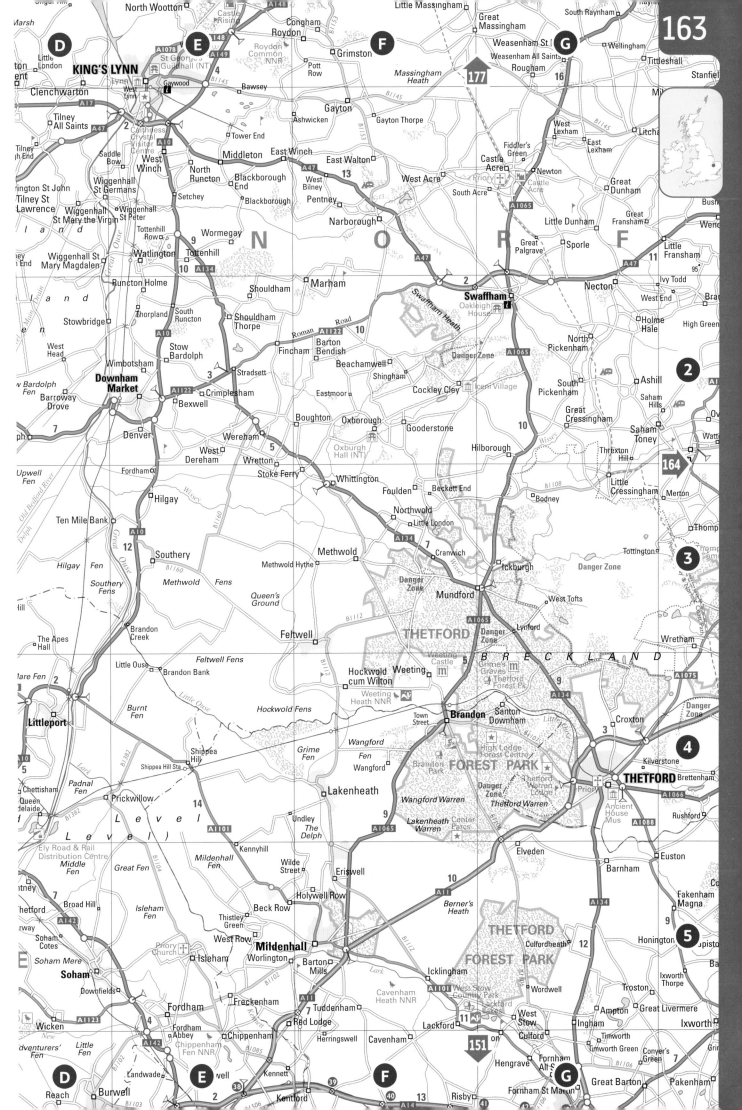

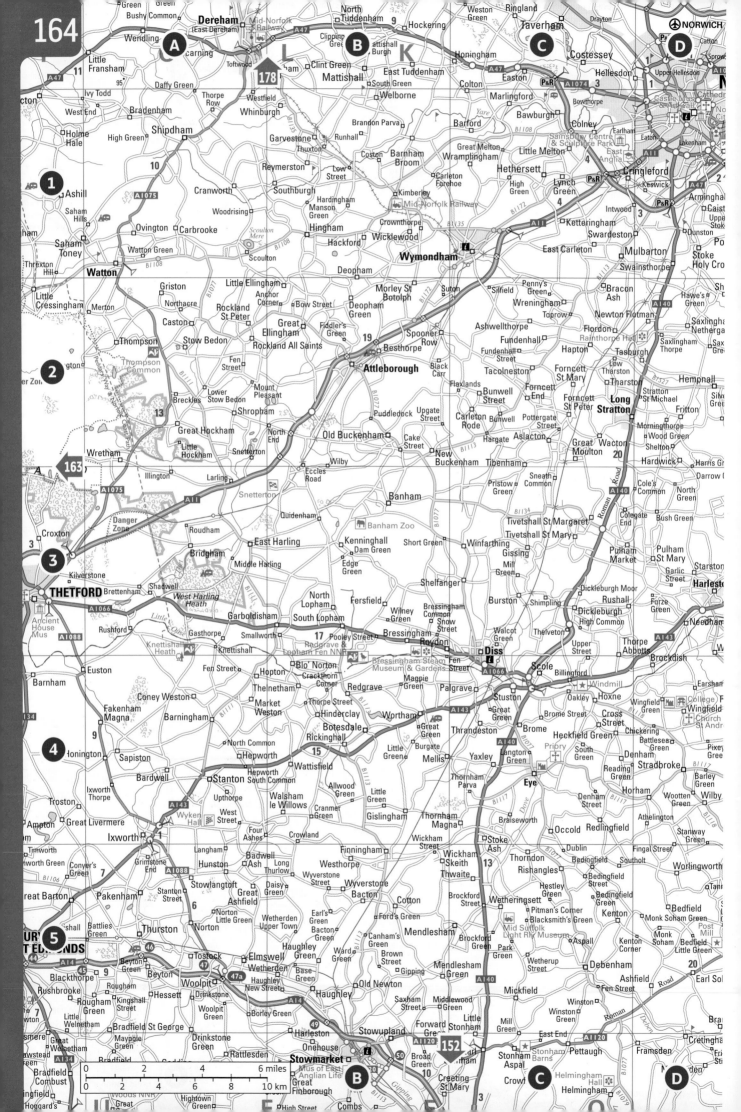

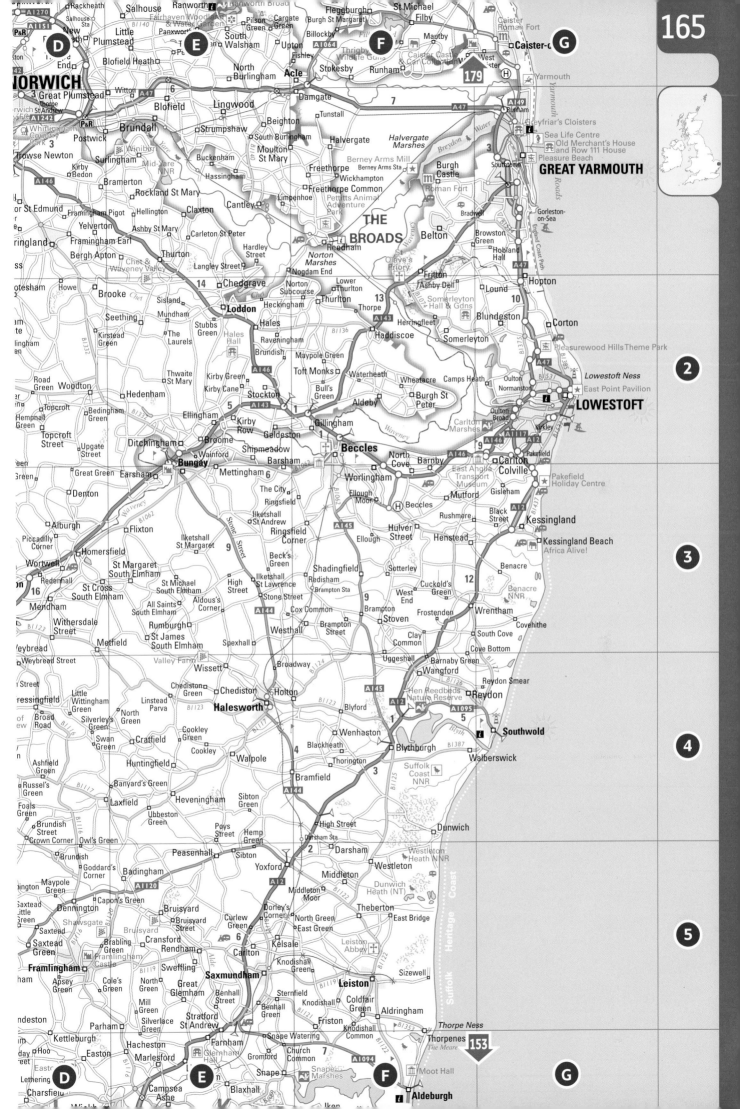

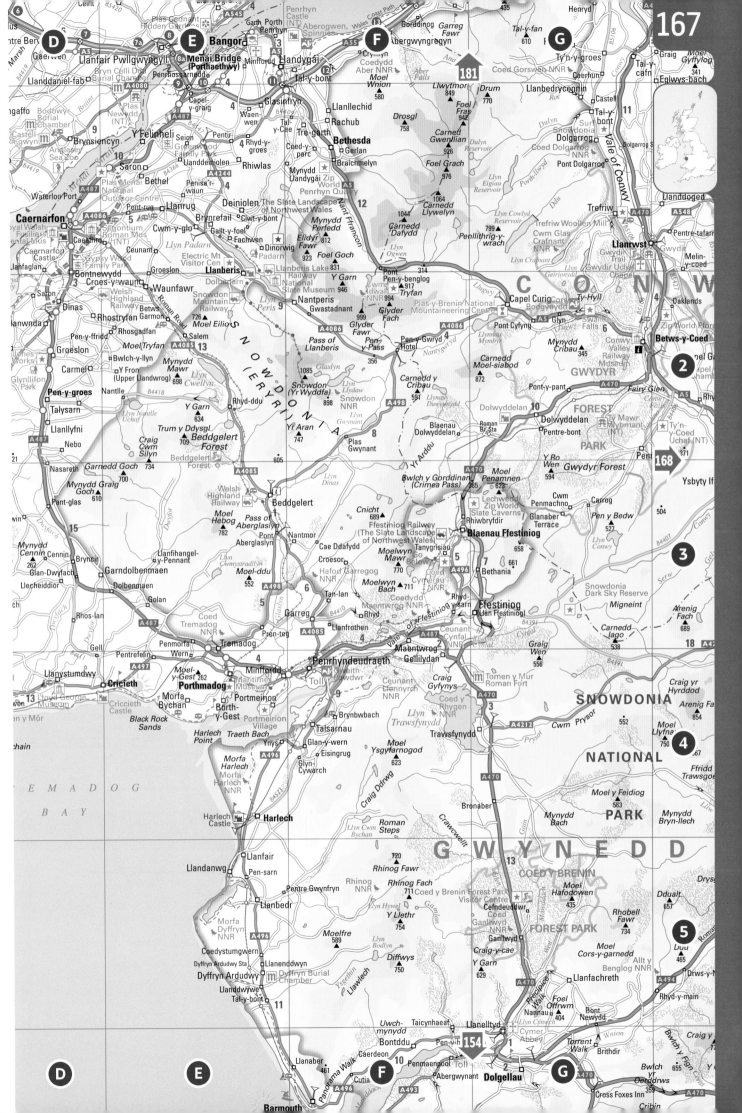

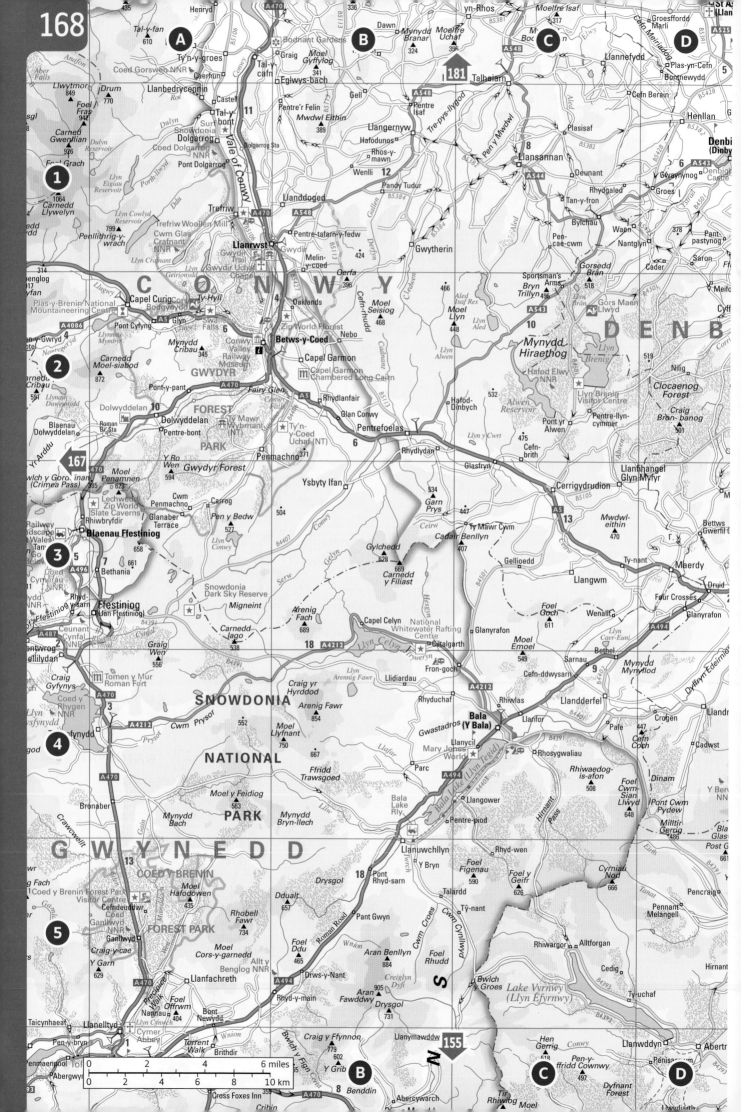

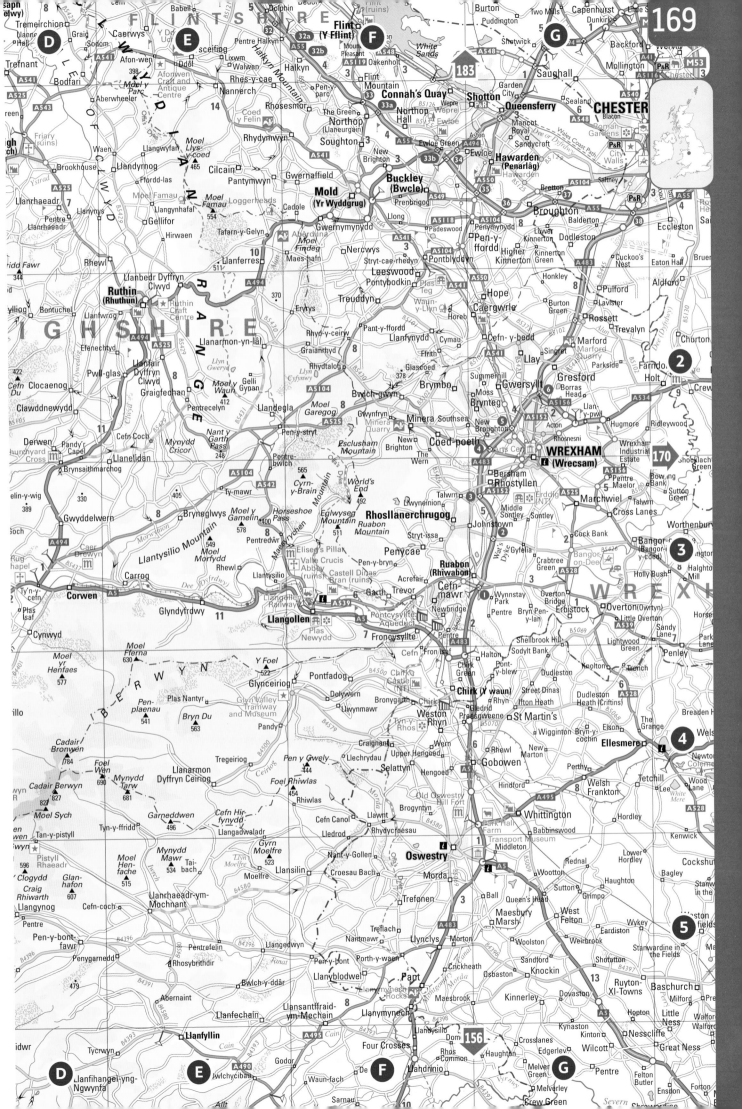

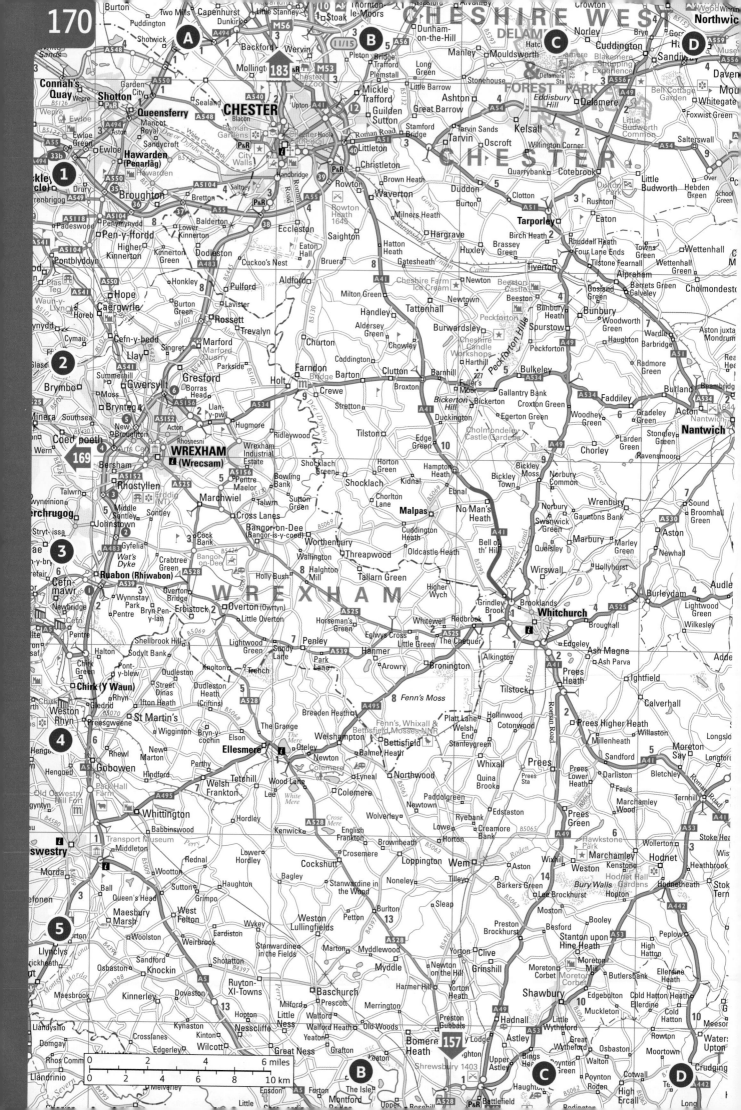

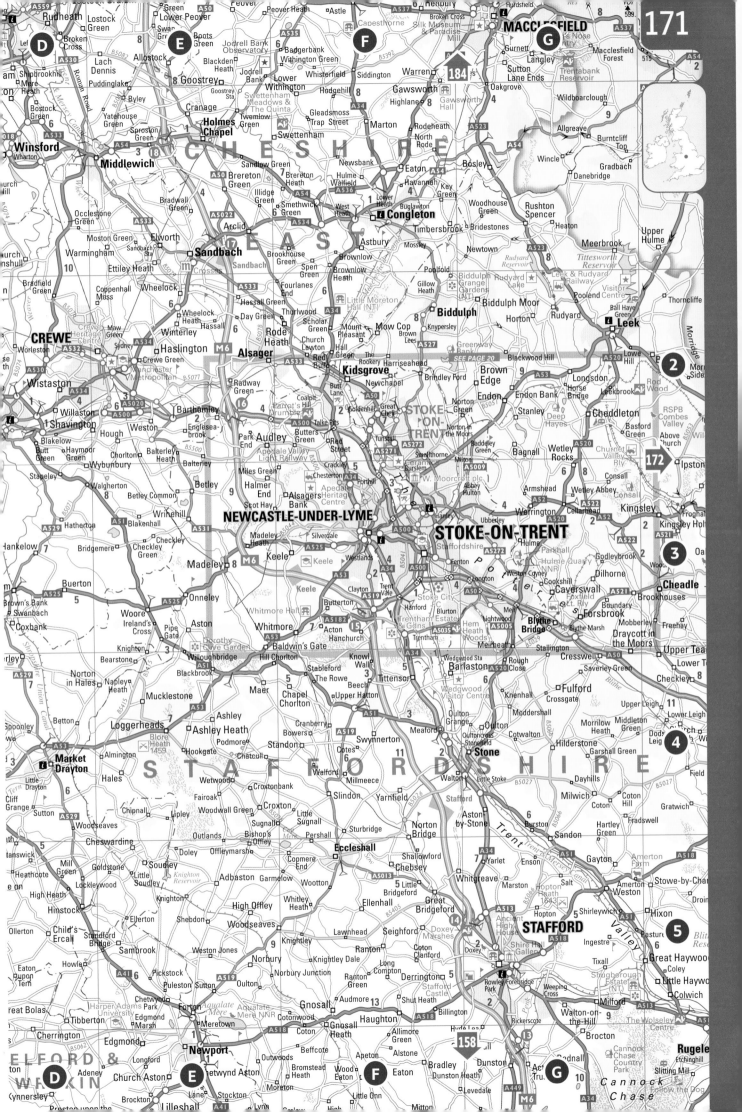

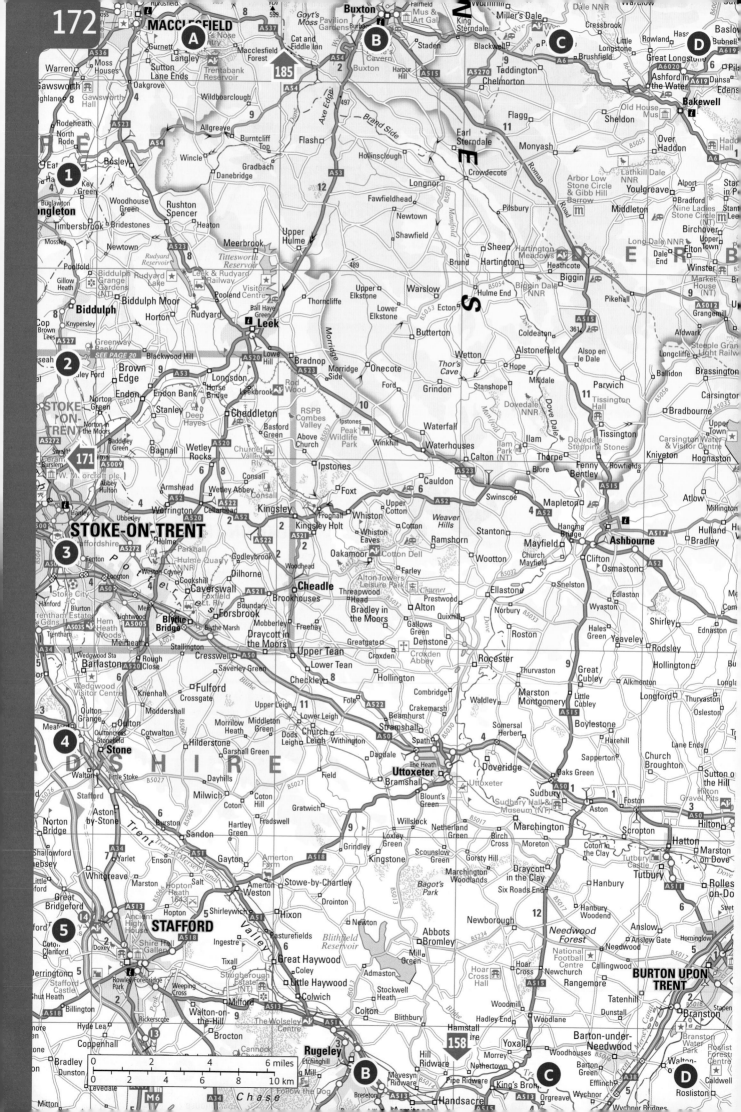

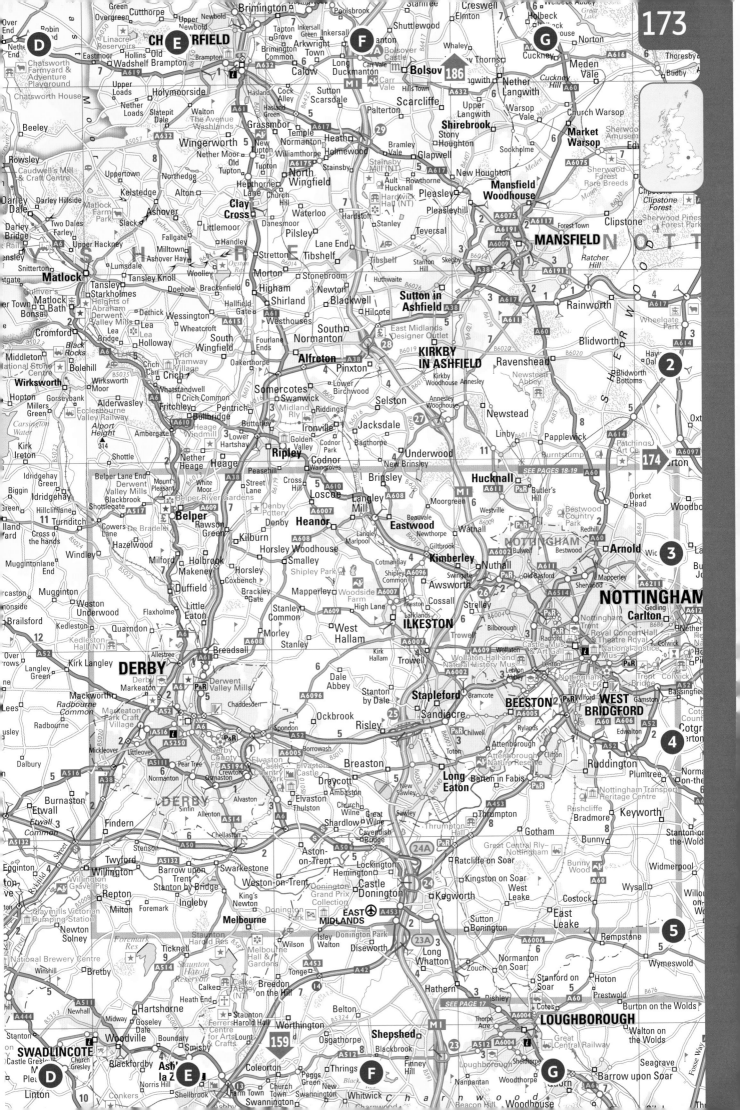

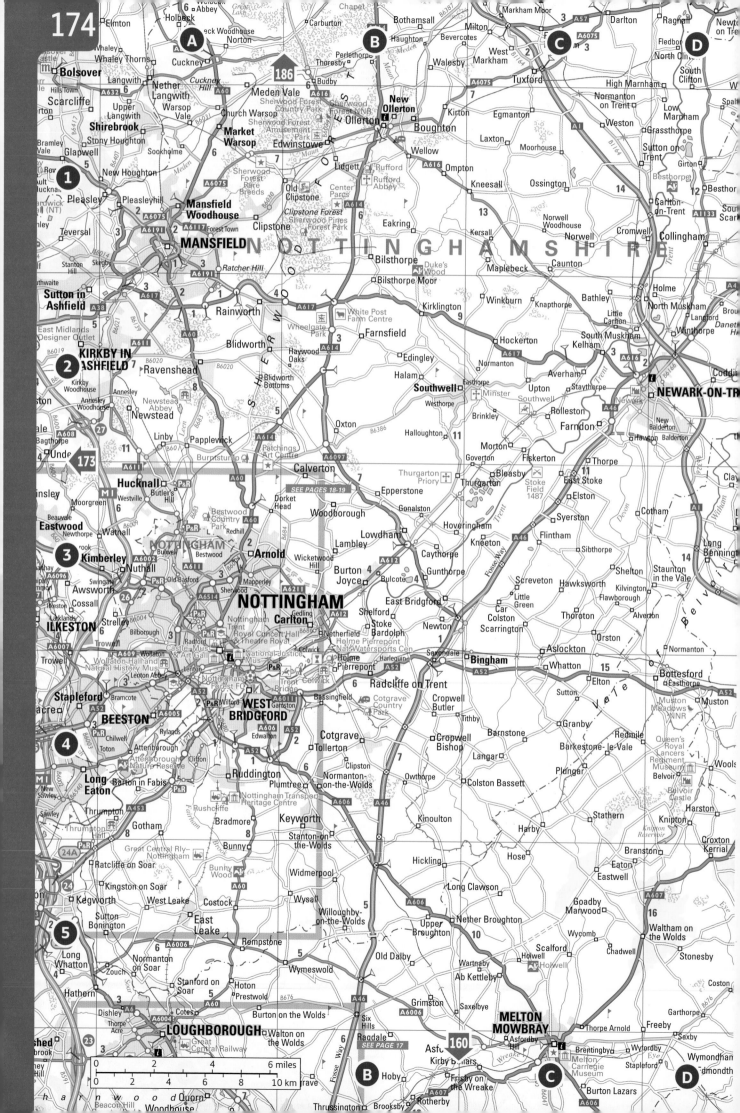

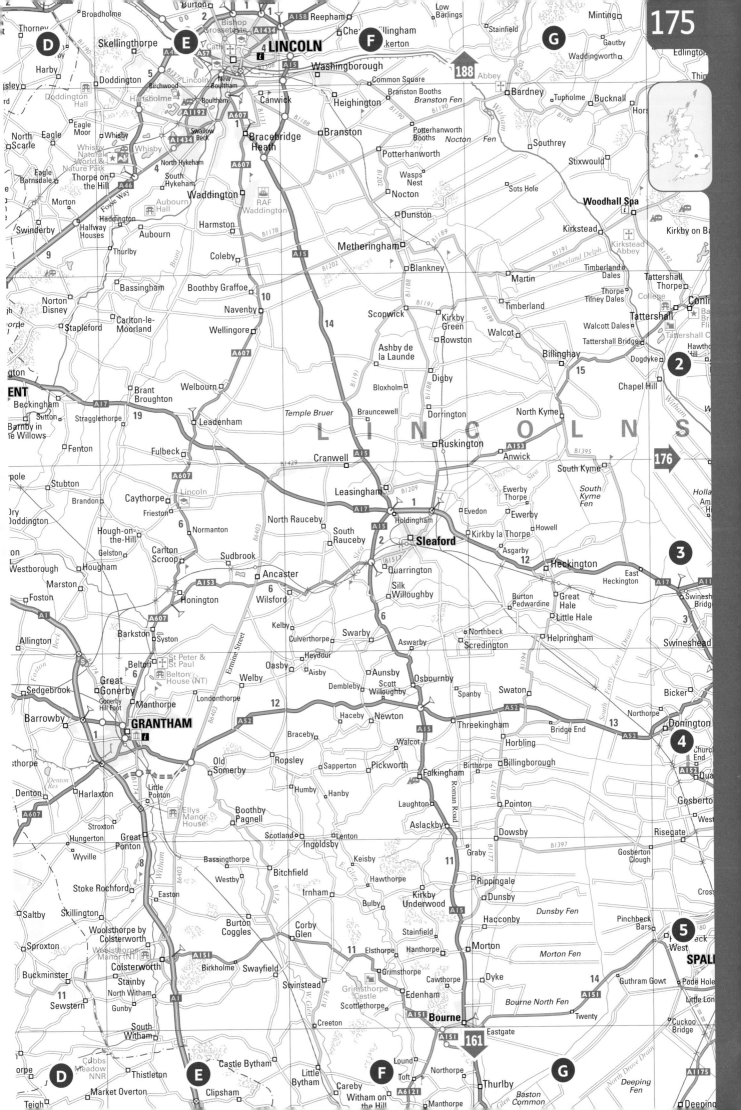

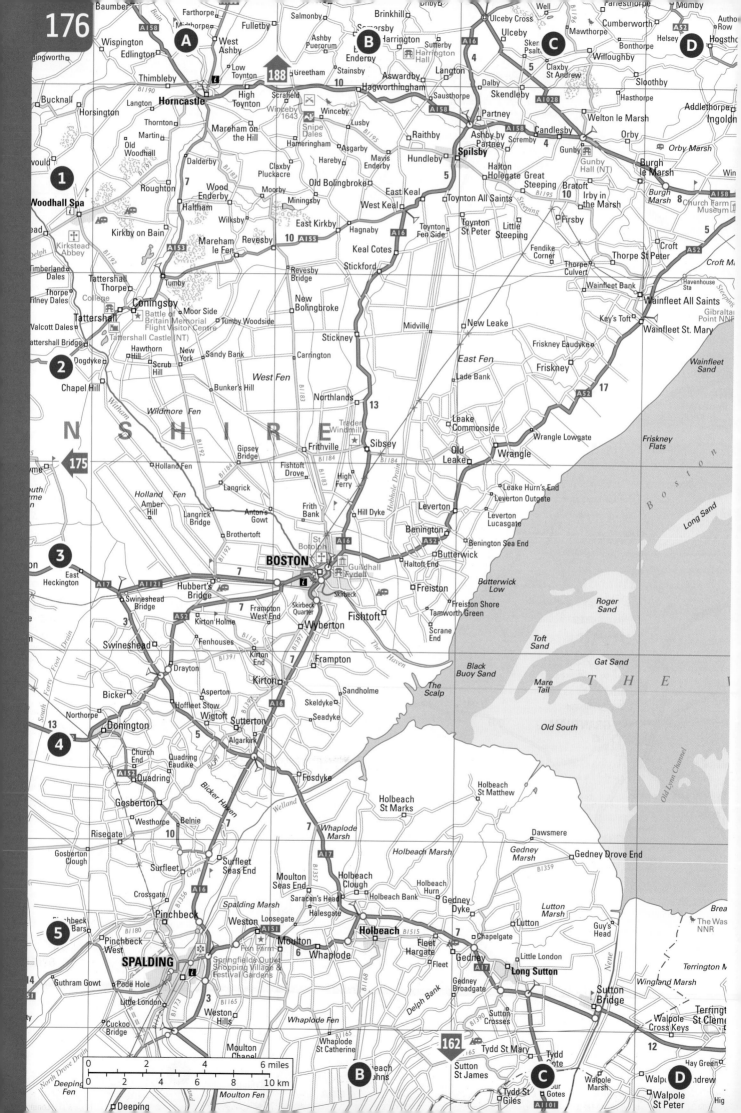

189

2

3

4

5

10

Ingoldmells
Point
Fantasy Island
Butlins Family
Entertainment Resort
Skegness Water
Leisure Park

hells

rpe

Thorpe

Seathorne

Skegness

Natureland
Seal Sanctuary

arsh   Seacroft

Gibraltar
Point NNR

Gibraltar

Gibraltar Pt

D e e p s

L y n n   D e e p s

North Norfolk
Heritage Coast

Scolt Head
Island
NNR

*Holkham
Bay*

Brancaster Bay

Norton

Holkham Bay
NNR

Holme Dunes
NNR

Holme next the Sea

Thornham   A149

Titchwell

Brancaster
Staithe

Burnham
Deepdale

Brancaster

Burnham
Norton

Burnham
Overy Staithe

Burnham
Overy Town

Holkham

Wells-ne

3

**Burnham
Market**

17

Burnham Thorpe

Holkham
Hall

Sea Life Centre

Hunstanton

Ringstead

*Peddars Way &
Norfolk Coast Path*

Creake
Abbey

Wight

Wells &
Walsingham
Lt. Rly

Summerfield

Norfolk
Lavender

Heacham

Eaton

Sedgeford

Docking

B1155

Stanhoe

North
Creake

South
Creake

B1454

Egmere
Shirehall
Museum

Shrine of Our Lady
of Walsingham

North
Barsh

Hou
St Gi

W A S H

Seal Sand

13

Snettisham

A149

Southgate

Ingoldisthorpe

Shernborne

Fring

Bircham
Newton

Great Bircham

Bircham
Tofts

B1153

Bagthorpe

Barmer

Syderstone

B1454

Sculthorpe

East
Barsham

West
Barsham

B1105

*Peter Black
Sand*

Dersingham

A149

Langham
Glass Ltd.

Tattersett

A148

Dunton
Shereford

178

Fakenh

Fakenh

B1440

Anmer

Houghton Hall

East Rudham

Coxford

Tatterford

Hempton

Toftrees

Colkir

A1065

5

Whissonsett

*Bulldog
Sand*

Dersingham
Bog NNR

Sandringham
House

Sandringham

West Newton

B1153

New Houghton

17

West Rudham

Helhoughton

West Raynham

East
Raynham

t Sand

Wolferton

St Mary
Magdalene
Chapel

Flitcham

A148

Harpley

Great
Massingham

South Raynham

Horningtoft

Godwick

Trinity
Hospital

Castle Rising

Hillington

Little Massingham

West Raynham

arsh

Ongar Hill

North Wootton

Castle
Rising

A148

Congham

Roydon

B1153

Roydon
Common
NNR

Weasenham St Peter

Weasenham All Saints

Rougham

16

Wellingham

Tittleshall

Little
London

St George's
Guildhall (NT)

South
Wootton

A1078

A149

KING'S LYNN

Gaywood

4

B1145

Grimston

Pott
Row

Stanfiel

Clenchwarton

A17

West
Lynn

Bawsey

Gayton

*Massingham
Heath*

B1145

163

Mileham

Tilney
ints
End

A47

2

Caithness
Crystal
Visitor
Centre

A10

D

Tower End

E

West

Middleton

East Winch

Ashwicken

n Thorpe

East Walton

B1153

F

Castle

Fiddler's
Green

East
Lexham

G

Litcham

Longh

Bitterl

Saddle
Row

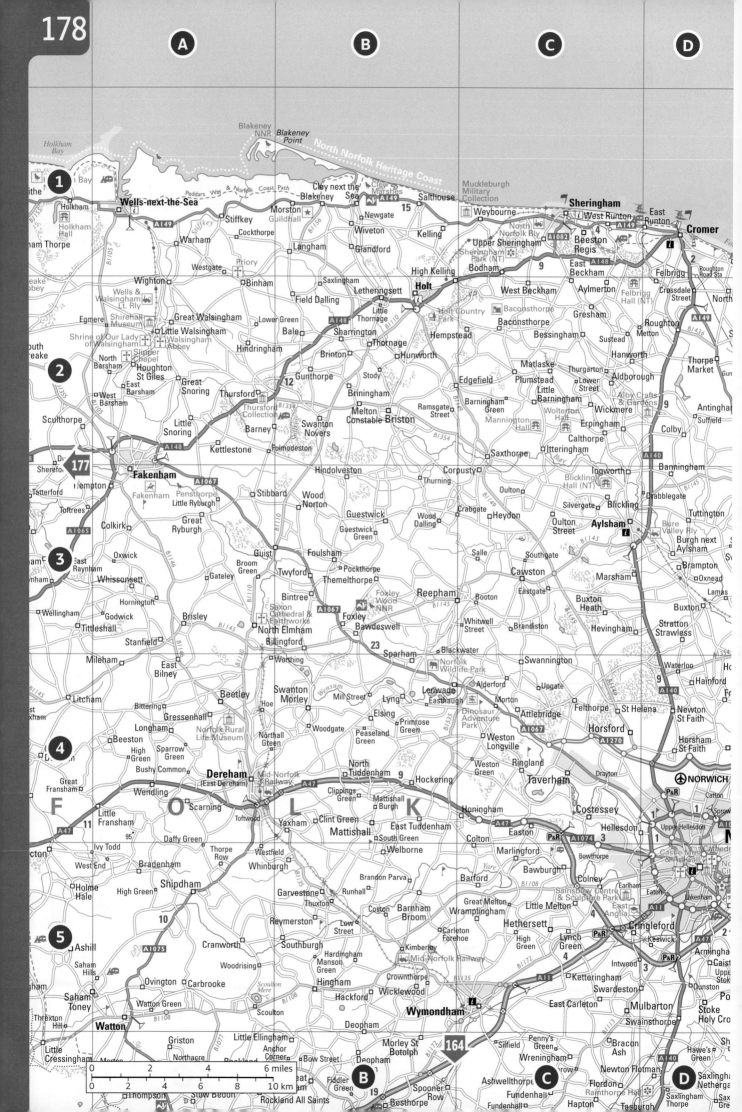

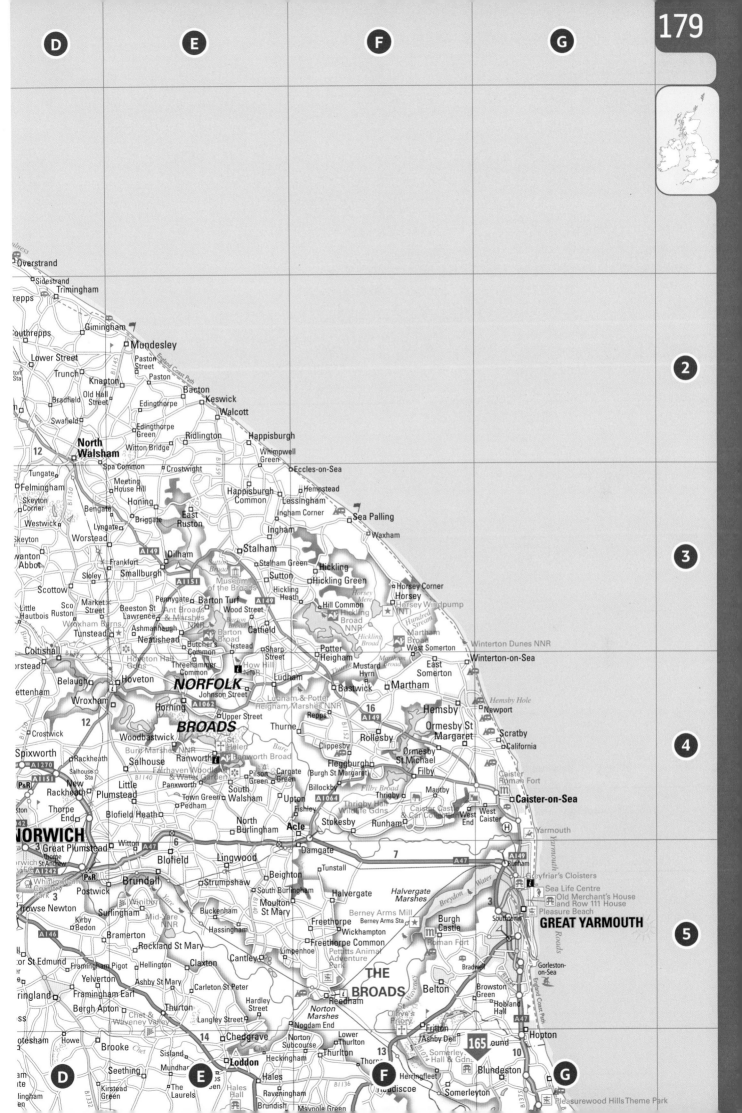

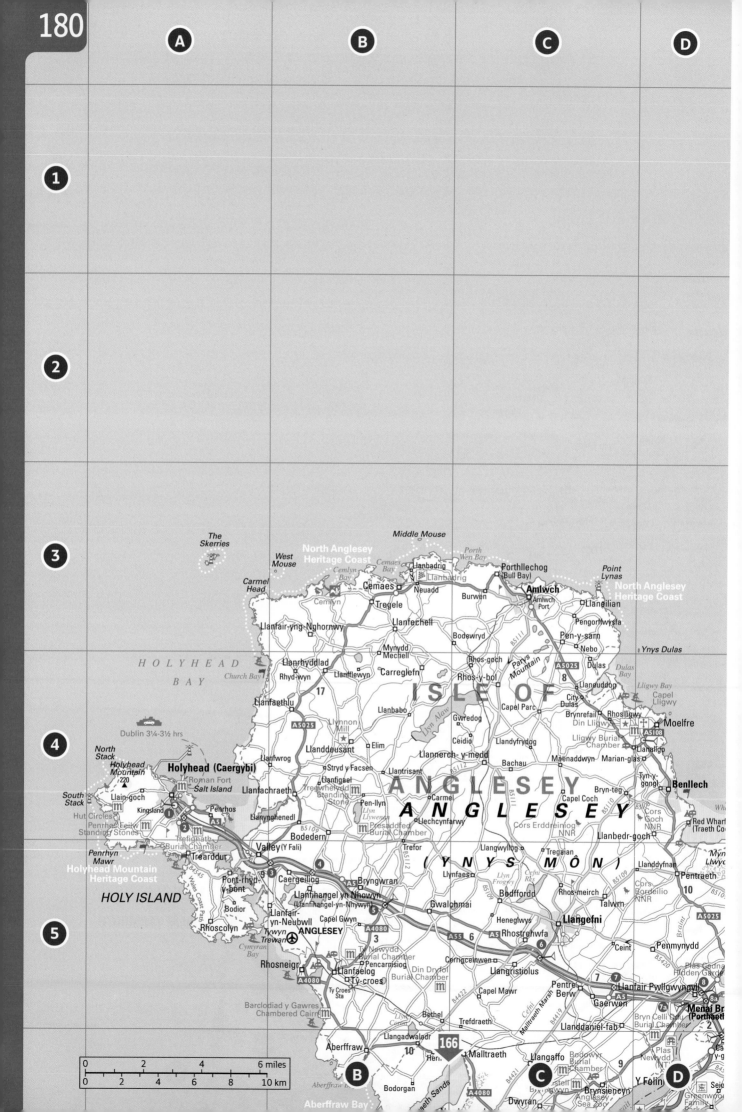

A   B   C   D

1

2

3

The Skerries
Middle Mouse
North Anglesey
Heritage Coast
West
Mouse
Cemaes
Bay
Porth
Wen Bay
Porthllechog
(Bull Bay)
Point
Lynas
Carmel
Head
Cemlyn
Bay
Llanbadrig
Llanbadrig
Amlwch
North Anglesey
Heritage Coast
Cemlyn
Cemaes
Neuadd
Burwen
Amlwch
Port
Llaneilian
Tregele
Llanfechell
Bodewryd
Pen-y-sarn
Pengorffwysfa
Llanfair-yng-Nghornwy
Mynydd
Mechell
Rhos-goch
Parys
Mountain
Nebo
Ynys Dulas

HOLYHEAD
BAY
Church Bay
Llanrhyddlad
Rhyd-wyn
Llanfflewyn
Carreglefn
Rhos-y-bol
A5025
Dulas
Dulas
Bay
Llligwy Bay
Capel
Lligwy
Llanfaethlu
17
Llanbabo
Llyn Alaw
Gwredog
Capel Parc
City
Dulas
Brynrefail
Din Lligwy
Rhosiligwy
Moelfre
A5025
Llynnon
Mill
Elim
Ceidio
Llandyfrydog
Lligwy Burial
Chamber
Llanaligo
A5108
Llanfwrog
Llanddeusant
Llannerch- y-medd
Bachau
Maenaddwyn
Marian-glas
Stryd y Facsen
Llantrisant
ANGLESEY
Bryn-teg
Tyn-y-
gongl
Benllech
Llanfigael
Trewelfryd
Standing
Stone
Pen-llyn
Carmel
Capel Coch
ANGLESEY
Cors
Goch
NNR
Llanfachraeth
Llechcynfarwy
Red Wharf
(Traeth Co
Llanynghenedl
Llyn
Llywenan
Presaddfed
Burial Chamber
(YNYS MÔN)
Cors Erddreiniog
NNR
Llanbedr-goch
Bodedern
Trefor
Llangwyllog
Tregaian
Llanddyfnan
Pentraeth
Valley (Y Fali)
Llynfaes
Llyn
Frogwy
Cefni
Res
Cors
Bordeilio
NNR
Myn
Lliwy
Caergeiliog
Bryngwran
Gwalchmai
Bodffordd
Rhos-meirch
10
Dublin 3¼-3½ hrs
North
Stack
Holyhead
Mountain
220
Holyhead (Caergybi)
Roman Fort
Salt Island
Heneglwys
A55
A5
Talwrn
A5025
Llangefni
South
Stack
Kingsland
Penrhos
Llanfihangel yn Nhowyn
(Llanfihangel-yn-Nhwyn)
Rhostrehwfa
Ceint
Penmynydd
Hut Circles
Penrhos Feilw
Standing Stones
Trefignath
Burial Chamber
Capel Gwyn
A4080
3
6
Pentre
Berw
7
Penrhyn
Mawr
Treaddur
Llanfair-
yn-Neubwll
Cerrigceinwen
Llangristiolus
Llanfair Pwllgwyngyll
Holyhead Mountain
Heritage Coast
HOLY ISLAND
Rhoscolyn
Tywyn
Trewan
Cymyran
Bay
ANGLESEY
Capel Mawr
Gaerwen
7b
Menai Br
(Porthaet
Bodior
Ty Newydd
Burial Chamber
Din Dryfol
Burial Chamber
B4422
Bryn Celli Ddu
Burial Chamber
Rhosneigr
Pencarnisiog
Llanfaelog
Tŷ-croes
Bethel
Llanddaniel-fab
Plas
Newydd
Plas
Ty Croes
Sta
B4421
Trefdraeth
Barclodiad y Gawres
Chambered Cairn
Cefni
Malltraeth Marsh
166
Aberffraw
Llangadwaladr
10
Hen
Malltraeth
Llangaffo
Bodowyr
Burial
Chamber
9
Y Felin
0   2   4   6 miles
0 2 4 6 8 10 km
Aberffraw B
Bodorgan
Aberffraw Bay
Dwyran
Brynsiencyn

4

5

B   C   D

Ⓐ Ⓑ Ⓒ Ⓓ

1

2

← 181

Liverpool
(Birkenhead) to   hours
Belfast..............................8
Liverpool to   hours
Douglas........2¾ (March-Nov)
Dublin......................7½-9½

3

L I V E R P O O L

B A Y

West
Hoyle
Bank

East
Hoyle
Bank

Mockb

Meols
Sta

A553

Manor Road Sta

Hoylake

Royal
Liverpool

Hoylake Sta

Red
Rocks
Marsh

Hilbre Island

West
Kirby
Sta

Grange

Frankby

West Kirby

Caldy

Irb
Hi

B5140

A540

4

Welsh Channel

Prestatyn
Sands
Holiday
Centre

Talacre

Point of
Ayr

Thurstaston

Dawpool
Bank

Prestatyn

Llawndy

Mostyn Bank

5

Gronant

Gwespyr

Ffynnongroyw

Pen-y-ffordd

A547

Rhyl

Sea Aquarium

Ffrith

SC

A548

Meliden
(Gallt Melyd)

Llanasa

Gym

Mostyn Quay

10

Mostyn

Glan-y-don

Kinmel Bay
(Bae Cinmel)

2

B5119

Bodrhyddan
Hall

Gwaenysgor

Tan-yr-
allt

Gop
Hill 8

Trelogan

Trelawnyd

A548

Axton

Whitford
(Chwitffordd)

A5151

Llannerch-y-môr

Holywell Bank

Penrhyn)

Abergele
Roads

A525

Wales Coast Path

Rhuddlan

Dyserth

Ochr-
y-foel

Cwm

Marian
Cwm

Maen
Achwyfaen

Lloc

Roman
Road

A5026

Carmel

Basingwerk
Abbey

Pantasaph
Friary

Greenfield Valley

Greenfield
(Maes-Glas)

St Winifred's Holy Well & Chap

wyn Bay
Colwyn)

22

10

23

Llanddulas

23a

Pensarn

Towyn

Plas
Morfa Llwyd

Rhuddlan
Castle and
Twthil

6

3

Cwm

8

Gorsedd

31

Pantasaph

Calcoed

2

Walwen

Whelston

Bagillt
Bank

Abergele

A547

Rhyd-y-foel

24

A55

St George

24a

Pengwern

A525

B5429

27a

28

Rhuallt

A55

29

30

Pen-y-
cefn

Babell

Dolphin

Brynford

A5026

Holywell (Treffynnon)

Bagillt

5

olwen

Betws-
yn-Rhos

6

Moelfre Isaf

Bodelwyddan

27

26

25

St Asaph
(Llanelwy)

Rhuallt

Roman

Caerwys

Y Dôl
Uchaf

Ysceifiog

Lixwm

Walwen

A5119

32b

Bedol

Flint
(Y Fflint)

32a

A55

4

Llanelian-
yn-Rhos

Rhyd-y-foel

A548

6

317

Mynydd
Bodrochwyn

Cefn Meiriadog

B5381

Groesffordd
Marli

B5382

Tremeirchion

Graig

Sodom

Afon-wen

Moel
y Parc

Afonwen
Craft and
Antique
Centre

Pentre Halkyn

Halkyn

Mount Pleasant

F L I N T S H I R E

Dawn

324

Mynydd
Branar

396

Moelfre Uchaf

Llannefydd

Plas-yn-Cefn

Llannerch
Hall

168

wheeler

338

Rhes-y-cae

Nannerch

Pen-y-
parc

33

Llanfair Talhaiarn

A548

A544

Trefnant

A525

A541

Bodfari

A543

V A L E   O F   C L W Y D

14

Coed
y Felin

Rhosesmor

The Green

rthop

Soughton

Cefn
Berain

Henllan

B5428

Green

Waen

Rhydymwyn

Aln

B5119

Pentre
Isaf

Elwy

Aled

Tre-pys-llygod

0   2   4   6 miles
0 2   4   6   8   10 km

Ⓑ   Ⓒ   Ⓓ

Denbigh
(Dinbych)

Friary
(ruins)

Llangwyfan

Moel
Llys-y-coed

Llansannan

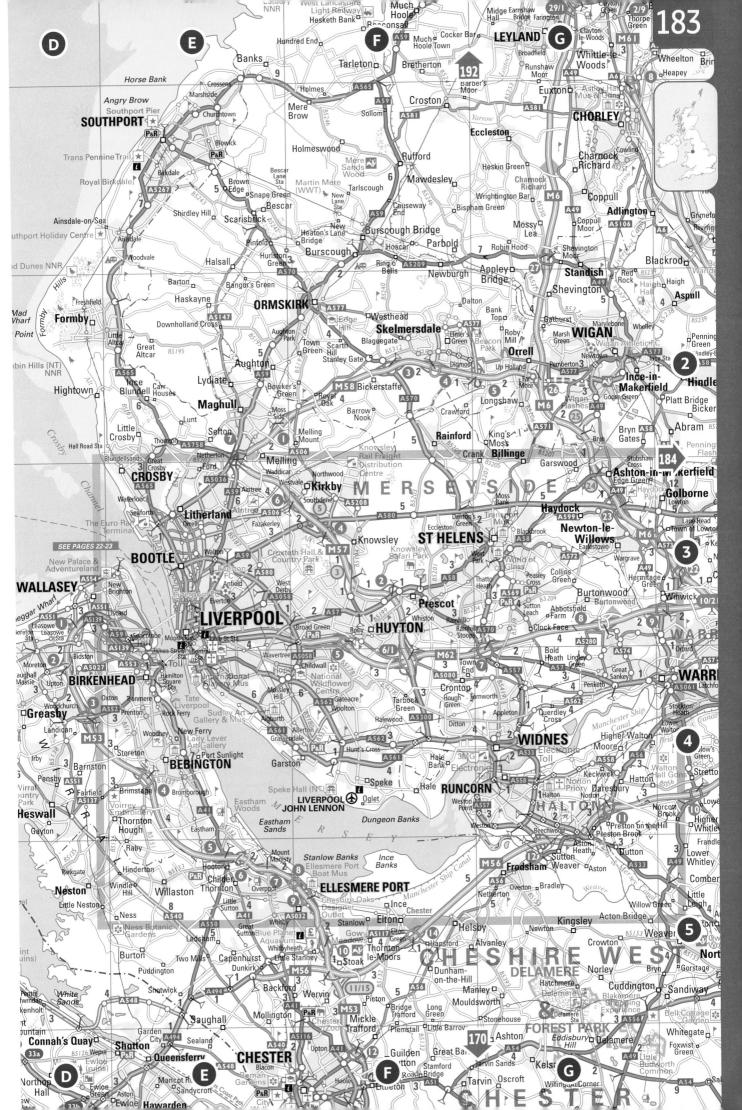

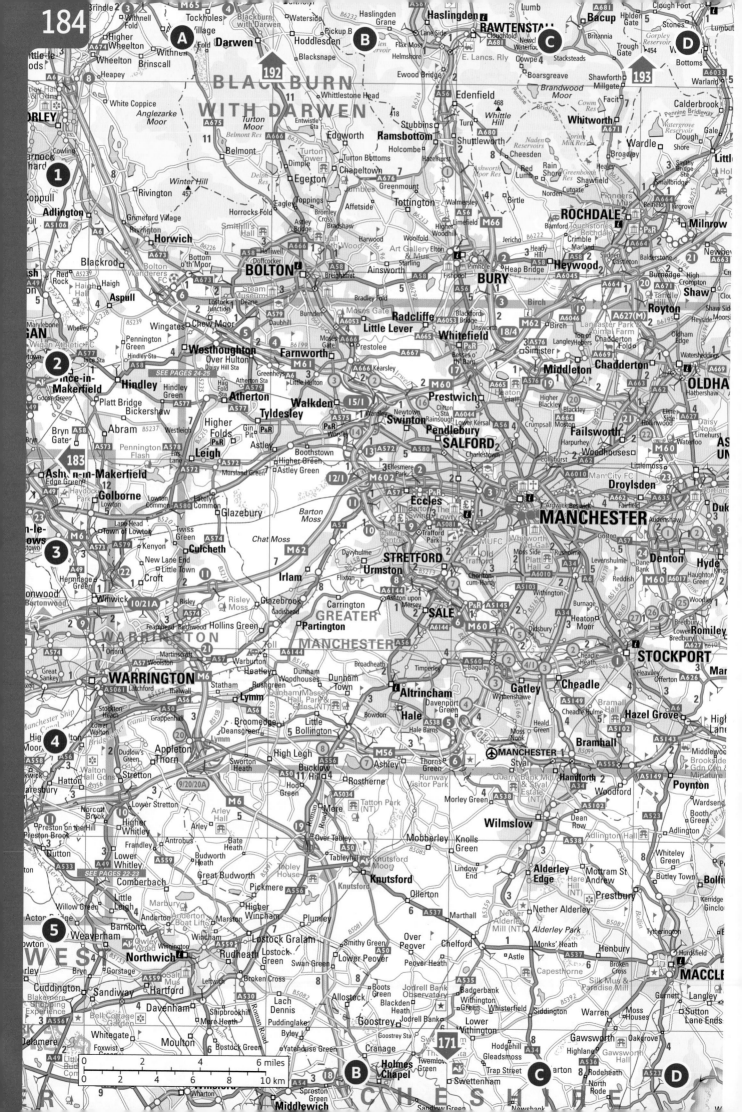

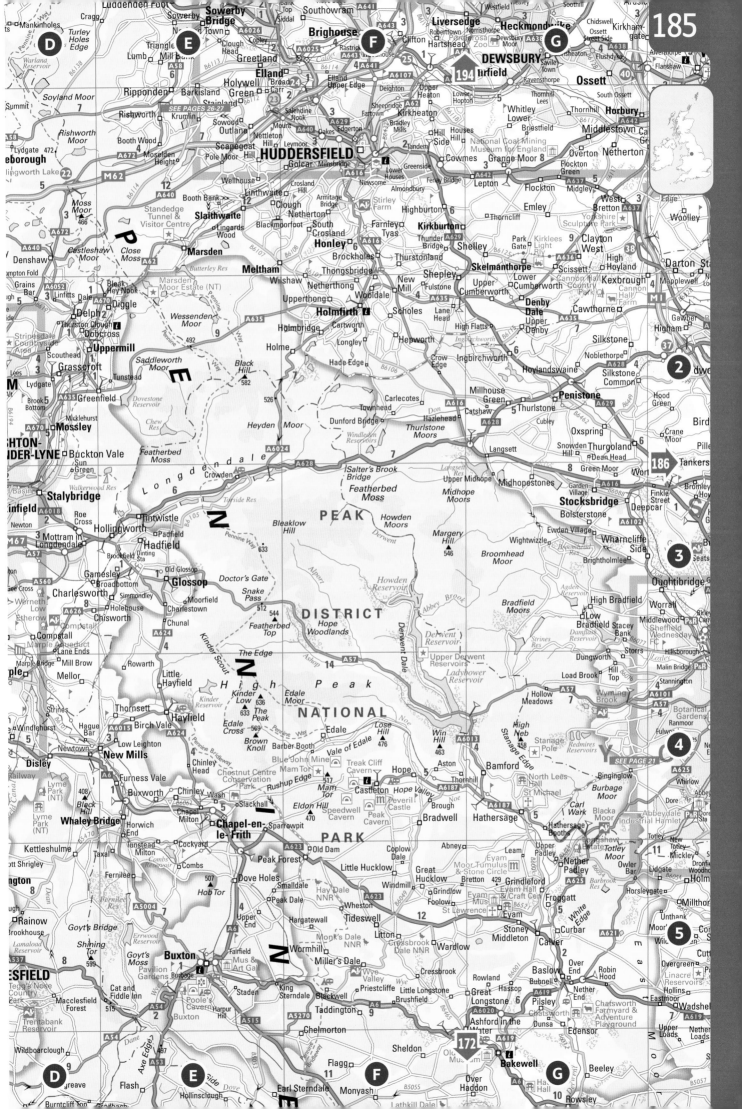

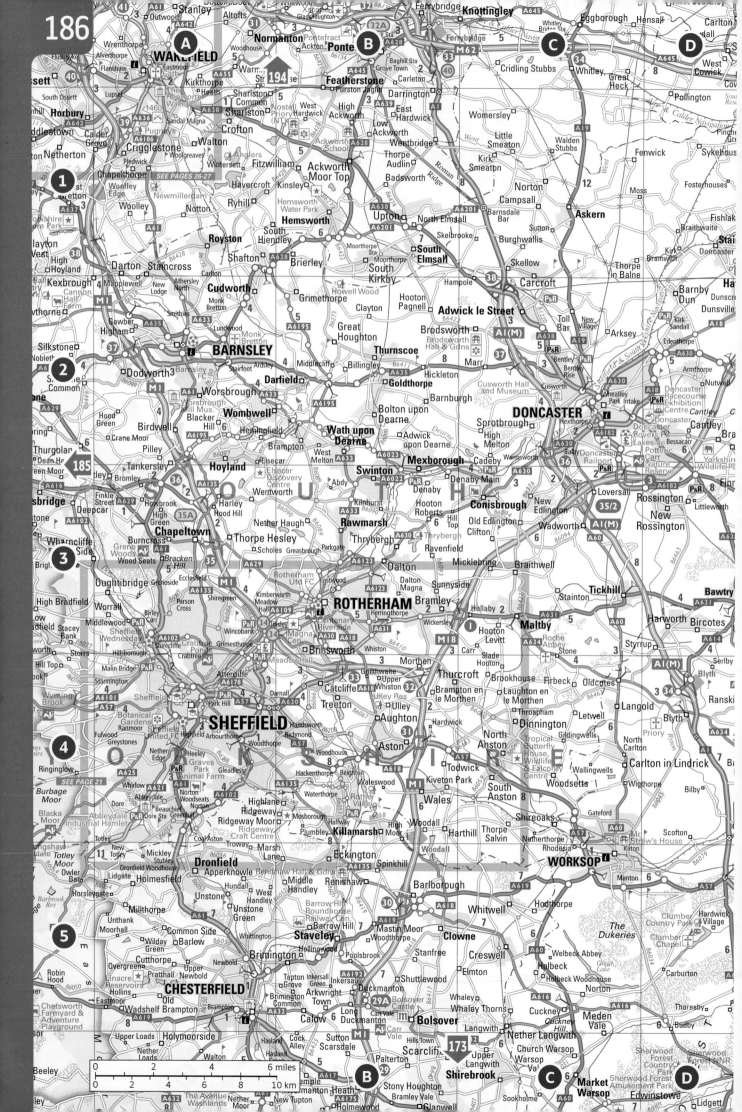

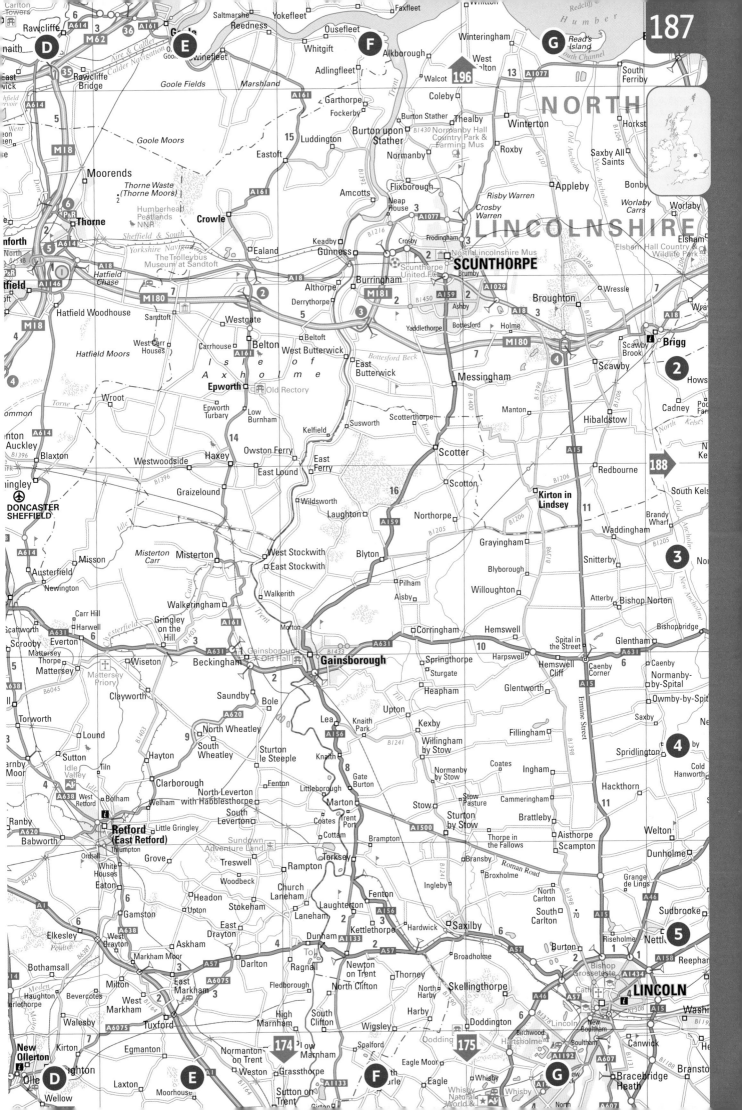

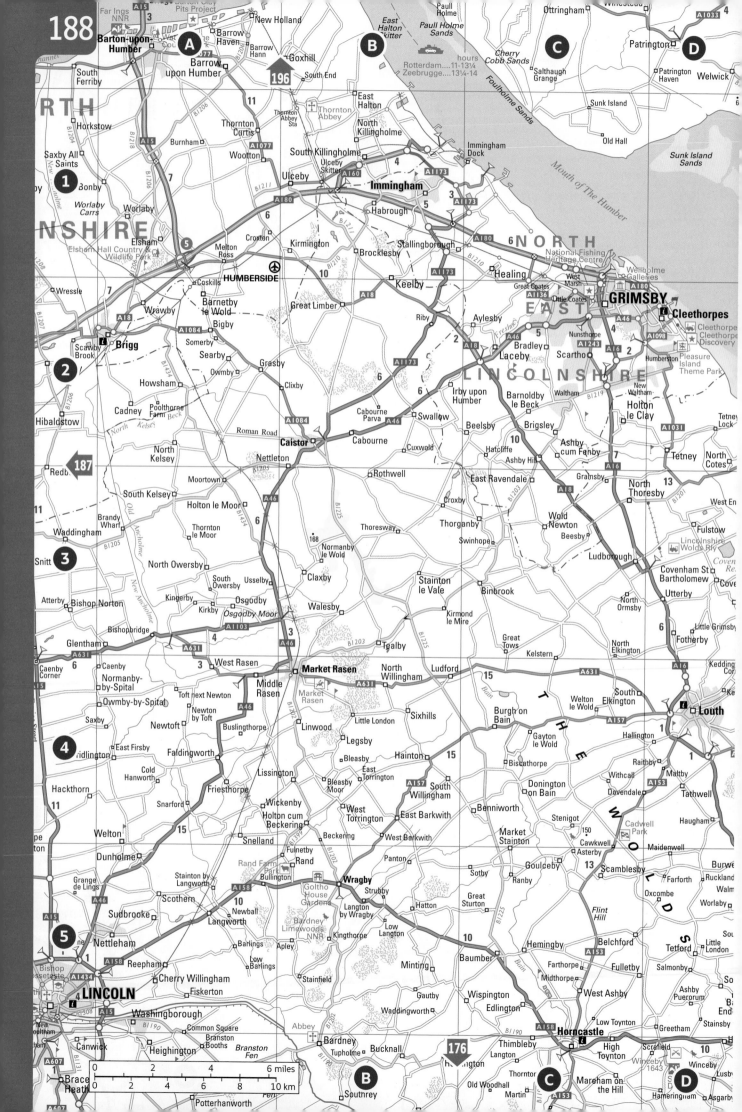

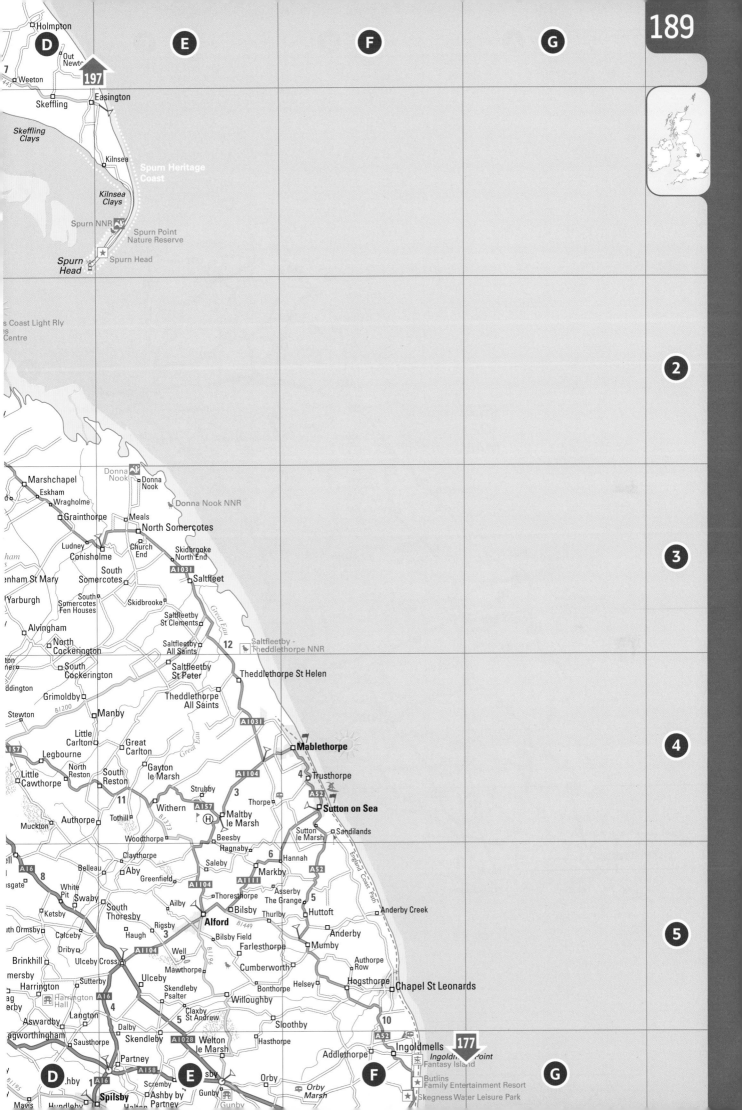

D · E · F · G

Holmpton
Out Newto
197
Weeton
Easington
Skeffling

Skeffling Clays

Kilnsea

Spurn Heritage Coast

Kilnsea Clays

Spurn NNR

Spurn Point Nature Reserve

Spurn Head
Spurn Head

s Coast Light Rly
Centre

2

Marshchapel
Eskham
Wragholme
Donna Nook
Donna Nook
Donna Nook NNR
Grainthorpe
Meals
North Somercotes
Ludney
Church End
Skidbrooke North End
Conisholme
South Somercotes
A1031
Saltfleet

enham St Mary
Yarburgh
South Somercotes Fen Houses
Skidbrooke
Saltfleetby St Clements
Great Eau
Alvingham
12
Saltfleetby - Theddlethorpe NNR
North Cockerington
Saltfleetby All Saints
ton
South Cockerington
Saltfleetby St Peter
Theddlethorpe St Helen
ddington
Grimoldby
B1200
Theddlethorpe All Saints
Stewton
Manby
A1031

3

4

Little Carlton
Great Carlton
Great Eau
A157
Legbourne
North Reston
Gayton le Marsh
Mablethorpe
Little Cawthorpe
South Reston
Strubby
4 Trusthorpe
11
Withern
A157
3
Thorpe
A52
Muckton
Authorpe
Tothill
Maltby le Marsh
H
Beesby
Sutton on Sea
Woodthorpe
Sutton le Marsh
Sandilands
Cl022
Claythorpe
Hagnaby
6
Hannah
Belleau
Aby
Saleby
A52
A16
8
Greenfield
Markby
5
White Pit
Swaby
Ailby
A1104
Asserby
5
Ketsby
Thoresthorpe
The Grange
South Thoresby
Bilsby
Thurlby
Huttoft
Anderby Creek
th Ormsby
Calceby
Rigsby
Alford
B1449
Driby
Haugh
3
Bilsby Field
Anderby
Brinkhill
A1104
Well
Farlesthorpe
Mumby
mersby
Sutterby
Ulceby Cross
Mawthorpe
Cumberworth
Authorpe Row
Harrington
Ulceby
Skendleby Psalter
Bonthorpe
Helsey
Hogsthorpe
Chapel St Leonards
ag
Harrington Hall
A16
4
Willoughby
Aswardby
Langton
Dalby
Claxby St Andrew
agworthingham
Sausthorpe
Skendleby
A1028
Welton le Marsh
Hasthorpe
Sloothby
10
A52
Partney
Addlethorpe
Ingoldmells
177
A158
Ingold Point
Fantasy Island
hby
1
Scremby
sby
Orby
Butlins Family Entertainment Resort
Spilsby
Gunby
Orby Marsh
Skegness Water Leisure Park
Mavis
Hundleby
Partney
Gunby

5

D · E · F · G

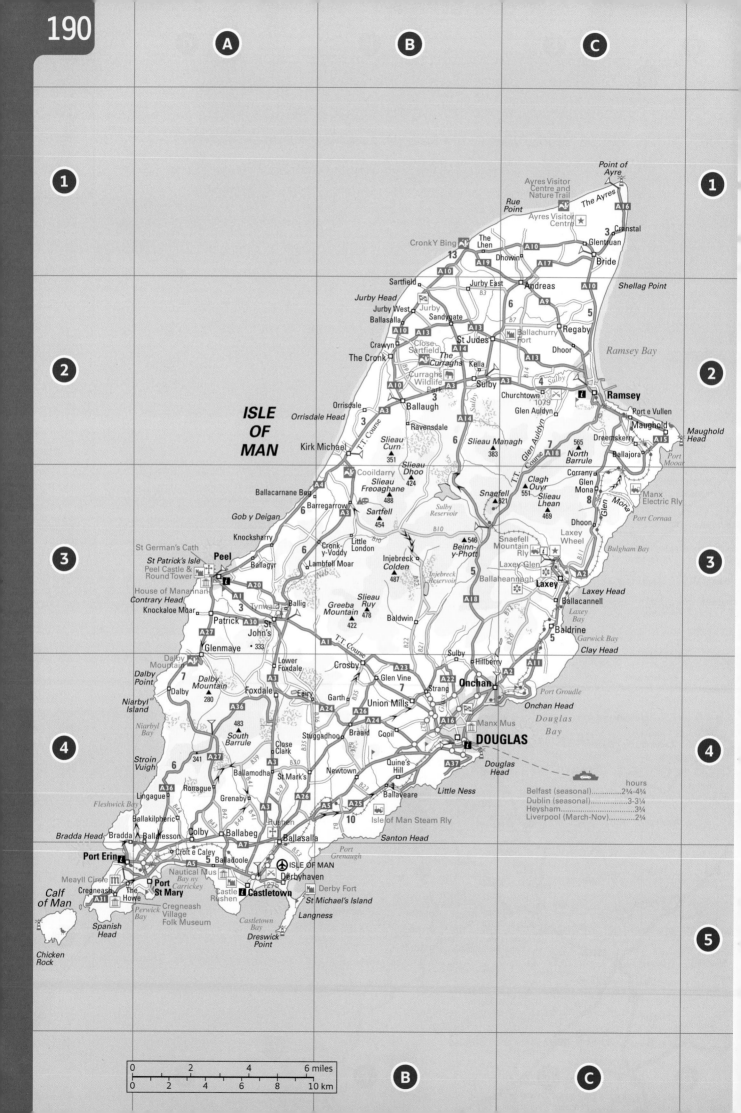

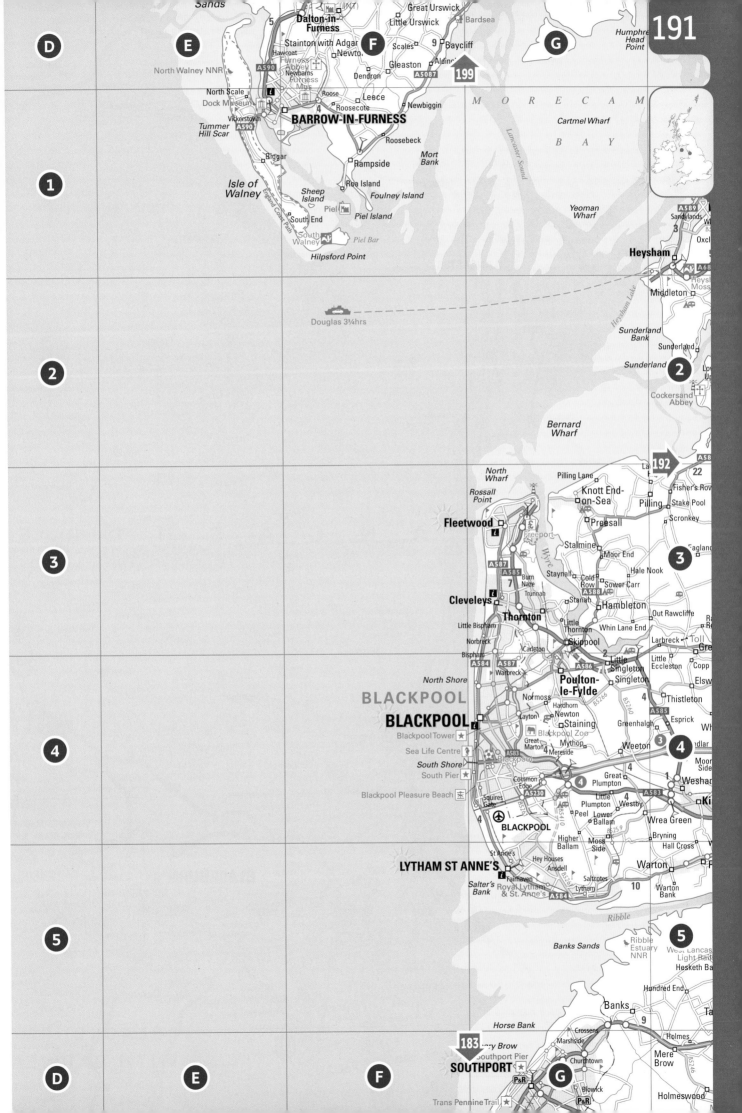

D **E** **F** **G**

Sands
Great Urswick
Little Urswick
Bardsea
Humphrey Head Point

Dalton-in-Furness
5
Stainton with Adgar
Newton
Scales
9 Baycliff

North Walney NNR
Hawcoat
A590
Furness Abbey
Newbarns
Furness Mus
Dendron
Aldingham
Gleaston

199

North Scale
Dock Museum
i
Roose
Leece
Roosecote
Newbiggin

MORECAM

BARROW-IN-FURNESS
Cartmel Wharf
BAY

Vickerstown
A590
Roosebeck

Tummer Hill Scar
Lancaster Sound

1
Rampside
Mort Bank

Isle of Walney
Biggar
Roa Island

Sheep Island
Foulney Island
Yeoman Wharf
Sandylands
Oxcl
A589

South End
Piel
Piel Island

South Walney
Piel Bar
Heysham
Heysham Moss
A68

Hilpsford Point
Middleton

Douglas 3¾hrs
Heysham Lake
Sunderland Bank
Sunderland

2
Sunderland
2

Cockersand Abbey

Bernard Wharf

192
A58
22

North Wharf
Pilling Lane
Fisher's Row

Rossall Point
Knott End-on-Sea
Pilling
Stake Pool

Fleetwood
Preesall
Scronkey

Freeport
Stalmine
aglano

Wyre
Moor End
Hale Nook

3
A587
A585
Burn Naze
Cold Row
Sower Carr
3

Staynall
Trunnah
Stanah

Cleveleys
i
Hambleton
Out Rawcliffe

Thornton
Little Thornton
Whin Lane End
Ra
Re

Little Bispham
Skippool
Larbreck
Toll

Norbreck
Carleton
2
Little Singleton
Little Eccleston
Copp
Gre

Bispham
A584
A586
Singleton
Elsw

North Shore
Warbreck
4
Thistleton

BLACKPOOL
Normoss
Poulton-le-Fylde

Hardhorn
Greenhalgh
Esprick

BLACKPOOL
i
Layton
Newton
Staining
Weeton
3
edlar
4
Blackpool Tower ★
Blackpool Zoo
Mythop

Sea Life Centre
Great Marton
Mereside
Moor Side

South Shore
Blackpool FC
A583
Great Plumpton
Wesha

South Pier
A583
Ki

Common Edge
4
Little Plumpton
Westby

Blackpool Pleasure Beach
A230
Peel
Lower Ballam
Wrea Green

Squires Gate
Higher Ballam
Moss Side
Bryning

BLACKPOOL
Hall Cross

St Anne's
Hey Houses
Warton

LYTHAM ST ANNE'S
Ansdell
Saltcotes
Warton Bank

Salter's Bank
Fairhaven
Royal Lytham & St. Anne's
Lytham
10

A584

Ribble

5
Banks Sands
Ribble Estuary NNR
West Lancs Light Rai
5
Hesketh Ba

Hundred End

Banks
Ta

Horse Bank
Crossens
9
Holmes

183
Marshside
Mere Brow

ry Brow
Southport Pier
Churchtown

SOUTHPORT
P&R
Blowick
Holmeswood

Trans Pennine Trail ★
P&R

D **E** **F** **G**

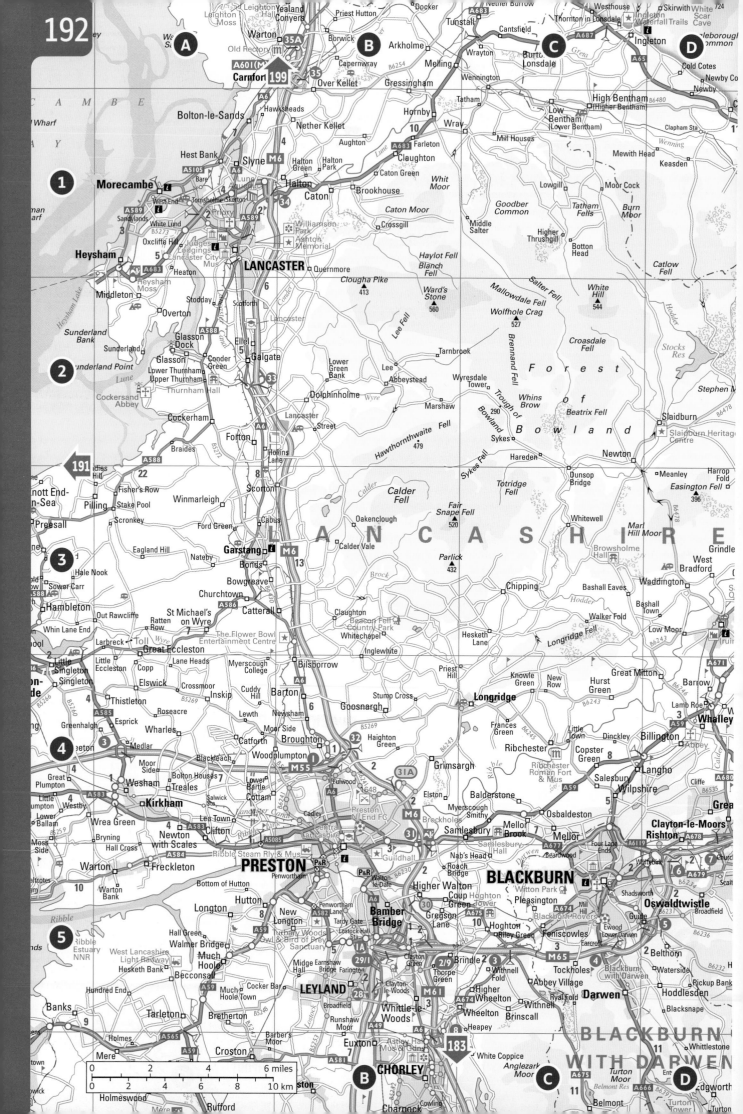

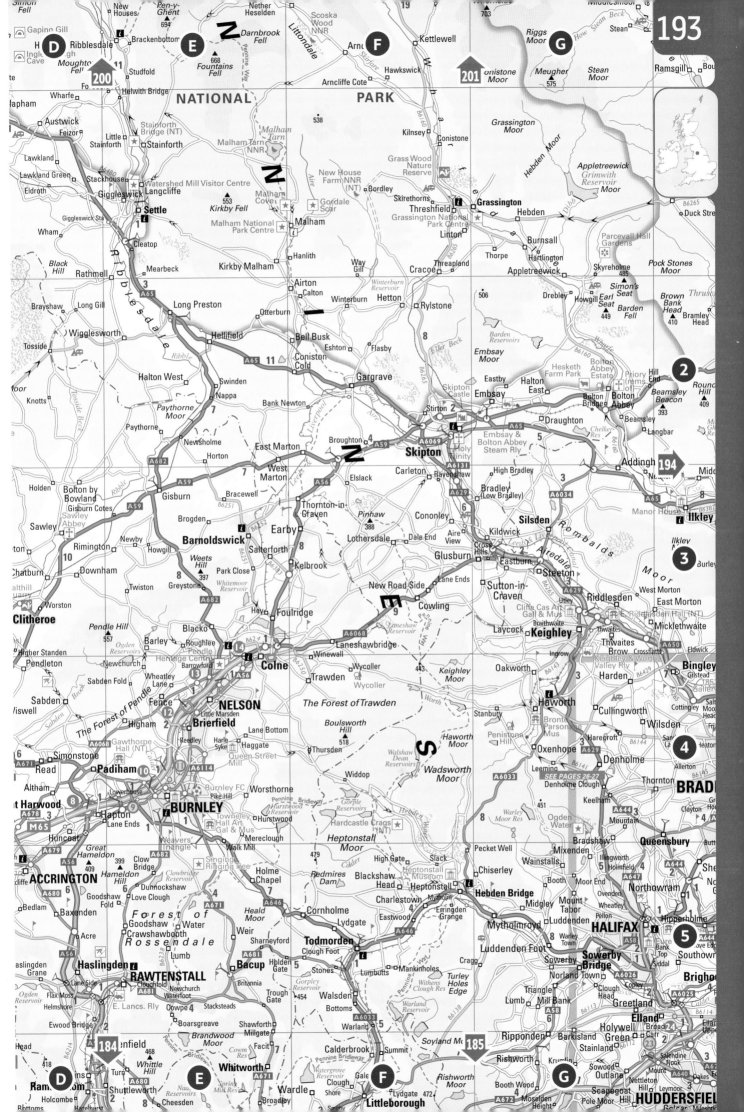

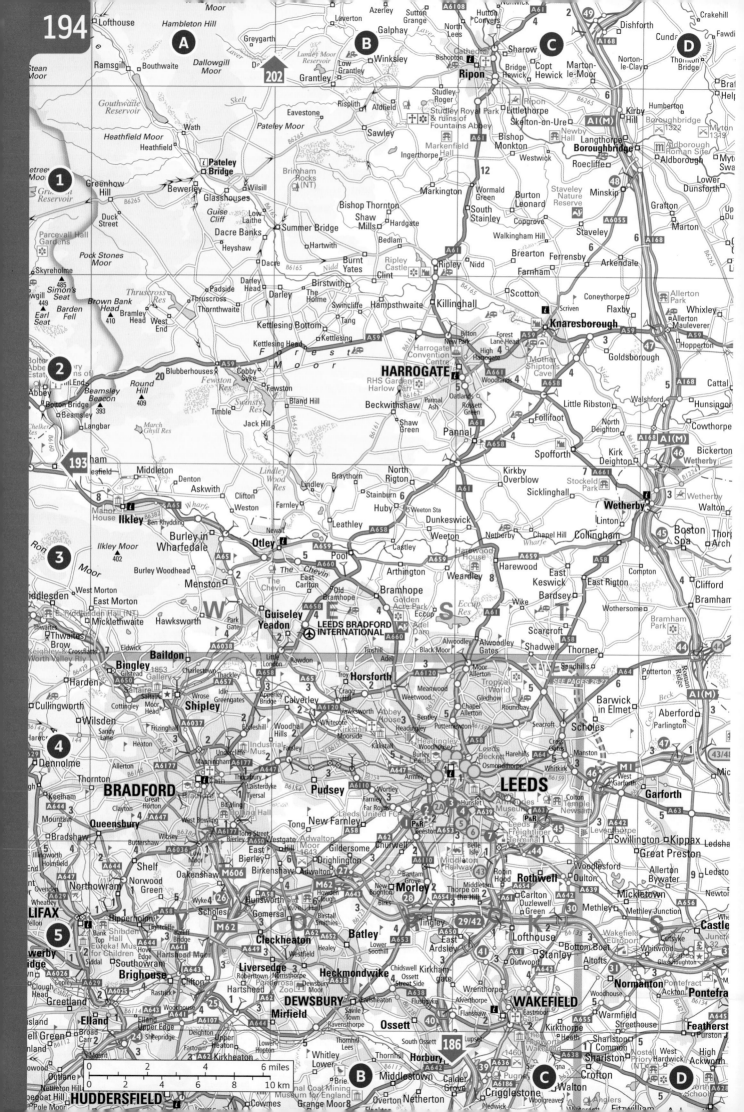

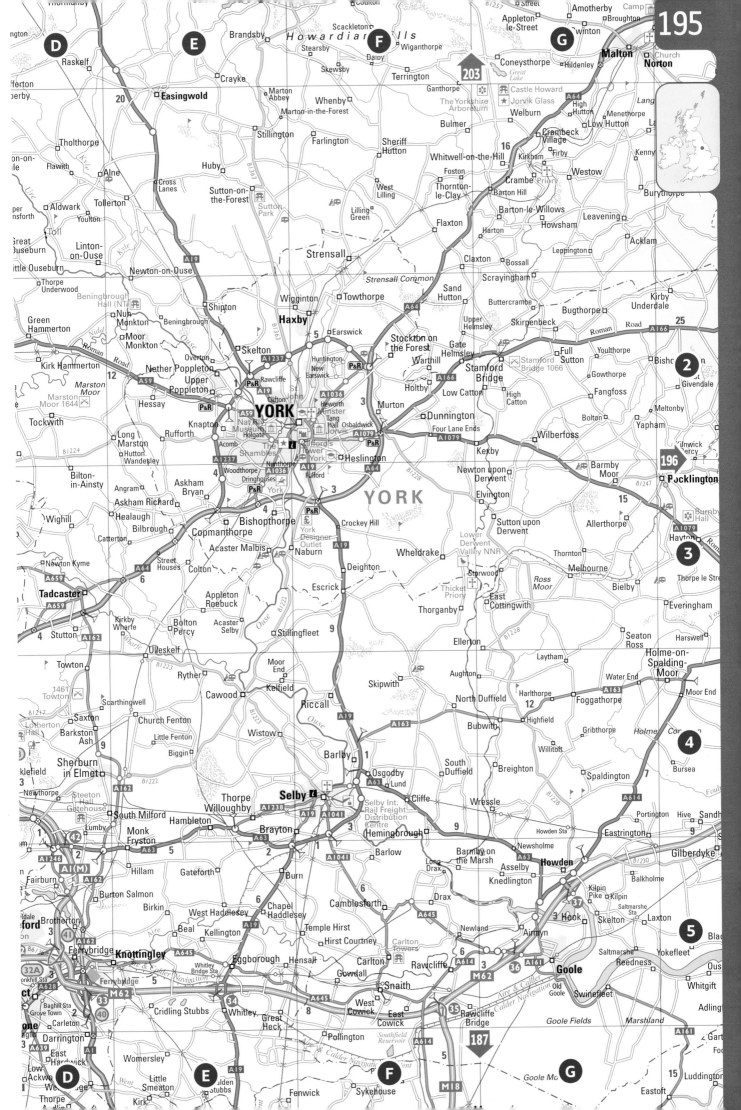

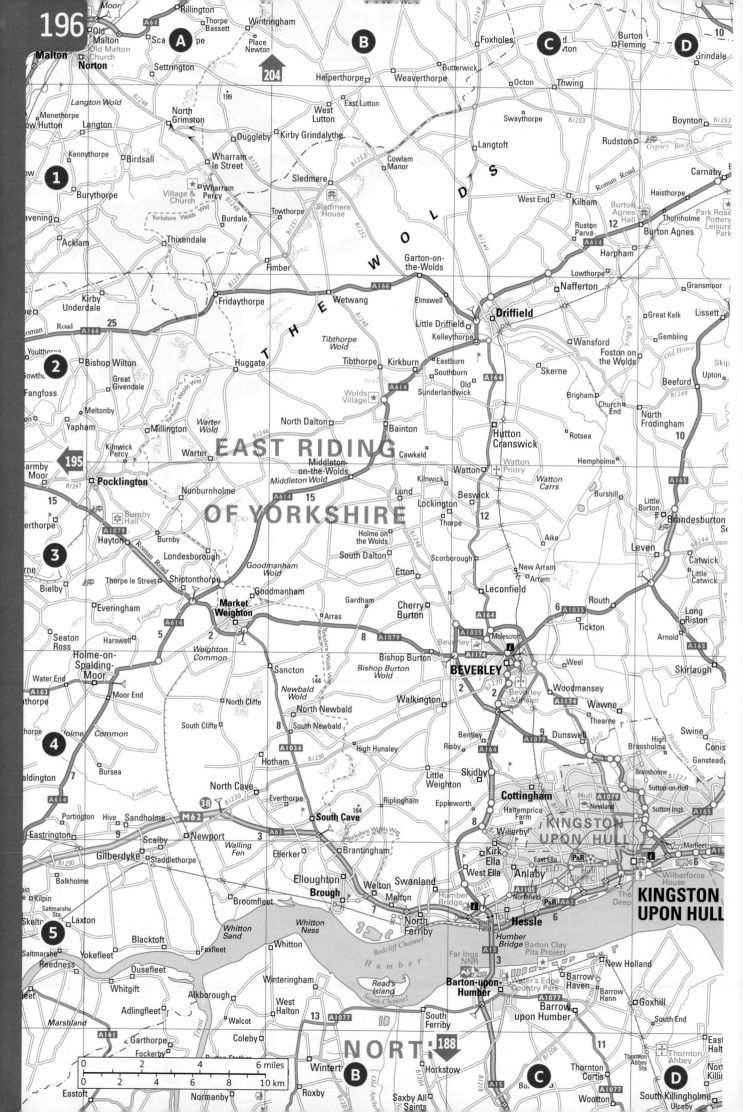

Speeton

Crab Rocks

RSPB
Bempton Cliffs
Seabird Centre

B1229

Buckton

Bempton

ough Cliffs
eserve

D **E** **F** **G**

A165

Flamborough
Head

urough

205

Sewerby Hall
& Gardens

B1255

B1259

Sewerby

Flamborough Headland
Heritage Coast

Bridlington

West Hill

essingby

Hilderthorpe

P&R

Wilsthorpe

*Carnaby
Moor*

6

Fraisthorpe

BRIDLINGTON

BAY

A165

Barmston

B1242

Ulrome

Skipsea

sea

Skipsea
Brough

B1242

Dunnington

North
End

Atwick

2

Bewholme

eaton

Hornsea

B1244

★ Trans Pennine Trail

*Hornsea
Mere*

Freeport

Hornsea Freeport

Sigglesthorne

Goxhill

Rolston

3

Little
Hatfield

Mappleton

B1242

Great Hatfield

Great Cowden

Rise

North End

25

Withernwick

New
Ellerby

Marton

West
Newton

East Newton

Old
Ellerby

Aldbrough

Etherdwick
Grange

B1242

12

Burton
Constable Hall

B1238

4

Burton
Constable

Flinton

Garton

Grimston

Thirtleby

Sproatley

Humbleton

Fitling

Hilston

Wyton

B1238

Danthorpe

Owstwick

Lelley

Bilton

B1240

Elstronwick

North End

Tunstall

B1239

Burton
Pidsea

Roos

B1242

Preston

East End

Dairy House

Waxholme

33

Hedon

Wadworth Hill

B1362

A1033

Burstwick

Rimswell

B1362

Withernsea

Thorngumbald

Halsham

East
End

Paull

Camerton

Keyingham

Hollym

5

Ryehill

11

Paull
Holme

Ottringham

Winestead

A1033

4

*East
Halton
Skitter*

*Paull Holme
Sands*

Holmpton

Patrington

hours

Rotterdam....11-13¼
Zeebrugge....13¼-14

*Cherry
Cobb Sands*

Salthaugh
Grange

Patrington
Haven

Welwick

7

Weeton

B1445

Foullholme Sands

Sunk Island

6

Skeffling

189 ington

gholme

D **E** **F** **G**

Immingham
Dock

Old Hall

*Sunk Island
Sands*

keffling
Clays

Spurn Heritage

Kilnsea

4

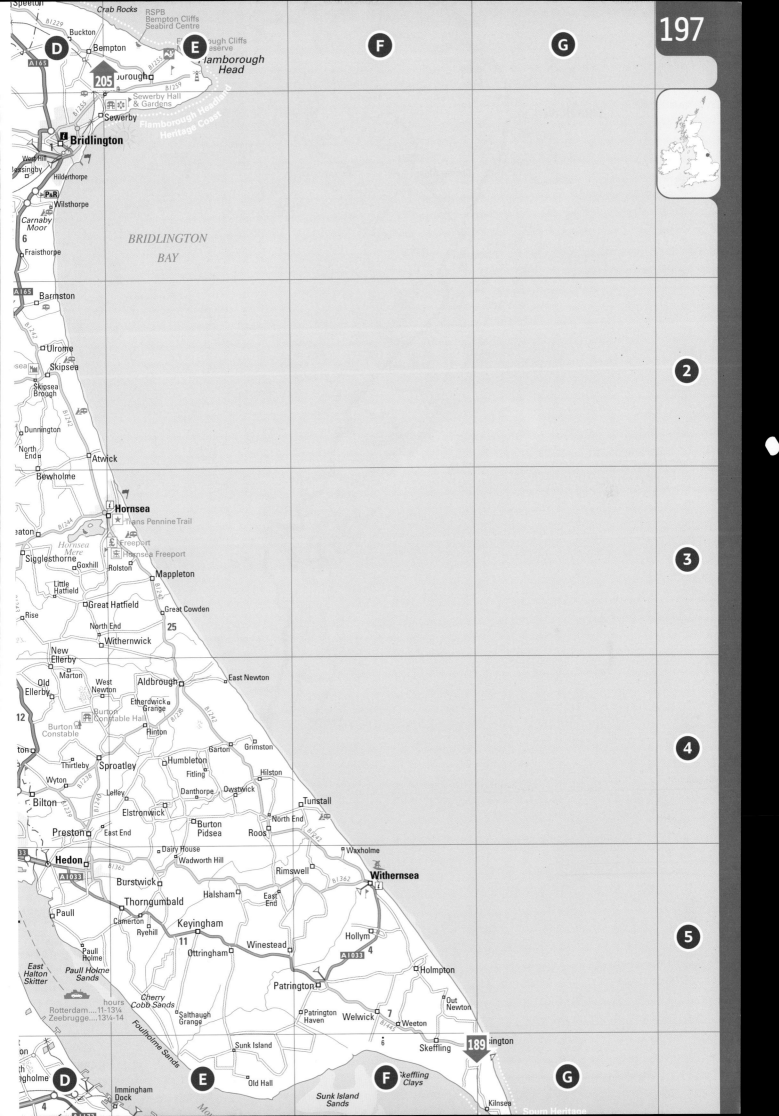

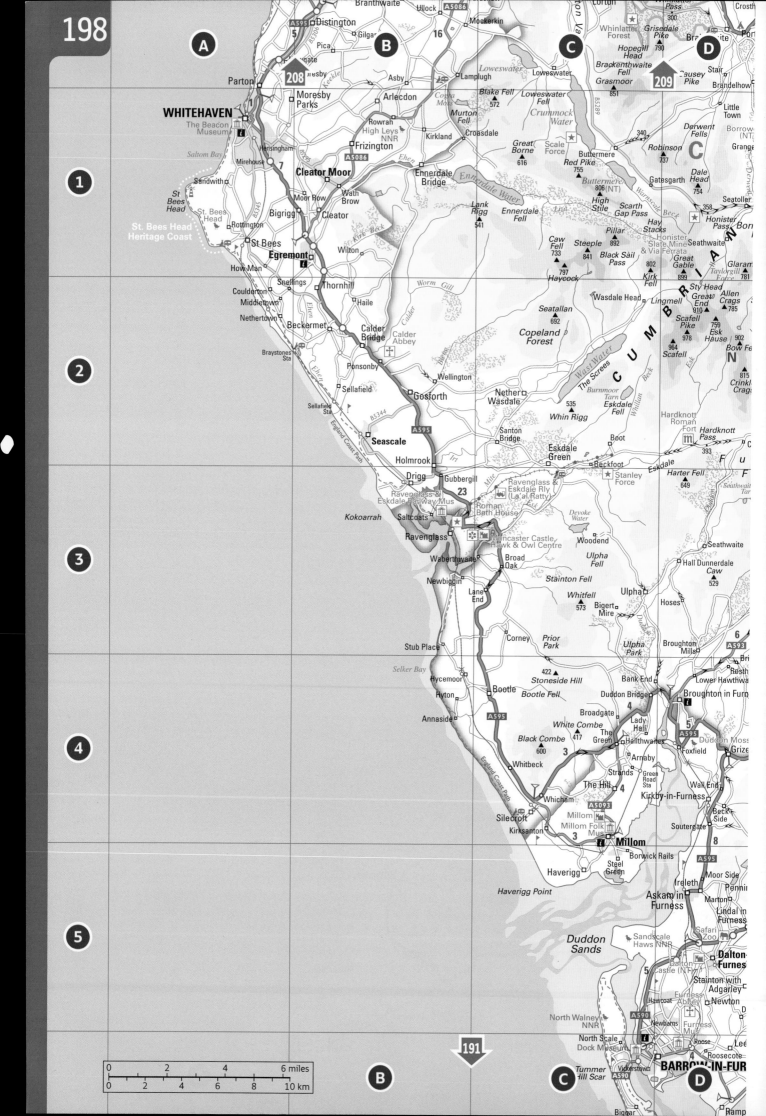

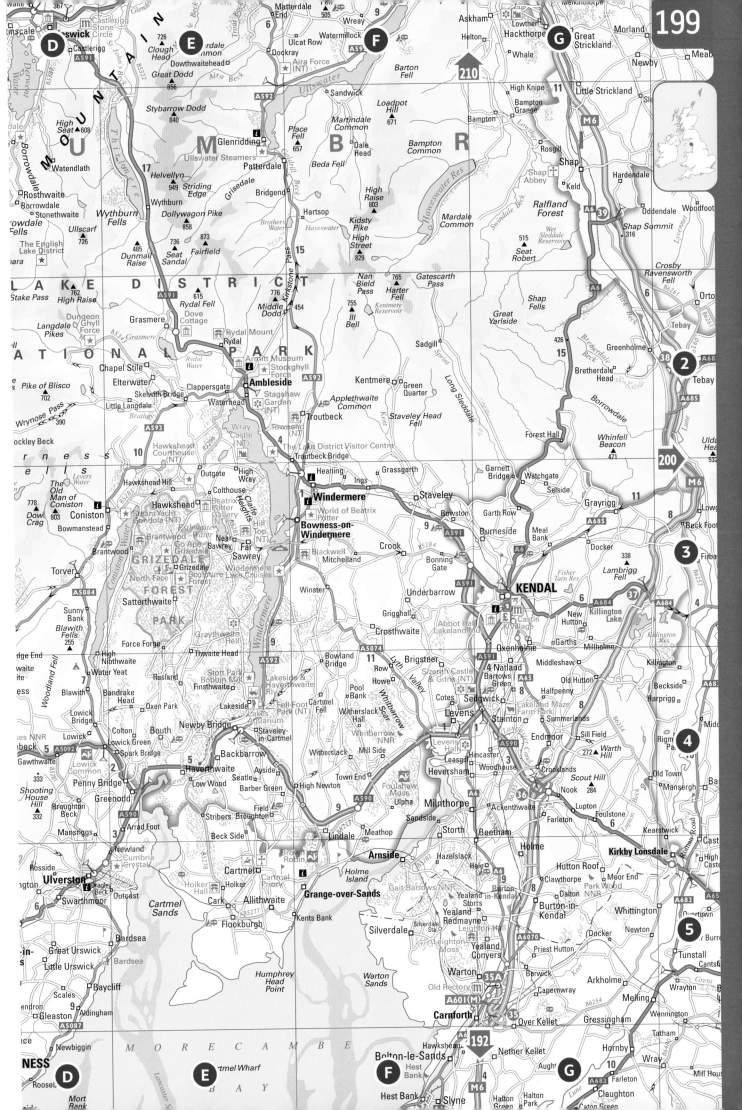

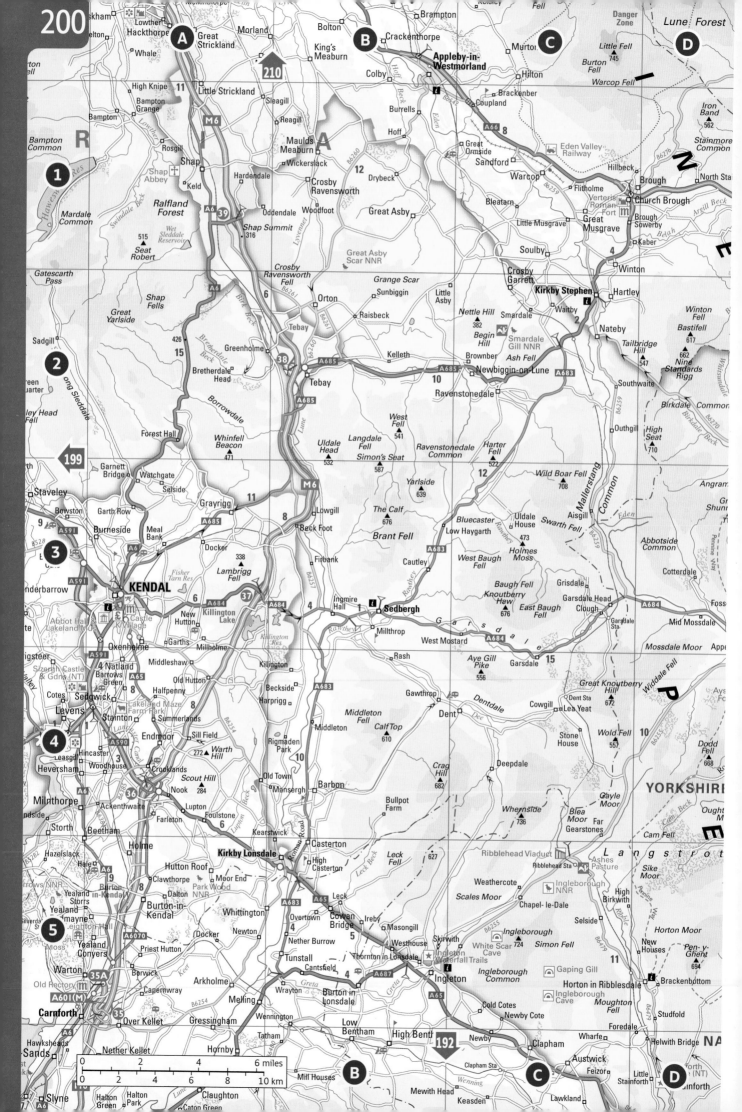

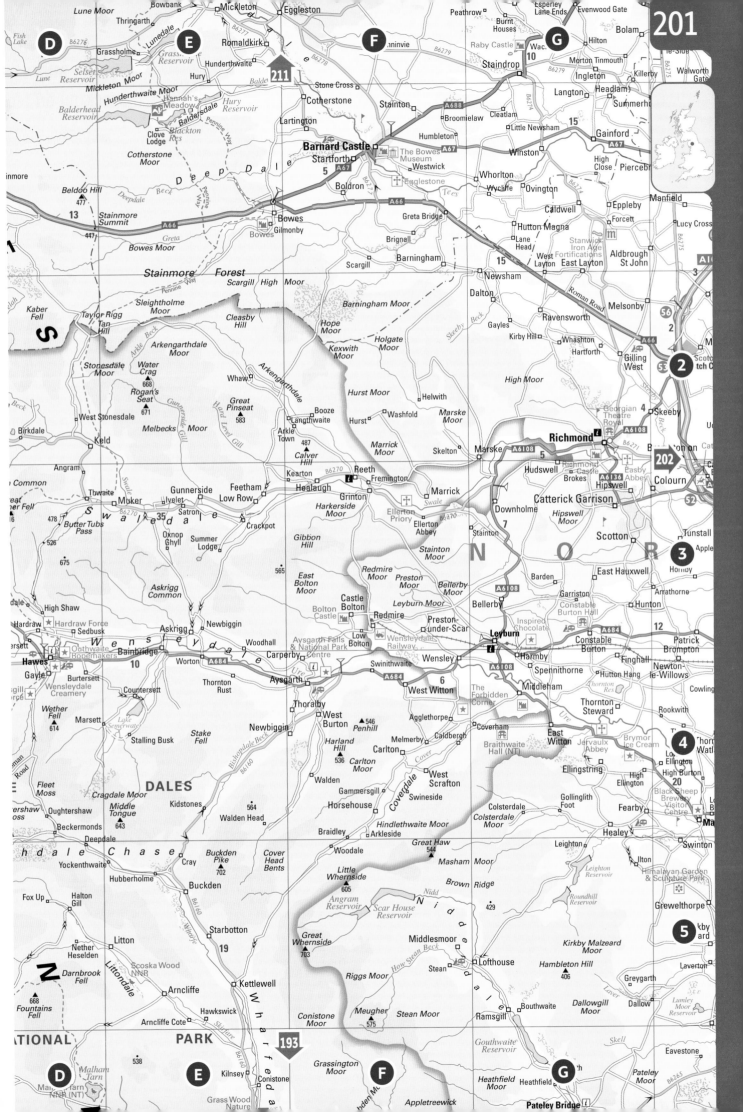

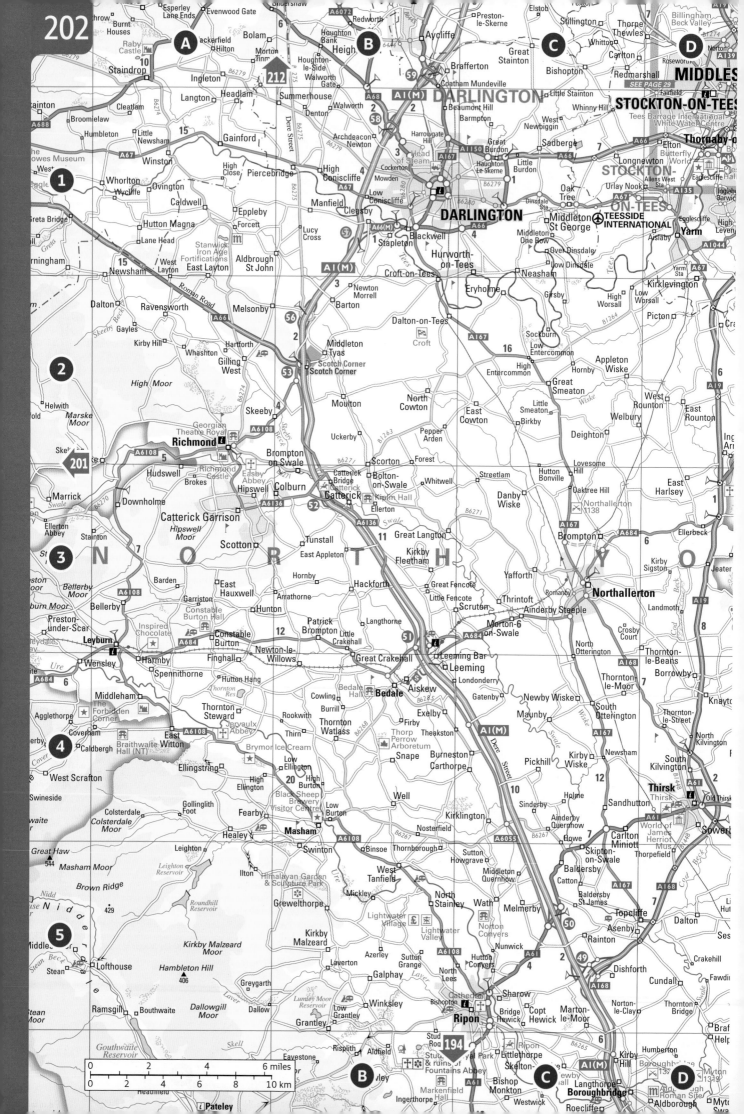

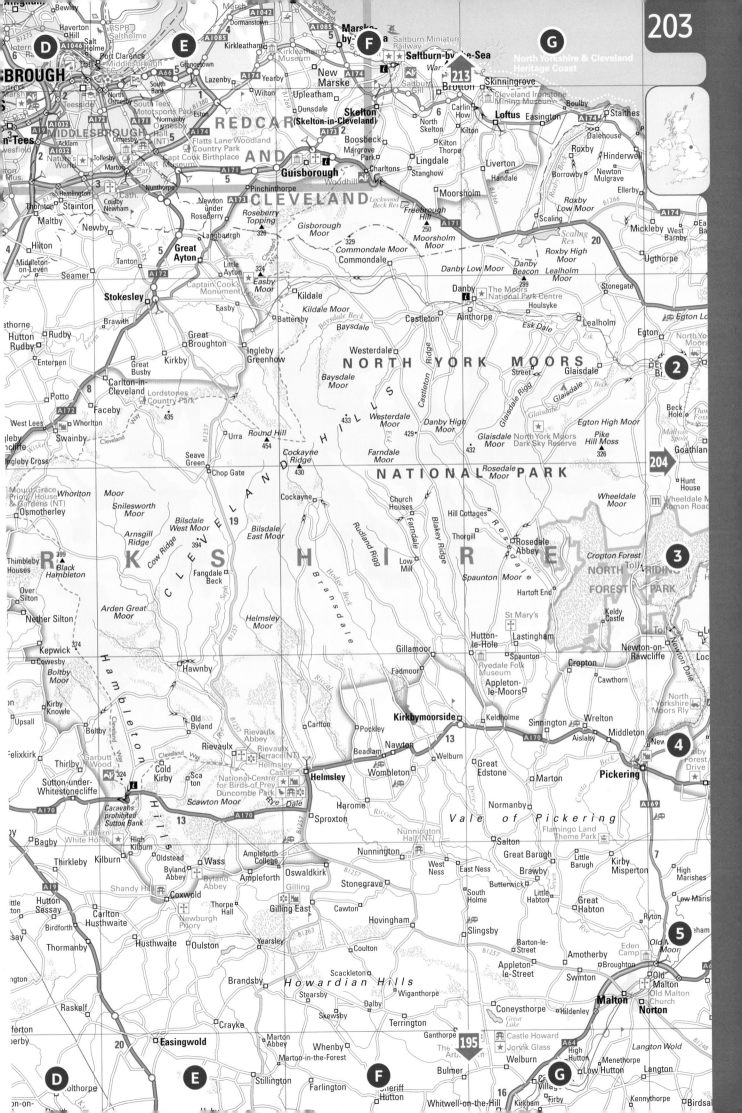

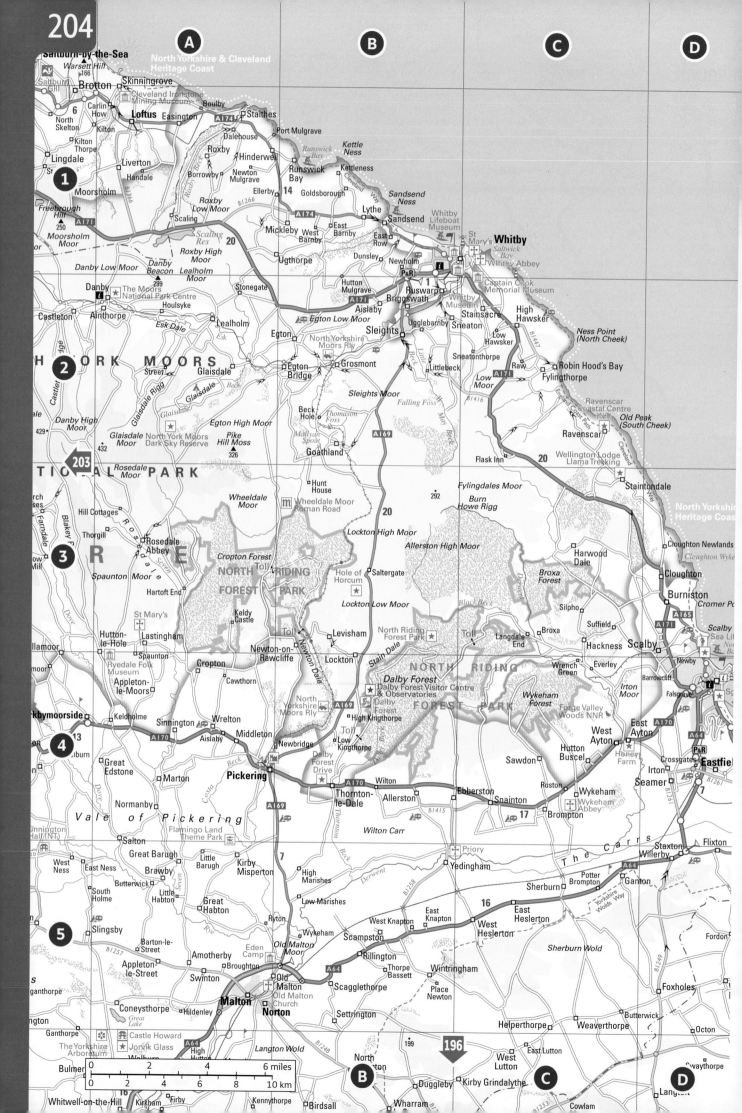

D **E** **F** **G**

2

3

& Cleveland

Ness Rocks
& Marine Sanctuary
North Bay
Miniature Railway

Scarborough Castle
SCARBOROUGH
Scarborough Art Gall
South Bay
Spa Complex
Black Rocks

3

P&R Osgodby
Cayton Bay
Cayton **7**
The Wyke
Lebberston
Gristhorpe
England Coast Path
Filey Brigg
Hertford **A165**
A1039 **Filey**
Folkton **6** *Filey Bay*
West Flotmanby Muston

4

Hunmanby

Reighton Sands
Reighton
Speeton
Crab Rocks
RSPB
Bempton Cliffs
Seabird Centre
B1229
Buckton
Flamborough Cliffs
Nature Reserve
Wold Newton
10
Burton Fleming
Bempton
B1255
Grindale
A165
Flamborough Head
Flamborough
B1255
Thwing
Marton
Sewerby Hall & Gardens
Flamborough Headland
B1253
Boynton **B1255**
Heritage Coast

5

197

D **E** Bridlington **F** **G**

Rudston
Gypsey Race
West Hill
Bessingby

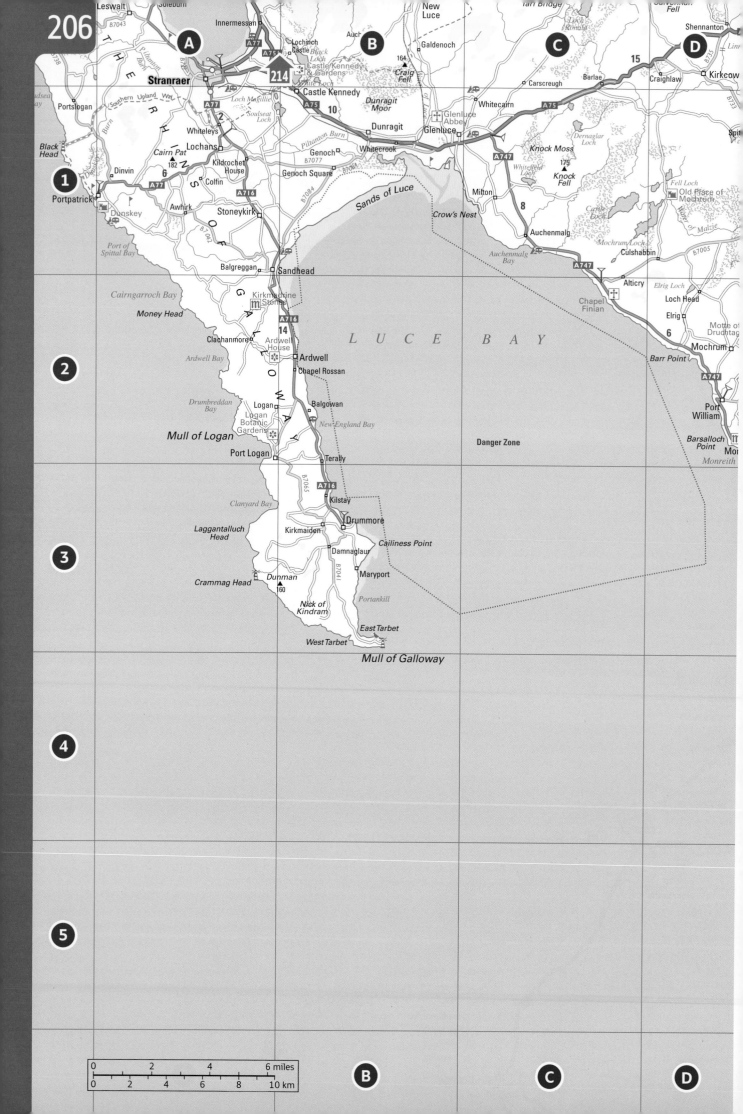

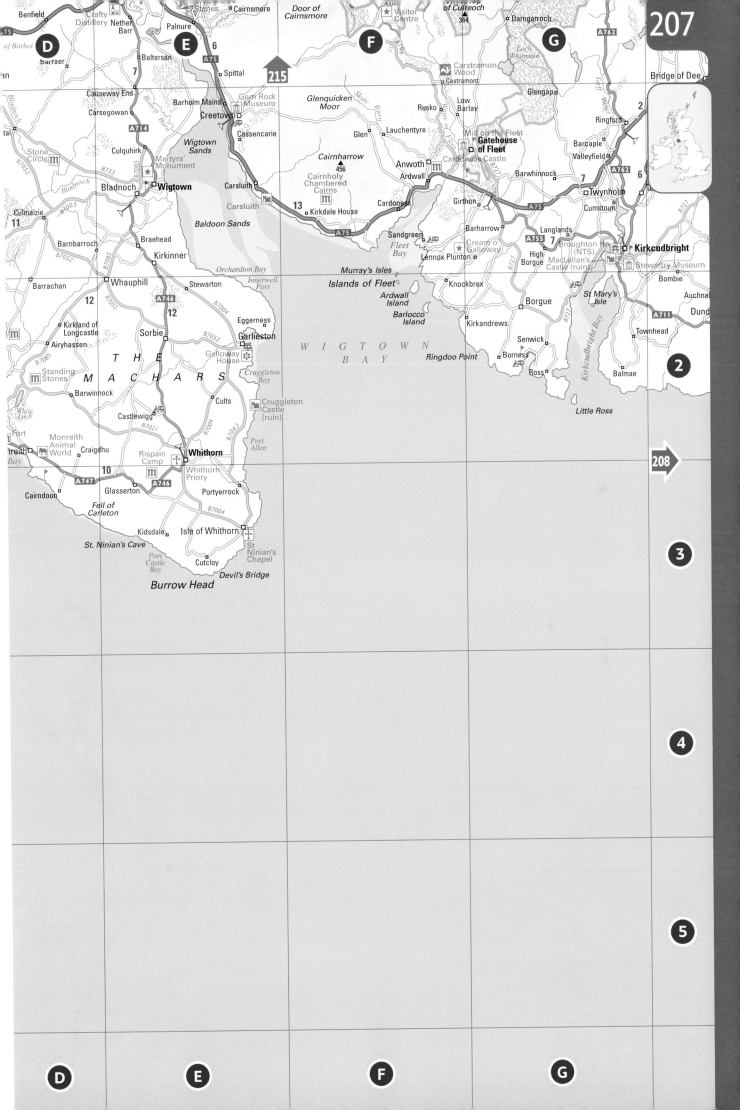

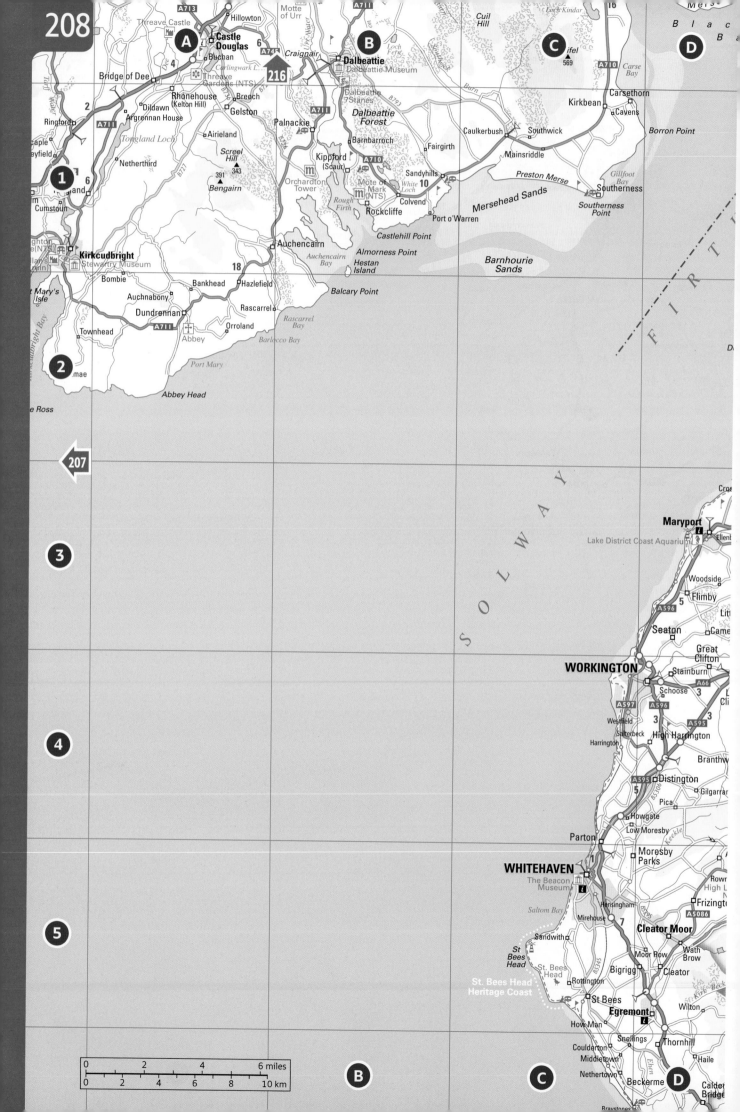

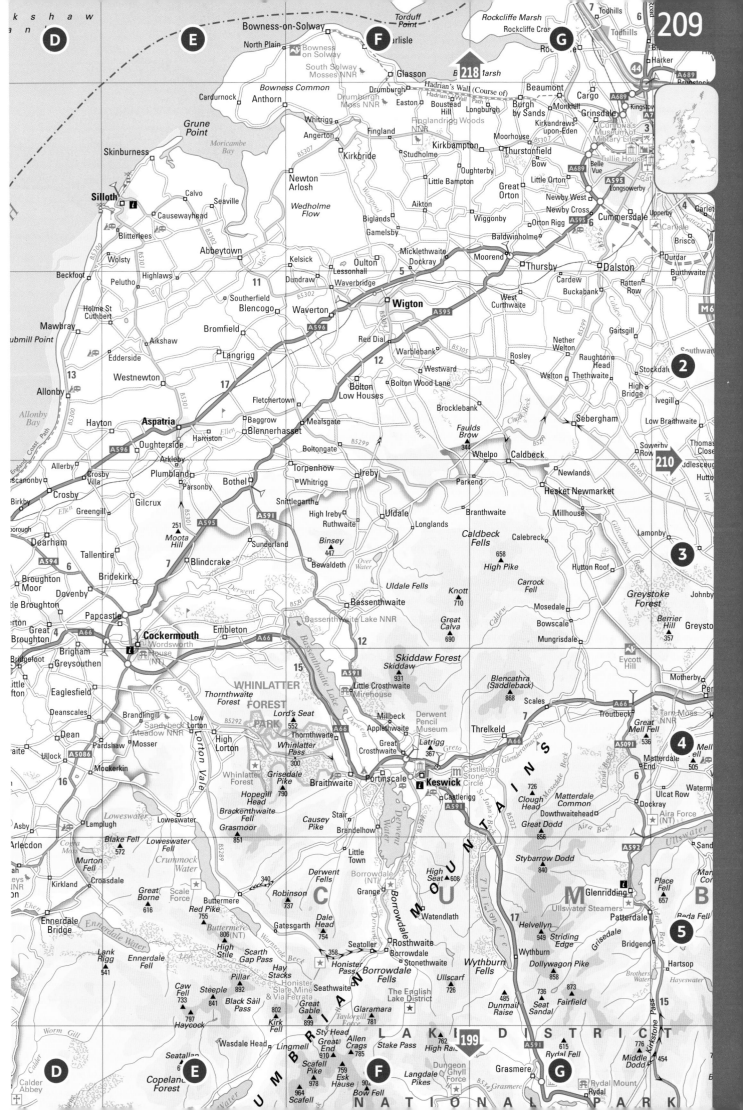

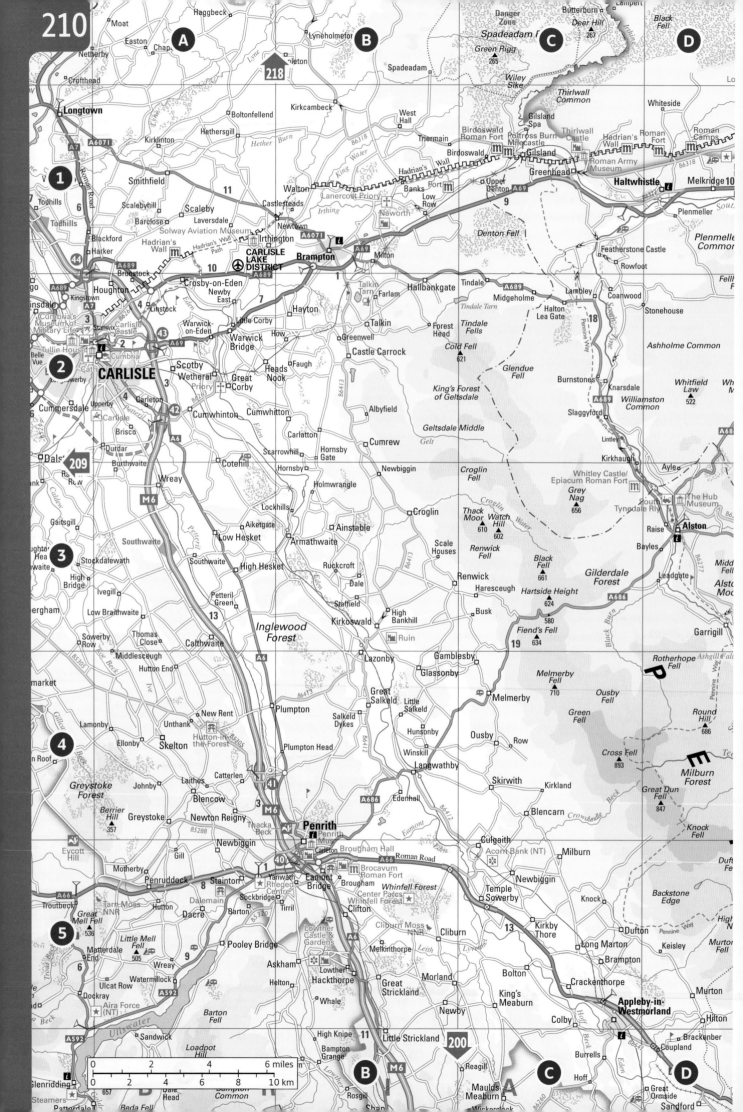

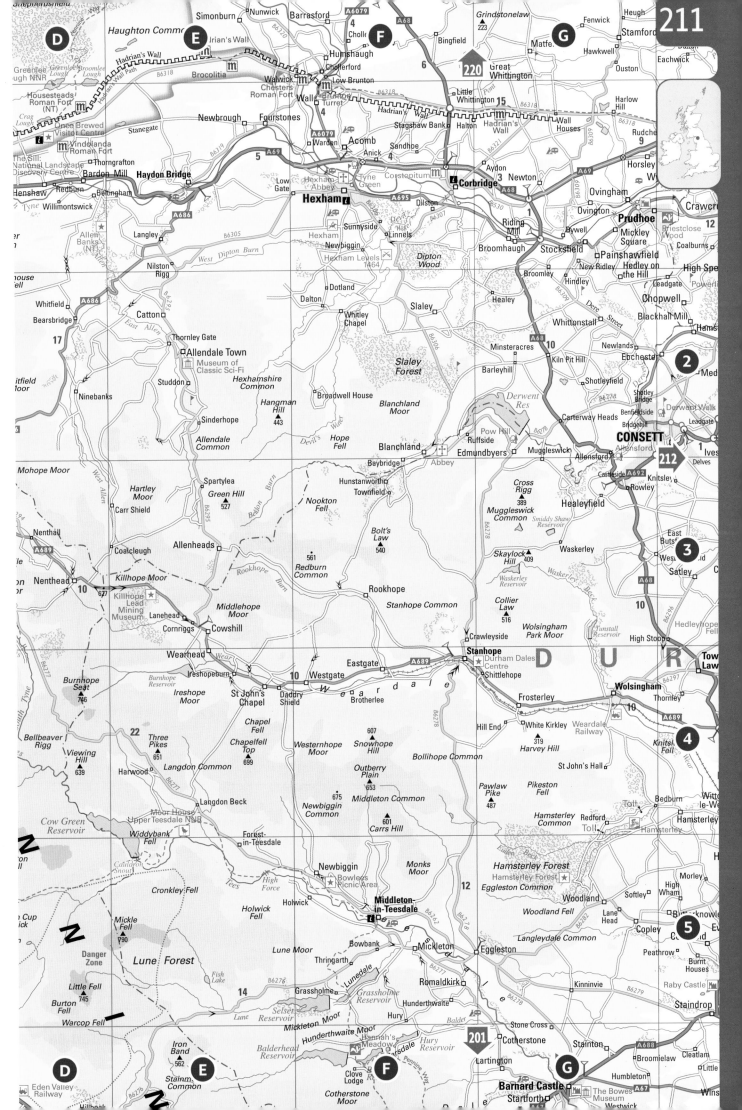

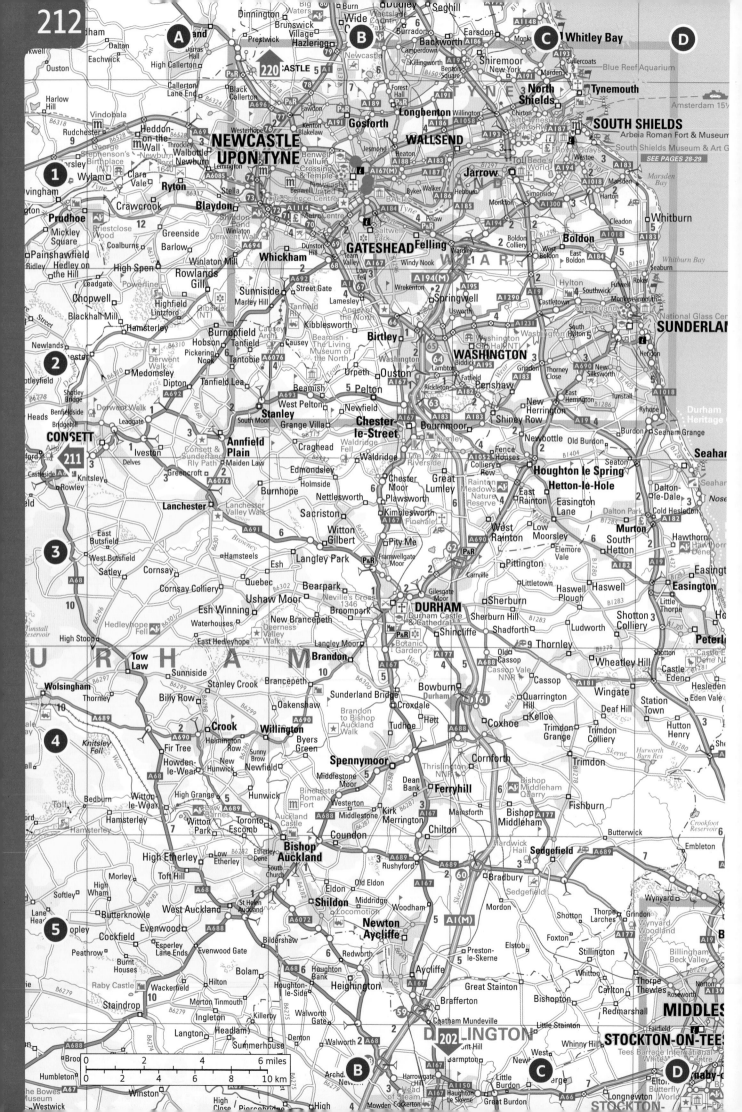

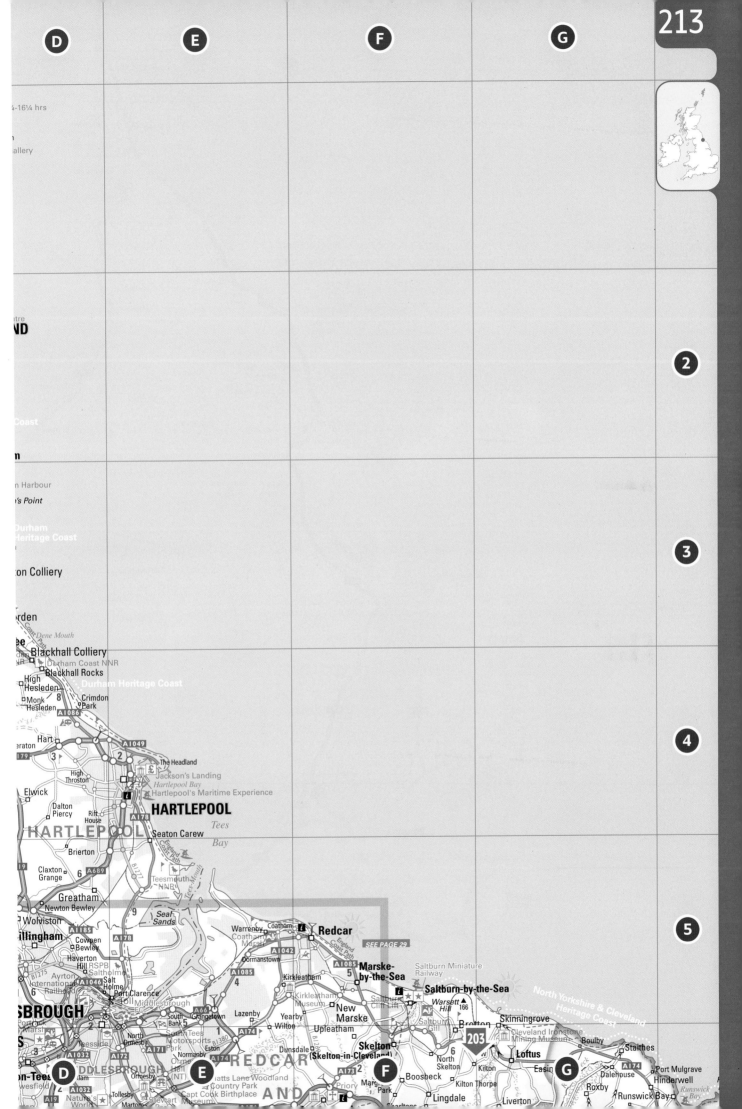

D E F G

2

3

4

5

4-16¼ hrs

...allery

...ND

...Coast

...n

...n Harbour
...'s Point

...Durham
...Heritage Coast

...on Colliery

...rden

Dene Mouth

Blackhall Colliery
NR Durham Coast NNR
Blackhall Rocks
High
Hesleden
Monk 8 Crimdon
Hesleden Park
A1086

Hart
...eraton A1049
3 High
Throston
Elwick The Headland
Jackson's Landing
Dalton Rift Hartlepool Bay
Piercy House Hartlepool's Maritime Experience

HARTLEPOOL Tees
A178 Bay
HARTLEPOOL Seaton Carew
Brierton
Claxton 6 A689
Grange
Greatham
Newton Bewley
Wolviston 9 Seal
Sands
illingham A1185 Warrenby Coatham Redcar
Cowpen Coatham
Bewley Marsh SEE PAGE 29
Haverton A1042 Dormanstown
Hill RSPB A1085 Marske-
Ayrton Saltholme 5 by-the-Sea
B1275 International Salt Kirkleatham Saltburn Miniature
Railway Holme Railway
A1046 Port Clarence Kirkleatham Saltburn-by-the-Sea
Toll Middlesbrough Museum Saltburn
SBROUGH A66 4 New Cliff Lift Warsett
South Marske Hill 166
Bank Grangetown Lazenby Yearby Upleatham Saltburn
...S North Wilton Gill Brotton Skinningrove
Ormesby South Tees 203 Cleveland Ironstone
A171 Motorsports 1 A174 Dunsdale 6 Mining Museum Boulby
A1032 Park Eston North Staithes
DDLESBROUGH Orme Skelton Kilton
...n-Tees A172 REDCAR (Skelton-in-Cleveland) Loftus Easin G Dalehouse
...esfield A1032 E Watts Lane Woodland Boosbeck Kilton Port Mulgrave
A19 Nature's Country Park F Kilton Thorpe Roxby Hinderwell
World Tollesby Capt Cook Birthplace AND Marg Priory Lingdale Liverton Runswick Bay
Marton Stewart Museum Park Runswick
...arltons Bay

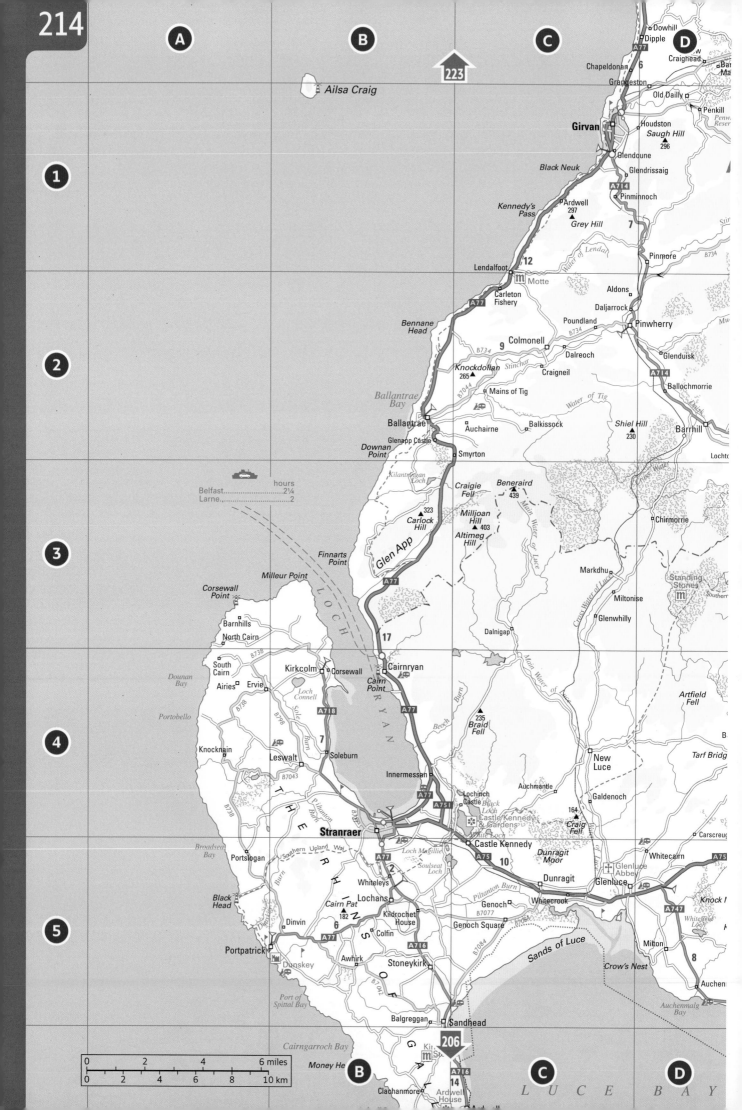

A B C D

223

Ailsa Craig

Girvan

1

Black Neuk

Kennedy's Pass

Ardwell
297
Grey Hill

12

Lendalfoot

Motte

Carleton
Fishery

Bennane
Head

2

Ballantrae
Bay

Colmonell
9

Knockdolian
265

Mains of Tig

Ballantrae

Glenapp Castle
Downan
Point

Smyrton

Kilantringan
Loch

Craigie
Fell

Beneraird
439

Carlock
Hill
323

Glen App

Milljoan
Hill
403
Altimeg
Hill

3

Milleur Point

Finnarts
Point

A77

Corsewall
Point

Barnhills

North Cairn

Dounan
Bay

South
Cairn

Airies Ervie

Kirkcolm

Corsewall

Loch
Connell

Cairnryan

Cairn
Point

17

A77

Dalnigap

Markdhu

Miltonise

Standing
Stones

Glenwhilly

Chirmorrie

4

Portobello

Knocknain

Leswalt

B798

Soleburn

7

Beoch
Burn

Braid
Fell
235

New
Luce

Auchmantle

Galdenoch

Artfield
Fell

Tarf Bridge

Innermessan

A77

Lochinch
Castle

Craig
Fell
164

A751

Castle Kennedy
& Gardens

White Loch

Stranraer

Loch Magillie

Castle Kennedy

Carscreug

Broadsea
Bay

Portslogan

Southern Upland Way

Whiteleys

Soulseat
Loch

A77

Dunragit
Moor

10

Whitecairn

A75

Glenluce
Abbey

Black
Head

Cairn Pat
182

Lochans

Dinvin

Colfin

Kildrochet
House

Genoch
Square

Whitecrook
Genoch

Dunragit

Glenluce

Knock

A747

Milton

5

Portpatrick

Dunskey

Awhirk

Stoneykirk

A716

B7084

Sands of Luce

Crow's Nest

Auchen

Port of
Spittal Bay

Balgreggan Sandhead

206

Auchenmalg
Bay

Cairngarroch Bay

0   2   4   6 miles
0 2 4 6 8 10 km

Money He

B   C   D

A716
14

Clachanmore

Ardwell
House

L U C E   B A Y

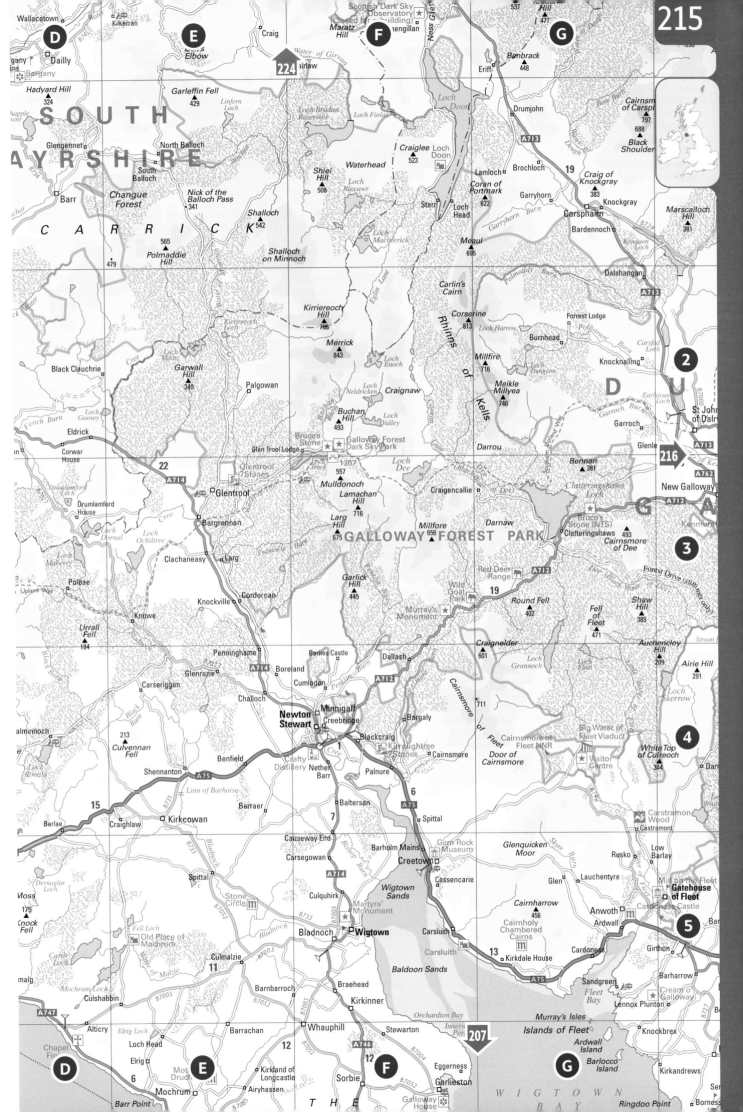

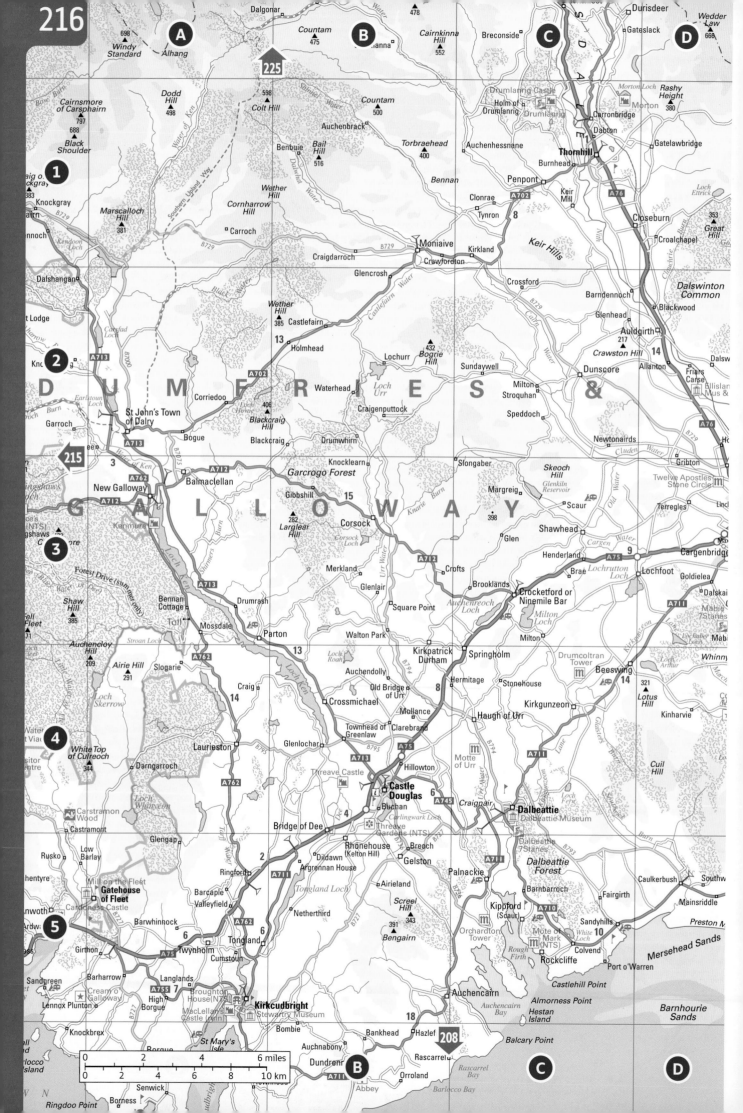

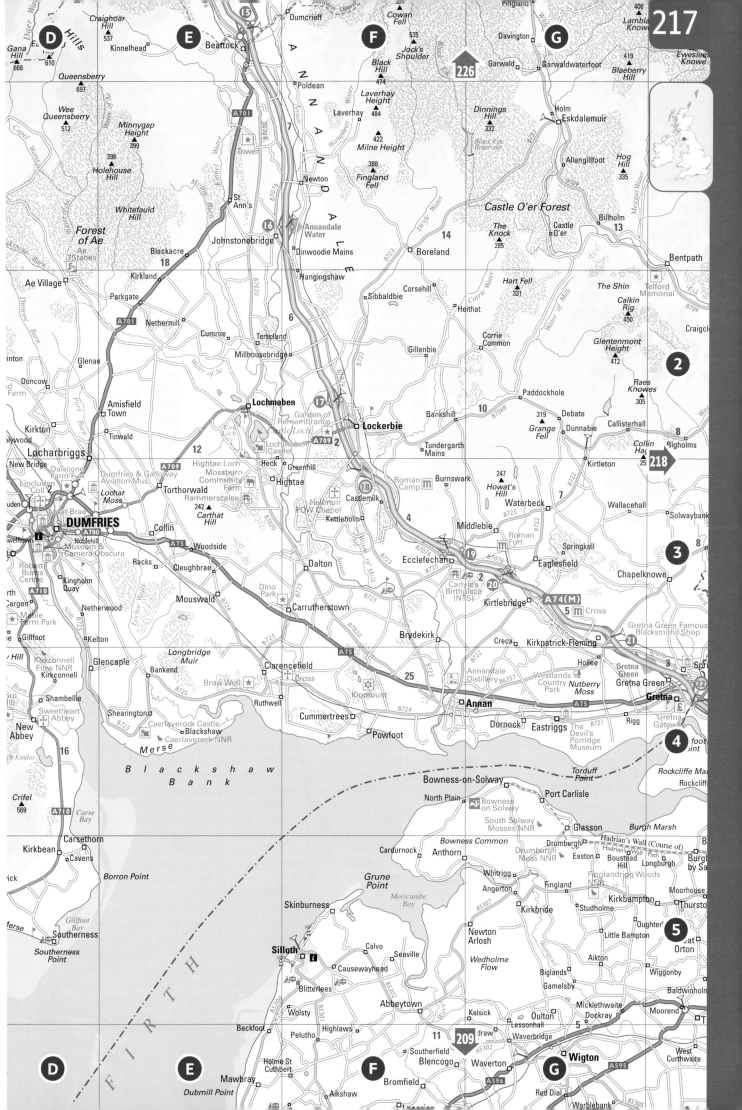

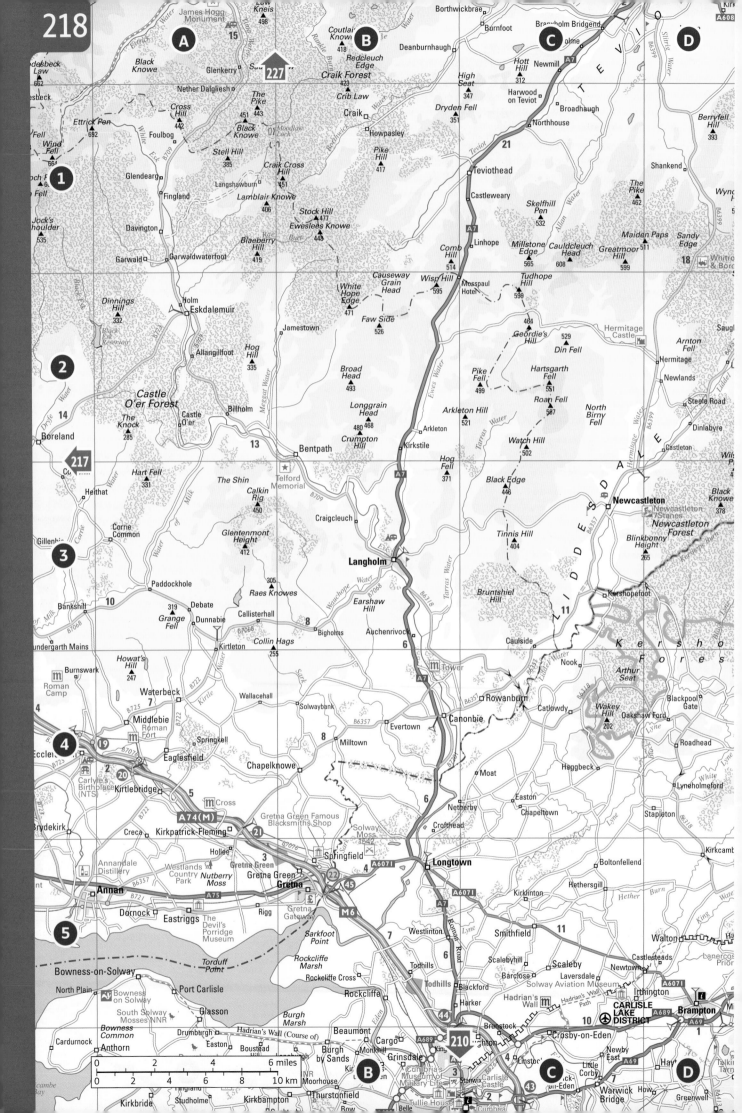

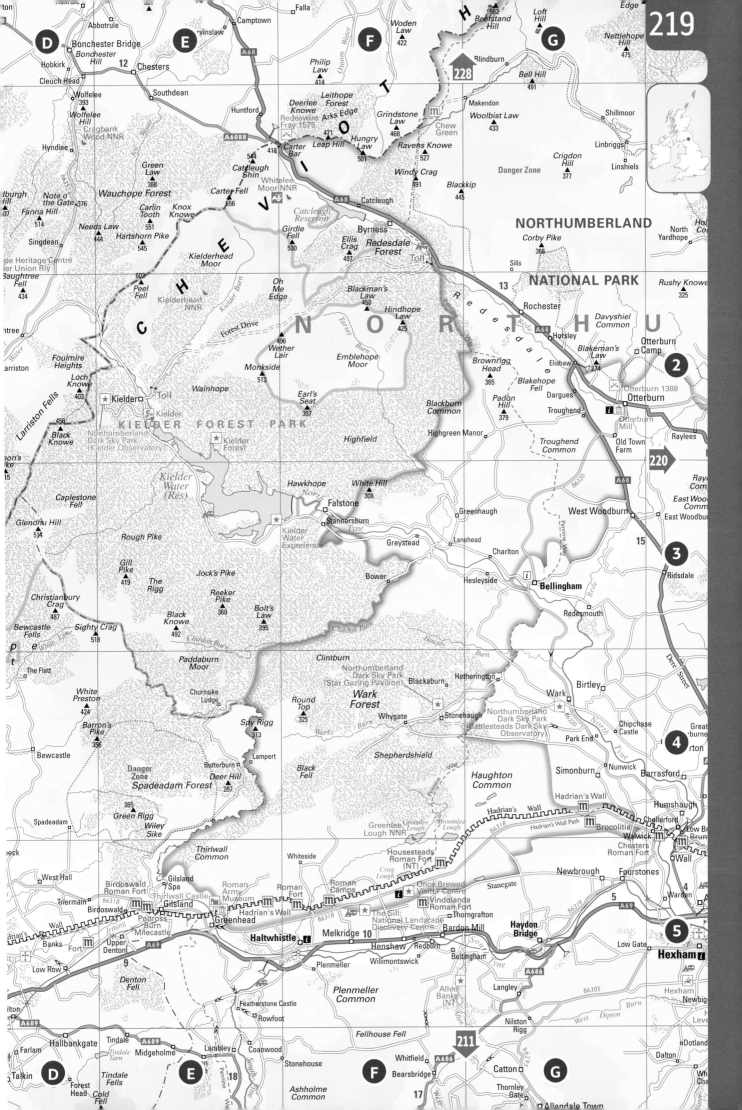

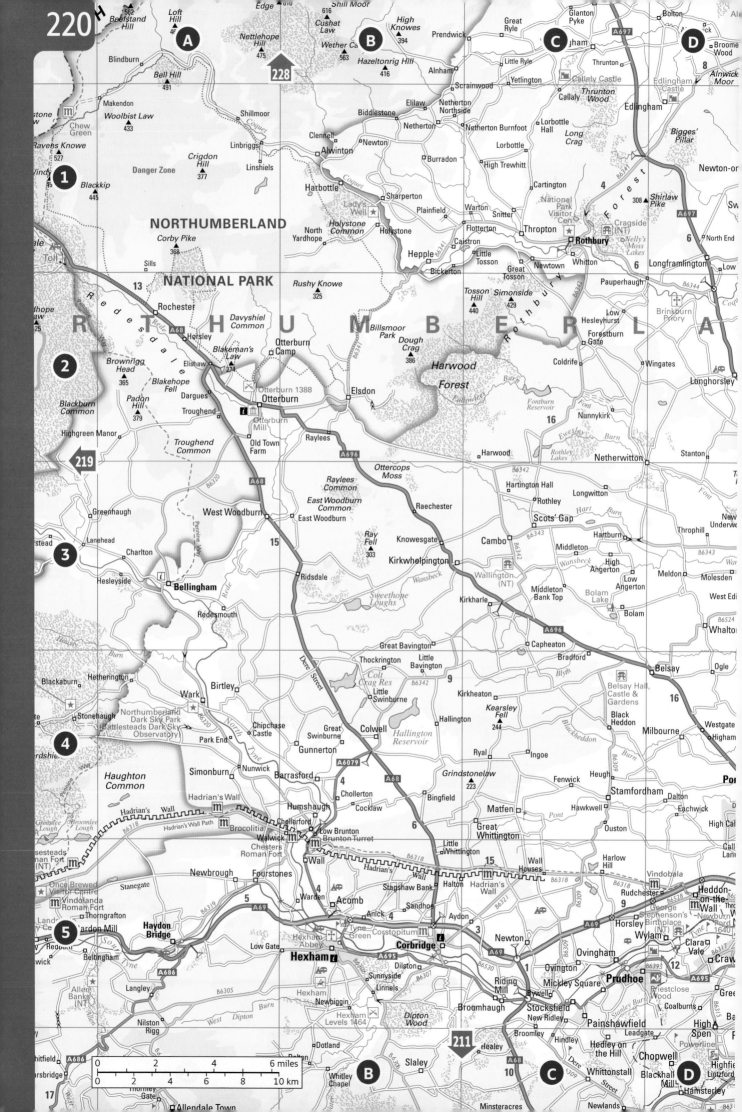

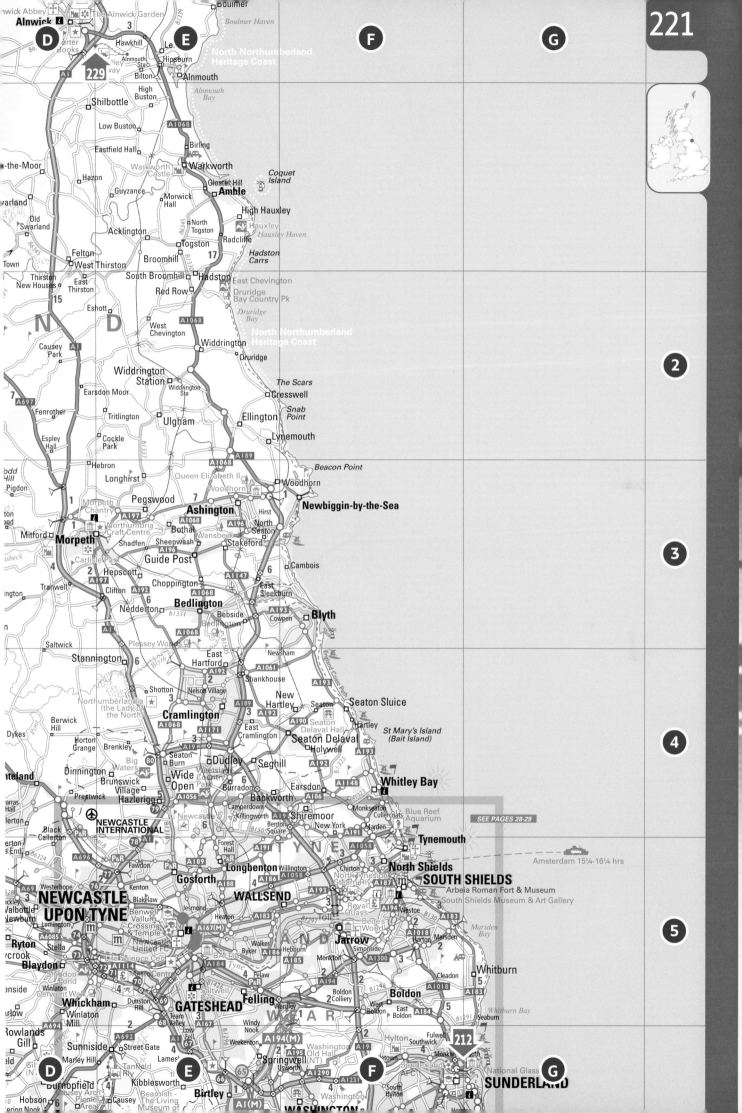

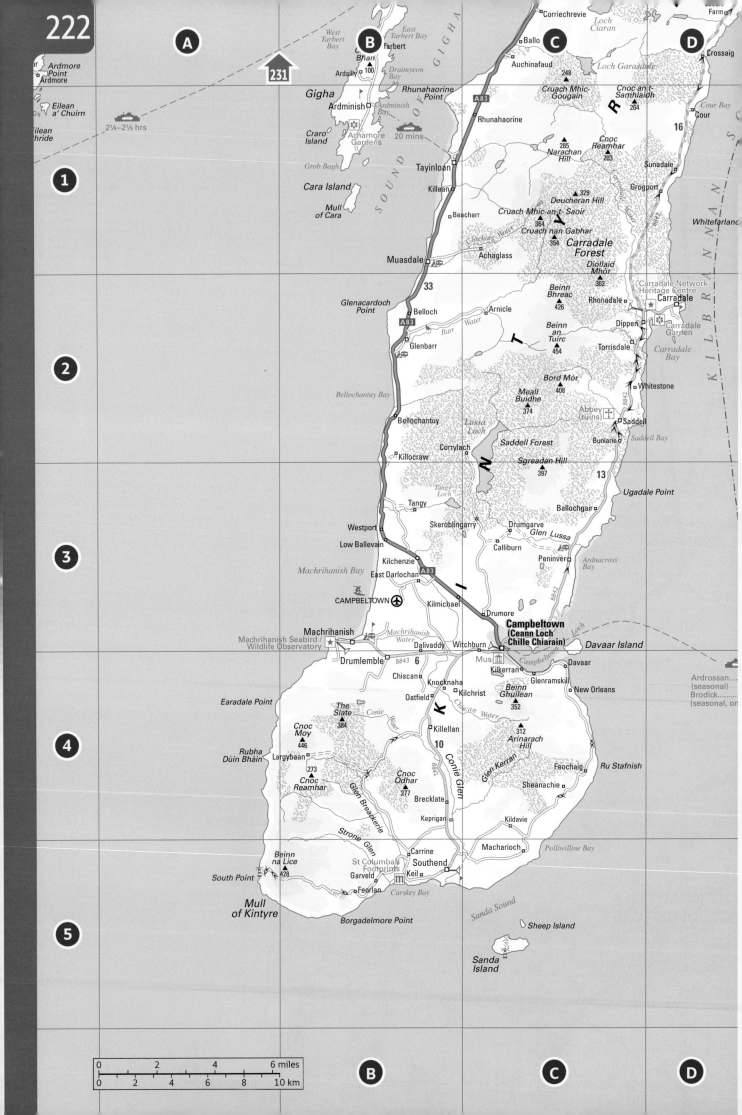

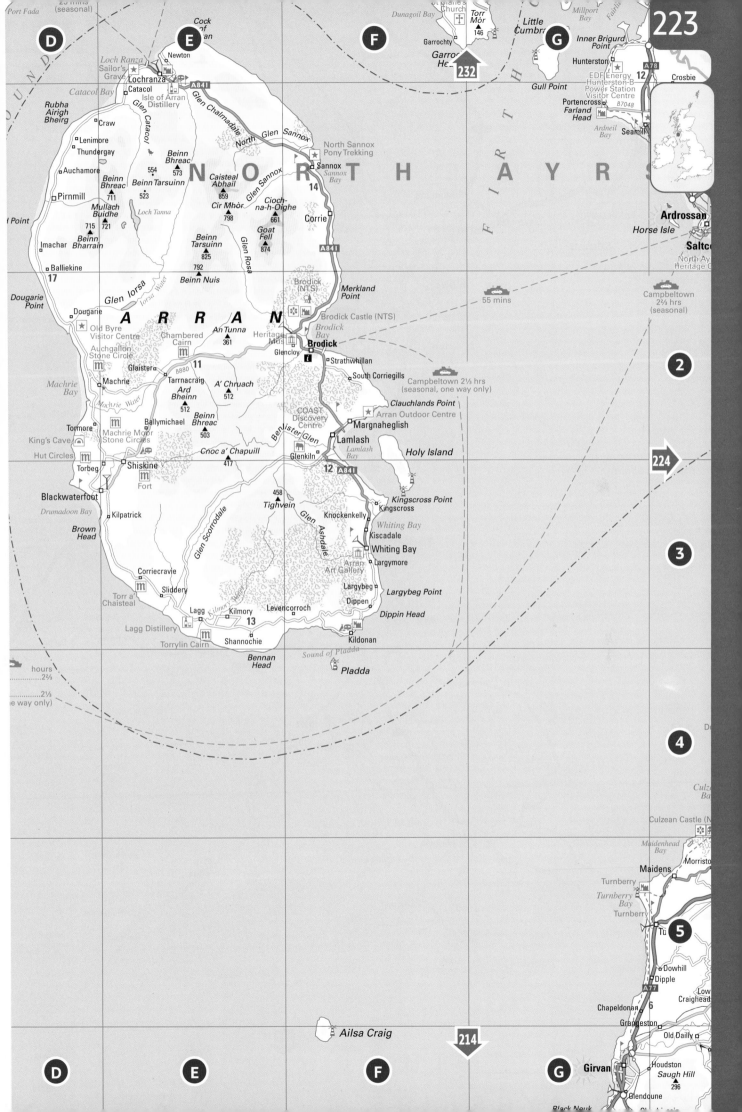

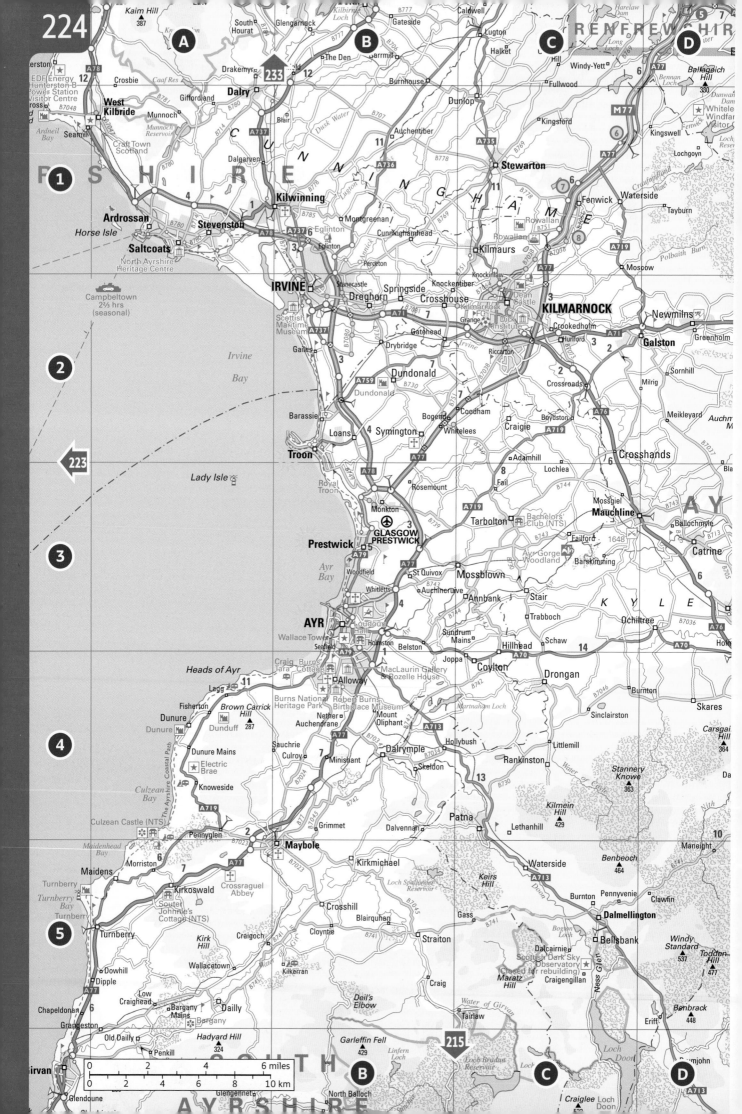

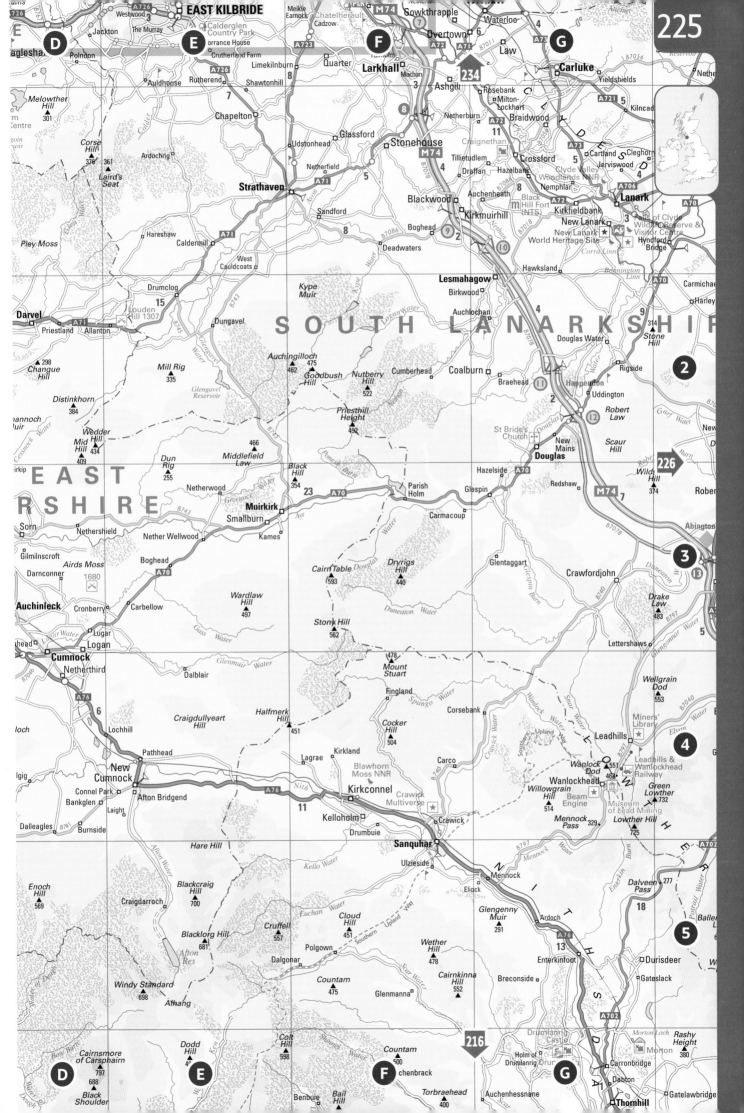

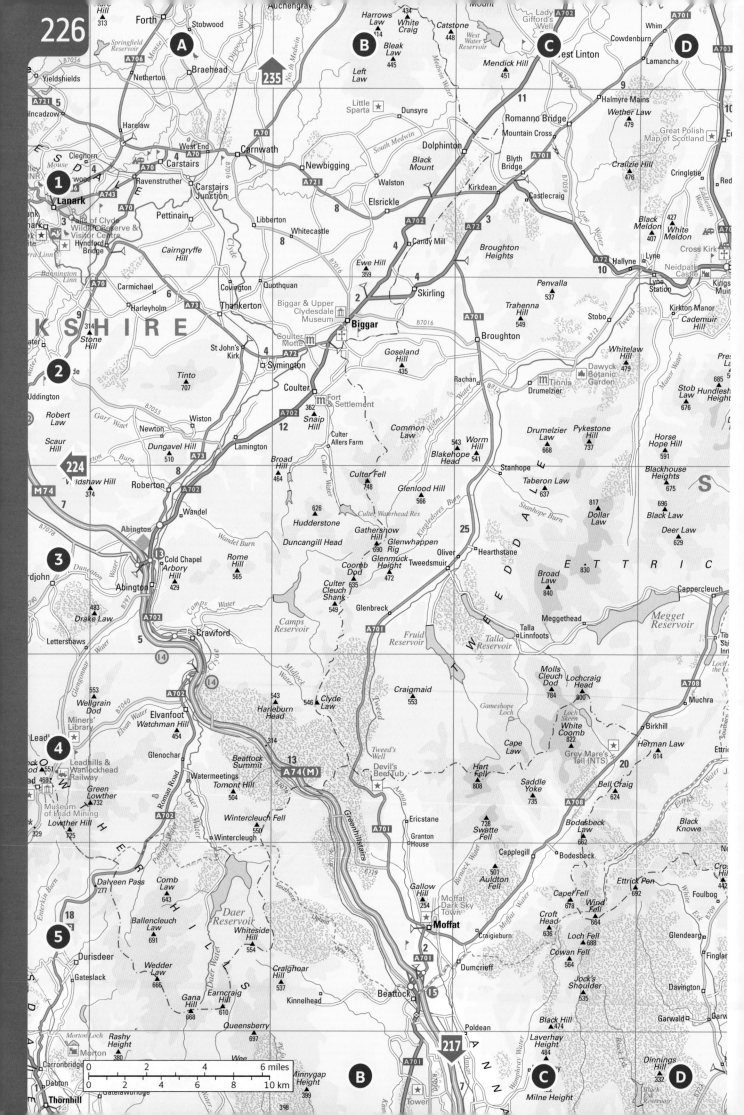

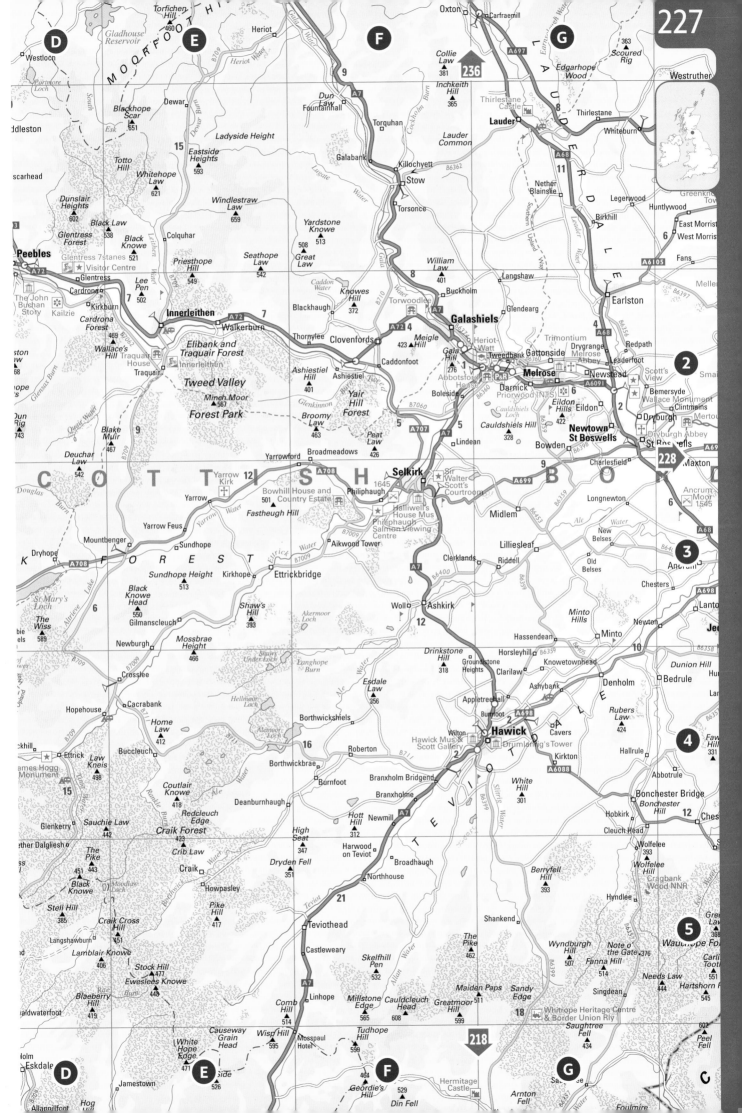

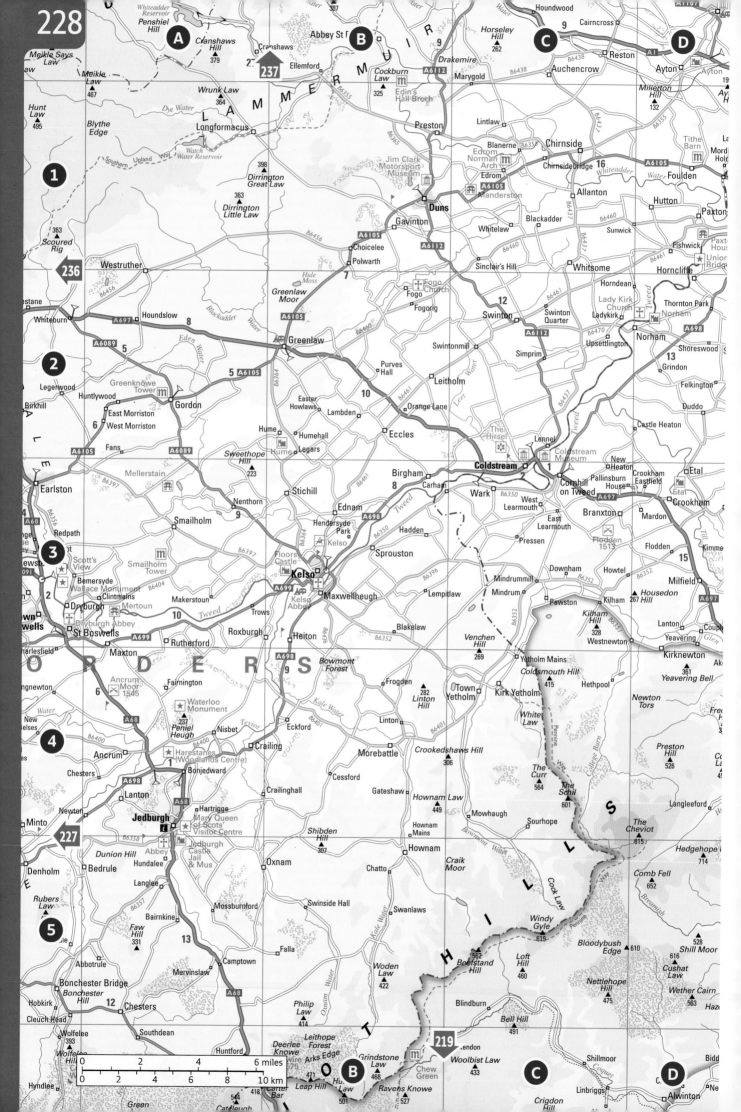

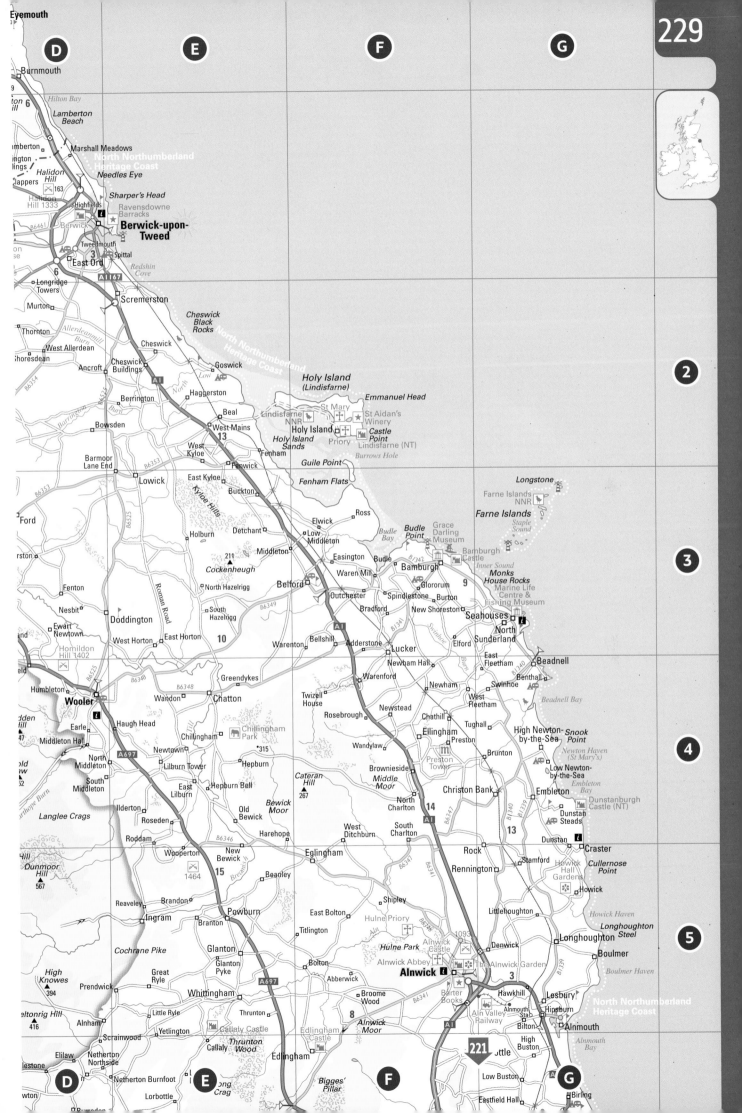

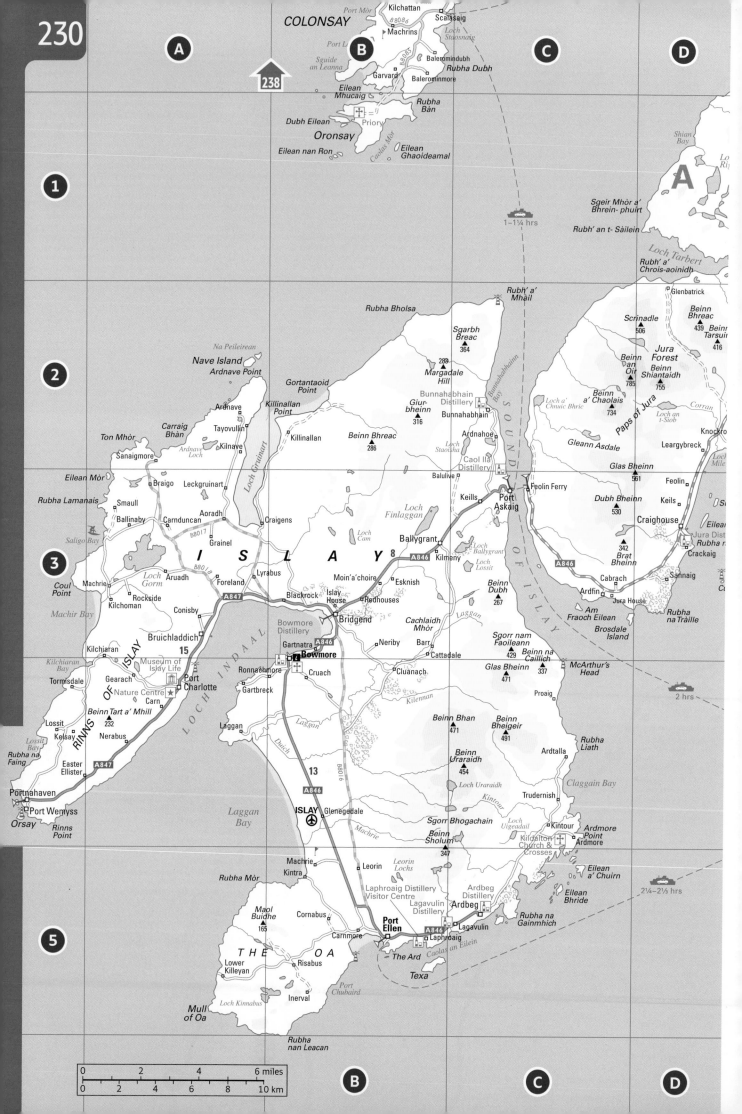

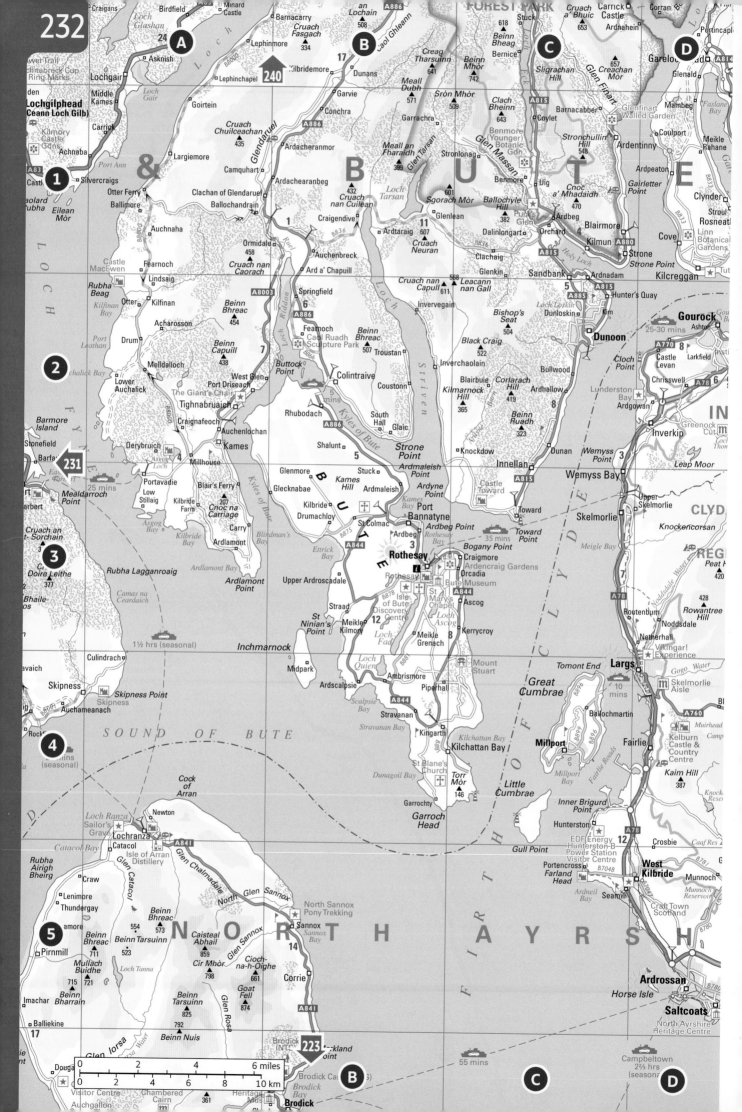

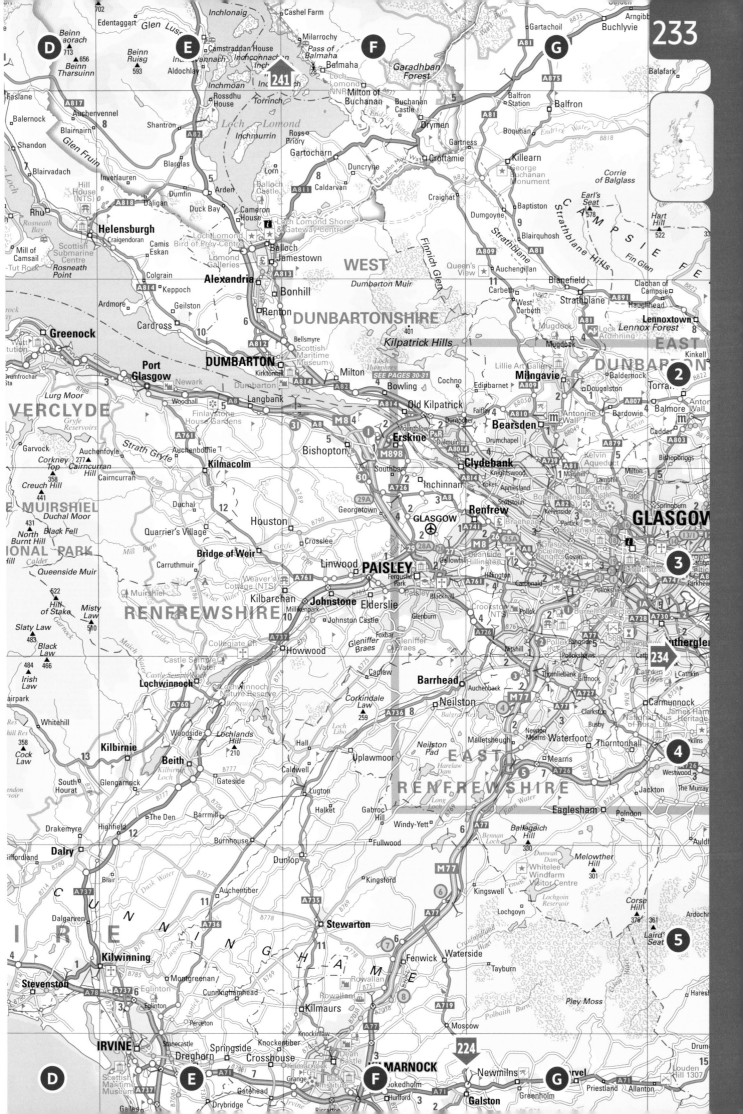

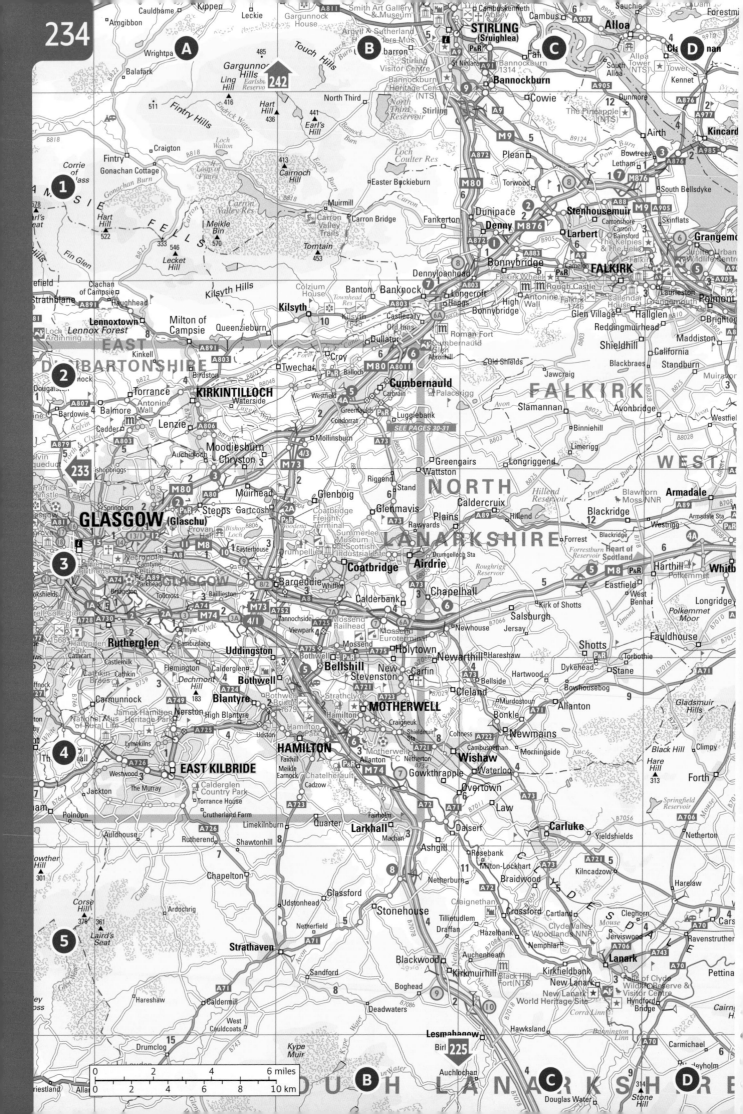

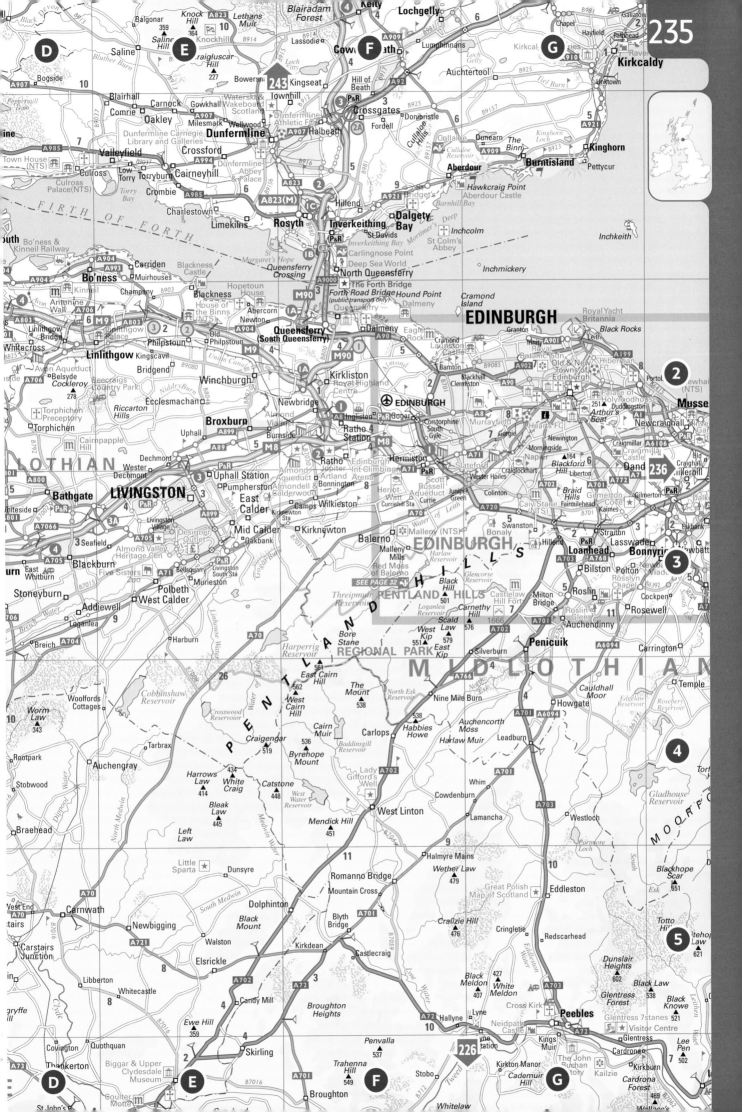

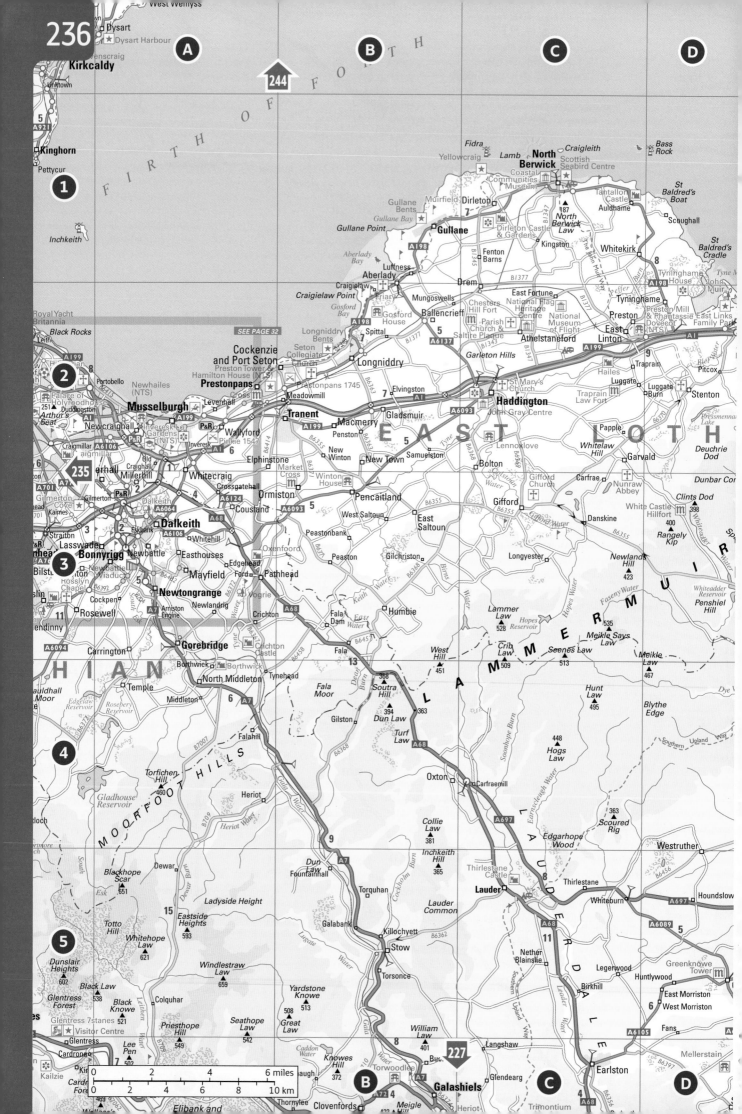

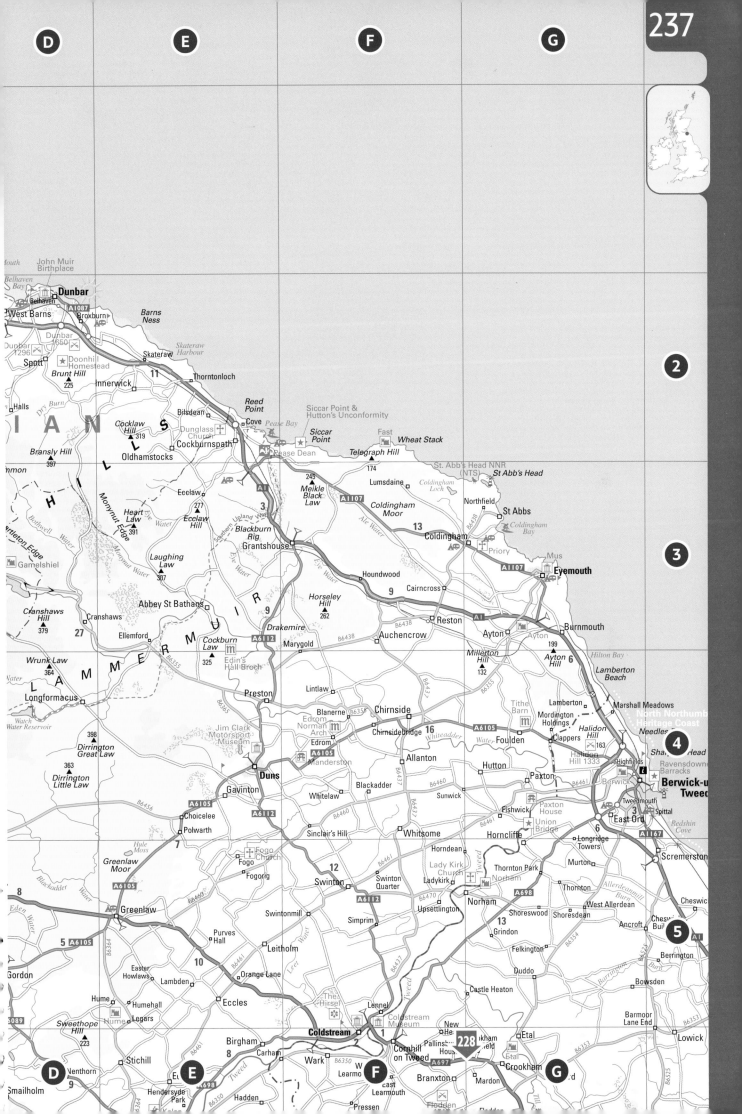

Treshnish Isles
Sgeir a' Chaisteil
Fladda
Lunga

Loch Tuath
Ruh
Fanmore
Ballygow
Ballyg
Kilbr

246

Rubha Chulinish
Eile Dioghl
Gometra House
Bèarnas
Beinn Chreagach
Beinn nan Gall
Laggan Bay

Bac Mòr (Dutchman's Cap)
Bac Beag

Gometra
Rubha Maol na Mine
306
▲313
Sheila's Cottage
ULVA
Ac
A' Chrannag

Maisgeir
Little Colonsay
Sama Islar

Staffa
Eilean Dubh
Staffa NNR (NTS)
Chapel
Inch Kenneth

Fingal's Cave
Fingal's Cave
Erisgeir
Balmeana

Creach Bheinn
▲491
Ardmeanach
Bearraich
▲432
Burg (NTS) ★
Aird na h-Iolaire
Carraig Mhic Thòmais
Port na Croise
LO

Réidh Eilean
Eilean Chalbha
Dùn I
▲100
Iona Abbey
Rubha nan Cearc
Ardchrishnish
20

Port an Duine Mhairbh
Maclean's Cross ★
Kintra
Beinn Chladan
81
Eorabus
Loch na Lathaich
Ardtun

Ruanaich
Baile Mòr
Fionnphort
Aridhglas
A849
Lee
Cruach Min
376

Stac an Aoineidh ★
IONA
Fidden
Ross of Mull
Bunessan

Rubha na Carraig-gèire
Iona (NTS)
Knockvologan
Torr Fada
Ardalanish
Uisken
Scoor

Soa Island
Erraid
87 ▲
Ardchiavaig
Port Mòr
Rubha nam Bràithean

Eilean Dubh
Aird Mòr ▲ 89
Eilean a' Chalmain
Eilean Mòr
Rubh' Ardalanish

Dearg Sgeir
Ruadh Sgeir

Torran Rocks
Na Torrain

West Reef
McPhail's Anvil
Torran Sgoilte

Sgeir Ghobhlach

Otter Rock

Dubh Artach

Eilean Dubh
Balnahard

Balnahard
Rubh' a'

Kiloran Bay

Colonsay Whale
Colonsay House Gardens
Loch an Sgoltaire
Colonsay House
Port Ceann a' Gharraidh

COLONSAY
Kiloran

Upper Kilchattan
B8086
Lower Kilchattan
Scalasaig

Port Mòr
Loch Fada
B8087

Machrins
Loch Staosnaig

Port Lotha
Balleromindubh
B8085

Sguide an Leanna
Garvard
Rubha Dubh
Balerominmore

230

Port Askaig 1–1¼

Eilean Mhucaig
Rubha Bàn

Dubh Eilean
Priory
Oronsay

Eilean nan Ron
Caolas Mòr
Eilean Ghaoideamal

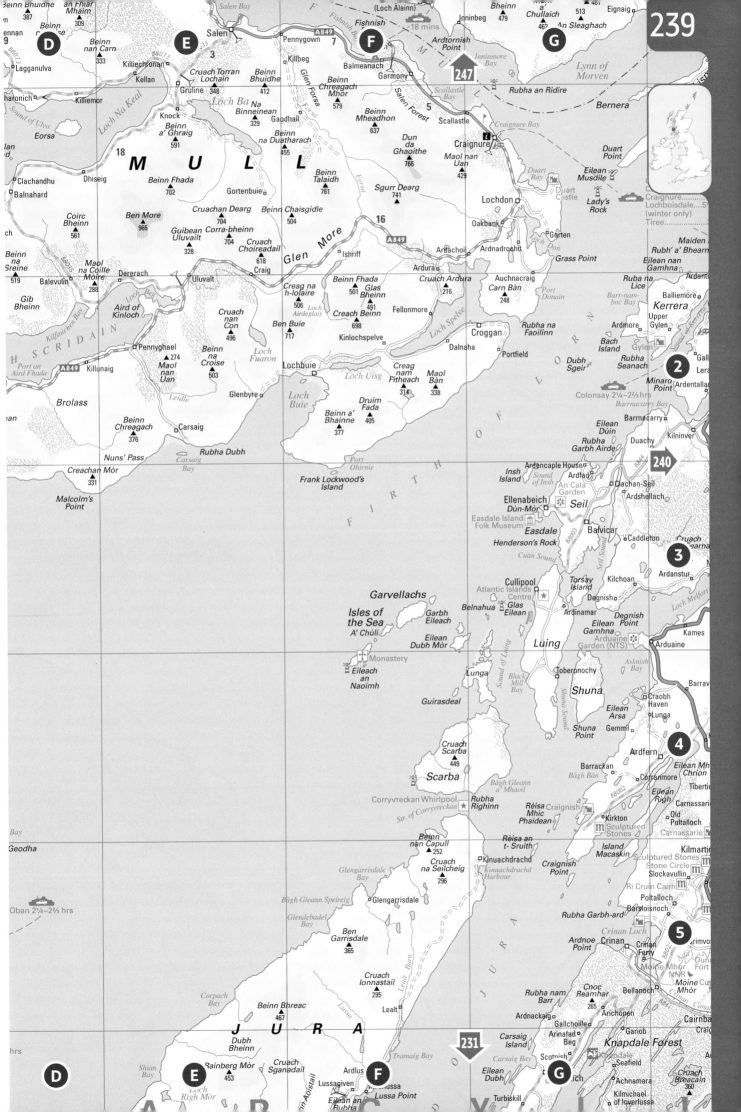

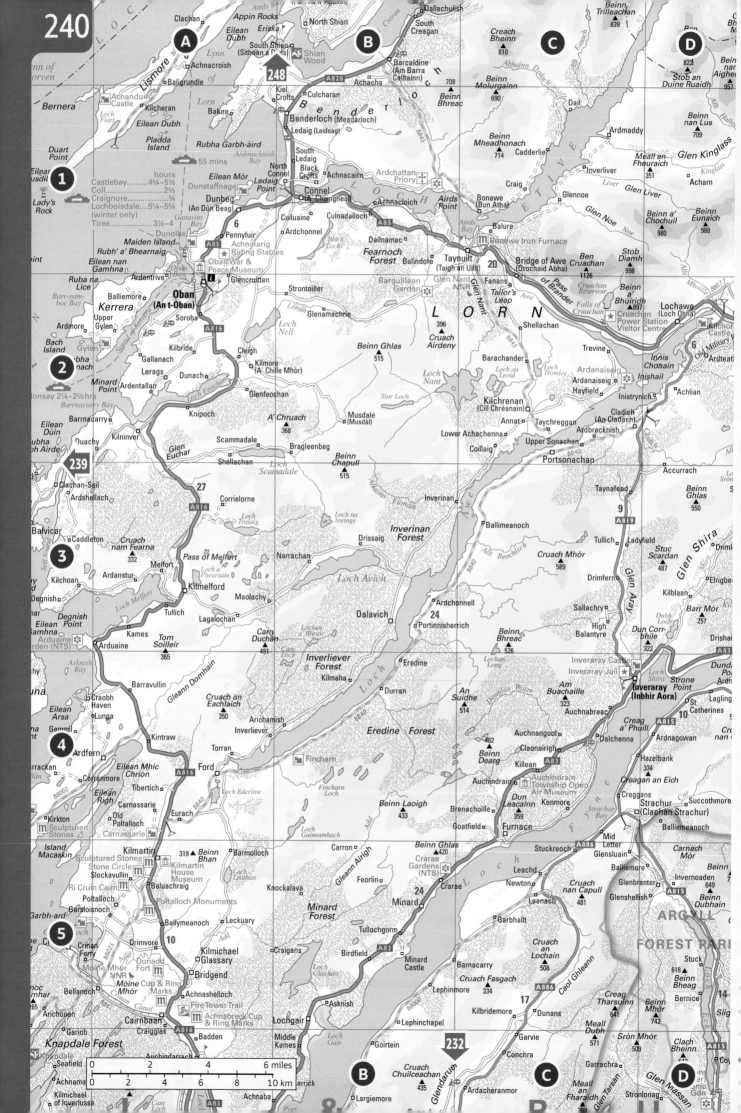

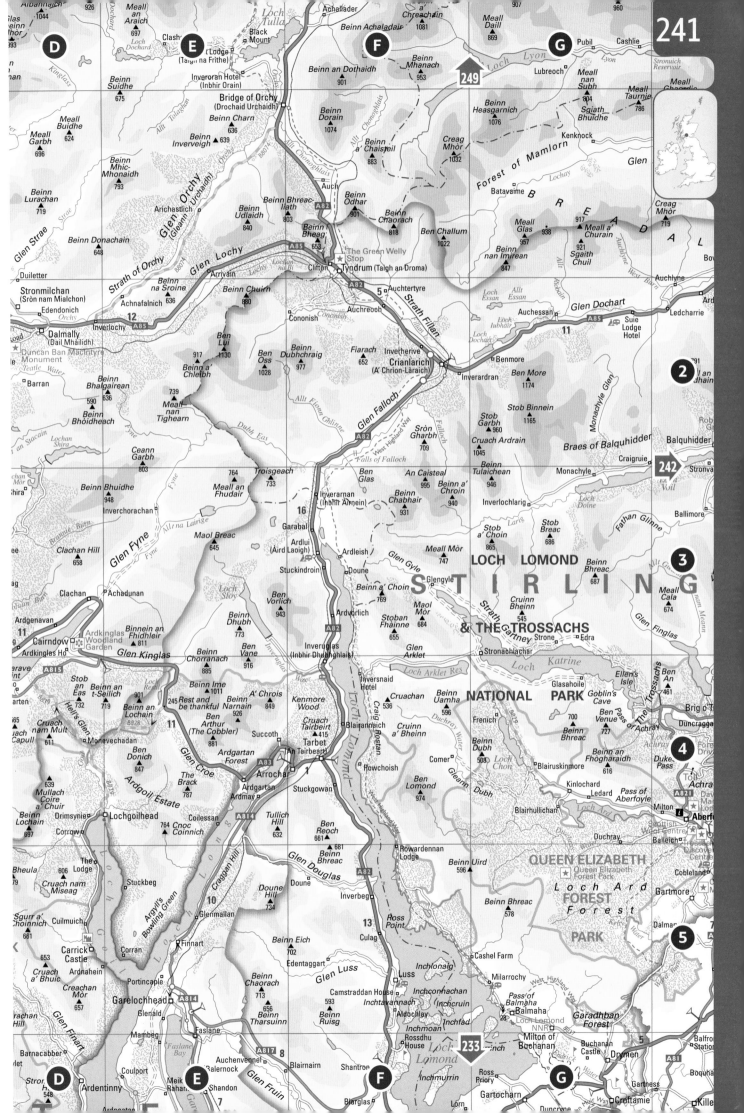

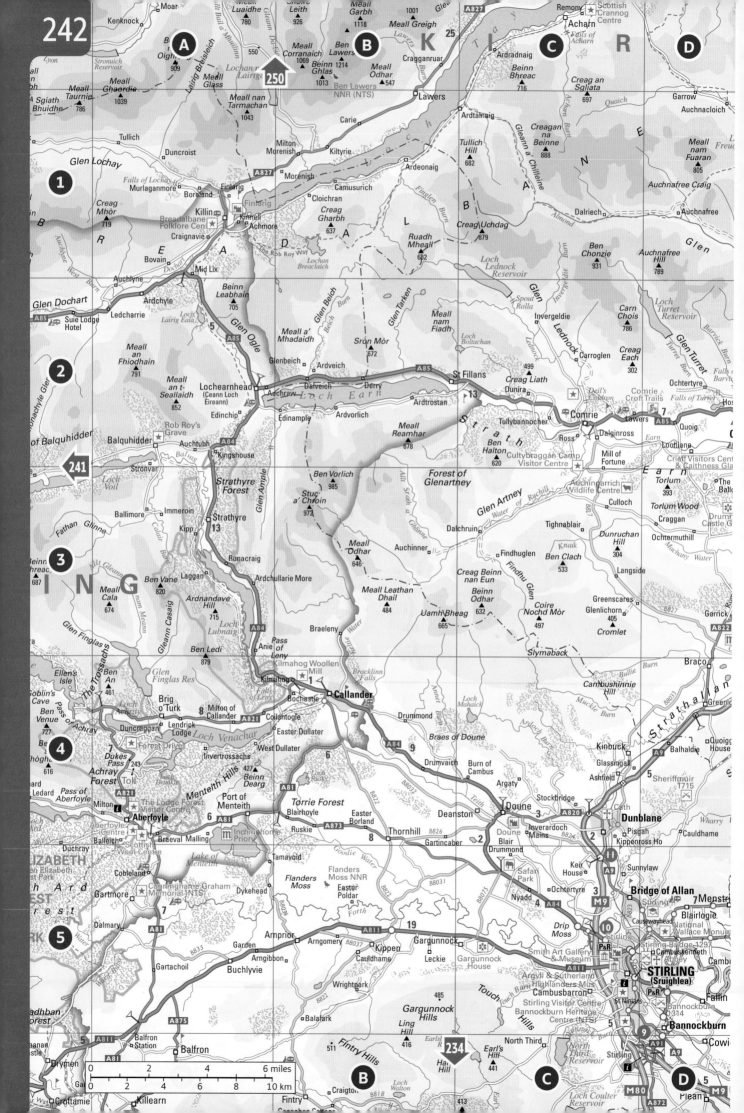

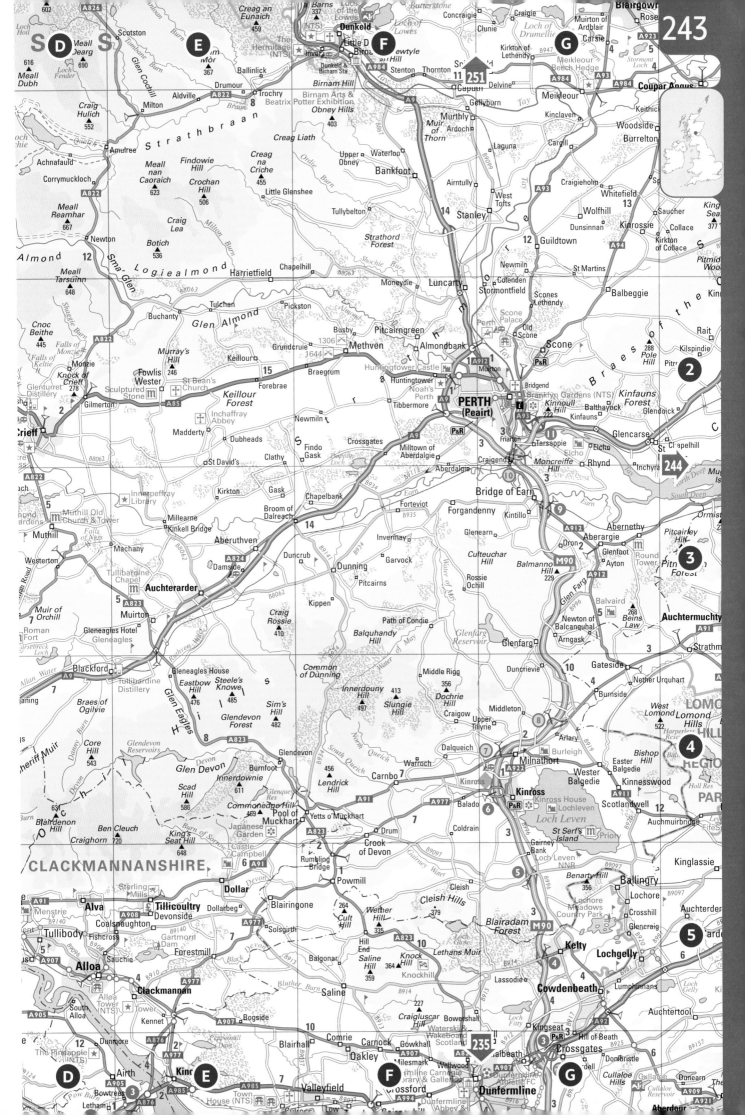

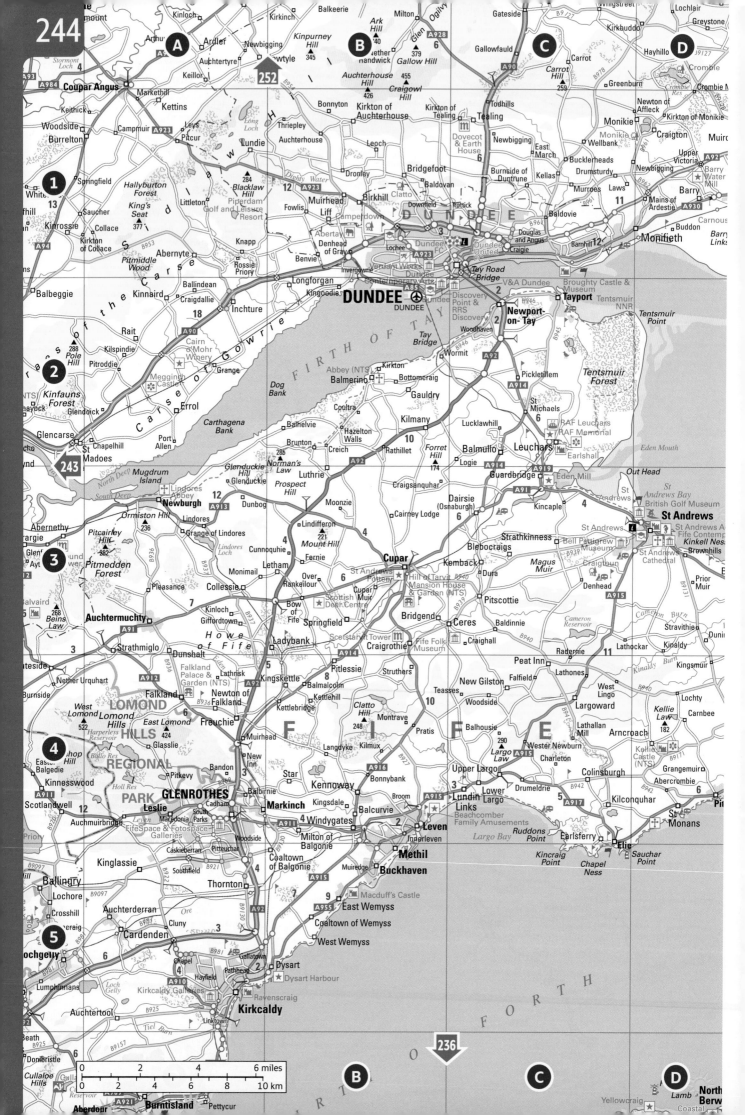

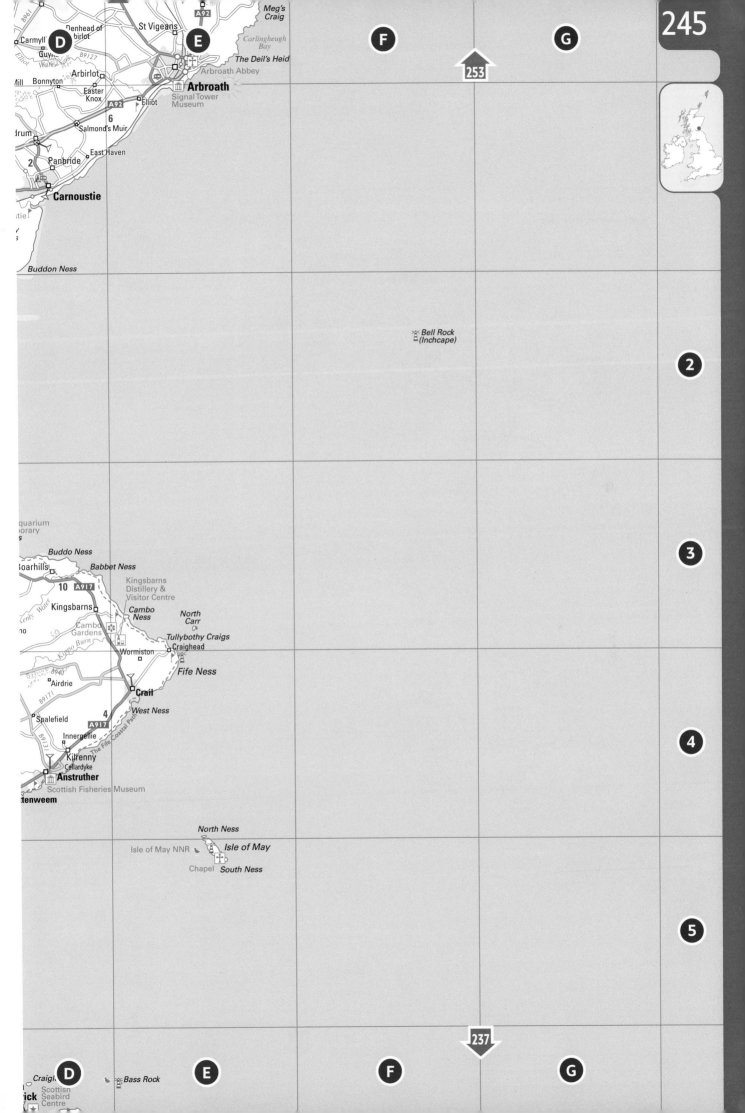

Denhead of birlot
Carmyll
Guy
D
St Vigeans
E
Meg's Craig
Carlingheugh Bay
F
G
The Deil's Heid
Arbirlot
Easter Knox
Bonnyton
Mill
drum
Salmond's Muir
6
Arbroath Abbey
Arbroath
Signal Tower Museum
Elliot
East Haven
Panbride
2
Carnoustie
253

Buddon Ness

Bell Rock (Inchcape)

2

quarium orary
Buddo Ness
Boarhills
Babbet Ness
3
10 A917
Kingsbarns
Kingsbarns Distillery & Visitor Centre
Cambo Ness
North Carr
Cambo Gardens
Tullybothy Craigs
Wormiston
Craighead
Airdrie
Fife Ness
Crail
Spalefield
West Ness
Innergellie
The Fife Coastal Path
4
Kilrenny
Cellardyke
Anstruther
Scottish Fisheries Museum
tenweem

North Ness
Isle of May NNR
Isle of May
Chapel
South Ness

5

237

Craig
D
Bass Rock
E
F
G
ick
Scottish Seabird Centre

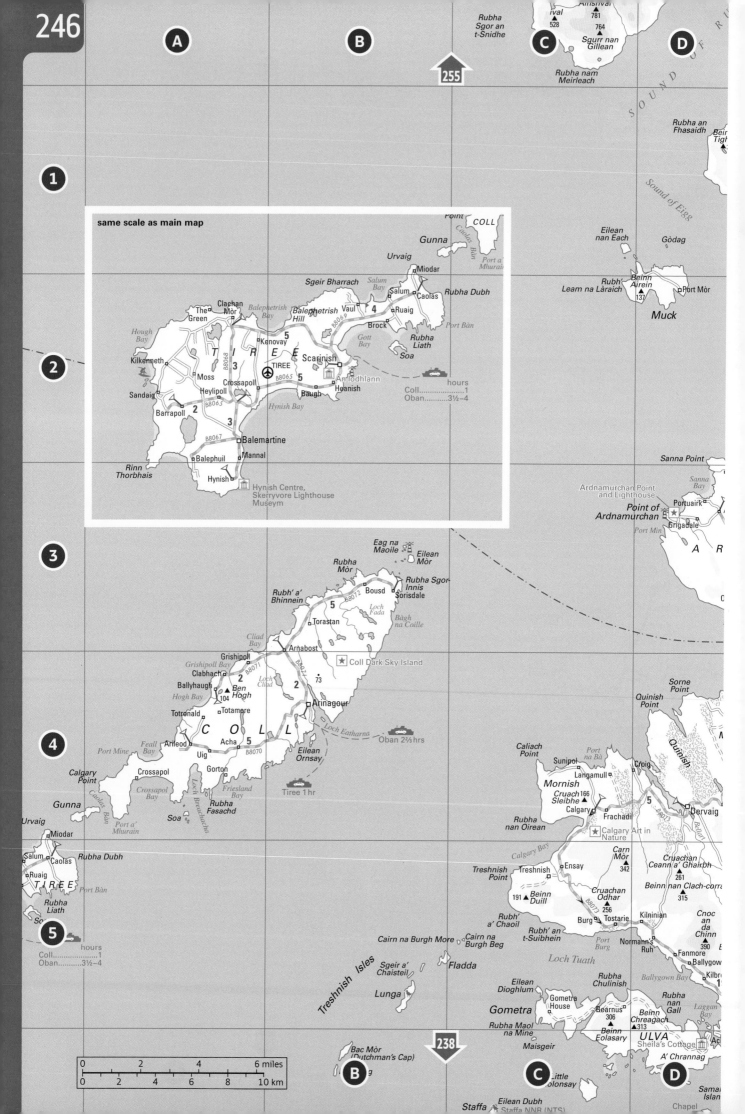

A　　B　　C　　D

255

Rubha Sgor an t-Snidhe

Rubha nam Meirleach

SOUND OF RÙM

Rubha an Fhasaidh

Beinn Tigh

Sound of Eigg

1

Eilean nan Each

Gòdag

Rubh' Leam na Làraich

Beinn Airein 137

Port Mòr

Muck

same scale as main map

Point **COLL**

Gunna

Urvaig Miodar

Sgeir Bharrach Salum

Salum Bay Caolas

Rubha Dubh

Clachan Mòr The Green

Balephetrish Bay Balephetrish Hill Vaul 4 Ruaig

Hough Bay B8069 Brock

Gott Bay Rubha Liath

T I R E E Kenovay 5 Scarinish Soa

Port Bàn

Kilkenneth 2 TIREE B8065 5

Moss Crossapoll An Iodhlann Coll.............1

Heylipoll B8065 3 Baugh Heanish Oban..........3½–4 hours

Sandaig 2

Barrapoll B8065 3 *Hynish Bay*

B8067 Balemartine

Balephuil Mannal

Rinn Thorbhais Hynish Hynish Centre, Skerryvore Lighthouse Museum

2

Sanna Point

Sanna Bay

Ardnamurchan Point and Lighthouse

Point of Ardnamurchan Portuairk

Port Min Grigadale

A R

Eag na Maoile Eilean Mòr

Rubha Mòr

Rubha Sgor-Innis

Rubh' a' Bhinnein Bousd Sorisdale

5 B8012 *Loch Fada* *Bàgh na Caille*

Torastan

Cliad Bay Arnabost

Grishipoll ★ Coll Dark Sky Island

Grishipoll Bay B8071 B8021

Clabhach *Loch Cliad*

Ballyhaugh ▲ Ben Hogh 2 73

Hogh Bay 104

Totronald Totamore Arinagour

C O L L *Loch Eatharna*

Arileod Acha 5 Oban 2⅔hrs

Feall Bay Uig B8070

Port Mine Gorton Eilean Ornsay

Calgary Point Crossapol

Crossapol Bay *Friesland Bay*

Gunna Rubha Fasachd

Urvaig *Caolas Bàn* Soa Tiree 1 hr

Miodar *Port a' Mhurain*

Salum Caolas *Rubha Dubh*

Ruaig

T I R E E *Port Bàn*

Rubha Liath

Soa

3

4

Sorne Point

Quinish Point

Quinish

Caliach Point Sunipol *Port na Bà* Croig

Langamull

Mornish Cruach Sleibhe 166 Calgary Frachadil Dervaig

5 B8073

Rubha nan Oirean ★ Calgary Art in Nature *Beltoir*

Calgary Bay

Treshnish Point Treshnish Ensay Carn Mòr 342 Cruachan Ceann a' Ghairbh 261 Cnoc an da Chinn 390

191 ▲ Beinn Duill Cruachan Odhar 256 Beinn nan Clach-corra 315

Rubh' a' Chaoil Burg Tostarie Kilninian Fanmore

Cairn na Burgh More Cairn na Burgh Beg *Rubh' an t-Suibhein* *Port Burg* Normann's Ruh Ballygown

Treshnish Isles Fladda *Loch Tuath* *Ballygown Bay*

Sgeir a' Chaisteil Eilean Dioghlum Rubha Chulinish Rubha nan Gall *Laggan Bay*

Lunga Gometra House Bearnus 306 Beinn Chreagach ▲ 313

Gometra Beinn Eolasay **ULVA**

Rubha Maol na Mine Sheila's Cottage

Bac Mòr (Dutchman's Cap) **Maisgeir** A' Chrannag

238

Samala Isle

5

Coll.............1 hours

Oban..........3½–4

A B C D

Staffa Eilean Dubh Chapel

Staffa NNR (NTS)

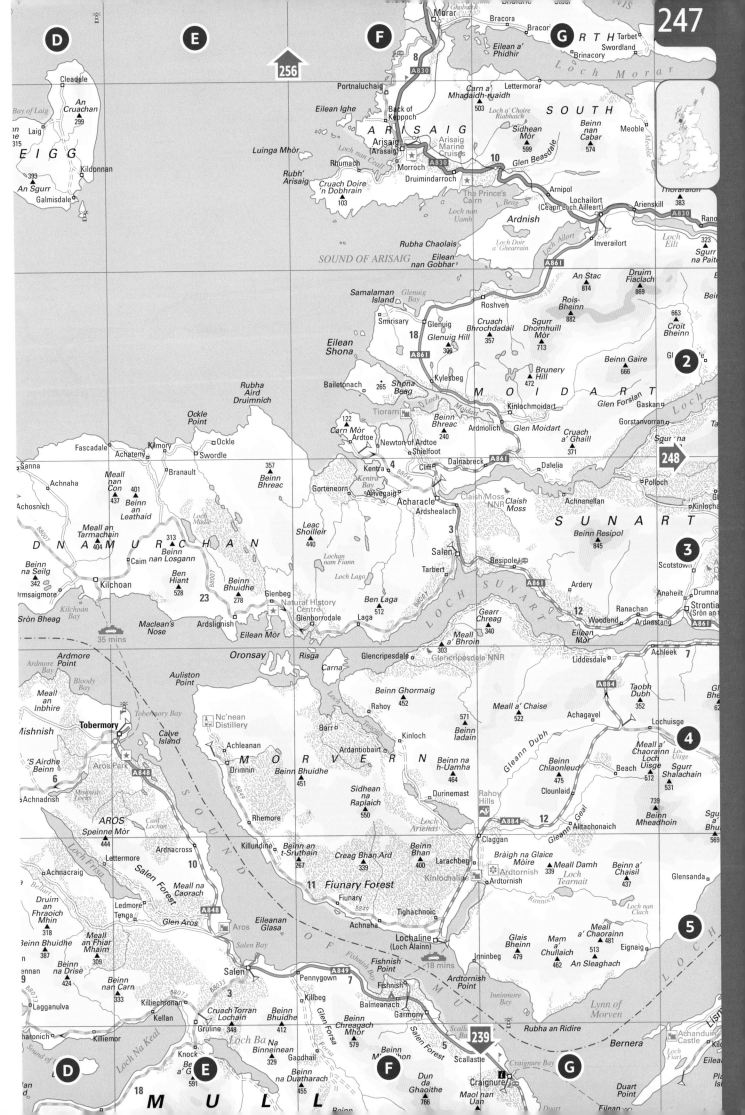

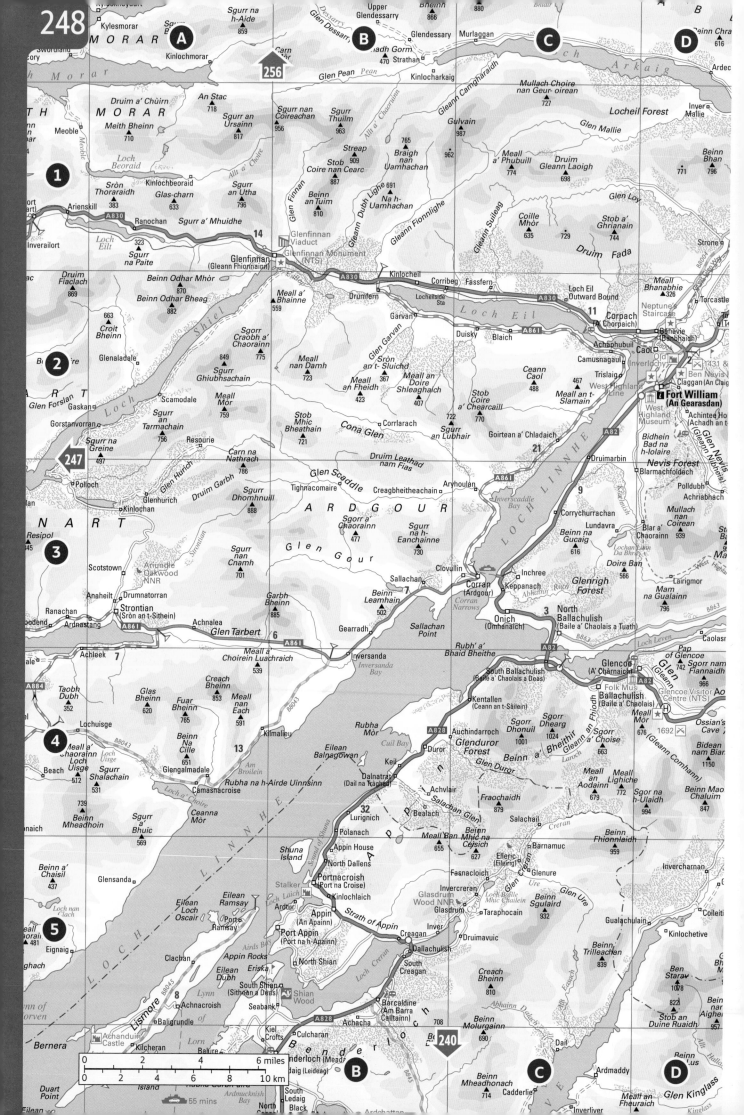

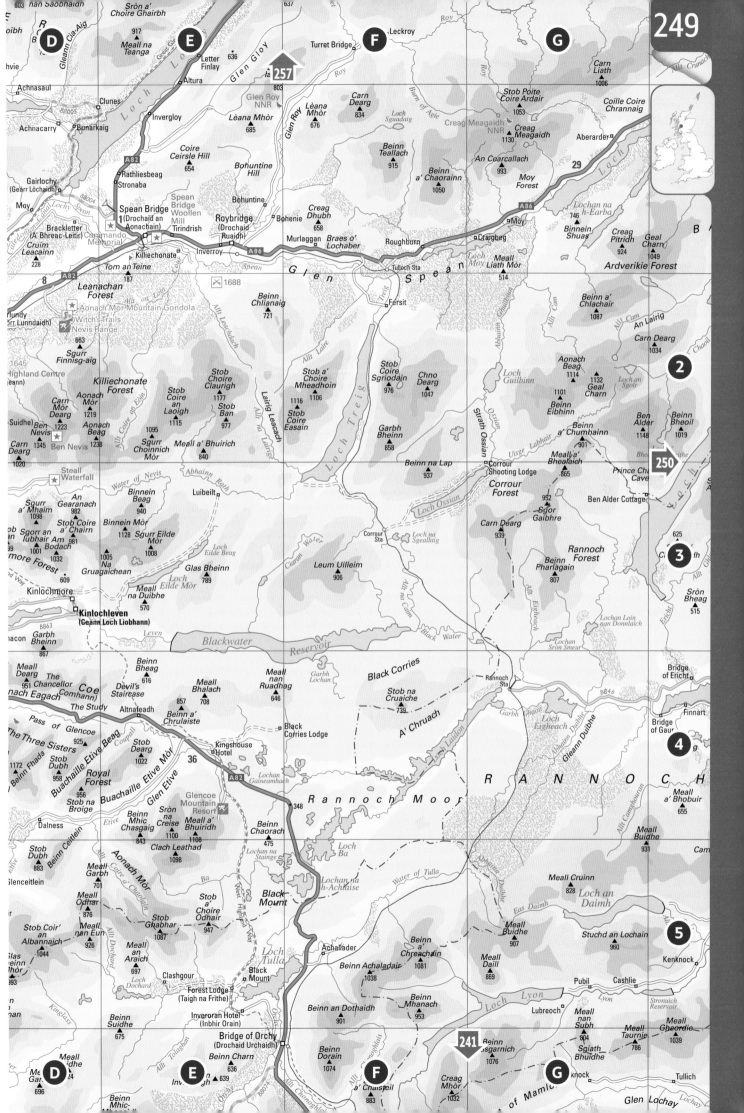

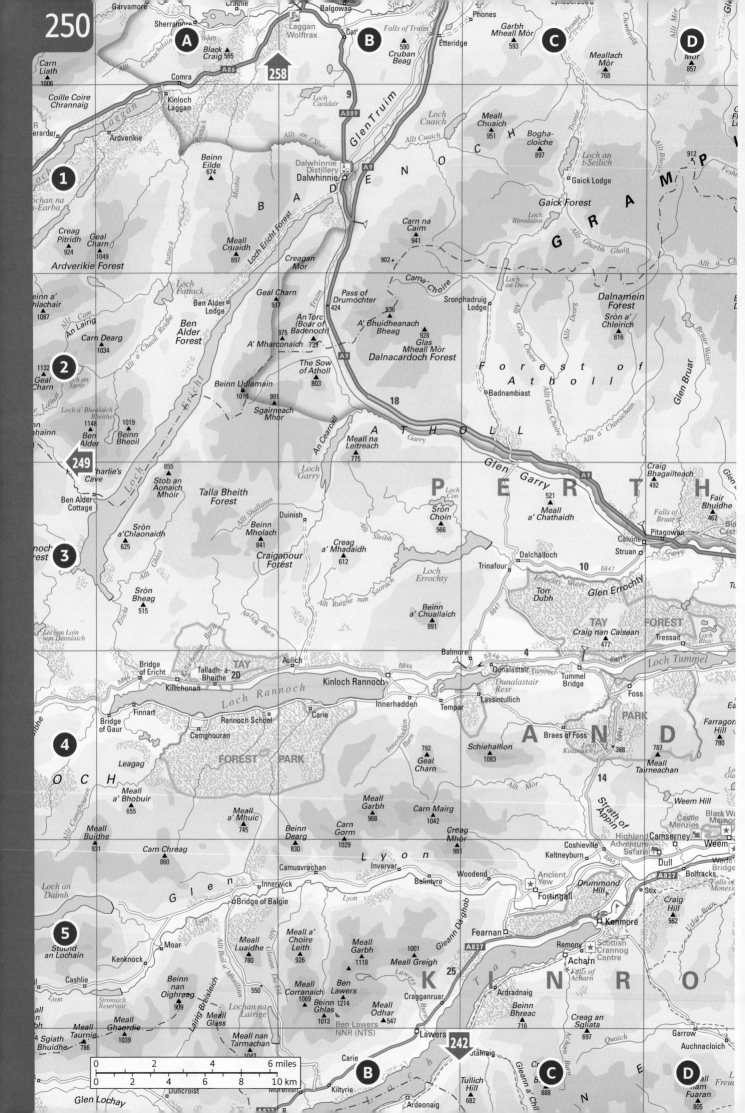

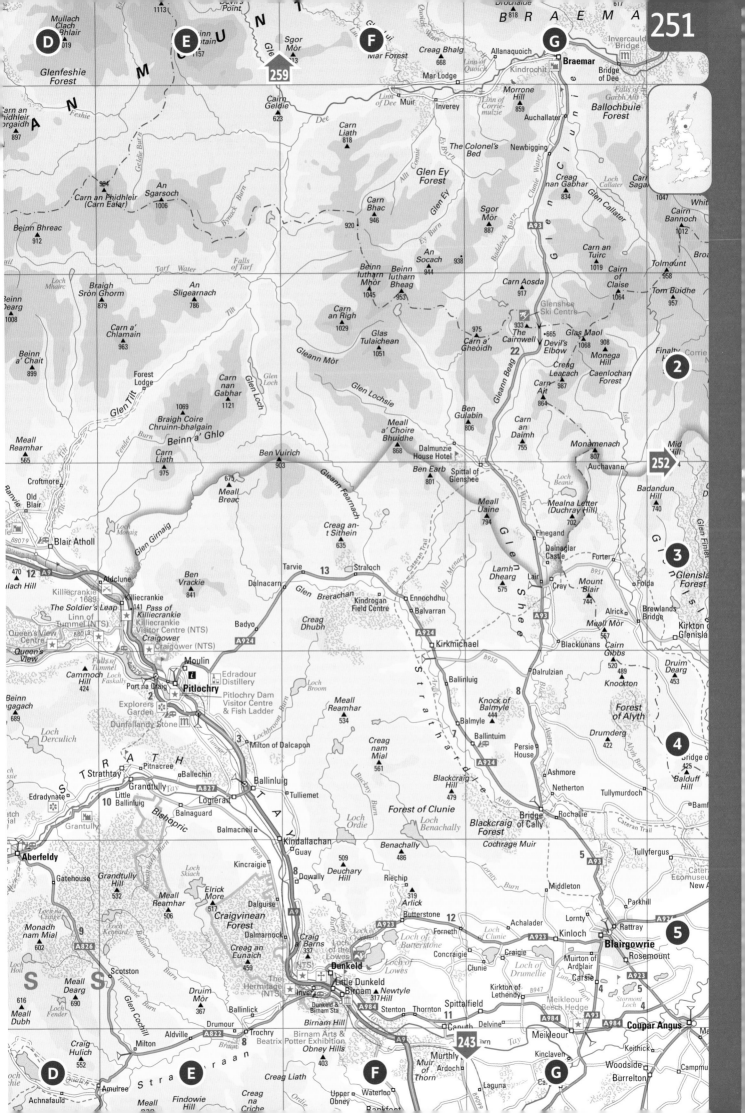

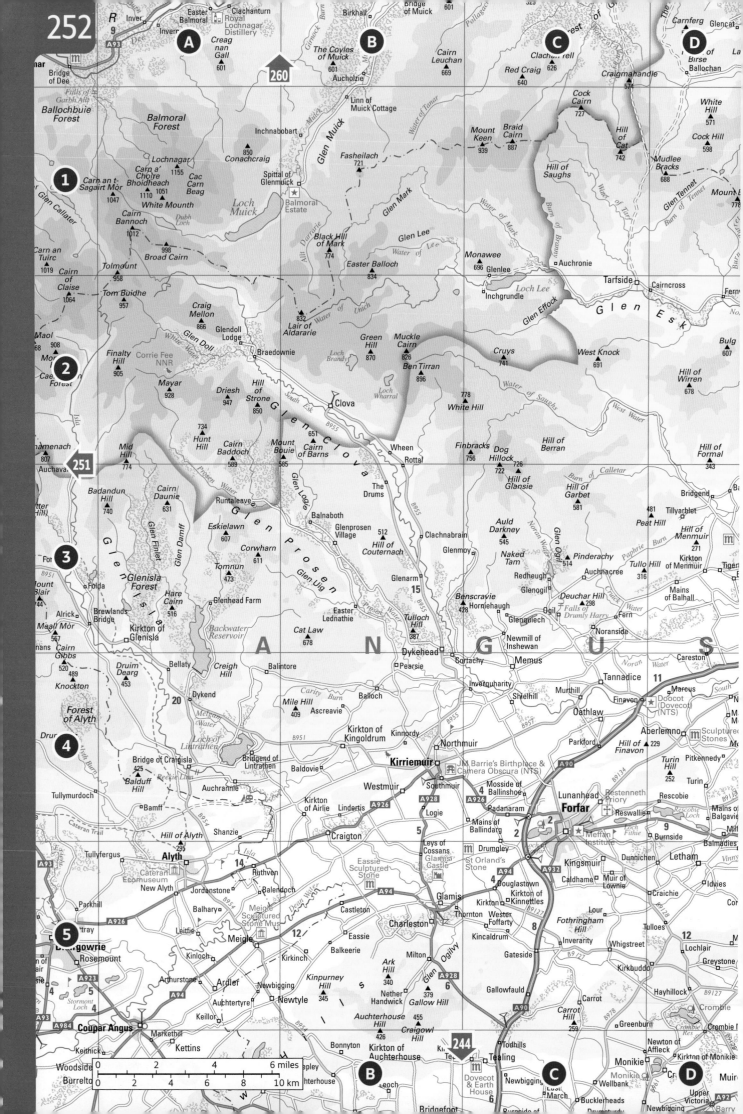

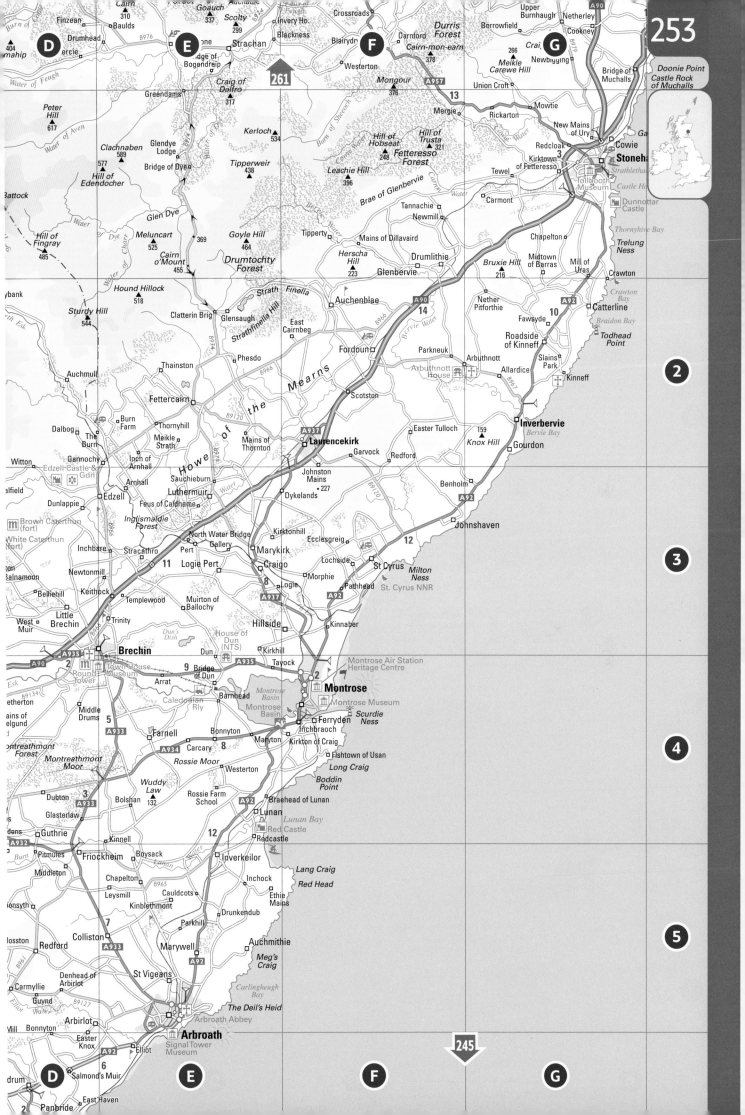

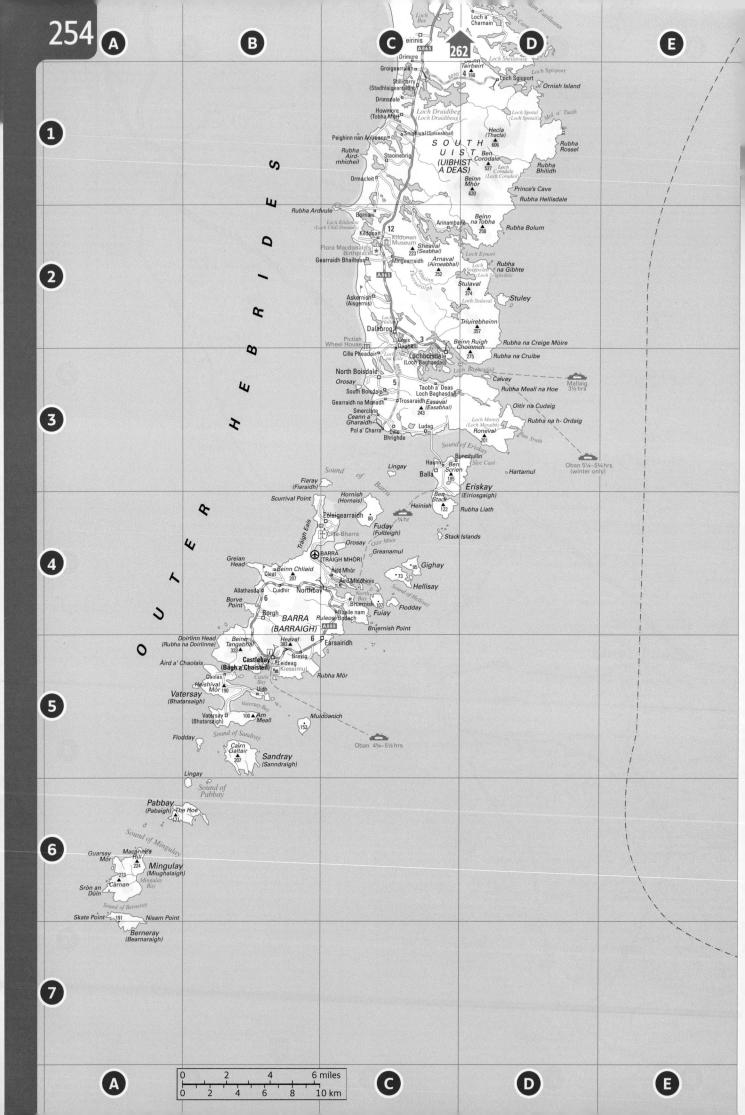

A B C D E

1

eirinis

Drimore

Groigearraidh

Stilligarry
(Stadhlaigearraidh)

Drimsdale

Howmore
(Tobha Mòr)

Peighinn nan Aoireann

Rubha Àird-mhicheil

Staoinebrig

Ormacleit

Loch Bee

Loch a' Charnain

Loch Sgioport

Loch Sheilbhaig

Beinn Tairbeirt
4 168

Loch Sgioport

Ornish Island

Loch Druidibeg
(Loch Druidibeag)

Snishival (Snìseabhal)

**SOUTH UIST
(UIBHIST A DEAS)**

Hecla
(Thacla)
606

Loch Spotal
(Loch Spotail)

Rubha Rossel

Ben Corodale
527

Loch Corodale
(Loch Coradail)

Rubha Bhilidh

Beinn Mhòr
620

Prince's Cave

Rubha Hellisdale

2

O U T E R   *H E B R I D E S*

Rubha Ardvule

Bornais

Loch Kildonan
(Loch Chill Donnain)

Kildonan

12

Flora Macdonald's Birthplace

Gearraidh Bhailteas

Kildonan Museum

Mingearraidh

Sheaval
(Seabhal)
223

Arnaval
(Airneabhal)
252

A865

Askernish
(Aisgernis)

Albannach

Allt Bhain

Beinn na Tobha
258

Rubha Bolum

Loch Eynort

Loch Snigisclett
(Loch Snigisgleit)

Rubha na Gibhte

Stulaval
374

Loch Stulaval

Stuley

Triuirebheinn
357

Rubha na Creige Mòire

3

Dalabrog

Pictish Wheel House

Crois Dùghaill

Cille Pheadair

Loch na Cille

North Boisdale

Orosay

South Boisdale

Gearraidh na Monadh

Smerclate

Ceann a Gharaidh

Pol a' Charra

Cille Bhrìghde

Lochboisdale
(Loch Baghasdail)

3

5

Taobh a' Deas
Loch Baghasdail

Trosaraidh

Easaval
(Easabhal)
243

Ludag

Beinn Ruigh Choinnich
275

Loch Baghasdail

Calvay

Rubha Meall na Hoe

Loch Moreef
(Loch Moraibh)

Roneval
201

Sound of Eriskay

Gleann Sruth

Rubha na Cruibe

Mallaig
3½ hrs

Oitir na Cudaig

Rubha na h- Ordaig

Oban 5¼–5½ hrs
(winter only)

4

Sound   of   Barra

Fiaray
(Fiaraidh)

Scurrival Point

Hornish
(Hornais)

Lingay

Haunn

Balla

Bunmhullin

Ben Scrien
185

Sloc Caol

Eriskay
(Eiriosgaigh)

Hartamul

Eòlaigearraidh

Cille Bharra

Orosay

Fuday
(Fuideigh)

¼ hr

Heinish

Ben Stack
122

Rubha Liath

Stack Islands

Greian Head

BARRA
(TRÀIGH MHÒR)

Cleat

Beinn Chliaid
207

Àird Mhòr

Àird Mhidhinis

Greanamul

95 Gighay

73

Hellisay

Allathasdal

Cuidhir

Northbay

North Bay

Floday

Sound of Hellisay

Borve Point

Borgh

BARRA
(BARRAIGH)

Ruleos

Buaile nam Bodach

A888

Fuiay

Bruernish

107

Bruernish Point

5

Doirlinn Head
(Rubha na Doirlinne)

Àird a' Chaolais

Beinn Tangabhal
333

Heaval
383

Brevig

6

Earsairidh

**Castlebay
(Bàgh a'Chaisteil)**

Leideag

Kiessimul

Caolas

Castle Bay

Rubha Mòr

Heishival Mòr
190

Uidh

**Vatersay
(Bhatarsaigh)**

Vatersay
(Bhatarsaigh)

100 Am Meall

Vatersay Bay

Muldoanich

153

Oban 4¾–5½ hrs

Floday

Sound of Sandray

Cairn Galtair
207

Sandray
(Sanndraigh)

Lingay

Sound of Pabbay

6

Pabbay
(Pabaigh)

The Hoe
171

Sound of Mingulay

Guarsay Mòr

Macphee's Hill
224

Mingulay
(Miughalaigh)

273

Càrnan

Mingulay Bay

Sròn an Dùin

Sound of Berneray

Skate Point

191

Nisam Point

Berneray
(Bearnaraigh)

7

A B C D E

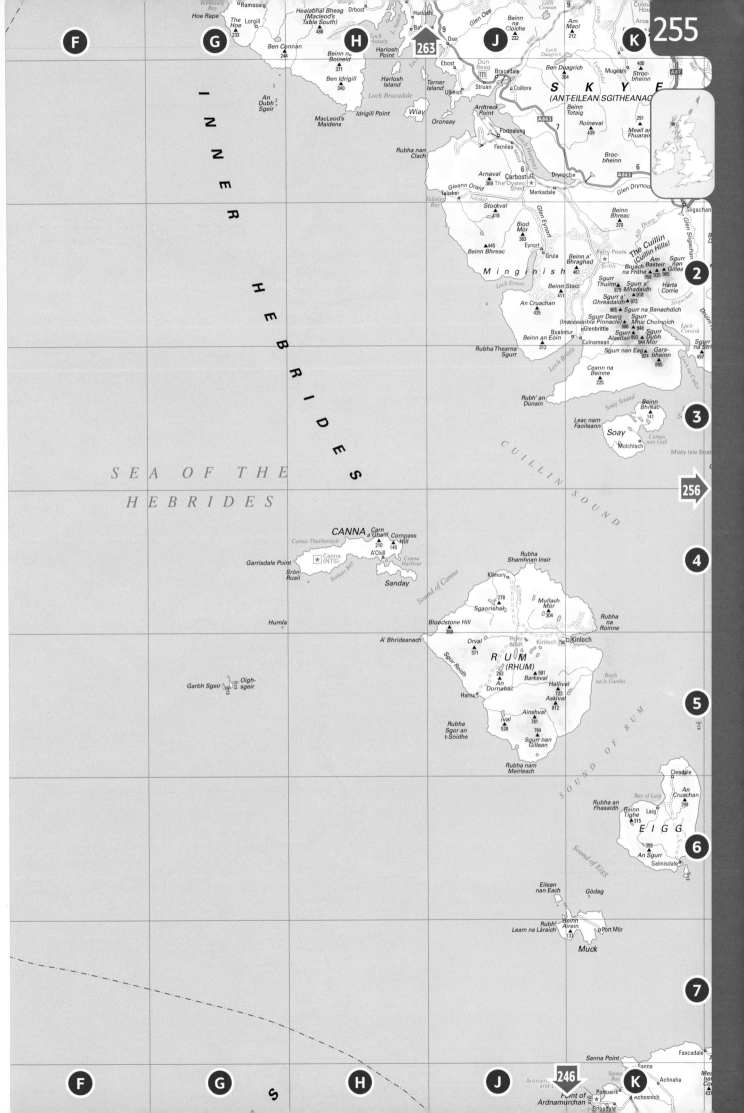

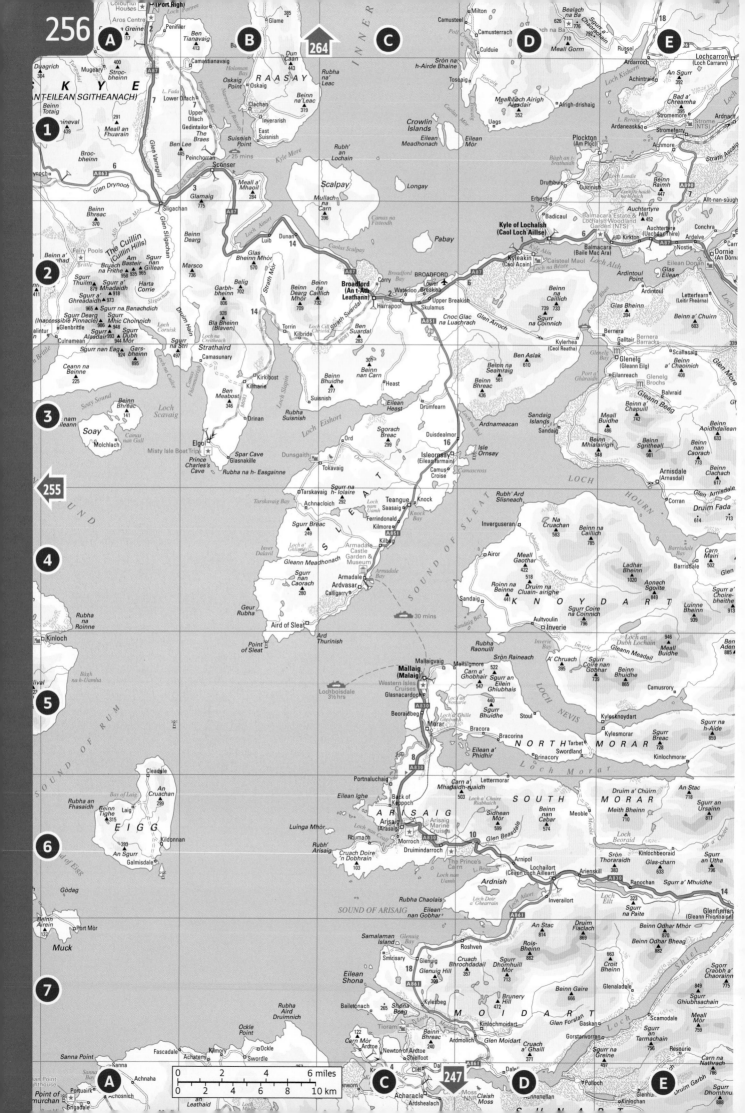

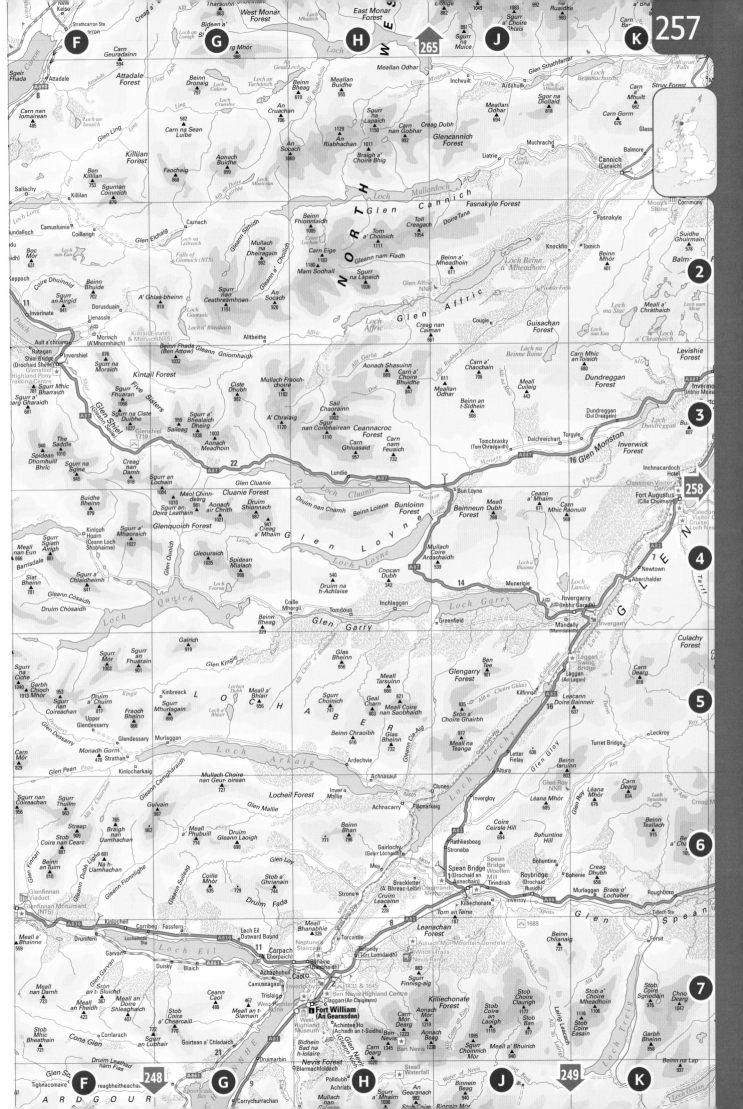

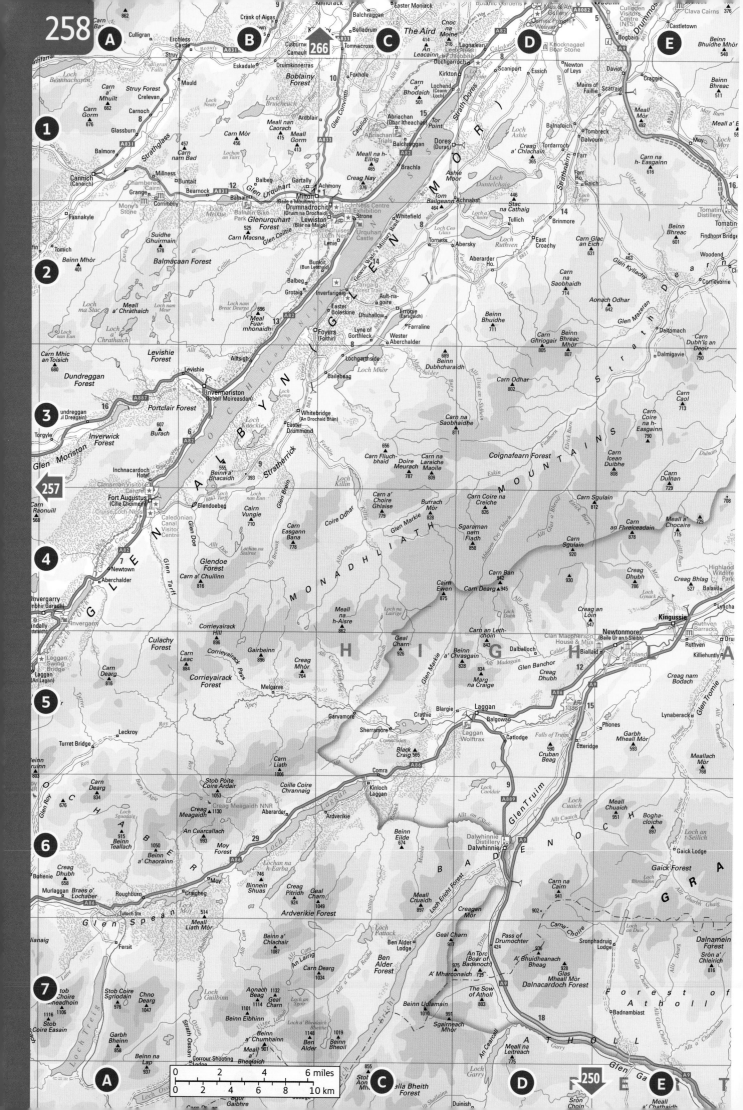

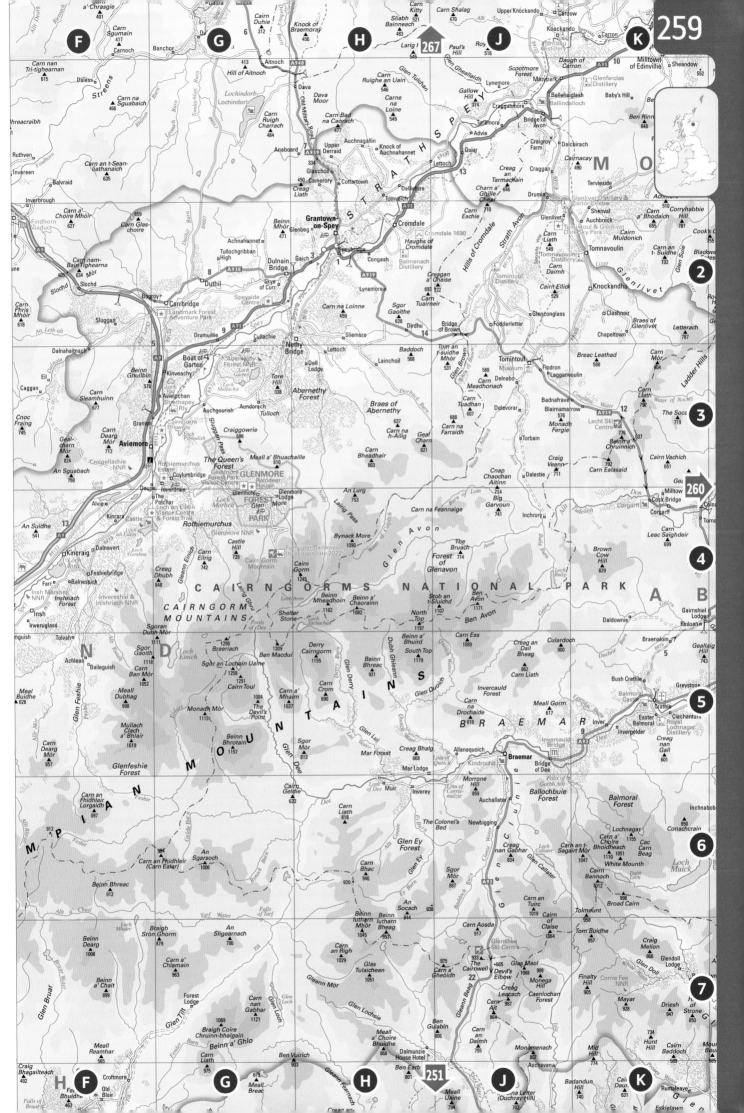

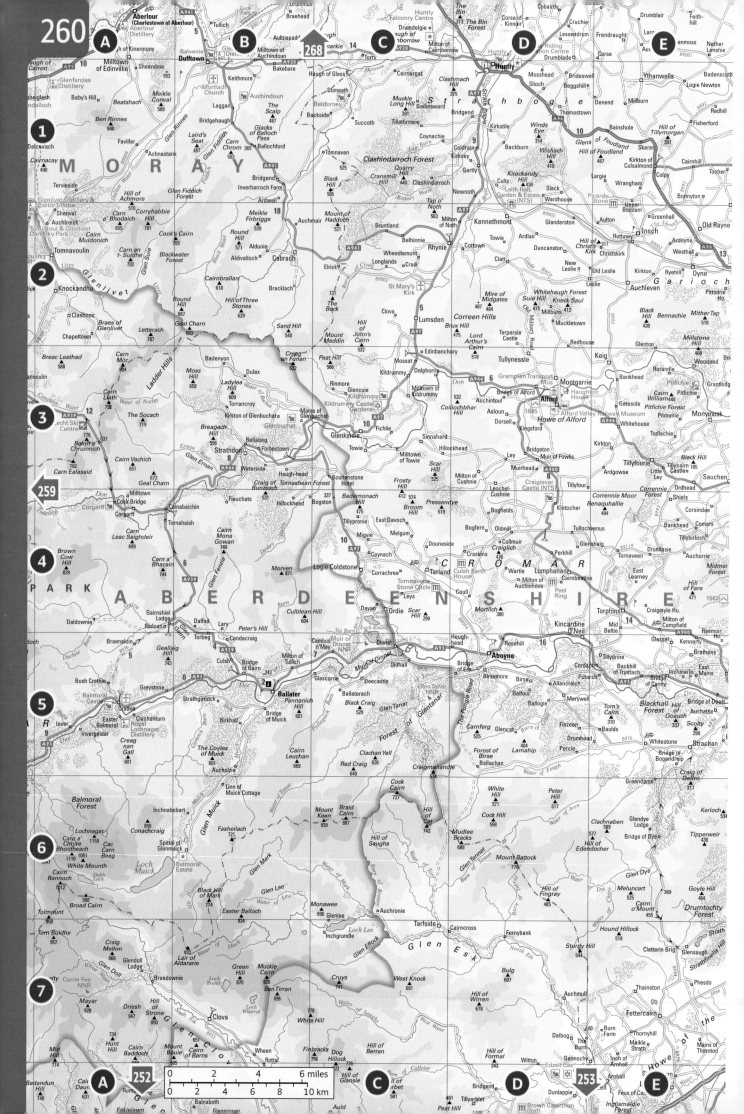

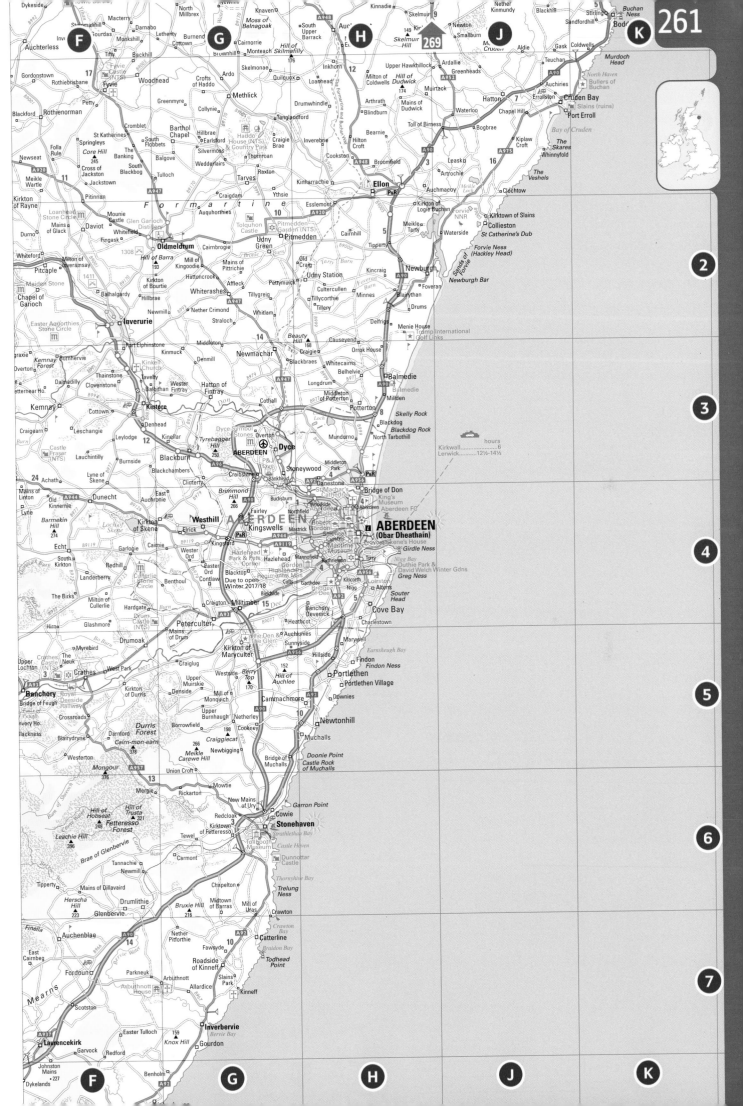

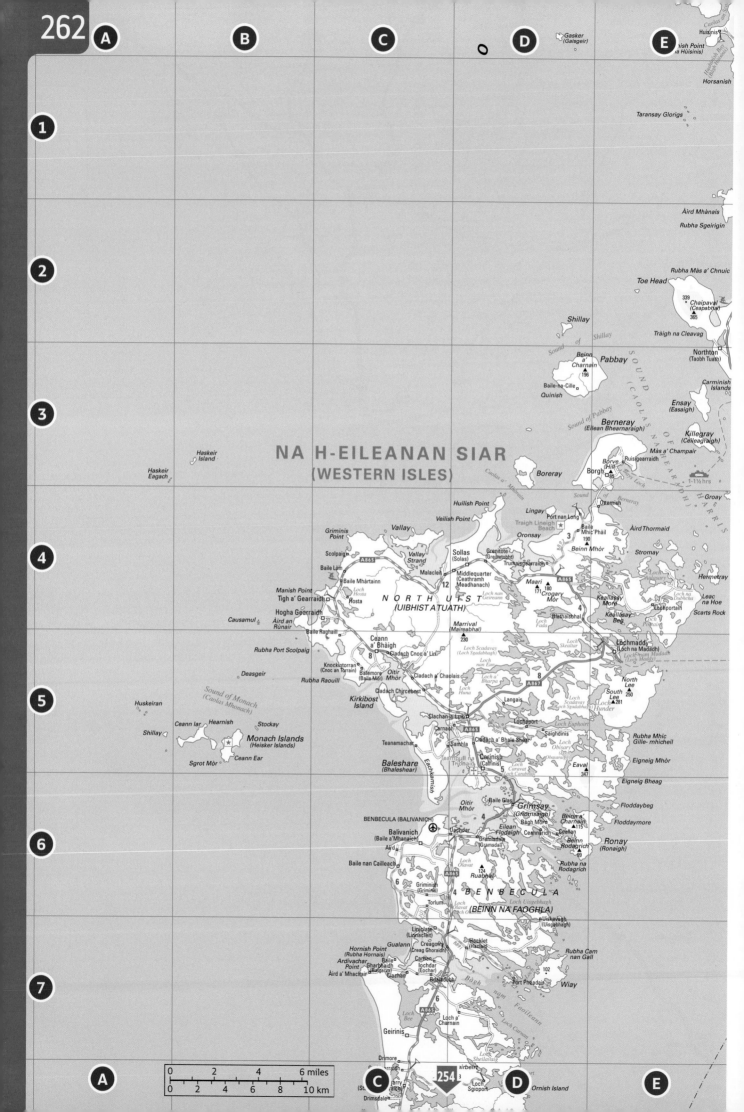

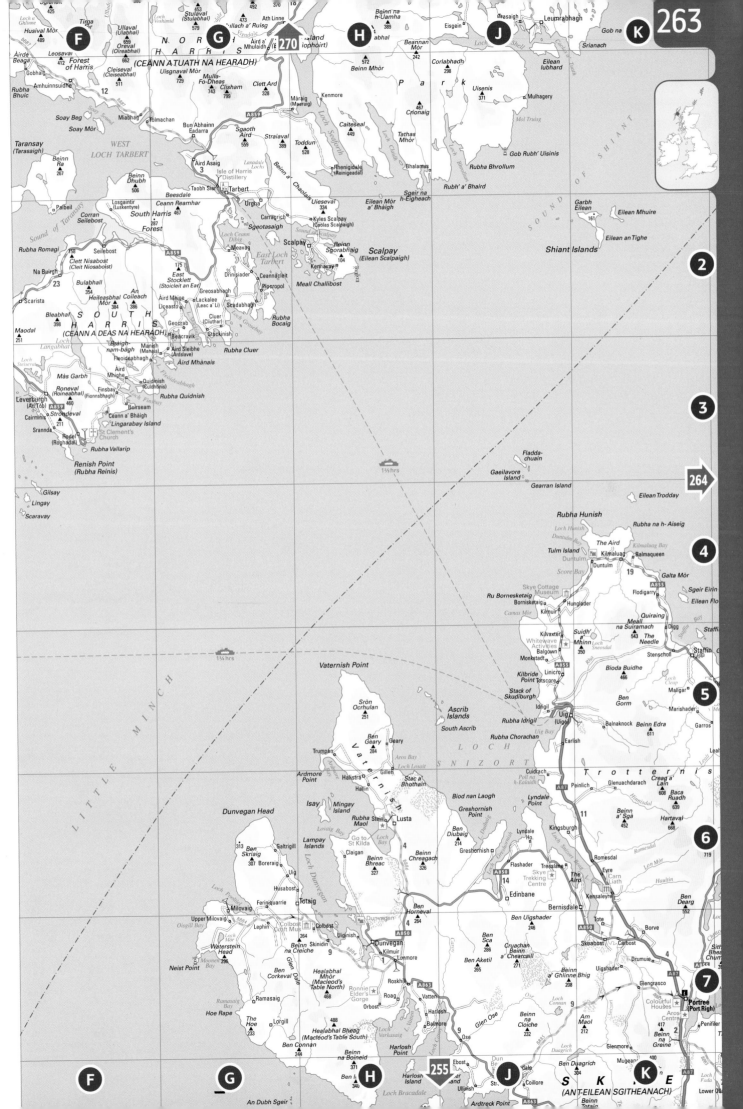

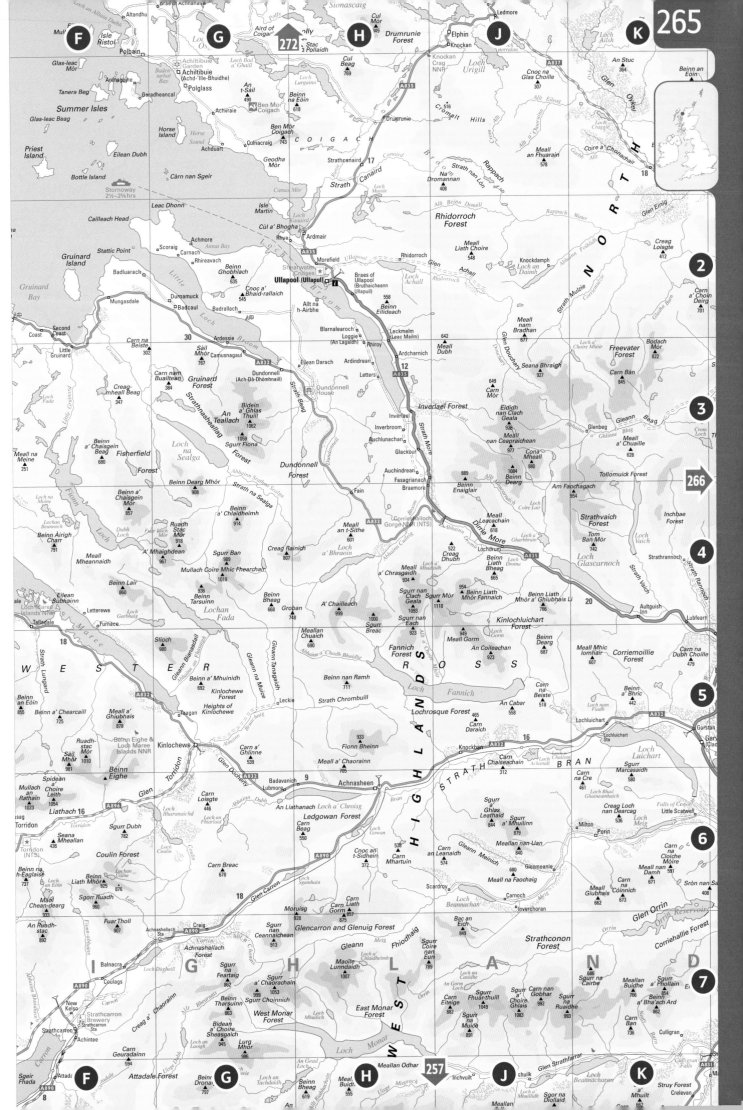

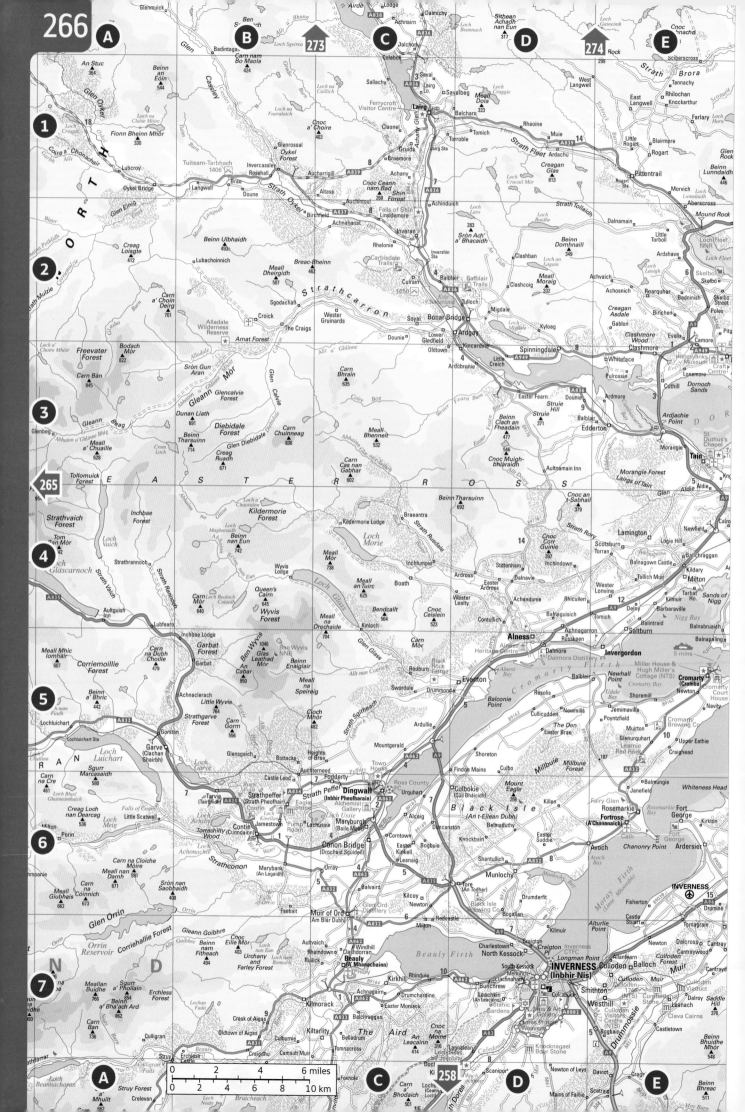

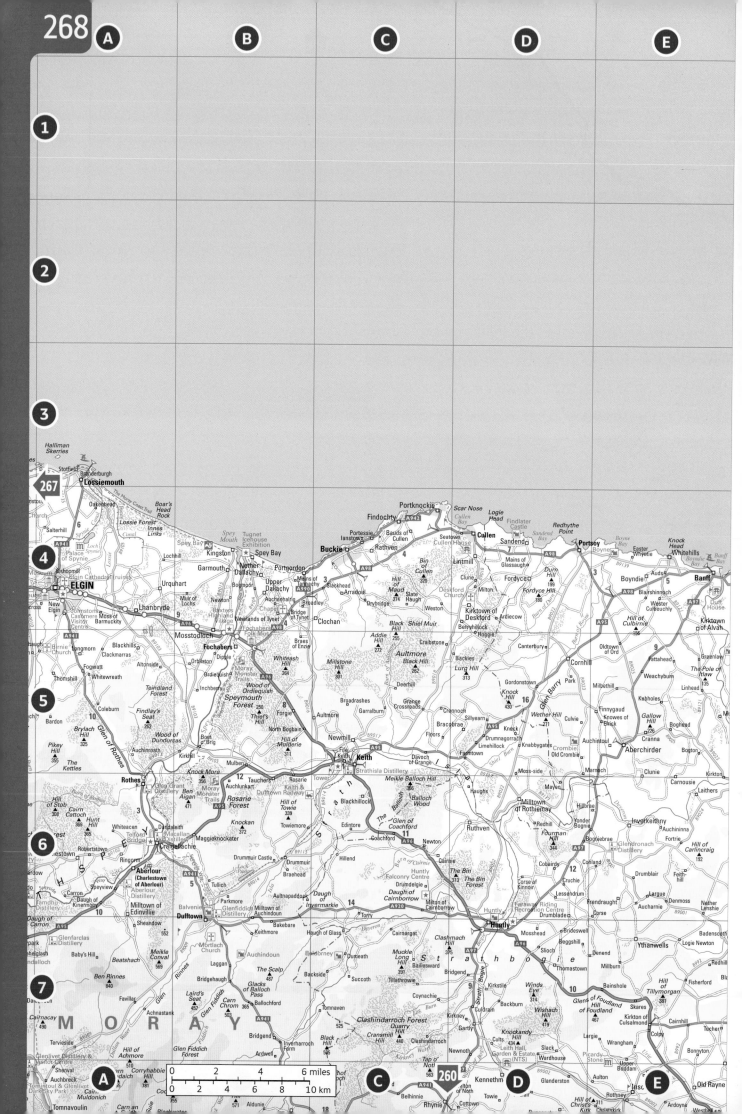

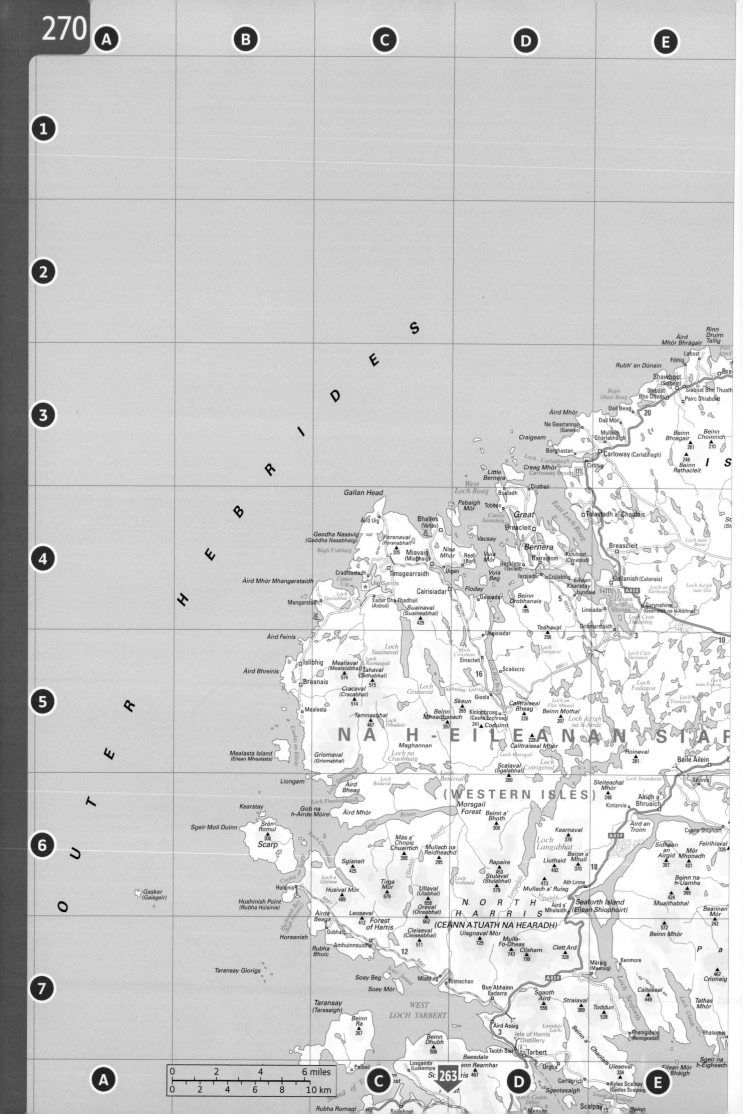

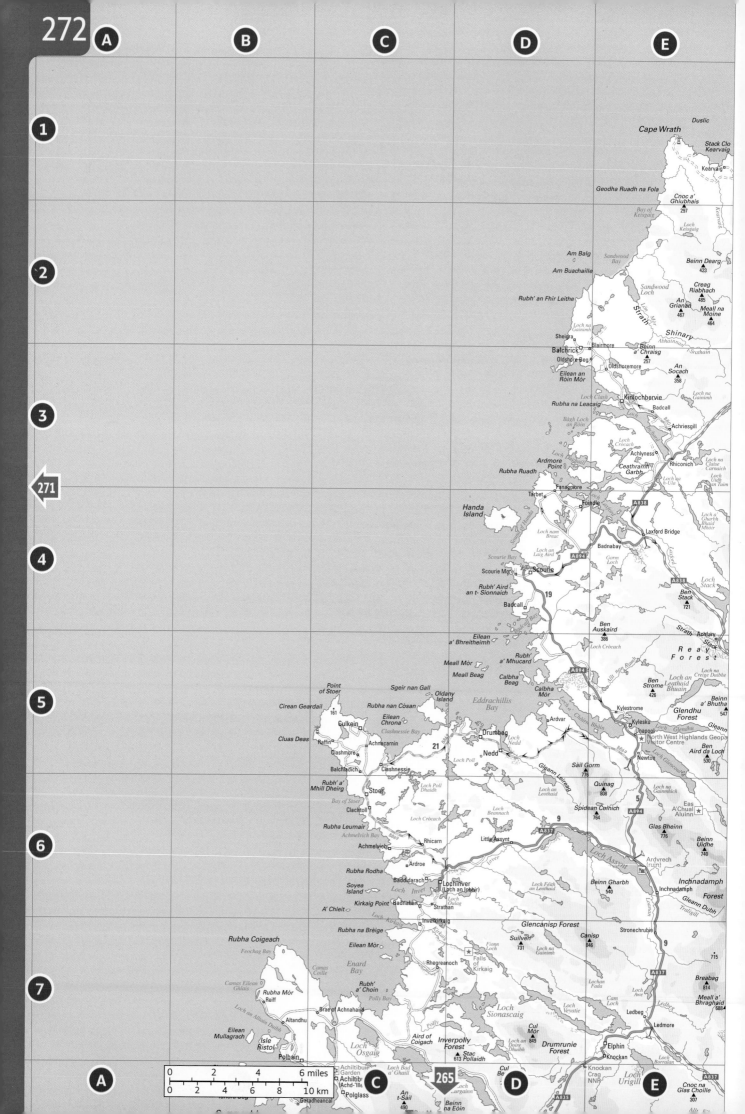

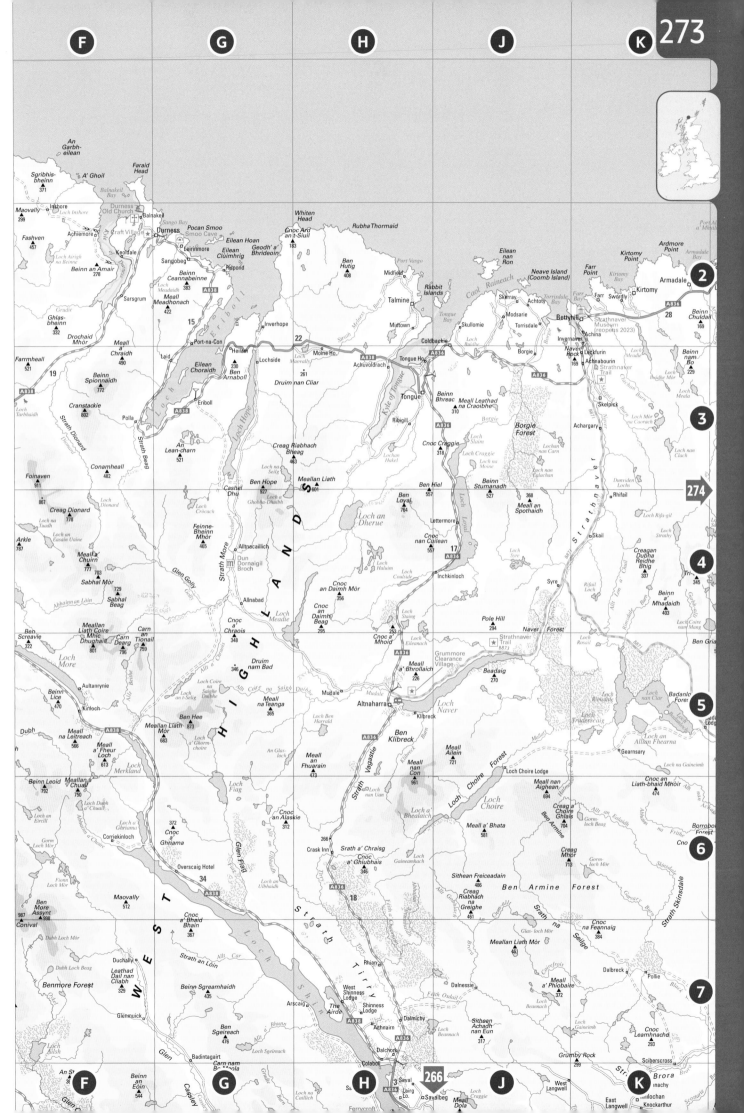

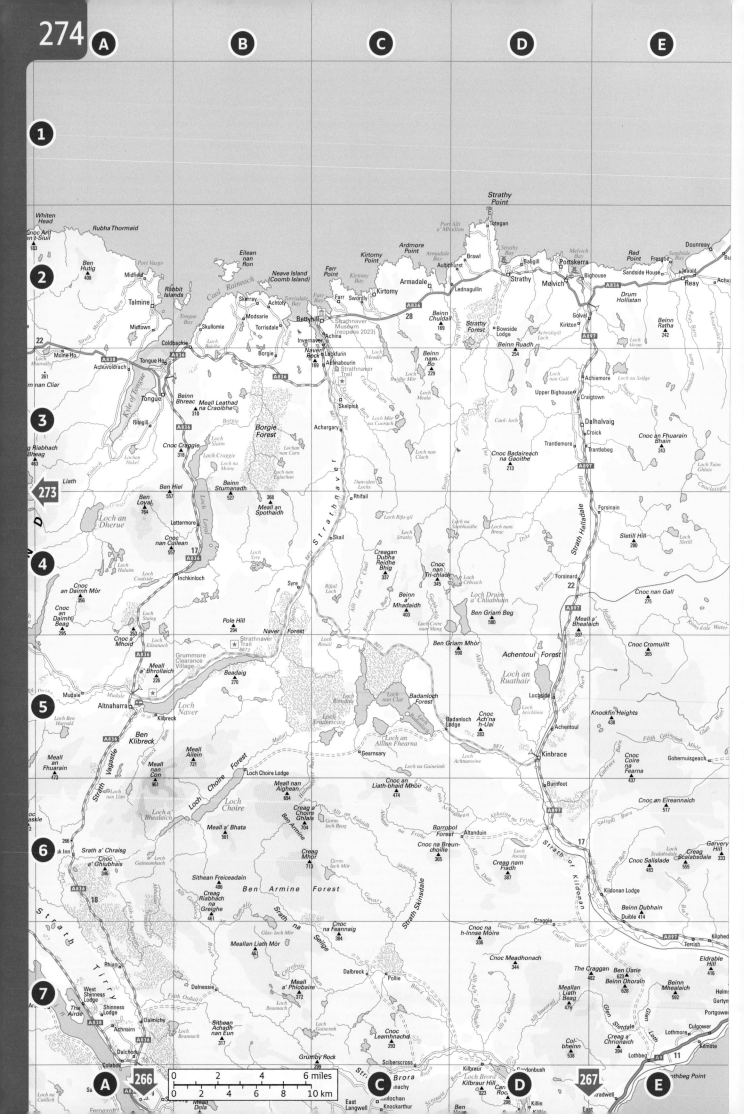

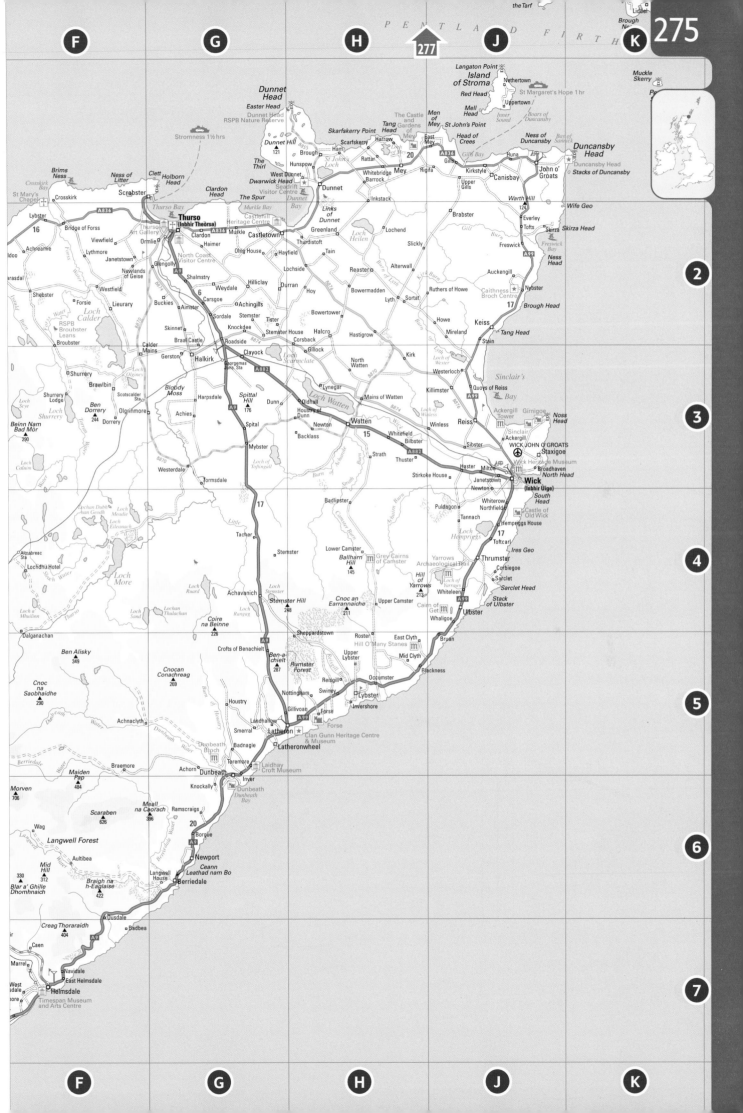

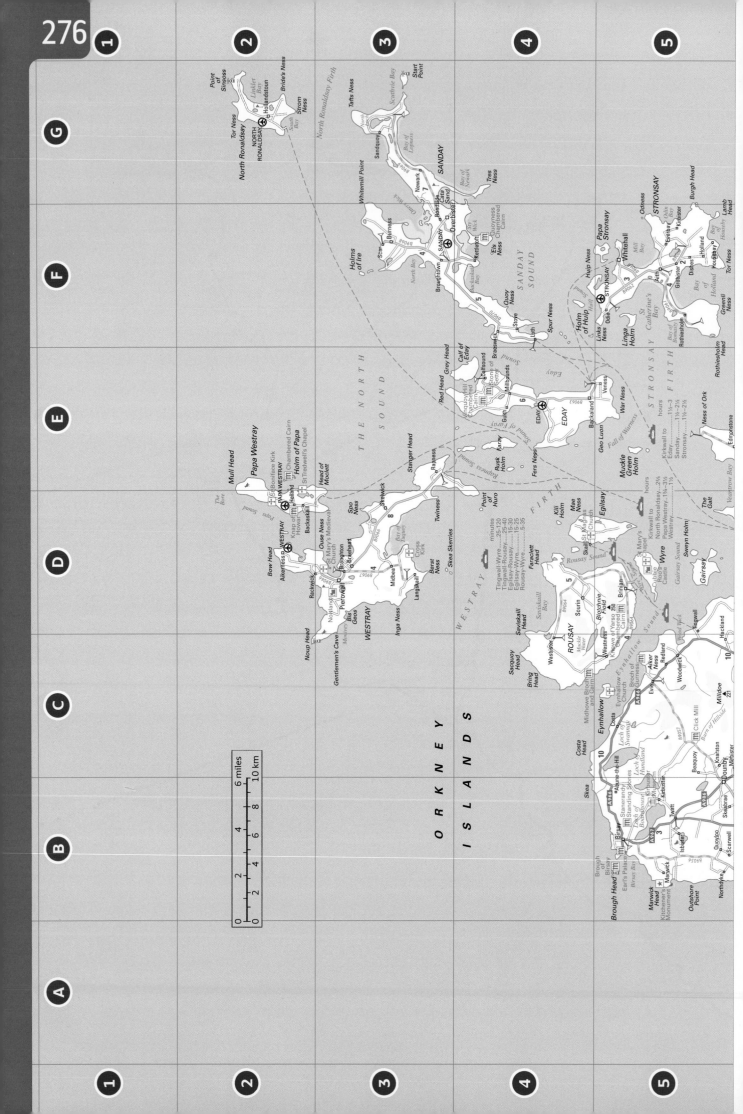

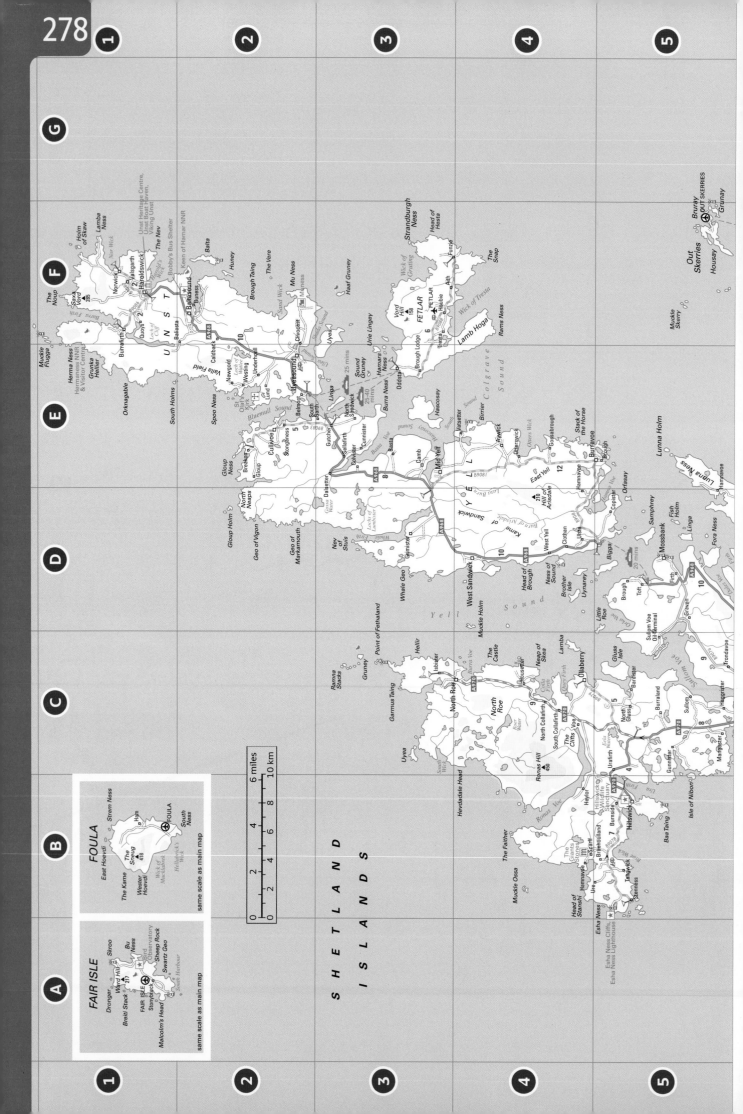

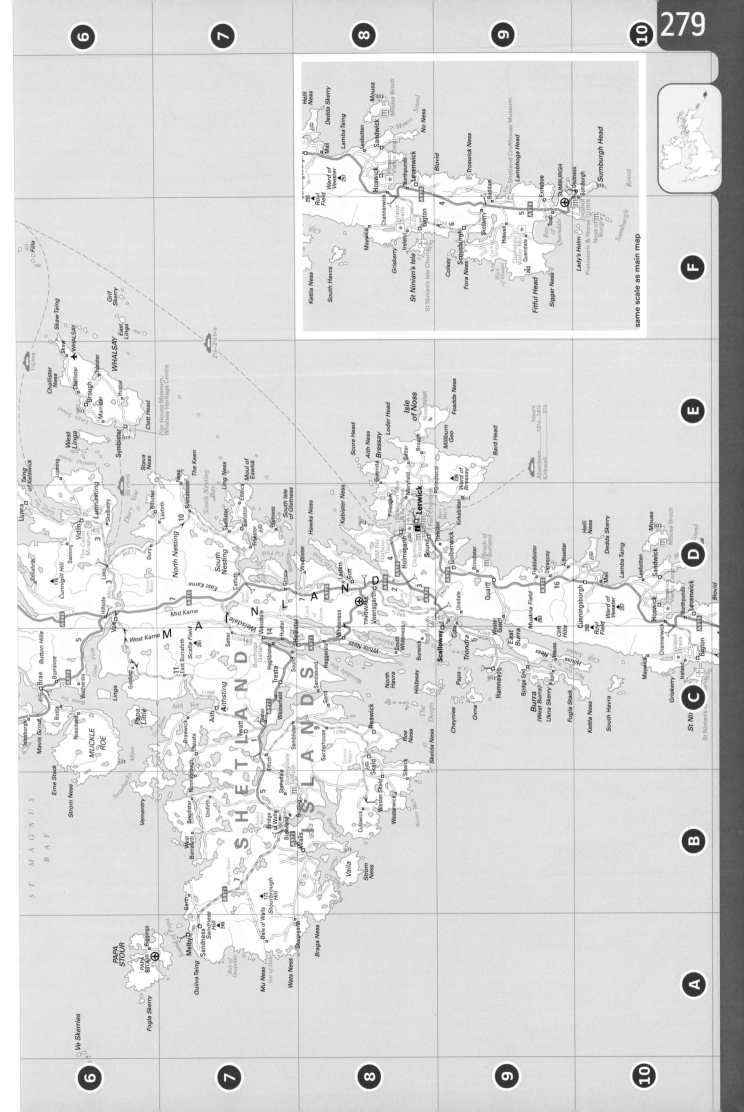

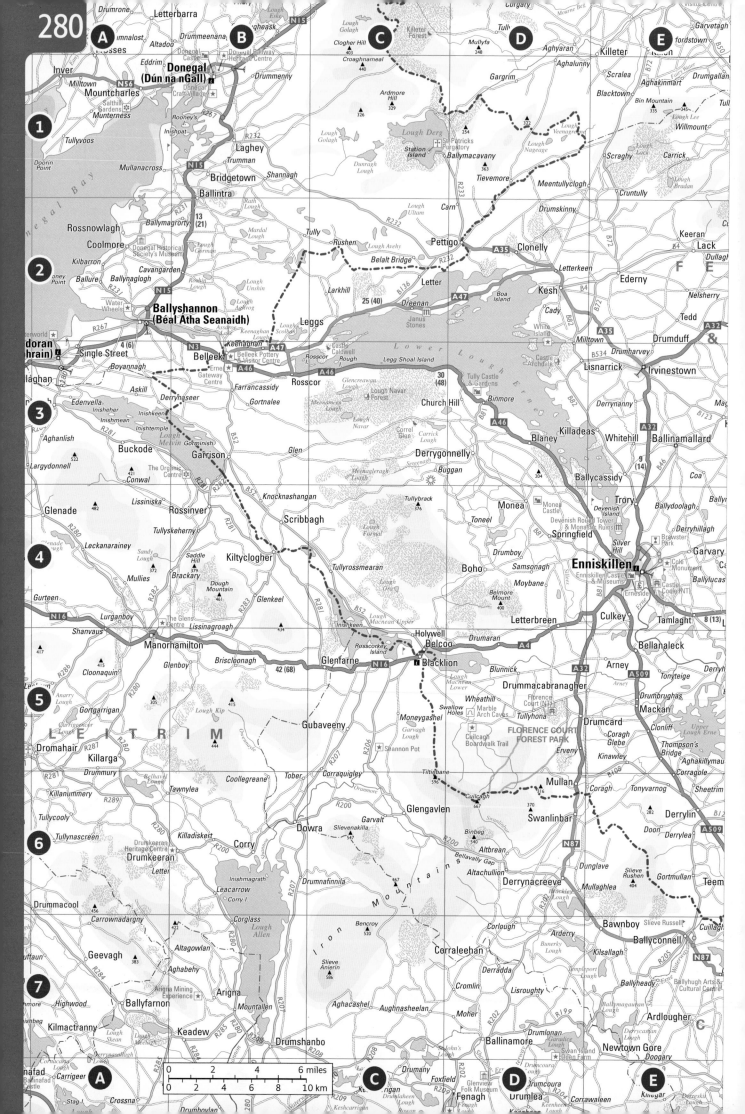

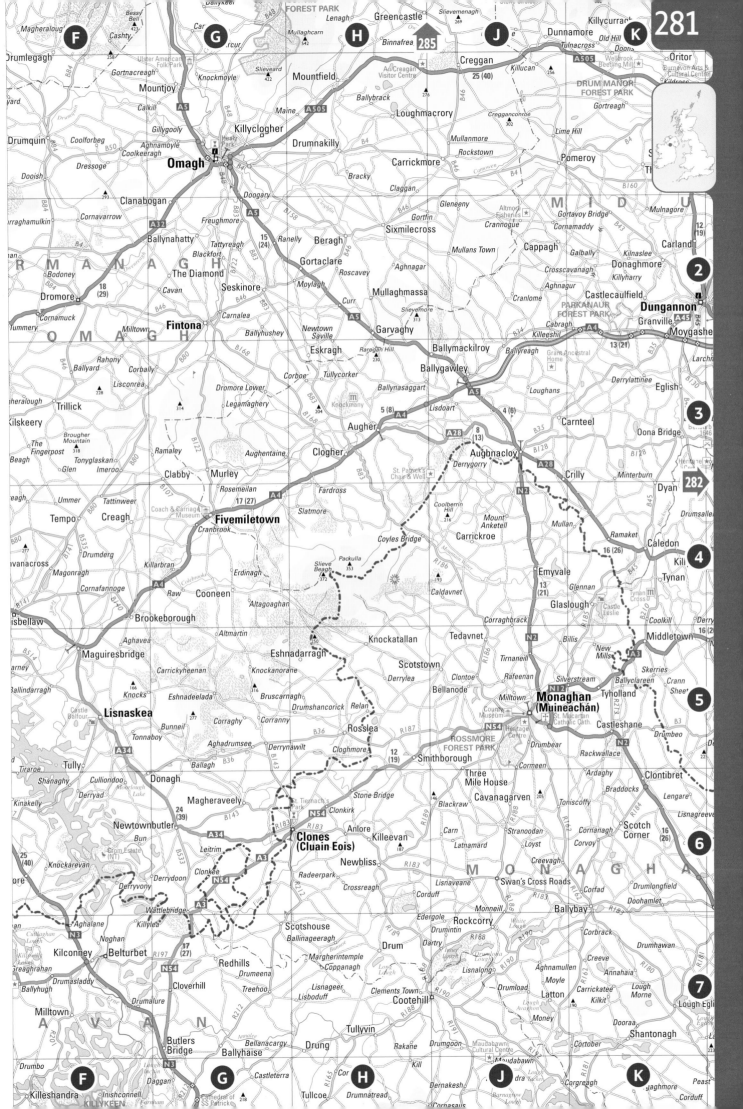

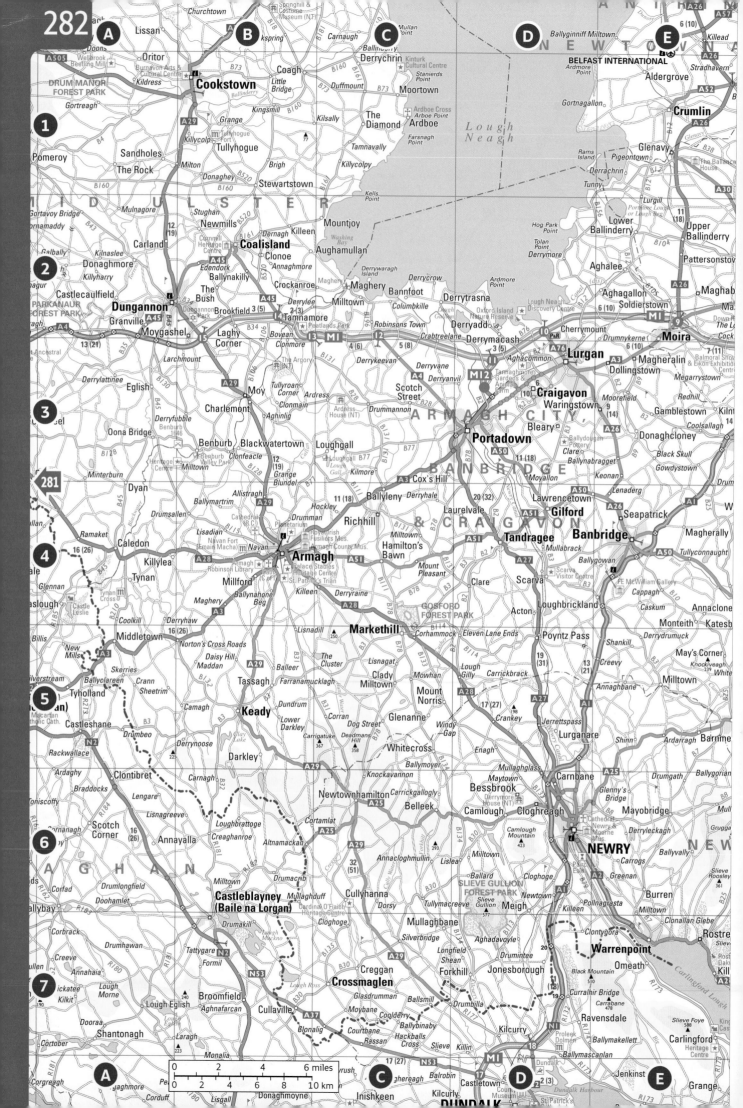

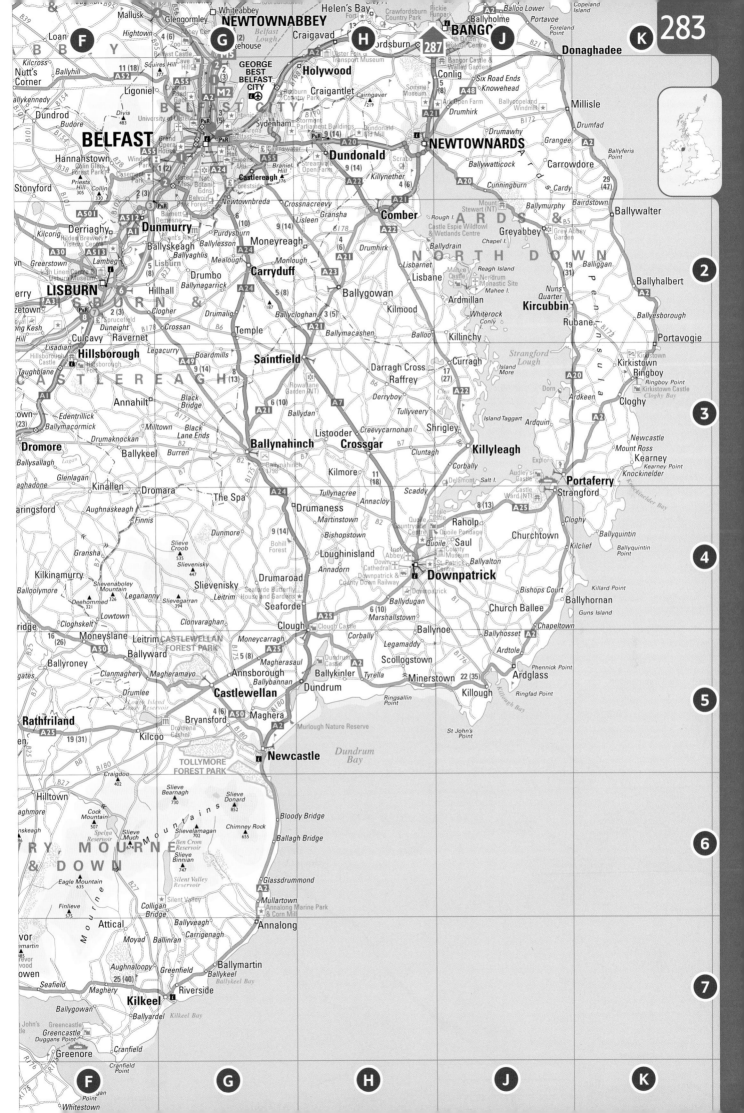

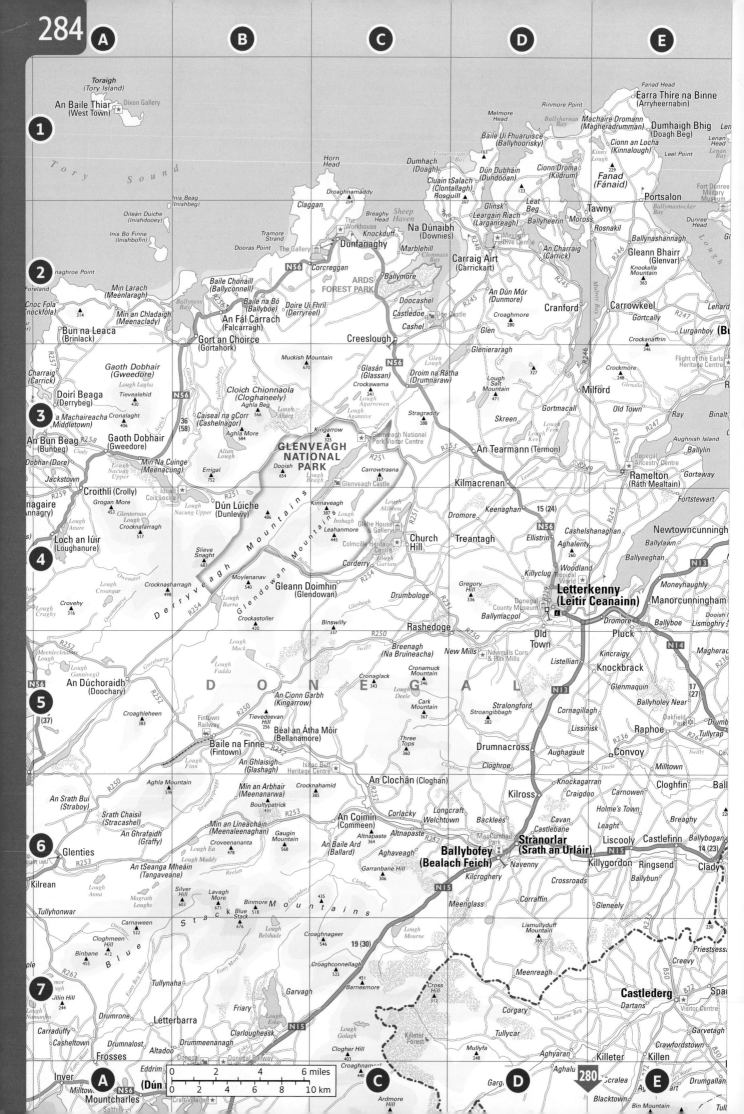

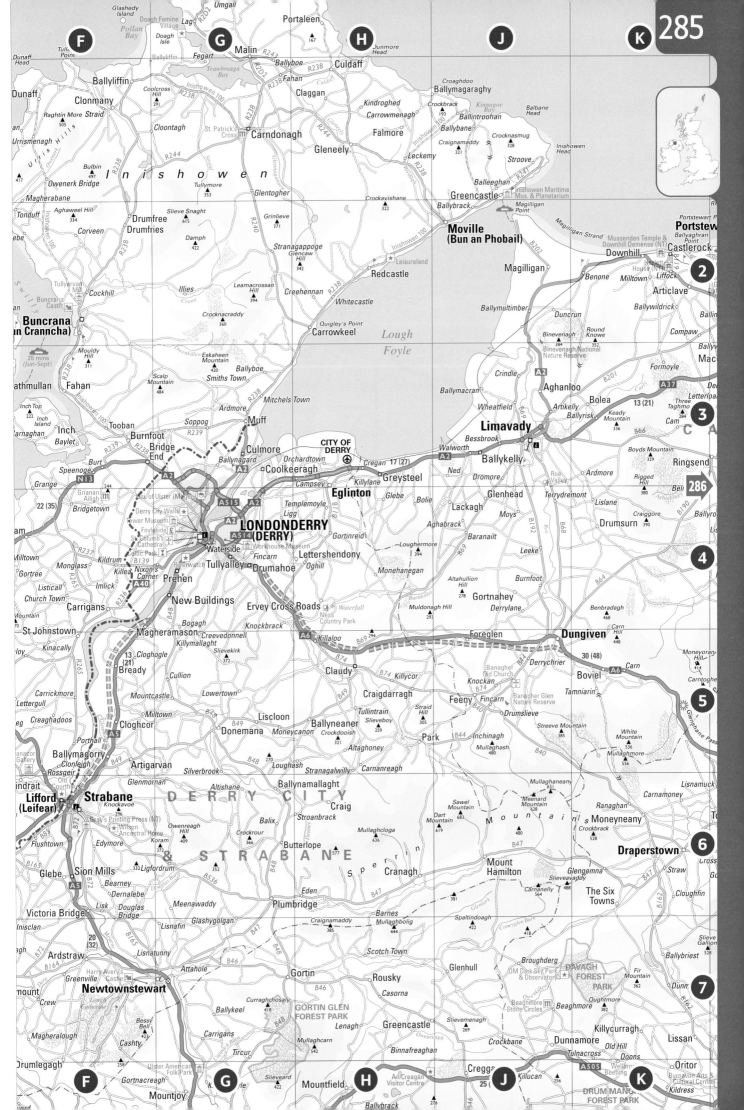

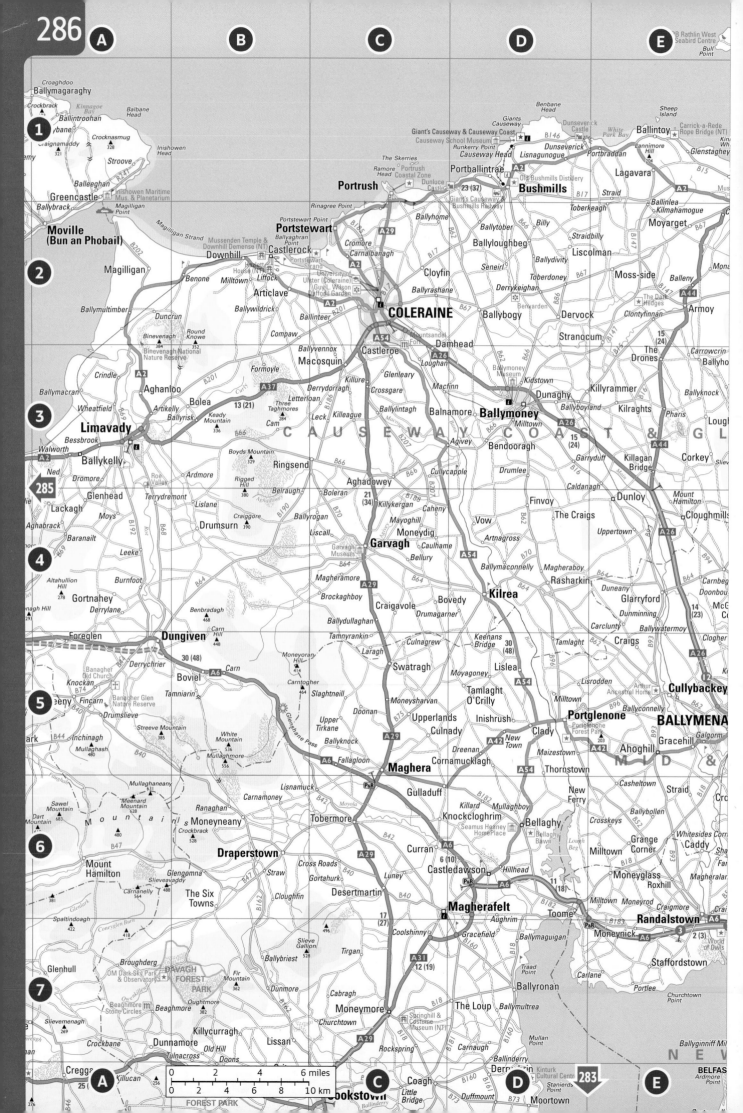

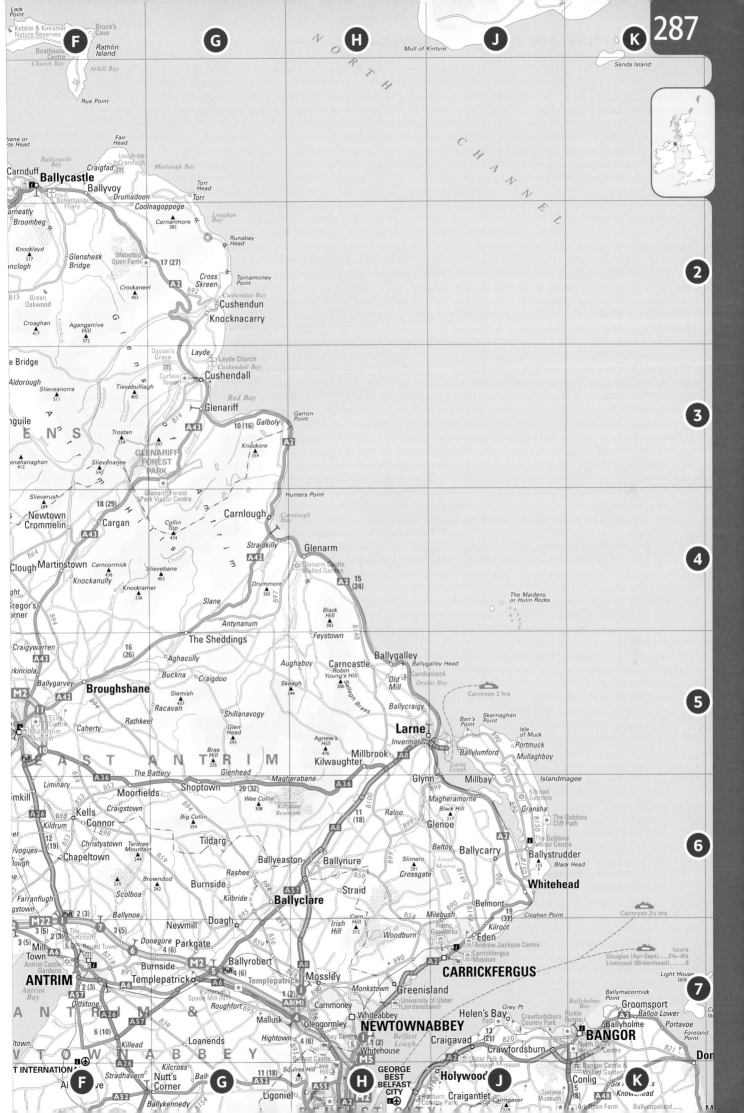

Place, place of interest and World Heritage Site names are followed by a **page number** and a grid reference in black type. The feature can be found on the map somewhere within the grid square shown.

Where two or more places have the same name the abbreviated *county* or *unitary authority* names are shown to distinguish between them.
A list of these abbreviated names appears below.

A selection of the most popular places of interest are shown within the index in blue type. Their postcode information is supplied after the county / unitary authority names to aid integration with satnav systems.

Sites with World Heritage Status are shown within the index in maroon type.

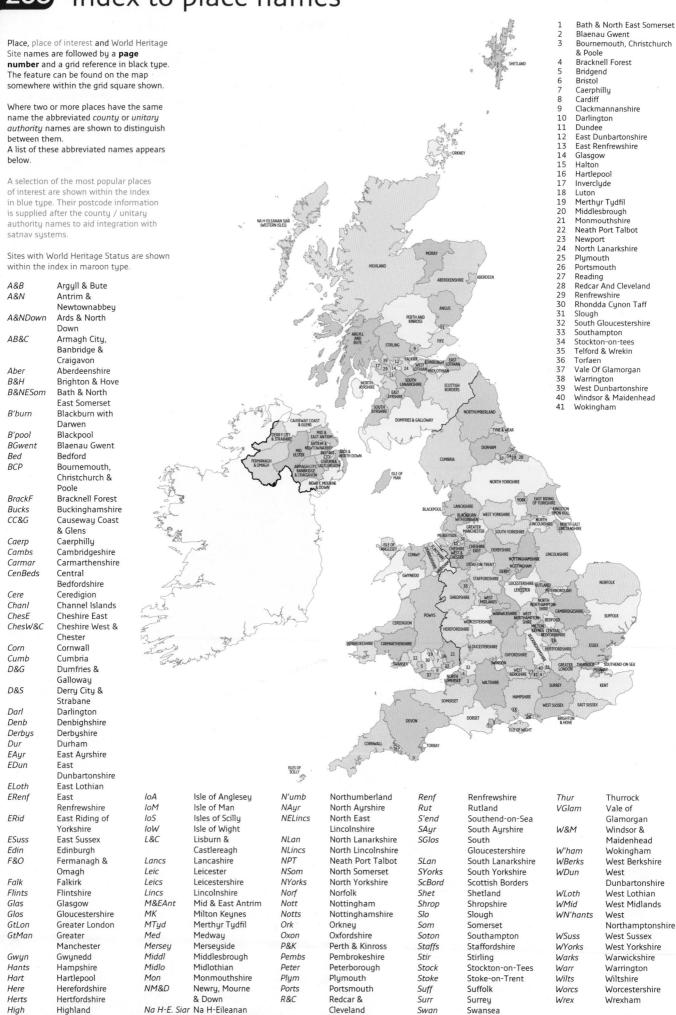

1	Bath & North East Somerset
2	Blaenau Gwent
3	Bournemouth, Christchurch & Poole
4	Bracknell Forest
5	Bridgend
6	Bristol
7	Caerphilly
8	Cardiff
9	Clackmannanshire
10	Darlington
11	Dundee
12	East Dunbartonshire
13	East Renfrewshire
14	Glasgow
15	Halton
16	Hartlepool
17	Inverclyde
18	Luton
19	Merthyr Tydfil
20	Middlesbrough
21	Monmouthshire
22	Neath Port Talbot
23	Newport
24	North Lanarkshire
25	Plymouth
26	Portsmouth
27	Reading
28	Redcar And Cleveland
29	Renfrewshire
30	Rhondda Cynon Taff
31	Slough
32	South Gloucestershire
33	Southampton
34	Stockton-on-tees
35	Telford & Wrekin
36	Torfaen
37	Vale Of Glamorgan
38	Warrington
39	West Dunbartonshire
40	Windsor & Maidenhead
41	Wokingham

A&B	Argyll & Bute
A&N	Antrim & Newtownabbey
A&NDown	Ards & North Down
AB&C	Armagh City, Banbridge & Craigavon
Aber	Aberdeenshire
B&H	Brighton & Hove
B&NESom	Bath & North East Somerset
B'burn	Blackburn with Darwen
B'pool	Blackpool
BGwent	Blaenau Gwent
Bed	Bedford
BCP	Bournemouth, Christchurch & Poole
BrackF	Bracknell Forest
Bucks	Buckinghamshire
CC&G	Causeway Coast & Glens
Caerp	Caerphilly
Cambs	Cambridgeshire
Carmar	Carmarthenshire
CenBeds	Central Bedfordshire
Cere	Ceredigion
Chanl	Channel Islands
ChesE	Cheshire East
ChesW&C	Cheshire West & Chester
Corn	Cornwall
Cumb	Cumbria
D&G	Dumfries & Galloway
D&S	Derry City & Strabane
Darl	Darlington
Denb	Denbighshire
Derbys	Derbyshire
Dur	Durham
EAyr	East Ayrshire
EDun	East Dunbartonshire
ELoth	East Lothian
ERenf	East Renfrewshire
ERid	East Riding of Yorkshire
ESuss	East Sussex
Edin	Edinburgh
F&O	Fermanagh & Omagh
Falk	Falkirk
Flints	Flintshire
Glas	Glasgow
Glos	Gloucestershire
GtLon	Greater London
GtMan	Greater Manchester
Gwyn	Gwynedd
Hants	Hampshire
Hart	Hartlepool
Here	Herefordshire
Herts	Hertfordshire
High	Highland
Hull	Kingston upon Hull
Invcly	Inverclyde

IoA	Isle of Anglesey
IoM	Isle of Man
IoS	Isles of Scilly
IoW	Isle of Wight
L&C	Lisburn & Castlereagh
Lancs	Lancashire
Leic	Leicester
Leics	Leicestershire
Lincs	Lincolnshire
M&EAnt	Mid & East Antrim
MK	Milton Keynes
MTyd	Merthyr Tydfil
Med	Medway
Mersey	Merseyside
Middl	Middlesbrough
Midlo	Midlothian
Mon	Monmouthshire
NM&D	Newry, Mourne & Down
Na H-E. Siar	Na H-Eileanan Siar (Western Isles)
NN'hants	North Northamptonshire

N'umb	Northumberland
NAyr	North Ayrshire
NELincs	North East Lincolnshire
NLan	North Lanarkshire
NLincs	North Lincolnshire
NPT	Neath Port Talbot
NSom	North Somerset
NYorks	North Yorkshire
Norf	Norfolk
Nott	Nottingham
Notts	Nottinghamshire
Ork	Orkney
Oxon	Oxfordshire
P&K	Perth & Kinross
Pembs	Pembrokeshire
Peter	Peterborough
Plym	Plymouth
Ports	Portsmouth
R&C	Redcar & Cleveland
RCT	Rhondda Cynon Taff
Read	Reading

Renf	Renfrewshire
Rut	Rutland
S'end	Southend-on-Sea
SAyr	South Ayrshire
SGlos	South Gloucestershire
SLan	South Lanarkshire
SYorks	South Yorkshire
ScBord	Scottish Borders
Shet	Shetland
Shrop	Shropshire
Slo	Slough
Som	Somerset
Soton	Southampton
Staffs	Staffordshire
Stir	Stirling
Stock	Stockton-on-Tees
Stoke	Stoke-on-Trent
Suff	Suffolk
Surr	Surrey
Swan	Swansea
Swin	Swindon
T&W	Tyne & Wear
Tel&W	Telford & Wrekin

Thur	Thurrock
VGlam	Vale of Glamorgan
W&M	Windsor & Maidenhead
W'ham	Wokingham
WBerks	West Berkshire
WDun	West Dunbartonshire
WLoth	West Lothian
WMid	West Midlands
WN'hants	West Northamptonshire
WSuss	West Sussex
WYorks	West Yorkshire
Warks	Warwickshire
Warr	Warrington
Wilts	Wiltshire
Worcs	Worcestershire
Wrex	Wrexham

1853 Gallery *WYorks* BD18 3LA 26 C1

A
Ab Kettleby 174 C5
Ab Lench 146 C2
Abbas Combe 117 E5
Abberley 145 G1
Abberley Common 145 G1
Abberton *Essex* 138 D1
Abberton *Worcs* 146 B2
Abberwick 229 F5
Abbess Roding 137 E1
Abbey Dore 144 C4
Abbey Hulton 171 G3
Abbey St. Bathans 237 E3
Abbey Village 192 B2
Abbey Wood 137 D5
Abbeycwmhir 155 G5
Abbeydale 186 A4
Abbeystead 192 B2
Abbeytown 209 E1
Abbotrule 228 A5
Abbots Bickington 113 D4
Abbots Bromley 172 B5
Abbots Langley 135 F2
Abbots Leigh 131 E5
Abbots Morton 146 C2
Abbots Ripton 162 A4
Abbot's Salford 146 C2
Abbots Worthy 119 F4
Abbotsbury 104 B4
Abbotsbury Swannery *Dorset* DT3 4JG 104 B4
Abbotsfield Farm 183 G3
Abbotsham 113 E3
Abbotskerswell 101 E1
Abbotsley 150 A2
Abbotstone 119 G4
Abbotts Ann 119 E3
Abbott's Barton 119 F4
Abbottswood 119 E5
Abdon 157 E4
Abdy 186 B3
Abenhall 131 F1
Aber *Cere* 142 A3
Aber *Powys* 144 A5
Aberaeron 142 A1
Aberangell 155 E2
Aberarad 141 G3
Aberarder 249 G1
Aberarder House 258 D2
Aberargie 243 F2
Aber-arth 142 A1
Aberavon 129 D3
Aber-banc 141 G3
Aberbargoed 130 B2
Aberbeeg 130 B2
Aberbowlan 142 C4
Aberbrân 143 F5
Abercanaid 129 G2
Aber-carn 130 B3
Abercastle 140 B4
Abercegir 155 E2
Aberchalder 257 K4
Aberchirder 268 E5
Abercorn 235 E2
Abercrave 129 E1
Abercregan 129 E3
Abercrombie 244 D4
Abercrychan 143 D4
Abercwmboi 129 G2
Abercych 141 F3
Abercynafon 129 G1
Abercynon 129 G3
Abercywarch 155 E2
Aberdalgie 243 F2
Aberdare 129 F2
Aberdaron 166 A5
Aberdeen (Obar Dheathain) 261 H4
Aberdeen Airport 261 G3
Aberdeen Art Gallery AB10 1FQ 63 Aberdeen
Aberdesach 166 D2
Aberdour 235 F1
Aberdovey (Aberdyfi) 154 C3
Aberduhonw 143 G3
Aberdulais 129 D3
Aberedw 143 G3
Abereiddy 140 A4
Aber-erch 166 C4
Aberfan 129 G2
Aberfeldy 251 D5
Aberffraw 166 C1
Aber-ffrwd 154 C5
Aberford 194 D4
Aberfoyle 242 A4
Abergavenny (Y Fenni) 130 B1
Abergele 182 A5
Abergiâr 142 B3
Abergorlech 142 B4
Abergwesyn 143 E2
Abergwili 142 A5
Abergwydol 155 D2
Abergwynant 154 C1
Abergwynfi 129 E3
Abergwyngregyn 181 E5
Abergynolwyn 154 C2
Aberhafesp 155 G3
Aberhosan 155 E3
Aberkenfig 129 E4
Aberlady 236 B1
Aberlemno 252 D4
Aberllefenni 155 D2
Aber-Ilia 129 F1
Aberlour (Charlestown of Aberlour) 267 K7
Abermad 154 B5
Abermeurig 142 B2
Abermule (Aber-miwl) 156 A3
Abernaint 169 E5
Aber-nant *Carmar* 141 G5
Aber-nant *RCT* 129 G2
Abernethy 243 G3
Abernyte 244 A1
Aberporth 141 F2
Aberscross 266 E2
Abersky 258 C2
Abersoch 166 C5
Abersychan 130 B2
Aberthin 129 G5
Abertillery 130 B2
Abertridwr *Caerp* 130 A4

Abertridwr *Powys* 155 G1
Abertysswg 130 A2
Aberuthven 243 E3
Aberwheeler 169 D1
Aberyscir 143 F5
Aberystwyth 154 B4
Aberystwyth Arts Centre *Cere* SY23 3DE 154 B4
Abingdon 133 G3
Abinger Common 121 G3
Abinger Hammer 121 F3
Abington 226 A3
Abington Pigotts 150 B3
Abingworth 108 D2
Ablington *Glos* 132 D2
Ablington *Wilts* 118 C3
Abney 185 F5
Above Church 172 B2
Aboyne 260 D5
Abram 184 A2
Abriachan (Obar Itheachan) 258 C1
Abridge 137 D3
Abronhill 234 B2
Abson 131 G5
Abthorpe 148 B3
Abune-the-Hill 276 B5
Aby 189 E5
Acaster Malbis 195 E3
Acaster Selby 195 E3
Accrington 193 D5
Accurrach 240 D2
Acha 246 A4
Achabraid 232 A2
Achacha 248 B5
Achadacaie 231 G3
Achadh-chaorrunn 231 F4
Achadunan 241 E3
Achagavel 247 G4
Achaglass 231 F5
Achahoish 231 F2
Achalader 251 G5
Achallader 249 F5
Achamore 231 D2
Achandunie 266 D4
Achany 266 C1
Achaphubuil 248 C2
Acharacle 247 F3
Achargary 274 C3
Acharn *A&B* 240 D1
Acharn *P&K* 250 C5
Acharonich 239 D1
Acharosson 232 A2
Achateny 247 E2
Achath 261 F2
Achavanich 275 G4
Achavraie 265 G1
Achddu 128 A2
Achduart 265 G1
Achentoul 274 D5
Achfary 272 E5
Achgarve 264 E2
Achiemore *High* 273 F2
Achiemore *High* 274 D3
Achies 275 G3
A'Chill 255 H4
Achiltibuie (Achd-'Ille-Bhuidhe) 265 G1
Achina 274 C2
Achindown 267 F7
Achinduich 266 C2
Achingills 275 G2
Achintee 265 H3
Achintee House (Achadh an t-Suidhe) 248 D2
Achintraid 256 E1
Achlean 259 F5
Achleanan 247 E4
Achleek 247 G4
Achlian 240 D2
Achluachrach 249 D1
Achlyness 272 E3
Achmelvich 272 C6
Achmony 258 C1
Achmore *High* 265 F2
Achmore *High* 265 G2
Achmore (Acha Mòr) 271 F5
Achmore *Stir* 242 A1
Achnaba 232 A1
Achnabat 258 C1
Achnabourin 274 C3
Achnacairn 240 B1
Achnacarnin 272 C5
Achnacarry 249 E1
Achnaclerach 266 B5
Achnacloich *A&B* 240 B1
Achnacloich *High* 256 B4
Achnaclyth 275 F5
Achnacraig 247 D5
Achnacroish 248 A4
Achnadrish 246 D4
Achnafalnich 241 E2
Achnafauld 243 D1
Achnagairn 266 C7
Achnagarron 266 D4
Achnaha *High* 247 F5
Achnaha *High* 247 D3
Achnahanat 266 C2
Achnahannet 259 G2
Achnairn 273 H7
Achnalea 248 A3
Achnamara 231 F1
Achnanellan 249 D2
Achnasaul 249 D1
Achnasheen 265 H6
Achnashelloch 240 A5
Achnastank 259 K1
Achorn 275 G4
Achosnich *High* 266 E2
Achosnich *High* 246 D3
Achreamie 275 F2
Achriabhach 248 D3
Achriesgill 272 E3
Achtoty 273 J2
Achurch 161 F4
Achuvoldrach 273 H3
Achvaich 266 E2
Achvarasdal 274 E2
Achvlair 248 B4
Achvraie 265 G1
Ackenthwaite 199 G4
Ackergill 275 J3
Acklam *Middl* 203 D1
Acklam *NYorks* 195 G1
Ackleton 157 G3
Acklington 221 E1
Ackton 194 D5
Ackworth Moor Top 186 B1
Acle 179 F4
Acock's Green 158 D4

Acol 125 F2
Acomb *N'umb* 211 F1
Acomb *York* 195 E2
Aconbury 145 E4
Acre 193 D5
Acrefair 169 F3
Acrise Place 125 D4
Acton *AB&C* 282 D4
Acton *ChesE* 170 D2
Acton *Dorset* 105 F5
Acton *GtLon* 136 A4
Acton *Shrop* 156 C4
Acton *Staffs* 171 F3
Acton *Suff* 151 G3
Acton *Worcs* 146 A1
Acton *Wrex* 170 A2
Acton Beauchamp 145 F2
Acton Bridge 183 G5
Acton Burnell 157 E2
Acton Green 145 F2
Acton Pigott 157 E2
Acton Round 157 F3
Acton Scott 157 D4
Acton Trussell 158 B1
Acton Turville 132 A4
Adamhill 224 C2
Adbaston 171 E5
Adber 116 C5
Adderbury 147 G4
Adderley 171 D4
Adderstone 229 F3
Addiewell 235 D3
Addingham 193 G3
Addington *Bucks* 148 C5
Addington *GtLon* 122 C2
Addington *Kent* 123 G2
Addiscombe 121 F1
Addlestone 121 F1
Addlethorpe 176 D1
Adel 194 B4
Adeney 157 G1
Adeyfield 135 F2
Adfa 155 G2
Adforton 156 D5
Adisham 125 D4
Adlestrop 147 E5
Adlingfleet 196 A5
Adlington *ChesE* 184 D4
Adlington *Lancs* 183 G1
Admaston *Staffs* 172 B5
Admaston *Tel&W* 157 F1
Admington 147 E3
Adsborough 115 F5
Adscombe 115 E4
Adstock 148 C4
Adstone 148 A2
Adversane 121 F5
Advie 259 J1
Adwalton 194 B5
Adwell 134 B3
Adwick le Street 186 C2
Adwick upon Dearne 186 B2
Adziel 269 H5
Ae Village 217 D2
Afan Forest Park *NPT* SA13 3HG 129 E3
Affetside 184 B1
Affleck 261 G2
Affpuddle 105 E3
Afon-wen *Flints* 182 C5
Afon-wen *Gwyn* 166 D4
Afonwen Craft & Antique Centre *Flints* CH7 5UB 182 C5
Africa Alive! *Suff* NR33 7TF 165 G3
Afton 106 C4
Afton Bridgend 225 E4
Agglethorpe 201 F4
Aghabrack 285 J4
Aghacommon 282 E3
Aghacully 287 G5
Aghadavoyle 282 D7
Aghadowey 286 C5
Aghadrumsee 281 G5
Aghalee 282 E2
Aghalunny 280 D1
Aghanloo 285 J3
Aghavea 281 F5
Aghinlig 282 B3
Aghnagar 281 H2
Aghnagur 281 J2
Aghnamoyle 281 G1
Aghyaran 284 D7
Agivey 286 C3
Ahoghill 286 E5
Aigburth 183 E4
Aiginis 271 G4
Aike 196 C3
Aikerness 276 D2
Aikers 277 D8
Aiketgate 210 A3
Aikshaw 209 E2
Aikton 209 F1
Aikwood Tower 227 F3
Ailby 189 E5
Ailey 144 C3
Ailsworth 161 G3
Aimes Green 136 D2
Aimster 275 G2
Ainderby Quernhow 202 C4
Ainderby Steeple 202 C3
Aingers Green 152 C5
Ainsdale 183 E1
Ainsdale-on-Sea 183 E1
Ainstable 210 B3
Ainsworth 184 B1
Ainthorpe 203 G2
Aintree 183 E3
Aird *Na H-E. Siar* 262 C6
Aird *Na H-E. Siar* 271 H4
Àird a' Mhachair 262 C7
Àird a' Mhulaidh 270 D6
Àird Asaig 270 D7
Àird Dhail 271 G1
Àird Mhidhinis 254 C4
Àird Mhighe 263 G2

Aird Mhighe 263 F3
Àrd Mhòr 254 C4
Aird of Sleat 256 B4
Àird Sleibhe (Ardslave) 263 G3
Aird Thunga 271 G4
Àird Uig 270 C4
Airdrie *Fife* 245 D3
Airdrie *NLan* 234 B3
Aire View 193 F3
Airidh a' Bhruaich 270 E6
Airieland 216 B5
Airies 214 A4
Airigh-drishaig 256 D1
Airmyn 195 G5
Airntully 243 F1
Airor 256 D4
Airth 234 C1
Airton 193 F2
Airyhassen 207 D2
Aisby *Lincs* 187 F3
Aisby *Lincs* 175 F4
Aisgill 200 C1
Aish *Devon* 100 C1
Aish *Devon* 101 E2
Aisholt 115 E4
Aiskew 202 B4
Aislaby *NYorks* 204 B2
Aislaby *NYorks* 203 G4
Aislaby *Stock* 202 D1
Aisthorpe 187 G4
Aith *Ork* 277 B6
Aith *Ork* 276 F5
Aith *Shet* 279 C7
Aith *Shet* 278 F3
Aithsetter 279 D9
Aitnoch 259 G1
Akeld 229 D4
Akeley 148 C4
Akenham 152 C3
Albaston 99 E3
Albecq 101 E5
Alberbury 156 C1
Albert Park TS1 3LB 78 Middlesbrough
Albert Town 126 C1
Albourne 109 E3
Albourne Green 109 E2
Albrighton *Shrop* 158 A2
Albrighton *Shrop* 157 D1
Alburgh 165 D2
Albury *Herts* 150 C5
Albury *Oxon* 134 B2
Albury *Surr* 121 F3
Albury End 150 C5
Albury Heath 121 F3
Albyfield 210 B2
Alcaig 266 C6
Alcaston 157 D4
Alciston 110 A3
Alcombe 114 C3
Alconbury 161 G5
Alconbury Hill 161 G5
Alconbury Weston 161 G5
Aldborough *Norf* 178 C2
Aldborough *NYorks* 194 D1
Aldbourne 133 E5
Aldbrough 197 E4
Aldbrough St. John 202 B1
Aldbury 135 E1
Aldclune 251 E3
Aldeburgh 153 F2
Aldeby 165 F2
Aldenham 136 A3
Aldenham Country Park *Herts* WD6 3AT 136 A3
Alderbury 118 C5
Alderford 178 C4
Aldergrove 282 E1
Alderholt 106 A1
Alderley 131 G3
Alderley Edge 184 C5
Aldermaston 119 G1
Aldermaston Wharf 120 B1
Alderminster 147 E3
Alderney 101 F4
Alderney Airport 101 F4
Alder's End 145 F4
Aldersey Green 170 B2
Aldershot 121 D2
Alderton *Glos* 146 B4
Alderton *Shrop* 157 D1
Alderton *Suff* 153 E3
Alderton *Wilts* 132 A4
Alderton *WN'hants* 148 C3
Alderwasley 173 E2
Aldfield 194 B1
Aldford 170 B2
Aldham *Essex* 152 A5
Aldham *Suff* 152 B3
Aldie *Aber* 269 J6
Aldie *High* 266 E3
Aldingbourne 108 B3
Aldingham 199 D5
Aldington *Kent* 124 C5
Aldington *Worcs* 146 C3
Aldivalloch 260 B2
Aldochlay 241 F5
Aldons 214 A2
Aldreth 162 C5
Aldridge 158 C2
Aldringham 153 F1
Aldsworth *Glos* 133 D2
Aldsworth *WSuss* 107 G2
Aldunie 260 B2
Aldville 243 E1
Aldwark *Derbys* 172 D2
Aldwark *NYorks* 195 D1
Aldwick 108 B4
Aldwincle 161 F4
Aldworth 134 A5
Alexandra Palace *GtLon* N22 7AY 12 A1
Alexandria 233 E2
Aley 115 E4
Aley Green 135 F1
Alfardisworthy 112 C4
Alfington 103 E3
Alfold 121 F4
Alfold Crossways 121 F4
Alfreton 173 F2
Alfrick 145 G2

Alfrick Pound 145 G2
Alfriston 110 A3
Algarkirk 176 A4
Alhampton 116 C4
Alkborough 196 A5
Alkerton 147 F3
Alkham 125 E4
Alkington 170 C4
Alkmonton 172 C4
All Cannings 118 B1
All Saints South Elmham 165 E2
All Stretton 157 D3
Allaleigh 101 E2
Allanaquoich 259 J5
Allancreich 260 D5
Allanfearn 266 E7
Allangillfoot 218 A2
Allanton *D&G* 216 D2
Allanton *EAyr* 225 E2
Allanton *NLan* 234 C4
Allanton *ScBord* 237 E3
Allanton *SLan* 234 B4
Allardice 253 G2
Allathasdal 254 B4
Allbrook 119 F5
Allendale Town 211 E2
Allenheads 211 E3
Allen's Green 137 D1
Allensford 211 G2
Allensmore 145 D4
Allenton 173 E4
Aller 116 B5
Allerby 209 D3
Allercombe 102 D3
Allerford *Devon* 99 E2
Allerford *Som* 114 C3
Allerston 204 B4
Allerthorpe 195 G3
Allerton *Mersey* 183 F4
Allerton *WYorks* 194 A4
Allerton Bywater 194 D5
Allerton Mauleverer 194 D2
Allesley 159 E4
Allestree 173 E4
Allet Common 96 B5
Allexton 160 D3
Allgreave 171 G1
Allhallows 124 A1
Allhallows-on-Sea 124 A1
Alligin Shuas 264 E6
Allimore Green 158 A1
Allington *Dorset* 104 A3
Allington *Lincs* 175 D3
Allington *Wilts* 118 B1
Allington *Wilts* 118 A5
Allington *Wilts* 132 A5
Allistragh 282 B4
Allithwaite 199 F5
Allnabad 273 G4
Alloa 243 D5
Allonby 209 D2
Allostock 184 B5
Alloway 224 B4
Allowenshay 103 G1
Allscot 157 G3
Allscott 157 F1
Allt na h-Airbhe 265 H2
Alltachonaich 247 G4
Alltbeithe 257 G2
Alltforgan 168 C5
Alltmawr 143 G3
Alltnacaillich 273 G4
Allt-nan-sùugh 257 F1
Alltsigh 258 B3
Alltwalis 142 A4
Allt-wen 128 D2
Alltyblaca 142 B3
Allwood Green 164 B4
Almeley 144 C2
Almeley Wootton 144 C2
Almer 105 F3
Almington 171 E4
Alminstone Cross 113 D3
Almiston Cross 113 D3
Almondbank 243 F2
Almondbury 185 F1
Almondell & Calderwood Country Park *WLoth* EH52 5PE 235 E3
Almondsbury 131 F4
Alne 195 D1
Alness 266 D5
Alnham 229 D5
Alnmouth 229 G5
Alnwick 229 F5
Alnwick Garden, The *N'umb* NE66 1YU 229 F5
Alperton 136 A4
Alphamstone 151 G4
Alpheton 151 G2
Alphington 102 C3
Alport 172 D1
Alpraham 170 C2
Alresford 152 B5
Alrewas 159 D1
Alrick 251 G3
Alsager 171 E2
Alsagers Bank 171 F3
Alsop en le Dale 172 C2
Alston *Cumb* 210 D3
Alston *Devon* 103 G2
Alston Sutton 116 B2
Alstone *Glos* 146 B4
Alstone *Som* 116 A3
Alstone *Staffs* 158 A1
Alstonefield 172 C2
Alswear 114 A5
Alt 184 D2
Altaghoney 285 H5
Altagoaghan 281 G4
Altandhu 272 B7
Altanduin 274 D6
Altarnun 97 G1
Altass 266 B2
Altens 261 H4
Alterwall 275 H2
Altham 193 D4
Althorne 138 C3
Althorp House *WN'hants* NN7 4HQ 148 B2
Althorpe 187 F2
Alticry 215 D5
Altmartin 281 G5
Altnafeadh 249 E4
Altnaharra 273 H5

Altnamackan 282 B6
Altofts 194 C5
Alton *Derbys* 173 E1
Alton *Hants* 120 C4
Alton *Staffs* 172 B3
Alton Barnes 118 C1
Alton Pancras 104 D2
Alton Priors 118 C1
Alton Towers Leisure Park *Staffs* ST10 4DB 172 B3
Alton Water Reservoir *Suff* IP9 2RY 152 C4
Altonside 267 K6
Altrincham 184 B4
Altura 257 J5
Alva 243 D5
Alvanley 183 F5
Alvaston 173 E4
Alvechurch 158 C5
Alvecote 159 E2
Alvediston 118 A5
Alveley 157 G4
Alverdiscott 113 F3
Alverstoke 107 F3
Alverstone 107 E4
Alverthorpe 194 C5
Alverton 174 C3
Alves 267 J5
Alvescot 133 E2
Alveston *SGlos* 131 F4
Alveston *Warks* 147 E2
Alvie 259 F4
Alvingham 189 D3
Alvington 131 F2
Alwalton 161 G3
Alweston 104 C1
Alwington 113 E3
Alwinton 220 B1
Alwoodley 194 C3
Alwoodley Gates 194 C3
Alyth 252 A5
Am Bac (Back) 271 G3
Amalebra 94 B3
Ambaston 173 E4
Amber Hill 176 A3
Ambergate 173 E2
Amberley *Glos* 132 A2
Amberley *WSuss* 108 C2
Amble 221 E1
Amblecote 158 A4
Ambleside 199 E3
Ambleston 140 D5
Ambrismore 232 B4
Ambrosden 134 B1
Amcotts 187 F1
Amersham 135 E3
Amerton 171 G5
Amerton Farm *Staffs* ST18 0LA 171 G5
Amesbury 118 C3
Ameysford 105 G2
Amhuinnsuidhe 270 C7
Amington 159 E2
Amisfield Town 217 E2
Amlwch 180 C3
Amlwch Port 180 C3
Ammanford (Rhydaman) 128 C1
Amotherby 203 G5
Ampfield 119 E5
Ampleforth 203 E5
Ampleforth College 203 E5
Ampney Crucis 132 C2
Ampney St. Mary 132 C2
Ampney St. Peter 132 C2
Amport 119 E3
Ampthill 149 F4
Ampton 163 G5
Amroth 127 E2
Amulree 243 D1
An Cnoc 271 G4
Anaboard 259 H1
Anahelt 248 A3
Ancaster 175 E3
Ancroft 237 G5
Ancrum 228 A4
Ancton 108 B3
Anderby 189 F5
Anderby Creek 189 F5
Andersea 116 A4
Andersfield 115 F4
Anderson 105 E3
Anderton 184 A5
Anderton Boat Lift *ChesW&C* CW9 6FW 184 A5
Andover 119 E3
Andover Down 119 E3
Andoversford 132 C1
Andreas 190 C2
Anelog 166 A5
Anfield 183 E3
Angarrack 94 C3
Angarrick 95 E3
Angelbank 157 E5
Angerton 209 F1
Angle 126 B2
Anglers Country Park *WYorks* WF4 2EB 186 A1
Angler's Retreat 154 D3
Anglesey (Ynys Môn) 180 B4
Anglesey Abbey & Gardens *Cambs* CB25 9EJ 150 D1
Anglesey Airport 180 B5
Angmering 108 C3
Angmering-on-Sea 108 C3
Angram *NYorks* 195 E3
Angram *NYorks* 201 D3
Anick 211 F1
Anie 242 A3
Ankerville 267 F4
Anlaby 196 C5
Anmer 177 F5
Anmore 107 F1
Anna Valley 119 E3
Annacloghmullin 282 C6
Annaclone 282 E4
Annaclay 283 H4
Annadorn 283 H4
Annaghbane 282 E5
Annaghmore 282 B2
Annahilt 283 F3
Annalong 283 G7

Annan 217 F4
Annaside 198 B4
Annat *A&B* 240 C2
Annat *High* 264 E6
Annbank 224 C3
Anne Hathaway's Cottage *Warks* CV37 9HH 147 D2
Annesley 173 G2
Annesley Woodhouse 173 F2
Annfield Plain 212 A2
Anniesland 233 G3
Annscroft 157 D2
Ansdell 191 G5
Ansford 116 D4
Ansley 173 E3
Anslow 172 D5
Anslow Gate 172 C5
Ansteadbrook 121 E4
Anstey *Herts* 150 C4
Anstey *Leics* 160 A2
Anstruther 245 D4
Ansty *Warks* 159 F4
Ansty *Wilts* 118 A5
Ansty *WSuss* 109 E1
Ansty Coombe 118 A5
Ansty Cross 105 D2
Anthill Common 107 F1
Anthorn 209 E1
Antingham 179 D2
Anton's Gowt 176 A3
Antonine Wall (Frontiers of the Roman Empire) *Central Scotland* 30 C2, 234 C2 etc.
Antony 99 D5
Antrim 287 F7
Antrim Castle Gardens *A&N* BT41 4LH 287 F7
Antrim Round Tower *A&N* BT41 1BL 287 F7
Antrobus 184 A5
Antynanum 287 F7
Anvil Corner 113 D5
Anvil Green 124 D3
Anwick 175 G2
Anwoth 215 G5
Aonach Mòr Mountain Gondola & Nevis Range Ski Centre *High* PH33 6SW 249 D2
Aoradh 230 A3
Apethorpe 161 F3
Apeton 158 A1
Apley 188 B5
Apperknowle 186 A5
Apperley 146 A5
Apperley Bridge 194 A4
Appersett 201 D3
Appin (An Apainn) 248 B5
Appin House 248 B5
Appleby 187 G1
Appleby Magna 159 F1
Appleby Parva 159 F2
Appleby-in-Westmorland 210 C5
Applecross 264 D7
Appledore *Devon* 113 E2
Appledore *Devon* 103 D1
Appledore *Kent* 111 F1
Appledore Heath 124 B5
Appleford 134 A3
Appleshaw 119 E3
Applethwaite 209 F4
Appleton *Halton* 183 G4
Appleton *Oxon* 133 G2
Appleton Roebuck 195 E3
Appleton Thorn 184 A4
Appleton Wiske 202 C2
Appleton-le-Moors 203 G5
Appleton-le-Street 203 G5
Appletreehall 227 G3
Appletreewick 193 G1
Appley 115 D5
Appley Bridge 183 G2
Apse Heath 107 E4
Apsey Green 153 D1
Apsley 135 F2
Apsley End 149 G4
Apuldram 108 A3
Arbeia Roman Fort & Museum (Frontiers of the Roman Empire) *T&W* NE33 2BB 28 E1
Arbirlot 253 E2
Arborfield 120 C1
Arborfield Cross 120 C1
Arborfield Garrison 120 C1
Arbourthorne 186 A4
Arbroath 253 F2
Arbuthnott 253 F2
Archdeacon Newton 202 B1
Archiestown 267 K7
Arclid 171 E1
Ard a' Chapuill 232 B1
Ardacheranbeg 232 B1
Ardacheranmor 232 B1
Ardachoil 239 G1
Ardachu 266 D1
Ardailly 231 E4
Ardalanish 238 C3
Ardallie 261 J1
Ardanaiseig 240 C2
Ardaneaskan 256 E1
Ardanstur 240 A3
Ardantiobairt 247 F4
Ardantrive 240 A2
Ardarragh 282 E5
Ardarroch 264 E7
Ardbeg *A&B* 232 B3
Ardbeg *A&B* 230 C5
Ardbeg *A&B* 232 C1
Ardblair 258 C1
Ardbrecknish 240 C2
Ardcharnich 265 H3
Ardchiavaig 238 C3
Ardchonnel 240 B1
Ardchrishnish 238 D2
Ardchronie 266 D3
Ardchuilk 257 J1
Ardchullarie More 242 A3
Ardchyle 242 A2

Arddleen 156 B1
Ardechvie 257 H5
Ardeley 150 B5
Ardelve 256 E2
Arden 233 E1
Ardencaple House 239 G3
Ardens Grafton 146 D2
Ardentallan 240 A2
Ardentinny 232 C1
Ardeonaig 242 B1
Ardery 247 G3
Ardessie 265 G3
Ardfad 239 G3
Ardfern 240 A4
Ardfin 230 C3
Ardgartan 241 E4
Ardgenavan 241 D3
Ardglass 283 J5
Ardgour (Corran) 248 C3
Ardgowan 232 D2
Ardgowse 260 E3
Ardgye 267 J5
Ardhallow 242 C2
Ardheslaig 264 D6
Ardiecow 268 D4
Ardindrean 265 H3
Ardingly 109 F1
Ardington 133 G4
Ardington Wick 133 G4
Ardintoul 256 E2
Ardkinglas House 241 D3
Ardkeen 283 K3
Ardlair 260 D2
Ardlamont 232 A3
Ardleigh 152 B5
Ardleigh Green 137 E4
Ardleigh Heath 152 B4
Ardleish 241 E4
Ardler 252 A5
Ardley 148 A5
Ardley End 137 E1
Ardlui (Àird Laoigh) 241 F3
Ardlussa 231 E1
Ardmaddy 240 C1
Ardmair 265 H2
Ardmaleish 232 B3
Ardmay 241 E4
Ardmenish 231 D2
Ardminish 231 E5
Ardmolich 247 G2
Ardmore *A&B* 230 C4
Ardmore *A&B* 239 G2
Ardmore *A&B* 233 E2
Ardmore *CC&G* 286 B3
Ardmore *High* 266 E3
Ardnackaig 239 G5
Ardnacross 247 E5
Ardnadrochit 239 G1
Ardnagoine 265 F1
Ardnagowan 240 D4
Ardnahein 241 D5
Ardnahoe 230 C2
Ardnastang 248 A3
Ardnave 230 A3
Ardno 241 D4
Ardo 261 G1
Ardoch *D&G* 225 G5
Ardoch *Moray* 267 J6
Ardoch *P&K* 243 F1
Ardochrig 234 A5
Ardoyne 260 E2
Ardpatrick 231 F3
Ardpeaton 232 D1
Ardquin 283 J3
Ardradnaig 250 C5
Ardress 282 C3
Ardrishaig 231 G1
Ardroe 272 C6
Ardross 263 H4
Ardrossan 232 D5
Ardscalpsie 232 B4
Ardshave 266 E2
Ardshealach 247 F3
Ardshellach 239 G3
Ardsley 186 A2
Ardslignish 247 E3
Ardstraw 285 F7
Ardtalla 230 C4
Ardtalnaig 242 C1
Ardtaraig 232 B1
Ardteatle 240 D2
Ardtoe 247 F2
Ardtole 283 J5
Ardtornish 247 G5
Ardtrostan 242 B2
Ardtur 248 B5
Arduaine 240 A3
Ardullie 266 C5
Ardura 239 F1
Ardvar 272 C5
Ardvasar 256 C4
Ardveich 242 B2
Ardverikie 250 A1
Ardvorlich *A&B* 241 F3
Ardvorlich *P&K* 242 B2
Ardwall 215 G3
Ardwell *D&G* 206 B2
Ardwell *Moray* 260 B1
Ardwell *SAyr* 214 C1
Ardwick 184 C3
Areley Kings 158 A5
Arford 120 D4
Argaty 242 C4
Argoed 130 A3
Argoed Mill 143 F1
Argos Hill 110 A1
Argrennan House 216 B5
Argyll & Sutherland
  Highlanders Museum
  Stir FK8 1EH 242 C5
Arichamish 240 B4
Arichastlich 241 E1
Arichonan 239 G5
Aridhglas 238 C2
Arienskill 247 G1
Arileod 246 A4
Arinacrinachd 264 D6
Arinafad Beg 231 F1
Arinagour 246 B4
Arinambane 254 C2
Arisaig (Àrasaig) 247 F3

Arivegaig 247 F3
Arkendale 194 C1
Arkesden 150 C4
Arkholme 199 G5
Arkle Town 201 F2
Arkleby 209 E3
Arkleside 201 F4
Arkleton 218 B2
Arkley 136 B3
Arksey 186 C2
Arkwright Town 186 B5
Arlary 243 G4
Arle 146 B5
Arlecdon 208 D5
Arlesey 149 G4
Arleston 157 F1
Arley 184 A4
Arlingham 131 G1
Arlington *Devon* 113 G1
Arlington *ESuss* 110 A3
Arlington *Glos* 132 C2
Arlington Beccott 113 G1
Armadale *High* 274 C2
Armadale *High* 256 C4
Armadale *WLoth* 234 D3
Armagh 282 C5
Armathwaite 210 B3
Arminghall 179 D5
Armitage 158 C1
Armitage Bridge 185 F1
Armley 194 B4
Armoy 286 E2
Armscote 147 E3
Armshead 171 G3
Armston 161 F4
Armthorpe 186 D2
Arnaby 198 C4
Arncliffe 201 E5
Arncliffe Cote 201 E5
Arncroach 244 D4
Arne 105 F4
Arnesby 160 B3
Arney 280 E5
Arngask 243 G3
Arngibbon 242 B5
Arngomery 242 B5
Arnhall 253 E3
Arnicle 222 C2
Arnipol 247 G1
Arnisdale
  (Arnasdal) 256 E3
Arnish 264 B7
Arniston Engine 236 A3
Arnol 271 F3
Arnold *ERid* 196 D3
Arnold *Notts* 173 G3
Arnolfini Gallery
  BS1 4QA 66 Bristol
Arnprior 242 B5
Arnside 199 F5
Aros Centre *High*
  IV51 9EU 263 K7
Arowry 170 B2
Arrad Foot 199 E4
Arradoul 268 C4
Arram 196 C3
Arran 223 E2
Arras 196 B3
Arrat 253 E4
Arrathorne 202 B3
Arreton 107 E4
Arrington 150 B2
Arrivain 241 E1
Arrochar 241 F4
Arrow 146 C2
Arscaig 273 H7
Arscott 156 D2
Arthington 194 B3
Arthingworth 160 C4
Arthog 154 C1
Arthrath 261 H1
Arthurstone 252 A5
Articlave 286 B2
Artigarvan 285 F5
Artikelly 285 J3
Artnagross 286 D4
Artrochie 261 J1
Aruadh 230 A3
Arundel 108 C3
Arundel Castle *WSuss*
  BN18 9AB 108 C3
Arundel Cathedral (R.C.)
  WSuss
  BN18 9AY 108 C3
Aryhoulan 248 C3
Asby 209 D4
Ascog 232 C3
Ascot 121 E1
Ascott 147 F4
Ascott d'Oyley 133 F1
Ascott Earl 133 E1
Ascott-under-
  Wychwood 133 F1
Ascreavie 252 B4
Asenby 202 D5
Asfordby 160 C1
Asfordby Hill 160 C1
Asgarby *Lincs* 176 B1
Asgarby *Lincs* 175 B3
Ash *Dorset* 105 E1
Ash *Kent* 125 E3
Ash *Kent* 123 F2
Ash *Som* 116 B5
Ash *Surr* 121 D2
Ash Barton 113 F5
Ash Bullayne 102 A2
Ash Green *Surr* 121 E3
Ash Green *Warks* 159 F4
Ash Magna 170 C4
Ash Mill 114 A5
Ash Parva 170 C4
Ash Priors 115 E5
Ash Street 152 B3
Ash Thomas 102 D1
Ash Vale 121 D2
Ashampstead 134 A5
Ashbocking 152 C2
Ashbourne 172 C3
Ashbrittle 115 D5
Ashburnham Place 110 B2
Ashburton 101 D1
Ashbury *Devon* 99 F1
Ashbury *Oxon* 133 D4
Ashby 188 A3
Ashby by Partney 176 C1
Ashby cum Fenby 188 C2
Ashby de la Launde 175 F2

Ashby de la Zouch 159 F1
Ashby Dell 165 F2
Ashby Folville 160 C1
Ashby Hill 188 C2
Ashby Magna 160 A3
Ashby Parva 160 A4
Ashby Puerorum 188 D5
Ashby St. Ledgers 148 A1
Ashby St. Mary 179 E5
Ashchurch 146 B4
Ashcombe *Devon* 102 C5
Ashcombe *NSom* 116 A1
Ashcott 116 A4
Ashdon 151 D3
Ashe 119 G3
Asheldham 138 C2
Ashen 151 F3
Ashenden 124 A5
Ashendon 134 C1
Ashens 231 G2
Ashey 107 E4
Ashfield *Here* 145 E5
Ashfield *Stir* 242 C4
Ashfield *Suff* 152 D1
Ashfield Green *Suff* 165 D4
Ashfield Green *Suff* 151 F2
Ashfold Crossways 109 E1
Ashford *Devon* 100 C3
Ashford *Devon* 113 F2
Ashford *Hants* 106 A1
Ashford *Kent* 124 C4
Ashford *Surr* 135 F5
Ashford Bowdler 157 E5
Ashford Carbonel 157 E5
Ashford Hill 119 G1
Ashford in the
  Water 185 F5
Ashgill 234 B4
Ashiestiel 227 F2
Ashill *Devon* 103 D1
Ashill *Norf* 163 G2
Ashill *Som* 103 G1
Ashingdon 138 B3
Ashington *N'umb* 221 E3
Ashington *Som* 116 C5
Ashington *WSuss* 108 D2
Ashkirk 227 F3
Ashlett 107 D2
Ashleworth 146 A5
Ashleworth Quay 146 A5
Ashley *Cambs* 151 E1
Ashley *ChesE* 184 B4
Ashley *Devon* 113 G4
Ashley *Glos* 132 B3
Ashley *Hants* 119 E4
Ashley *Hants* 106 B3
Ashley *Kent* 125 F4
Ashley *NN'hants* 160 C3
Ashley *Staffs* 171 E4
Ashley *Wilts* 117 F1
Ashley Down 155 E5
Ashley Green 135 E2
Ashley Heath
  Dorset 106 A2
Ashley Heath
  Staffs 171 E4
Ashmanhaugh 179 E3
Ashmansworth 119 F2
Ashmansworthy 112 D4
Ashmolean Museum
  Oxon OX1 2PH
  80 Oxford
Ashmore *Dorset* 105 F1
Ashmore *P&K* 251 G4
Ashmore Green 119 G1
Ashorne 147 F2
Ashover 173 E1
Ashover Hay 173 E1
Ashow 159 F5
Ashperton 145 F3
Ashprington 101 E2
Ashreigney 113 G4
Ashridge Estate *Herts*
  HP4 1LX 135 E1
Ashtead 121 G2
Ashton *ChesW&C* 170 C1
Ashton *Corn* 94 D4
Ashton *Corn* 99 D4
Ashton *Hants* 107 E1
Ashton *Here* 145 E1
Ashton *Invcly* 232 D2
Ashton *NN'hants* 161 F4
Ashton *Peter* 161 G2
Ashton *WN'hants* 148 C3
Ashton Common 117 F2
Ashton Court Estate
  NSom BS41 9JN 8 B3
Ashton Keynes 132 C3
Ashton under Hill 146 B4
Ashton upon
  Mersey 184 B3
Ashton-in-
  Makerfield 183 G3
Ashton-under-Lyne 184 D3
Ashurst *Hants* 106 C1
Ashurst *Kent* 123 E5
Ashurst *WSuss* 109 D2
Ashurst Bridge 106 C1
Ashurstwood 122 C5
Ashwater 99 D1
Ashwell *Herts* 150 A4
Ashwell *Rut* 161 D1
Ashwell End 150 A3
Ashwellthorpe 164 C2
Ashwick 116 D3
Ashwicken 163 F1
Ashybank 227 G4
Askam in Furness 198 D5
Askern 186 C1
Askernish
  (Aisgernis) 254 C2
Askerswell 104 B3
Askett 134 D2
Askham *Cumb* 210 B5
Askham *Notts* 187 E5
Askham Bryan 195 E3
Askham Richard 195 E3
Asknish 240 B5
Askrigg 201 E3
Askwith 194 A3
Aslackby 175 F4
Aslacton 164 C2
Aslockton 174 C3
Asloun 260 D3
Aspall 152 C1
Aspatria 209 E2
Aspenden 150 B5

Asperton 176 A4
Aspley Guise 149 E4
Aspley Heath 149 E4
Aspull 184 A2
Asselby 195 G5
Asserby 188 C5
Assington 152 A4
Assington Green 151 F2
Astbury 171 F1
Astcote 148 B2
Asterby 188 C5
Asterley 156 D2
Asterton 156 D3
Asthall 133 F1
Asthall Leigh 133 F1
Astle 184 C5
Astley *GtMan* 184 B2
Astley *Shrop* 157 E1
Astley *Warks* 159 F4
Astley *Worcs* 145 G1
Astley Abbotts 157 G3
Astley Bridge 184 B1
Astley Cross 146 A1
Astley Green 184 B3
Astley Lodge 157 E1
Aston *ChesE* 170 D3
Aston *ChesW&C* 183 G5
Aston *Derbys* 185 F4
Aston *Derbys* 172 C5
Aston *Flints* 170 A1
Aston *Here* 157 D5
Aston *Here* 145 D1
Aston *Herts* 150 A5
Aston *Oxon* 133 F2
Aston *Shrop* 170 C5
Aston *Shrop* 158 A3
Aston *Staffs* 171 E3
Aston *SYorks* 186 B4
Aston *Tel&W* 157 F2
Aston *W'ham* 134 C4
Aston *WMid* 158 C4
Aston Abbotts 149 D5
Aston Botterell 157 F4
Aston Cantlow 146 D2
Aston Clinton 135 D1
Aston Crews 145 F5
Aston Cross 146 B4
Aston End 150 A5
Aston Eyre 157 F3
Aston Fields 146 B1
Aston Flamville 159 G3
Aston Heath 183 G5
Aston Ingham 145 F5
Aston juxta
  Mondrum 171 D2
Aston le Walls 147 G2
Aston Magna 147 D4
Aston Munslow 157 E4
Aston on Carrant 146 B4
Aston on Clun 156 C4
Aston Pigott 156 C2
Aston Rogers 156 C2
Aston Rowant 134 C3
Aston Sandford 134 C2
Aston Somerville 146 C4
Aston Subedge 146 D3
Aston Tirrold 134 A4
Aston-by-Stone 171 G4
Aston-on-Trent 173 F5
Astwick 150 A4
Astwood 149 E3
Astwood Bank 146 C1
Aswarby 175 F3
Aswardby 189 D5
Aswick Grange 162 B1
Atch Lench 146 C2
Atcham 157 E2
Ath Linne 270 D6
Athelhampton 105 D3
Athelington 164 D4
Athelney 116 A5
Athelstaneford 236 C2
Atherfield Green 107 E5
Atherington *Devon* 113 F3
Atherington *WSuss* 108 C3
Atherstone 159 F3
Atherstone on Stour 147 E2
Atherton 184 A2
Atlow 172 D3
Attadale 257 D1
Attanhole 285 E2
Attenborough 173 G4
Attenborough Nature
  Reserve *Nott* NG9 6DY
  19 F4
Atterby 187 G3
Attercliffe 186 A4
Atterley 157 F3
Atterton 159 F3
Attical 283 F7
Attingham Park
  Shrop SY4 4TP 157 E1
Attleborough *Norf*
  164 B2
Attleborough
  Warks 159 F3
Attlebridge 178 C4
Attleton Green 151 F2
Atwick 197 D2
Atworth 117 F1
Auberrow 145 D3
Aubourn 175 E1
Auch 241 F1
Auchairne 214 C2
Auchallater 251 G1
Auchameanach 231 G4
Auchamore 231 G5
Aucharnie 268 E6
Aucharrigill 266 B1
Auchattie 260 E5
Auchavan 251 G3
Auchbraad 231 G1
Auchbreck 259 K2
Auchenback 233 G4
Auchenblae 253 F2
Auchenbothie 232 D2
Auchenbrack 216 B1
Auchenbreck 216 B4
Auchencairn 216 B5
Auchencrow 237 F3
Auchendinny 235 G3
Auchendolly 216 B4
Auchenfoyle 233 E2
Auchengillan 233 G1
Auchengray 235 D4
Auchenhalrig 268 B4
Auchenharvie 233 E5
Auchenheath 234 C5

Auchenhessnane 216 C1
Auchenlochan 232 A2
Auchenmalg 214 D5
Auchenrivock 218 B3
Auchentiber 233 E5
Auchenvennel 232 D1
Auchessan 241 G2
Auchgourish 259 G3
Auchinafaud 231 F4
Auchincruive 224 B3
Auchindarrach 231 G1
Auchindarroch 248 C4
Auchindrain 240 C4
Auchindrean 265 H3
Auchininna 268 E6
Auchinleck 234 A2
Auchinloch 234 A2
Auchinner 242 B3
Auchinroath 267 K6
Auchintoul *Aber* 260 D3
Auchintoul *Aber* 260 E5
Auchintoul *High* 266 C5
Auchiries 261 J1
Auchleven 260 E2
Auchlochan 225 G2
Auchlunachan 265 H3
Auchlunies 261 G5
Auchlunkart 268 B6
Auchlyne 242 A2
Auchmacoy 261 H1
Auchmair 260 B2
Auchmantle 214 C4
Auchmithie 253 E5
Auchmuirbridge 244 A4
Auchmull 253 E3
Auchnabony 208 A2
Auchnabreac 240 C4
Auchnacloich 242 D1
Auchnacraig 239 G1
Auchnacree 252 C3
Auchnafree 242 D1
Auchnagallin 259 H1
Auchnagatt 269 H6
Auchnaha 232 A1
Auchnangoul 240 C4
Auchnha 252 A4
Auchnotteroch 214 A4
Aucholzie 260 B5
Auchorrie 260 E4
Auchrannie 252 A4
Auchraw 242 A2
Auchreoch 241 F2
Auchronie 252 C2
Auchterarder 243 E3
Auchtercairn 264 E4
Auchterderran 244 A5
Auchterhouse 244 B1
Auchterless 269 F6
Auchtermuchty 244 A3
Auchterneed 266 B6
Auchtertool 244 A5
Auchtertyre *Angus* 252 A5
Auchtertyre (Uachdar Thire)
  High 256 E2
Auchtertyre *Moray* 267 J6
Auchtertyre *Stir* 241 F2
Auchtubh 242 A2
Auckengill 275 J2
Auckley 186 D2
Audenshaw 184 D3
Audlem 171 D3
Audley 171 E2
Audley End *Essex* 150 D4
Audley End *Essex* 151 G4
Audley End *Suff* 151 G2
Audmore 171 F1
Auds 268 E4
Aughaboy 287 H5
Aughamullan 282 B2
Aughentaine 281 G3
Augher 281 H3
Aughnacloy 281 J3
Aughnaloopy 283 F7
Aughnaskeagh 283 F4
Aughrim 286 D6
Aughton *ERid* 195 G4
Aughton *Lancs* 183 E2
Aughton *Lancs* 192 B1
Aughton *SYorks* 186 B4
Aughton *Wilts* 118 D2
Aughton Park 183 E2
Auldearn 267 G6
Aulden 145 D2
Auldgirth 216 D2
Auldhame 236 C1
Auldhouse 234 A4
Aulich 250 B4
Ault a'chruinn 257 F2
Ault Hucknall 173 F1
Aultanrynie 273 F5
Aultbea
  (An t-Allt Beithe) 264 E3
Aultgrishan 264 D3
Aultguish Inn 265 K4
Aultibea 275 F6
Aultiphurst 274 D2
Aultmore 268 C5
Ault-na-goire 258 C2
Aultnamain Inn 266 D4
Aultnapaddock 268 B6
Aulton 260 E2
Aultvaich 266 C7
Aultvoulin 256 D4
Aunby 161 F2
Aundorach 259 G3
Aunk 102 D2
Aunsby 175 F4
Auquharthies 261 G2
Aust 131 E4
Austerfield 187 D3
Austrey 159 E2
Austwick 193 D1
Authorpe 189 E4
Authorpe Row 189 F5
Avebury 132 D5
Avebury Ring (Stonehenge,
  Avebury & Associated Sites)
  Wilts SN8 1RF 132 D5
Aveley 137 E4
Avening 132 A3
Averham 174 C2
Avery Hill 136 D5
Aveton Gifford 100 C3
Avielochan 259 G3
Aviemore 259 F3
Avington *Hants* 119 G4
Avington *WBerks* 119 E5
Avoch 266 D6
Avon 106 A3

Avon Dassett 147 G2
Avon Heath Country Park
  Dorset BH24 2DA 3 E1
Avon Valley Railway *SGlos*
  BS30 6HD 8 E4
Avonbridge 234 D2
Avoncliff 117 F2
Avonmouth 131 E5
Avonwick 100 D2
Awbridge 119 E5
Awhirk 214 B5
Awkley 131 E4
Awliscombe 103 E2
Awre 131 G2
Awsworth 173 F3
Axbridge 116 B2
Axford *Hants* 120 B3
Axford *Wilts* 133 E5
Axminster 103 F3
Axmouth 103 F3
Axton 182 C4
Axtown 100 B1
Aycliffe 212 B5
Aydon 211 F1
Aylburton 131 F2
Ayle 210 D3
Aylesbeare 102 D3
Aylesbury 134 D1
Aylesby 188 C2
Aylesford 123 G3
Aylesham 125 E3
Aylestone 160 A2
Aylmerton 178 C2
Aylsham 178 C3
Aylton 145 F4
Aymestrey 144 D1
Aynho 148 A4
Ayot Green 136 B1
Ayot St. Lawrence 136 A1
Ayot St. Peter 136 B1
Ayr 224 B3
Aysgarth 201 F4
Aysgarth Falls & National
  Park Centre *NYorks*
  DL8 3TH 201 F4
Ayshford 102 D1
Ayside 199 E4
Ayston 161 D2
Aythorpe Roding 137 E1
Ayton *P&K* 243 G3
Ayton *ScBord* 237 G3
Aywick 278 E4
Azerley 202 B5

B
Babbacombe 101 F1
Babbacombe Model Village
  Torbay TQ1 3LA 101 F1
Babbinswood 170 A4
Babb's Green 136 C1
Babcary 116 C5
Babel 143 E4
Babell 182 C5
Babeny 99 G3
Bablock Hythe 133 G2
Babraham 150 D2
Babworth 187 D4
Baby's Hill 259 K1
Bachau 180 C4
Back of Keppoch 247 F1
Back Street 151 F2
Backaland 276 E4
Backaskaill 276 D2
Backbarrow 199 E4
Backburn 260 D1
Backe 127 F1
Backfolds 269 J5
Backford 183 F5
Backhill 261 F1
Backhill of
  Clackriach 269 H6
Backies *High* 267 F1
Backies *Moray* 268 D5
Backlass 275 H3
Backside 260 C1
Backwell 116 B1
Backworth 221 E4
Bacon End 137 F1
Baconend Green 137 F1
Baconsthorpe 178 C2
Bacton *Here* 144 C4
Bacton *Norf* 179 E2
Bacton *Suff* 152 B1
Bacton Green 152 B1
Bacup 193 E5
Badachro 264 D4
Badanloch Lodge 274 C5
Badavanich 265 H6
Badbea 275 F7
Badbury 133 D4
Badbury Wick 133 D4
Badby 148 A2
Badcall *High* 272 D3
Badcall *High* 272 E3
Badcaul 265 G2
Baddeley Green 171 G2
Baddesley Clinton 159 D5
Baddesley Clinton *Warks*
  B93 0DQ 159 D5
Baddesley Ensor 159 E3
Baddidarach 272 C6
Baddoch 251 F1
Badenscoth 261 F1
Badenyon 260 B3
Badgall 97 G1
Badger 157 G3
Badgerbank 184 C5
Badgers Mount 123 D2
Badgeworth 132 B1
Badgworth 116 A2
Badicaul 256 D2
Badingham 153 E1
Badintagairt 273 G7
Badlesmere 124 C3
Badley 152 B2
Badlipster 275 H4
Badluarach 265 F2
Badminton 132 A4
Badnaban 272 C6
Badnabay 272 E4
Badnafrave 259 K3
Badnagie 275 G5
Badnambiast 250 C2
Badninish 266 E2
Badrallach 265 G2
Badsey 146 C3
Badshot Lea 121 D3

Badsworth 186 B1
Badwell Ash 152 A1
Badworthy 100 C1
Badyo 251 E3
Bag Enderby 189 D5
Bagber 105 D1
Bagby 203 D4
Bagendon 132 C2
Bagginswood 157 F4
Baggrave Hall 160 B2
Baggrow 209 E2
Bàgh Mòr 262 D6
Bagillt 182 D5
Baginton 159 F5
Baglan 128 D3
Bagley *Shrop* 170 B5
Bagley *Som* 116 B3
Bagmore 120 B3
Bagnall 171 G2
Bagnor 119 F1
Bagpath 132 A3
Bagshot *Surr* 121 E1
Bagshot *Wilts* 119 E1
Bagstone 131 F4
Bagthorpe *Norf* 177 F4
Bagthorpe *Notts* 173 F2
Baguley 184 C4
Bagworth 159 G2
Bagwyllydiart 144 D5
Baildon 194 A4
Baile Ailein 270 E5
Baile an Truiseil
  (Ballantrushal) 271 F2
Baile Gharbhaidh (Balgarva)
  262 C7
Baile Glas 262 D6
Baile Lòin 262 C5
Baile Mhàrtainn 262 C4
Baile Mhic' Phàil 262 D4
Baile Mòr 238 B2
Baile nan Cailleach 262 C6
Baile Raghaill 262 C5
Bailebeag 258 C3
Baileguish 259 F5
Baile-na-Cille 262 D3
Bailetonach 247 F2
Bailiesward 260 C1
Bailiff Bridge 194 A5
Baillieston 234 A3
Bainbridge 201 E3
Bainsford 234 C1
Bainshole 260 E1
Bainton *ERid* 196 B2
Bainton *Oxon* 148 A5
Bainton *Peter* 161 F2
Bairdstown 283 K1
Bairnkine 228 A5
Bakebare 260 B1
Baker Street 137 F4
Baker's End 136 C1
Bakewell 172 D1
Bala (Y Bala) 168 C4
Balachulish 264 B7
Balado 243 F4
Balafark 242 B5
Balaldie 267 F4
Balavil 258 E4
Balbeg *High* 258 B1
Balbeg *High* 258 B2
Balbeggie 243 G2
Balbirnie 244 A4
Balblair 266 E5
Balblair *High* 266 C5
Balblair *High* 266 E3
Balby 186 C2
Balcharn 266 C1
Balcherry 267 F3
Balchers 269 F5
Balchladich 272 C5
Balchraggan *High* 266 C7
Balchraggan *High* 258 C1
Balchrick 272 D3
Balcombe 122 C5
Balcurvie 244 B4
Baldernock 233 G2
Baldersby 202 C5
Baldersby St. James
  202 C5
Balderstone
  GtMan 184 D1
Balderstone *Lancs* 192 C4
Balderton
  ChesW&C 170 A1
Balderton *Notts* 174 D2
Baldhu 96 B5
Baldinnie 244 C3
Baldock 150 A4
Baldovie *Angus* 252 B4
Baldovie *Dundee* 244 C1
Baldrine 190 C3
Baldslow 110 C2
Baldwin 190 B3
Baldwinholme 209 G1
Baldwin's Gate 171 E3
Baldwins Hill 122 C5
Bale 178 B2
Balemartine 246 A2
Balemore
  (Baile Mòr) 262 C5
Balendoch 252 A5
Balephuil 246 A2
Balerno 235 F3
Balernock 233 D1
Baleromindubh 238 C5
Baleromore 238 C5
Baleshare
  (Bhaleshear) 262 C5
Balevulin 238 C2
Balfield 252 D3
Balfour *Aber* 260 D5
Balfour *Ork* 277 D6
Balfron 233 G1
Balfron Station 233 G1
Balgaveny 268 E6
Balgonar 243 E5
Balgove 261 G1
Balgowan *D&G* 206 B2
Balgowan *High* 258 D5
Balgown 263 J5
Balgreen 269 F5
Balgreggan 214 B5
Balgy 264 E6
Balhaldie 242 D4

Balhalgardy 261 F2
Balham 136 B5
Balhary 252 A5
Balhelvie 244 B2
Baliasta 278 F2
Baligill 274 D2
Baligrundle 248 A5
Balindore 240 B1
Balintore Angus 252 A4
Balintore High 267 F4
Balintraid 266 E4
Balintyre 250 B5
Balivanich (Baile a'Mhanaich) 262 C6
Balix 285 G5
Balkeerie 252 B5
Balkholme 195 G5
Balkissock 214 C2
Ball 170 A5
Ball Haye Green 171 G2
Ball Hill 119 F1
Balla 254 C3
Ballabeg 190 A4
Ballacannell 190 C3
Ballacarnane Beg 190 A3
Ballachulish (Baile a' Chaolais) 248 D2
Balladoole 190 A5
Ballafesson 190 A4
Ballagh 281 G5
Ballagh Bridge 283 G6
Ballagyr 190 A3
Ballajora 190 C2
Ballakilpheric 190 A4
Ballamodha 190 A4
Ballantrae 214 B2
Ballard 282 D6
Ballards Gore 138 C3
Ballasalla IoM 190 A4
Ballasalla IoM 190 B2
Ballater 260 B5
Ballaterach 260 C5
Ballaugh 190 B2
Ballaveare 190 B4
Ballchraggan 266 E4
Ballechin 251 E4
Balleer 282 B5
Balleich 242 A4
Ballencrieff 236 B2
Balleny 286 C2
Ballidon 172 D2
Balliekine 251 D4
Balliemeanoch 240 D4
Balliemore A&B 240 D5
Balliemore A&B 240 A4
Ballig 190 A3
Balligan 283 K2
Ballimeanoch 240 C3
Ballimore A&B 232 A1
Ballimore Stir 242 A3
Ballinaby 230 A3
Ballinamallard 280 E3
Ballindarragh 281 F5
Ballindean 244 A2
Ballinderry 286 D7
Ballingdon 151 G3
Ballinger Common 135 E2
Ballingham 145 E4
Ballingry 243 G5
Ballinlea 286 E2
Ballinlick 251 E5
Ballinluig P&K 251 E4
Ballinluig P&K 251 F4
Ballinran 283 G7
Ballinteer 286 C2
Ballintoy 286 E1
Ballintuim 251 G4
Balloch Angus 252 B4
Balloch High 266 E7
Balloch NLan 234 B2
Balloch WDun 233 E1
Ballochan 260 D5
Ballochandrain 232 A1
Ballochford 260 B1
Ballochgair 222 C3
Ballochmartin 232 C4
Ballochmorrie 214 C2
Ballochmyle 224 D3
Ballochroy 231 F4
Ballogie 260 D5
Balloo 283 H2
Balloo Lower 287 K7
Balloolymore 282 A4
Balls Cross 121 E5
Balls Green Essex 152 B3
Ball's Green Glos 132 A3
Balls Hill 158 B3
Ballsmill 282 C7
Ballyaghlis 283 G2
Ballyalton 283 J4
Ballyard 281 F3
Ballyardel 283 F7
Ballyaurgan 231 F2
Ballybannan 283 G5
Ballybogy 286 D2
Ballybollen 286 E6
Ballyboyland 286 D3
Ballybrack 281 H1
Ballybriest 286 B7
Ballycarry 287 J6
Ballycassidy 280 E3
Ballycastle 287 F1
Ballyclare 287 G6
Ballycloghan 283 H2
Ballyconnelly 283 G2
Ballycraigy 287 H5
Ballydan 283 H3
Ballydivity 286 D2
Ballydoolagh 280 E4
Ballydrain 283 H2
Ballydugan 283 H4
Ballydullaghan 286 C5
Ballyeaston 282 G6
Ballyesborough 283 K3
Ballygarvey 287 F5
Ballygawley 281 J3
Ballyginniff Milltown 287 F7
Ballygordan 282 E6
Ballygowan A&NDown 283 H2
Ballygowan AB&C 282 E4
Ballygowan NM&D 283 F7
Ballygowan 246 D5
Ballygrant 230 B3
Ballyhalbert 283 K2

Ballyhaugh 246 A4
Ballyhill 283 F1
Ballyhoe Bridge 286 E3
Ballyholme 287 K7
Ballyhome 286 C2
Ballyhornan 283 J4
Ballyhosset 283 J5
Ballyhushey 281 G2
Ballykee F&O 285 G7
Ballykeel L&C 283 F3
Ballykeel NM&D 283 G7
Ballykelly 285 J3
Ballykennedy 283 F1
Ballykinler 283 H5
Ballyknock CC&G 286 E3
Ballyknock Mid Ulster 286 C5
Ballyleny 282 C4
Ballylesson 283 G2
Ballylintagh 286 C3
Ballyloughbeg 286 D2
Ballylucas 280 E4
Ballylumford 287 J5
Ballymacashen 283 H2
Ballymackilroy 281 J3
Ballymaconnelly 286 D4
Ballymacormick 283 F3
Ballymacran 285 J3
Ballymagorry 285 F5
Ballymaguigan 286 D7
Ballymartin NM&D 283 G7
Ballymartin AB&C 282 B4
Ballymena 287 F5
Ballymichael 223 E2
Ballymoney 286 D3
Ballymoyer 282 C5
Ballymultimber 285 J2
Ballymultrea 286 D7
Ballymurphy 283 J4
Ballynabragget 282 E3
Ballynagard 283 G3
Ballynagarrick 283 G3
Ballynahatty 281 G2
Ballynahinch 283 G3
Ballynahone Beg 282 B4
Ballynakilly 282 B2
Ballynamallaght 285 G6
Ballynasaggart 281 H3
Ballyneaner 285 H5
Ballynoe A&N 287 F6
Ballynoe NM&D 283 H5
Ballynure 287 H6
Ballyquintin 283 K4
Ballyrashane 286 C2
Ballyreagh F&O 281 F4
Ballyreagh Mid Ulster 281 J3
Ballyrisk 286 B3
Ballyrobert 287 G7
Ballyrogan 286 C4
Ballyronan 286 D7
Ballyroney 283 F3
Ballysallagh 283 F3
Ballyskeagh 283 F2
Ballystrudder 287 J6
Ballyvally 282 E6
Ballyveagh 283 G7
Ballyvennox 286 C3
Ballyvoy 287 F1
Ballywalter 283 K2
Ballyward 283 F3
Ballywatermoy 286 E5
Ballywatticock 283 J1
Ballywildrick 286 B2
Balmacara (Baile Mac Ara) 256 E3
Balmaclellan 216 A3
Balmacneil 251 E4
Balmadies 283 G2
Balmae 207 G2
Balmaha 241 G5
Balmalcolm 244 B4
Balmaqueen 263 K4
Balmedie 261 H3
Balmerino 244 B2
Balmerlawn 106 C2
Balminnoch 215 D4
Balmore EDun 234 A2
Balmore High 257 F3
Balmore High 257 K1
Balmore High 266 H7
Balmore P&K 250 C4
Balmullo 244 C2
Balmungie 266 E6
Balmyle 251 F4
Balnaboth 252 A3
Balnabruaich 266 E4
Balnacra 265 F7
Balnafoich 258 D1
Balnaguard 251 E4
Balnaguisich 266 D4
Balnahard A&B 238 D5
Balnahard A&B 239 D1
Balnain 258 B1
Balnakeil 273 F2
Balnaknock 263 K5
Balnamoon 252 D3
Balnamore 286 D3
Balnapaling 266 E5
Balnespick 259 F4
Balquhidder 242 A2
Balsall 159 E5
Balsall Common 159 E5
Balsall Heath 158 C4
Balscote 147 F3
Balsham 151 E3
Baltasound 278 F2
Balterley 171 E2
Balterley Heath 171 E2
Baltersan 215 F4
Balthangie 269 G5
Balthayock 243 G2
Baltonsborough 116 C2
Baluachraig 240 A5
Balulive 230 C3
Balure A&B 240 B1
Balure A&B 240 A1
Balvaird 266 C6
Balvarran 251 F3

Balvicar 239 G3
Balvraid High 256 E3
Balvraid High 259 F1
Bamber Bridge 192 B5
Bamber's Green 151 D5
Bamburgh 229 F3
Bamburgh Castle N'umb NE69 7DF 229 F3
Bamff 252 A4
Bamford Derbys 185 G4
Bamford GtMan 184 D1
Bampton Cumb 199 G1
Bampton Devon 114 C5
Bampton Oxon 133 F2
Bampton Grange 199 G1
Banavie (Banbhaidh) 248 D2
Banbridge 282 E4
Banbury 147 G3
Banbury Museum Oxon OX16 2PQ 147 G4
Bancffosfelen 128 A1
Banchor 267 G7
Banchory 261 F5
Banchory Devenick 261 H4
Bancycapel 128 A1
Bancyfelin 127 G1
Banc-y-ffordd 142 A4
Bandon 174 B1
Bandrake Head 199 E4
Banff 268 E4
Bangor A&NDown 287 K7
Bangor Gwynd 181 D5
Bangor-on-Dee (Bangor-is-y-coed) 170 A3
Bangor's Green 183 E2
Banham 164 B3
Banham Zoo Norf NR16 2HE 164 B3
Bank 106 B2
Bank End 198 C4
Bank Newton 193 F2
Bank Street 145 F1
Bank Top Lancs 183 G2
Bank Top WYorks 194 A5
Bankend 217 E4
Bankfoot 243 F1
Bankglen 225 D4
Bankhead Aber 260 E4
Bankhead Aber 260 E4
Bankhead Aberdeen 261 G3
Bankhead D&G 208 A2
Bankland 116 A5
Banknock 234 B2
Banks Cumb 210 B3
Banks Lancs 191 G5
Bankshill 217 F2
Banners Gate 158 C3
Banningham 178 D3
Bannister Green 151 E5
Bannockburn 242 D5
Banstead 122 B3
Bantam Grove 194 B5
Bantham 100 C3
Banton 234 B2
Banwell 116 A2
Banwen Pyrddin 129 G2
Banyard's Green 165 E4
Bapchild 124 B2
Baptiston 233 G1
Bapton 118 A4
Bar End 119 F5
Bar Hill 150 B1
Bar Hill Fort (Frontiers of the Roman Empire) EDun 31 G1
Barachander 240 C2
Baranailt 285 J4
Barassie 224 B2
Barbaraville 286 E4
Barber Booth 185 F4
Barber Green 189 E4
Barber's Moor 183 F1
Barbican Arts & Conference Centre GtLon EC2Y 8DS 45 J1
Barbon 200 B4
Barbridge 170 D2
Barbrook 114 A3
Barby 160 A5
Barcaldine (Am Barra Calltainn) 248 C2
Barcaple 216 A5
Barcheston 147 E4
Barclose 210 A1
Barcombe 109 G2
Barcombe Cross 109 G2
Barden 202 A3
Barden Park 123 E4
Bardennoch 215 G2
Bardfield End Green 151 E4
Bardfield Saling 151 E5
Bardister 278 C5
Bardney 175 G1
Bardon Leics 159 G1
Bardon Moray 267 K6
Bardon Mill 211 D2
Bardowie 233 G1
Bardsea 199 D5
Bardsey 194 C3
Bardsey Island (Ynys Enlli) 166 A5
Bardwell 164 A4

Barkham 120 C1
Barking GtLon 136 D4
Barking Suff 152 B2
Barking Tye 152 B2
Barkisland 193 G5
Barkston 175 E3
Barkston Ash 195 D4
Barkway 150 C4
Barlae 215 D4
Barland 144 B1
Barlaston 171 F4
Barlavington 108 B2
Barlborough 186 B5
Barlby 195 F4
Barley Herts 150 C4
Barley Lancs 193 E3
Barley Green 164 D4
Barleycroft End 150 C5
Barleyhill 211 G2
Barleythorpe 160 D2
Barling 138 C4
Barlings 188 A5
Barlow Derbys 186 A5
Barlow NYorks 195 F5
Barlow T&W 212 A1
Barmby Moor 195 G3
Barmby on the Marsh 195 F5
Barmer 177 G4
Barmolloch 240 A5
Barmoor Lane End 229 E3
Barmouth (Abermaw) 154 C1
Barmpton 202 C1
Barmston 197 D2
Barnaby Green 165 F4
Barnacabber 232 C1
Barnacarry 240 B5
Barnack 161 F2
Barnacle 159 F4
Barnamuc 248 C5
Barnard Castle 201 F1
Barnard Gate 133 G1
Barnardiston 151 F3
Barnard's Green 145 G3
Barnbarroch D&G 215 E5
Barnbarroch D&G 216 C5
Barnburgh 186 B2
Barnby 165 F3
Barnby Dun 186 D2
Barnby in the Willows 175 D2
Barnby Moor 187 D4
Barndennoch 216 C2
Barne Barton 100 A2
Barnehurst 137 E5
Barnes D&S 285 H6
Barnes GtLon 136 B5
Barnes Street 123 F4
Barnet 136 B3
Barnet Gate 136 B3
Barnetby le Beck 188 C2
Barnetby le Wold 188 A2
Barney 178 A2
Barnham Suff 163 G5
Barnham WSuss 108 B3
Barnham Broom 178 B5
Barnhead 253 E4
Barnhill ChesW&C 170 B2
Barnhill Dundee 244 C1
Barnhill Moray 267 J6
Barnhills 214 A3
Barningham Dur 201 F1
Barningham Suff 164 A4
Barningham Green 178 C2
Barnoldby le Beck 188 C2
Barnoldswick 193 E3
Barns Green 121 G5
Barnsdale Bar 186 C1
Barnsley Glos 132 C2
Barnsley SYorks 186 A2
Barnsole 125 E3
Barnstaple 113 F2
Barnston Essex 137 F1
Barnston Mersey 183 D5
Barnstone 174 C4
Barnt Green 158 C5
Barnton ChesW&C 184 A3
Barnton Edin 235 F2
Barnwell All Saints 161 F4
Barnwell Country Park N'hants PE8 5PB 161 F4
Barnwell St. Andrew 161 F4
Barnwood 146 A1
Barons' Cross 145 D2
Barr A&B 239 G4
Barr High 247 F4
Barr SAyr 215 D1
Barr Som 115 E5
Barr Hall 151 F4
Barra (Barraigh) 254 B4
Barra (Tràigh Mhòr) Airport 254 B4
Barrachan 207 D2
Barrackan 239 G4
Barraer 215 E4
Barraglom 270 D4
Barrahormid 231 F1
Barran 241 D2
Barrapoll 246 A2
Barrasford 220 B4
Barravullin 240 A4
Barregarrow 190 B3
Barrets Green 170 C2
Barrhead 233 G4
Barrhill 214 D2
Barrington Cambs 150 B3
Barrington Som 103 G1
Barripper 94 D3
Barrisdale 256 E4
Barrmill 233 F4
Barrnacarry 240 A2
Barrock 275 H1
Barrow Glos 146 A5
Barrow Lancs 192 D4
Barrow Rut 161 D1
Barrow Shrop 157 F2
Barrow Som 117 E4
Barrow Som 104 B5
Barrow Suff 151 F1
Barrow Gurney 116 C1
Barrow Hann 196 C5
Barrow Haven 196 C5
Barrow Hill 186 B5
Barrow Nook 183 F2
Barrow Street 117 F4

Barrow upon Humber 196 C5
Barrow upon Soar 160 A1
Barrow upon Trent 173 E5
Barroway Drove 163 D2
Barrowby 175 D4
Barrowcliff 204 D4
Barrowden 161 E2
Barrowford 193 E4
Barrow-in-Furness 191 F1
Barrows Green 199 G4
Barry Angus 244 D1
Barry VGlam 115 E1
Barry Island Pleasure Park VGlam CF62 5TR 115 E1
Barsby 160 B2
Barsham 165 E3
Barskimming 224 D3
Barston 159 E5
Barter Books, Alnwick N'umb NE66 2NP 229 F5
Bartestree 145 E3
Barthol Chapel 261 G1
Bartholomew Green 151 F5
Barthomley 171 E2
Bartley 106 C1
Bartley Green 158 C4
Bartlow 151 D3
Barton Cambs 150 C2
Barton ChesW&C 170 B2
Barton Cumb 210 A3
Barton Glos 146 C5
Barton Lancs 192 B4
Barton Lancs 183 E2
Barton NYorks 202 B2
Barton Oxon 134 A2
Barton Torbay 101 F1
Barton Warks 146 D2
Barton Bendish 163 F2
Barton End 132 A3
Barton Green 159 D1
Barton Hartshorn 148 B4
Barton Hill 195 G1
Barton in Fabis 173 G4
Barton in the Beans 159 F2
Barton Mills 163 F5
Barton-le-Clay 149 F4
Barton-le-Street 203 G5
Barton-le-Willows 195 G1
Barton-on-the-Heath 147 E4
Barton-under-Needwood 159 D1
Barton-upon-Humber 196 C5
Barvas (Barabhas) 271 F3
Barway 162 D5
Barwell 159 G3
Barwhinnock 216 A5
Barwick Herts 136 C1
Barwick Som 104 B1
Barwick in Elmet 194 C4
Barwinnock 207 D2
Baschurch 170 B5
Bascote 147 G1
Base Green 152 B1
Basford Green 171 G2
Bashall Eaves 192 C3
Bashall Town 192 D3
Bashley 106 B3
Basildon Essex 137 G4
Basildon WBerks 134 B5
Basingstoke 120 B2
Baslow 185 G5
Bason Bridge 116 A3
Bassaleg 130 B4
Bassenthwaite 209 F3
Bassett 106 D1
Bassingbourn 150 B3
Bassingfield 174 B4
Bassingham 175 E2
Bassingthorpe 175 E5
Basta 278 E3
Baston 161 G1
Bastonford 146 A2
Bastwick 179 F4
Batavaime 241 G1
Batch 116 A2
Batchley 146 C1
Batchworth 135 F3
Batchworth Heath 135 F3
Batcombe Dorset 104 C1
Batcombe Som 117 D4
Bate Heath 184 A5
Batemoor 186 A4
Bath 117 E1
Bath Abbey B&NESom BA1 1LT 63 Bath
Bathampton 117 E1
Bathealton 115 D5
Batheaston 117 E1
Bathford 117 E1
Bathgate 235 D2
Bathley 174 C2
Bathpool Corn 97 G2
Bathpool Som 115 F5
Bathway 116 C2
Batley 194 B5
Batsford 147 D4
Batson 100 D4
Battersby 203 E2
Battersea 136 B5
Battersea Cats & Dogs Home GtLon SW8 4AA 13 A5
Battersea Park Children's Zoo GtLon SW11 4NJ 13 A5
Battisborough Cross 100 C3
Battisford 152 B2
Battisford Tye 152 B2
Battle ESuss 110 C2
Battle Powys 143 G4
Battle ESuss TN33 0AD 110 C2
Battledown 146 B5
Battlefield 157 E1

Battlesbridge 137 G3
Battlesden 149 E5
Battlesea Green 164 D4
Battleton 114 C5
Battles Green 152 A1
Battramsley 106 C3
Batt's Corner 120 D3
Bauds of Cullen 268 C4
Baugh 246 B2
Baughton 146 A3
Baughurst 119 G1
Baulds 260 E5
Baulking 133 F3
Baumber 188 C5
Baunton 132 C2
Baveney Wood 157 F5
Baverstock 118 A4
Bawburgh 178 C5
Bawdeswell 178 B3
Bawdrip 116 A4
Bawdsey 153 E3
Bawdsey Manor 153 E4
Bawsey 163 E1
Bawtry 187 D3
Baxenden 193 D5
Baxterley 159 E3
Baxter's Green 151 F2
Baxters Highland Village Moray IV32 7LD 268 B4
Bay 117 F3
Baybridge 211 F3
Baycliff 199 D5
Baydon 133 E5
Bayford Herts 136 C2
Bayford Som 117 E5
Bayfordbury 136 C1
Bayham Abbey 123 F5
Bayles 210 D3
Baylham 152 C2
Baynards Green 148 A5
Bayles 210 D3
Bayston Hill 157 D2
Bayswater 136 B4
Baythorn End 151 F3
Bayton 157 F5
Bayworth 134 A2
Beach High 247 G4
Beach SGlos 131 G5
Beachampton 148 C4
Beachamwell 163 F2
Beacharr 231 E5
Beachley 131 E3
Beacon Devon 103 E2
Beacon Devon 103 F2
Beacon Fell Country Park Lancs PR3 2NL 192 B3
Beacon Hill Dorset 105 F3
Beacon Hill Essex 138 B1
Beacon Hill Surr 121 D4
Beacon Hill Country Park Leics LE12 8SR 17 A2
Beacon Park, Up Holland Lancs WN8 7RU 183 G2
Beacon's Bottom 134 C3
Beaconsfield 135 E3
Beacravik 263 G2
Beadlam 203 F4
Beadlow 149 G4
Beadnell 229 G4
Beaford 113 F4
Beal N'umb 229 E2
Beal NYorks 195 E5
Bealach 248 B4
Beale Park WBerks RG8 9NH 134 B5
Bealsmill 99 D3
Beambridge 170 D2
Beamhurst 172 B4
Beaminster 104 A2
Beamish 212 B2
Beamish - The Living Museum of the North Dur DH9 0RG 29 A1
Beamsley 193 G2
Bean 137 E5
Beanacre 118 A1
Beanley 229 E5
Beaquoy 276 C5
Beardon 99 F1
Beardwood 192 C5
Beare 102 C2
Beare Green 121 G3
Bearley 147 D1
Bearnie 261 H1
Bearnock 258 B1
Bearnus 246 C5
Bearpark 212 B3
Bearsbridge 211 D2
Bearsden 233 G2
Bearsted 123 G3
Bearstone 171 E4
Bearwood BCP 105 G3
Bearwood WMid 158 C4
Beattles Story Mersey L3 4AD 42 B5
Beattock 226 B5
Beauchamp Roding 137 E1
Beauchief 186 A4
Beaudesert 147 D1
Beaufort 130 A1
Beaulieu 106 C2
Beaulieu: National Motor Museum, Abbey & Palace House Hants SO42 7ZN 4 A5
Beauly (A' Mhanaichinn) 266 C7
Beaumaris (Biwmares) 181 E5
Beaumaris Castle (Castles & Town Walls of King Edward in Gwynedd) Gwyn LL58 8AP 181 E5
Beaumont Chani 100 C5
Beaumont Cumb 209 G1
Beaumont Essex 152 C5
Beaumont Hill 202 B1
Beaumont Leys 160 A2

Beauvale 173 F3
Beauworth 119 G5
Beaver Green 124 B4
Beaworthy 99 E1
Beazley End 151 F5
Bebington 183 E4
Bebside 221 E3
Beccles 165 F2
Beccles Heliport 165 F3
Becconsall 192 A5
Beck Foot 200 B3
Beck Hole 204 B2
Beck Row 163 E5
Beck Side Cumb 198 D4
Beck Side Cumb 199 E4
Beckbury 157 G2
Beckenham 122 C4
Beckering 188 B4
Beckermet 198 B2
Beckermonds 201 D4
Becket End 163 F3
Beckfoot Cumb 198 C2
Beckfoot Cumb 209 D2
Beckford 146 B3
Beckhampton 118 B3
Beckingham Lincs 175 D2
Beckingham Notts 187 E4
Beckington 117 F2
Beckley ESuss 111 E5
Beckley Oxon 134 A1
Beck's Green 165 E3
Beckside 200 B4
Beckton 136 D4
Beckwithshaw 194 B3
Becontree 137 D4
Bedale 202 B4
Bedburn 211 G4
Bedchester 105 E1
Beddau 129 G4
Beddgelert 167 E3
Beddingham 109 G3
Beddington 122 B2
Beddington Corner 122 B2
Bedfield 152 C1
Bedfield Little Green 152 C1
Bedford 149 F3
Bedgebury Cross 123 G5
Bedgrove 134 D1
Bedham 121 F5
Bedhampton 107 G2
Bedingfield 152 C1
Bedingfield Green 152 C1
Bedingfield Street 152 C1
Bedingham Green 165 D2
Bedlam Lancs 193 B1
Bedlam NYorks 194 B1
Bedlar's Green 150 D5
Bedlington 221 E3
Bedlinog 129 G2
Bedminster 131 E5
Bedmond 135 F2
Bednall 158 B1
Bedol 182 D5
Bedrule 228 A5
Bedstone 156 C5
Bedwas 130 A4
Bedwell 150 A5
Bedwellty 130 A2
Bedworth 159 F4
Bedworth Woodlands 159 F4
Beeby 160 B2
Beech Hants 120 B4
Beech Staffs 171 F4
Beech Hill 120 B1
Beechingstoke 118 B2
Beechwood 183 G4
Beecraigs Country Park WLoth EH49 6PL 235 D2
Beedon 133 G5
Beeford 196 D2
Beeley 173 D2
Beelsby 188 C2
Beenham 119 G1
Beeny 98 B1
Beer 103 F4
Beer Hackett 104 C1
Beercrocombe 116 A5
Beesands 101 E4
Beesby Lincs 189 E5
Beesby NELincs 188 C3
Beeson 101 E3
Beeston CenBeds 149 G3
Beeston ChesW&C 170 C2
Beeston Norf 178 A4
Beeston Notts 173 G4
Beeston WYorks 194 B4
Beeston Regis 178 C1
Beeston St. Lawrence 179 E3
Beeswing 216 C4
Beetham Cumb 199 F5
Beetham Som 103 F1
Beetley 178 A4
Beffcote 158 A1
Began 130 B4
Begbroke 133 G1
Begdale 162 C2
Begelly 127 E2
Beggar's Bush 144 B1
Beggearn Huish 114 D4
Beggshill 260 D1
Beguildy (Bugeildy) 156 A5
Beighton Norf 179 E5
Beighton SYorks 186 B4
Beili-glas 130 C2
Beith 233 E4
Bekesbourne 125 D3
Bekonscot Model Village Bucks HP9 2PL 135 E3
Belaugh 179 D4
Belbroughton 158 B5
Belchalwell 105 D2
Belchalwell Street 105 D2
Belchamp Otten 151 G3
Belchamp St. Paul 151 F3
Belchamp Walter 151 G3
Belchford 188 C5
Belcoo 280 C5
Belfast 283 G1
Belfast Castle Belfast City BT15 5GR 283 G1
Belfield 184 D1
Belford 229 F3
Belgrave 160 A2
Belhaven 237 D2

Belhelvie **261** H3
Belhinnie **260** C2
Bell Bar **136** B2
Bell Busk **193** F2
Bell End **158** B5
Bell Heath **158** B5
Bell o' th' Hill **170** C3
Bellabeg **260** B5
Belladrum **266** C7
Bellaghy **286** D6
Bellanaleck **280** E5
Bellanoch **240** A5
Bellaty **252** A4
Belle Isle **194** C5
Belle Vue **209** G1
Belleau **189** E5
Belleheiglash **259** J1
Belleek F&O **280** E3
Belleek NM&D **282** C6
Bellerby **202** A3
Bellever **99** G3
Bellfields **121** E2
Belliehill **253** D3
Bellingdon **135** E2
Bellingham GtLon **136** C5
Bellingham N'umb **220** A3
Belloch **222** B2
Bellochantuy **222** B2
Bell's Cross **152** C2
Bells Yew Green **123** F5
Bellsbank **224** C5
Bellshill N'umb **229** F3
Bellshill NLan **234** B3
Bellside **234** C4
Bellsmyre **233** F2
Bellsquarry **235** E3
Bellury **286** C4
Belmaduthy **266** D6
Belmesthorpe **161** F1
Belmont B'burn **184** A1
Belmont GtLon **122** B2
Belmont GtLon **136** A3
Belmont M&EAnt **287** J6
Belmont Shet **278** D1
Belnie **261** E2
Belowda **97** D3
Belper **173** E3
Belper Lane End **173** E3
Belraugh **286** B4
Belsay **220** D4
Belsford **101** D2
Belsize **135** F2
Belstead **152** C3
Belston **224** B3
Belstone **99** G1
Belstone Corner **99** G1
Belsyde **235** D2
Belthorn **192** D5
Beltinge **125** D2
Beltingham **211** D1
Beltoft **187** F2
Belton Leics **173** F5
Belton Lincs **175** E4
Belton NLincs **187** E2
Belton Norf **179** F5
Belton Rut **160** D2
Belton House Lincs
NG32 2LS **175** E4
Beltoy **287** J6
Beltring **123** F4
Belvedere **137** D5
Belvoir **174** D4
Bembridge **107** F4
Bemerton **118** C4
Bempton **205** E5
Ben Alder Cottage **249** G3
Ben Alder Lodge **250** A2
Ben Rhydding **194** A3
Benacre **165** G3
Benbecula (Beinn na
Faoghla) **262** D6
Benbecula (Balivanich)
Airport **262** C6
Benbuie **216** B1
Benburb **282** B3
Benderloch
(Meadarloch) **240** B1
Bendish **149** G5
Bendooragh **286** D3
Benenden **124** A5
Benfield **215** E4
Benfieldside **211** F2
Bengate **179** E3
Bengeo **136** C1
Bengeworth **146** C3
Benhall **146** B5
Benhall Green **153** E1
Benhall Street **153** E1
Benholm **253** G3
Beningbrough **195** E2
Benington Herts **150** A5
Benington Lincs **176** B3
Benington Sea End **176** B3
Benllech **180** D4
Benmore A&B **232** C1
Benmore Stir **241** G2
Bennacott **98** C1
Bennan Cottage **216** A3
Bennett End **134** C3
Bennetts End **135** F2
Benniworth **188** C4
Benone **286** B2
Benover **123** G4
Benson **134** B3
Benston **279** D7
Benthall N'umb **229** G4
Benthall Shrop **157** F2
Bentham **132** B1
Benthoul **261** G4
Bentlawnt **156** C2
Bentley ERid **196** C4
Bentley Essex **137** E3
Bentley Hants **120** C3
Bentley Suff **152** C3
Bentley Warks **159** E3
Bentley WMid **158** B3
Bentley WYorks **194** B4
Bentley Heath
Herts **136** B3
Bentley Heath
WMid **159** D3
Bentley Rise **186** C2
Benton **113** G2
Benton Square **221** F4

Bentpath **218** B2
Bentworth **120** B3
Benvie **244** B1
Benville Lane **104** B2
Benwell **212** B1
Benwell Vallum Crossing &
Temple (Frontiers of
the Roman Empire)
T&W NE15 6QP **28** A2
Benwick **162** B3
Beoley **146** C1
Beoraidbeg **256** C5
Bepton **108** A2
Beragh **281** H2
Berden **150** C5
Bere Alston **100** A1
Bere Ferrers **100** A1
Bere Regis **105** E3
Berea **140** A4
Berepper **95** D4
Bergh Apton **179** E5
Berinsfield **134** A3
Berkeley **131** F3
Berkhamsted **135** E2
Berkley **117** F3
Berkswell **159** E5
Bermondsey **136** C5
Bernera (Eilean
Bhearnaraigh) **262** E3
Berners Roding **137** F2
Bernice **240** D5
Bernisdale **263** K6
Berrick Prior **134** B3
Berrick Salome **134** B3
Berriedale **275** G6
Berrier **209** G4
Berriew (Aberriw) **156** A2
Berrington
N'umb **229** E2
Berrington Shrop **157** E2
Berrington Worcs **145** E1
Berrington Green **145** E1
Berriowbridge **97** G2
Berrow Som **115** F2
Berrow Worcs **145** G4
Berrow Green **145** G2
Berry Cross **113** E4
Berry Down Cross **113** F1
Berry Hill Glos **131** E1
Berry Hill Pembs **141** D3
Berry Pomeroy **101** E1
Berryhillock **268** D4
Berrynarbor **113** F1
Berry's Green **122** D3
Bersham **170** A3
Berstane **277** D6
Berth-lwyd **128** B3
Berwick **110** A3
Berwick Bassett **132** D5
Berwick Hill **221** E4
Berwick St. James **118** B4
Berwick St. John **117** F5
Berwick St. Leonard **118** A4
Berwick-upon-
Tweed **237** G4
Bescar **183** E1
Bescot **158** C3
Besford Shrop **170** C5
Besford Worcs **146** B3
Bessacarr **186** D2
Bessbrook CC&G **285** J3
Bessbrook NM&D **282** D6
Bessels Leigh **133** G2
Besses o' th' Barn **184** C2
Bessingby **197** D1
Bessingham **178** C2
Best Beech Hill **123** F5
Besthorpe Norf **164** B2
Besthorpe Notts **174** D1
Bestwood **173** G3
Bestwood Country Park
Notts NG6 8UF **19** G1
Beswick ERid **196** C3
Beswick GtMan **184** C3
Betchworth **122** B3
Bethania Cere **142** B1
Bethania Gwyn **167** E1
Bethania Gwyn **168** C4
Bethel Gwyn **167** E1
Bethel IoA **180** C5
Bethersden **124** B5
Bethesda Gwyn **167** F1
Bethesda Pembs **127** D1
Bethlehem **142** C5
Bethnal Green **136** C4
Betley **171** E3
Betley Common **171** E3
Betsham **137** F5
Betteshanger **125** F3
Bettiscombe **103** G3
Bettisfield **170** B4
Betton Shrop **156** C2
Betton Shrop **171** D4
Betton Strange **157** E2
Bettws Bridgend **129** F4
Bettws Newport **130** B3
Bettws Bledrws **142** B2
Bettws Cedewain **156** A3
Bettws Gwerfil
Goch **168** D3
Bettws Newydd **130** C2
Bettws-y-crwyn **156** B4
Bettyhill **274** C2
Betws CenBeds **149** E5
Betws (Y Betws) **142** B5
Betws Disserth **144** A2
Betws Garmon **167** E2
Betws Ifan **141** G3
Betws-y-Coed **168** A2
Betws-yn-Rhos **182** A5
Beulah Cere **141** F3
Beulah Powys **143** F2
Bevendean **109** F3
Bevercotes **187** D5
Beverley **196** C4
Beverston **132** A3
Bevington **131** F3
Bewaldeth **209** F3
Bewcastle **219** D4
Bewdley **157** G5
Bewerley **194** A1
Bewholme **197** D3
Bewl Water ESuss
TN3 8JH **123** F5
Bewley Common **118** A1
Bexhill **110** C3
Bexley **137** D5
Bexleyheath **137** D5
Bexwell **163** E2

Beyton **152** A1
Beyton Green **152** A1
Bhalamus **270** E7
Bhaltos (Valtos) **270** C4
Biallaid **258** E5
Bibury **132** D2
Bicester **148** A5
Bickenhall **103** F1
Bickenhill **159** D4
Bicker **176** A4
Bickershaw **184** A2
Bickerstaffe **183** F2
Bickerton
ChesW&C **170** C2
Bickerton Devon **101** E4
Bickerton N'umb **220** B1
Bickerton NYorks **195** D2
Bickford **158** A1
Bickham **114** C3
Bickham Bridge **100** D2
Bickham House **102** C4
Bickington Devon **113** F2
Bickington Devon **102** A5
Bickleigh Devon **100** B1
Bickleigh Devon **102** C2
Bickleton **113** F2
Bickley **122** D2
Bickley Moss **170** C3
Bickley Town **170** C3
Bicknacre **137** G2
Bicknoller **115** E4
Bicknor **124** A3
Bickton **106** A1
Bicton Here **145** D1
Bicton Shrop **156** D1
Bicton Shrop **156** B4
Bicton Heath **157** D1
Bicton Park Botanical
Gardens Devon
EX9 7BJ **103** D4
Bidborough **123** E4
Biddenden **124** A5
Biddenden Green **124** A4
Biddenham **149** F3
Biddestone **132** A5
Biddick **212** C2
Biddisham **116** A2
Biddlesden **148** B3
Biddlestone **220** B1
Biddulph **171** F2
Biddulph Moor **171** G2
Bideford **113** E3
Bidford-on-Avon **146** D2
Bidlake **99** E2
Bidston **183** D3
Bidwell **149** F5
Bielby **195** G3
Bieldside **261** G4
Bierley IoW **107** E5
Bierley WYorks **194** A4
Bierton **134** D1
Big Pit National Coal
Museum (Blaenavon
Industrial Landscape)
Torfaen NP4 9XP **130** B2
Big Sand **264** D4
Big Sheep, The Devon
EX39 5AP **113** E3
Big Sky Adventure Play
Peter PE2 7BU **161** G3
Bigbury **100** C3
Bigbury-on-Sea **100** C3
Bigby **188** A2
Bigert Mire **198** C3
Biggar Cumb **191** E1
Biggar SLan **226** B2
Biggin Derbys **172** C2
Biggin Derbys **172** C1
Biggin NYorks **195** E4
Biggings **279** A6
Biggin Hill **122** D3
Biggin Hill Airport **122** D2
Biggleswade **149** G3
Bigholms **218** B3
Bighouse **274** D2
Bighton **120** B4
Biglands **209** F1
Bignor **108** B2
Bigrigg **208** D5
Bigton **279** C10
Bilberry **97** E4
Bilborough **173** G3
Bilbrook Som **114** D3
Bilbrook Staffs **158** A2
Bilbrough **195** E3
Bilbster **275** H3
Bilby **186** D4
Bildershaw **212** A5
Bildeston **152** A3
Billacombe **100** B2
Billericay **137** F3
Billesdon **160** C2
Billesley **146** D2
Billholm **218** A2
Billingborough **175** G4
Billinge **183** G3
Billingford Norf **164** C4
Billingford Norf **178** B3
Billingham **213** D5
Billinghay **175** G2
Billingley **186** B2
Billingshurst **121** F5
Billingsley **157** G4
Billington CenBeds **149** E5
Billington Lancs **192** D4
Billington Staffs **171** F5
Billister **279** D6
Billockby **179** F4
Billy **286** D2
Billy Row **212** A4
Bilsborrow **192** B4
Bilsby **189** E5
Bilsby Field **189** E5
Bilsdean **237** E2
Bilsham **108** B3
Bilsington **124** C5
Bilson Green **131** F1
Bilsthorpe **174** B1
Bilsthorpe Moor **174** B2
Bilston Midlo **235** G3
Bilston WMid **158** B3
Bilstone **159** F2
Bilting **124** C4
Bilton ERid **197** D4
Bilton N'umb **229** G5
Bilton NYorks **194** C2
Bilton Warks **159** G5
Bilton-in-Ainsty **195** D3
Bimbister **277** C6

Binbrook **188** C3
Bincombe **104** C4
Bindal **267** G3
Bindon **115** E5
Bines Green **109** D2
Binfield **134** D5
Binfield Heath **134** C5
Bingfield **220** B4
Bingham **174** C4
Bingham's
Melcombe **105** D2
Bingley **194** A4
Bings Heath **157** E1
Binham **178** A2
Binley Hants **119** F2
Binley WMid **159** F5
Binmore **280** D3
Binnareaghan **285** H7
Binniehill **234** C2
Binsoe **202** B5
Binstead **107** E3
Binsted Hants **120** C3
Binsted WSuss **108** B3
Binton **146** D2
Bintree **178** B3
Binweston **156** C2
Birch Essex **152** A5
Birch GtMan **184** C2
Birch Cross **172** C4
Birch Green Essex **138** C1
Birch Green Herts **136** B1
Birch Grove **109** G1
Birch Heath **170** C1
Birch Vale **185** E4
Birch Wood **103** F1
Bircham Newton **177** F4
Bircham Tofts **177** F4
Birchanger **150** D5
Bircher **145** D1
Bircher Common **145** D1
Birchfield **266** B2
Birchgrove Cardiff **130** A4
Birchgrove Swan **128** D3
Birchington **125** F2
Birchmoor **159** E2
Birchover **172** D1
Birchwood Lincs **175** E1
Birchwood Warr **184** A3
Bircotes **186** D3
Bird Street **152** B2
Birdbrook **151** F3
Birdbush **118** A5
Birdfield **240** B5
Birdforth **203** D5
Birdham **108** A3
Birdingbury **147** G1
Birdland, Bourton-on-
the-Water Glos
GL54 2BN **147** D5
Birdlip **132** B1
Birdoswald **210** C7
Birdoswald Roman Fort
(Frontiers of the Roman
Empire) Cumb CA8 7DD
210 C1
Birds Green **137** E2
Birdsall **196** A1
Birdsgreen **157** G4
Birdsmoor Gate **103** G2
Birdston **234** A2
Birdwell **186** A2
Birdwood **131** G1
Birgham **228** B3
Birichen **266** E2
Birkby Cumb **209** D3
Birkby NYorks **202** C2
Birkdale Mersey **183** E1
Birkdale NYorks **201** E3
Birkenhead **183** E4
Birkenshaw **194** B5
Birkhall **260** B5
Birkhill Angus **244** B1
Birkhill ScBord **236** C5
Birkhill ScBord **226** D4
Birkholme **175** E5
Birkin **195** E5
Birks **194** B5
Birkwood **225** G2
Birley **145** D2
Birley Carr **186** A3
Birling Kent **123** F2
Birling N'umb **221** E1
Birling Gap **110** A4
Birlingham **146** B3
Birmingham **158** C4
Birmingham Airport
159 D4
Birmingham Botanical
Gardens WMid
B15 3TR **34** B7
Birmingham City Museum
& Art Gallery WMid
B3 3DH **35** E4
Birnam **251** F5
Birsay **276** B5
Birse **260** D5
Birstall **160** A2
Birstall Smithies **194** B5
Birstwith **194** B2
Birthorpe **175** G4
Birtle **184** C1
Birtley Here **144** C1
Birtley N'umb **220** B4
Birtley T&W **212** B2
Birts Street **145** G4
Birtsmorton **146** A4
Bisbrooke **161** D3
Bish Mill **114** A5
Bisham **135** D3
Bishampton **146** B2
Bishop Auckland **212** B5
Bishop Burton **196** B4
Bishop Middleham **212** C4
Bishop Monkton **194** C1
Bishop Norton **187** G3
Bishop Sutton **116** C2
Bishop Thornton **194** B1
Bishop Wilton **195** G2
Bishopbridge **188** A3
Bishopbriggs **234** A2
Bishopmill **267** K5
Bishops Cannings **118** B1

Bishop's Castle **156** C4
Bishop's Caundle **104** C1
Bishop's Cleeve **146** B5
Bishops Court **283** J4
Bishop's Frome **145** F3
Bishops Gate **135** E5
Bishop's Green
Essex **137** F1
Bishop's Green
Hants **119** E1
Bishop's Hull **115** F5
Bishop's Itchington
147 F2
Bishops Lydeard **115** E5
Bishop's Norton **146** A5
Bishops Nympton **114** A5
Bishop's Offley **171** E5
Bishop's Stortford **150** C5
Bishop's Sutton **120** B4
Bishop's Tachbrook **147** F1
Bishop's Tawton **113** F2
Bishop's Waltham **107** E1
Bishop's Wood **158** A2
Bishopsbourne **125** D3
Bishopsteignton **102** C5
Bishopstoke **107** D1
Bishopston Bristol **131** E5
Bishopston Swan **128** B4
Bishopstone Bucks **134** D1
Bishopstone ESuss **109** G3
Bishopstone Here **144** D3
Bishopstone Swin **133** E4
Bishopstone Wilts **118** B5
Bishopstown **283** H4
Bishopsworth **116** C1
Bishopthorpe **195** E3
Bishopton Darl **212** C5
Bishopton NYorks **202** B5
Bishopton Renf **233** F2
Bishopton Warks **147** D2
Bishton **130** C4
Bisley Glos **132** B2
Bisley Surr **121** E2
Bispham **191** G4
Bispham Green **183** F1
Bissoe **96** B5
Bisterne **106** A2
Bisterne Close **106** B2
Bitchet Green **123** E3
Bitchfield **175** E5
Bittadon **113** F1
Bittaford **100** C1
Bittering **178** A4
Bitterley **157** E5
Bitterne **107** D1
Bitteswell **160** A4
Bitton **117** D1
Bix **134** C4
Bixter **279** C7
Blaby **160** A3
Black Bourton **133** E2
Black Bridge L&C **283** G3
Black Bridge
Pembs **126** C2
Black Callerton **212** A1
Black Carr **164** B2
Black Clauchrie **215** D2
Black Corries Lodge **249** E4
Black Country Living
Museum WMid
DY1 4SQ **14** B2
Black Crofts **240** B1
Black Cross **96** D3
Black Dog **102** B2
Black Heddon **220** C4
Black Lane Ends **283** G3
Black Marsh **156** C3
Black Moor **194** B3
Black Mount **249** E5
Black Notley **151** F5
Black Park Country
Park Bucks
SL3 6DR **135** F4
Black Sheep Brewery
Visitor Centre NYorks
HG4 4EN **202** B5
Black Skull **282** E3
Black Street **165** G3
Black Swan Guild,
Frome Som
BA11 1BB **117** E3
Black Torrington **113** E5
Blackaburn **219** F4
Blackacre **217** E1
Blackadder **237** F4
Blackawton **101** D2
Blackborough
Devon **103** D2
Blackborough Norf **163** E1
Blackborough End **163** E1
Blackboys **110** A5
Blackbraes Aber **261** G3
Blackbraes Falk **234** D2
Blackbrook Derbys **173** E3
Blackbrook Leics **159** G4
Blackbrook Mersey **183** G3
Blackbrook Staffs **171** E4
Blackburn Aber **261** G3
Blackburn B'burn **192** C5
Blackburn WLoth **235** D3
Blackbushe **120** C2
Blackcastle **267** F6
Blackchambers **261** F3
Blackcraig D&G **215** F4
Blackcraig D&G **216** B2
Blackden Heath **184** B5
Blackdog **261** H3
Blackdown Devon **99** F3
Blackdown Dorset **103** G2
Blackdown Warks **147** F1
Blackfen **106** D2
Blackfield **106** D2
Blackford Cumb **218** B5
Blackford P&K **243** D4
Blackford Som **117** D3
Blackford Som **116** B3
Blackford Bridge **184** C2
Blackfordby **159** F1
Blackgang **107** D5
Blackgang Chine
IoW PO38 2HN **107** D5
Blackhall Edin **235** G2
Blackhall Renf **233** F4

Blackhall Renf **233** F3
Blackhall Colliery **213** D4
Blackhall Mill **212** A2
Blackhall Rocks **213** D4
Blackham **123** E5
Blackhaugh **227** F2
Blackheath Essex **152** B5
Blackheath GtLon **136** C5
Blackheath Suff **165** F4
Blackheath Surr **121** F3
Blackheath WMid
158 B4
Blackhill Aber **269** J5
Blackhill Aber **269** J6
Blackhillock **268** C6
Blackhills **267** K6
Blackland **114** B4
Blackleach **192** A4
Blackley **184** C2
Blacklunans **251** G3
Blackmill **129** F4
Blackmoor Hants **120** C4
Blackmoor Som **103** E1
Blackmoor Gate **113** G1
Blackmoorfoot **185** F2
Blackmore **137** F2
Blackmore End
Essex **151** F4
Blackmore End
Herts **136** A1
Blackness Aber **260** E5
Blackness Falk **235** E2
Blackness High **275** H5
Blacknest **120** C3
Blackney **104** A3
Blacko **193** E3
Blackpill **128** C3
Blackpool B'pool **191** G4
Blackpool Devon **101** E3
Blackpool Airport **191** G4
Blackpool Bridge **127** D1
Blackpool Gate **218** D4
Blackpool Piers B'pool
FY1 1BB **191** G4
Blackpool Pleasure
Beach B'pool
FY4 1PL **191** G4
Blackpool Tower
FY1 4BJ **64** Blackpool
Blackpool Zoo
B'pool FY3 8PP **191** G4
Blackridge **234** C3
Blackrock A&B **230** B3
Blackrock Mon **130** B1
Blackrod **184** A1
Blackshaw **217** E4
Blackshaw Head **193** F5
Blacksmith's Green **152** C1
Blacksnape **192** D5
Blackstone **109** E2
Blackthorn **134** B1
Blackthorpe **152** A1
Blacktoft **196** A5
Blacktop **261** G4
Blacktown
Newport **130** B4
Blackwater Corn **96** B5
Blackwater Hants **120** D2
Blackwater IoW **107** E4
Blackwater Norf **178** B3
Blackwater Som **103** F1
Blackwaterfoot **223** E3
Blackwatertown **282** B3
Blackwell Darl **202** B1
Blackwell Derbys **185** F5
Blackwell Derbys **173** F2
Blackwell Warks **147** E3
Blackwell Worcs **158** B5
Blackwell WSuss **122** C5
Blackwells End **145** G5
Blackwood (Coed-duon)
Caerp **130** A3
Blackwood D&G **216** D2
Blackwood SLan **234** B5
Blackwood Hill **171** G2
Blacon **170** A1
Bladbean **125** D4
Bladnoch **215** F5
Bladon **133** G1
Blaenannerch **141** F3
Blaenau
Dolwyddelan **167** F2
Blaenau Ffestiniog **167** F3
Blaenavon **130** B2
Blaenavon Industrial
Landscape Torfaen
130 B2
Blaenawey **130** B1
Blaencelyn **141** G2
Blaenclydach **129** F3
Blaencwm **129** F2
Blaendyryn **143** F4
Blaen-ffos **141** E4
Blaengarw **129** F3
Blaengeuffordd **154** C4
Blaengweche **128** C2
Blaen-gwrach **129** E2
Blaengwynfi **129** E3
Blaenllechau **129** G3
Blaenos **143** D4
Blaenpennal **142** C1
Blaen-plwyf **154** B5
Blaen-porth **141** F3
Blaenrhondda **129** F2
Blaen-waun **141** F5
Blaen-y-coed **141** G5
Blagdon NSom **116** B2
Blagdon Torbay **101** E1
Blagdon Hill **103** F1
Blaguegate **183** F2
Blaich **248** C2
Blaina **130** A2
Blair **233** E1
Blair Atholl **251** D3
Blair Castle P&K
PH18 5TL **251** D3
Blair Drummond **242** C5
Blair Drummond Safari &
Adventure Park Stir
FK9 4UR **242** C5
Blairannaich **241** F4

Blairbuie **232** C2
Blairgowrie **251** G5
Blairhall **235** E1
Blairhoyle **242** B4
Blairhullichan **241** G4
Blairingone **243** F5
Blairkip **224** D2
Blairlogie **242** D5
Blairmore A&B **232** C1
Blairmore High **266** E1
Blairmore High **272** D5
Blairnairn **233** D1
Blairnamarrow **259** K3
Blairpark **232** D4
Blairquhan **224** B5
Blairquhosh **233** G1
Blair's Ferry **232** B3
Blairshinnoch **268** E4
Blairuskinmore **241** G4
Blairvadach **233** D1
Blairydryne **261** F5
Blairythan **261** H2
Blaisdon **131** G1
Blake End **151** F5
Blake House Craft
Centre Essex
CM77 6RA **151** F5
Blakebrook **158** A5
Blakedown **158** A5
Blakelaw ScBord **228** B3
Blakelaw T&W **212** B1
Blakeley **158** A3
Blakelow **171** D2
Blakemere **144** C3
Blakemere Shopping
Experience ChesW&C
CW8 2EB **183** F5
Blakeney Glos **131** F2
Blakeney Norf **178** B1
Blakenhall
ChesE **171** E3
Blakenhall WMid **158** B3
Blakeshall **158** A4
Blakesley **148** B2
Blanchland **211** F2
Bland Hill **194** B2
Blandford Camp **105** F2
Blandford Forum **105** E2
Blandford St. Mary **105** E2
Blanefield **233** G1
Blanerne **237** F4
Blankney **175** F1
Blantyre **234** A4
Blar a' Chaorainn **248** D3
Blargie **258** E5
Blarglas **233** E1
Blarmachfoldach **248** C3
Blarnalearoch **265** H2
Blashford **106** A2
Blaston **160** D3
Blathaisbhal **262** D4
Blatherwycke **161** E3
Blawith **199** D4
Blaxhall **153** E2
Blaxton **187** D2
Blaydon **212** A1
Bleadney **116** B3
Bleadon **116** A2
Bleak Hey Nook **185** E2
Blean **124** D2
Bleary **282** D3
Bleasby Lincs **188** B4
Bleasby Notts **174** C3
Bleasby Moor **188** B4
Bleatarn **200** C1
Bleathwood
Common **145** E1
Blebocraigs **244** C3
Bleddfa **144** B1
Bledington **147** E5
Bledlow **134** C2
Bledlow Ridge **134** C3
Blencarn **210** C4
Blencogo **209** E2
Blencow **210** A4
Blendworth **107** G1
Blenheim Palace Oxon
OX20 1PP **133** G1
Blennerhasset **209** E2
Blervie Castle **267** H6
Bletchingdon **134** A1
Bletchingley **122** C3
Bletchley MK **149** D4
Bletchley Shrop **170** D4
Bletherston **141** D5
Bletsoe **149** F2
Blewbury **134** A4
Blickling **178** C3
Blickling Hall Norf
NR11 6NF **178** C3
Blidworth **173** G2
Blidworth
Bottoms **173** G2
Blindburn Aber **261** H1
Blindburn N'umb **228** C5
Blindcrake **209** E3
Blindley Heath **122** C4
Blisland **97** E2
Bliss Gate **157** G5
Blissford **106** A1
Blisworth **148** C2
Blithbury **172** B5
Blitterlees **209** E1
Blo' Norton **164** B4
Blockley **147** D4
Blofield **179** E5
Blofield Heath **179** E4
Bloody Bridge **283** G6
Blore **172** C3
Blossomfield **158** D5
Blount's Green **172** B4
Blowick **183** E1
Bloxham **147** G4
Bloxholm **175** F2
Bloxwich **158** B2
Bloxworth **105** E3
Blubberhouses **194** B2
Blue Anchor Corn **96** D4
Blue Anchor Som **114** D3
Blue Bell Hill **123** G2
Blue Planet Aquarium,
Ellesmere Port
ChesW&C
CH65 9LF **183** F5
Blue Reef Aquarium
ESuss TN34 3DW
75 Hastings

Blue Reef Aquarium, Newquay *Corn* TR7 1DU **96** C3
Blue Reef Aquarium, Southsea *Ports* PO5 3PB **5** G6
Blue Reef Aquarium, Tynemouth *T&W* NE30 4JF **28** E1
Bluebell Railway *WSuss* TN22 3QL **109** F1
Bluewater **137** E5
Blundellsands **183** E3
Blundeston **165** G2
Blunnick **280** D5
Blunsdon St. Andrew **132** D4
Bluntington **158** A5
Bluntisham **162** B5
Blunts **98** D4
Blurton **171** F3
Blyborough **187** G3
Blymhill **158** A1
Blymhill Common **157** G1
Blymhill Lawn **158** A1
Blyth *N'umb* **221** F3
Blyth *Notts* **186** D4
Blyth Bridge **235** F5
Blyth End **159** E3
Blythburgh **165** F4
Blythe Bridge **171** G3
Blythe Marsh **171** G3
Blyton **187** F3
Boardmills **283** G3
Boarhills **245** D3
Boarhunt **107** F2
Boars Hill **133** G2
Boarsgreave **193** E5
Boarshead **123** E4
Boarstall **134** B1
Boarzell **110** C1
Boasley Cross **99** F1
Boat o' Brig **268** B5
Boat of Garten **259** G3
Boath **266** C2
Bobbing **124** A2
Bobbington **158** A3
Bobbingworth **137** E2
Bocaddon **97** F4
Bochastle **242** B4
Bocketts Farm Park *Surr* KT22 9BS **121** G2
Bockhampton **133** F5
Bocking **151** F5
Bocking Churchstreet **151** F5
Bockleton **145** E1
Boconnoc **97** F3
Boddam *Aber* **269** K6
Boddam *Shet* **279** F9
Bodden **116** D3
Boddington **146** A5
Bodedern **180** B4
Bodelwyddan **182** B5
Bodenham *Here* **145** E2
Bodenham *Wilts* **118** C5
Bodenham Moor **145** E2
Bodesbeck **226** C5
Bodewryd **180** C3
Bodfari **182** B5
Bodffordd **180** C5
Bodham **178** C1
Bodiam **110** C1
Bodiam Castle *ESuss* TN32 5UA **110** C1
Bodicote **147** G4
Bodieve **97** D2
Bodinnick **97** F4
Bodior **180** A5
Bodle Street Green **110** B2
Bodleian Library *Oxon* OX1 3BG **80** Oxford
Bodmin **97** E3
Bodnant Garden *Conwy* LL28 5RE **181** G5
Bodney **163** G3
Bodoney **281** D2
Bodorgan **166** C1
Bodrane **97** G3
Bodsham **124** D4
Boduan **166** C4
Bodwen **97** E3
Bodymoor Heath **159** D3
Bogagh **285** G4
Bogallan **266** D6
Bogbain **266** E7
Bogbrae **261** J1
Bogbuie **266** C6
Bogend **224** B2
Bogfern **260** D4
Bogfields **260** D4
Bogfold **269** G5
Boghead *Aber* **268** E5
Boghead *EAyr* **225** E3
Boghead *SLan* **234** B5
Boghole Farm **267** G6
Bogmoor **268** B4
Bogniebrae **268** D6
Bognor Regis **108** B4
Bograxie **261** F3
Bogroy **259** G2
Bogside **243** G5
Bogston **260** B4
Bogton **268** E5
Bogue **216** A2
Bohemia **106** B1
Bohenie **249** E1
Bohetherick **100** A1
Boho **280** D4
Bohortha **95** F3
Bohuntine **249** E1
Boirseam **263** F3
Bojewyan **94** A3
Bokiddick **97** E3
Bolam *Dur* **212** A4
Bolam *N'umb* **220** C3
Bolam Lake Country Park *N'umb* NE20 0HE **220** C3
Bolberry **100** C4
Bold Heath **183** G4
Bolderwood **106** B2
Boldon **212** C1
Boldon Colliery **212** C1
Boldre **106** C3

Boldron **201** F1
Bole **187** E4
Bolea **286** B3
Bolehill **173** D2
Boleigh **94** B4
Bolenowe **95** D3
Boleran **286** C4
Boleside **227** F2
Bolfracks **250** D5
Bolgoed **128** C2
Bolham *Devon* **102** C1
Bolham *Notts* **187** E4
Bolham Water **103** E1
Bolie **285** H4
Bolingey **96** B4
Bollington **184** D5
Bolney **109** E1
Bolnhurst **149** F2
Bolshan **253** E4
Bolsover **186** B5
Bolsterstone **185** G3
Bolstone **145** E4
Boltby **203** D4
Bolter End **134** C3
Bolton *Cumb* **210** C5
Bolton *ELoth* **236** C2
Bolton *ERid* **195** G2
Bolton *GtMan* **184** B2
Bolton *N'umb* **229** F3
Bolton Abbey **193** G2
Bolton Abbey Estate *NYorks* BD23 6EX **193** G2
Bolton Bridge **193** G2
Bolton by Bowland **193** D3
Bolton Houses **192** A4
Bolton Low Houses **209** F2
Bolton Museum & Art Gallery *GtMan* BL1 1SE **184** B2
Bolton Percy **195** E3
Bolton Priory *NYorks* BD23 6EX **193** G2
Bolton upon Dearne **186** B2
Bolton Wood Lane **209** F2
Boltonfellend **210** A1
Boltongate **209** F2
Bolton-le-Sands **192** A1
Bolton-on-Swale **202** B3
Bolventor **97** F2
Bombie **208** A2
Bomere Heath **157** D1
Bonar Bridge **266** D2
Bonawe (Bun Atha) **240** C1
Bonby **188** A1
Boncath **141** F4
Bonchester Bridge **227** G4
Bonchurch **107** E5
Bondleigh **113** G4
Bonds **192** A4
Bonehill **159** D2
Bonhill **233** E2
Boningale **158** A2
Bonjedward **228** A4
Bonkle **234** C4
Bonning Gate **199** F3
Bonnington *Edin* **235** F3
Bonnington *Kent* **124** D5
Bonnybank **244** B4
Bonnybridge **234** C1
Bonnykelly **269** G5
Bonnyrigg **236** A3
Bonnyton *Aber* **260** E1
Bonnyton *Angus* **245** D1
Bonnyton *Angus* **253** E4
Bonnyton *Angus* **244** B1
Bonsall **173** D2
Bont **130** C1
Bont Dolgadfan **155** E2
Bont Newydd **168** A5
Bontddu **154** C1
Bont-goch (Elerch) **154** C4
Bonthorpe **189** E5
Bontnewydd *Conwy* **182** B5
Bontnewydd *Gwyn* **167** D1
Bontuchel **169** D2
Bonvilston **129** G5
Bôn-y-maen **128** C3
Boode **113** F2
Boohay **101** F2
Booker **134** C3
Booley **170** C5
Boor **264** E3
Boorley Green **107** E1
Boosbeck **203** F1
Boose's Green **151** E4
Boot **198** C2
Boot Street **152** D3
Booth **193** G5
Booth Bank **185** E1
Booth Green **184** D4
Booth Wood **185** E1
Boothby Graffoe **175** E2
Boothby Pagnell **175** F4
Boothstown **184** B2
Boothville **148** C1
Bootle *Cumb* **198** C4
Bootle *Mersey* **183** E3
Booton **178** C3
Boots Green **184** B5
Booze **201** F2
Boquhan **233** G1
Boraston **157** F5
Bordeaux **101** F4
Borden *Kent* **124** A2
Borden *WSuss* **120** D5
Bordley **193** F1
Bordon **120** C4
Boreham *Essex* **137** G2
Boreham *Wilts* **117** F3
Boreham Street **110** B2
Borehamwood **136** A3
Boreland *D&G* **217** F1
Boreland *D&G* **215** E4
Boreland *Stir* **242** A1
Boreley **146** A1
Boreraig **263** G6
Borgh *Na H-E. Siar* **262** E3
Borgh *Na H-E. Siar* **254** B4
Borghastan **270** D3
Borgie **273** J3
Borgue *D&G* **207** G2
Borgue *High* **275** G6
Borley **151** G3
Borley Green *Essex* **151** G3

Borley Green *Suff* **152** A1
Bornais **254** C2
Borness **207** G2
Bornisketaig **263** J4
Borough Green **123** F3
Boroughbridge **194** C1
Borras Head **170** A2
Borrowash **173** F4
Borrowby *NYorks* **203** G1
Borrowby *NYorks* **202** D4
Borrowdale **209** F5
Borrowfield **261** G5
Borstal **123** G2
Borth **154** C4
Borthwick **236** A4
Borthwickbrae **227** F4
Borthwickshiels **227** F4
Borth-y-Gest **167** E4
Borve (Borgh) *Na H-E. Siar* **271** G2
Borve *High* **263** K7
Borwick **199** G5
Borwick Rails **198** C5
Bosavern **94** A3
Bosbury **145** F3
Boscarne **97** E3
Boscastle **98** C1
Boscastle Pottery *Corn* PL35 0HE **98** B1
Boscombe *BCP* **106** A3
Boscombe *Wilts* **118** D4
Bosham **108** A3
Bosham Hoe **108** A3
Bosherston **126** C3
Bosley **171** G1
Bossall **195** G1
Bossiney **97** E1
Bossingham **125** D4
Bossington *Hants* **119** E4
Bossington *Som* **114** B3
Bostadh **270** D4
Bostock Green **171** D1
Boston **176** B3
Boston Spa **194** D3
Boswarthan **94** B3
Boswinger **97** D5
Bosworth Battlefield Country Park *Leics* CV13 0AD **159** F3
Botallack **94** A3
Botanic Garden *Oxon* OX1 4AZ **80** Oxford
Botany Bay **136** C3
Botcheston **159** G2
Botesdale **164** B4
Bothal **221** E3
Bothamsall **187** D5
Bothel **209** E3
Bothenhampton **104** A3
Bothwell **234** B4
Botley *Bucks* **135** E2
Botley *Hants* **107** E1
Botley *Oxon* **133** G2
Botloe's Green **145** G5
Botolph Claydon **148** C5
Botolphs **109** D3
Botolph's Bridge **124** D5
Bottacks **266** B5
Bottesford *Leics* **174** D4
Bottesford *NLincs* **187** F2
Bottisham **150** D1
Bottlesford **118** C2
Bottom Boat **194** C5
Bottom of Hutton **192** A5
Bottom o'th'Moor **184** A1
Bottomcraig **244** B2
Bottoms **193** F5
Botton Head **192** C1
Botusfleming **100** A1
Botwnnog **166** B4
Bough Beech **123** D4
Boughrood **144** A4
Boughspring **131** E3
Boughton Aluph **124** C4
Boughton Lees **124** C4
Boughton Malherbe **124** A4
Boughton Monchelsea **123** G3
Boughton Street **124** C3
Boulby **203** G1
Bouldnor **106** C4
Bouldon **157** E4
Boulge **153** D2
Boulmer **229** G5
Boulston **126** C1
Boultenstone Hotel **260** C3
Boultham **175** E1
Boundary *Derbys* **159** F1
Boundary *Staffs* **171** G3
Bourn **150** B2
Bourne **175** F5
Bourne End *Bucks* **135** D4
Bourne End *CenBeds* **149** E3
Bourne End *Herts* **135** F2
Bournebridge **137** E3
Bournemouth **105** G3
Bournemouth Airport **106** A3
Bournemouth International Centre BH2 5BH **64** Bournemouth
Bournheath **158** B5
Bournmoor **212** C2
Bournville **158** C4
Bourton *Bucks* **148** C4
Bourton *Dorset* **117** E4
Bourton *Oxon* **133** E4
Bourton *Shrop* **157** E3
Bourton *Wilts* **118** B1
Bourton on Dunsmore **159** G5
Bourton-on-the-Hill **147** D4
Bourton-on-the-Water **147** D5
Bousd **246** B3
Boustead Hill **209** F1
Bouth **199** E4
Bouthwaite **202** A5
Bovain **242** A1
Bovean **282** B2

Bovedy **286** C4
Boveney **135** E5
Boveridge **105** G1
Boverton **114** C1
Bovey Tracey **102** B5
Boviel **286** B5
Bovingdon **135** F2
Bovinger **137** E2
Bovington Camp **105** E4
Bow *Cumb* **209** G1
Bow *Devon* **102** A2
Bow *Devon* **101** E2
Bow *Ork* **277** C8
Bow Brickhill **149** E4
Bow Street *Devon* **101** E2
Bow Street *Norf* **164** B2
Bowbank **211** F5
Bowburn **212** C4
Bowcombe **107** D4
Bowd **103** E3
Bowden *Devon* **101** E3
Bowden *ScBord* **227** G2
Bowden Hill **118** A1
Bowdon **184** B4
Bower **219** F3
Bower Hinton **104** A1
Bower House Tye **152** A3
Bowerchalke **118** B5
Bowerhill **118** A1
Bowermadden **275** H2
Bowers **171** F4
Bowers Gifford **137** G4
Bowershall **243** F5
Bowertower **275** H2
Bowes **201** E1
Bowgreave **192** A3
Bowhousebog **234** C4
Bowithick **97** F1
Bowker's Green **183** F2
Bowland Bridge **199** F4
Bowley **145** E2
Bowley Town **145** E2
Bowlhead Green **121** E4
Bowling *WDun* **233** F2
Bowling *WYorks* **194** A4
Bowling Bank **170** A3
Bowmanstead **199** E3
Bowmore **230** B3
Bowness-on-Solway **218** A5
Bowness-on-Windermere **199** F3
Bowscale **209** G3
Bowsden **237** G5
Bowside Lodge **274** D2
Bowston **199** F3
Bowthorpe **178** C5
Bowtrees **234** D1
Box *Glos* **132** A2
Box *Wilts* **117** F1
Box End **149** F3
Boxbush *Glos* **131** G1
Boxbush *Glos* **145** F5
Boxford *Suff* **152** A3
Boxford *WBerks* **133** G5
Boxgrove **108** A3
Boxley **123** G3
Boxmoor **135** F2
Box's Shop **112** C5
Boxted *Essex* **152** A4
Boxted *Suff* **151** G2
Boxted Cross **152** A4
Boxwell **132** A3
Boxworth **150** B1
Boxworth End **150** B1
Boyden Gate **125** E2
Boydston **224** C2
Boylestone **172** C4
Boyndie **268** E4
Boynton **196** D1
Boys Hill **104** C2
Boysack **253** E5
Boyton *Corn* **98** D1
Boyton *Suff* **153** E3
Boyton *Wilts* **118** A4
Boyton Cross **137** F2
Boyton End **151** F3
Bozeat **149** E2
Braaid **190** B4
Braal Castle **275** G2
Brabling Green **153** D1
Brabourne **124** C4
Brabourne Lees **124** C4
Brabster **275** J2
Bracadale **255** J1
Braceborough **161** F2
Bracebridge Heath **175** E1
Braceby **175** F4
Bracewell **193** E3
Brachla **258** C1
Brackenber **200** C1
Brackenbottom **200** D5
Brackenfield **173** E1
Brackens **269** F5
Bracklach **260** B2
Bracklamore **269** G5
Bracklesham **108** A4
Brackletter (A' Bhreac-Leitir) **249** E1
Brackley *N'hants* **148** A4
Brackley *High* **267** F6
Brackley Gate **173** E3
Brackley Hatch **148** B3
Bracknell **121** D1
Braco **242** D4
Bracon Ash **164** C2
Bracora **256** D5
Bracorina **256** D5
Bradbourne **172** D2
Bradbury **212** C5
Bradda **190** A4
Bradden **148** B3
Braddock **97** F3
Bradenham *Bucks* **134** D3
Bradenham *Norf* **178** A5
Bradenstoke **132** C5
Bradfield *Essex* **152** C4
Bradfield *Norf* **179** D2
Bradfield *WBerks* **134** B5

Bradfield Combust **151** G2
Bradfield Green **171** D2
Bradfield Heath **152** C5
Bradfield St. Clare **152** A2
Bradfield St. George **152** A1
Bradfield Southend (Southend) **134** A5
Bradford *Corn* **97** F2
Bradford *Derbys* **172** D1
Bradford *Devon* **113** E5
Bradford *N'umb* **229** F3
Bradford *WYorks* **194** A4
Bradford Abbas **104** B1
Bradford Cathedral Church of St. Peter *WYorks* BD1 4EH **65** Bradford
Bradford Leigh **117** F1
Bradford Peverell **104** C3
Bradford-on-Avon **117** F1
Bradford-on-Tone **115** E3
Bradgate Park *Leics* LE6 0HE **17** B3
Bradiford **113** F2
Brading **107** F4
Bradley *ChesW&C* **183** G5
Bradley *Derbys* **172** D3
Bradley *Hants* **120** B3
Bradley *NELincs* **188** C2
Bradley (Low Bradley) *NYorks* **193** G3
Bradley *Staffs* **158** A1
Bradley *WMid* **158** B3
Bradley Green *Warks* **159** E2
Bradley Green *Worcs* **146** B1
Bradley in the Moors **172** B3
Bradley Mills **185** F1
Bradley Stoke **131** F4
Bradmore *Notts* **173** G4
Bradmore *WMid* **158** A3
Bradney **116** A4
Bradninch **102** D2
Bradnop **172** B2
Bradnor Green **144** B2
Bradpole **104** A3
Bradshaw *GtMan* **184** B1
Bradshaw *WYorks* **193** G4
Bradstone **99** D2
Bradwall Green **171** E1
Bradwell *Derbys* **185** F4
Bradwell *Devon* **113** E1
Bradwell *Essex* **151** G5
Bradwell *MK* **148** D4
Bradwell *Norf* **179** G5
Bradwell Grove **133** E2
Bradwell Waterside **138** C2
Bradwell-on-Sea **138** D2
Bradworthy **112** D4
Brae *D&G* **216** C3
Brae *High* **266** B1
Brae *Shet* **279** D6
Brae of Achnahaird **272** C7
Braeantra **266** C4
Braedownie **252** A2
Braeface **269** F6
Braegrum **243** F2
Braehead *D&G* **215** F5
Braehead *Glas* **233** G3
Braehead *Moray* **268** B6
Braehead *Ork* **276** D7
Braehead *Ork* **276** D5
Braehead *SLan* **225** G2
Braehead *SLan* **235** D4
Braehead of Lunan **253** E4
Braehoulland **278** B4
Braeleny **242** B3
Braemar **259** J6
Braemore *High* **266** C1
Braemore *High* **275** F5
Braemore *High* **265** H4
Braenaloin **259** K5
Braes of Enzie **268** B5
Braes of Foss **250** C4
Braes of Ullapool (Bruthaichean Ullapuil) **265** H2
Braeswick **276** F4
Braeval **242** A4
Brafferton *Darl* **212** B5
Brafferton *NYorks* **202** D5
Brafield-on-the-Green **148** D2
Bragar **270** E3
Bragbury End **150** A5
Bragenham **149** E5
Bragleenbeg **240** B2
Braichmelyn **167** F1
Braides **192** A2
Braidley **201** F4
Braidwood **234** C5
Braigo **230** A3
Brailsford **173** D3
Brain's Green **131** F2
Braintree **151** F5
Braiseworth **164** C4
Braishfield **119** E5
Braithwaite *SYorks* **186** D1
Braithwaite *WYorks* **193** G3
Braithwell **186** C3
Braken *Kent* **125** D4
Bramber **109** D2
Brambletye **122** D5
Brambridge **119** F5
Bramcote *Notts* **173** G4
Bramcote *Warks* **159** G4
Bramdean **120** B5
Bramerton **179** D5
Bramfield *Herts* **136** B1
Bramfield *Suff* **165** E4
Bramford **152** C3
Bramhall **184** C4
Bramham **194** D3
Bramhope **194** B3
Bramley *Hants* **120** B2
Bramley *SYorks* **186** B3
Bramley *Surr* **121** F3
Bramley Corner **120** B2
Bramley Head **194** A2
Bramley Vale **173** F1
Bramling **125** E3

Brampford Speke **102** C3
Brampton *Cambs* **162** A5
Brampton *Cumb* **210** B1
Brampton *Cumb* **210** C5
Brampton *Derbys* **186** A5
Brampton *Lincs* **187** F5
Brampton *Norf* **178** D3
Brampton *Suff* **165** F3
Brampton *SYorks* **186** B2
Brampton Abbotts **145** E5
Brampton Ash **160** C4
Brampton Bryan **156** C5
Brampton en le Morthen **186** B4
Brampton Street **165** F3
Brampton Valley Way Country Park *WN'hants* NN6 9DG **160** C5
Bramshall **172** B4
Bramshaw **106** B1
Bramshill **120** C1
Bramshott **120** D4
Bramwell **116** B5
Bran End **151** E5
Branault **247** E3
Brancaster **177** F3
Brancaster Staithe **177** F3
Brancepeth **212** B4
Branchill **267** H6
Brand Green **145** G5
Brandelhow **209** F4
Branderburgh **267** K4
Brandesburton **196** D3
Brandeston **152** D1
Brandis Corner **113** E5
Brandiston **178** C3
Brandlingill **209** E4
Brandon *Dur* **212** B4
Brandon *Lincs* **175** E3
Brandon *N'umb* **229** E5
Brandon *Suff* **163** F4
Brandon *Warks* **159** G5
Brandon Bank **163** E4
Brandon Creek **163** E3
Brandon Park *Suff* IP27 0SU **164** A4
Brandon Parva **178** B5
Brandsby **203** E5
Brandy Wharf **188** A3
Brane **94** B4
Branksome **105** G3
Branksome Park **105** G3
Bransbury **119** F3
Bransby **187** F5
Branscombe **103** E4
Bransford **145** G2
Bransford Bridge **146** A2
Bransgore **106** A3
Bransholme **196** C4
Branson's Cross **158** C5
Branston *Leics* **174** D5
Branston *Lincs* **175** F1
Branston *Staffs* **172** D5
Branston Booths **175** F1
Branston Water Park *Staffs* DE14 3EZ **172** D5
Brant Broughton **175** E2
Brantham **152** C4
Branthwaite *Cumb* **209** F3
Branthwaite *Cumb* **209** D4
Brantingham **196** B5
Branton *N'umb* **229** E5
Branton *SYorks* **186** D2
Brantwood **199** E3
Branxholm Bridge **227** F4
Branxholme **227** F4
Branxton **228** C3
Brassey Green **170** C1
Brassington **172** D2
Brasted **123** D3
Brasted Chart **123** D3
Brathens **260** E5
Bratoft **176** C1
Brattleby **187** G4
Bratton *Som* **114** B3
Bratton *Tel&W* **157** F1
Bratton *Wilts* **118** A2
Bratton Clovelly **99** E1
Bratton Fleming **113** G2
Bratton Seymour **117** D5
Braughing **150** B5
Brauncewell **175** F2
Braunston *Rut* **160** D2
Braunston *WN'hants* **148** A1
Braunstone **160** A2
Braunton **113** E2
Brawby **203** G5
Brawdy **140** B5
Brawith **203** E2
Brawl **274** D2
Brawlbin **275** F3
Bray **135** E5
Bray Shop **98** D3
Bray Wick **135** D5
Braybrooke **160** C4
Braydon Side **132** C4
Brayford **113** G2
Brayshaw **193** D2
Braythorn **194** B3
Brayton **195** F4
Braywoodside **135** D5
Brazacott **98** C1
Brea **96** A5
Breach *Kent* **125** D4
Breach *Kent* **124** A2
Breachwood Green **149** G5
Breacleit **270** D4
Breaden Heath **170** B4
Breadsall **173** E4
Breadstone **131** G2
Bready **285** F3
Breage **94** D4
Breakon **278** E2
Bream **131** F2
Breamore **106** A1
Brean **115** F2
Breanais **270** B5
Brearton **194** C1
Breascleit **270** E4
Breaston **173** F4
Brechfa **142** B4
Brechin **253** E3
Breck of Cruan **277** C6
Breckles **164** A2

Breckles **164** A2
Brecon (Aberhonddu) **143** G5
Brecon Beacons Dark Sky Reserve *Carmar./Powys* **129** E1
Brecon Beacons Visitor Centre *Powys* LD3 8ER **143** F5
Breconside **225** G5
Bredbury **184** D3
Brede **110** D2
Bredenbury **145** F2
Bredfield **153** D2
Bredgar **124** A2
Bredhurst **123** G2
Bredon **146** B4
Bredon's Hardwick **146** B4
Bredon's Norton **146** B4
Bredwardine **144** C3
Breedon on the Hill **173** F5
Breibhig **271** G4
Breich **235** D3
Breightmet **184** B2
Breighton **195** G4
Breinton **145** D4
Breinton Common **145** D4
Bremhill **132** B5
Bremhill Wick **132** B5
Brenachoille **240** C4
Brenchley **123** F4
Brendon *Devon* **114** A3
Brendon *Devon* **113** D5
Brendon *Devon* **113** D5
Brenkley **221** E4
Brent Eleigh **152** A3
Brent Knoll **116** A2
Brent Pelham **150** C4
Brentford **136** A5
Brentingby **160** C1
Brentwood **137** E3
Brenzett **111** F1
Brenzett Green **111** F1
Breoch **216** B5
Brereton **158** C1
Brereton Green **171** E1
Brereton Heath **171** F1
Breretonhill **158** C1
Bressay **279** E8
Bressingham **164** B3
Bressingham Common **164** B3
Bressingham Steam Museum & Gardens *Norf* IP22 2AA **164** B3
Bretby **173** D5
Bretford **159** G5
Bretforton **146** C3
Bretherdale Head **199** G2
Bretherton **192** A5
Brettabister **279** D7
Brettenham *Norf* **164** A3
Brettenham *Suff* **152** A2
Bretton *Derbys* **185** F5
Bretton *Flints* **170** A1
Bretton *Peter* **161** G2
Brevig **254** C4
Brewlands Bridge **251** G3
Brewood **158** A2
Briach **267** H6
Briantspuddle **105** E3
Brick End **151** D5
Brickendon **136** C2
Bricket Wood **136** A2
Brickhill **151** F4
Brickkiln Green **151** F4
Bricklehampton **146** B3
Bride **190** C2
Bridekirk **209** E3
Bridell **141** E3
Bridestones **171** G1
Bridestowe **99** F2
Brideswell **260** D1
Bridford **102** B4
Bridge *Corn* **96** A5
Bridge *Kent* **125** D3
Bridge End *Cumb* **198** D4
Bridge End *Devon* **100** C3
Bridge End *Essex* **151** E4
Bridge End *Lincs* **175** G4
Bridge End *Shet* **279** C9
Bridge Hewick **202** C5
Bridge of Alford **260** D3
Bridge of Allan **242** C5
Bridge of Avon **259** J1
Bridge of Awe (Drochaid Abha) **240** C1
Bridge of Balgie **250** A5
Bridge of Bogendreip **260** E5
Bridge of Brown **259** J2
Bridge of Cally **251** G4
Bridge of Canny **260** E5
Bridge of Craigisla **252** A4
Bridge of Dee *Aber* **259** J5
Bridge of Dee *Aber* **260** D5
Bridge of Dee *D&G* **216** B4
Bridge of Don **261** H4
Bridge of Dun **253** E4
Bridge of Dye **253** E1
Bridge of Earn **243** G3
Bridge of Ericht **250** A4
Bridge of Ess **260** D5
Bridge of Feugh **260** E5
Bridge of Forss **275** F2
Bridge of Gairn **260** B5
Bridge of Gaur **250** A4
Bridge of Muchalls **261** G5
Bridge of Muick **260** B5
Bridge of Orchy (Drochaid Urchaidh) **241** E1
Bridge of Tynet **268** B4
Bridge of Walls **279** B7
Bridge of Weir **233** E3
Bridge Reeve **113** G4
Bridge Sollers **144** D3
Bridge Street **151** G3
Bridge Trafford **183** F5
Bridgefoot *Angus* **244** B1
Bridgefoot *Cambs* **150** C3
Bridgefoot *Cumb* **209** D4
Bridgehampton **116** C5
Bridgehaugh **260** B1
Bridgehill **211** G2
Bridgemary **107** E2
Bridgemere **171** E3
Bridgend *A&B* **230** B3
Bridgend *A&B* **240** C5
Bridgend *Aber* **260** D1

Bridgend *Aber* 269 F6
Bridgend *Angus* 252 D3
Bridgend (Pen-y-bont ar Ogwr) *Bridgend* 129 F5
Bridgend *Corn* 97 F4
Bridgend *Cumb* 199 F1
Bridgend *Fife* 244 B3
Bridgend *Moray* 260 B1
Bridgend *P&K* 243 G2
Bridgend *WLoth* 235 E2
Bridgend of Lintrathen 252 A4
Bridgerule 112 C5
Bridges 156 C3
Bridgeton *Aber* 260 D3
Bridgeton *Glas* 234 A3
Bridgetown *Corn* 98 D2
Bridgetown *Som* 114 C4
Bridgewater Hall, Manchester *GtMan* M2 3WS 46 B4
Bridgeyate 131 F5
Bridgham 164 A3
Bridgnorth 157 G3
Bridgnorth Cliff Railway *Shrop* WV16 4AH 157 G3
Bridgtown 158 B2
Bridgwater 115 F4
Bridlington 197 D1
Bridport 104 A3
Bridstow 145 E5
Brierfield 193 E4
Brierley *Glos* 131 F1
Brierley *Here* 145 D2
Brierley *SYorks* 186 B1
Brierley Hill 158 B4
Brierton 213 D5
Briestfield 185 G1
Brig o'Turk 242 A4
Brigg 188 B1
Briggate 179 E2
Briggswath 204 B2
Brigh 282 B1
Brigham *Cumb* 209 D3
Brigham *ERid* 196 C2
Brighouse 194 B4
Brightgate 173 D2
Brighthampton 133 F2
Brightholmlee 185 G3
Brightling 110 B1
Brightlingsea 139 E1
Brighton *B&H* 109 F3
Brighton *Corn* 96 D4
Brighton Centre, The *B&H* BN1 2GR 65 Brighton
Brighton City (Shoreham) Airport 109 D3
Brighton Museum & Art Gallery *B&H* BN1 1EE 65 Brighton
Brighton Pier *B&H* BN2 1TW 65 Brighton
Brightons 234 D2
Brightwalton 133 G5
Brightwalton Green 133 G5
Brightwell 152 D3
Brightwell Baldwin 134 B3
Brightwell Upperton 134 B3
Brightwell-cum-Sotwell 134 A3
Brignall 201 F1
Brigsley 188 C2
Brigsteer 199 F4
Brigstock 161 E4
Brill *Bucks* 134 B1
Brill *Corn* 95 E4
Brilley 144 B4
Brilley Mountain 144 B2
Brimaston 140 C5
Brimfield 145 E1
Brimington 186 B5
Brimington Common 186 B5
Brimley 102 B5
Brimpsfield 132 B1
Brimpton 119 G1
Brims 277 B9
Brimscombe 132 A2
Brimstage 183 E4
Brinacory 256 D5
Brindham 115 F3
Brindister *Shet* 279 D9
Brindister *Shet* 279 B7
Brindle 192 B5
Brindley Ford 171 F2
Brineton 158 A1
Bringhurst 160 D3
Brington 161 F5
Brinian 276 D5
Briningham 178 B2
Brinkhill 189 D5
Brinkley *Cambs* 151 E2
Brinkley *Notts* 174 C2
Brinklow 159 G5
Brinkworth 132 C4
Brinmore 258 C2
Brinscall 192 C5
Brinsea 116 B1
Brinsley 173 F3
Brinsop 144 D3
Brinsworth 186 B3
Brinton 178 B2
Brisco 210 A2
Brisley 178 A3
Brislington 131 F5
Brissenden Green 124 B5
Bristol 131 E5
Bristol Airport 116 C1
Bristol Beacon BS1 5AR 66 Bristol
Bristol Cathedral BS1 5TJ 66 Bristol
Bristol City Museum & Art Gallery *Bristol* BS8 1RL 8 B3
Bristol Zoo *Bristol* BS8 3HA 8 B3
Briston 178 B2
Britford 118 C5
Brithdir *Caerp* 130 A2
Brithdir *Gwyn* 155 D1
Brithem Bottom 102 D1

British Empire & Commonwealth Museum BS1 6QH 66 Bristol
British Library (St. Pancras) *GtLon* NW1 2DB 12 B4
British Museum *GtLon* WC1B 3DG 44 E2
Briton Ferry (Llansawel) 128 D3
Britwell 135 E4
Britwell Salome 134 B3
Brixham 101 F2
Brixton *Devon* 100 B2
Brixton *GtLon* 136 C5
Brixton Deverill 117 F4
Brixworth 160 C5
Brixworth Country Park *W'hants* NN6 9DG 160 C5
Brize Norton 133 E2
Broad Alley 146 A1
Broad Blunsdon 133 D3
Broad Campden 147 D4
Broad Carr 185 E1
Broad Chalke 118 B5
Broad Ford 123 G5
Broad Green *Cambs* 151 E2
Broad Green *CenBeds* 149 E3
Broad Green *Essex* 151 G5
Broad Green *Essex* 150 C4
Broad Green *Mersey* 183 F3
Broad Green *Suff* 152 B2
Broad Green *Worcs* 145 G2
Broad Haven 126 B1
Broad Hill 163 D5
Broad Hinton 132 D5
Broad Laying 119 F1
Broad Marston 146 D3
Broad Oak *Cumb* 198 C3
Broad Oak *ESuss* 110 D2
Broad Oak *ESuss* 110 B1
Broad Oak *Here* 145 D5
Broad Road 165 D4
Broad Street *ESuss* 111 D2
Broad Street *Kent* 124 A3
Broad Street *Wilts* 118 C2
Broad Street Green 138 B2
Broad Town 132 C5
Broadbottom 185 D3
Broadbridge 108 A3
Broadbridge Heath 121 G4
Broadclyst 102 C3
Broadfield *Lancs* 192 D5
Broadfield *Lancs* 192 B5
Broadford (An t-Ath Leathann) 256 C2
Broadford Airport 256 C2
Broadford Bridge 121 F5
Broadgate 198 C4
Broadhaugh 227 F5
Broadhaven 275 H1
Broadheath *GtMan* 184 B4
Broadheath *Worcs* 145 F1
Broadhembury 103 E2
Broadhempston 101 E1
Broadholme 187 F5
Broadland Row 110 D2
Broadlay 127 G5
Broadley *Lancs* 184 C1
Broadley *Moray* 268 B4
Broadley Common 136 D2
Broadmayne 104 D4
Broadmeadows 227 F2
Broadmere 120 B3
Broadmoor 127 D2
Broadnymett 102 A2
Broadoak *Dorset* 104 A3
Broadoak *Glos* 131 F1
Broadoak *Kent* 125 D2
Broadoak End 136 C1
Broadrashes 268 C5
Broad's Green 137 F1
Broadsea 269 H4
Broadstairs 125 F2
Broadstone *BCP* 105 G3
Broadstone *Shrop* 157 E4
Broadstreet Common 130 C2
Broadwas 145 G2
Broadwater *Herts* 150 A5
Broadwater *WSuss* 108 D3
Broadwater Down 123 E5
Broadwaters 158 A5
Broadway *Carmar* 127 G2
Broadway *Carmar* 127 F1
Broadway *Pembs* 126 B1
Broadway *Som* 103 G1
Broadway *Suff* 165 E4
Broadway *Worcs* 146 D4
Broadwell *Glos* 147 G5
Broadwell *Oxon* 133 E2
Broadwell *Warks* 147 G1
Broadwell House 211 F2
Broadwey 104 C4
Broadwindsor 104 A2
Broadwood Kelly 113 G5
Broadwoodwidger 99 E2
Brobury 144 C3
Brocastle 129 F5
Brochel 264 B7
Brochloch 215 G1
Brock 246 B2
Brockaghboy 286 C4
Brockamin 145 G2
Brockbridge 107 F1
Brockdish 164 D4
Brockenhurst 106 B2
Brockford Green 152 C1
Brockford Street 152 C1
Brockhall 148 B1
Brockham 121 G3
Brockhampton *Glos* 146 C5
Brockhampton *Glos* 146 B5
Brockhampton *Here* 145 E4
Brockhampton *Here* 145 F2
Brockhampton Green 104 D2
Brockholes 185 F1
Brockholes *Lancs* PR5 0AG 192 B4

Brockhurst *Hants* 107 E2
Brockhurst *WSuss* 122 D5
Brocklebank 209 G2
Brocklesby 188 B1
Brockley *NSom* 116 B1
Brockley *Suff* 151 G2
Brockley Green 151 F3
Brock's Green 119 F1
Brockton *Shrop* 157 E3
Brockton *Shrop* 157 G2
Brockton *Shrop* 156 C1
Brockton *Shrop* 156 D4
Brockton *Tel&W* 157 G1
Brockton 203 F1
Brockweir 131 E2
Brockwood Park 120 B5
Brockworth 132 A1
Brocolitia (Frontiers of the Roman Empire) *N'umb* 220 A4
Brocton 158 B1
Brodick 223 F2
Brodsworth 186 C2
Brogaig 263 G5
Brogborough 149 E4
Brogden 193 E3
Brogyntyn 169 F4
Broken Cross *ChesW&C* 184 C5
Broken Cross *ChesW&C* 184 A5
Brokenborough 132 B4
Brokes 202 A3
Bromborough 183 E4
Brome 164 C4
Brome Street 164 C4
Bromeswell 153 E2
Bromfield *Cumb* 209 E2
Bromfield *Shrop* 157 D5
Bromham *Bed* 149 F2
Bromham *Wilts* 118 A1
Bromley *GtLon* 122 D2
Bromley *SYorks* 186 A3
Bromley Green 124 B5
Bromley Cross 184 B1
Brompton *Med* 123 G2
Brompton *NYorks* 202 C3
Brompton *NYorks* 204 C4
Brompton *Shrop* 157 E2
Brompton on Swale 202 B3
Brompton Ralph 115 D4
Brompton Regis 114 C4
Bromsash 145 F5
Bromsberrow 145 G4
Bromsberrow Heath 145 G4
Bromsgrove 158 B5
Bromstead Heath 158 A1
Bromyard 145 F2
Bromyard Downs 145 F2
Bronaber 168 A4
Bronant 142 C1
Brondesbury 136 B4
Bronington 170 B4
Bronllys 144 A3
Bronnant 142 A5
Bron-y-gaer 127 G1
Brongydd 144 B3
Bronwydd Arms 142 A5
Bronydd 144 B3
Brook *Hants* 106 B1
Brook *Hants* 106 C4
Brook *Hants* 119 E5
Brook *IoW* 106 C4
Brook *Kent* 124 C4
Brook *Surr* 121 E4
Brook *Surr* 121 F3
Brook Bottom 185 D3
Brook End *Bed* 149 F1
Brook End *Herts* 150 B5
Brook End *MK* 149 E2
Brook End *Worcs* 146 A3
Brook Hill 106 B1
Brook Street *Essex* 137 E3
Brook Street *Kent* 124 B5
Brook Street *Suff* 151 G3
Brook Street *WSuss* 109 F1
Brooke *Norf* 165 D2
Brooke *Rut* 160 D2
Brookeborough 281 F4
Brookend *Glos* 131 G5
Brookend *Glos* 131 F2
Brookfield *Derbys* 185 E3
Brookfield *Mid Ulster* 282 B2
Brookhampton 134 D1
Brookhouse *ChesE* 184 D5
Brookhouse *Denb* 169 D1
Brookhouse *Lancs* 192 B4
Brookhouse *SYorks* 186 C4
Brookhouse Green 171 F1
Brookhouses 171 G3
Brookland 111 E1
Brooklands *D&G* 216 C3
Brooklands *Shrop* 170 C3
Brooklands Museum *Surr* KT13 0QN 121 F1
Brookmans Park 136 B2
Brooks 156 A3
Brooks Green 121 G5
Brooksby 160 B1
Brookside Miniature Railway *ChesE* SK12 1BZ 25 G6
Brookthorpe 132 A1
Brookwood 121 E2
Broom *CenBeds* 149 G3
Broom *Fife* 244 B4
Broom *Warks* 146 C2
Broom Green 178 A3
Broom Hill *Dorset* 105 G2
Broom Hill *Worcs* 158 B5
Broom of Dalreach 243 F3
Broombjberg 283 G5
Broomcroft 157 E2
Broome *Norf* 165 E2
Broome *Shrop* 156 D4
Broome *Worcs* 158 B5
Broome Wood 229 F5
Broomedge 184 B4
Broomer's Corner 121 G5
Broomfield *Aber* 261 H1
Broomfield *Essex* 137 G1
Broomfield *Kent* 125 D2
Broomfield *Kent* 124 A3
Broomfield *Som* 115 F4
Broomfleet 196 A5
Broomhall Green 170 D3
Broomhaugh 211 G1
Broomhead 269 H4

Broomhill *Bristol* 131 F5
Broomhill *N'umb* 221 E1
Broomielaw 201 F1
Broomley 211 G1
Broompark 212 B3
Broom's Green 145 G4
Brora 267 G1
Broseley 157 F2
Brotherlee 211 F4
Brotherton 176 A3
Brotherton 195 D5
Brotton 203 F1
Broubster 275 F2
Brough *Cumb* 200 C1
Brough *Derbys* 185 F4
Brough *ERid* 196 B5
Brough *High* 275 H1
Brough *Notts* 174 D2
Brough *Ork* 277 C6
Brough *Shet* 279 D7
Brough *Shet* 278 D5
Brough *Shet* 279 E6
Brough *Shet* 278 B3
Brough Lodge 278 E3
Brough Sowerby 200 C1
Broughall 170 C3
Brougham 210 B5
Brougham Hall *Cumb* CA10 2DE 210 B5
Broughderg 285 J7
Broughshane 287 F5
Broughton *Bucks* 134 D1
Broughton *Cambs* 162 A5
Broughton *Flints* 170 A5
Broughton *Hants* 119 E4
Broughton *Lancs* 192 B4
Broughton *MK* 149 D3
Broughton *NLincs* 187 G2
Broughton *NN'hants* 160 D5
Broughton *NYorks* 203 G5
Broughton *NYorks* 193 F2
Broughton *Ork* 276 F2
Broughton *ScBord* 226 C2
Broughton *VGlam* 129 E5
Broughton Astley 160 A3
Broughton Beck 199 D4
Broughton Gifford 117 F1
Broughton Green 146 B1
Broughton Hackett 146 B2
Broughton in Furness 198 D3
Broughton Mills 198 D3
Broughton Moor 209 D3
Broughton Poggs 133 E2
Broughtown 276 F3
Broughty Ferry 244 C1
Browland 279 B7
Brown Candover 119 G4
Brown Edge *Lancs* 183 E1
Brown Edge *Staffs* 171 G1
Brown Heath 170 B1
Brown Lees 171 F2
Brown Street 152 B1
Brownber 200 C2
Browndown 107 E3
Brownheath 178 B5
Brownhill 269 G6
Brownhills *Fife* 244 D4
Brownhills *WMid* 158 C2
Brownieside 229 F4
Brownlow 171 F1
Brownlow Heath 171 F1
Brown's Bank 170 D3
Brownsea Island *Dorset* BH13 7EE 105 G4
Brownshill 132 A2
Brownshill Green 159 F4
Brownsover 160 A5
Brownston 100 C2
Browston Green 179 F5
Broxa 204 C3
Broxbourne 136 C2
Broxburn *ELoth* 237 D2
Broxburn *WLoth* 235 E2
Broxholme 187 G5
Broxted 151 E4
Broxton 170 B2
Broxwood 144 C2
Broyle Side 109 G2
Bruachmary 267 F7
Bruan 275 J5
Bruar (Brù) 271 F3
Bruera 170 B1
Bruern 147 E5
Bruernish 254 C4
Bruichladdich 230 A3
Bruisyard 153 E1
Bruisyard Street 153 E1
Brumby 187 G2
Brund 172 C1
Brundall 179 E5
Brundish *Norf* 165 E2
Brundish *Suff* 153 D1
Brundish Street 165 E2
Brunery 247 G1
Brunswick Village 221 E4
Bruntingthorpe 160 B3
Bruntland 260 C2
Brunton *Fife* 244 B2
Brunton *N'umb* 229 G4
Brunton *Wilts* 118 D1
Brunton Turret (Frontiers of the Roman Empire) *N'umb* NE46 4EE 220 A4
Bruscarnagh 281 H5
Brushfield 185 F5
Brushford *Devon* 113 G5
Brushford *Som* 114 C5
Bruton 117 D4
Bryansford 283 G5
Bryanston 105 E2
Bryant's Bottom 135 D3
Brydekirk 217 F3
Brymbo 169 F2
Brymor Ice Cream *NYorks* HG4 4PG 202 A4
Brympton 104 B1
Bryn *Caerp* 130 A3
Bryn *Carmar* 128 B2
Bryn *ChesW&C* 184 A5
Bryn *GtMan* 183 G2
Bryn *NPT* 129 E3
Bryn *Shrop* 156 B4
Bryn Bach Country Park *BGwent* NP22 3AY 130 A2
Bugle 97 E4

Bryn Gates 183 G2
Bryn Pen-y-lan 170 A3
Brynaman 128 D1
Brynbwbach 167 F4
Brynberian 141 E4
Bryn-cae 129 F4
Bryncethin 129 F4
Bryncir 167 D3
Bryn-coch *Bridgend* 129 F4
Bryn-coch *NPT* 128 D3
Bryncroes 166 B4
Bryn-crug 154 C2
Bryneglwys 169 E3
Brynford 182 C2
Bryngwran 180 B5
Bryngwyn *Mon* 130 C2
Bryngwyn *Powys* 144 A3
Brynhenllan 140 D4
Brynhoffnant 141 G2
Bryning 192 A4
Brynithel 130 B2
Bryn-mawr *BGwent* 130 A1
Bryn-mawr *Gwyn* 166 B4
Brynmelyn 156 A5
Brynmenyn 129 F4
Brynna 129 F4
Brynnau Gwynion 129 F4
Brynog 142 B2
Bryn-penarth 156 A2
Brynrefail *Gwyn* 167 E1
Brynrefail *IoA* 180 C4
Brynsadler 129 G4
Brynsaithmarchog 169 D2
Brynsiencyn 167 D1
Bryn-teg *IoA* 180 C4
Brynteg *Wrex* 170 A2
Brynygwenin 130 C1
Bryn-y-cochin 170 A4
Bryn-y-maen 181 F5
Buaile nan Bodach 254 C4
Bualadubh 262 C7
Bualintur 255 K2
Bualnaluib 264 D7
Bubbenhall 159 F5
Bubnell 185 G5
Bubwith 195 G4
Buccleuch 227 E4
Buchan 216 B4
Buchanan Castle 233 F1
Buchanhaven 269 K6
Buchanty 243 E2
Buchlyvie 242 A5
Buckabank 209 G2
Buckby Wharf 148 B1
Buckden *Cambs* 149 G1
Buckden *NYorks* 201 E5
Buckenham 179 E5
Buckerell 103 E2
Buckfast 100 D1
Buckfast Abbey *Devon* TQ11 0EE 100 D1
Buckfastleigh 100 D1
Buckhaven 244 B5
Buckholm 227 F2
Buckholt 131 E1
Buckhorn Weston 117 E5
Buckhurst Hill 136 D3
Buckie 268 C4
Buckies 275 G2
Buckingham 148 B4
Buckingham Palace *GtLon* SW1A 1AA 44 B4
Buckland *Bucks* 135 D1
Buckland *Devon* 100 C3
Buckland *Glos* 146 C4
Buckland *Hants* 106 C3
Buckland *Here* 145 E2
Buckland *Herts* 150 B4
Buckland *Kent* 125 F4
Buckland *Oxon* 133 F3
Buckland *Surr* 122 B3
Buckland Brewer 113 E3
Buckland Common 135 E2
Buckland Dinham 117 E2
Buckland Filleigh 113 E5
Buckland in the Moor 102 A5
Buckland Monachorum 100 A1
Buckland Newton 104 C2
Buckland Ripers 104 C4
Buckland St. Mary 103 F1
Buckland-tout-Saints 101 D3
Bucklebury 134 A5
Bucklerheads 244 C1
Bucklers Hard 106 C3
Bucklesham 152 D3
Buckley (Bwcle) 169 F1
Buckley Green 147 D1
Bucklow Hill 184 B4
Buckman Corner 121 G5
Buckminster 175 D5
Buckna 287 D5
Bucknall 175 G1
Bucknall *Oxon* 148 A5
Bucknell *Shrop* 156 C5
Buckridge 157 G5
Buck's Cross 112 D3
Bucks Green 121 F4
Bucks Hill 135 F2
Bucks Horn Oak 120 D3
Buck's Mills 113 D3
Buckspool 126 C3
Buckton *ERid* 205 E5
Buckton *Here* 156 C5
Buckton *N'umb* 229 E3
Buckton Vale 185 D2
Buckworth 161 G5
Budbrooke 147 E1
Budby 186 B5
Buddon 244 D1
Buddle 112 C5
Budge's Shop 98 D5
Budlake 102 C2
Budle 229 F3
Budleigh Salterton 103 D4
Budock Water 95 E3
Budworth Heath 184 A5
Buerton 171 D4
Bugbrooke 148 B2
Buggan 280 C2
Buglawton 171 F1

Bugthorpe 195 G2
Building End 150 C4
Buildwas 157 F2
Builth Road 143 G2
Builth Wells (Llanfair-ym-Muallt) 143 G2
Bulby 175 F5
Bulcote 174 B3
Buldoo 274 E2
Bulford 118 C3
Bulford Camp 118 C3
Bulkeley 170 C2
Bulkington *Warks* 159 F4
Bulkington *Wilts* 118 A2
Bulkworthy 113 D4
Bull Green 124 B5
Bullamoor 202 C3
Bull Green 136 B1
Bullbridge 173 E2
Bullbrook 121 D1
Bullen's Green 136 B2
Bulley 131 G1
Bullington 188 A5
Bullpot Farm 200 B4
Bulls Cross 136 C3
Bull's Green *Herts* 136 B1
Bull's Green *Norf* 165 F2
Bullwood 232 C2
Bulmer *Essex* 151 G3
Bulmer *NYorks* 195 F1
Bulmer Tye 151 G4
Bulphan 137 E4
Bulstone 103 E4
Bulverhythe 110 C3
Bulwark 269 H6
Bulwell 173 G3
Bulwick 161 E3
Bumble's Green 136 D2
Bun 281 F6
Bun Abhainn Eadarra 270 D7
Bun Loyne 257 J4
Bunarkaig 249 D1
Bunbury 170 C2
Bunbury Heath 170 C2
Bunchrew 266 D7
Bundalloch 256 E2
Bunessan 238 C2
Bungay 165 E3
Bunker's Hill 176 A2
Bunlarie 222 C2
Bunloit (Bun Leothaid) 258 C2
Bunmhullin 254 C3
Bunnahabhain 230 C2
Bunneil 281 G5
Buntait 257 K1
Buntingford 150 B5
Bunwell 164 C2
Bunwell Street 164 C2
Burbage *Derbys* 185 E5
Burbage *Leics* 159 G3
Burbage *Wilts* 118 D1
Burbage Abbey *Leics* LE10 3DD 159 G3
Burchett's Green 134 D4
Burcombe 118 B4
Burcot *Oxon* 134 A3
Burcot *Worcs* 158 B5
Burcott 149 D5
Burdale 196 A1
Burdocks 121 F5
Burdon 212 C2
Burdrop 147 F4
Bures 152 A4
Bures Green 152 A4
Burfa 144 B1
Burford *Oxon* 133 E1
Burford *Shrop* 145 E1
Burg 246 B2
Burgate 164 B4
Burge End 149 G4
Burgess Hill 109 F2
Burgh 152 D2
Burgh by Sands 209 G1
Burgh Castle 179 F5
Burgh Heath 122 B3
Burgh le Marsh 176 C1
Burgh next Aylsham 178 D3
Burgh on Bain 188 C4
Burgh St. Margaret (Fleggburgh) 179 F4
Burgh St. Peter 165 F2
Burghclere 119 F1
Burghead 267 J5
Burghfield 120 B1
Burghfield Common 120 B1
Burghfield Hill 120 B1
Burghill 145 D3
Burghwallis 186 C1
Burham 123 G2
Buriton 120 C5
Burland 170 D2
Burlawn 97 D3
Burleigh 121 E1
Burlescombe 103 D1
Burleston 105 D3
Burley *Hants* 106 B2
Burley *Rut* 161 D2
Burley *WYorks* 194 B4
Burley Gate 145 E3
Burley in Wharfedale 194 A3
Burley Street 106 B2
Burley Woodhead 194 A3
Burleydam 170 D2
Burlingjobb 144 B2
Burlow 110 A2
Burlton 170 B5
Burmarsh 124 D5
Burmington 147 E4
Burn 195 E5
Burn Farm 253 E2
Burn Naze 191 G3
Burn of Cambus 242 C4
Burnage 184 C3
Burnaston 173 D4
Burnby 196 A3
Burncross 186 A3
Burnedge 184 D1
Burnend 269 G6
Burneside 199 G3
Burness 276 F3
Burneston 202 C4
Burnett 117 D1
Burnfoot *CC&G* 285 J4
Burnfoot *High* 274 D6
Burnfoot *P&K* 243 E4
Burnfoot *ScBord* 227 G4
Burnfoot *ScBord* 227 F4
Burnham *Bucks* 135 E4
Burnham *NLincs* 188 A1
Burnham Deepdale 177 G3
Burnham Green 136 B1
Burnham Market 177 G3
Burnham Norton 177 G3
Burnham Overy Staithe 177 G3
Burnham Overy Town 177 G3
Burnham Thorpe 177 G3
Burnham-on-Crouch 138 C3
Burnham-on-Sea 116 A3
Burnhaven 269 K6
Burnhead *D&G* 215 G2
Burnhead *D&G* 216 C1
Burnhervie 261 F3
Burnhill Green 157 G2
Burnhope 212 A3
Burnhouse 233 E4
Burniston 204 D3
Burnley 193 E4
Burnmouth 237 G3
Burnopfield 212 A3
Burn's Green 150 B5
Burns National Heritage Park *SAyr* KA7 4PQ 224 B4
Burnside *A&N* 287 G7
Burnside *A&N* 287 F6
Burnside *Aber* 261 F3
Burnside *EAyr* 225 D4
Burnside *EAyr* 224 C5
Burnside *Fife* 243 G4
Burnside *Shet* 278 B5
Burnside *WLoth* 235 E2
Burnside of Duntrune 244 C1
Burnstones 210 C4
Burnswark 217 F3
Burnt Hill 134 A5
Burnt Houses 212 A5
Burnt Oak 136 B3
Burnt Yates 194 B1
Burntcliff Top 171 G1
Burntisland 235 F1
Burntstalls 194 C4
Burntwood 158 C2
Burntwood Green 158 C2
Burnworthy 103 E1
Burpham *Surr* 121 F2
Burpham *WSuss* 108 C3
Burra 279 C9
Burradon *N'umb* 220 B1
Burradon *T&W* 221 E4
Burrafirth 278 F1
Burraland 278 C5
Burras 95 D3
Burraton *Corn* 100 A1
Burraton *Corn* 100 A2
Burravoe *Shet* 278 E5
Burravoe *Shet* 279 C6
Burray 277 D8
Burrells 200 C1
Burrelton 244 A1
Burren *L&C* 283 G3
Burren *NM&D* 282 E6
Burridge *Devon* 103 E1
Burridge *Hants* 107 E1
Burrill 202 B4
Burringham 187 F2
Burrington *Devon* 113 G4
Burrington *Here* 156 D5
Burrington *NSom* 116 B2
Burrough Green 151 E2
Burrough on the Hill 160 C1
Burrow *Som* 114 C3
Burrow *Som* 104 A1
Burrow Bridge 116 A4
Burrowhill 121 E1
Burrows Cross 121 F3
Burry 128 A3
Burry Green 128 A3
Burry Port 128 A2
Burscough 183 F1
Burscough Bridge 183 F1
Bursea 196 A4
Burshill 196 C3
Bursledon 107 D2
Burslem 171 F3
Burstall 152 C3
Burstock 104 A2
Burston *Norf* 164 C3
Burston *Staffs* 171 G4
Burstow 122 C4
Burstwick 197 E5
Burtersett 201 D4
Burthorpe 151 F1
Burthwaite 210 A3
Burtle 116 B3
Burtle Hill 116 A3
Burton *BCP* 106 A3
Burton *ChesW&C* 183 E5
Burton *ChesW&C* 170 B5
Burton *Lincs* 187 G5
Burton *N'umb* 229 F3
Burton *Pembs* 126 C2
Burton *Som* 115 E3
Burton *Wilts* 132 A5
Burton *Wilts* 117 F5
Burton Agnes 196 D1
Burton Bradstock 104 A4
Burton Coggles 175 E5
Burton End 150 D5
Burton Ferry 126 C2
Burton Fleming 205 D5
Burton Green *Warks* 159 E5
Burton Green *Wrex* 170 A2
Burton Hastings 159 G4
Burton in Lonsdale 200 B5
Burton Joyce 174 B3
Burton Latimer 161 E5

Burton Lazars **160** C1
Burton Leonard **194** C1
Burton on the
  Wolds **173** G5
Burton Overy **160** B3
Burton Pedwardine **175** G3
Burton Pidsea **197** E4
Burton Salmon **195** D5
Burton Stather **187** F1
Burton upon
  Stather **187** F1
Burton upon Trent **172** D5
Burton's Green **151** G1
Burtonwood **183** G3
Burwardsley **170** C2
Burwarton **157** F4
Burwash **110** B1
Burwash Common **110** B1
Burwash Weald **110** B1
Burwell *Cambs* **151** D1
Burwell *Lincs* **189** D5
Burwen **180** C2
Burwick *Ork* **277** D9
Burwick *Shet* **279** C8
Bury *Cambs* **162** A4
Bury *GtMan* **184** C1
Bury *Som* **114** C5
Bury *WSuss* **108** C2
Bury End **146** C4
Bury Green **150** C5
Buryas Bridge **94** B4
Burythorpe **195** G1
Busbridge **121** E3
Busby *ERenf* **233** G4
Busby *P&K* **243** F2
Buscot **133** E3
Bush **112** C5
Bush Bank **145** D2
Bush Green **164** A4
Bushbury **158** B2
Bushby **160** B2
Bushey **136** A3
Bushey Heath **136** A3
Bushley **146** A4
Bushley Green **146** A4
Bushmills **286** D1
Bushton **132** C5
Bushy Common **178** A4
Business Design Centre,
  Islington *GtLon*
  N1 0QH **12** B3
Busk **210** C3
Buslingthorpe **188** A4
Bussage **132** A2
Busta **279** C6
Butcher's Common **179** E3
Butcher's Cross **110** A1
Butcher's Pasture **151** E5
Butcombe **116** C1
Bute **232** B3
Bute Town **130** A2
Buthill **267** J5
Butleigh **116** C4
Butleigh Wootton **116** C4
Butler's Cross **134** D2
Butler's Hill **173** G3
Butlers Marston **147** F3
Butlersbank **170** C4
Butley **153** E2
Butley Abbey **153** E3
Butley Low Corner **153** E3
Butley Mills **153** E2
Butley Town **184** D5
Butt Green **171** D2
Butt Lane **171** F2
Butterburn **219** E4
Buttercrambe **195** G2
Butterknowle **212** A5
Butterleigh **102** C2
Butterley **173** F2
Butterlope **285** G6
Buttermere *Cumb* **209** E5
Buttermere *Wilts* **119** E1
Butters Green **171** F2
Buttershaw **194** A4
Butterstone **251** F5
Butterton *Staffs* **172** B2
Butterton *Staffs* **171** F3
Butterwick *Dur* **212** C5
Butterwick *Lincs* **176** B3
Butterwick *NYorks* **204** C5
Butterwick *NYorks* **203** G5
Buttington **156** B2
Buttonbridge **157** G5
Buttonoak **157** G5
Buttons' Green **152** A2
Butts **102** B4
Butt's Green *Essex* **137** G2
Butt's Green
  Hants **119** D5
Buttsash **106** D2
Buxhall **152** B2
Buxted **109** G1
Buxton *Derbys* **185** E5
Buxton *Norf* **178** D3
Buxton Heath **178** C3
Buxworth **185** E4
Bwlch **141** E4
Bwlch-clawdd **141** G4
Bwlchderwin **167** D3
Bwlch-gwyn **169** F2
Bwlch-llan **142** B2
Bwlchnewydd **141** G5
Bwlchtocyn **166** C5
Bwlchycibau **156** A1
Bwlch-y-ddâr **169** E5
Bwlchyfadfa **142** A3
Bwlch-y-ffridd **155** G3
Bwlch-y-groes **141** F4
Bwlch-y-llyn **167** E2
Bwlchymynydd **128** B3
Bwlchysarnau **155** G5
Byers Green **212** B4
Byfield **148** A2
Byfleet **121** F1
Byford **144** C3
Bygrave **150** A4
Byker **212** B1
Byland Abbey **203** E5
Bylane End **97** G4
Bylchau **168** C1
Byley **171** F5
Bynea **128** B3
Byrness **219** F1
Bystock **102** D4

Bythorn **161** F5
Byton **144** C1
Bywell **211** G1
Byworth **121** E5

C
Cabharstadh **271** F5
Cabourne **188** B2
Cabourne Parva **188** B2
Cabrach *A&B* **230** C3
Cabrach *Moray* **260** B2
Cabragh *Mid Ulster* **281** K2
Cabragh *Mid Ulster* **286** C7
Cabus **192** A3
Cackle Street
  ESuss **110** D2
Cackle Street
  ESuss **109** G1
Cacrabank **227** E4
Cadboll **267** F4
Cadbury **102** C2
Cadbury Barton **113** G4
Cadbury Heath **131** F5
Cadbury World *WMid*
  B30 1JR **15** E4
Cadder **234** A2
Cadderlie **240** C1
Caddington **135** F2
Caddleton **189** E1
Caddonfoot **227** F2
Caddy **286** D6
Cade Street **110** B1
Cadeby *Leics* **159** G2
Cadeby *SYorks* **186** C2
Cadeleigh **102** C2
Cader **169** F1
Cadgwith **95** E5
Cadham **244** A4
Cadishead **184** B3
Cadle **128** C3
Cadley *Lancs* **192** B4
Cadley *Wilts* **118** D1
Cadnam **106** B1
Cadney **188** A2
Cadole **169** F2
Cadover Bridge **100** B1
Cadwell **149** E4
Cadwst **168** D4
Cady **280** D2
Cadzow **234** B4
Cae Ddafydd **167** F3
Caeathro **167** E1
Caehopkin **129** E1
Caen **275** F7
Caenby **188** A4
Caenby Corner **187** G4
Caeo (Caio) **142** C4
Caer Llan **131** D2
Caerau *Bridgend* **129** E3
Caerau *Cardiff* **130** A5
Caerdeon **154** C1
Caerfarchell **140** A5
Caergeiliog **180** B5
Caergwrle **170** A2
Caerhun **181** F5
Caer'n-lan **129** E1
Caerleon **130** C3
Caernarfon **167** D1
Caernarfon Castle (Castles
  & Town Walls of King
  Edward in Gwynedd)
  Gwyn LL55 2AY **167** D1
Caerphilly **130** A4
Caersws **155** G3
Caerwedros **141** G2
Caer-went **131** D4
Caerwys **182** C5
Caethle Farm **154** C3
Caggan **259** F3
Caggle Street **130** C1
Caheny **286** C4
Caherty **287** F5
Caim *High* **247** E3
Caim *IoA* **181** E4
Cairisiadar **270** C4
Cairminis **263** F3
Cairnargat **260** C1
Cairnbaan **240** A5
Cairnbrogie **261** G2
Cairnbulg **269** J4
Cairncross *Angus* **252** D2
Cairncross *ScBord* **237** F3
Cairncurran **233** E3
Cairndoon **207** D3
Cairndow **241** D3
Cairness **269** J4
Cairney Lodge **244** B3
Cairneyhill **235** E1
Cairngorm Mountain *High*
  PH22 1RB **259** G4
Cairnhill *Aber* **261** H2
Cairnhill *Aber* **260** E1
Cairnie *Aber* **261** G4
Cairnie *Aber* **268** C6
Cairnorrie **269** G6
Cairnryan **214** B4
Cairnsmore **215** F4
Caister-on-Sea **179** G4
Caistor **188** B2
Caistor St. Edmund **178** D5
Caistron **220** B1
Caithness Crystal Visitor
  Centre *Norf*
  PE30 4NE **163** E1
Cake Street **164** B2
Cakebole **158** A5
Calbost **271** G6
Calbourne **106** C4
Calceby **189** D5
Calcoed **182** C5
Calcot **134** B5
Calcott *Kent* **125** E3
Calcott *Shrop* **156** C1
Calcotts Green **131** G1
Calcutt **132** D3
Caldanagh **286** E3
Caldback **278** E2
Caldbeck **209** G3
Caldecote *Cambs* **150** B2
Caldecote *Cambs* **161** G4
Caldecote *Herts* **150** A4

Caldecote *Warks* **159** F3
Caldecote *WN'hants*
  148 B2
Caldecott *NN'hants*
  149 E1
Caldecott *Oxon* **133** G3
Caldecott *Rut* **161** D3
Calder Bridge **198** B2
Calder Grove **186** A1
Calder Vale **192** B3
Calder Mains **275** F3
Calderbank **234** B3
Calderbrook **184** D1
Caldercruix **234** C3
Calderglen Country Park
  SLan G75 0QZ **31** E6
Caldermill **234** A5
Caldey Island **127** E3
Caldhame **252** C5
Caldicot **131** D4
Caldwell *Derbys* **159** E1
Caldwell *ERenf* **233** F4
Caldwell *NYorks* **202** A1
Caldy **182** B4
Calebreck **209** G3
Caledon **282** A4
Caledrhydiau **142** A2
Calford Green **151** E3
Calfsound **276** E4
Calgary **246** C4
Califer **267** H6
California *Falk* **234** D2
California *Norf* **179** G4
California *Suff* **152** D3
California Country Park
  W'ham
  RG40 4HT **120** C1
Calke **173** E5
Calke Abbey *Derbys*
  DE73 7LE **173** E5
Calkill **281** G1
Callakille **264** C6
Callaly **220** C1
Callander **242** B4
Callanish (Calanais) **270** E4
Callaughton **157** F3
Callerton Lane End **212** A1
Calliburn **222** C3
Calligarry **256** C4
Callington **99** D3
Callingwood **172** C5
Callisterhall **218** A3
Callow **145** D4
Callow End **146** A3
Callow Hill *Wilts* **132** C4
Callow Hill *Worcs* **157** G5
Callow Hill *Worcs* **146** C1
Callows Grave **145** E1
Calmore **106** C1
Calmsden **132** C2
Calow **186** B5
Calrossie **266** E4
Calshot **107** D2
Calstock **100** A1
Calstone
  Wellington **118** B1
Calthorpe **178** C2
Calthwaite **210** A3
Calton *NYorks* **193** F2
Calton *Staffs* **172** C2
Calveley **170** C2
Calver **185** G5
Calver Hill **144** C3
Calverhall **170** D4
Calverleigh **102** C1
Calverley **194** B4
Calvert **148** B5
Calverton *MK* **148** C4
Calverton *Notts* **174** B3
Calvine **250** C3
Calvo **209** E1
Cam *CC&G* **286** B3
Cam *Glos* **131** G3
Camaghy **286** B5
Camasnacroise **248** A4
Camastianavaig **256** B1
Camasunary **256** B3
Camault Muir **266** C7
Camb **278** E3
Camber **111** E2
Camberley **121** D1
Camberwell **136** C5
Camblesforth **195** F5
Cambo **220** C3
Cambois **221** F3
Camborne **96** A4
Camborne & Redruth Mining
  District (Cornwall & West
  Devon Mining Landscape)
  Corn **95** D2
Cambourne **150** B2
Cambridge *Cambs* **150** C2
Cambridge *Glos* **131** G2
Cambridge American
  Military Cemetery &
  Memorial *Cambs*
  CB23 7PH **150** B2
Cambridge International
  Airport *Cambs* **150** C2
Cambridge University
  Botanic Garden *Cambs*
  CB2 1JF **150** C2
Cambus **234** D1
Cambus o'May **260** C5
Cambusbarron **242** C5
Cambuskenneth **242** D5
Cambuslang **234** A3
Cambusnethan **234** C4
Camden Town **136** B4
Camel Hill **116** C5
Camelford **97** D2
Cameley **116** D2
Camelon **234** C1
Camelsdale **121** D4
Camer **123** F2
Cameron House **233** F1
Camerory **259** F4
Camerton
  B&NESom **117** D2
Camerton *Cumb* **208** D3
Camerton *ERid* **197** F5
Camghouran **250** A4
Camis Eskan **233** E1

Camlough **282** D6
Cammachmore **261** H5
Cammeringham **187** G4
Camore **266** E2
Camp Hill *Pembs* **127** E1
Camp Hill *Warks* **159** F3
Campbeltown (Ceann Loch
  Chille Chiarain) **222** C3
Campbeltown
  Airport **222** B3
Camperdown **221** E4
Camperdown Country
  Park *Dundee*
  DD2 4TF **244** B1
Campmuir **244** A1
Camps **235** F5
Camps End **151** E3
Camps Heath **165** G2
Campsall **186** C1
Campsea Ashe **153** E2
Campsey **285** H3
Campton **149** G4
Camptown **228** A5
Camrose **126** C1
Camserney **250** D5
Camstraddan
  House **241** F5
Camus Croise **256** C3
Camus-luinie **257** F2
Camusnagaul *High* **248** C2
Camusnagaul *High* **265** K6
Camusrory **256** E5
Camusteel **264** D7
Camusterrach **264** D7
Camusurich **242** B1
Camusvrachan **250** B5
Canada **106** B1
Canaston Bridge **127** D1
Candacraig **260** B5
Candlesby **176** C1
Candy Mill **235** E5
Cane End **134** B5
Canewdon **138** B3
Canfield End **151** D5
Canford Bottom **105** G2
Canford Cliffs **105** G4
Canford Heath **105** G3
Canford Magna **105** G3
Canham's Green **152** B1
Canisbay **275** J1
Canley **159** F5
Cann **117** F5
Cann Common **117** F5
Canna **255** H4
Cannard's Grave **116** D3
Cannich (Canaich) **257** K1
Canning Town **136** D4
Cannington **115** F4
Cannock **158** B2
Cannock Wood **158** C1
Cannon Hall Country Park
  SYorks S75 4AT **185** G2
Cannon Hall Farm *SYorks*
  S75 4AT **185** G2
Cannon Hill Park *WMid*
  B13 8RD **15** E4
Cannop **131** F1
Canon Bridge **144** D3
Canon Frome **145** F3
Canon Pyon **145** D3
Canonbie **218** A4
Canons Ashby **148** A2
Canon's Town **94** C3
Canterbury *Aber* **268** D5
Canterbury *Kent* **124** D3
Canterbury Cathedral
  (Canterbury Cathedral,
  St Augustine's Abbey,
  & St Martin's Church)
  Kent CT1 2EH
  125 D3
Canterbury Tales, The
  Kent CT1 2TG
  67 Canterbury
Cantley *Norf* **179** E5
Cantley *SYorks* **186** D2
Cantlop **157** E2
Canton **130** A5
Cantray **266** E7
Cantraydoune **266** E7
Cantraywood **266** E7
Cantsfield **200** B5
Canvey Island **137** G4
Canwell Hall **158** D2
Canwick **175** E1
Canworthy Water **98** C1
Caol **248** D2
Caolas *A&B* **246** B2
Caolas *Na H-E. Siar* **254** B5
Caolasnacon **248** D3
Capel *Kent* **123** F4
Capel *Surr* **121** G3
Capel Bangor **154** C4
Capel Betws Lleucu
  142 C2
Capel Carmel **166** A5
Capel Celyn **168** B3
Capel Coch **180** C4
Capel Curig **168** A2
Capel Cynon **142** A3
Capel Dewi *Carmar* **142** A5
Capel Dewi *Cere* **154** C4
Capel Dewi *Cere* **142** A3
Capel Garmon **168** B2
Capel Gwyn
  Carmar **142** A5
Capel Gwyn *IoA* **180** B5
Capel Gwynfe **142** D5
Capel Hendre **128** C1
Capel Isaac **142** B5
Capel Iwan **141** F4
Capel le Ferne **125** E5
Capel Llanilltern **129** G5
Capel Mawr **180** C5
Capel Parc **180** C3
Capel Sain Silin **142** B2
Capel St. Andrew **153** E3
Capel St. Mary **152** B4
Capel Seion **154** C5
Capel Tygwydd **141** F3
Capel Uchaf **166** D3
Capelulo **181** F5
Capel-y-ffin **144** B4
Capel-y-graig **167** E1
Capenhurst **183** E5
Capernwray **199** G5
Capheaton **220** C3

Caplaw **233** F4
Capon's Green **153** D1
Cappagh *AB&C* **282** E4
Cappagh *Mid Ulster* **281** J2
Cappercleuch **226** D3
Capplegill **226** C5
Capstone **123** G2
Capton *Devon* **101** E2
Capton *Som* **115** D4
Caputh **251** E5
Car Colston **174** C3
Caradon Mining District
  (Cornwall & West Devon
  Mining Landscape)
  Corn **97** G3
Caradon Town **97** G2
Carbellow **225** F3
Carbeth **233** G1
Carbis Bay **94** C3
Carbost *High* **263** K7
Carbost *High* **255** J1
Carbrain **234** B2
Carbrooke **178** A5
Carburton **186** D5
Carcary **253** E4
Carco **225** F4
Carcluny **286** E4
Carcroft **186** A5
Cardenden **244** A5
Cardeston **156** C1
Cardew **209** G1
Cardiff
  (Caerdydd) **130** A5
Cardiff Bay Visitor Centre
  Cardiff CF10 4PA **7** C4
Cardiff Castle & Museum
  Cardiff CF10 3RB **67** Cardiff
Cardiff Airport **115** D1
Cardigan (Aberteifi) **141** E3
Cardinal's Green **151** D3
Cardington *Bed* **149** F3
Cardington *Shrop* **157** E3
Cardinham **97** F3
Cardno **269** H4
Cardonald **233** G3
Cardoness **215** G5
Cardow **267** J7
Cardross **233** E2
Cardurnock **209** E1
Cardy **283** J3
Careby **161** F1
Careston **252** D4
Carew **126** D2
Carew Cheriton **126** D2
Carew Newton **126** D2
Carey **145** E4
Carfin **234** B4
Carfrae **236** C3
Carfraemill **236** C4
Cargan **287** F4
Cargate Green **179** E4
Cargen **217** D3
Cargenbridge **217** D3
Cargill **243** G1
Cargo **209** G1
Cargreen **100** A1
Carham **228** B3
Carhampton **114** D3
Carharrack **96** B5
Carie *P&K* **250** B4
Carie *P&K* **242** B1
Carines **96** B4
Carinish (Cairinis) **262** D5
Carisbrooke **107** D4
Carisbrooke Castle &
  Museum *IoW*
  PO30 1XY **107** D4
Cark **199** E5
Carkeel **100** A1
Carland **282** A2
Carland Cross **96** C4
Carlane **286** E7
Carlatton **210** B2
Carlby **161** F1
Carlcotes **185** F2
Carleen **94** D4
Carleton *Cumb* **210** A2
Carleton *Cumb* **210** B5
Carleton *Lancs* **191** G3
Carleton *NYorks* **193** F3
Carleton *WYorks* **195** D5
Carleton Fishery **214** C2
Carleton Forehoe **178** B5
Carleton Rode **164** C2
Carleton St. Peter **179** E5
Carlin How **203** F1
Carlincraig **268** E6
Carlisle **210** A1
Carlisle Cathedral
  Cumb CA3 8TZ
  68 Carlisle
Carlisle Lake District Airport
  210 A1
Carlisle Park,
  Morpeth *N'umb*
  NE61 1YD **221** D3
Carloggas **96** C3
Carlops **235** F4
Carlow
  (Càrlabhagh) **270** E3
Carlton *Bed* **149** E2
Carlton *Cambs* **151** E2
Carlton *Leics* **159** F2
Carlton *Notts* **174** B3
Carlton *NYorks* **195** F4
Carlton *NYorks* **201** F4
Carlton *NYorks* **203** F4
Carlton *Stock* **212** C5
Carlton *Suff* **153** E1
Carlton *SYorks* **186** A1
Carlton *WYorks* **194** C5
Carlton Colville **165** G2
Carlton Curlieu **160** B3
Carlton Green **151** E2
Carlton Husthwaite **203** E5
Carlton in Lindrick **186** C4
Carlton Miniott **202** C4
Carlton Scroop **175** E3
Carlton-in-
  Cleveland **203** E2
Carlton-le-
  Moorland **175** E2
Carlton-on-Trent **174** D1
Carluke **234** C4
Carlyon Bay **97** E4
Carmacoup **225** F3
Carmarthen
  (Caerfyrddin) **142** A5

Carmel *Carmar* **128** B1
Carmel *Flints* **182** C5
Carmel *Gwyn* **167** D2
Carmel *IoA* **180** B4
Carmichael **226** A2
Carmont **253** G1
Carmunnock **233** G4
Carmyle **234** A3
Carmyllie **253** D5
Carn *A&B* **230** A4
Carn *CC&G* **286** B5
Carn Brea Village **96** A5
Carn Dearg **264** D4
Carnaby **196** D1
Carnach *High* **257** G2
Carnach *High* **265** G2
Carnach *Na H-E. Siar*
  262 D5
Carnagh **282** B6
Carnalbanagh **286** C2
Carnamoney **286** B6
Carnan **262** C7
Carnanreagh **285** H5
Carnassarie **240** A4
Carnbee **244** D4
Carnbo **243** F4
Carncastle **287** F5
Carndu **256** E2
Carnduff **286** E1
Carnduncan **230** A3
Carneatly **286** E2
Carnforth **199** F5
Carnhedryn **140** B5
Carnhell Green **94** D3
Carnichal **269** H5
Carnkie *Corn* **95** D3
Carnkie *Corn* **95** E3
Carnlough **287** G4
Carnmoney **287** H7
Carnmore **230** B5
Carno **155** F3
Carnoch *High* **257** K1
Carnoch *High* **265** J6
Carnoch *High* **267** F7
Carnock **235** E1
Carnon Downs **96** C5
Carnousie **268** E5
Carnoustie **245** D1
Carnteel **282** B5
Carntyne **234** A3
Carnwath **235** D5
Carnyorth **94** A3
Carol Green **159** E5
Carperby **201** F4
Carr **186** C3
Carr Hill **187** D3
Carr Houses **183** E2
Carr Shield **211** E3
Carr Vale **186** B5
Carradale **222** D2
Carragrich **263** G2
Carrbridge **259** G2
Carrefour Selous **100** C5
Carreglefn **180** B4
Carreg-wen **141** F3
Carrhouse **187** E2
Carrick *A&B* **232** A1
Carrick *F&O* **280** E1
Carrick Castle **241** D5
Carrick-a-Rede
  Rope Bridge (NT) *CC&G*
  BT54 6LS **286** E1
Carrickbrack **282** D5
Carrickfergus *M&EAnt*
  BT38 7BG **287** J7
Carrickgallogly **282** C6
Carrickmore **281** J1
Carrickyheenan **281** G5
Carriden **235** E1
Carrigans **285** G7
Carrigenagh **283** G7
Carrine **222** B5
Carrington *GtMan* **184** B3
Carrington *Lincs* **176** B2
Carrington *Midlo* **236** A3
Carroch **216** A1
Carrog *Conwy* **168** A3
Carrog *Denb* **169** E3
Carroglen **242** C2
Carrogs **282** E6
Carrol **267** F1
Carron *A&B* **240** B5
Carron *Falk* **234** C1
Carron *Moray* **267** K7
Carron Bridge **234** B1
Carronshore **234** C1
Carrot **252** C5
Carrow Hill **130** D3
Carrowcrin **286** E3
Carrowdore **283** J1
Carrutherstown **217** F3
Carruthmuir **233** E3
Carrville **212** B3
Carry **232** A3
Carryduff **283** G2
Carsaig **239** E2
Carscreugh **214** D4
Carse **231** F3
Carse of Ardersier **267** F6
Carsegowan **215** F5
Carseriggan **215** E4
Carsethorn **217** D5
Carsgoe **275** G2
Carshalton **122** B2
Carshalton Beeches **122** B2
Carsie **251** G5
Carsington **173** D2
Carsington Water *Derbys*
  DE6 1ST **172** D2
Carsluith **215** F5
Carsphairn **215** G1
Carstairs **234** D5
Carstairs Junction **235** D5
Carswell Marsh **133** F3
Carter's Clay **119** D5
Carterton **133** E2
Carterway Heads **211** G2
Carthew **97** E4
Cartland **234** C5
Cartmel **199** E5

Cartmel Fell **199** F4
Cartworth **185** F2
Carwe (Carway) **128** A2
Cascades Adventure
  Pool *Devon*
  EX33 1NZ **113** E2
Cascob **144** B1
Cashel Farm **241** G5
Casheltown **286** E6
Cashes Green **132** A2
Cashlie **249** G5
Cashmoor **105** F1
Cashty **285** F7
Caskieberran **244** A4
Caskum **282** E4
Casorna **285** H7
Cassencarie **215** F5
Cassington **133** G1
Cassop **212** C4
Castell **168** A1
Castell Gorfod **141** F5
Castell Howell **142** A3
Castellau **129** G4
Castell-y-bwch **130** B3
Casterton **200** B5
Castle Acre **163** G1
Castle Ashby *NN'hants*
  NN7 1LQ **148** D2
Castle Bolton **201** F3
Castle Bromwich **158** D4
Castle Bytham **161** E1
Castle Caereinion **156** A2
Castle Camps **151** E3
Castle Carrock **210** B2
Castle Cary **116** D4
Castle Combe **132** A5
Castle Donington **173** F5
Castle Douglas **216** B4
Castle Drogo *Devon*
  EX6 6PB **102** A3
Castle Eaton **132** D3
Castle Eden **212** D4
Castle Eden Dene National
  Nature Reserve *Dur*
  SR8 1NJ **212** D4
Castle End **159** E5
Castle Frome **145** F3
Castle Gate **94** B3
Castle Goring **108** D3
Castle Green **121** E1
Castle Gresley **159** E1
Castle Heaton **237** G5
Castle Hedingham **151** F4
Castle Hill *Kent* **123** F4
Castle Hill *Suff* **152** C3
Castle Howard *NYorks*
  YO60 7DA **195** G1
Castle Kennedy **214** C5
Castle Leod **266** B6
Castle Levan **232** D2
Castle Madoc **143** G4
Castle Morris **140** C4
Castle O'er **218** A2
Castle Rising **177** E5
Castle Semple Water
  Country Park *Renf*
  PA12 4HJ **233** E4
Castle Stuart **266** E7
Castlebay (Bàgh
  a'Chaisteil) **254** B5
Castlebythe **140** D5
Castlecary **234** B2
Castlecaulfield **282** A2
Castlecraig *High* **267** F5
Castlecraig *ScBord* **235** F5
Castledawson **286** D6
Castlederg **284** E7
Castlefairn **216** B2
Castleford **194** D5
Castlemartin **126** C3
Castlemilk *D&G* **217** F3
Castlemilk *Glas* **234** A4
Castlemorton **145** G4
Castlereagh **283** G1
Castlerigg **209** F4
Castlerock **286** B2
Castleroe **286** C3
Castleside **211** G3
Castlesteads **210** B1
Castlethorpe **148** C3
Castleton *A&B* **231** G1
Castleton *Aber* **269** F5
Castleton *Angus* **252** B5
Castleton *Derbys* **185** F4
Castleton *GtMan* **184** C1
Castleton *Newport* **130** B4
Castleton *NYorks* **203** F2
Castleton *ScBord* **218** C5
Castleton *Dorset* **104** C3
Castletown *High* **275** G2
Castletown *High* **265** F2
Castletown *IoM* **190** A5
Castletown *T&W* **212** C2
Castleweary **227** F5
Castlewellan **283** G5
Castlewigg **207** E2
Castley **194** B3
Caston **164** A2
Castor **161** G3
Castramont **215** G4
Caswell **128** B4
Cat & Fiddle Inn **185** E5
Catacol **232** A5
Catbrain **131** E4
Catbrook **131** E2
Catchall **94** B4
Catcleugh **219** F1
Catcliffe **186** B4
Catcott **116** A4
Caterham **122** C3
Catfield **179** E3
Catford **136** C5
Catforth **192** A4
Cathays **130** A5
Cathcart **233** G3
Cathedine **144** A5
Catherine-de-
  Barnes **159** D4
Catherington **107** F1
Catherston
  Leweston **103** G3
Catherton **157** F5
Cathkin **234** A4
Catisfield **107** E2
Catlodge **258** C5
Catlowdy **218** C4
Catmere End **150** C4
Catmore **133** G4

Caton *Devon* 102 A5
Caton *Lancs* 192 B1
Caton Green 192 B1
Cator Court 99 G3
Catrine 224 D3
Catsfield 110 C2
Catsfield Stream 110 C2
Catshaw 185 G2
Catshill 158 B5
Cattadale 230 B3
Cattal 194 D2
Cattawade 152 B4
Catterall 192 B3
Catterick 202 B3
Catterick Bridge 202 B3
Catterick Garrison 202 A3
Catterlen 210 A4
Catterline 253 G2
Catterton 195 E3
Catteshall 121 E3
Catthorpe 160 A5
Cattishall 161 E1
Cattistock 104 B2
Catton *N'umb* 211 E2
Catton *Norf* 178 D4
Catton *NYorks* 202 C5
Catton Hall 159 E1
Catwick 196 D3
Catworth 161 F5
Caudle Green 132 B1
Caudwell's Mill & Craft
   Centre *Derbys*
   DE4 2EB 173 G1
Caulcott *CenBeds* 149 F3
Caulcott *Oxon* 148 A5
Cauldcots 253 E5
Cauldhame *Stir* 242 B5
Cauldhame *Stir* 242 D4
Cauldon 172 B3
Caulhame 286 C4
Caulkerbush 216 D5
Caulside 218 C3
Caundle Marsh 104 C1
Caunsall 158 A4
Caunton 174 C1
Causeway
   D&G 215 F4
Causeway End
   Essex 137 F1
Causeway End
   Lancs 183 F1
Causewayhead
   Cumb 209 E1
Causeway Head 286 D1
Causewayhead *Stir* 242 D5
Causey 212 B2
Causey Arch Picnic Area
   Dur NE16 5EG 28 A4
Causey Park 221 D2
Causeyend 261 H3
Cautley 200 B3
Cavan 281 G2
Cavanacross 280 E4
Cavendish 151 G3
Cavendish Bridge 173 F5
Cavenham 151 F1
Cavens 217 D5
Cavers 227 G4
Caversfield 148 A5
Caversham 134 C5
Caverswall 171 G4
Cawdor 267 F6
Cawkeld 196 B2
Cawkwell 188 C4
Cawood 195 E4
Cawsand 100 A3
Cawston *Norf* 178 C3
Cawston *Warks* 159 G5
Cawthorn 203 G4
Cawthorne 185 G2
Cawthorpe 175 F5
Cawton 203 F5
Caxton 150 B2
Caxton Gibbet 150 A1
Caynham 157 E5
Caythorpe *Lincs* 175 E3
Caythorpe *Notts* 174 B3
Cayton 205 D4
CC2000 *Pembs*
   SA67 8DD 127 D1
Ceallan 262 D6
Ceann a' Bhàigh
   Na H-E. Siar 262 C5
Ceann a' Bhàigh
   Na H-E. Siar 263 F3
Ceann Shiphoirt 270 E6
Ceannacleit 263 D2
Ceannaridh 262 D6
Cearsiadair 271 F6
Cedig 167 E3
Cefn (Pontcysyllte Aqueduct
   & Canal) *Denb/Powys*
   Wrex 169 F3
Cefn Berain 168 C1
Cefn Canol 169 F4
Cefn Cantref 143 G5
Cefn Coch *Denb* 169 E2
Cefn Coch *Powys* 155 G2
Cefn Cross 129 E4
Cefn Einion 156 B4
Cefn Hengoed 130 A3
Cefn Rhigos 129 F2
Cefn-brith 168 C2
Cefn-caer-Ferch 166 D3
Cefn-coch 169 E5
Cefncoedycymmer 129 G2
Cefncribwr 129 E4
Cefn-ddwysarn 168 C3
Cefndeuddwr 168 A5
Cefneithin 128 B1
Cefngorwydd 143 F3
Cefn-gwyn 156 A4
Cefn-mawr 169 F3
Cefnpennar 129 G2
Cefn-y-bedd 170 A2
Cefn-y-pant 141 E5
Ceidio 180 C4
Ceidio Fawr 166 B4
Ceint 180 C5
Cellan 142 C3
Cellardyke 245 D4
Cellarhead 171 G4
Cemaes 180 B3
Cemmaes 155 E2
Cemmaes Road
   (Glantwymyn) 155 E2
Cenarth 141 F3

Cennin 167 D3
Centre for Life
   T&W NE1 4EP
   79 Newcastle upon Tyne
Ceramica *Stoke*
   ST6 3DS 20 C2
Ceres 244 C3
Cerist 155 F4
Cerne Abbas 104 C2
Cerney Wick 132 C3
Cerrigceinwen 180 C5
Cerrigydrudion 168 C3
Cessford 228 B4
Ceunant 167 E1
Chaceley 146 A4
Chacewater 96 B5
Chackmore 148 B4
Chacombe 147 G3
Chad Valley 158 C4
Chadderton 184 D2
Chadderton Fold 184 C2
Chaddesden 173 E4
Chaddesley Corbett 158 A5
Chaddlewortth 133 G5
Chadlington 147 F5
Chadshunt 147 F2
Chadstone 149 D2
Chadwell *Leics* 174 C5
Chadwell *Shrop* 157 G1
Chadwell Heath 137 D4
Chadwell St. Mary 137 F5
Chadwick End 159 E5
Chaffcombe 103 G1
Chafford Hundred 137 F5
Chagford 102 A4
Chailey 109 F2
Chainhurst 123 G4
Chalbury 105 G2
Chalbury Common 105 G2
Chaldon 122 C3
Chaldon Herring (East
   Chaldon) 105 D4
Chale 107 D5
Chale Green 107 D4
Chalfont Common 135 F3
Chalfont St. Giles 135 F3
Chalfont St. Peter 135 F3
Chalford *Glos* 132 A2
Chalford *Wilts* 117 F3
Chalgrave 149 E5
Chalgrove 134 B3
Chalk 137 F5
Chalk End 137 F1
Challaborough 100 C3
Challacombe 113 G1
Challister 279 E6
Challoch 215 E4
Challock 124 C3
Chalmington 104 B2
Chalton *CenBeds* 149 F5
Chalton *Hants* 107 G1
Chalvey 135 E5
Chalvington 110 A3
Champany 235 E2
Chancery 154 B5
Chandler's Cross 135 F3
Chandler's Ford 119 F5
Channel Islands 100 A5
Channel's End 149 G2
Channerwick 279 D10
Chantry *Som* 117 E3
Chantry *Suff* 152 C3
Chapel 244 A5
Chapel Allerton
   Som 116 B2
Chapel Allerton
   WYorks 194 C4
Chapel Amble 97 D2
Chapel Brampton 148 C1
Chapel Chorlton 171 F4
Chapel Cleeve 114 D3
Chapel Cross 110 B1
Chapel End 149 F3
Chapel Green
   Warks 159 E4
Chapel Green
   Warks 147 G1
Chapel Haddlesey 195 E5
Chapel Hill *Aber* 261 J1
Chapel Hill *Lincs* 176 A2
Chapel Hill *Mon* 131 E2
Chapel Hill *NYorks* 194 C3
Chapel Knapp 117 F1
Chapel Lawn 156 C5
Chapel Leigh 115 E5
Chapel Milton 185 E4
Chapel of Garioch 261 F2
Chapel Rossan 206 B2
Chapel Row
   Essex 137 G2
Chapel Row
   WBerks 119 G1
Chapel St. Leonards 189 F5
Chapel Stile 199 E2
Chapel Town 96 C4
Chapelbank 243 F3
Chapeldonan 223 G5
Chapelend Way 151 F4
Chapel-en-le-Frith 185 E4
Chapelgate 176 C5
Chapelhall 234 B3
Chapelhill *High* 267 F4
Chapelhill *P&K* 244 A3
Chapelhill *P&K* 243 F3
Chapelknowe 218 B4
Chapelthorpe 186 A1
Chapelton *Aber* 253 G1
Chapelton *Angus* 253 E5
Chapelton *Devon* 113 F3
Chapelton *SLan* 234 A5
Chapeltown *B'burn* 184 B1
Chapeltown *Cumb* 218 C4
Chapeltown
   M&EAnt 287 F6
Chapeltown *Moray* 259 K2
Chapeltown *NM&D* 283 J4
Chapeltown *SYorks* 186 A3
Chapmans Well 99 E1
Chapmanslade 117 F3
Chapmore End 136 C1
Chappel 151 G5
Charaton 98 D4
Chard 103 G2
Chard Junction 103 G3
Chardleigh Green 103 G1
Chardstock 103 G2
Charfield 131 G3
Charing 124 B4
Charing Cross 106 A1

Charing Heath 124 B4
Charingworth 147 D4
Charlbury 133 F1
Charlcombe 117 E1
Charlecote 147 E2
Charlemont 282 B3
Charles 113 G2
Charles Tye 152 B2
Charlesfield 227 G3
Charleston 252 B5
Charlestown *Aber* 269 J4
Charlestown
   Aberdeen 261 H4
Charlestown *Corn* 97 E4
Charlestown
   Derbys 185 E3
Charlestown
   Dorset 104 C5
Charlestown *Fife* 235 E1
Charlestown
   GtMan 184 C2
Charlestown
   High 264 E4
Charlestown
   High 266 D7
Charlestown
   WYorks 194 A4
Charlestown
   WYorks 193 F5
Charlestown (Cornwall
   & West Devon Mining
   Landscape) *Corn* 96 E4
Charlestown of Aberlour
   (Aberlour) *Moray* 267 K7
Charlesworth 185 E3
Charleton 244 C4
Charlinch 115 F4
Charlotteville 121 F3
Charlton *GtLon* 136 D5
Charlton *Hants* 119 E3
Charlton *Herts* 149 G5
Charlton *N'umb* 220 A3
Charlton *Oxon* 133 G4
Charlton *Som* 117 D2
Charlton *Som* 116 D3
Charlton *Som* 115 F5
Charlton *Tel&W* 157 E1
Charlton *Wilts* 118 A5
Charlton *Wilts* 132 B4
Charlton *Wilts* 118 C2
Charlton *WN'hants* 148 A4
Charlton *Worcs* 146 C3
Charlton *WSuss* 108 A2
Charlton Abbots 146 C5
Charlton Adam 116 C5
Charlton Down 104 C3
Charlton
   Horethorne 117 D5
Charlton Kings 146 B5
Charlton Mackrell 116 C5
Charlton Marshall 105 E2
Charlton Musgrove 117 E5
Charlton on the Hill 105 E2
Charlton-All-Saints 118 C5
Charlton-on-
   Otmoor 134 A1
Charlons 203 F1
Charlwood 122 B4
Charminster 104 C3
Charmouth 103 G3
Charndon 148 B5
Charney Bassett 133 F3
Charnock Richard 183 G1
Charsfield 153 D2
Chart Corner 123 G4
Chart Sutton 124 A4
Charter Alley 119 G2
Charterhouse 116 B2
Charterville
   Allotments 133 F2
Chartham 124 D3
Chartham Hatch 124 D3
Chartridge 135 E2
Chartwell
   Kent TN16 1PS 123 D3
Charvil 134 C5
Charwelton 148 A2
Chase End Street 145 G4
Chase Terrace 158 C2
Chasetown 158 C2
Chastleton 147 E5
Chasty 112 D5
Chatburn 193 D3
Chatcull 171 E4
Chatelherault Country
   Park *SLan*
   ML3 7UE 31 G6
Chatham 123 G2
Chatham Green 137 G1
Chatham Historic
   Dockyard *Med*
   ME4 4TZ 123 G2
Chathill 229 F4
Chatsworth Farmyard &
   Adventure Playground
   Derbys
   DE45 1PP 185 G5
Chatsworth House *Derbys*
   DE45 1PP 185 G5
Chattenden 137 G5
Chatteris 162 B4
Chattisham 152 B3
Chatto 228 B5
Chatton 229 E4
Chaul End 149 F5
Chavey Down 121 E1
Chawleigh 102 A1
Chawley 133 G2
Chawston 149 G2
Chawton 120 C4
Chazey Heath 134 B5
Cheadle *GtMan* 184 C4
Cheadle *Staffs* 172 B3
Cheadle Heath 184 C4
Cheadle Hulme 184 C4
Cheam 122 B2
Cheapside 121 E1
Chearsley 134 C1
Chebsey 171 F5
Checkendon 134 B4
Checkley *ChesE* 171 E3
Checkley *Here* 145 E4
Checkley *Staffs* 172 B4
Checkley Green 171 E3
Chedburgh 151 F2
Cheddar 116 B2
Cheddar Caves & Gorge
   Som BS27 3QF 116 B2
Cheddington 135 E1

Cheddleton 171 G2
Cheddon Fitzpaine 115 F5
Chedglow 132 B3
Chedgrave 165 E2
Chedington 104 A2
Chediston 165 E4
Chediston Green 165 E4
Chedworth 132 C1
Chedzoy 115 F4
Cheesden 184 C1
Cheeseman's Green 124 C5
Cheetham Hill 184 C2
Cheglinch 113 F1
Cheldon 102 A1
Chelford 184 C5
Chellaston 173 E4
Chells 150 A5
Chelmarsh 157 G4
Chelmondiston 152 D4
Chelmorton 172 C1
Chelmsford 137 G2
Chelmsford Cathedral
   Essex CM1 1TY 137 G2
Chelmsley Wood 159 D4
Chelsea 136 B5
Chelsfield 123 D2
Chelsham 122 C3
Chelston Heath 115 E5
Chelsworth 152 A3
Cheltenham 146 B5
Chelveston 149 E1
Chelvey 116 B1
Chelwood 116 D1
Chelwood Common 109 G1
Chelwood Gate 109 G1
Chelworth 132 B3
Cheney Longville 156 D4
Chenies 135 F3
Chepstow
   (Cas-gwent) 131 E3
Cherhill 132 C5
Cherington *Glos* 132 B3
Cherington *Warks* 147 E4
Cheriton *Devon* 114 A3
Cheriton *Hants* 119 G5
Cheriton *Kent* 125 D5
Cheriton *Pembs* 126 C3
Cheriton *Swan* 128 A3
Cheriton Bishop 102 A3
Cheriton Cross 102 A3
Cheriton Fitzpaine 102 B2
Cherrington 171 D5
Cherry Burton 196 B3
Cherry Green 151 D5
Cherry Hinton 150 C2
Cherry Willingham 188 A5
Cherrymount 282 D2
Chertsey 121 F1
Cheselbourne 105 D3
Chesham 135 E2
Chesham Bois 135 F3
Cheshire Farm Ice Cream,
   Tattenhall *ChesW&C*
   CH3 9NE 170 B1
Cheshunt 136 C2
Cheslyn Hay 158 B2
Chessington 121 G1
Chessington World of
   Adventures *GtLon*
   KT9 2NE 121 G1
Chestall 158 C1
Chester 170 B1
Chester Cathedral
   ChesW&C CH1 2HU
   69 Chester
Chester Moor 212 B3
Chester Zoo *ChesW&C*
   CH2 1LH 183 F5
Chesterblade 117 D3
Chesterfield
   Derbys 186 A5
Chesterfield *Staffs* 158 D2
Chester-le-Street 212 B2
Chesters *ScBord* 228 A5
Chesters *ScBord* 228 A4
Chesters Roman Fort
   (Frontiers of the Roman
   Empire) *N'umb* NE46 4EU
   220 B5
Chesterton *Cambs* 150 C1
Chesterton *Cambs* 161 G3
Chesterton *Oxon* 148 A5
Chesterton *Shrop* 157 G3
Chesterton *Staffs* 171 F3
Chesterton *Warks* 147 F2
Chesterton Green 147 F2
Chestfield 124 D2
Cheston 100 C2
Cheswardine 171 E5
Cheswick 229 E2
Cheswick Buildings 229 E2
Cheswick Green 158 D5
Chetnole 104 C2
Chettiscombe 102 C1
Chettisham 162 D4
Chettle 105 F1
Chetton 157 F3
Chetwode 148 B5
Chetwynd Aston 157 G1
Chetwynd Park 171 E5
Cheveley 151 E1
Chevening 123 D3
Cheverell's Green 135 F1
Chevin Forest Park *WYorks*
   LS21 3JL 194 B3
Chevington 151 F2
Chevithorne 102 C1
Chew Magna 116 C1
Chew Moor 184 A2
Chew Stoke 116 C1
Chewton
   Keynsham 116 D1
Chewton Mendip 116 C2
Chicacott 99 G1
Chicheley 149 E3
Chichester 108 A3
Chichester Cathedral *WSuss*
   PO19 1PX 108 A3
Chickerell 104 C4
Chickering 164 D4
Chicklade 118 A4
Chicksands 149 G4
Chidden 107 F1
Chiddingfold 121 E4
Chiddingly 110 A2
Chiddingstone 123 D4

Chiddingstone
   Causeway 123 E4
Chiddingstone
   Hoath 123 D4
Chideock 104 A3
Chidham 107 G2
Chidswell 194 B5
Chieveley 133 G5
Chignall St. James 137 F2
Chignall Smealy 137 F1
Chigwell 136 D3
Chigwell Row 137 D3
Chilbolton 119 E3
Chilcomb 119 G5
Chilcombe 104 B3
Chilcompton 117 D2
Chilcote 159 E1
Child Okeford 105 E1
Child Thornton 183 E5
Childerditch 137 F4
Childrey 133 F4
Child's Ercall 171 D5
Childswickham 146 C4
Childwall 183 F4
Childwick Green 136 A1
Chilfrome 104 B3
Chilgrove 108 A2
Chilham 124 C3
Chilhampton 118 B4
Chilla 118 C5
Chillaton 99 E2
Chillenden 125 E3
Chillerton 107 D4
Chillesford 153 E2
Chilley 101 D2
Chillingham 229 E4
Chillington *Devon* 101 D3
Chillington *Som* 103 G1
Chilmark 118 A4
Chilson *Oxon* 133 F1
Chilson *Som* 103 G2
Chilsworthy *Corn* 99 E3
Chilsworthy *Devon* 112 D5
Chilthorne Domer 104 A1
Chilton *Bucks* 134 B1
Chilton *Devon* 102 B2
Chilton *Dur* 212 B5
Chilton *Oxon* 133 G4
Chilton *Suff* 151 G3
Chilton Candover 119 G4
Chilton Cantelo 116 C5
Chilton Foliat 133 F5
Chilton Polden 116 A4
Chilton Street 151 F3
Chilton Trinity 115 F4
Chilvers Coton 159 F3
Chilwell 173 G4
Chilworth *Hants* 106 D1
Chilworth *Surr* 121 F3
Chimney 133 F2
Chimney Street 151 F3
Chineham 120 B2
Chingford 136 C3
Chinley 185 E4
Chinley Head 185 E4
Chinnor 134 C2
Chipchase Castle 220 A4
Chipley 115 E5
Chipnall 171 E4
Chippenham
   Cambs 151 E1
Chippenham *Wilts* 132 B5
Chipperfield 135 F2
Chipping *Herts* 150 B4
Chipping *Lancs* 192 C3
Chipping Campden 147 D4
Chipping Hill 138 B1
Chipping Norton 147 F5
Chipping Ongar 137 E2
Chipping Sodbury 131 G4
Chipping Warden 147 G3
Chipstable 114 D5
Chipstead *Kent* 123 D3
Chipstead *Surr* 122 B3
Chirbury 156 B2
Chirk (Y Waun) 169 F4
Chirk (Pontcysyllte Aqueduct
   & Canal) *Denb/Powys*
   Wrex 169 F4
Chirk Green 169 F4
Chirmorrie 214 D3
Chirnside 237 F4
Chirnsidebridge 237 F4
Chirton *T&W* 212 C1
Chirton *Wilts* 118 B2
Chisbury 119 D1
Chiscan 222 B4
Chiselborough 104 A1
Chiseldon 133 D5
Chiserley 193 G5
Chislehampton 134 A3
Chislehurst 136 D5
Chislet 125 E2
Chiswell 104 C5
Chiswell Green 136 A2
Chiswick 136 B5
Chiswick End 150 B3
Chisworth 185 D3
Chithurst 120 D5
Chittering 162 C5
Chitterne 118 A3
Chittlehamholt 113 G3
Chittlehampton 113 G3
Chittoe 118 A1
Chivelstone 101 D4
Chivenor 113 F2
Chobham 121 E1
Cholderton 118 D3
Cholesbury 135 E2
Chollerford 220 B4
Chollerton 220 B4
Cholsey 134 A4
Cholstrey 145 D2
Cholwell
   B&NESom 116 D1
Cholwell *Devon* 99 E3
Chop Gate 203 E3
Choppington 221 E3
Chopwell 212 A2
Chorley *ChesE* 170 C2
Chorley *Lancs* 183 G1
Chorley *Shrop* 157 F4
Chorley *Staffs* 158 C1
Chorleywood 135 F3
Chorlton 171 E2
Chorlton Lane 170 B3

Chorlton-cum-
   Hardy 184 C3
Chowley 170 B2
Chrishall 150 C4
Chrishall Grange 150 C3
Chrisswell 232 D2
Christ Church *Oxon*
   OX1 1DP 80 Oxford
Christchurch
   BCP 106 A3
Christchurch
   Cambs 162 C3
Christchurch
   Newport 130 C4
Christian Malford 132 B5
Christleton 170 B1
Christmas Common 134 C3
Christon 116 A2
Christon Bank 229 G4
Christow 102 B4
Christskirk 260 E2
Christystown 287 F6
Chryston 234 A2
Chudleigh 102 B5
Chudleigh Knighton 102 B5
Chulmleigh 113 G4
Chunal 185 E3
Church 192 D5
Church Aston 157 G1
Church Ballee 283 J4
Church Brampton 148 C1
Church Brough 200 C1
Church Broughton 172 D4
Church Charwelton 148 A2
Church Common 153 E2
Church Crookham 120 D2
Church Eaton 158 A1
Church End *Cambs* 162 B2
Church End *Cambs* 162 B5
Church End *Cambs* 162 A4
Church End
   CenBeds 149 G4
Church End
   CenBeds 149 E5
Church End
   CenBeds 149 G2
Church End
   CenBeds 149 E4
Church End
   CenBeds 149 E4
Church End *ERid* 196 C2
Church End *Essex* 151 D3
Church End *Essex* 151 F5
Church End *Glos* 146 A4
Church End *Hants* 120 B2
Church End *Herts* 136 A1
Church End *Herts* 150 C5
Church End *Lincs* 176 A4
Church End *Lincs* 176 B3
Church End *Warks* 159 E3
Church End *Wilts* 132 C5
Church Enstone 147 F5
Church Fenton 195 E4
Church Green 103 E3
Church Gresley 159 E1
Church
   Hanborough 133 G1
Church Hill
   ChesW&C 170 D1
Church Hill *Derbys* 173 F1
Church Hill *F&O* 281 G3
Church Houses 203 F3
Church Knowle 105 F4
Church Laneham 187 F5
Church Langley 137 D2
Church Langton 160 C3
Church Lawford 159 G5
Church Lawton 171 F2
Church Leigh 172 B4
Church Lench 146 C2
Church Mayfield 172 C3
Church Minshull 171 D1
Church Norton 108 A4
Church of St. Mary-
   in-Castro *Kent*
   CT16 1HU 70 Dover
Church Preen 157 E3
Church Pulverbatch 156 D2
Church Stoke 156 B3
Church Stowe 148 B2
Church Street
   Essex 151 F3
Church Street *Kent* 137 G5
Church Stretton 157 D3
Church Town *Leics* 159 F1
Church Town *Surr* 122 C3
Church Village 129 G4
Church Warsop 173 G1
Church Westcote 147 E5
Church Wilne 173 F4
Churcham 131 G1
Churchdown 132 A1
Churchend *Essex* 138 D3
Churchend *Essex* 151 F5
Churchend *SGlos* 131 G3
Churchfield 158 C3
Churchgate 136 C2
Churchgate Street 137 D1
Churchill *Devon* 113 F1
Churchill *Devon* 103 F2
Churchill *NSom* 116 B2
Churchill *Oxon* 147 E5
Churchill *Worcs* 146 B2
Churchill *Worcs* 158 A5
Churchill Museum &
   Cabinet War Rooms
   GtLon SW1A 2AQ 44 D5
Churchingford 103 F1
Churchover 160 A4
Churchstanton 103 E1
Churchstow 100 D3
Churchtown *Devon* 113 G1
Churchtown *IoM* 190 C2
Churchtown *Lancs* 192 A3
Churchtown
   Mersey 183 E1
Churchtown *Mid Ulster*
   286 C7
Churchtown *NM&D* 283 J4
Churnsike Lodge 219 E4
Churston Ferrers 101 F2
Churt 121 D4
Churton 170 B2
Churwell 194 B5
Chute Cadley 119 E2
Chute Standen 119 E2
Chwilog 166 D4

Chyandour 94 B3
Chysauster 94 B3
Cilan Uchaf 166 B5
Cilcain 169 E1
Cilcennin 142 B1
Cilcewydd 156 B2
Cilfrew 129 D2
Cilfynydd 129 G3
Cilgerran 141 E4
Cilgwyn *Carmar* 142 D4
Cilgwyn *Pembs* 141 D4
Ciliau Aeron 142 B2
Cille Bhrighde 254 C3
Cille Pheadair 254 C3
Cilmaen-gwyn 128 D2
Cilmery 143 G2
Cilrhedyn 141 F4
Cilrhedyn Bridge 140 D2
Cilsan 142 C4
Ciltalgarth 168 B3
Cilwendeg 141 E4
Cilybebyll 128 D2
Cil-y-cwm 143 D3
Cimla 129 D3
Cinderford 131 F1
Cippenham 135 E4
Cippyn 141 E3
Cirbhig 270 D3
Cirencester 132 C2
City *GtLon* 136 C4
City *VGlam* 129 F5
City Airport 136 D4
City Dulas 180 C4
City of Bath
   B&NESom 117 E1
City of Coventry Stadium
   (Coventry City F.C.)
   WMid CV6 6GE 16 D2
Clabby 281 G3
Clabhach 246 A4
Clachaig 232 C1
Clachan *A&B* 232 C1
Clachan *A&B* 248 A5
Clachan *A&B* 231 F4
Clachan *High* 256 B1
Clachan *Na H-E. Siar*
   262 C7
Clachan Mòr 246 A2
Clachan of
   Campsie 234 A2
Clachan of
   Glendaruel 232 A1
Clachan-a-Luib 262 D5
Clachandhu 239 D1
Clachaneasy 215 E3
Clachanmore 206 A2
Clachan-Seil 239 G2
Clachanturn 259 K5
Clachbreck 231 F2
Clachnabrain 252 B3
Clachnaharry 266 D7
Clachtoll 272 C6
Clackmannan 243 E5
Clackmarras 267 K6
Clacton Pier *Essex*
   CO15 1QX 139 E1
Clacton-on-Sea 139 E1
Cladach a' Bhale
   Shear 262 D5
Cladach a' Chaolais 262 C5
Cladach Chircebost 262 C5
Cladach Cnoc a' Lòin
   262 C7
Cladich (An Cladach)
   240 C1
Cladswell 146 C2
Clady *D&S* 284 E6
Clady *Mid Ulster* 286 D5
Clady Milltown 282 C5
Claggan *F&O* 281 H1
Claggan (An Claigeann)
   High 248 C3
Claggan *High* 247 G5
Claigan 263 H6
Claines 146 A2
Clambers Play Centre
   ESuss TN34 1LD
   75 Hastings
Clanabogan 281 G2
Clandown 117 D2
Clanfield *Hants* 107 G1
Clanfield *Oxon* 133 E2
Clanmaghery 283 F5
Clannaborough
   Barton 102 A2
Clanville 119 E3
Claonaig 231 G4
Claonairigh 240 C4
Claonel 266 C1
Clapgate 150 C5
Clapham *Bed* 149 F2
Clapham *Devon* 102 B4
Clapham *GtLon* 136 B5
Clapham *NYorks* 192 D1
Clapham *WSuss* 108 C3
Clapham Green 149 F2
Clapham Hill 124 D2
Clappers 237 G3
Clappersgate 199 E2
Clapton *Som* 104 A2
Clapton *Som* 116 D2
Clapton-in-
   Gordano 131 D5
Clapton-on-
   the-Hill 133 D1
Clapworthy 113 G3
Clara Vale 212 A1
Clarach 154 C4
Clarbeston 141 D5
Clarbeston Road 140 D5
Clarborough 187 E4
Clardon 275 G2
Clare *AB&C* 282 D3
Clare *AB&C* 282 D4
Clare *Suff* 151 F3
Clare Castle Country Park
   Suff CO10 8NJ 151 F3
Clarebrand 216 B4
Claremont Landscape
   Garden *Surr*
   KT10 9JG 121 G1
Clarencefield 217 E4
Clarilaw 227 G4
Clark's Green 121 G4
Clarkston 233 G4
Clashban 266 D2
Clashcoig 266 D2
Clashdorran 266 C7

Clashgour 249 E5
Clashindarroch 260 C1
Clashmore High 266 E3
Clashmore High 272 C5
Clashnessie 272 C5
Clatford 118 C1
Clathy 243 E2
Clatt 260 D2
Clatter 155 F3
Clattercote 147 G3
Clatterford 107 D4
Clatterford End 137 E2
Clatterin Brig 253 E2
Clatteringshaws 215 G3
Clatworthy 115 F4
Claudy 285 H5
Claughton Lancs 192 B1
Claughton Lancs 192 B3
Clavelshay 115 F4
Claverdon 147 D1
Claverham 116 B1
Clavering 150 C4
Claverley 157 F3
Claverton 117 E1
Claverton Down 117 E1
Clawdd-coch 129 G5
Clawddnewydd 169 D2
Clawfin 224 D5
Clawthorpe 199 G5
Clawton 99 G1
Claxby 188 B3
Claxby Pluckacre 176 B1
Claxby St. Andrew 189 E5
Claxton Norf 179 E5
Claxton NYorks 195 F1
Claxton Grange 213 D5
Clay Common 165 F3
Clay Coton 160 A5
Clay Cross 173 E1
Clay End 150 B5
Clay Hill 131 F1
Clay of Allan 267 F4
Claybrooke Magna 159 G4
Claybrooke Parva 159 G4
Claydene 123 D4
Claydon Oxon 147 G2
Claydon Suff 152 D2
Claygate Devon 114 D5
Claygate Kent 123 G4
Claygate Surr 121 F1
Claygate Cross 123 F3
Clayhanger Devon 114 D5
Clayhanger WMid 158 C2
Clayhidon 103 E1
Clayhill ESuss 110 D1
Clayhill Hants 106 C2
Clayhithe 150 D1
Clayock 275 G3
Claypit Hill 150 B2
Claypits 131 G2
Claypole 174 D3
Claythorpe 189 E5
Clayton Staffs 171 F3
Clayton SYorks 186 B2
Clayton WSuss 109 E2
Clayton WYorks 194 A4
Clayton Green 192 B5
Clayton West 185 G1
Clayton-le-Moors 192 D4
Clayton-le-Woods 192 B5
Clayworth 187 E4
Cleadale 247 D1
Cleadon 212 C1
Clearbrook 100 B1
Clearwell 131 E2
Cleasby 202 B1
Cleat Ork 277 D9
Cleat Na H-E. Siar 254 B4
Cleatlam 202 A1
Cleatop 193 F1
Cleator 208 D5
Cleator Moor 208 D5
Cleckheaton 194 A5
Clee St. Margaret 157 E4
Cleedownton 157 E4
Cleehill 157 E5
Cleestanton 157 E5
Cleethorpes 188 D2
Cleeve NSom 116 B1
Cleeve Oxon 134 B4
Cleeve Hill 146 B5
Cleeve Prior 146
Clehonger 145 D4
Cleish 243 F5
Cleland 234 B4
Clement's End 135 F1
Clemsfold 121 G4
Clench Common 118 C1
Clenchwarton 177 D5
Clennell 220 B1
Clent 158 B5
Cleobury Mortimer 157 F5
Cleobury North 157 F4
Clephanton 267 F6
Clerklands 227 G3
Clermiston 235 F2
Clestrain 277 C7
Cleuch Head 227 G4
Cleughbrae 217 E3
Clevancy 132 C5
Clevedon 130 D5
Cleveley 147 F5
Cleveleys 191 G3
Clevelode 146 A3
Cleverton 132 B4
Clewer 116 B2
Clewer Green 135 E5
Clewer Village 135 E5
Cliburn 210 B5
Cliddesden 120 B3
Cliff Carmar 127 G2
Cliff High 247 F3
Cliff End 111 D2
Cliff Grange 170 D4
Cliffe Lancs 192 D4
Cliffe Med 137 G5
Cliffe NYorks 195 F3

Cliffe Woods 137 G5
Clifford Here 144 B3
Clifford WYorks 194 D3
Clifford Chambers 147 D2
Clifford's Mesne 145 F5
Clifford's Tower
  YO1 9SA 90 York
Cliffs End 125 E3
Clifton Bristol 131 E5
Clifton CenBeds 149 G4
Clifton Cumb 210 B5
Clifton Derbys 172 C3
Clifton Devon 113 F1
Clifton Lancs 192 A4
Clifton N'umb 221 E3
Clifton Nott 173 G4
Clifton NYorks 194 A3
Clifton Oxon 147 G4
Clifton Stir 241 F1
Clifton SYorks 186 C3
Clifton Worcs 146 A3
Clifton WYorks 194 A5
Clifton York 195 E2
Clifton Campville 159 E1
Clifton Hampden 134 A3
Clifton Maybank 104 B1
Clifton Park Museum
  SYorks S65 2AA 21 D1
Clifton Reynes 149 E2
Clifton upon
  Dunsmore 160 A5
Clifton upon Teme 145 G1
Cliftonville 125 F3
Climping 108 C3
Climpy 234 D4
Clink 117 E3
Clint 194 B2
Clint Green 178 B4
Clinterty 261 G3
Clintmains 228 A3
Clippesby 179 F4
Clippings Green 178 B4
Clipsham 161 E1
Clipston Notts 174 B4
Clipston WN'hants 160 C4
Clipstone 173 G1
Clitheroe 192 D3
Clive 170 C5
Cliveden Garden & Maze
  Bucks SL6 0JA 135 E4
Clivocast 278 F2
Clixby 188 B2
Clocaenog 169 D2
Clochan 268 C4
Clochtow 261 J1
Clock Face 183 G3
Clockhill 269 G6
Cloddach 267 J6
Cloddiau 156 A2
Cloford 117 E3
Cloghcor 285 F5
Clogher M&EAnt 286 E5
Clogher Mid Ulster 281 H3
Clogher L&C 282 E7
Cloghmore 281 H5
Cloghoge NM&D 282 C7
Cloghoge NM&D 282 D6
Cloghogle 285 F5
Cloghskelt 283 F4
Cloghy A&NDown 283 K3
Cloghy NM&D 283 J4
Cloichran 242 B1
Clola 269 J6
Clonalig 282 C7
Clonallan Glebe 282 E7
Clonelly 280 D2
Clonfeacle 282 B3
Clonliff 280 E5
Clonmain 282 B3
Clonmore 282 B3
Clonoe 282 B2
Clonrae 216 C1
Clontyfinnan 286 E2
Clontygora 282 D7
Clonvaraghan 283 G4
Clophill 149 F4
Clopton 161 F4
Clopton Corner 152 D2
Clopton Green Suff 151 F2
Clopton Green Suff 152 D2
Close Clark 190 A4
Closeburn 216 C1
Closworth 104 B1
Clothall 150 A4
Clothan 278 D4
Clotton 170 C1
Clough Cumb 200 C3
Clough GtMan 184 D1
Clough GtMan 184 D1
Clough M&EAnt 286 E4
Clough NM&D 283 H4
Clough WYorks 185 F1
Clough Foot 193 F5
Clough Head 193 G5
Cloughfin 286 B6
Cloughfold 193 E5
Cloughmills 286 E4
Cloughreagh 282 D6
Cloughton 204 D3
Cloughton
  Newlands 204 D3
Clounlaid 247 G4
Clousta 279 C7
Clouston 277 C6
Clova Aber 260 C2
Clova Angus 252 B2
Clove Lodge 201 E1
Clovelly 112 D3
Clovelly Cross 112 D3
Clovelly Village Devon
  EX39 5TA 112 D3
Clovenfords 227 F2
Clovenstone 261 F3
Cloves 267 J5
Clovullin 248 C3
Clow Bridge 193 E5
Clowne 186 B5
Clows Top 157 F5
Cliburn 210 B5
Cly next the Sea 178 B1
Cliburn 210 B5
Cliddesden 120 B3
Cliff Carmar 127 G2
Cliff High 247 F3
Cliff End 111 D2
Cliff Grange 170 D4
Cliffe Lancs 192 D4
Cliffe Med 137 G5
Cliffe NYorks 195 E3

Clunas 267 F7
Clunbury 156 C4
Clunderwen 127 E1
Clune High 258 E2
Clune Moray 268 E5
Clunes 249 E1
Clungunford 156 C5
Clunie Aber 268 E5
Clunie P&K 251 G5
Cluntagh 283 H3
Clunton 156 C4
Cluny 244 A5
Clutton B&NESom 116 D2
Clutton ChesW&C 170 B2
Clwt-y-bont 167 E1
Clwydyfagwyr 129 G2
Clydach Mon 130 B1
Clydach Swan 128 C2
Clydach Terrace 130 A1
Clydach Vale 129 F3
Clydau 141 F4
Clydebank 233 F2
Clyffe Pypard 132 C5
Clynder 232 D1
Clyne 129 G2
Clynelish 266 E1
Clynfyw 141 F4
Clynnog Fawr 166 D3
Clyro 144 B3
Clyst Honiton 102 C3
Clyst Hydon 102 D2
Clyst St. George 102 C4
Clyst St. Lawrence 102 D2
Clyst St. Mary 102 C4
Clyst William 103 D2
Cnewr 143 E5
Cnwch-coch 154 C5
Coa 280 E3
Coachford 268 C6
Coad's Green 97 G2
Coagh 282 B2
Coal Aston 186 A5
Coalbrookdale 157 F2
Coalbrookvale 130 A2
Coalburn 225 G2
Coalburns 212 A1
Coalcleugh 211 E3
Coaley 131 G2
Coalisland 282 B2
Coalmoor 157 F2
Coalpit Heath 131 F4
Coalpit Hill 171 F2
Coalport 157 G2
Coalsnaughton 243 E5
Coaltown of
  Balgonie 244 B5
Coaltown of
  Wemyss 244 B5
Coalville 159 G1
Coalway 131 E1
Coanwood 210 C2
Coast 265 G2
Coat 116 B5
Coatbridge 234 B3
Coate Swin 133 D4
Coate Wilts 118 B1
Coates Cambs 162 B3
Coates Glos 132 B2
Coates Lincs 187 G4
Coates Notts 187 F4
Coates WSuss 108 B2
Coatham 213 E5
Coatham
  Mundeville 212 B5
Cobairdy 268 D6
Cobbaton 113 G3
Cobbler's Plain 131 D2
Cobby Syke 194 A2
Cobden 102 D3
Coberley 132 B1
Cobhall Common 145 D4
Cobham Kent 123 F2
Cobham Surr 121 G1
Cobleland 242 A5
Cobley Hill 158 C5
Cobnash 145 D1
Coburty 269 H4
Cock Alley 173 F1
Cock Bank 170 A3
Cock Bevington 146 C2
Cock Bridge 259 K4
Cock Clarks 138 B2
Cock Green 137 G1
Cock Hill 283 F2
Cock Marling 111 D2
Cockayne 203 F3
Cockayne Hatley 150 A3
Cockburnspath 237 E2
Cockenzie & Port
  Seton 236 B2
Cocker Bar 192 B5
Cockerham 192 A2
Cockermouth 209 E3
Cockernhoe 149 G5
Cockerton 202 B1
Cockett 128 C3
Cockfield Dur 212 A5
Cockfield Suff 152 A2
Cockfosters 136 B3
Cocking 108 A2
Cockington 101 E1
Cocklake 116 B3
Cocklaw 220 B5
Cockle Park 221 E3
Cockleford 132 B1
Cockley Beck 198 D3
Cockley Cley 163 F2
Cockpen 236 A3
Cockpole Green 134 C4
Cockshutt 170 B5
Cockthorpe 178 A1
Cockwood Devon 102 C4
Cockwood Som 115 F3
Cockyard 185 E4
Codda 97 F2
Coddenham 152 C2
Coddington
  ChesW&C 170 B2
Coddington Here 145 G3
Coddington Notts 174 D2
Codford St. Mary 118 A4
Codford St. Peter 118 A4
Codicote 136 B1
Codmore Hill 108 C2

Codnor 173 F3
Codnor Park 173 F2
Codrington 131 G5
Codsall 158 A2
Codsall Wood 158 A2
Coed Morgan 130 C1
Coedcae 130 B2
Coedkernew 130 B4
Coedely 129 G4
Coed-poeth 169 F2
Coedway 156 C1
Coed-y-bryn 141 G3
Coedycaerau 130 C3
Coed-y-paen 130 C3
Coed-yr-ynys 144 A5
Coedstumgwern 167 E5
Coelbren 129 E1
Cofton 102 C4
Cofton Hackett 158 C5
Cogan 130 A5
Cogenhoe 148 D1
Coggeshall 151 G5
Coggeshall
  Hamlet 151 G5
Coggins Mill 110 A1
Coig Peighinnean 271 H1
Coilantogle 242 A4
Coileitir 248 D5
Coilessan 241 E4
Coillaig 240 C2
Coille Mhorgil 257 G4
Coille-righ 257 F2
Coillore 255 J1
Coity 129 F4
Col 271 G4
Col Uarach 271 G4
Colaboll 273 H7
Colan 96 C3
Colaton Raleigh 103 D4
Colbost 263 H7
Colburn 202 B3
Colbury 106 C1
Colby Cumb 210 C5
Colby IoM 190 A4
Colby Norf 179 D2
Colchester 152 A5
Colchester Castle Museum
  Essex CO11 1TJ 152 A5
Colchester Green 152 A2
Colchester Zoo Essex
  CO3 0SL 152 A5
Colcot 115 E1
Cold Ash 119 G1
Cold Ashby 160 B5
Cold Ashton 131 G5
Cold Aston 132 D1
Cold Blow 127 E1
Cold Brayfield 149 E2
Cold Chapel 226 A3
Cold Cotes 200 C5
Cold Hanworth 188 A4
Cold Harbour 134 B4
Cold Hatton 170 D5
Cold Hatton Heath 170 D5
Cold Hesledon 212 D3
Cold Higham 148 B2
Cold Inn 127 E2
Cold Kirby 203 E4
Cold Newton 160 C2
Cold Northcott 97 G1
Cold Norton 138 B2
Cold Overton 160 D2
Cold Row 191 G3
Coldbackie 273 J2
Coldblow 137 E5
Coldean 109 F3
Coldeast 102 B5
Coldeaton 172 C2
Colden 193 F5
Colden Common 119 F5
Coldfair Green 153 F1
Coldham 162 C2
Coldharbour Glos 131 E2
Coldharbour Surr 121 G3
Coldingham 237 G3
Coldrain 243 F4
Coldred 125 E4
Coldrey 120 C3
Coldridge 113 G5
Coldrife 220 C2
Coldstream 228 C3
Coldvreath 97 D4
Coldwaltham 108 C2
Coldwells 269 K6
Cole 116 D4
Cole End 159 D4
Cole Green 136 B1
Cole Henley 119 F2
Colebatch 156 C4
Colebrook 102 D2
Colebrooke 102 A2
Coleburn 267 K6
Coleby Lincs 175 E1
Coleby NLincs 187 F1
Coleford Devon 102 A2
Coleford Glos 131 E1
Coleford Som 117 D3
Colegate End 164 C3
Colehill 105 G2
Coleman Green 136 A1
Coleman's Hatch 122 D5
Colemere 170 B4
Colemore 120 C4
Colemore Green 157 G3
Colenden 243 G2
Coleorton 159 G1
Colerne 132 A5
Cole's Common 164 D3
Cole's Cross 101 D3
Cole's Green 153 D1
Colesbourne 132 C1
Colesden 149 G2
Coleshill Bucks 135 E3
Coleshill Oxon 133 E3
Coleshill Warks 159 E4
Colestocks 103 D2
Coley B&NESom 116 C2
Coley Staffs 172 A5
Colfin 214 B5
Colgate 122 B5
Colgrain 233 E2
Colinsburgh 244 C4
Colinton 235 G3
Colintraive 232 B2

Colkirk 178 A3
Coll 246 A4
Collace 244 A1
Collafirth 279 D6
Collamoor Head 98 B1
Collaton St. Mary 101 E1
Coll Dark Sky Island Argyll
  & Bute 246 B4
Collessie 244 A3
Colleton Mills 113 G4
Collett's Green 146 A2
Collier Row 137 E3
Collier Street 123 G4
Collier's End 150 B5
Collier's Wood 136 B5
Colliery Row 212 C3
Colliston 253 E5
Colliton 103 D2
Colligan Bridge 283 G6
Collin 217 E3
Collingbourne
  Ducis 118 D2
Collingbourne
  Kingston 118 D2
Collingham Notts 174 D1
Collingham WYorks 194 C3
Collington 145 F1
Collingtree 148 C2
Collins End 134 B5
Collins Green
  Worcs 145 G2
Collins Green Warr 183 G3
Colliston 253 E5
Colliton 103 D2
Collmuir 260 D4
Collycroft 159 F4
Collyhurst 184 C2
Collynie 261 G1
Collyweston 161 E2
Colmonell 214 C2
Colmworth 149 G2
Colnabaichin 259 K4
Colnbrook 135 F5
Colne Cambs 162 B5
Colne Lancs 193 E4
Colne Engaine 151 G4
Colney 178 C5
Colney Heath 136 B2
Colney Street 136 A2
Colonsay 238 C5
Colonsay House 238 C5
Colpy 260 E1
Colquhar 236 A5
Colsterdale 202 A4
Colsterworth 175 E5
Colston Bassett 174 C4
Coltfield 267 J5
Colthouse 199 E3
Coltishall 179 D4
Coltness 234 C4
Colton Cumb 199 E4
Colton Norf 178 C5
Colton NYorks 195 E3
Colton Staffs 172 A5
Colton WYorks 194 C4
Columbkille 282 C2
Colva 144 B2
Colvend 216 C5
Colvister 278 E3
Colwall 145 G3
Colwall Green 145 G3
Colwall Stone 145 G3
Colwell 220 B4
Colwich 172 B5
Colwick 174 B3
Colwinston 129 F5
Colworth 108 B3
Colwyn Bay
  (Bae Colwyn) 181 G5
Colyford 103 F3
Colyton 103 F3
Combe Here 144 C1
Combe Oxon 133 G1
Combe Som 116 B5
Combe WBerks 119 E1
Combe Common 121 E4
Combe Cross 102 B5
Combe Down 117 E1
Combe Florey 115 E4
Combe Hay 117 E2
Combe Martin 113 G1
Combe Martin Wildlife &
  Dinosaur Park Devon
  EX34 0NG 113 G1
Combe Pafford 101 F1
Combe Raleigh 103 E2
Combe St. Nicholas
  103 G1
Combeinteignhead 102 B5
Comber 283 H2
Comberbach 184 A5
Comberford 159 D2
Comberton Cambs 150 B2
Comberton Here 145 D1
Combpyne 103 F3
Combridge 172 B4
Combrook 147 F2
Combs Derbys 185 E5
Combs Suff 152 B2
Combs Ford 152 B2
Combwich 115 F3
Comer 241 F4
Comers 260 E4
Comhampton 146 A1
Comins-coch 154 C4
Commercial End 151 D1
Commins Coch 155 E2
Common Edge 191 G4
Common Moor 97 G2
Common Platt 132 D4
Common Side 188 A5
Common Square 188 A5
Commondale 203 F1
Commonside 172 D3
Compaw 286 B2
Compstall 185 D3
Compton Devon 101 E1
Compton Hants 119 F5
Compton Plym 100 A2
Compton Staffs 158 A4
Compton Surr 121 E3
Compton WBerks 134 A4
Compton Wilts 118 C2
Compton WSuss 107 G2
Compton WYorks 194 D3
Compton Abbas 105 E1

Compton Abdale 132 C1
Compton Bassett 132 C5
Compton
  Beauchamp 133 E4
Compton Bishop 116 A2
Compton Dando 116 D1
Compton Dundon 116 B4
Compton Martin 116 C2
Compton
  Pauncefoot 116 D5
Compton Valence 104 B3
Compton Verney 147 F2
Compton Wynyates 147 F3
Comra 258 C5
Comrie Fife 235 E1
Comrie P&K 242 C2
Conchra Arg 232 B1
Conchra High 256 E2
Concraigie 251 G5
Conder Green 192 A2
Conderton 146 B4
Condicote 146 D5
Condorrat 234 B2
Condover 157 D2
Coney Weston 164 A4
Coneyhurst 121 G5
Coneysthorpe 203 G5
Coneythorpe 194 C2
Conford 120 D4
Congash 259 H2
Congdon's Shop 97 G2
Congerstone 159 F2
Congham 177 F5
Congl-y-wal 168 A3
Congleton 171 F1
Congresbury 116 B1
Congreve 158 B1
Conicavel 267 G6
Coningsby 176 A2
Conington Cambs 161 G4
Conington Cambs 150 B1
Conisbrough 186 C3
Conisby 230 A3
Conisholme 189 E3
Coniston Cumb 199 E3
Coniston ERid 197 D4
Coniston Cold 193 F2
Conistone 193 F1
Conland 268 E6
Conlig 283 J1
Connah's Quay 169 F1
Connel
  (A' Choingheal) 240 B1
Connel Park 225 E4
Connor 287 F6
Connor Downs 94 C3
Conock 118 B2
Conon Bridge (Drochaid
  Sgùideil) 266 C6
Cononish 241 F2
Cononley 193 F3
Cononsyth 253 D5
Consall 171 G3
Consett 212 A2
Constable Burton 202 A3
Constantine 95 E4
Constantine Bay 96 C2
Contin
  (Cunndainn) 266 B6
Contlaw 261 G4
Contullich 266 D4
Conwy 181 F5
Conwy Castle (Castles
  & Town Walls of King
  Edward in Gwynedd)
  Conwy LL32 8AY 181 F5
Conyer 124 B2
Conyer's Green 151 G1
Cooden 110 C3
Coodham 224 C2
Cooil 190 B4
Cookbury 113 E5
Cookbury Wick 113 D5
Cookham 135 D4
Cookham Dean 135 D4
Cookham Rise 135 D4
Cookhill 146 C2
Cookley Suff 165 E4
Cookley Worcs 158 A4
Cookley Green Oxon 134 B3
Cookley Green Suff 165 E4
Cookney 261 G5
Cook's Green 152 A2
Cooksbridge 109 F2
Cooksey Green 146 B1
Cookshill 171 G3
Cooksmill Green 137 F2
Cookston 261 H1
Cookstown 282 A2
Coolderry 282 C7
Coolforbeg 281 F1
Coolham 121 G5
Cooling 137 G5
Cooling Street 137 G5
Coolkeeragh D&S 285 F2
Coolkeeragh F&O 281 F1
Coolkill 282 A4
Coolnagoppoge 287 F2
Coolsallagh 282 F2
Coolshinny 286 C7
Coombe Corn 97 D4
Coombe Corn 112 C4
Coombe Corn 96 A5
Coombe Corn 96 C5
Coombe Devon 101 D3
Coombe Devon 102 A3
Coombe Devon 103 E3
Coombe Som 115 F5
Coombe Som 104 A2
Coombe Wilts 118 C2
Coombe Bissett 118 C5
Coombe Country Park
  Warks CV3 2AB 16 D3
Coombe End 114 D5
Coombe Hill 146 A5
Coombe Keynes 105 E4
Coombes 109 D3
Coombes Moor 144 C1
Cooneen 281 G4
Cooper's Corner
  ESuss 110 C1
Cooper's Corner
  Kent 123 D4
Cooper's Green 136 A2
Coopersale 137 D2

Coopersale Street 137 D2
Cootham 108 C2
Cop Street 125 E3
Copdock 152 C3
Copford Green 152 A5
Copgrove 194 C1
Copister 278 D5
Cople 149 G3
Copley Dur 211 G5
Copley WYorks 193 G5
Coplow Dale 185 F5
Copmanthorpe 195 E3
Copmere End 171 F5
Copp 192 A4
Coppathorne 112 C5
Coppenhall 158 B1
Coppenhall Moss 171 E2
Copperhouse 94 C3
Coppicegate 157 G4
Coppingford 161 G4
Copplebridge 117 F5
Copplestone 102 A2
Coppull 183 G1
Coppull Moor 183 G1
Copsale 121 G5
Copse Hill 122 B2
Copster Green 192 C4
Copston Magna 159 G4
Copt Heath 159 D5
Copt Hewick 202 C5
Copt Oak 159 G1
Copthall Green 136 D2
Copthorne 122 C5
Copy Lake 113 G4
Copythorne 106 C1
Coragh 280 E5
Coragh Glebe 280 E5
Coralhill 269 J4
Corbally F&O 281 G3
Corbally NM&D 283 H5
Corbally NM&D 283 J3
Corbets Tey 137 E4
Corbiegoe 275 J4
Corbridge 211 F1
Corby 161 D4
Corby Glen 175 F5
Corcord 260 D4
Cordorcan 215 E3
Coreley 157 F4
Corfcott Green 98 D1
Corfe 103 F1
Corfe Castle Dorset
  BH20 5EZ 105 F4
Corfe Mullen 105 F3
Corfton 157 D4
Corgarff 259 K4
Corgary 284 D7
Corhammock 282 C2
Corkey 286 E3
Corley 159 F4
Corley Ash 159 E4
Corley Moor 159 E4
Corn Exchange Cambs
  CB2 3QB 66 Cambridge
Cornabus 230 B5
Cornafannoge 281 F4
Cornamaddy 281 J2
Cornamuck 281 F2
Cornamucklagh 286 D5
Cornard Tye 152 A3
Cornavarrow 281 F4
Corndon 99 G2
Corney 198 C3
Cornforth 212 C4
Cornhill 268 D5
Cornhill on Tweed 228 C3
Cornholme 193 F5
Cornish Gold & Treasure
  Park Corn
  TR16 4HN 96 A5
Cornish Hall End 151 E4
Cornquoy 277 E7
Cornriggs 211 E3
Cornsay 212 A3
Cornsay Colliery 212 A3
Corntown High 266 C6
Corntown VGlam 129 F5
Cornwall Airport Newquay
  96 C3
Cornwell 147 E5
Cornwood 100 C2
Cornworthy 101 E2
Corpach
  (A' Chorpaich) 248 D2
Corpusty 178 C3
Corrachree 260 C4
Corraghy 281 G5
Corragole 280 E6
Corran A&B 241 E5
Corran AB&C 282 C5
Corran High 256 E2
Corran (Ardgour)
  High 248 C3
Corranbuie 231 G3
Corranmore 239 G4
Corranny 281 G5
Corrany 190 C3
Corribeg 248 B2
Corrie 232 B5
Corrie Common 218 A3
Corriechrevie 231 F4
Corriecravie 223 E3
Corriedoo 216 A2
Corriekinloch 273 F6
Corrielorne 240 A3
Corrievorrie 258 E2
Corrimony 257 K1
Corringham Lincs 187 F3
Corringham Thur 137 G4
Corris 154 D2
Corris Uchaf 154 D2
Corrlarach 248 B2
Corscombe 104 B2
Corse Aber 268 E6
Corse Glos 145 G5
Corse Lawn 146 A4
Corse of Kinnoir 268 D6

Corsebank **225** G4
Corsegight **269** G5
Corsehill **217** F2
Corsewall **214** B5
Corsham **132** A5
Corsindae **260** E4
Corsley **117** F3
Corsley Heath **117** F3
Corsock **216** B3
Corston *B&NESom* **117** D1
Corston *Wilts* **132** B4
Corstorphine **235** F2
Cortachy **252** B4
Cortamlat **282** B6
Corton *Suff* **165** G2
Corton *Wilts* **118** A3
Corton Denham **116** D5
Corwar House **215** G4
Corwen **169** D3
Coryton *Devon* **99** F3
Coryton *Thur* **137** G4
Cosby **160** A3
Coscote **134** A4
Coseley **158** B3
Cosford *Shrop* **157** G2
Cosford *Warks* **160** A5
Cosham **107** F2
Cosheston **126** D2
Coshieville **250** C5
Coskills **188** A2
Cosmeston **131** E5
Cosmeston Lakes Country
Park *VGlam*
CF64 5UY **115** E1
Cossall **173** F3
Cossington *Leics* **160** B1
Cossington *Som* **116** A3
Costa **276** C5
Costessey **178** C4
Costock **173** G5
Coston *Leics* **174** D5
Coston *Norf* **178** C5
Cote *Oxon* **133** F2
Cote *Som* **116** A3
Cotebrook **170** C1
Cotehill **210** A2
Cotes *Cumb* **199** F4
Cotes *Leics* **173** G5
Cotes *Staffs* **171** F4
Cotesbach **160** A4
Cotford St. Luke **115** E5
Cotgrave **174** B3
Cotham **174** C3
Cothelstone **115** E4
Cotheridge **145** G2
Cotherstone **201** F1
Cothill **133** G3
Cotleigh **103** F2
Cotmanhay **173** F3
Coton *Cambs* **150** C2
Coton *Staffs* **171** G4
Coton *Staffs* **159** D2
Coton *Staffs* **171** F5
Coton *WN'hants* **160** B5
Coton Clanford **171** F5
Coton Hill **171** G4
Coton in the Clay **172** C5
Coton in the Elms **159** E1
Cotonwood *Shrop* **170** C4
Cotonwood *Staffs* **171** F5
Cotswold Country Park
& Beach *Glos* GL7 6DF
132 C3
Cotswold Wildlife Park
Oxon OX18 4JP **133** E2
Cott **101** D1
Cottam *Lancs* **192** A4
Cottam *Notts* **187** F4
Cottartown **259** H1
Cottenham **150** C1
Cotterdale **200** D3
Cottered **150** B5
Cotteridge **158** C5
Cotterstock **161** F3
Cottesbrooke **160** C5
Cottesmore **161** E1
Cottingham
NN'hants **160** D3
Cottingley **194** A4
Cottisford **148** A4
Cotton *Staffs* **172** B3
Cotton *Suff* **152** B1
Cotton End **149** D3
Cottonworth **119** E4
Cottown *Aber* **260** D2
Cottown *Aber* **269** G6
Cottown *Aber* **261** F3
Cotts **100** A1
Cottwood **113** G4
Cotwall **157** F1
Cotwalton **171** G4
Couch's Mill **97** F4
Coughton *Here* **145** E3
Coughton *Warks* **146** C1
Cougie **257** J2
Coulaghailtro **231** F3
Coulags **265** F2
Coulby Newham **203** E1
Coulderton **198** A2
Coull **260** D4
Coulport **232** D1
Coulsdon **122** B3
Coulston **118** A2
Coulter **226** B2
Coultershaw Bridge
108 B2
Coultings **115** F3
Coulton **203** F5
Coultra **244** F5
Cound **157** E2
Coundlane **157** E2
Coundon *Dur* **212** B4
Coundon *WMid* **159** F4
Countersett **201** E4
Countess Wear **102** C3
Countesthorpe **160** A3
Countisbury **114** A3
Coup Green **192** B5
Coupar Angus **252** A5
Coupland *Cumb* **200** C1
Coupland *N'umb* **228** D3
Cour **231** G5
Court Colman **129** E4
Court House Green **159** F4
Court-at-Street **124** C5

Courtauld Institute of Art
Gallery *GtLon*
WC2R 0RN **45** F3
Courteenhall **148** C2
Courtsend **138** D3
Courtway **115** F4
Cousland **236** A3
Cousley Wood **123** F5
Coustion **232** B2
Cove *A&B* **232** D1
Cove *Devon* **102** C1
Cove *Hants* **120** D2
Cove *High* **264** E2
Cove *ScBord* **237** E2
Cove Bay **261** H4
Cove Bottom **165** F3
Covehithe **165** G3
Coven **158** B2
Coveney **162** C4
Covenham
St. Bartholomew **188** D3
Covenham St. Mary **188** D3
Coventry **159** F5
Coventry Airport **159** F5
Coventry Cathedral *WMid*
CV1 5AB **69** Coventry
Coventry Transport Museum
WMid CV1 1JG
69 Coventry
Coverack **95** E5
Coverham **202** A4
Covesea **267** J4
Covingham **133** D4
Covington *Cambs* **161** F5
Covington *SLan* **226** A2
Cowan Bridge **200** B5
Cowbeech **110** B3
Cowbit **162** A1
Cowbridge *Som* **114** C3
Cowbridge *VGlam* **129** F5
Cowden **123** D4
Cowden Pound **123** D4
Cowdenbeath **243** G1
Cowdenburn **235** G4
Cowers Lane **173** E3
Cowes **107** D3
Cowesby **203** D4
Cowesfield Green **119** D5
Cowey Green **152** B5
Cowfold **109** E1
Cowgill **200** C4
Cowie *Aber* **253** G1
Cowie *Stir* **234** C1
Cowlam Manor **196** B1
Cowley *Devon* **102** C3
Cowley *Glos* **132** B1
Cowley *GtLon* **135** F4
Cowley *Oxon* **134** A2
Cowling *Lancs* **183** G1
Cowling *NYorks* **193** F3
Cowling *NYorks* **202** B4
Cowlinge **151** F2
Cowmes **185** F1
Cowpe **193** E5
Cowpen **221** E3
Cowpen Bewley **213** D5
Cowplain **107** F1
Cowsden **146** B2
Cowshill **211** E3
Cowthorpe **194** D2
Cox Common **165** E3
Coxbank **171** E3
Coxbench **173** E3
Coxbridge **116** C4
Coxford **177** G5
Coxheath **123** G3
Coxhoe **212** C4
Coxley **116** C3
Coxley Wick **116** C3
Coxpark **99** E3
Coxtie Green **137** E3
Coxwold **203** E5
Coychurch **129** F5
Coylton **224** C4
Coylumbridge **259** G4
Coynach **260** C4
Coynachie **260** C1
Coytrahen **129** E4
Crabbet Park **122** C5
Crabgate **178** B3
Crabtree *Plym* **100** B2
Crabtree *SYorks* **186** A4
Crabtree *WSuss* **109** E1
Crabtree Green **170** A3
Crabtreelane **282** C3
Crackaig **230** D3
Crackenthorpe **210** C5
Crackington **98** B1
Crackington Haven **98** B1
Crackley **171** F2
Crackleybank **157** G1
Crackpot **201** E3
Crackthorn Corner **164** B4
Cracoe **193** F1
Craddock **103** D1
Cradhlastadh **270** C4
Cradley *Here* **145** G3
Cradley *WMid* **158** B4
Cradley Heath **158** B4
Crafthole **99** D5
Crafton **135** D1
Cragg **193** G5
Cragg Hill **194** B4
Craggan *Moray* **259** J1
Craggan *P&K* **242** D3
Cragganmore **259** J1
Cragganruair **259** J1
Craggie *High* **258** E1
Craggie *High* **266** D7
Craghead **212** B2
Cragside *N'umb*
NE65 7PX **220** D1
Crai **143** E5
Craibstone
Aberdeen **261** G4
Craibstone *Moray* **268** C5
Craichie **252** D5
Craig *A&B* **240** C1
Craig *A&B* **239** E1
Craig *D&G* **216** A4
Craig *D&S* **285** H6
Craig *High* **264** D5
Craig *High* **265** G7
Craig *SAyr* **224** B5
Craigans **240** A5

Craigavad **287** J7
Craigavole **286** C4
Craigavon **282** D3
Craigbeg **291** G1
Craig-berth-lwyd **129** G3
Craig-cefn-parc **128** C2
Craigcleuch **218** B3
Craigdallie **244** A2
Craigdam **261** G1
Craigdarragh **285** H5
Craigdarroch *D&G* **216** B1
Craigdarroch *EAyr* **225** E5
Craigdhu *D&G* **207** D3
Craigdhu *High* **266** B7
Craigdoo **287** G5
Craigearn **261** F3
Craigellachie **267** K7
Craigellie **269** J4
Craigend *Moray* **267** J6
Craigend *P&K* **243** G2
Craigendive **232** B1
Craigendoran **233** E1
Craigengillan **224** C3
Craigenputtock **216** B2
Craigens **230** B3
Craigfad **287** F1
Craigglas **240** A5
Craighall **244** C3
Craighat **233** F1
Craighead *Fife* **245** E3
Craighead *High* **266** E5
Craighlaw **215** E4
Craighouse **230** D3
Craigie *Dundee* **244** C1
Craigie *P&K* **251** G5
Craigie *SAyr* **224** C2
Craigie Brae **261** G1
Craigieburn **217** E4
Craigieholm **243** G1
Craigielaw **236** B2
Craiglockhart **235** G2
Craiglug **261** G5
Craigmaud **269** G5
Craigmillar **235** G2
Craigmore *A&N* **286** E6
Craigmyle House **260** E4
Craignafeoch **232** A2
Craignant **169** F4
Craignavie **242** A1
Craigneil **214** C2
Craigneuk **234** B4
Craignure **239** G1
Craigo **253** E2
Craigoch **224** A5
Craigow **243** F4
Craigrothie **244** B3
Craigroy **267** J6
Craigroy Farm **259** J1
Craigruie **241** G2
Craigs **286** E5
Craigsanquhar **244** B3
Craigston *A&N* **286** E6
Craigstown *M&EAnt*
287 F6
Craigton *Aberdeen* **261** G4
Craigton *Angus* **244** D1
Craigton *Angus* **252** B4
Craigton *High* **266** E7
Craigton *Stir* **234** A1
Craigtown **274** D3
Craig-y-nos **129** E1
Craigywarren **287** F5
Craik *Aber* **260** C2
Craik *ScBord* **227** E5
Crail **245** E4
Crailing **228** A4
Crailinghall **228** A4
Crakehill **202** D5
Crakemarsh **172** B4
Crambe **195** G1
Crambeck Village **195** G1
Cramlington **221** E4
Cramond **235** F2
Cranage **171** E1
Cranberry **171** F4
Cranborne **105** G1
Cranbourne **135** E4
Cranbrook *Plym* **100** B2
Cranbrook *GtLon* **136** D4
Cranbrook *Kent* **123** G5
Cranbrook Common **123** G5
Crane Moor **186** A2
Crane Park Island *Gt Lon*
N1C 4PW **11** A7
Cranfield *CenBeds* **149** E3
Cranfield *NM&D* **283** F7
Cranford *Devon* **112** D3
Cranford *GtLon* **136** A5
Cranford St. Andrew **161** E5
Cranford St. John **161** E5
Cranham *Glos* **132** A1
Cranham *GtLon* **137** E4
Crank **183** G3
Crankey **282** D5
Cranleigh **121** F4
Cranlome **281** J2
Cranmer Green **164** B4
Cranmore *IoW* **106** C4
Cranmore *Som* **117** D3
Crann **282** A5
Cranna **268** E5
Crannoch **268** C5
Crannogue **281** J2
Cranoe **160** C3
Cransford **153** E1
Cranshaws **237** D3
Cranstal **190** C1
Crantock **96** B3
Cranwell **175** F3
Cranwich **163** F3
Cranworth **178** A5
Craobh Haven **239** G4
Crapstone **100** B1
Crarae **240** B5
Crask Inn **273** H2
Crask of Aigas **266** C7
Craskins **260** D4
Craster **229** F4
Crateford **158** B2
Cratfield **165** E4
Crathes **261** F5
Crathie *Aber* **259** K5

Crathie *High* **258** C5
Crathorne **202** D2
Craven Arms **156** D4
Craw **231** G5
Crawcrook **212** A1
Crawford *Lancs* **183** F2
Crawford *SLan* **226** A3
Crawfordjohn **225** G3
Crawfordsburn **287** G2
Crawfordstown **284** J7
Crawick **225** F4
Crawley *Devon* **103** F2
Crawley *Hants* **119** F4
Crawley *Oxon* **133** F1
Crawley *WSuss* **122** B5
Crawley Down **122** C5
Crawleyside **211** F3
Crawshawbooth **193** E5
Crawton **253** G2
Crawyn **190** B2
Cray *P&K* **251** G3
Crayford **137** E5
Crayke **203** E5
Crays Hill **137** G3
Cray's Pond **134** B4
Crazies Hill **134** C4
Creacombe **102** B1
Creag-goch **140** B4
Creagan **248** B5
Creagbheitheachain **248** B3
Creagh **281** F4
Creagorry
(Creag Ghoraidh) **262** C7
Crealy Theme Park & Resort
Devon EX5 1DR **102** C3
Creamore Bank **170** C4
Creaton **160** C5
Creca **218** A4
Credenhill **145** D3
Crediton **102** B2
Creebridge **215** F4
Creech Heathfield **115** F5
Creech St. Michael **115** F5
Creed **96** D5
Creedy Park **102** B2
Creekmoor **105** F3
Creekmouth **137** D4
Creeting St. Mary **152** B2
Creeton **175** F5
Creetown **215** F5
Creevedonnell **285** G5
Creevy *AB&C* **282** D2
Creevy *D&S* **284** E7
Creevycarnonan **283** H3
Cregan *CC&G* **285** H3
Creggan *NM&D* **282** C7
Creggan *F&O* **281** J1
Creggans **240** C4
Cregneash **190** A5
Cregrina **144** A2
Creich **244** B2
Creigau **131** E1
Creigiau **129** G4
Crelevan **257** K1
Crelly **95** E4
Cremyll **100** A3
Crendell **105** G1
Cressage **157** E2
Cressbrook **185** F5
Cresselly **127** D2
Cressing **151** F5
Cresswell *N'umb* **221** E2
Cresswell *Staffs* **171** G4
Cresswell Quay **127** D2
Creswell **186** C5
Cretingham **152** D2
Cretshengan **231** F3
Crew **285** J2
Crew Green **156** C1
Crewe *ChesE* **171** E2
Crewe *ChesW&C* **170** B2
Crewe Green **171** E2
Crewkerne **104** A2
Crew's Hole **117** F5
Crewton **173** E4
Crianlarich (A' Chrion-
Làraich) **241** F2
Cribbs Causeway **131** E4
Cribyn **142** B2
Crich **173** E2
Crich Carr **173** E2
Crich Common **173** E2
Crich Tramway Village
Derbys DE4 5DP **173** E2
Crichie **269** H6
Crichton **236** A3
Crickadarn **143** G3
Cricket Hill **120** D1
Cricket St. Thomas **103** G2
Crickham **116** B3
Crickheath **169** F5
Crickhowell **130** B1
Cricklade **132** D3
Cricklewood **136** B4
Crickley Hill Country Park
Glos GL4 8JY **132** B1
Crick's Green **145** F2
Criddlestyle **106** A1
Cridling Stubbs **195** E5
Criftins (Dudleston
Heath) **170** A4
Criggan **97** E3
Criggion **156** B1
Crigglestone **186** A1
Crilly **281** J3
Crimble **184** C1
Crimchard **103** G2
Crimdon Park **213** D4
Crimond **269** J5
Crimonmogate **269** J5
Crimplesham **163** E2
Crinan **239** G5
Crinan Ferry **239** G5
Crindle **285** J4
Cringleford **178** C5
Cringletie **235** G5
Crinow **127** E1
Cripplestyle **105** G1
Cripp's Corner **110** C1
Crix **137** G1

Crathie *High* **258** C5
Croalchapel **216** D1
Croasdale **209** D5
Crock Street **103** G1
Crockanore **282** C6
Crockenhill **123** E2
Crockerhill **107** E2
Crocker End **134** C4
Crockernwell **102** A3
Crockerton **117** F3
Crockerton Green **117** F3
Crocketford
(Ninemile Bar) **216** C3
Crockey Hill **195** F3
Crockham Hill **122** D3
Crockhurst Street **123** F4
Crockleford Heath **152** B5
Croesau Bach **169** F5
Croeserw **129** E3
Croes-goch **140** B4
Croes-hywel **130** C1
Croes-lan **141** G3
Croesor **167** E2
Croespenmaen **130** A3
Croesyceiliog
Carmar **128** A1
Croesyceiliog
Torfaen **130** C3
Croes-y-pant **130** C2
Croes-y-waun **167** E2
Croford **115** E5
Croft *Here* **145** D1
Croft *Leics* **160** A3
Croft *Lincs* **176** D1
Croft *Warr* **184** A3
Croftamie **233** F1
Crofthead **218** B4
Croftmore **251** D3
Crofton *Wilts* **119** D1
Crofton *WYorks* **186** A1
Croft-on-Tees **202** B2
Crofts **216** B4
Crofts of Benachielt **275** G5
Crofts of Buinach **267** J6
Crofts of Haddo **261** G1
Crofty **128** B3
Crogen **168** D4
Croggan **239** G2
Croglin **210** B3
Croick *High* **266** B2
Croick *High* **274** D3
Croig **246** D2
Crois Dùghaill **254** C3
Croit e Caley **190** A5
Cromarty (Cromba) **266** E5
Crombie **235** E1
Crombie Country Park
Angus DD5 3QL **252** D5
Crombie Mill **244** D1
Cromblet **261** F1
Cromdale **259** H2
Cromer *Herts* **150** A5
Cromer *Norf* **178** D1
Cromford **173** D2
Cromhall **131** F3
Cromhall Common **131** F4
Cromkill **287** D2
Cromor
Na H-E. Siar **271** G5
Crompton Fold **185** D1
Cromwell **174** C1
Cronberry **225** E3
Crondall **120** D3
Cronk-y-Voddy **190** B3
Cronton **183** F4
Crook *Cumb* **199** F3
Crook *Dur* **212** A4
Crook of Devon **243** F4
Crooked Soley **133** F5
Crookedholm **224** C2
Crookham *N'umb* **228** C3
Crookham *WBerks* **119** G1
Crookham Eastfield **228** D3
Crookham Village **120** C2
Crooklands **199** G4
Cropredy **147** G3
Cropston **160** A1
Cropthorne **146** B3
Cropton **203** G4
Cropwell Bishop **174** B4
Cropwell Butler **174** B4
Crosbie **232** D5
Crosbost **271** F5
Crosby *Cumb* **209** D3
Crosby *IoM* **190** B4
Crosby *Mersey* **183** E3
Crosby *NLincs* **187** F1
Crosby Court **202** D3
Crosby Garrett **200** C2
Crosby
Ravensworth **200** B1
Crosby Villa **209** D3
Crosby-on-Eden **210** A2
Croscombe **116** C3
Crosemere **170** B5
Crosland Hill **185** F1
Cross *Som* **116** B2
Cross (Cros) *Na H-E. Siar*
271 H1
Cross Ash **130** D1
Cross Bank **157** G5
Cross End *Bed* **149** F2
Cross End *Essex* **151** G4
Cross Foxes Inn **155** D1
Cross Gates **194** C4
Cross Green *Devon* **99** D2
Cross Green *Staffs* **158** B2
Cross Green *Suff* **152** A2
Cross Green *Suff* **151** G2
Cross Green *Suff* **151** G2
Cross Hands
Carmar **128** C1
Cross Hands
Pembs **127** D1
Cross Hill **173** F3
Cross Hills **193** G3
Cross Houses **157** E2
Cross in Hand **110** A1
Cross Inn *Cere* **141** G2
Cross Inn *Cere* **142** B1
Cross Inn *RCT* **129** G4
Cross Keys **123** E3
Cross Lane Head **157** G3
Cross Lanes *Corn* **96** B5
Cross Lanes *Corn* **95** D5

Cross Lanes *NYorks* **195** E1
Cross Lanes *Wrex* **170** A3
Cross of Jackston **261** F1
Cross Roads **286** C6
Cross Street **164** C4
Crossaig **231** G4
Crossan **283** G2
Crossapol **246** A4
Crossapoll **246** A2
Cross-at-Hand **123** G4
Crossbush **108** C3
Crosscanonby **209** D3
Crosscavanagh **281** K2
Crossdale Street **178** D2
Crossens **183** E1
Crossflatts **194** A3
Crossford *D&G* **216** C3
Crossford *Fife* **235** E1
Crossford *SLan* **234** B5
Crossgar **283** H3
Crossgare **286** C3
Crossgate *Lincs* **176** A5
Crossgate *M&EAnt* **287** J6
Crossgate *Staffs* **171** G4
Crossgatehall **236** A3
Crossgates *Fife* **235** F1
Crossgates *NYorks* **204** D4
Crossgates *P&K* **243** F2
Crossgates *Powys* **143** G1
Crossgill **192** B2
Crosshands *Carmar* **128** C2
Crosshands *EAyr* **224** D2
Crosshill *Fife* **243** G5
Crosshill *SAyr* **224** B5
Crosshouse **224** B2
Crosskeys *Caerp* **130** B3
Crosskeys *M&EAnt* **286** E6
Crosskirk **275** F1
Crosslanes **156** C1
Crosslee *Renf* **233** F3
Crosslee *ScBord* **227** E4
Crossmaglen **282** C7
Crossmichael **216** B4
Crossmoor **192** A4
Crossnacreevy **283** G2
Crossroads *Aber* **261** F5
Crossroads *EAyr* **224** C2
Crossway *Mon* **130** C1
Crossway *Powys* **143** G1
Crossway Green
Mon **131** E3
Crossway Green
Worcs **146** A1
Crossways *Dorset* **105** D4
Crossways *Glos* **131** E1
Crosswell **141** E4
Crosthwaite **199** F3
Croston **183** F1
Crostwick **179** D4
Crostwight **179** E3
Crothair **270** D4
Crouch **123** F3
Crouch End **136** B4
Crouch Hill **104** D1
Croucheston **118** B5
Croughton **148** A4
Crovie **269** G4
Crow **106** A2
Crow Edge **185** F2
Crow Green **137** E3
Crow Hill **145** F5
Crowan **94** D3
Crowborough **123** E5
Crowborough
Warren **123** E5
Crowcombe **115** E4
Crowdecote **172** C1
Crowden **185** E3
Crowdhill **119** F5
Crowell **134** C3
Crowfield *Suff* **152** C2
Crowfield *WN'hants*
148 B3
Crowhurst *ESuss* **110** C2
Crowhurst *Surr* **122** C4
Crowhurst Lane End
122 C4
Crowland *Lincs* **162** A1
Crowland *Suff* **164** B4
Crowlas **94** C3
Crowle *NLincs* **187** E1
Crowle *Worcs* **146** B2
Crowle Green **146** B2
Crowmarsh Gifford **134** B4
Crown Corner **165** D4
Crownhill **100** A2
Crownthorpe **178** B5
Crowntown **94** D3
Crow's Nest **97** G3
Crowsnest **156** C2
Crowthorne **120** D1
Crowton **183** G5
Croxall **159** E1
Croxby **188** B3
Croxdale **212** B4
Croxden **172** B4
Croxley Green **135** F3
Croxteth Country Park
Mersey L12 0HB **22** C2
Croxteth Hall *Mersey*
L12 0HB **22** C2
Croxton *Cambs* **150** A2
Croxton *NLincs* **188** A1
Croxton *Norf* **163** G4
Croxton *Staffs* **171** F4
Croxton *Staffs* **170** C2
Croxton Kerrial **174** D5
Croxtonbank **171** F4
Croy *High* **266** E7
Croy *NLan* **234** B2
Croyde **113** E2
Croydon *Cambs* **150** B3
Croydon *GtLon* **122** C2
Cruach **230** B4
Cruchie **268** D6
Cruckmeole **156** D2
Cruckton **156** D1
Cruden Bay **261** J1
Crudgington **157** F1
Crudwell **132** B3
Crug **156** A5
Crugmeer **96** D2
Crug-y-bar **142** C4
Crùlabhig **270** D4
Crumlin *A&N* **282** E1

Crumlin *BGwent* **130** B3
Crumpsall **184** C2
Crumpsbrook **157** F5
Crundale *Kent* **124** C4
Crundale *Pembs* **126** C1
Cruntully **280** D1
Crunwere Farm **127** E1
Crutherland Farm **234** A4
Cruwys Morchard **102** B1
Crux Easton **119** F2
Crwbin **128** C2
Cryers Hill **135** D3
Crymlyn **181** E5
Crymych **141** E4
Crynant **129** D2
Crystal Palace **136** C5
Crystal Palace Park
GtLon SE20 8DT **13** C7
Cuaig **264** D6
Cubbington **147** F1
Cubert **96** B4
Cubley **185** G2
Cublington *Bucks* **148** C5
Cublington *Here* **144** D4
Cuckfield **109** F1
Cucklington **117** E5
Cuckney **186** C5
Cuckold's Green **165** F3
Cuckoo Bridge **176** A5
Cuckoo's Corner **120** C3
Cuckoo's Nest **170** A1
Cuddesdon **134** B2
Cuddington *Bucks* **134** C1
Cuddington
ChesW&C **183** G5
Cuddington Heath **170** B3
Cuddy Hill **192** A4
Cudham **122** D3
Cudlipptown **99** F3
Cudmore Grove Country
Park *Essex*
CO5 8UE **139** G1
Cudworth *Som* **103** G1
Cudworth *SYorks* **186** A2
Cuerdley Cross **183** G4
Cuffley **136** C2
Cuidhaseadair **271** H2
Cuidhir **254** B4
Cuidrach **263** J6
Cuilcagh Boardwalk Trail
F&O BT92 1EW **280** D5
Cuilmuich **241** D5
Cuil-uaine **240** B1
Culag **241** F5
Culbo **266** D5
Culbokie
(Cùil Bhàicidh) **266** D6
Culbone **114** B3
Culburnie **266** B7
Culcabock **266** D7
Culcavy **283** F2
Culcharan **240** B1
Culcharry **267** F6
Culcheth **184** A3
Culdrain **260** D1
Culduie **264** D7
Culford **151** G4
Culfordheath **163** G5
Culgaith **210** C5
Culgower **274** F7
Culham **134** A3
Culindrach **232** A4
Culkein **272** C5
Culkerton **132** B3
Culkey **280** E4
Cullachie **259** G2
Cullaville **282** B7
Cullen **268** D4
Cullercoats **221** F4
Cullicudden **266** D5
Culligran **265** K7
Cullingworth **193** G4
Cullion **285** G5
Culliondoo **281** F6
Cullipool **239** G3
Cullivoe **278** E3
Culloch **242** C3
Culloden **266** E7
Cullompton **102** D2
Culmaily **267** F2
Culmalzie **215** E5
Culmington **157** E5
Culmore **285** H4
Culmstock **103** E1
Culnacnoc **264** B5
Culnacraig **265** G1
Culnadalloch **240** B1
Culnady **286** C5
Culnagrew **286** C5
Culnaknock **264** B5
Culnamean **255** K2
Culpho **152** D3
Culquhirk **215** E5
Culrain **266** C2
Culross **235** D1
Culroy **224** B4
Culsh **260** B5
Culshabbin **215** E5
Culswick **279** B8
Culter Allers Farm **226** B2
Cultercullen **261** H2
Cults *Aber* **260** D1
Cults *Aberdeen* **261** G4
Cults *D&G* **207** D3
Cultybraggan Camp Visitor
Centre *P&K* PH6 2AB
242 C3
Culverhouse Cross **130** A5
Culverstone Green **123** F2
Culverthorpe **175** F3
Culvie **268** D5
Culworth **148** A3
Culzean Castle & Country
Park *SAyr*
KA19 8LE **224** A4
Cumberhead **225** F2
Cumberlow Green **150** B4
Cumbernauld **234** B2
Cumbernworth **189** F5
Cumbria Crystal,
Ulverston *Cumb*
LA12 7LB **199** E5
Cuminestown **269** G6
Cumloden **215** F4
Cummersdale **209** G1
Cummertrees **217** F4

Cummingstown 267 J5
Cumnock 225 D3
Cumnor 133 G2
Cumrew 210 B2
Cumrue 217 E2
Cumstoun 216 A5
Cumwhinton 210 A2
Cumwhitton 210 B2
Cundall 202 D5
Cunningburn 283 J1
Cunninghamhead 233 E5
Cunningsburgh 279 D10
Cunnister 278 E3
Cunnoquhie 244 B3
Cupar 244 B3
Cupar Muir 244 B3
Curbar 185 G5
Curborough 158 D1
Curbridge Hants 107 E1
Curbridge Oxon 133 F2
Curdridge 107 E1
Curdworth 159 D3
Curland 103 F1
Curlew Green 153 E1
Curling Tye Green 138 B2
Curload 116 A5
Curr 281 H2
Curragh 283 J3
Curraghamulkin 281 F2
Curran 286 C6
Curridge 133 G5
Currie 235 F3
Curry Mallet 116 A5
Curry Rivel 116 A5
Curteis' Corner 124 A5
Curtisden Green 123 G4
Curtisknowle 100 D2
Cury 95 D4
Cusgarne 96 B5
Cushendall 287 G3
Cushendun 287 G2
Cushnie 269 F4
Cushuish 115 E4
Cusop 144 B3
Cusworth 186 C2
Cutcloy 207 E3
Cutcombe 114 C4
Cutgate 184 C1
Cuthill 266 E3
Cutiau 154 C1
Cutlers Green 151 D4
Cutnall Green 146 A1
Cutsdean 146 C4
Cutsyke 194 D5
Cutthorpe 186 A5
Cutts 279 D9
Cuttyhill 269 J5
Cuxham 134 B3
Cuxton 123 G2
Cuxwold 188 B2
Cwm BGwent 130 A2
Cwm Denb 182 B5
Cwm Gwaun 140 D4
Cwm Gwyn 128 C3
Cwm Head 156 D4
Cwm Irfon 143 E3
Cwm Llinau (Cwmlline) 155 E2
Cwm Penmachno 168 A3
Cwm Plysgog 141 E3
Cwmafan 129 D3
Cwmaman 129 G3
Cwm-ann 142 B3
Cwm-bach Carmar 141 F5
Cwm-bach Carmar 128 A2
Cwm-bach Powys 144 A4
Cwm-bach RCT 129 G2
Cwmbach Llechrhyd Powys 143 G2
Cwmbelan 155 F4
Cwmbrân 130 B3
Cwmbrwyno 154 D4
Cwm-carn 130 B3
Cwmcarvan 131 D2
Cwmcewydd 155 E1
Cwm-cou 141 F3
Cwmcrawnon 130 A1
Cwmdare 129 F2
Cwm-du Carmar 142 C4
Cwmdu Powys 144 A5
Cwmduad 141 G4
Cwmerfyn 154 D4
Cwmfelin 129 G2
Cwmfelin-boeth 127 E1
Cwmfelin-fach 130 A3
Cwmfelinmynach 141 F5
Cwm-ffrwd 128 A1
Cwm-ffrwd-oer 130 B2
Cwmgiedd 129 D1
Cwm-gors 128 D1
Cwmgwili 128 B1
Cwm-gwrach 129 E2
Cwmhiraeth 141 G4
Cwmifor 142 C5
Cwmisfael 128 A1
Cwmllyfri 127 G1
Cwmllynfell 128 D1
Cwm-mawr 128 B1
Cwm-miles 141 E5
Cwm-morgan 141 F4
Cwm-parc 129 F3
Cwm-pen-graig 141 G4
Cwmpennar 129 G2
Cwmsychbant 142 A3
Cwmsymlog 154 C4
Cwmtillery 130 B2
Cwm-twrch Isaf 129 D1
Cwm-twrch Uchaf 129 D1
Cwm-y-glo 167 E1
Cwmyoy 144 C5
Cwm-yr-Eglwys 140 D3
Cwmyrhaiadr 155 D3
Cwmystwyth 155 D5
Cwrt 154 C2
Cwrt-henri 142 B5
Cwrtnewydd 142 A3
Cwrtycadno 142 C3
Cwrt-y-gollen 130 B1
Cyffylliog 169 D2
Cyfronydd 156 A2
Cymau 169 F2
Cymmer NPT 129 E3
Cymmer RCT 129 G3
Cyncoed 130 A4
Cynghordy 143 E4
Cynheidre 128 A2
Cynwyd 169 D3
Cynwyl Elfed 141 G5

D
Dabton 216 C1
Daccombe 101 F1
Dacre Cumb 210 A5
Dacre NYorks 194 A1
Dacre Banks 194 A1
Daddry Shield 211 E4
Dadford 148 B4
Dadlington 159 G3
Dafen 128 B2
Daffy Green 178 A5
Dagdale 172 B4
Dagenham 137 D4
Daggons 106 A1
Daglingworth 132 B2
Dagnall 135 E1
Dail 240 C1
Dail Beag 270 E3
Dail Mòr 270 E3
Dailly 224 A5
Dailnamac 240 B1
Dainton 101 E1
Dairsie (Osnaburgh) 244 C3
Dairy House 197 E5
Daisy Bank 158 C3
Daisy Green 152 B1
Daisy Hill 282 B5
Dalabrog 254 C2
Dalavich 240 B3
Dalballoch 258 D5
Dalbeattie 216 C4
Dalblair 225 E4
Dalbog 253 D2
Dalbreck 274 C7
Dalbury 173 D4
Dalby IoM 190 A4
Dalby Lincs 176 C1
Dalby NYorks 203 F5
Dalby Forest Drive NYorks YO18 7LT 204 B4
Dalcairnie 224 C5
Dalchalloch 250 C3
Dalchalm 267 G1
Dalchenna 240 C4
Dalchirach 259 J1
Dalchork 273 H7
Dalchreichart 257 J3
Dalchruin 242 C3
Dalcross 266 E7
Dalderby 176 A1
Dalditch 102 D4
Daldownie 259 K4
Dale Cumb 210 B3
Dale GtMan 185 D2
Dale Pembs 126 B2
Dale Abbey 173 F4
Dale End Derbys 172 D1
Dale End NYorks 193 F3
Dale Head 199 F1
Dale of Walls 279 A7
Dale Park 108 B2
Dalehouse 203 G1
Dalelia 247 G3
Daless 259 F1
Dalestie 259 J3
Dalfad 260 B4
Dalganachan 275 F4
Dalgarven 233 D5
Dalgety Bay 235 F1
Dalgig 225 D4
Dalginross 242 C2
Dalgonar 225 F5
Dalguise 251 E5
Dalhalvaig 274 D3
Dalham 151 F1
Daligan 233 E1
Dalinlongart 232 C1
Dalivaddy 222 B3
Daljarrock 214 C2
Dalkeith 236 A3
Dallachulish 248 B5
Dallas 267 J6
Dallaschyle 267 F7
Dallash 215 F4
Dalleagles 225 D4
Dallinghoo 153 D2
Dallington ESuss 110 B2
Dallington WN'hants 148 C1
Dallow 202 A5
Dalmadilly 261 F3
Dalmally (Dail Mhàilidh) 241 D2
Dalmarnock 251 F5
Dalmary 242 A5
Dalmellington 224 C5
Dalmeny 235 F2
Dalmichy 273 H7
Dalmigavie 258 E3
Dalmore 266 D5
Dalmuir 233 F2
Dalmunzie House Hotel 251 F2
Dalnabreck 247 G3
Dalnacarn 251 F3
Dalnaglar Castle 251 G3
Dalnaha 239 F2
Dalnahaitnach 259 F3
Dalnamain 266 E2
Dalnatrat (Dail na Tràghad) 248 B4
Dalnavert 259 F4
Dalnavie 266 D4
Dalness 249 D4
Dalnessie 273 J7
Dalnigap 214 C3
Dalqueich 243 F4
Dalreoch 214 C2
Dalriech 242 C1
Dalroy 266 E7
Dalrulzian 251 G4
Dalry 233 D5
Dalrymple 224 B4
Dalscote 148 B2
Dalserf 234 B4
Dalsetter 278 E3
Dalshangan 215 G2
Dalskairth 216 D3
Dalston 209 G1
Dalswinton 216 D2
Daltomach 258 E2
Dalton Cumb 199 G5
Dalton D&G 217 F3
Dalton Lancs 183 F2
Dalton N'umb 220 D4
Dalton N'umb 211 F2
Dalton NYorks 202 D5
Dalton NYorks 202 A2
Dalton SYorks 186 B3
Dalton Magna 186 B3
Dalton Piercy 213 D4
Dalton-in-Furness 198 D5
Dalton-le-Dale 212 D3
Dalton-on-Tees 202 B2
Daltote 231 F1
Daltra 267 G7
Dalveich 242 B2
Dalvennan 224 B4
Dalvourn 258 D1
Dalwhinnie 250 B1
Dalwood 103 F2
Dam Green 164 B3
Damask Green 150 A5
Damerham 106 A1
Damgate 179 F5
Damhead 286 C3
Damnaglaur 206 B3
Damside 243 E3
Danaway 124 A2
Danbury 137 G2
Danby 203 G2
Danby Wiske 202 C3
Dancers Hill 136 B3
Dandaleith 267 K7
Danderhall 236 A3
Dane Bank 184 D3
Dane End 150 B5
Dane Hills 160 A2
Danebridge 171 G1
Danehill 109 G1
Danesmoor 173 F1
Danestone 261 H3
Daniel's Water 124 B4
Danskine 236 C3
Danthorpe 197 E4
Danzey Green 146 D1
Darby End 158 B4
Darby Green 120 D1
Darenth 137 E5
Daresbury 183 G4
Darfield 186 B2
Dargate 124 C2
Dargues 220 A2
Darite 97 G3
Darkley 282 B5
Darland 123 G2
Darlaston 158 B3
Darley 194 B2
Darley Bridge 173 D1
Darley Dale 173 D1
Darley Head 194 A2
Darley Hillside 173 D1
Darlingscott 147 E3
Darlington 202 B1
Darliston 170 C4
Darlton 187 E5
Darnabo 269 F6
Darnall 186 A4
Darnconner 225 D3
Darnford 261 F5
Darngarroch 216 A4
Darnick 227 G2
Darowen 155 E2
Darra 269 F6
Darracott 112 C4
Darragh Cross 283 H3
Darras Hall 221 D4
Darrington 186 B1
Darrow Green 165 D3
Darsham 153 F1
Dartans 284 E7
Dartfield 269 J5
Dartford 137 E5
Dartington 101 D1
Dartington Crystal Devon EX38 7AN 113 E4
Dartmeet 99 G3
Dartmouth 101 E2
Dartmouth Steam Railway Torbay TQ4 6AF 101 E2
Darton 186 A1
Darvel 225 D2
Darwell 110 C1
Darwell Hole 110 B2
Darwen 192 C5
Datchet 135 E5
Datchworth 136 B1
Datchworth Green 136 B1
Daubhill 184 A2
Daugh of Kinermony 267 K7
Dauntsey 132 B4
Dauntsey Green 132 B4
Dauntsey Lock 132 B4
Dava 259 H1
Davaar 222 C4
Davan 260 C4
Davenham 184 A5
Davenport Green 184 C4
Daventry 148 A1
Daventry Country Park WN'hants NN11 2JB 148 A1
Davidstow 97 F1
Davington 226 D5
Daviot Aber 261 F2
Daviot High 258 E1
Davoch of Grange 268 C5
Davyhulme 184 B3
Dawley 157 F2
Dawlish 102 C5
Dawn 181 G5
Daws Heath 138 B4
Daw's House 98 D2
Dawsmere 176 C4
Day Green 171 E2
Dayhills 171 G4
Dayhouse Bank 158 B5
Daylesford 147 E5
Ddôl 182 C5
Deadman's Cross 149 G3
Deadwaters 234 B5
Deaf Hill 212 C4
Deal 125 F3
Deal Hall 138 D3
Dean Cumb 209 D4
Dean Devon 100 D1
Dean Dorset 105 F1
Dean Hants 107 E1
Dean Oxon 147 F5
Dean Som 117 D3
Dean Bank 212 B4
Dean Castle & Country Park EAyr KA3 1XB 224 C2
Dean Cross 113 F1
Dean Head 185 G2
Dean Prior 100 D1
Dean Row 184 C4
Dean Street 123 G3
Deanburnhaugh 227 E4
Deane GtMan 184 A2
Deane Hants 119 G2
Deanland 105 F1
Deanlane End 107 G1
Deans Bottom 124 A2
Deanscales 209 D4
Deansgreen 184 A4
Deanshanger 148 C4
Deanston 242 C4
Dearham 209 D3
Debach 152 D2
Debate 218 A3
Debden 151 D4
Debden Cross 151 D4
Debden Green Essex 51 D4
Debden Green Essex 136 D3
Debenham 152 C1
Deblin's Green 146 A3
Dechmont 235 E2
Decker Hill 157 G1
Deddington 147 G4
Dedham 152 B4
Dedham Heath 152 B4
Dedworth 135 E5
Deecastle 260 C5
Deene 161 E3
Deenethorpe 161 E3
Deep, The HU1 4DP 76 Kingston upon Hull
Deep Sea World, North Queensferry Fife KY11 1JR 235 F1
Deepcar 185 G3
Deepcut 121 E2
Deepdale Cumb 200 C4
Deepdale NYorks 201 D5
Deeping Gate 161 G2
Deeping St. James 161 G2
Deeping St. Nicholas 162 A1
Deepweir 131 D4
Deerhill 268 C5
Deerhurst 146 A5
Deerhurst Walton 146 A5
Deerness Valley Walk Dur DH7 7RJ 212 A3
Deerton Street 124 B2
Defford 146 B3
Defynnog 143 F5
Deganwy 181 F5
Degnish 239 G3
Deighton NYorks 202 C2
Deighton WYorks 185 F1
Deighton York 195 F3
Deiniolen 167 E1
Delabole 97 E1
Delamere 170 C1
Delavorar 259 J3
Delfrigs 261 H2
Dell Lodge 259 H3
Dell Quay 108 A3
Delliefure 259 H1
Delly End 133 F1
Delnabo 259 J3
Delny 266 E4
Delph 185 D2
Delphorrie 260 C3
Delves 212 A3
Delvine 251 G5
Dembleby 175 F4
Denaby 186 B3
Denaby Main 186 B3
Denbies Wine Estate Surr RH5 6AA 121 G2
Denbigh (Dinbych) 168 D1
Denbury 101 E1
Denby 173 E3
Denby Dale 185 G2
Denby Pottery Derbys DE5 8NX 18 C1
Denchworth 133 F3
Dendron 198 D5
Denend 260 E1
Denford 161 E5
Dengie 138 C2
Denham Bucks 135 F4
Denham Suff 164 C4
Denham Suff 151 F1
Denham Green 135 F4
Denham Street 164 C4
Denhead Aber 261 F3
Denhead Aber 269 J5
Denhead Fife 244 C3
Denhead of Arbirlot 253 D5
Denhead of Gray 244 B1
Denholm 227 G4
Denholme 193 G4
Denholme Clough 193 G4
Denio 166 C4
Denmead 107 F1
Denmill 261 G3
Denmoss 268 E6
Dennington 153 D1
Denny 234 C1
Dennyloanhead 234 C1
Denshaw 185 D1
Denside 261 G5
Densole 125 E4
Denston 151 F2
Denstone 172 B3
Dent 200 C4
Denton Cambs 161 G4
Denton Darl 202 B1
Denton ESuss 109 G3
Denton GtMan 184 D3
Denton Kent 125 E4
Denton Kent 137 F5
Denton Lincs 175 D4
Denton Norf 165 D3
Denton NYorks 194 A3
Denton Oxon 134 A2
Denton WN'hants 148 D2
Denton's Green 183 F3
Denver 163 E2
Denvilles 107 G2
Denwick 229 G5
Deopham 178 B5
Deopham Green 164 B2
Depden 151 F2
Depden Green 151 F2
Deptford GtLon 136 C5
Deptford Wilts 118 B4
Derby 173 E4
Derby City Museum & Art Gallery DE1 1BS 70 Derby
Derbyhaven 190 A5
Dereham (East Dereham) 178 A4
Dererach 239 E2
Deri 130 A2
Dernagh 282 B2
Dernalebe 285 F6
Derrachrin 282 E1
Derriaghy 283 F2
Derril 112 D5
Derringstone 125 E4
Derrington 171 F5
Derriton 112 D5
Derry 242 B2
Derry City Walls D&S BT48 6PR 285 G4
Derry Hill 132 B5
Derryad 281 F6
Derryadd 282 D2
Derryanvil 282 D3
Derryboy 283 H3
Derrychrier 285 J5
Derrychrin 282 C1
Derrycrow 282 C2
Derrydoon 281 F6
Derrydorragh 286 C3
Derrydrumuck 282 E5
Derryfubble 282 B3
Derrygonnelly 280 D3
Derryhale 282 C4
Derryharney 281 F5
Derryhaw 282 A4
Derryhillagh 280 E4
Derrykeevan 282 C3
Derrykeighan 286 D2
Derrylane 285 J4
Derrylattinee 282 A3
Derrylea 280 E6
Derryleckagh 282 E6
Derrylee 282 B2
Derrylin 280 E6
Derrymacash 282 D2
Derrymore 282 D2
Derrynanny 280 E3
Derrynawilt 281 G5
Derrynoose 282 B5
Derryraine 282 C4
Derrythorpe 187 F2
Derrytrasna 282 C2
Derryvane 282 C3
Dersingham 177 E4
Dervaig 246 D4
Dervock 286 D2
Derwen 169 D2
Derwen-fawr (Broad Oak) 142 B5
Derwen-las 154 D3
Derwent Valley Mills Derbys DE4 3RQ 173 E3
Derwent Walk Country Park Dur NE16 3BN 28 A3
Derwydd 128 C1
Derybruich 232 A2
Desborough 160 D4
Desertmartin 286 C6
Desford 159 G2
Detchant 229 E3
Dethick 173 E2
Detling 123 G3
Deuddwr 156 B1
Deunant 168 C1
Deuxhill 157 F4
Devauden 131 D3
Devil's Bridge (Pontarfynach) 154 D5
Devitts Green 159 E3
Devizes 118 B1
Devon Guild of Craftsmen Devon TQ13 9AF 102 B5
Devonport 100 A2
Devonside 243 E5
Devoran 95 E3
Devoran & Perran (Cornwall & West Devon Mining Landscape) Corn 95 E3
Dewar 236 A5
Dewlish 105 D3
Dewsall Court 145 D4
Dewsbury 194 B5
Dewsbury Moor 194 B5
Dhiseig 239 D1
Dhoon 190 C3
Dhoor 190 C2
Dhowin 190 C1
Dhuhallow 258 C2
Dial Green 121 E5
Dial Post 109 D2
Dibden 106 D2
Dibden Hill 135 E3
Dibden Purlieu 106 D2
Dick Institute EAyr KA1 3BU 224 C2
Dickleburgh 164 C3
Dickleburgh Moor 164 C3
Didbrook 146 C4
Didcot 134 A3
Diddington 149 G1
Diddlebury 157 E4
Didley 145 D4
Didling 108 A2
Didmarton 132 A4
Didsbury 184 C3
Didworthy 100 C1
Digby 175 F2
Digg 263 K5
Diggle 185 E2
Digmoor 183 F2
Digswell 136 B1
Dihewyd 142 A2
Dildawn 216 B5
Dilham 179 E3
Dilhorne 171 G3
Dillington 149 G1
Dilston 211 F1
Dilton Marsh 117 F3
Dilwyn 144 D2
Dilwyn Common 144 D2
Dimple 184 B1
Dinas Carmar 141 F4
Dinas Gwyn 167 D2
Dinas Gwyn 166 B4
Dinas Cross 140 D4
Dinas Dinlle 166 D2
Dinas Mawddwy 155 E1
Dinas Powys 130 A5
Dinckley 192 C4
Dinder 116 C3
Dinedor 145 E4
Dingestow 131 D1
Dingley 160 C4
Dingwall (Inbhir Pheofharain) 266 C6
Dinlabyre 218 D2
Dinnet 260 C5
Dinnington Som 104 A1
Dinnington SYorks 186 C4
Dinnington T&W 221 E4
Dinorwig 167 E1
Dinosaur Adventure Park Norf NR9 5JW 178 C4
Dinosaur Museum, Dorchester Dorset DT1 1EW 104 C3
Dinton Bucks 134 C1
Dinton Wilts 118 B4
Dinton Pastures Country Park W'ham RG10 0TH 134 C5
Dinvin 214 B5
Dinwoodie Mains 217 F1
Dinworthy 112 D4
Dipford 115 F5
Dippen A&B 222 C2
Dippen NAyr 223 F3
Dippenhall 120 D3
Dipple Moray 268 B5
Dipple SAyr 224 A5
Diptford 100 D2
Dipton 212 A2
Dirdhu 259 H2
Dirleton 236 C1
Discoed 144 B1
Discovery Museum T&W NE1 4JA 79 Newcastle upon Tyne
Diseworth 173 F5
Dishes 276 F5
Dishforth 202 C5
Dishley 173 G5
Disley 185 D4
Diss 164 C3
Disserth 143 G2
Distington 208 D4
Ditcheat 116 D4
Ditchingham 165 E2
Ditchley 147 F5
Ditchling 109 F2
Ditteridge 117 F1
Dittisham 101 E2
Ditton Halton 183 F4
Ditton Kent 123 G3
Ditton Green 151 E2
Ditton Priors 157 F4
Dixton Glos 146 B4
Dixton Mon 131 E1
Doagh 287 G7
Dobcross 185 D2
Dobwalls 97 G3
Doccombe 102 A4
Dochgarroch 258 D1
Dock Museum, Barrow-in-Furness Cumb LA14 2PW 191 E1
Dockenfield 120 D3
Docker Cumb 199 G3
Docker Lancs 199 G5
Docking 177 F4
Docklow 145 E2
Dockray Cumb 209 G4
Dockray Cumb 209 F1
Dodbrooke 100 D3
Doddenham 145 G2
Doddinghurst 137 E3
Doddington Cambs 162 C3
Doddington Kent 124 B3
Doddington Lincs 187 G5
Doddington N'umb 229 D3
Doddington Shrop 157 F5
Doddiscombsleigh 102 B4
Doddycross 98 D4
Dodford WN'hants 148 B1
Dodford Worcs 158 B5
Dodington SGlos 131 G4
Dodington Som 115 E3
Dodington Ash 131 G5
Dodleston 170 A1
Dods Leigh 172 B4
Dodscott 113 F4
Dodworth 186 A2
Doehole 173 E2
Doffcocker 184 A1
Dog Street 282 C5
Dog Village 102 C3
Dogdyke 176 A2
Dogmersfield 120 C2
Dogsthorpe 162 A2
Dol Fawr 155 E2
Dolanog 155 G1
Dolau Powys 144 A1
Dolau RCT 129 G4
Dolbenmaen 167 E3
Doley 171 E5
Dolfach 155 F5
Dolfor 156 A4
Dolgarreg 142 D4
Dolgarrog 168 A1
Dolgellau 154 D1
Dôl-goch 154 C2
Dolgran 142 A4
Doll 267 F1
Dollar 243 E5
Dollarbeg 243 E5
Dollingstown 282 E3
Dolphin 182 C5
Dolphinholme 192 B2
Dolphinton 235 F5
Dolton 113 F4
Dolwen Conwy 181 G5
Dolwen Powys 155 F2
Dolwyddelan 168 A2
Dôl-y-bont 154 C4
Dolycannau 144 A3
Dolyhir 144 B2
Dolywern 169 F4
Domgay 156 B1
Donagh 281 F6
Donaghadee 283 J1
Donaghcloney 282 E3
Donaghey 282 B1
Donaghmore 282 A2
Doncaster 186 C2
Doncaster Racecourse Exhibition Centre SYorks DN2 6BB 186 D2
Doncaster Sheffield Airport 187 D3
Donegore 287 G7
Donemana 285 G5
Donhead St. Andrew 118 A5
Donhead St. Mary 118 A5
Donibristle 235 F1
Doniford 115 D3
Donington Lincs 176 A4
Donington Shrop 158 A2
Donington le Heath 159 G1
Donington on Bain 188 C4
Donisthorpe 159 F1
Donkey Sanctuary, Salcombe Regis Devon EX10 0NU 103 E4
Donna Nook 189 E3
Donnington Glos 147 D5
Donnington Here 145 G4
Donnington Shrop 157 E2
Donnington Tel&W 157 G1
Donnington WBerks 119 F1
Donnington WSuss 108 A3
Donyatt 103 G1
Doogary 281 G2
Dooish 281 F1
Doon 280 E6
Doonan 286 C5
Doonbought 287 F4
Doons 281 K1
Dorchester Dorset 104 C3
Dorchester Oxon 134 A3
Dorchester Abbey Oxon OX10 7HH 134 A3
Dordon 159 E2
Dore 186 A4
Dores (Duras) 258 C1
Dorket Head 173 G3
Dorking 121 G3
Dorley's Corner 153 E1
Dormans Park 122 C4
Dormansland 122 D4
Dormanstown 213 E5
Dormer's Wells 136 A4
Dormington 145 E3
Dormston 146 B2
Dorn 147 E4
Dorney 135 E5
Dorney Reach 135 E5
Dornie (An Dòrnaidh) 256 E2
Dornoch 266 E3
Dornock 218 A5
Dorrery 275 F3
Dorridge 159 D5
Dorrington Lincs 175 F2
Dorrington Shrop 157 D2
Dorsell 260 D3
Dorset & East Devon Coast Dorset 105 E5
Dorsington 146 D3
Dorstone 144 C3
Dorsy 282 C6
Dorton 134 B1
Dorusduain 257 F2
Dosthill 159 E3
Dotland 211 F2
Dottery 104 A3
Doublebois 97 F3
Dougalston 233 G2
Dougarie 223 D2
Doughton 132 A3
Douglas IoM 190 B4
Douglas SLan 225 G2
Douglas & Angus 244 C1
Douglas Bridge 285 F7
Douglas Water 225 G2
Douglastown 252 C5
Doulting 116 D3
Dounby 276 B5
Doune A&B 241 F5
Doune A&B 241 F3
Doune High 259 F3
Doune High 266 B1
Doune Stir 242 C4
Dounepark 269 F4
Douneside 260 C4
Dounie High 266 D3
Dounie High 266 C2
Dounreay 274 E2
Dousland 100 B1
Dovaston 170 A5
Dove Holes 185 E5
Dovenby 209 D3
Dovendale 188 D4
Dover 125 F4
Dover Castle Kent CT16 1HU 70 Dover
Dovercourt 152 D4
Doverdale 146 A1
Doveridge 172 C4
Doversgreen 122 B4
Dowally 251 F5
Dowdeswell 146 C5
Dowhill 224 A5
Dowlais 129 G2
Dowland 113 F4
Dowlands 103 F3
Dowlish Ford 103 G1
Dowlish Wake 103 G1
Down Ampney 132 D3
Down County Museum NM&D BT30 6AH 283 H4
Down End 116 A3
Down Hatherley 146 A5
Down St. Mary 102 A2
Down Thomas 100 B3
Downderry 98 D5
Downe 122 D2
Downend IoW 107 E4
Downend SGlos 131 F5
Downend WBerks 133 G5
Downfield 244 B1
Downfields 163 E5
Downgate 99 D3
Downham Essex 137 G3
Downham Lancs 193 D3
Downham N'umb 228 C3
Downham Market 163 E2
Downhead Corn 97 G1
Downhead Som 117 D3
Downhead Som 116 C5

Downhill **286** B2
Downholland Cross **183** E2
Downholme **202** A3
Downies **261** H5
Downley **135** D3
Downpatrick **283** H4
Downs **130** A5
Downside *NSom* **116** B1
Downside *Som* **116** D3
Downside *Som* **116** D2
Downside *Surr* **121** G2
Downton *Devon* **99** F2
Downton *Devon* **101** E2
Downton *Hants* **106** B3
Downton *Wilts* **118** C5
Downton on the
   Rock **156** D5
Dowsby **175** G5
Dowthwaitehead **209** G4
Doxey **171** G5
Doynton **131** G5
Drabblegate **178** D3
Draethen **130** B4
Draffan **234** B5
Dragley Beck **199** D5
Drakeland Corner **100** B2
Drakelow **158** A4
Drakemyre **233** D4
Drakes Broughton **146** B3
Drakes Cross **158** C5
Draperstown **286** B6
Draughton *NYorks* **193** G2
Draughton *WN'hants*
   160 C5
Drax **195** F5
Draycot Foliat **133** D5
Draycote **147** G1
Draycott *Derbys* **173** F4
Draycott *Glos* **147** D4
Draycott *Shrop* **158** A3
Draycott *Som* **116** B2
Draycott *Worcs* **146** A3
Draycott in the Clay
   172 C5
Draycott in the Moors
   171 G4
Drayford **102** A1
Draynes **97** G3
Drayton *Leics* **160** D3
Drayton *Lincs* **176** A4
Drayton *Norf* **178** C4
Drayton *Oxon* **147** G3
Drayton *Oxon* **133** G3
Drayton *Ports* **107** F2
Drayton *Som* **116** B5
Drayton *Warks* **147** D2
Drayton *Worcs* **158** B5
Drayton Bassett **159** D2
Drayton Beauchamp
   135 E1
Drayton Manor Park *Staffs*
   B78 3TW **159** D2
Drayton Parslow **148** D5
Drayton
   St. Leonard **134** A3
Drebley **193** G2
Dreemskerry **190** C2
Dreenan *F&O* **280** C2
Dreenan *Mid Ulster* **286** D5
Dreenhill **126** C1
Dre-fach *Carmar* **141** G4
Dre-fach *Carmar* **128** B1
Dre-fach *Cere* **142** B3
Drefelin **141** G4
Dreghorn **224** B2
Drem **236** C2
Dressoge **281** F1
Drewsteignton **102** A3
Driby **189** D5
Driffield *ERid* **196** C2
Driffield *Glos* **132** C3
Drigg **198** B3
Drighlington **194** B5
Drimfern **240** C3
Drimlee **240** D3
Drimnin **247** E4
Drimore **262** C7
Drimpton **104** A2
Drimsdale **254** C1
Drimsynie **241** D4
Drimvore **240** A5
Drinan **256** B3
Dringhouses **195** E2
Drinisiader **263** G2
Drinkstone **152** A1
Drinkstone Green **152** A1
Drishaig **241** D3
Drissaig **240** B3
Drointon **172** B5
Droitwich Spa **146** A1
Dromara **283** F3
Dromore *AB&C* **283** F3
Dromore *CC&G* **285** J3
Dromore *F&O* **281** F2
Dron **243** G3
Dronfield **186** A5
Dronfield
   Woodhouse **186** A5
Drongan **224** C4
Dronley **244** B1
Droop **105** D2
Dropmore **135** E4
Droxford **107** F1
Droylsden **184** D3
Druid **168** D2
Druidston **126** B1
Druimarbin **248** C2
Druimavuic **248** C5
Druimdrishaig **231** F2
Druimindarroch **247** F1
Druimkinnerras **258** B1
Drum *A&B* **232** A2
Drum *P&K* **243** F4
Drumachloy **232** B3
Drumadoon **287** F1
Drumagarner **286** D4
Drumaghadone **283** F3
Drumahoe **285** G4
Drumaknockan **283** F3
Drumalig **283** G3
Drumaness **283** G4
Drumaran **280** D5
Drumaroad **283** G4
Drumawhy **283** J1
Drumbeg **272** D5
Drumblade **268** D6
Drumblair **268** E6
Drumbo **283** G2

Drumboy **280** D4
Drumbrughas **280** E5
Drumbuie *D&G* **225** F4
Drumbuie *High* **256** D1
Drumburgh **209** F2
Drumcard **280** D5
Drumchapel **233** G2
Drumchardine **266** C7
Drumchork **264** E3
Drumclog **225** E2
Drumdelgie **268** C6
Drumderfit **266** D6
Drumderg **281** F4
Drumduff **280** E3
Drumeldrie **244** C4
Drumelzier **226** C2
Drumena Cashel *NM&D*
   BT34 5JX **283** G5
Drumfad **283** K1
Drumfearn **256** C3
Drumfern **248** B2
Drumgallan **280** E1
Drumgath **282** E6
Drumgley **252** C4
Drumguish **258** E5
Drumharvey **280** E3
Drumhead **260** E5
Drumhirr *A&NDown*
   283 H2
Drumhirr *A&NDown*
   283 J1
Drumin **259** J1
Drumine **266** E6
Drumintee **282** E7
Drumjohn **215** G1
Drumlamford
   House **215** D3
Drumlasie **260** C4
Drumlee *AB&C* **283** F5
Drumlee *CC&G* **286** D3
Drumlegagh **285** F7
Drumlemble **282** B4
Drumlithie **253** F1
Drummacabranagher
   280 E5
Drumman **282** B4
Drummannon **282** C3
Drummond *High* **266** D5
Drummond *Stir* **242** B4
Drummore **206** B3
Drummuir **268** B6
Drummuir Castle **268** B6
Drumnadrochit (Druim na
   Drochaid) **258** C2
Drumnagorrach **268** D5
Drumnakilly **281** H1
Drumnatorran **248** A3
Drumnykerne **282** E2
Drumoak **261** F5
Drumore **222** C3
Drumour **283** F3
Drumpellier Country Park
   NLan ML5 1RX **31** G3
Drumquin **281** F1
Drumrash **216** A3
Drumrunie **265** H1
Drums **261** H2
Drumsallen **281** H5
Drumskinny **280** D2
Drumsleve **285** J5
Drumsturdy **244** C1
Drumsurn **286** B4
Drumuie **263** F7
Drumuillie **259** G2
Drumvaich **242** B4
Drumwhindle **261** H2
Drumwhirn **216** B2
Drunkendub **253** E5
Druridge **221** E2
Druridge Bay Country
   Park *N'umb*
   NE61 5BX **221** E2
Drury **169** F1
Drusillas Park *ESuss*
   BN26 5QS **110** A3
Drws-y-nant **168** B5
Dry Doddington **174** D3
Dry Drayton **150** B1
Dry Harbour **264** C6
Dry Sandford **133** G2
Dry Street **137** F4
Drybeck **200** B1
Drybridge *Moray* **268** C4
Drybridge *NAyr* **224** B2
Drybrook **131** F1
Dryburgh **227** G2
Drygrange **227** G2
Dryhope **227** D3
Drymen **233** F1
Drymuir **269** H6
Drynoch **255** K1
Dryslwyn **142** B5
Dryton **157** E2
Duachy **240** A2
Dubford **269** F4
Dubhchladach **231** G3
Dubheads **243** E2
Dublin **152** C1
Dubton **253** D4
Duchal **233** E1
Duchray **241** G4
Duck Bay **233** E1
Duck End *Bed* **149** F3
Duck End *Cambs* **150** A1
Duck End *Essex* **151** E5
Duck Street **194** A1
Duckington **170** B2
Ducklington **133** F2
Duckmanton **186** B5
Duck's Cross **149** F2
Ducks Island **136** B3
Duddenhoe End **150** C4
Duddingston **235** G2
Duddington **161** E2
Duddlestone **115** F5
Duddleswell **109** G1
Duddo **237** G5
Duddon **170** C1
Duddon Bridge **198** C4
Dudleston **170** A4
Dudleston Heath
   (Criftins) **170** A4
Dudley *T&W* **221** E4
Dudley *WMid* **158** B3
Dudley Port **158** B3

Dudley Zoo & Castle
   WMid DY1 4QB **14** B3
Dudlow's Green **184** A4
Dudsbury **105** G3
Duffield **173** E3
Duffryn **129** E3
Duffus **267** J5
Duggleby **196** A1
Duiar **259** J1
Duible **274** E6
Duiletter **241** D2
Duinish **250** B3
Duirinish **256** D1
Duisdalemor **256** C3
Duisky **248** C2
Duke End **159** F4
Dukestown **130** A1
Dukinfield **184** D3
Dulas **180** C4
Dulax **260** B3
Dulcote **116** C3
Dulford **103** D2
Dull **250** B4
Dullaghan **281** F2
Dullatur **234** B2
Dullingham **151** E2
Dullingham Ley **151** E2
Dulnain Bridge **259** G2
Duloe *Bed* **149** G1
Duloe *Corn* **97** G4
Dulsie **267** G2
Dulverton **114** C5
Dulwich **136** C5
Dulwich Picture Gallery
   GtLon SE21 7AD **13** C7
Dumbarton **233** E1
Dumbleton **146** C4
Dumcrieff **226** D3
Dumeath **260** C1
Dumfin **233** E1
Dumfries **217** D3
Dumgoyne **233** G1
Dummer **119** G3
Dun **253** E4
Dunach **240** A2
Dunaghy **286** D3
Dunalastair **250** C4
Dunan *A&B* **232** C2
Dunan *High* **256** B2
Dunans **240** C5
Dunball **116** A3
Dunbar **237** D2
Dunbeath **275** G5
Dunbeg
   (An Dùn Beag) **240** A1
Dunblane **242** C4
Dunbog **244** A3
Dunbridge **119** E5
Duncanston *Aber* **260** D2
Duncanston *High* **266** C6
Dunchideock **102** B4
Dunchurch **159** G5
Duncote **148** B2
Duncow **217** D2
Duncraggan **242** A4
Duncrievie **243** G4
Duncroist **242** A1
Duncrub **243** F3
Duncrun **285** J2
Duncryne **233** F1
Duncton **108** B2
Dundee **244** C1
Dundee Airport **244** B2
Dundee Contemporary Arts
   DD1 4DY **71** Dundee
Dundon **116** B4
Dundon Hayes **116** B4
Dundonald *L&C* **283** H1
Dundonald *SAyr* **224** B2
Dundonnell (Ach-Dà-
   Dhòmhnaill) **265** H2
Dundraw **209** F2
Dundreggan
   (Dul Dreagain) **257** K3
Dundrennan **208** A2
Dundridge **107** E1
Dundrod **28** E1
Dundrum *AB&C* **282** B5
Dundrum *NM&D* **283** H5
Dundry **116** C1
Duneany **286** E4
Dunearn **235** G1
Dunecht **261** F4
Duneight **283** F2
Dunfield **132** D3
Dunford Bridge **185** F2
Dungannon **282** A2
Dungate **124** B3
Dungavel **225** E2
Dungiven **285** J5
Dungworth **185** G3
Dunham *A&B* **240** B4
Dunham Massey Hall,
   Park & Gardens *GtMan*
   WA14 4SJ **24** C3
Dunham Town **184** B4
Dunham
   Woodhouses **184** B4
Dunham-on-the-
   Hill **183** D5
Dunhampton **146** A1
Dunholme **188** A5
Dunino **244** D3
Dunipace **234** C1
Dunira **242** C2
Dunkeld **251** F5
Dunkerton **117** E2
Dunkeswell **103** E2
Dunkeswick **194** C3
Dunkirk *ChesW&C* **183** E5
Dunkirk *Kent* **124** C3
Dunk's Green **123** F3
Dunlappie **253** D3
Dunley *Hants* **119** F3
Dunley *Worcs* **145** G1
Dunlop **233** F5
Dunloskin **232** C2
Dunloy **286** E4
Dunluce Castle *CC&G*
   BT57 8UY **286** D1
Dunmere **97** E3
Dunminning **286** E4
Dunmore *A&B* **231** F3
Dunmore *Falk* **234** C1
Dyke *Devon* **112** D3

Dunmore *Mid Ulster*
   286 B7
Dunmore *NM&D* **283** G4
Dunmurry **283** F2
Dunn **275** G3
Dunn Street **123** G2
Dunnabie **218** A3
Dunnamore **285** J7
Dunnet **275** H1
Dunnichen **252** D5
Dunning **243** F3
Dunnington *ERid* **197** D2
Dunnington *Warks* **146** C2
Dunnington *York* **195** F2
Dunnockshaw **193** E5
Dunoon **232** C2
Dunragit **214** C5
Dunrostan **231** F1
Duns **237** E4
Duns Tew **147** G5
Dunsa **185** G5
Dunsby **175** G5
Dunscore **216** C2
Dunscroft **187** D2
Dunsdale **203** F1
Dunsden Green **134** C5
Dunsfold **121** F4
Dunsford *Devon* **102** B4
Dunsford *Devon* EX6 7EG
   102 B4
Dunshalt **244** A3
Dunshill **146** A4
Dunsinnan **243** G1
Dunsland Cross **113** E5
Dunsley *NYorks* **204** B1
Dunsley *Staffs* **158** A4
Dunsmore **135** D2
Dunsop Bridge **192** C2
Dunstable **149** E5
Dunstable Downs *CenBeds*
   LU6 2GY **149** E5
Dunstall **172** C5
Dunstall Green **151** F1
Dunstan **229** G5
Dunstan Steads **229** G4
Dunster **114** C3
Dunster Castle & Gardens
   Som TA24 6SL **114** C3
Dunston *Lincs* **175** F1
Dunston *Norf* **178** D5
Dunston *Staffs* **158** B1
Dunston Heath **158** B1
Dunston Hill **212** B1
Dunstone *Devon* **102** A5
Dunstone *Devon* **100** B2
Dunsville **187** D2
Dunswell **196** C4
Dunsyre **235** E5
Dunterton **99** D3
Duntisbourne
   Abbots **132** B2
Duntisbourne Leer **132** B2
Duntisbourne
   Rouse **132** B2
Duntish **104** C2
Duntocher **233** F2
Dunton *Bucks* **148** D5
Dunton *CenBeds* **150** A3
Dunton *Norf* **177** G4
Dunton Bassett **160** A3
Dunton Green **123** E3
Dunton Wayletts **137** F3
Duntulm **263** K4
Dunure **224** A4
Dunure Mains **224** A4
Dunvant **128** B3
Dunvegan **263** H7
Dunvegan Castle *High*
   IV55 8WF **263** H7
Dunwich **165** F4
Dura **244** C3
Durdar **210** A2
Durgan **95** E4
Durgates **123** F5
Durham **212** B3
Durham Castle and
   Cathedral *Dur* DH1 3RW &
   DH1 3EH **212** B3
Durham Dales Centre *Dur*
   DL13 2FJ **211** G4
Durinemast **247** F4
Durisdeer **225** G5
Durleigh **115** F4
Durley *Hants* **107** E1
Durley *Wilts* **118** D1
Durley Street **107** E1
Durlow Common **145** F4
Durlston Country
   Park *Dorset*
   BH19 2JL **105** G5
Durmacmuck **265** G2
Durness **273** J3
Durno **261** F2
Duror **248** B4
Durran *A&B* **240** B4
Durran *High* **275** G2
Durrants **107** G2
Durrington *Wilts* **118** C3
Durrington *WSuss* **108** D3
Dursley **131** G3
Dursley Cross **131** F1
Durston **115** F5
Durweston **105** E2
Dury **279** D6
Duston **148** C1
Dutlas **156** B5
Duton Hill **151** E5
Dutson **98** D2
Duxford **183** G5
Dwygyfylchi **181** F5
Dwyran **166** D1
Dyan **282** A4
Dyce **261** G3
Dyfatty **128** A2
Dyffryn *Bridgend* **129** E3
Dyffryn *Pembs* **126** C1
Dyffryn *VGlam* **129** G5
Dyffryn Ardudwy **167** E5
Dyffryn Castell **155** D4
Dyffryn Ceidrych **142** D5
Dyffryn Cellwen **129** E1
Dyke *Devon* **112** D3

Dyke *Lincs* **175** G5
Dyke *Moray* **267** G6
Dykehead *Angus* **252** B3
Dykehead *NLan* **234** C4
Dykehead *Stir* **242** A5
Dykelands **253** F3
Dykend **252** A4
Dykeside **269** F6
Dylan Thomas Centre
   SA1 1RR **86** Swansea
Dylife **155** E3
Dymchurch **111** G1
Dymock **145** G4
Dynamic Earth *Edin*
   EH8 8AS **37** J4
Dyrham **131** G5
Dyrham Park *SGlos*
   SN14 8ER **8** E2
Dysart **244** B5
Dyserth **182** B5

E

Eachwick **220** D4
Eadar Dha Fhadhail
   (Ardroil) **270** C4
Eagland Hill **192** A3
Eagle **175** D1
Eagle Barnsdale **175** D1
Eagle Moor **175** D1
Eaglescliffe **202** D1
Eaglesfield *Cumb* **209** D4
Eaglesfield *D&G* **218** A4
Eaglesham **233** G4
Eaglethorpe **161** F3
Eagley **184** B1
Eairy **190** B1
Eakley **148** D2
Eakring **174** B1
Ealand **187** E1
Ealing **136** A4
Eamont Bridge **210** B5
Earby **193** F3
Earcroft **192** C5
Eardington **157** G3
Eardisland **144** D3
Eardisley **144** C3
Eardiston *Shrop* **170** A5
Eardiston *Worcs* **145** F1
Earith **162** C5
Earl Shilton **159** G3
Earl Soham **152** D1
Earl Sterndale **172** B1
Earl Stonham **152** C2
Earle **229** D4
Earlestown **183** G3
Earley **134** C5
Earlham **178** C5
Earls Barton **149** D1
Earls Colne **151** G5
Earl's Common **146** B2
Earl's Court **136** B5
Earl's Croome **146** A3
Earl's Green **152** B1
Earlsdon **159** F5
Earlsferry **244** C4
Earlsford **261** G1
Earlsheaton **194** B5
Earlston **227** G2
Earlswood *Mon* **131** D3
Earlswood *Surr* **122** B4
Earlswood *Warks* **158** D5
Earnley **108** A4
Earnshaw Bridge **192** B5
Earsairidh **254** C5
Earsdon **221** F1
Earsdon Moor **221** D2
Earsham **165** E3
Earsham Street **164** D3
Earswick **195** F2
Eartham **108** B3
Earthcott Green **131** F4
Easby **203** E1
Easdale **239** G3
Easebourne **121** D5
Easenhall **159** G5
Eashing **121** E3
Easington *Bucks* **134** B1
Easington *Dur* **212** D3
Easington *ERid* **189** D1
Easington *N'umb* **229** F3
Easington *Oxon* **134** D1
Easington *Oxon* **147** G4
Easington *R&C* **203** G1
Easington Colliery **212** D3
Easington Lane **212** C4
Easingwold **195** E1
Easole Street **125** E3
Eassie **252** B5
East Aberthaw **114** D1
East Acton **136** B4
East Allington **101** D3
East Anstey **114** C4
East Anton **119** E3
East Appleton **202** B3
East Ardsley **194** C5
East Ashling **108** A3
East Auchronie **261** G4
East Ayton **204** C4
East Barkwith **188** B4
East Barming **123** G3
East Barnby **204** B1
East Barnet **136** B3
East Barsham **178** A2
East Beckham **178** C2
East Bedfont **135** F5
East Bergholt **152** B4
East Bierley **194** B5
East Bilney **178** A4
East Blatchington **109** G4
East Boldon **212** C1
East Boldre **106** C2
East Bolton **229** F5
East Bower **116** A4
East Brent **116** A2
East Bridge **153** F1
East Bridgford **174** B3
East Brora **267** G1
East Buckland **113** G2
East Budleigh **103** D4
East Burnham **135** E4
East Burra **279** C9
East Burrafirth **279** C7
East Burton **105** E4
East Butsfield **212** A3
East Butterleigh **102** C2
East Butterwick **187** F2
East Cairnbeg **253** F2

East Calder **235** E3
East Carleton **178** C5
East Carlton
   NN'hants **160** D4
East Carlton
   WYorks **194** B3
East Chaldon (Chaldon
   Herring) **105** D4
East Challow **133** G4
East Charleton **101** D3
East Chelborough **104** B2
East Chiltington **109** F2
East Chinnock **104** A1
East Chisenbury **118** C2
East Clandon **121** F2
East Claydon **148** C5
East Clyne **267** G1
East Clyth **275** H5
East Coker **104** B1
East Compton
   Dorset **105** E1
East Compton
   Som **116** D3
East Coombe **102** B2
East Cornworthy **101** E2
East Cottingwith **195** G3
East Cowes **107** E3
East Cowick **195** F5
East Cowton **202** C2
East Cramlington **221** E4
East Cranmore **117** D3
East Creech **105** F4
East Croachy **258** D2
East Darlochan **222** B3
East Davoch **260** C4
East Dean *ESuss* **110** A4
East Dean *Hants* **119** D5
East Dean *WSuss* **108** B2
East Dereham
   (Dereham) **178** A4
East Down **113** F1
East Drayton **187** E5
East Ella **196** C5
East End *BCP* **105** F3
East End *ERid* **197** D4
East End *ERid* **197** E5
East End *Essex* **138** C2
East End *Hants* **119** F1
East End *Hants* **106** C3
East End *Herts* **150** C5
East End *Kent* **124** A5
East End *Kent* **124** B1
East End *MK* **149** E3
East End *NSom* **131** D5
East End *Oxon* **133** F1
East End *Som* **116** C2
East End *Suff* **152** C2
East End *Suff* **152** C1
East Farleigh **123** G3
East Farndon **160** C4
East Ferry **187** F3
East Firsby **188** A4
East Fleetham **229** G4
East Fortune **236** C2
East Garston **133** F5
East Ginge **133** G4
East Goscote **160** B1
East Grafton **119** D1
East Green *Suff* **153** F1
East Green *Suff* **151** E2
East Grimstead **118** C5
East Grinstead **122** C5
East Guldeford **111** E1
East Haddon **148** B1
East Hagbourne **134** A4
East Halton **188** B1
East Ham **136** D4
East Hanney **133** G3
East Hanningfield **137** G2
East Hardwick **186** B1
East Harling **164** A3
East Harlsey **202** D3
East Harnham **118** C5
East Harptree **116** C2
East Hartford **221** E4
East Harting **107** G1
East Hatch **118** A5
East Hatley **150** A2
East Hauxwell **202** A3
East Haven **245** D1
East Heckington **175** G3
East Hedleyhope **212** A3
East Helmsdale **275** F7
East Hendred **133** G4
East Herrington **212** C2
East Heslerton **204** C5
East Hewish **116** B1
East Hoathly **110** A2
East Holme **105** F4
East Horndon **137** F4
East Horrington **116** C3
East Horsley **121** F2
East Horton **229** E3
East Howe **105** G3
East Huntspill **116** A3
East Hyde **136** A1
East Ilsley **133** G4
East Keal **176** B1
East Kennett **118** C1
East Keswick **194** C3
East Kilbride **234** A4
East Kimber **99** E1
East Kirkby **176** B1
East Knapton **204** B5
East Knighton **105** E4
East Knowstone **114** B5
East Knoyle **117** F4
East Kyloe **229** E3
East Lambrook **104** A1
East Langdon **125** F4
East Langton **160** C3
East Langwell **266** E1
East Lavant **108** A3
East Lavington **108** B2
East Layton **202** A1
East Leake **173** G5
East Learmouth **228** C3
East Learney **260** E4
East Leigh *Devon* **102** A3
East Leigh *Devon* **102** A1
East Leigh *Devon* **101** D3
East Leigh *Devon* **100** C2

East Lexham **163** G1
East Lilburn **229** E4
East Linton **236** C2
East Liss **120** C5
East Lockinge **133** G4
East Looe **97** G4
East Lound **187** E2
East Lulworth **105** E4
East Lutton **196** B1
East Lydford **116** C4
East Lyn **114** A3
East Lyng **116** A5
East Mains **260** E5
East Malling **123** G3
East Malling Heath
   123 F3
East March **244** C1
East Marden **108** A2
East Markham **187** E5
East Martin **105** G1
East Marton **193** F2
East Meon **120** B5
East Mere **102** C1
East Mersea **139** D1
East Mey **275** J1
East Midlands
   Airport **173** F5
East Molesey **121** G1
East Moor **194** C5
East Morden **105** F3
East Morriston **236** D5
East Morton **194** A3
East Ness **203** F5
East Newton **197** E4
East Norton **160** D2
East Oakley **119** G2
East Ogwell **102** B5
East Orchard **105** E1
East Ord **237** G4
East Panson **99** D1
East Parley **106** A3
East Peckham **123** F4
East Pennard **116** C4
East Point Pavilion,
   Lowestoft *Suff*
   NR33 0AP **165** G2
East Portlemouth **100** D4
East Prawle **101** D4
East Preston **108** C3
East Pulham **104** C2
East Putford **113** D4
East Quantoxhead **115** E3
East Rainton **212** C3
East Ravendale **188** C3
East Raynham **177** G5
East Retford
   (Retford) **187** E4
East Rigton **194** C3
East Rolstone **116** A1
East Rounton **202** D2
East Row **204** B1
East Rudham **177** G5
East Runton **178** D1
East Ruston **179** E3
East Saltoun **236** B3
East Shefford **133** F5
East Sleekburn **221** E3
East Somerton **179** F4
East Stockwith **187** E3
East Stoke *Dorset* **105** E4
East Stoke *Notts* **174** C3
East Stour **117** F5
East Stourmouth **125** E2
East Stratton **119** G3
East Street **116** C4
East Studdal **125** F4
East Suisnish **256** B1
East Taphouse **97** F3
East Thirston **221** D2
East Tilbury **137** F5
East Tisted **120** C4
East Torrington **188** B4
East Town **116** D3
East Trewent **126** D3
East Tuddenham **178** B4
East Tytherley **119** D5
East Tytherton **132** B5
East Village **102** B2
East Wall **157** E3
East Walton **163** F1
East Wellow **119** E5
East Whitburn **235** D3
East Wickham **137** D5
East Williamston **127** D2
East Winch **163** F1
East Winterslow **118** D4
East Wittering **107** G3
East Witton **202** A4
East Woodburn **220** B3
East Woodhay **119** F1
East Woodlands **117** E3
East Worldham **120** C4
East Worlington **102** A1
East Youlstone **112** C4
Eastacott **113** G3
Eastbourne **110** B4
Eastbourne Pier *ESuss*
   BN21 3EL **72** Eastbourne
Eastbrook **130** A5
Eastburn *ERid* **196** B2
Eastburn *WYorks* **193** G3
Eastbury *Herts* **136** A3
Eastbury *WBerks* **133** F5
Eastby **193** G2
Eastchurch **124** B1
Eastcombe *Glos* **132** A2
Eastcombe *Som* **115** E4
Eastcote *GtLon* **136** A4
Eastcote *WMid* **159** D5
Eastcote *WN'hants* **148** B2
Eastcott *Corn* **112** C4
Eastcott *Wilts* **118** B2
Eastcourt **132** B3
Eastdown **101** E3
Eastend **147** F5
Easter Ardross **266** D4
Easter Balgedie **243** G4
Easter Balmoral **259** K5
Easter Boleskine **258** C2
Easter Borland **242** B4
Easter Brae **266** D5
Easter Buckieburn **234** B1
Easter Compton **131** E4
Easter Drummond **258** B3
Easter Dullater **242** A4
Easter Ellister **230** A4
Easter Fearn **266** D3

Easter Galcantray 267 F7
Easter Howlaws 237 E5
Easter Kinkell 266 C6
Easter Knox 253 D5
Easter Lednathie 252 B3
Easter Moniack 266 C7
Easter Ord 261 G4
Easter Poldar 242 B5
Easter Skeld (Skeld) 279 C8
Easter Suddie 266 D6
Easter Tulloch 253 F2
Easter Whyntie 268 E4
Eastergate 108 B3
Easterhouse 234 A3
Easterton 118 B2
Easterton Sands 118 B2
Eastertown 116 A2
Eastfield Bristol 131 E5
Eastfield NLan 234 C3
Eastfield NYorks 204 D4
Eastfield Hall 221 D2
Eastgate Dur 211 F4
Eastgate Lincs 161 G1
Eastgate Norf 178 C3
Easthall 150 A5
Eastham Mersey 183 E4
Eastham Worcs 145 F1
Easthampstead 121 D1
Easthampton 144 D1
Easthaugh 178 B4
Eastheath 120 D1
Easthope 157 E3
Easthorpe Essex 152 A5
Easthorpe Leics 174 D4
Easthorpe Notts 174 C2
Easthouses 236 A3
Eastington Devon 102 A2
Eastington Glos 132 D1
Eastington Glos 131 G2
Eastleach Martin 133 E2
Eastleach Turville 133 E2
Eastleigh Devon 113 E3
Eastleigh Hants 106 D1
Eastling 124 B3
Eastmoor Derbys 186 A5
Eastmoor Norf 163 F2
Eastnor 145 G4
Eastoft 187 F1
Eastoke 107 G3
Easton Cambs 161 G5
Easton Cumb 218 C4
Easton Cumb 209 F1
Easton Devon 102 A4
Easton Dorset 104 C5
Easton Hants 119 G4
Easton IoW 106 C4
Easton Lincs 175 D4
Easton Norf 178 C4
Easton Som 116 C3
Easton Suff 153 D2
Easton Wilts 132 A5
Easton Grey 132 A4
Easton Maudit 149 D2
Easton on the Hill 161 F2
Easton Royal 118 D1
Easton-in-Gordano 131 E5
Eastrea 162 A3
Eastriggs 218 C4
Eastrington 195 G4
Eastry 125 F3
Eastside 277 D8
East-the-Water 113 E3
Eastville 154 C1
Eastwell 174 C5
Eastwick 136 D1
Eastwood Notts 173 F3
Eastwood S'end 138 B4
Eastwood SYorks 186 B3
Eastwood WYorks 193 F5
Eastwood End 162 C3
Eathorpe 147 F4
Eaton ChesE 171 F1
Eaton ChesW&C 170 C1
Eaton Leics 174 C4
Eaton Norf 178 D5
Eaton Norf 177 F2
Eaton Notts 187 E5
Eaton Oxon 133 G2
Eaton Shrop 157 E3
Eaton Shrop 156 C4
Eaton Bishop 144 D4
Eaton Bray 149 E5
Eaton Constantine 157 F2
Eaton Ford 149 G2
Eaton Hall 170 B1
Eaton Hastings 133 E3
Eaton Socon 149 G2
Eaton upon Tern 171 D5
Eaves Green 159 E4
Eavestone 194 B1
Ebberston 204 B4
Ebbesborne Wake 118 A5
Ebbw Vale
   (Glyn Ebwy) 130 A2
Ebchester 212 A2
Ebdon 116 A1
Ebford 102 C4
Ebley 132 A2
Ebnal 170 B3
Ebost 255 J1
Ebrington 147 D3
Ebsworthy Town 99 F1
Ecchinswell 119 F2
Ecclaw 237 E3
Ecclefechan 217 F3
Eccles GtMan 184 B3
Eccles Kent 123 G2
Eccles ScBord 237 E5
Eccles Green 144 C3
Eccles Road 164 B2
Ecclesfield 186 A3
Ecclesgreig 253 F3
Eccleshall 171 F5
Eccleshill 194 A4
Ecclesmachan 235 E2
Eccles-on-Sea 179 F3
Eccleston
   ChesW&C 170 B1
Eccleston Lancs 183 G1
Eccleston Mersey 183 F3
Eccup 194 B3
Echt 261 F4
Eckford 228 B4
Eckington Derbys 186 B5
Eckington Worcs 146 B3
Ecton NN'hants 148 D1
Ecton Staffs 172 B2
Edale 185 F4

Eday 276 E4
Eday Airfield 276 E4
Edburton 109 E2
Edderside 209 E2
Edderton 266 E3
Eddington 119 E1
Eddleston 235 G5
Eden M&EAnt 287 J7
Eden Camp NYorks
   YO17 6RT 204 B5
Eden Park 122 C2
Edenbridge 122 D4
Edendonich 241 D2
Edendork 282 B2
Edenfield 184 B1
Edenhall 210 B4
Edenham 175 F5
Edensor 185 G5
Edentaggart 241 F5
Edenthorpe 186 D2
Edentrillick 283 F3
Edern 166 B4
Ederny 280 C2
Edgarley 116 C4
Edgbaston 158 C4
Edgcote 148 A3
Edgcott Bucks 148 B5
Edgcott Som 114 B4
Edgcumbe 95 E3
Edge Glos 132 A2
Edge Shrop 156 C2
Edge End 131 E1
Edge Green
   ChesW&C 170 B2
Edge Green GtMan 183 G3
Edge Green Norf 164 B3
Edgebolton 170 C5
Edgefield 178 B2
Edgefield Street 178 B2
Edgeley 170 C3
Edgerley 156 C1
Edgerton 185 F1
Edgeworth 132 B2
Edginswell 101 E1
Edgmond 157 G1
Edgmond Marsh 171 E5
Edgton 156 C4
Edgware 136 B3
Edgworth 184 B1
Edinample 242 B2
Edinbanchory 260 C3
Edinbane 263 J6
Edinbarnet 233 G2
Edinburgh 235 G2
Edinburgh Airport 235 F2
Edinburgh Castle Edin
   EH1 2NG 37 E4
Edinburgh Zoo Edin
   EH12 6TS 32 B2
Edinchip 242 A2
Edingale 159 E1
Edingley 174 B2
Edingthorpe 179 E2
Edingthorpe Green 179 E2
Edington Som 116 A4
Edington Wilts 118 A2
Edintore 268 C6
Edinvale 267 J6
Edistone 112 C3
Edith Weston 161 E2
Edithmead 116 A3
Edlaston 172 C3
Edlesborough 135 E1
Edlingham 220 D1
Edlington 187 D5
Edmondsham 105 G1
Edmondsley 212 B3
Edmondstown 129 G3
Edmondthorpe 161 D1
Edmonstone 276 E5
Edmonton Corn 97 D2
Edmonton GtLon 136 C3
Edmundbyers 211 G2
Ednam 228 B3
Ednaston 172 D3
Edney Common 137 F2
Edra 241 G3
Edradynate 251 D4
Edrom 237 F4
Edstaston 170 C4
Edstone 147 D1
Edvin Loach 145 F2
Edwalton 173 G4
Edwardstone 152 A3
Edwardsville 129 G3
Edwinsford 142 C4
Edwinstowe 174 B1
Edworth 150 A3
Edwyn Ralph 145 F2
Edzell 253 E3
Efail-fach 129 D3
Efailisaf 129 G3
Efailnewydd 166 C4
Efail-wen 141 E5
Efenechtyd 169 G2
Effingham 121 G2
Effirth 279 C7
Efflinch 159 D1
Efford 102 B2
Egbury 119 F2
Egdean 121 E5
Egdon 146 B2
Egerton GtMan 184 B1
Egerton Kent 124 B4
Egerton Forstal 124 A4
Egerton Green 170 C2
Egg Buckland 100 A2
Eggb(o)rough 195 E5
Eggerness 207 E2
Eggesford Barton 113 G4
Eggington 149 E5
Egginton 173 D5
Egglescliffe 202 D1
Eggleston 211 F5
Egham 135 E4
Egham Wick 135 E4
Egilsay 276 D5
Egleton 161 D2
Eglingham 229 F5
Eglinton D&S 285 H3
Eglinton NAyr 233 E5
Eglish 282 A3
Egloshayle 97 E2

Egloskerry 97 G1
Eglwys Cross 170 B3
Eglwys Nunydd 129 E4
Eglwys-Brewis 114 D1
Eglwys-bach 181 E5
Eglwys-fach 154 C3
Eglwyswrw 141 E4
Egmanton 174 C1
Egmere 178 A2
Egremont 208 D5
Egton 204 B2
Egton Bridge 204 B2
Egypt 119 F3
Eight Ash Green 152 A5
Eignaig 247 G5
Eil 259 F3
Eilanreach 256 E3
Eildon 227 G4
Eilean Darach 265 H3
Eilean Shona 247 F2
Einacleit 270 C4
Eisgein 271 F6
Eisingrug 167 F4
Eisteddfa Gurig 155 D4
Elan Valley Visitor Centre
   Powys LD6 5HP 143 F1
Elan Village 143 F1
Elberton 131 F4
Elborough 116 A2
Elburton 100 B2
Elcho 243 G2
Elcombe 132 D4
Elder Street 151 D4
Eldernell 162 B3
Eldersfield 145 G4
Elderslie 233 F2
Eldon 212 B5
Eldrick 215 D2
Eldroth 193 D1
Eldwick 194 A3
Elemore Vale 212 C3
Eleven Lane Ends 282 D5
Elford N'umb 229 F3
Elford Staffs 159 D1
Elford Closes 162 D5
Elgin 267 K5
Elgol 256 B3
Elham 125 D4
Elie 244 C4
Elilaw 220 B1
Elim 180 B4
Eling Hants 106 C1
Eling WBerks 134 A5
Eliock 225 G5
Elishaw 220 B1
Elkesley 187 D5
Elkington 160 B5
Elkstone 132 B1
Elland 194 A5
Elland Upper Edge
   194 A5
Ellary 231 F2
Ellastone 172 C3
Ellbridge 100 A1
Ellel 192 A2
Ellemford 237 E3
Ellenabeich 239 G3
Ellenborough 208 D3
Ellenhall 171 F5
Ellen's Green 121 F4
Ellerbeck 202 D3
Ellerby 203 G1
Ellerdine 170 D5
Ellerdine Heath 170 D5
Elleric (Eileirig) 248 C5
Ellerker 196 B5
Ellerton ERid 195 G3
Ellerton NYorks 202 B3
Ellerton Shrop 171 E5
Ellerton Abbey 201 F3
Ellesborough 134 D2
Ellesmere 170 A4
Ellesmere Park 184 B3
Ellesmere Port 183 F5
Ellingham Hants 106 A2
Ellingham N'umb 229 F5
Ellingham Norf 165 E2
Ellingstring 202 A4
Ellington Cambs 161 G5
Ellington N'umb 221 E2
Ellington Thorpe 161 G5
Elliot 245 E1
Elliot's Green 117 E3
Ellisfield 120 B3
Ellishadder 263 K5
Ellistown 159 G1
Ellon 261 H1
Ellonby 210 A4
Ellough 165 F3
Ellough Moor 165 F3
Elloughton 196 B5
Ellwood 131 E2
Elm 162 C2
Elm Park 137 E4
Elmbridge 146 B1
Elmdon Essex 150 C4
Elmdon WMid 159 D4
Elmdon Heath 159 D4
Elmers End 122 C2
Elmer's Green 183 F2
Elmesthorpe 159 G3
Elmhurst 158 D1
Elmley Castle 146 B3
Elmley Lovett 146 A1
Elmore 131 G1
Elmore Back 131 G1
Elmscott 112 C3
Elmsett 152 B3
Elmstead Essex 152 B5
Elmstead GtLon 136 D5
Elmstead Market 152 B5
Elmstone 125 E2
Elmstone
   Hardwicke 146 B5
Elmswell ERid 196 B2
Elmswell Suff 152 A1
Elmton 186 C5
Elphin 272 E7
Elphinstone 236 A2
Elrick Aber 261 G4
Elrick Moray 260 C3
Elrig 206 D2
Elrigbeag 240 D3

Elsdon 220 B2
Elsecar 186 A2
Elsecar Heritage Centre
   SYorks S74 8HJ 186 A3
Elsenham 150 D5
Elsfield 134 A1
Elsham 188 A1
Elsing 178 B4
Elslack 193 G3
Elson Hants 107 F2
Elson Shrop 170 A4
Elsrickle 235 E5
Elstead 121 E3
Elsted 108 A2
Elsthorpe 175 F5
Elstob 212 C5
Elston Lancs 192 B4
Elston Notts 174 C3
Elstone 113 G4
Elstow 149 F3
Elstree 136 A3
Elstronwick 197 E4
Elswick 192 A4
Elsworth 150 B1
Elterwater 199 E2
Eltham 136 D5
Eltisley 150 A2
Elton Cambs 161 F3
Elton ChesW&C 183 F5
Elton Derbys 172 D1
Elton Glos 131 G1
Elton Here 145 D1
Elton Notts 174 C4
Elton Stock 202 D1
Elton Green 183 F5
Elvanfoot 226 A4
Elvaston 173 F4
Elveden 163 G5
Elvingston 236 B2
Elvington Kent 125 E3
Elvington York 195 G3
Elwick Hart 213 D4
Elwick N'umb 229 F3
Elworth 171 E1
Elworthy 115 D4
Ely Cambs 162 D5
Ely Cardiff 130 A5
Emberton 149 D3
Emberton Country Park
   MK MK46 5FJ 149 D2
Embleton Cumb 209 E3
Embleton Hart 212 D5
Embleton N'umb 229 G4
Embo 267 F4
Embo Street 267 F2
Emborough 116 D2
Embsay 193 G2
Embsay & Bolton Abbey
   Steam Railway NYorks
   BD23 6AF 193 G2
Emerson Park 137 E4
Emery Down 106 B2
Emley 185 G1
Emmington 134 C2
Emneth 162 C2
Emneth Hungate 162 D2
Empingham 161 E2
Empshott 120 C4
Empshott Green 120 C4
Emsworth 107 G2
Enagh 282 D5
Enborne 119 F1
Enborne Row 119 F1
Enchmarsh 157 E3
Enderby 160 A3
Endmoor 199 G4
Endon 171 G2
Endon Bank 171 G2
Enfield 136 C3
Enfield Wash 136 C3
Enford 118 C2
Engine Common 131 F4
Englefield 134 B5
Englefield Green 135 E4
Englesea-brook 171 E2
English Bicknor 131 E1
English Frankton 170 B5
Englishcombe 117 E1
Enham Alamein 119 E3
Enmore 115 F4
Ennerdale Bridge 209 D5
Enniscaven 97 D4
Enniskillen 280 E4
Enniskillen Castle &
   Museums F&O
   BT74 7ER 280 E4
Ennochdhu 251 F3
Ensay 246 C5
Ensdon 156 D1
Ensis 113 F3
Enson 171 G5
Enstone 147 F5
Enterkinfoot 225 G5
Enterpen 203 D2
Enton Green 121 E3
Epney 131 G1
Epperstone 174 B3
Epping 137 D2
Epping Green
   Essex 136 D2
Epping Green
   Herts 136 B2
Epping Upland 136 D2
Eppleby 202 A1
Eppleworth 196 C4
Epsom 122 B2
Epwell 147 F3
Epworth 187 F2
Epworth Turbary 187 E2
Erbistock 170 A3
Erbusaig 256 D2
Erchless Castle 266 B7
Erdinagh 281 F1
Erdington 158 D3
Eredine 240 B4
Ericstane 226 B4
Eridge Green 123 E5
Eriff 224 D5
Erines 231 G2

Erisey Barton 95 E5
Eriskay
   (Eiriosgaigh) 254 C3
Eriswell 163 F5
Erith 137 E5
Erlestoke 118 A2
Ermington 100 C2
Ernesettle 100 A1
Erpingham 178 C2
Erringden Grange 193 F5
Errogie (Earagaidh) 258 C2
Errol 243 G2
Errollston 261 J1
Ervey Cross Roads 285 H4
Ervie 214 A4
Erwarton 152 D4
Erwood 143 G3
Eryholme 202 C2
Eryrys 169 F2
Escart 231 G3
Escart Farm 231 G4
Escomb 212 A5
Escrick 195 F3
Esgair 141 G5
Esgairgeiliog Ceinws
   155 D3
Esgyryn 181 G5
Esh 212 A3
Esh Winning 212 A3
Esher 121 G1
Eshnadarragh 281 H5
Eshnadeelada 281 H5
Eshott 221 E2
Eshton 193 G2
Esinge 258 B2
Essendine 161 F1
Essendon 136 B2
Essich 258 D1
Essington 158 B2
Esslemont 261 H2
Eston 203 E1
Eswick 279 D7
Etal 228 D3
Etchilhampton 118 B1
Etchingham 110 C1
Etchinghill Kent 125 D5
Etchinghill Staffs 158 C1
Etherdwick Grange 197 E4
Etherley Dene 212 A5
Ethie Mains 253 E5
Eton 135 E5
Eton Wick 135 E5
Etteridge 258 D5
Ettiley Heath 171 E1
Ettington 147 E3
Etton ERid 196 B3
Etton Peter 161 G2
Ettrick 227 D4
Ettrickbridge 227 E3
Ettrickhill 227 D4
Etwall 173 D4
Eudon George 157 F4
Euorach 240 A4
Euston 163 G5
Euxton 183 G1
Evanstown 129 F4
Evanton 266 D5
Evedon 175 F3
Evelix 266 E2
Evenjobb 144 B1
Evenley 148 A4
Evenlode 147 E5
Evenwood 212 A5
Evenwood Gate 212 A5
Everbay 276 F5
Evercreech 116 D4
Everdon 148 A2
Everingham 196 A3
Everleigh 118 D2
Everley High 275 J2
Everley NYorks 204 C4
Eversholt 149 E4
Evershot 104 B2
Eversley 120 C1
Eversley Cross 120 C1
Everthorpe 196 B4
Everton CenBeds 150 A2
Everton Hants 106 B3
Everton Mersey 183 E3
Everton Notts 187 D3
Evertown 218 B4
Eves Corner 138 C3
Evesbatch 145 F3
Evesham 146 C3
Evesham Country Park
   Shopping & Garden
   Centre Worcs
   WR11 4TP 146 C3
Evie 276 C5
Evington 160 B2
Ewart Newtown 229 D3
Ewden Village 185 G3
Ewell 122 B2
Ewell Minnis 125 E4
Ewelme 134 B3
Ewen 132 C3
Ewenny 129 F5
Ewerby 175 G3
Ewerby Thorpe 175 G3
Ewhurst 121 F3
Ewhurst Green
   ESuss 110 C1
Ewhurst Green
   Surr 121 F4
Ewloe 170 A1
Ewloe Green 169 F1
Ewood 192 C5
Ewood Bridge 193 D5
Eworthy 99 F1
Ewshot 120 D3
Ewyas Harold 144 C5
Ewyn 224 D5

Exbury 106 D2
Exbury Gardens Hants
   SO45 1AZ 4 B6
Exceat 110 A4
Exebridge 114 C5
Exelby 202 B4
Exeter 102 C3
Exeter Airport 102 C3
Exeter Cathedral Devon
   EX1 1HS 72 Exeter
Exford 114 B4
Exfords Green 157 D2
Exhall Warks 146 D2
Exhall Warks 159 F4
Exlade Street 134 B4
Exminster 102 C4
Exmoor Dark Sky Reserve
   Devon/Som 114 A3
Exmouth 102 D4
Exnaboe 279 F9
Exning 151 E1
Explore-At-Bristol
   BS1 5DB 66 Bristol
Exton Devon 102 C4
Exton Hants 120 B5
Exton Rut 161 E1
Exton Som 114 C4
Exwick 102 C3
Eyam 185 G5
Eydon 148 A3
Eye Here 145 D1
Eye Peter 162 A2
Eye Suff 164 C4
Eye Green 162 A2
Eyemouth 237 G3
Eyeworth 150 A3
Eyhorne Street 124 A3
Eyke 153 E2
Eynesbury 149 G2
Eynort 255 J2
Eynsford 123 E2
Eynsham 133 G2
Eype 104 A3
Eyre 263 K6
Eythorne 125 E4
Eyton Here 145 D1
Eyton Shrop 156 C4
Eyton on Severn 157 E2
Eyton upon the Weald
   Moors 157 F1
Eywood 144 C2

F
Faccombe 119 E2
Faceby 203 D2
Fachwen 167 E1
Facit 184 C1
Faddiley 170 C2
Fadmoor 203 F4
Faebait 266 B6
Faerdre 128 C2
Faifley 233 G2
Fail 224 C3
Failand 131 E5
Failford 224 C3
Failsworth 184 C2
Fain 265 H4
Fair Isle 278 A1
Fair Isle Airstrip 278 A1
Fair Oak Devon 102 C1
Fair Oak Hants 107 D1
Fair Oak Hants 119 G3
Fair Oak Green 120 B1
Fairbourne 154 C1
Fairburn 195 D5
Fairfield Derbys 185 E5
Fairfield GtMan 184 D3
Fairfield Kent 111 E1
Fairfield Mersey 183 D4
Fairfield Stock 202 D1
Fairfield Worcs 158 B5
Fairfield Halls, Croydon
   GtLon CR9 1DG 122 C2
Fairford 132 D2
Fairgirth 216 C5
Fairhaven 191 G5
Fairhill 234 B4
Fairholm 234 B4
Fairlands Valley Park Herts
   SG2 0BL 150 A5
Fairley 261 G4
Fairlie 232 D4
Fairlight 111 D2
Fairlight Cove 111 D2
Fairmile Devon 103 D3
Fairmile Surr 121 G1
Fairmilehead 235 G3
Fairnington 228 A4
Fairoak 171 E4
Fairseat 123 F2
Fairstead 137 G1
Fairwarp 109 G1
Fairwater 130 A5
Fairy Cross 113 E3
Fairyhill 128 A3
Fakenham 178 A3
Fakenham Magna 164 A4
Fala 236 B3
Fala Dam 236 B3
Falahill 236 A4
Faldingworth 188 A4
Falfield Fife 244 C4
Falfield SGlos 131 F3
Falkenham 153 D4
Falkirk 234 C2
Falkirk Wheel Falk
   FK1 4RS 234 B2
Falkland 244 A4
Falla 228 B5
Fallgate 173 E1
Fallagloon 286 C5
Fallin 242 D5
Falmer 109 F3
Falmouth 95 F3
Falsgrave 204 D4
Falstone 219 F3
Famous Grouse Experience,
   Glenturret Distillery
   P&K PH7 4HA 243 D2
Fanagmore 272 D4
Fanans 240 C2
Fancott 149 F5
Fangdale Beck 203 E3
Fangfoss 195 G2
Fankerton 234 B1
Fanmore 246 D5
Fanner's Green 137 F1
Fans 236 D5

Fantasy Island Lincs
   PE25 1RH 177 D1
Far Cotton 148 C2
Far Forest 157 G5
Far Gearstones 200 C4
Far Green 131 G2
Far Moor 183 G2
Far Oakridge 132 B2
Far Royds 194 B4
Far Sawrey 199 E3
Farcet 162 A3
Farden 157 E5
Fardross 281 H4
Fareham 107 E2
Farewell 158 C1
Farforth 188 D5
Faringdon 133 E3
Farington 192 B5
Farlam 210 B2
Farlary 266 E1
Farleigh NSom 116 C1
Farleigh Surr 122 C2
Farleigh Hungerford 117 F2
Farleigh Wallop 120 B3
Farlesthorpe 189 E5
Farleton Cumb 199 G4
Farleton Lancs 192 B3
Farley Derbys 173 D1
Farley Shrop 156 C2
Farley Staffs 172 B3
Farley Wilts 118 D5
Farley Green Suff 151 F2
Farley Green Surr 121 F3
Farley Hill 120 C1
Farleys End 131 G1
Farlington 195 F1
Farlow 157 F4
Farm Town 159 F1
Farmborough 117 D1
Farmcote 146 C5
Farmington 132 D1
Farmoor 133 G2
Farmtown 268 D5
Farnborough
   GtLon 122 D2
Farnborough
   Hants 121 D2
Farnborough
   Warks 147 G3
Farnborough
   WBerks 133 G4
Farnborough Street 121 D2
Farncombe 121 E3
Farndish 149 E1
Farndon ChesW&C 170 B2
Farndon Notts 174 C2
Farne Islands 229 G3
Farnell 253 E4
Farnham Dorset 105 F1
Farnham Essex 150 C5
Farnham NYorks 194 C1
Farnham Suff 153 E1
Farnham Surr 120 D3
Farnham Common 135 E4
Farnham Green 150 C5
Farnham Royal 135 E4
Farningham 123 E2
Farnley NYorks 194 B3
Farnley WYorks 194 B4
Farnley Tyas 185 F1
Farnsfield 174 B2
Farnworth GtMan 184 B2
Farnworth Halton 183 G4
Farr High 274 C2
Farr High 258 D1
Farr High 259 F4
Farr House 258 D1
Farraline 258 C2
Farranamucklagh 282 B5
Farrancassidy 280 D2
Farranflugh 287 F6
Farrington 102 D3
Farrington Gurney 116 D2
Farsley 194 B4
Farthing Corner 124 A2
Farthing Green 124 A4
Farthinghoe 148 A4
Farthingstone 148 B2
Farthorpe 188 C5
Fartown 185 F1
Farway 103 E3
Fasag 264 E6
Fasagrianach 265 H3
Fascadale 247 E2
Fasnacloich 248 C5
Fasnakyle 257 K2
Fassfern 248 C1
Fatfield 212 C2
Fattahead 268 E5
Faugh 210 B2
Fauldhouse 234 D3
Faulkbourne 137 G1
Faulkland 117 E2
Fauls 170 C4
Faulston 118 B5
Faversham 124 C2
Favillar 259 K1
Fawdington 202 D5
Fawdon 212 B2
Fawfieldhead 172 B1
Fawkham Green 123 E2
Fawler 133 F1
Fawley Bucks 134 C4
Fawley Hants 107 D2
Fawley WBerks 133 F4
Fawley Chapel 145 E5
Fawside 253 G2
Faxfleet 196 A5
Faxton 160 C5
Faygate 122 B5
Fazakerley 183 E3
Fazeley 159 E2
Fearby 202 A4
Fearn 267 F4
Fearnan 250 C5
Fearnbeg 264 D6
Fearnhead 184 A3
Fearnmore 264 D5
Fearnoch A&B 232 B2
Fearnoch A&B 232 A1
Featherstone
   Staffs 158 B2
Featherstone
   WYorks 194 D5

Featherstone
Castle **210** C1
Feckenham **146** C1
Feeny **285** J5
Feering **151** G5
Feetham **201** E3
Feith-hill **268** E6
Feizor **193** D1
Felbridge **122** C5
Felcourt **122** C4
Felden **135** F2
Felhampton **156** D4
Felindre Carmar **142** D5
Felindre Carmar **142** B5
Felindre Carmar **141** G4
Felindre Carmar **142** C4
Felindre Cere **142** B2
Felindre Powys **144** A5
Felindre Powys **156** A4
Felindre Powys **144** A4
Felindre Swan **128** C2
Felindre Farchog **141** D4
Felin-fach Cere **142** B2
Felin-fach Powys **143** G4
Felin-foel **128** C3
Felin-gwm Isaf **142** B5
Felin-gwm Uchaf **142** B5
Felinwnda **141** G3
Felixkirk **203** D4
Felixstowe **153** E4
Felixstowe Ferry **153** E4
Felkington **237** E5
Felldownhead **99** D2
Felling **212** B1
Fellonmore **239** F2
Felmersham **149** E2
Felmingham **179** D3
Felpham **108** B4
Felsham **152** A2
Felsted **151** E5
Feltham **136** A5
Felthamhill **136** A5
Felthorpe **178** C4
Felton Here **145** E3
Felton N'umb **221** D1
Felton NSom **116** C1
Felton Butler **156** C1
Feltwell **163** F3
Fen Ditton **150** C1
Fen Drayton **150** B1
Fen End **159** E5
Fen Street Norf **164** A2
Fen Street Norf **164** B4
Fen Street Suff **164** A4
Fen Street Suff **152** C1
Fenay Bridge **185** F1
Fence **193** E4
Fence Houses **212** C2
Fencott **134** A1
Fendike Corner **176** C1
Fenham **229** E2
Fenhouses **176** A3
Feniscowles **192** C5
Feniton **103** E3
Fenn Street **137** G5
Fenni-fach **143** G5
Fenny Bentley **172** C2
Fenny Bridges **103** E3
Fenny Compton **147** G2
Fenny Drayton **159** F3
Fenny Stratford **149** D4
Fenrother **221** D2
Fenstanton **150** B1
Fenton Cambs **162** B5
Fenton Lincs **187** F5
Fenton Lincs **175** D2
Fenton N'umb **229** D3
Fenton Notts **187** E4
Fenton Stoke **171** F3
Fenton Barns **236** C1
Fenwick EAyr **233** F5
Fenwick N'umb **220** C4
Fenwick N'umb **229** E2
Fenwick SYorks **186** C1
Feochaig **222** C4
Feock **95** F3
Feolin **230** D3
Feolin Ferry **230** C3
Feorlan **222** B5
Feorlin **240** B5
Ferens Art Gallery HU1 3RA
76 Kingston upon Hull
Ferguslie Park **233** F4
Feriniquarrie **263** G6
Fern **252** C3
Ferndale **129** F3
Ferndown **105** G2
Ferness **267** G7
Fernham **133** E3
Fernhill Heath **146** A2
Fernhurst **121** D5
Fernie **244** B3
Fernilea **255** J1
Fernilee **185** E5
Fernybank **252** D2
Ferrensby **194** C1
Ferrers Centre for Arts &
Crafts Leics
LE65 1RU **173** E5
Ferrindonald **256** C4
Ferring **108** C3
Ferry Hill **162** B4
Ferrybridge **195** D5
Ferryden **253** F4
Ferryhill **212** B4
Ferryside
(Glanyferi) **127** G1
Fersfield **164** B3
Fersit **249** F2
Feshiebridge **259** F4
Festival Park BGwent
NP23 8FP **130** A2
Fetcham **121** G2
Fetlar **278** F3
Fetlar Airport **278** F3
Fetterangus **269** H5
Fettercairn **253** E2
Fetternear House **261** F3
Feus of Caldhame **253** E3
Fewcott **148** A5
Fewston **194** A2
Feystown **287** H5
Ffair-fach **142** C5
Ffair-Rhos **142** D1
Ffaldybrenin **142** C3
Ffarmers **142** C3
Ffawyddog **130** B1

Ffestiniog
(Llan Ffestiniog) **168** A3
Ffestiniog Railway (The
Slate Landscape of
Northwest Wales) Gwyn
LL49 9NF **167** F3
Fforddlas Denb **169** D1
Fforddlas Powys **144** B4
Fforest **128** B2
Fforest-fach **128** C3
Fforest **128** B2
Ffostrasol **141** G3
Ffos-y-ffin **142** A1
Ffrith Denb **182** B4
Ffrith Flints **169** F2
Ffrwdgrech **143** G5
Ffynnon **127** G1
Ffynnongroyw **182** C4
Fibhig **270** E3
Fichlie **260** C3
Fidden **238** C2
Fiddington Glos **146** B4
Fiddington Som **115** F3
Fiddler's Green
Glos **146** B5
Fiddler's Green
Here **145** E3
Fiddler's Green
Norf **163** G1
Fiddler's Green
Norf **164** B2
Fiddlers Hamlet **137** D2
Field **172** B4
Field Broughton **199** E4
Field Dalling **178** B2
Field Head **159** G2
Fife Keith **268** C5
Fifehead Magdalen **117** E5
Fifehead Neville **105** D1
Fifehead
St. Quintin **105** D1
Fifield Oxon **133** E1
Fifield W&M **135** E5
Fifield Bavant **118** B5
Figheldean **118** C3
Filby **179** F4
Filey **205** E4
Filgrave **149** D3
Filham **100** C2
Filkins **133** E2
Filleigh Devon **113** F3
Filleigh Devon **102** A1
Fillingham **187** F4
Fillongley **159** E4
Filmore Hill **120** B5
Filton **131** F5
Fimber **196** A1
Finavon **252** C4
Fincham **163** E2
Finchampstead **120** C1
Finchdean **107** G1
Finchingfield **151** E4
Finchley **136** B3
Findern **173** E4
Findhorn **267** H5
Findhorn Bridge **259** F2
Findhuglen **242** C3
Findo Gask **243** F2
Findochty **268** C4
Findon Aber **261** H5
Findon WSuss **108** D3
Findon Mains **266** D5
Findon Valley **108** D3
Findrassie **267** J5
Findron **161** E5
Finedon **161** E5
Finegand **251** G3
Fingal Street **164** C3
Fingland Cumb **209** F1
Fingland D&G **225** F2
Fingland D&G **225** F4
Finglesham **125** F4
Fingringhoe **152** B5
Finlarig **242** A1
Finmere **148** B4
Finnart A&B **241** E5
Finnart P&K **250** A4
Finney Hill **159** G1
Finningham **152** B1
Finningley **187** D3
Finnis **283** F4
Finnygaud **268** E5
Finsbay
(Fionnsbhagh) **263** F3
Finsbury **136** C4
Finstall **158** B5
Finsthwaite **199** E4
Finstock **133** F1
Finstown **277** C6
Fintona **281** G2
Fintry Aber **269** F5
Fintry Stir **234** A1
Finvoy **286** D4
Finwood **147** D1
Finzean **260** D5
Fionnphort **238** B2
Fir Tree **212** A4
Firbank **200** B3
Firbeck **186** C4
Firby NYorks **202** B4
Firby NYorks **195** G1
Firgrove **184** D1
Firs Lane **184** A2
Firsby **176** C1
Firsdown **118** D4
Firth **278** D5
Fishbourne IoW **107** E3
Fishbourne WSuss
108 A3
Fishburn **212** C4
Fishcross **243** E5
Fisherford **269** E6
Fishers Farm Park WSuss
RH14 0EG **121** F5
Fisher's Pond **119** F5
Fisher's Row **192** A4
Fishersgate **109** E3
Fisherstreet **121** E4
Fisherton High **266** E6
Fisherton SAyr **224** A4

Fisherton de la
Mere **118** A4
Fishguard
(Abergwaun) **140** C4
Fishlake **187** D1
Fishleigh Barton **113** F3
Fishley **179** F4
Fishnish **247** F5
Fishpond Bottom **103** G3
Fishponds **131** F5
Fishpool **184** C2
Fishtoft **176** B3
Fishtoft Drove **176** B3
Fishtown of Usan **253** F4
Fishwick **237** G4
Fiskerton Lincs **188** A5
Fiskerton Notts **174** C2
Fitling **197** E4
Fittleton **118** C3
Fittleworth **108** C2
Fitton End **162** C1
Fitz **156** D1
Fitzhead **115** E4
Fitzroy **115** E5
Fitzwilliam **186** B1
Fitzwilliam Museum
Cambs CB2 1RB
66 Cambridge
Fiunary **247** F5
Five Acres **131** E1
Five Ash Down **109** G1
Five Ashes **110** A1
Five Bridges **145** F3
Five Houses **106** D4
Five Lanes **130** D3
Five Oak Green **123** F4
Five Oaks Chanl **100** C5
Five Oaks WSuss **121** F5
Five Roads **128** A2
Five Turnings **156** B5
Five Wents **124** A3
Fivehead **116** A5
Fivelanes **97** G1
Fivemiletown **281** G4
Flack's Green **137** G1
Flackwell Heath **135** D4
Fladbury **146** B2
Fladdabister **279** D9
Flagg **172** C1
Flamborough **205** F5
Flamborough Cliffs Nature
Reserve ERid YO15 1BJ
205 F5
Flamingo Land Theme
Park NYorks
YO17 6UX **203** G4
Flamingo Park,
Hastings ESuss
TN34 3AR **110** D3
Flamstead **135** F1
Flamstead End **136** C2
Flansham **108** B3
Flanshaw **194** C5
Flasby **193** F2
Flash **172** B1
Flashader **263** J6
Flask Inn **204** C2
Flatts Lane Woodland
Country Park R&C
TS6 0NN **203** E1
Flaunden **135** F2
Flawborough **174** C3
Flawith **195** D1
Flax Bourton **116** C1
Flax Moss **193** E5
Flaxby **194** C2
Flaxholme **173** E3
Flaxlands **164** C2
Flaxley **131** F1
Flaxton **195** F1
Flaxpool **115** E4
Fleckney **160** B3
Flecknoe **148** A1
Fledborough **187** F5
Fleet Hants **120** D2
Fleet Hants **107** G2
Fleet Lincs **176** B5
Fleet Air Arm Museum
Som BA22 8HT **116** C5
Fleet Hargate **176** B5
Fleetville **136** A2
Fleetwood **191** G3
Fleggburgh (Burgh St.
Margaret) **179** F4
Flemingston **129** G5
Flemington **234** A4
Flempton **151** G1
Fleoideabhagh **263** F3
Flesherin **271** H4
Fletchersbridge **97** F3
Fletchertown **209** F2
Fletching **109** G1
Fleuchats **260** B4
Fleur-de-lis **130** A3
Flexbury **112** C5
Flexford **121** E2
Flimby **208** D3
Flimwell **123** G5
Flint (Y Fflint) **182** D5
Flint Cross **150** C3
Flint Mountain **182** D5
Flintham **174** C3
Flinton **197** E4
Flint's Green **159** E4
Flishinghurst **123** G5
Flitcham **177** F5
Flitholme **200** C1
Flitton **149** F4
Flitwick **149** F4
Flixborough **187** F1
Flixton GtMan **184** B3
Flixton NYorks **204** D5
Flixton Suff **165** E3
Flockton **185** F1
Flockton Green **185** F1
Flodden **229** D3
Flodigarry **263** K4
Flood's Ferry **162** B3
Flookburgh **199** E5
Floors **268** C5
Flordon **164** C2
Flore **148** B1
Florence Court F&O
BT92 1DB **280** D5
Flotta **277** C8
Flotterton **220** C1

Flowton **152** B3
Flushdyke **194** B5
Flushing Aber **269** J6
Flushing Corn **95** F3
Flushing Corn **95** E4
Flushtown **285** F6
Fluxton **103** D3
Flyford Flavell **146** B2
Foals Green **165** D4
Fobbing **137** G4
Fochabers **268** B5
Fochriw **130** A2
Fockerby **187** F1
Fodderletter **259** J2
Fodderty **266** C6
Foddington **116** C5
Foel **155** F1
Foelgastell **128** B1
Fogo **237** E5
Fogorig **237** E5
Fogwatt **267** K6
Foindle **272** D4
Folda **251** G3
Fole **172** B4
Foleshill **159** F4
Folke **104** C1
Folkestone **125** E5
Folkingham **175** F4
Folkington **110** A3
Folksworth **161** G4
Folkton **205** D5
Folla Rule **261** F1
Follifoot **194** C2
Folly Dorset **104** D2
Folly Pembs **140** C5
Folly Farm, Begelly Pembs
SA68 0XA **127** E2
Folly Gate **99** F1
Fonmon **115** D1
Fonthill Bishop **118** A4
Fonthill Gifford **118** A4
Fontmell Magna **105** E1
Fontmell Parva **105** D1
Fontwell **108** B3
Font-y-gary **115** D1
Foolow **185** F5
Footherley **158** D2
Foots Cray **137** D5
Forbestown **260** B3
Force Forge **199** E3
Force Green **122** D3
Forcett **202** A1
Forches Cross **102** A2
Ford A&B **240** A4
Ford Bucks **134** C2
Ford Devon **101** D1
Ford Devon **113** E3
Ford Devon **101** F5
Ford Glos **146** C5
Ford Mersey **183** E3
Ford Midlo **236** A3
Ford N'umb **229** D3
Ford Pembs **140** C5
Ford Plym **100** A2
Ford Shrop **156** D1
Ford Som **115** D5
Ford Staffs **172** B2
Ford Wilts **132** A5
Ford WSuss **108** B3
Ford End **137** F1
Ford Green **192** A3
Ford Heath **156** D1
Ford Street **103** E1
Forda **99** F1
Fordbridge **159** E4
Fordcombe **123** E4
Fordell **235** F1
Forden (Forddun) **156** B2
Forder Green **101** D1
Fordgate **116** A4
Fordham Cambs **163** E5
Fordham Essex **152** A5
Fordham Norf **163** E3
Fordham Abbey **163** E5
Fordham Heath **152** A5
Fordhouses **158** B2
Fordingbridge **106** A1
Fordon **205** D5
Fordoun **253** F2
Ford's Green **152** B1
Fordstreet **152** A5
Fordwells **133** F1
Fordwich **125** D3
Fordyce **268** D4
Forebrae **243** E2
Foredale **193** E1
Foregate **146** A1
Foreglen **285** J5
Foreland **230** A3
Foremark **173** E4
Foremark Reservoir Derbys
DE65 6EG **173** E4
Forest **202** B2
Forest Coal Pit **144** B5
Forest Gate **136** D4
Forest Green **121** G3
Forest Hall Cumb **199** G2
Forest Hall T&W **212** B1
Forest Head **210** B2
Forest Hill GtLon **136** C5
Forest Hill Oxon **134** A2
Forest Lane Head **194** C2
Forest Lodge (Taigh na
Frithe) A&B **249** E1
Forest Lodge P&K **251** E2
Forest Row **123** D5
Forest Side **107** D4
Forest Town **173** G1
Forestburn Gate **220** C2
Forest-in-Teesdale **211** E4
Forestmill **243** E5
Forestside **107** G1
Forfar **252** C4
Forfar Loch Country Park
Angus DD8 1BT **252** C4
Forgandenny **243** F3
Forge **155** D3
Forgie **268** B5
Forhill **158** C5
Forkill **282** D7
Forres **267** H6
Formby **183** D2
Formoyle **286** B3
Forncett End **164** C2
Forncett St. Mary **164** C2
Forncett St. Peter **164** C2
Forneth **251** F5
Fornham All Saints **151** G1

Fornham St. Martin
151 G1
Fornighty **267** G6
Forres **267** H6
Forrest **234** C3
Forrest Lodge **215** G2
Forsbrook **171** G3
Forse **275** H5
Forsie **275** F2
Forsinain **274** E1
Forsinard **274** E1
Forston **104** C3
Fort Augustus (Cille
Chuimein) **257** K4
Fort William
(An Gearasdan) **248** D2
Fort George **266** E6
Fort Fun, Eastbourne
ESuss BN22 7LQ **110** B3
Forter **251** G3
Forteviot **243** F3
Forth **234** D4
Forthampton **146** A4
Fortingall **250** C5
Fortis Green **136** B4
Forton Hants **119** F3
Forton Lancs **192** A2
Forton Shrop **156** D1
Forton Som **103** G2
Forton Staffs **171** E5
Fortrie **268** E6
Fortrose
(A'Chananaich) **266** E6
Fortuneswell **104** C5
Forty Green **135** E3
Forty Hill **136** C3
Forward Green **152** B2
Fosbury **119** E2
Foscot **147** E5
Fosdyke **176** B4
Foss **250** C4
Foss Cross **132** C2
Fossdale **201** D3
Fossebridge **132** C1
Foster Street **137** D2
Fosterhouses **186** D1
Foster's Booth **148** B2
Foston Derbys **172** C4
Foston Leics **160** B3
Foston Lincs **175** D3
Foston NYorks **195** F1
Foston on the
Wolds **196** D2
Fotherby **188** D3
Fotheringhay **161** F3
Foubister **277** E7
Foul Mile **110** B2
Foula **278** B1
Foula Airstrip **278** B1
Foulbog **226** D5
Foulden Norf **163** F3
Foulden ScBord **237** G4
Foulness Island **138** D3
Foulridge **193** E3
Foulsham **178** B3
Fountainhall **236** B5
Four Ashes Staffs **158** B5
Four Ashes Staffs **158** A4
Four Ashes Suff **164** A4
Four Crosses
Denb **168** D3
Four Crosses
Powys **156** B1
Four Crosses
Powys **155** G2
Four Crosses
Staffs **158** B2
Four Elms **123** D4
Four Forks **115** F4
Four Gotes **162** C1
Four Lane Ends
B'burn **192** C5
Four Lane Ends
ChesW&C **170** C2
Four Lane Ends
York **195** E2
Four Lanes **95** D3
Four Marks **120** B4
Four Oaks ESuss **111** D1
Four Oaks Glos **145** F5
Four Oaks WMid **159** E4
Four Oaks WMid **158** D3
Four Oaks Park **158** D3
Four Roads **128** A2
Four Throws **110** C1
Fourlane Ends **173** E2
Fourlanes End **171** F2
Fourpenny **267** F2
Fourstones **211** E1
Fovant **118** B5
Foveran **261** H2
Fowey **97** F4
Fowlis **244** B1
Fowlis Wester **243** E2
Fowlmere **150** C3
Fownhope **145** E4
Fox Hatch **137** E3
Fox Lane **121** D2
Fox Street **152** B5
Fox Up **201** D5
Foxbar **233** F3
Foxcombe Hill **133** G2
Foxcote Glos **132** C1
Foxcote Som **117** E2
Foxdale **190** A4
Foxearth **151** G3
Foxfield **198** D4
Foxham **132** B5
Foxhole Corn **97** D4
Foxhole High **258** C1
Foxholes **204** D5
Foxhunt Green **110** A2
Foxley Here **144** D3
Foxley Norf **178** B3
Foxley Wilts **132** A4
Foxley WN'hants **148** B2
Foxt **172** B3
Foxton Cambs **150** C3
Foxton Dur **212** C5
Foxton Leics **160** B3
Foxton Locks Leics
LE16 7RA **160** B3
Foxup **201** D5
Foxwist Green **170** D1
Foy **145** E5
Foyers (Foithir) **258** C2
Frachadil **246** C4

Fraddam **94** C3
Fraddon **96** D4
Fradley **159** D1
Fradswell **171** G4
Fraisthorpe **197** D1
Framfield **109** G1
Framingham Earl **179** D5
Framingham Pigot **179** D5
Framlingham **153** D1
Frampton Dorset **104** C3
Frampton Lincs **176** B4
Frampton Cotterell **131** F4
Frampton Mansell **132** B2
Frampton on
Severn **131** G2
Frampton West
End **176** A3
Framsden **152** D2
Framwellgate Moor **212** B3
France Lynch **132** B2
Frances Green **192** A5
Franche **158** A5
Frandley **184** A5
Frankby **182** D4
Frankfort **179** E3
Frankley **158** B4
Franksbridge **144** A2
Frankton **159** G5
Frant **123** E5
Fraserburgh **269** H4
Frating **152** B5
Fratton **107** F2
Freasley **159** E3
Freathy **99** D5
Freckenham **163** E5
Freckleton **192** A5
Freeby **174** D5
Freefolk **119** F3
Freehay **172** B3
Freeland **133** G1
Freester **279** D7
Freethorpe
Common **179** F5
Freiston **176** B3
Freiston Shore **176** B3
Fremington Devon **113** F2
Fremington NYorks **201** F3
French Brothers Cruises
W&M SL4 5JH **135** E5
Frenchay **131** F5
Frenchbeer **99** G2
Frendraught **268** E6
Frenich **241** G4
Frensham **120** D4
Fresgoe **274** E2
Freshbrook **132** D4
Freshfield **183** D2
Freshford **117** E2
Freshwater **106** C4
Freshwater Bay **106** C4
Freshwater East **126** D3
Fressingfield **165** D4
Freston **152** C3
Fretherne **131** G2
Frettenham **178** D4
Freuchie **244** A4
Freughmore **281** G2
Freystrop Cross **126** C1
Friars, The, Aylesford Kent
ME20 7BX **123** G3
Friars Carse **216** D2
Friar's Gate **123** D5
Friarton **243** G2
Friday Bridge **162** C2
Friday Street ESuss **110** B3
Friday Street Suff **152** D2
Friday Street Suff **153** E2
Friday Street Surr **121** G3
Fridaythorpe **196** A2
Friern Barnet **136** B3
Friesthorpe **188** A4
Frieston **175** E3
Frieth **134** C3
Frilford **133** G3
Frilsham **134** A5
Frimley **121** D2
Frimley Green **121** D2
Frindsbury **123** G2
Fring **177** F4
Fringford **148** B5
Friningham **124** A3
Frinsted **124** A3
Frinton-on-Sea **139** F1
Friockheim **253** D5
Friog **154** C1
Frisby on the
Wreake **160** B1
Friskney **176** C2
Friskney
Eaudyke **176** C2
Friston ESuss **110** A4
Friston Suff **153** F1
Fritchley **173** E2
Frith **124** B3
Frith Bank **176** B3
Frith Common **145** F1
Fritham **106** B1
Frithelstock **113** E4
Frithelstock Stone **113** E4
Frithville **176** B2
Frittenden **124** A4
Frittiscombe **101** E3
Fritton Norf **164** C2
Fritton Norf **179** F5
Fritwell **148** A5
Frizinghall **194** A4
Frizington **208** D5
Frocester **132** A2
Frochas **156** B2
Frodesley **157** E2
Frodesley Lane **157** E2
Frodingham **187** F1
Frodsham **183** G5
Frog End **150** C2
Frog Pool **145** G1
Frogden **228** B4
Froggatt **185** G5
Froghall **172** B3
Frogham **106** A1
Frogland Cross **131** F4
Frogmore Devon **101** D3
Frogmore Hants **120** D2
Frogmore Herts **136** A2
Frogwell **98** D4
Frolesworth **160** A3
Frome **117** E3

Frome Market **117** F2
Frome St. Quintin **104** B2
Frome Whitfield **104** C3
Fromes Hill **145** F3
Fron Gwyn **166** C4
Fron Powys **156** B2
Fron Powys **156** A3
Fron Isaf **169** F4
Froncysyllte **169** F4
Fron-goch **168** C4
Frostenden **165** F3
Frosterley **211** G4
Froxfield **119** E1
Froxfield Green **120** C5
Fruitmarket Gallery Edin
EH1 1DF **37** G4
Fryerning **137** F2
Fugglestone
St. Peter **118** C4
Fulbeck **175** E2
Fulbourn **150** D2
Fulbrook **133** E1
Fulflood **119** F5
Fulford Som **115** F5
Fulford Staffs **171** G4
Fulford York **195** F3
Fulham **136** B5
Fulking **109** E2
Full Sutton **195** G2
Fullaford **113** G2
Fuller Street **137** G1
Fuller's Moor **170** B2
Fullerton **119** E4
Fulletby **188** C5
Fullwood **233** F4
Fulmer **135** F4
Fulmodeston **178** A2
Fulnetby **188** B5
Fulready **147** E3
Fulstone **185** F2
Fulstow **188** D3
Fulwell Oxon **147** F5
Fulwell T&W **212** C2
Fulwood Lancs **192** B4
Fulwood SYorks **186** A4
Fun Farm, Spalding Lincs
PE12 6JU **176** A5
Fundenhall **164** C2
Fundenhall
Street **164** C2
Funtington **108** A3
Funtley **107** E2
Funzie **278** F3
Furley **103** F2
Furnace A&B **240** C4
Furnace Carmar **128** B2
Furnace Cere **154** C3
Furnace High **265** H4
Furnace End **159** E3
Furner's Green **109** G1
Furness Vale **185** E4
Furneux Pelham **150** C5
Furnham **103** G2
Further Quarter **124** A5
Furtho **148** C3
Furze Green **164** D3
Furze Platt **135** D4
Furzehill Devon **114** A3
Furzehill Dorset **105** G2
Furzeley Corner **107** F1
Furzley **106** B1
Fyfett **103** F1
Fyfield Essex **137** E2
Fyfield Glos **133** E2
Fyfield Hants **119** D3
Fyfield Oxon **133** G3
Fyfield Wilts **118** C1
Fyfield Wilts **118** C1
Fylingthorpe **204** C2
Fyning **120** D5
Fyvie **261** F1

G
Gabalfa **130** A5
Gabhsann Bho
Dheas **271** G2
Gabhsann Bho
Thuath **271** G2
Gablon **266** E2
Gabroc Hill **233** F4
Gaddesby **160** B1
Gaddesden Row **135** F1
Gadebridge **135** F2
Gadshill **137** G5
Gaer Newport **130** B4
Gaer Powys **144** A5
Gaer-fawr **130** D3
Gaerllwyd **130** D3
Gaerwen **180** C5
Gagingwell **147** G5
Gaich High **259** H2
Gaich High **258** D1
Gaick Lodge **250** C1
Gailes **224** B2
Gailey **158** B1
Gainford **202** A1
Gainsborough **187** F3
Gainsford End **151** F4
Gairloch
(Gearrloch) **264** D4
Gairlochy (Gearr
Lòchaidh) **249** D1
Gairney Bank **243** G5
Gairnshiel Lodge **259** K4
Gaitsgill **209** G2
Galabank **236** B5
Galashiels **227** F2
Galbally **281** K2
Galboly **287** G5
Galdenoch **214** C4
Gale **184** D1
Galgate **192** A2
Galgorm **286** E5
Galhampton **116** D5
Gallanach **240** A2
Gallantry Bank **170** C2
Gallatown **244** A5
Gallchoille **239** G5
Gallery **253** E3
Gallery of Modern Art,
Glasgow Glas
G1 3AH **39** F4
Galley Common **159** F3
Galleyend **137** G2
Galleywood **137** G2

Galloway Forest Dark Sky
Park *D & G* 215 F2
Gallowfauld 252 C5
Gallowhill 233 F3
Gallows Green 172 B3
Gallowstree
Common 134 B4
Gallowstree Elm 158 A4
Galltair 256 E2
Gallt-y-foel 167 E1
Galmington 115 F5
Galmisdale 247 D1
Galmpton *Devon* 100 C3
Galmpton *Torbay* 101 E2
Galmpton
Warborough 101 E2
Galphay 202 B5
Galston 224 C2
Galtrigill 263 G6
Gamble's Green 137 G1
Gamblesby 210 C4
Gamblestown 282 E3
Gamelsby 209 F1
Gamesley 185 E3
Gamlingay 150 A2
Gamlingay Cinques 150 A2
Gamlingay Great
Heath 150 A2
Gammaton 113 E3
Gammaton Moor 113 E3
Gammersgill 201 F4
Gamrie 269 F4
Gamston *Notts* 187 E5
Gamston *Notts* 174 B4
Ganarew 131 E1
Gang 98 D4
Ganllwyd 168 A5
Gannochy 253 E2
Ganstead 197 D4
Ganthorpe 203 F5
Ganton 204 C5
Ganwick Corner 136 B3
Gaodhail 239 F1
Gappah 102 B5
Gara Bridge 100 D2
Garabal 241 F3
Garadheancal 265 F1
Garbat 266 B5
Garbhallt 240 C5
Garboldisham 164 B3
Garden 242 A5
Garden City 170 A1
Garden Village 185 G3
Gardeners Green 120 D1
Gardenstown 269 D1
Garderhouse 279 C8
Gardham 196 B3
Gare Hill 117 E3
Garelochhead 241 E5
Garford 133 G3
Garforth 194 D4
Gargrave 193 F2
Gargrim 280 D1
Gargunnock 242 C5
Gariob 231 F1
Garlic Street 164 D3
Garlies Castle 215 F4
Garlieston 207 E2
Garlinge Green 124 D3
Garlogie 261 F4
Garmelow 171 F5
Garmond 269 G5
Garmony 247 F5
Garmouth 268 B4
Garmston 157 F2
Garnant 128 C1
Garndolbenmaen 167 D3
Garneddwen 155 D2
Garnett Bridge 199 G3
Garnfadrun 166 B4
Garnswllt 128 C2
Garrabost 271 H4
Garrachra 232 B1
Garralburn 268 C5
Garras 95 E4
Garreg 167 F3
Garreg Bank 156 B1
Garrett's Green 159 D4
Garrick 242 C3
Garrigill 210 D3
Garrison 280 B3
Garriston 202 A3
Garroch 215 G2
Garrochty 232 B4
Garros 263 K5
Garrow 242 D1
Garryduff 286 D3
Garryhorn 215 G1
Garsdale 200 C4
Garsdale Head 200 C3
Garsdon 132 B4
Garshall Green 171 G4
Garsington 134 A2
Garstang 192 A3
Garston 183 F4
Garswood 183 G3
Gartachoil 242 A5
Gartally 258 B1
Gartavaich 231 G4
Gartbreck 230 A4
Gartcosh 234 A3
Garth *Bridgend* 129 E3
Garth *Cere* 154 C4
Garth *Gwyn* 181 D5
Garth *IoM* 190 B4
Garth *Powys* 143 F3
Garth *Shet* 279 B7
Garth Row 199 G3
Garthbrengy 143 G4
Garthdee 261 H4
Gartheli 142 B2
Garthmyl 156 A3
Garthorpe *Leics* 174 D5
Garthorpe *NLincs* 187 F1
Garths 199 G3
Garthynty 142 D3
Gartincaber 242 B4
Gartly 260 D1
Gartmore 242 A5
Gartnagrenach 231 F4
Gartnatra 230 B3
Gartness 233 G1
Gartocharn 233 F1
Garton 197 F4
Garton-on-the-
Wolds 196 B1

Gartymore 275 F7
Garvagh 286 C4
Garvaghy 281 H2
Garvald 236 C2
Garvamore 258 C5
Garvan 248 C2
Garvard 238 C5
Garvary 280 B4
Garve (Clachan
Ghairbh) 265 K5
Garveld 222 B5
Garvestone 178 B5
Garvetagh 284 E7
Garvie 232 B1
Garvock *Aber* 253 F2
Garvock *Invcly* 233 D2
Garvock *P&K* 243 E3
Garwald 276 D5
Garwaldwaterfoot 226 D5
Garway 145 D5
Garway Hill 144 D5
Garynahine (Gearraidh na
h-Aibhne) 270 C4
Gask *Aber* 269 J6
Gask *Aber* 269 F6
Gask *P&K* 243 E3
Gaskan 248 A2
Gass 224 C5
Gastard 117 F1
Gasthorpe 164 A3
Gaston Green 137 E1
Gatcombe 107 D4
Gate Burton 187 F4
Gate Helmsley 195 F2
Gate House 231 D2
Gateacre 183 F4
Gateford 186 C4
Gateforth 195 E5
Gatehead 224 B2
Gatehouse 178 B3
Gatehouse of Fleet 216 A5
Gatelawbridge 216 D1
Gateley 178 A3
Gatenby 202 C4
Gatesgarth 209 E5
Gateshaw 228 B4
Gateshead 212 B1
Gatesheath 170 B1
Gateside *Aber* 260 E3
Gateside *Angus* 252 C5
Gateside *Fife* 243 G4
Gateside *NAyr* 233 E4
Gateslack 225 G5
Gathurst 183 G2
Gatley 184 C4
Gattonside 227 G2
Gaufron 143 G2
Gaulby 160 B2
Gauldry 244 B3
Gauntons Bank 170 C3
Gaunt's Common 105 G2
Gaunt's Earthcott 131 F4
Gautby 188 B5
Gavinton 237 E4
Gawber 186 A2
Gawcott 148 B4
Gawsworth 184 C5
Gawthorp 200 B4
Gawthwaite 199 D4
Gay Bowers 137 G2
Gay Street 121 F5
Gaydon 147 F2
Gayhurst 148 D3
Gayle 201 D4
Gayles 202 A2
Gayton *Mersey* 183 D4
Gayton *Norf* 163 F1
Gayton *Staffs* 171 G5
Gayton le Marsh 189 E4
Gayton le Wold 188 C4
Gayton Thorpe 163 F1
Gaywood 177 E5
Gazeley 151 F1
Geanies House 267 F5
Gearach 230 A4
Gearnsary 274 C5
Gearradh 248 B3
Gearraidh Bhailteas
254 C2
Gearraidh Bhaird 271 F5
Gearraidh na
Monadh 254 C3
Geary 263 H5
Gedding 152 A2
Geddington 161 D4
Gedgrave Hall 153 F3
Gedintailor 256 B2
Gedling 174 B3
Gedney 176 C5
Gedney Broadgate 176 C5
Gedney Drove End 176 C5
Gedney Dyke 176 C5
Gedney Hill 162 B1
Gee Cross 185 D3
Geilston 233 E2
Geirinis 262 C7
Geisiadar 270 C4
Geldeston 165 E2
Gell *Conwy* 168 B1
Gell *Gwyn* 167 E2
Gelli *Pembs* 127 D1
Gelli *RCT* 129 F3
Gelli-aur (Golden Grove)
128 B1
Gelli Aur Country Park
Carmar SA32 8LR 142 C3
Gelli Gynan 169 E2
Gelli-deg 129 G2
Gellifor 169 E1
Gelli-gaer 130 B1
Gellilydan 167 F3
Gellinudd 128 D2
Gelli-wen 141 F5
Gellyburn 243 A1
Gelston *D&G* 216 B5
Gelston *Lincs* 175 E3
Gembling 196 D2
Gemmil 239 G4
Genoch 214 C5
Genoch Square 214 C5
Gentleshaw 158 C1
Geocrab 263 G2
George Green 135 F4
George Nympton 114 A5
Georgeham 113 E2
Georgetown 233 F3

Gerlan 167 F1
Germansweek 99 E1
Germoe 94 C4
Gerrans 95 F3
Gerrards Cross 135 F4
Gerston 275 G1
Gestingthorpe 151 G4
Geuffordd 156 B1
Geufron 155 E4
Giant's Causeway &
Causeway Coast *CC&G*
BT57 8SU 286 D1
Giant's Ring *Belfast City*
BT8 8LE 283 G2
Gibbet Hill 117 E3
Gibbshill 216 B3
Gibraltar *Lincs* 177 D2
Gibraltar *Suff* 165 D3
Gibraltar Point National
Nature Reserve *Lincs*
PE24 4SU 177 D2
Gibside *T&W*
NE16 6BG 212 A1
Giddeahall 132 A5
Giddy Green 105 E4
Gidea Park 137 E4
Gidleigh 99 G2
Giffnock 233 G4
Gifford 236 C3
Giffordland 233 D5
Giffordtown 244 A3
Giggleswick 193 E1
Gigha 231 F5
Gilberdyke 196 A5
Gilbert's End 146 A3
Gilchriston 236 B3
Gilcrux 209 E3
Gildersome 194 B5
Gildingwells 186 C4
Gileston 114 D1
Gilfach 130 A1
Gilfach Goch 129 F4
Gilfachreda 142 A2
Gilford 282 C2
Gilgarran 208 D4
Gill 210 A5
Gillamoor 203 F4
Gillan 95 E4
Gillen 263 H5
Gillenbie 217 F2
Gillfoot 217 D3
Gilling East 203 F5
Gilling West 202 A2
Gillingham *Dorset* 117 F5
Gillingham *Med* 123 G2
Gillingham *Norf* 165 F2
Gillivoan 275 G5
Gillock 275 H3
Gillow Heath 171 F2
Gills 275 J1
Gill's Green 123 G5
Gillygooly 281 G1
Gilmanscleuch 227 E3
Gilmerton *Edin* 235 G3
Gilmerton *P&K* 243 D2
Gilmilnscroft 225 D3
Gilmonby 201 E1
Gilmorton 160 A3
Gilsland 210 C1
Gilsland Spa 210 C1
Gilson 159 D3
Gilstead 194 A4
Gilston *Herts* 137 D1
Gilston *ScBord* 236 B4
Gilston Park 136 D1
Giltbrook 173 F3
Gilwern 130 B1
Gimingham 179 D2
Gin Pit 184 A2
Ginclough 185 D5
Ginger's Green 110 B2
Giosla 270 D5
Gipping 152 B1
Gipsey Bridge 176 A3
Girlsta 279 D7
Girsby 202 C2
Girthon 216 A5
Girton *Cambs* 150 C1
Girton *Notts* 174 D1
Girvan 214 C1
Gisburn 193 E3
Gisburn Cotes 193 E3
Gisleham 165 G3
Gislingham 164 B4
Gissing 164 C3
Gittisham 103 E3
Givons Grove 121 G2
Glackour 265 H3
Gladestry 144 B2
Gladsmuir 236 B2
Glaic 232 B2
Glais 128 D2
Glaisdale 203 G2
Glaister 223 E2
Glame 264 B7
Glamis 252 B5
Glamis Castle *Angus*
DD8 1QJ 252 B5
Glan Conwy 168 B2
Glanaber Terrace 168 A3
Glanaman 128 C1
Glanbran 143 E4
Glan-Denys 142 B3
Glanderston 260 D2
Glandford 178 B1
Glanduar 142 B3
Glandwr *Shet* 141 E5
Glan-Dwyfach 167 D3
Glangrwyney 130 B1
Glanllynfi 129 E4
Glanmule 156 A3
Glan-rhyd *NPT* 129 D2
Glan-rhyd *Pembs* 141 E3
Glanton 229 E5
Glanton Pyke 229 E5
Glanvilles Wootton 104 C2
Glan-wern 154 C4
Glanwydden 181 G4
Glan-y-don 182 C5
Glan-y-llyn 130 A4
Glan-y-nant 155 F4
Glanyrafon *Gwyn* 168 C3
Glanyrafon *Gwyn* 168 D3
Glanyrafon *IoA* 181 E4
Glan-y-wern 167 F4
Glapthorn 161 F3
Glapwell 173 F1

Glarryford 286 E4
Glasahoile 241 G4
Glasbury 144 A4
Glaschoil 259 H1
Glascoed *Mon* 130 C2
Glascoed *Wrex* 169 F2
Glascorrie 260 C5
Glascote 159 E2
Glascwm 144 A2
Glasdrum 248 C5
Glasdrumman 282 C7
Glasfryn 168 C2
Glasgow (Glaschu) 233 G3
Glasgow Airport 233 F3
Glasgow Botanic
Garden *Glas*
G12 0UE 30 C3
Glasgow Prestwick
Airport 224 B3
Glasgow Royal Concert Hall
Glas G2 3NY 39 F3
Glasgow Science Centre
Glas G51 1EA 38 A4
Glashmore 261 F4
Glashygolgan 285 G6
Glasinfryn 167 E1
Glasnacardoch 256 C5
Glasnakille 256 B3
Glaspant 141 E4
Glaspwll 154 D3
Glass Studio, Eastbourne
Pier *ESuss*
BN21 3EL 110 B4
Glassburn 257 K1
Glassel 260 E5
Glassenbury 123 G5
Glasserton 207 E3
Glassford 234 B5
Glasshouse 145 G5
Glasshouses 194 A1
Glassingall 242 C4
Glassnall 242 A4
Glasslie 244 A4
Glasson *A&B* 232 B3
Glasson *Cumb* 218 A5
Glasson *Lancs* 192 A3
Glasson Dock 192 A3
Glassonby 210 B4
Glasterlaw 253 D4
Glaston 161 D2
Glastonbury 116 B4
Glastonbury Abbey *Som*
BA6 9EL 116 C4
Glatton 161 G3
Glazebrook 184 A3
Glazebury 184 A3
Glazeley 157 G4
Gleadless 186 A4
Gleadsmoss 171 F1
Gleann Tholastaidh
271 H3
Gleaston 199 D5
Glebe *CC&G* 285 H4
Glebe *D&S* 285 F6
Glecknabae 232 B3
Gledhow 194 C4
Gledrid 169 F4
Glemsford 151 G3
Glen *D&G* 216 C3
Glen *D&G* 215 G5
Glen *F&O* 280 D3
Glen *F&O* 281 F3
Glen Auldyn 190 C2
Glen Mona 190 C3
Glen Parva 160 A3
Glen Trool Lodge 215 F2
Glen Village 234 C2
Glen Vine 190 B4
Glenae 217 D2
Glenaladale 248 A2
Glenald 241 E5
Glenamachrie 240 B2
Glenanane 282 C5
Glenapp Castle 214 B2
Glenariff 287 G3
Glenarm *Angus* 252 B3
Glenarm *M&EAnt* 287 H4
Glenavy 282 E1
Glenbarr 222 B2
Glenbatrick 230 D2
Glenbeg *High* 265 K3
Glenbeg *High* 259 H2
Glenbeg *High* 247 F3
Glenbeich 242 A2
Glenbervie 253 F1
Glenboig 234 B3
Glenborrodale 247 F2
Glenbranter 240 D5
Glenbreck 226 B3
Glenbrittle 255 F2
Glenburn 233 F3
Glenbyre 239 E2
Glencaple 217 D4
Glencarse 243 G2
Glencat 260 D5
Glenceitlein 248 D5
Glencloy 223 F2
Glencoe
(A' Chàrnaich) 248 D4
Glencoe Visitor Centre
High PH49 4LA 248 D4
Glenconglass 259 J2
Glencraig 243 G5
Glencripesdale 247 F4
Glencrosh 216 B2
Glencruitten 240 A2
Glencuie 260 C3
Glendye Lodge 253 E1
Glendearg *D&G* 226 D2
Glendearg *ScBord* 227 G2
Glendessary 257 F5
Glendevon 243 E4
Glendoebeg 258 B4
Glendoick 244 A2
Glendoll Lodge 252 B2
Glendoune 214 C1
Glendrissaig 214 C1
Glenduckie 244 A3
Glenduisk 214 C2
Gleneagles Hotel 243 E3
Gleneagles House 243 E4
Glenearn 243 G3
Gleneeny 281 J2
Glenegedale 230 B4
Glenelg
(Gleann Eilg) 256 E3
Glengolly 275 G2
Glengormley 287 H7
Glenfarg 243 G3

Glenfeochan 240 A2
Glenfield 160 A2
Glenfinnan (Gleann
Fhionnain) 248 B1
Glenfoot 243 G3
Glengalmadale 248 A4
Glengap 216 A5
Glengarnock 233 E4
Glengarrisdale 239 F5
Glengolly 275 G2
Glengrasco 263 K7
Glengyle 241 F2
Glenhead *CC&G* 285 J4
Glenhead *D&G* 216 C2
Glenhead *M&EAnt* 287 G6
Glenhead Farm 252 B3
Glenhull 285 J7
Glenhurich 248 A3
Gleniffer Braes Country Park
Renf PA2 8TE 30 A4
Glenkerry 227 D4
Glenkiln 223 F2
Glenkin 232 C1
Glenkindie 260 C3
Glenlagan 283 F3
Glenlair 216 B3
Glenlatterach 267 K6
Glenlean 232 B1
Glenleary 286 C3
Glenlee *Angus* 252 C2
Glenlee *D&G* 216 A2
Glenlichorn 242 C3
Glenlivet 259 J1
Glenlochar 216 B4
Glenluce 214 C5
Glenmallan 241 E5
Glenmanna 225 F5
Glenmavis 234 B3
Glenmaye 190 A4
Glenmeanie 265 J6
Glenmore *A&B* 232 B3
Glenmore *High* 263 K7
Glenmore *High* 259 G4
Glenmore Forest Park
Visitor Centre *High*
PH22 1QY 259 G3
Glenmore Lodge 259 G4
Glenmornan 285 G6
Glenmoy 252 C3
Glenmuick 273 F7
Glennoe 240 C1
Glenny's Bridge 282 E6
Glenochar 226 A4
Glenoe 287 H6
Glenogil 252 C3
Glenprosen
Village 252 B3
Glenquiech 252 C3
Glenramskill 222 C4
Glenrazie 215 E4
Glenridding 209 G5
Glenrisdell 231 G4
Glenrossal 266 C2
Glenrothes 244 A4
Glensanda 248 A5
Glensaugh 253 E2
Glensgaich 266 B5
Glenshalg 260 D4
Glenshesk Bridge 287 F2
Glenshellish 240 D5
Glensluain 240 C5
Glenstaghey 286 E1
Glentaggart 225 G3
Glentham 188 A3
Glenton 260 E2
Glentress 227 D2
Glentress 7stanes *ScBord*
EH45 8NB 235 G5
Glentress Forest
Visitor Centre *ScBord*
EH45 8NB 235 G5
Glentrool 215 E3
Glentruan 190 C1
Glentworth 187 G4
Glenuachdarach 263 K6
Glenuig 247 F2
Glenure 248 C5
Glenurquhart 266 E5
Glenwhilly 214 C3
Glespin 225 G3
Gletness 279 D7
Glewstone 145 E5
Glinton 161 G2
Glogue 141 F4
Glooston 160 C3
Glororum 229 H3
Glossop 185 E3
Gloster Hill 221 E1
Gloucester 132 A1
Gloucester Cathedral
Glos GL1 2LR
73 Gloucester
Gloucester Historic
Docks *Glos* GL1 2ER
73 Gloucester
Gloucestershire
Airport 146 A5
Gloucestershire &
Warwickshire Railway
Glos GL54 5DT 146 B5
Gloup 278 E2
Gloweth 96 B5
Glusburn 193 G3
Glympton 147 G5
Glyn 168 A2
Glynarthen 141 G3
Glynceiriog 169 F4
Glyncoch 129 G3
Glyncorrwg 129 E3
Glyn-Cywarch 167 F4
Glynde 109 G3
Glyndebourne 109 G2
Glyndyfrdwy 169 E3
Glynn 287 J6
Glynneath
(Glyn-Nedd) 129 E2
Glynogwr 129 F4
Glyntaff 129 G4
Gnosall 171 F5
Gnosall Heath 171 F5
Go Bananas, Colchester
Essex CO1 1BX 152 A5
Goadby 160 C2
Goadby Marwood 174 C5
Goatacre 132 C5
Goatfield 240 C4
Goathill 104 C1

Goathland 204 B2
Goathurst 115 F4
Gobernuisgeach 274 E5
Gobhaig 270 C7
Gobowen 170 A4
Godalming 121 G3
Goddard's Corner 153 D1
Goddards Green 109 E1
Godden Green 123 E3
Goddington 123 D2
Godford Cross 103 E2
Godington 148 B5
Godleybrook 171 G3
Godmanchester 162 A5
Godmanstone 104 C3
Godmersham 124 C3
Godney 116 B3
Godolphin Cross 94 D3
Godor 156 B1
Godre'r-graig 129 D2
Godshill *Hants* 106 A1
Godshill *IoW* 107 E4
Godstone 122 C3
Godstone Farm *Surr*
RH9 8LX 122 C3
Godwick 178 A3
Goetre 130 C2
Goff's Oak 136 C2
Gogar 235 F2
Gogarth 181 F4
Goginan 154 C4
Goirtean a'
Chladaich 248 C2
Goirtein 232 A1
Golan 167 E3
Golant 97 F4
Golberdon 98 D3
Golborne 184 A3
Golcar 185 F1
Gold Hill *Cambs* 162 D3
Gold Hill *Dorset* 105 E1
Goldcliff 130 C4
Golden Acre Park
WYorks
LS16 8BQ 194 B3
Golden Cross 110 A2
Golden Green 123 F4
Golden Pot 120 C3
Golden Valley
Derbys 173 F2
Golden Valley *Glos* 146 B5
Goldenhill 171 F2
Golders Green 136 B4
Goldhanger 138 C2
Goldielea 216 D3
Golding 157 E2
Goldington 149 F2
Goldsborough
NYorks 204 B1
Goldsborough
NYorks 194 C2
Goldsithney 94 C3
Goldstone 171 E5
Goldthorn Park 158 B3
Goldthorpe 186 B2
Goldworthy 113 D3
Goleulong 2000 Lightship,
Cardiff *Cardiff*
CF10 4PA 7 C4
Golford 123 G5
Gollanfield 267 F6
Gollinglith Foot 202 A4
Golspie 267 F2
Golval 274 D2
Gomeldon 118 C4
Gomersal 194 B5
Gometra 246 C5
Gometra House 246 C5
Gomshall 121 G3
Gonachan Cottage 234 A1
Gonalston 174 B3
Gonerby Hill Foot 175 E4
Gonfirth 279 C6
Good Easter 137 F1
Gooderstone 163 F2
Goodleigh 113 G2
Goodmanham 196 A3
Goodmayes 137 D4
Goodnestone *Kent* 125 E3
Goodnestone *Kent* 124 C3
Goodrich 131 E1
Goodrington 101 E2
Goodshaw 193 E5
Goodshaw Fold 193 E5
Goodwick (Wdig) 140 C4
Goodworth Clatford 119 E3
Goodyers End 159 F4
Goole 195 G5
Goom's Hill 146 C2
Goonbell 96 B5
Goonhavern 96 B4
Goonvrea 96 B5
Goose Green *Essex* 152 C5
Goose Green *Essex* 152 C5
Goose Green
GtMan 183 G2
Goose Green *Kent* 123 F3
Goose Green *SGlos* 131 F5
Goose Pool 145 D3
Gooseham 112 C4
Goosehill Green 146 B1
Goosewell 100 B5
Goosey 133 F3
Goosnargh 192 B4
Goostrey 184 B5
Gorcott Hill 146 C1
Gorddinog 181 E5
Gordon 236 D5
Gordonbush 267 F1
Gordonstoun 267 J5
Gordonstown *Aber* 268 D5
Gordonstown *Aber* 261 F1
Gore Cross 118 B2
Gore End 119 F1
Gore Street 125 E2
Gorebridge 236 A3
Gorefield 162 C1
Gorey 100 D5
Gorgie 235 G2
Goring 134 B4
Goring Heath 134 B5
Goring-by-Sea 108 D3
Gorllwyn 141 G4
Gornalwood 158 B3
Gorrachie 269 F5
Gorran Churchtown 97 D5

Gorran Haven 97 E5
Gorsedd 182 C5
Gorseinon 128 B3
Gorseness 277 D6
Gorseybank 173 D2
Gors-goch 142 A2
Gors-las 128 B1
Gorsley 145 F5
Gorsley Common 145 F5
Gorstage 184 A5
Gorstan 265 K5
Gorstanvorran 248 A2
Gorsty Hill 172 C5
Gortaclare 281 H2
Gortahurk 286 C6
Gortavoy Bridge 281 K2
Gorten 239 G1
Gortenbuie 239 E1
Gorteneorn 247 F2
Gortfin 281 H2
Gortin 285 G7
Gortinreid 285 H4
Gortmullan 280 E6
Gortnacreagh 281 G1
Gortnagallon 282 E1
Gortnahey 285 J4
Gortnalee 280 B3
Gorton *A&B* 246 A4
Gorton *GtMan* 184 C3
Gortreagh 281 K1
Gosbeck 152 C2
Gosberton 176 A4
Gosberton Clough 175 G5
Goseley Dale 173 E5
Gosfield 151 F5
Gosford *Here* 145 E1
Gosford *Oxon* 134 A1
Gosforth *Cumb* 198 B2
Gosforth *T&W* 212 B1
Gosland Green 170 C2
Gosmore 149 G5
Gospel End 158 A3
Gosport 107 F3
Gossabrough 278 E4
Gossington 131 G2
Gossops Green 122 B5
Goswick 229 E2
Gotham 173 G4
Gotherington 146 B5
Gothers 97 D4
Gott 279 D8
Gotton 115 F5
Goudhurst 123 G5
Goulceby 188 C5
Gourdas 269 F6
Gourdon 253 G2
Gourock 232 D2
Govan 233 G3
Goverton 174 C2
Goveton 101 D4
Govilon 130 B1
Gowanhill 269 J4
Gowdall 195 F5
Gowdystown 282 E3
Gowerton 128 B3
Gowkhall 235 E1
Gowkthrapple 234 B4
Gowthorpe 195 G2
Goxhill *ERid* 197 D3
Goxhill *NLincs* 196 D5
Goytre 129 D4
Gozzard's Ford 133 G3
Grabhair 271 F6
Graby 175 F5
Gracefield 286 D7
Gracehill 286 E5
Gradbach 171 G1
Grade 95 E5
Gradeley Green 170 C2
Graffham 108 B2
Grafham *Cambs* 149 G1
Grafham *Surr* 121 F3
Grafham Water *Cambs*
PE28 0BH 149 G1
Grafton *Here* 145 D4
Grafton *NYorks* 194 D1
Grafton *Oxon* 133 E2
Grafton *Shrop* 156 D1
Grafton *Worcs* 145 E1
Grafton *Worcs* 146 B4
Grafton Flyford 146 B2
Grafton Regis 148 C3
Grafton Underwood 161 E4
Grafty Green 124 A4
Graianrhyd 169 F2
Graig *Carmar* 128 A2
Graig *Conwy* 181 G5
Graig *Denb* 182 B5
Graigfechan 169 E2
Grain 124 A1
Grainel 230 A3
Grainhow 269 G6
Grains Bar 185 D2
Grainsby 188 C3
Grainthorpe 189 D3
Graizelound 187 E3
Gramisdale
(Gramsdal) 262 D6
Grampound 96 D5
Grampound Road 96 C4
Granborough 148 C5
Granby 174 C4
Grand Pier, Teignmouth
Devon
TQ14 8BB 102 C5
Grandborough 147 G1
Grandes Rocques 101 F4
Grandtully 251 E4
Grange *Cumb* 209 F5
Grange *EAyr* 224 C2
Grange *High* 257 K1
Grange *Med* 123 G2
Grange *Mersey* 182 D4
Grange *Mid Ulster* 282 B1
Grange *P&K* 244 A2
Grange Blundel 282 B2
Grange Corner 286 E6
Grange Crossroads 268 C5
Grange de Lings 187 G5
Grange Hall 267 H5
Grange Hill 136 D3
Grange Moor 185 G1
Grange of Lindores 244 A3
Grange Villa 212 B2
Grangee 283 J1
Grangemill 172 D2
Grangemouth 234 D1
Grangemuir 244 D4

Grange-over-Sands 199 F5
Grangeston 214 D1
Grangetown
  Cardiff 130 A5
Grangetown R&C 213 E5
Granish 259 G3
Gransha AB&C 283 F4
Gransha L&C 283 H2
Gransha M&EAnt 287 J6
Gransmoor 196 C3
Granston 140 B4
Grantchester 150 C2
Grantham 175 E4
Grantley 202 B5
Grantlodge 261 F3
Granton 235 G2
Granton House 226 B5
Grantown-on-Spey 259 H2
Grantsfield 145 E1
Grantshouse 237 F3
Granville 282 D7
Grappenhall 184 A4
Grasby 188 C2
Grasmere 199 E2
Grass Green 151 F4
Grasscroft 185 D2
Grassendale 183 E4
Grassgarth 199 F3
Grassholme 211 F5
Grassington 193 G1
Grassmoor 173 F1
Grassthorpe 174 C1
Grateley 119 D3
Gratwich 172 B4
Gravel Hill 135 F3
Graveley Cambs 150 A1
Graveley Herts 150 A5
Gravelly Hill 158 D3
Gravels 156 C2
Graven 278 D5
Gravesend 137 F5
Grayingham 187 G3
Grayrigg 199 G3
Grays 137 F5
Grayshott 121 D4
Grayswood 121 E4
Grazeley 120 B1
Greasbrough 186 B3
Greasby 183 D4
Great Aberystwyth Camera
  Obscura Cere
  SY23 2DN 154 B4
Great Abington 150 D3
Great Addington 161 E5
Great Altcar 183 E2
Great Alne 146 D2
Great Amwell 136 C1
Great Asby 200 B1
Great Ashfield 152 A1
Great Ayton 203 E1
Great Baddow 137 G2
Great Badfield 151 E4
Great Barford 149 G2
Great Barr 158 C3
Great Barrington 133 E1
Great Barrow 170 B1
Great Barton 151 G1
Great Barugh 203 G5
Great Bavington 220 B3
Great Bealings 152 D3
Great Bedwyn 119 D1
Great Bentley 152 C5
Great Bernera 270 D4
Great Billing 148 D1
Great Bircham 177 F4
Great Blakenham 152 C2
Great Bolas 170 D5
Great Bookham 121 G2
Great Bourton 147 G3
Great Bowden 160 C4
Great Bradley 151 E2
Great Braxted 138 B1
Great Bricett 152 B2
Great Brickhill 149 E4
Great Bridgeford 171 F5
Great Brington 148 B1
Great Bromley 152 B5
Great Broughton
  Cumb 209 D3
Great Broughton
  NYorks 203 E2
Great Buckland 123 F2
Great Budworth 184 A5
Great Burdon 202 C1
Great Burstead 137 F3
Great Busby 203 E2
Great Cambourne 150 B2
Great Canfield 137 E1
Great Canney 138 B2
Great Carlton 189 E4
Great Casterton 161 F2
Great Chalfield 117 F1
Great Chart 124 B4
Great Chatwell 157 G1
Great Chell 171 F2
Great Chesterford 150 D3
Great Cheverell 118 A2
Great Chishill 150 C4
Great Clacton 139 E1
Great Clifton 208 D4
Great Coates 188 C2
Great Comberton 146 B3
Great Corby 210 A2
Great Cornard 151 G3
Great Cowden 197 E3
Great Coxwell 133 E3
Great Crakehall 202 B4
Great Cransley 160 D5
Great
  Cressingham 163 G2
Great Crosby 183 E2
Great Crosthwaite 209 F4
Great Cubley 172 C4
Great Cumbrae 232 C4
Great Dalby 160 C1
Great Doddington 149 D1
Great Doward 131 E1
Great Dunham 163 G1
Great Dunmow 151 E5
Great Durnford 118 C4
Great Easton Essex 151 E5
Great Easton Leics 160 D3
Great Eccleston 192 A3
Great Edstone 203 G4
Great Ellingham 164 B2
Great Elm 117 E3
Great Eversden 150 B3

Great Fencote 202 B3
Great Finborough 152 B2
Great Fransham 163 G1
Great Gaddesden 135 F1
Great Gidding 161 G4
Great Givendale 196 A2
Great Glemham 153 E1
Great Glen 160 B3
Great Gonerby 175 D4
Great Gransden 150 A2
Great Green
  Cambs 150 A3
Great Green Norf 165 D3
Great Green Suff 152 A2
Great Green Suff 164 C4
Great Green Suff 164 B4
Great Habton 203 G5
Great Hale 175 G3
Great Hall Hants
  SO23 8UJ
  89 Winchester
Great Hallingbury 137 E1
Great Hampden 134 D2
Great Harrowden 161 D5
Great Harwood 192 D4
Great Haseley 134 B2
Great Hatfield 197 D3
Great Haywood 172 B5
Great Heath 159 F4
Great Heck 195 E5
Great Henny 151 G4
Great Hinton 118 A2
Great Hockham 164 A2
Great Holland 139 F1
Great Horkesley 152 A4
Great Hormead 150 C4
Great Horton 194 A4
Great Horwood 148 C4
Great Houghton
  SYorks 186 B3
Great Houghton
  WN'hants 148 C2
Great Hucklow 185 F5
Great Kelk 196 D2
Great Kimble 134 D2
Great Kingshill 135 D3
Great Langton 202 B3
Great Leighs 151 G1
Great Limber 188 B2
Great Linford 148 D3
Great Livermere 163 G5
Great Longstone 185 G5
Great Lumley 212 B3
Great Lyth 157 D2
Great Malvern 152 A2
Great Maplestead 151 G4
Great Marton 191 G4
Great Massingham 177 F5
Great Melton 178 C3
Great Missenden 135 D2
Great Mitton 192 D3
Great Mongeham 125 F3
Great Moulton 164 C3
Great Munden 150 B5
Great Musgrave 200 C1
Great Ness 156 C1
Great Notley 151 F5
Great Nurcot 114 C4
Great Oak 130 C2
Great Oakley Essex 152 C5
Great Oakley
  NN'hants 161 D4
Great Offley 149 G5
Great Ormside 200 C1
Great Orton 209 G1
Great Ouseburn 194 D1
Great Oxendon 160 C4
Great Oxney Green 137 F2
Great Palgrave 163 G1
Great Parndon 136 D2
Great Paxton 150 A1
Great Plumpton 191 G4
Great Plumstead 179 E5
Great Ponton 175 E4
Great Potheridge 113 F4
Great Preston 194 C5
Great Purston 148 A4
Great Raveley 162 A4
Great Rissington 133 D1
Great Rollright 147 F4
Great Ryburgh 178 A3
Great Ryle 229 E5
Great Ryton 157 D2
Great St. Mary's Church
  Cambs CB2 3PQ
  66 Cambridge
Great Saling 151 F5
Great Salkeld 210 B4
Great Sampford 151 E4
Great Sankey 183 G4
Great Saredon 158 B2
Great Saxham 151 F1
Great Shefford 133 F5
Great Shelford 150 C2
Great Smeaton 202 C2
Great Snoring 178 A2
Great Somerford 132 B4
Great Stainton 212 C5
Great Stambridge 138 C3
Great Staughton 149 G1
Great Steeping 176 C1
Great Stonar 125 F3
Great Strickland 210 B5
Great Stukeley 162 A5
Great Sturton 188 C5
Great Sutton
  ChesW&C 183 E5
Great Sutton Shrop 157 E4
Great Swinburne 220 B4
Great Tew 147 F5
Great Tey 151 G5
Great Thorness 107 D3
Great Thurlow 151 E3
Great Torr 100 C3
Great Torrington 113 E4
Great Tosson 220 C1
Great Totham
  Essex 138 B1
Great Totham
  Essex 138 B1
Great Tows 188 C3
Great Urswick 199 D5
Great Wakering 138 C4
Great Waldingfield 152 A3

Great Walsingham 178 A2
Great Waltham 137 F1
Great Warley 137 E3
Great Washbourne 146 B4
Great Weeke 102 B4
Great Welnetham 151 G2
Great Wenham 152 B4
Great Whittington 220 C4
Great Wigborough 138 C1
Great Wigsell 110 C1
Great Wilbraham 150 D2
Great Wilne 173 F4
Great Wishford 118 B4
Great Witcombe 132 B1
Great Witley 145 G1
Great Wolford 147 E4
Great Wratting 151 E3
Great Wymondley 150 A5
Great Wyrley 158 B2
Great Wytheford 157 E1
Great Yarmouth 179 G5
Great Yeldham 151 F4
Greatford 161 F1
Greatgate 172 B3
Greatham Hants 120 C4
Greatham Hart 213 D5
Greatham WSuss 108 C2
Greatness 123 E3
Greatstone-on-Sea 111 F1
Greatworth 148 A3
Green 169 G2
Green Cross 121 D4
Green End Bed 149 G2
Green End Bucks 149 E4
Green End Cambs 162 A5
Green End Cambs 162 B5
Green End Herts 150 B5
Green End Herts 150 C5
Green End Warks 159 E4
Green Hammerton 195 D2
Green Hill 132 C4
Green Lane 146 C1
Green Moor 185 G3
Green Ore 116 B3
Green Quarter 199 F2
Green Street ESuss 110 C3
Green Street Herts 136 A3
Green Street Herts 150 C5
Green Street Worcs 146 A3
Green Street
  WSuss 121 G5
Green Street Green
  GtLon 137 D5
Green Street Green
  Kent 137 E5
Green Tye 136 D1
Greenan 282 E6
Greenburn 252 C5
Greencastle F&O 285 H7
Greencastle NM&D 283 F7
Greencroft 212 A3
Greendams 253 E1
Greendykes 229 E4
Greenend 147 F5
Greenfaulds 234 B2
Greenfield CenBeds 149 F4
Greenfield (Maes-Glas)
  Flints 182 C5
Greenfield GtMan 185 E2
Greenfield High 257 J4
Greenfield Lincs 189 E5
Greenfield NM&D 283 G2
Greenfield Oxon 134 C3
Greenford 136 A4
Greengairs 234 B2
Greengates 194 A4
Greengill 209 E3
Greenhalgh 192 A4
Greenhall 260 E2
Greenham 119 F1
Greenhaugh 219 F3
Greenhead 210 C1
Greenheads 261 J1
Greenheys 184 B3
Greenhill D&G 217 F3
Greenhill GtLon 136 A4
Greenhill High 267 J4
Greenhill SYorks 186 A4
Greenhithe 137 E5
Greenholm 224 D2
Greenholme 199 G2
Greenhow Hill 194 A1
Greenigo 277 D7
Greenland 275 H2
Greenlands 134 C4
Greenlaw Aber 268 E5
Greenlaw ScBord 237 E5
Greenloaning 242 C4
Greenmeadow 130 B3
Greenmoor Hill 134 B4
Greenmount 184 B1
Greenmyre 261 G3
Greenock 233 D2
Greenodd 199 E4
Greens Norton 148 B3
Greenscares 242 C3
Greenside T&W 212 A1
Greenside WYorks 185 F1
Greenstead 152 B5
Greenstead Green 151 G5
Greensted 137 E2
Greensted Green 137 E2
Greenville 285 F7
Greenway Pembs 141 D4
Greenway Som 116 A5
Greenwell 210 B2
Greenwich 136 C5
Greenwood Forest Park,
  Y Felinheli Gwyn
  LL56 4QN 167 E1
Greenstown 283 F2
Greet 146 C4
Greete 157 E5
Greetham Lincs 188 D5
Greetham Rut 161 E1
Greetland 193 G5
Gregson Lane 192 B5
Greinton 116 B4
Grenaby 190 A4
Grendon N'hants 149 D1
Grendon Warks 159 E3
Grendon Common 159 E3
Grendon Green 145 E2
Grendon
  Underwood 148 B5
Grenitote
  (Greinetobht) 262 D4

Grenofen 99 E3
Grenoside 186 A3
Greosabhagh 263 G2
Gresford 170 A2
Gresham 178 C2
Greshornish 263 J6
Gress (Griais) 271 G3
Gressenhall 178 A4
Gressingham 192 B1
Greta Bridge 201 F1
Gretna 218 B5
Gretna Green 218 B5
Gretna Green Famous
  Blacksmith's Shop, D&G
  DG16 5DY 218 B5
Gretton Glos 146 C4
Gretton NN'hants 161 E3
Gretton Shrop 157 E3
Grewelthorpe 202 B5
Greyabbey 283 J2
Greygarth 202 A5
Greylake 116 A4
Greys Green 134 C4
Greysouthen 209 D4
Greystead 219 F3
Greysteel 285 H3
Greystoke 210 A4
Greystone Aber 259 K5
Greystone Angus 252 D5
Greystone Lancs 193 E3
Greystones 186 A4
Greywell 120 C2
Gribthorpe 195 G4
Gribton 216 D2
Griff 159 F4
Griffithstown 130 B3
Grigadale 246 D3
Grigghall 199 F3
Grimeford Village 184 A1
Grimethorpe 186 B2
Grimister 278 D3
Grimley 146 A1
Grimmet 224 B4
Grimness 277 D8
Grimoldby 189 E4
Grimpo 170 A5
Grimsargh 192 B4
Grimsay
  (Griomasaigh) 262 D6
Grimsbury 147 G3
Grimsby 188 C2
Grimscote 148 B2
Grimscott 112 C5
Grimshader
  (Griomsiadar) 271 G5
Grimsthorpe 175 F5
Grimston Leics 174 B5
Grimston Norf 177 F5
Grimstone 104 C3
Grimstone End 152 A1
Grindale 196 D5
Grindiscol 279 D9
Grindle 157 G2
Grindleford 185 G5
Grindleton 193 D3
Grindley 172 B5
Grindley Brook 170 C3
Grindlow 185 F5
Grindon N'umb 237 G5
Grindon Staffs 172 B2
Grindon Stock 212 C5
Grindon T&W 212 C2
Gringley on the Hill 187 E3
Grinsdale 209 G1
Grinshill 170 C5
Grinton 201 F3
Griomarstaidh 270 E4
Grisdale 200 C3
Grishipoll 246 A4
Gristhorpe 205 D4
Griston 164 A2
Gritley 277 E7
Grittenham 132 C4
Grittleton 132 A5
Grizebeck 198 D4
Grizedale 199 E3
Grobister 276 F5
Groby 160 A2
Groes 168 D1
Groes-faen 129 G4
Groesffordd 166 B4
Groesffordd Marli 182 B5
Groeslon Gwyn 167 D2
Groeslon Gwyn 167 E1
Groes-lwyd 156 B1
Groes-wen 130 A4
Grogport 231 G5
Groigearraidh 254 C1
Gromford 153 E2
Gronant 182 B4
Groombridge 123 E5
Groombridge Place Gardens
  Kent TN3 9QG 123 E5
Groomsport 283 J1
Grosmont Mon 144 D5
Grosmont NYorks 204 B2
Grotaig 258 B2
Groton 152 A3
Groundistone
  Heights 227 G4
Grouville 100 C3
Grove Bucks 149 E5
Grove Dorset 104 C5
Grove Kent 125 E2
Grove Notts 187 E5
Grove Oxon 133 G3
Grove End 124 A2
Grove Green 123 G3
Grove Park 136 D5
Grove Town 195 D5
Grovehill 135 F2
Grovesend SGlos 131 F4
Grovesend Swan 128 B2
Gruids 266 C2
Gruinard 255 J2
Grula 255 J2
Gruline 247 E5
Grumbla 94 B4
Grundcruie 243 F2
Grundisburgh 152 D2
Gruting 279 B8
Grutness 279 G10
Gualachulain 248 D5
Guardbridge 244 C3

Guarlford 146 A3
Guay 251 F5
Gubberill 198 B3
Gubblecote 135 E1
Guernsey 101 F5
Guernsey Airport 101 E5
Guestling Green 111 D3
Guestling Thorn 111 D2
Guestwick 178 B3
Guestwick Green 178 B3
Guide 192 D5
Guide Post 221 E3
Guilden Down 156 C4
Guilden Morden 150 A3
Guilden Sutton 170 B1
Guildford 121 E3
Guildford House Gallery
  Surr GU1 3AJ
  74 Guildford
Guildtown 243 G1
Guilsborough 160 B5
Guilsfield (Cegidfa) 156 B1
Guilthwaite 186 B4
Guisborough 203 F1
Guiseley 194 A3
Guist 178 B3
Guith 276 E4
Guiting Power 146 C5
Gulberwick 279 D9
Gulladuff 286 C6
Gullane 236 B1
Gullane Bents ELoth
  EH31 2AZ 236 B1
Gulval 94 B3
Gulworthy 99 E3
Gumfreston 127 E2
Gumley 160 B3
Gunby Lincs 175 E5
Gunby Lincs 176 C1
Gundleton 120 B4
Gunn 113 G2
Gunnersbury 136 A5
Gunnerside 201 E3
Gunnerton 220 B4
Gunness 187 F1
Gunnislake 99 E3
Gunnista 279 E8
Gunstone 158 A2
Gunter's Bridge 121 E5
Gunthorpe Norf 178 B2
Gunthorpe Notts 174 B3
Gunthorpe Rut 161 D2
Gunville 107 D4
Gunwalloe 95 D4
Gupworthy 114 C4
Gurnard 107 D3
Gurnett 184 D5
Gurney Slade 116 D3
Gurnos MTyd 129 G2
Gurnos Powys 129 D2
Gushmere 124 C3
Gussage All Saints 105 G1
Gussage St. Andrew 105 F1
Gussage St. Michael 105 F1
Guston 125 F4
Gutcher 278 E3
Guthram Gowt 175 G5
Guthrie 253 D4
Guyhirn 162 B2
Guynd 253 D5
Guy's Head 176 C5
Guy's Marsh 117 F5
Guyzance 221 E1
Gwaelod-y-garth 130 A4
Gwaenysgor 182 B4
Gwaithla 144 B2
Gwalchmai 180 B5
Gwastad 140 D5
Gwastadnant 167 F2
Gwauncaegurwen 128 D1
Gwaynynog 168 D1
Gwbert 141 E3
Gweek 95 E4
Gwehelog 130 C2
Gwenddwr 143 G3
Gwendreath 95 E5
Gwennap 96 B5
Gwennap Mining District
  (Cornwall & West Devon
  Mining Landscape) Corn
  96 B5
Gwenter 95 E5
Gwernaffield 169 F1
Gwernesney 130 D2
Gwernogle 142 B4
Gwernymynydd 169 F1
Gwern-y-Steeple 129 G5
Gwersyllt 170 A2
Gwespyr 182 C4
Gwinear 94 C3
Gwithian 94 C2
Gwredog 180 C4
Gwrhay 130 A3
Gwyddelwern 169 D3
Gwyddgrug 142 A4
Gwynfryn 169 F2
Gwystre 143 E1
Gwytherin 168 B1
Gyfelia 170 A2
Gyre 277 C7
Gyrn Goch 166 D3

H
H.M.S. Belfast GtLon
  SE1 2JH 12 C4
H.M.S. Victory PO1 3PX
  82 Portsmouth
H.M.S. Warrior PO1 3QX
  82 Portsmouth
Habberley 156 C2
Habin 120 D5
Habost (Tabost) 271 F6
Habrough 188 B1
Haccombe 102 B5
Hacconby 175 G5
Haceby 175 F4
Hacheston 153 E2
Hackbridge 122 B2
Hackenthorpe 186 B4
Hackford 178 B5
Hackforth 202 B3
Hackland 276 C5
Hackleton 148 D2
Hacklete (Haclait) 262 D7
Hacklete (Tacleit) 270 D4
Hackleton 148 D2
Hacklinge 125 F3
Hackness NYorks 204 C3
Hackness Ork 277 C8

Hackney 136 C4
Hackthorn 187 G4
Hackthorpe 210 B5
Hacton 137 E4
Hadden 228 B3
Haddenham Bucks 134 C2
Haddenham
  Cambs 162 C5
Haddington ELoth 236 C2
Haddington Lincs 175 E1
Haddiscoe 165 F2
Haddo Country Park Aber
  AB41 7EQ 261 G1
Haddon 161 G3
Hade Edge 185 F2
Hademore 159 D2
Hadfield 185 E3
Hadham Cross 136 D1
Hadham Ford 150 C5
Hadleigh Essex 138 B4
Hadleigh Suff 152 B3
Hadleigh Castle Country
  Park Essex
  SS7 2PP 138 B4
Hadleigh Farm Essex
  SS7 2AP 138 B4
Hadleigh Heath 152 A3
Hadley Tel&W 157 F1
Hadley Worcs 146 A1
Hadley End 172 C5
Hadley Wood 136 B3
Hadlow 123 F4
Hadlow Down 110 A1
Hadnall 170 C5
Hadrian's Wall
  (Frontiers of the Roman
  Empire) Cumb/N'umb
  210 C1 & 211 G1
Hadspen 117 D4
Hadstock 151 D3
Hadston 221 E2
Hadzor 146 B1
Haffenden Quarter 124 A4
Hafod Bridge 142 C4
Hafod-Dinbych 168 B2
Hafodunos 168 B1
Hafodyrynys 130 B3
Haggate 193 E4
Haggbeck 218 C4
Haggerston 136 C4
Haggerston N'umb 229 E2
Haggrister 278 C5
Haggs 234 C2
Hagley Here 145 E3
Hagley Worcs 158 B4
Hagnaby Lincs 176 B1
Hagnaby Lincs 189 E5
Hague Bar 185 D4
Hagworthingham 176 B1
Haigh 184 A2
Haigh Hall Country Park
  GtMan
  WN2 1PE 183 G2
Haighton Green 192 B4
Hail Weston 149 G1
Haile 198 B2
Hailes 146 C4
Hailey Herts 136 C1
Hailey Oxon 134 B4
Hailey Oxon 133 F1
Hailsham 110 A3
Haimer 275 G2
Hainault 137 D3
Hainault Forest Country
  Park Essex
  IG7 4QN 137 D3
Haine 125 F2
Hainford 178 D4
Hainton 188 B4
Haisthorpe 196 D1
Hakin 126 B2
Halam 174 B2
Halbeath 235 F1
Halberton 102 D1
Halcro 275 G3
Hale GtMan 184 B4
Hale Halton 183 F4
Hale Hants 106 A1
Hale Surr 120 D3
Hale Bank 183 F4
Hale Barns 184 B4
Hale Nook 191 G3
Hale Street 123 F4
Hales Norf 165 E2
Hales Staffs 171 E4
Hales Green 172 C3
Hales Place 124 D3
Halesgate 176 B5
Halesowen 158 B4
Halesworth 165 E4
Halewood 183 F4
Half Way Inn 102 B3
Halford Devon 102 B5
Halford Shrop 156 D4
Halford Warks 147 E3
Halfpenny 199 G4
Halfpenny Green 158 A3
Halfway Carmar 142 C4
Halfway Carmar 128 B2
Halfway Powys 143 E4
Halfway WBerks 119 F1
Halfway SYorks 186 B4
Halfway Bridge 121 E5
Halfway House 156 C1
Halfway Houses
  Kent 124 B1
Halfway Houses
  Lincs 175 D1
Halghton Mill 170 B3
Halifax 193 G5
Halistra 263 H6
Halket 233 F4
Halkirk 275 G3
Halkyn 182 D5
Hall 233 F4
Hall Cross 192 A5
Hall Dunnerdale 198 D3
Hall Green ChesE 171 F2
Hall Green Lancs 192 A5
Hall Green WMid 158 D4
Hall Grove 136 B1
Hall of the Forest 156 B4
Halland 110 A2
Hallaton 160 C3
Hallatrow 116 D2

Hallbankgate 210 B2
Hallen 131 E4
Hallfield Gate 173 E2
Hallglen 234 C2
Hallin 263 H6
Halling 123 G2
Hallington Lincs 188 D4
Hallington N'umb 220 B4
Halliwell 184 A1
Halloughton 174 B2
Hallow 146 A2
Hallow Heath 146 A2
Hallrule 227 G4
Halls 237 D2
Halls Green Essex 136 D2
Hall's Green Herts 150 A5
Hallsands 101 E4
Hallthwaites 198 C4
Hallwood Green 145 F4
Hallworthy 97 F1
Hallyne 235 F5
Halmer End 171 E3
Halmond's Frome 145 F3
Halmore 131 F2
Halmyre Mains 235 F5
Halnaker 108 A3
Halsall 183 E1
Halse Som 115 E5
Halse WN'hants 148 A3
Halsetown 94 C3
Halsham 197 E5
Halsinger 113 F2
Halstead Essex 151 G4
Halstead Kent 123 D2
Halstead Leics 160 C2
Halstock 104 B2
Halsway 115 E4
Haltemprice Farm 196 C4
Haltham 176 A1
Haltoft End 176 B3
Halton Bucks 135 D1
Halton Halton 183 G4
Halton Lancs 192 B1
Halton N'umb 211 F1
Halton Wrex 170 A4
Halton East 193 G2
Halton Gill 201 D5
Halton Green 192 B1
Halton Holegate 176 C1
Halton Lea Gate 210 C2
Halton Park 192 B1
Halton West 193 E2
Haltwhistle 210 D1
Halvergate 179 F5
Halwell 101 D2
Halwill 99 E1
Halwill Junction 99 E1
Ham Glos 131 F2
Ham Glos 146 B5
Ham GtLon 136 A5
Ham High 275 H1
Ham Kent 125 F3
Ham Plym 100 A2
Ham Shet 278 B1
Ham Som 115 F5
Ham Som 103 F1
Ham Wilts 119 E1
Ham Common 117 F5
Ham Green Here 145 G3
Ham Green Kent 124 A2
Ham Green Kent 111 D1
Ham Green NSom 131 E5
Ham Green Worcs 146 C1
Ham Hill 123 F2
Ham Hill Country Park
  Som TA14 6RW 104 A1
Ham Street 116 C4
Hambleden 134 C4
Hambledon Hants 107 F3
Hambledon Surr 121 E4
Hamble-le-Rice 107 D2
Hambleton Lancs 191 G3
Hambleton NYorks 195 E4
Hambridge 116 A5
Hambrook SGlos 131 F5
Hambrook WSuss 107 G2
Hameringham 176 B1
Hamerton 161 G4
Hamilton 234 B4
Hamilton's Bawn 282 C4
Hamlet Devon 103 F3
Hamlet Dorset 104 B2
Hammer 121 D4
Hammerpot 108 C3
Hammersmith 136 B5
Hammersmith Apollo
  GtLon W6 9QH 11 B5
Hammerwich 158 C2
Hammerwood 122 D5
Hammond Street 136 C2
Hammoon 105 E1
Hamnavoe Shet 279 C9
Hamnavoe Shet 278 B4
Hamnavoe Shet 278 B3
Hamnavoe Shet 278 D5
Hamnish Clifford 145 E2
Hamp 115 F4
Hampden Park 110 B3
Hampden Park Stadium
  Glas G42 9BA 30 D4
Hamperden End 151 D4
Hampnett 132 C1
Hampole 186 C2
Hampreston 105 G3
Hampstead 136 B4
Hampstead
  Norreys 134 A4
Hampsthwaite 194 B2
Hampton Devon 103 F3
Hampton GtLon 121 G1
Hampton Kent 125 D2
Hampton Peter 161 G3
Hampton Shrop 157 G4
Hampton Swin 133 D3
Hampton Worcs 146 C3
Hampton Bishop 145 E4
Hampton Court Palace &
  Garden GtLon
  KT8 9AU 11 B8
Hampton Fields 132 A3
Hampton Heath 170 B3
Hampton in Arden 159 E4
Hampton Lovett 146 A1
Hampton Lucy 147 E2
Hampton on the Hill
  147 E1

Hampton Poyle **134** A1
Hampton Wick **121** G1
Hamptworth **106** B1
Hamsey **109** G2
Hamstall Ridware **158** D1
Hamstead **106** C3
Hamstead Marshall **119** F1
Hamsteels **212** A4
Hamsterley *Dur* **212** A4
Hamsterley *Dur* **212** A2
Hamsterley Forest *Dur*
  DL13 3NL **211** G5
Hamstreet **124** C5
Hamworthy **105** F3
Hanbury *Staffs* **172** C5
Hanbury *Worcs* **146** B1
Hanbury Woodend **172** C5
Hanby **175** F4
Hanchurch **171** F3
Handa Island **272** D4
Handale **203** G1
Handbridge **170** B1
Handcross **122** B5
Handforth **184** C4
Handley *ChesW&C* **170** B2
Handley *Derbys* **173** E1
Handley Green **137** F2
Handsacre **158** D1
Handside **136** B1
Handsworth *SYorks* **186** B4
Handsworth *WMid* **158** C3
Handwoodbank **156** D1
Handy Cross **135** D3
Hanford *Dorset* **105** E1
Hanford *Stoke* **171** F3
Hanging Bridge **172** C3
Hanging Houghton **160** C5
Hanging Langford **118** B4
Hangingshaw **217** F2
Hanham **131** F5
Hankelow **171** D3
Hankerton **132** B3
Hankham **110** B3
Hanley **171** F3
Hanley Castle **146** A3
Hanley Child **145** F1
Hanley Swan **146** A3
Hanley William **145** F1
Hanlith **193** F1
Hanmer **170** B4
Hannah **189** E5
Hannahstown **283** F1
Hannington *Hants* **119** G2
Hannington *Swin* **133** D2
Hannington *WN'hants*
  160 D5
Hannington Wick **133** D3
Hanslope **148** D3
Hanthorpe **175** F5
Hanwell *GtLon* **136** A4
Hanwell *Oxon* **147** G3
Hanwood **156** D2
Hanworth *GtLon* **136** A5
Hanworth *Norf* **178** C2
Happisburgh **179** E2
Happisburgh
  Common **179** E3
Hapsford **183** F5
Hapton *Lancs* **193** D4
Hapton *Norf* **164** C2
Harberton **101** D2
Harbertonford **101** D2
Harbledown **124** D3
Harborne **158** C4
Harborough Magna **159** G5
Harbottle **220** B1
Harbour Park Amusements,
  Littlehampton *WSuss*
  BN17 5LL **108** C3
Harbourneford **100** D1
Harbridge **106** A1
Harbridge Green **106** A1
Harburn **235** E3
Harbury **147** F2
Harby *Leics* **174** C4
Harby *Notts* **187** F5
Harcombe **103** E3
Harcombe Bottom **103** G3
Harden *WMid* **158** C2
Harden *WYorks* **193** G4
Hardendale **199** G1
Hardenhuish **132** B5
Hardgate *Aber* **261** F4
Hardgate *NYorks* **194** B1
Hardham **108** C2
Hardhorn **191** G4
Hardingham **178** B5
Hardingstone **148** C2
Hardington **117** E2
Hardington
  Mandeville **104** B1
Hardington Marsh **104** A1
Hardington Moor **104** B1
Hardley **106** D2
Hardley Street **179** E5
Hardmead **149** E3
Hardraw **201** D3
Hardstoft **173** F1
Hardway *Hants* **107** F2
Hardway *Som* **117** E4
Hardwick *Bucks* **134** D1
Hardwick *Cambs* **150** B2
Hardwick *Lincs* **187** F5
Hardwick *NN'hants*
  149 D1
Hardwick *Norf* **164** D2
Hardwick *Oxon* **133** D2
Hardwick *Oxon* **148** A5
Hardwick *SYorks* **186** B4
Hardwick *WMid* **158** C3
Hardwick Hall *Derbys*
  S44 5QJ **173** F1
Hardwick Hall Country Park,
  Sedgefield *Dur*
  TS21 2EH **212** C5
Hardwick Village **186** D5
Hardwicke *Glos* **146** B5
Hardwicke *Glos* **131** G1
Hardwicke *Here* **144** B3
Hardy's Green **152** A4
Hare Green **152** B5
Hare Hatch **134** C4
Hare Street *Herts* **150** B5
Hare Street *Herts* **150** B5
Hareby **176** B1
Harecroft **193** G4
Hareden **192** C3
Harefield **135** F3

Harehill **172** C4
Harehills **194** C4
Harehope **229** E4
Harelaw **234** D5
Hareplain **124** A5
Haresceugh **210** C3
Harescombe **132** A1
Haresfield **132** A1
Hareshaw *NLan* **234** C3
Hareshaw *SLan* **234** A5
Harestock **119** F4
Harewood **194** C3
Harewood End **145** E5
Harewood House *WYorks*
  LS17 9LG **194** C3
Harford *Devon* **100** C2
Harford *Devon* **102** B3
Hargate **164** C2
Hargatewall **185** F5
Hargrave *ChesW&C* **170** B1
Hargrave *NN'hants* **161** F5
Hargrave *Suff* **151** F2
Hargrave Green **151** F2
Harker **218** A5
Harkstead **152** C4
Harlaston **159** E1
Harlaxton **175** D4
Harle Syke **193** E4
Harlech **167** E4
Harlech Castle
  (Castles & Town Walls of
  King Edward in Gwynedd)
  Gwyn LL46 2YH **167** E4
Harlequin **174** B4
Harlescott **157** E1
Harlesden **136** B4
Harleston *Devon* **101** D3
Harleston *Norf* **164** D3
Harleston *Suff* **152** B1
Harlestone **148** C1
Harley *Shrop* **157** E2
Harley *SYorks* **186** A3
Harleyholm **226** A2
Harlington
  CenBeds **149** F4
Harlington *GtLon* **135** F5
Harlosh **263** H7
Harlow **136** D2
Harlow Hill **211** G1
Harlthorpe **195** G4
Harlton **150** B2
Harlyn **96** C2
Harman's Cross **105** F4
Harmby **202** A4
Harmer Green **136** B1
Harmer Hill **170** B5
Harmondsworth **135** F5
Harmston **175** E1
Harnage **157** E2
Harnham **118** C5
Harnhill **132** C2
Harold Hill **137** E3
Harold Park **137** E3
Harold Wood **137** E3
Haroldston West **126** B1
Haroldswick **278** F1
Harome **203** F4
Harpenden **136** A1
Harpford **103** D3
Harpham **196** C1
Harpley *Norf* **177** F5
Harpley *Worcs* **145** F1
Harpole **148** B1
Harprigg **200** B4
Harpsdale **275** G3
Harpsden **134** C4
Harpswell **187** G4
Harpur Hill **185** E5
Harpurhey **184** C2
Harracott **113** F3
Harrapool **256** C2
Harrietfield **243** E2
Harrietsham **124** A3
Harringay **136** C4
Harrington *Cumb* **208** C4
Harrington *Lincs* **189** D5
Harrington *NN'hants*
  160 C5
Harringworth **161** E3
Harris **255** J5
Harris Green **164** D2
Harris Museum & Art
  Gallery, Preston *Lancs*
  PR1 2PP **192** B5
Harriseahead **171** F2
Harriston **209** E2
Harrogate **194** C2
Harrogate Convention
  Centre *NYorks* HG1 5LA
  74 Harrogate
Harrold **149** E2
Harrold-Odell Country Park
  Bed MK43 7DS **149** E2
Harrop Fold **192** D3
Harrow *GtLon* **136** A4
Harrow *High* **275** H1
Harrow Green **151** G2
Harrow Museum *GtLon*
  HA2 6PX **10** B1
Harrow on the Hill
  136 A4
Harrow Weald **136** A3
Harrowbarrow **99** E3
Harrowden **149** F3
Harrowgate Hill **202** B1
Harry Stoke **131** F5
Harston *Cambs* **150** C2
Harston *Leics* **174** D4
Harswell **196** A3
Hart **213** D4
Hartburn **220** C3
Hartest **151** G2
Hartfield *ESuss* **123** D5
Hartfield *High* **264** D7
Hartford *Cambs* **162** A5
Hartford *ChesW&C* **184** A5
Hartford *Som* **114** C5
Hartford End **137** F1
Hartfordbridge **120** C2
Hartforth **202** A2
Hartgrove **105** E1
Harthill *ChesW&C* **170** C2
Harthill *NLan* **234** D3
Harthill *SYorks* **186** B4
Hartington **172** C1
Hartington Hall **220** C3
Hartland **112** C3
Hartland Quay **112** C3

Hartlebury **158** A5
Hartlepool **213** E4
Hartlepool's Maritime
  Experience *Hart*
  TS24 0XZ **213** E4
Hartley *Cumb* **200** C2
Hartley *Kent* **123** F2
Hartley *Kent* **123** G5
Hartley Green **171** G5
Hartley *Staffs* **171** F5
Hartley Mauditt **120** B2
Hartley Wespall **120** B2
Hartley Wintney **120** C2
Hartlington **193** G1
Hartlip **124** A2
Hartoft End **203** G3
Harton *NYorks* **195** G1
Harton *Shrop* **157** D4
Harton *T&W* **212** C1
Hartpury **146** A5
Hartrigg **228** A4
Hartshead **194** A5
Hartshill **159** F3
Hartsholme Country Park
  Lincs LN6 0EY **175** E1
Hartshorne **173** E5
Hartsop **199** F1
Hartwell *Bucks* **134** C1
Hartwell *NN'hants* **148** C2
Hartwith **194** B1
Hartwood **234** C4
Harvel **123** F2
Harvington *Worcs* **146** C3
Harvington *Worcs* **158** A5
Harwell *Notts* **187** D3
Harwell *Oxon* **133** G4
Harwich **152** D4
Harwood *Dur* **211** E4
Harwood *GtMan* **184** B1
Harwood *N'umb* **220** D3
Harwood Dale **204** C3
Harwood on
  Teviot **227** F5
Harworth **186** D3
Hasbury **158** B4
Hascombe **121** F3
Haselbech **160** C5
Haseley
  Plucknett **104** A1
Haseley **147** E1
Haseley Knob **159** E5
Haselor **146** D2
Hasfield **146** A5
Hasguard **126** B2
Haskayne **183** E2
Hasketon **153** D2
Hasland **173** E1
Hasland Green **173** E1
Haslemere **121** E4
Haslingden **193** D5
Haslingden Grane **193** D5
Haslingfield **150** C2
Haslington **171** E2
Hassall **171** E2
Hassall Green **171** E2
Hassell Street **124** C4
Hassendean **227** G3
Hassingham **179** E5
Hassocks **109** F2
Hassop **185** G5
Haster **275** J3
Hasthorpe **176** C1
Hastigrow **275** H2
Hastingleigh **124** C4
Hastings *ESuss* **110** D3
Hastings *Som* **103** G1
Hastings Fishermen's
  Museum *ESuss*
  TN34 3DW **75** Hastings
Hastingwood **137** D2
Hastoe **135** E2
Haswell **212** C3
Haswell Plough **212** C3
Hatch *CenBeds* **149** G3
Hatch *Hants* **120** B2
Hatch Beauchamp **116** A5
Hatch End **136** A3
Hatch Green **103** G1
Hatching Green **136** A1
Hatchmere **183** G5
Hatcliffe **188** C2
Hatfield *Here* **145** E2
Hatfield *Herts* **136** B2
Hatfield *SYorks* **187** D2
Hatfield Broad Oak **137** E1
Hatfield Heath **137** E1
Hatfield House *Herts*
  AL9 5NF **136** B2
Hatfield
  Woodhouse **187** D2
Hatford **133** F3
Hatherden **119** E2
Hatherleigh **113** F5
Hathern **173** F5
Hatherop **133** D2
Hathersage **185** G4
Hathersage Booths
  185 G4
Hathershaw **184** D2
Hatherton *ChesE* **171** D3
Hatherton *Staffs* **158** B1
Hatley St. George **150** A2
Hatt **99** D4
Hattingley **120** B4
Hatton *Aber* **261** J1
Hatton *Derbys* **172** D5
Hatton *GtLon* **136** A5
Hatton *Lincs* **188** B5
Hatton *Shrop* **157** D3
Hatton *Warks* **147** E1
Hatton Castle **269** F6
Hatton Country World
  Warks CV35 8XA
  147 E1
Hatton Heath **170** B1
Hatton of Fintray **261** G3
Hattoncrook **261** G2
Haugh **189** E5
Haugh Head **229** E4
Haugh of Glass **260** C1
Haugh of Urr **216** C4
Haugham **188** D4
Haughhead **234** A2
Haughley **152** B1
Haughley Green **152** B1

Haughley New
  Street **152** B1
Haughs **268** D6
Haughton *ChesE* **170** C2
Haughton *Notts* **187** D5
Haughton *Powys* **156** C1
Haughton *Shrop* **157** F3
Haughton *Shrop* **157** E1
Haughton *Shrop* **170** A5
Haughton *Staffs* **171** F5
Haughton Green **184** D3
Haughton Le Skerne **202** C1
Haultwick **150** B5
Haunn **254** C3
Haunton **159** E1
Hauxton **150** C2
Havannah **171** F1
Havant **107** G2
Haven **144** D2
Havenstreet **107** E3
Havercroft **186** A1
Haverfordwest
  (Hwlffordd) **126** C1
Haverhill **151** E3
Haverigg **198** C5
Havering Park **137** D3
Havering-atte-
  Bower **137** E3
Haversham **148** D3
Haverthwaite **199** E4
Haverton Hill **213** D5
Haviker Street **123** G4
Havyat **116** C4
Hawarden
  (Penarlâg) **170** A1
Hawbridge **146** B3
Hawbush Green **151** F5
Hawcoat **198** D5
Hawes **201** D4
Hawe's Green **164** D2
Hawick **227** G4
Hawkchurch **103** G2
Hawkedon **151** F2
Hawkenbury *Kent* **123** E5
Hawkenbury *Kent* **124** A4
Hawkeridge **117** F2
Hawkerland **103** D4
Hawkes End **159** E4
Hawkesbury *Notts* **131** G4
Hawkesbury
  Upton **131** G4
Hawkhill **229** G5
Hawkhurst **123** G5
Hawkinge **125** E4
Hawkley **120** C5
Hawkridge **114** B4
Hawkshead **199** E3
Hawkshead Hill **199** E3
Hawksheads **192** A1
Hawksland **234** A1
Hawkswick **201** E5
Hawksworth *Notts* **174** C3
Hawksworth
  WYorks **194** A3
Hawkwell *Essex* **138** B3
Hawkwell *N'umb* **220** C4
Hawley *Hants* **121** D2
Hawley *Kent* **137** E5
Hawley's Corner **122** D3
Hawling **146** C5
Hawnby **203** E4
Haworth **193** G4
Hawstead **151** G2
Hawstead Green **151** G2
Hawthorn *Dur* **212** D3
Hawthorn *Hants* **120** B4
Hawthorn *RCT* **129** G4
Hawthorn *Wilts* **117** F1
Hawthorn Hill
  BrackF **135** D5
Hawthorn Hill
  Lincs **176** A2
Hawthorpe **175** F5
Hawton **174** C2
Haxby **195** F2
Haxey **187** E2
Haxted **122** D4
Haxton **118** C3
Hay Green **162** D1
Hay Mills **158** D4
Hay Street **150** B5
Haydock **183** G3
Haydon *Dorset* **104** C1
Haydon *Swin* **132** D4
Haydon Bridge **211** E1
Haydon Wick **132** D4
Hayes *GtLon* **135** F4
Hayes *GtLon* **122** D2
Hayes End **135** F4
Hayfield *A&B* **240** C2
Hayfield *Derbys* **185** E4
Hayfield *Fife* **244** A5
Hayfield *High* **275** G2
Haygrove **115** F4
Hayhillock **252** D5
Hayle **94** C3
Hayling Island **107** G2
Haymoor Green **171** D2
Hayne **102** C1
Haynes **149** G3
Haynes Church End **149** F3
Haynes West End **149** F3
Hay-on-Wye (Y Gelli
  Gandryll) **144** B3
Hayscastle **140** B5
Hayscastle Cross **140** C5
Hayton *Cumb* **210** B2
Hayton *Cumb* **209** E2
Hayton *ERid* **196** A3
Hayton *Notts* **187** E4
Hayton's Bent **157** E4
Haytor Vale **102** A5
Haytown **113** D4

Hazelside **225** G3
Hazelslack **199** F5
Hazelslade **158** C1
Hazelton Walls **244** B2
Hazelwood *Derbys* **173** E3
Hazelwood *GtLon* **122** D2
Hazlefield **208** A2
Hazlehead *Aber* **261** G4
Hazlehead *SYorks* **185** F2
Hazlemere **135** D2
Hazlerigg **221** E4
Hazleton **132** C1
Hazon **221** D1
Heacham **177** E4
Head Bridge **113** G4
Headbourne
  Worthy **119** F4
Headcorn **124** A4
Headingley **194** B4
Headington **134** A2
Headlam **202** A1
Headless Cross **146** C1
Headley *Hants* **120** D4
Headley *Hants* **119** G1
Headley *Surr* **122** B3
Headley Down **120** D4
Headley Heath **158** C5
Headon **187** E5
Heads Nook **210** A2
Heady Hill **184** C1
Heage **173** E2
Healabhal Bheag **263** H7
Healaugh *NYorks* **201** F3
Healaugh *NYorks* **195** E3
Heald Green **184** C4
Heale *Devon* **113** G1
Heale *Som* **116** A5
Healey *Lancs* **184** C1
Healey *N'umb* **211** G2
Healey *NYorks* **202** A4
Healey *WYorks* **194** B5
Healeyfield **211** G3
Healing **188** C1
Heamoor **94** B3
Heaning **199** F3
Heanish **246** B2
Heanor **173** F3
Heanton
  Punchardon **113** F2
Heanton Satchville **113** F4
Heap Bridge **184** C1
Heapey **192** C5
Heapham **187** F4
Hearn **120** D4
Heart of Neolithic Orkney
  Ork **277** C6
Heart of the Country
  Centre *Staffs*
  WS14 9QR **158** D2
Hearthstane **226** C3
Heasley Mill **114** A4
Heast **256** C3
Heath *Cardiff* **130** A4
Heath *Derbys* **173** F1
Heath *WYorks* **186** A1
Heath & Reach **149** E5
Heath End *Derbys* **173** E5
Heath End *Hants* **119** G1
Heath End *Hants* **119** F1
Heath End *Surr* **120** D3
Heath Hayes **158** C1
Heath Hill **157** G1
Heath House **116** B3
Heath Town **158** B3
Heathbrook **170** D5
Heathcote *Derbys* **172** C1
Heathcote *Shrop* **171** D5
Heathencote **148** C3
Heather **159** F1
Heatherton Activity Park
  Pembs
  SA70 8RJ **127** D2
Heathfield *Devon* **102** B5
Heathfield *ESuss* **110** A1
Heathfield *NYorks* **194** A1
Heathfield *Som* **115** E5
Heathrow Airport **135** F5
Heathton **158** A3
Heatley **184** B4
Heaton *Lancs* **192** A1
Heaton *Staffs* **171** G1
Heaton *T&W* **212** B1
Heaton *WYorks* **194** A4
Heaton Moor **184** C3
Heaton Park *GtMan*
  M25 2SW **25** E2
Heaton's Bridge **183** F1
Heaverham **123** E3
Heaviley **184** D4
Heavitree **102** C3
Hebburn **212** C1
Hebden **193** G1
Hebden Bridge **193** G5
Hebden Green **170** D1
Hebing End **150** B5
Hebron *Carmar* **141** E5
Hebron *N'umb* **221** D3
Heck **217** E2
Heckfield **120** C1
Heckfield Green **164** C4
Heckfordbridge **152** A5
Heckington **165** E2
Heckmondwike **194** B5
Heddington **118** A1
Heddle **277** C6
Heddon-on-the-
  Wall **212** A1
Hedenham **165** E2
Hedge End **107** D1
Hedgerley **135** E4
Hedging **116** A5
Hedley on the Hill **211** G2
Hednesford **158** C1
Hedon **197** D5
Hedsor **135** E4
Heeley **186** A4
Heglibister **279** C7
Heighington *Darl* **212** B5
Heighington *Lincs* **175** F1
Heightington **157** G5
Heiton **228** B3
Hele *Devon* **113** F1
Hele *Devon* **102** C2
Hele *Devon* **98** D1
Hele *Devon* **102** A5
Hele *Som* **115** E5
Hele *Torbay* **101** F1
Hele Bridge **113** F5
Hele Lane **102** A1
Helebridge **112** C5
Helensburgh **233** D1
Helford **95** E4
Helford Passage **95** E4
Helhoughton **177** G5
Helions Bumpstead **151** E3
Hell Corner **119** E1
Hellaby **186** C3
Helland *Corn* **97** F3
Helland *Som* **116** A5
Hellandbridge **97** E2
Hellesdon **178** D4
Hellidon **148** A2
Hellifield **193** F2
Hellingly **110** A2
Hellington **179** E5
Hellister **279** C8
Helmdon **148** A3
Helmingham **152** C2
Helmington Row **212** A4
Helmsdale **275** F7
Helmshore **193** D5
Helmsley **203** F4
Helperby **194** D1
Helperthorpe **204** C5
Helpringham **175** G3
Helpston **161** G2
Helsby **183** F5
Helsey **189** F5
Helston **95** D4
Helstone **97** E1
Helton **210** B5
Helwith **201** F2
Helwith Bridge **193** E1
Hem **156** B2
Hemborough Post **101** E2
Hemel Hempstead **135** F2
Hemerdon **100** B2
Hemingbrough **195** F4
Hemingby **188** C5
Hemingfield **186** A2
Hemingford Abbots **162** A5
Hemingford Grey **162** A5
Hemingstone **152** C2
Hemington *Leics* **173** F5
Hemington
  N'hants **161** F4
Hemington *Som* **117** E2
Hemley **153** D3
Hemlington **203** D1
Hemp Green **153** E1
Hempholme **196** C2
Hempnall **164** D2
Hempnall Green **164** D2
Hempriggs **267** J5
Hempriggs House **275** J4
Hempstead *Essex* **151** E4
Hempstead *Med* **123** G2
Hempstead *Norf* **179** E3
Hempstead *Norf* **178** C2
Hempsted **132** A1
Hempton *Norf* **178** A3
Hempton *Oxon* **147** G4
Hemsby **179** F4
Hemswell **187** G3
Hemswell Cliff **187** G4
Hemsworth **186** B1
Hemyock **103** E2
Henbury *Bristol* **131** E5
Henbury *ChesE* **184** C5
Henderland **216** C3
Hendersyde Park **228** B3
Hendham **100** D2
Hendon *GtLon* **136** B4
Hendon *T&W* **212** C2
Hendraburnick **97** F1
Hendre *Bridgend* **129** F4
Hendre *Gwyn* **166** C4
Hendreforgan **129** F4
Heneglwys **180** C5
Henfield *SGlos* **131** F5
Henfield *WSuss* **109** E2
Henford **99** D1
Hengherst **124** B5
Hengoed *Caerp* **130** A3
Hengoed *Powys* **144** B2
Hengoed *Shrop* **169** F4
Hengrave **151** G1
Henham **150** D5
Heniarth **156** A2
Henlade **115** F5
Henley *Dorset* **104** C2
Henley *Shrop* **157** E5
Henley *Som* **116** B4
Henley *Som* **104** A2
Henley *Suff* **152** C2
Henley *WSuss* **121** D5
Henley Corner **116** B4
Henley Park **121** E2
Henley-in-Arden **147** D1
Henley-on-Thames **134** C4
Henley's Down **110** C2
Henllan *Carmar* **141** G3
Henllan *Denb* **168** D1
Henllan Amgoed **141** E5
Henllys **130** B3
Henlow **149** G4
Hennock **102** B4
Henny Street **151** G4
Henryd **181** F5
Henry's Moat **140** D5
Hensall **195** E5
Henshaw **211** D1
Hensingham **208** C5
Henstead **165** F3
Hensting **119** F5
Henstridge **104** D1
Henstridge Ash **104** D1
Henstridge
  Bowden **117** D5
Henton *Oxon* **134** C2
Henton *Som* **116** B3
Henwood **97** G2
Heogan **279** D8
Heol Senni **143** F5
Heolgerrig **129** G2
Heol-y-cyw **129** F4
Hepburn **229** E4

Hepburn Bell **229** E4
Hepple **220** B1
Hepscott **221** E3
Hepthorne Lane **173** F1
Heptonstall **193** F5
Hepworth *Suff* **164** A4
Hepworth *WYorks* **185** F2
Hepworth South
  Common **164** A4
Herbrandston **126** B2
Hereford **145** E3
Hereford Cathedral
  Here HR1 2NG
  75 Hereford
Heriot **236** A4
Heritage Motor Centre,
  Gaydon *Warks*
  CV35 0BJ **147** F2
Herm **101** G3
Hermiston **235** F2
Hermitage *D&G* **216** B4
Hermitage *Dorset* **104** C2
Hermitage *ScBord* **218** D3
Hermitage *WBerks* **134** A5
Hermitage *WSuss* **107** G2
Hermitage Green **184** A3
Hermon *Carmar* **141** G4
Hermon *IoA* **166** C1
Hermon *Pembs* **141** F4
Herne **125** D2
Herne Bay **125** D2
Herne Common **125** D2
Herne Pound **123** F3
Herner **113** F3
Hernhill **124** C2
Herodsfoot **97** G3
Herongate **137** F3
Heron's Ghyll **109** G1
Heronsgate **135** F3
Herriard **120** B3
Herringfleet **165** F2
Herring's Green **149** F3
Herringswell **151** F1
Herringthorpe **186** B3
Hersden **125** D2
Hersham *Corn* **112** C5
Hersham *Surr* **121** G1
Herstmonceux **110** B2
Herston **277** D8
Hertford **136** C1
Hertford Heath **136** C1
Hertingfordbury **136** C1
Hesket Newmarket
  209 H3
Hesketh Bank **192** A5
Hesketh Lane **192** C3
Heskin Green **183** G1
Hesleden **212** D4
Hesleyside **220** A3
Heslington **195** F2
Hessay **195** E2
Hessenford **98** D5
Hessett **152** A1
Hessle **196** C5
Hest Bank **192** A1
Hester's Way **146** B1
Hestley Green **152** C1
Heston **136** A5
Heswall **183** D4
Hethe **148** A5
Hethelpit Cross **145** G5
Hetherington **220** A4
Hethersett **178** C5
Hethersgill **210** A1
Hethpool **228** C4
Hett **212** B4
Hetton **193** F2
Hetton-le-Hole **212** C3
Heugh **220** C4
Heugh-head *Aber* **260** B3
Heugh-head *Aber* **260** D5
Heveningham **165** E4
Hever **123** D4
Hever Castle & Gardens
  Kent TN8 7NG **123** D4
Heversham **199** F4
Hevingham **178** C3
Hewas Water **97** D5
Hewell Grange **146** C1
Hewell Lane **146** C1
Hewelsfield **131** E2
Hewelsfield
  Common **131** E2
Hewish *NSom* **116** B1
Hewish *Som* **104** A2
Hewood **103** G2
Heworth **195** F2
Hewton **99** F1
Hexham **211** F1
Hexham Abbey *N'umb*
  NE46 3JN **211** F1
Hextable **137** E5
Hexthorpe **186** C2
Hexton **149** G4
Hexworthy **99** G3
Hey **193** E3
Hey Houses **191** G5
Heybridge *Essex* **137** G3
Heybridge *Essex* **138** B2
Heybridge Basin **138** B2
Heybrook Bay **100** A3
Heydon *Cambs* **150** C3
Heydon *Norf* **178** C3
Heydour **175** F4
Heylipoll **246** A2
Heylor **278** B4
Heyop **156** B5
Heysham **192** A1
Heyshaw **194** A1
Heyshott **108** A2
Heyside **184** D2
Heytesbury **118** A3
Heythrop **147** F5
Heywood *GtMan* **184** C1
Heywood *Wilts* **117** F2
Hibaldstow **187** G2
Hibb's Green **151** G2
Hickleton **186** B2
Hickling *Norf* **179** F3
Hickling *Notts* **174** B5
Hickling Green **179** F3
Hickling Heath **179** F3
Hickstead **109** E1
Hidcote Bartrim **147** D3
Hidcote Boyce **147** D3
Hidcote Manor Garden
  Glos GL55 6LR **147** D3
High Ackworth **186** B1

305

High Angerton 220 C3
High Balantyre 240 C3
High Bankhill 210 B3
High Beach 136 D3
High Bentham (Higher
  Bentham) 192 C1
High Bickington 113 F3
High Birkwith 200 C5
High Blantyre 234 A4
High Bonnybridge 234 C2
High Borgue 216 A5
High Borve (Bail Àrd Bhuirgh)
  271 G2
High Bradfield 185 G3
High Bradley 193 G3
High Bransholme 196 D4
High Bray 113 G2
High Bridge 209 G2
High Brooms 123 E4
High Bullen 113 F3
High Burton 202 B4
High Buston 221 E1
High Callerton 221 D4
High Casterton 200 B5
High Catton 195 G2
High Close 202 A1
High Cogges 133 F2
High Common 164 C3
High Coniscliffe 202 B1
High Crompton 184 D2
High Cross Hants 120 C5
High Cross Herts 136 C1
High Cross WSuss 109 E2
High Easter 137 F1
High Ellington 202 A4
High Entercommon
  202 C2
High Ercall 157 E1
High Etherley 212 A5
High Ferry 176 B3
High Flatts 185 G2
High Garrett 151 F5
High Gate 193 F5
High Grange 212 A4
High Green Norf 178 C5
High Green Norf 178 A4
High Green Norf 178 A5
High Green Suff 151 G1
High Green SYorks 186 A3
High Green Worcs 146 A3
High Halden 124 A5
High Halstow 137 G5
High Ham 116 B4
High Harrington 208 D4
High Harrogate 194 C2
High Hatton 170 D5
High Hauxley 221 E1
High Hawsker 204 C2
High Heath Shrop 171 D5
High Heath WMid 158 C2
High Hesket 210 A3
High Hesleden 213 D4
High Hoyland 185 G1
High Hunsley 196 B4
High Hurstwood 109 G1
High Hutton 195 G1
High Ireby 209 F3
High Kelling 178 B2
High Kilburn 203 E5
High Kingthorpe 204 B4
High Knipe 199 G3
High Lane Derbys 173 F3
High Lane GtMan 185 D4
High Lane Worcs 145 F1
High Laver 137 E2
High Legh 184 B4
High Leven 203 D1
High Littleton 116 D2
High Lodge Forest Centre
  Suff IP27 0AF 163 G4
High Lorton 209 E4
High Marishes 204 B5
High Marnham 187 F5
High Melton 186 C2
High Moor 186 B4
High Moorland Visitor
  Centre, Princetown Devon
  PL20 6QF 99 F3
High Newton 199 F4
High Newton-by-the-
  Sea 229 G4
High Nibthwaite 199 D3
High Offley 171 E5
High Ongar 137 E2
High Onn 158 A1
High Park Corner 152 B5
High Roding 137 F1
High Shaw 201 D3
High Spen 212 A1
High Stoop 212 A3
High Street Corn 97 D4
High Street Kent 123 G5
High Street Suff 153 F2
High Street Suff 165 F4
High Street Suff 151 G3
High Street Green 152 B2
High Throston 213 D4
High Town 158 B1
High Toynton 176 A1
High Trewhitt 220 C1
High Wham 212 A5
High Wigsell 110 C1
High Woods Country Park
  Essex CO4 5JR 152 B5
High Woolaston 131 E3
High Worsall 202 C2
High Wray 199 E3
High Wych 197 D1
High Wycombe 135 G2
Higham Derbys 173 E2
Higham Kent 137 G5
Higham Lancs 193 E4
Higham Suff 151 F1
Higham Suff 152 B4
Higham SYorks 186 A2
Higham Borough 125 E2
Higham Dykes 220 D4
Higham Ferrers 149 E1
Higham Gobion 149 G4
Higham on the Hill 159 F3
Higham Wood 123 F4
Highampton 113 E5
Highams Park 136 C3
Highbridge Hants 119 F5
Highbridge Som 116 A3
Highbrook 122 C5
Highburton 185 F1
Highbury 117 D3

Highclere 119 F1
Highcliffe 106 B3
Higher Alham 117 D3
Higher Ansty 105 D2
Higher Ashton 102 B4
Higher Ballam 191 G4
Higher Bentham (High
  Bentham) 192 C1
Higher Blackley 184 C2
Higher Brixham 101 F2
Higher Cheriton 103 E2
Higher Combe 114 C4
Higher Folds 184 A2
Higher Gabwell 101 F1
Higher Green 184 B3
Higher Halstock
  Leigh 104 B2
Higher Kingcombe 104 B3
Higher Kinnerton 170 A1
Higher Muddiford 113 F2
Higher Nyland 117 E5
Higher Prestacott 99 D1
Higher Standen 193 D3
Higher Tale 103 D2
Higher Town Corn 97 E3
Higher Town IoS 96 B1
Higher Walreddon 99 E3
Higher Walton
  Lancs 192 B5
Higher Walton
  Warr 183 G4
Higher Wambrook 103 F2
Higher Whatcombe 105 E2
Higher Wheelton 192 C5
Higher Whiteleigh 98 C1
Higher Whitley 184 A4
Higher Wincham 184 A5
Higher Woodhill 184 B1
Higher Woodsford 105 D4
Higher Wraxall 104 B2
Higher Wych 170 B3
Highfield ERid 195 G4
Highfield NAyr 233 E4
Highfield Oxon 148 A5
Highfield SYorks 186 A4
Highfield T&W 212 A2
Highfields Cambs 150 B2
Highfields N'umb 237 G4
Highgate ESuss 122 D5
Highgate GtLon 136 B4
Highgreen Manor 220 A2
Highlane ChesE 171 F1
Highlane Derbys 186 B4
Highlaws 209 E2
Highleadon 145 G5
Highleigh Devon 114 C5
Highleigh WSuss 108 A4
Highley 157 G4
Highmead 142 B3
Highmoor Cross 134 B4
Highmoor Hill 131 D4
Highnam 146 A1
Highstead 125 E2
Highsted 124 B2
Highstreet Green
  Essex 151 F4
Highstreet Green
  Surr 121 E4
Hightae 217 E3
Highter's Heath 158 C5
Hightown A&N 287 H7
Hightown Hants 106 A3
Hightown Mersey 183 D2
Hightown Green 152 A2
Highway 132 C5
Highweek 102 B5
Highwood 145 F1
Highwood Hill 136 B3
Highworth 133 E3
Hilborough 163 G2
Hilcote 173 F2
Hilcott 118 C2
Hilden Park 123 E4
Hildenborough 123 E4
Hildenley 203 G5
Hildersham 150 D3
Hilderstone 171 G4
Hilderthorpe 197 D1
Hilfield 104 C2
Hilgay 163 E3
Hill SGlos 131 F3
Hill Warks 147 G1
Hill Worcs 146 B3
Hill Brow 120 C5
Hill Chorlton 171 E4
Hill Common 179 F3
Hill Cottages 203 G3
Hill Croome 146 A3
Hill Deverill 117 F3
Hill Dyke 176 B3
Hill End Dur 211 G4
Hill End Fife 243 F5
Hill End Glos 146 A4
Hill End GtLon 135 F3
Hill End NYorks 193 G2
Hill Green 150 C4
Hill Head 157 F5
Hill Houses 157 F5
Hill Mountain 126 C2
Hill of Beath 235 F1
Hill of Fearn 267 F4
Hill Ridware 158 C1
Hill Row 162 C5
Hill Side 185 F1
Hill Street 106 C3
Hill Top Hants 106 D2
Hill Top SYorks 186 B3
Hill Top SYorks 185 G4
Hill View 105 F3
Hill Wootton 147 F1
Hillam 195 E5
Hillbeck 200 C1
Hillberry 190 B4
Hillborough 125 E2
Hillbrae Aber 268 E6
Hillbrae Aber 261 F2
Hillbrae Aber 261 G1
Hillbutts 105 F2
Hillclifflane 173 D3
Hillend Aber 268 C6
Hillend Fife 235 F1
Hillend Midlo 235 G4
Hillend NLan 234 C3
Hillend Swan 128 A3
Hillend Green 145 G5
Hillersland 131 E1

Hillesden 148 B5
Hillesley 131 G4
Hillfarrance 115 E5
Hillfoot End 149 G4
Hillhall 283 F2
Hillhead Devon 101 F2
Hillhead Mid Ulster 286 D6
Hillhead SAyr 224 C3
Hillhead of
  Auchentumb 269 H5
Hillhead of
  Cocklaw 269 J6
Hilliard's Cross 159 D1
Hilliclay 275 G2
Hillingdon 135 F4
Hillington Glas 233 G3
Hillington Norf 177 F5
Hillmorton 160 A5
Hillockhead Aber 260 B4
Hillockhead Aber 260 C3
Hillowton 216 B4
Hillpound 107 E1
Hill's End 149 E4
Hills Town 173 F1
Hillsborough L&C
  283 F3
Hillsborough SYorks
  186 A3
Hillsborough Castle L&C
  BT26 6AG 283 F3
Hillsford Bridge 114 A3
Hillside Aber 261 H5
Hillside Angus 253 F3
Hillside Moray 267 J5
Hillside Shet 279 D6
Hillside Worcs 145 G1
Hillswick 278 B5
Hilltown 283 F6
Hillway 107 F4
Hillwell 279 F9
Hillyfields 106 C1
Hilmarton 132 C5
Hilperton 117 F2
Hilsea 107 F2
Hilston 197 E4
Hilton Cambs 150 A1
Hilton Cumb 210 D5
Hilton Derbys 172 D4
Hilton Dorset 105 D2
Hilton Dur 212 A5
Hilton High 267 G3
Hilton Shrop 157 G3
Hilton Staffs 158 C2
Hilton Stock 203 D1
Hilton Croft 261 H1
Hilton of Cadboll 267 F4
Hilton of Delnies 267 F6
Himbleton 146 B2
Himley 158 A3
Himley Hall & Park
  WMid DY3 4DF 14 A2
Hincaster 199 G4
Hinchley Wood 121 G1
Hinckley 159 G3
Hinderclay 164 B4
Hinderton 183 E5
Hinderwell 203 G1
Hindford 170 A4
Hindhead 121 D4
Hindley GtMan 184 A2
Hindley N'umb 211 G2
Hindley Green 184 A2
Hindlip 146 A2
Hindolveston 178 B3
Hindon Som 114 C3
Hindon Wilts 118 A4
Hindringham 178 A2
Hingham 178 B5
Hinksford 158 A4
Hinstock 171 D5
Hintlesham 152 B3
Hinton Glos 131 F2
Hinton Hants 106 B3
Hinton Here 144 C4
Hinton SGlos 131 G5
Hinton Shrop 156 D2
Hinton WN'hants 148 A2
Hinton Admiral 106 B3
Hinton Ampner 119 G5
Hinton Blewett 116 C2
Hinton
  Charterhouse 117 E2
Hinton Martell 105 G2
Hinton on the
  Green 146 C3
Hinton Parva
  Dorset 105 F2
Hinton Parva Swin 133 E4
Hinton St. George 104 A1
Hinton St. Mary 105 D1
Hinton Waldrist 133 F3
Hinton-in-the-
  Hedges 148 A4
Hints Shrop 157 F5
Hints Staffs 159 D2
Hinwick 149 E1
Hinxhill 124 C4
Hinxton 150 C3
Hinxworth 150 A3
Hipperholme 194 A5
Hipsburn 229 G5
Hipswell 202 A3
Hirn 261 F4
Hirnant 169 D5
Hirst 221 E3
Hirst Courtney 195 F5
Hirwaen 169 E1
Hirwaun 129 F2
Hiscott 113 F3
Histon 150 C1
Hitcham Bucks 135 E4
Hitcham Suff 152 A2
Hitchin 149 G5
Hither Green 136 C5
Hittisleigh 102 A3
Hittisleigh Barton 102 A3
Hive 196 A4
Hixon 172 B5
Hoaden 125 E3
Hoaldalbert 144 C5
Hoar Cross 172 C5
Hoar Park Craft Centre
  Warks
  CV10 0QU 159 E3
Hoarwithy 145 E5
Hoath 125 E2
Hobarris 156 C5
Hobbister 277 C7
Hobbs Cross 136 D2
Hobbs Cross 137 D3

Hobbledown Adventure Farm
  Park and Zoo Surr
  KT19 8PT 121 G1
Hobbles Green 151 F2
Hobbs Cross 136 D2
Hobbs Cross 137 D3
Hobbs Lots Bridge 162 B2
Hobkirk 227 G4
Hobland Hall 179 G5
Hoby 160 B1
Hockerill 150 C5
Hockering 178 B4
Hockerton 174 C2
Hockley AB&C 282 C4
Hockley Essex 138 B3
Hockley Heath 159 D5
Hockliffe 149 E5
Hockwold cum
  Wilton 163 F4
Hockworthy 102 D1
Hoddesdon 136 C2
Hoddlesden 192 D5
Hodgehill 171 F1
Hodgeston 126 D3
Hodnet 170 D5
Hodnetheath 170 D5
Hodsoll Street 123 F2
Hodson 133 D4
Hodthorpe 186 C5
Hoe 178 A4
Hoe Gate 107 F1
Hoff 200 B1
Hoffleet Stow 176 A4
Hoggard's Green 151 G2
Hoggeston 148 D5
Hoggie 268 D5
Hoggrill's End 159 E3
Hoghton 192 C5
Hognaston 172 D2
Hogsthorpe 189 F5
Holbeach 176 B5
Holbeach Bank 176 B5
Holbeach Clough 176 B5
Holbeach Drove 162 B1
Holbeach Hurn 176 B5
Holbeach St. Johns 162 B1
Holbeach St. Marks 176 B4
Holbeach St. Matthew 176 C4
Holbeck 186 C5
Holbeck
  Woodhouse 186 C5
Holberrow Green 146 C2
Holbeton 100 C2
Holborough 123 G2
Holbrook Derbys 173 E3
Holbrook Suff 152 C4
Holbrooks 159 F4
Holburn 229 E3
Holbury 106 D2
Holcombe Devon 102 C5
Holcombe GtMan 184 B1
Holcombe Som 117 D3
Holcombe Burnell
  Barton 102 B3
Holcombe Rogus 103 D1
Holcot 148 C1
Holden 193 D3
Holden Gate 193 E5
Holdenby 148 B1
Holdenhurst 106 A3
Holder's Green 151 E5
Holders Hill 136 B4
Holdgate 157 E4
Holdingham 175 F3
Holditch 103 G2
Hole 103 E1
Hole Park 124 A5
Holehouse 185 E4
Hole-in-the-Wall 145 F5
Holford 115 E3
Holgate 195 E2
Holker 199 E5
Holkham 177 G3
Hollacombe Devon 113 D5
Hollacombe Devon 102 B2
Hollacombe Town 113 G4
Holland Ork 276 D2
Holland Ork 276 F5
Holland Surr 122 D3
Holland Fen 176 A3
Holland-on-Sea 139 E1
Hollandstoun 276 G1
Hollee 218 A5
Hollesley 153 E3
Hollicombe 101 F1
Hollingbourne 124 A3
Hollingbury 109 F3
Hollingrove 110 B1
Hollington Derbys 172 D4
Hollington ESuss 110 C2
Hollington Staffs 172 B4
Hollingwood 186 B5
Hollingworth 185 E3
Hollins 186 A5
Hollins Green 184 A3
Hollins Lane 192 A3
Hollinsclough 172 B1
Hollinwood GtMan 184 D2
Hollinwood Shrop 170 C4
Hollocombe 113 G4
Hollow Meadows 185 G4
Holloway 173 E2
Hollowell 160 B5
Holly Bush 170 B3
Holly End 162 C2
Holly Green 134 C2
Hollybush Caerp 130 A2
Hollybush EAyr 224 B4
Hollybush Worcs 145 G4
Hollyhurst 170 C3
Hollym 197 F5
Hollywater 120 D4
Hollywood 158 C5
Holm D&G 218 D2
Holm (Tolm) Na H-E. Siar
  271 G4
Holm of Drumlanrig 216 C1
Holmbridge 185 F2
Holmbury St. Mary 121 G3
Holmbush 122 B5
Holme Cambs 161 G4
Holme Cumb 199 G5
Holme NLincs 187 G5
Holme Notts 174 D2
Holme NYorks 202 C4
Holme WYorks 185 F2
Holme Chapel 193 E5

Holme Hale 163 G2
Holme Lacy 145 E4
Holme Marsh 144 C2
Holme next the Sea 177 F3
Holme on the
  Wolds 196 B3
Holme Pierrepont 174 B4
Holme St. Cuthbert 209 E2
Holme-on-Spalding-
  Moor 196 A4
Holmer 145 E3
Holmer Green 135 E3
Holmes 183 F1
Holmes Chapel 171 E1
Holme's Hill 110 A2
Holmesfield 186 A5
Holmeswood 183 F1
Holmewood 173 F1
Holmfield 193 G5
Holmfirth 185 F2
Holmhead D&G 216 B2
Holmhead EAyr 225 D3
Holmpton 197 F5
Holmrook 198 B2
Holmsgarth 279 D8
Holmsleigh Green 103 F2
Holmston 224 B3
Holmwrangle 210 B3
Holne 100 D1
Holnest 104 C2
Holnicote 114 C3
Holsworthy 112 D5
Holsworthy Beacon 113 D5
Holt Dorset 105 G2
Holt Norf 178 B2
Holt Wilts 117 F1
Holt Worcs 146 A1
Holt Wrex 170 B2
Holt End Hants 120 B4
Holt End Worcs 146 C1
Holt Fleet 146 A1
Holt Heath Dorset 105 G2
Holt Heath Worcs 146 A1
Holt Wood 105 G2
Holtby 195 F2
Holton Oxon 134 B2
Holton Som 117 D5
Holton Suff 165 F4
Holton cum
  Beckering 188 B4
Holton Heath 105 F3
Holton le Clay 188 C2
Holton le Moor 188 A3
Holton St. Mary 152 B4
Holtspur 135 E4
Holtye 123 D5
Holtye Common 123 D5
Holway 115 F5
Holwell Dorset 104 C1
Holwell Herts 149 G4
Holwell Leics 174 C5
Holwell Oxon 133 E2
Holwell Som 117 E3
Holwick 211 F5
Holworth 105 D4
Holy Cross 158 B5
Holy Island IoA 180 A5
Holy Island (Lindisfarne)
  N'umb 229 F2
Holy Trinity Church,
  Skipton NYorks
  BD23 1NJ 193 F2
Holy Trinity Church,
  Stratford-upon-Avon
  Warks CV37 6BG
  85 Stratford-upon-Avon
Holybourne 120 C3
Holyfield 136 C2
Holyhead
  (Caergybi) 180 A4
Holymoorside 173 E1
Holyport 135 D5
Holystone 220 B1
Holytown 234 B3
Holywell Cambs 162 B5
Holywell Corn 96 B4
Holywell Dorset 104 B2
Holywell ESuss 110 B4
Holywell F&O 280 C5
Holywell (Treffynnon)
  Flints 182 C5
Holywell N'umb 221 F4
Holywell Bay Fun Park
  Corn TR8 5PW 96 B4
Holywell Green 185 E1
Holywell Lake 115 E5
Holywell Row 163 F5
Holywood A&NDown
  283 H1
Holywood D&G 216 D2
Hom Green 145 E5
Homer 157 F2
Homer Row 137 G2
Homersfield 165 D3
Homington 118 C5
Honey Hill 124 D2
Honey Street 118 C1
Honey Tye 152 A4
Honeyborough 126 C2
Honeybourne 146 D3
Honeychurch 113 G5
Honicknowle 100 A2
Honiley 159 E5
Honing 179 E3
Honingham 178 C4
Honington Lincs 175 E3
Honington Suff 164 A4
Honington Warks 147 E3
Honiton 103 E2
Honkley 170 A2
Honley 185 F1
Hoo 155 F2
Hoo Green 184 B4
Hoo Meavy 100 B1
Hoo St Werburgh 137 G5
Hood Green 186 A2
Hood Hill 186 A4
Hooe ESuss 110 B3
Hooe Plym 100 B2
Hooe Common 110 B2
Hook Cambs 162 B3
Hook ERid 195 G5
Hook Hants 120 C1
Hook Hants 107 E2
Hook Pembs 126 C1
Hook Wilts 132 C4
Hook Green Kent 123 F5

Hook Green Kent 123 F2
Hook Green Kent 137 F5
Hook Green Kent 137 F3
Hook Norton 147 F4
Hook-a-Gate 157 D2
Hooke 104 B2
Hookgate 171 E4
Hookway 102 B3
Hookwood 122 B4
Hoole 170 B1
Hooley 122 B3
Hoop 131 E2
Hooton 183 E5
Hooton Levitt 186 C3
Hooton Pagnell 186 B2
Hooton Roberts 186 B3
Hop Farm, The Kent
  TN12 6PY 123 F4
Hop Pocket, The Here
  WR6 5BT 145 F3
Hop Pole 161 G1
Hopcrofts Holt 147 G5
Hope Derbys 185 F4
Hope Devon 100 C4
Hope Flints 170 A2
Hope Powys 156 B2
Hope Shrop 156 C2
Hope Staffs 172 C2
Hope Bagot 157 E5
Hope Bowdler 157 D3
Hope End Green 151 D5
Hope Mansell 131 F1
Hope under
  Dinmore 145 E2
Hopehouse 227 D4
Hopeman 267 J5
Hope's Green 137 G4
Hopesay 156 C4
Hopkinstown 129 G3
Hopley's Green 144 C2
Hopperton 194 C2
Hopstone 157 G3
Hopton Derbys 173 D2
Hopton Norf 165 G2
Hopton Shrop 170 C5
Hopton Shrop 170 A5
Hopton Staffs 171 G5
Hopton Suff 164 A4
Hopton Cangeford 157 E4
Hopton Castle 156 C5
Hopton Wafers 157 F5
Hoptonheath 156 C5
Hopwas 159 D2
Hopwood 158 C5
Horam 110 A2
Horbling 175 G4
Horbury 185 G1
Horden 212 D3
Horderley 156 D4
Hordle 106 B3
Hordley 170 A4
Horeb Carmar 128 A2
Horeb Cere 141 G3
Horeb Flints 169 F2
Horfield 131 E5
Horham 164 D4
Horkesley Heath 152 A5
Horkstow 187 G1
Horley Oxon 147 G3
Horley Surr 122 B4
Horn Hill 135 F3
Hornblotton 116 C4
Hornblotton Green 116 C4
Hornby Lancs 192 B1
Hornby NYorks 202 B3
Hornby NYorks 202 C2
Horncastle 176 A1
Hornchurch 137 E4
Horncliffe 237 G5
Horndean Hants 107 G1
Horndean ScBord 237 G5
Horndon 99 F2
Horndon on the Hill 137 F4
Horne 122 C4
Horne Row 137 G2
Horner 114 B3
Horniehaugh 252 C3
Horning 179 E4
Horninghold 160 D3
Horninglow 172 D5
Horningsea 150 C1
Horningsham 117 F3
Horningtoft 178 A3
Horningtops 97 G3
Horns Cross Devon 113 D3
Horns Cross ESuss 110 D1
Horns Green 123 D3
Hornsbury 103 G1
Hornsby 210 B3
Hornsby Gate 210 B2
Hornsea 197 E3
Hornsea Freeport ERid
  HU18 1UT 197 E3
Hornsey 136 C4
Hornton 147 F3
Horrabridge 100 B1
Horridge 102 A3
Horringer 151 G1
Horrocks Fold 184 B1
Horse Bridge 171 G2
Horseback 158 A1
Horsebridge Devon 99 E3
Horsebridge Hants 119 E4
Horsebrook 158 A1
Horsecastle 116 B1
Horsehay 157 F2
Horseheath 151 E3
Horsehouse 201 F4
Horsell 121 E2
Horseman's Green 170 B3
Horsenden 134 C2
Horseshoe Green 123 D4
Horseway 162 C4
Horsey 179 F3
Horsey Corner 179 F3
Horsford 178 C4
Horsforth 194 B4
Horsham Worcs 145 G2
Horsham WSuss 121 G4
Horsham St. Faith 178 D4
Horsington Lincs 175 G1
Horsington Som 117 E5
Horsington Marsh 117 E5
Horsley Derbys 173 E3
Horsley Glos 132 A3
Horsley N'umb 211 G1

Horsley N'umb 220 A2
Horsley Cross 152 C5
Horsley Woodhouse 173 E3
Horsleycross Street 152 C5
Horsleygate 186 A5
Horsleyhill 227 G4
Horsmonden 123 F4
Horspath 134 A2
Horstead 179 D4
Horsted Keynes 109 F1
Horton Bucks 135 E1
Horton Dorset 105 G2
Horton Lancs 193 E3
Horton SGlos 131 G4
Horton Shrop 170 B5
Horton Som 103 G1
Horton Staffs 171 G2
Horton Swan 128 A4
Horton Tel&W 157 E1
Horton W&M 135 F5
Horton Wilts 118 B1
Horton WN'hants 148 D2
Horton Cross 103 G1
Horton Grange 221 E4
Horton Green 170 B3
Horton Heath 107 D1
Horton in
  Ribblesdale 200 C5
Horton Inn 105 G2
Horton Kirby 123 E2
Horton-cum-
  Studley 134 B1
Horwich 184 A1
Horwich End 185 E4
Horwood 113 F3
Hoscar 183 F1
Hose 174 C5
Hoses 198 D3
Hosh 243 D2
Hosta 262 C4
Hoswick 279 D10
Hotham 196 A4
Hothfield 124 B4
Hoton 173 G5
Houbie 278 F3
Houdston 214 C1
Hough 171 E2
Hough Green 183 F4
Hougham 175 D3
Hough-on-the-Hill 175 E3
Houghton Cambs 162 A5
Houghton Cumb 210 A2
Houghton Devon 100 C3
Houghton Hants 119 E4
Houghton Pembs 126 C2
Houghton WSuss 108 C2
Houghton Bank 212 B5
Houghton Conquest 149 F3
Houghton le Spring 212 C3
Houghton on the
  Hill 160 B2
Houghton Regis 149 F5
Houghton St. Giles 178 A2
Houghton-le-Side 212 B5
Houlsyke 203 G2
Hound 107 D2
Hound Green 120 C2
Houndslow 236 D5
Houndsmoor 115 E5
Houndwood 237 F3
Hounslow 136 A5
House of Marbles & Teign
  Valley Glass Devon
  TQ13 9DS 102 B5
Housebay 276 F5
Househill 267 F6
Houses Hill 185 F1
Houses of Parliament
  (Palace of Westminster)
  (Palace of Westminster &
  Westminster Abbey inc.
  St Margaret's Church)
  GtLon SW1A 0AA 13 B5
Housesteads Roman
  Fort (Frontiers of the
  Roman Empire) N'umb
  NE47 6NN 211 D1
Housetter 278 C4
Housham Tye 137 E1
Houss 279 C9
Houston 233 F3
Houstry 275 G4
Houstry of Dunn 275 H3
Houton 277 C7
Hove 109 E3
Hove Edge 194 A5
Hoveringham 174 B3
Hoveton 179 E4
Hovingham 203 F5
How 210 B2
How Caple 145 F4
How End 149 F3
How Green 123 D4
How Man 208 C3
Howbrook 186 A3
Howden 195 G5
Howden Clough 194 B5
Howden-le-Wear 212 A4
Howe Cumb 199 F4
Howe High 275 J2
Howe Norf 165 D2
Howe NYorks 202 C4
Howe Green 137 G2
Howe of Teuchar 269 F6
Howe Street Essex 137 F1
Howe Street Essex 151 F2
Howegreen 138 B2
Howell 175 G3
Howey 143 G2
Howgate Cumb 208 C4
Howgate Midlo 235 G4
Howgill Lancs 193 E3
Howgill NYorks 193 G2
Howick 229 G5
Howle 171 D5
Howle Hill 145 F5
Howlett End 151 D4
Howletts Wild Animal Park
  Kent CT4 5EL 125 D3
Howley 103 F2
Howmore
  (Tobha Mòr) 254 C1
Hownam 228 B5
Hownam Mains 228 B4
Howpasley 227 E5
Howsham NLincs 188 A2
Howsham NYorks 195 G1

Howt Green 124 A2
Howtel 228 C3
Howton 144 D5
Howwood 233 F3
Hoxa 277 D8
Hoxne 164 C4
Hoy High 275 H2
Hoy Ork 277 B8
Hoylake 182 D4
Hoyland 186 A2
Hoylandswaine 185 G2
Hoyle 108 B2
Hubberholme 201 E5
Hubberston 126 B2
Hubbert's Bridge 176 A3
Huby NYorks 195 E1
Huby NYorks 194 B3
Hucclecote 132 A1
Hucking 124 A3
Hucknall 173 G3
Huddersfield 185 F1
Huddington 146 B2
Huddlesford 158 D2
Hudnall 135 F1
Hudscott 113 G3
Hudswell 202 A3
Huggate 196 A2
Hugglescote 159 G1
Hugh Town 96 B1
Hughenden Valley 135 D3
Hughley 157 E3
Hugmore 170 A2
Hugus 96 B5
Huish Devon 113 F4
Huish Wilts 118 C1
Huish Champflower 114 D5
Huisinis 270 B6
Hulcote 149 E4
Hulcott 135 D1
Hull 196 D5
Hulland 172 D3
Hulland Ward 173 D3
Hullavington 132 A4
Hullbridge 138 B3
Hulme 171 G3
Hulme End 172 C2
Hulme Walfield 171 F1
Hulver Street 165 F3
Hulverstone 106 C4
Humber Devon 102 B5
Humber Here 145 E2
Humber Bridge Country
  Park ERid
  HU13 0LN 196 D5
Humberside Airport 188 A1
Humberston 188 D2
Humberstone 160 B2
Humberton 194 D1
Humbie 236 B3
Humbleton Dur 201 F4
Humbleton ERid 197 E4
Humbleton N'umb 229 D4
Humby 175 F4
Hume 237 E5
Humehall 237 E5
Hummer 104 B1
Humshaugh 220 B4
Huna 275 J1
Huncoat 193 D4
Huncote 160 A3
Hundalee 228 A5
Hundall 186 A5
Hunderthwaite 211 F5
Hundleby 176 B1
Hundleton 126 C2
Hundon 151 F3
Hundred Acres 107 E1
Hundred End 192 A5
Hundred House 144 A2
Hungarton 160 B2
Hungate End 148 C3
Hungerford Hants 106 A1
Hungerford Shrop 157 E4
Hungerford WBerks 119 E1
Hungerford
  Newtown 133 F5
Hungerton 175 D5
Hunglader 263 J4
Hunmanby 205 D5
Hunningham 147 F1
Hunningham Hill 147 F1
Hunny Hill 107 D4
Hunsdon 136 D1
Hunsingore 194 D2
Hunslet 194 C4
Hunsonby 210 B4
Hunspow 275 H1
Hunstanton 177 E3
Hunston Suff 152 A1
Hunston WSuss 108 A3
Hunsworth 194 A5
Hunt End 146 C1
Hunt House 204 B3
Huntercombe End 134 B4
Hunters Forstal 125 D2
Hunter's Inn 113 G1
Hunter's Quay 232 C2
Hunterston 232 C3
Huntford 219 G2
Huntham 116 A5
Huntingdon 162 A5
Huntingfield 165 E4
Huntingford 117 F4
Huntington Here 144 B2
Huntington Here 145 D3
Huntington Staffs 158 B1
Huntington Tel&W 157 F2
Huntington York 195 F2
Huntingtower 243 F2
Huntley 131 G1
Huntly 260 D1
Huntlywood 236 B5
Hunton Hants 119 F3
Hunton Kent 123 G4
Hunton NYorks 202 A3
Hunton Bridge 135 F2
Hunt's Cross 183 F4
Huntscott 114 C3
Huntsham 114 D5
Huntshaw 113 F3
Huntshaw Cross 113 F3
Huntshaw Water 113 F3
Huntspill 116 A3
Huntworth 116 A4
Hunwick 212 A4
Hunworth 178 B2

Hurcott Som 116 C5
Hurcott Som 103 G1
Hurdley 116 B3
Hurdsfield 184 D5
Hurley W&M 134 D4
Hurley Warks 159 F3
Hurley Bottom 134 D4
Hurlford 224 C2
Hurliness 277 B9
Hurlston Green 183 E1
Hurn 106 A3
Hursley 119 F5
Hurst NYorks 201 F2
Hurst W'ham 134 C5
Hurst Green Essex 139 D1
Hurst Green ESuss 110 C1
Hurst Green Lancs 192 C4
Hurst Green Surr 122 C3
Hurst Wickham 109 E2
Hurstbourne
  Tarrant 119 E2
Hurstpierpoint 109 E2
Hurstwood 193 E4
Hurtmore 121 E3
Hury 211 F5
Husabost 263 G6
Husbands Bosworth
  160 B4
Husborne Crawley 149 E4
Husthwaite 203 E5
Hutcherleigh 101 D2
Huthwaite 173 F2
Huttoft 189 F5
Hutton Cumb 210 A5
Hutton Essex 137 F3
Hutton Lancs 192 A5
Hutton NSom 116 A2
Hutton ScBord 237 G4
Hutton Bonville 202 C2
Hutton Buscel 204 C4
Hutton Conyers 202 C5
Hutton Cranswick 196 C2
Hutton End 210 A4
Hutton Hang 202 A4
Hutton Henry 212 D4
Hutton Magna 202 A1
Hutton Mount 137 F3
Hutton Mulgrave 204 B2
Hutton Roof Cumb 199 G5
Hutton Roof Cumb 209 G3
Hutton Rudby 203 D2
Hutton Sessay 203 D5
Hutton Wandesley 195 E2
Hutton-le-Hole 203 G3
Huxham 102 C3
Huxham Green 116 C4
Huxley 170 C1
Huxter Shet 279 C7
Huxter Shet 279 E6
Huyton 183 F3
Hycemoor 198 B4
Hyde Glos 132 A2
Hyde End W'ham 120 C1
Hyde End WBerks 119 G1
Hyde Heath 135 E2
Hyde Lea 158 B1
Hydestile 121 E3
Hylands Park Essex
  CM2 8WQ 137 F2
Hyndford Bridge 234 D5
Hyndlee 227 G5
Hynish 246 A3
Hyssington 156 C3
Hythe Hants 106 D2
Hythe Kent 125 D5
Hythe End 135 F5
Hythie 269 J5
Hyton 198 B4

I
Ianstown 268 C4
Iarsiadar 270 D4
Ibberton 105 D2
Ible 172 D2
Ibsley 106 A2
Ibstock 159 G1
Ibstone 134 B3
Ibthorpe 119 E2
Ibworth 119 G2
Icelton 116 A1
Ickburgh 163 G3
Ickenham 135 F4
Ickford 134 B2
Ickham 125 E3
Ickleford 149 G4
Icklesham 111 D2
Ickleton 150 C3
Icklingham 163 F5
Ickwell Green 149 G3
Icomb 147 E5
Idbury 147 E5
Iddesleigh 113 F5
Ide 102 C3
Ide Hill 123 D3
Ideford 102 B5
Iden 111 E1
Iden Green Kent 123 G5
Iden Green Kent 124 A5
Idle 194 A4
Idless 96 C5
Idlicote 147 E3
Idmiston 118 C4
Idridgehay 173 D3
Idridgehay Green 173 D3
Idrigil 263 J5
Idstone 133 E4
Idvies 252 D5
Iffley 134 A2
Ifield 122 B5
Ifieldwood 122 B5
Ifold 121 F4
Iford BCP 106 A3
Iford ESuss 109 G3
Ifton 131 D4
Ifton Heath 170 A4
Ightfield 170 C4
Ightham 123 E3
Ightham Mote Kent
  TN15 0NT 123 E3
Iken 153 F2
Ilam 172 C2
Ilchester 116 C5
Ilderton 229 E4
Ilford 136 D4
Ilfracombe 113 F1

Ilkeston 173 F3
Ilketshall
  St. Andrew 165 E3
Ilketshall
  St. Lawrence 165 E3
Ilketshall
  St. Margaret 165 E3
Ilkley 194 A3
Illey 158 B4
Illidge Green 171 E1
Illington 164 A3
Illingworth 193 G5
Illogan 96 A5
Illston on the Hill 160 C3
Ilmer 134 C2
Ilmington 147 E3
Ilminster 103 G1
Ilston NYorks 202 A5
Ilton Som 103 G1
Imachar 231 G5
Imber 118 A3
Imeroo 242 A3
Immingham 188 B1
Immingham Dock 188 C1
Impington 150 C1
Ince 183 F1
Ince Blundell 183 E2
Ince-in-Makerfield 183 G2
Inch Kenneth 238 D1
Inchbae Lodge 266 B5
Inchbare 253 E3
Inchberry 268 B5
Inchbraoch 253 F4
Inchgrundle 252 C2
Inchinnan 233 F3
Inchindown 266 D4
Inchinnan 233 F3
Inchkinloch 273 J4
Inchlaggan 257 H4
Inchlumpie 266 C4
Inchmarlo 260 E5
Inchmarnock 232 B4
Inchnabobart 252 B1
Inchnacardoch
  Hotel 257 K3
Inchnadamph 272 E6
Inchock 253 E5
Inchree 248 C3
Inchrory 259 J4
Inchture 244 A2
Inchvuilt 257 J1
Inchyra 243 G2
Indian Queens 96 D4
Inerval 230 B5
Ingatestone 137 F3
Ingbirchworth 185 G2
Ingerthorpe 194 B3
Ingestre 171 G5
Ingham Lincs 187 G4
Ingham Norf 179 E3
Ingham Suff 163 G5
Ingham Corner 179 E3
Ingleborough 162 C1
Ingleby Derbys 173 E5
Ingleby Lincs 187 F5
Ingleby Arncliffe 202 D2
Ingleby Barwick 202 D1
Ingleby Cross 202 D2
Ingleby Greenhow 203 E2
Ingleigh Green 113 G5
Inglesbatch 117 E1
Inglesham 133 E3
Ingleton Dur 212 A1
Ingleton NYorks 200 B5
Inglewhite 192 B4
Ingliston 235 F2
Ingmire Hall 200 B3
Ingoe 220 C4
Ingoldisthorpe 177 E4
Ingoldmells 177 D1
Ingoldsby 175 F4
Ingon 147 D2
Ingram 229 E5
Ingrave 137 F3
Ingrow 193 G4
Ings 199 F3
Ingst 131 E4
Ingworth 178 C3
Inham Hall 161 F5
Inhurst 119 G1
Iniscaan 284 E7
Inisrush 286 D5
Inistrynich 240 D2
Injebreck 190 B3
Inkberrow 146 C2
Inkersall 186 B5
Inkersall Green 186 B5
Inkhorn 261 H1
Inkpen 119 E1
Inkstack 275 H1
Inmarsh 118 A1
Innellan 232 C3
Innergellie 245 D4
Innerhadden 250 B4
Innerleithen 227 E2
Innerleven 244 B4
Innermessan 214 B4
Innerwick ELoth 237 E2
Innerwick P&K 250 A5
Inninbeg 247 E5
Innsworth 146 A5
Insch 260 E2
Insh 259 F4
Inshore 273 F2
Inskip 192 A4
Instow 113 E2
Intake 186 C2
International Centre, The,
  Telford Tel&W
  TF3 4JH 157 G2
Intwood 178 C5
Inver A&B 248 B5
Inver Aber 259 K5
Inver High 267 F3
Inver High 275 G5

Inver P&K 251 F5
Inver Mallie 248 D1
Inverailort 247 G1
Inveralligin 264 E6
Inverallochy 269 J4
Inveran 266 C2
Inverarary
  (Inbhir Aora) 240 C4
Inverarndoch Mains 242 C4
Inverardran 241 F2
Inverarish 256 B1
Inverarity 252 C5
Inverarnan
  (Inbhir Àirnein) 241 F4
Inverasdale 264 E3
Inverbain 264 D6
Inverbeg 241 F5
Inverbervie 253 G2
Inverbroom 265 H3
Inverbrough 259 F2
Invercassley 266 B1
Inverchaolain 232 B2
Invercharnan 248 D5
Inverchoran 241 E3
Invercreran 248 C5
Inverdruie 259 G3
Inverebrie 261 H1
Invereen 258 C1
Inverernan 241 J6
Inveresk 236 A2
Inverey 251 F1
Inverfarigaig 258 C2
Invergarry
  (Inbhir Garadh) 257 K4
Invergelder 259 K5
Invergeldie 242 C2
Invergloy 249 E1
Invergordon 266 E5
Invergowrie 244 B1
Inverguseran 256 D4
Inverharroch Farm 260 B1
Inverhevie 241 F2
Inverhope 273 G2
Inverie 256 D4
Inverinan 240 B3
Inverinate 257 F2
Inverkeilor 253 E5
Inverkeithing 235 F1
Inverkeithny 268 E6
Inverkip 232 D2
Inverkirkaig 272 C7
Inverlael 265 H3
Inverlauren 233 E1
Inverliever 240 A4
Inverliver 240 C1
Inverlochlarig 241 G3
Inverlochy 241 D2
Inverlussa 231 G1
Invermay 243 F3
Invermoidart 247 F2
Invermoriston (Inbhir
  Moireasdan) 258 B3
Invernaver 274 C2
Inverneil 231 G1
Inverness
  (Inbhir Nis) 266 D7
Inverness Airport 266 E6
Invernettie 269 K6
Invernoaden 240 D5
Inveroran Hotel (Inbhir
  Orain) 249 E5
Inverquharity 252 C4
Inverquhomery 269 J6
Inverroy 249 E1
Inversanda 248 B4
Invershiel 257 F3
Invershore 275 H5
Inversnaid Hotel 241 F4
Invertrossachs 242 A4
Inverugie 269 K6
Inveruglas (Inbhir
  Dhubhghlais) 241 F4
Inveruglass 259 F4
Inverurie 261 F2
Invervar 250 B5
Invervegain 232 B2
Invery House 260 E5
Inverythan 269 F5
Inwardleigh 99 F1
Inworth 138 B1
Iochdar (Eochar) 262 C7
Iping 120 C5
Ipplepen 101 E1
Ipsden 134 B4
Ipstones 172 B3
Ipswich 152 C3
Irby 183 D4
Irby Hill 183 D4
Irby in the Marsh 176 C1
Irby upon Humber 188 B2
Irchester 149 E1
Ireby Cumb 209 F3
Ireby Lancs 200 B5
Ireland Ork 277 C7
Ireland Shet 279 C10
Ireland's Cross 171 E3
Ireleth 198 D5
Ireshopeburn 211 E4
Irlam 184 B3
Irnham 175 F5
Iron Acton 131 F4
Iron Cross 146 C2
Ironbridge 157 F2
Ironbridge Gorge Tel&W
  TF8 7DQ 157 F2
Irons Bottom 122 B4
Ironville 173 F2
Irstead 179 E3
Irthington 210 A1
Irthlingborough 161 E5
Irton 204 D4
Irvine 224 B2
Irvinestown 280 G3
Isauld 274 E2
Isbister Ork 277 C6
Isbister Ork 276 B5
Isbister Shet 279 E6
Isbister Shet 278 C3
Isfield 109 G2
Isham 161 D5
Ishriff 239 F1

Isington 120 C3
Island of Stroma 275 J1
Islaw'r-dref 154 C1
Islay 230 A3
Islay Airport 230 B4
Islay House 230 B3
Isle Brewers 116 A5
Isle Abbotts 116 A5
Isle of Bute Discovery Centre
  A&B PA20 0AH 232 B3
Isle of Lewis (Eilean
  Leodhais) 271 F3
Isle of Man 190 B3
Isle of Man Airport 190 A5
Isle of May 245 E5
Isle of Noss 279 E8
Isle of Sheppey 124 B1
Isle of Walney 191 E1
Isle of Whithorn 207 E3
Isle of Wight 107 D4
Isle of Wight (Sandown)
  Airport 107 E4
Isle of Wight Pearl IoW
  PO30 4DD 106 D4
Isle of Wight Zoo IoW
  PO36 8QB 107 F4
Isles of Scilly
  (Scilly Isles) 96 B1
Islesburgh 279 C6
Islesteps 217 D3
Isleworth 136 A5
Isley Walton 173 F5
Islibhig 270 B5
Islip NN'hants 161 E5
Islip Oxon 134 A1
Isombridge 157 F1
Istead Rise 123 F2
Itchen 106 D1
Itchen Abbas 119 G4
Itchen Valley Country Park
  Hants SO30 3HQ 4 C3
Itchingfield 121 F5
Itchington 131 F4
Itteringham 178 C2
Itton Devon 99 G1
Itton Mon 131 D3
Itton Common 131 D3
Ivegill 210 A3
Ivelet 201 E3
Iver 135 F4
Iver Heath 135 F4
Iveston 212 A2
Ivetsey Bank 158 A1
Ivinghoe 135 E1
Ivinghoe Aston 135 E1
Ivington 145 D2
Ivington Green 145 D2
Ivy Hatch 123 E3
Ivy Todd 163 G2
Ivybridge 100 C2
Ivychurch 111 F1
Iwade 124 B2
Iwerne Courtney
  (Shroton) 105 E1
Iwerne Minster 105 E1
Ixworth 164 A4
Ixworth Thorpe 164 A4

J
Jack Hill 194 A2
Jackfield 157 F2
Jacksdale 173 F2
Jackstown 261 F1
Jackton 233 G4
Jacobstow 98 B1
Jacobstowe 113 F4
Jacobswell 121 E2
James Hamilton
  Heritage Park SLan
  G74 5LB 31 E5
James Pringle Weavers
  of Inverness High
  IV2 4RB 266 D7
Jameston 127 D3
Jamestown D&G 218 A2
Jamestown High 266 B6
Jamestown WDun 233 E1
Janefield 266 E6
Janetstown High 275 F2
Janetstown High 275 J3
Janus Stones F&O
  BT93 8AA 280 C2
Jarrow 212 C1
Jarvis Brook 123 E5
Jasper's Green 151 F5
Jawcraig 234 C2
Jayes Park 121 G3
Jaywick 139 E1
Jealott's Hill 135 D5
Jeater Houses 202 D3
Jedburgh 228 A4
Jeffreyston 127 D2
Jemimaville 266 E5
Jephson Gardens Warks
  CV32 4ER 16 B6
Jericho 184 C1
Jerrettspass 282 D5
Jersay 234 C3
Jersey 100 C5
Jersey Airport 100 B5
Jersey Marine 128 D3
Jerviswood 234 C5
Jesmond 212 B1
Jevington 110 A3
Jinney Ring Craft Centre,
  The Worcs
  B60 4BU 146 B1
Jockey End 135 F1
Jodrell Bank 184 B5
Jodrell Bank Observatory
  ChesE SK11 9DL
  184 B5
John Muir Country Park
  ELoth
  EH42 1UW 236 D2
John o' Groats 275 J1
Johnby 210 A4
John's Cross 110 C1
Johnshaven 253 F3
Johnson Street 179 E4
Johnston 126 C1
Johnston Mains 253 F2
Johnstone 233 F3
Johnstone Castle 233 F3
Johnstonebridge 217 E1

Isington 120 C3
Johnstons Cashmere Visitor
  Centre Moray
  IV30 4AF 267 K5
Johnstown
  Carmar 127 G1
Johnstown Wrex 170 A3
Jonesborough 282 D7
Joppa 224 C4
Jordans 135 E3
Jordanston 140 C4
Jordanstone 252 A5
Jorvik Glass NYorks
  YO60 7DA 195 G1
Jorvik YO1 9WT 90 York
Joy's Green 131 F1
Jumpers Common 106 A3
Juniper Green 235 F3
Juniper Hill 148 A4
Jura 231 D1
Jura House 230 C3
Jurby East 190 B2
Jurby West 190 B2

K
Kaber 200 C1
Kaimes 235 G3
Kames A&B 232 A2
Kames A&B 240 A3
Kames EAyr 225 E3
Katesbridge 283 F4
Kea 96 C5
Keadby 187 G2
Keady 282 B5
Keal Cotes 176 B1
Kearney 283 K3
Kearnsey 125 E4
Kearsley 184 B2
Kearstwick 200 B5
Kearton 201 F3
Kearvaig 272 E1
Keasden 192 D1
Kebholes 268 E5
Keckwick 183 G4
Keddington 188 D4
Keddington Corner 189 D4
Kedington 151 F3
Kedleston 173 E3
Keelby 188 B1
Keele 171 F3
Keeley Green 149 F3
Keelham 193 G4
Keenagham 280 B3
Keenans Bridge 286 D5
Keenthorne 115 F4
Keeran 280 E2
Keeres Green 137 E1
Keeston 126 B1
Keevil 118 A2
Kegworth 173 F5
Kehelland 96 A5
Keig 260 E3
Keighley 193 G3
Keighley & Worth Valley
  Railway WYorks
  BD22 8NJ 193 G3
Keil Cumb 199 G5
Keil High 248 B5
Keilhill 269 F5
Keillmore 231 E1
Keillor 252 A5
Keillour 243 E2
Keills 230 C3
Keils 230 C3
Keinton Mandeville 116 C4
Keir House 242 B5
Keir Mill 216 C1
Keisby 175 F5
Keisley 210 D5
Keiss 275 J2
Keith 268 C5
Keithick 244 A1
Keithmore 260 B1
Keithock 253 E3
Kelbrook 193 F3
Kelby 175 F3
Keld Cumb 199 G3
Keld NYorks 201 D2
Keldholme 203 G4
Keldy Castle 203 G3
Kelfield NLincs 187 F2
Kelfield NYorks 195 E4
Kelham 174 C2
Kella 190 B2
Kellacott 99 E2
Kellan 247 E5
Kellas Angus 244 C1
Kellas Moray 267 J6
Kellaton 101 D4
Kellaways 132 B5
Kelleythorpe 196 C2
Kelling 178 B1
Kellington 195 E5
Kelloe 212 C4
Kelloholm 225 F4
Kelly Corn 97 E2
Kelly Devon 99 D2
Kelly Bray 99 D3
Kelmarsh 160 C5
Kelmscott 133 E3
Kelsale 153 E1
Kelsall 170 C1
Kelsay 230 A4
Kelshall 150 B4
Kelsick 209 F1
Kelso 228 B3
Kelstedge 173 E1
Kelstern 188 C3
Kelston 117 E1
Keltneyburn 250 C5
Kelton 217 D3
Kelton Hill
  (Rhonehouse) 216 B5
Kelty 243 G5
Kelvedon 138 B1
Kelvedon Hatch 137 E3
Kelvin Hall Glas
  G3 8AW 38 A2
Kelvingrove Art Gallery &
  Museum Glas
  G3 8AG 38 A2
Kelvinside 233 G3
Kelynack 94 A4
Kemacott 113 G1
Kemback 244 C3
Kemberton 157 G2
Kemble 132 B3
Kemerton 146 B3

Kemeys
  Commander 130 C2
Kemeys Inferior 130 C3
Kemnay 261 F3
Kemp Town 109 F3
Kempe's Corner 124 C4
Kempley 145 F5
Kempley Green 145 F5
Kemps Green 158 D5
Kempsey 146 A2
Kempsford 133 D3
Kempshott 119 G3
Kempston 149 F3
Kempston Hardwick 149 F3
Kempston West End 149 E3
Kempton 156 C4
Kemsing 123 E3
Kemsley 124 B2
Kenardington 124 B5
Kenchester 144 D3
Kencot 133 E2
Kendal 199 G3
Kenderchurch 144 D5
Kendleshire 131 F5
Kenfig 129 E4
Kenfig Hill 129 E4
Kenidjack 94 A3
Kenilworth 159 E5
Kenilworth Castle Warks
  CV8 1NE 16 A4
Kenknock P&K 250 A5
Kenknock Stir 241 G1
Kenley GtLon 122 C2
Kenley Shrop 157 E2
Kenmore A&B 240 C4
Kenmore High 264 D6
Kenmore P&K 250 C5
Kenmore Na H-E. Siar
  270 E7
Kenn Devon 102 C4
Kenn NSom 116 B1
Kennacraig 231 G3
Kennall Vale
  (Cornwall & West Devon
  Mining Landscape) Corn
  95 E3
Kennards House 97 G1
Kennavay 263 H3
Kenneggy Downs 94 C4
Kennerleigh 102 B2
Kennerty 260 E5
Kennet 243 E5
Kennethmont 260 D2
Kennett 151 E1
Kennford 102 C4
Kenninghall 164 B3
Kennington Kent 124 C4
Kennington Oxon 134 A2
Kennoway 244 B4
Kenny 103 G1
Kennythorpe 195 G1
Kenovay 246 A2
Kensaleyre 263 K6
Kensington 136 B4
Kensington Palace GtLon
  W8 4PX 10 E4
Kenstone 170 C5
Kensworth 135 F1
Kent & East Sussex Railway
  Kent TN30 6HE 124 A5
Kent Street ESuss 110 C2
Kent Street Kent 123 F3
Kentallen (Ceann an t-
  Sàilein) 248 C3
Kentchurch 144 D5
Kentford 151 F1
Kentisbeare 103 D2
Kentisbury 113 G1
Kentisbury Ford 113 G1
Kentish Town 136 B4
Kentmere 199 F2
Kenton Devon 102 C4
Kenton Suff 152 C1
Kenton T&W 212 B1
Kenton Corner 152 D1
Kentra 247 F3
Kents Bank 199 E5
Kent's Green 145 G5
Kent's Oak 119 E5
Kenwick 170 B4
Kenwood House GtLon
  NW3 7JR 10 F2
Kenwyn 96 C5
Kenyon 184 A3
Keoldale 273 F2
Keonan 282 E3
Keose (Ceòs) 271 F5
Keppanach 248 C3
Keppoch A&B 233 E2
Keppoch High 256 E2
Keprigan 222 B4
Kepwick 203 D3
Keresley 159 F4
Kernborough 101 D3
Kerrera 240 A2
Kerridge 184 D5
Kerris 94 B4
Kerry (Ceri) 156 A3
Kerrycroy 232 C3
Kerry's Gate 144 C4
Kerrysdale 264 E3
Kersall 174 C1
Kersey 152 B3
Kersey Vale 152 B3
Kershopefoot 218 C3
Kerswell 103 D2
Kerswell Green 146 A3
Kerthen Wood 94 C3
Kesgrave 152 D3
Kesh 280 D2
Kessingland 165 G3
Kessingland Beach 165 G3
Kestle 97 D5
Kestle Mill 96 C4
Keston 122 D2
Keswick Cumb 209 F4
Keswick Norf 178 D5
Keswick Norf 179 E2
Ketley Bank 157 F1
Ketsby 189 D5
Kettering 161 D5
Ketteringham 178 C5
Kettins 244 A1
Kettle Corner 123 G3
Kettlebaston 152 A2
Kettlebridge 244 B4
Kettlebrook 159 E2

Kettleburgh 153 D1
Kettlehill 244 B4
Kettleholm 217 F3
Kettleness 204 B1
Kettleshulme 185 D5
Kettlesing 194 B2
Kettlesing Bottom 194 B2
Kettlesing Head 194 B2
Kettlestone 178 A2
Kettlethorpe 187 F5
Kettletoft 276 F4
Kettlewell 201 E5
Ketton 161 E2
Kevingtown 123 D2
Kew 136 A5
Kewstoke 116 A1
Kexbrough 186 A2
Kexby Lincs 187 F4
Kexby York 195 G2
Key Green 171 F1
Keyham 160 B2
Keyhaven 106 C3
Keyingham 197 E5
Keymer 109 F2
Keynsham 117 D1
Key's Toft 176 C2
Keysoe 149 F1
Keysoe Row 149 F1
Keyston 161 F5
Keyworth 174 B4
Kibblesworth 212 B2
Kibworth Beauchamp 160 B3
Kibworth Harcourt 160 B3
Kidbrooke 136 D5
Kiddemore Green 158 A2
Kidderminster 158 A5
Kiddington 147 G5
Kidlington 133 G1
Kidmore End 134 B5
Kidnal 170 B3
Kidsdale 207 E3
Kidsgrove 171 F2
Kidstones 201 E4
Kidstown 286 D3
Kidwelly (Cydweli) 128 A2
Kiel Crofts 240 A1
Kielder 219 E2
Kielder Forest N'umb NE48 1ER 219 E2
Kielder Water N'umb NE48 1BX 219 F3
Kilbarchan 233 F3
Kilbeg 256 C4
Kilberry 231 F3
Kilbirnie 233 E4
Kilblaan 240 D3
Kilbraur 274 D7
Kilbrennan 246 D5
Kilbride A&B 240 A2
Kilbride A&B 232 B3
Kilbride A&N 287 G6
Kilbride High 256 B2
Kilbride Farm 232 A3
Kilbridemore 240 C5
Kilburn Derbys 173 E3
Kilburn GtLon 136 B4
Kilburn NYorks 203 E5
Kilby 160 B3
Kilchattan Bay 232 C4
Kilchenzie 222 B3
Kilcheran 240 A1
Kilchiaran 230 A3
Kilchoan A&B 239 G3
Kilchoan High 247 D3
Kilchoman 230 A3
Kilchrenan (Cill Chrèanain) 240 C2
Kilchrist 222 B4
Kilclief 283 J4
Kilcoo 283 F5
Kilconquhar 244 C4
Kilcorig 283 F2
Kilcot 145 F5
Kilcoy 266 C6
Kilcreggan 232 D1
Kilcross 283 F1
Kildale 203 F2
Kildary 266 E4
Kildavie 222 C4
Kildermorie Lodge 266 C4
Kildonan NAyr 223 F3
Kildonan Na H-E. Siar 254 C2
Kildonan Lodge 274 E6
Kildonnan 247 D1
Kildress 282 A1
Kildrochet House 214 B5
Kildrum 287 F6
Kildrummy 260 C3
Kildwick 193 G3
Kilfinan 232 A2
Kilfinnan 257 J5
Kilgetty 127 E2
Kilgwrrwg Common 131 D3
Kilham ERid 196 C1
Kilham N'umb 228 C3
Kilkeel 283 G7
Kilkenneth 246 A2
Kilkenny 132 C1
Kilkerran A&B 222 C4
Kilkerran SAyr 224 B5
Kilkhampton 112 C4
Kilkinamurry 283 F4
Killadeas 280 E3
Killagan Bridge 286 E3
Killaloo 285 H5
Killamarsh 186 B4
Killarbran 281 G4
Killard 286 D6
Killay 128 C3
Killbeg 247 F5
Killead 287 F7
Killeague 286 C3
Killean A&B 231 E5
Killean A&B 240 C4
Killearn 233 G1
Killeen AB&C 282 C4
Killeen Mid Ulster 282 B2
Killeen NM&D 282 D6
Killeeshil 281 J3
Killellan 222 B4
Killen D&S 284 E7
Killen High 266 D6
Killerby 212 A5
Killerton 102 C2
Killerton Devon EX5 3LE 102 C2
Killeter 284 E7
Killichonan 250 A4
Killiechonate 249 E1
Killiechronan 247 E5
Killiecrankie 251 E3
Killiehuntly 258 E5
Killiemor 239 D1
Killilan 257 F1
Killimster 275 J3
Killin High 267 F1
Killin Stir 242 A1
Killinallan 230 B2
Killinchy 283 J2
Killinghall 194 B2
Killington Cumb 200 B4
Killington Devon 113 G1
Killingworth 221 E4
Killochyett 236 B5
Killocraw 222 B2
Killough 283 J5
Killowen 282 E7
Killucan 281 J1
Killunaig 239 D2
Killundine 247 E5
Killure 286 C3
Killyclogher 281 G1
Killycolp 282 B1
Killycolpy 282 C1
Killycor 285 H5
Killycurragh 286 B7
Killyharry 281 K2
Killykergan 286 C4
Killylane 285 H3
Killylea AB&C 282 A4
Killyleagh 283 J3
Killymallaght 285 G5
Killynether 283 H1
Killyrammer 286 D3
Kilmacolm 233 E3
Kilmaha 240 B4
Kilmahamogue 286 E2
Kilmahog 242 B4
Kilmalieu 248 A4
Kilmaluag 263 K4
Kilmany 244 B2
Kilmarie 256 B3
Kilmarnock 224 C2
Kilmartin 240 A5
Kilmaurs 233 F5
Kilmelford 240 A3
Kilmeny 230 B3
Kilmersdon 117 D2
Kilmeston 119 G5
Kilmichael 222 B3
Kilmichael Glassary 240 A5
Kilmichael of Inverlussa 231 F1
Kilmington Devon 103 F3
Kilmington Wilts 117 E4
Kilmington Common 117 E4
Kilmood 283 H2
Kilmorack 266 B7
Kilmore (A' Chille Mhòr) A&B 240 A2
Kilmore AB&C 282 C3
Kilmore High 256 C4
Kilmore NM&D 283 H3
Kilmory A&B 231 F1
Kilmory A&B 231 F2
Kilmory High 255 J4
Kilmory High 247 E2
Kilmory NAyr 223 E3
Kilmote 274 E7
Kilmuir High 263 H7
Kilmuir High 266 D7
Kilmuir High 266 E4
Kilmuir High 263 J4
Kilmun 232 C1
Kilmux 244 B4
Kiln Green Here 131 F1
Kiln Green W'ham 134 D5
Kiln Pit Hill 211 G2
Kilnaslee 281 K2
Kilnave 230 A2
Kilncadzow 234 C5
Kilndown 123 G5
Kilnhurst 186 B3
Kilninian 246 D5
Kilninver 240 A2
Kilnsea 189 E1
Kilnsey 193 F1
Kilntown 282 E3
Kilnwick 196 B3
Kilnwick Percy 196 A2
Kiloran 238 C5
Kilpatrick 223 E3
Kilpeck 144 D4
Kilphedir 274 E7
Kilpin 195 G5
Kilpin Pike 195 G5
Kilraghts 286 E3
Kilrea 286 D4
Kilrenny 245 D4
Kilroot 287 J7
Kilsally 282 B1
Kilsby 160 A5
Kilskeery 280 E3
Kilspindie 244 A2
Kilstay 206 B3
Kilsyth 234 B2
Kiltarlity 266 C7
Kilton Notts 186 C5
Kilton R&C 203 F1
Kilton Som 115 E3
Kilton Thorpe 203 F1
Kiltyrie 242 B1
Kilvaxter 263 J5
Kilve 115 E3
Kilverstone 163 G4
Kilvington 174 D3
Kilwaughter 287 H5
Kilwinning 233 E5
Kimberley Norf 178 B5
Kimberley Notts 173 G3
Kimberworth 186 B3
Kimble Wick 134 D2
Kimblesworth 212 B3
Kimbolton Cambs 149 F1
Kimbolton Here 145 E1
Kimbridge 119 E5
Kimcote 160 A4
Kimmeridge 105 F5
Kimmerston 229 D3
Kimpton Hants 119 D3
Kimpton Herts 136 A1
Kinakelly 281 F6
Kinaldy 244 D3
Kinallen 283 F4
Kinawley 280 E5
Kinblethmont 253 E5
Kinbrace 274 D5
Kinbreack 257 G5
Kinbuck 242 C4
Kincaldrum 252 C5
Kincaple 244 C3
Kincardine Fife 234 D1
Kincardine High 266 D3
Kincardine O'Neil 260 D5
Kinclaven 243 G1
Kincorth 261 H4
Kincraig Aber 261 H2
Kincraig High 259 F4
Kincraigie 251 E5
Kindallachan 251 E4
Kindrogan Field Centre 251 F3
Kinellar 261 G3
Kineton Glos 146 C5
Kineton Warks 147 F2
Kineton Green 158 D4
Kinfauns 243 G2
King Sterndale 185 E5
Kingarth 232 B4
Kingcoed 130 D2
Kingerby 188 A3
Kingham 147 E5
Kingholm Quay 217 D3
Kinghorn 235 G1
Kinglassie 244 A5
Kingoodie 244 B2
King's Acre 145 D3
King's Bank 111 D1
King's Bromley 158 D1
Kings Caple 145 E5
King's Cliffe 161 F3
King's College Chapel, Cambridge Cambs CB2 1ST 150 C2
King's Coughton 146 C2
King's Green 145 G4
King's Heath 158 C4
Kings Hill Kent 123 F3
King's Hill Warks 159 F5
King's Hill WMid 158 B3
Kings Langley 135 F2
King's Lynn 177 E5
King's Meaburn 210 C5
Kings Mills 101 E5
King's Moss 183 G2
Kings Muir 227 D2
King's Newnham 159 G5
King's Newton 173 E5
King's Norton Leics 160 B2
King's Norton WMid 158 C5
Kings Nympton 113 G4
King's Pyon 144 D2
Kings Ripton 162 A5
King's Somborne 119 E4
King's Stag 104 D1
King's Stanley 132 A2
King's Sutton 147 G4
King's Tamerton 100 A2
King's Walden 149 G5
Kings Worthy 119 F4
Kingsand 100 A2
Kingsbarns 245 D3
Kingsbridge Devon 100 D3
Kingsbridge Som 114 C4
Kingsburgh 263 J6
Kingsbury GtLon 136 A4
Kingsbury Warks 159 E3
Kingsbury Episcopi 116 B5
Kingsbury Water Park Warks B76 0DY 159 E3
Kingscavil 235 E2
Kingsclere 119 G2
Kingscote 132 A3
Kingscott 113 F4
Kingscross 223 F3
Kingsdale 244 B4
Kingsdon 116 C5
Kingsdown Kent 125 F4
Kingsdown Swin 133 D4
Kingsdown Wilts 117 F1
Kingseat 243 G5
Kingsey 134 C2
Kingsfold Pembs 126 C3
Kingsfold WSuss 121 G4
Kingsford Aber 269 F6
Kingsford Aber 260 D3
Kingsford Aberdeen 261 G4
Kingsford EAyr 233 F5
Kingsford Worcs 158 A4
Kingsgate 125 F1
Kingshall Street 152 A1
Kingsheanton 113 F2
Kingshouse 242 A2
Kingshouse Hotel 249 E4
Kingshurst 159 D4
Kingskerswell 101 E1
Kingskettle 244 B4
Kingsland Here 144 D1
Kingsland IoA 180 A4
Kingsley ChesW&C 183 G5
Kingsley Hants 120 C4
Kingsley Staffs 172 B3
Kingsley Green 121 D4
Kingsley Holt 172 B3
Kingslow 157 G3
Kingsmill 282 B1
Kingsmoor 136 D2
Kingsmuir Angus 252 C5
Kingsmuir Fife 244 D4
Kingsnorth 124 C5
Kingstanding 158 C3
Kingsteignton 102 B5
Kingsteps 267 G6
Kingsthorne 145 D4
Kingsthorpe 148 C1
Kingston Cambs 150 B2
Kingston Corn 99 D3
Kingston Devon 100 C3
Kingston Devon 103 D4
Kingston Dorset 104 D2
Kingston Dorset 105 F5
Kingston ELoth 236 C1
Kingston GtMan 184 D3
Kingston Hants 106 A2
Kingston IoW 107 D4
Kingston Kent 125 D3
Kingston MK 149 E4
Kingston Moray 268 B4
Kingston WSuss 108 C3
Kingston Bagpuize 133 G3
Kingston Blount 134 C3
Kingston by Sea 109 E3
Kingston Deverill 117 F4
Kingston Gorse 108 C3
Kingston Lacy Dorset BH21 4EA 3 A1
Kingston Lisle 133 F4
Kingston Maurward 104 D3
Kingston near Lewes 109 F3
Kingston on Soar 173 G5
Kingston Russell 104 B3
Kingston St. Mary 115 F5
Kingston Seymour 116 B1
Kingston Stert 134 C2
Kingston upon Hull 196 D5
Kingston upon Thames 121 G1
Kingston Warren 133 F4
Kingstone Here 144 D4
Kingstone Here 145 F5
Kingstone Som 103 G1
Kingstone Staffs 172 B5
Kingstone Winslow 133 E4
Kingstown 209 G1
Kingswear 101 E2
Kingswell 233 G5
Kingswells 261 G4
Kingswinford 158 A4
Kingswood Bucks 134 B1
Kingswood Glos 131 G3
Kingswood Here 144 B2
Kingswood Kent 124 A3
Kingswood Powys 156 B2
Kingswood SGlos 131 F5
Kingswood Som 115 E4
Kingswood Surr 122 B3
Kingswood Warks 159 D5
Kingthorpe 188 B5
Kington Here 144 B2
Kington Worcs 146 B2
Kington Langley 132 B5
Kington Magna 117 E5
Kington St. Michael 132 B5
Kingussie 258 E4
Kingweston 116 C4
Kinharrachie 261 H1
Kinharvie 216 D4
Kinkell 234 A2
Kinkell Bridge 243 E3
Kinknockie 269 J6
Kinlet 157 G4
Kinloch Fife 244 A3
Kinloch High 273 F5
Kinloch High 247 F4
Kinloch High 255 K5
Kinloch High 266 C4
Kinloch P&K 252 A5
Kinloch P&K 251 G5
Kinloch Hourn (Ceann Loch Shubhairne) 257 F4
Kinloch Laggan 250 A1
Kinloch Rannoch 250 B4
Kinlochan 248 A3
Kinlochard 241 G4
Kinlocharkaig 257 F5
Kinlochbeoraid 248 A1
Kinlochbervie 272 E3
Kinlocheil 248 B2
Kinlochetive 248 D5
Kinlochewe 265 G5
Kinlochlaich 248 B5
Kinlochleven (Ceann Loch Lìobhann) 249 D3
Kinlochmoidart 247 G2
Kinlochmorar 256 E5
Kinlochmore 249 D3
Kinlochroag (Ceann Lochroag) 270 D5
Kinlochspelve 239 F2
Kinloss 267 H5
Kinmel Bay (Bae Cinmel) 182 A4
Kinmuck 261 G3
Kinnaber 253 F3
Kinnadie 269 H6
Kinnaird 244 A2
Kinneff 253 G2
Kinnelhead 226 B5
Kinnell Angus 253 E4
Kinnell Stir 242 A1
Kinnerley 170 A5
Kinnersley Here 144 C3
Kinnersley Worcs 146 A3
Kinnerton 144 B1
Kinnerton Green 170 A1
Kinnesswood 243 G4
Kinninvie 211 G5
Kinnordy 252 B4
Kinoulton 174 B4
Kinrara 259 F4
Kinross 243 G4
Kinrossie 243 G1
Kinsbourne Green 136 A1
Kinsham Here 144 C1
Kinsham Worcs 146 B4
Kinsley 186 B1
Kinson 105 G3
Kintarvie 270 E6
Kintbury 119 E1
Kintessack 267 G5
Kintillo 243 G3
Kintocher 260 D4
Kinton Here 156 D5
Kinton Shrop 156 C1
Kintore 261 F3
Kintour 230 C4
Kintra A&B 230 B5
Kintra A&B 238 C2
Kintradwell 267 G1
Kintraw 240 A4
Kinuachdrachd 239 G5
Kinveachy 259 G3
Kinver 158 A4
Kinwarton 146 D2
Kiplaw Croft 261 J1
Kipp 242 A3
Kippax 194 D4
Kippen P&K 243 F3
Kippen Stir 242 B5
Kippenross House 242 C4
Kippford (Scaur) 216 C5
Kipping's Cross 123 F4
Kippington 123 E3
Kirbister Ork 277 C7
Kirbister Ork 276 F5
Kirbuster 276 B5
Kirby Bedon 179 D5
Kirby Bellars 160 C1
Kirby Cane 165 E2
Kirby Corner 159 E5
Kirby Cross 152 D5
Kirby Fields 160 A2
Kirby Green 165 E2
Kirby Grindalythe 196 B1
Kirby Hill NYorks 202 A2
Kirby Hill NYorks 194 C1
Kirby Knowle 203 D4
Kirby le Soken 152 D5
Kirby Misperton 203 G5
Kirby Muxloe 160 A2
Kirby Row 165 E2
Kirby Sigston 202 D3
Kirby Underdale 196 A2
Kirby Wiske 202 C4
Kircubbin 283 J2
Kirdford 121 F5
Kirk 275 H3
Kirk Bramwith 186 D1
Kirk Deighton 194 C2
Kirk Ella 196 C5
Kirk Hallam 173 F3
Kirk Hammerton 195 D2
Kirk Ireton 173 D2
Kirk Langley 173 D4
Kirk Merrington 212 B4
Kirk Michael 190 B2
Kirk of Shotts 234 C3
Kirk Sandall 186 D2
Kirk Smeaton 186 C1
Kirk Yetholm 228 C4
Kirkabister 279 D9
Kirkandrews 207 G2
Kirkandrews-upon-Eden 209 G1
Kirkbampton 209 G1
Kirkbean 217 D5
Kirkbride 209 F1
Kirkbuddo 252 D5
Kirkburn ERid 196 B2
Kirkburn ScBord 227 D2
Kirkburton 185 F1
Kirkby Lincs 188 A3
Kirkby Mersey 183 F3
Kirkby NYorks 203 E2
Kirkby Fleetham 202 B3
Kirkby Green 175 F2
Kirkby in Ashfield 173 F2
Kirkby la Thorpe 175 F3
Kirkby Lonsdale 200 B5
Kirkby Malham 193 E1
Kirkby Mallory 159 G2
Kirkby Malzeard 202 B5
Kirkby on Bain 176 A1
Kirkby Overblow 194 C3
Kirkby Stephen 200 C2
Kirkby Thore 210 C5
Kirkby Underwood 175 F5
Kirkby Wharfe 195 E3
Kirkby Woodhouse 173 F2
Kirkby-in-Furness 198 D4
Kirkbymoorside 203 F4
Kirkcaldy 244 A5
Kirkcambeck 210 B1
Kirkcolm 214 B4
Kirkconnel 225 F4
Kirkconnell 217 D4
Kirkcowan 215 E4
Kirkcudbright 216 A5
Kirkdale House 215 G5
Kirkdean 235 F5
Kirkfieldbank 234 C5
Kirkgunzeon 216 C4
Kirkham Lancs 192 A4
Kirkham NYorks 195 G1
Kirkhamgate 194 C5
Kirkharle 220 C3
Kirkhaugh 210 C3
Kirkheaton N'umb 220 C4
Kirkheaton WYorks 185 F1
Kirkhill Angus 253 E3
Kirkhill High 266 C7
Kirkhill Moray 268 B5
Kirkhope 227 E3
Kirkibost High 256 B3
Kirkibost (Circebost) Na H-E. Siar 270 D4
Kirkinch 252 B5
Kirkinner 215 F5
Kirkinriola 287 F5
Kirkintilloch 234 A2
Kirkistown 283 K3
Kirkland Cumb 210 C4
Kirkland Cumb 209 D5
Kirkland D&G 216 C1
Kirkland D&G 225 F4
Kirkland D&G 217 E2
Kirkland of Longcastle 207 D2
Kirkleatham 213 E5
Kirklevington 202 D1
Kirkley 165 G2
Kirklington Notts 174 B2
Kirklington NYorks 202 C4
Kirklinton 210 A1
Kirkliston 235 F2
Kirkmaiden 206 B3
Kirkmichael P&K 251 F3
Kirkmichael SAyr 224 B5
Kirkmuirhill 234 B5
Kirknewton N'umb 228 D3
Kirknewton WLoth 235 F3
Kirkney 260 D1
Kirkoswald Cumb 210 B3
Kirkoswald SAyr 224 A5
Kirkpatrick Durham 216 B3
Kirkpatrick-Fleming 218 A4
Kirksanton 198 C4
Kirkstall 194 B4
Kirkstead 175 G1
Kirkstile Aber 260 D1
Kirkstile D&G 218 B2
Kirkstyle 275 J1
Kirkthorpe 194 C5
Kirkton A&B 239 G4
Kirkton Aber 260 E2
Kirkton Aber 268 E5
Kirkton Aber 260 E3
Kirkton Angus 252 C5
Kirkton D&G 217 D2
Kirkton Fife 244 B2
Kirkton High 258 D1
Kirkton High 266 E2
Kirkton High 266 E6
Kirkton High 274 D2
Kirkton High 256 E2
Kirkton P&K 243 E3
Kirkton ScBord 227 G4
Kirkton Manor 226 D2
Kirkton of Airlie 252 B4
Kirkton of Auchterhouse 244 B1
Kirkton of Barevan 267 F7
Kirkton of Bourtie 261 G2
Kirkton of Collace 243 G1
Kirkton of Craig 253 F4
Kirkton of Culsalmond 260 E1
Kirkton of Durris 261 F5
Kirkton of Glenbuchat 260 B3
Kirkton of Glenisla 252 A3
Kirkton of Kingoldrum 252 B4
Kirkton of Kinnettles 252 C5
Kirkton of Lethendy 251 G5
Kirkton of Logie Buchan 261 H2
Kirkton of Maryculter 261 G5
Kirkton of Menmuir 252 D3
Kirkton of Monikie 244 D1
Kirkton of Rayne 260 E1
Kirkton of Skene 261 G4
Kirkton of Tealing 244 C1
Kirktonhill Aber 253 E3
Kirktonhill WDun 233 E2
Kirktown 269 J5
Kirktown of Alvah 268 E4
Kirktown of Deskford 268 D4
Kirktown of Fetteresso 253 G1
Kirktown of Slains 261 J2
Kirkwall 277 D6
Kirkwall Airport 277 D7
Kirkwhelpington 220 B3
Kirmington 188 B1
Kirmond le Mire 188 B3
Kirn 232 C2
Kirriemuir 252 B4
Kirstead Green 165 D2
Kirtlebridge 218 A4
Kirtleton 218 A3
Kirtling 151 E2
Kirtling Green 151 E2
Kirtlington 134 A1
Kirtomy 274 C2
Kirton Lincs 176 B4
Kirton Notts 174 B1
Kirton Suff 153 D4
Kirton End 176 A3
Kirton Holme 176 A3
Kirton in Lindsey 187 G3
Kiscadale 223 F3
Kislingbury 148 B2
Kismeldon Bridge 113 D4
Kit Hill Country Park Corn PL17 8AX 99 D3
Kites Hardwick 147 G1
Kitley 100 B2
Kittisford 115 D5
Kittisford Barton 115 D5
Kittle 128 B4
Kitt's End 136 B3
Kitt's Green 159 D4
Kitwood 120 B4
Kivernoll 145 D4
Kiveton Park 186 B4
Klibreck 273 H5
Knabbygates 268 D5
Knaith 187 F4
Knaith Park 187 F4
Knap Corner 117 F5
Knaphill 121 E2
Knaplock 114 B4
Knapp P&K 244 A1
Knapp Som 116 A5
Knapthorpe 174 C2
Knaptoft 160 B4
Knapton Norf 179 E2
Knapton York 195 E2
Knapton Green 144 D2
Knapwell 150 B1
Knaresborough 194 C2
Knarsdale 210 C2
Knarston 276 C5
Knaven 269 G6
Knayton 202 D4
Knebworth 150 A5
Knebworth House Herts SG3 6PY 150 A5
Knedlington 195 G5
Kneesall 174 C1
Kneesworth 150 B3
Kneeton 174 C3
Knelston 128 A4
Knenhall 171 G4
Knettishall 164 A3
Knettishall Heath Country Park Suff IP22 2TQ 164 A3
Knightacott 113 G2
Knightcote 147 G2
Knightley 171 F5
Knightley Dale 171 F5
Knighton BCP 105 G3
Knighton Devon 100 B3
Knighton Dorset 104 C1
Knighton Leic 160 A2
Knighton (Tref-y-clawdd) Powys 156 B5
Knighton Som 115 E3
Knighton Staffs 171 E5
Knighton Staffs 171 E3
Knighton Wilts 133 E5
Knighton on Teme 157 F5
Knightswood 233 G3
Knightwick 145 G2
Knill 144 B1
Knipoch 240 A2
Knipton 174 D4
Knitsley 212 A3
Kniveton 172 D2
Knock A&B 239 E1
Knock Cumb 210 C5
Knock High 256 C4
Knock Moray 268 D5
Knock of Auchnahannet 259 H1
Knockalava 240 B5
Knockally 275 G6
Knockaloe Moar 190 A3
Knockan CC&G 285 J5
Knockan High 272 E7
Knockandhu 259 K2
Knockando 267 J7
Knockanorane 281 G5
Knockanully 287 F4
Knockarevan 281 F6
Knockarthur 266 E1
Knockavannon 282 C6
Knockbain 266 D6
Knockban 265 J5
Knockbrack D&S 285 G4
Knockbreck 266 E3
Knockbrex 207 F2
Knockcloghrim 286 C6
Knockdamph 265 J2
Knockdee 275 G2
Knockdow 232 C2
Knockdown 132 A4
Knockenkelly 223 F3
Knockentiber 224 B2
Knockfin 257 K2
Knockgray 215 G1
Knockholt 123 D3
Knockholt Pound 123 D3
Knockin 170 A5
Knockinelder 283 K3
Knockinlaw 224 C2
Knockintorran (Cnoc an Torrain) 262 C5
Knocklearn 216 B3
Knockmany Passage Grave Mid Ulster BT76 0XJ 281 H3
Knockmill 123 E2
Knockmoyle 281 G1
Knocknacarry 287 G2
Knocknaha 222 B4
Knocknain 214 A4
Knocknalling 215 G2
Knocknashangan 280 B4
Knockrome 231 D2
Knocks 281 F5
Knocksharry 190 A3
Knockville 215 E3
Knockvologan 238 C3
Knodishall 153 F1
Knodishall Common 153 F1
Knodishall Green 153 F1
Knole 116 B5
Knolls Green 184 C5
Knolton 170 A4
Knook 118 A3
Knossington 160 D2
Knott End-on-Sea 191 G3
Knotting 149 F1
Knotting Green 149 F1
Knottingley 195 E5
Knotts 193 D2
Knotty Green 135 E3
Knowbury 157 E5
Knowe 215 E3
Knowehead 283 J1
Knowes of Elrick 268 E5
Knowesgate 220 B3
Knoweside 224 A4
Knowetownhead 227 G4
Knowhead 269 H5
Knowl Green 151 F3
Knowl Hill 134 D5
Knowl Wall 171 F4
Knowle Bristol 131 F5
Knowle Devon 102 A2
Knowle Devon 113 E2
Knowle Devon 103 D4
Knowle Shrop 157 E5
Knowle Som 114 C3
Knowle WMid 159 D5
Knowle Cross 102 D3
Knowle Green 192 C4
Knowle Hall 116 A3
Knowle St. Giles 103 G1
Knowlton Dorset 105 G1
Knowlton Kent 125 E3
Knowsley 183 F3
Knowsley Safari Park Mersey L34 4AN 23 E2
Knowstone 114 B5
Knox Bridge 123 G4
Knucklas (Cnwclas) 156 B5
Knutsford 184 B5
Knypersley 171 F2
Krumlin 185 E1
Kuggar 95 E5
Kyle of Lochalsh (Caol Loch Aillse) 256 D2
Kyleakin (Caol Acain) 256 D2
Kylerhea (Ceol Reatha) 256 D2
Kyles Scalpay (Caolas Scalpaigh) 263 H2
Kylesbeg 247 F2
Kylesknoydart 256 E5
Kylesku 272 E5
Kylesmorar 256 E5
Kylestrome 272 E5
Kyloag 266 D2
Kynaston 170 A5
Kynnersley 157 F1
Kyre Park 145 F1

L
Labost 270 E3
Lacasaigh 271 F5
Lace Market Centre NG1 1HF 80 Nottingham
Laceby 188 C2
Lacey Green 134 D2
Lach Dennis 184 B5
Lack 280 E2
Lackagh 285 J4
Lackalee (Leac a' Li) 263 G2
Lackford 163 F5
Lacock 118 A1
Ladbroke 147 G2
Laddingford 123 F4
Lade Bank 176 B2
Ladies Hill 192 A3
Ladock 96 C4
Lady Hall 198 C4

Lady Lever Art Gallery *Mersey* CH62 5EQ **22** B4
Ladybank **244** B3
Ladycross **98** D2
Ladyfield **240** C3
Ladykirk **237** F5
Ladysford **269** H4
Ladywood **146** A1
Laga **247** F4
Lagalochan **240** A3
Lagavara **286** E1
Lagg *A&B* **231** D2
Lagg *NAyr* **223** E3
Lagg *SAyr* **224** A4
Laggan *A&B* **230** A4
Laggan (An Lagan) *High* **257** J5
Laggan *High* **258** D5
Laggan *Moray* **260** B1
Laggan *Stir* **242** A3
Lagganulva **247** D5
Lagganvoulin **259** J3
Laghy Corner **282** B2
Laglingarten **240** D4
Lagnalean **266** D7
Lagrae **225** F4
Laguna **243** G1
Laid **273** G3
Laide **265** F2
Laig **247** D1
Laight **225** F4
Lainchoil **259** H3
Laindon **137** F4
Laing Art Gallery *T&W* NE1 8AG **79** Newcastle upon Tyne
Lair **251** G3
Lairg **266** C1
Lairg Lodge **266** C1
Laisterdyke **194** A4
Laithers **268** E6
Laithes **210** A4
Lake *Devon* **113** F2
Lake *Devon* **100** B1
Lake *IoW* **107** E4
Lake *Wilts* **118** C4
Lake District Visitor Centre at Brockhole *Cumb* LA23 1LJ **199** E2
Lakenham **178** D5
Lakenheath **163** F4
Lakes Aquarium *Cumb* LA12 8AS **199** E4
Lakes End **162** D3
Lakeside *Cumb* **199** E4
Lakeside *Thur* **137** E5
Lakeside & Haverthwaite Railway *Cumb* LA12 8AL **199** E4
Laleham **121** F1
Laleston **129** E5
Lamancha **235** G4
Lamarsh **151** G4
Lamas **178** D3
Lamb Corner **152** B4
Lamb Roe **192** B4
Lambden **237** E5
Lambeg **283** F2
Lamberhurst **123** F5
Lamberhurst Quarter **123** F5
Lamberton **237** F3
Lambfell Moor **190** A3
Lambley *N'umb* **210** C2
Lambley *Notts* **174** B3
Lambourn **133** F5
Lambourn Woodlands **133** F5
Lambourne End **137** D3
Lambs Green **122** B5
Lambston **126** C1
Lambton **212** B2
Lamellion **97** G3
Lamerton **99** E3
Lamesley **212** B2
Lamington *High* **266** E4
Lamington *SLan* **226** A2
Lamlash **223** F2
Lamloch **215** G1
Lamonby **210** A4
Lamorna **94** B4
Lamorran **96** C5
Lampert **219** E4
Lampeter (Llanbedr Pont Steffan) **142** B3
Lampeter Velfrey **127** E1
Lamphey **126** D2
Lamplugh **209** D4
Lamport **160** C5
Lamyatt **117** D4
Lana *Devon* **98** D1
Lana *Devon* **112** D5
Lanark **234** C5
Lanarth **95** E4
Lancaster **192** A1
Lancaster Leisure Park *Lancs* LA1 3LA **192** A1
Lancaster Priory *Lancs* LA1 1YZ **192** A1
Lanchester **212** A3
Lancing **109** D3
Landbeach **150** C1
Landcross **113** E3
Landerberry **261** F4
Landewednack **95** E5
Landford **106** B1
Landhallow **275** G5
Landican **183** D4
Landimore **128** A3
Landkey **113** F2
Landmoth **202** D3
Landore **128** C3
Landrake **99** D4
Land's End *Corn* TR19 7AA **94** A4
Land's End Airport **94** A4
Landscove **101** D1
Landshipping **126** D1
Landulph **100** A1
Landwade **151** E1
Landywood **158** B2
Lane Bottom **193** E4
Lane End *Bucks* **134** D3
Lane End *Cumb* **198** C3
Lane End *Derbys* **173** F1

Lane End *Dorset* **105** E3
Lane End *Hants* **119** G5
Lane End *Here* **131** F1
Lane End *Kent* **137** E5
Lane End *Wilts* **117** F3
Lane Ends *Derbys* **172** D4
Lane Ends *GtMan* **185** D3
Lane Ends *Lancs* **193** D4
Lane Ends *NYorks* **193** F3
Lane Green **158** A2
Lane Head *Dur* **202** A1
Lane Head *Dur* **211** G5
Lane Head *GtMan* **184** A3
Lane Head *WYorks* **185** F2
Lane Heads **192** A4
Lane Side **193** D5
Laneast **97** G1
Lane-end **97** E3
Laneham **187** F5
Lanehead *Dur* **211** E3
Lanehead *N'umb* **219** F3
Lanesend **127** D2
Lanesfield **158** B3
Laneshawbridge **193** F3
Langais **262** D5
Langamull **246** C4
Langar **174** C4
Langbank **233** E2
Langbar **193** G2
Langbaurgh **203** E1
Langcliffe **193** E1
Langdale End **204** C3
Langdon *Corn* **98** C1
Langdon *Corn* **98** D2
Langdon Beck **211** E4
Langdon Hills **137** F4
Langdon Hills Country Park *Essex* SS17 9NH **137** F4
Langdon House **102** C3
Langdyke **244** B4
Langford *CenBeds* **149** G3
Langford *Essex* **138** B2
Langford *Notts* **174** D2
Langford *Oxon* **133** E2
Langford Budville **115** E5
Langham *Essex* **152** B4
Langham *Norf* **178** B1
Langham *Rut* **160** D2
Langham *Suff* **152** A1
Langham Moor **152** B4
Langho **192** C4
Langholm **218** B3
Langland **128** C4
Langlands **216** A5
Langlee **228** D4
Langleeford **228** D4
Langley *ChesE* **184** D5
Langley *Derbys* **173** F3
Langley *Essex* **150** C4
Langley *Glos* **146** C5
Langley *GtMan* **184** C2
Langley *Hants* **106** D2
Langley *Herts* **150** A5
Langley *Kent* **123** G3
Langley *N'umb* **211** E1
Langley *Oxon* **133** F1
Langley *Slo* **135** F5
Langley *Som* **115** D5
Langley *Warks* **147** D1
Langley *WSuss* **120** D5
Langley Burrell **132** B5
Langley Corner **135** F4
Langley Green *Derbys* **173** D4
Langley Green *Warks* **147** E1
Langley Green *WSuss* **122** B5
Langley Heath **124** A3
Langley Marsh **115** D5
Langley Mill **173** F3
Langley Moor **212** B3
Langley Park *Bucks* SL3 6DW **135** F4
Langley Street **179** E5
Langney **110** B3
Langold **186** C4
Langore **97** G1
Langport **116** B5
Langrick **176** A3
Langrick Bridge **176** A3
Langridge *B&NESom* **117** E1
Langridge *Devon* **113** F3
Langridgeford **113** F3
Langrigg **209** E2
Langrish **120** C5
Langsett **185** G2
Langshaw **227** G2
Langshawburn **227** D5
Langside *Glas* **233** G3
Langside *P&K* **242** C3
Langskaill **276** D5
Langstone *Hants* **107** G2
Langstone *Newport* **130** C3
Langthorne **202** B3
Langthorpe **194** C1
Langthwaite **201** F2
Langtoft *ERid* **196** C1
Langtoft *Lincs* **161** G1
Langton *Dur* **202** A1
Langton *Lincs* **189** D5
Langton *Lincs* **176** A1
Langton *NYorks* **195** G1
Langton by Wragby **188** B5
Langton Green *Kent* **123** E5
Langton Green *Suff* **164** C3
Langton Herring **104** C3
Langton Long Blandford **105** E2
Langton Matravers **105** F5
Langtree **113** E4
Langtree Week **113** E4
Langwathby **210** B4
Langwell **266** B1
Langwell House **275** G6
Langwith **186** C5
Langworth **188** A5
Lanhydrock *Corn* PL30 5AD **97** E3
Lanivet **97** E3
Lank **97** E2
Lanlivery **97** E4
Lanner **96** B5
Lanoy **97** G2
Lanreath **97** F4

Lansallos **97** F4
Lansdown **117** E1
Lanteglos **97** E1
Lanteglos Highway **97** F4
Lanton *N'umb* **228** D3
Lanton *ScBord* **228** A4
Lanvean **96** C3
Lapford **102** A2
Laphroaig **230** B5
Lapley **158** A1
Lapworth **159** D5
Larach na Gaibhre **231** F2
Larachbeg **247** F5
Laragh **286** C5
Larbert **234** C1
Larbreck **192** A3
Larchmount **282** B3
Larden Green **170** C2
Larg **215** E3
Largie **260** E1
Largiemore **232** A1
Largoward **244** C4
Largs **232** D4
Largue **268** E6
Larguebaan **222** B4
Largybeg **223** F3
Largymore **223** F3
Lark Hall **151** D3
Larkfield **232** D2
Larkhall **234** B4
Larkhill *Wilts* **118** C3
Larklands **173** F3
Larling **164** A3
Larne **287** H5
Larriston **218** D2
Lartington **201** F1
Lary **260** B4
Lasborough **132** A3
Lasham **120** B3
Lashbrook **113** E5
Lashenden **124** A4
Lassington **145** G5
Lassintullich **250** C4
Lassodie **243** G5
Lasswade **236** A3
Lastingham **203** G3
Latchford *Herts* **150** C5
Latchford *Oxon* **134** B2
Latchingdon **138** B2
Latchley **99** E3
Lately Common **184** A3
Lathallan Mill **244** C4
Lathbury **149** D3
Latheron **275** G5
Latheronwheel **275** G5
Lathockar **244** C3
Lathones **244** C4
Lathrisk **244** A4
Latimer **135** F3
Latteridge **131** F4
Lattiford **117** D5
Latton **132** C3
Lauchentyre **215** F5
Lauchintilly **261** F3
Lauder **236** C5
Laugharne (Lacharn) **127** G1
Laughterton **187** F5
Laughton *ESuss* **110** A2
Laughton *Leics* **160** B4
Laughton *Lincs* **175** F4
Laughton *Lincs* **187** F3
Laughton en le Morthen **186** C4
Launcells **112** C5
Launcells Cross **112** C5
Launceston **98** D2
Launde Abbey **160** C2
Launton **148** B5
Laurelvale **282** D2
Laurencekirk **253** F2
Laurieston *D&G* **216** A4
Laurieston *Falk* **234** D2
Lavendon **149** E2
Lavenham **152** A3
Laverhay **227** F1
Lavernock **115** E1
Laversdale **210** A1
Laverstock **118** C4
Laverstoke **119** F3
Laverton *Glos* **146** C4
Laverton *NYorks* **202** B5
Laverton *Som* **117** E2
Lavister **170** A2
Law **234** C4
Lawers *P&K* **242** C2
Lawers *P&K* **242** B1
Lawford *Essex* **152** B4
Lawford *Som* **115** E4
Lawhitton **99** D2
Lawkland **193** D1
Lawkland Green **193** D1
Lawley **157** F2
Lawnhead **171** F5
Lawrence Weston **131** E5
Lawrencetown **282** D4
Lawrenny **126** D2
Laws **244** C1
Lawshall **151** G2
Lawshall Green **151** G2
Lawton **148** D1
Laxdale (Lacasdal) **271** G4
Laxey **190** C3
Laxfield **165** D4
Laxfirth *Shet* **279** D7
Laxfirth *Shet* **279** D8
Laxford Bridge **272** E4
Laxo **279** D6
Laxton *ERid* **195** G5
Laxton *NN'hants* **161** E3
Laxton *Notts* **174** C1
Laycock **193** G3
Layde **287** G3
Layer Breton **138** C1
Layer de la Haye **138** C1
Layer Marney **138** C1
Layham **152** B3
Laymore **103** G2
Layter's Green **135** E3
Laytham **195** G4
Layton **191** G4
Lazenby **213** E5
Lazonby **210** B4
Lea *Derbys* **173** D2
Lea *Here* **145** F5
Lea *Lincs* **187** F4
Lea *Shrop* **156** C4
Lea *Shrop* **156** D2

Lea *Wilts* **132** B4
Lea Bridge **173** E2
Lea Green **145** F1
Lea Marston **159** E3
Lea Town **192** A4
Lea Yeat **200** C4
Leachd **240** C5
Leachkin (An Leacainn) **266** D7
Leadburn **235** G4
Leaden Roding **137** E1
Leadenham **175** E2
Leaderfoot **227** G2
Leadgate *Cumb* **210** D3
Leadgate *Dur* **212** A2
Leadgate *N'umb* **212** A2
Leadhills **225** G4
Leadingcross Green **124** A3
Leafield **133** F1
Leagrave **149** F5
Leake Commonside **176** B2
Leake Hurn's End **176** C3
Lealands **110** A2
Lealholm **203** G2
Lealt *A&B* **239** F5
Lealt *High* **264** B5
Leam **185** G5
Leamington Hastings **147** G1
Leamington Spa **147** G1
Leamington Spa Art Gallery & Museum *Warks* CV32 4AA **16** B6
Leamoor Common **156** D4
Leanach *A&B* **240** C5
Leanach *High* **266** E7
Leanaig **266** C6
Leanoch **267** J6
Leargybreck **230** D2
Leasgill **199** F4
Leasingham **175** F3
Leasowe **183** D4
Leason **128** A3
Leat **98** D2
Leatherhead **121** G2
Leathley **194** B3
Leaton *Shrop* **157** D1
Leaton *Tel&W* **157** F1
Leaveland **124** C3
Leavenheath **152** A4
Leavening **195** G1
Leaves Green **122** D2
Leavesden Green **136** A2
Lebberston **205** D4
Lechlade-on-Thames **133** E3
Leck *CC&G* **286** C2
Leck *Lancs* **200** B5
Leckford **119** E4
Leckfurin **274** C3
Leckgruinart **230** A3
Leckhampstead *Bucks* **148** C4
Leckhampstead *WBerks* **133** G5
Leckhampstead Thicket **133** G5
Leckhampton **132** B1
Leckie *High* **265** G5
Leckie *Stir* **242** B5
Leckmelm (Leac Mailm) **265** H3
Leckroy **257** K5
Leckuary **240** A5
Leckwith **130** A5
Leconfield **196** C3
Ledaig (Leideag) **240** B1
Ledard **241** G4
Ledbeg **272** E7
Ledburn **149** D5
Ledbury **145** G4
Ledcharrie **242** A2
Ledgemoor **144** D2
Ledicot **144** D1
Ledmore *A&B* **247** E5
Ledmore *High* **272** E7
Lednagullin **274** C2
Ledsham *ChesW&C* **183** E5
Ledsham *WYorks* **195** D5
Ledston **194** D5
Ledstone **100** D3
Ledwell **147** G5
Lee *Devon* **113** E1
Lee *Hants* **106** C1
Lee *Lancs* **192** B2
Lee *Shrop* **170** B4
Lee Brockhurst **170** C5
Lee Chapel **137** F4
Lee Clump **135** E2
Lee Mill Bridge **100** B2
Lee Moor **100** B1
Lee Valley Park *Essex* EN9 1XQ **136** C2
Leebotten **279** D10
Leebotwood **157** D3
Leece **191** F1
Leeds *Kent* **124** A3
Leeds *WYorks* **194** B4
Leeds Art Gallery *WYorks* LS1 3AA **40** B3
Leeds Bradford International Airport **194** B3
Leeds Castle & Gardens *Kent* ME17 1PL **124** A3
Leedstown **94** D3
Leegomery **157** F1
Leek **171** G2
Leek Wootton **147** E1
Leekbrook **171** G2
Leeke **285** J3
Leeming *NYorks* **202** B4
Leeming *WYorks* **193** G4
Leeming Bar **202** B4
Lee-on-the-Solent **107** E2
Lees *Derbys* **173** D4
Lees *GtMan* **185** D2
Leeswood **169** F2
Leftwich **184** A5
Legacurry **283** F3
Legamaddy **283** H5
Leganany **283** F4
Legars **237** E5
Legbourne **189** D4
Legerwood **236** C5

Leggs **280** C2
Legoland Windsor *W&M* SL4 4AY **135** E5
Legsby **188** B4
Leicester **160** A2
Leicester Forest East **160** A2
Leideag **254** B5
Leigh *Dorset* **104** C2
Leigh *Dorset* **105** G3
Leigh *GtMan* **184** A2
Leigh *Kent* **123** E4
Leigh *Shrop* **156** C2
Leigh *Surr* **122** B4
Leigh *Wilts* **132** C3
Leigh *Worcs* **145** G2
Leigh Beck **138** B4
Leigh Common **117** E5
Leigh Delamere **132** A5
Leigh Green **124** B5
Leigh Park **107** G2
Leigh Sinton **145** G2
Leigh upon Mendip **117** D3
Leigh Woods **131** E5
Leigham **100** B2
Leighland Chapel **114** D4
Leigh-on-Sea **138** B4
Leighterton **132** A3
Leighton (Tre'r Llai) *Powys* **156** B2
Leighton *Shrop* **157** F2
Leighton *Som* **117** E3
Leighton Bromswold **161** G5
Leighton Buzzard **149** E5
Leinthall Earls **144** D1
Leinthall Starkes **144** D1
Leintwardine **156** D5
Leire **160** A4
Leirinmore **273** G2
Leiston **153** F1
Leitfie **252** A5
Leith **235** G2
Leitholm **237** E5
Leitir *F&O* **281** G6
Leitrim *NM&D* **283** G4
Leitrim *NM&D* **283** G5
Lelant **94** C3
Lelley **197** E4
Lemington **212** A1
Lemnas **269** G4
Lempitlaw **228** B3
Lemsford **136** B1
Lenaderg **282** E2
Lenagh **285** H7
Lenchwick **146** C2
Lendalfoot **214** C1
Lendrick Lodge **242** A4
Lenham **124** A3
Lenham Heath **124** B4
Lenie **258** C2
Lenimore **231** G5
Lennel **237** E5
Lennox Plunton **216** A5
Lent Rise **135** E4
Lenton *Lincs* **175** F4
Lenton *Nott* **173** G4
Lenton Abbey **173** G4
Lenwade **178** B4
Lenzie **234** A2
Leoch **244** B1
Leochel-Cushnie **260** D3
Leominster **145** D2
Leonard Stanley **132** A2
Leorin **230** B5
Lepe **106** D3
Lephin **263** G7
Lephinchapel **240** B5
Lephinmore **240** B5
Leppington **195** G1
Lepton **185** G1
Lerags **240** C2
Lerryn **97** F4
Lerwick **279** D8
Lesbury **229** G5
Leschangie **261** F3
Leslie *Aber* **260** D2
Leslie *Fife* **244** A4
Lesmahagow **225** G2
Lesnewth **98** B1
Lessendrum **268** D6
Lessingham **179** E3
Lessness Heath **137** D5
Lessonhall **209** F1
Leswalt **214** B4
Letchmore Heath **136** A3
Letchworth Garden City **150** A4
Letcombe Bassett **133** F4
Letcombe Regis **133** F4
Letham *Angus* **252** D5
Letham *Falk* **234** C1
Letham *Fife* **244** B3
Lethanhill **224** C4
Lethenty **269** G6
Letheringham **153** D2
Letheringsett **178** B2
Lettaford **102** A4
Letter **261** F3
Letter Finlay **257** J5
Letterbreen **280** D4
Letterewe **265** F4
Letterfearn (Leitir Fhearna) **256** E2
Letterkeen **280** D2
Letterloan **286** C2
Lettermorar **247** G1
Lettermore *A&B* **247** D5
Lettermore *High* **273** J4
Letters **265** H3
Lettershaws **225** G3
Lettershendony **285** H4
Letterston **140** C5
Lettoch *High* **259** H3
Lettoch *High* **259** J1
Letton *Here* **156** C1
Letton *Here* **144** C3
Letty Green **136** B1
Letwell **186** C4
Leuchars **244** C2
Leumrabhagh **271** F6
Leurbost (Liurbost) **271** F5
Leusdon **102** A5
Levedale **158** A1
Level's Green **150** C5

Leven *ERid* **196** D3
Leven *Fife* **244** B4
Levencorroch **223** F3
Levenhall **236** A2
Levens **199** F4
Levens Green **150** B5
Levenshulme **184** C3
Levenwick **279** D10
Leverburgh **263** F3
Leverington **162** C1
Leverstock Green **135** F2
Leverton **176** B3
Leverton Lucasgate **176** C3
Leverton Outgate **176** C3
Levington **152** D4
Levisham **204** B3
Levishie **258** B3
Lew **133** F2
Lewannick **97** G1
Lewcombe **104** B2
Lewdown **99** E2
Lewes **109** G2
Leweston **140** C5
Lewisham **136** C5
Lewiston (Blàr na Maigh) **258** C2
Lewistown **129** F4
Lewknor **134** C3
Leworthy **113** G2
Lewson Street **124** B2
Lewth **192** A4
Lewtrenchard **99** E2
Ley *Aber* **260** D3
Ley *Corn* **97** F3
Ley Green **149** G5
Leybourne **123** F3
Leyburn **202** A3
Leyland **192** B5
Leylodge **261** F3
Leymoor **185** F1
Leys *Aber* **269** J5
Leys *Aber* **260** C4
Leys *P&K* **244** A1
Leys of Cossans **252** B5
Leysdown-on-Sea **124** C1
Leysmill **253** E5
Leysters **145** E1
Leyton **136** C4
Leytonstone **136** C4
Lezant **98** D3
Lezerea **95** D3
Lhanbryde **267** K5
Liatrie **257** J1
Libanus **143** F5
Libberton **235** D5
Libbery **146** B2
Liberton **235** G3
Liceasto **263** G2
Lichfield **158** D2
Lichfield Cathedral *Staffs* WS13 7LD **158** D2
Lickey **158** B5
Lickey End **158** B5
Lickey Hills Country Park *Worcs* B45 8ER **14** C6
Lickfold **121** E5
Liddaton Green **99** E2
Liddel **277** D9
Liddesdale **247** G4
Liddington **133** E4
Lidgate *Derbys* **186** A5
Lidgate *Suff* **151** F2
Lidgett **174** B1
Lidlington **149** E4
Lidsey **108** B3
Lidsing **123** G2
Lienassie **257** F2
Lieurary **275** F2
Liff **244** B1
Liffock **286** B2
Lifton **99** D2
Liftondown **99** D2
Ligfordrum **285** G6
Lightcliffe **194** A5
Lighthorne **147** F2
Lighthorne Heath **147** F2
Lighthouse, The, Glasgow *Glas* G1 3NU **39** E4
Lighthouse, The - Poole's Centre for the Arts *BCP* BH15 1UG **3** B4
Lightwater Valley *NYorks* HG4 3HT **202** B5
Lightwater **121** E1
Lightwood **171** G3
Lightwood Green *ChesE* **170** D3
Lightwood Green *Wrex* **170** A3
Ligoniel **283** G1
Lilbourne **160** A5
Lilburn Tower **229** E4
Lilleshall **157** G1
Lilley *Herts* **149** G5
Lilley *WBerks* **133** G5
Lilliesleaf **227** G3
Lilling Green **195** F1
Lillingstone Dayrell **148** C3
Lillingstone Lovell **148** C3
Lillington *Dorset* **104** C3
Lillington *Warks* **147** F1
Lilliput **105** G4
Lilstock **115** E3
Lilyhurst **157** G1
Limavady **285** J3
Limbury **149** F5
Lime Hill **281** J1
Lime Side **184** D2
Limefield **184** C1
Limehillock **268** D5
Limehurst **184** D2
Limekilnburn **234** B4
Limekilns **235** E1
Limerigg **234** C2
Limerstone **106** D4
Liminary **287** F6
Limington **116** C5
Limpenhoe **179** E5
Limpley Stoke **117** E1
Limpsfield **122** C3
Limpsfield Chart **122** D3
Linacre Reservoirs *Derbys* S42 7JW **186** A5

Linbriggs **220** A1
Linby **173** G2
Linchmere **121** D4
Lincluden **217** D3
Lincoln **187** G5
Lincoln Castle *Lincs* LN1 3AA **77** Lincoln
Lincoln Cathedral *Lincs* LN2 1PL **77** Lincoln
Lincomb **146** A1
Lincombe *Devon* **100** D2
Lincombe *Devon* **100** D3
Lindal in Furness **199** D5
Lindale **199** F4
Lindean **227** F2
Lindertis **252** B4
Lindfield **109** F1
Lindford **120** D4
Lindifferon **244** B3
Lindisfarne (Holy Island) **229** F2
Lindley **194** B3
Lindores **244** A3
Lindow End **184** C5
Lindridge **145** F1
Lindsaig **232** A2
Lindsell **151** E5
Lindsey **152** A3
Lindsey Tye **152** A3
Linfitts **185** D2
Linford *Hants* **106** A2
Linford *Thur* **137** F5
Linford Wood **148** D3
Lingague **190** A4
Lingards Wood **185** E1
Lingdale **203** F1
Lingen **144** C1
Lingfield **122** C4
Lingley Green **183** G4
Lingwood **179** E5
Linhead **268** E5
Linhope **227** F5
Liniclate (Lionacleit) **262** C7
Linicro **263** J5
Linkend **146** A4
Linkenholt **119** E2
Linkhill **110** D1
Linkinhorne **98** D3
Linklater **277** D9
Linksness *Ork* **277** B7
Linksness *Ork* **277** E6
Linktown **244** A5
Linley *Shrop* **156** C3
Linley *Shrop* **157** F3
Linley Green **145** F2
Linlithgow **235** E2
Linlithgow Bridge **235** D2
Linn of Muick Cottage **252** B1
Linnels **211** F1
Linney **126** B3
Linshiels **220** A1
Linsiadar **270** E4
Linsidemore **266** C2
Linslade **149** E5
Linstead Parva **165** E4
Linstock **210** A2
Linthwaite **185** F1
Lintlaw **237** F4
Lintmill **268** D4
Linton *Cambs* **151** D3
Linton *Derbys* **159** E1
Linton *Here* **145** F5
Linton *Kent* **123** G3
Linton *NYorks* **193** F2
Linton *ScBord* **228** B4
Linton *WYorks* **194** C3
Linton-on-Ouse **195** D1
Lintzford **212** A2
Linwood *Hants* **106** A2
Linwood *Lincs* **188** B5
Linwood *Renf* **233** F3
Lionel (Lional) **271** H1
Liphook **120** D4
Lipley **171** F4
Lisadian *AB&C* **282** B4
Lisadian *L&C* **283** F3
Lisbane **283** H2
Lisbarnet **283** H2
Lisbellaw **281** F4
Lisburn **283** F2
Liscall **286** C4
Liscard **183** E3
Liscloon **285** G5
Liscolman **286** D1
Liscombe **114** B4
Lisconrea **281** F3
Lisdoart **281** J3
Lisk **285** F6
Liskeard **97** G3
Lislane **286** B4
Lislea *Mid Ulster* **286** D5
Lislea *NM&D* **282** D6
Lisleen **283** H2
L'Islet **101** F4
Lismore **240** A1
Lisnadill **282** B5
Lisnafin **285** G7
Lisnagat **282** C5
Lisnagunogue **286** D1
Lisnamuck **286** C6
Lisnarick **280** D3
Lisnaskea **281** F5
Lisnatunny **285** F7
Lisrodden **286** D5
Liss **120** C5
Liss Forest **120** C5
Lissan **286** B7
Lissett **196** D2
Lissington **188** B4
Liston **151** G3
Listooder **283** H3
Lisvane **130** A4
Liswerry **130** C4
Litcham **163** G1
Litchborough **148** B2
Litchfield **119** F2
Litherland **183** E3
Litlington *Cambs* **150** B3
Litlington *ESuss* **110** A3
Little Abington **150** D3
Little Addington **161** E5
Little Alne **146** D1
Little Altcar **183** E2
Little Amwell **136** C1
Little Ann **119** E3
Little Asby **200** B2

Little Assynt 272 D6
Little Aston 158 C3
Little Atherfield 107 D5
Little Ayton 203 E1
Little Baddow 137 G2
Little Badminton 132 A4
Little Ballinluig 251 E4
Little Bampton 209 F1
Little Bardfield 151 E4
Little Barford 149 G2
Little Barningham 178 C2
Little Barrington 133 E1
Little Barrow 170 B1
Little Barugh 203 G5
Little Bavington 220 B4
Little Bealings 152 D3
Little Bedwyn 119 D1
Little Beeby 160 B2
Little Bentley 152 C5
Little Berkhamsted 136 B2
Little Billing 148 D1
Little Birch 145 E4
Little Bispham 191 G3
Little Blakenham 152 C3
Little Bloxwich 158 C2
Little Bollington 184 B4
Little Bookham 121 G2
Little Bourton 147 G3
Little Bowden 160 C4
Little Bradley 151 E2
Little Brampton 156 C4
Little Braxted 138 B1
Little Brechin 253 D3
Little Brickhill 149 E4
Little Bridge 282 B1
Little Bridgeford 171 F5
Little Brington 148 B1
Little Bromley 152 B5
Little Broughton 209 D3
Little Budworth 170 C1
Little Burdon 202 C1
Little Burstead 137 F3
Little Burton 196 D3
Little Bytham 161 F1
Little Canford 105 G3
Little Carlton Lincs 189 D4
Little Carlton Notts 174 C2
Little Casterton 161 F1
Little Catwick 196 D3
Little Catworth 161 F5
Little Cawthorpe 189 D4
Little Chalfield 117 F1
Little Chalfont 135 E3
Little Chart 124 B4
Little Chesterford 150 D3
Little Chesterton 148 A5
Little Cheverell 118 A2
Little Clacton 139 E1
Little Clanfield 133 E2
Little Clifton 209 D4
Little Coates 188 C2
Little Comberton 146 B3
Little Common 110 C3
Little Compton 147 E4
Little Corby 210 A2
Little Cornard 151 G4
Little Cowarne 145 F2
Little Coxwell 133 E3
Little Crakehall 202 B3
Little Cransley 160 D5
Little Crawley 149 E3
Little Creaton 160 C5
Little Creich 266 D3
Little Cressingham 163 G3
Little Crosby 183 E2
Little Crosthwaite 209 F4
Little Cubley 172 C4
Little Dalby 160 C1
Little Dens 269 J6
Little Dewchurch 145 E4
Little Ditton 151 E2
Little Doward 131 E1
Little Down 119 E2
Little Downham 162 D4
Little Drayton 171 D4
Little Driffield 196 C2
Little Dunham 163 G1
Little Dunkeld 251 F5
Little Dunmow 151 E5
Little Durnford 118 C4
Little Easton 151 E5
Little Eaton 173 E3
Little Eccleston 192 A4
Little Ellingham 164 B2
Little End 137 E2
Little Everdon 148 A3
Little Eversden 150 B2
Little Faringdon 133 E2
Little Fencote 202 B3
Little Finborough 152 B2
Little Fransham 178 A4
Little Gaddesden 135 E1
Little Garway 144 D5
Little Gidding 161 G4
Little Glemham 153 E2
Little Glenshee 243 E1
Little Gorsley 145 F5
Little Gransden 150 A2
Little Green Cambs 150 A3
Little Green Notts 174 C3
Little Green Suff 164 B4
Little Green Suff 164 B4
Little Green Wrex 170 B3
Little Grimsby 188 D3
Little Gringley 187 E4
Little Gruinard 265 F3
Little Habton 203 G5
Little Hadham 150 C5
Little Hale 175 G3
Little Hallingbury 137 D1
Little Hampden 135 D2
Little Haresfield 132 A2
Little Harrowden 161 D5
Little Haseley 134 B2
Little Hatfield 197 D3
Little Hautbois 179 D3
Little Haven
  Pembs 126 B1
Little Haven
  WSuss 121 G4
Little Hay 158 D2
Little Hayfield 185 E4
Little Haywood 172 B5
Little Heath 159 F4
Little Hereford 145 E1
Little Hockham 164 A4
Little Horkesley 152 A4

Little Hormead 150 C5
Little Horsted 109 G2
Little Horton 118 B1
Little Horwood 148 C4
Little Houghton 148 D2
Little Hucklow 185 F5
Little Hulton 184 B2
Little Hungerford 134 A5
Little Irchester 149 E1
Little Keyford 117 E3
Little Kimble 134 D2
Little Kineton 147 F2
Little Kingshill 135 D3
Little Langdale 199 E2
Little Langford 118 B4
Little Laver 137 E2
Little Lawford 159 G5
Little Leigh 184 A5
Little Leighs 137 G1
Little Lever 184 B2
Little Ley 260 E3
Little Linford 148 D3
Little Linton 151 D3
Little London
  Bucks 134 B1
Little London
  Essex 150 C5
Little London
  ESuss 110 A2
Little London
  Hants 119 E3
Little London
  Hants 120 B1
Little London IoM 190 B3
Little London Lincs 176 C5
Little London Lincs 176 A5
Little London Lincs 188 D5
Little London Lincs 188 B4
Little London Norf 177 D5
Little London Norf 163 F3
Little London Oxon 134 A2
Little London
  Powys 155 G4
Little London Suff 152 B2
Little London
  WYorks 194 B4
Little Longstone 185 F5
Little Lyth 157 D2
Little Malvern 145 G3
Little Maplestead 151 G4
Little Marcle 145 F4
Little Marland 113 F4
Little Marlow 135 D4
Little Marsden 193 E4
Little Massingham 177 F5
Little Melton 178 C3
Little Milford 126 C1
Little Mill 130 C2
Little Milton 134 B2
Little Missenden 135 E3
Little Musgrave 200 C1
Little Ness 157 D1
Little Neston 183 D5
Little Newcastle 140 D5
Little Newsham 202 A1
Little Oakley
  Essex 152 D5
Little Oakley
  NN'hants 161 D4
Little Odell 149 E2
Little Offley 149 G5
Little Onn 158 A1
Little Orton Cumb 209 G1
Little Orton Leics 159 F2
Little Ouse 163 E4
Little Ouseburn 194 D1
Little Packington 159 E4
Little Parndon 136 D1
Little Paxton 149 G1
Little Petherick 96 D2
Little Plumpton 191 G4
Little Plumstead 179 E4
Little Ponton 175 E4
Little Posbrook 107 E2
Little Potheridge 113 F4
Little Preston 148 A2
Little Raveley 162 A4
Little Ribston 194 C2
Little Rissington 133 D1
Little Rogart 266 E1
Little Rollright 147 E4
Little Ryburgh 178 A3
Little Ryle 229 E5
Little Ryton 157 D2
Little Salkeld 210 B4
Little Sampford 151 E4
Little Saxham 151 G1
Little Scatwell 265 K6
Little Shelford 150 C2
Little Shrawardine 156 C1
Little Silver 102 C2
Little Singleton 191 G4
Little Smeaton
  NYorks 186 C1
Little Smeaton
  NYorks 202 C1
Little Snoring 178 A2
Little Sodbury 131 G4
Little Sodbury End 131 G4
Little Somborne 119 E4
Little Somerford 132 B4
Little Soudley 171 E5
Little Stainforth 193 E1
Little Stainton 202 C1
Little Stanney 183 F5
Little Staughton 149 G1
Little Steeping 176 C1
Little Stoke 171 G4
Little Stonham 152 C2
Little Street 162 D4
Little Stretton Leics 160 B2
Little Stretton
  Shrop 156 D3
Little Strickland 199 G1
Little Stukeley 162 A5
Little Sugnall 171 F4
Little Sutton 183 E5
Little Swinburne 220 B4
Little Tarrington 145 F3
Little Tew 147 F5
Little Tey 151 G4
Little Thetford 162 D5
Little Thornage 178 B3
Little Thornton 191 G3
Little Thorpe 212 D3
Little Thurlow 151 E2

Little Thurlow
  Green 151 E2
Little Thurrock 137 F5
Little Torboll 266 E2
Little Torrington 113 E4
Little Tosson 220 C1
Little Totham 138 B1
Little Town Cumb 209 F5
Little Town Lancs 192 C4
Little Town Warr 184 A3
Little Twycross 159 F2
Little Urswick 199 D5
Little Wakering 138 C4
Little Walden 150 D3
Little Waldingfield 152 A3
Little Walsingham 178 A2
Little Waltham 137 G1
Little Warley 137 F3
Little Washbourne 146 B4
Little Weighton 196 B4
Little Welland 146 A4
Little Welnetham 151 G1
Little Wenham 152 B4
Little Wenlock 157 F2
Little Whittington 211 F1
Little Wilbraham 150 D2
Little Wishford 118 B4
Little Witcombe 132 B1
Little Witley 145 G1
Little Wittenham 134 A3
Little Wittingham
  Green 165 D4
Little Wolford 147 E4
Little Woodcote 122 B4
Little Wratting 151 E3
Little Wymington 149 E1
Little Wymondley 150 A5
Little Wyrley 158 C2
Little Wytheford 157 E1
Little Yeldham 151 F4
Littlebeck 204 B2
Littleborough
  Devon 102 B1
Littleborough
  GtMan 184 D1
Littleborough
  Notts 187 F4
Littlebourne 125 E3
Littlebredy 104 A3
Littlebury 150 D4
Littlebury Green 150 C4
Littledean 131 F1
Littleferry 267 F2
Littleham Devon 113 E3
Littleham Devon 102 D4
Littlehampton 108 C3
Littlehempston 101 E1
Littlehoughton 229 G5
Littlemill EAyr 224 C4
Littlemill High 267 G6
Littlemoor Derbys 173 E1
Littlemoor Dorset 104 C4
Littlemoore 134 A2
Littlemoss 184 D3
Littleover 173 E4
Littleport 163 D4
Littlestead Green 134 C5
Littlestone-on-Sea 111 F1
Littlethorpe 194 C1
Littleton ChesW&C 170 B1
Littleton Hants 119 F4
Littleton P&K 244 A1
Littleton Som 116 B4
Littleton Surr 121 F1
Littleton Drew 132 A4
Littleton Panell 118 B2
Littletown Dur 212 C2
Littletown IoW 107 E3
Littlewick Green 134 D5
Littlewindsor 104 A2
Littleworth Glos 146 D4
Littleworth Oxon 133 F3
Littleworth Staffs 158 C1
Littleworth SYorks 186 D3
Littleworth Worcs 146 A3
Littley Green 137 F1
Litton Derbys 185 F5
Litton NYorks 201 E5
Litton Som 116 C3
Litton Cheney 104 B3
Liverpool 183 E3
Liverpool Cathedral
  Mersey L1 7AZ 42 E6
Liverpool John Lennon
  Airport 183 F4
Liverpool Metropolitan
  Cathedral (RC) Mersey
  L3 5TQ 43 E4
Liversedge 194 B5
Liverton Devon 102 B5
Liverton R&C 203 G1
Liverton Street 124 A4
Livingston 235 E3
Livingston Village 235 E3
Lixwim 182 C5
Lizard 95 E5
Llaingarreglwyd 142 A2
Llain-goch 180 A4
Llaithddu 155 G4
Llampha 129 F5
Llan 155 E2
Llanaber 154 C1
Llanaelhaearn 166 C3
Llanaeron 142 A1
Llanafan 154 C5
Llanafan-fawr 143 F2
Llanallgo 180 C4
Llanarmon 166 C4
Llanarmon Dyffryn
  Ceiriog 169 E4
Llanarmon-yn-Iâl 169 E2
Llanarth Cere 142 A2
Llanarth Mon 130 C1
Llanarthne 142 B5
Llanasa 182 C4
Llanbabo 180 B4
Llanbadarn Fawr 154 B4
Llanbadarn
  Fynydd 155 G5
Llanbadarn-y-
  garreg 144 A3
Llanbadoc 130 C2
Llanbadrig 180 B3
Llanbeder 130 C3
Llanbedr Gwyn 167 E5
Llanbedr Powys 144 B5
Llanbedr Powys 144 A3

Llanbedr Dyffryn
  Clwyd 169 E2
Llanbedr-goch 180 D4
Llanbedrcennin 168 A1
Llanberis 167 E2
Llanbethery 111 D1
Llanbister 156 A5
Llanblethian 129 F5
Llanboidy 141 F5
Llanbradach 130 A4
Llanbrynmair 155 E2
Llancadle 114 D1
Llancarfan 129 G5
Llancayo 130 C2
Llancynfelyn 154 C3
Llandafal 130 A2
Llandaff 130 A5
Llandaff North 130 A5
Llandanwg 167 E5
Llandawke 127 F1
Llanddaniel-fab 180 C5
Llanddarog 128 A3
Llanddeiniol 154 B5
Llanddeiniolen 167 E1
Llandderfel 168 C4
Llanddeusant
  Carmar 143 D4
Llanddeusant IoA 180 B4
Llan-ddew 143 G4
Llanddewi 128 A4
Llanddewi Brefi 142 C2
Llanddewi
  Rhydderch 130 C1
Llanddewi
  Skirrid 130 C1
Llanddewi Velfrey 127 E1
Llanddewi
  Ystradenni 144 A1
Llanddewi'r-cwm 143 G3
Llanddoged 168 B5
Llanddona 181 D5
Llanddowror 127 F1
Llanddulas 181 G5
Llanddwywe 167 E5
Llanddyfnan 180 D5
Llandefaelog Fach 143 G4
Llandefaelog-
  tre'r-graig 144 A5
Llandefalle 144 A4
Llandegfan 181 D5
Llandegla 169 E2
Llandegley 144 A1
Llandegveth 130 C3
Llandeilo 142 C5
Llandeilo
  Abercywyn 127 G1
Llandeilo Graban 143 G3
Llandeilo'r-Fan 143 E4
Llandeloy 140 B5
Llandevaud 130 D3
Llandevenny 130 D4
Llandinabo 145 E5
Llandinam 155 G4
Llandissilio 141 E5
Llandogo 131 E2
Llandough VGlam 130 A5
Llandough VGlam 129 F5
Llandovery
  (Llanymddyfri) 143 D4
Llandow 129 E5
Llandre Carmar 142 C3
Llandre Carmar 141 E5
Llandre Cere 154 C4
Llandrillo 168 D4
Llandrindod Wells 143 G1
Llandrinio 156 B1
Llandudno 181 F4
Llandudno Junction 181 F5
Llandwrog 167 D2
Llandybie 128 C1
Llandyfaelog 128 A1
Llandyfân 128 C1
Llandyfriog 141 G3
Llandyfrydog 180 C4
Llandygai 181 D5
Llandygwydd 141 F3
Llandynan 169 E3
Llandyrnog 169 E1
Llandysilio 156 B1
Llandyssil 156 A3
Llandysul 142 A3
Llanedeyrn 130 B4
Llanedi 128 B2
Llaneglwys 143 G4
Llanegryn 154 C2
Llanegwad 142 B5
Llaneilian 180 C3
Llanelian-yn-Rhos 181 G5
Llanelidan 169 E2
Llanelieu 144 A4
Llanelli 128 B2
Llanelli Millennium Coastal
  Park Carmar
  SA15 2LF 128 A3
Llanelltyd 154 D1
Llanelly 130 B1
Llanelly Hill 130 B1
Llanelwedd 143 G2
Llanenddwyn 167 E5
Llanengan 166 B5
Llanerfyl 155 G2
Llaneuddog 180 C4
Llanfachraeth 180 B4
Llanfachreth 168 A5
Llanfaelog 180 B5
Llanfaelrhys 166 B5
Llanfaenor 130 D1
Llan-faes IoA 181 E5
Llan-faes Powys 143 G5
Llanfaethlu 180 B4
Llanfaglan 167 D1
Llanfair 167 E5
Llanfair Caereinion 156 A2
Llanfair Clydogau 142 C2
Llanfair Dyffryn
  Clwyd 169 E2
Llanfair Talhaiarn 182 A5
Llanfair Waterdine 156 B5
Llanfairfechan 181 E5
Llanfair-Nant-Gwyn 141 E4

Llanfairorllwyn 141 G3
Llanfair-yng-Nghornwy
  180 B3
Llanfair-yn-Neubwll 180 B5
Llanfallteg 127 E1
Llanfaredd 143 G2
Llanfarian 154 B5
Llanfechain 169 E5
Llanfechan 143 F2
Llanfechell 180 B3
Llanfendigaid 154 B2
Llanferres 169 E1
Llanfflewyn 180 B4
Llanfigael 180 B4
Llanfihangel Glyn
  Myfyr 168 C2
Llanfihangel Nant
  Brân 143 F4
Llanfihangel Nant
  Melan 144 A2
Llanfihangel
  Rhydithon 144 A1
Llanfihangel Rogiet 130 D4
Llanfihangel
  Tal-y-llyn 144 A5
Llanfihangel yn
  Nhowyn 180 B5
Llanfihangel Ystrad
  Llewern 130 D1
Llanfihangel-
  ar-arth 142 A3
Llanfihangel-uwch-
  Gwili 142 A5
Llanfihangel-y-
  Creuddyn 154 C5
Llanfihangel-yng-
  Ngwynfa 155 G1
Llanfihangel-y-Pennant
  Gwyn 167 E3
Llanfihangel-y-Pennant
  Gwyn 154 C2
Llanfilo 144 A4
Llanfoist 130 B1
Llanfor 168 C4
Llanfrechfa 130 C3
Llanfrothen 167 F3
Llanfrynach 143 G5
Llanfwrog IoA 180 B4
Llanfyllin 156 A1
Llanfynydd Carmar 142 B5
Llanfynydd Flints 169 F2
Llanfyrnach 141 F4
Llangadfan 155 G1
Llangadog 142 D5
Llangadwaladr IoA 166 C1
Llangadwaladr
  Powys 169 E4
Llangaffo 166 C1
Llangammarch
  Wells 143 F3
Llangan 129 F5
Llangarron 145 E5
Llangasty-Talyllyn 144 A5
Llangathen 142 B5
Llangattock 130 B1
Llangattock
  Lingoed 130 C1
Llangattock-Vibon-
  Avel 130 D1
Llangedwyn 169 E5
Llangeinor 129 F4
Llangeitho 142 C2
Llangeler 141 G4
Llangelynin 154 B2
Llangendeirne 128 A1
Llangennech 128 B2
Llangennith 128 A3
Llangenny 130 B1
Llangernyw 168 B5
Llangian 166 B5
Llangiwg 128 D2
Llanglofan 140 C4
Llanglydwen 141 E5
Llangoed 181 E5
Llangoedmor 141 E3
Llangollen 169 F3
Llangollen Railway Denb
  LL20 8SN 169 F3
Llangolman 141 E5
Llan-gors 144 A5
Llangorwen 154 C4
Llangovan 131 D2
Llangower 168 B4
Llangranog 141 F3
Llangristiolus 180 C5
Llangrove 131 E1
Llangua 144 C5
Llangunllo 156 B5
Llangunnor 142 A5
Llangurig 155 F5
Llangwm Conwy 168 C3
Llangwm Mon 130 D2
Llangwm Pembs 126 C2
Llangwnnadl 166 B4
Llangwyfan 169 E1
Llangwyllog 180 C5
Llangwyryfon 154 C5
Llangybi Cere 142 C2
Llangybi Gwyn 166 D3
Llangybi Mon 130 C3
Llangyfelach 128 C3
Llangynhafal 169 E1
Llangynidr 130 A1
Llangynin 127 F1
Llangynllo 142 A3
Llangynog Carmar 127 G1
Llangynog Powys 169 D5
Llangynwyd 129 E4
Llanhamlach 143 G5
Llanharan 129 G4
Llanharry 129 G4
Llanhennock 130 C3
Llanhilleth 130 B2
Llanidloes 155 F4
Llaniestyn 166 B4
Llanigon 144 B4
Llanilar 154 C5
Llanilid 129 F4
Llanishen Cardiff 130 A4
Llanishen Mon 131 D2
Llanllawddog 142 A5
Llanllechid 167 F1
Llanlleonfel 143 F2
Llanllugan 155 G2

Llan-llwch 127 G1
Llanllwchaiarn 156 A3
Llanllwni 142 A3
Llanllyfni 167 D2
Llanllywel 130 C3
Llanmadoc 128 A3
Llanmaes 114 D1
Llanmartin 130 C4
Llanmerewig 156 A3
Llanmihangel 129 F5
Llan-mill 127 E1
Llanmiloe 127 F2
Llanmorlais 128 B3
Llannefydd 182 A5
Llannerch Hall 182 B5
Llannerch-y-medd 180 C4
Llannerch-y-môr 182 C5
Llan-non Carmar 128 B2
Llan-non Cere 142 B1
Llannor 166 C4
Llanover 130 C1
Llanpumsaint 142 A5
Llanreithan 140 C5
Llanrhaeadr 169 D1
Llanrhaeadr-ym-
  Mochnant 169 E5
Llanrhian 140 B4
Llanrhidian 128 A3
Llanrhyddlad 180 B4
Llanrhystud 142 B1
Llanrothal 131 D1
Llanrug 167 E1
Llanrumney 130 B4
Llanrwst 168 A1
Llansadurnen 127 F1
Llansadwrn Carmar 142 C4
Llansadwrn IoA 181 D5
Llansaint 127 G2
Llansamlet 128 C3
Llansanffraid Glan
  Conwy 181 G5
Llansannan 168 C1
Llansannor 129 F5
Llansantffraed 144 A5
Llansantffraed-
  Cwmdeuddwr 143 F1
Llansantffraed-in-
  Elwel 143 G2
Llansantffraid-ym-
  Mechain 169 E5
Llansawel 142 C4
Llansilin 169 F5
Llansoy 130 D2
Llanspyddid 143 G5
Llanstadwell 126 C2
Llansteffan 127 G1
Llanstephan 144 A3
Llantarnam 130 C3
Llanteg 127 E1
Llanthony 144 B5
Llantilio Crossenny
  130 C1
Llantilio Pertholey 130 C1
Llantood 141 E3
Llantrisant IoA 180 B4
Llantrisant Mon 130 C3
Llantrisant RCT 129 G4
Llantrithyd 129 G5
Llantwit Fardre 129 G4
Llantwit Major 114 D1
Llantysilio 169 E3
Llanuwchllyn 168 B5
Llanvaches 130 D3
Llanvair-Discoed 130 D3
Llanvapley 130 C1
Llanvetherine 130 C1
Llanveynoe 144 C4
Llanvihangel Crucorney
  (Llanfihangel Crucornau)
  144 C5
Llanvihangel
  Gobion 130 C2
Llanvithyn 129 G5
Llanwarne 145 E5
Llanwddyn 155 G1
Llanwenog 142 A3
Llan-wern 130 C4
Llanwinio 141 F5
Llanwnda Gwyn 167 D2
Llanwnda Pembs 140 C4
Llanwnnen 142 B3
Llanwnog 155 G3
Llanwrda 142 D4
Llanwrin 155 D2
Llanwrthwl 143 F1
Llanwrtyd Wells 143 E3
Llanwyddelan 155 G2
Llanyblodwel 169 F5
Llan-y-bri 127 G1
Llanybydder 142 B3
Llan-y-cefn 141 E5
Llanychaer 140 C4
Llanycil 168 C4
Llanycrwys 142 C3
Llanymawddwy 155 E1
Llanymynech 169 F5
Llanynghenedl 180 B4
Llanynys 169 E1
Llan-y-pwll 170 A2
Llanyre 143 G1
Llanystumdwy 167 D4
Llan-y-wern 144 A5
Llawhaden 127 D1
Llawndy 182 C4
Llawnt 169 F4
Llawr-y-dref 166 B5
Llawr-y-glyn 155 F3
Llay 170 A2
Llechcynfarwy 180 B4
Llecheiddior 167 D3
Llechfaen 143 G5
Llechryd Caerp 130 A2
Llechryd Cere 141 F3
Llechrydau 169 F4
Llechwedd /Zip World
  Slate Caverns Gwyn
  LL41 3NB 168 A3
Lledrod Cere 154 C5
Lledrod Powys 169 F5
Llethryd 128 B3
Llidiad-Nenog 142 B4
Llidiardau 168 B4
Llithfaen 166 C3
Lloc 182 C5
Llong 169 F1

Llowes 144 A3
Lloyney 156 B5
Llundain-fach 142 B2
Llwydcoed 129 F3
Llwydiarth 155 G1
Llwyn 156 B4
Llwyncelyn 142 A2
Llwyn-croes 142 A5
Llwyndafydd 141 G2
Llwynderw 156 B2
Llwyn-drain 141 F4
Llwynduris 166 C3
Llwyneinion 169 F3
Llwyn-Madoc 143 F2
Llwynmawr 169 F4
Llwyn-onn Cere 142 A1
Llwyn-onn MTyd 129 G2
Llwyn-y-brain
  Carmar 127 E1
Llwyn-y-brain
  Carmar 142 A1
Llwyn-y-groes 142 B2
Llwynypia 129 F3
Llyn Brenig Conwy
  LL21 9TT 168 C2
Llyn Llech Owain Country
  Park Carmar
  SA14 7NF 128 B1
Llynclys 169 F5
Llynfaes 180 C5
Llysfaen 181 G5
Llys-wen 144 A4
Llysworney 129 F5
Llys-y-frân 140 D5
Llywel 143 F4
Load Brook 185 G4
Loandhu 267 F4
Loanends 287 G7
Loanhead Aber 261 H1
Loanhead Midlo 235 G3
Loans 224 C2
Lobb 113 E2
Lobhillcross 99 E2
Loch a' Charnain 262 D7
Loch an Eilein Visitor Centre
  & Forest Trail High
  PH22 1QT 259 F4
Loch Choire Lodge 273 J5
Loch Eil Outward
  Bound 248 C2
Loch Head D&G 206 D2
Loch Head D&G 215 F1
Loch Lomond Shores &
  Gateway Centre WDun
  G83 8QL 233 E4
Loch Ness Exhibition Centre
  High IV63 6TU 258 C2
Loch of the Lowes P&K
  PH8 0HH 251 F5
Loch Sgioport 254 D1
Lochailort (Ceann Loch
  Ailleart) 247 G1
Lochaline
  (Loch Àlainn) 247 F5
Lochans 214 B5
Locharbriggs 217 D3
Lochawe
  (Loch Obha) 240 D2
Lochboisdale (Loch
  Baghasdail) 254 C3
Lochbuie 239 F2
Lochcarron
  (Loch Carrann) 264 C5
Lochdhu Hotel 275 F4
Lochdon 239 G1
Lochdrum 265 J4
Lochearnhead (Ceann Loch
  Èireann) 242 A2
Lochee 244 B1
Lochend High 275 H2
Lochend (Ceann Loch)
  High 258 C1
Locheport 262 D5
Lochfoot 216 D3
Lochgair 240 B5
Lochgarthside 258 C3
Lochgelly 243 F5
Lochgilphead (Ceann Loch
  Gilb) 231 G2
Lochgoilhead 241 E4
Lochgoyn 233 G5
Lochhill EAyr 225 D4
Lochhill Moray 267 K5
Lochinch Castle 214 C4
Lochinver
  (Loch an Inbhir) 272 C6
Lochlair 252 D5
Lochlane 242 D5
Lochlea 224 C2
Lochluichart 265 K5
Lochmaben 217 E2
Lochmaddy 262 E5
Lochore 243 F5
Lochore Meadows Country
  Park Fife
  KY5 8BA 243 G5
Lochportain 262 E4
Lochranza 232 A3
Lochside Aber 253 F3
Lochside High 273 G3
Lochside High 274 D5
Lochside High 275 H2
Lochslin 267 F3
Lochton 215 D2
Lochty 244 D4
Lochuisge 247 G4
Lochurr 216 B2
Lochussie 266 B6
Lochwinnoch 233 E4
Lockengate 97 E3
Lockerbie 217 F2
Lockeridge 118 C1
Lockerley 119 D5
Lockhills 210 B3
Locking 116 A2
Lockington ERid 196 B3
Lockington Leics 173 F5
Lockleywood 171 E5
Locks Heath 107 E2
Locksbottom 122 D2
Lockton 204 B4
Locomotion: The National
  Railway Museum at
  Shildon Dur
  DL4 2QP 212 B5
Loddington Leics 160 C2

Loddington
  NN'hants **160** D5
Loddiswell **100** D3
Loddon **165** E2
Lode **150** D1
Loders **104** A3
Lodsworth **121** E5
Lofthouse NYorks **202** A5
Lofthouse WYorks **194** C5
Loftus **203** G1
Logan D&G **206** A2
Logan EAyr **225** D3
Loganlea **235** D3
Loggerheads **171** E4
Loggerheads Country Park
  Denb CH7 5LH **169** E1
Loggie (An Lagaidh) **265** H2
Logie Angus **253** E3
Logie Angus **252** B4
Logie Fife **253** G5
Logie Coldstone **260** C4
Logie Hill **266** E4
Logie Newton **260** E1
Logie Pert **253** E4
Login **141** E5
Lolworth **150** B1
Lonbain **264** C6
Londesborough **196** A3
London **136** C4
London Apprentice **97** E5
London Ashford
  Airport **111** F1
London Beach **124** A5
London Biggin Hill
  Airport **122** D2
London City
  Airport **136** C4
London Colney **136** A2
London Eye GtLon
  SE1 7PB **45** F5
London Gatwick
  Airport **122** B4
London Heathrow
  Airport **135** F5
London Luton
  Airport **149** G5
London Minstead **106** B1
London Oxford
  Airport **133** G1
London Southend
  Airport **138** B4
London Stansted
  Airport **150** D5
London Transport Museum
  GtLon WC2E 7BB **45** E3
Londonderry (Derry)
  D&S **285** G4
Londonderry
  NYorks **202** B4
Londubh **264** E3
Lonemore **266** E3
Long Ashton **131** E5
Long Bennington **174** D3
Long Bank **157** G5
Long Bredy **104** B3
Long Buckby **148** B1
Long Clawson **174** C5
Long Compton
  Staffs **171** F5
Long Compton
  Warks **147** F5
Long Crendon **134** B2
Long Crichel **105** F1
Long Dean **132** A5
Long Downs **95** E3
Long Drax **195** F5
Long Duckmanton **186** B5
Long Eaton **173** F4
Long Gill **193** D2
Long Green
  ChesW&C **183** F5
Long Green Essex **152** A5
Long Green Worcs **146** A4
Long Hanborough **133** G1
Long Itchington **147** G1
Long Lane **157** F1
Long Lawford **159** G5
Long Load **116** B5
Long Marston Herts **135** D1
Long Marston
  NYorks **195** E2
Long Marston
  Warks **147** D3
Long Marton **210** B4
Long Meadowend **156** D4
Long Melford **151** G3
Long Newnton **132** B3
Long Preston **193** E2
Long Riston **196** D3
Long Stratton **164** C2
Long Street **148** C3
Long Sutton Hants **120** C3
Long Sutton Lincs **176** C4
Long Sutton Som **116** B5
Long Thurlow **152** B1
Long Whatton **173** F5
Long Wittenham **134** A3
Longbenton **212** B1
Longborough **147** D5
Longbridge Plym **100** B2
Longbridge Warks **147** E1
Longbridge WMid **158** C5
Longbridge Deverill **117** F3
Longburgh **209** G1
Longburton **104** C1
Longcliffe **172** D2
Longcombe **101** E2
Longcot **133** E3
Longcroft **234** B2
Longcross Devon **99** E3
Longcross Surr **121** F1
Longden **156** D2
Longdon Staffs **158** C1
Longdon Worcs **146** A4
Longdon Green **158** C1
Longdon upon Tern **157** F1
Longdown **102** B3
Longdrum **261** H3
Longfield Kent **123** F2
Longfield Hill **123** F2
Longfleet **105** G3
Longford Derbys **172** D4
Longford Glos **146** A5
Longford GtLon **135** F5
Longford Shrop **170** D4
Longford Tel&W **157** G1
Longford WMid **159** F4
Longforgan **244** B2
Longformacus **237** D4
Longham Dorset **105** G3
Longham Norf **178** A4
Longhill **269** H5
Longhirst **221** E3
Longhope Glos **131** F1
Longhope Ork **277** C8
Longhorsley **220** D2
Longhoughton **229** G5
Longlands Aber **260** C2
Longlands Cumb **209** F3
Longlands GtLon **136** D5
Longlane Derbys **173** D4
Longlane WBerks **133** G5
Longleat House Wilts
  BA12 7NW **117** F3
Longleat Safari Park Wilts
  BA12 7NW **117** F3
Longlevens **132** A1
Longley **185** F2
Longley Green **145** G2
Longmanhill **269** F4
Longmoor Camp **120** C4
Longmorn **267** K6
Longnewton ScBord **227** G3
Longnewton Stock **202** C1
Longney **131** G1
Longniddry **236** B2
Longniddry Bents ELoth
  EH32 0PX **236** B2
Longnor Shrop **157** D2
Longnor Staffs **172** B1
Longparish **119** F3
Longridge Lancs **192** C4
Longridge Staffs **158** B1
Longridge WLoth **235** D3
Longridge End **146** A5
Longridge Towers **237** G4
Longriggend **234** C2
Longrock **94** C3
Longsdon **171** G2
Longshaw **183** G2
Longside **269** J6
Longslow **171** D4
Longsowerby **209** G1
Longstanton **150** C1
Longstock **119** E4
Longstone **94** C3
Longstowe **150** B2
Longstreet **118** C2
Longthorpe **161** G3
Longton Lancs **192** A5
Longton Stoke **171** G3
Longtown Cumb **218** B5
Longtown Here **144** C5
Longville in the
  Dale **157** E3
Longwell Green **131** F5
Longwick **134** C2
Longwitton **220** C3
Longworth **133** F3
Longyester **236** C3
Lonmay **269** J5
Lonmore **263** H7
Looe **97** G4
Look Out Discovery Park,
  Bracknell BrackF
  RG12 7QW **121** D1
Loose **123** G3
Loosebeare **102** A2
Loosegate **176** B5
Loosley Row **134** D2
Lopcombe Corner **119** D4
Lopen **104** A1
Loppington **170** B5
Lorbottle **220** D1
Lorbottle Hall **220** C1
Lordington **107** G2
Lord's Cricket Ground &
  Museum GtLon
  NW8 8QN **10** F4
Lord's Hill **106** C1
Lorgill **263** G7
Lorn **233** E1
Lornty **251** G5
Loscoe **173** F3
Loscombe **104** A3
Losgaintir (Luskentyre)
  263 F2
Lossiemouth **267** K4
Lossit **230** A3
Lostock Gralam **184** A5
Lostock Green **184** A5
Lostock
  Junction **184** A2
Lostwithiel **97** F4
Loth **276** F4
Lothbeg **274** E7
Lothersdale **193** F3
Lotherton Hall Estate
  WYorks
  LS25 3EB **195** D4
Lothmore **274** E7
Loudwater **135** E3
Lough Gilly **282** D5
Loughan **286** C3
Loughans **281** J3
Loughash **285** H5
Loughborough **160** A1
Loughbrickland **282** E4
Loughgall **282** C3
Loughguile **286** E3
Loughinisland **283** H4
Loughmacrory **281** H1
Loughor **128** B3
Loughton Essex **136** D3
Loughton MK **148** D4
Loughton Shrop **157** F4
Louis Tussaud's Waxworks
  FY1 5AA **64** Blackpool
Lound Lincs **161** F1
Lound Notts **187** D4
Lound Suff **165** G2
Lount **159** F2
Lour **252** C5
Louth **188** D4
Love Clough **193** E5
LOVE Gorgie Farm Edin
  EH11 2LA **36** B7
Lovedean **107** F3
Loversall **186** C3
Loves Green **137** F2
Lovesome Hill **202** C3
Loveston **127** D2
Lovington **116** C4
Low Ackworth **186** B1
Low Angerton **220** C3
Low Ballevain **222** B3
Low Barlay **215** G5
Low Barlings **188** A5
Low Bentham (Lower
  Bentham) **192** C1
Low Bolton **201** F3
Low Bradfield **185** G3
Low Bradley
  (Bradley) **193** G3
Low Braithwaite **210** A3
Low Brunton **220** B4
Low Burnham **187** E2
Low Burton **202** B4
Low Buston **221** E1
Low Catton **195** G2
Low Coniscliffe **202** B1
Low Craighead **224** A5
Low Dinsdale **202** C1
Low Ellington **202** B4
Low Entercommon **202** C2
Low Etherley **212** A5
Low Fell **212** B2
Low Gate **211** F1
Low Grantley **202** B5
Low Green **194** A2
Low Habberley **158** A5
Low Ham **116** B5
Low Hawsker **204** C2
Low Haygarth **200** B3
Low Hesket **210** A3
Low Hesleyhurst **220** C2
Low Hutton **195** G1
Low Kingthorpe **204** B4
Low Laithe **194** A1
Low Langton **188** B5
Low Leighton **185** E4
Low Lorton **209** E4
Low Marishes **204** B5
Low Marnham **174** D1
Low Middleton **229** F3
Low Mill **203** F3
Low Moor Lancs **192** D3
Low Moor WYorks **194** A5
Low Moorsley **212** C3
Low Moresby **208** C4
Low Newton-by-
  the-Sea **229** G4
Low Row Cumb **210** B1
Low Row NYorks **201** E3
Low Stillaig **232** A3
Low Street **178** B5
Low Tharston **164** C2
Low Torry **235** E1
Low Town **220** D1
Low Toynton **188** C5
Low Wood **199** E4
Low Worsall **202** C2
Lowbands **145** G4
Lowdham **174** B3
Lowe **170** C4
Lowe Hill **171** G2
Lower Achachenna **240** C2
Lower Aisholt **115** F4
Lower Apperley **146** A5
Lower Arncott **134** B1
Lower Ashtead **121** G2
Lower Ashton **102** B4
Lower Assendon **134** C4
Lower Auchalick **232** A2
Lower Ballam **191** G4
Lower Ballinderry **282** D2
Lower Barewood **144** C2
Lower Bartle **192** A4
Lower Bayble
  (Pabail Iarach) **271** H4
Lower Beeding **109** E1
Lower Benefield **161** E4
Lower Bentham (Low
  Bentham) **192** C1
Lower Bentley **146** B1
Lower Berry Hill **131** E1
Lower Birchwood **173** F2
Lower Boddington **147** G2
Lower Boscaswell **94** A3
Lower Bourne **120** D3
Lower Brailes **147** F4
Lower Breakish **256** C2
Lower Bredbury **184** D3
Lower Broadheath **146** A2
Lower Brynamman **128** D1
Lower Bullingham **145** E4
Lower Bullington **119** F3
Lower Burgate **106** A1
Lower Burrow **116** B5
Lower Burton **144** D2
Lower Caldecote **149** G3
Lower Cam **131** G2
Lower Cambourne **150** B2
Lower Camster **275** H4
Lower Chapel **143** G4
Lower Cheriton **103** E2
Lower Chicksgrove **118** A4
Lower Chute **119** E2
Lower Clent **158** B4
Lower Creedy **102** B2
Lower
  Cumberworth **185** G2
Lower Darkley **282** B5
Lower Darwen **192** C5
Lower Dean **149** F1
Lower Diabaig **264** D5
Lower Dicker **110** A2
Lower Dinchope **157** D4
Lower Down **156** C4
Lower Drift **94** B4
Lower Dunsforth **194** D1
Lower Earley **134** C5
Lower Edmonton **136** C3
Lower Elkstone **172** B2
Lower End Bucks **134** B2
Lower End MK **149** E4
Lower End NN'hants
  149 D1
Lower Everleigh **118** C2
Lower Eythorne **125** E4
Lower Failand **131** E5
Lower Farringdon **120** C4
Lower Foxdale **190** A4
Lower Freystrop **126** C1
Lower Froyle **120** C3
Lower Gabwell **101** F1
Lower Gledfield **266** C2
Lower Godney **116** B3
Lower Gravenhurst **149** G4
Lower Green Essex **150** C4
Lower Green Herts **149** G5
Lower Green Kent **123** E5
Lower Green Norf **178** A2
Lower Green Staffs **158** B2
Lower Green Bank **192** B2
Lower Halstock Leigh
  104 B2
Lower Halstow **124** A2
Lower Hardres **124** D3
Lower Harpton **144** B1
Lower Hartshay **173** E2
Lower Hartwell **134** C1
Lower Hawthwaite **198** D4
Lower Haysden **123** E4
Lower Hayton **157** E4
Lower Heath **171** F1
Lower Hergest **144** B2
Lower Heyford **147** G5
Lower Higham **137** G5
Lower Holbrook **152** C4
Lower Hopton **185** G1
Lower Hordley **170** A5
Lower Horncroft **108** C2
Lower Horsebridge **110** A2
Lower Houses **185** F1
Lower Howsell **145** G3
Lower Kilchattan **238** C5
Lower Kilcott **131** G4
Lower Killeyan **230** A5
Lower Kingcombe **104** B3
Lower Kingswood **122** B3
Lower Kinnerton **170** A1
Lower Langford **116** B1
Lower Largo **244** C4
Lower Leigh **172** B4
Lower Lemington **147** E4
Lower Lovacott **113** F3
Lower Loxhore **113** G2
Lower Lydbrook **131** E1
Lower Lye **144** D1
Lower Machen **130** A5
Lower Maes-coed **144** C4
Lower Mannington **105** G2
Lower Middleton
  Cheney **148** A3
Lower Milton **116** B3
Lower Moor **146** B3
Lower Morton **131** F3
Lower Nash **126** D2
Lower Nazeing **136** C2
Lower Netchwood **157** F3
Lower Nyland **117** E5
Lower Oddington **147** E5
Lower Ollach **256** B1
Lower Penarth **130** A5
Lower Penn **158** A3
Lower Pennington **106** C3
Lower Peover **184** B5
Lower Pollicott **134** C1
Lower Quinton **147** D3
Lower Race **130** B2
Lower Rainham **124** A2
Lower Roadwater **114** D4
Lower Sapey **145** F1
Lower Seagry **132** B4
Lower Shelton **149** E3
Lower Shiplake **134** C5
Lower Shuckburgh **147** G1
Lower Slaughter **147** D5
Lower Soothill **194** B5
Lower Stanton
  St. Quintin **132** B4
Lower Stoke **124** A1
Lower Stondon **149** G4
Lower Stone **131** F3
Lower Stonnall **158** C2
Lower Stow Bedon **164** A2
Lower Street ESuss **110** C3
Lower Street Norf **179** D2
Lower Street Norf **178** C2
Lower Street Suff **152** C3
Lower Stretton **184** A4
Lower Sundon **149** F5
Lower Swanwick **107** D2
Lower Swell **147** D5
Lower Tadmarton **147** G4
Lower Tale **103** D2
Lower Tean **172** B4
Lower Thurlton **165** F2
Lower Thurnham **192** A2
Lower Town Corn **95** D4
Lower Town Devon **102** A5
Lower Town IoS **96** B1
Lower Town Pembs **140** C4
Lower Trebullett **98** D2
Lower Tysoe **147** F3
Lower Upcott **102** B4
Lower Upham **107** E1
Lower Upnor **137** G5
Lower Vexford **115** E4
Lower Wallop **156** C2
Lower Walton **184** A4
Lower Waterhay **132** C3
Lower Weald **148** C4
Lower Wear **102** C4
Lower Weare **116** B2
Lower Welson **144** B2
Lower Whatley **117** E3
Lower Whitley **184** A5
Lower Wick **146** A2
Lower Wield **120** B3
Lower Withington **171** F1
Lower Woodend **134** D4
Lower Woodford **118** C4
Lower Wyche **145** G3
Lower Wych **117** E3

Lowry, The GtMan
  M50 3AZ **24** D3
Lowsonford **147** D1
Lowther **210** B5
Lowthorpe **196** C1
Lowton Devon **113** G5
Lowton GtMan **184** A3
Lowton Som **103** E1
Lowton Common **184** A3
Lowtown **283** F4
Loxbeare **102** C1
Loxhill **121** F4
Loxhore **113** G2
Loxley **147** E2
Loxley Green **172** B4
Loxton **116** A2
Loxwood **121** F4
Lubachoinnich **266** B2
Lubcroy **265** K1
Lubenham **160** C4
Lubfearn **265** K4
Lubmore **265** G5
Lubreoch **249** G5
Luccombe **114** C3
Luccombe Village **107** E4
Lucker **229** F3
Luckett **99** D3
Luckington **132** A4
Lucklawhill **244** C2
Luckwell Bridge **114** C4
Lucton **144** D1
Lucy Cross **202** B1
Ludag **254** C3
Ludborough **188** C3
Ludbrook **100** C2
Ludchurch **127** E1
Luddenden **193** G5
Luddenden Foot **193** G5
Luddenham Court **124** B2
Luddesdown **123** F2
Luddington NLincs **187** F1
Luddington Warks **147** D2
Luddington in the
  Brook **161** G4
Ludford Lincs **188** B4
Ludford Shrop **157** E5
Ludgershall Bucks **134** B1
Ludgershall Wilts **119** D2
Ludgvan **94** C3
Ludham **179** E4
Ludlow **157** D5
Ludney **189** D3
Ludstock **145** F4
Ludstone **158** A3
Ludwell **118** A5
Ludworth **212** C3
Luffincott **98** D1
Luffness **236** B1
Lufton **104** B1
Lugar **225** D3
Luggate Burn **236** D2
Luggiebank **234** B2
Lugton **233** F4
Lugwardine **145** E3
Luib **256** B2
Luibeilt **249** E5
Luing **239** G3
Lulham **144** D3
Lullington Derbys **159** E1
Lullington Som **117** E2
Lulsgate Bottom **116** C1
Lulsley **145** G2
Lulworth Camp **105** E4
Lulworth Cove Visitor
  Centre Dorset
  BH20 5RQ **105** E5
Lumb Lancs **193** E5
Lumb WYorks **193** G5
Lumbutts **193** F5
Lumby **195** D4
Lumphanan **260** D4
Lumphinnans **243** G5
Lumsdaine **237** F3
Lumsdale **173** E1
Lumsden **260** C2
Lunan **253** E4
Lunanhead **252** C4
Luncarty **243** F2
Lund ERid **196** B3
Lund NYorks **195** F4
Lund Shet **278** E2
Lundale **270** D4
Lundavra **248** C3
Lunderston Bay Inv cly
  PA16 0DN **232** D2
Lunderton **269** K6
Lundie Angus **244** A3
Lundie High **257** H3
Lundin Links **244** C4
Lundwood **186** A2
Lundy **112** B1
Luney **286** C6
Lunga **240** A4
Lunna **279** D6
Lunning **279** E6
Lunnon **128** B4
Lunsford's Cross **110** C2
Lunt **183** E2
Luntley **144** C2
Luppitt **103** E2
Lupset **186** A1
Lupton **199** G4
Lurgan **282** D2
Lurganare **282** D5
Lurgashall **121** E5
Lurgill **282** E1
Lurignich **248** B3
Lusby **176** B1
Luss **241** F5
Lussagiven **231** E1
Lusta **263** H6
Lustleigh **102** A4
Luston **145** D1
Luthermuir **253** E3
Luthrie **244** B3
Luton Devon **103** D3
Luton Devon **102** C5
Luton Luton **149** G5
Luton Med **123** G2
Luton Airport **149** G5
Lutterworth **160** A4
Lutton Devon **100** B2
Lutton Dorset **105** F4
Lutton Lincs **176** C5
Lutton NN'hants **161** G4
Luxborough **114** C4
Luxulyan **97** E4

Lybster High **275** F2
Lybster High **275** H5
Lydacott **113** E5
Lydbury North **156** C4
Lydcott **113** G2
Lydd **125** E4
Lydden **125** E4
Lydden **125** E4
Lyddington **161** D3
Lydd-on-Sea **111** F1
Lyde Green **131** F5
Lydeard
  St. Lawrence **115** E4
Lydford **99** F2
Lydford-on-Fosse **116** C4
Lydgate GtMan **185** E1
Lydgate GtMan **185** D2
Lydgate WYorks **193** F5
Lydham **156** C3
Lydiard Millicent **132** C4
Lydiard Tregoze **132** D4
Lydiate **183** E2
Lydlinch **104** D1
Lydney **131** F2
Lydstep **127** D3
Lye **158** B4
Lye Cross **116** B1
Lye Green Bucks **135** E2
Lye Green ESuss **123** E5
Lye Green Warks **147** D1
Lye's Green **117** F3
Lyford **133** F3
Lymbridge Green **124** D4
Lyme Regis **103** G3
Lymekilns **234** A4
Lyminge **125** D4
Lymington **106** C3
Lyminster **108** C3
Lymm **184** A4
Lymore **106** B3
Lympne **124** D5
Lympsham **116** A2
Lympstone **102** C4
Lynaberack **258** E5
Lynch **114** B3
Lynch Green **178** C5
Lyndale House **263** J6
Lyndhurst **106** B2
Lyndon **161** D2
Lyne Aber **261** F4
Lyne ScBord **235** G5
Lyne Surr **121** F1
Lyne Down **145** F4
Lyne of Gorthleck **258** C2
Lyne of Skene **261** F3
Lyneal **170** B4
Lyneham Oxon **147** E5
Lyneham Wilts **132** C5
Lyneholmeford **218** D4
Lynemore High **259** H2
Lynemore Moray **259** J1
Lynemouth **221** E2
Lyness **277** C8
Lynford **163** G3
Lyng **178** B4
Lyngate **179** E3
Lynmouth **114** A3
Lynn **157** G1
Lynsted **124** B2
Lynstone **112** C5
Lynton **114** A3
Lynton & Lynmouth Cliff
  Railway Devon
  EX35 6EP **114** A3
Lyon's Gate **104** C2
Lyonshall **144** C2
Lyrabus **230** A3
Lytchett Matravers **105** F3
Lytchett Minster **105** F3
Lyth **275** H2
Lytham **191** G5
Lytham St. Anne's **191** G5
Lythe **204** B1
Lythe Hill **121** E4
Lythes **277** D9
Lythmore **275** F2

Maendy VGlam **129** G5
Maenporth **95** E4
Maentwrog **167** F3
Maen-y-groes **141** G2
Maer Corn **112** C5
Maer Staffs **171** E4
Maerdy Carmar **142** C5
Maerdy Carmar **142** C5
Maerdy Conwy **168** D3
Maerdy RCT **129** F3
Maesbrook **169** F5
Maesbury Marsh **170** A5
Maes-glas **130** B3
Maesgwynne **141** F5
Maes-hafn **169** F1
Maeshowe (Heart of
  Neolithic Orkney) Ork
  KW16 3LB **277** C6
Maes-Treylow **144** B1
Maesybont **128** B1
Maesycrugiau **142** A3
Maesycwmmer **130** A3
Magdalen Laver **137** E2
Maggieknockater **268** B6
Maggots End **150** C5
Maghaberry **282** E2
Magham Down **110** B2
Maghera Mid Ulster
  286 C5
Maghera NM&D **283** G5
Magheraboy **287** G6
Magheraboy **286** D4
Magherafelt **286** C6
Magheralane **286** E6
Magheralin **282** E3
Magherally **282** E4
Magheralough D&S **285** F7
Magheralough F&O **281** F3
Magheramason **285** F4
Magheramorne **287** J6
Magheramore **286** C4
Magherasaul **283** G5
Magheraveely **281** F6
Maghery AB&C **282** B4
Maghery AB&C **282** C2
Maghery NM&D **283** F7
Maghull **183** E2
Magilligan **285** J2
Magna Centre, Rotherham
  SYorks S60 1DX **21** C1
Magna Park **160** A4
Magonragh **281** D4
Magor **130** D4
Magpie Green **164** B4
Maguiresbridge **281** F5
Maiden Bradley **117** E4
Maiden Head **116** C1
Maiden Law **212** A3
Maiden Newton **104** B3
Maiden Wells **126** C3
Maidencombe **101** F1
Maidenhayne **103** F3
Maidenhead **135** D4
Maidens **224** A5
Maiden's Green **135** D5
Maidensgrove **134** C4
Maidenwell Corn **97** F2
Maidenwell Lincs **188** D5
Maidford **148** B2
Maids' Moreton **148** C4
Maidstone **123** G3
Maidwell **160** C5
Mail **279** D10
Maindee **130** C4
Maindy Cardiff **130** A5
Maine **281** H1
Mains of Ardestie **244** D1
Mains of Balgavies **252** D4
Mains of Balhall **252** D3
Mains of Ballindarg **252** C4
Mainsbrook **149** D5
Mains of Burgie **267** H6
Mains of Culsh **269** G6
Mains of Dillavaird **253** F1
Mains of Drum **261** G4
Mains of Dudwick **261** H1
Mains of Faillie **258** E1
Mains of Fedderate **269** G6
Mains of Glack **261** F2
Mains of Glassaugh **268** D4
Mains of
  Glenbuchat **260** B3
Mains of Linton **261** F3
Mains of Melgund **252** D4
Mains of Pitfour **269** H6
Mains of Pittrichie **261** G2
Mains of Sluie **267** H6
Mains of Tannachy **268** D4
Mains of Thornton **253** E2
Mains of Tig **214** C2
Mains of Watten **275** H3
Mainsforth **212** C4
Mainsriddle **216** D5
Mainstone **156** B4
Maisemore **146** A5
Maizestown **286** D5
Major's Green **158** D5
Makendon **220** A1
Makeney **173** E3
Makerstoun **228** A3
Malacleit **262** C4
Malborough **100** D4
Malden Rushett **121** G1
Maldon **138** B2
Malham **193** F1
Maligar **263** K5
Malin Bridge **186** A4
Mallaig (Malaig) **256** C5
Mallaigmore **256** C5
Mallaigvaig **256** C5
Malleny Mills **235** F3
Malletsheugh **233** G4
Malling **242** A4
Mallows Green **150** C5
Mallusk **287** G7
Mallwyd **155** E1
Malmesbury **132** B4
Malmsmead **114** A3
Malpas ChesW&C **170** B3
Malpas Corn **96** C5
Malpas Newport **130** C3
Maltby Lincs **188** D4

Maltby *Stock* 203 D1
Maltby *SYorks* 186 C3
Maltby le Marsh 189 E4
Malting End 151 F2
Malting Green 138 C1
Maltman's Hill 124 A4
Malton 203 G5
Malvern Link 145 G3
Malvern Wells 145 G3
Mamberg 232 D1
Mamble 157 F5
Mamhead 102 C4
Mamhilad 130 A2
Manaccan 95 E4
Manadon 100 A2
Manaton 102 A4
Manby 189 D4
Mancetter 159 F3
Manchester 184 C4
Manchester Airport 184 C4
Manchester Apollo *GtMan*
M12 6AP 47 H6
Manchester Art Gallery
GtMan M2 3JL 47 E4
Manchester Central *GtMan*
M2 3GX 46 D5
Manchester Craft & Design
Centre *GtMan*
M4 5JD 47 F3
Manchester Museum
GtMan M13 9PL 47 F7
Manchester United Museum
& Stadium Tour Centre
GtMan M16 ORA 24 D3
Mancot Royal 170 A1
Mandally
(Manndalaidh) 257 J4
Manea 162 C4
Maneight 224 D5
Manfield 202 B1
Mangaster 278 C5
Mangerton 104 A3
Mangotsfield 131 F5
Manish (Manais) 263 G3
Mankinholes 193 F3
Manley 183 G5
Man-moel 130 A2
Mannal 246 C2
Manningford
Abbots 118 C2
Manningford
Bohune 118 C2
Manningford Bruce 118 C2
Manningham 194 A4
Mannings Amusement Park
Suff IP11 2DW 153 D4
Mannings Heath 109 E1
Mannington 105 E1
Manningtree 152 C4
Mannofield 261 H4
Manor Farm Country Park
Hants SO30 2ER 4 D3
Manor Park 135 E4
Manorbier 127 D3
Manorbier Newton 126 D2
Manordeifi 141 F3
Manordeilo 142 C5
Manorowen 140 C4
Mansell Gamage 144 C3
Mansell Lacy 144 D3
Mansergh 200 B4
Mansfield 173 G1
Mansfield
Woodhouse 173 G1
Manson Green 178 B5
Mansriggs 199 D4
Manston *Dorset* 105 E1
Manston *Kent* 125 F2
Manston *WYorks* 194 C4
Manswood 105 F2
Manthorpe *Lincs* 161 F1
Manthorpe *Lincs* 175 E4
Manton *NLincs* 187 F2
Manton *Notts* 186 C5
Manton *Rut* 161 D2
Manton *Wilts* 118 C1
Manuden 150 C5
Manwood Green 137 E1
Maolachy 240 A3
Maperton 117 D5
Maple Cross 135 F3
Maplebeck 174 C1
Mapledurham 134 B5
Mapledurwell 120 B2
Maplehurst 121 G5
Maplescombe 123 E2
Mapleton 172 C3
Mapperley *Derbys* 173 F3
Mapperley *Notts* 173 G3
Mapperton *Dorset* 104 B3
Mapperton *Dorset* 105 F3
Mappleborough
Green 146 C1
Mappleton 197 E3
Mapplewell 186 A2
Mappowder 104 D2
Mar Lodge 259 F1
Màraig (Maaruig) 270 E7
Marazion 95 D3
Marbhig 271 G6
Marbury 170 C3
Marbury Country Park
ChesW&C
CW9 6AT 184 A5
March 162 C3
Marcham 133 G3
Marchamley 170 C5
Marchamley Wood 170 C4
Marchington 172 C4
Marchington
Woodlands 172 C5
Marchwiel 170 A3
Marchwood 106 C1
Marcross 114 C1
Marcus 252 D4
Marden *Here* 145 E3
Marden *Kent* 123 G4
Marden *T&W* 221 F4
Marden *Wilts* 118 B2
Marden Ash 137 E2
Marden Beech 123 G4
Marden Thorn 123 G4
Marden's Hill 123 D5
Mardon 228 D3
Mardy 130 C1

Mare Green 116 A5
Marefield 160 C2
Mareham le Fen 176 A1
Mareham on
the Hill 176 A1
Maresfield 109 G1
Marfleet 196 C4
Marford 170 A2
Margam 129 D4
Margam Country Park
NPT SA13 2TJ 129 E4
Margaret Marsh 105 E1
Margaret Roding 137 E1
Margaretting 137 F2
Margaretting Tye 137 F2
Margate 125 F1
Margnaheglish 223 F2
Margreig 216 C3
Margrove Park 203 F1
Marham 163 F2
Marhamchurch 112 C5
Marholm 161 F2
Marian Cwm 182 B5
Mariandyrys 181 E4
Marian-glas 180 D4
Mariansleigh 114 A5
Marishader 263 K5
Maristow House 100 A1
Maritime Greenwich *GtLon*
SE10 9NF 13 D4
Mark 116 A3
Mark Causeway 116 A3
Mark Cross 123 E5
Markbeech 123 D4
Markby 189 E5
Markeaton 173 E4
Markeaton Park Craft Village
Derby DE22 3BG 18 A4
Market Bosworth 159 G2
Market Bosworth Country
Park *Leics*
CV13 OLP 159 G2
Market Deeping 161 G1
Market Drayton 171 D4
Market Harborough 160 C4
Market Lavington 118 B2
Market Overton 161 D1
Market Rasen 188 B4
Market Stainton 188 C5
Market Street 179 D3
Market Warsop 173 G1
Market Weighton 196 A3
Market Weston 164 A4
Markethill *P&K* 244 A1
Markethill *AB&C* 282 C5
Markfield 159 G1
Markham 130 A2
Markham Moor 187 E5
Markington 194 B1
Marks Gate 137 D3
Marks Tey 152 A5
Markwell 99 D5
Markyate 135 F1
Marl Bank 145 G3
Marland 184 C1
Marlborough 118 C1
Marlbrook 158 B5
Marlcliff 146 C2
Marldon 101 E1
Marle Green 110 A5
Marlesford 153 E2
Marley Green 170 C3
Marley Hill 212 B2
Marlingford 178 C5
Marloes 126 A2
Marlow *Bucks* 135 D4
Marlow *Here* 156 D5
Marlpit Hill 123 D4
Marlpool 173 F3
Marnhull 105 D1
Marnoch 268 D5
Marple 185 D4
Marple Bridge 185 D4
Marr 186 C2
Marrick 201 F3
Marrister 279 E6
Marros 127 F2
Marsden *T&W* 212 C1
Marsden *WYorks* 185 E1
Marsett 201 E4
Marsh 103 F1
Marsh Baldon 134 A3
Marsh Gibbon 148 B5
Marsh Green
Devon 102 D3
Marsh Green
GtMan 183 G2
Marsh Green *Kent* 122 D4
Marsh Green
Tel&W 157 F1
Marsh Lane 186 B5
Marsh Street 114 C3
Marshall Meadows 237 G3
Marshalswton 283 H4
Marshalsea 103 G2
Marshalswick 136 A2
Marsham 178 C3
Marshaw 192 B2
Marshborough 125 F3
Marshbrook 156 D4
Marshchapel 189 D3
Marshfield
Newport 130 B4
Marshfield *SGlos* 131 G5
Marshgate 98 B1
Marshland
St. James 162 D2
Marshside 183 E1
Marshwood 103 G3
Marske 202 A2
Marske-by-the-Sea 213 F5
Marsland Green 184 A3
Marston *ChesW&C* 184 A5
Marston *Here* 144 C2
Marston *Lincs* 175 D3
Marston *Oxon* 134 A2
Marston *Staffs* 171 G5
Marston *Staffs* 158 A1
Marston *Warks* 159 E3
Marston *Wilts* 118 A2

Marston Doles 147 G2
Marston Green 159 D4
Marston Magna 116 C5
Marston Meysey 132 D3
Marston
Montgomery 172 C4
Marston Moretaine 149 E3
Marston on Dove 172 D5
Marston
St. Lawrence 148 A3
Marston Stannett 145 E2
Marston Trussell 160 B4
Marstow 131 E1
Marsworth 135 E1
Marten 119 D1
Marthall 184 B5
Martham 179 F4
Martin *Hants* 105 G1
Martin *Lincs* 175 G2
Martin *Lincs* 176 A1
Martin Drove End 118 B5
Martin Hussingtree 146 A1
Martin Mere *Lancs*
L40 OTA 183 F1
Martinhoe 113 G1
Martinscroft 184 A4
Martinstown *Dorset*
104 C4
Martinstown *M&EAnt*
287 F4
Martinstown *NM&D*
283 H4
Martlesham 152 D3
Martlesham Heath 152 D3
Martletwy 126 D1
Martley 145 G1
Martock 104 A1
Marton *ChesE* 171 F1
Marton *Cumb* 198 D5
Marton *ERid* 197 D4
Marton *ERid* 197 F3
Marton *Lincs* 187 F4
Marton *Middl* 203 E1
Marton *NYorks* 194 D1
Marton *NYorks* 203 G4
Marton *Shrop* 156 B2
Marton *Shrop* 170 B5
Marton *Warks* 147 G1
Marton Abbey 195 E1
Marton-in-the-
Forest 195 E1
Marton-le-Moor 202 C5
Martyr Worthy 119 G4
Martyr's Green 121 F2
Marwell Zoo *Hants*
SO21 1JH 4 D1
Marwick 276 B5
Marwood 113 F2
Mary Rose *PO1 3LX*
82 Portsmouth
Mary Tavy 99 F3
Marybank (An Lagaidh)
High 266 B6
Marybank *Na H-E. Siar*
271 G4
Maryburgh
(Baile Mairi) 266 C6
Maryfield *Corn* 100 A2
Maryfield *Shet* 279 D8
Marygold 237 F4
Maryhill *Aber* 261 G3
Maryhill *Glas* 233 G3
Marykirk 253 E3
Marylebone *GtLon* 136 B4
Marylebone *GtMan* 183 G2
Marypark 259 J1
Maryport *Cumb* 208 D3
Maryport *D&G* 206 B3
Marystow 99 E2
Maryton 253 E4
Marywell *Aber* 261 H5
Marywell *Aber* 260 D5
Marywell *Angus* 253 E5
Masham 202 B4
Mashbury 137 F1
Masongill 200 B5
Mastin Moor 186 B5
Mastrick 261 H4
Matchborough 146 C1
Matching 137 E1
Matching Green 137 E1
Matching Tye 137 E1
Matfen 220 C4
Matfield 123 F4
Mathern 131 E3
Mathon 145 G3
Mathry 140 B4
Matlaske 178 C2
Matlock 173 E1
Matlock Bank 173 E1
Matlock Bath 173 D2
Matson 132 A1
Matterdale End 209 G4
Mattersey 187 D4
Mattersey Thorpe 187 D4
Mattingley 120 C2
Mattishall 178 B4
Mattishall Burgh 178 B4
Mauchline 224 C3
Maud 269 H6
Maufant 100 C5
Maugersbury 147 D5
Maughold 190 C2
Mauld 257 K1
Maulden 149 F4
Maulds Meaburn 200 B1
Maunby 202 C4
Maund Bryan 145 E2
Maundown 115 D1
Mautby 179 F4
Mavesyn Ridware 158 C1
Mavis Enderby 176 B1
Mawbray 209 D2
Mawdesley 183 F1
Mawdlam 129 E4
Mawgan 95 E4
Mawgan Porth 96 C3
Mawla 96 B5
Mawnan 95 E4
Mawnan Smith 95 E4
Mawsley 160 D5
Mawthorpe 189 E5
Maxey 161 G2
Maxstoke 159 E4

Maxted Street 124 D4
Maxton *Kent* 125 F4
Maxton *ScBord* 228 A3
Maxwellheugh 228 B3
Maxwelltown 217 D3
Maxworthy 98 C1
May Hill 145 G5
Mayals 128 C3
Maybole 224 B5
Maybury 121 F2
Mayen 268 D6
Mayfair 136 B4
Mayfield *ESuss* 110 A1
Mayfield *Midlo* 236 A3
Mayfield *Staffs* 172 C3
Mayford 121 E2
Mayland 138 C2
Maylandsea 138 C2
Maynard's Green 110 A2
Mayobridge 282 E6
Mayoghill 286 C4
Maypole *IoS* 96 B1
Maypole *Kent* 125 D2
Maypole *Mon* 131 D1
Maypole Green
Essex 152 A5
Maypole Green
Norf 165 F2
Maypole Green
Suff 153 D1
Maypole Green
Suff 152 A2
May's Corner 282 E5
May's Green *NSom* 116 A1
Mays Green *Oxon* 134 C4
Maytown 282 D6
Maywick 279 C10
Mazetown 283 F2
McGregor's Corner 287 F4
Mead 112 C4
Mead End 118 B5
Meadgate 117 D2
Meadle 134 D2
Meadow Green 145 G2
Meadowhall 186 A3
Meadowmill 236 B2
Meadowtown 156 C2
Meadwell 99 E2
Meaford 171 F4
Meal Bank 199 G3
Mealabost (Mealabost) 271 G4
Mealabost Borve
(Mealabost) 271 G2
Mealrigg 209 E3
Mealsgate 209 F2
Meanley 192 D3
Meanwood 194 B4
Mearbeck 193 E1
Meare 116 B3
Meare Green 115 G5
Mears Ashby 148 D1
Measham 159 F1
Meathop 199 F4
Meavag *Na H-E. Siar*
263 G2
Meavy 100 B1
Medbourne 160 D3
Meddon 112 C4
Meden Vale 173 G1
Medlar 192 A4
Medmenham 134 D4
Medomsley 212 A2
Medstead 120 B4
Meerbrook 171 G1
Meer End 159 E5
Meerbrook 171 G1
Meesden 150 C4
Meeson 171 D5
Meeth 113 F5
Meggethead 226 C3
Meidrim 141 F5
Meifod *Denb* 168 C3
Meifod *Powys* 156 A1
Meigh 282 D6
Meigle 252 A5
Meikle Earnock 234 B4
Meikle Grenach 232 B3
Meikle Kilmory 232 B3
Meikle Rahane 233 D1
Meikle Strath 253 E2
Meikle Tarty 261 H2
Meikle Wartle 261 F1
Meikleour 243 G1
Meikleyard 224 D2
Meinciau 128 A1
Meir 171 G3
Meirheath 171 G3
Melbost (Mealabost) 271 G4
Melbost Borve
(Mealabost) 271 G2
Melbourn 150 B3
Melbourne *Derbys* 173 E5
Melbourne *ERid* 195 G3
Melbury 112 C4
Melbury Abbas 105 E1
Melbury Bubb 104 B2
Melbury Osmond 104 B2
Melbury Sampford 104 B2
Melby 279 A7
Melchbourne 149 F1
Melcombe
Bingham 105 D2
Melcombe Regis 104 C4
Meldon *Devon* 99 F1
Meldon *N'umb* 220 D3
Meldreth 150 B3
Meledor 96 D4
Melfort 240 A3
Melgarve 258 B5
Melgum 260 C4
Meliden
(Gallt Melyd) 182 B4
Melincourt 129 E2
Melin-y-coed 168 B1
Melin-y-ddol 155 G2
Melin-y-grug 155 G2
Melin-y-wig 168 D3
Melkinthorpe 210 B5
Melkridge 210 D1
Melksham 118 A1
Melksham Forest 118 A1
Melldalloch 232 A2
Melling *Lancs* 199 G5
Melling *Mersey* 183 E2

Melling Mount 183 F2
Mellis 164 B4
Mellon Charles 264 E2
Mellon Udrigle 264 E2
Mellor *GtMan* 185 D4
Mellor *Lancs* 192 C4
Mellor Brook 192 C4
Mells 117 E3
Melmerby *Cumb* 210 C4
Melmerby *NYorks* 201 E4
Melmerby *NYorks* 202 C5
Melplash 104 A3
Melrose *Aber* 269 F4
Melrose *ScBord* 227 G2
Melsetter 277 B9
Melsonby 202 A2
Meltham 185 E1
Melton *ERid* 196 B5
Melton *Suff* 153 D2
Melton Constable 178 B2
Melton Mowbray 160 C1
Melton Ross 188 A1
Meltonby 195 G2
Melvaig 264 D3
Melverley 156 C1
Melverley Green 156 C1
Melvich 274 D2
Membury 103 F2
Memsie 269 H4
Memus 252 C4
Menabilly 97 E4
Menai Bridge
(Porthaethwy) 181 D5
Mendham 165 D3
Mendlesham 152 C1
Mendlesham Green 152 B1
Menethorpe 195 G1
Menheniot 97 G3
Menithwood 145 G1
Mennock 225 G5
Menston 194 A3
Menstrie 242 D5
Mentmore 135 E1
Meoble 247 G1
Meole Brace 157 D1
Meols 182 A4
Meon 107 E2
Meonstoke 107 F1
Meopham 123 F2
Meopham Green 123 F2
Mepal 162 C4
Meppershall 149 G4
Merbach 144 C3
Mercaston 173 D3
Mere *ChesE* 184 B4
Mere *Wilts* 117 F4
Mere Brow 183 F1
Mere Green 158 D3
Mere Heath 184 A5
Mereclough 193 E4
Meresloe 191 G4
Meretown 171 E5
Mereworth 123 F3
Mergie 253 F1
Meriden 159 E4
Merkadale 255 J1
Merkinch 266 D7
Merkland 216 B3
Merley 105 G3
Merlin's Bridge 126 C1
Merridge 115 F4
Merrifield 101 E3
Merrington 170 B5
Merrion 126 C3
Merriott 104 A1
Merrivale 99 F3
Merrow 121 F2
Merry Hill *Herts* 136 A3
Merry Hill *WMid* 158 B4
Merry Hill *WMid* 158 A3
Merrymeet 97 G3
Mersea Island 138 D1
Mersey Ferries *Mersey*
CH44 6QY 42 A4
Merseyside Maritime
Museum *Mersey*
L3 4AQ 42 B5
Mersham 124 C5
Merstham 122 B3
Merston 108 A3
Merstone 107 E4
Merther 96 C5
Merthyr 141 G5
Merthyr Cynog 143 F4
Merthyr Dyfan 115 E1
Merthyr Mawr 129 E5
Merthyr Tydfil 129 G2
Merthyr Vale 129 G3
Merton *Devon* 113 F4
Merton *Norf* 164 A2
Merton *Oxon* 134 A1
Mervinslaw 228 B5
Meshaw 102 A1
Messing 138 C1
Messingham 187 F2
Metcombe 103 D3
Metfield 165 D3
Metherell 100 A1
Metheringham 175 F1
Methil 244 B5
Methlem 166 A4
Methley 194 C5
Methley Junction 194 C5
Methlick 261 G1
Methven 243 F2
Methwold 163 F3
Methwold Hythe 163 F3
MetroCentre 212 B1
Mettingham 165 E3
Metton 178 C2
Mevagissey 97 E5
Mewith Head 192 D1
Mexborough 186 B3
Mey 275 H1
Meysey Hampton 132 D2
Miabhaig *Na H-E. Siar*
270 C7
Mial 264 D3
Miavaig (Miabhaig)
270 C7
Michaelchurch 145 E5
Michaelchurch
Escley 144 C4
Michaelchurch-on-
Arrow 144 B2
Michaelston-le-Pit 130 A5
Michaelston-super-
Ely 130 A5

Michaelston-y-
Fedw 130 B4
Michaelston 97 E2
Michelcombe 100 C1
Micheldever 119 G4
Michelmersh 119 E5
Mickfield 152 C1
Mickle Trafford 170 B1
Micklebring 186 C3
Mickleby 204 B1
Micklefield 194 D4
Micklefield Green 135 F3
Mickleham 121 G2
Micklehurst 185 D2
Mickleover 173 E4
Micklethwaite
Cumb 209 F1
Micklethwaite
WYorks 193 G3
Mickleton *Dur* 211 F5
Mickleton *Glos* 147 D3
Mickletown 194 C5
Mickley *Derbys* 186 A5
Mickley *NYorks* 202 B5
Mickley Green 151 G2
Mickley Square 211 G1
Mid Ardlaw 269 H4
Mid Beltie 260 E4
Mid Calder 235 E3
Mid Clyth 275 H5
Mid Hants Railway
Hants SO24 9JG 120 B4
Mid Lambrook 104 A1
Mid Lavant 108 A3
Mid Letter 240 C4
Mid Lix 242 A1
Mid Mossdale 200 D3
Mid Yell 278 D3
Midbea 276 D3
Middle Assendon 134 C4
Middle Aston 147 G5
Middle Barton 147 G5
Middle Bickenhill 159 E4
Middle
Bockhampton 106 A3
Middle Claydon 148 C5
Middle Drift 97 F3
Middle Drums 253 D4
Middle
Duntisbourne 132 B2
Middle Handley 186 B5
Middle Harling 164 A3
Middle Kames 232 A1
Middle Littleton 146 C3
Middle Maes-coed 144 C4
Middle Marwood 113 F2
Middle Mill 140 B5
Middle Quarter 124 A5
Middle Rasen 188 A4
Middle Rigg 243 F4
Middle Salter 192 C1
Middle Sontley 170 A3
Middle Stoford 115 E5
Middle Taphouse 97 F3
Middle Town 96 B1
Middle Tysoe 147 F3
Middle Wallop 119 D4
Middle Winterslow 118 D4
Middle Woodford 118 C4
Middlebie 218 A4
Middlecliff 186 B2
Middlecott 113 E5
Middleham 202 A4
Middlehill *Aber* 269 G6
Middlehill *Corn* 97 G3
Middlehope 157 E4
Middlemarsh 104 C2
Middlemoor 99 E3
Middlequarter (Ceathramh
Meadhanach) 262 D4
Middlesbrough 213 D5
Middlesceugh 210 A3
Middleshaw 199 G4
Middlestone 212 B4
Middlestone Moor 212 B4
Middlestown 185 G1
Middleton *Aber* 261 G3
Middleton *Angus* 253 D5
Middleton *Cumb* 200 B4
Middleton *Derbys* 172 D2
Middleton *Derbys* 172 C1
Middleton *Essex* 151 G3
Middleton *GtMan* 184 C2
Middleton *Hants* 119 F3
Middleton *Here* 145 E1
Middleton *IoW* 106 C4
Middleton *Lancs* 192 A2
Middleton *Midlo* 236 A4
Middleton *Norf* 163 E1
Middleton *N'hants*
160 D4
Middleton *N'umb* 220 C3
Middleton *N'umb* 229 E3
Middleton *Norf* 163 E1
Middleton *NYorks* 203 G4
Middleton *P&K* 243 G4
Middleton *P&K* 251 G5
Middleton *Shrop* 156 B3
Middleton *Shrop* 157 E5
Middleton *Shrop* 170 A5
Middleton *Suff* 153 F1
Middleton *Swan* 128 A4
Middleton *Warks* 159 D3
Middleton *WYorks* 194 A3
Middleton *WYorks* 194 B5
Middleton Baggot 157 F3
Middleton Bank Top 220 C3
Middleton Cheney 147 G3
Middleton Green 171 G4
Middleton Hall 229 D4
Middleton Moor 153 F1
Middleton of
Potterton 261 H3
Middleton on the
Hill 145 E1
Middleton
One Row 202 C1
Middleton Park 261 H3
Middleton Priors 157 F4
Middleton
Quernhow 202 C5
Middleton
St. George 202 C1
Middleton Scriven 157 F4
Middleton Stoney 148 A5
Middleton Tyas 202 B2
Middleton-in-
Teesdale 211 F5

Middleton-on-
Leven 203 D1
Middleton-on-Sea 108 B3
Middleton-on-the-
Wolds 196 B3
Middletown *AB&C* 282 A5
Middletown *Cumb* 198 A2
Middletown *Powys* 156 C1
Middlewich 171 E1
Middlewood *ChesE* 184 D4
Middlewood *SYorks* 186 A3
Middlewood Green 152 B1
Middlezoy 116 A4
Middridge 212 B5
Midfield 273 H2
Midford 117 E1
Midge Hall 192 B5
Midgeholme 210 C2
Midgham 119 G1
Midgley *WYorks* 185 G1
Midgley *WYorks* 193 G5
Midhopestones 185 G3
Midhurst 121 D5
Midland Railway Centre
Derbys DE5 3QZ 173 F2
Midlem 227 G3
Midloe Grange 149 G1
Midpark 232 B4
Midsomer Norton 117 D2
Midthorpe 188 D3
Midtown *High* 273 H2
Midtown *High* 264 E3
Midtown of Barras 253 G2
Midville 176 B2
Midway 173 E5
Migdale 266 D2
Migvie 260 C4
Milarrochy 241 G5
Milber 102 B5
Milbethill 268 E5
Milborne Port 104 C1
Milborne
St. Andrew 105 D3
Milborne Wick 117 D5
Milbourne
N'umb 220 D3
Milbourne *Wilts* 132 B4
Milburn 210 C5
Milbury Heath 131 F3
Milcombe 147 G4
Milden 152 A3
Mildenhall *Suff* 163 F5
Mildenhall *Wilts* 118 D1
Mile Elm 118 A1
Mile End *Essex* 152 A5
Mile End *Glos* 131 E1
Mile End Park *GtLon*
E3 4HL 12 D4
Mile Oak 123 F4
Mile Town 124 B1
Milebrook 156 C5
Milebush *Kent* 123 G4
Milebush *M&EAnt* 287 J7
Mileham 178 A4
Miles Green 171 F3
Miles Hope 145 E1
Milesmark 235 E1
Miles's Green 119 G1
Milfield 228 D3
Milford *Derbys* 173 E3
Milford *Devon* 112 C3
Milford *Shrop* 170 B5
Milford *Staffs* 171 G5
Milford *Surr* 121 E3
Milford Haven
(Aberdaugleddau)
126 B2
Milford on Sea 106 B3
Milkwall 131 E2
Mill Bank 193 G5
Mill Brow 185 D4
Mill End *Bucks* 134 C4
Mill End *Cambs* 151 E2
Mill End *Herts* 150 B4
Mill End *Herts* 151 E5
Mill Green *Cambs* 151 E3
Mill Green *Essex* 137 F2
Mill Green *Herts* 136 B2
Mill Green *Norf* 164 C3
Mill Green *Shrop* 171 D5
Mill Green *Staffs* 158 C1
Mill Green *Suff* 153 E1
Mill Green *Suff* 152 B3
Mill Green *Suff* 152 A2
Mill Green *WMid* 158 C2
Mill Hill *B'burn* 192 C5
Mill Hill *Cambs* 150 A2
Mill Hill *GtLon* 136 B3
Mill Houses 192 C1
Mill Lane 120 C2
Mill of Camsail 233 D1
Mill of Colp 269 F6
Mill of Elrick 269 H6
Mill of Fortune 242 C2
Mill of Kingoodie 261 G2
Mill of Monquich 261 G5
Mill of Uras 253 G1
Mill Side 199 F4
Mill Street *Kent* 123 F3
Mill Street *Norf* 178 B4
Mill Town 277 F7
Milland 120 D5
Millbank 269 J5
Millbay 287 J6
Millbeck 209 F4
Millbounds 276 E4
Millbreck 269 J6
Millbridge 120 D3
Millbrook *CenBeds* 149 F4
Millbrook *Corn* 100 A2
Millbrook *M&EAnt* 287 H5
Millbrook *Soton* 106 C1
Millburn *Aber* 260 E2
Millburn *Aber* 260 E1
Millcombe 101 E2
Millcorner 110 D1
Milldale 172 C2
Millden 261 H3
Milldens 252 D4
Millearne 243 E3
Millend 147 F3
Millenheath 170 C4
Millennium Seed Bank,
Wakehurst Place *WSuss*
RH17 6TN 122 C5
Millerhill 236 A3
Miller's Dale 185 F5

Mil - Nas

Millers Green Derbys 173 D2
Miller's Green Essex 137 E2
Millford 282 B4
Millgate 193 E5
Millhalf 144 B3
Millhayes Devon 103 E1
Millhayes Devon 103 F2
Millholme 199 G3
Millhouse A&B 232 A2
Millhouse Cumb 209 G3
Millhouse Green 185 G2
Millhousebridge 217 F2
Millikenpark 233 F3
Millin Cross 126 C1
Millington 196 A2
Millington Green 173 D3
Millisle 283 J1
Millmeece 171 F4
Millness 257 K1
Millom 198 C4
Millow 150 A3
Millpool 97 F2
Millport 232 C4
Millthorpe 186 A5
Millthrop 200 B3
Milltimber 261 G4
Milltown A&N 286 E6
Milltown AB&C 282 B3
Milltown AB&C 282 C2
Milltown AB&C 282 C4
Milltown AB&C 282 E5
Milltown Aber 259 K4
Milltown CC&G 286 B2
Milltown CC&G 286 D3
Milltown Corn 97 F4
Milltown D&G 218 B4
Milltown D&S 285 F5
Milltown Derbys 173 E1
Milltown Devon 113 F2
Milltown F&O 280 D3
Milltown F&O 281 F2
Milltown High 267 G7
Milltown L&C 283 F3
Milltown M&EAnt 286 D5
Milltown M&EAnt 286 E6
Milltown NM&D 282 D6
Milltown NM&D 282 E6
Milltown of Aberdalgie 243 F2
Milltown of Auchindoun 260 B1
Milltown of Craigston 269 F5
Milltown of Edinvillie 267 K7
Milltown of Kildrummy 260 C3
Milltown of Rothiemay 268 D6
Milltown of Towie 260 C3
Milnathort 243 G4
Milners Heath 170 B1
Milngavie 233 G2
Milnrow 184 D1
Milnsbridge 185 F1
Milnthorpe 199 F4
Milovaig 263 G6
Milrig 224 D2
Milson 157 F5
Milstead 124 B3
Milston 118 C3
Milton Angus 252 B5
Milton Cambs 150 C1
Milton Cumb 210 B1
Milton D&G 216 C2
Milton D&G 216 C3
Milton D&G 214 D5
Milton Derbys 173 E5
Milton High 265 K6
Milton High 266 E4
Milton High 267 G6
Milton High 264 D7
Milton High 266 C7
Milton High 275 J3
Milton (Baile a' Mhuilinn) High 258 B1
Milton Mid Ulster 282 A1
Milton Moray 268 D4
Milton Newport 130 C4
Milton Notts 187 E5
Milton NSom 116 A1
Milton Oxon 147 G4
Milton Oxon 133 G3
Milton P&K 243 E1
Milton Pembs 126 D2
Milton Ports 107 F3
Milton Som 116 B5
Milton Stir 242 A4
Milton Stoke 171 G2
Milton WDun 233 F2
Milton Abbas 105 E2
Milton Abbot 99 E3
Milton Bridge 235 G3
Milton Bryan 149 E4
Milton Clevedon 117 D4
Milton Combe 100 A1
Milton Country Park Cambs CB24 6AZ 150 C1
Milton Damerel 113 D4
Milton End 131 G1
Milton Ernest 149 F2
Milton Green 170 B2
Milton Hill 133 G3
Milton Keynes 149 D4
Milton Keynes Village 149 D4
Milton Lilbourne 118 C1
Milton Malsor 148 C2
Milton Morenish 242 B1
Milton of Auchinhove 260 D4
Milton of Balgonie 244 B4
Milton of Buchanan 241 G5
Milton of Cairnborrow 268 C6
Milton of Callander 242 A4
Milton of Campfield 260 E4
Milton of Campsie 234 A2
Milton of Coldwells 261 H1
Milton of Cullerlie 261 F4
Milton of Cushnie 260 D3
Milton of Dalcapon 251 E4
Milton of Inveramsay 261 F2
Milton of Noth 260 D2
Milton of Tullich 260 B5
Milton on Stour 117 E5
Milton Regis 124 A2
Milton Street 110 A3
Miltonduff 267 J5
Miltonhill 267 H5
Miltonise 214 C3
Milton-Lockhart 234 C5
Milton-under-Wychwood 133 E1
Milverton Som 115 E5
Milverton Warks 147 F1
Milwich 171 G4
Mimbridge 121 E1
Minack Theatre Corn TR19 6JU 94 A4
Minard 240 B5
Minard Castle 240 B5
Minchington 105 F1
Minchinhampton 132 A2
Mindrum 228 C3
Mindrummill 228 C3
Minehead 114 C3
Minera 169 F2
Minerstown 283 H5
Minety 132 C3
Minety Lower Moor 132 C3
Minffordd Gwyn 154 D1
Minffordd Gwyn 167 E4
Minffordd Gwyn 181 D5
Mingearraidh 254 C2
Miningsby 176 B1
Minions 97 G2
Minishant 224 B4
Minley Manor 120 D2
Minllyn 155 E1
Minnes 261 H2
Minnigaff 215 F4
Minnonie 269 F4
Minskip 194 C1
Minstead 106 B1
Minsted 121 D5
Minster Kent 124 B1
Minster Kent 125 F2
Minster Lovell 133 F1
Minsteracres 211 G2
Minsterley 156 C2
Minsterworth 131 G1
Minterburn 281 K3
Minterne Magna 104 C2
Minterne Parva 104 C2
Minting 188 B5
Mintlaw 269 J6
Minto 227 G3
Minton 156 D3
Minwear 126 D1
Minworth 159 D3
Miodar 246 B1
Mirbister 277 C6
Mirehouse 208 C5
Mireland 275 J2
Mirfield 194 B5
Miserden 132 B2
Miskin RCT 129 G4
Miskin RCT 129 G3
Misselfore 118 B5
Misson 187 D3
Misterton Leics 160 A4
Misterton Notts 187 E3
Misterton Som 104 A2
Mistley 152 C4
Mitcham 122 B2
Mitchel Troy 131 D1
Mitcheldean 131 F1
Mitchell 96 C4
Mitchelland 199 F3
Mitcheltroy Common 131 D2
Mitford 221 D3
Mithian 96 B4
Mitton 158 A1
Mixbury 148 B4
Mixenden 193 G5
Moar 250 A5
Moat 218 C4
Moats Tye 152 B2
Mobberley ChesE 184 B5
Mobberley Staffs 172 B3
Moccas 144 C3
Mochdre Conwy 181 G5
Mochdre Powys 155 G4
Mochrum 206 D2
Mockbeggar Hants 106 A2
Mockbeggar Kent 123 G4
Mockerkin 209 D4
Modbury 100 C2
Moddershall 171 G4
Modern Art Oxford Oxon OX1 1BP 80 Oxford
Modsarie 273 J2
Moel Famau Country Park Denb LL15 1US 169 E1
Moelfre IoA 180 D4
Moelfre Powys 169 E5
Moffat 226 B5
Mogerhanger 149 G3
Moin'a'choire 230 B3
Moine House 273 H3
Moira L&C 282 E5
Moira Leic 159 F1
Molash 124 C3
Mol-chlach 255 K3
Mold (Yr Wyddgrug) 169 F1
Molehill Green Essex 151 D5
Molehill Green Essex 151 F5
Molescroft 196 C3
Molesden 220 D3
Molesworth 161 F5
Mollance 216 B4
Molland 114 B5
Mollington ChesW&C 183 E5
Mollington Oxon 147 G3
Mollinsburn 234 B2
Monach Islands (Heisker Islands) 262 B5
Monachty 142 B1
Monachyle 241 G3
Monanclogh 286 E2
Monea 280 D4
Monehanegan 285 H4
Monevechadan 241 D4
Monewden 152 D2
Moneycanon 285 G5
Moneycarragh 283 G5
Moneydie 243 F2
Moneydig 286 C4
Moneyglass 286 E6
Moneymore 286 C7
Moneyneany 286 B6
Moneynick 286 E7
Moneyreagh 283 H2
Moneyrod 286 E6
Moneyrow Green 135 D5
Moneysharvan 286 C5
Moneyslane 283 F5
Moniaive 216 B1
Monifieth 244 D1
Monikie 244 D1
Monikie Country Park Angus DD5 3QN 244 C1
Monimail 244 A3
Monington 141 E3
Monk Bretton 186 A2
Monk Fryston 195 E5
Monk Hesleden 213 D4
Monk Sherborne 120 B2
Monk Soham 152 D1
Monk Soham Green 152 D1
Monk Street 151 E5
Monken Hadley 136 B3
Monkerton 102 C3
Monkey Mates W'ham RG41 1JA 134 C5
Monkey World, Wareham Dorset BH20 6HH 105 E4
Monkhide 145 F3
Monkhill 209 G1
Monkhopton 157 F3
Monkland 145 D2
Monkleigh 113 E3
Monknash 129 F5
Monkokehampton 113 F5
Monks Eleigh 152 A3
Monks Eleigh Tye 152 A3
Monk's Gate 109 E1
Monks' Heath 184 C5
Monk's Hill 124 A4
Monks Horton 124 D5
Monks Kirby 159 G4
Monks Risborough 134 D2
Monkscross 99 D3
Monkseaton 221 F4
Monkshill 269 F6
Monksilver 115 D4
Monkstadt 263 J5
Monkstown 287 H7
Monkswood 130 C2
Monkton Devon 103 E2
Monkton Kent 125 E2
Monkton Pembs 126 C2
Monkton SAyr 224 B3
Monkton T&W 212 C1
Monkton VGlam 129 F5
Monkton Combe 117 E1
Monkton Deverill 117 F4
Monkton Farleigh 117 F1
Monkton Heathfield 115 F5
Monkton Up Wimborne 105 G1
Monkton Wyld 103 G3
Monkwearmouth 212 C2
Monkwood 120 B4
Monlough 283 G2
Monmouth (Trefynwy) 131 E1
Monnington Court 144 C4
Monnington on Wye 144 C3
Monreith 207 D2
Montacute 104 B1
Montacute House Som TA15 6XP 104 B1
Monteach 269 G6
Monteith 282 E4
Montford 156 D1
Montford Bridge 156 D1
Montgarrie 260 D3
Montgomery (Trefaldwyn) 156 B3
Montgreenan 233 E5
Montpellier Gallery Warks CV37 6EP 85 Stratford-upon-Avon
Montrave 244 B4
Montrose 253 F4
Monxton 119 E3
Monyash 172 C1
Monymusk 260 E3
Monzie 243 D2
Moodiesburn 234 A2
Moons Moat North 146 C1
Moonzie 244 B3
Moor Allerton 194 C4
Moor Cock 192 C1
Moor Crichel 105 F2
Moor End Bed 149 F2
Moor End CenBeds 149 E5
Moor End Cumb 199 G5
Moor End ERid 196 A4
Moor End Lancs 191 G3
Moor End NYorks 195 E4
Moor End WYorks 193 G5
Moor Green Wilts 117 F1
Moor Green WMid 158 C4
Moor Head 194 A4
Moor Monkton 195 E2
Moor Row 208 D5
Moor Side Cumb 198 D5
Moor Side Lancs 192 A4
Moor Side Lancs 192 A4
Moor Side Lincs 176 A2
Moor Street 124 A2
Moorby 176 A1
Moorcot 144 C2
Moordown 105 G3
Moore 183 G4
Moorefield 282 E3
Moorend 209 G1
Moorends 187 D1
Moorfield 185 E3
Moorfields 287 F6
Moorgreen 173 F3
Moorhall 186 A5
Moorhampton 144 C3
Moorhouse Cumb 209 G1
Moorhouse Notts 174 C1
Moorland (Northmoor Green) 116 A4
Moorlinch 116 A4
Moors Valley Country Park Dorset BH24 2ET 106 A2
Moors Valley Railway Dorset BH24 2ET 105 G2
Moorsholm 203 F1
Moorside Dorset 105 D1
Moorside GtMan 185 D2
Moorside WYorks 194 B4
Moorthorpe 186 B1
Moortown IoW 106 D4
Moortown Lincs 188 A3
Moortown Mid Ulster 282 C1
Moortown Tel&W 157 F1
Morangie 266 E3
Morar 256 C5
Morborne 161 G3
Morchard Bishop 102 A2
Morcombelake 104 A3
Morcott 161 E2
Morda 169 F5
Morden Dorset 105 F3
Morden GtLon 122 B2
Morden Hall Park GtLon SM4 5JD 11 F8
Morden Park 122 B2
Mordiford 145 E4
Mordington Holdings 237 G4
Mordon 212 C5
More 156 C3
Morebath 114 C5
Morebattle 228 B4
Morecambe 192 A1
Morefield 265 H2
Moreleigh 101 D2
Morenish 242 B1
Moresby Parks 208 C5
Morestead 119 G5
Moreton Dorset 105 E4
Moreton Essex 137 E2
Moreton Here 145 E1
Moreton Mersey 183 D4
Moreton Oxon 134 B2
Moreton Staffs 172 C4
Moreton Staffs 157 G1
Moreton Corbet 170 C5
Moreton Jeffries 145 F3
Moreton Mill 170 C5
Moreton Morrell 147 F2
Moreton on Lugg 145 E3
Moreton Paddox 147 F2
Moreton Pinkney 148 A3
Moreton Say 170 D4
Moreton Valence 131 G2
Moretonhampstead 102 A4
Moreton-in-Marsh 147 E4
Morfa Carmar 128 B1
Morfa Cere 141 G2
Morfa Bychan 167 E4
Morfa Glas 129 E2
Morfa Nefyn 166 B3
Morgan's Vale 118 C5
Morganstown 130 A4
Mork 131 E2
Morland 210 B5
Morley Derbys 173 E3
Morley Dur 212 A5
Morley WYorks 194 B5
Morley Green 184 C4
Morley St. Botolph 164 B2
Mornick 98 D3
Morningside Edin 235 G2
Morningside NLan 234 C4
Morningthorpe 164 D2
Morpeth 221 E3
Morphie 253 F3
Morrey 158 D1
Morridge Side 172 B2
Morrilow Heath 171 G4
Morriston SAyr 224 A5
Morriston Swan 128 C3
Morristown 130 A5
Morroch 247 F1
Morston 178 B1
Mortehoe 113 E1
Morthen 186 B4
Mortimer 120 B1
Mortimer West End 120 B1
Mortimer's Cross 144 D1
Mortlake 136 B5
Morton Derbys 173 F1
Morton Lincs 175 F5
Morton Lincs 187 F3
Morton Lincs 175 D1
Morton Notts 174 C2
Morton SGlos 131 F3
Morton Shrop 169 F5
Morton Bagot 146 D1
Morton on the Hill 178 C4
Morton Tinmouth 212 A5
Morton-on-Swale 202 C3
Morvah 94 B3
Morval 97 G4
Morvich (A'Mhormhaich) High 257 F2
Morvich High 266 E1
Morvil 140 D4
Morville 157 F3
Morwellham 100 A1
Morwellham Quay Museum Devon PL19 8JL 99 E3
Morwenstow 112 C4
Morwick Hall 221 E1
Mosborough 186 B4
Moscow 233 F5
Mosedale 209 G3
Moselden Height 185 E1
Moseley WMid 158 B3
Moseley Worcs 146 A2
Moses Gate 184 B2
Moss A&B 246 A2
Moss SYorks 186 C1
Moss Wrex 170 A2
Moss Bank 183 G3
Moss Houses 184 C5
Moss Nook 184 C4
Moss of Barmuckity 267 K5
Moss Side GtMan 184 C3
Moss Side Lancs 191 G4
Moss Side Mersey 183 E2
Mossat 260 C3
Mossbank 278 D5
Mossblown 224 C3
Mossburnford 228 A5
Mossdale 216 A3
Mossend 234 B3
Mosser 209 E4
Mossgiel 224 C3
Mosshead 260 D1
Mosside of Ballinshoe 252 C4
Mossley A&N 287 H7
Mossley ChesE 171 F1
Mossley GtMan 185 D2
Mossley Hill 183 E4
Mosspaul Hotel 218 B2
Moss-side CC&G 286 E2
Moss-side High 267 F6
Moss-side Moray 268 D5
Mosstodloch 268 B4
Mosston 252 D5
Mossy Lea 183 G1
Mosterton 104 A2
Moston GtMan 184 C2
Moston Shrop 170 C5
Moston Green 171 E1
Mostyn 182 C4
Motcombe 117 F5
Mothecombe 100 C3
Mother Shipton's Cave NYorks HG5 8DD 194 C2
Motherby 210 A5
Motherwell 234 B4
Mottingham 136 D5
Mottisfont 119 E5
Mottisfont Abbey Hants SO51 0LP 119 E5
Mottistone 106 D4
Mottram in Longdendale 185 D3
Mottram St. Andrew 184 C5
Mouldsworth 183 G5
Moulin 251 E4
Moulsecoomb 109 F3
Moulsford 134 A4
Moulsham 137 G2
Moulsoe 149 E3
Moulton ChesW&C 171 D1
Moulton Lincs 176 B5
Moulton NYorks 202 B2
Moulton Suff 151 E1
Moulton VGlam 129 G5
Moulton WN'hants 148 C1
Moulton Chapel 162 A1
Moulton St. Mary 179 F5
Moulton Seas End 176 B5
Mounie Castle 261 F2
Mount Corn 96 B4
Mount Corn 97 F3
Mount High 267 G7
Mount Kent 125 D4
Mount WYorks 185 F1
Mount Ambrose 96 B5
Mount Bures 152 A4
Mount Charles 97 E4
Mount Edgcumbe Country Park Corn PL10 1HZ 2 B3
Mount Hamilton CC&G 286 E4
Mount Hamilton D&S 285 J6
Mount Hawke 96 B5
Mount Manisty 183 E5
Mount Norris 282 C5
Mount Oliphant 224 B4
Mount Pleasant AB&C 282 C4
Mount Pleasant ChesE 171 F2
Mount Pleasant Derbys 173 E3
Mount Pleasant Derbys 159 E1
Mount Pleasant ESuss 109 G2
Mount Pleasant Flints 182 D5
Mount Pleasant GtLon 135 F3
Mount Pleasant Hants 106 C3
Mount Pleasant Norf 164 A2
Mount Pleasant Suff 151 F3
Mount Ross 283 K3
Mount Sorrel 118 B5
Mount Stewart A&NDown BT22 2AN 283 J2
Mount Tabor 193 G5
Mountain 193 G4
Mountain Ash (Aberpennar) 129 G3
Mountain Cross 235 F5
Mountain Water 140 C5
Mountbenger 227 E3
Mountblairy 268 E5
Mountblow 233 F2
Mountcastle 285 G5
Mountfield ESuss 110 C1
Mountfield F&O 281 H1
Mountgerald 266 C5
Mountjoy Corn 96 C3
Mountjoy F&O 281 G1
Mountjoy Mid Ulster 282 C2
Mountnessing 137 F3
Mounton 131 E3
Mountsandel Fort CC&G BT52 1TW 286 C2
Mountsorrel 160 A1
Mousa 279 D10
Mousehole 94 B4
Mouswald 217 E3
Mow Cop 171 F2
Mowden 202 B1
Mowhan 282 C5
Mowhaugh 228 C4
Mowsley 160 B4
Mowtie 253 G1
Moxley 158 B3
Moy High 249 D1
Moy High 249 G1
Moy High 258 E1
Moy Mid Ulster 282 B3
Moy House 267 H6
Moyad 283 F7
Moyagoney 286 D5
Moyallon 282 D3
Moyarget 286 E2
Moybane F&O 280 D4
Moybane NM&D 282 C7
Moygashel 282 B2
Moylagh 281 H2
Moylgrove 141 E3
Moys 285 J4
Muasdale 231 E5
Much Birch 145 E4
Much Cowarne 145 F3
Much Dewchurch 145 D4
Much Hadham 136 D1
Much Hoole 192 A5
Much Hoole Town 192 A5
Much Marcle 145 F4
Much Wenlock 157 F2
Muchalls 261 H5
Muchelney 116 B5
Muchelney Ham 116 B5
Muchlarnick 97 G4
Muchra 226 D4
Muchrachd 257 J1
Muck 246 D2
Mucking 137 F4
Muckle Roe 279 C6
Muckleford 104 C3
Mucklestone 171 E4
Muckleton 170 C5
Muckletown 260 D2
Muckley 157 F3
Muckley Corner 158 C2
Muckton 189 D4
Mudale 273 H5
Muddiford 113 F2
Muddles Green 110 A2
Muddleswood 109 E2
Mudeford 106 A3
Mudford 104 B1
Mudgley 116 B3
Mugdock 233 G2
Mugdock Country Park Stir G62 8EL 30 C1
Mugeary 255 K1
Mugginton 173 D3
Muggintonlane End 173 D3
Muggleswick 211 G3
Mugswell 122 B3
Muie 266 D1
Muir 251 F1
Muir of Fowlis 260 D3
Muir of Lochs 268 B4
Muir of Lownie 252 C5
Muir of Ord (Am Blàr Dubh) 266 C6
Muiravonside Country Park Falk EH49 6LW 235 D2
Muirden 269 F5
Muirdrum 245 D1
Muiredge 244 B5
Muirhead Aber 260 D3
Muirhead Angus 244 B1
Muirhead Fife 244 A4
Muirhead Moray 267 H5
Muirhead NLan 234 A3
Muirhouses 235 E1
Muirkirk 225 E3
Muirmill 234 B1
Muirtack Aber 261 H1
Muirtack Aber 269 G6
Muirton High 266 E5
Muirton P&K 243 E3
Muirton P&K 243 G2
Muirton of Ardblair 251 G5
Muirton of Ballochy 253 E3
Muirtown 267 G6
Muiryfold 269 F5
Muker 201 E3
Mulbarton 178 C5
Mulben 268 B5
Mulhagery 271 F7
Mull 239 E1
Mullabrack 282 D4
Mullach Chàrlabhaigh 270 E3
Mullacott Cross 113 F1
Mullaghbane 282 C7
Mullaghboy M&EAnt 287 J5
Mullaghboy Mid Ulster 286 D6
Mullaghduff 282 B6
Mullaghglass 282 D6
Mullaghmassa 281 H2
Mullaghmore 282 E6
Mullan 280 D6
Mullanmore 281 J1
Mullans Town 281 J2
Mullartown 283 G6
Mullion 95 D5
Mullion Cove 95 D5
Mulnagore 282 A2
Mumbles (Y Mwmbwls) 128 C4
Mumby 189 F5
Munderfield Row 145 F2
Munderfield Stocks 145 F2
Mundesley 179 E2
Mundford 163 G3
Mundham 165 E2
Mundon 138 B2
Mundurno 261 H3
Munerigie 257 J4
Mungasdale 265 F2
Mungoswells 236 B2
Mungrisdale 209 G3
Munlochy 266 D6
Munnoch 232 D5
Munsley 145 F3
Munslow 157 E4
Murchington 99 G2
Murcott Oxon 134 A1
Murcott Wilts 132 B3
Murdostoun 234 C4
Murieston 235 E3
Murkle 275 G2
Murlaganmore 242 A1
Murlaggan High 257 G5
Murlaggan High 249 F1
Murley 281 G3
Murra 277 B7
Murrell Green 120 C2
Murroes 244 C1
Murrow 162 B2
Mursley 148 D5
Murston 124 B2
Murthill 252 C4
Murthly 243 F1
Murton Cumb 210 D5
Murton Dur 212 C3
Murton N'umb 237 G5
Murton Swan 128 B4
Murton York 195 F2
Musbury 103 F3
Muscliff 105 G3
Musdale (Musdàl) 240 B2
Museum in Docklands GtLon E14 4AL 12 D4
Museum of Childhood, Edinburgh Edin EH1 1TG 37 G4
Museum of Childhood, London GtLon E2 9PA 12 C4
Museum of Flight ELoth EH39 5LF 236 C2
Museum of Garden History, London GtLon SE1 7LB 45 F7
Museum of London GtLon EC2Y 5HN 45 J2
Museum of Science & Industry, Manchester GtMan M3 4FP 46 C4
Museum of Transport, Glasgow Glas G3 8DP 38 A2
Musselburgh 236 A2
Mussenden Temple & Downhill Demesne CC&G BT51 4RP 286 B2
Mustard Hyrn 179 F4
Muston Leics 174 D4
Muston NYorks 205 D5
Mustow Green 158 A5
Mutford 165 F3
Muthill 243 D3
Mutley 100 A2
Mutterton 102 D2
Muxton 157 G1
Mybster 275 G3
Myddfai 143 D4
Myddle 170 B5
Myddlewood 170 B5
Mydroilyn 142 A2
Myerscough College 192 A4
Myerscough Smithy 192 C4
Mylor 95 F3
Mylor Bridge 95 F3
Mynachdy 130 A5
Mynachlog-ddu 141 E4
Myndtown 156 C4
Mynydd Llandygái 167 F1
Mynydd Mechell 180 B4
Mynydd y Garreg 128 A2
Mynydd-bach Mon 131 D3
Mynydd-bach Swan 128 C3
Mynytho 166 C4
Myrebird 261 F5
Mytchett 121 D2
Mytholm 193 F5
Mytholmroyd 193 G5
Mythop 191 G4
Myton-on-Swale 194 D1
Mytton 156 D1

N
Na Gearrannan (Garenin) 270 D3
Naast 264 E3
Nab's Head 192 C5
Na Buirgh 263 F2
Naburn 195 E3
Nackington 125 D3
Nacton 152 D3
Nadderwater 102 B3
Nafferton 196 C2
Nailbridge 131 F1
Nailsbourne 115 F5
Nailsea 131 D5
Nailstone 159 G2
Nailsworth 132 A3
Nairn 267 F6
Nancegollan 94 D3
Nancekuke 96 A5
Nancledra 94 B3
Nanhoron 166 B4
Nannau 168 A5
Nannerch 169 E1
Nanpantan 160 A1
Nanpean 97 D4
Nansledan 96 C3
Nanstallon 97 E3
Nant-ddu 129 G1
Nanternis 141 G2
Nantgaredig 142 A5
Nantgarw 130 A4
Nant-glas 143 F1
Nantglyn 168 D1
Nantgwyn 155 F5
Nantlle 167 E2
Nantmawr 169 F5
Nantmel 143 G1
Nantmor 167 F3
Nantperis 167 F2
Nantwich 170 D2
Nant-y-caws 128 A1
Nant-y-derry 130 C2
Nant-y-dugoed 155 F1
Nantyffyllon 129 E3
Nant-y-glo 130 A1
Nant-y-Gollen 169 F5
Nant-y-groes 143 G1
Nant-y-moel 129 F3
Nant-y-Pandy 181 E5
Naphill 135 D3
Napley Heath 171 E4
Nappa 193 E2
Napton on the Hill 147 G1
Narberth (Arberth) 127 E1
Narborough Leics 160 A3
Narborough Norf 163 F1
Narkurs 98 D5
Narrachan 240 B3
Nasareth 167 D3
Naseby 160 B5
Nash Bucks 148 C4
Nash Here 144 C1
Nash Newport 130 C4
Nash Shrop 157 F5
Nash Street 123 F2
Nassington 161 F3
Nasty 150 B5

Nateby Cumb 200 C2
Nateby Lancs 192 A3
Nately Scures 120 C2
National Agricultural Centre, Stoneleigh Warks CV8 2LZ 16 B5
National Army Museum GtLon SW3 4HT 13 A5
National Botanic Garden of Wales Carmar SA32 8HG 128 B1
National Botanic Gardens Belfast City BT7 1LP 283 G1
National Coal Mining Museum for England WYorks WF4 4RH 27 F6
National Exhibition Centre WMid B40 1NT 15 H4
National Fishing Heritage Centre, Grimsby NELincs DN31 1UZ 188 C2
National Gallery GtLon WC2N 5DN 44 D4
National Gallery of Scotland Edin EH2 2EL 37 F4
National Indoor Arena, Birmingham WMid B1 2AA 34 D4
National Marine Aquarium PL4 0LF 81 Plymouth
National Maritime Museum Cornwall Corn TR11 3QY 95 F3
National Maritime Museum, Greenwich GtLon SE10 9NF 13 D5
National Media Museum WYorks BD1 1NQ 65 Bradford
National Memorial Arboretum, Alrewas Staffs DE13 7AR 159 D1
National Motorcycle Museum, Solihull WMid B92 0EJ 159 E4
National Museum Cardiff CF10 3NP 67 Cardiff
National Museum of Scotland Edin EH1 1JF 37 G5
National Portrait Gallery GtLon WC2H 0HE 44 D4
National Railway Museum YO26 4XJ 90 York
National Sea Life Centre, Birmingham WMid B1 2JB 34 D4
National Seal Sanctuary Corn TR12 6UG 95 E4
National Slate Museum, Llanberis Gwyn LL55 4TY 167 E2
National Space Centre, Leicester Leic LE4 5NS 17 C4
National Wallace Monument Stir FK9 5LF 242 D5
National War Museum, Edinburgh Edin EH1 2NG 37 E4
National Waterfront Museum SA1 3RD 86 Swansea
National Wildflower Centre, Liverpool Mersey L16 3NA 22 D3
Natland 199 G4
Natural History Museum at Tring Herts HP23 6AP 135 E1
Natural History Museum, London GtLon SW7 5BD 11 F5
Natureland Seal Sanctuary Lincs PE25 1DB 177 D1
Naughton 152 B3
Naunton Glos 146 D5
Naunton Worcs 146 A4
Naunton Beauchamp 146 B2
Navan 282 B4
Navan Fort AB&C BT60 4LD 282 B4
Navenby 175 E2
Navestock 137 E3
Navestock Side 137 E3
Navidale 275 F7
Navity 266 E5
Nawton 203 F4
Nayland 152 A4
Nazeing 136 D2
Neacroft 106 A3
Neal's Green 159 F4
Neap 279 E7
Neap House 187 F1
Near Sawrey 199 E3
Nearton End 148 D5
Neasden 136 B4
Neasham 202 C1
Neat Enstone 147 F5
Neath (Castell-nedd) 129 D3
Neatham 120 C3
Neatishead 179 E3
Nebo Cere 142 B1
Nebo Conwy 168 B2
Nebo Gwyn 167 D2
Nebo IoA 180 C3
Necton 163 G2
Ned 285 J3
Nedd 272 D5
Nedderton 221 E3
Nedging 152 A3
Nedging Tye 152 B3
Needham 164 D3
Needham Lake Suff IP6 8NU 152 B2
Needham Market 152 B2
Needham Street 151 F1
Needingworth 162 B5
Needles Pleasure Park IoW PO39 0JD 106 C4
Needwood 172 C5
Neen Savage 157 F5
Neen Sollars 157 F5
Neenton 157 F4
Nefyn 166 C3
Neighbourne 116 D3
Neilston 233 F4
Neithrop 147 G3
Nelsherry 280 E2
Nelson Caerp 130 A3
Nelson Lancs 193 E4
Nelson Village 221 E4
Nemphlar 234 C5
Nempnett Thrubwell 116 C1
Nenthall 211 D3
Nenthead 211 D3
Nenthorn 228 A3
Neopardy 102 A3
Nerabus 230 A4
Nercwys 169 F1
Neriby 230 B3
Nerston 234 A4
Nesbit 229 D3
Nesfield 193 G3
Ness 183 E5
Ness Botanic Gardens ChesW&C CH64 4AY 183 E5
Ness of Tenston 277 B6
Nesscliffe 156 C1
Neston ChesW&C 183 D5
Neston Wilts 117 F1
Nether Alderley 184 C5
Nether Auchendrane 224 B4
Nether Barr 215 F4
Nether Blainslie 236 C5
Nether Broughton 174 B5
Nether Burrow 200 B5
Nether Cerne 104 C3
Nether Compton 104 B1
Nether Crimond 261 G2
Nether Dalgliesh 227 D5
Nether Dallachy 268 B4
Nether Edge 186 A4
Nether End 185 G5
Nether Exe 102 C3
Nether Glasslaw 269 G5
Nether Handwick 252 B5
Nether Haugh 186 B3
Nether Heage 173 E2
Nether Heselden 201 D5
Nether Heyford 148 B2
Nether Kellet 192 B1
Nether Kinmundy 269 J6
Nether Langwith 186 C5
Nether Lenshie 268 E6
Nether Loads 173 E1
Nether Moor 173 E1
Nether Padley 185 G5
Nether Pitforthie 253 G2
Nether Poppleton 195 E2
Nether Silton 203 D3
Nether Skyborry 156 B5
Nether Stowey 115 E4
Nether Urquhart 243 G4
Nether Wallop 119 E4
Nether Wasdale 198 C2
Nether Wellwood 225 E3
Nether Welton 209 G2
Nether Westcote 147 E5
Nether Whitacre 159 E3
Nether Winchendon (Lower Winchendon) 134 C1
Nether Worton 147 G5
Netheravon 118 C3
Netherbrae 269 F5
Netherbrough 277 C6
Netherburn 234 C5
Netherbury 104 A3
Netherby Cumb 218 B4
Netherby NYorks 194 C3
Nethercott 147 G5
Netherfield ESuss 110 C2
Netherfield Notts 174 B3
Netherfield SLan 234 B5
Netherhall 232 D3
Netherhampton 118 C5
Netherhay 104 A2
Netherland Green 172 C4
Netherley 261 G5
Nethermill 217 E2
Nethermuir 269 H6
Netherseal 159 E1
Nethershield 225 D3
Netherstreet 118 A1
Netherthird D&G 216 B5
Netherthird EAyr 225 D4
Netherthong 185 F2
Netherthorpe 186 C4
Netherton Angus 252 D4
Netherton ChesW&C 183 G5
Netherton Devon 102 B5
Netherton Hants 119 E2
Netherton Mersey 183 E2
Netherton N'umb 220 B1
Netherton NLan 234 B4
Netherton Oxon 133 G2
Netherton P&K 251 G4
Netherton SLan 234 D4
Netherton WMid 158 B4
Netherton Worcs 146 B3
Netherton WYorks 185 G1
Netherton WYorks 185 F1
Netherton Burnfoot 220 B1
Netherton Northside 220 B1
Nethertown Cumb 198 A2
Nethertown Ork 275 J1
Nethertown Staffs 158 D1
Netherwitton 220 D2
Netherwood D&G 217 D3
Netherwood EAyr 225 E3
Nethy Bridge 259 H2
Netley Abbey 107 D2
Netley Marsh 106 C1
Nettlebed 134 B4
Nettlebridge 116 D3
Nettlecombe Dorset 104 B3
Nettlecombe IoW 107 E5
Nettlecombe Som 115 D4
Nettleden 135 F1
Nettleham 188 A5
Nettlestead Kent 123 F3
Nettlestead Suff 152 B3
Nettlestead Green 123 F3
Nettlestone 107 F3
Nettlesworth 212 B3
Nettleton Lincs 188 B2
Nettleton Wilts 132 A5
Nettleton Hill 185 E1
Netton Devon 100 B3
Netton Wilts 118 C4
Neuadd Cere 142 A2
Neuadd IoA 180 B3
Neuadd Powys 143 F3
Nevendon 137 G3
Nevern 141 D4
Nevill Holt 160 D3
New Abbey 217 D4
New Aberdour 269 G4
New Addington 122 C2
New Alresford 119 G4
New Alyth 252 A5
New Arley 159 E3
New Arram 196 C3
New Ash Green 123 F2
New Balderton 174 D2
New Barn 123 F2
New Belses 227 G3
New Bewick 229 E4
New Bolingbroke 176 B2
New Boultham 187 G5
New Bradwell 148 D3
New Brancepeth 212 B3
New Bridge D&G 216 D3
New Bridge Devon 102 A5
New Brighton Flints 169 F1
New Brighton Hants 107 G2
New Brighton Mersey 183 E3
New Brighton Wrex 169 F2
New Brighton WYorks 194 B5
New Brinsley 173 F2
New Broughton 170 A2
New Buckenham 164 B2
New Buildings 285 G4
New Byth 269 G5
New Cheriton 119 G5
New Cross Cere 154 C5
New Cross GtLon 136 C5
New Cumnock 225 E4
New Deer 269 G6
New Duston 148 C1
New Earswick 195 F2
New Edlington 186 C3
New Elgin 267 K5
New Ellerby 197 D4
New Eltham 136 D5
New End 146 C1
New England 161 G2
New Farnley 194 B4
New Ferry Mersey 183 E4
New Ferry M&EAnt 286 D6
New Galloway 216 A3
New Gilston 244 C4
New Greens 136 A2
New Grimsby 96 A1
New Hartley 221 F4
New Haw 121 F1
New Heaton 228 C3
New Hedges 127 E2
New Herrington 212 C2
New Hinksey 134 A2
New Holland 196 C5
New Houghton Derbys 173 G1
New Houghton Norf 177 F5
New Houses 200 D5
New Hunwick 212 A4
New Hutton 199 G3
New Hythe 123 G3
New Inn Carmar 142 A4
New Inn Fife 244 A4
New Inn Mon 131 D2
New Inn Torfaen 130 B3
New Invention Shrop 156 B5
New Invention WMid 158 B2
New Kelso 265 F7
New Lanark 234 C5
New Lanark SLan ML11 9DB 234 C5
New Lane 183 F1
New Lane End 184 A3
New Leake 176 C2
New Leeds 269 H5
New Leslie 260 D2
New Lodge 186 A2
New Longton 192 B5
New Luce 214 C4
New Mains 225 G2
New Mains of Ury 253 G1
New Malden 122 B2
New Marske 213 F5
New Marton 170 A4
New Mill Corn 94 B3
New Mill Herts 135 E1
New Mill WYorks 185 F2
New Mill End 136 A1
New Mills Corn 96 C4
New Mills Derbys 185 E4
New Mills Glos 131 F2
New Mills Mon 131 E2
New Mills (Y Felin Newydd) Powys 155 G2
New Milton 106 B3
New Mistley 152 C4
New Moat 141 D5
New Ollerton 174 B1
New Orleans 222 C4
New Oscott 158 C3
New Palace & Adventureland, New Brighton Mersey CH45 2JX 22 A2
New Park Corn 97 F1
New Park NYorks 194 B2
New Pitsligo 269 G5
New Polzeath 96 D2
New Quay (Ceinewydd) 141 G1
New Rackheath 179 D4
New Radnor (Maesyfed) 144 B1
New Rent 210 A4
New Ridley 211 G1
New Road Side 193 F3
New Romney 111 F1
New Rossington 186 D3
New Row Cere 154 D5
New Row Lancs 192 C4
New Sawley 173 F4
New Shoreston 229 F3
New Silksworth 212 C2
New Stevenston 234 B4
New Swannington 159 G1
New Totley 186 A5
New Town CenBeds 149 G3
New Town Cere 141 E3
New Town Dorset 105 F1
New Town Dorset 105 F2
New Town ELoth 236 B2
New Town ESuss 109 G1
New Town Glos 146 C4
New Town Mid Ulster 286 D5
New Tredegar 130 A2
New Tupton 173 E1
New Ulva 231 F1
New Valley 271 G4
New Village 186 C2
New Walk Museum & Art Gallery LE1 7EA 77 Leicester
New Walsoken 162 C2
New Waltham 188 C2
New Walton Pier Essex CO14 8ES 153 D5
New Winton 236 B2
New World 162 B3
New Yatt 133 F1
New York Lincs 176 A2
New York T&W 221 F4
Newall 194 B3
Newark Ork 276 G3
Newark Peter 162 A2
Newark Castle, Newark-on-Trent Notts NG24 1BG 174 C2
Newark-on-Trent 174 D2
Newarthill 234 B4
Newball 188 A5
Newbarn 125 D5
Newbarns 198 D5
Newbattle 236 A3
Newbiggin Cumb 210 A5
Newbiggin Cumb 210 C5
Newbiggin Cumb 210 B3
Newbiggin Cumb 191 F1
Newbiggin Cumb 198 B3
Newbiggin Dur 212 A5
Newbiggin N'umb 211 F1
Newbiggin NYorks 201 F4
Newbiggin NYorks 201 E3
Newbiggin-by-the-Sea 221 F3
Newbigging Aber 261 G5
Newbigging Aber 251 G1
Newbigging Angus 244 C1
Newbigging Angus 244 C1
Newbigging Angus 252 A5
Newbigging SLan 235 E5
Newbiggin-on-Lune 200 C2
Newbold Derbys 186 A5
Newbold Leics 159 G1
Newbold on Avon 159 G5
Newbold on Stour 147 E3
Newbold Pacey 147 E2
Newbold Verdon 159 G2
Newborough (Niwbwrch) IoA 166 D1
Newborough Peter 162 A2
Newborough Staffs 172 C5
Newbottle T&W 212 C2
Newbottle WN'hants 148 A4
Newbourne 153 D3
Newbridge (Cefn Bychan) Caerp 130 B3
Newbridge Corn 94 B3
Newbridge Corn 98 D4
Newbridge Edin 235 F2
Newbridge ESuss 123 D5
Newbridge Hants 106 B1
Newbridge IoW 106 D4
Newbridge NYorks 204 B4
Newbridge Oxon 133 G2
Newbridge Pembs 140 C4
Newbridge Wrex 169 F3
Newbridge Green 146 A4
Newbridge on Usk 130 C3
Newbridge on Wye 143 G2
Newbrough 211 E1
Newbuildings 102 A2
Newburgh Aber 269 H5
Newburgh Aber 261 H2
Newburgh Fife 244 A3
Newburgh Lancs 183 F1
Newburgh ScBord 227 E3
Newburn 212 A1
Newbury Som 117 D2
Newbury WBerks 119 F1
Newbury Wilts 117 F3
Newbury Park 136 D4
Newby Cumb 210 B5
Newby Lancs 193 E3
Newby NYorks 203 E1
Newby NYorks 192 D1
Newby NYorks 204 D4
Newby Bridge 199 E4
Newby Cote 200 C5
Newby Cross 209 G1
Newby East 210 A2
Newby Hall NYorks HG4 5AE 194 C1
Newby West 209 G1
Newby Wiske 202 C4
Newcastle A&NDown 283 K3
Newcastle Bridgend 129 E5
Newcastle Mon 130 D1
Newcastle NM&D 283 G5
Newcastle Shrop 156 B4
Newcastle Emlyn (Castell Newydd Emlyn) 141 G3
Newcastle International Airport 221 D4
Newcastle upon Tyne 212 B1
Newcastleton 218 C3
Newcastle-under-Lyme 171 F3
Newchapel Pembs 141 F4
Newchapel Staffs 171 F2
Newchapel Surr 122 C4
Newchurch Carmar 141 G5
Newchurch IoW 107 E4
Newchurch Kent 124 C5
Newchurch Lancs 193 E5
Newchurch Lancs 193 E4
Newchurch Mon 131 D3
Newchurch Powys 144 B2
Newchurch Staffs 172 C5
Newcott 103 F2
Newcraighall 236 A2
Newdigate 121 G3
Newell Green 135 D5
Newenden 110 D1
Newent 145 G5
Newerne 131 F2
Newfield Dur 212 B4
Newfield Dur 212 B2
Newfield High 266 E4
Newfound 119 G2
Newgale 140 B5
Newgate 178 B1
Newgate Street 136 C2
Newgord 278 E2
Newhall ChesE 170 D3
Newhall Derbys 173 D5
Newham 229 F4
Newham Hall 229 F4
Newhaven 109 G3
Newhey 184 D1
Newholm 204 B1
Newhouse 234 B3
Newick 109 G1
Newingreen 124 D5
Newington Edin 235 G2
Newington Kent 125 D5
Newington Kent 124 A2
Newington Notts 187 D3
Newington Oxon 134 B3
Newington Bagpath 132 A3
Newland Cumb 199 E5
Newland Glos 131 E2
Newland Hull 196 C4
Newland NYorks 195 F5
Newland Oxon 133 F1
Newland Worcs 145 G3
Newlandrig 236 A3
Newlands Cumb 209 G3
Newlands Essex 138 B4
Newlands N'umb 211 G2
Newlands ScBord 218 D2
Newland's Corner 121 F3
Newlands of Geise 275 F2
Newlands of Tynet 268 B4
Newlyn 94 B4
Newmachar 261 G3
Newmains 234 C4
Newman's End 137 E1
Newman's Green 151 G3
Newmarket Suff 151 E1
Newmarket Na H-E. Siar 271 G4
Newmill A&N 287 G7
Newmill Aber 253 F1
Newmill Aber 269 G6
Newmill Aber 261 G2
Newmill Moray 268 C5
Newmill ScBord 227 F4
Newmill of Inshewan 252 C3
Newmillerdam 186 A1
Newmillerdam Country Park WYorks WF2 6QP 27 H6
Newmills High 266 D5
Newmills Mid Ulster 282 B2
Newmiln P&K 243 G1
Newmiln P&K 243 F2
Newmilns 224 D2
Newney Green 137 F2
Newnham Glos 131 F1
Newnham Hants 120 C2
Newnham Herts 150 A4
Newnham Kent 124 B3
Newnham WN'hants 148 A2
Newnham Bridge 145 F1
Newnham Paddox 159 G4
Newnoth 260 D1
Newport Corn 98 D2
Newport Devon 113 F2
Newport ERid 196 A4
Newport Essex 150 D4
Newport Glos 131 F3
Newport High 275 G6
Newport IoW 107 E4
Newport (Casnewydd) Newport 130 C4
Newport Norf 179 G4
Newport (Trefdraeth) Pembs 141 D4
Newport Som 116 A5
Newport Tel&W 157 G1
Newport Pagnell 149 D3
Newport-on-Tay 244 C2
Newpound Common 121 F5
Newquay 96 C3
Newquay Zoo Corn TR7 2LZ 96 C3
Newry 282 D6
Newsbank 171 F1
Newseat 261 F1
Newsells 150 B4
Newsham Lancs 192 B4
Newsham N'umb 221 E4
Newsham NYorks 202 A1
Newsham NYorks 202 C4
Newsholme ERid 195 G5
Newsholme Lancs 193 E2
Newsome 185 F1
Newstead N'umb 229 F4
Newstead Notts 173 G2
Newstead ScBord 227 G2
Newstead Abbey Notts NG15 8NA 173 G2
Newthorpe Notts 173 F3
Newthorpe NYorks 195 D4
Newtoft 188 A4
Newton A&B 240 C5
Newton Aber 268 C6
Newton Aber 269 J6
Newton Bridgend 129 E5
Newton Cambs 150 C3
Newton Cardiff 130 B5
Newton ChesW&C 170 C2
Newton ChesW&C 183 G5
Newton Cumb 198 D5
Newton D&G 217 F1
Newton Derbys 173 F2
Newton GtMan 185 D3
Newton Here 144 C1
Newton Here 145 E2
Newton Here 144 C4
Newton High 275 J3
Newton High 266 E7
Newton High 275 H3
Newton High 272 E5
Newton High 266 C6
Newton High 266 E5
Newton Lancs 192 C2
Newton Lancs 199 G5
Newton Lancs 191 G4
Newton Lincs 175 F4
Newton Moray 268 B4
Newton NN'hants 161 D4
Newton N'umb 211 G1
Newton N'umb 220 B1
Newton NAyr 232 A4
Newton Norf 163 G1
Newton Notts 174 B3
Newton P&K 243 D1
Newton Pembs 140 B5
Newton Pembs 126 C2
Newton ScBord 228 A4
Newton SGlos 131 F3
Newton Shrop 170 B4
Newton SLan 226 A2
Newton Som 115 E4
Newton Staffs 172 B5
Newton Suff 152 A3
Newton Swan 128 C4
Newton Warks 160 A5
Newton Wilts 118 D5
Newton WLoth 235 E2
Newton WYorks 194 D5
Newton Abbot 102 B5
Newton Arlosh 209 F1
Newton Aycliffe 212 B5
Newton Bewley 213 D5
Newton Blossomville 149 E2
Newton Bromswold 149 E1
Newton Burgoland 159 F2
Newton by Toft 188 A4
Newton Ferrers 100 B3
Newton Flotman 164 D2
Newton Green 131 E3
Newton Harcourt 160 B3
Newton Kyme 195 D3
Newton Longville 148 D4
Newton Mearns 233 G4
Newton Morrell NYorks 202 B2
Newton Morrell Oxon 148 B5
Newton Mountain 126 C2
Newton Mulgrave 203 G1
Newton of Affleck 244 C1
Newton of Ardtoe 247 F2
Newton of Balcanquhal 243 G3
Newton of Dalvey 267 H6
Newton of Falkland 244 A4
Newton of Leys 258 D1
Newton on the Hill 170 B5
Newton on Trent 187 F5
Newton Poppleford 103 D4
Newton Purcell 148 B4
Newton Regis 159 E2
Newton Reigny 210 A4
Newton St. Cyres 102 B3
Newton St. Faith 178 D4
Newton St. Loe 117 E1
Newton St. Petrock 113 E4
Newton Solney 173 D5
Newton Stacey 119 F3
Newton Stewart 215 F4
Newton Tony 118 D3
Newton Tracey 113 F3
Newton under Roseberry 203 E1
Newton Underwood 221 D3
Newton upon Derwent 195 G3
Newton Valence 120 C4
Newton with Scales 192 A4
Newtonairds 216 C2
Newtongrange 236 A3
Newtonhill 261 H5
Newton-in-the-Isle 162 C1
Newton-le-Willows Mersey 183 G3
Newton-le-Willows NYorks 202 B4
Newtonmill 253 E3
Newtonmore (Baile Ùr an t-Slèibh) 258 E5
Newton-on-Ouse 195 E2
Newton-on-Rawcliffe 204 B3
Newton-on-the-Moor 221 D1
Newtown Bucks 135 E2
Newtown ChesW&C 170 C2
Newtown Corn 97 G2
Newtown Corn 94 C4
Newtown Cumb 210 B1
Newtown Derbys 185 D4
Newtown Devon 114 A5
Newtown Devon 103 D3
Newtown Dorset 104 A2
Newtown Glos 131 F2
Newtown GtMan 183 G2
Newtown GtMan 184 B2
Newtown Hants 107 F1
Newtown Hants 119 F1
Newtown Hants 106 B1
Newtown Hants 119 E5
Newtown Hants 107 E1
Newtown Here 145 F3
Newtown Here 145 D2
Newtown High 257 K4
Newtown IoM 190 B4
Newtown IoW 106 D3
Newtown NM&D 282 D6
Newtown N'umb 220 C1
Newtown N'umb 229 E4
Newtown Oxon 134 C4
Newtown (Y Drenewydd) Powys 156 A3
Newtown RCT 129 G3
Newtown Shrop 170 B4
Newtown Som 115 F4
Newtown Som 103 F1
Newtown Staffs 171 G1
Newtown Staffs 172 B1
Newtown Staffs 158 B2
Newtown Wilts 118 A5
Newtown Wilts 119 E1
Newtown Crommelin 287 F4
Newtown Linford 160 A2
Newtown St. Boswells 227 G2
Newtown Saville 281 H3
Newtown Unthank 159 G2
Newtownabbey 287 H7
Newtownards 283 H1
Newtownbreda 283 G1
Newtownbutler 281 G6
Newtownhamilton 282 C6
Newtown-in-Saint-Martin 95 E4
Newtownstewart 285 G7
Newtyle 252 A5
Newyears Green 135 F4
Neyland 126 C2
Nibley Glos 131 F2
Nibley SGlos 131 F4
Nibley Green 131 G3
Nicholashayne 103 E1
Nicholaston 128 B4
Nidd 194 C1
Nigg Aberdeen 261 H4
Nigg High 267 F4
Nightcott 114 B5
Nilig 168 D2
Nilston Rigg 211 E1
Nimlet 131 G5
Nine Ashes 137 E2
Nine Elms 132 D4
Nine Mile Burn 235 F4
Ninebanks 211 D2
Ninemile Bar (Crocketford) 216 C3
Nineveh 145 F1
Ninfield 110 C2
Ningwood 106 D4
Nisbet 228 A4
Niton 107 E5
Nitshill 233 G3
Nixon's Corner 285 G4
Nizels 123 E3
No Man's Heath ChesW&C 170 C3
No Man's Heath Warks 159 E2
No Man's Land 97 G4
Noah's Ark 123 E3
Noak Hill 137 E3
Noblehill 217 D3
Noblethorpe 185 G2
Nobottle 148 B1
Nocton 175 F1
Noddsdale 232 D3
Nogdam End 179 E5
Noke 134 A1
Nolton 126 B1
Nolton Haven 126 B1
Nomansland Devon 102 B1
Nomansland Wilts 106 B1
Noneley 170 B5
Nonington 125 E3
Nook Cumb 218 C4
Nook Cumb 199 G4
Noonsbrough 279 B7
Noranside 252 C3
Norbreck 191 G3
Norbury ChesE 170 C3
Norbury Derbys 172 C3
Norbury GtLon 136 C5
Norbury Shrop 156 C3
Norbury Staffs 171 E5
Norbury Common 170 C3
Norbury Junction 171 E5
Norchard 127 D3
Norcott Brook 184 A4
Nordelph 163 D2
Norden Dorset 105 F4
Norden GtMan 184 C1
Nordley 157 F3
Norfolk Lavender, Heacham Norf PE31 7JE 177 E4
Norham 237 G5
Norland Town 193 G5
Norley 183 G5
Norleywood 106 C3
Norlington 109 G2
Norman Cross 161 G3
Normanby NLincs 187 F1
Normanby NYorks 203 G4
Normanby R&C 203 E1
Normanby by Stow 187 F4
Normanby Hall Country Park NLincs DN15 9HU 187 F1
Normanby le Wold 188 B3
Normanby-by-Spital 188 A4
Normandy 121 E2
Normann's Ruh 246 D5
Norman's Bay 110 B3
Norman's Green 103 D2
Normanston 165 G2
Normanton Derby 173 E4
Normanton Leics 174 D3
Normanton Lincs 175 E3
Normanton Notts 174 C2
Normanton Rut 161 E2
Normanton WYorks 194 C5
Normanton le Heath 159 F1
Normanton on Soar 173 G5
Normanton on Trent 174 C1
Normanton-on-the-Wolds 174 B4
Normoss 191 G4
Norrington Common 117 F1
Norris Green 100 A1
Norris Hill 159 F1

Norristhorpe 194 B5
North Acton 136 B4
North Anston 186 C4
North Ascot 121 E1
North Aston 147 G5
North Baddesley 106 C1
North Ballachulish
(Baile a' Chaolais a
Tuath) 248 C3
North Balloch 215 E1
North Barrow 116 D5
North Barsham 178 A2
North Bay Miniature
Railway NYorks
YO12 6PF 204 D3
North Benfleet 137 G4
North Bersted 108 B3
North Berwick 236 C1
North Boarhunt 107 F1
North Bogbain 268 B5
North Boisdale 254 C3
North Bovey 102 A4
North Bradley 117 F2
North Brentor 99 E2
North Brewham 117 E4
North Bridge 121 E4
North Buckland 113 E1
North Burlingham 179 E4
North Cadbury 116 D5
North Cairn 214 A3
North Camp 121 D2
North Carlton Lincs 187 G5
North Carlton
Notts 186 C4
North Cave 196 A4
North Cerney 132 C2
North Chailey 109 F1
North Charford 106 A1
North Charlton 229 F4
North Cheriton 117 D5
North Chideock 104 A3
North Cliffe 196 A4
North Clifton 187 F5
North Cockerington 189 D3
North Coker 104 B1
North Collafirth 278 C4
North Common
SGlos 131 F5
North Common
Suff 164 A4
North Commonty 269 G6
North Connel 240 B1
North Coombe 102 B2
North Cornelly 129 E4
North Corner 131 F4
North Cotes 188 D2
North Cove 165 F3
North Cowton 202 B2
North Crawley 149 E3
North Cray 137 D5
North Creake 177 G4
North Curry 116 A5
North Dallens 248 B5
North Dalton 196 B2
North Dawn 277 D7
North Deighton 194 C2
North Dell (Dail Bho
Thuath) 271 G1
North Duffield 195 F4
North Elkington 188 C3
North Elmham 178 A3
North Elmsall 186 B1
North End
Bucks 148 D5
North End Dorset 117 F5
North End ERid 197 D2
North End ERid 197 D3
North End ERid 197 E4
North End Essex 137 F1
North End Hants 119 G5
North End Hants 106 A1
North End Leics 160 A1
North End N'umb 220 D1
North End Norf 164 B2
North End NSom 116 B1
North End Ports 107 F2
North End WSuss 108 A5
North End WSuss 108 B3
North Erradale 264 D3
North Essie 269 J5
North Fambridge 138 B3
North Ferriby 196 B5
North Frodingham 196 D2
North Gluss 278 C5
North Gorley 106 A1
North Green Norf 164 D3
North Green Suff 165 E4
North Green Suff 153 E1
North Green Suff 153 E1
North Grimston 196 A1
North Halling 123 G2
North Harby 187 F5
North Hayling 107 G2
North Hazelrigg 229 E3
North Heasley 114 A4
North Heath
WBerks 133 G5
North Heath
WSuss 121 F5
North Hill 97 G2
North Hillington 135 F4
North Hinksey 133 G2
North Holmwood 121 G3
North Houghton 119 E4
North Huish 100 D2
North Hykeham 175 E1
North Johnston 126 C1
North Kelsey 188 A2
North Kessock 266 D7
North Killingholme 188 B1
North Kilvington 202 D4
North Kilworth 160 B4
North Kingston 106 A2
North Kyme 175 G2
North Lancing 109 D3
North Lee 134 D2
North Lees 202 C5
North Leigh 133 F1
North Leverton with
Habblesthorpe 187 E4
North Littleton 146 C3
North Lopham 164 B3
North Luffenham 161 E2
North Marden
Midlo 236 A4
North Marston 148 C5
North Middleton
N'umb 229 E4

North Millbrex 269 G6
North Molton 114 A5
North Moreton 134 A4
North Mundham 108 A3
North Muskham 174 C2
North Newbald 196 B4
North Newington 147 G4
North Newnton 118 C1
North Newton 115 F4
North Nibley 131 G3
North Norfolk Railway
Norf NR26 8RA 178 C1
North Oakley 119 G2
North Ockendon 137 E4
North Ormesby 203 E1
North Ormsby 188 C3
North Otterington 202 C4
North Owersby 188 A3
North Perrott 104 A2
North Petherton 115 F4
North Petherwin 97 G1
North Pickenham 163 G2
North Piddle 146 B2
North Plain 217 F4
North Pool 101 D3
North Poorton 104 B3
North Quarme 114 C4
North Queensferry 235 F1
North Radworthy 114 A4
North Rauceby 175 F3
North Reston 189 D4
North Riding Forest Park
NYorks
YO18 7LT 204 B3
North Rigton 194 B3
North Rode 171 F1
North Roe 278 C4
North Ronaldsay 276 G2
North Ronaldsay
Airfield 276 G2
North Runcton 163 E2
North Sandwick 278 E3
North Scale 191 E4
North Scarle 175 D1
North Seaton 221 E3
North Shian (Sithean a
Tuath) 248 B5
North Shields 212 C1
North Shoebury 138 C4
North Side 162 A3
North Skelton 203 F1
North Somercotes 189 E3
North Stainley 202 B5
North Stainmore 200 D1
North Stifford 137 F4
North Stoke
B&NESom 117 E1
North Stoke Oxon 134 B4
North Stoke WSuss 108 C2
North Stoneham 106 D1
North Street
Hants 120 B4
North Street Kent 124 C3
North Street Med 124 A1
North Street
WBerks 134 B5
North Sunderland 229 G3
North Tamerton 98 D1
North Tarbothill 261 H3
North Tawton 113 G5
North Third 234 B1
North Tidworth 118 D3
North Togston 221 E1
North Town Devon 113 F5
North Town Hants 121 D2
North Town W&M 135 D4
North Tuddenham 178 B4
North Uist (Uibhist a
Tuath) 262 D4
North Walsham 179 D2
North Waltham 119 G3
North
Warnborough 120 C2
North Water Bridge
253 E3
North Watten 275 H3
North Weald
Bassett 137 D2
North Wembley 136 A4
North Wheatley 187 E4
North Whilborough 101 E1
North Wick 116 C1
North Widcombe 116 C2
North Willingham 188 B4
North Wingfield 173 F1
North Witham 175 E5
North Wootton
Dorset 104 C3
North Wootton
Norf 177 E5
North Wootton
Som 116 C3
North Wraxall 132 A5
North Wroughton 132 D4
North Yardhope 220 B1
North Yorkshire Moors
Railway NYorks
YO18 7AJ 204 B4
Northacre 164 A2
Northall 149 E5
Northall Green 178 A4
Northallerton 202 C3
Northam Devon 113 E3
Northam Soton 106 D1
Northam Burrows Country
Park Devon
EX39 1XR 113 E2
Northampton 148 C1
Northaw 136 B2
Northay Devon 103 G2
Northay Som 103 F1
Northbay 254 C4
Northbeck 175 F3
Northborough 161 G2
Northbourne Kent 125 F3
Northbourne Oxon 134 A4
Northbridge Street 110 C1
Northbrook Hants 119 F4
Northbrook Oxon 147 G5
Northchapel 121 E5
Northchurch 135 E2
Northcote Manor 113 G4
Northcott 98 D1
Northcourt 134 A3
Northdyke 276 B5
Northedge 173 E1

Northend
B&NESom 117 E1
Northend Bucks 134 C3
Northend Warks 147 F2
Northfield Aber 269 G4
Northfield
Aberdeen 261 H4
Northfield High 275 J4
Northfield Hull 196 C5
Northfield ScBord 237 G3
Northfield Som 115 F4
Northfield WMid 158 C5
Northfields 161 F2
Northfleet 137 F5
Northhouse 227 F5
Northiam 110 D1
Northill 149 G3
Northington Glos 131 G2
Northington Hants 119 G4
Northlands 176 B2
Northleach 132 D1
Northleigh Devon 103 E3
Northleigh Devon 113 G2
Northlew 99 F1
Northmoor 133 G2
Northmoor Green
(Moorland) 116 A4
Northmuir 252 B4
Northney 107 G2
Northolt 136 A4
Northop
(Llaneurgain) 169 F1
Northop Hall 169 F1
Northorpe Lincs 176 A4
Northorpe Lincs 187 F3
Northorpe Lincs 161 F1
Northover Som 116 C5
Northover Som 116 B4
Northowram 194 A5
Northport 105 F4
Northpunds 279 D10
Northrepps 178 D2
Northstowe 150 C1
Northton
(Taobh Tuath) 262 E3
Northtown 277 D8
Northumberland Dark Sky
Park N'umb 219 F4
Northumbria Craft Centre,
Morpeth N'umb
NE61 1PD 221 E3
Northway Glos 146 B4
Northway Som 115 E5
Northwich 184 A5
Northwick SGlos 131 E5
Northwick Som 116 A3
Northwick Worcs 146 A2
Northwold 163 F3
Northwood GtLon 136 A3
Northwood IoW 107 D3
Northwood Kent 125 F2
Northwood Mersey 183 F3
Northwood Shrop 170 B4
Northwood Green 131 G1
Northwood Hills 136 A3
Norton Glos 146 A5
Norton Halton 183 G4
Norton Herts 150 A4
Norton IoW 106 C4
Norton Mon 144 D5
Norton Notts 186 C5
Norton NYorks 203 G5
Norton Powys 144 C1
Norton Shrop 157 E2
Norton Shrop 157 G2
Norton Shrop 157 D4
Norton Stock 212 D5
Norton Suff 152 A1
Norton Swan 128 C2
Norton SYorks 186 C1
Norton SYorks 186 A4
Norton VGlam 129 E5
Norton Wilts 132 A4
Norton WMid 158 A4
Norton Worcs 146 A2
Norton Worcs 146 C3
Norton WSuss 108 B3
Norton WSuss 108 A4
Norton Bavant 118 A3
Norton Bridge 171 F4
Norton Canes 158 C2
Norton Canon 144 C3
Norton Disney 175 D2
Norton Ferris 117 E4
Norton Fitzwarren 115 E5
Norton Green
Herts 150 A5
Norton Green IoW 106 C4
Norton Green
Stoke 171 G2
Norton Hawkfield 116 C1
Norton Heath 137 F2
Norton in Hales 171 E4
Norton in the
Moors 171 F2
Norton Lindsey 147 E1
Norton Little Green 152 A1
Norton Malreward 116 C1
Norton Mandeville 137 E2
Norton St. Philip 117 E2
Norton Subcourse 165 F2
Norton Wood 144 C3
Norton Woodseats 186 A4
Norton-Juxta-
Twycross 159 F2
Norton-le-Clay 202 D5
Norton's Cross Roads
282 D5
Norton-sub-
Hamdon 104 A1
Norwell 174 C1
Norwell Woodhouse 174 C1
Norwich 178 D5
Norwich Airport 178 D4
Norwich Castle Museum &
Art Gallery Norf
NR1 3JU 79 Norwich
Norwich Cathedral Norf
NR1 4DH 79 Norwich
Norwick 278 F1
Norwood End 137 E2
Norwood Green
GtLon 136 A5
Norwood Green
WYorks 194 A5
Norwood Hill 122 B4

Norwood Park 116 C4
Noseley 160 C3
Noss Mayo 100 B3
Nosterfield 202 B4
Nosterfield End 151 E3
Nostie 256 E2
Notgrove 146 D5
Nottage 129 E5
Notting Hill 136 B4
Nottingham Nott 173 G3
Nottingham Castle Museum
& Art Gallery NG1 6EL
80 Nottingham
Nottington 104 C4
Notton Wilts 118 A1
Notton WYorks 186 A1
Nottswood Hill 131 G1
Nounsley 137 G1
Noutard's Green 145 G1
Nowton 151 G1
Nox 156 D1
Noyadd Trefawr 141 F3
Nuffield 134 B4
Nun Monkton 195 E2
Nunburnholme 196 A3
Nuneaton 159 F3
Nuneham
Courtenay 134 A3
Nunney 117 E3
Nunnington
NYorks 203 F5
Nunnington Park 115 D5
Nunnykirk 220 C2
Nunsthorpe 188 C2
Nunthorpe Middl 203 E1
Nunthorpe York 195 E3
Nunton 118 C5
Nunwick N'umb 220 A4
Nunwick NYorks 202 C5
Nup End 136 B1
Nupend 131 G2
Nursling 106 C1
Nursted 120 C5
Nurton 158 A3
Nutbourne WSuss 108 C2
Nutbourne WSuss 107 G2
Nutfield 122 C3
Nuthall 173 G3
Nuthampstead 150 C4
Nuthurst Warks 159 D5
Nuthurst WSuss 121 G5
Nutley ESuss 109 G1
Nutley Hants 120 B3
Nutt's Corner 283 F1
Nutwell 186 D2
Nyadd 242 C5
Nybster 275 J2
Nyetimber 108 A4
Nyewood 120 C5
Nymans WSuss
RH17 6EB 109 E1
Nymet Rowland 102 A2
Nymet Tracey 102 A2
Nympsfield 132 A2
Nynehead 115 E5
Nythe 116 B4
Nyton 108 B3

O
O2, The GtLon
SE10 0BB 13 E5
Oad Street 124 A2
Oadby 160 B2
Oak Cross 99 F1
Oak Tree 202 C1
Oakamoor 172 B3
Oakbank A&B 239 G1
Oakbank WLoth 235 E3
Oakdale BCP 105 G3
Oakdale Caerp 130 A3
Oake 115 E5
Oaken 158 A2
Oakenclough 192 B3
Oakengates 157 G1
Oakenhead 267 K5
Oakenholt 183 D5
Oakenshaw Dur 212 B4
Oakenshaw
WYorks 194 A5
Oakerthorpe 173 E2
Oakes 185 F1
Oakfield IoW 107 E3
Oakfield Torfaen 130 B3
Oakford Cere 142 A2
Oakford Devon 114 C5
Oakfordbridge 114 C5
Oakgrove 171 G1
Oakham 161 D2
Oakhanger 120 C4
Oakhill 116 D3
Oakington 150 C1
Oaklands Conwy 168 B2
Oaklands Herts 136 B1
Oakle Street 131 G1
Oakley BCP 105 G3
Oakley Bed 149 F2
Oakley Bucks 134 B1
Oakley Fife 235 E1
Oakley Hants 119 G2
Oakley Oxon 134 C2
Oakley Poole 105 G3
Oakley Suff 164 C4
Oakley Green 135 E5
Oakley Park 155 F3
Oakridge Lynch 132 B2
Oaks 156 D2
Oaks Green 172 C4
Oaksey 132 B3
Oakshaw Ford 218 D4
Oakshott 120 C5
Oakthorpe 159 F1
Oaktree Hill 202 C3
Oakwell Hall & Country Park
WYorks
WF17 9LG 27 E4
Oakwood Leisure Park
Pembs
SA67 8DE 127 D1
Oakwoodhill 121 G4
Oakworth 193 G4
Oare Kent 124 C2
Oare Som 114 B3
Oare Wilts 118 C1
Oasby 175 F4

Oatfield 222 B4
Oath 116 A5
Oathlaw 252 C4
Oatlands 194 C2
Oban (An t-Òban) 240 A2
Obley 156 C5
Oborne 104 C1
Obthorpe 161 F1
Occlestone Green 171 D1
Occold 164 C4
Occumster 275 H5
Oceanarium BH2 5AA
64 Bournemouth
Ochiltree 224 D3
Ochtermuthill 242 D2
Ochtertyre P&K 242 D2
Ochtertyre Stir 242 C5
Ockbrook 173 F4
Ockeridge 145 G1
Ockham 121 F2
Ockle 247 D2
Ockley 121 G4
Ocle Pychard 145 E3
Octon 204 D5
Odcombe 104 B1
Odd Down 117 E1
Oddendale 200 B1
Oddingley 146 B2
Oddington 134 A1
Odds Farm Park Bucks
HP10 0LX 135 E4
Oddsta 278 E3
Odell 149 E2
Odham 113 E5
Odie 276 F5
Odiham 120 C2
Odsey 150 A4
Odstock 118 C5
Odstone 159 F1
Offchurch 147 F1
Offenham 146 C3
Offerton 184 D4
Offham ESuss 109 F2
Offham Kent 123 F3
Offham WSuss 108 C3
Offley Hoo 149 G5
Offleymarsh 171 E5
Offord Cluny 150 A1
Offord D'Arcy 150 A1
Offton 152 B3
Offwell 103 E3
Ogbourne Maizey 133 D5
Ogbourne
St. Andrew 133 D5
Ogbourne
St. George 133 D5
Oghill 285 H4
Ogil 252 C3
Ogle 220 D4
Ogmore 129 E5
Ogmore Vale 129 F3
Ogmore-by-Sea 129 E5
Ogston Reservoir Derbys
DE55 6EL 173 E1
Oil Terminal 277 C8
Okeford Fitzpaine 105 E1
Okehampton 99 F1
Okehampton Camp 99 F1
Okraquoy 279 D9
Olchard 102 B5
Olchfa 128 C3
Old 160 C5
Old Aberdeen 261 H4
Old Alresford 119 G4
Old & New Towns of
Edinburgh Edin 32 C2
Old Arley 159 E3
Old Basford 173 G3
Old Basing 120 B2
Old Belses 227 G3
Old Bewick 229 E4
Old Blair 251 D3
Old Bolingbroke 176 B1
Old Bramhope 194 B3
Old Brampton 186 A5
Old Bridge of Urr 216 B4
Old Buckenham 164 B2
Old Burdon 212 C2
Old Burghclere 119 F2
Old Bushmills Distillery
CC&G BT1 2LB 286 D1
Old Byland 203 E4
Old Cassop 212 C4
Old Church Stoke 156 B3
Old Cleeve 114 D3
Old Clipstone 174 B1
Old Colwyn 181 G5
Old Craig 261 H2
Old Craighall 236 A2
Old Crombie 268 D5
Old Dailly 214 D1
Old Dalby 174 B5
Old Dam 185 F5
Old Deer 269 H6
Old Dilton 117 F3
Old Down SGlos 131 F4
Old Down Som 116 D2
Old Edlington 186 C3
Old Eldon 212 B5
Old Ellerby 197 D4
Old Felixstowe 153 E4
Old Fletton 161 G3
Old Ford 136 C4
Old Glossop 185 E3
Old Goginan 154 C4
Old Goole 195 G5
Old Gore 145 F5
Old Grimsby 96 A1
Old Hall 188 C1
Old Hall Green 150 B5
Old Hall Street 179 E2
Old Harlow 137 D1
Old Heath 152 B5
Old Heathfield 110 A1
Old Hill WMid 158 B4
Old Hurst 162 B5
Old Hutton 199 G4
Old Kea 96 C5
Old Kilpatrick 233 F2
Old Kinnernie 261 F4
Old Knebworth 150 A5
Old Leake 176 C2
Old Leslie 260 D2

Old Malton 204 B5
Old Mill 287 H5
Old Milton 106 B3
Old Milverton 147 E1
Old Montsale 138 D3
Old Netley 107 D1
Old Newton 152 B1
Old Philpstoun 235 E2
Old Poltalloch 240 A4
Old Radnor
(Pencraig) 144 B2
Old Rattray 269 J5
Old Rayne 260 E2
Old Romney 111 F1
Old Royal Naval College,
Greenwich GtLon
SE10 9LW 13 D5
Old Scone 243 G2
Old Shields 234 C3
Old Sodbury 131 G4
Old Somerby 175 E4
Old Station, The, Tintern
Parva Mon
NP16 7NX 131 E2
Old Stratford 148 C3
Old Sunderlandwick
196 C2
Old Swarland 221 D1
Old Swinford 158 B4
Old Thirsk 202 D4
Old Tupton 173 E1
Old Warden 149 G3
Old Weston 161 F5
Old Windsor 135 E5
Old Wives Lees 124 C3
Old Woking 121 F2
Old Woodhall 176 A1
Old Woods 170 B5
Oldberrow 146 D1
Oldborough 102 A2
Oldbury Kent 123 E3
Oldbury Shrop 157 G3
Oldbury Warks 159 F3
Oldbury WMid 158 B3
Oldbury Court Estate
Bristol BS16 2JH 8 D2
Oldbury Naite 131 F3
Oldbury on the Hill 132 A4
Oldbury-on-Severn 131 F3
Oldcastle Bridgend 129 F5
Oldcastle Mon 144 C3
Oldcastle Heath 170 B3
Oldcotes 186 C4
Oldcroft 131 F2
Oldeamere 162 B3
Oldfield 146 A1
Oldford 117 E2
Oldhall Aber 260 C5
Oldhall High 275 H3
Oldham 184 D2
Oldham Edge 184 D2
Oldhamstocks 237 E2
Oldland 131 F5
Oldmeldrum 261 G2
Oldmill 260 D4
Oldpark 157 F2
Oldridge 102 B3
Oldshore Beg 272 D3
Oldshoremore 272 E3
Oldstead 203 E5
Oldstone 287 F7
Oldtown 266 C3
Oldtown of Aigas 266 B7
Oldtown of Ord 268 E5
Oldwalls 128 A3
Oldways End 114 B5
Oldwhat 269 G5
Oldwich Lane 159 E5
Olgrinmore 275 G3
Oliver 226 C3
Oliver's Battery 119 F5
Ollaberry 278 C4
Ollerton ChesE 184 B5
Ollerton Notts 174 B1
Ollerton Shrop 170 D5
Olmstead Green 151 E3
Olney 149 D2
Olrig House 275 D2
Olton 158 D4
Olveston 131 F4
Olympia GtLon
W14 8UX 11 B5
Omagh 281 G1
Ombersley 146 A1
Ompton 174 B1
Onchan 190 B4
Onecote 172 B2
Onehouse 152 B2
Ongar Hill 177 D5
Ongar Street 144 C1
Onibury 157 D5
Onich
(Omhanaich) 248 C3
Onllwyn 129 E1
Onneley 171 E3
Onslow Green 137 F1
Onslow Village 121 E3
Oona Bridge 282 A3
Opinan High 264 D3
Opinan High 264 D4
Orange Lane 237 E5
Orasaigh 271 F6
Orbliston 268 B5
Orbost 263 H7
Orby 176 C1
Orcadia 232 C3
Orchard 232 C1
Orchard Portman 115 F5
Orchardton 285 H3
Orcheston 118 B3
Orcop 145 D5
Orcop Hill 145 D5
Ord 256 C3
Ordhead 260 E3
Ordie 260 C4
Ordiequish 268 B5
Ordsall 187 D5
Ore 110 D2
Oreham Common 109 E2
Oreston 100 B2
Oreton 157 F4
Orford Suff 153 F3
Orford Warr 184 A3
Organford 105 F3
Orgreave 158 D1

Orlton 282 A1
Orlestone 124 B5
Orleton Here 145 E1
Orleton Worcs 145 F1
Orleton Common 145 D1
Orlingbury 161 D5
Ormacleit 254 C1
Ormesby 203 E1
Ormesby
St. Margaret 179 F4
Ormesby
St. Michael 179 F4
Ormidale 232 B1
Ormiscaig 264 D2
Ormiston 236 B3
Ormlie 275 G2
Ormsaigmore 247 D3
Ormsary 231 F2
Ormskirk 183 F2
Ormsay 230 B1
Orphir 277 C7
Orpington 123 D2
Orrell GtMan 183 G2
Orrell Mersey 183 E3
Orrisdale 190 B2
Orrok House 261 H3
Orroland 208 A2
Orsett 137 F4
Orsett Heath 137 F4
Orslow 158 A1
Orston 174 C3
Orton Cumb 200 B1
Orton N'hants 160 D5
Orton Longueville 161 G3
Orton Rigg 209 G1
Orton Waterville 161 G3
Orton-on-the-Hill 159 F2
Orwell 150 B2
Osbaldeston 192 C4
Osbaldwick 195 F2
Osbaston Leics 159 G2
Osbaston Shrop 170 A5
Osbaston Tel&W 157 E1
Osbaston Hollow 159 G2
Osborne 107 E3
Osborne House IoW
PO32 6JX 107 E3
Osbournby 175 F4
Oscroft 170 C1
Ose 263 J7
Osgathorpe 159 G1
Osgodby Lincs 188 B3
Osgodby NYorks 195 F4
Osgodby NYorks 205 D4
Oskaig 256 B1
Osleston 172 D4
Osmaston Derby 173 E4
Osmaston Derbys 172 C3
Osmington 104 D4
Osmington Mills 104 D4
Osmondthorpe 194 C4
Osmotherley 203 D3
Osnaburgh (Dairsie)
244 C3
Ospringe 124 C2
Ossett 194 B5
Ossett Street Side 194 B5
Ossian's Grave CC&G
BT44 0TG 287 G3
Ossington 174 C1
Ostend 138 C3
Osterley 136 A5
Osterley Park & House
GtLon TW7 4RB 11 B5
Oswaldkirk 203 E5
Oswaldtwistle 192 D5
Oswestry 169 F4
Oteley 170 B4
Otford 123 E3
Otham 123 G3
Otherton 158 B1
Othery 116 A4
Otley Suff 152 D2
Otley WYorks 194 B3
Otter 232 A2
Otter Ferry 232 A1
Otterbourne 119 F5
Otterburn N'umb 220 A2
Otterburn NYorks 193 E2
Otterburn Camp 220 A2
Otterden Place 124 B3
Otterham 98 B1
Otterham Quay 124 A2
Otterhampton 115 F3
Otternish 262 E4
Ottershaw 121 F1
Otterswick 278 E4
Otterton 103 D4
Otterton Mill Devon
EX9 7HG 103 D4
Otterwood 106 D2
Ottery St. Mary 103 D3
Ottinge 125 D4
Ottringham 197 E5
Oughterby 209 F1
Oughtershaw 201 D4
Oughterside 209 E2
Oughtibridge 186 A3
Oulston 203 E5
Oulton Cumb 209 F1
Oulton Norf 178 C3
Oulton Staffs 171 G4
Oulton Staffs 171 G4
Oulton Suff 165 G2
Oulton WYorks 194 C5
Oulton Broad 165 G2
Oulton Grange 171 G4
Oulton Street 178 C3
Oultoncross 171 G4
Oundle 161 F4
Ousby 210 C4
Ousdale 275 F6
Ousden 151 F2
Ouston Dur 212 B2
Ouston N'umb 220 C4
Out Newton 197 F5
Out Rawcliffe 192 A3
Out Skerries
Airstrip 278 F5
Outcast 199 E5
Outchester 229 F3
Outertown 277 B7
Outgate 199 E3
Outhgill 200 C2
Outhwaite Ropemakers
NYorks DL8 3NT 201 D4

Outlands 171 E5
Outlane 185 E1
Outwell 162 D2
Outwood Surr 122 C4
Outwood WYorks 194 C5
Outwoods 185 F2
Ouzlewell Green 194 C5
Ovenden 193 G5
Over Cambs 162 B5
Over ChesW&C 170 D1
Over Glos 132 A1
Over SGlos 131 E4
Over Burrows 173 D4
Over Compton 104 B1
Over Dinsdale 202 C1
Over End 185 G5
Over Green 159 D3
Over Haddon 172 D1
Over Hulton 184 A2
Over Kellet 192 B4
Over Kiddington 147 G5
Over Monnow 131 D1
Over Norton 147 F5
Over Peover 184 B5
Over Rankeilour 244 B3
Over Silton 203 D3
Over Stowey 115 E4
Over Stratton 104 A1
Over Tabley 184 B4
Over Wallop 119 D4
Over Whitacre 159 E2
Over Winchendon (Upper
  Winchendon) 134 C1
Over Worton 147 G5
Overbister 276 F3
Overbrae 269 G5
Overbury 146 B4
Overcombe 104 C4
Overgreen 186 A5
Overleigh 116 B4
Overpool 183 E5
Overscaig Hotel 273 G6
Overseal 159 G5
Overslade 159 G5
Oversland 124 C3
Oversley Green 146 C2
Overstone 148 B1
Overstrand 178 D1
Overthorpe 147 G3
Overton Aber 261 F3
Overton Aberdeen 261 G3
Overton ChesW&C 183 G5
Overton Hants 119 G3
Overton Lancs 192 A2
Overton NYorks 195 E2
Overton Shrop 157 E5
Overton Swan 128 A4
Overton (Owrtyn)
  Wrex 170 A3
Overton WYorks 185 G1
Overtown Lancs 200 B5
Overtown NLan 234 C4
Overtown Swin 133 D5
Overy 134 A3
Oving Bucks 134 C1
Oving WSuss 108 B3
Ovingdean 109 F3
Ovingham 211 G1
Ovington Dur 202 A1
Ovington Essex 151 F3
Ovington Hants 119 G4
Ovington N'umb 211 G1
Ovington Norf 178 A5
Ower Hants 106 C1
Ower Hants 107 D2
Owermoigne 105 D4
Owler Bar 185 G5
Owlpen 131 G3
Owl's Green 153 D1
Owlswick 134 C2
Owmby 188 A2
Owmby-by-Spital 188 A4
Owslebury 119 G5
Owston 160 C2
Owston Ferry 187 F2
Owstwick 197 E4
Owthorpe 174 B4
Oxborough 163 F2
Oxcliffe Hill 192 A1
Oxcombe 188 D5
Oxen End 151 E5
Oxen Park 199 E4
Oxencombe 102 B4
Oxenhall 145 G4
Oxenholme 199 G3
Oxenhope 193 G4
Oxenpill 116 B3
Oxenton 146 B4
Oxenwood 119 E2
Oxford 134 A2
Oxford Cathedral Oxon
  OX1 1AB 80 Oxford
Oxford Story Oxon
  OX1 3AJ 80 Oxford
Oxford University Museum
  of Natural History
  Oxon OX1 3PW
  80 Oxford
Oxhey 136 A3
Oxhill 147 F3
Oxley 158 B2
Oxley Green 138 C1
Oxley's Green 110 B1
Oxnam 228 B5
Oxnead 178 D3
Oxnop Ghyll 201 E3
Oxshott 121 G1
Oxspring 185 G2
Oxton 122 C3
Oxton Mersey 183 E4
Oxton Notts 174 B2
Oxton ScBord 236 B4
Oxwich 128 A4
Oxwich Green 128 A4
Oxwick 178 A3
Oykel Bridge 265 K1
Oyne 260 E2
Ozleworth 131 G3

P
Pabbay 262 D3
Packington 159 F1
Packwood 159 D5
Padanaram 252 C4
Padarn Country Park
  Gwyn
  LL55 4TY 167 E1

Padbury 148 C4
Paddington 136 B4
Paddlesworth 125 D4
Paddock 124 B3
Paddock Wood 123 F4
Paddockhaugh 267 K6
Paddolgreen 170 C5
Padeswood 169 F1
Padfield 185 E3
Padiham 193 D4
Padside 194 A2
Padstow 96 D2
Padworth 120 B1
Paganhill 132 A2
Pagham 108 A4
Paglesham
  Churchend 138 C3
Paglesham Eastend
  138 C3
Paible 263 F2
Paignton 101 E1
Paignton Pier
  Torbay
  TQ4 6BW 101 E1
Paignton Zoo
  Torbay
  TQ4 7EU 101 E2
Pailton 159 G4
Paine's Corner 110 B1
Painscastle 144 A3
Painshawfield 211 G1
Painswick 132 A2
Pairc Shiabost 270 E3
Paisley 233 F3
Pakefield 165 G2
Pakenham 152 A1
Palace of Holyroodhouse
  Edin EH8 8DX 37 J4
Palace of Westminster
  (Houses of Parliament)
  (Palace of Westminster &
  Westminster Abbey inc.
  St Margaret's Church)
  GtLon SW1A 0AA 13 B5
Palacerigg Country Park
  NLan G67 3HU 234 B2
Pale 168 C4
Palehouse
  Common 109 G2
Palestine 119 D3
Paley Street 135 D5
Palgowan 215 F2
Palgrave 164 C4
Pallinsburn House 228 C3
Palmarsh 124 D5
Palmers Cross 121 F3
Palmers Green 136 C4
Palmerscross 267 K5
Palmerston 130 A5
Palnackie 216 C5
Palnure 215 F4
Palterton 173 F1
Pamber End 120 B2
Pamber Green 120 B2
Pamber Heath 120 B1
Pamington 146 B4
Pamphill 105 F2
Pampisford 150 C3
Pan 277 C8
Panborough 116 B3
Panbride 245 D1
Pancrasweek 112 C5
Pancross 114 D1
Pandy Gwyn 154 C2
Pandy Mon 144 C3
Pandy Powys 155 F2
Pandy Wrex 169 E4
Pandy Tudur 168 B1
Pandy'r Capel 169 D2
Panfield 151 F5
Pangbourne 134 B5
Pannal 194 C2
Pannal Ash 194 B2
Panshanger 136 B1
Pant 169 F5
Pant Gwyn 168 B5
Pant Mawr 155 E4
Pantasaph 182 C5
Panteg 169 E2
Pant-glas Gwyn 167 D3
Pantglas Powys 155 D3
Pantgwyn Carmar 142 B5
Pantgwyn Cere 141 F3
Pant-lasau 128 C2
Panton 188 B5
Pant-pastynog 168 D1
Pantperthog 154 D2
Pant-y-dwr 155 F5
Pant-y-ffordd 169 F2
Pant-y-ffridd 156 A2
Pantyffynnon 128 C1
Pantygasseg 130 B3
Pantygelli 130 C1
Pant-y-mwyn 169 E1
Panxworth 179 E4
Papa Stour 279 A6
Papa Stour Airstrip 279 A6
Papa Westray 276 D2
Papa Westray
  Airfield 276 D2
Papcastle 209 E3
Papil 279 C9
Papple 236 C2
Papplewick 173 G2
Papworth Everard 150 A1
Papworth St. Agnes 150 A1
Par 97 E4
Paradise Park, Newhaven
  ESuss BN9 0DH 109 G3
Paradise Wildlife Park,
  Broxbourne Herts
  EN10 7QA 136 C2
Parbold 183 F1
Parbrook Som 116 C4
Parbrook WSuss 121 F5
Parc 168 B4
Parc Seymour 130 D3
Parc-llyn 141 F3
Parcrhydderch 142 C2
Parc-y-rhos 142 B3
Pardshaw 209 D4
Parham 153 E1
Parish Holm 225 F3
Park Aber 260 E5
Park Close 193 E3
Park Corner ESuss 123 E5

Park Corner Oxon 134 B4
Park End N'umb 220 A4
Park End Staffs 171 E2
Park End Worcs 157 G5
Park Gate Hants 107 E2
Park Gate Worcs 158 B5
Park Gate WYorks 194 A3
Park Gate WYorks 185 G1
Park Green 152 C1
Park Hill 186 A4
Park Lane 170 B4
Park Langley 122 C2
Park Rose Pottery & Leisure
  Park ERid
  YO15 3QF 196 D1
Park Street 136 A2
Parkend Cumb 209 G3
Parkeston 152 C4
Parkfield Corn 98 D4
Parkfield SGlos 131 F5
Parkfield WMid 158 B4
Parkford 252 C2
Parkgate A&N 287 G7
Parkgate ChesW&C 183 D5
Parkgate D&G 217 E2
Parkgate Kent 124 A5
Parkgate Surr 122 B4
Parkgate SYorks 186 B3
Parkham 113 D3
Parkham Ash 113 D3
Parkhead 234 A3
Parkhill Angus 253 E5
Parkhill P&K 251 G5
Parkhouse 131 D2
Parkhurst 107 D3
Parkmill 128 B4
Parkmore 268 B6
Parkneuk 253 F2
Parkside 170 A2
Parkstone 105 G3
Parkway 116 C5
Parley Cross 105 G3
Parley Green 106 A3
Parlington 194 D4
Parracombe 113 G1
Parrog 140 D4
Parson Cross 186 A3
Parson Drove 162 B2
Parsonage Green 137 F1
Parsonby 209 E3
Partick 233 G3
Partington 184 B3
Partney 176 C1
Parton Cumb 208 C4
Parton D&G 216 B3
Partridge Green 109 D2
Parwich 172 C2
Paslow Wood
  Common 137 E2
Passenham 148 C4
Passfield 120 D4
Passingford Bridge 137 E3
Paston 179 E2
Paston Street 179 E2
Pasturefields 171 G5
Patchacott 99 E1
Patcham 109 F3
Patchetts Green 136 A3
Patching 108 C3
Patchole 113 G1
Patchway 131 F4
Pateley Bridge 194 A1
Path of Condie 243 F3
Pathe 116 A4
Pathfinder Village 102 B3
Pathhead Aber 253 F3
Pathhead EAyr 225 E4
Pathhead Fife 244 A5
Pathhead Midlo 236 A3
Pathlow 147 D2
Patmore Heath 150 C5
Patna 224 C4
Patney 118 B2
Patrick 190 A3
Patrick Brompton 202 B3
Patrington 197 F5
Patrington Haven 197 F5
Patrishow 144 B5
Patrixbourne 125 D3
Patterdale 209 G5
Pattersonstown 282 E2
Pattingham 158 A3
Pattishall 148 B2
Pattiswick 151 G5
Paul 94 B4
Paulerspury 148 C3
Paull 197 D5
Paull Holme 197 D5
Paul's Green 94 D3
Paulton 117 D2
Paultons Park Hants
  SO51 6AL 106 C1
Pauperhaugh 220 C2
Pave Lane 157 G2
Pavenham 149 E2
Pavilion Gardens, Buxton
  Derbys
  SK17 6XN 185 E5
Pawlett 116 A3
Pawston 228 C3
Paxford 147 D4
Paxhill Park 109 F1
Paxton 237 G4
Payden Street 124 B3
Payhembury 103 D2
Paythorne 193 E2
Peacehaven 109 G3
Peacemarsh 117 F5
Peachley 146 A2
Peak Dale 185 E5
Peak Forest 185 F5
Peakirk 161 G2
Pean Hill 124 D2
Pearsie 252 B4
Pearson's Green 123 F4
Peartree 136 B1
Peartree Green
  Essex 137 E3
Peartree Green
  Here 145 F4
Pease Pottage 122 B5
Peasedown
  St. John 117 E2
Peasehill 173 F3
Peaseland Green 178 B4

Peasemore 133 G5
Peasenhall 153 E1
Peaslake 121 F3
Peasley Cross 183 G3
Peasmarsh ESuss 111 D1
Peasmarsh Surr 121 E3
Peaston 236 B3
Peastonbank 236 B3
Peat Inn 244 C4
Peathill 269 H4
Peatling Magna 160 A3
Peatling Parva 160 A4
Pebble Coombe 122 B3
Pecket Well 193 F5
Peckforton 170 C2
Peckham 136 C5
Peckleton 159 G2
Pedham 179 E4
Pedmore 158 B4
Pedwell 116 B4
Peebles 235 G5
Peel IoM 190 A3
Peel Lancs 191 G4
Peening Quarter 111 D1
Peggs Green 159 G1
Pegsdon 149 G4
Pegswood 221 E3
Pegwell 125 F2
Peighinn nan
  Aoireann 254 C1
Peinchorran 256 B1
Peinlich 263 K6
Pelaw 212 B1
Pelcomb 126 C1
Pelcomb Bridge 126 C1
Pelcomb Cross 126 C1
Peldon 138 C1
Pellon 193 G5
Pelsall 158 C2
Pelton 212 B2
Pelutho 209 E2
Pelynt 97 G4
Pemberton 183 G2
Pembrey (Pen-bre) 128 A2
Pembrey Country Park
  Carmar
  SA16 0EJ 128 A2
Pembridge 144 C2
Pembroke (Penfro) 126 C2
Pembroke Dock
  (Doc Penfro) 126 C2
Pembury 123 E4
Pen-allt 131 E1
Penally 127 E3
Penalt 145 E5
Penare 97 D5
Penarron 156 A4
Penarth 130 A5
Pen-bont
  Rhydybeddau 154 C4
Pen-boyr 141 G4
Penbryn 141 F2
Pencader 142 A4
Pen-cae-cwm 168 C1
Pencaenewydd 166 D3
Pencaitland 236 B3
Pencarnisiog 180 B5
Pencarreg 142 B3
Pencarrow 97 F1
Pencelli 143 G5
Pen-clawdd 128 B3
Pencoed 129 F4
Pencombe 145 E2
Pencoyd 145 E5
Pencraig Here 145 E5
Pencraig Powys 168 D5
Pendeen 94 A3
Penderyn 129 F2
Pendlebury 184 B2
Pendleton 193 D4
Pendock 145 G4
Pendoggett 97 E2
Pendomer 104 B1
Pendoylan 129 G5
Penegoes 155 D2
Penelewey 96 C5
Pen-ffordd 141 D5
Pengam 130 A3
Penge 136 C5
Pengenffordd 144 A5
Pengorffwysfa 180 C3
Pengover Green 97 G3
Pengroesoped 130 C2
Pengwern 182 B5
Penhale 95 D5
Penhallow 96 B4
Penhalvean 95 E3
Penhelig 154 C3
Penhill 133 D4
Penhow 130 D3
Penhurst 110 B2
Peniarth 154 C2
Penicuik 235 G3
Peniel 142 A5
Penifiler 263 K7
Peninver 222 C3
Penisa'r-waun 167 E1
Penisarcwm 155 G1
Penishawain 143 G4
Penistone 185 G2
Penjerrick 95 E3
Penketh 183 G4
Penkill 214 D1
Penkridge 158 B1
Penley 170 B4
Penllech 166 B4
Penllergaer 128 C3
Pen-llyn IoA 180 B4
Penllyn VGlam 129 F5
Pen-lôn 166 D1
Penmachno 168 A2
Penmaen 128 B4
Penmaenan 181 F5
Penmaenmawr 181 F5
Penmaenpool (Llyn
  Penmaen) 154 C1
Penmaen-Rhôs 181 G5
Penmark 115 D1
Penmon 181 E4
Penmorfa 167 E3
Penmynydd 180 D5

Penn Bucks 135 E3
Penn WMid 158 A3
Penn Street 135 E3
Pennal 154 D2
Pennal-isaf 154 D2
Pennan 269 G4
Pennance 96 B5
Pennant Cere 142 B1
Pennant Powys 155 E3
Pennant Melangell 168 D5
Pennar 126 C2
Pennard 128 B4
Pennerley 156 C3
Penninghame 215 E4
Pennington Cumb 199 D5
Pennington Hants 106 C3
Pennington Green 184 A2
Pennington Flash Country
  Park
  WN7 3PA 184 A3
Pennorth 144 A5
Pennsylvania 131 G5
Penny Bridge 199 E4
Pennycross 100 A2
Pennyfuir 240 A1
Pennygate 179 E3
Pennyghael 239 E2
Pennyglen 224 A4
Pennygown 247 F5
Pennymoor 102 B1
Penny's Green 164 C2
Pennyvenie 224 C5
Pen-parc Cere 141 F3
Penparc Pembs 140 B4
Penparcau 154 B4
Penpedairheol 130 C2
Penpethy 97 E1
Penpillick 97 E4
Penpol 95 F4
Penpoll 97 F4
Penponds 94 D3
Penpont D&G 216 C1
Pen-pont Powys 143 F5
Penprysg 129 F4
Penquit 100 C2
Penrherber 141 F4
Penrhiw 141 F3
Penrhiwceiber 129 G3
Penrhiw-goch 128 B1
Penrhiw-llan 141 G3
Penrhiwpâl 141 G3
Penrhiwtyn 128 D3
Penrhos Gwyn 166 C4
Pen-rhos Mon 130 D1
Pen-rhos Powys 129 E1
Penrhosgarnedd 181 D5
Penrhyn Bay
  (Bae Penrhyn) 181 G4
Penrhyn Castle Gwyn
  LL57 4HN 181 E5
Penrhyn-coch 154 C4
Penrhyndeudraeth 167 F4
Penrhyn-side 181 G4
Pen-rhys 129 G3
Penrice 128 A4
Penrith 210 B5
Penrose Corn 96 C2
Penrose Corn 97 G1
Penruddock 210 A5
Penryn 95 E3
Pen-sarn Carmar 128 A1
Pensarn Conwy 182 A5
Pen-sarn Gwyn 167 E5
Pen-sarn Gwyn 166 B3
Pensax 145 G1
Pensby 183 D4
Penselwood 117 E4
Pensford 116 D1
Pensham 146 B3
Penshaw 212 C2
Penshurst 123 E4
Pensilva 97 G3
Pensnett 158 B4
Penston 236 B2
Pentewan 97 E5
Pentir 167 E1
Pentire 96 B3
Pentireglaze 96 D2
Pentlepoir 127 E2
Pentlow 151 G3
Pentlow Street 151 G3
Pentney 163 F1
Penton Mewsey 119 E3
Pentonville 136 C4
Pentraeth 180 D5
Pentre Powys 169 D5
Pentre Powys 155 F5
Pentre Powys 155 F3
Pentre Powys 144 B1
Pentre Powys 156 B3
Pentre Powys 156 A4
Pentre RCT 129 F3
Pentre Shrop 156 C5
Pentre Shrop 156 C1
Pentre Wrex 169 F5
Pentre Wrex 170 A3
Pentre Berw 180 C5
Pentre Ffwrndan 183 D5
Pentre Galar 141 E4
Pentre Gwenlais 128 C1
Pentre Gwynfryn 167 E5
Pentre Halkyn 182 D5
Pentre Isaf 168 B1
Pentre Llanrhaeadr 169 D1
Pentre Llifior 156 A3
Pentre Maelor 170 A3
Pentre Meyrick 129 F5
Pentre Poeth 128 C3
Pentre-bach Cere 142 B3
Pentre-bach MTyd 129 G2
Pentre-bach Powys 143 F4
Pentre-bach RCT 129 G3
Pentre-bach Swan 128 B2
Pentrebach Swan 128 A4
Pentre-bont 168 A2
Pentrebwlch 169 E3
Pentrecagal 141 G3
Pentrecelyn Denb 169 E2
Pentre-celyn
  Powys 155 E2
Pentre-chwyth 128 C3
Pentreclwydau 129 E2
Pentre-cwrt 141 G4
Pentre-Dolau-
  Honddu 143 F3
Pentredwr Denb 169 E3
Pentre-dwr Swan 128 C3
Pentrefelin Carmar 142 C5
Pentrefelin Cere 142 C3
Pentrefelin Conwy 181 G5
Pentrefelin Gwyn 167 E4

Pentrefelin Powys 169 E5
Pentrefoelas 168 B2
Pentregat 141 G2
Pentregwenlais 128 C1
Pentreheyling 156 B3
Pentre-llwyn-
  llwyd 143 F2
Pentre-llyn Cere 154 C5
Pentre-llyn-
  cymmer 168 C2
Pentre-piod 168 B4
Pentre-poeth 130 A4
Pentre'r Felin 168 B1
Pentre'r-beirdd 156 A1
Pentre'r-felin 143 E4
Pentre-tafarn-y-
  fedw 168 B1
Pentre-ty-gwyn 143 E4
Pentrich 173 E2
Pentridge 105 G1
Pen-twyn Caerp 130 A2
Pen-twyn Caerp 130 B2
Pentwyn Cardiff 130 A4
Pen-twyn Mon 131 E2
Pentwyn-mawr 130 A3
Pentyrch 130 A4
Pen-uwch 142 B1
Penwithick 97 E4
Penwood 119 F1
Penwortham 192 B5
Penwortham Lane 192 B5
Pen-wyllt 129 E1
Pen-y-banc 142 C5
Pen-y-bont
  Carmar 143 D4
Pen-y-bont
  Carmar 141 G5
Pen-y-bont Powys 155 G1
Pen-y-bont Powys 169 F5
Pen-y-bont Powys 144 A1
Pen-y-bont-fawr 169 D5
Pen-y-bryn Caerp 130 A3
Pen-y-bryn Gwyn 154 C1
Pen-y-bryn Pembs 141 E3
Pen-y-bryn Wrex 169 F3
Pen-y-cae Powys 129 E1
Penycae Wrex 169 F3
Pen-y-cae-mawr 130 D3
Pen-y-cefn 182 C5
Penycoedcae 129 G4
Pen-y-clawdd 130 D2
Pen-y-cwm 140 B5
Pen-y-darren 129 G2
Pen-y-fai 129 E4
Pen-y-ffordd Flints 170 A1
Pen-y-ffordd Flints 182 C5
Pen-y-ffridd 167 E2
Pen-y-gaer 144 A5
Pen-y-garn Carmar 142 B4
Pen-y-garn Cere 154 C4
Penygarnedd 169 E5
Pen-y-garreg 143 G3
Pen-y-graig Gwyn 166 B4
Pen-y-graig RCT 129 G3
Pen-y-groes Carmar
  128 B1
Pen-y-groes Gwyn 167 D2
Pen-y-Gwryd Hotel 167 F2
Pen-y-lan 129 F4
Pen-y-Mynydd
  Carmar 128 A2
Penymynydd
  Flints 170 A1
Pen-y-parc 169 F1
Pen-yr-Park 144 B3
Penyrenglyn 129 F3
Pen-yr-heol Mon 130 D1
Penyrheol Swan 128 B3
Pen-y-sarn 180 C3
Pen-y-stryt 169 E2
Pen-y-waun 129 F2
Penzance 94 B3
Penzance Heliport 94 B3
People's Palace & Winter
  Gardens Glas
  G40 1AT 39 H6
Peopleton 146 B2
Peover Heath 184 B5
Peper Harow 121 E3
Peplow 170 D5
Pepper Arden 202 B2
Pepper's Green 137 F1
Perceton 233 E5
Percie 260 D5
Percyhorner 269 H4
Perham Down 119 D3
Periton 114 C3
Perivale 136 A4
Perkhill 260 D4
Perkins Beach 156 C2
Perkin's Village 102 D3
Perlethorpe 186 D5
Perran Downs 94 C3
Perranarworthal 95 E3
Perranporth 96 B4
Perranuthnoe 94 C4
Perranzabuloe 96 B4
Perrott's Brook 132 C2
Perry Barr 158 C3
Perry Crofts 159 E2
Perry Green Essex 151 G5
Perry Green Herts 136 D1
Perry Green Wilts 132 B4
Perry Street 137 F5
Perrymead 117 E1
Pershall 171 E1
Pershore 146 B3
Persie House 251 G4
Pert 253 E3
Pertenhall 149 F1
Perth (Peairt) 243 G2
Perthcelyn 129 G3
Perthy 170 A4
Perton 158 A3
Pestalozzi Children's
  Village 110 C2
Peter Tavy 99 F3
Peterborough 161 G3
Peterburn 264 D3
Peterchurch 144 C4
Peterculter 261 G4
Peterhead 269 K6
Peterlee 212 D3
Peter's Green 136 A1
Peters Marland 113 E4
Peters Port
  (Port Pheadair) 262 D7

Petersfield 120 C5
Petersfinger 118 C5
Peterstone
  Wentlooge 130 B4
Peterston-super-
  Ely 129 G5
Peterstow 145 E5
Petham 124 D3
Petrockstowe 113 F5
Pett 111 D2
Pettaugh 152 C2
Petteril Green 210 A3
Pettigo 280 D2
Pettinain 235 D5
Pettistree 153 D2
Petton Devon 114 C5
Petton Shrop 170 B5
Petts Wood 122 D2
Petty 261 F1
Petty France 131 G4
Pettycur 235 G1
Pettymuick 261 H2
Petworth 121 E5
Pevensey 110 B3
Pevensey Bay 110 B3
Peverell 100 A2
Pewsey 118 C1
Pharis 286 E3
Pheasant's Hill 134 C3
Phesdo 253 E2
Philham 112 C3
Philharmonic Hall, Liverpool
  Mersey L1 9BP 43 E5
Philiphaugh 227 F3
Phillack 94 C3
Philleigh 95 F3
Philpstoun 235 E2
Phocle Green 145 F5
Phoenix Green 120 C2
Phones 258 E5
Phorp 267 H6
Photographer's Gallery, The,
  London GtLon
  WC2H 7HY 44 E3
Pibsbury 116 B5
Pica 208 D4
Piccadilly Corner 165 D3
Pickerells 137 E2
Pickering 203 G4
Pickering Nook 212 A2
Picket Piece 119 E3
Picket Post 106 A2
Pickford Green 159 E4
Pickhill 202 C4
Picklescott 156 D3
Pickletillem 244 C2
Pickmere 184 A5
Pickney 115 F4
Pickstock 171 E5
Pickston 243 E2
Pickup Bank 192 D5
Pickwell Devon 113 E1
Pickwell Leics 160 C1
Pickworth Lincs 175 F4
Pickworth Rut 161 E1
Picton ChesW&C 183 F5
Picton NYorks 202 D2
Piddinghoe 109 G3
Piddington Bucks 134 D3
Piddington Oxon 134 B1
Piddington
  WN'hants 148 D2
Piddlehinton 104 D3
Piddletrenthide 104 D3
Pidley 162 B5
Piece Hall, Halifax WYorks
  HX1 1RE 26 B5
Piercebridge 202 B1
Pierowall 276 D3
Pigdon 221 D2
Pigeontown 282 E1
Pike Hill 193 E4
Pikehall 172 C2
Pikeshill 106 B2
Pilgrims Hatch 137 E3
Pilham 187 F3
Pill 131 E5
Pillaton Corn 99 D4
Pillaton Staffs 158 B1
Pillerton Hersey 147 E3
Pillerton Priors 147 E3
Pilleth 144 B1
Pilley Hants 106 C3
Pilley SYorks 186 A2
Pilling 192 A3
Pilling Lane 191 G3
Pillowell 131 F2
Pilning 131 E4
Pilsbury 172 B1
Pilsdon 104 A3
Pilsgate 161 F2
Pilsley Derbys 173 F1
Pilsley Derbys 185 G5
Pilson Green 179 E4
Piltdown 109 G1
Pilton Devon 113 F2
Pilton NN'hants 161 F4
Pilton Rut 161 E2
Pilton Som 116 D3
Pilton Swan 128 A4
Pilton Green 128 A4
Pimhole 184 C1
Pimlico 135 F2
Pimperne 105 F2
Pin Mill 152 D4
Pinchbeck 176 A5
Pinchbeck Bars 176 A5
Pinchbeck West 176 A5
Pincheon Green 187 D1
Pinchinthorpe 203 E1
Pindon End 148 C3
Pinehurst 132 D4
Pinfold 183 E1
Pinged 128 A2
Pinhay 103 G3
Pinhoe 102 C3
Pinkneys Green 135 D4
Pinley Green 147 E1
Pinminnoch 214 C1
Pinn 103 E4
Pinner 136 A4
Pinner Green 136 A3
Pinvin 146 B3
Pinwherry 214 C2
Pinxton 173 F2
Pipe & Lyde 145 E3
Pipe Gate 171 E4

Pipe Ridware 158 C1
Pipehill 158 C2
Piperhall 232 B4
Piperhill 267 F6
Pipers Pool 97 G1
Pipewell 160 D4
Pippacott 113 F2
Pipton 144 A4
Pirbright 121 E2
Pirnmill 231 G5
Pirton Herts 149 G4
Pirton Worcs 146 A3
Pisgah 242 C4
Pishill 134 C4
Pistyll 166 C3
Pitagowan 250 D3
Pitblae 269 H4
Pitcairngreen 243 F2
Pitcairns 243 F3
Pitcaple 261 F2
Pitch Green 134 C2
Pitch Place Surr 121 E2
Pitch Place Surr 121 D4
Pitchcombe 132 A2
Pitchcott 148 C5
Pitchford 157 E2
Pitcombe 117 D4
Pitcot 129 E5
Pitcox 236 D2
Pitcur 244 A1
Pitfichie 260 E3
Pitgrudy 266 E2
Pitinnan 261 F1
Pitkennedy 252 D4
Pitkevy 244 A4
Pitlessie 244 B4
Pitlochry 251 E4
Pitman's Corner 152 C1
Pitmedden 261 G2
Pitminster 103 F1
Pitmuies 253 D5
Pitnacree 251 E4
Pitney 116 B5
Pitroddie 244 A2
Pitscottie 244 C3
Pitsea 137 G4
Pitsford 148 C1
Pitsford Hill 115 D4
Pitstone 135 E2
Pitt Devon 102 D1
Pitt Hants 119 F5
Pitt Rivers Museum Oxon
  OX1 3PP 80 Oxford
Pittendreich 267 J5
Pittentrail 266 E1
Pittenweem 244 D4
Pitteuchar 244 A5
Pittington 212 C3
Pittodrie House 260 E2
Pitton Swan 128 A4
Pitton Wilts 118 D4
Pittulie 269 H4
Pittville 146 B5
Pity Me 212 B3
Pityme 96 C2
Pixey Green 164 D4
Pixley 145 F4
Place Newton 204 B5
Plaidy 269 F5
Plain Dealings 127 D1
Plainfield 220 B1
Plains 234 B3
Plainsfield 115 E4
Plaish 157 E3
Plaistow GtLon 136 C4
Plaistow WSuss 121 F4
Plaitford 106 B1
Plaitford Green 119 D5
Plas 142 A5
Plas Gwynant 167 F2
Plas Isaf 169 D4
Plas Llwyd 182 A5
Plas Llwyngwern 155 D2
Plas Nantyr 169 E4
Plashett 127 F2
Plasisaf 168 C1
Plas-rhiw-Saeson 155 F2
Plastow Green 119 G1
Plas-yn-Cefn 182 B5
Platt 123 F3
Platt Bridge 184 A2
Platt Lane 170 C4
Platt's Heath 124 A3
Plawsworth 212 B3
Plaxtol 123 F3
Play Hatch 134 C5
Playden 111 E1
Playford 152 D3
Playing Place 96 C5
Playley Green 145 G4
Plealey 156 D2
Plean 234 C1
Pleasance 244 A3
Pleasant Valley 150 D4
Pleasington 192 C5
Pleasley 173 G1
Pleasleyhill 173 G1
Pleasure Beach, Great
  Yarmouth Norf
  NR30 3EH 199 H5
Pleasure Island Theme Park
  NELincs
  DN35 0PL 188 D2
Pleasurewood Hills Theme
  Park Suff
  NR32 5DZ 165 G2
Pleck Dorset 104 D1
Pleck WMid 158 B3
Pledgdon Green 151 E5
Pledwick 186 A1
Plemstall 183 F5
Plenmeller 210 D1
Pleshey 137 F1
Plessey Woods Country
  Park N'umb
  NE22 6AN 221 E3
Plockton
  (Am Ploc) 256 E1
Plocrapol 263 G2
Plomer's Hill 135 D2
Plot Gate 116 C4
Plough Hill 159 F3
Plowden 156 C4
Ploxgreen 156 C1
Pluckley 124 B4
Pluckley Thorne 124 B4

Plucks Gutter 125 E2
Plumbland 209 E3
Plumbley 186 B4
Plumbridge 285 G6
Plumley 184 B4
Plumpton Cumb 210 A4
Plumpton ESuss 109 F2
Plumpton WN'hants
  148 B3
Plumpton Green 109 F2
Plumpton Head 210 B4
Plumstead GtLon 137 D5
Plumstead Norf 178 C2
Plumtree 174 B4
Plungar 174 C4
Plush 104 D2
Plusha 98 D3
Plushabridge 98 D3
Plwmp 141 G2
Plym Bridge 100 B2
Plymouth 100 A2
Plymouth Pavilions
  PL1 3LF 81 Plymouth
Plympton 100 B2
Plymstock 100 B2
Plymtree 103 D2
Pockley 203 F4
Pocklington 196 A3
Pocombe Bridge 102 B3
Pode Hole 176 A5
Podimore 116 C5
Podington 149 E1
Podmore 171 E4
Podsmead 132 A1
Poffley End 133 F1
Point Clear 139 D1
Pointon 175 G4
Pol a' Charra 254 C3
Polanach 248 B4
Polapit Tamar 98 D2
Polbae 215 D3
Polbain 272 B7
Polbathic 98 D5
Polbeth 235 E3
Poldean 217 F1
Pole Moor 185 E1
Polebrook 161 F4
Polegate 110 A3
Poles 266 E2
Polesden Lacey Surr
  RH5 6BD 121 G2
Polesworth 159 E2
Polglass 265 G1
Polgooth 97 D4
Polgown 225 F5
Poling 108 C3
Poling Corner 108 C3
Polkemmet Country Park
  WLoth EH47 0AD
  234 D3
Polkerris 97 E4
Polla 273 G3
Pollardras 94 D3
Polldubh 248 D3
Pollie 274 C7
Pollington 186 D1
Pollnagrasta 282 D6
Polloch 247 G3
Pollok 233 G3
Pollokshaws 233 G3
Pollokshields 233 G3
Polmassick 97 D5
Polmont 234 D2
Polnoon 233 G4
Polperro 97 G4
Polruan 97 F4
Polsham 116 C3
Polstead 152 A3
Polstead Heath 152 A3
Poltalloch 240 A5
Poltimore 102 C2
Polton 235 G3

Pontllyfni 166 D2
Pontlottyn 130 A2
Pontneddfechan 129 F2
Pontrhydfendigaid 142 D1
Pont-rhyd-y-bont 180 A5
Pontrhydyfen 129 D3
Pont-rhyd-y-groes
  154 D5
Pontrhydyrun 130 B3
Pontrilas 144 C5
Pontrobert 156 A1
Pont-rug 167 E1
Ponts Green 110 B2
Pontshill 145 F5
Pontsiân 142 A3
Pontsticill 129 G1
Pont-tyweli (Pontwelly)
  142 A4
Pontyates
  (Pont-iets) 128 A2
Pontyberem 128 B1
Pont-y-blew 170 A4
Pontybodkin 169 F2
Pont-y-clun 129 G4
Pontycymer 129 F3
Pontygwaith 129 G3
Pontymister 130 B3
Pontymoel 130 B2
Pontypool 130 B2
Pont-y-pant 168 A2
Pontypridd 129 G3
Pont-y-rhyl 129 F4
Pont-y-waun 130 B3
Pooksgreen 106 C1
Pool Corn 96 A3
Pool WYorks 194 B3
Pool Bank 199 F4
Pool Green 158 C2
Pool Head 145 E2
Pool Quay 156 B1
Pool Street 151 F4
Poole 105 G3
Poole Keynes 132 B3
Poolend 171 G2
Poolewe 264 E3
Pooley Bridge 210 A5
Pooley Street 164 B3
Poolfold 171 F2
Poolhill 145 G5
Poolsbrook 186 B5
Poolthorne Farm 188 A2
Pope Hill 126 C1
Popeswood 120 D1
Popham 119 G3
Poplar 136 C4
Porchfield 106 D3
Porin 265 K6
Poringland 179 D5
Porkellis 95 D3
Porlock 114 B3
Porlock Weir 114 B3
Port Allen 244 A2
Port Appin (Port na
  h-Apainn) 248 B5
Port Askaig 230 C3
Port Bannatyne 232 B3
Port Carlisle 218 A5
Port Charlotte 230 A4
Port Clarence 213 E5
Port Driseach 232 A2
Port e Vullen 190 C2
Port Ellen 230 B5
Port Elphinstone 261 F3
Port Erin 190 A5
Port Erroll 261 J1
Port Eynon 128 A4
Port Gaverne 97 E1
Port Glasgow 233 E2
Port Henderson 264 D4
Port Isaac 97 D1
Port Logan 206 A2
Port Lympne Wild Animal
  Park Kent
  CT21 4PD 124 D5
Port Mòr 246 D2
Port Mulgrave 203 G1
Port na Craig 251 E4
Port nan Long 262 D4
Port of Menteith 242 A4
Port of Ness
  (Port Nis) 271 H1
Port o'Warren 216 C5
Port Quin 97 D1
Port Ramsay 248 A5
Port St. Mary 190 A5
Port Solent 107 F2
Port Sunlight 183 E4
Port Talbot 129 D4
Port Tennant 128 C3
Port Wemyss 230 A4
Port William 206 D2
Portachoillan 231 F4
Portadown 282 D3
Portaferry 283 J3
Portavadie 232 A3
Portavoe 287 K7
Portavogie 283 K3
Portballintrae 286 D1
Portbraddan 286 E1
Portbury 131 E5
Portchester 107 F2
Portencross 232 C5
Portesham 104 C4
Portessie 268 C4
Portfield A&B 239 G2
Portfield WSuss 108 A3
Portfield Gate 126 C1
Portgate 99 E2
Portglenone 286 D5
Portglenone Forest Park
  M&EAnt
  BT44 8BN 286 D5
Portgordon 268 B4
Portgower 275 F7
Porth Corn 96 C3
Porth RCT 129 G3
Porth Colmon 166 A4
Porth Navas 95 E4
Porth Penrhyn 181 D5
Porthallow Corn 95 E4
Porthallow Corn 97 G4
Porthcawl 129 E5
Porthcothan 96 C3
Porthcurno 94 A4
Porth-gain 140 B4
Porthill 171 F3
Porthkerry 115 D1

Porthkerry Country Park
  VGlam
  CF62 3BY 115 D1
Porthleven 94 D4
Porthlechog (Bull Bay)
  180 C1
Porthmadog 167 E4
Porthmeor 94 B3
Portholland 97 D5
Porthoustock 95 F4
Porthpean 97 E4
Porthtowan 96 A5
Porth-y-waen 241 G5
Portincaple 241 G5
Portington 195 G4
Portinnisherrich 240 B3
Portinscale 209 F4
Portishead 131 D5
Portknockie 268 C4
Portland Basin Museum
  GtMan OL7 0QA 25 H3
Portlee 286 E7
Portlethen 261 H5
Portlethen Village 261 H5
Portloe 95 G3
Portlooe 97 G4
Portmahomack 267 G3
Portmellon 97 E5
Portmore 106 C3
Portmuck 287 J5
Port-na-Con 273 G2
Portnacroish
  (Port na Croise) 248 B5
Portnaguran (Port nan
  Giùran) 271 H4
Portnahaven 230 A4
Portnalong 255 J1
Portnaluchaig 247 F1
Portobello 236 A2
Porton 118 C4
Portpatrick 214 B5
Portreath 96 A5
Portreath Harbour
  (Cornwall & West Devon
  Mining Landscape) Corn
  96 A5
Portree (Port Righ) 263 K7
Portrush 286 C1
Portscatho 95 F3
Portsea 107 F3
Portskerra 274 D2
Portslade 109 E3
Portslade-by-Sea 109 E3
Portslogan 214 A5
Portsmouth 107 F3
Portsmouth Guildhall
  PO1 2AB
  82 Portsmouth
Portsmouth Historic
  Dockyard PO1 3LJ
  82 Portsmouth
Portsonachan 240 B2
Portsoy 268 D4
Portstewart 286 C2
Portuairk 246 D3
Portvoller 271 H4
Portway Here 144 C3
Portway Here 145 D3
Portway Here 145 D4
Portway Worcs 158 C5
Portwrinkle 98 D5
Portyerrock 207 E3
Posenhall 157 F2
Poslingford 151 F3
Postbridge 99 G3
Postcombe 134 C3
Postling 124 D5
Postwick 179 D5
Potarch 260 E5
Potsgrove 149 E5
Pott Row 177 E5
Pott Shrigley 184 D5
Potten End 135 F2
Potter Brompton 204 C5
Potter Heigham 179 F4
Potter Street 137 D2
Pottergate Street 164 C3
Potterhanworth 175 F1
Potterhanworth
  Booths 175 F1
Potteries Museum & Art
  Gallery ST1 3DW
  85 Stoke-on-Trent
Potterne 118 A2
Potterne Wick 118 B2
Potternewton 194 B4
Potters Bar 136 B2
Potters Crouch 136 A2
Potter's Green 159 F4
Potters Marston 159 G3
Potterspury 148 C3
Potterton N'umb 261 H3
Potterton WYorks 194 D4
Pottle Street 117 F3
Potto 203 D2
Potton 150 A3
Pott's Green 152 A5
Poughill Corn 112 C5
Poughill Devon 102 B2
Poulshot 118 A2
Poulton 132 D2
Poulton-le-Fylde 191 G4
Pound Bank 145 G3
Pound Green ESuss 110 A1
Pound Green Suff 151 F2
Pound Green
  Worcs 157 G5
Pound Hill 122 B5
Pound Street 119 F1
Poundbury 104 C3
Poundffald 128 B3
Poundfield 123 E5
Poundgate 109 G1
Poundland 214 C2
Poundon 148 B5
Poundsbridge 123 E4
Poundsgate 102 A5
Poundstock 98 C1
Povey Cross 122 B4
Pow Green 145 G3

Powburn 229 E5
Powderham 102 C4
Powderham Castle Devon
  EX6 8JQ 102 C4
Powerstock 104 B3
Powfoot 217 F4
Powick 146 A2
Poxwell 104 D4
Poyle 135 F5
Poynings 109 E2
Poynington 117 D5
Poyntington 117 D5
Poynton ChesE 184 D4
Poynton Tel&W 157 E1
Poynton Green 157 E1
Poyntz Pass 282 D5
Poyntzfield 266 E5
Poys Street 165 E4
Poyston 126 C1
Poyston Cross 126 C1
Poystreet Green 152 A2
Praa Sands 94 C4
Pratis 244 B4
Pratt's Bottom 123 D2
Praze-an-Beeble 94 D3
Predannack Wollas 95 D5
Prees 170 C4
Prees Green 170 C4
Prees Heath 170 C4
Prees Higher Heath 170 C4
Prees Lower Heath 170 C4
Preesall 191 G3
Preesgweene 169 F4
Prehen 285 G4
Prenbrigog 169 F1
Prendergast 126 C1
Prendwick 229 E5
Pren-gwyn 142 A3
Pren-teg 167 E3
Prenton 183 E4
Prescot 183 F3
Prescott Shrop 170 B5
Prescott Shrop 157 E3
Presley 267 H6
Pressen 228 C3
Prestatyn 182 B4
Prestbury ChesE 184 D5
Prestbury Glos 146 B5
Presteigne
  (Llanandras) 144 C1
Presthope 157 E3
Prestleigh 116 D3
Prestolee 184 B2
Preston B&H 109 F3
Preston Devon 102 B5
Preston Dorset 104 D4
Preston ELoth 236 C2
Preston ERid 197 D4
Preston Glos 145 F4
Preston Glos 132 C2
Preston Herts 149 G5
Preston Kent 124 C2
Preston Kent 125 E2
Preston Lancs 192 B5
Preston N'umb 229 F4
Preston Rut 161 D2
Preston ScBord 237 E4
Preston Shrop 157 E1
Preston Som 115 D4
Preston Suff 152 A2
Preston Torbay 101 E1
Preston Wilts 132 C5
Preston Bagot 147 D1
Preston Bissett 148 B4
Preston Bowyer 115 E5
Preston Brockhurst 170 C5
Preston Brook 183 G4
Preston Candover 120 B3
Preston Capes 148 A3
Preston Deanery 148 C2
Preston Gubbals 157 D1
Preston Guildhall Lancs
  PR1 1HT 192 B5
Preston on Stour 147 E3
Preston on the Hill 183 G4
Preston on Wye 144 C3
Preston Plucknett 104 B1
Preston upon the Weald
  Moors 157 F1
Preston Wynne 145 E3
Preston-le-Skerne 212 C5
Prestonpans 236 A2
Preston-under-Scar 201 F3
Prestwich N'umb 221 E1
Prestwich WYorks 184 C2
Prestwick SAyr 224 B3
Prestwold 173 G5
Prestwood Bucks 135 D2
Prestwood Staffs 172 C3
Price Town 129 F3
Prickwillow 163 D4
Priddy 116 C2
Priest Hill 192 C4
Priest Hutton 199 G5
Priest Weston 156 B2
Priestcliffe 185 F5
Priestland 225 D2
Priestsessagh 284 E7
Priestwood 123 F2
Primethorpe 160 A3
Primrose Green 178 B4
Primrose Hill 184 B4
Princes End 158 B3
Princes Gate 127 E1
Princes Risborough 134 C2
Princetown Caerp 130 A1
Princetown Devon 99 F3
Principality Stadium
  CF10 1GE 67 Cardiff
Prior Muir 244 D3
Prior's Frome 145 E4
Priors Halton 157 D5
Priors Hardwick 147 G2
Priors Marston 147 G2
Prior's Norton 146 A5
Priors Park 146 A4
Priorslee 157 F1
Priory Country Park Bed
  MK41 9SH 149 F2
Priory Wood 144 B3
Priston 117 D1
Pristow Green 164 C3
Prittlewell 138 B4

Privett 120 B5
Prixford 113 F2
Proaig 230 C4
Probus 96 C5
Protstonhill 269 G4
Provand's Lordship Glas
  G4 0RH 39 H3
Prudhoe 211 G1
Prussia Cove 94 C4
Pubil 249 G5
Publow 116 D1
Puckeridge 150 B5
Puckington 103 G1
Pucklechurch 131 F5
Pucknall 119 E5
Puckrup 146 A4
Puddinglake 171 E1
Puddington
  ChesW&C 183 E5
Puddington
  Devon 102 B1
Puddlebrook 131 F1
Puddledock 164 B2
Puddletown 105 D3
Pudleston 145 E2
Pudsey 194 B4
Pugneys Country Park
  WYorks WF2 7EQ 27 G6
Pulborough 108 C2
Pulborough Brooks RSPB
  Nature Reserve WSuss
  RH20 2EL 108 C2
Puldagon 275 J4
Puleston 171 E5
Pulford 170 A2
Pulham 116 A3
Pulham Market 164 C3
Pulham St. Mary 164 D3
Pulley 157 D2
Pulloxhill 149 F4
Pulrossie 266 E3
Pulverbatch 156 D2
Pumpherston 235 E3
Pumsaint 142 C3
Puncheston 140 D5
Puncknowle 104 B4
Punnett's Town 110 B1
Purbrook 107 F2
Puriton 116 A3
Purleigh 138 B2
Purley 122 C2
Purley on Thames 134 B5
Purlogue 156 B5
Purlpit 117 F1
Purls Bridge 162 C4
Purse Caundle 104 C1
Purslow 156 C4
Purston Jaglin 186 B1
Purtington 103 G2
Purton Glos 131 F2
Purton Glos 131 F2
Purton Wilts 132 C4
Purton Stoke 132 C3
Purves Hall 237 E5
Pury End 148 C3
Pusey 133 F3
Putley 145 F4
Putley Green 145 F4
Putney 136 B5
Putsborough 113 E1
Puttenham Herts 135 D1
Puttenham Surr 121 E3
Puttock End 151 G3
Putts Corner 103 E2
Puxton 116 B1
Pwll 128 A2
Pwllcrochan 126 C2
Pwlldefaid 166 A5
Pwll-glas 169 E2
Pwllgloyw 143 G4
Pwllheli 166 C4
Pwll-Mawr 130 B5
Pwllmeyric 131 E3
Pwll-trap 127 F1
Pwll-y-glaw 129 D3
Pye Corner Kent 124 A4
Pye Corner
  Newport 130 C4
Pye Green 158 B1
Pyecombe 109 E2
Pyle Bridgend 129 E4
Pyle IoW 107 D5
Pyleigh 115 E4
Pylle 116 D4
Pymoor (Pymore) 162 C4
Pymore (Pymoor)
  Cambs 162 C4
Pymore Dorset 104 A3
Pyrford 121 F2
Pyrford Green 121 F2
Pyrton 134 B3
Pytchley 161 D5
Pyworthy 112 D5

Q
Quabbs 156 B4
Quadring 176 A4
Quadring Eaudike 176 A4
Quainton 148 C5
Quarff 279 D9
Quarley 119 D3
Quarndon 173 E3
Quarr Hill 107 E3
Quarrier's Village 233 E3
Quarrington 175 F3
Quarrington Hill 212 C4
Quarry Bank 158 B4
Quarry Bank Mill & Styal
  Estate ChesE
  SK9 4LA 184 C4
Quarrybank 170 C1
Quarrywood 267 J5
Quarter 234 B4
Quatford 157 G3
Quatt 157 G4
Quebec 212 A3
Quedgeley 132 A1
Queen Adelaide 163 D4
Queen Camel 116 C5
Queen Charlton 116 D1
Queen Dart 102 B1

Queen Elizabeth Forest Park
  Stir FK8 3SX 241 G5
Queen Elizabeth Hall
  GtLon SE1 8XX 45 F4
Queen Elizabeth Olympic
  Park GtLon
  E20 2ST 12 D3
Queen Elizabeth II
  Conference Centre GtLon
  SW1P 3EE 44 D6
Queen Elizabeth II Country
  Park, Ashington N'umb
  NE63 9YF 221 E3
Queen Oak 117 E4
Queen Street 232 B3
Queen's Bower 107 E4
Queen's Gallery,
  Buckingham Palace
  GtLon SW1A 1AA 44 B6
Queen's Hall, Edinburgh
  Edin EH8 9JG 37 H6
Queen's Head 127 E1
Queen's View Centre P&K
  PH16 5NR 251 D3
Queensbury GtLon 136 A4
Queensbury
  WYorks 194 A4
Queensferry (South
  Queensferry)
  Edin 235 F2
Queensferry Flints 170 A1
Queenswood Country Park
  Here HR6 0PY 145 D2
Queenzieburn 234 A3
Quemerford 118 B1
Quendale 279 F18
Quendon 150 D4
Queniborough 160 B1
Quenington 132 D2
Quernmore 192 B1
Queslett 158 C3
Quethiock 98 D4
Quholm 277 B6
Quick's Green 134 A5
Quidenham 164 B3
Quidhampton 119 G2
Quidinish
  (Cuidhtinis) 263 F3
Quilquox 261 H1
Quina Brook 170 C4
Quindry 277 D8
Quine's Hill 190 B4
Quinhill 231 F4
Quinton WMid 158 B4
Quinton WN'hants 148 C3
Quinton Green 148 C2
Quintrell Downs 96 C3
Quixhill 172 C3
Quoditch 99 E1
Quoig 242 D2
Quoiggs House 242 D4
Quoile 283 J4
Quoisley 170 C3
Quorn (Quorndon) 160 A1
Quorndon (Quorn) 160 A1
Quothquan 226 A2
Quoyloo 276 B5
Quoys 278 F1
Quoys of Reiss 275 J3

R
R.A.F. Museum, Cosford
  Shrop TF11 8UP 157 G2
R.A.F. Museum, Hendon
  GtLon
  NW9 5LL 10 D1
R.H.S. Garden Harlow Carr
  NYorks
  HG3 1QB 194 B2
R.H.S. Garden Hyde Hall
  Essex CM3 8ET 137 G3
R.H.S. Garden Rosemoor
  Devon EX38 8PH 113 F4
R.H.S. Garden Wisley Surr
  GU23 6QB 121 F2
Raasay 264 C5
Raby 183 E5
Racavan 287 G5
Rachan 226 C2
Rachub 167 F1
Rackenford 102 B1
Rackham 108 C2
Rackheath 179 D4
Racks 217 F3
Rackwick Ork 277 B8
Rackwick Ork 276 B3
Radbourne 173 E4
Radcliffe GtMan 184 B2
Radcliffe N'umb 221 E1
Radcliffe on Trent 174 B4
Radclive 148 B4
Radcot 133 E3
Raddington 114 D5
Radernie 244 C4
Radford B&NESom 117 D2
Radford Nott 173 G3
Radford Oxon 147 G5
Radford WMid 159 F4
Radford Semele 147 F1
Radipole 104 C4
Radlett 136 A2
Radley 134 A3
Radley Green 137 F2
Radmore Green 170 C2
Radnage 134 C3
Radstock 117 D2
Radstone 148 A3
Radway 147 F3
Radway Green 171 E2
Radwell Bed 149 F2
Radwell Herts 150 A4
Radwinter 151 E4
Radyr 130 A4
Raechester 220 B3
Raemoir House 260 E5
Raffin 272 C5
Rafford 267 H6
Raffrey 283 H3
Ragdale 160 B1
Ragged Appleshaw 119 E3
Raglan 130 D2
Ragnall 187 F5
Raholp 283 J4
Rahony 281 F3
Rahoy 247 F4
Rain Shore 184 C1
Rainford 183 F2

317

Rainham GtLon 137 E4
Rainham Med 124 A2
Rainhill 183 F3
Rainhill Stoops 183 G3
Rainow 185 D5
Rainsough 184 B2
Rainton 202 C5
Rainworth 173 G2
Raisbeck 200 B2
Raise 210 D3
Rait 244 A2
Raithby Lincs 176 B1
Raithby Lincs 188 D4
Rake 120 D5
Raleigh's Cross 114 C4
Ram 142 B3
Ram Alley 118 D1
Ram Lane 124 B4
Ramaket 281 K4
Ramaley 281 G3
Ramasaig 263 G7
Rame Corn 95 E3
Rame Corn 100 A3
Rampisham 104 B2
Rampside 191 F1
Rampton Cambs 150 C1
Rampton Notts 187 F5
Ramsbottom 184 B4
Ramsbury 133 E5
Ramscraigs 275 G6
Ramsdean 120 C5
Ramsdell 119 G2
Ramsden 133 F1
Ramsden Bellhouse 137 G3
Ramsden Heath 137 G3
Ramsey Cambs 162 A4
Ramsey Essex 152 D4
Ramsey IoM 190 C2
Ramsey Forty Foot 162 B4
Ramsey Heights 162 A4
Ramsey Island
   Essex 138 C2
Ramsey Island
   Pembs 140 A5
Ramsey Mereside 162 A4
Ramsey St. Mary's 162 A4
Ramsgate 125 F2
Ramsgate Street 178 B2
Ramsgill 202 A5
Ramsholt 153 E3
Ramshorn 172 B3
Ramsnest Common 121 E4
Ranachan 247 G3
Ranaghan 286 B6
Ranby Lincs 188 C5
Ranby Notts 187 D4
Rand 188 B5
Rand Farm Park Lincs
   LN8 5NJ 188 B5
Randalstown 286 E6
Randwick 132 A2
Ranelly 281 G2
Rangemore 172 C5
Rangeworthy 131 F4
Ranish (Ranais) 271 G5
Rankinston 224 C4
Rank's Green 137 G1
Ranmoor 186 A4
Ranmore Common 121 G2
Rannoch School 250 A4
Ranochan 248 A1
Ranscombe 114 C3
Ranskill 187 D4
Ranton 171 F5
Ranton Green 171 F5
Ranworth 179 E4
Rapness 276 E3
Rapps 103 G1
Rascarrel 208 A2
Rash 200 B4
Rasharkin 286 D4
Rashee 287 G6
Rashwood 146 B1
Raskelf 203 D5
Rassau 130 A1
Rastrick 194 A5
Ratagan 257 F3
Ratby 160 A2
Ratcliffe Culey 159 F3
Ratcliffe on Soar 173 F5
Ratcliffe on the
   Wreake 160 B1
Ratford Bridge 126 B1
Ratfyn 118 C3
Rathen 269 H4
Rathfriland 282 E5
Rathillet 244 B2
Rathliesbeag 249 E1
Rathkeel 287 F5
Rathmell 193 E1
Ratho 235 F2
Ratho Station 235 F2
Rathven 268 C4
Ratley 147 F3
Ratling 125 E3
Ratlinghope 156 D3
Ratsloe 102 C3
Rattar 275 H1
Ratten Row Cumb 209 G2
Ratten Row Lancs 192 A3
Rattery 100 D1
Rattlesden 152 A2
Rattray 251 G5
Raughton Head 209 G2
Raunds 161 E5
Ravenfield 186 B3
Ravenglass 198 B3
Ravenglass & Eskdale
   Railway (La'al Ratty)
   Cumb CA18 1SW
   198 C3
Raveningham 165 E2
Raven's Green 152 C5
Ravensdale 190 B2
Ravenshaw 193 F3
Ravenshayes 102 C3
Ravenshead 173 G2
Ravensmoor 170 C2
Ravensthorpe
   WN'hants 160 B5
Ravensthorpe
   WYorks 194 B5
Ravenstone Leics 159 G1
Ravenstone MK 149 D3
Ravenstonedale 200 C2
Ravenstruther 234 D5

Ravensworth 202 A2
Ravernet 283 F2
Raw F&O 281 G4
Raw NYorks 204 C2
Rawcliffe ERid 195 F5
Rawcliffe York 195 E2
Rawcliffe Bridge 195 F5
Rawdon 194 B4
Rawmarsh 186 B3
Rawnsley 158 C1
Rawreth 137 G3
Rawridge 103 F2
Rawson Green 173 E3
Rawyards 234 B3
Raxton 261 G1
Raydon 152 B4
Raylees 220 B2
Rayleigh 138 B3
Raymond's Hill 103 G3
Rayne 151 F5
Rayners Park 122 B2
Rayne's Lane 136 A4
Reach 151 D1
Read 193 D4
Reading 134 C5
Reading Green 164 C4
Reading Street 124 B5
Reagill 200 B1
Real Mary King's Close, The
   Edin EH1 1PG 37 F4
Rearquhar 266 E2
Rearsby 160 B1
Rease Heath 170 D2
Reaster 275 H2
Reaveley 229 E5
Reawick 279 C8
Reay 274 E2
Reculver 125 E2
Red Ball 103 D1
Red Bull 171 F2
Red Dial 209 G2
Red Hill Hants 107 G1
Red Hill Warks 146 D2
Red Lodge 163 E5
Red Lumb 184 C1
Red Oaks Hill 151 D4
Red Point 264 D5
Red Post Corn 112 C5
Red Post Devon 101 E5
Red Rail 145 E5
Red Rock 183 G2
Red Roses 127 F1
Red Row 221 E2
Red Street 171 F2
Red Wharf Bay
   (Traeth Coch) 180 D4
Redberth 127 D2
Redbourn 136 A1
Redbourne 187 G3
Redbrook Glos 131 E1
Redbrook Wrex 170 C3
Redbrook Street 124 B5
Redburn High 266 C5
Redburn High 267 G7
Redburn N'umb 211 D1
Redcar 213 F5
Redcastle Angus 253 E4
Redcastle High 266 C7
Redcliff Bay 130 D5
Redcloak 253 G2
Reddingmuirhead 234 D2
Reddish 184 C3
Redditch 146 C1
Rede 151 G2
Redenhall 165 D3
Redesmouth 220 A3
Redford Aber 253 F2
Redford Angus 253 D5
Redford Dur 211 G4
Redford WSuss 121 D5
Redgrave 164 B4
Redheugh 252 C3
Redhill Aber 260 E1
Redhill Aber 261 F4
Redhill L&C 282 E3
Redhill Moray 268 D6
Redhill Notts 173 G3
Redhill NSom 116 B1
Redhill Surr 122 B3
Redhill Aerodrome &
   Heliport 122 B4
Redhouse A&B 231 G3
Redhouse Aber 260 D2
Redhouses 230 B3
Redisham 165 F3
Redland Bristol 131 E5
Redland Ork 276 C5
Redlingfield 164 C4
Redlynch Som 117 E4
Redlynch Wilts 118 D5
Redmarley D'Abitot 145 G4
Redmarshall 212 C5
Redmile 174 C4
Redmire 201 F3
Redmoor 97 E3
Rednal 170 A5
Redpath 227 G2
Redruth 96 A5
Redscarhead 235 G5
Redshaw 225 G3
Redstone Bank 127 E1
Redwick Newport 130 D4
Redwick SGlos 131 E4
Redworth 212 B5
Reed 150 B4
Reed End 150 B4
Reedham 179 F5
Reedley 193 E4
Reedness 195 G5
Reef (Riof) 270 D4
Reepham Lincs 188 A5
Reepham Norf 178 B3
Reeth 201 F3
Regaby 190 C2
Regil 116 C1
Regoul 267 F6
Reiff 272 B7
Reigate 122 B3
Reighton 205 E5
Reisgill 275 H5
Reiss 275 J3
Rejerrah 96 C4
Relan 281 H5
Releath 95 D3
Relubbus 94 C3
Relugas 267 G7
Remenham 134 C4

Remenham Hill 134 C4
Remony 250 C5
Rempstone 173 G5
Rendcomb 132 C1
Rendham 153 E1
Rendlesham 153 E2
Renfrew 233 G3
Renhold 149 F2
Renishaw 186 B5
Rennington 229 G5
Renton 233 E2
Renwick 210 B3
Repps 179 F4
Repton 173 E5
Rescobie 252 D4
Rescorla 97 E4
Resipole 247 G3
Resolfen 129 E2
Resolis 266 D5
Resolven 129 E2
Resourie 248 A2
Respryn 97 F3
Reston 237 F3
Restormel 97 F3
Reswallie 252 D4
Reterth 96 D4
Retew 96 D4
Retford
   (East Retford) 187 E4
Rettendon 137 G3
Rettendon Place 137 G3
Retyn 96 C4
Revesby 176 A1
Revesby Bridge 176 B1
Rew 102 A5
Rew Street 107 D3
Rewe Devon 102 C3
Rewe Devon 102 B3
Reybridge 118 A1
Reydon 165 F4
Reydon Smear 165 G4
Reymerston 178 B5
Reynalton 127 D2
Reynoldston 128 A4
Rezare 99 D3
Rhadyr 130 C2
Rhandir-mwyn 143 D3
Rhaoine 266 D1
Rhayader
   (Rhaeadr Gwy) 143 F1
Rhedyn 166 B4
Rheola 159 E1
Rhes-y-cae 169 E1
Rhewl Denb 169 E3
Rhewl Denb 169 E1
Rhewl Shrop 170 A4
Rhian 273 H7
Rhicarn 272 C6
Rhiconich 272 E3
Rhicullen 266 D4
Rhidorroch 265 H2
Rhifail 274 C4
Rhigos 129 F2
Rhilochan 266 E1
Rhinduie 266 C7
Rhireavach 265 G2
Rhiroy 265 H3
Rhiston 156 B3
Rhiw 166 B4
Rhiwargor 168 C5
Rhiwbina 130 A4
Rhiwbryfdir 167 F3
Rhiwderin 130 B4
Rhiwinder 129 G4
Rhiwlas Gwyn 167 E1
Rhiwlas Gwyn 168 B4
Rhiwlas Powys 169 F4
Rhode 115 F4
Rhodes Minnis 124 D4
Rhodesia 186 C5
Rhodiad-y-brenin 140 A5
Rhodmad 154 B5
Rhonadale 222 C2
Rhonehouse
   (Kelton Hill) 216 B5
Rhoose 115 D1
Rhôs Carmar 141 G4
Rhôs NPT 128 D2
Rhos Common 156 B1
Rhosaman 128 D1
Rhoscolyn 180 A5
Rhoscrowther 126 C2
Rhosesmor 169 F1
Rhos-fawr 166 C4
Rhosgadfan 167 E2
Rhos-goch IoA 180 C4
Rhos-goch Powys 144 A3
Rhos-hill 141 E3
Rhoshirwaun 166 A5
Rhos-lan 167 E2
Rhoslefain 154 B2
Rhosllanerchrugog 169 F3
Rhoslligwy 180 C4
Rhos-maen 142 C5
Rhos-meirch 180 C5
Rhosneigr 180 B5
Rhosnesni 170 A2
Rhôs-on-Sea 181 G4
Rhossili 128 A4
Rhosson 140 A5
Rhostrehwfa 180 C5
Rhostryfan 167 D2
Rhostyllen 170 A3
Rhos-y-bol 180 C4
Rhosybrithdir 169 E5
Rhosycaerau 140 C4
Rhos-y-garth 154 C5
Rhos-y-llan 166 B4
Rhos-y-mawn 168 B3
Rhos-y-meirch 144 B1
Rhu 233 D1
Rhuallt 182 B5
Rhubodach 232 B2
Rhuddall Heath 170 C1
Rhuddlan 182 B5
Rhue 265 H2
Rhulen 144 A3
Rhumach 247 F1
Rhunahaorine 231 F5

Rhyd Gwyn 167 F3
Rhyd Powys 155 F2
Ripple Kent 125 F4
Ripple Worcs 146 A4
Ripponden 185 E1
Risabus 230 B5
Risbury 145 E2
Risby ERid 196 C4
Risby Suff 151 F1
Risca 130 A3
Rise 197 D3
Riseden 123 G5
Risegate 175 F4
Riseholme 187 G5
Riseley Bed 149 F1
Riseley W'ham 120 C1
Rishangles 152 C1
Rishton 192 D4
Rishworth 185 E1
Risinghurst 134 A2
Risley Derbys 173 F4
Risley Warr 184 A3
Risplith 194 B1
Rispond 273 G2
Rivar 119 E2
Rivenhall 138 B1
Rivenhall End 138 B1
River Kent 125 F4
River WSuss 121 E5
River Bank 150 D1
River Bridge 116 A3
Riverford Bridge 101 D2
Riverhead 123 E3
Riverside Cardiff 130 A5
Riverside NM&D 283 G7
Riverview Park 137 F5
Rivington 184 A1
Roa Island 191 F1
Roach Bridge 192 B5
Road Green 165 D2
Road Weedon 148 B2
Roade 148 C2
Roadhead 218 D4
Roadside High 275 G2
Roadside Ork 276 F3
Roadside of Kinneff 253 G2
Roadwater 114 D4
Roag 263 H7
Roast Green 150 C4
Roath 130 A5
Robert Burns Birthplace
   Museum SAyr
   KA7 4PQ 224 B4
Roberton ScBord 227 F4
Roberton SLan 225 G3
Robertsbridge 110 C1
Robertstown
   Moray 267 K7
Robertstown RCT 129 G2
Roberttown 194 A5
Robeston Cross 126 B2
Robeston Wathen 127 D1
Robeston West 126 B2
Robin Hill Countryside
   Adventure Park IoW
   PO30 2NU 107 E4
Robin Hood
   Derbys 185 G5
Robin Hood Lancs 183 G1
Robin Hood WYorks 194 C5
Robin Hood's Bay 204 C2
Robinhood End 151 F4
Robins 120 D5
Robinson's Town 282 C5
Roborough Devon 113 F4
Roborough Plym 100 B1
Roby 183 F3
Roby Mill 183 G2
Rocester 172 C4
Roch 140 B5
Roch Bridge 140 B5
Roch Gate 140 B5
Rochallie 251 G4
Rochdale 184 C1
Roche 97 D3
Rochester Med 123 G2
Rochester N'umb 220 A2
Rochester Cathedral Med
   ME1 1SX 123 G2
Rochford Essex 138 B3
Rochford Worcs 145 F1
Rock Corn 96 D2
Rock N'umb 229 G5
Rock Worcs 157 G5
Rock Ferry 183 E4
Rockbeare 102 D3
Rockbourne 106 A1
Rockcliffe Cumb 218 B5
Rockcliffe D&G 216 C5
Rockcliffe Cross 218 B5
Rockfield A&B 231 G4
Rockfield High 267 G3
Rockfield Mon 131 D1
Rockford 106 A2
Rockhampton 131 F3
Rockhead 97 E1
Rockingham 161 D3
Rockland All Saints 164 A2
Rockland St. Mary 179 E5
Rockland St. Peter 164 A2
Rockley 133 D5
Rockside 230 A3
Rockspring 286 C7
Rockstown 281 J1
Rockwell End 134 C4
Rockwell Green 103 E1
Rodborough 132 A2
Rodbourne 132 B4
Rodbridge Corner 151 G3
Rodd 144 C1
Roddam 229 E4
Rodden 104 C4
Rode 117 F2
Rode Heath 171 F2
Rodeheath 171 F1
Roden 157 E1
Rodel (Roghadal) 263 F3

Roden 157 E1
Rodhuish 114 D4
Rodington 157 E1
Rodington Heath 157 E1
Rodley 131 G1
Rodmarton 132 B3
Rodmell 109 G3
Rodmersham 124 B2
Rodmersham Green 124 B2
Rodney Stoke 116 B2
Rodsley 172 D3
Rodway 131 G5
Roe Cross 185 D3
Roe Green 150 B4
Roecliffe 194 C1
Roehampton 136 B5
Roesound 279 C6
Roffey 121 G4
Rogart 266 E1
Rogate 120 D5
Rogerstone 130 B4
Rogiet 131 D4
Rokemarsh 134 B3
Roker 212 D2
Rollesby 179 F4
Rolleston Leics 160 C2
Rolleston Notts 174 C2
Rollestone 118 B3
Rolleston-on-Dove 172 D5
Rolston 197 E3
Rolstone 116 A1
Rolvenden 124 A5
Rolvenden Layne 124 A5
Romaldkirk 211 F5
Roman Bath House
   (Frontiers of the Roman
   Empire) EDun 30 C4
Roman Baths B&NESom
   BA1 1LZ 117 E1
Roman Fort (Frontiers of
   the Roman Empire) Falk
   234 B2
Romanby 202 C3
Romanno Bridge 235 F5
Romansleigh 114 A5
Romesdal 263 K6
Romford Dorset 105 G2
Romford GtLon 137 E4
Romiley 184 D3
Romney, Hythe &
   Dymchurch Railway
   Kent TN28 8PL 124 D5
Romney Street 123 E2
Romsey 119 E5
Romsley Shrop 157 G4
Romsley Worcs 158 B5
Rona 264 C6
Ronachan 231 F4
Ronague 190 A4
Ronnachmore 230 B4
Rood End 158 C4
Rookhope 211 F3
Rookley 107 E4
Rookley Green 107 E4
Rooks Bridge 116 A2
Rook's Nest 115 D4
Rookwith 202 B4
Roos 197 E4
Roose 191 F1
Roosebeck 191 F1
Roosecote 191 F1
Rootham's Green 149 F2
Rootpark 235 D4
Ropley 120 B4
Ropley Dean 120 B4
Ropley Soke 120 B4
Ropsley 175 E4
Rora 269 J5
Rorandle 260 E3
Rorrington 156 C2
Rosarie 268 B6
Roscavey 281 H2
Rose 96 B4
Rose Ash 114 A5
Rose Green Essex 152 A5
Rose Green WSuss 108 B4
Rose Hill 109 G2
Roseacre Kent 123 G3
Roseacre Lancs 192 A4
Rosebank 234 C5
Rosebrough 229 F4
Rosebush 141 D5
Rosecare 98 B1
Rosecliston 96 C4
Rosedale Abbey 203 G3
Roseden 229 E4
Rosehall 266 B1
Rosehearty 269 H4
Rosehill Aber 260 D5
Rosehill Shrop 157 E4
Roseisle 267 J5
Roselands 110 B3
Rosemarket 126 C2
Rosemarkie 266 E6
Rosemary Lane 103 E2
Rosemeilan 281 G2
Rosemount P&K 251 G5
Rosemount SAyr 224 B3
Rosenannon 97 D3
Rosenithon 95 F4
Rosepool 126 B1
Rosevean 97 E4
Roseville 158 B3
Rosewell 235 G3
Roseworth 212 D5
Rosgill 199 G1
Roshven 247 G2
Roskhill 263 H7
Roskorwell 95 E4
Rosley 209 G2
Roslin 235 G3
Rosliston 159 E1
Rosliston Forestry Centre
   Derbys
   DE12 8JX 159 E1
Rosneath 233 D1
Ross D&G 207 G2
Ross N'umb 229 F3
Ross P&K 242 C2
Ross Priory 233 F1
Rosscor 280 B3
Rossdhu House 233 E1
Rossett 170 A2
Rossett Green 194 C2
Rosside 199 D5
Rossie Farm School 253 E4
Rossie Ochill 243 F3
Rossie Priory 244 A1

Rossington 186 D3
Rosskeen 266 D5
Rosslea 281 H5
Rosslyn Chapel Midlo
   EH25 9PU 32 D4
Rossmore 105 G3
Ross-on-Wye 145 F4
Roster 275 H5
Rostherne 184 B4
Rosthwaite Cumb 209 F5
Rosthwaite Cumb 198 D4
Roston 172 C3
Rostrevor 282 E7
Rosudgeon 94 C4
Rosyth 235 F1
Rothbury 220 C1
Rother Valley Country Park
   SYorks S26 5PQ 21 E3
Rotherby 160 B1
Rotherfield 123 E5
Rotherfield Greys 134 C4
Rotherfield Peppard
   134 C4
Rotherham 186 B3
Rothersthorpe 148 C2
Rotherwick 120 C2
Rothes 267 K7
Rothesay 232 B3
Rothiebrisbane 261 F1
Rothiemurchus High
   PH22 1QH 259 G4
Rothienorman 261 F1
Rothiesholm 276 F5
Rothley Leics 160 A1
Rothley N'umb 220 C3
Rothney 260 E2
Rothwell Lincs 188 B3
Rothwell NN'hants 160 C4
Rothwell WYorks 194 C5
Rotsea 196 C2
Rottal 252 B3
Rotten Row Bucks 134 C4
Rotten Row WMid 159 D5
Rottingdean 109 F3
Rottington 208 C5
Roud 107 E4
Roudham 164 A3
Rough Castle (Frontiers of
   the Roman Empire)
   Falk 234 C2
Rough Close 171 G4
Rough Common 124 D3
Rougham Norf 177 G5
Rougham Suff 152 A1
Rougham Green 152 A1
Roughburn 249 F1
Roughfort 287 G7
Roughlee 193 E3
Roughley 158 D3
Roughton Lincs 176 A1
Roughton Norf 178 D2
Roughton Shrop 157 G3
Round Bush 136 A3
Roundbush Green 137 E1
Roundham 104 A2
Roundhay 194 C4
Roundstreet
   Common 121 F5
Roundway 118 B1
Rous Lench 146 C2
Rousay 276 D4
Rousdon 103 F3
Rousham 147 G5
Rousky 285 H7
Routenburn 232 C3
Routh 196 C3
Rout's Green 134 C3
Row Corn 97 E2
Row Cumb 199 F4
Row Cumb 210 C4
Row Heath 139 E1
Row Town 121 F1
Rowanburn 218 C4
Rowardennan
   Lodge 241 F5
Rowarth 185 E4
Rowbarton 115 F5
Rowberrow 116 B2
Rowchoish 241 F4
Rowde 118 A1
Rowden 99 G1
Rowen 181 F5
Rowfields 172 C3
Rowfoot 210 C1
Rowhedge 152 B5
Rowhook 121 G4
Rowington 147 E1
Rowland 185 G5
Rowland's Castle 107 G1
Rowlands Gill 212 A2
Rowledge 120 D3
Rowlestone 144 C5
Rowley Devon 102 A1
Rowley Dur 211 G3
Rowley Shrop 156 C2
Rowley Park 171 G5
Rowley Regis 158 B4
Rowly 121 F3
Rowner 107 E2
Rowney Green 158 C5
Rownhams 106 C1
Rowrah 209 D5
Rowsham 135 D1
Rowsley 173 D1
Rowstock 133 G4
Rowston 175 F2
Rowthorne 173 F1
Rowton ChesW&C 170 B1
Rowton Shrop 156 C1
Rowton Tel&W 157 F1
Roxburgh 228 B3
Roxby NLincs 187 G1
Roxby NYorks 203 G1
Roxhill 286 E6
Roxton 149 G2
Roxwell 137 F2
Royal Academy of Arts
   GtLon W1J 0BD 44 C4
Royal Albert Hall GtLon
   SW7 2AP 11 F5
Royal Albert Memorial
   Museum & Art Gallery
   Devon EX4 3RX
   72 Exeter
Royal Armouries Museum,
   Leeds WYorks
   LS10 1LT 41 G5

Royal Artillery Barracks
GtLon SE18 5DP **13** F5
Royal Bath & West
Showground *Som*
BA4 6QN **116** D4
Royal Botanic Garden,
Edinburgh *Edin*
EH3 5LR **36** D1
Royal Botanic Gardens,
Kew *GtLon*
TW9 3AE **11** C6
Royal British Legion
Village **123** G3
Royal Centre NG1 5ND
80 Nottingham
Royal Cornwall Museum
Corn TR1 2SJ **4** D4
Royal Festival Hall *GtLon*
SE1 8XX **45** F5
Royal Highland Centre *Edin*
EH28 8NB **32** A2
Royal Horticultural Halls
GtLon SW1P 2PB **44** D7
Royal Hospital Chelsea
GtLon SW3 4SR **13** A5
Royal Leamington
Spa **147** F1
Royal Mews, Buckingham
Palace *GtLon*
SW1W 0QH **44** B6
Royal Naval Museum
PO1 3NH
82 Portsmouth
Royal Oak **183** F2
Royal Observatory
Greenwich *GtLon*
SE10 8XJ **13** D5
Royal Opera House *GtLon*
WC2E 9DD **45** E3
Royal Pavilion *B&H*
BN1 1EE **65** Brighton
Royal Scots Regimental
Museum, The *Edin*
EH1 2YT **37** F4
Royal Scottish Academy
Edin EH2 2EL **37** F4
Royal Tunbridge
Wells **123** E5
Royal Victoria Country Park
Hants SO31 5GA **4** C4
Royal Welch Fusiliers
Regimental Museum
Gwyn LL55 2AY **167** D1
Royal Wootton
Bassett **132** C4
Royal Yacht Britannia
Edin EH6 6JJ **32** C1
Roybridge (Drochaid
Ruaidh) **249** E1
Roydon *Essex* **136** D1
Roydon *Norf* **164** B3
Roydon *Norf* **177** F5
Roydon Hamlet **136** D2
Royston *Herts* **150** B3
Royston *SYorks* **186** A1
Royton **184** D2
Rozel **100** C5
Ruabon (Rhiwabon) **170** A3
Ruaig **246** B2
Ruan Lanihorne **96** C5
Ruan Major **95** D5
Ruan Minor **95** E5
Ruanaich **238** B2
Ruardean **131** F1
Ruardean Hill **131** F1
Ruardean Woodside **131** F1
Rubane **283** K2
Rubery **158** B5
Ruckcroft **210** B3
Ruckinge **124** C5
Ruckland **188** D5
Rucklers Lane **135** F2
Ruckley **157** E2
Rudbaxton **140** C5
Rudby **203** D2
Rudchester **212** A1
Ruddington **173** G4
Ruddlemoor **97** E4
Rudford **145** G5
Rudge **117** F2
Rudgeway **131** F4
Rudgwick **121** F4
Rudhall **145** F5
Rudheath **184** A5
Rudley Green **138** B2
Rudloe **117** F1
Rudry **130** A4
Rudston **196** C1
Rudyard **172** B2
Rudyard Lake *Staffs*
ST13 8RT **171** G2
Rufford **183** F1
Rufford Country Park *Notts*
NG22 9DF **174** B1
Rufforth **195** E2
Ruffside **211** F4
Rugby **160** A5
Rugby Football Union,
Twickenham *GtLon*
TW1 1DZ **11** B6
Rugeley **158** C1
Ruilick **266** C7
Ruishton **115** F5
Ruisigearraidh **262** E3
Ruislip **135** F4
Ruislip Gardens **135** F4
Ruislip Manor **136** A4
Rum **255** J5
Rumbling Bridge **243** F5
Rumburgh **165** E3
Rumford **96** C2
Rumleigh **100** A1
Rumney **130** B5
Rumwell **115** E5
Runacraig **242** A3
Runcorn **183** G4
Runcton **108** A3
Runcton Holme **163** E2
Rundlestone **99** F3
Runfold **121** D3
Runhall **178** B5
Runham *Norf* **179** F4
Runham *Norf* **179** G5
Runnington **115** E5
Runsell Green **137** G2
Runshaw Moor **183** G1
Runswick Bay **204** B1
Runtaleave **252** A3

Runway Visitor Park
GtMan M90 1QX **25** E6
Runwell **137** G3
Ruscombe *Glos* **132** A2
Ruscombe *W'ham* **134** C5
Rush Green
GtLon **137** E4
Rush Green
Herts **150** A5
Rushall *Here* **145** F4
Rushall *Norf* **164** C3
Rushall *Wilts* **118** C2
Rushall *WMid* **158** C2
Rushbrooke **151** G1
Rushbury **157** E3
Rushden *Herts* **150** B4
Rushden *NN'hants* **149** E1
Rushford *Devon* **99** E3
Rushford *Norf* **164** A3
Rushgreen **184** A4
Rushlake Green **110** B2
Rushmere **165** F3
Rushmere
St. Andrew **152** D3
Rushmoor **121** D3
Rushock **158** A5
Rusholme **184** C3
Rushton *ChesW&C*
170 C1
Rushton *NN'hants* **160** D4
Rushton *Shrop* **157** F2
Rushton Spencer **171** G1
Rushwick **146** A2
Rushy Green **109** G2
Rushyford **212** B5
Ruskie **242** B4
Ruskington **175** F2
Rusko **215** G5
Rusland **199** E4
Rusper **122** B5
Ruspidge **131** F1
Russ Hill **122** B4
Russel **264** E7
Russell Green **137** G1
Russell's Green **110** C2
Russell's Water **134** C3
Russel's Green **165** D4
Rusthall **123** E5
Rustington **108** C3
Ruston **204** C4
Ruston Parva **196** C1
Ruswarp **204** B2
Rutherend **234** A4
Rutherford **228** A3
Rutherglen **234** A3
Ruthernbridge **97** E3
Ruthers of Howe **275** J2
Ruthin (Rhuthun)
Denb **169** D2
Ruthin *VGlam* **129** F5
Ruthrieston **261** H4
Ruthven *Aber* **268** D6
Ruthven *Angus* **252** A5
Ruthven *High* **259** F1
Ruthven *High* **258** E5
Ruthvoes **96** D3
Ruthwaite **209** F3
Ruthwell **217** E4
Rutland Water *Rut*
LE15 8QL **161** D2
Ruyton-XI-Towns **170** A5
Ryal **220** C4
Ryal Fold **192** C5
Ryall *Dorset* **104** A3
Ryall *Worcs* **146** A3
Ryarsh **123** F3
Rydal **199** E2
Ryde **107** E3
Rydon **112** D5
Rye **111** E1
Rye Foreign **111** D1
Rye Harbour **111** E2
Rye Park **136** C2
Rye Street **145** G4
Ryebank **170** C4
Ryeford **145** F5
Ryehill *Aber* **260** E2
Ryehill *ERid* **197** E5
Ryhall **161** F1
Ryhill **186** A1
Ryhope **212** D2
Rylands **173** G4
Rylstone **193** F2
Ryme Intrinseca **104** B1
Ryther **195** E4
Ryton *Glos* **145** G4
Ryton *NYorks* **203** G5
Ryton *Shrop* **157** G2
Ryton *T&W* **212** A1
Ryton-on-
Dunsmore **159** F5

S

S.S. Great Britain *Bristol*
BS1 6TY **8** B3
Saasaig **256** C4
Sabden **193** D4
Sabden Fold **193** E4
Sackers Green **152** A4
Sacombe **136** C1
Sacombe Green **136** C1
Sacriston **212** B2
Sadberge **202** C1
Saddell **222** C2
Saddington **160** B3
Saddle Bole **163** E1
Sadgill **199** F2
Safari Zoo *Cumb*
LA15 8JR **198** D5
Saffron Walden **150** D4
Sageston **127** D2
Saham Hills **178** A5
Saham Toney **163** G2
Saighdinis **262** D5
Saighton **170** B1
St. Abbs **237** G3
St. Agnes **96** B4
St. Agnes Mining District
(Cornwall & West Devon
Mining Landscape) *Corn*
95 E1
St. Aidan's Winery *N'umb*
TD15 2RX **229** F2
St. Albans **136** A2
St. Albans Cathedral *Herts*
AL1 1BY **136** A2

St. Allen **96** C4
St. Andrews **244** D3
St Andrew's & Blackfriars
Halls *Norf* NR3 1AU
79 Norwich
St. Andrews Major **130** A5
St. Anne **101** G4
St. Anne's **191** G5
St. Ann's **217** E1
St. Ann's Chapel
Corn **99** E3
St. Ann's Chapel
Devon **100** C3
St. Anthony **95** F3
St. Anthony's Hill **110** B3
St. Anthony-in-
Meneage **95** E4
St. Arvans **131** E3
St. Asaph
(Llanelwy) **182** B5
St. Athan **114** D1
St. Aubin **100** C5
St. Audries **115** E3
St. Austell **96** C4
St. Bees **208** C5
St. Blazey **97** E4
St. Blazey Gate **97** E4
St. Boswells **227** G2
St. Botolph's Church,
Boston *Lincs* PE21 6NP
176 B3
St. Brelade **100** B5
St. Breock **97** D2
St. Breward **97** D1
St. Briavels **131** E1
St. Brides **126** B1
St. Brides Major **129** E5
St. Bride's
Netherwent **130** D4
St. Brides
Wentlooge **130** B4
St. Bride's-super-
Ely **129** G5
St. Budeaux **100** A2
St. Buryan **94** B4
St. Catherine **117** E1
St. Catherines **240** C4
St. Clears (Sanclêr) **127** F1
St. Cleer **97** G3
St. Clement *Chanl* **100** C5
St. Clement *Corn* **96** C5
St. Clether **97** G1
St. Colmac **232** B3
St. Columb Major **96** D3
St. Columb Minor **96** C3
St. Columb Road **96** D4
St. Combs **269** J4
St. Cross South
Elmham **165** D3
St. Cyrus **253** F3
St. Davids *Fife* **235** F1
St. David's *P&K* **243** E2
St. David's (Tyddewi)
Pembs **140** A5
St. David's Hall CF10 1AH
67 Cardiff
St. Day **96** B5
St. Decumans **115** D3
St. Dennis **97** D4
St. Denys **106** D1
St. Dogmaels
(Llandudoch) **141** E3
St. Dogwells **140** C5
St. Dominick **100** A1
St. Donats **114** C1
St. Edith's Marsh **118** A1
St. Endellion **97** D2
St. Enoder **96** C4
St. Erme **96** C5
St. Erney **99** D5
St. Erth **94** C3
St. Erth Praze **94** C3
St. Ervan **96** C2
St. Eval **96** C3
St. Ewe **97** D5
St. Fagans **130** A5
St. Fagans National Museum
of History *Cardiff*
CF5 6XB **7** A4
St. Fergus **269** J5
St. Fillans **242** B2
St. Florence **127** D2
St. Gennys **98** B1
St. George *Bristol* **131** F5
St. George *Conwy* **182** A5
St. Georges *NSom* **116** A1
St. George's *Tel&W* **157** G1
St. George's *VGlam* **129** G5
St. George's Hall, Liverpool
Mersey L1 1JJ **42** D3
St. Germans **99** D5
St. Giles' Cathedral,
Edinburgh *Edin*
EH1 1RE **37** F4
St. Giles in the
Wood **113** F4
St. Giles on the
Heath **99** D1
St. Harmon **155** F4
St. Helen Auckland **212** A4
St. Helena **178** C4
St. Helen's *ESuss* **110** D2
St. Helens *IoW* **107** F4
St. Helens *Mersey* **183** G3
St. Helier *Chanl* **100** C5
St. Helier *GtLon* **122** B2
St. Hilary *Corn* **94** C3
St. Hilary *VGlam* **129** G5
St. Hill **122** C5
St. Ibbs **149** G5
St. Illtyd **130** B2
St. Ippollitts **149** G5
St. Ishmael **127** G2
St. Ishmael's **126** B2
St. Issey **96** D2
St. Ive **99** D5
St. Ives *Cambs* **162** B5
St. Ives *Corn* **94** C2
St. Ives *Dorset* **106** A2
St. James South
Elmham **165** D4
St. John *Chanl* **100** C4
St. John *Corn* **100** A2

St. John the Baptist Church,
Cirencester *Glos*
GL7 2NX **132** C2
St. John *GtLon* **136** C5
St. John's *IoM* **190** A3
St. John's *Surr* **121** E2
St. John's *Worcs* **146** A2
St. John's Chapel
Devon **113** F3
St. John's Chapel
Dur **211** E4
St. John's Fen End **162** D1
St. John's Hall **211** G4
St. John's Highway **162** D1
St. John's Kirk **226** A2
St. John's Town of
Dalry **216** A2
St. Judes **190** B2
St. Just **94** A3
St. Just in Roseland **95** F3
St. Just Mining District
(Cornwall & West Devon
Mining Landscape)
Corn **94** A3
St. Katherines **261** F1
St. Keverne **95** E4
St. Kew **97** E2
St. Kew Highway **97** E2
St. Keyne **97** G3
St. Lawrence *Corn* **97** E3
St. Lawrence *Essex* **138** C2
St. Lawrence *IoW* **107** E5
St. Lawrence's Church,
Eyam *Derbys*
S32 5QH **185** G5
St. Leonards *Bucks* **135** E2
St. Leonards
Dorset **106** A2
St. Leonards
ESuss **110** D3
St. Leonards
Grange **106** D3
St. Leonard's
Street **123** F3
St. Levan **94** A4
St. Lythans **130** A4
St. Madoes **243** G2
St. Margaret South
Elmham **165** E3
St. Margarets *Here* **144** C4
St. Margarets *Herts* **136** C1
St. Margarets *Wilts* **118** D1
St. Margaret's at
Cliffe **125** F4
St Margaret's Church
(Palace of Westminster &
Westminster Abbey inc.
St Margaret's Church)
GtLon SW1P 3JX **44** D6
St. Margaret's Hope **277** D8
St. Mark's **190** A4
St. Martin *Chanl* **101** F5
St. Martin *Chanl* **100** C5
St. Martin *Corn* **97** G4
St. Martin *Corn* **95** E4
St. Martin-in-the-Fields
Church *GtLon*
WC2N 4JH **44** E4
St. Martin's *IoS* **96** B1
St. Martins *P&K* **243** G1
St. Martin's *Shrop* **170** A4
St Martin's Church
(Canterbury Cathedral,
St Augustine's Abbey,
& St Martin's Church)
Kent CT1 1PW **125** D3
St. Mary **100** C5
St. Mary Bourne **119** F2
St. Mary Church **129** G5
St. Mary Cray **123** D2
St. Mary Hill **129** F5
St. Mary Hoo **137** G5
St. Mary in the
Marsh **111** F1
St. Mary Magdalene Chapel,
Sandringham *Norf*
PE35 6EH **177** E5
St. Mary the Virgin Church,
Holy Island *N'umb*
TD15 2RX **229** F2
St. Mary the Virgin Church,
Oxford *Oxon*
OX1 4AH **134** A2
St. Mary the Virgin Church,
Rye *ESuss*
TN31 7HE **111** E2
St. Marychurch **101** F1
St. Mary's *IoS* **96** B1
St. Mary's *Ork* **277** D7
St. Mary's Airport **96** B1
St. Mary's Bay **111** F1
St. Mary's Church, Whitby
NYorks
YO22 4JT **204** C1
St. Mary's Grove **116** B1
St. Maughans
Green **131** D1
St. Mawes **95** F3
St. Mawgan **96** C3
St. Mellion **99** D4
St. Mellons **130** B5
St. Merryn **96** C2
St. Mewan **97** D4
St. Michael
Caerhays **97** D5
St. Michael Church **116** A4
St. Michael Penkevil **96** C5
St. Michael South
Elmham **165** E4
St. Michaels *Fife* **244** C2
St. Michaels *IoW* **190** B2
St. Michaels *Worcs* **145** E1
St. Michael's Church,
Hathersage *Derbys*
S32 1AJ **185** G4
St. Michael's Mount *Corn*
TR17 0HT **94** C4
St. Michael's on
Wyre **192** A3
St. Mildred's Church,
Whippingham *IoW*
PO32 6LP **107** E3
St. Minver **97** D2
St. Monans **244** D4
St. Mungo Museum of
Religious Life & Art
Glas G4 0RH **39** H3

St. Mungo's Cathedral,
Glasgow *Glas*
G4 0QZ **39** J3
St. Neot **97** F3
St. Neots **149** G1
St. Newlyn East **96** C4
St. Nicholas *Pembs* **140** C4
St. Nicholas *VGlam* **129** G5
St. Nicholas at
Wade **125** E2
St. Ninians **242** C5
St. Osyth **138** D1
St. Ouen **100** B5
St. Owen's Cross **145** E5
St. Paul's Cathedral,
London *GtLon*
EC4M 8AD **45** J3
St. Paul's Cray **123** D2
St. Paul's Walden **149** G5
St. Peter **100** C5
St. Peter Port **101** F5
St. Peter's **125** F5
St. Petrox **126** C3
St. Pinnock **97** G3
St. Quivox **224** B3
St. Ruan **95** E5
St. Sampson **101** F4
St. Saviour *Chanl* **101** E5
St. Saviour *Chanl* **100** C5
St. Stephen **96** D4
St. Stephens *Corn* **100** A2
St. Stephens *Corn* **98** D2
St. Stephens *Herts* **136** A2
St. Teath **97** E1
St. Thomas **102** C3
St. Tudy **97** E2
St. Twynnells **126** C3
St. Veep **97** F4
St. Vigeans **253** E5
St. Wenn **97** D3
St. Weonards **145** D5
St. Winnow **97** F4
St. Winwaloe's Church,
Gunwalloe *Corn*
TR12 7QE **95** D4
Saintbury **146** D4
Saintfield **283** H3
Salachail **248** C4
Salcombe **100** D4
Salcombe Regis **103** E4
Salcott **138** C1
Sale **184** B3
Sale Green **146** B2
Saleby **189** E5
Salehurst **110** C1
Salem *Carmar* **142** C5
Salem *Cere* **154** C4
Salen *Gwyn* **167** G5
Salen *A&B* **247** E5
Salen *High* **247** F3
Salendine Nook **185** F1
Salesbury **192** C4
Saleway **146** B2
Salford *CenBeds* **149** E4
Salford *GtMan* **184** C3
Salford *Oxon* **147** E5
Salford Priors **146** C2
Salfords **122** B4
Salhouse **179** E4
Saligo **230** A3
Saline **243** F5
Salisbury **118** C5
Salisbury Cathedral
Wilts SP1 2EF
83 Salisbury
Salkeld Dykes **210** B5
Sallachan **248** B3
Sallachy *High* **266** C1
Sallachy *High* **257** F1
Salle **178** C3
Sally Lunn's House
B&NESom BA1 1NX
63 Bath
Salmonby **188** D5
Salmond's Muir **245** D1
Salperton **146** C5
Salph End **149** F2
Salsburgh **234** C3
Salt **171** G3
Salt Hill **135** E4
Salt Holme **213** D5
Saltaire **194** A4
Saltash **100** A2
Saltburn *High* **266** E4
Saltburn-by-the-
Sea **213** D5
Saltburn Cliff Lift
R&C TS12 1DP **213** F5
Saltby **175** D5
Saltcoats *Cumb* **198** B3
Saltcoats *NAyr* **232** D5
Saltcotes **191** G5
Saltdean **109** F3
Salterbeck **208** C4
Salterforth **193** E3
Saltergate **204** B3
Salterhill **267** K5
Salterswall **170** D1
Saltfleet **189** E3
Saltfleetby All
Saints **189** E3
Saltfleetby
St. Clements **189** E3
Saltfleetby
St. Peter **189** E4
Saltford **117** D1
Salthaugh Grange **197** E5
Salthouse **178** B1
Saltley **158** C4
Saltmarshe **195** G5
Saltness **277** B8
Saltney **170** A1
Salton **203** G4
Saltrens **113** E3
Salum **246** B2
Salwarpe **146** A1
Salwayash **104** A3
Sambourne **146** C1
Sambrook **171** E5
Samhla **262** C5
Samlesbury **192** C4

Sampford Arundel **103** E1
Sampford Brett **115** D3
Sampford
Courtenay **113** G5
Sampford Moor **103** E1
Sampford Peverell **102** D1
Sampford Spiney **99** F3
Samsonagh **280** D4
Samuelston **236** B2
Sanaigmore **230** A2
Sancreed **94** B4
Sancton **196** B4
Sand *Shet* **279** C8
Sand *Som* **116** B2
Sand Hutton **195** F2
Sandaig *A&B* **246** A2
Sandaig *High* **256** D3
Sandaig *High* **256** D3
Sandal Magna **186** A1
Sanday **276** E2
Sanday Airfield **276** E3
Sandbach **171** E1
Sandbank **232** C1
Sandbanks **105** G4
Sandend **268** D4
Sanderstead **122** C2
Sandford *Cumb* **200** C1
Sandford *Devon* **102** B2
Sandford *Dorset* **105** F4
Sandford *IoW* **107** E4
Sandford *NSom* **116** B2
Sandford *Shrop* **170** C4
Sandford *Shrop* **170** A5
Sandford *SLan* **234** B5
Sandford Orcas **116** D5
Sandford St. Martin **147** G5
Sandfordhill **269** K6
Sandford-on-
Thames **134** A2
Sandgarth **277** E6
Sandgate **125** D4
Sandgreen **215** G5
Sandhaven **269** H4
Sandhead **214** B5
Sandhills *Dorset* **104** C1
Sandhills *Dorset* **104** B2
Sandhills *Surr* **121** E4
Sandhills *WYorks* **194** C4
Sandhoe **211** F1
Sandholes **282** A1
Sandholme *ERid* **196** A4
Sandholme *Lincs* **176** B4
Sandhurst *BrackF* **120** D1
Sandhurst *Glos* **146** A5
Sandhurst *Kent* **110** C1
Sandhurst Cross **110** C1
Sandhutton **202** C4
Sandiacre **173** F4
Sandilands **189** F4
Sandiway **184** A5
Sandleheath **106** A1
Sandleigh **133** G2
Sandling **123** G3
Sandlow Green **171** E1
Sandness **279** A7
Sandon *Essex* **137** G2
Sandon *Herts* **150** B4
Sandon *Staffs* **171** G5
Sandown **107** F4
Sandplace **97** G4
Sandquoy **276** G3
Sandridge *Devon* **101** E2
Sandridge *Herts* **136** A1
Sandridge *Wilts* **118** A1
Sandringham **177** E5
Sandrocks **109** F1
Sandsend **204** B1
Sandside House **274** E2
Sandsound **279** C8
Sandtoft **187** E2
Sanduck **102** A4
Sandway **124** A3
Sandwell **158** C4
Sandwell Park Farm *WMid*
B71 4BG **14** D2
Sandwell Valley Country
Park *WMid*
B71 4BG **14** D2
Sandwich **125** F3
Sandwick *Cumb* **199** F1
Sandwick *Shet* **279** D10
Sandwick (Sanndabhaig)
Na H-E. Siar **271** G4
Sandwith **208** C5
Sandy *Carmar* **128** A2
Sandy *CenBeds* **149** G3
Sandy Bank **176** A2
Sandy Haven **126** B2
Sandy Lane *Wilts* **118** A1
Sandy Lane *Wrex* **170** B3
Sandy Lane
WYorks **194** A4
Sandy Way **107** D4
Sandycroft **170** A1
Sandygate *Devon* **102** B5
Sandygate *IoM* **190** B2
Sandyhills **216** C5
Sandylands **192** A1
Sandypark **102** A4
Sandyway **145** D5
Sangobeg **273** G2
Sankyn's Green **145** G1
Sanna **247** D3
Sannaig **230** D3
Sannox **232** B5
Sanquhar **225** F5
Santon Bridge **198** C2
Santon Downham **163** G4
Sapcote **159** G3
Sapey Common **145** G1
Sapiston **164** A4
Sapperton *Derbys* **172** C4
Sapperton *Glos* **132** B2
Sapperton *Lincs* **175** F4
Saracen's Head **176** B5
Sarclet **275** J4
Sardis **126** C2
Sarisbury **107** E2
Sark **101** G5
Sark Dark Sky Island **101** G5
Sarn *Bridgend* **129** F4
Sarn *Powys* **156** B3
Sarn Bach **166** C5
Sarn Mellteyrn **166** B4
Sarnau *Carmar* **127** G1
Sarnau *Cere* **141** G2

Sarnau *Gwyn* **168** A3
Sarnau *Powys* **156** B1
Sarnau *Powys* **143** G4
Sarnesfield **144** C2
Saron *Carmar* **128** C1
Saron *Carmar* **141** G4
Saron *Denb* **168** D2
Saron *Gwyn* **167** E1
Saron *Gwyn* **167** D2
Sarratt **135** F3
Sarre **125** E2
Sarsden **147** E5
Sarsgrum **273** F2
Sartfield **190** B2
Satley **212** A3
Satron **201** E3
Satterleigh **113** G3
Satterthwaite **199** E3
Sauchen **260** E3
Saucher **243** G1
Sauchie **243** D5
Sauchieburn **253** E3
Sauchrie **224** B4
Saughall **183** E5
Saughall Massie **183** D4
Saughtree **219** D2
Saul *Glos* **131** G2
Saul *NM&D* **283** J4
Saundby **187** E4
Saundersfoot **127** E2
Saunton **113** E2
Sausthorpe **176** B1
Saval **266** C1
Savalbeg **266** C1
Saverley Green **171** G4
Savile Town **194** B5
Sawbridge **148** A1
Sawbridgeworth **137** D1
Sawdon **204** C4
Sawley *Derbys* **173** F4
Sawley *Lancs* **193** D3
Sawley *NYorks* **194** B1
Sawston **150** C3
Sawtry **161** G4
Saxby *Leics* **160** D1
Saxby *Lincs* **188** A4
Saxby All Saints **187** G1
Saxelbye **174** B5
Saxham Street **152** B1
Saxilby **187** F5
Saxlingham **178** B2
Saxlingham Green **164** D2
Saxlingham
Nethergate **164** D2
Saxlingham
Thorpe **164** D2
Saxmundham **153** E1
Saxon Street **151** E2
Saxondale **174** B4
Saxtead **153** D1
Saxtead Green **153** D1
Saxtead Little
Green **153** D1
Saxthorpe **178** C2
Saxton **195** D4
Sayers Common **109** E2
Scackleton **203** F5
Scadabhagh **263** G2
Scaddy **283** H3
Scaftworth **187** D3
Scagglethorpe **204** B5
Scaitcliffe **193** D5
Scalasaig **238** C5
Scalby *ERid* **196** A5
Scalby *NYorks* **204** D3
Scaldwell **160** C5
Scale Houses **210** B3
Scaleby **210** A1
Scalebyhill **210** A1
Scales *Cumb* **209** G4
Scales *Cumb* **199** D5
Scalford **174** C5
Scaling **203** G1
Scaliscro **270** D5
Scallasaig **256** E3
Scallastle **239** G1
Scalloway **279** C9
Scalpay (Eilean
Scalpaigh) **263** H2
Scamblesby **188** C5
Scammadale **240** A2
Scamodale **248** A2
Scampston **204** B5
Scampton **187** G5
Scaniport **258** D1
Scapa **277** D7
Scapegoat Hill **185** E1
Scar **276** F3
Scarborough **204** D4
Scarborough Sea Life &
Marine Sanctuary
NYorks
YO12 6RP **204** D3
Scarcewater **96** D4
Scarcliffe **173** F1
Scarcroft **194** C3
Scardroy **265** J6
Scarff **278** B4
Scarfskerry **275** H1
Scargill **201** F1
Scarinish **246** B2
Scarisbrick **183** E1
Scarista **263** F2
Scarning **178** A4
Scarrington **174** C3
Scarrowhill **210** B2
Scarth Hill **183** F2
Scarthingwell **195** D4
Scartho **188** C2
Scarva **282** D4
Scarwell **276** B5
Scatraig **258** E1
Schaw **224** C3
Scholar Green **171** F2
Scholes *SYorks* **186** A3
Scholes *WYorks* **194** C4
Scholes *WYorks* **185** F2
Scholes *WYorks* **194** A5
School Green **170** D1

School House 103 G2
Schoose 208 D4
Sciberscross 266 E1
Science Museum GtLon SW7 2DD 11 F5
Scilly Isles (Isles of Scilly) 96 B1
Scissett 185 G1
Scleddau 140 C4
Sco Ruston 179 D3
Scofton 186 D4
Scolboa 287 F6
Scole 164 C4
Scollogstown 283 H5
Scolpaig 262 C4
Scone 243 G2
Scones Lethendy 243 G2
Sconser 256 B1
Scoor 238 D3
Scopwick 175 F2
Scoraig 265 G2
Scorborough 196 C3
Scorrier 96 B5
Scorriton 100 D1
Scorton Lancs 192 B3
Scorton NYorks 202 B2
Scot Hay 171 E3
Scotby 210 A2
Scotch Corner 202 B2
Scotch Street 282 C3
Scotch Town 285 H7
Scotch Whisky Heritage Centre Edin EH1 2NE 37 F4
Scotforth 192 A2
Scothern 188 A5
Scotland 175 F4
Scotland End 147 F4
Scotland Street 152 A4
Scotland Street School Museum of Education Glas G5 8QB 38 C6
Scotlandwell 243 G4
Scotnish 231 F1
Scots' Gap 220 C3
Scotsburn 266 E4
Scotston Aber 253 F2
Scotston P&K 251 E5
Scotstoun 233 G3
Scotstown 248 A3
Scott Willoughby 175 F4
Scotter 187 F2
Scotterthorpe 187 F2
Scottish Exhibition & Conference Centre (S.E.C.C.) Glas G3 8YW 38 B4
Scottish National Gallery of Modern Art (Modern One) Edin EH4 3DR 36 B4
Scottish National Gallery of Modern Art (Modern Two) Edin EH4 3DS 36 B4
Scottish National Portrait Gallery Edin EH2 1JD 37 F3
Scottish Parliament Edin EH99 1SP 37 H4
Scottish Seabird Centre, North Berwick ELoth EH39 4SS 236 C1
Scottish Wool Centre, Aberfoyle Stir FK8 3UQ 242 A4
Scottlethorpe 175 F5
Scotton Lincs 187 F3
Scotton NYorks 202 A3
Scotton NYorks 194 C2
Scottow 179 D3
Scoughall 236 D1
Scoulton 178 A5
Scounslow Green 172 B5
Scourie 272 D4
Scourie More 272 D4
Scousburgh 279 F9
Scouthead 185 D2
Scrabster 275 G1
Scrafield 176 B1
Scraghy 280 E1
Scrainwood 220 B1
Scralea 280 E1
Scrane End 176 B3
Scraptoft 160 B2
Scratby 179 G4
Scrayingham 195 G2
Scredington 175 F3
Scremby 176 C1
Scremerston 229 E2
Screveton 174 C3
Scribbagh 280 B4
Scriven 194 C2
Scronkey 192 A3
Scrooby 187 D3
Scropton 172 C4
Scrub Hill 176 A2
Scruton 202 C3
Sculthorpe 177 G4
Scunthorpe 187 F1
Scurlage 128 A4
Sea 103 G1
Sea Life Centre, Blackpool FY1 5AA 64 Blackpool
Sea Life Centre, Brighton B&H BN2 1TB 65 Brighton
Sea Life Centre, Great Yarmouth Norf NR30 3AH 179 G5
Sea Life London Aquarium GtLon SE1 7PD 45 F5
Sea Life Sanctuary, Hunstanton Norf PE36 5BH 177 E3
Sea Mills 131 E5
Sea Palling 179 F3
Seabank 248 B5
Seaborough 104 A2
Seaburn 212 D1
Seacombe 183 E3
Seacroft Lincs 177 D1
Seacroft WYorks 194 C4
Seadyke 176 B4
Seafield A&B 231 F1
Seafield NM&D 283 F7
Seafield SAyr 224 B3
Seafield WLoth 235 E3
Seaford 109 G4
Seaforde 283 H4
Seaforth 183 E3
Seagrave 160 B1
Seagry Heath 132 B4
Seaham 212 D3
Seaham Grange 212 D2
Seahouses 229 G3
Seal 123 E3
Sealand 170 A1
Seale 121 D3
Sea-Life Adventure, Southend-on-Sea S'end SS1 2ER 138 B4
Sealyham 140 C5
Seamer NYorks 203 D1
Seamer NYorks 204 D4
Seamill 232 C5
Seapatrick 282 E4
SeaQuarium, Rhyl Denb LL18 3AF 182 B4
Searby 188 A2
Seasalter 124 C2
Seascale 198 B2
Seathorne 177 D1
Seathwaite Cumb 209 F5
Seathwaite Cumb 198 D3
Seatle 199 E4
Seatoller 209 F5
Seaton Corn 98 D5
Seaton Cumb 208 D3
Seaton Devon 103 F3
Seaton Dur 212 C2
Seaton ERid 197 D3
Seaton N'umb 221 F4
Seaton Rut 161 E3
Seaton Burn 221 E4
Seaton Carew 213 E5
Seaton Delaval 221 F4
Seaton Junction 103 F3
Seaton Ross 195 G3
Seaton Sluice 221 F4
Seaton Tramway Devon EX12 2NQ 103 F3
Seatown Aber 269 J5
Seatown Dorset 104 A3
Seatown Moray 268 D4
Seave Green 203 E2
Seaview 107 F3
Seaville 209 E1
Seavington St. Mary 104 A1
Seavington St. Michael 104 A1
Seawick 139 E1
Sebastopol 130 B3
Sebergham 209 G2
Seckington 159 E2
Second Coast 265 F2
Sedbergh 200 B3
Sedbury 131 E3
Sedbusk 201 D3
Seddington 149 G3
Sedgeberrow 146 C4
Sedgebrook 175 D4
Sedgefield 212 C5
Sedgeford 177 F4
Sedgehill 117 F5
Sedgemere 159 E5
Sedgley 158 B3
Sedgwick 199 G4
Sedlescombe 110 C2
Sedlescombe Street 110 C2
Seend 118 A1
Seend Cleeve 118 A1
Seer Green 135 E3
Seething 165 E2
Sefton 183 E2
Seghill 221 E4
Seifton 157 D4
Seighford 171 F5
Seil 239 G3
Seilebost 263 F2
Seion 167 E1
Seisdon 158 A3
Seisiadar 271 H4
Seized! Revenue & Customs Uncovered Mersey L3 4AQ 42 B5
Selattyn 169 F4
Selborne 120 C4
Selby 195 F4
Selham 121 E5
Selhurst 122 C2
Selkirk 227 F3
Sellack 145 E5
Sellafield 198 B2
Sellafirth 278 E3
Sellindge 124 D5
Selling 124 C3
Sells Green 118 A1
Selly Oak 158 C4
Selmeston 110 A3
Selsdon 122 C2
Selsey 108 A4
Selsfield Common 122 C5
Selside Cumb 199 G3
Selside NYorks 200 C5
Selsley 132 A2
Selstead 125 E4
Selston 173 F2
Selworthy 114 C3
Semblister 279 C7
Semer 152 A3
Semington 117 F1
Semley 117 F5
Send 121 F2
Send Marsh 121 F2
Seneirl 286 E2
Senghenydd 130 A3
Sennen 94 A4
Sennen Cove 94 A4
Sennybridge 143 F5
Senwick 207 G2
Sequer's Bridge 100 C2
Serlby 186 D4
Serpentine Gallery GtLon W2 3XA 11 F5
Serrington 118 B4
Seskinore 281 G2
Sessay 203 D5
Setchey 163 E1
Setley 106 C2
Setter Shet 279 E8
Setter Shet 279 C7
Settiscarth 277 C6
Settle 193 E1
Settrington 204 B5
Seven Ash 115 E4
Seven Bridges 132 D3
Seven Kings 137 D4
Seven Sisters 129 E2
Seven Springs 132 B1
Sevenhampton Glos 146 C5
Sevenhampton Swin 133 E3
Sevenoaks 123 E3
Sevenoaks Weald 123 E3
Severn Beach 131 E4
Severn Stoke 146 A3
Severn Valley Railway Shrop DY12 1BG 157 G4
Sevick End 149 F2
Sevington 124 C4
Sewards End 151 D4
Sewardstone 136 C3
Sewerby 197 D1
Sewerby Hall & Gardens ERid YO15 1EA 197 E1
Seworgan 95 E3
Sewstern 175 D5
Seymour Villas 113 E1
Sezincote 147 D4
Sgiogarstaigh (Skigersta) 271 H1
Sgodachail 266 B2
Shabbington 134 B2
Shackerley 158 A2
Shackerstone 159 F2
Shackleford 121 E3
Shadfen 221 E3
Shadforth 212 C3
Shadingfield 165 F3
Shadoxhurst 124 B5
Shadsworth 192 D5
Shadwell Norf 164 A3
Shadwell WYorks 194 C3
Shaftenhoe End 150 C4
Shaftesbury 117 F5
Shafton 186 A1
Shakespeare's Birthplace Warks CV37 6QW 85 Stratford-upon-Avon
Shakespeare's Globe Theatre GtLon SE1 9DT 45 J4
Shalbourne 119 E1
Shalcombe 106 C4
Shalden 120 B3
Shalden Green 120 C3
Shaldon 102 C5
Shalfleet 106 D4
Shalford Essex 151 F5
Shalford Surr 121 F3
Shalford Green 151 F5
Shallowford Devon 114 A3
Shallowford Staffs 171 F5
Shalmsford Street 124 C3
Shalmstry 275 G2
Shalstone 148 B4
Shalunt 232 B2
Shambellie 217 D4
Shamley Green 121 F3
Shanaghy 281 F6
Shandon 233 D1
Shandwick 267 F4
Shangton 160 C3
Shankend 227 G5
Shankhouse 221 E4
Shankill 282 E5
Shanklin 107 E4
Shanklin Chine IoW PO37 6BW 107 E4
Shannochie 223 E3
Shantron 233 E1
Shantullich 266 D6
Shanzie 252 A4
Shap 199 G1
Shapinsay 277 E6
Shapwick Dorset 105 F2
Shapwick Som 116 B4
Sharcott 118 C2
Shard End 159 D4
Shardlow 173 F4
Shareshill 158 B2
Sharlston 186 A1
Sharlston Common 186 A1
Sharnal Street 137 G5
Sharnbrook 149 E2
Sharneyford 193 E5
Sharnford 159 G3
Sharnhill Green 104 D2
Sharow 202 C5
Sharp Street 179 E3
Sharpenhoe 149 F4
Sharperton 220 B1
Sharpham House 101 E2
Sharpness 131 F2
Sharpthorne 122 C5
Sharrington 178 B2
Sharvogues 287 F6
Shatterford 157 G4
Shatterling 125 E3
Shaugh Prior 100 B1
Shave Cross 104 A3
Shavington 171 E2
Shaw GtMan 184 D2
Shaw Swin 132 D4
Shaw WBerks 119 F1
Shaw Wilts 117 F1
Shaw Green Herts 150 A4
Shaw Green NYorks 194 B2
Shaw Mills 194 B1
Shaw Side 184 D2
Shawbost (Siabost) 270 E3
Shawbury 170 C5
Shawell 160 A4
Shawfield GtMan 184 C1
Shawfield Staffs 172 B1
Shawford 119 F5
Shawforth 193 E5
Shawhead 216 C3
Shawtonhill 234 A5
Shean 282 D7
Sheanachie 222 C4
Sheandow 259 K1
Shearington 217 E4
Shearsby 160 B3
Shebbear 113 E5
Shebdon 171 E5
Shebster 275 F2
Shedfield 107 E1
Sheen 172 C1
Sheepridge 185 F1
Sheepscombe 132 A1
Sheepstor 100 B1
Sheepwash Devon 113 E5
Sheepwash N'umb 221 E3
Sheepway 131 D5
Sheepy Magna 159 F2
Sheepy Parva 159 F2
Sheering 137 E1
Sheerness 124 B1
Sheet 120 C5
Sheetrim AB&C 282 A5
Sheetrim F&O 280 E6
Sheffield 186 A4
Sheffield Botanic Gardens SYorks S10 2LN 21 B3
Sheffield Bottom 120 B1
Sheffield Green 109 G1
Sheffield Park Garden ESuss TN22 3QX 109 G1
Shefford 149 G4
Shefford Woodlands 133 F5
Sheigra 272 D2
Sheinton 157 F2
Shelderton 156 D5
Sheldon Derbys 172 C1
Sheldon Devon 103 E2
Sheldon WMid 158 D4
Sheldwich 124 C3
Sheldwich Lees 124 C3
Shelf Bridgend 129 F4
Shelf WYorks 194 A5
Shelfanger 164 C3
Shelfield Warks 146 D1
Shelfield WMid 158 C2
Shelfield Green 146 D1
Shelford 174 B3
Shellachan A&B 240 A2
Shellachan A&B 240 C2
Shellbrook 159 F1
Shellbrook Hill 170 A3
Shelley Essex 137 E2
Shelley Suff 152 B4
Shelley WYorks 185 G1
Shellingford 133 F3
Shellow Bowells 137 F2
Shelsley Beauchamp 145 G1
Shelsley Walsh 145 G1
Shelswell 148 B4
Shelthorpe 160 A1
Shelton Bed 149 F1
Shelton Norf 164 D2
Shelton Notts 174 C3
Shelton Shrop 157 D1
Shelve 156 C3
Shelwick 145 E3
Shelwick Green 145 E3
Shenfield 137 F3
Shenington 147 F3
Shenley 136 A2
Shenley Brook End 148 D4
Shenley Church End 148 D4
Shenleybury 136 A2
Shenmore 144 C4
Shennanton 215 E4
Shenstone Staffs 158 D2
Shenstone Worcs 158 A5
Shenstone Woodend 158 D2
Shenton 159 F2
Shenval 259 K2
Shepeau Stow 162 B1
Shephall 150 A5
Shepherd's Bush 136 B5
Shepherd's Green 134 C4
Shepherd's Patch 131 G2
Shepherdswell (Sibertswold) 125 E4
Shepley 185 F2
Sheppardstown 275 H5
Shepperdine 131 F3
Shepperton 121 F1
Shepreth 150 B3
Shepreth Wildlife Park Cambs SG8 6PZ 150 B3
Shepshed 159 G1
Shepton Beauchamp 104 A1
Shepton Mallet 116 D3
Shepton Montague 117 D4
Shepway 123 G3
Sheraton 212 D4
Sherborne Dorset 104 C1
Sherborne Glos 133 D1
Sherborne St. John 120 B2
Sherbourne 147 E1
Sherbourne Street 152 A3
Sherburn Dur 212 C3
Sherburn NYorks 204 C5
Sherburn Hill 212 C3
Sherburn in Elmet 195 D4
Shere 121 F3
Shereford 177 G5
Sherfield English 119 D5
Sherfield on oddon 120 B2
Sherford Devon 101 D3
Sherford Som 115 F5
Sheriff Hutton 195 F1
Sheriffhales 157 G1
Sheringham 178 C1
Sheringham Park Norf NR26 8TL 178 C1
Sherington 149 D3
Shernal Green 146 B1
Shernborne 177 F4
Sherramore 258 C5
Sherrington 118 A4
Sherston 132 A4
Sherwood 173 G3
Sherwood Forest Country Park Notts NG21 9HN 174 B1
Sherwood Forest Fun Park Notts NG21 9QA 174 B1
Sherwood Green 113 F3
Sherwood Pines Forest Park Notts NG21 9JL 174 B1
Shetland Islands 279 B7
Shevington 183 G2
Shevington Moor 183 G1
Sheviock 99 D5
Shide 107 E4
Shiel Bridge (Drochaid Sheile) 257 F3
Shieldaig High 264 E6
Shieldaig High 264 E4
Shieldhill 234 C2
Shielfoot 247 F2
Shielhill 252 C4
Shiels 260 E4
Shifford 133 F2
Shifnal 157 G2
Shilbottle 221 D1
Shildon 212 B5
Shillanavogy 287 G5
Shillingford Devon 114 C5
Shillingford Oxon 134 A3
Shillingford Abbot 102 C4
Shillingford St. George 102 C4
Shillingstone 105 E1
Shillington 149 G4
Shillmoor 220 A1
Shilstone 113 F5
Shilton Oxon 133 E2
Shilton Warks 159 G4
Shimpling Norf 164 C3
Shimpling Suff 151 G2
Shimpling Street 151 G2
Shincliffe 212 B3
Shiney Row 212 C2
Shinfield 120 C1
Shingay 150 B3
Shingham 163 F2
Shingle Street 153 E3
Shinn 282 E5
Shinness Lodge 273 H7
Shipbourne 123 E3
Shipbrookhill 184 A5
Shipdham 178 A5
Shipham 116 B2
Shiphay 101 E1
Shiplake 134 C5
Shiplake Row 134 C5
Shipley N'umb 229 F5
Shipley Shrop 158 A3
Shipley WSuss 121 G5
Shipley WYorks 194 A4
Shipley Bridge Devon 100 C1
Shipley Bridge Surr 122 C4
Shipley Common 173 F3
Shipley Country Park Derbys DE75 7GX 18 D2
Shipmeadow 165 E2
Shippea Hill 163 E4
Shippon 133 G3
Shipston on Stour 147 E3
Shipton Glos 132 C1
Shipton NYorks 195 E2
Shipton Shrop 157 E3
Shipton Bellinger 118 D3
Shipton Gorge 104 A3
Shipton Green 108 A3
Shipton Moyne 132 A4
Shipton Oliffe 132 C1
Shipton Solers 132 C1
Shipton-on-Cherwell 133 G1
Shiptonthorpe 196 A3
Shipton-under-Wychwood 133 E1
Shira 241 D3
Shirburn 134 B3
Shirdley Hill 183 E1
Shire Hall Gallery, Stafford Staffs ST16 2LD 171 G5
Shire Oak 158 C2
Shirebrook 173 G1
Shirecliffe 186 A3
Shiregreen 186 A3
Shirehampton 131 E5
Shiremoor 221 F4
Shirenewton 131 D3
Shireoaks 186 C4
Shirl Heath 144 D2
Shirland 173 E2
Shirley Derbys 172 D3
Shirley GtLon 122 C2
Shirley Hants 106 A3
Shirley Soton 106 D1
Shirley WMid 158 D5
Shirley Heath 158 D5
Shirley Warren 106 C1
Shirleywich 171 G5
Shirrell Heath 107 E1
Shirwell 113 F2
Shirwell Cross 113 F2
Shiskine 223 E3
Shittlehope 211 G4
Shobdon 144 C1
Shobley 106 A2
Shobrooke 102 B2
Shocklach 170 B3
Shocklach Green 170 B3
Shoeburyness 138 C4
Sholden 125 F3
Sholing 107 D1
Shoot Hill 156 D1
Shooter's Hill 136 D5
Shop Corn 96 C2
Shop Corn 112 C4
Shop Corner 152 D4
Shopnoller 115 E4
Shoptown 287 G6
Shore 184 D1
Shoreditch 136 C4
Shoreham 123 E2
Shoreham-by-Sea 109 E3
Shoremill 266 E5
Shoresdean 237 G5
Shoreswood 237 G5
Shoreton 266 D5
Shorley 119 G5
Shorncote 132 C3
Shorne 137 F5
Shorne Ridgeway 137 F5
Short Cross 156 B2
Short Green 164 B3
Short Heath Derbys 159 F1
Short Heath WMid 158 C3
Shortacombe 99 F2
Shortbridge 109 G1
Shortfield Common 120 D3
Shortgate 109 G2
Shortgrove 150 D4
Shorthampton 147 F5
Shortlands 122 C2
Shortlanesend 96 C5
Shorton 101 E1
Shorwell 107 D4
Shoscombe 117 E2
Shotatton 170 A5
Shotesham 164 D2
Shotgate 137 G3
Shotley N'hants 161 E3
Shotley Suff 152 D4
Shotley Bridge 211 G2
Shotley Gate 152 D4
Shotleyfield 211 G2
Shottenden 124 C3
Shottermill 121 D4
Shottery 147 D2
Shotteswell 147 G3
Shottisham 153 E3
Shottle 173 E2
Shottlegate 173 E3
Shotton Dur 212 D4
Shotton Dur 212 C5
Shotton Flints 170 A1
Shotton N'umb 221 E4
Shotton Colliery 212 C3
Shotts 234 C3
Shotwick 183 E5
Shouldham 163 E2
Shouldham Thorpe 163 E2
Shoulton 146 A2
Shover's Green 123 F5
Shrawardine 156 C1
Shrawley 146 A1
Shreding Green 135 F4
Shrewley 147 E1
Shrewsbury 157 D1
Shrewton 118 B3
Shri Venkateswara (Balaji) Temple of the United Kingdom WMid B69 3DU 14 C3
Shrigley 283 J3
Shrine of Our Lady of Walsingham (Anglican) Norf NR22 6EF 178 A2
Shripney 108 B3
Shrivenham 133 E4
Shropham 164 A2
Shroton (Iwerne Courtney) 105 E1
Shrub End 152 A5
Shucknall 145 E3
Shudy Camps 151 E3
Shugborough Estate Staffs ST17 0XB 171 G5
Shurdington 132 B1
Shurlock Row 134 D5
Shurnock 146 C1
Shurrery 275 F3
Shurrery Lodge 275 F3
Shurton 115 F3
Shustoke 159 E3
Shut Heath 171 F5
Shute Devon 103 F3
Shute Devon 102 B2
Shutford 147 F3
Shuthonger 146 A4
Shutlanger 148 C3
Shutt Green 158 A2
Shuttington 159 E2
Shuttlewood 186 B5
Shuttleworth 184 B1
Siabost Bho Dheas 270 E3
Siabost Bho Thuath 270 E3
Siadar Iarach 271 F2
Siadar Uarach 271 F2
Sibbaldbie 217 F2
Sibbertoft 160 B4
Sibdon Carwood 156 D4
Sibertswold (Shepherdswell) 125 E4
Sibford Ferris 147 F4
Sibford Gower 147 F4
Sible Hedingham 151 F4
Sibley's Green 151 E5
Sibsey 176 B2
Sibson Cambs 161 F3
Sibson Leics 159 F2
Sibster 275 J3
Sibthorpe 174 C3
Sibton 153 E1
Sibton Green 165 E4
Sicklesmere 151 G1
Sicklinghall 194 C3
Sidbury Devon 103 E3
Sidbury Shrop 157 F4
Sidcot 116 B2
Sidcup 137 D5
Siddal 194 A5
Siddington ChesE 184 C5
Siddington Glos 132 C3
Sidemoor 158 B5
Sidestrand 179 D2
Sidford 103 E3
Sidlesham 108 A4
Sidley 110 C3
Sidlow 122 B4
Sidmouth 103 E4
Sigford 102 A5
Sigglesthorne 197 D3
Sigingstone 129 F5
Signet 133 E1
Silbury Hill (Stonehenge, Avebury & Associated Sites) Wilts SN8 1QH 118 C1
Silchester 120 B1
Sildinis 270 E6
Sileby 160 B1
Silecroft 198 C4
Silent Valley NM&D BT33 0HU 283 G6
Silfield 164 C2
Silian 142 B2
Silk Willoughby 175 F3
Silkstead 119 F5
Silkstone 185 G2
Silkstone Common 185 G2
Sill Field 199 G4
Silloth 209 E1
Sills 220 A1
Sillyearn 268 D5
Silpho 204 C3
Silsden 193 G3
Silsoe 149 F4
Silver End CenBeds 149 G3
Silver End Essex 151 G5
Silver Green 165 D2
Silver Hill 280 E4
Silver Street Kent 124 A2
Silver Street Som 116 C4
Silverbridge 282 C7
Silverbrook 285 G5
Silverburn 235 G3
Silvercraigs 231 G1
Silverdale Lancs 199 F5
Silverdale Staffs 171 F3
Silvergate 178 C3
Silverhill 110 C2
Silverlace Green 153 E2
Silverley's Green 165 D4
Silvermoss 261 G1
Silverstone 148 B3
Silverton 102 C2
Silvington 157 F5
Silwick 279 B8
Simister 184 C2
Simmondley 185 E3
Simonburn 220 A4
Simonsbath 114 A4
Simonside 212 C1
Simonstone Bridgend 129 F4
Simonstone Lancs 193 D4
Simprim 237 F5
Simpson 149 D4
Sinclair's Hill 237 F4
Sinclairston 224 C4
Sinderby 202 C4
Sinderhope 211 E2
Sindlesham 120 C1
Sinfin 173 E4
Singdean 227 G5
Singleton Lancs 191 G4
Singleton WSuss 108 A2
Singlewell 137 F5
Singret 170 A2
Sinkhurst Green 124 A4
Sinnahard 260 C3
Sinnington 203 G4
Sion Mills 285 F6
Sinton Green 146 A1
Sipson 135 F5
Sirhowy 130 A1
Sirhowy Valley Country Park Caerp NP11 7BD 130 A3
Sisland 165 E2
Sissinghurst 123 G5
Sissinghurst Castle Garden Kent TN17 2AB 124 A5
Siston 131 F5
Sithney 94 D4
Sittingbourne 124 B2
Six Ashes 157 G4
Six Hills 174 B5
Six Mile Bottom 151 D2
Six Road Ends 283 J1
Six Roads End 172 C5
Sixhills 188 B4
Sixmile 124 D4
Sixmilecross 281 H2
Sixpenny Handley 105 G1
Sizewell 153 F1
Skail 274 C4
Skaill Ork 277 B6
Skaill Ork 277 E7
Skaill Ork 276 D4
Skara Brae (Heart of Neolithic Orkney) Ork KW16 3LR 277 B6
Skares Aber 260 E1
Skares EAyr 224 D4
Skarpigarth 279 A7
Skateraw 237 E2
Skaw 279 E6
Skeabost 263 K7
Skeabrae 276 B5
Skeeby 202 B2
Skeffington 160 C2
Skeffling 189 D1
Skegby 173 G1
Skegness 177 D1
Skegness Water Leisure Park Lincs PE25 1JF 177 D1
Skelberry Shet 279 F9
Skelberry Shet 279 D6
Skelbo 266 E2
Skelbo Street 266 E2
Skelbrooke 186 C1
Skeld (Easter Skeld) 279 C8
Skeldon 224 B4
Skeldyke 176 B4
Skellingthorpe 187 G5
Skellister 279 D7
Skellow 186 C1
Skelmanthorpe 185 G1
Skelmersdale 183 F2
Skelmonae 261 G1
Skelmorlie 232 C3
Skelmuir 269 H6
Skelpick 274 C3
Skelton Cumb 210 A4
Skelton ERid 195 G5
Skelton NYorks 201 F2
Skelton (Skelton-in-Cleveland) R&C 203 F1
Skelton York 195 E2
Skelton-in-Cleveland (Skelton) 203 F1
Skelton-on-Ure 194 C1
Skelwick 276 D3
Skelwith Bridge 199 E2
Skendleby 176 C1
Skendleby Psalter 189 E5
Skenfrith 145 D5
Skerne 196 C2
Skeroblingarry 222 C3
Skerray 273 J2
Skerries 282 A5
Skerton 192 A1
Sketchley 159 G3
Sketty 128 C3
Skewen 128 D3
Skewsby 203 F5
Skeyton 178 D3
Skeyton Corner 179 D3
Skidbrooke 189 E3
Skidbrooke North End 189 E3
Skidby 196 C4
Skilgate 114 C5
Skillington 175 D5
Skinburness 209 E1
Skinflats 234 D1
Skinidin 263 H7
Skinnet 275 G2
Skinningrove 203 G1

Skipness **231** G4
Skippool **191** G3
Skipsea **197** D2
Skipsea Brough **197** D2
Skipton **193** F2
Skipton Castle *NYorks* BD23 1AW **193** F2
Skipton-on-Swale **202** C5
Skipwith **195** F4
Skirbeck **176** B3
Skirbeck Quarter **176** B3
Skirethorns **193** F1
Skirlaugh **196** D4
Skirling **226** B2
Skirmett **134** C4
Skirpenbeck **195** G2
Skirwith *Cumb* **210** C4
Skirwith *NYorks* **200** C5
Skirza **275** J2
Skittle Green **134** C2
Skomer Island **126** A2
Skulamus **256** C2
Skullomie **273** J2
Skyborry Green **156** B5
Skye **255** K1
Skye Green **151** G5
Skye of Curr **259** G2
Skyreholme **193** G1
Slack *Aber* **260** D1
Slack *Derbys* **173** E1
Slack *WYorks* **193** F5
Slackhall **185** E4
Slackhead **268** C4
Slad **132** A2
Slade *Devon* **113** F1
Slade *Devon* **103** E2
Slade *Pembs* **126** C1
Slade *Swan* **128** A4
Slade Green **137** E5
Slade Hooton **186** C4
Sladesbridge **97** E2
Slaggyford **210** C2
Slaghtneill **286** C5
Slaidburn **192** D2
Slains Park **253** G2
Slaithwaite **185** E1
Slaley **211** F2
Slamannan **234** C2
Slane **287** G4
Slapton *Bucks* **149** E5
Slapton *Devon* **101** E3
Slapton *WN'hants* **148** B3
Slate Haugh **268** C4
Slatepit Dale **173** E1
Slatmore **281** H4
Slattadale **264** E4
Slaugham **109** E1
Slaughden **153** F2
Slaughterford **132** A5
Slawston **160** C3
Sleaford *Hants* **120** D4
Sleaford *Lincs* **175** F3
Sleagill **199** G1
Sleap **170** B5
Sledge Green **146** A4
Sledmere **196** B1
Sleights **204** B2
Slepe **105** F3
Slerra **112** D3
Slickly **275** H2
Sliddery **223** E3
Sliemore **259** H2
Slievenisky **283** G4
Sligachan **255** K2
Slimbridge **131** G2
Slimbridge Wildfowl & Wetlands Trust *Glos* GL2 7BT **131** G2
Slindon *Staffs* **171** F4
Slindon *WSuss* **108** B3
Slinfold **121** G4
Sling **131** E2
Slingsby **203** F5
Slioch **260** D1
Slip End *CenBeds* **135** F1
Slip End *Herts* **150** A4
Slipper Chapel, Houghton St. Giles *Norf* NR22 6AL **178** A2
Slipton **161** E5
Slitting Mill **158** C1
Slochd **259** F2
Slockavullin **240** A5
Slogarie **216** A4
Sloley **179** D3
Slongaber **216** C3
Sloothby **189** E5
Slough **135** E4
Slough Green *Som* **115** F5
Slough Green *WSuss* **109** E1
Sluggan **259** F2
Slyne **192** A1
Smailholm **228** A3
Small Dole **109** E2
Small Hythe **124** A5
Smallbridge **184** D1
Smallbrook **102** B3
Smallburgh **179** E3
Smallburn *Aber* **269** J6
Smallburn *EAyr* **225** E3
Smalldale **185** E5
Smalley **173** F3
Smallfield **122** C4
Smallford **136** A2
Smallridge **103** F2
Smallthorne **171** F2
Smallworth **164** B3
Smannell **119** E3
Smardale **200** C2
Smarden **124** A4
Smaull **230** A3
Smeatharpe **103** E1
Smeeth **124** C5
Smeeton Westerby **160** B3
Smerclet **254** C3
Smerral **275** G5
Smestow **158** A3
Smethwick **158** C4
Smethwick Green **171** F1
Smirisary **247** F2
Smisby **159** F1
Smith End Green **145** G2
Smithfield **210** A1
Smithies **186** A2
Smithincott **103** D1
Smith's End **150** B4
Smith's Green *Essex* **151** D5
Smith's Green *Essex* **151** E3
Smithstown **264** D4
Smithton **266** E7
Smithy Green **184** B5
Smockington **159** G4
Smugglers Adventure *ESuss* TN34 3HY **75** Hastings
Smyrton **214** C2
Smythe's Green **138** C1
Snailbeach **156** C2
Snailwell **151** E1
Snainton **204** C4
Snaith **195** F5
Snape *NYorks* **202** B4
Snape *Suff* **153** E2
Snape Green **183** E1
Snape Watering **153** E2
Snarestone **159** F2
Snarford **188** A4
Snargate **111** E1
Snave **111** F1
Sneachill **146** B2
Snead **156** C3
Snead's Green **146** A1
Sneath Common **164** C3
Sneaton **204** B2
Sneatonthorpe **204** C2
Snelland **188** A4
Snellings **198** A2
Snelston **172** C3
Snetterton **164** A2
Snettisham **177** E4
Snipeshill **124** B2
Snishival (Sniseabhal) **254** C1
Snitter **220** C1
Snitterby **187** G3
Snitterfield **147** E2
Snitterton **173** D1
Snittlegarth **209** F3
Snitton **157** E5
Snodhill **144** C3
Snodland **123** G2
Snow End **150** C4
Snow Street **164** B3
Snowden Hill **185** G2
Snowdon Mountain Railway *Gwyn* LL55 4TY **167** E2
Snowshill **146** C4
Snowshill Manor & Gardens *Glos* WR12 7JU **146** C4
Soar *Cardiff* **129** G4
Soar *Carmar* **142** C5
Soar *Devon* **100** D4
Soay **255** K3
Soberton **107** F1
Soberton Heath **107** F1
Sockbridge **210** B5
Sockburn **202** C2
Sodom **182** B5
Sodylt Bank **170** A4
Softley **211** G5
Soham **163** D5
Soham Cotes **163** D5
Soldierstown **282** E2
Soldon **112** D4
Soldon Cross **112** D4
Soldridge **120** B4
Sole Street *Kent* **124** C4
Sole Street *Kent* **123** F2
Soleburn **214** B4
Solihull **159** D5
Solihull Lodge **158** C5
Sollas (Solas) **262** D4
Sollers Dilwyn **144** D2
Sollers Hope **145** F4
Sollom **183** F1
Solomon's Tump **131** G1
Solsgirth **243** E5
Solva **140** A5
Solwaybank **218** B4
Somerby *Leics* **160** C1
Somerby *Lincs* **188** A2
Somercotes **173** F2
Somerford **158** B2
Somerford Keynes **132** C3
Somerley **108** A4
Somerleyton **165** F2
Somersal Herbert **172** C4
Somersby **188** D5
Somerset House *GtLon* WC2R 1LA **45** F3
Somersham *Cambs* **162** B5
Somersham *Suff* **152** B3
Somerton *Newport* **130** C4
Somerton *Oxon* **147** G5
Somerton *Som* **116** B5
Somerton *Suff* **151** G2
Sompting **109** D3
Sompting Abbotts **109** D3
Sonning **134** C5
Sonning Common **134** C4
Sonning Eye **134** C5
Sontley **170** A3
Sookholme **173** G1
Sopley **106** A3
Sopworth **132** A4
Sorbie **207** E2
Sordale **275** G2
Sorisdale **246** B3
Sorn **225** D3
Sornhill **224** D2
Soroba **240** A2
Sortat **275** H2
Sotby **188** C5
Sots Hole **175** G1
Sotterley **165** F3
Soudley **171** E5
Soughton **169** F1
Soulbury **149** D5
Soulby **200** C1
Souldern **148** A4
Souldrop **149** E1
Sound *ChesE* **170** D3
Sound *Shet* **279** D8
Sound *Shet* **279** C7
Sourhope **228** C4
Sourin **276** D4
Sourton **99** F1
Soutergate **198** D4
South Acre **163** G1
South Acton **136** A5
South Alkham **125** E4
South Allington **101** D4
South Alloa **243** D5
South Ambersham **121** E5
South Anston **186** C4
South Ascot **121** E1
South Baddesley **106** C3
South Ballachulish (Baile a' Chaolais a Deas) **248** C4
South Balloch **215** E1
South Bank **213** E5
South Barrow **116** D5
South Bellsdyke **234** D1
South Benfleet **137** G4
South Bersted **108** B3
South Blackbog **261** F1
South Bockhampton **106** A3
South Boisdale **254** C3
South Bowood **104** A3
South Brent **100** C1
South Brentor **99** E2
South Brewham **117** E4
South Broomhill **221** E2
South Burlingham **179** E5
South Cadbury **116** D5
South Cairn **214** A4
South Carlton **187** G5
South Cave **196** B4
South Cerney **132** C3
South Chard **103** G2
South Charlton **229** F4
South Cheriton **117** D5
South Church **212** B5
South Cliffe **196** A4
South Clifton **187** F5
South Cockerington **189** D4
South Collafirth **278** C4
South Common **109** F2
South Cornelly **129** E4
South Corriegills **223** F2
South Cove **165** F3
South Creagan **248** B5
South Creake **177** G4
South Crosland **185** F1
South Croxton **160** B1
South Croydon **122** C2
South Dalton **196** B3
South Darenth **137** E5
South Dell (Dail Bho Dheas) **271** G1
South Duffield **195** F4
South Elkington **188** C4
South Elmsall **186** B1
South End *Bucks* **149** D5
South End *Cumb* **191** F1
South End *Hants* **106** A1
South End *NLincs* **196** D5
South Erradale **264** D4
South Fambridge **138** B3
South Fawley **133** F4
South Ferriby **196** B5
South Field **196** C5
South Flobbets **261** F1
South Garth **278** E3
South Godstone **122** C4
South Gorley **106** A1
South Green *Essex* **137** F3
South Green *Essex* **138** D1
South Green *Norf* **178** B4
South Green *Suff* **164** C4
South Gyle **235** F2
South Hall **232** B2
South Hanningfield **137** G3
South Harefield **135** F4
South Harting **107** G1
South Hayling **107** G3
South Hazelrigg **229** E3
South Heath **135** E2
South Heighton **109** G3
South Hetton **212** C3
South Hiendley **186** A1
South Hill **98** D3
South Hinksey **134** A2
South Hole **112** C4
South Holme **203** F5
South Holmwood **121** G3
South Hornchurch **137** E4
South Hourat **233** D4
South Huish **100** C3
South Hykeham **175** E1
South Hylton **212** C2
South Kelsey **188** A3
South Kessock **266** D7
South Killingholme **188** B1
South Kilvington **202** D4
South Kilworth **160** B4
South Kirkby **186** B1
South Kirkton **261** F4
South Knighton **102** B5
South Kyme **175** G3
South Lancing **109** D3
South Ledaig **240** B1
South Leigh **133** F2
South Leverton **187** E4
South Littleton **146** C3
South Lopham **164** B3
South Luffenham **161** E2
South Malling **109** G2
South Marston **133** D4
South Middleton **229** D4
South Milford **195** D4
South Milton **100** C3
South Mimms **136** B2
South Molton **114** A5
South Moor **212** A2
South Moreton **134** A4
South Mundham **108** A3
South Muskham **174** C2
South Newbald **196** B4
South Newington **147** G4
South Newton **118** B4
South Normanton **173** F2
South Norwood **122** C2
South Nutfield **122** C4
South Ockendon **137** E4
South Ormsby **189** D5
South Ossett **185** G1
South Otterington **202** C4
South Owersby **188** A3
South Oxhey **136** A3
South Park **122** B4
South Parks **244** A4
South Perrott **104** A2
South Petherton **104** A1
South Petherwin **98** D2
South Pickenham **163** G2
South Pool **101** D3
South Queensferry (Queensferry) **235** F2
South Radworthy **114** A4
South Rauceby **175** F3
South Raynham **177** G5
South Redbriggs **269** F6
South Reston **189** E4
South Ronaldsay **277** D9
South Ruislip **136** A4
South Runcton **163** E2
South Scarle **174** D1
South Shian (Sithean a Deas) **248** B5
South Shields **212** C1
South Shields Museum & Art Gallery *T&W* NE33 2JA **28** E2
South Somercotes **189** E3
South Somercotes Fen Houses **189** E3
South Stainley **194** C1
South Stoke *B&NESom* **117** E1
South Stoke *Oxon* **134** B4
South Stoke *WSuss* **108** C3
South Street *ESuss* **109** F2
South Street *GtLon* **122** D3
South Street *Kent* **123** F2
South Street *Kent* **124** D2
South Street *Kent* **124** A2
South Tawton **99** G1
South Thoresby **189** E5
South Tidworth **118** D3
South Tottenham **136** C4
South Town *Devon* **102** C4
South Town *Hants* **120** B4
South Uist (Uibhist a Deas) **254** C1
South Upper Barrack **269** H6
South View **120** B2
South Walsham **179** E4
South Warnborough **120** C3
South Weald **137** E3
South Weston **134** C3
South Wheatley *Corn* **98** C1
South Wheatley *Notts* **187** E4
South Whiteness **279** C8
South Wigston **160** A3
South Willingham **188** B4
South Wingfield **173** E2
South Witham **161** E1
South Wonston **119** F4
South Woodham Ferrers **138** B3
South Wootton **177** E5
South Wraxall **117** F1
South Yardle **158** D4
South Zeal **99** G1
Southall **136** A4
Southam *Glos* **146** B5
Southam *Warks* **147** G1
Southampton **106** D1
Southampton Airport **107** D1
Southbar **233** F3
Southborough *GtLon* **122** D2
Southborough *Kent* **123** E4
Southbourne *BCP* **106** A3
Southbourne *WSuss* **107** G2
Southbrook **102** D3
Southburgh **178** B5
Southburn **196** B2
Southchurch **138** C4
Southcott *Devon* **99** F1
Southcott *Wilts* **118** C2
Southcourt **134** D1
Southdean **219** E1
Southdene **183** F3
Southease **109** G3
Southend *A&B* **222** B5
Southend *Aber* **269** F6
Southend *Bucks* **134** C4
Southend (Bradfield Southend) *WBerks* **134** A5
Southend *Wilts* **133** D5
Southend Airport **138** B4
Southend Pier *S'end* SS1 1EE **138** B4
Southend-on-Sea **138** B4
Southerfield **209** E2
Southerly **99** F2
Southern Green **150** B4
Southerndown **129** E5
Southerness **217** D5
Southery **163** E3
Southfield **244** A5
Southfields **136** B5
Southfleet **137** F5
Southgate *Cere* **154** B4
Southgate *GtLon* **136** C3
Southgate *Norf* **178** C3
Southgate *Norf* **177** E4
Southgate *Swan* **128** B4
Southill **149** G3
Southington **119** G3
Southleigh **103** F3
Southmarsh **117** E4
Southminster **138** C3
Southmoor **133** F3
Southmuir **252** B4
Southoe **149** G1
Southolt **152** C1
Southorpe **161** F2
Southowram **194** A5
Southport **183** E1
Southport Pier *Mersey* PR8 1QX **183** E1
Southrepps **179** D2
Southrey **175** G1
Southrop **133** D2
Southrope **120** B3
Southsea *Ports* **107** F3
Southsea *Wrex* **169** F2
Southtown *Norf* **179** G5
Southtown *Ork* **277** D8
Southwaite *Cumb* **200** C2
Southwaite *Cumb* **210** A3
Southwark Cathedral *GtLon* SE1 9DA **12** B4
Southwater **121** G5
Southwater Street **121** G5
Southway **116** C3
Southwell *Dorset* **104** C5
Southwell *Notts* **174** B2
Southwell Minster *Notts* NG25 0HD **174** C2
Southwick *D&G* **216** D5
Southwick *Hants* **107** F2
Southwick *N'hants* **161** F3
Southwick *Som* **116** A3
Southwick *T&W* **212** C2
Southwick *Wilts* **117** F2
Southwick *WSuss* **109** E3
Southwold **165** G4
Southwood **116** C4
Sowden **102** C4
Sower Carr **191** G3
Sowerby *NYorks* **202** D4
Sowerby *WYorks* **193** G5
Sowerby Bridge **193** G5
Sowerby Row **209** G2
Sowerhill **114** B5
Sowley Green **151** F2
Sowood **185** E1
Sowton **102** C3
Soyal **266** C2
Spa Common **179** D2
Spa Complex *NYorks* YO11 2HD **83** Scarborough
Spadeadam **219** D4
Spalding **176** A5
Spaldington **195** G4
Spaldwick **161** G5
Spalefield **245** D4
Spalford **174** D1
Spamount **284** E7
Spanby **175** F4
Sparham **178** B4
Spark Bridge **199** E4
Sparkford **116** D5
Sparkhill **158** C4
Sparkwell **100** B2
Sparrow Green **178** A4
Sparrowpit **185** E4
Sparrow's Green **123** F5
Sparsholt *Hants* **119** F4
Sparsholt *Oxon* **133** F4
Spartylea **211** E3
Spath **172** B4
Spaunton **203** G4
Spaxton **115** F4
Spean Bridge (Drochaid an Aonachain) **249** E1
Spean Bridge Woollen Mill *High* PH34 4EP **249** E1
Spear Hill **108** D2
Speddoch **216** C2
Speedwell **131** F5
Speen *Bucks* **134** D2
Speen *WBerks* **119** F1
Speeton **205** E5
Speke **183** F4
Speldhurst **123** E4
Spellbrook **137** D1
Spelsbury **147** F5
Spen Green **171** F1
Spencers Wood **120** C1
Spennithorne **202** A4
Spennymoor **212** B4
Spernall **146** C1
Spetchley **146** A2
Spetisbury **105** F2
Spexhall **165** E3
Spey Bay **268** B4
Speybridge **259** H2
Speyview **267** K7
Spilsby **176** B1
Spindlestone **229** F3
Spinkhill **186** B5
Spinnaker Tower PO1 3TN **82** Portsmouth
Spinningdale **266** D3
Spirthill **132** B5
Spital *High* **275** G3
Spital *W&M* **135** E5
Spital in the Street **187** G3
Spitalbrook **136** C2
Spitfire & Hurricane Memorial, R.A.F. Manston *Kent* CT12 5DF **125** F2
Spithurst **109** G2
Spittal *D&G* **215** F4
Spittal *D&G* **215** E5
Spittal *ELoth* **236** B2
Spittal *N'umb* **229** E1
Spittal *Pembs* **140** C5
Spittal of Glenmuick **252** B1
Spittal of Glenshee **251** G3
Spittalfield **251** G5
Spixworth **178** D4
Splayne's Green **109** G1
Splott **130** B5
Spofforth **194** C2
Spondon **173** F4
Spooner Row **164** B2
Spoonley **171** D4
Sporle **163** G1
Sportsman's Arms **168** C2
Spott **237** D2
Spratton **160** C5
Spreakley **120** D3
Spreyton **99** G1
Spriddlestone **100** B2
Spridlington **188** A4
Spring Grove **136** A5
Spring Vale **107** F3
Springburn **234** A3
Springfield *A&B* **232** B2
Springfield *D&G* **218** B5
Springfield *F&O* **280** D4
Springfield *Fife* **244** B3
Springfield *Moray* **267** H6
Springfield *P&K* **243** G1
Springfield *WMid* **158** C4
Springhill *Staffs* **158** C2
Springhill *Staffs* **158** B2
Springholm **216** C4
Springkell **218** A4
Springleys **261** F1
Springside **224** B2
Springthorpe **187** F4
Springwell **212** B2
Sproatley **197** D4
Sproston Green **171** E1
Sprotbrough **186** C2
Sproughton **152** C3
Sprouston **228** B3
Sprowston **178** D4
Sproxton *Leics* **175** D5
Sproxton *NYorks* **203** F4
Sprytown **99** E2
Spurlands End **135** D3
Spurstow **170** C2
Spyway **104** B3
Square Point **216** B3
Squires Gate **191** G4
Srannda **263** F3
Sròndoire **231** G2
Sronphadruig Lodge **250** C2
Stableford *Shrop* **157** G3
Stableford *Staffs* **171** F4
Stacey Bank **185** G3
Stackhouse **193** E1
Stackpole **126** C3
Stacksteads **193** E5
Staddiscombe **100** B2
Staddlethorpe **196** A5
Staden **185** E5
Stadhampton **134** B3
Staffield **210** B3
Staffin **263** K5
Stafford **171** G5
Staffordstown **286** E7
Stagden Cross **137** F1
Stagsden **149** E3
Stagshaw Bank **211** F1
Stain **275** J2
Stainburn *Cumb* **208** D4
Stainburn *NYorks* **194** B3
Stainby **175** E5
Staincross **186** A1
Staindrop **212** A5
Staines-upon-Thames **135** F5
Stainfield *Lincs* **175** F5
Stainfield *Lincs* **188** B5
Stainforth *NYorks* **193** E1
Stainforth *SYorks* **186** D1
Staining **191** G4
Stainland **185** E1
Stainsacre **204** C2
Stainsby *Derbys* **173** F1
Stainsby *Lincs* **188** D5
Stainton *Cumb* **199** G4
Stainton *Cumb* **210** A5
Stainton *Dur* **201** F1
Stainton *Middl* **203** D1
Stainton *NYorks* **202** A3
Stainton *SYorks* **186** C3
Stainton by Langworth **188** A5
Stainton le Vale **188** B3
Stainton with Adgarley **198** D5
Staintondale **204** C3
Stair *Cumb* **209** F4
Stair *EAyr* **224** C3
Stairfoot **186** A2
Staithes **203** G1
Stake Pool **192** A3
Stakeford **221** E3
Stakes **107** F2
Stalbridge **104** D1
Stalbridge Weston **104** D1
Stalham **179** E3
Stalham Green **179** E3
Stalisfield Green **124** B3
Stalling Busk **201** E4
Stallingborough **188** B1
Stallington **171** G4
Stalmine **191** G3
Stalybridge **185** D3
Stambourne **151** F4
Stamford *Lincs* **161** F2
Stamford *N'umb* **229** G5
Stamford Bridge *ChesW&C* **170** B1
Stamford Bridge *ERid* **195** G2
Stamfordham **220** C4
Stanah **191** G3
Stanborough **136** B1
Stanborough Park *Herts* AL8 6XF **136** B1
Stanbridge *CenBeds* **149** E5
Stanbridge *Dorset* **105** G2
Stanbridge Earls **119** E5
Stanbury **193** G4
Stand **234** B3
Standalone Farm, Letchworth Garden City *Herts* SG6 4JN **150** A4
Standburn **234** D2
Standedge Tunnel & Visitor Centre *WYorks* HD7 6NQ **185** E1
Standeford **158** B2
Standen **124** A5
Standen Street **124** A5
Standerwick **117** F2
Standford **120** D4
Standford Bridge **171** E5
Standish *Glos* **132** A2
Standish *GtMan* **183** G1
Standlake **133** F2
Standon *Hants* **119** F5
Standon *Herts* **150** B5
Standon *Staffs* **171** F4
Standon Green End **136** C1
Stane **234** C4
Stanecastle **224** B2
Stanfield **178** A3
Stanford *CenBeds* **149** G3
Stanford *Kent* **124** D5
Stanford *Shrop* **156** C1
Stanford Bishop **145** F2
Stanford Bridge **145** G1
Stanford Dingley **134** A5
Stanford End **120** C1
Stanford in the Vale **133** F3
Stanford on Avon **160** A5
Stanford on Soar **173** G5
Stanford on Teme **145** G1
Stanford Rivers **137** E2
Stanford-le-Hope **137** F4
Stanfree **186** B5
Stanghow **203** F1
Stanground **162** A3
Stanhoe **177** G4
Stanhope *Dur* **211** F4
Stanhope *ScBord* **226** C3
Stanion **161** E4
Stanklyn **158** A5
Stanley *Derbys* **173** F3
Stanley *Dur* **212** A2
Stanley *Notts* **173** F1
Stanley *P&K* **243** G1
Stanley *Staffs* **171** G2
Stanley *Wilts* **132** B5
Stanley *WYorks* **194** C5
Stanley Common **173** F3
Stanley Crook **212** A4
Stanley Gate **183** F2
Stanley Hill **145** F3
Stanleygreen **170** C4
Stanlow *ChesW&C* **183** F5
Stanlow *Shrop* **157** G3
Stanmer **109** F2
Stanmore *GtLon* **136** A3
Stanmore *WBerks* **133** G5
Stannersburn **219** F3
Stanningfield **151** G2
Stannington *N'umb* **221** E4
Stannington *SYorks* **186** A4
Stansbatch **144** C1
Stansfield **151** F2
Stanshope **172** C2
Stanstead **151** G3
Stanstead Abbotts **136** C1
Stansted **123** F2
Stansted Mountfitchet **150** D5
Stanton *Derbys* **159** E1
Stanton *Glos* **146** C4
Stanton *N'umb* **220** D2
Stanton *Staffs* **172** C3
Stanton *Suff* **164** A4
Stanton by Bridge **173** E5
Stanton by Dale **173** F4
Stanton Drew **116** C1
Stanton Fitzwarren **133** D3
Stanton Harcourt **133** G2
Stanton Hill **173** F1
Stanton in Peak **172** D1
Stanton Lacy **157** D5
Stanton Lees **173** D1
Stanton Long **157** E3
Stanton Prior **117** D1
Stanton St. Bernard **118** B1
Stanton St. John **134** A2
Stanton St. Quintin **132** B5
Stanton Street **152** A1
Stanton under Bardon **159** G1
Stanton upon Hine Heath **170** C5
Stanton Wick **116** D1
Stanton-on-the-Wolds **174** B4
Stanwardine in the Fields **170** B5
Stanwardine in the Wood **170** B5
Stanway *Essex* **152** A5
Stanway *Glos* **146** C4
Stanway Green *Essex* **152** A5
Stanway Green *Suff* **164** D4
Stanwell **135** F5
Stanwell Moor **135** F5
Stanwick **161** E5
Stanwix **210** A2
Stanydale **279** B7
Staoinebrig **254** C1
Stapeley **171** D3
Stapenhill **173** D5
Staple *Kent* **125** E3
Staple *Som* **115** E3
Staple Cross **114** D5
Staple Fitzpaine **103** F1
Staplecross **110** C1
Staplefield **109** E1
Stapleford *Cambs* **150** C2
Stapleford *Herts* **136** C1
Stapleford *Leics* **160** D1
Stapleford *Lincs* **175** D2
Stapleford *Notts* **173** F4
Stapleford *Wilts* **118** B4
Stapleford Abbotts **137** D3
Stapleford Tawney **137** E3
Staplegrove **115** F5
Staplehay **115** F5
Staplehurst **123** G4
Staplers **107** E4
Staplestreet **124** C2
Stapleton *Cumb* **218** D4
Stapleton *Here* **144** C1
Stapleton *Leics* **159** G3
Stapleton *NYorks* **202** B1
Stapleton *Shrop* **157** D2
Stapleton *Som* **116** B5
Stapley **103** E1
Staploe **149** G1
Staplow **145** F3
Star *Fife* **244** B4
Star *Pembs* **141** F4
Star *Som* **116** B2
Starbotton **201** E5
Starcross **102** C4
Stareton **159** F5
Starkholmes **173** E2
Starling **184** B1
Starling's Green **150** C4
Starr **215** F1
Starston **164** D3
Startforth **201** F1
Startley **132** B4
Statham **184** A4
Stathe **116** A5
Stathern **174** C4
Station Town **212** D4
Staughton Green **149** G1
Staughton Highway **149** G1
Staunton *Glos* **131** E1
Staunton *Glos* **145** G5
Staunton Harold Hall **173** E5
Staunton Harold Reservoir *Derbys* DE73 8DN **173** E5
Staunton in the Vale **174** D3
Staunton on Arrow **144** C1
Staunton on Wye **144** C3
Staveley *Cumb* **199** F3

Staveley Derbys 186 B5
Staveley NYorks 194 C1
Staveley-in-Cartmel 199 E4
Staverton Devon 101 D1
Staverton Glos 146 A5
Staverton Wilts 117 F1
Staverton WN'hants 148 A1
Staverton Bridge 146 A5
Stawell 116 A4
Stawley 115 D5
Staxigoe 275 J3
Staxton 204 D5
Staylittle (Penffordd-las) 155 E3
Staynall 191 D4
Staythorpe 174 C2
Stean 201 F5
Steane 148 A4
Stearsby 203 F5
Steart 115 F3
Stebbing 151 E5
Stebbing Green 151 E5
Stechford 158 D4
Stedham 121 D5
Steel Cross 123 E5
Steel Green 198 C5
Steele Road 218 D2
Steen's Bridge 145 E2
Steep 120 C5
Steep Marsh 120 C5
Steeple Dorset 105 F4
Steeple Essex 138 C2
Steeple Ashton 118 A2
Steeple Aston 147 G5
Steeple Barton 147 G5
Steeple Bumpstead 151 F4
Steeple Claydon 148 B5
Steeple Gidding 161 G4
Steeple Langford 118 B4
Steeple Morden 150 A3
Steeraway 157 F2
Steeton 193 G3
Stein 263 H6
Steinis 271 G4
Steinmanhill 269 F6
Stella 212 A1
Stelling Minnis 124 D4
Stembridge 116 B5
Stemster High 275 G2
Stemster High 275 G4
Stemster House 275 G2
Stenalees 97 D4
Stenhill 103 D1
Stenhousemuir 234 C1
Stenigot 188 C4
Stenness 278 B5
Stenscholl 263 K5
Stenson 173 E5
Stenton ELoth 236 D2
Stenton P&K 251 F5
Stepaside Pembs 127 E2
Stepaside Powys 155 G4
Stepney 136 C4
Steppingley 149 F4
Stepps 234 A3
Sternfield 153 E1
Sterridge 113 F1
Stert 118 B2
Stetchworth 151 E2
Stevenage 150 A4
Stevenston 233 D5
Steventon Hants 119 G3
Steventon Oxon 133 G3
Steventon End 151 E3
Stevington 149 E2
Stewart Park, Middlesbrough
Middl TS7 8AR 29 C4
Stewartby 149 F3
Stewarton D&G 207 G2
Stewarton EAyr 233 F5
Stewartstown 282 B1
Stewkley 149 D5
Stewley 103 G1
Stewton 189 D4
Steynton 126 C2
Stibb 112 C4
Stibb Cross 113 E4
Stibb Green 118 D1
Stibbard 178 A3
Stibbington 161 F3
Stichill 228 B3
Sticker 97 D4
Stickford 176 B1
Sticklepath Devon 99 G1
Sticklepath Som 103 G1
Stickling Green 150 C4
Stickney 176 B2
Stiff Street 124 A2
Stiffkey 178 A1
Stifford's Bridge 145 G3
Stileway 116 B3
Stilligarry (Stadhlaigearraidh) 254 C1
Stillingfleet 195 E3
Stillington NYorks 195 E1
Stillington Stock 212 C5
Stilton 161 G4
Stinchcombe 131 G3
Stinsford 104 D3
Stirchley Tel&W 157 G2
Stirchley WMid 158 C4
Stirkoke House 275 J3
Stirling Aber 269 K6
Stirling (Sruighlea)
Stir 242 C5
Stirling Castle Stir
FK8 1EJ 242 C5
Stirling Visitor Centre Stir
FK8 1EH 242 C5
Stirton 193 F2
Stisted 151 G5
Stitchcombe 118 D1
Stithians 95 E3
Stittenham 266 D4
Stivichall 159 F5
Stix 250 C5
Stixwould 175 G1
Stoak 183 F5
Stobo 226 C2
Stoborough 105 F4
Stoborough Green 105 F4
Stobwood 235 D4
Stock 137 F3
Stock Green 146 B2
Stock Lane 133 E5
Stock Wood 146 C2

Stockbridge Hants 119 E4
Stockbridge Stir 242 C4
Stockbridge WSuss 108 A3
Stockbury 124 A2
Stockcross 119 F1
Stockdale 95 E3
Stockdalewath 209 G2
Stockerston 160 D3
Stockgrove Country Park
CenBeds
LU7 0BA 149 E4
Stocking Green Essex 151 D4
Stocking Green MK 148 D3
Stocking Pelham 150 C5
Stockingford 159 F3
Stockinish 263 G2
Stockland Cardiff 130 A5
Stockland Devon 103 F2
Stockland Bristol 115 E3
Stockleigh English 102 B2
Stockleigh Pomeroy 102 B2
Stockley 118 B1
Stocklinch 103 G1
Stockport 184 C3
Stocksbridge 185 G3
Stocksfield 211 G1
Stockton Here 145 E1
Stockton Norf 165 E2
Stockton Shrop 157 G3
Stockton Shrop 156 B2
Stockton Tel&W 157 G1
Stockton Warks 147 G1
Stockton Wilts 118 A4
Stockton Heath 184 A4
Stockton on Teme 145 G1
Stockton on the Forest 195 F2
Stockton-on-Tees 202 D1
Stockwell Heath 172 B5
Stockwood Bristol 116 D1
Stockwood Dorset 104 B2
Stodday 192 A2
Stodd001 125 E2
Stody 178 B2
Stoer 272 C6
Stoford Som 104 B1
Stoford Wilts 118 B4
Stogumber 115 D4
Stogursey 115 F3
Stoke Devon 112 C3
Stoke Hants 119 F2
Stoke Hants 107 G2
Stoke Med 124 A1
Stoke Plym 100 A2
Stoke WMid 159 F5
Stoke Abbott 104 A2
Stoke Albany 160 D4
Stoke Ash 164 C4
Stoke Bardolph 174 B3
Stoke Bishop 131 E5
Stoke Bliss 145 F1
Stoke Bruerne 148 C2
Stoke by Clare 151 F3
Stoke Canon 102 C3
Stoke Charity 119 F4
Stoke Climsland 99 D3
Stoke D'Abernon 121 G2
Stoke Doyle 161 F4
Stoke Dry 161 D3
Stoke Edith 145 F3
Stoke Farthing 118 B5
Stoke Ferry 163 F3
Stoke Fleming 101 E3
Stoke Gabriel 101 E2
Stoke Golding 159 F3
Stoke Goldington 148 D3
Stoke Green 135 E4
Stoke Hammond 149 D5
Stoke Heath Shrop 171 D5
Stoke Heath Worcs 146 B1
Stoke Holy Cross 178 D5
Stoke Lacy 145 F3
Stoke Lyne 148 A5
Stoke Mandeville 134 D1
Stoke Newington 136 C4
Stoke on Tern 170 D5
Stoke Orchard 146 B5
Stoke Pero 114 B3
Stoke Poges 135 E4
Stoke Pound 146 B1
Stoke Prior Here 145 E2
Stoke Prior Worcs 146 B1
Stoke Rivers 113 G2
Stoke Rochford 175 E5
Stoke Row 134 B4
Stoke St. Gregory 116 A5
Stoke St. Mary 115 F5
Stoke St. Michael 117 D3
Stoke St.
Milborough 157 E4
Stoke sub Hamdon 104 A1
Stoke Talmage 134 B3
Stoke Trister 117 E5
Stoke Villice 116 C1
Stoke Wake 105 D2
Stoke-by-Nayland 152 A4
Stokeford 105 E4
Stokeham 187 E5
Stokeinteignhead 102 C5
Stokenchurch 134 C3
Stokenham 101 E3
Stokes-on-Trent 171 F4
Stokesay 156 D4
Stokesby 179 F4
Stokesley 203 E2
Stolford 115 F3
Ston Easton 116 D2
Stondon Massey 137 E2
Stone Bucks 134 C1
Stone Glos 131 F3
Stone Kent 137 E5
Stone Kent 111 E1
Stone Som 116 C4
Stone Staffs 171 G4
Stone SYorks 186 C4
Stone Worcs 158 A5
Stone Allerton 116 B2
Stone Cross Dur 201 F1
Stone Cross ESuss 110 C3
Stone Cross ESuss 110 A1
Stone Cross Kent 124 B5
Stone Cross Kent 123 E5
Stone House 200 C4

Stone Street Kent 123 E3
Stone Street Suff 165 E3
Stone Street Suff 152 A4
Stonea 162 C3
Stonebridge ESuss 110 A1
Stonebridge NSom 116 A2
Stonebridge Warks 159 E4
Stonebroom 173 F2
Stonecross Green 151 G2
Stonefield A&B 231 G2
Stonefield Staffs 171 G4
Stonegate ESuss 110 B1
Stonegate NYorks 203 G2
Stonegrave 203 F5
Stonehaugh 219 F4
Stonehaven 253 G1
Stonehenge (Stonehenge,
Avebury & Associated Sites)
Wilts SP4 7DE 118 C3
Stonehill 121 E1
Stonehouse
ChesW&C 183 G5
Stonehouse D&G 216 C4
Stonehouse Glos 132 A2
Stonehouse N'umb 210 C2
Stonehouse Plym 100 A2
Stonehouse SLan 234 B5
Stoneleigh Surr 122 B2
Stoneleigh Warks 159 F5
Stoneley Green 170 D2
Stonely 149 G1
Stoner Hill 120 C5
Stones 193 F5
Stones Green 152 C5
Stonesby 174 D5
Stonesfield 133 F1
Stonestreet Green 124 C5
Stonethwaite 209 F5
Stoney Cross 106 B1
Stoney Middleton 185 G5
Stoney Stanton 159 G3
Stoney Stoke 117 E4
Stoney Stratton 117 D4
Stoney Stretton 156 C2
Stoneyburn 235 D3
Stoneyford 103 D4
Stoneygate 160 B2
Stoneyhills 138 C3
Stoneykirk 214 B5
Stoneywood 261 G3
Stonganess 278 E2
Stonham Aspal 152 C2
Stonham Barns Suff
IP14 6AT 152 C2
Stonnall 158 C2
Stonor 134 C4
Stonton Wyville 160 C3
Stony Houghton 173 F1
Stony Stratford 148 C3
Stonybreck 278 A1
Stonyfield 283 F1
Stoodleigh Devon 102 C1
Stoodleigh Devon 113 G2
Stopham 108 C2
Stopsley 149 G5
Stoptide 96 D2
Storeton 183 E4
Stormontfield 243 G2
Stornoway
(Steòrnabhagh) 271 G4
Stornoway Airport 271 G4
Storridge 145 G3
Storrington 108 C2
Storrs 185 G4
Storth 199 F4
Storwood 195 G3
Stotfield 268 B5
Stotfold 150 A4
Stottesdon 157 F4
Stoughton Leics 160 B2
Stoughton Surr 121 E2
Stoughton WSuss 107 G1
Stoughton Cross 116 B3
Stoul 256 D5
Stoulton 146 B3
Stour Provost 117 E5
Stour Row 117 F5
Stourbridge 158 A4
Stourhead Wilts
BA12 6QD 117 E4
Stourpaine 105 E2
Stourport-on-Severn 158 A5
Stourton Staffs 158 A4
Stourton Warks 147 E4
Stourton Wilts 117 E4
Stourton Caundle 104 D1
Stove 276 F4
Stoven 165 F3
Stow Lincs 187 F4
Stow ScBord 236 B5
Stow Bardolph 163 E2
Stow Bedon 164 A2
Stow cum Quy 150 D1
Stow Longa 161 G5
Stow Maries 138 B3
Stow Pasture 187 F4
Stowbridge 163 D2
Stowe Glos 131 E2
Stowe Shrop 156 C5
Stowe Staffs 158 C1
Stowe Landscape Gardens
Bucks
MK18 5DQ 148 B4
Stowe-by-Chartley 172 B5
Stowehill 148 B2
Stowell Glos 132 C1
Stowell Som 117 D5
Stowey 116 C2
Stowford Devon 99 D4
Stowford Devon 113 G3
Stowford Devon 103 E4
Stowlangtoft 152 A1
Stowmarket 152 B2
Stowting 124 D4
Stowupland 152 B2
Straad 232 B3
Stracathro 253 E3
Strachan 260 E5
Strachur (Clachan
Strachur) 240 C4
Stradbroke 164 D4
Stradishall 151 F2

Stradsett 163 E2
Stragglethorpe 175 E2
Straid A&N 287 H6
Straid CC&G 286 E1
Straid M&EAnt 286 E6
Straidbilly 286 D2
Straidkilly 287 G4
Straight Soley 133 F5
Straiton Edin 235 G3
Straiton SAyr 224 B5
Straloch Aber 261 G2
Straloch P&K 251 F3
Stramshall 172 B4
Stranagalwilly 285 H5
Strands 198 C4
Strang 190 B4
Strangford Here 145 E5
Strangford NM&D 283 J4
Stranocum 286 E1
Stranraer 214 B4
Strata Florida 142 D1
Stratfield Mortimer 120 B1
Stratfield Saye 120 B1
Stratfield Turgis 120 B2
Stratford CenBeds 149 G3
Stratford Glos 146 A4
Stratford GtLon 136 C4
Stratford St. Andrew 153 E1
Stratford St. Mary 152 B4
Stratford sub Castle 118 C4
Stratford Tony 118 B5
Stratford-upon-Avon 147 E2
Stratford-upon-Avon
Butterfly Farm
Warks CV37 7LS
85 Stratford-upon-Avon
Strath 275 H3
Strathan High 272 C6
Strathan High 257 F5
Strathaven 234 B5
Strathblane 233 G2
Strathcanaird 265 H1
Strathcarron 265 F7
Strathclyde Country Park
NLan ML1 3ED 31 G5
Strathdon 260 B3
Strathgirnock 260 B5
Strathkinness 244 C3
Strathmiglo 244 A3
Strathpeffer (Strath
Pheofhair) 266 B6
Strathrannoch 265 K4
Strathtay 251 E4
Strathwhillan 223 F2
Strathy 274 D2
Strathyre 242 A3
Stratton Corn 112 C5
Stratton Dorset 104 C3
Stratton Glos 132 C2
Stratton Audley 148 B5
Stratton Hall 152 D4
Stratton St.
Margaret 133 D4
Stratton St. Michael 164 D2
Stratton Strawless 178 D3
Stratton-on-the-Fosse 117 D2
Stravanan 232 B4
Stravithie 244 D3
Straw 286 B6
Strawberry Hill 136 A5
Stream 115 D4
Streat 109 F2
Streatham 136 B5
Streatham Vale 136 B5
Streatham Ice and Leisure
Centre GtLon
SW16 6HX 13 B7
Streatley CenBeds 149 F5
Streatley WBerks 134 A4
Street Devon 103 E4
Street Lancs 192 B2
Street NYorks 203 G2
Street Som 116 B4
Street Som 103 G2
Street Ashton 159 G4
Street Dinas 170 A4
Street End 108 A4
Street Gate 212 B2
Street Houses 195 E3
Street Lane 173 E3
Street on the Fosse 116 D4
Streethay 158 D1
Streethouse 194 C5
Streetlam 202 C3
Streetly 158 C3
Streetly End 151 E3
Strefford 156 D4
Strelley 173 G3
Strensall 195 F1
Strensham 146 B3
Stretcholt 115 F3
Strete 101 E3
Stretford GtMan 184 B3
Stretford Here 144 D2
Stretford Here 145 E2
Strethall 150 C4
Stretham 162 D5
Strettington 108 A3
Stretton ChesW&C 170 B2
Stretton Derbys 173 E1
Stretton Rut 161 E1
Stretton Staffs 158 A1
Stretton Staffs 173 D5
Stretton Warr 184 A4
Stretton en le Field 159 F1
Stretton Grandison 145 F3
Stretton Heath 156 C1
Stretton Sugwas 145 D3
Stretton under
Fosse 159 G4
Stretton Westwood 157 E3
Stretton-on-
Dunsmore 159 G5
Stretton-on-Fosse 147 E4
Stribers 199 E4
Strichen 269 H5
Strines 185 D4
Strinesdale Countryside
Area GtMan
OL4 2JJ 25 H1
Stringston 115 E3
Strixton 149 E1
Stroanbrack 285 H6
Stroat 131 E2
Stromeferry 256 E1
Stromemore 256 E1
Stromness 277 B7

Stronaba 249 E1
Stronachlachar 241 G3
Strone A&B 232 C1
Strone A&B 232 C1
Strone High 258 C2
Strone High 248 C3
Strone Stir 241 G3
Stronechrubie 272 E7
Stronlonag 232 C1
Stronmilchan (Sròn nam
Mialchon) 241 D2
Stronsay 276 F5
Stronsay Airport 276 F5
Strontian (Sròn an
t-Sìthein) 248 A3
Strood 123 G2
Strood Green Surr 122 B4
Strood Green WSuss 121 F5
Strood Green WSuss 121 G4
Stroquhan 216 C2
Stroud Glos 132 A2
Stroud Hants 120 C5
Stroud Common 121 F3
Stroud Green Essex 138 B3
Stroud Green WSuss 132 A2
Stroude 121 F1
Stroul 232 D1
Stroxton 175 E4
Struan High 255 J1
Struan P&K 250 C3
Strubby Lincs 189 E4
Strubby Lincs 188 B5
Strumpshaw 179 E5
Struthers 244 B4
Struy 258 B1
Stryd 169 F1
Stryd-y-Facsen 180 B4
Stryt-cae-rhedyn 169 F1
Stryt-issa 169 F3
Stuart & Waterford Crystal
Factory Shop, Crieff P&K
PH7 4HQ 243 D2
Stuart Line Cruises, Exmouth
Devon EX8 1EJ 102 D4
Stuartfield 269 H6
Stub Place 198 B3
Stubber's Green 158 C2
Stubbington 107 E2
Stubbins 184 B1
Stubbs Green 165 E2
Stubhampton 105 F1
Stubley 186 A5
Stubshaw Cross 183 G2
Stubton 175 D2
Stuck A&B 232 B3
Stuck A&B 240 D5
Stuckbeg 241 E5
Stuckgowan 241 F4
Stuckindroin 241 F3
Stuckreoch 240 C5
Stuckton 106 A1
Stud Green 135 D5
Studdon 211 E2
Studfold 200 D5
Studham 135 F1
Studholme 209 F1
Studland 105 G4
Studland & Godlingston
Heath NNR Dorset
BH19 3AX 105 G4
Studley Warks 146 C1
Studley Wilts 132 B5
Studley Common 146 C1
Studley Green 134 C3
Studley Roger 202 B5
Studley Royal Park & Ruins
of Fountains Abbey
NYorks HG4 3DY 194 B1
Stuggadhoo 190 B4
Stughan 282 B2
Stump Cross Essex 150 D3
Stump Cross Lancs 192 B5
Stuntney 163 D5
Stunts Green 110 B2
Sturbridge 171 F4
Sturgate 187 F4
Sturmer 151 E3
Sturminster
Common 105 D1
Sturminster
Marshall 105 F2
Sturminster
Newton 105 D1
Sturry 125 E2
Sturton by Stow 187 F4
Sturton le Steeple 187 E4
Stuston 164 C4
Stutton NYorks 195 D3
Stutton Suff 152 C4
Styal 184 C4
Stydd 192 C4
Styrrup 186 D3
Suardail 271 G4
Succoth A&B 241 E4
Succoth Aber 260 C1
Succothmore 240 D4
Suckley 145 G2
Suckley Green 145 G2
Suckley Knowl 145 G2
Sudborough 161 E4
Sudbourne 153 F2
Sudbrook Lincs 175 E3
Sudbrook Mon 131 E4
Sudbrooke 188 A5
Sudbury Derbys 172 C4
Sudbury GtLon 136 A4
Sudbury Suff 151 G3
Sudbury Hall Derbys
DE6 5HT 172 C4
Sudden 184 C1
Sudgrove 132 B2
Suffield Norf 178 D2
Suffield NYorks 204 C3
Sugnall 171 F4
Sugwas Pool 145 D3
Suie Lodge Hotel 241 G2
Suisnish 256 B3
Sulaisiadar 271 H4
Sulby IoM 190 B2
Sulby IoM 190 B4
Sulgrave 148 A3
Sulham 134 B5
Sulhamstead 120 B1
Sullington 108 C2
Sullom 278 C5
Sullom Voe Oil
Terminal 278 C5

Sully 115 E1
Sumburgh 279 F10
Sumburgh Airport 279 F9
Summer Bridge 194 B1
Summer Isles 265 F1
Summer Lodge 201 E3
Summercourt 96 C4
Summerfield Norf 177 F4
Summerfield Worcs 158 A5
Summerhill 170 A2
Summerhouse 202 B1
Summerleaze 130 D4
Summerlands 199 G4
Summertown 134 A2
Summit 184 D1
Sun Green 185 D3
Sunadale 231 G5
Sunbiggin 200 B2
Sunbury-on-Thames 121 G1
Sundaywell 216 C2
Sunderland Cumb 209 F3
Sunderland Lancs 192 A2
Sunderland T&W 212 C2
Sunderland Bridge 212 B4
Sunderland Museum &
Winter Gardens
T&W SR1 1PP
86 Sunderland
Sundhope 227 E3
Sundon Park 149 F5
Sundridge 123 D3
Sundrum Mains 224 C3
Sunhill 132 D2
Sunipol 246 C4
Sunk Island 188 C1
Sunningdale 121 E1
Sunninghill 121 E1
Sunningwell 133 G2
Sunniside Dur 212 A4
Sunniside T&W 212 B2
Sunny Bank 199 D3
Sunny Brow 212 A4
Sunnylaw 242 C5
Sunnyside N'umb 211 F3
Sunnyside SYorks 186 B3
Sunnyside WSuss 122 C5
Sunton 118 D2
Surbiton 121 G1
Surfleet 176 A5
Surfleet Seas End 176 A5
Surlingham 179 E5
Sustead 178 C2
Susworth 187 F2
Sutcombe 112 D4
Sutcombemill 112 D4
Suton 164 B2
Sutors of Cromarty 267 F5
Sutterby 189 D5
Sutterton 176 A4
Sutton Cambs 162 C5
Sutton CenBeds 150 A3
Sutton Devon 102 D5
Sutton Devon 100 D3
Sutton GtLon 122 B2
Sutton Kent 125 F4
Sutton Lincs 175 D2
Sutton Norf 179 E3
Sutton Notts 174 C4
Sutton Notts 187 D4
Sutton Oxon 133 G2
Sutton Pembs 126 C1
Sutton Peter 161 F3
Sutton Shrop 157 G4
Sutton Shrop 171 D4
Sutton Shrop 157 G1
Sutton Shrop 170 A5
Sutton Staffs 171 E5
Sutton Suff 153 E3
Sutton SYorks 186 C1
Sutton WSuss 108 B2
Sutton Abinger 121 G3
Sutton at Hone 137 E5
Sutton Bank National Park
Centre NYorks
YO7 2EH 203 E4
Sutton Bassett 160 C4
Sutton Benger 132 B5
Sutton Bingham 104 B1
Sutton Bonington 173 G5
Sutton Bridge 176 C5
Sutton Cheney 159 G2
Sutton Coldfield 158 D3
Sutton Courtenay 134 A3
Sutton Crosses 176 C5
Sutton Grange 202 B5
Sutton Green Oxon 133 G2
Sutton Green Surr 121 F2
Sutton Green Wrex 170 B3
Sutton Holms 105 G2
Sutton Hoo Suff
IP12 3DJ 153 E3
Sutton Howgrave 202 B5
Sutton in Ashfield 173 F2
Sutton in the Elms 160 A3
Sutton Ings 196 D4
Sutton Lane Ends 184 D5
Sutton le Marsh 189 F4
Sutton Leach 183 G3
Sutton Maddock 157 G2
Sutton Mallet 116 A4
Sutton Mandeville 118 A5
Sutton Montis 116 D5
Sutton on Sea 189 F4
Sutton on the Hill 172 D4
Sutton on Trent 174 C1
Sutton Poyntz 104 D4
Sutton St. Edmund 162 B1
Sutton St. James 162 C1
Sutton St. Nicholas 145 E3
Sutton Scarsdale 173 F1
Sutton Scotney 119 F4
Sutton upon Derwent 195 G3
Sutton Valence 124 A4
Sutton Veny 117 F3
Sutton Waldron 105 E1
Sutton Weaver 183 G5
Sutton Wick
B&NESom 116 C2
Sutton Wick Oxon 133 G3
Sutton-in-Craven 193 G3
Sutton-on-Hull 196 D4
Sutton-on-the-Forest 195 E1

Sutton-under-Brailes 147 F4
Sutton-under-
Whitestonecliffe 203 D4
Swaby 189 D5
Swadlincote 159 F1
Swaffham 163 G2
Swaffham Bulbeck 151 D1
Swaffham Prior 151 D1
Swafield 179 E2
Swainbost
(Suaineabost) 271 H1
Swainby 203 D2
Swainshill 145 D3
Swainsthorpe 178 D5
Swainswick 117 E1
Swalcliffe 147 F4
Swalecliffe 125 E2
Swallow 188 B2
Swallow Beck 175 E1
Swallow Falls Conwy
LL24 0DW 168 A2
Swallowcliffe 118 A5
Swallowfield 120 C1
Swallows Cross 137 F3
Swampton 119 F2
Swan Green
ChesW&C 184 B5
Swan Green Suff 165 D4
Swan Street 151 G5
Swanage 105 G5
Swanage Railway Dorset
BH19 1HB 105 G5
Swanbach 171 D3
Swanbourne 148 D5
Swanbridge 115 E1
Swancote 157 G3
Swanland 196 B5
Swanlaws 228 B5
Swanley 123 E2
Swanley Village 123 E2
Swanmore Hants 107 E1
Swanmore IoW 107 E3
Swannington Leics 159 G1
Swannington Norf 178 C4
Swanscombe 137 F5
Swansea
(Abertawe) 128 C3
Swansea Museum SA1 1SN
86 Swansea
Swanston 235 G3
Swanton Abbot 179 D3
Swanton Morley 178 B4
Swanton Novers 178 B2
Swanton Street 124 A3
Swanwick Derbys 173 F2
Swanwick Hants 107 E2
Swanwick Green 170 C3
Swarby 175 F3
Swardeston 178 D5
Swarkestone 173 E5
Swarland 221 D1
Swarraton 119 G4
Swarthmoor 199 D5
Swaton 175 G4
Swavesey 150 B1
Sway 106 C3
Swayfield 175 E5
Swaything 106 D1
Swaythorpe 196 C1
Sweetham 102 B3
Sweethay 115 F5
Sweetshouse 97 E3
Sweffling 153 E1
Swell 116 A5
Swepstone 159 F1
Swerford 147 F4
Swettenham 171 F1
Swffryd 130 B3
Swift's Green 124 A4
Swiftsden 110 C1
Swilland 152 C2
Swillington 194 C4
Swimbridge 113 G2
Swimbridge Newland 113 F2
Swinbrook 133 E1
Swincliffe 194 B2
Swincombe 113 G1
Swinden 193 E2
Swinderby 175 D1
Swindon Staffs 158 A3
Swindon Swin 133 D4
Swindon Village 146 B5
Swine 196 D4
Swinefleet 195 G5
Swineford 117 D1
Swineshead Bed 149 F1
Swineshead Lincs 176 A3
Swineshead Bridge 176 A3
Swineside 201 F4
Swiney 275 H5
Swinford Leics 160 A5
Swinford Oxon 133 G2
Swingate 173 G3
Swingfield Minnis 125 E4
Swingleton Green 152 A3
Swinhoe 229 G4
Swinhope 188 C3
Swining 279 D6
Swinithwaite 201 F4
Swinscoe 172 C3
Swinside Hall 228 B5
Swinstead 175 F5
Swinton GtMan 184 B2
Swinton NYorks 203 G5
Swinton NYorks 202 B5
Swinton ScBord 237 F5
Swinton SYorks 186 B3
Swinton Quarter 237 F5
Swintonmill 237 F5
Swithland 160 A1
Swordale 266 C5
Swordland 256 D5
Swordle 247 E2
Swordly 274 C2
Sworton Heath 184 A4
Swydffynnon 142 C1
Swyncombe 134 B3
Swynnerton 171 F4
Swyre 104 B4
Sychnant 155 F5
Syde 132 B1
Sydenham
Belfast City 283 G1
Sydenham GtLon 136 C5
Sydenham Oxon 134 C2

Sydenham Damerel 99 E3
Syderstone 177 G4
Sydling St. Nicholas 104 C3
Sydmonton 119 F2
Sydney 171 E2
Syerston 174 C3
Sykehouse 186 D1
Sykes 192 C2
Sylen 128 B2
Symbister 279 E6
Symington SAyr 224 B2
Symington SLan 226 A2
Symonds Yat 131 E1
Symondsbury 104 A3
Synod Inn (Post-mawr) 142 A2
Syre 273 J4
Syreford 146 C5
Syresham 148 B3
Syston Leics 160 B1
Syston Lincs 175 E3
Sytchampton 146 A1
Sywell 148 D1
Sywell Country Park NN'hants NN6 0QX 148 D1

T
Taagan 265 G5
Tableyhill 184 B5
Tabost (Habost) 271 F6
Tachbrook Mallory 147 F1
Tacher 275 G4
Tackley 147 G5
Tacolneston 164 C2
Tadcaster 195 D3
Tadden 105 F2
Taddington Derbys 185 F5
Taddington Glos 146 C4
Taddiport 113 E4
Tadley 120 B1
Tadlow 150 A3
Tadmarton 147 F4
Tadpole Bridge 133 F2
Tadworth 122 B3
Tafarnau-bach 130 A1
Tafarn-y-bwlch 141 D4
Tafarn-y-Gelyn 169 E1
Taff Merthyr Garden Village 130 A3
Taff's Well (Ffynnon Taf) 130 A4
Tafolwern 155 E2
Taibach NPT 129 D4
Tai-bach Powys 169 E5
Taicynhaeaf 154 C1
Tain High 275 H2
Tain High 266 E3
Tai'n Lôn 166 D3
Tai'r Bull 143 F5
Tai'r-gwaith 128 D1
Tai'r-heol 130 A3
Tairlaw 224 C5
Tai'r-ysgol 128 C2
Takeley 151 D5
Takeley Street 150 D5
Talachddu 143 G4
Talacre 182 C4
Talardd 168 B5
Talaton 103 D3
Talbenny 126 B1
Talbot Green 129 G4
Talbot Village 105 G3
Talerddig 155 F2
Talgarreg 142 A2
Talgarth 144 A4
Talisker 255 J1
Talke Pits 171 F2
Talkin 210 B2
Talkin Tarn Country Park Cumb CA8 1HN 210 B2
Talla Linnfoots 226 C3
Talladale 265 F4
Talladh-a-Bheithe 250 A4
Talland 97 G4
Tallarn Green 170 B3
Tallentire 209 E3
Talley (Talyllychau) 142 C4
Tallington 161 F2
Talmine 273 H2
Talog 141 G5
Tal-sarn 142 B2
Talsarnau 167 F4
Talskiddy 96 D3
Talwrn IoA 180 C5
Talwrn Wrex 169 F3
Talwrn Wrex 170 A3
Tal-y-bont Cere 154 C4
Tal-y-bont Conwy 168 A1
Tal-y-bont Gwyn 167 E5
Tal-y-bont Gwyn 181 E5
Talybont-on-Usk 144 A5
Tal-y-Cae 167 F1
Tal-y-cafn 181 F5
Tal-y-coed 130 D1
Talygarn 129 G4
Tal-y-llyn Gwyn 154 D2
Tal-y-llyn Powys 144 A5
Talyllyn Railway (The Slate Landscape of Northwest Wales) Gwyn 154 C2
Talysarn 167 G2
Tal-y-wern 155 E2
Tamar Valley Mining District (Cornwall & West Devon Mining Landscape) Corn/Devon 99 E3
Tamavoid 242 A5
Tamerton Foliot 100 A1
Tamlaght CC&G 286 D5
Tamlaght F&O 280 E4
Tamlaght O'Crilly 286 D5
Tamnamore 282 B5
Tamnavally 282 C1
Tamniarin 286 B5
Tamnyrankin 286 C5
Tamworth 159 E2
Tamworth Green 176 B3
Tan Office Green 151 F2
Tandem 185 F1
Tandragee 282 D4
Tandridge 122 C3
Tanerdy 142 A5
Tanfield 212 A2
Tanfield Lea 212 A2
Tang 194 B2

Tang Hall 195 F2
Tangiers 126 C1
Tanglandford 261 G1
Tangley 119 E2
Tangmere 108 B3
Tangwick 278 B5
Tangy 222 B3
Tank Museum, Bovington Dorset BH20 6JG 105 E4
Tankerness 277 E7
Tankersley 186 A2
Tankerton 124 D2
Tan-lan 167 F3
Tannach 275 J4
Tannachie 253 F1
Tannadice 252 C4
Tannington 152 D1
Tannochside 234 A3
Tansley 173 E2
Tansley Knoll 173 E2
Tansor 161 F2
Tantobie 212 A2
Tanton 203 E1
Tanworth in Arden 158 D5
Tan-y-fron 168 C1
Tangyrisiau 167 F4
Tan-y-graig 166 C4
Tan-y-groes 141 F3
Tan-y-pistyll 169 D5
Tan-yr-allt 182 B4
Taobh a' Deas Loch Baghasdail 254 C3
Taobh Siar 270 D7
Tapeley 113 E3
Taplow 135 E4
Tapton Grove 186 B5
Taransay (Tarasaigh) 270 C7
Taraphocain 248 C5
Tarbat House 266 E4
Tarbert A&B 231 G4
Tarbert A&B 231 G3
Tarbert A&B 231 E1
Tarbert High 247 F3
Tarbert Na H-E. Siar 270 D7
Tarbet (An Tairbeart) A&B 241 F4
Tarbet High 256 D5
Tarbet High 272 D4
Tarbock Green 183 F4
Tarbolton 224 C3
Tarbrax 235 E4
Tardebigge 146 B1
Tardy Gate 192 B5
Tarfside 252 C2
Tarland 260 C4
Tarleton 192 A5
Tarlscough 183 F1
Tarlton 132 B3
Tarnbrook 192 B2
Tarnock 116 A2
Tarporley 170 C1
Tarr 115 E4
Tarrant Crawford 105 F2
Tarrant Gunville 105 F1
Tarrant Hinton 105 F1
Tarrant Keyneston 105 F2
Tarrant Launceston 105 F2
Tarrant Monkton 105 F2
Tarrant Rawston 105 F2
Tarrant Rushton 105 F2
Tarrel 267 F3
Tarring Neville 109 G3
Tarrington 145 F3
Tarnacraig 223 E2
Tarsappie 243 G2
Tarskavaig 256 B3
Tarves 261 G1
Tarvie (Tairbhidh) High 266 B6
Tarvie P&K 251 F3
Tarvin 170 B1
Tarvin Sands 170 B1
Tasburgh 164 D2
Tasley 157 F3
Tassagh 282 B5
Taston 147 F5
Tate Britain GtLon SW1P 4RG 13 B5
Tate Liverpool Mersey L3 4BB 42 B5
Tate Modern GtLon SE1 9TG 45 H4
Tate St. Ives Corn TR26 1TG 94 C2
Tatenhill 172 D5
Tathall End 148 D3
Tatham 192 C1
Tathwell 188 D4
Tatsfield 122 D3
Tattenhall 170 B2
Tattenhoe 148 D4
Tatterford 177 G5
Tattersett 177 G4
Tattershall 176 A2
Tattershall Bridge 175 G2
Tattershall Thorpe 176 A2
Tattingstone 152 C4
Tattinweer 281 F2
Tatton Park ChesE WA16 6QN 184 B4
Tattyreagh 281 G2
Tatworth 103 G2
Tauchers 268 B6
Taughbatee 283 F3
Taunton 115 F5
Tavelty 261 F3
Taverham 178 C4
Tavernspite 127 E1
Tavistock 99 E3
Tavistock (Cornwall & West Devon Mining Landscape) Devon 99 E3
Taw Bridge 113 G5
Taw Green 99 G1
Tawstock 113 F3
Taxal 185 E5
Tayburn 233 G5
Taychreggan 240 C2
Tayinloan 231 E5
Taylors Cross 112 C4
Taynafead 240 C3
Taynish 231 F1

Taynton Glos 145 G5
Taynton Oxon 133 E1
Taynuilt (Taigh an Uillt) 240 C1
Tayock 253 E4
Tayovullin 230 A2
Tayport 244 C2
Tayvallich 231 F1
Tea Green 149 G5
Tealby 188 B3
Tealing 244 C1
Team Valley 212 B1
Teanamachar 262 C5
Teangue 256 C4
Teasses 244 C4
Tebay 200 B2
Tebworth 149 E5
Tedburn St. Mary 102 B3
Tedd 280 E2
Teddington Glos 146 B5
Teddington GtLon 136 A5
Tedstone Delamere 145 F2
Tedstone Wafre 145 F2
Teemore 281 F6
Teeton 160 B5
Teffont Evias 118 A4
Teffont Magna 118 A4
Tegryn 141 F4
Tehidy Country Park Corn TR14 0HA 96 A5
Teifi Marshes Nature Reserve Pembs SA43 2TB 141 E3
Teigh 161 D1
Teign Village 102 B4
Teigngrace 102 B5
Teignmouth 102 C5
Telford 157 F2
Telford Wonderland Tel&W TF3 4AY 157 G2
Telham 110 C2
Tellisford 117 F2
Telscombe 109 G3
Telscombe Cliffs 109 G3
Tempar 250 B4
Templand 217 E2
Temple Corn 97 F2
Temple L&C 283 G2
Temple Midlo 236 A4
Temple Balsall 159 E5
Temple Bar 142 B2
Temple Cloud 116 D2
Temple End 151 E2
Temple Ewell 125 E4
Temple Grafton 146 D2
Temple Guiting 146 C5
Temple Herdewyke 147 F2
Temple Hirst 195 F5
Temple Newsam WYorks LS15 0AE 27 M7
Temple Normanton 173 F1
Temple Sowerby 210 C5
Templecombe 117 E5
Templemoyle 285 H4
Templepatrick 287 G7
Templeton Devon 102 B1
Templeton Pembs 127 E1
Templeton Bridge 102 B1
Templewood 253 E3
Tempo 281 F4
Ten Mile Bank 163 E3
Tenbury Wells 145 E1
Tenby (Dinbych-y-pysgod) 127 E2
Tendring 152 C5
Tendring Green 152 C5
Tenga 247 E5
Tenterden 124 A5
Tepersie Castle 260 D2
Terally 106 B2
Terling 137 G1
Tern 157 F1
Ternhill 170 D4
Terregles 216 D3
Terriers 135 E3
Terrington 203 F5
Terrington St. Clement 177 D5
Terrington St. John 162 D1
Terrydermont 285 J4
Terry's Green 158 D5
Tervieside 259 K1
Teston 123 G3
Testwood 106 C1
Tetbury 132 A3
Tetbury Upton 132 A3
Tetchill 170 A4
Tetcott 98 D1
Tetford 188 D5
Tetney 188 D2
Tetney Lock 188 D2
Tetsworth 134 B2
Tettenhall 158 A2
Tettenhall Wood 158 A3
Tetworth 150 A2
Teuchan 261 J1
Teversal 173 F1
Teversham 150 C2
Teviothead 227 F5
Tewel 253 G1
Tewin 136 B1
Tewkesbury 146 A4
Tewkesbury Abbey Glos GL20 5RZ 146 A4
Teynham 124 B2
Thackley 194 A4
Thainston 253 E2
Thainstone 261 F3
Thakeham 108 D2
Thame 134 C2
Thames Ditton 121 G1
Thames Haven 137 G4
Thamesmead 137 D4
Thanington 124 D3
Thankerton 226 A2
Tharston 164 C2
Thatcham 119 G1
Thatto Heath 183 G3
Thaxted 151 E4
The Apes Hall 163 D3
The Bage 144 B3
The Balloch 242 D3

The Banking 261 F1
The Bar 121 G5
The Battery 287 G6
The Birks 261 F4
The Bog 156 C3
The Bourne 120 D3
The Bratch 158 A3
The Broad 145 D1
The Bryn 130 C2
The Burf 146 A1
The Burn 253 D2
The Bush 282 B2
The Butts 117 E3
The Camp 132 B2
The Chequer 170 B3
The City Bucks 134 C3
The City Suff 165 E3
The Cluster 282 C5
The Common Wilts 118 D4
The Common Wilts 132 C4
The Craigs CC&G 286 C5
The Craigs High 266 B2
The Cronk 190 B2
The Dark Hedges CC&G BT53 8PX 286 C2
The Delves 158 C3
The Den 233 E4
The Den & The Glen Aber AB12 5FT 261 G5
The Diamond F&O 281 G2
The Diamond Mid Ulster 282 C1
The Dicker 110 A3
The Down 157 F3
The Drones 286 B3
The Drums 252 B3
The Eaves 131 F2
The English Lake District 199 E2
The Fingerpost 281 F7
The Flatt 219 D4
The Folly 136 A1
The Forge 144 C1
The Forstal ESuss 123 E5
The Forstal Kent 124 C5
The Forth Bridge Fife/WLoth EH30 9SF 235 F2
The Gobbins Visitor Centre M&EAnt BT40 3SL 287 J6
The Grange Lincs 189 F5
The Grange Shrop 170 A4
The Grange Surr 122 A2
The Green A&B 246 A2
The Green Cumb 198 C4
The Green Essex 137 E1
The Green Flints 169 F1
The Green Wilts 117 F4
The Grove 146 A3
The Haven 121 F4
The Headland 213 E4
The Heath 178 C2
The Herberts 129 F5
The Hermitage 122 B3
The Hill 198 C4
The Holme 194 B2
The Howe 190 A5
The Isle 157 D1
The Laurels 165 E2
The Leacon 124 B5
The Lee 135 D2
The Leigh 146 A5
The Lhen 190 B1
The Lodge 241 D5
The Lodge Forest Visitor Centre Stir FK8 3SX 242 A4
The Long Kesh 283 F3
The Loup 286 D7
The Luxulyan Valley (Cornwall & West Devon Mining Landscape) Corn 97 E4
The Marsh 156 C3
The Milky Way Adventure Park Devon EX39 5RY 112 D3
The Moor ESuss 110 D3
The Moor Kent 110 C1
The Moors National Park Centre, Danby NYorks YO21 2NB 203 G2
The Murray 234 A4
The Mythe 146 A4
The Narth 131 E2
The Neuk 261 F5
The Node 136 B1
The Oval 117 E1
The Polchar 259 G4
The Port of Hayle (Cornwall & West Devon Mining Landscape) Corn 94 C3
The Quarter 124 A4
The Reddings 146 B5
The Rhos 126 D1
The Rock 282 A1
The Rookery 171 F2
The Rowe 171 F4
The Sale 159 D1
The Sands 121 D3
The Sheddings 287 G5
The Shoe 132 A5
The Six Towns 286 B6
The Slade 134 A5
The Slate Landscape of Northwest Wales Conwy/Gwyn 167 E1
The Smithies 157 F3
The Spa 283 G4
The Stocks 111 E1
The Swillett 135 F3
The Thrift 150 B4
The Vauld 145 E3
The Wern 169 F2
The Wyke 157 G2
Theakston 202 C4
Thealby 187 F1
Theale Som 116 B3
Theale WBerks 134 B5
Thearne 196 C4
Theberton 153 F1
Thedden Grange 120 B4
Theddingworth 160 B4
Theddlethorpe All Saints 189 E4
Theddlethorpe St. Helen 189 E4
Thelbridge Barton 102 A1

Thelbridge Cross 102 A1
Thelnetham 164 B4
Thelveton 164 C3
Thelwall 184 A1
Themelthorpe 178 B3
Thenford 148 A4
Therfield 150 B4
Thetford Lincs 161 G1
Thetford Norf 163 G4
Thetford Forest Park Norf IP27 0TJ 163 G4
Thethwaite 209 G2
Theydon Bois 136 D3
Theydon Garnon 137 D3
Theydon Mount 137 D3
Thickwood 132 A5
Thimbleby Lincs 176 A1
Thimbleby NYorks 202 D3
Thingley 117 F1
Thirkleby 203 D5
Thirlby 203 D4
Thirlestane 236 C5
Thirn 202 B4
Thirsk 202 D4
Thirston New Houses 221 D2
Thirtleby 197 D4
Thistleton Lancs 192 A4
Thistleton Rut 161 E1
Thistley Green 163 E5
Thixendale 196 A1
Thockrington 220 B4
Tholomas Drove 162 B2
Tholthorpe 195 D1
Thomas Chapel 127 E2
Thomas Close 210 A3
Thomastown 260 D1
Thompson 164 A2
Thompson's Bridge 280 E5
Thomshill 267 K6
Thong 137 F5
Thongsbridge 185 F2
Thoralby 201 F4
Thoresby 186 D5
Thoresthorpe 189 E5
Thoresway 188 B3
Thorganby Lincs 188 C3
Thorganby NYorks 195 F3
Thorgill 203 G3
Thorington 165 F4
Thorington Street 152 B4
Thorley 137 D1
Thorley Houses 150 C5
Thorley Street Herts 137 D1
Thorley Street IoW 106 C4
Thormanby 203 D5
Thornaby-on-Tees 203 D1
Thornage 178 B2
Thornborough Bucks 148 C4
Thornborough NYorks 202 B5
Thornbury Devon 113 D5
Thornbury Here 145 F2
Thornbury SGlos 131 F3
Thornbury WYorks 194 A4
Thornby 160 B5
Thorncliff 185 G1
Thorncliffe 172 B2
Thorncombe 103 G2
Thorncombe Street 121 F3
Thorncote Green 149 G3
Thorncross 106 D4
Thorndon 152 C1
Thorndon Country Park Essex CM13 3RZ 137 F3
Thorndon Cross 99 F1
Thorne 187 D1
Thorne St. Margaret 115 D5
Thorner 194 C4
Thorney Bucks 135 F5
Thorney Notts 187 F5
Thorney Peter 162 A2
Thorney Som 116 B5
Thorney Close 212 C2
Thorney Hill 106 B3
Thornfalcon 115 F5
Thornford 104 C1
Thorngrafton 211 D1
Thorngrove 116 A4
Thorngumbald 197 E5
Thornham 177 F3
Thornham Magna 164 C4
Thornham Parva 164 C4
Thornhaugh 161 F2
Thornhill Cardiff 130 A4
Thornhill Cumb 198 B2
Thornhill D&G 216 C1
Thornhill Derbys 185 F4
Thornhill Soton 107 D1
Thornhill Stir 242 B4
Thornhill WYorks 185 G1
Thornhill Lees 185 G1
Thornholme 196 D1
Thornicombe 105 E2
Thornley Dur 212 C4
Thornley Dur 212 A4
Thornley Gate 211 E2
Thornliebank 233 G4
Thornroan 261 G1
Thorns 151 F2
Thorns Green 184 B4
Thornsett 185 E4
Thornton Angus 252 B5
Thornton Bucks 148 C4
Thornton ERid 195 G3
Thornton Fife 244 A5
Thornton Lancs 191 G3
Thornton Leics 159 G2
Thornton Lincs 176 A1
Thornton Mersey 183 E2
Thornton Middl 203 D1
Thornton N'umb 237 D5
Thornton P&K 251 F5
Thornton Pembs 126 C2
Thornton WYorks 194 A4
Thornton Bridge 202 D5
Thornton Curtis 188 A1
Thornton Heath 122 C2
Thornton Hough 183 E4
Thornton in Lonsdale 200 B5
Thornton le Moor 188 A3
Thornton Park 237 G5
Thornton Rust 201 F4
Thornton Steward 202 A4
Thornton Watlass 202 B4

Thornton-in-Craven 193 F3
Thornton-le-Beans 202 D3
Thornton-le-Clay 195 F1
Thornton-le-Dale 204 B4
Thornton-le-Moor 202 D4
Thornton-le-Moors 183 F5
Thornton-le-Street 202 D4
Thornton-loch 237 E2
Thornwood 137 D2
Thornyhill 253 E2
Thornylee 227 F2
Thoroton 174 C3
Thorp Arch 194 D3
Thorpe Derbys 172 C2
Thorpe ERid 196 B3
Thorpe Lincs 189 E4
Thorpe Norf 165 F2
Thorpe Notts 174 C2
Thorpe NYorks 193 G1
Thorpe Surr 121 F1
Thorpe Abbotts 164 C3
Thorpe Acre 173 G4
Thorpe Arnold 174 C5
Thorpe Audlin 186 B1
Thorpe Bassett 204 B5
Thorpe Bay 138 C4
Thorpe Constantine 159 E2
Thorpe Culvert 176 C1
Thorpe End 179 D4
Thorpe Green Essex 152 C5
Thorpe Green Lancs 192 B5
Thorpe Green Suff 152 A2
Thorpe Hall 203 E5
Thorpe Hesley 186 A3
Thorpe in Balne 186 C1
Thorpe in the Fallows 187 G4
Thorpe Langton 160 C3
Thorpe Larches 212 C5
Thorpe le Street 196 A3
Thorpe Malsor 160 D5
Thorpe Mandeville 148 A3
Thorpe Market 178 D2
Thorpe Morieux 152 A2
Thorpe on the Hill Lincs 175 E1
Thorpe on the Hill WYorks 194 C5
Thorpe Park Surr KT16 8PN 121 F1
Thorpe Row 178 A5
Thorpe St. Andrew 179 D5
Thorpe St. Peter 176 C1
Thorpe Salvin 186 C4
Thorpe Satchville 160 C1
Thorpe Street 164 B4
Thorpe Thewles 212 D5
Thorpe Tilney Dales 175 G2
Thorpe Underwood NN'hants 160 C4
Thorpe Underwood NYorks 195 D2
Thorpe Waterville 161 F4
Thorpe Willoughby 195 E4
Thorpefield 202 D5
Thorpe-le-Soken 152 C5
Thorpeness 153 F1
Thorpland 163 E2
Thorrington 152 B5
Thorverton 102 C2
Thrandeston 164 B4
Thrapston 161 E5
Threapland 193 F1
Threapwood 170 B3
Threapwood Head 172 B3
Three Ashes 117 D3
Three Bridges 122 B5
Three Burrows 96 B5
Three Chimneys 124 A5
Three Cocks (Aberllynfi) 144 A4
Three Counties Showground Worcs WR13 6NW 145 G3
Three Crosses 128 B3
Three Cups Corner 110 B1
Three Hammers 97 G1
Three Holes 162 D2
Three Leg Cross 123 F5
Three Legged Cross 105 G2
Three Mile Cross 120 C1
Three Oaks 110 D2
Threehammer Common 179 E4
Threekingham 175 F4
Threemilestone 96 B5
Threlkeld 209 G4
Threshfield 193 F1
Threxton Hill 163 G2
Thriepley 244 B1
Thrigby 179 F4
Thrigby Hall Wildlife Gardens Norf NR29 3DR 179 F4
Thringarth 211 F5
Thringstone 159 G1
Thrintoft 202 C3
Thriplow 150 C3
Throapham 186 C4
Throckenholt 162 B2
Throcking 150 B4
Throckley 212 A1
Throckmorton 146 B3
Throop 105 G3
Throphill 220 D3
Thropton 220 C1
Througham 132 B2
Throwleigh 99 G2
Throwley 124 B3
Throws 151 E5
Thrumpton Notts 173 G4
Thrumpton Notts 187 E5
Thrumster 275 J4
Thrunton 229 E5
Thrupp Glos 132 A2
Thrupp Oxon 133 G1
Thrupp Oxon 133 E3
Thruscross 194 A2
Thrushelton 99 E2
Thrussington 160 B1
Thruxton Hants 119 D3
Thruxton Here 144 D4
Thrybergh 186 B3
Thrybergh Country Park SYorks S65 4NU 186 B3
Thulston 173 F5
Thunder Bridge 185 F1
Thundergay 231 G5
Thundersley 138 B4

Thunderton 269 J6
Thundridge 136 C1
Thurcaston 160 A1
Thurcroft 186 B4
Thurdistoft 275 H2
Thurdon 112 C4
Thurgarton Norf 178 C2
Thurgarton Notts 174 B3
Thurgoland 185 G2
Thurlaston Leics 160 A3
Thurlaston Warks 159 G5
Thurlbear 115 F5
Thurlby Lincs 161 G1
Thurlby Lincs 175 E1
Thurlby Lincs 189 E5
Thurleigh 149 F2
Thurlestone 100 C3
Thurloxton 115 F4
Thurlstone 185 G2
Thurlton 165 F2
Thurlwood 171 F2
Thurmaston 160 B2
Thurnby 160 B2
Thurne 179 F4
Thurnham 124 A3
Thurning NN'hants 161 F4
Thurning Norf 178 B3
Thurnscoe 186 B2
Thursby 209 G1
Thursden 193 F4
Thursford 178 A2
Thursford Collection Norf NR21 0AS 178 A2
Thursley 121 E4
Thurso (Inbhir Theòrsa) 275 G2
Thurstaston 182 D4
Thurston 152 A1
Thurston Clough 185 D2
Thurstonfield 209 G1
Thurstonland 185 F1
Thurton 179 E5
Thurvaston Derbys 172 D4
Thurvaston Derbys 172 C4
Thuster 275 H3
Thuxton 178 B5
Thwaite NYorks 201 D3
Thwaite Suff 152 C1
Thwaite Head 199 E3
Thwaite St. Mary 165 E2
Thwaites 193 G3
Thwaites Brow 193 G3
Thwing 205 D5
Tibbermore 243 F2
Tibberton Glos 145 G5
Tibberton Tel&W 171 D5
Tibberton Worcs 146 B2
Tibbie Shiels Inn 226 C3
Tibenham 164 C2
Tibertich 240 A4
Tibshelf 173 F1
Tibthorpe 196 B2
Ticehurst 123 F5
Tichborne 119 G4
Tickencote 161 F2
Tickenham 131 D5
Tickford End 149 D3
Tickhill 186 C3
Ticklerton 157 D3
Ticknall 173 E5
Tickton 196 C3
Tidbury Green 158 D5
Tidcombe 119 D2
Tiddington Oxon 134 B2
Tiddington Warks 147 E2
Tiddleywink 132 A5
Tidebrook 110 B1
Tideford 98 D5
Tideford Cross 98 D4
Tidenham 131 E3
Tidenham Chase 131 E3
Tideswell 185 F5
Tidmarsh 134 B5
Tidmington 147 E4
Tidpit 105 G1
Tidworth 118 D3
Tiers Cross 126 C1
Tiffield 148 B2
Tifty 269 F6
Tigerton 252 D3
Tigh a' Gearraidh 262 C4
Tighachnoic 247 F5
Tighnabat 242 C3
Tighnabruaich 232 A2
Tighnacomaire 248 B3
Tigley 101 D1
Tilbrook 149 F1
Tilbury 137 F5
Tilbury Green 151 F3
Tildarg 287 G6
Tile Hill 159 E5
Tilehurst 134 B5
Tilford 121 D3
Tilgate 122 B5
Tilgate Forest Row 122 B5
Tilgate Park WSuss RH10 5PQ 122 B5
Tillathrowie 260 C1
Tillers' Green 145 F4
Tillery 261 H2
Tilley 170 C5
Tillicoultry 243 E5
Tillietudlem 225 G1
Tillingham 138 C2
Tillington Here 145 D3
Tillington WSuss 121 E5
Tillington Common 145 D3
Tillyarblet 252 D3
Tillybirloch 260 E4
Tillycairn Castle 260 E3
Tillycorthie 261 H2
Tillydrine 260 E5
Tillyfar 269 G6
Tillyfour 260 D3
Tillyfourie 260 E3
Tillygreig 261 G2
Tillypronie 260 C4
Tilmanstone 125 F3
Tiln 187 E4
Tilney All Saints 163 D1
Tilney Fen End 162 D1
Tilney High End 163 D1
Tilney St. Lawrence 162 D1
Tilshead 118 B3
Tilstock 170 C4
Tilston 170 B2
Tilstone Fearnall 170 C1
Tilsworth 149 E5

Tilton on the Hill 160 C2
Tiltups End 132 A3
Timberland 175 F1
Timberland Dales 175 G1
Timbersbrook 171 F1
Timberscombe 114 C3
Timble 194 A2
Timewell 114 C5
Timperley 184 B4
Timsbury
  B&NESom 117 D2
Timsbury Hants 119 E5
Timsgearraidh 270 C4
Timworth 151 G1
Timworth Green 151 G1
Tincleton 105 D3
Tindale 210 C2
Tindon End 151 E4
Tingewick 148 B4
Tingley 194 B5
Tingrith 149 F4
Tingwall 276 D5
Tingwall (Lerwick)
  Airport 279 D8
Tinhay 99 D2
Tinney 98 C1
Tinshill 194 B4
Tinsley 186 B3
Tinsley Green 122 B5
Tintagel 97 E1
Tintagel Castle Corn
  PL34 0HE 97 E1
Tintern 131 E2
Tintinhull 104 A1
Tintwistle 185 E3
Tinwald 217 E2
Tinwell 161 F2
Tippacott 114 A3
Tipperty Aber 253 F1
Tipperty Aber 261 H2
Tipps End 162 C3
Tiptoe 106 B3
Tipton 158 B3
Tipton St. John 103 D3
Tiptree 138 C1
Tiptree Heath 138 B1
Tiptree Museum Essex
  CO5 0RF 138 C1
Tirabad 143 E3
Tiraroe 281 F6
Tircur 285 G7
Tiree 246 A2
Tiree Airport 246 B2
Tirgan 286 C7
Tirindrish 249 E1
Tirley 146 A5
Tir-phil 130 A2
Tirril 210 B5
Tir-y-dail 128 C2
Tisbury 118 A5
Tisman's Common 121 F4
Tissington 172 C2
Tister 275 G2
Titanic Belfast BT3 9EP
  63 Belfast
Titchberry 112 C3
Titchfield 107 E2
Titchmarsh 161 F5
Titchwell 177 F3
Titchwell Marsh Norf
  PE31 8BB 177 F3
Tithby 174 B4
Titley 144 C1
Titlington 229 F5
Titmore Green 150 A5
Titsey 122 D3
Titson 112 C5
Tittensor 171 F4
Tittesworth Reservoir & Visitor
  Centre Staffs
  ST13 8TQ 171 G2
Tittleshall 177 G5
Tiverton ChesW&C 170 C1
Tiverton Devon 102 C1
Tivetshall
  St. Margaret 164 C3
Tivetshall St. Mary 164 C3
Tivington 114 C3
Tixall 171 G5
Tixover 161 E2
Toab Ork 277 E7
Toab Shet 279 F9
Toberdoney 286 D2
Toberkeagh 286 D2
Tobermory 247 E4
Toberonochy 239 G4
Tobson 270 D4
Tocher 260 E1
Tockenham 132 C5
Tockenham Wick 132 C4
Tockholes 192 C5
Tockington 131 F4
Tockwith 195 D2
Todber 117 E5
Toddington CenBeds 149 F5
Toddington Glos 146 C4
Todenham 147 E4
Todhills Angus 244 C1
Todhills Cumb 218 B5
Todlachie 260 E3
Todmorden 193 F5
Todwick 186 B4
Toft Cambs 150 B2
Toft Lincs 161 F1
Toft Shet 278 D5
Toft Hill 212 A4
Toft Monks 165 F2
Toft next Newton 188 A4
Toftcarl 275 J4
Toftrees 177 G5
Tofts 275 J2
Toftwood 178 A4
Togston 221 E1
Tokavaig 256 C3
Tokers Green 134 B5
Tolastadh a' Chaolais 270 D4
Tolastadh Bho Thuath
  271 H3
Tolastadh Ur 271 H3
Toll Bar 186 C2
Toll of Birness 261 J1
Tolland 114 C4
Tollard Farnham 105 F1
Tollard Royal 105 F1
Tollcross 234 A3
Toller Down Gate 104 B2
Toller Fratrum 104 B3

Toller Porcorum 104 B3
Toller Whelme 104 B2
Tollerton Notts 174 B3
Tollerton NYorks 195 E1
Tollesbury 138 C1
Tollesby 203 E1
Tolleshunt D'Arcy 138 C1
Tolleshunt Knights 138 C1
Tolleshunt Major 138 B1
Tolmachan 270 C7
Tolpuddle 105 D3
Tolvah 259 F5
Tolworth 121 G1
Tom an Fhuadain 271 F6
Tomatin 259 F2
Tombreck 258 D1
Tomchrasky
  (Tom Chrasgaidh) 257 J3
Tomdoun 257 H4
Tomdow 267 H7
Tomich High 257 K2
Tomich High 266 E4
Tomich High 266 D1
Tomintoul 259 J3
Tomnacross 266 C7
Tomnamoon 267 H6
Tomnaven 260 C1
Tomnavoulin 259 K2
Tomvaich 259 H1
Ton Pentre 129 F3
Tonbridge 123 E4
Ton-du 129 E4
Tonedale 115 E5
Toneel 280 D4
Tonfanau 154 B2
Tong Kent 124 A4
Tong Shrop 157 G2
Tong WYorks 194 B4
Tong Norton 157 G2
Tong Street 194 A4
Tonge 173 F5
Tongham 121 D3
Tongland 216 A5
Tongue 273 H3
Tongue House 273 H3
Tongwynlais 130 A4
Ton-mawr 129 E3
Tonna 129 D3
Tonnaboy 281 F5
Tonwell 136 C1
Tonyglaskan 281 F5
Tonypandy 129 F3
Tonyrefail 129 G4
Tonyteige 280 E5
Tonyvarnog 280 E6
Toome 286 D6
Toot Baldon 134 A2
Toot Hill 137 E2
Toothill Hants 106 C1
Toothill Swin 132 D4
Tooting Graveney 136 B5
Top End 149 F1
Top of Hebers 184 C2
Topcliffe 202 D5
Topcroft 165 D2
Topcroft Street 165 D2
Toppesfield 151 F4
Toppings 184 B1
Toprow 164 C2
Topsham 102 C4
Topsham Bridge 100 D2
Torastan 246 B3
Torbain 259 J3
Torbeg Aber 260 B5
Torbeg NAyr 223 E3
Torbothie 234 C4
Torbryan 101 E1
Torcastle 248 D2
Torcross 101 E3
Tordarroch 258 D1
Tore (An Todhar) 266 D6
Toreduff 267 J5
Toremore High 259 J1
Toremore High 275 G5
Torfrey 97 F4
Torgyle 257 K3
Torksey 187 F5
Torlum 262 C6
Torlundy
  (Tòrr Lunndaidh) 248 D2
Tormarton 131 G5
Tormisdale 230 A4
Tormore 223 D2
Tormsdale 275 G3
Tornagrain 266 E6
Tornahaish 259 K4
Tornaveen 260 E4
Torness 258 C2
Toronto 212 A4
Torpenhow 209 F3
Torphichen 235 D2
Torphins 260 E4
Torpoint 100 A2
Torquay 101 F1
Torquay's Dinosaur World
  TQ1 2BB 101 F1
Torquhan 236 B3
Torr CC&G 287 G1
Torr Devon 100 B2
Torran A&B 240 A4
Torran High 266 E4
Torran High 264 B7
Torrance 234 A2
Torrance House 234 A4
Torrancroy 260 B3
Torre Som 114 D3
Torre Torbay 101 F1
Torrich 267 F6
Torridon 264 E6
Torrin 256 B2
Torrisdale A&B 222 C2
Torrisdale High 273 J2
Torrish 274 E7
Torrisholme 192 A1
Torroble 266 C1
Torry Aber 268 C6
Torry Aberdeen 261 H4
Torryburn 235 E1
Torsonce 236 B3
Torterston 269 J6
Torthorwald 217 E3
Tortington 108 B3
Torton 158 A5
Tortworth 131 G3
Torvaig 263 K7
Torver 199 D3
Torwood 234 C1
Torworth 187 D4

Tosberry 112 C3
Toscaig 256 D1
Toseland 150 A1
Tosside 193 F2
Tostarie 246 C5
Tostock 152 A1
Totaig 263 G6
Tote 263 K7
Tote Hill 121 D5
Totford 119 G4
Totham Hill 138 B1
Tothill 189 E4
Totland 106 C4
Totley 186 A5
Totnes 101 E1
Toton 173 G4
Totronald 246 A4
Totscore 263 J5
Tottenham 136 C3
Tottenhill 163 E1
Tottenhill Row 163 E1
Totteridge Bucks 135 D3
Totteridge GtLon 136 B3
Totternhoe 149 E5
Tottington GtMan 184 B1
Tottington Norf 163 G3
Totton 106 C1
Toulston 195 E3
Toulton 115 E4
Tournaig 264 E3
Toux 269 H5
Tovil 123 G3
Tow Law 212 A4
Towan Cross 96 B5
Toward 232 C3
Towcester 148 B3
Towednack 94 B3
Tower Bridge Exhibition
  GtLon SE1 2UP 12 C4
Tower End 163 E1
Tower of London GtLon
  EC3N 4AB 12 C4
Towersey 134 C2
Towie Aber 269 G4
Towie Aber 260 D2
Towie Aber 260 C3
Towiemore 268 B6
Town End Cambs 162 C3
Town End Cumb 199 F4
Town End Mersey 183 F4
Town Green Lancs 183 F2
Town Green Norf 179 E4
Town of Lowton 184 A3
Town Row 123 E5
Town Street 163 F4
Town Yetholm 228 C4
Townend 211 F3
Townfield 211 F3
Townhead D&G 207 G2
Townhead SYorks 185 F2
Townhead of
  Greenlaw 216 B4
Townhill Fife 235 F1
Townhill Swan 128 C3
Towns End 119 G2
Towns Green 170 D1
Townshend 94 C3
Towthorpe ERid 196 B1
Towthorpe York 195 F2
Towton 195 E3
Towyn 182 A5
Toynton All Saints 176 B1
Toynton Fen Side 176 B1
Toynton St. Peter 176 C1
Toy's Hill 123 D3
Trabboch 224 C3
Traboe 95 E4
Tradespark High 267 F6
Tradespark Ork 277 D7
Trafford Centre 184 B3
Trafford Centre
  GtMan M17 8AA 184 B3
Trafford Park 184 B3
Trago Mills, Newton Abbot
  Devon TQ12 6JD 102 B5
Trallong 143 F5
Trallwn 128 C3
Tram Inn 145 D4
Tranent 236 B2
Tranmere 183 E4
Trantlebeg 274 D3
Trantlemore 274 D3
Tranwell 221 D3
Trap 128 C1
Trap Street 171 F1
Traprain 236 C2
Trap's Green 146 D1
Trawden 193 F4
Trawscoed
  (Crosswood) 154 C5
Trawsfynydd 168 A4
Tre Taliesin 154 C3
Trealaw 129 G3
Treales 192 A4
Trearddur 180 A5
Tre-Aubrey 129 G5
Trebah Garden Corn
  TR11 5JZ 95 E4
Trebanog 129 G3
Trebanos 128 D2
Trebarrow 98 C1
Trebartha 97 G2
Trebarvah 95 E3
Trebarwith 97 E1
Trebeath 97 G1
Trebetherick 96 D2
Trebister 278 D9
Tre-boeth 128 C3
Treborough 114 D4
Trebudannon 96 C3
Trebullett 98 D3
Treburley 98 D3
Treburrick 96 C2
Trebyan 97 E3
Trecastle 143 E5
Trecott 113 G5
Trecrogo 98 D3
Trecwn 140 C4
Trecynon 129 F2
Tredaule 97 G2
Tredavoe 94 B4
Treddiog 140 B5
Tredegar 130 A2

Tredington Glos 146 B5
Tredington Warks 147 E3
Tredinnick Corn 98 C1
Tredinnick Corn 97 G4
Tredogan 115 D1
Tredomen 144 A4
Tredrissi 141 E3
Tredunnock 130 C3
Tredustan 144 A4
Tredworth 132 A1
Treen Corn 94 A4
Treen Corn 94 B3
Treesmill 97 E4
Treeton 186 B4
Trefasser 140 B4
Trefdraeth 180 C5
Trefecca 144 A4
Trefechan 129 G2
Trefeglwys 155 F3
Trefenter 142 C1
Treffgarne 140 C5
Treffynnon 140 B5
Trefgarn Owen 140 B5
Trefil 130 A1
Trefilan 142 B2
Tre-fin 140 B4
Treflach 169 F5
Trefnanney 156 B1
Trefnant 182 B5
Trefonen 169 F5
Trefor Gwyn 166 C3
Trefor IoA 180 B4
Treforest 129 G4
Treforest Industrial
  Estate 130 A4
Trefriw 168 A1
Tregadillett 97 G1
Tregaian 180 C5
Tregare 130 D1
Tregarland 97 G4
Tregaron 142 C2
Tregarth 167 F1
Tregaswith 96 C3
Tregavethan 96 B5
Tregear 96 C4
Tregeare 97 G1
Tregeiriog 169 E4
Tregele 180 B3
Tregidden 95 E4
Tregiskey 97 E5
Treglemais 140 B5
Tregolds 96 C2
Tregole 98 B1
Tregonetha 97 D3
Tregonning & Gwinear Mining
  Districts (Cornwall & West
  Devon Mining Landscape)
  Corn 94 C3
Tregony 96 D5
Tregoodwell 97 F1
Tregoss 97 D3
Tregowris 96 E4
Tregoyd 144 A4
Tregrehan Mills 97 E4
Tre-groes 142 A3
Treguff 129 G5
Tregullon 97 E3
Tregunnon 97 G1
Tregurrian 96 C3
Tregynon 155 G3
Trehafod 129 G3
Trehan 100 A2
Treharris 129 G3
Treherbert 129 F3
Tre-hill 129 G5
Trekenner 98 D3
Treknow 97 E1
Trelan 95 E5
Trelash 98 B1
Trelassick 96 C4
Trelawnyd 182 B5
Tre-lech 141 F4
Treleddyd-fawr 140 A5
Trelewis 130 A3
Treligga 97 E1
Trelights 97 D2
Trelill 97 E2
Trelissick 95 F3
Trelissick Corn
  TR3 6QL 95 F3
Trelleck 131 E2
Trelleck Grange 131 D2
Trelogan 182 C4
Trelowla 97 G4
Trelystan 156 B2
Tremadog 167 E3
Tremail 97 F1
Tre-main 141 F3
Tremaine 97 G1
Tremar 97 G3
Trematon 99 D5
Tremeirchion 182 B5
Tremethick Cross 94 B3
Tremore 97 E3
Trenance Corn 96 C3
Trenance Corn 96 D2
Trenarren 97 E5
Trench Tel&W 157 F1
Trench Wrex 170 A4
Trencreek 96 C3
Trenear 95 D3
Treneglos 97 G1
Trenewan 97 F4
Trengune 98 B1
Trent 104 B1
Trent Port 187 F4
Trent Vale 171 F3
Trentham 171 F3
Trentishoe 113 G1
Trenwheal 94 D3
Treoes 129 F5
Treowen 130 B3
Trequite 97 E2
Tre'r-ddôl 154 C3
Trerhyngyll 129 G5
Tre-Rhys 141 E3
Trerulefoot 98 D5
Tre-saith 141 F3
Tresco 96 A1
Trescott 158 A3
Trescowe 94 C3
Tresean 96 B4
Tresham 131 G3
Tresillian 96 C5
Tresillian 96 C5
Tresinney 97 F1

Tresinwen 140 B3
Treskerby 96 B5
Treskinnick Cross 98 C1
Treslea 97 F3
Tresmeer 97 G1
Tresowes Green 94 D4
Tresparrett 98 B1
Tresparrett Posts 98 B1
Tressait 250 D3
Tresta Shet 278 F3
Tresta Shet 279 C7
Treswell 187 E5
Trethewey 94 A4
Trethomas 130 A4
Trethurgy 97 E4
Tretio 140 A5
Tretire 145 E5
Tretower 144 A5
Treuddyn 169 F2
Trevadlock 97 G2
Trevalga 98 A1
Trevalyn 170 A2
Trevanson 97 D2
Trevarnon 94 C3
Trevarrack 94 B3
Trevarren 96 D3
Trevarrian 96 C3
Trevarrick 97 D5
Trevaughan Carmar 141 E3
Trevaughan Carmar 127 E1
Treveighan 97 E2
Trevellas 96 B4
Trevelmond 97 G3
Trevenen 95 D4
Treverva 95 E3
Trevescan 94 A4
Trevethin 130 B2
Trevigro 98 D4
Trevine 240 C2
Treviscoe 96 C4
Trevivian 97 G2
Trevone 96 C2
Trevor 97 F3
Trewalder 97 E1
Trewarmett 97 E1
Trewarthenick 96 D5
Trewassa 97 F1
Trewellard 94 A3
Trewen Corn 97 G1
Trewen Here 131 F1
Trewennack 95 D4
Trewern 156 B1
Trewethern 97 E2
Trewidland 97 G4
Trewilym 141 E3
Trewint Corn 97 G1
Trewint Corn 97 G1
Trewithian 96 C4
Trewoon 97 D4
Treworga 96 C5
Treworlas 95 F3
Treworlas 95 F3
Treworthal 95 F3
Trewyn 144 C5
Treyarnon 96 C2
Treyford 108 A2
Trezaise 97 D4
Triangle 193 G5
Trickett's Cross 105 G2
Triermain 210 B1
Trillick 281 F3
Trimdon 212 C4
Trimdon Colliery 212 C4
Trimdon Grange 212 C4
Trimingham 179 D2
Trimley Lower Street 153 D4
Trimley St. Martin 153 D4
Trimley St. Mary 153 D4
Trimpley 157 G5
Trimsaran 128 A2
Trimstone 113 E1
Trinafour 250 C3
Trinant 130 B3
Tring 135 E1
Trinity Angus 253 E3
Trinity Chanl 100 C1
Trinity Edin 235 G2
Trisant 154 D5
Triscombe Som 114 C4
Triscombe Som 115 E4
Trislaig 248 C2
Trispen 96 C4
Tritlington 221 E2
Trochry 243 E1
Troed-yr-aur 141 G3
Troed-y-rhiw 129 G2
Trofarth 181 G5
Trondavoe 278 C5
Troon Corn 95 D3
Troon SAyr 224 B2
Tropical Butterfly House,
  Wildlife & Falconry Centre
  SYorks S25 4EQ 21 F3
Tropical World, Roundhay
  WYorks LS8 2ER 27 G1
Trory 280 E4
Trosaraidh 254 C3
Troston 163 G5
Troswell 98 C1
Trottick 244 C1
Trottiscliffe 123 F2
Trotton 120 D5
Trough Gate 193 E5
Troughend 220 B2
Troustan 232 B2
Troutbeck Cumb 199 F2
Troutbeck Cumb 209 G4
Troutbeck Bridge 199 F2
Trow Green 131 F2
Troway 186 A5
Trowbridge Cardiff 130 B4
Trowbridge Wilts 117 F2
Trowell 173 F4
Trowle Common 117 F2
Trowley Bottom 135 F1
Trows 228 A3
Trowse Newton 178 D5
Troy 194 B4
Trudernish 230 C4
Trudoxhill 117 E3
Trull 115 F5
Trumaisgearraidh 262 D4
Trumpan 263 H5
Trumpet 145 F4
Trumpington 150 C2
Trumps Green 121 E1
Trunch 179 D2
Trunnah 191 G3
Truro 96 C5
Tweedbank 227 G3

Truro Cathedral Corn
  TR1 2AF 96 C5
Truscott 98 D2
Trusham 102 B4
Trusley 173 D4
Trusthorpe 189 F4
Truthan 96 C4
Trusmadees 111 C3

Tubney 133 G3
Tuckenhay 101 E2
Tuckhill 157 G4
Tuckingmill 96 A5
Tuddenham Suff 152 C3
Tuddenham Suff 163 F5
Tudeley 123 F4
Tudeley Hale 123 F4
Tudhoe 212 B4
Tudweiliog 166 B4
Tuesley 121 E3
Tuffley 132 A1
Tufton Hants 119 F3
Tufton Pembs 140 D5
Tugby 160 C2
Tugford 157 E4
Tughall 229 G4
Tulchan 243 E2
Tulleys Farm ·WSuss
  RH10 4PE 122 C5
Tullibardine Distillery P&K
  PH4 1QG 243 E3
Tullibody 243 D5
Tullich A&B 240 C1
Tullich A&B 240 A3
Tullich High 267 F4
Tullich High 258 D2
Tullich Moray 268 B6
Tullich Muir 266 E4
Tullie House Museum & Art
  Gallery Cumb CA3 8TP
  68 Carlisle
Tulliemet 251 F4
Tullintrain 285 H5
Tulloch Aber 261 G1
Tulloch High 266 G2
Tulloch Moray 267 H6
Tullochgorm 240 B6
Tullochgribban High 259 G2
Tullochvenus 260 D4
Tulloes 252 D5
Tully F&O 281 F5
Tullyalley 285 G4
Tullyard 281 F1
Tullybannocher 242 C2
Tullybelton 243 F1
Tullycar 284 D2
Tullyconnaught 282 E4
Tullycorker 281 H3
Tullyfergus 252 A5
Tullyhogue 282 B1
Tullyhona 280 D5
Tullymacreeve 282 C6
Tullymurdoch 251 G4
Tullynacree 283 H4
Tullynessle 260 D3
Tullyroan Corner 282 B3
Tullyrossmearan 280 C4
Tullyveery 283 H3
Tulnacross 286 B7
Tulse Hill 136 C5
Tumble (Y Tymbl) 128 B1
Tumby 176 A2
Tumby Woodside 176 A2
Tummel Bridge 250 C4
Tummery 280 E2
Tunbridge Wells 123 E5
Tundergarth Mains 217 F2
Tunga 271 G4
Tungate 179 D3
Tunley 117 D2
Tunny 282 E1
Tunstall ERid 197 F4
Tunstall Kent 124 A2
Tunstall Lancs 200 B5
Tunstall Norf 179 F5
Tunstall NYorks 202 B3
Tunstall Stoke 171 F2
Tunstall Suff 153 E2
Tunstall T&W 212 C2
Tunstead GtMan 185 E2
Tunstead Norf 179 E3
Tunstead Milton 185 E3
Tunworth 120 B3
Tupholme 175 G1
Tupsley 145 E3
Tupton 173 E1
Tur Langton 160 C3
Turbiskill 231 F1
Turclossie 269 G5
Turgis Green 120 B2
Turin 252 D4
Turkdean 132 D1
Turleigh 117 F1
Turn 184 C1
Turnastone 144 C4
Turnberry 224 A5
Turnchapel 100 A2
Turnditch 173 D3
Turner's Green 147 D1
Turners Hill 122 C5
Turners Puddle 105 E3
Turnford 136 C2
Turnworth 105 E2
Turret Bridge 257 K5
Turriff 269 F6
Turton Bottoms 184 B1
Turvey 149 E2
Turville 134 C3
Turville Heath 134 C3
Turweston 148 B4
Tutankhamun Exhibition,
  Dorchester Dorset
  DT1 1UW 104 C3
Tutbury 172 D5
Tutbury Castle Staffs DE13
  9JF 172 D5
Tutnall 158 B5
Tutshill 131 E3
Tuttington 178 D3
Tutts Clump 134 A5
Tutwell 99 D3
Tuxford 187 E5
Twatt Ork 276 B5
Twatt Shet 279 C7
Twechar 234 B2
Tweedbank 227 G3

Tweedmouth 237 G4
Tweedsmuir 226 B3
Twelve Oaks 110 B1
Twelveheads 96 B5
Twemlow Green 171 E1
Twenty 175 G5
Twickenham 136 A5
Twigworth 146 A5
Twineham 109 E1
Twineham Green 109 E1
Twinhoe 117 E2
Twinstead 151 G4
Twiss Green 184 A3
Twiston 193 E3
Twitchen Devon 114 A4
Twitchen Shrop 156 C5
Twitton 123 E2
Twizell House 229 F3
Two Bridges Devon 99 G3
Two Bridges Glos 131 F2
Two Dales 173 D1
Two Gates 159 E2
Two Mills 183 E5
Twycross 159 F2
Twycross Zoo Leics
  CV9 3PX 159 F2
Twyford Bucks 148 B5
Twyford Derbys 173 E5
Twyford Dorset 105 E1
Twyford Hants 119 F5
Twyford Leics 160 C1
Twyford Norf 178 B3
Twyford Oxon 147 G4
Twyford W'ham 134 C5
Twyford Common 145 E4
Twyn Shôn-Ifan 130 A3
Twynholm 216 A5
Twynllanan 143 D5
Twyn-yr-odyn 130 A5
Twynysheriff 130 D2
Twywell 161 E5
Tŷ-croes 180 B5
Ty Mawr Cwm Conwy 168 C3
Tyberton 144 C4
Tycroes 128 C1
Tycrwyn 156 A1
Tydd Gote 162 C1
Tydd St. Giles 162 C1
Tydd St. Mary 162 C1
Tye Common 137 F2
Tye Green Essex 151 F5
Tye Green Essex 150 D5
Tye Green Essex 137 F1
Tye Green Essex 136 D2
Tyersal 194 A4
Ty-hen 166 A4
Tyle-garw 129 G4
Tyler Hill 124 D2
Tylers Green Bucks 135 E3
Tyler's Green Essex 137 E1
Tylorstown 129 G3
Tylwch 155 F5
Ty-mawr Denb 169 E3
Tynan 282 A3
Ty-nant Conwy 168 C3
Tŷ-nant Gwyn 168 C5
Tyndrum
  (Taigh an Droma) 241 F1
Tyne Green Country Park
  N'umb NE46 3RY 211 F1
Tyneham 105 E4
Tynehead 236 A4
Tynemouth 212 C1
Tynewydd 129 F3
Tyningname 236 D2
Tynron 216 C3
Tyntesfield 131 E5
Ty'n-y-cefn 169 D3
Ty'n-y-cwm 155 E4
Tyn-y-ffridd 169 E4
Tyn-y-garn 129 E4
Tyn-y-gongl 180 D4
Tyn-y-graig Cere 142 C1
Tyn-y-graig
  Powys 143 G3
Ty'n-y-groes 181 F5
Tyrella 283 H5
Tyrie 269 H4
Tyringham 149 D3
Tyseley 158 D4
Tythegston 129 E5
Tytherington ChesE 184 D5
Tytherington SGlos 131 F4
Tytherington Som 117 E3
Tytherington Wilts 118 A3
Tytherton Lucas 132 B5
Tyttenhanger 136 A2
Ty-uchaf 168 C5
Tywardreath 97 E4
Tywardreath Highway 97 E4
Tywyn 154 B2

U
Uachdar 262 D6
Uags 256 D1
Ubberley 171 G3
Ubbeston Green 165 E4
Ubley 116 C2
Uckerby 202 B2
Uckfield 109 G1
Uckinghall 146 A4
Uckington 146 B5
Uddingston 234 A3
Uddington 225 G2
Udimore 111 D2
Udley 116 B1
Udny Green 261 G2
Udny Station 261 H2
Udstonhead 234 B4
Uffcott 132 D5
Uffculme 103 D1
Uffington Lincs 161 F2
Uffington Oxon 133 F4
Uffington Shrop 157 E1
Ufford Peter 161 F2
Ufford Suff 153 D2
Ufton 147 G1
Ufton Green 120 B1
Ufton Nervet 120 B1
Ugborough 100 C2
Ugford 118 B4
Uggeshall 165 F3
Ugglebarnby 204 B2
Ugley 150 D5
Ugley Green 150 D5

Ugthorpe 203 G1
Uidh 254 B5
Uig A&B 246 A4
Uig A&B 232 C1
Uig (Uige) High 263 J5
Uig High 263 G6
Uigen 270 C4
Uiginish 263 H7
Uigshader 263 K7
Uisken 238 C3
Uiskevagh (Uisgebhagh) 262 D6
Ulbster 275 J4
Ulcat Row 210 A5
Ulceby Lincs 189 E5
Ulceby NLincs 188 B1
Ulceby Cross 189 E5
Ulceby Skitter 188 B1
Ulcombe 124 A4
Uldale 209 F3
Uldale House 200 C3
Uley 131 G3
Ulgham 221 E2
Ullapool (Ullapul) 265 H2
Ullenhall 146 D1
Ullenwood 132 B1
Ulleskelf 195 E4
Ullesthorpe 160 A4
Ulley 186 B4
Ulley Reservoir Country Park SYorks S26 3XL 21 E2
Ullingswick 145 E3
Ullinish 255 J1
Ullock 209 D4
Ullswater Steamers Cumb CA11 0US 209 G5
Ulpha Cumb 198 C3
Ulpha Cumb 199 F4
Ulrome 197 D2
Ulsta 278 D4
Ulster American Folk Park F&O BT78 5QU 281 G1
Ulster Folk & Transport Museum A&NDown BT18 0EU 287 J7
Ulting 138 B2
Uluvalt 239 E1
Ulva 238 D1
Ulverston 199 D5
Ulwell 105 G4
Ulzieside 225 F5
Umberleigh 113 G3
Ummer 281 F4
Unapool 272 E5
Underbarrow 199 F3
Undercliffe 194 A4
Underhill 136 B3
Underhoull 278 E2
Underling Green 123 G4
Underriver 123 E3
Underwood Newport 130 C4
Underwood Notts 173 F2
Underwood Plym 100 B2
Undley 163 E4
Undy 130 D4
Ungisiadar 270 D5
Unifirth 279 B7
Union Croft 261 G5
Union Mills 190 B4
Union Street 123 G5
University of Glasgow Visitor Centre Glas G12 8QQ 38 B1
Unst 278 F1
Unst Airport 278 F2
Unstone 186 A5
Unstone Green 186 A5
Unsworth 184 C2
Unthank Cumb 210 A4
Unthank Derbys 186 A5
Up Cerne 104 C2
Up Exe 102 C2
Up Hatherley 146 B5
Up Holland 183 G2
Up Marden 107 G1
Up Mudford 104 B1
Up Nately 120 B2
Up Somborne 119 E4
Up Sydling 104 C2
Upavon 118 C2
Upchurch 124 A2
Upcott Devon 99 E1
Upcott Devon 113 F2
Upcott Here 144 C2
Upcott Som 114 C5
Upend 151 E2
Upgate 178 C4
Upgate Street Norf 164 B2
Upgate Street Norf 165 D2
Uphall Dorset 104 B2
Uphall WLoth 235 E2
Uphall Station 235 E3
Upham Devon 102 B2
Upham Hants 119 G5
Uphampton Here 144 C1
Uphampton Worcs 146 A1
Uphempston 101 E1
Uphill 116 A2
Uplands Glos 132 A2
Uplands Swan 128 C3
Uplawmoor 233 F4
Upleadon 145 G5
Upleatham 203 F1
Uplees 124 C2
Uploders 104 B3
Uplowman 102 D1
Uplyme 103 G3
Upminster 137 E4
Upottery 103 F2
Upper Affcot 156 D4
Upper Ardroscadale 232 B3
Upper Arley 157 G4
Upper Arncott 134 B1
Upper Astley 157 E1
Upper Aston 158 A3
Upper Astrop 148 A4
Upper Ballinderry 282 E2
Upper Barvas 271 F2
Upper Basildon 134 B5
Upper Bayble (Pabail Uarach) 271 H4
Upper Beeding 109 D2
Upper Benefield 161 E4
Upper Bentley 146 B1
Upper Berwick 157 D1
Upper Bighouse 274 D3
Upper Boat 130 A4
Upper Boddam 260 E1
Upper Boddington 147 G2
Upper Borth 154 C4
Upper Boyndlie 269 H4
Upper Brailes 147 F4
Upper Breakish 256 C2
Upper Breinton 145 D3
Upper Broadheath 146 A2
Upper Broughton 174 B5
Upper Brynamman 128 D1
Upper Bucklebury 119 G1
Upper Burgate 106 A1
Upper Burnhaugh 261 G5
Upper Caldecote 149 G3
Upper Camster 275 H4
Upper Canada 116 A2
Upper Catesby 148 A2
Upper Catshill 158 B5
Upper Chapel 143 G3
Upper Cheddon 115 F5
Upper Chicksgrove 118 A4
Upper Chute 119 D2
Upper Clatford 119 E3
Upper Coberley 132 B1
Upper Colwall 145 G3
Upper Cotton 172 B3
Upper Cound 157 E2
Upper Cumberworth 185 G2
Upper Cwmbran 130 B3
Upper Dallachy 268 B4
Upper Dean 149 F1
Upper Denby 185 G2
Upper Denton 210 C1
Upper Derraid 259 H1
Upper Derwent Reservoirs Derbys S33 0AQ 185 F4
Upper Diabaig 264 E5
Upper Dicker 110 A2
Upper Dovercourt 152 D4
Upper Dunsforth 194 D1
Upper Dunsley 135 E1
Upper Eastern Green 159 E4
Upper Eathie 266 E5
Upper Egleton 145 F3
Upper Elkstone 172 B2
Upper End 185 E5
Upper Enham 119 E3
Upper Farringdon 120 C4
Upper Framilode 131 G1
Upper Froyle 120 C3
Upper Gills 275 J1
Upper Glendessarry 257 F5
Upper Godney 116 B3
Upper Gornal 158 B3
Upper Gravenhurst 149 G4
Upper Green Essex 150 C4
Upper Green Essex 151 D4
Upper Green Mon 130 C1
Upper Green WBerks 119 E1
Upper Grove Common 145 E5
Upper Gylen 240 A2
Upper Hackney 173 D1
Upper Halliford 121 F1
Upper Halling 123 F2
Upper Hambleton 161 E2
Upper Harbledown 124 D3
Upper Hardres Court 125 D3
Upper Hartfield 123 D5
Upper Hatton 171 F4
Upper Hawkhillock 261 J1
Upper Hayesden 123 E4
Upper Hayton 157 E4
Upper Heath 157 E4
Upper Heaton 185 F1
Upper Hellesdon 178 D4
Upper Helmsley 195 F2
Upper Hengoed 169 F4
Upper Hergest 144 B2
Upper Heyford Oxon 147 G5
Upper Heyford WN'hants 148 B2
Upper Hill Here 145 D2
Upper Hill SGlos 131 F3
Upper Horsebridge 110 A2
Upper Howsell 145 G3
Upper Hulme 172 B1
Upper Inglesham 133 E3
Upper Kilchattan 238 C5
Upper Killay 128 B3
Upper Knockando 267 J7
Upper Lambourn 133 F4
Upper Langford 116 B2
Upper Langwith 173 G1
Upper Largo 244 C4
Upper Leigh 172 B4
Upper Ley 131 G1
Upper Loads 173 E1
Upper Lochton 260 E5
Upper Longdon 158 C1
Upper Longwood 157 F2
Upper Ludstone 158 A3
Upper Lybster 275 H5
Upper Lydbrook 131 F1
Upper Lyde 145 D3
Upper Lye 144 C1
Upper Maes-coed 144 C4
Upper Midhope 185 G3
Upper Milovaig 263 G7
Upper Milton 133 E1
Upper Minety 132 C3
Upper Moor 146 B3
Upper Morton 131 F3
Upper Muirskie 261 G5
Upper Nash 126 D2
Upper Newbold 186 A5
Upper North Dean 135 D3
Upper Norwood 136 C5
Upper Obney 243 F1
Upper Oddington 147 E5
Upper Ollach 256 B1
Upper Padley 185 G5
Upper Pennington 106 B3
Upper Pollicott 134 C1
Upper Poppleton 195 E2
Upper Quinton 147 D3
Upper Ratley 119 E5
Upper Ridinghill 269 J5
Upper Rissington 147 E5
Upper Rochford 145 F1
Upper Sanday 277 E7
Upper Sapey 145 F1
Upper Scolton 140 C5
Upper Seagry 132 B4
Upper Shelton 149 E3
Upper Sheringham 178 C1
Upper Shuckburgh 147 G1
Upper Siddington 132 C3
Upper Skelmorlie 232 D3
Upper Slaughter 147 D5
Upper Sonachan 240 C2
Upper Soudley 131 F1
Upper Staploe 149 G2
Upper Stoke 179 D5
Upper Stondon 149 G4
Upper Stowe 148 B2
Upper Street Hants 106 A1
Upper Street Norf 179 E4
Upper Street Norf 164 C4
Upper Street Suff 152 C4
Upper Street Suff 152 C2
Upper Strensham 146 B4
Upper Sundon 149 F5
Upper Swanmore 107 E1
Upper Swell 147 D5
Upper Tean 172 B4
Upper Thurnham 192 A2
Upper Tillyrie 243 G4
Upper Tirkane 286 C5
Upper Tooting 136 B5
Upper Town Derbys 172 D1
Upper Town Derbys 173 D2
Upper Town Derbys 172 D2
Upper Town Here 145 E3
Upper Town NSom 116 C1
Upper Tysoe 147 F3
Upper Upham 133 E5
Upper Upnor 137 G5
Upper Victoria 244 D1
Upper Vobster 117 E3
Upper Wardington 147 G3
Upper Waterhay 132 C3
Upper Weald 148 D4
Upper Weedon 148 B2
Upper Welson 144 B2
Upper Weston 117 E1
Upper Whiston 186 B4
Upper Wick 146 A2
Upper Wield 120 B4
Upper Winchendon (Over Winchendon) 134 C1
Upper Witton 158 C3
Upper Woodford 118 C4
Upper Woolhampton 119 G1
Upper Wootton 119 G2
Upper Wraxall 132 A5
Upper Wyche 145 G3
Upperby 210 A2
Upperlands 286 C5
Uppermill 185 D2
Upperthong 185 F2
Upperton 121 E5
Uppertown CC&G 286 E4
Uppertown Derbys 173 E1
Uppertown Ork 275 J1
Uppingham 161 D2
Uppington 157 E2
Upsall 203 D4
Upsettlington 237 F5
Upshire 136 D2
Upstreet 125 E2
Upthorpe 164 A4
Upton Bucks 134 C1
Upton Cambs 161 G5
Upton ChesW&C 170 B1
Upton Corn 97 G2
Upton Corn 112 C5
Upton Devon 103 D2
Upton Devon 100 D3
Upton Dorset 105 F3
Upton Dorset 104 D4
Upton ERid 196 D2
Upton Hants 119 E2
Upton Hants 106 C1
Upton Leics 159 F3
Upton Lincs 187 F4
Upton Mersey 183 D4
Upton Norf 179 E4
Upton Notts 187 E5
Upton Notts 174 C2
Upton Oxon 134 A4
Upton Oxon 133 E1
Upton Pembs 126 D2
Upton Peter 161 G2
Upton Slo 135 E5
Upton Som 114 C5
Upton Som 116 B5
Upton Wilts 117 F4
Upton WN'hants 148 C1
Upton WYorks 186 B1
Upton Bishop 145 F5
Upton Cheyney 117 D1
Upton Country Park BCP BH17 7BJ 3 A3
Upton Cressett 157 F3
Upton Crews 145 F5
Upton Cross 97 G2
Upton End 149 G4
Upton Grey 120 B3
Upton Hellions 102 B2
Upton Lovell 118 A3
Upton Magna 157 E1
Upton Noble 117 E4
Upton Park 136 D4
Upton Pyne 102 C3
Upton St. Leonards 132 A1
Upton Scudamore 117 F3
Upton Snodsbury 146 B2
Upton upon Severn 146 A3
Upton Warren 146 B1
Upwaltham 108 B2
Upware 162 D5
Upwell 162 D2
Upwey 104 C4
Upwick Green 150 C5
Upwood 162 A4
Uradale 279 D9
Urafirth 278 C5
Urbis, Manchester GtMan M4 3BG 47 E2
Urchany 267 F7
Urchfont 118 B2
Urdimarsh 145 E3
Ure 278 B5
Urgha 263 G2
Urlay Nook 202 D1
Urmston 184 B3
Urpeth 212 B2
Urquhart High 266 C6
Urquhart Moray 267 K5
Urquhart Castle High IV63 6XJ 258 C2
Urra 203 E2
Urray 266 C6
Ushaw Moor 212 B3
Usher Hall, Edinburgh Edin EH1 2EA 36 E5
Usk (Brynbuga) 130 C2
Usselby 188 A3
Usworth 212 C2
Utley 193 G3
Uton 102 B3
Utterby 188 D3
Uttoxeter 172 B4
Uwchmynydd 166 A5
Uxbridge 135 F4
Uyeasound 278 E2
Uzmaston 126 C1

V
V & A Dundee Dundee DD1 4EZ 71 Dundee
Valley (Y Fali) 180 A5
Valley Truckle 97 F1
Valleyfield D&G 216 A5
Valleyfield Fife 235 E1
Valsgarth 278 F1
Vange 137 G4
Varteg (Y Farteg) 130 B2
Vatersay (Bhatarsaigh) 254 B5
Vatsetter 278 E4
Vatten 263 H7
Vaul 246 B2
Vaynor 129 G1
Vaynor Park 156 A2
Veaullt 144 A2
Veensgarth 279 D8
Vellow 115 D4
Veness 276 E5
Venn 100 D3
Venn Ottery 103 D3
Venngreen 113 D4
Vennington 156 C2
Venny Tedburn 102 B3
Venterdon 99 D3
Ventnor 107 E5
Ventnor Botanic Gardens IoW PO38 1UL 107 E5
Venton 100 B2
Venue Cymru, Llandudno Conwy LL30 1BB 181 F4
Vernham Dean 119 E2
Vernham Street 119 E2
Vernolds Common 157 D4
Verwood 105 G2
Veryan 95 G3
Veryan Green 96 D5
Vickerstown 191 E1
Victoria 97 D3
Victoria & Albert Museum GtLon SW7 2RL 11 F5
Victoria Bridge 285 F6
Vidlin 279 D6
Viewfield 275 F2
Viewpark 234 B3
Vigo 158 C2
Vigo Village 123 F2
Villavin 113 F4
Vindobala (Frontiers of the Roman Empire) N'umb 212 A1
Vindolanda Roman Fort (Frontiers of the Roman Empire) N'umb NE47 7JN 211 D1
Vinehall Street 110 C1
Vine's Cross 110 A2
Viney Hill 131 F2
Virginia Water 121 E1
Virginstow 99 D1
Virley 138 C1
Vobster 117 E3
Voe Shet 279 D6
Voe Shet 278 C4
Vogrie Country Park Midlo EH23 4NU 32 F4
Voirrey Embroidery Mersey CH63 6JA 22 A5
Volks Electric Railway B&H BN2 1EN 109 F3
Vow 286 D4
Vowchurch 144 C4
Voy 277 B6
Vron Gate 156 C2

W
Waberthwaite 198 C3
Wackerfield 212 A5
Wacton 164 C2
Wadbister 279 D8
Wadborough 146 B3
Waddesdon 134 C1
Waddesdon Manor Bucks HP18 0JH 134 C1
Waddeton 101 E2
Waddicar 183 E3
Waddingham 187 G3
Waddington Lancs 192 D3
Waddington Lincs 175 E1
Waddingworth 188 B5
Waddon Devon 102 B5
Waddon GtLon 122 C2
Wadebridge 97 D2
Wadeford 103 G1
Wadenhoe 161 F4
Wadesmill 136 C1
Wadhurst 123 F5
Wadshelf 186 A5
Wadworth 186 C3
Wadworth Hill 197 E5
Waen Denb 169 E1
Waen Denb 168 C1
Waen-wen 167 E1
Wag 275 F6
Wainfleet All Saints 176 C2
Wainfleet Bank 176 C2
Wainfleet St. Mary 176 C2
Wainford 165 E2
Waingroves 173 F3
Wainhouse Corner 98 B1
Wainscott 137 G5
Wainstalls 193 G5
Waitby 200 C2
Wakefield 194 C5
Wakehurst Place WSuss RH17 6TN 122 C5
Wakerley 161 E3
Wakes Colne 151 G5
Walberswick 165 F4
Walberton 108 B3
Walbottle 212 A1
Walcot Lincs 175 F4
Walcot Lincs 175 G2
Walcot NLincs 196 A5
Walcot Shrop 156 C4
Walcot Tel&W 157 E1
Walcot Green 164 C3
Walcote Leics 160 A4
Walcote Warks 146 D2
Walcott 179 E2
Walcott Dales 175 G2
Walden 201 F4
Walden Head 201 E4
Walden Stubbs 186 C1
Walderslade 123 G2
Walderton 107 G1
Walditch 104 A3
Waldley 172 C4
Waldridge 212 B3
Waldringfield 153 D3
Waldron 110 A2
Wales 186 B4
Wales Millennium Centre, Cardiff Cardiff CF10 5AL 130 A5
Walesby Lincs 188 B3
Walesby Notts 187 D5
Waleswood 186 B4
Walford Here 156 C5
Walford Here 145 E5
Walford Shrop 170 B5
Walford Staffs 171 F4
Walford Heath 156 D1
Walgherton 171 D3
Walgrave 160 D5
Walhampton 106 C3
Walk Mill 193 E4
Walkden 184 B2
Walker 212 B1
Walker Art Gallery, Liverpool Mersey L3 8EL 42 D3
Walker Fold 192 C3
Walkerburn 227 E2
Walkeringham 187 E3
Walkerith 187 E3
Walkern 150 A5
Walker's Green 145 E3
Walkford 106 B3
Walkhampton 100 B1
Walkingham Hill 194 C1
Walkington 196 B4
Walkwood 146 C1
Wall Corn 94 D3
Wall N'umb 211 F1
Wall Staffs 158 D2
Wall End 198 D4
Wall Heath 158 A4
Wall Houses 211 G1
Wall under Heywood 157 E3
Wallace Collection, London GtLon W1U 3BN 44 A2
Wallacehall 218 A4
Wallacetown 224 A5
Wallasey 183 D3
Wallaston Green 126 C2
Wallend 124 A1
Waller's Green 145 F4
Wallingford 134 B4
Wallington GtLon 122 B2
Wallington Hants 107 E2
Wallington Herts 150 A4
Wallington Wrex 170 B3
Wallingwells 186 C4
Wallis 140 D5
Wallisdown 105 G3
Walliswood 121 G4
Walls 279 B8
Wallsend 212 C1
Wallyford 236 A2
Walmer 125 F3
Walmer Bridge 192 A5
Walmersley 184 C1
Walmley 158 D3
Walmsgate 189 D5
Walpole 165 E4
Walpole Cross Keys 162 D1
Walpole Highway 162 D1
Walpole Marsh 162 C1
Walpole St. Andrew 162 D1
Walpole St. Peter 162 D1
Walrond's Park 116 A5
Walrow 116 A3
Walsall 158 C3
Walsall Arboretum Illuminations WMid WS1 2AB 14 D1
Walsall Wood 158 C2
Walsden 193 F5
Walsgrave on Sowe 159 F4
Walsham le Willows 164 B4
Walshford 194 D2
Walsoken 162 C1
Walston 235 E5
Walsworth 149 G4
Walter's Ash 134 D3
Walterston 129 G5
Walterstone 144 C5
Waltham Kent 124 D4
Waltham NELincs 188 C2
Waltham Abbey 136 C2
Waltham Chase 107 E1
Waltham Cross 136 C2
Waltham on the Wolds 174 C5
Waltham St. Lawrence 134 D5
Walthamstow 136 C4
Walton Bucks 134 D1
Walton Cumb 210 B1
Walton Derbys 173 E1
Walton Leics 160 A4
Walton Mersey 183 E3
Walton MK 149 D4
Walton Peter 161 G2
Walton Powys 144 B2
Walton Shrop 157 D5
Walton Som 116 B4
Walton Staffs 171 F4
Walton Suff 153 E4
Walton Tel&W 157 E1
Walton Warks 147 E2
Walton WYorks 186 A1
Walton WYorks 194 D3
Walton Cardiff 146 B4
Walton East 140 D5
Walton Elm 105 D1
Walton Hall Gardens Warr WA4 6SN 23 H4
Walton Highway 162 C1
Walton Lower Street 153 D4
Walton on the Hill 122 B3
Walton on the Naze 153 D5
Walton on the Wolds 160 A1
Walton Park D&G 216 B3
Walton Park NSom 130 D5
Walton West 126 B1
Walton-in-Gordano 130 D5
Walton-le-Dale 192 B5
Walton-on-Thames 121 G1
Walton-on-the-Hill 171 G5
Walton-on-Trent 159 E1
Walwen Flints 182 C5
Walwen Flints 182 D5
Walwick 220 B4
Walworth 212 B5
Walworth CC&G 285 J3
Walworth Darl 202 B1
Walworth Gate 212 B5
Walwyn's Castle 126 B1
Wambrook 103 F2
Wanborough Surr 121 E3
Wanborough Swin 133 E4
Wandel 226 A3
Wandon 229 E4
Wandon End 149 G5
Wandsworth 136 B5
Wandylaw 229 F4
Wangford Suff 165 F4
Wangford Suff 163 F4
Wanlip 160 A1
Wanlockhead 225 G4
Wannock 110 A3
Wansbeck Riverside Park N'umb NE63 8TX 221 E3
Wansford ERid 196 C2
Wansford Peter 161 F3
Wanshurst Green 123 G4
Wanstrow 117 E3
Wanswell 131 F2
Wantage 133 F4
Wapley 131 G5
Wappenbury 147 F1
Wappenham 148 B3
Warblebank 209 F2
Warbleton 110 B2
Warblington 107 G2
Warborough 134 A3
Warboys 162 B4
Warbreck 191 G4
Warbstow 98 C1
Warburton 184 A4
Warcop 200 C1
Ward End 158 D4
Ward Green 152 B1
Warden Kent 124 C1
Warden N'umb 211 F1
Warden Hill 146 B5
Warden Street 149 G3
Wardhouse 260 D1
Wardington 147 G3
Wardle ChesE 170 D2
Wardle GtMan 184 D1
Wardley GtMan 184 B2
Wardley Rut 160 D2
Wardley T&W 212 C1
Wardlow 185 F5
Wardsend 184 D4
Wardy Hill 162 C4
Ware Herts 136 C1
Ware Kent 125 E2
Wareham 105 F4
Warehorne 124 B5
Waren Mill 229 F3
Warenford 229 F4
Warenton 229 F3
Wareside 136 C1
Waresley Cambs 150 A2
Waresley Worcs 158 A5
Warfield 135 D5
Wargrave Mersey 183 G3
Wargrave W'ham 134 C5
Warham Here 145 D4
Warham Norf 178 A1
Waringsford 283 F4
Waringstown 282 E3
Wark N'umb 220 A4
Wark N'umb 228 C3
Warkleigh 113 G3
Warkton 161 D5
Warkworth N'umb 221 E1
Warkworth WN'hants 147 G3
Warland 193 F5
Warleggan 97 F3
Warley Essex 137 E3
Warley WMid 158 C4
Warley Town 193 G5
Warlingham 122 C3
Warmfield 194 C5
Warmingham 171 E1
Warminghurst 108 D2
Warmington NN'hants 161 F3
Warmington Warks 147 G3
Warminster 117 F3
Warmlake 124 A4
Warmley 131 F5
Warmley Hill 131 F5
Warmsworth 186 C2
Warmwell 105 D4
Warndon 146 A2
Warners End 135 F2
Warnford 120 B5
Warnham 121 G4
Warningcamp 108 C3
Warninglid 109 E1
Warren ChesE 184 C5
Warren Pembs 126 C3
Warren House 99 G2
Warren Row 134 D4
Warren Street 124 B3
Warrenby 213 E5
Warrenpoint 282 E7
Warren's Green 150 A5
Warrington MK 149 D2
Warrington Warr 184 A4
Warroch 243 F4
Warsash 107 D2
Warslow 172 B2
Warsop Vale 173 G1
Warter 196 A2
Warthill 195 F2
Wartle 260 D4
Wartling 110 B3
Wartnaby 174 C5
Warton Lancs 199 G5
Warton Lancs 192 A5
Warton N'umb 220 C1
Warton Warks 159 E2
Warton Bank 192 A5
Warwick 147 E1
Warwick Bridge 210 A2
Warwick Castle Warks CV34 4QU 16 A6
Warwick Wold 122 C3
Warwick-on-Eden 210 A2
Wasbister 276 C4
Wasdale Head 198 C2
Waseley Hills Country Park Worcs B45 9AT 14 C6
Wash 185 E4
Wash Common 119 F1
Washall Green 150 C4
Washaway 97 E3
Washbourne 101 D2
Washbrook 116 B3
Washfield 102 C1
Washfold 201 F2
Washford Som 114 D3
Washford Warks 146 C1
Washford Pyne 102 B1
Washingborough 188 A5
Washington T&W 212 C2
Washington WSuss 108 D2
Washmere Green 152 A3
Wasing 119 G1
Waskerley 211 G3
Wasperton 147 E2
Wasps Nest 175 F1
Wass 203 E5
Wat Tyler Country Park Essex SS16 4UH 137 G4
Watchet 115 D3
Watchfield Oxon 133 E3
Watchfield Som 116 A3
Watchgate 199 G3
Watcombe 101 F1
Watendlath 209 F5
Water 193 E5
Water Eaton MK 149 D4
Water Eaton Oxon 134 A1
Water End Bed 149 G3
Water End CenBeds 149 F4
Water End ERid 195 G4
Water End Essex 151 D3
Water End Herts 136 B2
Water End Herts 135 F1
Water Newton 161 G3
Water Orton 159 D3
Water Stratford 148 B4
Water Yeat 199 D4
Waterbeach 150 C1
Waterbeck 218 A4
Watercombe 105 D4
Waterend 134 C3
Waterfall 172 B2
Waterfoot ERenf 233 G4
Waterfoot Lancs 193 E5
Waterford 136 C1
Watergate 97 F1
Waterhead Cumb 199 E2
Waterhead D&G 216 B2
Waterheath 165 F2
Waterhill of Bruxie 269 H6
Waterhouses Dur 212 A3
Waterhouses Staffs 172 B2
Wateringbury 123 F3
Waterlane 132 B2
Waterloo Aber 261 J1
Waterloo BCP 105 G3
Waterloo (Ty'nycoedcae) Caerp 130 A4
Waterloo Derbys 173 F1
Waterloo GtMan 184 D2
Waterloo High 256 C2
Waterloo Mersey 183 E3
Waterloo NLan 234 C4
Waterloo Norf 178 D4
Waterloo P&K 243 F1
Waterloo Pembs 126 C2
Waterloo Cross 103 D1
Waterloo Port 167 D1
Waterlooville 107 F1
Watermead Country Park Leics LE7 4PF 17 C3
Watermeetings 226 A4
Watermillock 210 A5
Watermouth Castle Devon EX34 9SL 113 F1
Waterperry 134 B2
Waterperry Oxon OX33 1JZ 134 B2
Waterrow 115 D5
Waters Upton 157 F1
Watersfield 108 C2
Watershed Mill Visitor Centre, Settle NYorks BD24 9LR 193 E1
Watersheddings 184 D2
Waterside Aber 260 B3
Waterside Aber 261 J2
Waterside B'burn 192 D5
Waterside Bucks 135 E2
Waterside D&S 285 G4
Waterside EAyr 224 C5
Waterside EAyr 233 F5
Waterside EDun 234 A2
Watersmeet House Devon EX35 6NT 114 A3
Waterstock 134 B2
Waterston 126 C2
Waterthorpe 186 B4
Waterworld, Hanley ST1 5PU 85 Stoke-on-Trent
Watford Herts 136 A3
Watford WN'hants 148 B1
Watford Park 130 A4
Wath NYorks 202 C5
Wath NYorks 194 A1
Wath Brow 208 D5
Wath upon Dearne 186 B2
Watley's End 131 F4
Watlington Norf 163 E1
Watlington Oxon 134 B3
Watnall 173 G3
Watten 275 H3
Wattisfield 164 B4
Wattisham 152 B2
Wattlebridge 281 G6
Watton Dorset 104 A3
Watton ERid 196 C3
Watton Norf 178 A5
Watton at Stone 136 C1
Watton Green 178 A5
Watton's Green 137 E3
Wattston 234 B3
Wattstown 129 G3

Wattsville **130** B3
Waughtonhill **269** H5
Waun y Clyn **128** A2
Waunarlwydd **128** C3
Waunclunda **142** C4
Waun-fach **156** B1
Waunfawr *Cere* **154** C4
Waunfawr *Gwyn* **167** E2
Waun-Lwyd **130** A2
Wavendon **149** E4
Waverbridge **209** F2
Waverton *ChesW&C* **170** B1
Waverton *Cumb* **209** F2
Wavertree **183** E4
Wawne **196** C4
Waxham **179** F3
Waxholme **197** F5
Way Gill **193** F1
Way Village **102** B1
Way Wick **116** A1
Waytown **104** A3
Weachyburn **268** E5
Weacombe **115** E3
Weald **133** F2
Weald & Downland Living
  Museum *WSuss*
  PO18 0EU **108** A2
Weald Country Park *Essex*
  CM14 5QS **137** E3
Wealdstone **136** A3
Weardley **194** B3
Weare **116** B2
Weare Giffard **113** E3
Wearhead **211** E4
Wearne **116** B5
Weasenham All Saints **177** G5
Weasenham St. Peter **177** G5
Weathercote **200** C5
Weatheroak Hill **158** C5
Weaverham **184** A5
Weaverthorpe **204** C5
Webheath **146** C1
Webton **144** D4
Wedderlairs **261** G1
Weddington **159** F3
Wedmore **116** B3
Wednesbury **158** B3
Wednesfield **158** B3
Weedon **134** D1
Weedon Bec **148** B2
Weedon Lois **148** B3
Weeford **158** D2
Week *Devon* **102** A1
Week *Devon* **101** D1
Week *Som* **114** C4
Week Orchard **112** C5
Week St. Mary **98** C1
Weeke **119** F4
Weekley **161** D4
Weel **196** C4
Weeley **152** C5
Weeley Heath **152** C5
Weem **250** D4
Weeping Cross **171** G5
Weethley **146** D1
Weeting **163** F4
Weeton *ERid* **197** F5
Weeton *Lancs* **191** G4
Weeton *NYorks* **194** B3
Weetwood **194** B4
Weir *Essex* **138** B4
Weir *Lancs* **193** E5
Weir Quay **100** A1
Weirbrook **170** A5
Weisdale **279** C7
Welbeck Abbey **186** C5
Welborne **178** B5
Welbourn **175** E2
Welburn *NYorks* **195** G1
Welburn *NYorks* **203** E4
Welbury **202** C2
Welby **175** E4
Welches Dam **162** C4
Welcombe **112** C4
Weldon **161** E4
Welford *WBerks* **133** G5
Welford *WN'hants* **160** B4
Welford-on-Avon **146** D2
Welham *Leics* **160** C3
Welham *Notts* **187** E4
Welham Green **136** B2
Well *Hants* **120** C3
Well *Lincs* **189** E5
Well *NYorks* **202** B4
Well End *Bucks* **135** D4
Well End *Herts* **136** B3
Well Hill **123** D2
Well Street **123** F3
Well Town **102** C2
Welland **145** G3
Wellbank **244** C1
Wellesbourne **147** E2
Wellhill **267** G5
Welling **137** D5
Wellingborough **149** D1
Wellingham **177** G5
Wellingore **175** E2
Wellington *Cumb* **198** B2
Wellington *Here* **145** D3
Wellington *Som* **115** E5
Wellington *Tel&W* **157** F1
Wellington Heath **145** G3
Wellington Marsh **145** D3
Wellow *B&NESom* **117** E2
Wellow *IoW* **106** C4
Wellow *Notts* **174** B1
Wells **116** C3
Wells Cathedral *Som*
  BA5 2UE **116** C3
Wells Green **158** D4
Wellsborough **159** F2
Wellswood **101** F1
Wellwood **235** E1
Welney **162** D3
Welsh Bicknor **131** E1
Welsh End **170** C4
Welsh Frankton **170** A4
Welsh Hook **140** C5
Welsh Mountain Zoo *Conwy*
  LL28 5UY **181** G5
Welsh Newton **131** D1
Welsh St. Donats **129** G5
Welshampton **170** B4
Welshpool
  (Y Trallwng) **156** B2
Welton *B&NESom* **117** D2
Welton *Cumb* **209** G2
Welton *ERid* **196** B5
Welton *Lincs* **188** A4
Welton *WN'hants* **148** A1
Welton le Marsh **176** C1
Welton le Wold **188** C4
Welwick **197** F5
Welwyn **136** B1
Welwyn Garden City **136** B1
Wem **170** C5
Wembdon **115** F4
Wembley **136** A4
Wembley *GtLon*
  HA9 0WS **10** C3
Wembley Park **136** A4
Wembury **100** B3
Wembworthy **113** G4
Wemyss Bay **232** C3
Wenallt *Cere* **154** C5
Wenallt *Gwyn* **168** C3
Wendens Ambo **150** D4
Wendlebury **134** A1
Wendling **178** A4
Wendover **135** D2
Wendover Dean **135** D2
Wendron **95** D3
Wendy **150** B3
Wenfordbridge **97** E2
Wenhaston **165** F4
Wenlli **168** B1
Wennington *Cambs* **162** A5
Wennington *GtLon* **137** E4
Wennington *Lancs* **200** B5
Wensley *Derbys* **173** D1
Wensley *NYorks* **201** F4
Wensleydale Creamery,
  Hawes *NYorks*
  DL8 3RN **201** D4
Wentbridge **186** B1
Wentnor **156** C3
Wentworth *Cambs* **162** C5
Wentworth *SYorks* **186** A3
Wenvoe **130** A5
Weobley **144** C2
Weobley Marsh **144** D2
Wooley Castle **158** C4
Wepham **108** B3
Wepre **169** F1
Wepre Country Park *Flints*
  CH5 4HL **169** F1
Wereham **163** E2
Wergs **158** A2
Wern *Gwyn* **167** E4
Wern *Powys* **156** B1
Wern *Powys* **130** A1
Wern *Shrop* **169** F4
Wernffrwd **128** B3
Wernolau **128** B2
Wernrheolydd **130** C1
Wern-y-cwrt **130** C2
Werrington *Corn* **98** D2
Werrington *Peter* **161** G2
Werrington *Staffs* **171** G3
Wervil Grange **141** G2
Wervin **183** F5
Wesham **192** A4
Wessington **173** E2
West Aberthaw **114** D1
West Acre **163** F1
West Acton **136** A4
West Allerdean **237** G5
West Alvington **100** D3
West Amesbury **118** C3
West Anstey **114** B5
West Ashby **188** C5
West Ashford **113** F2
West Ashling **108** A3
West Ashton **117** F2
West Auckland **212** A5
West Ayton **204** C4
West Bagborough **115** E4
West Barkwith **188** B4
West Barnby **204** B1
West Barns **237** D2
West Barsham **178** A2
West Bay **104** A3
West Beckham **178** C2
West Benhar **234** C3
West Bergholt **152** A5
West Bexington **104** B4
West Bilney **163** F1
West Blatchington **109** E3
West Boldon **212** C1
West Bourton **117** E5
West Bowling **194** A4
West Brabourne **124** C4
West Bradford **192** D3
West Bradley **116** C4
West Bretton **185** G1
West Bridgford **173** G4
West Bromwich **158** C3
West Buckland *Devon* **113** G2
West Buckland *Som* **115** E5
West Burrafirth **279** B7
West Burton *NYorks* **201** F4
West Burton *WSuss* **108** B2
West Butsfield **211** G3
West Butterwick **187** F2
West Byfleet **121** F1
West Cairncake **269** G6
West Caister **179** G4
West Calder **235** E3
West Camel **116** C5
West Carbeth **233** G2
West Carr Houses **187** E2
West Cauldcoats **234** A5
West Chaldon **105** D4
West Challow **133** F4
West Charleton **101** D3
West Chevington **221** E2
West Chiltington **108** C2
West Chiltington
  Common **108** C2
West Chinnock **104** A1
West Chisenbury **118** C2
West Clandon **121** F2
West Cliffe **125** F3
West Clyne **267** F1
West Compton
  Dorset **104** B3
West Compton *Som* **116** C3
West Cowick **195** F5
West Cross **128** C4
West Crudwell **132** B3
West Curry **98** C1
West Curthwaite **209** G2
West Dean *Wilts* **119** D5
West Dean *WSuss* **108** A2
West Deeping **161** G1
West Derby **183** E3
West Dereham **163** E2
West Ditchburn **229** F4
West Down **113** F1
West Drayton *GtLon* **135** F5
West Drayton *Notts* **187** E5
West Dullater **242** A4
West Dunnet **275** H1
West Edington **221** D3
West Ella **196** C5
West End *Bed* **149** E2
West End *BrackF* **135** D5
West End *Caerp* **130** B3
West End *Cambs* **162** C3
West End *ERid* **196** C1
West End *Hants* **107** D1
West End *Herts* **136** B2
West End *Kent* **125** D2
West End *Lancs* **192** A1
West End *Lincs* **189** D3
West End *Norf* **179** F4
West End *Norf* **178** A5
West End *NSom* **116** B1
West End *NYorks* **194** A2
West End *Oxon* **133** G2
West End *Oxon* **134** A4
West End *SLan* **235** D5
West End *Suff* **165** F3
West End *Surr* **121** G1
West End *Surr* **121** E1
West End *Wilts* **132** B3
West End *Wilts* **118** A5
West End *Wilts* **118** C4
West End Green **120** B1
West Farleigh **123** G3
West Farndon **148** A2
West Felton **170** A5
West Firle **109** G3
West Fleetham **229** F4
West Flotmanby **205** D5
West Garforth **194** C4
West Ginge **133** G4
West Glen **232** A2
West Grafton **118** D1
West Green *GtLon* **136** C4
West Green *Hants* **120** C2
West Grimstead **118** D5
West Grinstead **121** G5
West Haddlesey **195** E5
West Haddon **160** B5
West Hagbourne **134** A4
West Hagley **158** B4
West Hall **210** B1
West Hallam **173** F3
West Halton **196** B5
West Ham **136** C4
West Handley **186** A5
West Hanney **133** G3
West Hanningfield **137** G3
West Hardwick **186** B1
West Harnham **118** C5
West Harptree **116** C2
West Harrow **136** A4
West Harting **120** C5
West Hatch *Som* **115** F5
West Hatch *Wilts* **118** A5
West Head **163** E2
West Heath *ChesE* **171** F1
West Heath *GtLon* **135** D5
West Heath *Hants* **121** D5
West Heath *Hants* **119** G2
West Heath *WMid* **158** C5
West Helmsdale **275** F7
West Hendon **136** B4
West Hendred **133** G4
West Heslerton **204** C5
West Hewish **116** A1
West Hill *Devon* **103** D3
West Hill *ERid* **197** D1
West Hill *NSom* **131** D5
West Hoathly **122** C5
West Holme **105** E4
West Horndon **137** F4
West Horrington **116** C3
West Horsley **121** F2
West Horton **229** E3
West Hougham **125** E5
West Howe **105** G3
West Howetown **114** C4
West Huntspill **116** A3
West Hyde **135** F3
West Hythe **124** D5
West Ilsley **133** G4
West Itchenor **107** G3
West Keal **176** B1
West Kennett **118** C1
West Kennett Long Barrow
  (Stonehenge, Avebury &
  Associated Sites) *Wilts*
  SN8 1QH **118** C1
West Kilbride **232** D5
West Kingsdown **123** E2
West Kington **132** A5
West Kington Wick **132** A5
West Kirby **182** D2
West Knapton **204** B5
West Knighton **104** D4
West Knoyle **117** F4
West Kyloe **229** E2
West Lambrook **104** A1
West Langdon **125** F4
West Langwell **266** D1
West Lavington
  Wilts **118** B2
West Lavington
  WSuss **121** D5
West Layton **202** A2
West Leake **173** G5
West Learmouth **228** C3
West Lees **203** D2
West Leigh *Devon* **113** G5
West Leigh *Devon* **101** D1
West Leigh *Som* **115** E4
West Leith **135** E1
West Lexham **163** G1
West Lilling **195** F1
West Lingo **244** C4
West Linton **235** F4
West Liss **120** C5
West Littleton **131** G5
West Lockinge **133** G4
West Looe **97** G4
West Lulworth **105** E4
West Lutton **196** B1
West Lydford **116** C4
West Lyn **114** A3
West Lyng **116** A5
West Lynn **163** E1
West Mains **229** E2
West Malling **123** F3
West Malvern **145** G3
West Marden **107** G1
West Markham **187** E5
West Marsh **188** C2
West Marton **193** E2
West Melbury **117** F5
West Melton **186** B2
West Meon **120** B5
West Meon Hut **120** B5
West Mersea **138** D1
West Milton **104** A3
West Minster **124** B1
West Molesey **121** G1
West Monkton **115** F5
West Moors **105** G2
West Morden **105** F3
West Morriston **236** C5
West Morton **193** G3
West Mostard **200** C3
West Mudford **116** C5
West Muir **253** D3
West Ness **203** F5
West Newbiggin **202** C1
West Newton *ERid* **197** D4
West Newton *Norf* **177** E5
West Norwood **136** C5
West Ogwell **101** E1
West Orchard **105** E1
West Overton **118** C1
West Panson **98** D1
West Park *Aber* **261** F5
West Park *Mersey* **183** G3
West Parley **105** G3
West Peckham **123** F3
West Pelton **212** B2
West Pennard **116** C4
West Pentire **96** B3
West Perry **149** G1
West Porlock **114** B3
West Prawle **101** D4
West Preston **108** C3
West Pulham **104** D2
West Putford **113** D4
West Quantoxhead **115** E3
West Raddon **102** B2
West Rainton **212** C3
West Rasen **188** A4
West Raynham **177** G5
West Retford **187** D4
West Rounton **202** D2
West Row **163** E5
West Rudham **177** G5
West Runton **178** C1
West Saltoun **236** B3
West Sandford **102** B2
West Sandwick **278** D4
West Scrafton **201** F4
West Shepton **116** D3
West Shinness
  Lodge **273** H7
West Somerset Railway *Som*
  TA24 5BG **115** D4
West Somerton **179** F4
West Stafford **104** D4
West Stockwith **187** E3
West Stoke **108** A3
West Stonesdale **201** D2
West Stoughton **116** B3
West Stour **117** E5
West Stourmouth **125** E2
West Stow **163** G5
West Stow Country Park *Suff*
  IP28 6HG **163** F5
West Stowell **118** C1
West Stratton **119** G3
West Street *Kent* **124** B3
West Street *Med* **137** G5
West Street *Suff* **164** A4
West Tanfield **202** B5
West Taphouse **97** F3
West Tarbert **231** G3
West Tarring **108** D3
West Thirston **221** D1
West Thorney **107** G2
West Thurrock **137** E5
West Tilbury **137** F5
West Tisted **120** B5
West Tofts *Norf* **163** G3
West Tofts *P&K* **243** G1
West Torrington **188** B4
West Town *B&NESom* **116** C1
West Town *Hants* **107** G3
West Town *NSom* **116** B1
West Town *Som* **116** C1
West Tytherley **119** D5
West Walton **162** C1
West Wellow **106** B1
West Wembury **100** B3
West Wemyss **244** B5
West Wick **116** A1
West Wickham
  Cambs **151** E3
West Wickham *GtLon* **122** C2
West Williamston **126** D2
West Winch **163** E1
West Winterslow **118** D4
West Wittering **107** G3
West Witton **201** F4
West Woodburn **220** A3
West Woodhay **119** F1
West Woodlands **117** E3
West Worldham **120** C4
West Worlington **102** A1
West Worthing **108** D3
West Wratting **151** E2
West Wycombe **134** D3
West Yatton **132** A5
West Yell **278** D4
West Youlstone **112** C4
Westbere **125** E2
Westborough **174** D3
Westbourne *BCP* **105** G3
Westbourne *WSuss* **107** G2
Westbourne Green **136** B4
Westbrook *Kent* **125** F1
Westbrook *WBerks* **133** G5
Westbrook *Wilts* **118** A1
Westbury *Bucks* **148** B4
Westbury *Shrop* **156** C2
Westbury *Wilts* **117** F2
Westbury Leigh **117** F2
Westbury on Trym **131** E5
Westbury-on-Severn **131** G1
Westbury-sub-Mendip **116** C3
Westby *Lancs* **191** G4
Westby *Lincs* **175** G4
Westcliff-on-Sea **138** B4
Westcombe **117** D4
Westcot **133** F4
Westcott *Bucks* **134** C1
Westcott *Devon* **102** D2
Westcott *Surr* **121** G3
Westcott Barton **147** G5
Westcourt **118** D1
Westcroft **148** D4
Westdean **110** A4
Westdowns **97** E1
Westend Town **211** D2
Wester Aberchalder **258** C2
Wester Balgedie **243** F4
Wester Culbeuchly **268** E4
Wester Dechmont **235** E2
Wester Fintray **261** F3
Wester Foffarty **252** C5
Wester Greenskares **269** F3
Wester Gruinards **266** C2
Wester Hailes **235** F3
Wester Lealty **266** D4
Wester Lonvine **266** E4
Wester Newburn **244** C4
Wester Ord **261** G4
Wester Quarff **279** D9
Wester Skeld **279** B8
Westerdale *High* **275** G3
Westerdale *NYorks* **203** F2
Westerfield *Suff* **152** C3
Westerfield *Shet* **279** C7
Westergate **108** B3
Westerham **122** D3
Westerhope **212** A1
Westerleigh **131** F5
Westerloch **275** J3
Westerton *Aber* **261** F5
Westerton *Angus* **253** E4
Westerton *Dur* **212** B3
Westerton *P&K* **243** D3
Westerwick **279** B8
Westfield *Cumb* **208** C4
Westfield *ESuss* **110** D2
Westfield *High* **275** F2
Westfield *NLan* **234** B2
Westfield *Norf* **178** A5
Westfield *WLoth* **234** D2
Westfield *WYorks* **194** B5
Westfield Sole **123** G2
Westgate *Dur* **211** F4
Westgate *N'umb* **220** D4
Westgate *NLincs* **187** E2
Westgate *Norf* **178** A1
Westgate Hill **194** B5
Westgate on Sea **125** F1
Westhall *Aber* **260** E1
Westhall *Suff* **165** F3
Westham *Dorset* **104** C5
Westham *ESuss* **110** B3
Westham *Som* **116** B3
Westhampnett **108** A3
Westhay *Devon* **103** G2
Westhay *Som* **116** B3
Westhead **183** F2
Westhide **145** E3
Westhill *Aber* **261** G4
Westhill *High* **266** E7
Westhope *Here* **145** D2
Westhope *Shrop* **157** D4
Westhorp **148** A2
Westhorpe *Lincs* **176** A4
Westhorpe *Notts* **174** B2
Westhorpe *Suff* **152** B1
Westhoughton **184** A2
Westhouse **200** B5
Westhouses **173** F2
Westhumble **121** G2
Westing **278** E2
Westlake **100** C2
Westlands **171** F3
Westlea **132** D4
Westleigh *Devon* **113** E3
Westleigh *Devon* **103** D1
Westleigh *GtMan* **184** A2
Westleton **153** F1
Westley *Shrop* **156** C2
Westley *Suff* **151** G1
Westley Heights **137** F4
Westley Waterless **151** E2
Westlington **134** C1
Westlinton **218** B5
Westloch **235** G4
Westmancote **146** B4
Westmarsh **125** E2
Westmeston **109** F2
Westmill **150** B5
Westminster **136** B5
Westminster Abbey
  (Palace of Westminster &
  Westminster Abbey inc.
  St Margaret's Church)
  GtLon SW1P 3PA **44** E6
Westminster Abbey - Chapter
  House & Pyx Chamber
  GtLon SW1P 3PA **44** E6
Westminster Cathedral
  GtLon SW1P 2QW **44** C7
Westmuir **252** B4
Westness **276** D5
Westnewton *Cumb* **209** E2
Westnewton *N'umb* **228** D3
Westoe **212** C1
Weston *B&NESom* **117** E1
Weston *ChesE* **171** E1
Weston *Devon* **103** E4
Weston *Devon* **103** E2
Weston *Dorset* **104** C5
Weston *Halton* **183** G4
Weston *Hants* **120** C5
Weston *Here* **144** C2
Weston *Herts* **150** A4
Weston *Lincs* **176** A5
Weston *Moray* **268** C4
Weston *Notts* **174** B1
Weston *NYorks* **194** A3
Weston *Shrop* **170** C5
Weston *Shrop* **157** E3
Weston *Shrop* **156** C5
Weston *Soton* **107** D1
Weston *Staffs* **171** G5
Weston *WBerks* **133** G5
Weston *WN'hants* **148** A3
Weston Bampfylde **116** D5
Weston Beggard **145** E3
Weston by Welland **160** C3
Weston Colville **151** E2
Weston Corbett **120** B3
Weston Coyney **171** G3
Weston Favell **148** C1
Weston Green *Cambs* **151** E2
Weston Green *Norf* **178** C4
Weston Heath **157** G1
Weston Hills **176** A5
Weston in Arden **159** F4
Weston Jones **171** E5
Weston Longville **178** C4
Weston Lullingfields **170** B5
Weston Park *Staffs*
  TF11 8LE **158** A1
Weston Patrick **120** B3
Weston Point **183** F4
Weston Rhyn **169** F4
Weston Subedge **146** D3
Weston Town **117** E3
Weston Turville **135** D1
Weston under
  Penyard **145** F5
Weston under
  Wetherley **147** F1
Weston Underwood
  Derbys **173** D3
Weston Underwood
  MK **149** D2
Westonbirt **132** A4
Westonbirt - The National
  Arboretum *Glos*
  GL8 8QS **132** A4
Westoning **149** F4
Weston-in-Gordano **131** D5
Weston-on-Avon **147** D2
Weston-on-the-Green **134** A1
Weston-on-Trent **173** F5
Weston-super-Mare **116** A1
Weston-under-Lizard **158** A1
Westonzoyland **116** A4
Westow **195** G1
Westport *A&B* **222** B3
Westport *Som* **116** A5
Westra **130** A5
Westray **276** D2
Westray Airfield **276** D2
Westruther **236** D5
Westry **162** B3
Westside **276** D5
Westvale **183** F3
Westville **173** G3
Westward **209** F2
Westward Ho! **113** E3
Westwell *Kent* **124** B4
Westwell *Oxon* **133** E2
Westwell Leacon **124** B4
Westwick *Cambs* **150** C1
Westwick *Dur* **201** F1
Westwick *Norf* **179** D3
Westwood *Devon* **102** D3
Westwood *Peter* **161** G3
Westwood *SLan* **234** A4
Westwood *Wilts* **117** F2
Westwood Heath **159** E5
Westwoodside **187** E3
Wetham Green **124** A2
Wetheral **210** A2
Wetherby **194** D3
Wetherden **152** B1
Wetheringsett **152** C1
Wethersfield **151** F4
Wethersta **279** C6
Wetherup Street **152** C1
Wetley Abbey **171** G3
Wetley Rocks **171** G3
Wettenhall **170** D1
Wettenhall Green **170** D1
Wetton **172** C2
Wetwang **196** B2
Wetwood **171** E4
Wexcombe **119** D2
Wexham Street **135** E4
Weybourne *Norf* **178** C1
Weybourne *Surr* **121** D3
Weybread **165** D4
Weybread Street **165** D4
Weybridge **121** F1
Weycroft **103** G2
Weydale **275** G2
Weyhill **119** E3
Weymouth **104** C5
Weymouth Sea Life Adventure
  Park & Marine Sanctuary
  Dorset DT4 7SX **104** C4
Whaddon *Bucks* **148** D4
Whaddon *Cambs* **150** B3
Whaddon *Glos* **132** A1
Whaddon *Glos* **146** B5
Whaddon *Wilts* **118** C5
Whaddon *Wilts* **117** F1
Whaddon Gap **150** B3
Whale **210** B5
Whaley **186** C5
Whaley Bridge **185** E4
Whaley Thorns **186** C5
Whaligoe **275** J4
Whalley **192** D4
Whalsay **279** E6
Whalsay Airport **279** E6
Whalton **220** D3
Wham **193** D1
Whaplode **176** B5
Whaplode Drove **162** B1
Whaplode
  St. Catherine **162** B1
Wharfe **193** D1
Wharles **192** A4
Wharley End **149** E3
Wharncliffe Side **185** G3
Wharram le Street **196** B1
Wharram Percy **196** A1
Wharton
  ChesW&C **171** D1
Wharton *Here* **145** E2
Whashton **202** A2
Whatcote **147** F3
Whateley **159** E3
Whatfield **152** B3
Whatley **117** E3
Whatlington **110** C2
Whatsole Street **124** C4
Whatstandwell **173** E2
Whatton **174** C4
Whauphill **207** E2
Whaw **201** E2
Wheal Peevor
  (Cornwall & West Devon
  Mining Landscape) *Corn*
  95 C2
Wheatacre **165** F2
Wheatcroft **173** E2
Wheatfield *CC&G* **285** J3
Wheatfield *Oxon* **134** B3
Wheathampstead **136** A1
Wheathill *F&O* **280** D5
Wheathill *Shrop* **157** F4
Wheathill *Som* **116** C4
Wheatley *Hants* **120** C4
Wheatley *Oxon* **134** B2
Wheatley *WYorks* **193** G5
Wheatley Hill **212** C4
Wheatley Lane **193** E4
Wheatley Park **186** C2
Wheaton Aston **158** A1
Wheddon Cross **114** C4
Wheedlemont **260** C2
Wheelerstreet **121** E4
Wheelock **171** E2
Wheelock Heath **171** E2
Wheelton **192** C5
Wheen **252** B2
Wheldale **195** D5
Wheldrake **195** F3
Whelford **133** D3
Whelley **183** G2
Whelpley Hill **135** E2
Whelpo **209** G3
Whelston **182** D5
Whenby **195** F1
Whepstead **151** G2
Wherstead **152** C3
Wherwell **119** E3
Wheston **185** F5
Whetley Cross **104** A2
Whetstone *GtLon* **136** B3
Whetstone *Leics* **160** A3
Whicham **198** C4
Whichford **147** F4
Whickham **212** B1
Whiddon **113** E5
Whiddon Down **99** G1
Whifflet **234** B3
Whigstreet **252** C5
Whilton **148** B1
Whim **235** G4
Whimble **112** D5
Whimple **102** D3
Whimpwell Green **179** E3
Whin Lane End **191** G3
Whinburgh **178** B5
Whinlatter Forest *Cumb*
  CA12 5TW **209** E4
Whinny Hill **202** C1
Whinnyfold **261** J1
Whippingham **107** E3
Whipsnade **135** F1
Whipsnade Zoo *CenBeds*
  LU6 2LF **135** F1
Whipton **102** C3
Whirlow **186** A4
Whisby **175** E1
Whissendine **160** D1
Whissonsett **178** A3
Whisterfield **184** C5
Whistley Green **134** C5
Whiston *Mersey* **183** F3
Whiston *Staffs* **172** B3
Whiston *Staffs* **158** A1
Whiston *SYorks* **186** B3
Whiston *WN'hants* **148** D1
Whiston Cross **157** G2
Whiston Eaves **172** B3
Whitacre Fields **159** E3
Whitacre Heath **159** E3
Whitbeck **198** C4
Whitbourne **145** G2
Whitburn *T&W* **212** D1
Whitburn *WLoth* **234** D3
Whitby *ChesW&C* **183** E5
Whitby *NYorks* **204** B1
Whitby Abbey *NYorks*
  YO22 4JT **204** C1
Whitby Lifeboat Museum
  NYorks YO21 3PU **204** B1
Whitbyheath **183** E5
Whitchurch
  B&NESom **116** D1
Whitchurch *Bucks* **148** D5
Whitchurch *Cardiff* **130** A4
Whitchurch *Devon* **99** E3
Whitchurch *Hants* **119** F3
Whitchurch *Here* **131** E1
Whitchurch *Pembs* **140** A5
Whitchurch *Shrop* **170** C3
Whitchurch *Warks* **147** E3
Whitchurch
  Canonicorum **103** G2
Whitchurch Hill **134** B5
Whitchurch-on-
  Thames **134** B5
Whitcombe **104** D4
Whitcott Keysett **156** B4
White Ball **103** D1
White Cliffs of Dover *Kent*
  CT16 1HJ **125** F4
White Colne **151** G5
White Coppice **184** A1
White Cross *Corn* **96** C4
White Cross *Devon* **103** D2
White Cross *Here* **145** D3
White Cross *Wilts* **117** E4
White Cube *GtLon*
  N1 6PB **12** C4
White End **146** A5
White Hill **117** F4
White Houses **187** E5
White Kirkley **211** G4

White Lackington **104** D3
White Ladies Aston **146** B2
White Lund **192** A1
White Moor **173** E3
White Notley **137** G1
White Ox Mead **117** E2
White Pit **189** D5
White Post Farm Centre,
  Farnsfield *Notts*
  NG22 8HL **174** B2
White Rocks **144** D5
White Roding **137** E1
White Waltham **134** D5
Whiteabbey **287** H7
Whiteacen **287** K7
Whitebirk **192** D5
Whitebog **269** H5
Whitebridge *High* **275** H1
Whitebridge (An Drochaid
  Bhàn) *High* **258** B3
Whitebrook **131** E2
Whiteburn **236** C5
Whitecairn **214** D5
Whitecairns **261** H3
Whitecastle **235** E5
Whitechapel **192** B3
Whitechurch **141** E4
Whitecote **194** B4
Whitecraig **236** A2
Whitecroft **131** F2
Whitecrook **214** C5
Whitecross *Corn* **94** C3
Whitecross *Corn* **97** D2
Whitecross *Dorset* **104** A3
Whitecross *Falk* **235** D2
Whitecross *NM&D* **282** C5
Whiteface **266** E3
Whitefield *Aber* **261** F2
Whitefield *Devon* **114** A4
Whitefield *Dorset* **105** F3
Whitefield *GtMan* **184** C2
Whitefield *High* **258** C2
Whitefield *High* **275** H3
Whitefield *P&K* **243** G1
Whiteford **261** F2
Whitegate **170** D1
Whitegates **283** F5
Whitehall *Devon* **103** E5
Whitehall *Hants* **120** C2
Whitehall *Ork* **279** F6
Whitehall *WSuss* **121** G5
Whitehaven **208** C5
Whitehead **287** J6
Whitehill *Aber* **269** H5
Whitehill *F&O* **280** E3
Whitehill *Hants* **120** C4
Whitehill *Kent* **124** B3
Whitehill *Midlo* **236** A3
Whitehill *NAyr* **233** D4
Whitehills **268** E4
Whitehouse *A&B* **231** G3
Whitehouse *A&N* **287** H7
Whitehouse *Aber* **260** E3
Whitehouse Common **158** D3
Whitekirk **236** C1
Whitelackington **103** G1
Whitelaw **237** F4
Whiteleen **275** J4
Whitelees **224** B2
Whiteley **107** E2
Whiteley Bank **107** E4
Whiteley Green **184** D5
Whiteley Village **121** F1
Whiteleys **214** B5
Whitemans Green **109** F1
Whitemire **267** G6
Whitemoor **97** D4
Whiteness **279** C8
Whiteoak Green **133** F1
Whiteparish **118** D5
Whiterashes **261** G2
Whiterock **283** J2
Whiterow **275** J4
Whiteshill **132** A2
Whiteside *N'umb* **210** D1
Whiteside *WLoth* **235** D3
Whitesides Corner **286** E6
Whitesmith **110** A2
Whitestaunton **103** F1
Whitestone *A&B* **222** C2
Whitestone *Aber* **260** E5
Whitestone *Devon* **102** B3
Whitestreet Green **152** A4
Whitestripe **269** H5
Whiteway **132** B1
Whitewell *Aber* **269** H4
Whitewell *Lancs* **192** C3
Whitewell *Wrex* **170** B3
Whiteworks **99** G3
Whitewreath **267** K6
Whitfield *Here* **144** D4
Whitfield *Kent* **125** E4
Whitfield *N'umb* **211** D2
Whitfield *SGlos* **131** F3
Whitfield *WN'hants* **148** B4
Whitford *Devon* **103** F3
Whitford (Chwitffordd)
  Flints **182** C5
Whitgift **196** A5
Whitgreave **171** F5
Whithorn **207** E2
Whiting Bay **223** F3
Whitkirk **194** C4
Whitlam **261** G2
Whitland
  (Hendy-Gwyn) **127** F1
Whitland Abbey **127** F1
Whitleigh **100** A1
Whitletts **224** B3
Whitley *NYorks* **195** E5
Whitley *Read* **120** C1
Whitley *Wilts* **117** F1
Whitley Bay **12** F4
Whitley Chapel **211** F2
Whitley Heath **171** F5
Whitley Lower **185** G1
Whitley Row **123** D3
Whitlock's End **158** D5
Whitminster **131** G2
Whitmore *Dorset* **105** G2
Whitmore *Staffs* **171** F3
Whitnage **102** D1
Whitnash **147** F1
Whitnell **115** F3
Whitney-on-Wye **144** B3

Whitrigg *Cumb* **209** F1
Whitrigg *Cumb* **209** F3
Whitsbury **106** A1
Whitsome **237** F4
Whitson **130** C4
Whitstable **124** D2
Whitstone **98** C1
Whittingham **229** E5
Whittingslow **156** D4
Whittington *Derbys* **186** A5
Whittington *Glos* **146** C5
Whittington *Lancs* **200** B5
Whittington *Norf* **163** F3
Whittington *Shrop* **170** A4
Whittington *Staffs* **158** A4
Whittington *Staffs* **159** D2
Whittington *Worcs* **146** A2
Whittlebury **148** B3
Whittle-le-Woods **192** B5
Whittlesey **162** A3
Whittlesford **150** C3
Whittlestone Head **184** B1
Whitton *GtLon* **136** A5
Whitton *N'umb* **220** C2
Whitton *NLincs* **196** B5
Whitton *Powys* **144** B1
Whitton *Shrop* **157** E5
Whitton *Stock* **212** C5
Whitton *Suff* **152** C3
Whittonditch **133** E5
Whittonstall **211** G2
Whitway **119** G2
Whitwell *Derbys* **186** C5
Whitwell *Herts* **149** G5
Whitwell *IoW* **107** E5
Whitwell *NYorks* **202** B3
Whitwell *Rut* **161** E2
Whitwell Street **178** C3
Whitwell-on-the-Hill **195** G1
Whitwick **159** G1
Whitwood **194** D5
Whitworth **184** C1
Whitworth Art Gallery,
  Manchester *GtMan*
  M15 6ER **25** E4
Whixall **170** C4
Whixley **194** D2
Whorlton *Dur* **202** A1
Whorlton *NYorks* **203** D2
Whygate **219** F4
Whyle **145** E1
Whyteleafe **122** C3
Wibdon **131** E3
Wibsey **194** A4
Wibtoft **159** G4
Wichelstowe **132** D4
Wichenford **145** G1
Wichling **124** B3
Wick *BCP* **106** A3
Wick *Devon* **103** E2
Wick (Inbhir Ùige)
  High **275** J3
Wick *SGlos* **131** G5
Wick *Som* **115** F3
Wick *Som* **116** C4
Wick *VGlam* **129** F5
Wick *Wilts* **118** C5
Wick *Worcs* **146** B3
Wick *WSuss* **108** C3
Wick John O'Groats Airport
  275 J3
Wick Hill *Kent* **124** A4
Wick Hill *W'ham* **120** C1
Wick St. Lawrence **116** A1
Wicken *Cambs* **163** D5
Wicken *WN'hants* **148** C4
Wicken Bonhunt **150** C4
Wickenby **188** A4
Wicker Street Green **152** A3
Wickerslack **200** D2
Wickersley **186** B3
Wicketwood Hill **174** B3
Wickford **137** G3
Wickham *Hants* **107** E1
Wickham *WBerks* **133** F5
Wickham Bishops **138** B1
Wickham Heath **119** F1
Wickham Market **153** E2
Wickham St. Paul **151** G4
Wickham Skeith **152** B1
Wickham Street *Suff* **151** F2
Wickham Street *Suff* **152** B1
Wickhambreaux **125** E3
Wickhambrook **151** F2
Wickhamford **146** C4
Wickhampton **179** F5
Wicklewood **178** B5
Wickmere **178** C2
Wicksteed Park *NN'hants*
  NN15 6NJ **161** D5
Wickstreet **110** A3
Wickwar **131** G4
Widcombe **117** E1
Widdington **150** D4
Widdrington **221** E2
Widdrington Station **221** E2
Wide Open **221** E4
Widecombe in the
  Moor **102** A5
Widegates **97** G4
Widemouth Bay **112** C5
Widewall **277** D8
Widford *Essex* **137** F2
Widford *Herts* **136** D1
Widford *Oxon* **133** E1
Widham Green **151** E2
Widmer End **135** D3
Widmerpool **174** B5
Widnes **183** F4
Widworthy **103** F3
Wigan **183** G1
Wiganthorpe **203** F5
Wigborough **104** A1
Wiggaton **103** E3
Wiggenhall
  St. Germans **163** D1
Wiggenhall St. Mary
  Magdalen **163** D1
Wiggenhall St. Mary the
  Virgin **163** D1
Wiggenhall St. Peter **163** E1
Wiggens Green **151** E3
Wigginton *Herts* **135** E1
Wigginton *Oxon* **147** F4
Wigginton *Shrop* **170** A4
Wigginton *Staffs* **159** E2
Wigginton *York* **195** F2

Wigglesworth **193** E2
Wiggonby **209** G1
Wiggonholt **108** C2
Wighill **195** D3
Wighton **178** A2
Wightwizzle **185** G3
Wigley **106** C1
Wigmore *Here* **144** D1
Wigmore *Med* **124** A2
Wigsley **187** F5
Wigsthorpe **161** F4
Wigston **160** B3
Wigston Parva **159** G4
Wigthorpe **186** C4
Wigtoft **176** A4
Wigton **209** F2
Wigtown **215** F5
Wike **194** C3
Wilbarston **160** D4
Wilberfoss **195** G2
Wilburton **162** C5
Wilby *NN'hants* **149** D1
Wilby *Norf* **164** C3
Wilby *Suff* **164** D4
Wilcot **118** C1
Wilcott **156** C1
Wilcrick **130** D4
Wilday Green **186** A5
Wildboarclough **171** G1
Wilde Street **163** F5
Wilden *Bed* **149** F2
Wilden *Worcs* **158** A5
Wildern **119** E2
Wildhill **136** B2
Wildmoor **158** B5
Wildsworth **187** F3
Wilford **173** G4
Wilkesley **170** D3
Wilkhaven **267** G3
Wilkieston **235** F3
Wilksby **176** A1
Willand *Devon* **102** D1
Willand *Som* **103** E1
Willaston *ChesE* **171** D2
Willaston *ChesW&C* **183** E5
Willaston *Shrop* **170** C4
Willen **149** D3
Willen Lakeside Park *MK*
  MK15 9HQ **9** D2
Willenhall *WMid* **158** B3
Willenhall *WMid* **159** F5
Willerby *ERid* **196** C5
Willerby *NYorks* **204** D5
Willersey **146** D4
Willersley **144** C3
Willesborough **124** C4
Willesborough Lees **124** C4
Willesden **136** B4
Willesleigh **113** F2
Willesley **132** A4
Willett **115** E4
Willey *Shrop* **157** F3
Willey *Warks* **159** G4
Willey Green **121** E2
William's Green **152** A3
Williamscot **147** G3
Williamsthorpe **173** F1
Willian **150** A1
Willimontswick **211** D1
Willingale **137** E2
Willingdon **110** A3
Willingham **162** B5
Willingham by Stow **187** F4
Willingham Green **151** E2
Willington *Bed* **149** G2
Willington *Derbys* **173** D5
Willington *Dur* **212** A4
Willington *Kent* **123** G3
Willington *T&W* **212** C1
Willington *Warks* **147** E4
Willington Corner **170** C1
Willisham **152** B2
Willitoft **195** G4
Williton **115** D3
Willmount **280** E1
Willoughbridge **171** E3
Willoughby *Lincs* **189** E5
Willoughby *Warks* **148** A1
Willoughby Waterleys **160** A3
Willoughby-on-the-
  Wolds **174** B5
Willoughton **187** G3
Willow Green **184** A5
Willows Farm Village *Herts*
  AL2 1BB **136** A2
Willows Green **137** G1
Willsbridge **131** F5
Willslock **172** B4
Willsworthy **99** F2
Willtown **116** A5
Wilmcote **147** D2
Wilmington
  B&NESom **117** D1
Wilmington *Devon* **103** F2
Wilmington *ESuss* **110** A3
Wilmington *Kent* **137** E5
Wilmslow **184** C4
Wilnecote **159** E2
Wilney Green **164** B3
Wilpshire **192** C4
Wilsden **193** G4
Wilsford *Lincs* **175** F3
Wilsford *Wilts* **118** C4
Wilsford *Wilts* **118** C2
Wilsham **114** A3
Wilshaw **185** F2
Wilsill **194** A1
Wilsley Green **123** G5
Wilsley Pound **123** G5
Wilson **173** F5
Wilstead **149** F3
Wilsthorpe *ERid* **197** D1
Wilsthorpe *Lincs* **161** F1
Wilstone **135** E1
Wilton *Cumb* **208** D5
Wilton *Here* **145** E5
Wilton *NYorks* **204** B4
Wilton *R&C* **203** E1
Wilton *ScBord* **227** F4
Wilton *Wilts* **119** D1
Wilton *Wilts* **118** B3
Wilton House *Wilts*
  SP2 0BJ **118** B4
Wiltown **103** E1
Wimbish **151** D4
Wimbish Green **151** E4

Wimblebury **158** C1
Wimbledon **136** B5
Wimbledon All England Lawn
  Tennis & Croquet Club
  GtLon SW19 5AG **11** E7
Wimblington **162** C3
Wimborne Minster **105** G2
Wimborne Minster *Dorset*
  BH21 1HT **3** B2
Wimborne St. Giles **105** G1
Wimbotsham **163** E2
Wimpole **150** B3
Wimpole Home Farm *Cambs*
  SG8 0BW **150** B3
Wimpole Lodge **150** B3
Wimpstone **147** E3
Wincanton **117** E5
Winceby **176** B1
Wincham **184** A5
Winchburgh **235** E2
Winchcombe **146** C5
Winchelsea **111** E2
Winchelsea Beach **111** E2
Winchester **119** F5
Winchester Cathedral
  Hants SO23 9LS
  89 Winchester
Winchet Hill **123** G4
Winchfield **120** C2
Winchmore Hill *Bucks* **135** E3
Winchmore Hill *GtLon* **136** C3
Wincle **171** G1
Wincobank **186** A3
Windermere **199** F3
Winderton **147** F3
Windhill **266** C7
Windle Hill **183** E5
Windlehurst **185** D4
Windlesham **121** E1
Windley **173** E3
Windmill **185** F5
Windmill Hill *ESuss* **110** B2
Windmill Hill *Som* **103** G1
Windmill Hill *Worcs* **146** B3
Windmill Hill (Stonehenge,
  Avebury & Associated Sites),
  Wilts SN4 9NW **132** C5
Windrush **133** D1
Windsor **135** E5
Windsor Castle *W&M*
  SL4 1NJ **89** Windsor
Windsor Green **151** G2
Windy Gap **285** D5
Windy Nook **212** B1
Windygates **244** B4
Windy-Yett **233** F4
Wineham **109** E1
Winestead **197** E5
Winewall **193** F4
Winfarthing **164** C3
Winford *IoW* **107** E4
Winford *NSom* **116** C1
Winforton **144** B3
Winfrith Newburgh **105** E4
Wing *Bucks* **149** D5
Wing *Rut* **161** D2
Wingate **212** C4
Wingates *GtMan* **184** A2
Wingates *N'umb* **220** C2
Wingerworth **173** E1
Wingfield *CenBeds* **149** F5
Wingfield *Suff* **164** D4
Wingfield *Wilts* **117** F2
Wingfield Green **164** D4
Wingham **125** E3
Wingham Well **125** E3
Wingmore **125** D4
Wingrave **135** D1
Winkburn **174** C2
Winkfield **135** E5
Winkfield Row **135** D5
Winkhill **172** B2
Winkleigh **113** G5
Winksley **202** B5
Winkton **106** A3
Winlaton **212** A1
Winlaton Mill **212** A1
Winless **275** J3
Winmarleigh **192** A3
Winnard's Perch **96** D3
Winnersh **134** C5
Winnington **184** A5
Winscombe **116** B2
Winsford *ChesW&C* **171** D1
Winsford *Som* **114** C4
Winsham *Devon* **113** E2
Winsham *Som* **103** G2
Winshill **173** D5
Winsh-wen **128** C3
Winskill **210** B4
Winslade **120** B3
Winsley **117** F1
Winslow **148** C5
Winson **132** C2
Winsor **106** C1
Winster *Cumb* **199** F3
Winster *Derbys* **172** D2
Winston *Dur* **202** A1
Winston *Suff* **152** C1
Winston Green **152** C1
Winstone **132** B2
Winswell **113** E4
Winter Gardens FY1 1HW
  64 Blackpool
Winter Gardens *NSom*
  BS23 1AJ
  88 Weston-super-Mare
Winterborne Came **104** D4
Winterborne Clenston **105** E2
Winterborne
  Herringston **104** C4
Winterborne
  Houghton **105** E2
Winterborne Kingston **105** E3
Winterborne Monkton **104** C4
Winterborne Stickland **105** E2
Winterborne
  Whitechurch **105** E2
Winterborne Zelston **105** E3
Winterbourne *SGlos* **131** F4
Winterbourne *WBerks* **133** G5
Winterbourne Abbas **104** C3
Winterbourne Bassett **132** D5

Winterbourne
  Dauntsey **118** C4
Winterbourne Earls **118** C4
Winterbourne Gunner **118** C4
Winterbourne
  Monkton **132** D5
Winterbourne
  Steepleton **104** C4
Winterbourne Stoke **118** B3
Winterburn **193** F2
Wintercleugh **226** A3
Winteringham **196** B5
Winterley **171** E2
Wintersett **186** A1
Wintershill **107** E1
Winterslow **118** D4
Winterton **187** G1
Winterton-on-Sea **179** F4
Winthorpe *Lincs* **177** D1
Winthorpe *Notts* **174** D2
Winton *BCP* **105** G3
Winton *Cumb* **200** C1
Wintringham **204** B5
Winwick *Cambs* **161** G4
Winwick *Warr* **184** A3
Winwick *WN'hants* **160** B5
Wirksworth **173** D2
Wirksworth Moor **173** E2
Wirral Country Park *Mersey*
  CH61 0HN **182** D4
Wirswall **170** C3
Wisbech **162** C2
Wisbech St. Mary **162** C2
Wisborough Green **121** F5
Wiseton **187** E4
Wishaw *NLan* **234** B4
Wishaw *Warks* **159** D3
Wisley **121** F2
Wispington **188** C5
Wissett **165** E4
Wissington **152** A4
Wistanstow **156** D4
Wistanswick **171** D5
Wistaston **171** D2
Wiston *Pembs* **126** A1
Wiston *SLan* **226** A2
Wiston *WSuss* **108** D2
Wistow *Cambs* **162** A4
Wistow *NYorks* **195** E4
Wistow *Norf* **164** D2
Wiswell **192** D4
Witcham **162** C5
Witchampton **105** F2
Witchburn **222** C3
Witchford **162** D5
Witcombe **116** B5
Witham **138** B1
Witham Friary **117** E3
Witham on the Hill **161** F1
Withcall **188** C4
Withcote **160** C2
Withdean **109** F3
Witherenden Hill **110** B1
Witheridge **102** B1
Witherley **159** F3
Withern **189** E4
Withernsea **197** F5
Withernwick **197** D3
Withersdale Street **165** D3
Withersfield **151** E3
Witherslack **199** F4
Witherslack Hall **199** F4
Withiel **97** D3
Withiel Florey **114** C4
Withielgoose **97** E3
Withington *Glos* **132** C1
Withington *GtMan* **184** C3
Withington *Here* **145** E3
Withington *Shrop* **157** E1
Withington *Staffs* **172** B4
Withington Green **184** C5
Withington Marsh **145** E3
Withleigh **102** C1
Withnell **192** C5
Withnell Fold **192** C5
Withybrook *Som* **117** D3
Withybrook *Warks* **159** G4
Withycombe **102** D4
Withycombe Raleigh **102** D4
Withyham **123** D5
Withypool **114** B4
Witley **121** E4
Witnesham **152** C2
Witney **133** F2
Wittering **161** F2
Wittersham **111** D1
Witton *Angus* **253** D2
Witton *Norf* **179** E5
Witton *Worcs* **146** A1
Witton Bridge **179** E2
Witton Gilbert **212** B3
Witton Park **212** A4
Witton-le-Wear **212** A4
Wiveliscombe **115** D5
Wivelrod **120** B4
Wivelsfield **109** F2
Wivelsfield Green **109** F2
Wivenhoe **152** B5
Wiveton **178** B1
Wix **152** C5
Wixford **146** C2
Wixhill **170** C5
Wixoe **151** F3
Woburn **149** E4
Woburn Safari Park *CenBeds*
  MK17 9QN **9** F3
Woburn Sands **149** E4
Wokefield Park **120** B1
Woking **121** F2
Wokingham **120** D1
Wolborough **102** B5
Wold Newton *ERid* **204** D5
Wold Newton *NELincs* **188** C3
Woldingham **122** C3
Wolds Village, Bainton *ERid*
  YO25 9EF **196** B3
Wolfelee **227** G5
Wolferlow **145** F1
Wolferton **177** E5
Wolfhampcote **148** A1
Wolfhill **243** G1
Wolfpits **144** B2
Wolf's Castle **140** C5
Wolfsdale **140** C5
Woll **227** F4
Wollaston *NN'hants* **149** E1
Wollaston *Shrop* **156** C1
Wollaston *WMid* **158** A4

Wollaton **173** G4
Wollerton **170** D5
Wollescote **158** B4
Wolsingham **211** G4
Wolston **159** G5
Wolvercote **134** A2
Wolverhampton **158** B3
Wolverhampton Art Gallery
  WMid WV1 1DU **14** A1
Wolverley *Shrop* **170** B4
Wolverley *Worcs* **158** A5
Wolvers Hill **116** A1
Wolverton *Hants* **119** G2
Wolverton *MK* **148** D3
Wolverton *Warks* **147** E1
Wolverton *Wilts* **117** E4
Wolverton Common **119** G2
Wolvesnewton **131** D3
Wolvey **159** G4
Wolvey Heath **159** G4
Wolviston **213** D5
Womaston **144** B1
Wombleton **203** F4
Wombourne **158** A3
Wombwell **186** A2
Womenswold **125** E3
Womersley **186** C1
Wonastow **131** D1
Wonersh **121** F3
Wonford **102** C3
Wonson **99** G2
Wonston **119** F4
Wooburn **135** E4
Wooburn Green **135** E4
Wood Bevington **146** C2
Wood Burcote **148** B3
Wood Dalling **178** B3
Wood Eaton **158** A1
Wood End *Bed* **149** F3
Wood End *Bed* **149** F1
Wood End *Bucks* **148** C3
Wood End *Herts* **150** B5
Wood End *Warks* **159** D5
Wood End *Warks* **158** D5
Wood End *Warks* **159** E4
Wood End *WMid* **158** B2
Wood Enderby **176** A1
Wood Green *GtLon* **136** C3
Wood Green *Norf* **164** D2
Wood Green Animal Shelter,
  Godmanchester *Cambs*
  PE29 2NH **150** A1
Wood Lane **170** B4
Wood Norton **178** B3
Wood Seats **186** A3
Wood Stanway **146** C4
Wood Street **179** E3
Wood Street Village **121** E2
Woodacott **113** D5
Woodale **201** F5
Woodall **186** B4
Woodbastwick **179** E4
Woodbeck **187** E5
Woodborough *Notts* **174** B3
Woodborough *Wilts* **118** C2
Woodbridge *Devon* **103** E3
Woodbridge *Dorset* **104** D1
Woodbridge *Suff* **153** D3
Woodburn **287** H7
Woodbury *Devon* **102** D4
Woodbury *Som* **116** C3
Woodbury Salterton **102** D4
Woodchester **132** A2
Woodchurch *Kent* **124** B5
Woodchurch *Mersey* **183** D4
Woodcombe **114** C3
Woodcote *Oxon* **134** B4
Woodcote *Tel&W* **157** G1
Woodcote Green **158** B5
Woodcott **119** F2
Woodcroft **131** E3
Woodcutts **105** F1
Wooddltton **151** F2
Woodeaton **134** A1
Woodend *Aber* **260** E3
Woodend *Cumb* **198** C2
Woodend *High* **258** E2
Woodend *High* **247** G3
Woodend *P&K* **250** C2
Woodend *WN'hants* **148** B3
Woodend *WSuss* **108** A3
Woodend Green **151** D5
Woodfalls **118** C5
Woodfield *Oxon* **148** A5
Woodfield *SAyr* **224** B3
Woodford **200** B1
Woodford *Corn* **112** C4
Woodford *Devon* **101** D2
Woodford *Glos* **131** F3
Woodford *GtLon* **136** D3
Woodford *GtMan* **184** C3
Woodford *NN'hants* **161** E5
Woodford *Som* **115** D4
Woodford Bridge **136** D3
Woodford Green **136** D3
Woodford Halse **148** A2
Woodgate *Devon* **103** E1
Woodgate *Norf* **178** B4
Woodgate *WMid* **158** B4
Woodgate *Worcs* **146** B1
Woodgate *WSuss* **108** B3
Woodgreen **106** A1
Woodhall *Invclyd* **233** D2
Woodhall *NYorks* **201** E3
Woodhall Hills **194** A4
Woodhall Spa **175** G1
Woodham *Bucks* **134** B1
Woodham *Dur* **212** B5
Woodham *Surr* **121** F2
Woodham Ferrers **137** G3
Woodham Mortimer **138** B2
Woodham Walter **138** B2
Woodhaven **244** C2
Woodhead *Aber* **261** F1
Woodhead *Staffs* **172** B3
Woodhenge (Stonehenge,
  Avebury & Associated Sites)
  Wilts SP4 7AR **118** C3
Woodhey **183** E4
Woodhey Green **170** C2
Woodhill *Shrop* **157** G4
Woodhill *Som* **116** A5
Woodhorn **221** E3
Woodhouse *Cumb* **199** G4
Woodhouse *Leics* **160** A1
Woodhouse *SYorks* **186** B4
Woodhouse *WYorks* **194** B4

Woodhouse *WYorks* **194** C5
Woodhouse *WYorks* **194** C5
Woodhouse Down **131** F4
Woodhouse Eaves **160** A1
Woodhouse Green **171** G1
Woodhouses *GtMan* **185** D1
Woodhouses *Staffs* **159** D1
Woodhouses *Staffs* **158** C2
Woodhuish **101** F2
Woodhurst **162** B5
Woodingdean **109** F3
Woodington **119** F5
Woodland *Devon* **101** D1
Woodland *Kent* **124** D4
Woodland Head **102** A3
Woodlands *Dorset* **105** G2
Woodlands *Hants* **106** C1
Woodlands *NYorks* **157** C3
Woodlands *Shrop* **157** F4
Woodlands *Som* **115** E3
Woodlands Family Theme Park,
  Dartmouth *Devon*
  TQ9 7DQ **101** E2
Woodlands Park **135** D5
Woodlands St. Mary **133** F4
Woodlane **172** C5
Woodleigh **100** D3
Woodlesford **194** C5
Woodley *GtMan* **185** D1
Woodley *W'ham* **134** C5
Woodmancote *Glos* **132** C2
Woodmancote *Glos* **146** B5
Woodmancote *Glos* **131** G3
Woodmancote *WSuss*
  109 E2
Woodmancote *WSuss*
  107 G2
Woodmancott **119** G3
Woodmansey **196** C4
Woodmansterne **122** B3
Woodmanton **102** D4
Woodmill **172** C5
Woodminton **118** B5
Woodmoor **156** B2
Woodnesborough **125** F3
Woodnewton **161** F3
Woodperry **134** A1
Woodplumpton **192** B4
Woodrising **178** A5
Woodrow **105** D1
Wood's Corner **110** B2
Woods Eaves **144** B3
Wood's Green **123** F5
Woodseaves *Shrop* **171** D4
Woodseaves *Staffs* **171** E5
Woodsend **133** E5
Woodsetts **186** C4
Woodsford **105** D3
Woodside *Aberdeen* **261** H4
Woodside *BrackF* **135** E5
Woodside *CenBeds* **135** F1
Woodside *Cumb* **208** D3
Woodside *D&G* **217** E3
Woodside *Fife* **244** C4
Woodside *Fife* **244** A4
Woodside *GtLon* **122** C2
Woodside *Hants* **106** C3
Woodside *Herts* **136** B2
Woodside *NAyr* **233** E4
Woodside *P&K* **243** G1
Woodside *Shrop* **156** C1
Woodside *WMid* **158** B4
Woodside Animal Farm &
  Leisure Park *CenBeds*
  LU1 4DG **135** F1
Woodside Green **124** B3
Woodstock *Oxon* **133** G1
Woodstock *Pembs* **140** D5
Woodthorpe *Derbys* **186** B5
Woodthorpe *Leics* **160** A1
Woodthorpe *Lincs* **189** E4
Woodthorpe *SYorks* **186** A4
Woodthorpe *York* **195** E3
Woodton **165** D2
Woodtown **113** E3
Woodvale **183** E1
Woodville **159** F1
Woodwall Green **171** E4
Woodwalton **162** A4
Woodwick **276** C5
Woodworth Green **170** C2
Woodyates **105** G1
Woofferton **145** E1
Wookey **116** C3
Wookey Hole **116** C3
Wookey Hole Caves &
  Papermill *Som*
  BA5 1BB **116** C3
Wool **105** E4
Woolacombe **113** E1
Woolage Green **125** E4
Woolage Village **125** E3
Woolaston **131** E2
Woolaston Slade **131** E2
Woolavington **116** A3
Woolbeding **121** D5
Woolcotts **114** C4
Wooldale **185** F2
Wooler **229** D4
Woolfardisworthy
  Devon **102** B2
Woolfardisworthy
  Devon **112** D3
Woolfold **184** B1
Woolfords Cottages
  235 E4
Woolgarston **105** F4
Woolgreaves **186** A1
Woolhampton **119** G1
Woolhope **145** F4
Woolland **105** D2
Woollard **116** D1
Woollaton **113** E4
Woollensbrook **136** C2
Woolley *B&NESom* **117** E1
Woolley *Cambs* **161** G5
Woolley *Corn* **112** C4
Woolley *Derbys* **173** E1
Woolley *WYorks* **186** A1
Woolley Green *W&M* **135** D5
Woolley Green *Wilts* **117** F1
Woolmer Green **136** B1
Woolmere Green **146** B1
Woolmersdon **115** F4
Woolpit **152** A1
Woolpit Green **152** A1
Woolscott **147** G1

Woolsgrove 102 A2
Woolstaston 157 D3
Woolsthorpe 174 D4
Woolsthorpe by
  Colsterworth 175 E5
Woolston Devon 100 D3
Woolston Shrop 170 A5
Woolston Shrop 156 D4
Woolston Soton 106 D1
Woolston Warr 184 A4
Woolston Green 101 D1
Woolstone Glos 146 B4
Woolstone MK 149 D4
Woolstone Oxon 133 E4
Woolton 183 F4
Woolton Hill 119 F1
Woolverstone 152 C4
Woolverton 117 E2
Woolwich 136 D5
Woonton 144 C2
Wooperton 229 E5
Woore 171 E3
Wootten Green 164 D4
Wootton Bed 149 F3
Wootton Hants 106 B3
Wootton IoW 107 E3
Wootton Kent 125 E4
Wootton NLincs 188 A1
Wootton Oxon 133 G1
Wootton Oxon 133 G2
Wootton Shrop 157 D5
Wootton Shrop 170 A5
Wootton Staffs 171 F5
Wootton Staffs 172 C3
Wootton WN'hants 148 C2
Wootton Bassett 132 C4
Wootton Bridge 107 E3
Wootton Common 107 E3
Wootton Courtenay 114 C3
Wootton Fitzpaine 103 G3
Wootton Green 149 F3
Wootton Rivers 118 C1
Wootton St. Lawrence
  119 G2
Wootton Wawen 147 D1
Worcester 146 A2
Worcester Cathedral Worcs
  WR1 2LH 90 Worcester
Worcester Park 122 B2
Worcester Woods Country Park
  Worcs WR5 2LG 146 A2
Wordsley 158 A4
Wordwell 163 G5
Worfield 157 G3
Worgret 105 F4
Work 277 D6
Workhouse End 149 G2
Workington 208 D4
Worksop 186 C5
Worlaby Lincs 188 D5
Worlaby NLincs 188 A1
World Museum Liverpool
  Mersey L3 8EN 42 D3
World of Beatrix Potter
  Attraction Cumb
  LA23 3BX 199 F3
World of James Herriot, Thirsk
  NYorks YO7 1PL 202 D4
World's End Bucks 135 D2

Worlds End Hants 107 F1
World's End
  WBerks 133 G5
Worlds End WMid 158 D4
Worle 116 A1
Worleston 171 D2
Worlingham 165 F3
Worlington 163 E5
Worlingworth 152 D1
Wormald Green 194 C1
Wormbridge 144 D4
Wormegay 163 E1
Wormelow Tump 145 D4
Wormhill 185 F5
Wormingford 152 A4
Worminghall 134 B2
Wormington 146 C4
Worminster 116 C3
Wormiston 245 D4
Wormit 244 B2
Wormleighton 147 G2
Wormley Herts 136 C2
Wormley Surr 121 E4
Wormley West End 136 C2
Wormshill 124 A3
Wormsley 184 B2
Worplesdon 121 E2
Worrall 186 A3
Worsbrough 186 A2
Worsley 184 B2
Worstead 179 E3
Worsted Lodge 150 D2
Worsthorne 193 E4
Worston 193 D3
Worswell 100 B3
Worth Kent 125 F3
Worth WSuss 122 B5
Worth Matravers 105 F5
Wortham 164 B4
Worthen 156 C2
Worthenbury 170 B3
Worthing Norf 178 A4
Worthing WSuss 108 D3
Worthington 173 F5
Worting 120 B2
Wortley Glos 131 G3
Wortley SYorks 186 A3
Wortley WYorks 194 B4
Worton NYorks 201 E4
Worton Wilts 118 A2
Wortwell 165 D3
Wothersome 194 D3
Wotherton 156 B2
Wotter 100 B1
Wotton 121 G3
Wotton Underwood 134 B1
Wotton-under-Edge 131 G3
Woughton on the
  Green 149 D4
Wouldham 123 G2
Wrabness 152 C4
Wrae 269 F5
Wrafton 113 E2
Wragby 188 B5
Wragholme 189 D3
Wramplingham 178 C5
Wrangaton 100 C2
Wrangham 260 E1
Wrangle 176 C2

Wrangle Lowgate 176 C2
Wrangway 103 E1
Wrantage 116 A5
Wrawby 188 A2
Wraxall NSom 131 D5
Wraxall Som 116 D4
Wray 192 C1
Wrays 122 B4
Wraysbury 135 F5
Wrayton 200 B5
Wrea Green 191 G4
Wreay Cumb 210 A5
Wreay Cumb 210 A3
Wrecclesham 120 D3
Wrekenton 212 B2
Wrelton 203 G4
Wrenbury 170 C3
Wrench Green 204 C4
Wreningham 164 C2
Wrentham 165 F3
Wrenthorpe 194 C5
Wrentnall 156 D2
Wressle ERid 195 G4
Wressle NLincs 187 G2
Wrestlingworth 150 A3
Wretham 164 A2
Wretton 163 E2
Wrexham (Wrecsam) 170 A3
Wrexham Arts Centre Wrex
  LL11 1AU 170 A2
Wrexham Industrial
  Estate 170 A3
Wribbenhall 157 G5
Wrightington Bar 183 G1
Wrightpark 242 B5
Wright's Green 137 E1
Wrinehill 171 E3
Wrington 116 B1
Writhlington 117 D2
Writtle 137 F2
Wrockwardine 157 F1
Wroot 187 E2
Wrose 194 A4
Wrotham 123 F3
Wrotham Heath 123 F3
Wrotham Hill Park 123 F2
Wrottesley 158 A2
Wroughton 132 D4
Wroxall IoW 107 E5
Wroxall Warks 159 E5
Wroxeter 157 E2
Wroxham 179 E4
Wroxham Barns Norf
  NR12 8QU 179 E3
Wroxton 147 G3
Wstrws 141 G3
Wyaston 172 C3
Wyberton 176 B3
Wyboston 149 G2
Wybunbury 171 D2
Wych Cross 122 D5
Wychbold 146 B1
Wychnor 159 D1
Wychnor Bridges 159 D1
Wyck 120 C4
Wyck Rissington 147 D2
Wycliffe 202 A1

Wycoller 193 F4
Wycoller Country Park
  Lancs BB8 8SY 193 F4
Wycomb 174 C5
Wycombe Marsh 135 D3
Wyddial 150 B4
Wye 124 C4
Wyesham 131 E1
Wyfordby 160 C1
Wyke Devon 102 B3
Wyke Dorset 117 E5
Wyke Shrop 157 F2
Wyke Surr 121 E2
Wyke WYorks 194 A5
Wyke
  Champflower 117 D4
Wyke Regis 104 C5
Wykeham NYorks 204 C4
Wykeham NYorks 204 B5
Wyken Shrop 157 G3
Wyken WMid 159 F4
Wykey 170 A5
Wylam 212 A1
Wylde Green 158 D3
Wyllie 130 A3
Wylye 118 B4
Wymering 107 F2
Wymeswold 174 B5
Wymington 149 E1
Wymondham Leics 161 D1
Wymondham Norf 178 C5
Wyndham 129 F3
Wynford Eagle 104 B3
Wynnstay Park 170 A3
Wynyard 212 D5
Wynyard Woodland Park
  Stock TS21 3JG 212 C5
Wyre Forest Worcs
  DY14 9XQ 157 G5
Wyre Piddle 146 B3
Wyresdale Tower 192 C2
Wysall 174 B5
Wyson 145 E1
Wythall 158 C5
Wytham 133 G2
Wythburn 209 G5
Wythenshawe 184 C4
Wyton Cambs 162 A5
Wyton ERid 197 D4
Wyverstone 152 B1
Wyverstone Street 152 B1
Wyville 175 D5
Wyvis Lodge 266 B4

X
Xscape Castleford WYorks
  WF10 4DA 194 D5

Y
Y Bryn 168 B5
Y Fan 155 F4
Y Felinheli 167 E1
Y Ferwig 141 E3
Y Ffôr 166 C4
Y Fron (Upper
  Llandwrog) 167 E2
Y Gors 154 C5
Yaddlethorpe 187 F2
Yafford 106 D4

Yafforth 202 C3
Yalberton 101 E2
Yalding 123 F4
Yanley 116 C1
Yanwath 210 B5
Yanworth 132 C1
Yapham 195 G2
Yapton 108 B3
Yarburgh 188 D3
Yarcombe 103 F2
Yardley 158 D4
Yardley Gobion 148 C3
Yardley Hastings 149 D2
Yardro 144 B2
Yarford 115 F5
Yarkhill 145 F3
Yarlet 171 G5
Yarley 116 C3
Yarlington 117 D5
Yarm 202 D1
Yarmouth 106 C4
Yarnacott 113 G2
Yarnbrook 117 F2
Yarnfield 171 F4
Yarnscombe 113 F3
Yarnton 133 G1
Yarpole 145 D1
Yarrow ScBord 227 D3
Yarrow Som 116 A3
Yarrow Feus 227 E3
Yarrowford 227 F3
Yarsop 144 D3
Yarwell 161 F3
Yate 131 G4
Yatehouse Green 171 E1
Yateley 120 D1
Yatesbury 132 C5
Yattendon 134 A5
Yatton Here 144 D1
Yatton NSom 116 B1
Yatton Keynell 132 A5
Yaverland 107 F4
Yawl 103 G3
Yaxham 178 B4
Yaxley Cambs 161 G3
Yaxley Suff 164 C4
Yazor 144 D3
Ye Olde Pork Pie Shoppe,
  Melton Mowbray Leics
  LE13 1NW 160 C1
Yeabridge 104 A1
Yeading 136 A4
Yeadon 194 B3
Yealand Conyers 199 G5
Yealand Redmayne 199 G5
Yealand Storrs 199 G5
Yealmbridge 100 B2
Yealmpton 100 B2
Yearby 213 F5
Yearsley 203 E5
Yeaton 156 D1
Yeaveley 172 C3
Yeavering 228 D3
Yedingham 204 B5
Yelford 133 F2
Yell 278 D4
Yelland Devon 113 E2
Yelland Devon 99 F1
Yelling 150 A1

Yellowcraig ELoth
  EH39 5DS 236 C1
Yelvertoft 160 A5
Yelverton Devon 100 B1
Yelverton Norf 179 D5
Yenston 117 E5
Yeo Mill 114 B5
Yeo Vale 113 E3
Yeoford 102 A3
Yeolmbridge 98 D2
Yeomadon 112 D5
Yeovil 104 B1
Yeovil Country Park Som
  BA20 1QZ 104 B1
Yeovil Marsh 104 B1
Yeovilton 116 C5
Yerbeston 127 D2
Yesnaby 277 B6
Yesterday's World, Battle
  ESuss TN33 0AQ 110 C2
Yetholm Mains 228 C4
Yetlington 229 E5
Yetminster 104 B1
Yettington 103 D4
Yetts o'Muckhart 243 F4
Yew Green 147 E1
Yielden 149 F1
Yieldshields 234 C4
Ynys 167 E4
Ynys Tachwedd 154 C3
Ynysboeth 129 G3
Ynys-ddu 130 A3
Ynyshir 129 G3
Ynys-las 154 C3
Ynysmaerdy 129 G4
Ynysmeudwy 128 D2
Ynystawe 128 C2
Ynyswen 129 F3
Ynysybwl 129 G3
Yockenthwaite 201 E5
Yockleton 156 C1
Yokefleet 196 A5
Yoker 233 G3
Yonder Bognie 268 E6
York 195 F2
York Castle Museum
  YO1 9SA 90 York
York Dungeon
  YO1 9RD 90 York
York Minster
  YO1 7HH 90 York
Yorkletts 124 C2
Yorkley 131 F2
Yorkshire Museum
  YO1 7FR 90 York
Yorkshire Sculpture Park
  WYorks WF4 4LG 185 G1
Yorton 170 C5
Yorton Heath 170 C5
Youldon 112 D5
Youldonmoor Cross 112 D5
Youlgreave 172 D1
Youlthorpe 195 G2
Youlton 195 D1
Young's End 137 G1
Yoxall 158 D1
Yoxford 153 E1
Yr Hendy 128 B2
Ysbyty Cynfyn 155 D5

Ysbyty Ifan 168 B3
Ysbyty Ystwyth 154 D5
Ysceifiog 182 C5
Ysgubor-y-coed 154 C3
Ystalyfera 129 D2
Ystrad 129 F3
Ystrad Mynach 130 A3
Ystradaeron 142 B2
Ystradfellte 129 F1
Ystradffin 143 D3
Ystradgynlais 129 D1
Ystradmeurig 142 D1
Ystradowen Carmar 128 D1
Ystradowen VGlam 129 G5
Ystumtuen 154 D5
Ythanwells 260 E1
Ythsie 261 G1

Z
Zeal Monachorum 102 A2
Zeals 117 E4
Zelah 96 C4
Zennor 94 B3
Zouch 173 G5
ZSL London Zoo GtLon
  NW1 4RY 12 A3